# FAMILY GUIDE TO THE LAW

*The rights and responsibilities of the motorist
and his family under the laws of England and Wales*

Adapted, with an expanded section on motoring law, from
*Reader's Digest Family Guide to the Law*

## MEMBERS' EDITION

PUBLISHED BY DRIVE PUBLICATIONS LIMITED FOR THE AUTOMOBILE ASSOCIATION

FAMILY GUIDE TO THE LAW
AA Members' Edition

was edited and designed by
Drive Publications Limited
Berkeley Square House, London W1X 5PD
for the Automobile Association
Fanum House, Leicester Square, London WC2H 7LY
Second edition © 1972 The Reader's Digest Association Limited

Printed in Great Britain

# FAMILY GUIDE TO THE LAW

## CONSULTANT EDITOR

Michael Zander, B.A., LL.B., LL.M.,
*Solicitor; Reader in Law at London University*

## CONTRIBUTORS

Trevor M. Aldridge, M.A., *Solicitor*
Bryan Anns, B.A., *Barrister*
A. G. Beavis, R.TECH.ENG., A.M.I.R.T.E.,
M.I.M.I., FULL TECH.CERT. C. & G., *Senior
Lecturer, Department of Automobile Engineering,
Willesden College of Technology*
Harry Saul Bloom, B.A., LL.B., *Barrister;
Senior Lecturer in Law, University of Kent*
Richard Bourne
C. D. Brandreth, *Solicitor; Legal Adviser,
The Automobile Association*
Ian Brownlie, *Barrister; Fellow of Wadham
College, Oxford*
H. Cardno
Mrs E. M. Chapman, *Travel Information, The
Automobile Association*
Anthony Dimitriades, *Solicitor*
Bruce Douglas-Mann, M.P., *Solicitor*
D. R. Galley, *Solicitor*
C. Glasser, *Solicitor*
D. A. K. Hughes, *Solicitor*
Neville A. Joseph, F.C.A., F.C.I.S., F.T.I.I.,
*Chartered Accountant in public practice*
John R. Lambert, B.A., *Senior Research
Associate, Centre for Urban and Regional
Studies, Birmingham University*
L. L. Loewe, M.A., *Barrister*
John Long, F.R.I.C.S.

Tony Lynes
Ian A. Macdonald, M.A., LL.B., *Barrister*
Anthony R. Mellows, T.D., B.D., LL.M., PH.D.,
A.K.C., *Solicitor; Director of Conveyancing
Studies, King's College, London*
David S. Morris, LL.B., *Solicitor*
R. S. Nock, LL.M., *Barrister; Lecturer in
Law, London School of Economics*
Michael Perring, F.R.I.B.A.
Vincent Powell-Smith, LL.M., LL.B., J.C.B.,
DIP.COM., *Lecturer in Law, University of
Aston in Birmingham; Special Lecturer and
Consultant to the Construction Industry
Training Board*
Mrs Margaret Puxon, M.D., *Barrister*
Mrs Judith Reid, LL.B., *Barrister; Lecturer
in Law, London School of Economics*
M. J. Russ, *Travel Information, The Automobile
Association*
L. J. Sapper, LL.B., *Barrister*
Raymond S. Sim, LL.B., CERT. ED., F.R.S.A.,
*Barrister; Member of the Board of Examiners
of the Institute of Legal Executives and
Examiner to the Institute in Commercial Law*
J. Leahy Taylor, M.B., B.S., D.M.J.
D. A. Thomas, M.A., LL.B., *University of
Cambridge Institute of Criminology*
David Widdicombe, Q.C.

The publishers are indebted to the following people and organisations
for their assistance in checking the accuracy of the information in this book:

Bank of England
Barclays Bank Ltd
E. M. Barendt, B.A., B.C.L., *Barrister*
Geoffrey Bindman, B.C.L., M.A., *Solicitor*
Alastair Black, *Solicitor; Deputy Sheriff of
Greater London*
Professor Gordon J. Borrie, LL.M., *Barrister;
Professor of English Law, University of
Birmingham*

British Insurance Association
Professor L. Neville Brown, M.A., LL.B.,
*Solicitor; Professor of Comparative Law, Dean of
the Faculty of Law, University of Birmingham*
Michael Burtonshaw, D.M.S., F.C.I.I.,
*General Manager, Automobile Association
Insurance Services Group*
Ian Campbell, LL.B., *Barrister; Secretary,
Commons Preservation Society*

continued

R. K. Carrick, *Organisation and Legal Officer, Conservative and Unionist Central Office*

C. Clubley

The Consumer Council

Professor W. R. Cornish, LL.B., B.C.L., *Barrister; Professor of English Law, University of London*

Country Landowners' Association

Criminal Injuries Compensation Board

Customs and Excise

Decimal Currency Board

Department of Employment

Department of the Environment

Department of Health and Social Security

E. A. Doyle, *Director, Financial Collection Agencies* (UK) *Ltd*

David Field, B.A.

Foreign and Commonwealth Office

Professor J. F. Garner, LL.D., *Solicitor; Professor of Public Law, University of Nottingham*

General Register Office

John Gilmartin, B.A., B.COM., D.P.A., *Lecturer in Law, College for the Distributive Trades*

Bryan Harris, M.A.

G. Hawes, *Secretary, Space Housing Society* (RH) *Ltd*

Sir Desmond Heap, LL.M., *Comptroller and City Solicitor, Corporation of London*

Professor Brian Hogan, *Professor of Law, University of Leeds*

C. F. Holt, C.ENG., M.I.C.E., F.I.MUN.E., *Borough Engineer and Surveyor, London Borough of Havering*

Home Office

Muir Hunter, Q.C., M.A., M.R.I.

A. M. Jepson, LL.B., A.T.I.I.

Peter Kandler, LL.B., *Principal Solicitor, North Kensington Neighbourhood Law Centre*

Land Commission

The Law Society

J. Philip Lawton, M.A., LL.M., *Solicitor*

London Electricity Board

Lord Chancellor's Department

J. G. Mackley, B.A., *Regional Chief Officer (North), The Housing Corporation*

Metropolitan Water Board

Edward Moeran, *Solicitor*

National Giro

National Savings Bank

Nationwide Building Society

North Thames Gas Board

R. T. Oerton, *Solicitor*

John O'Keefe, O.B.E., B.SC.(ECON.), LL.B., *Barrister*

F. E. Perry, LL.B., F.I.B., *Hon. Lecturer in Law, City of London Polytechnic; Moderator, Institute of Bankers*

Andrew Phelan, M.A., *Barrister*

Post Office Corporation

Pre-School Playgroups Association

Principal Probate Registry

James Pyke, B.A., *Barrister; Lecturer in Law, University of Birmingham*

The Royal Institution of Chartered Surveyors

A. D. Russell, *Solicitor*

G. Sandys-Winsch, B.A., *Solicitor*

M. F. Saunders, F.C.I.I.

G. Spittle

Oliver Stanley, M.A., *Barrister; Director, Gray Dawes & Company Ltd, Merchant Bankers*

Professor Harry Street, LL.B., LL.M., PH.D., F.B.A., *Professor of English Law, University of Manchester*

John Vallat, M.A.

Professor K. W. Wedderburn, M.A., LL.B., *Barrister; Cassel Professor of Commercial Law, University of London*

Professor G. S. A. Wheatcroft, M.A., *Solicitor; Professor Emeritus of English Law, London University*

L. F. W. White, PH.D., B.SC., *Barrister*

W. Whittlesea-Webster, *Officer to the Sheriffs of Greater London, and the County of Surrey; Hon. Secretary, the Sheriffs' Officers' Association*

D. G. T. Williams, M.A., LL.B., LL.M., *Lecturer in Law, Cambridge University*

H. W. Wollaston, *Barrister*

# CONTENTS

# YOUR CAR

Continued

# YOUR HOME

# YOUR FAMILY

# YOUR MONEY

Continued

# YOUR JOB

# YOUR SOCIAL LIFE AND POLITICS

# YOUR BUSINESS

# THE MACHINERY OF THE LAW

# ABC OF CRIME AND PUNISHMENT

# THE LAW OUR SAFEGUARD

*By knowing the law we can assure ourselves of its protection; by ignoring it we put our rights in jeopardy*

*How the legal system provides a framework for our daily lives*

MOST people go through their lives without ever being arrested or involved in a court case; many never even have occasion to consult a solicitor. But no one can live in a modern industrial society without meeting the law in many different ways each day.

Every time we go shopping, or travel by bus or train, we are involved in the law of contract. Every time we drive a car we must pay attention not only to the criminal law but also to the requirements of the civil law of negligence. Every time a visitor enters our homes we become legally responsible for his safety—we owe him what the lawyers call 'a duty of care', whether we know it or not.

Even the most private and natural parts of our lives—birth, marriage and death—have significant legal aspects; and the law regulates the everyday events of ordinary life, such as taking a job, drawing Social Security benefits, renting a flat or buying a house.

In all these ways the law is a framework for the actions of citizens. In its most familiar form it tells us not to do something. The criminal law supports these prohibitions by an elaborate system of threatened penalties; and civil law often has a similar purpose—it compensates the person injured by someone else's negligence, and so indirectly discourages negligent conduct.

But law is more than a network of rules saying 'Thou shalt not'. It also enables people to do the things they wish to do—getting married or divorced, adopting a child or making a will, for instance. It lays down the requirements for licences—a licence to drive a car, for example, or a licence to sell wines and spirits in a restaurant. It provides the rules for the relationship between garages and their customers, between manufacturers and the people who use their products, between estate agents and people who wish to buy or sell houses.

The law marks out the limits of the power of individuals to control their affairs. A man may play a musical instrument—provided he does not play it too loudly. He can marry the woman of his choice—provided she is not within the prohibited degree of relationship. He can enlarge his home—provided he can show in his application for planning permission that his plans will not diminish the value of his neighbours' homes or damage the environment.

It is well known that ignorance of the law is no excuse; but in our modern society, where the law touches so many steps of our daily lives, ignorance of the law is also a positive risk—for it often deprives people of their legal rights.

Tenants leave their homes in response to a notice to quit —unaware that they have legal protection. Consumers fail to appreciate that they have legal remedies against the retailer who has sold them defective goods; they sign manufacturers' 'guarantees' which deprive them of their legal rights; they are hoodwinked by debt-collecting agencies who send them official-looking forms.

People injured in accidents refrain from taking proceedings against the person responsible because they do not know that it is possible to get damages for pain and suffering, or because they do not realise that even relatively minor injuries may be worth £50–£100.

Knowledge of the law, therefore, is not merely an agreeable social and intellectual advantage. Knowledge of the law is the way in which we can safeguard ourselves and our families by assuring ourselves of the rights and remedies which the legal system provides.

T HE English legal system has developed gradually since before the Norman Conquest. The early courts were set up by the feudal barons, and guilt or innocence was decided by ordeals in which it was believed that God intervened, revealing the wrongdoer and upholding the righteous. For instance, in the ordeal by water a priest admonished the water not to accept a liar. The person whose oath was being tested was then thrown in. If he floated, his oath was deemed to have been perjured.

**The birth of our law**
*The legal system's remote origins were in the era of feudal authority and superstitious customs*

In 1215 the Church decided that trial by ordeal was superstition; priests were forbidden to take part. A new method of trial was needed and the jury system emerged.

The jury at first was not convened to consider evidence but to say the truth (to give its verdict) on the basis of its own knowledge of local affairs. It was not until centuries later that the jury assumed its modern role of deciding facts on the basis of what it heard in court.

The introduction of jurymen meant that the old system of trial, in which a formal claim was met by a formal denial and the issue was decided by ordeal or combat, had to be enlarged to admit arguments about the facts. By this time, a class of professional advisers and spokesmen—the future legal profession—had started to develop.

From the early 13th century, there began a process of centralisation which eventually drove the feudal courts out of business. A single uniform system of justice was established throughout the country, enforced by judges travelling out from London on tours known as assizes. This system continued for 700 years—to be replaced in 1972 by the Crown Court in permanent session in large towns and cities.

Our present legal system is in a state of flux, and many of its familiar landmarks may be modified, or drastically altered, in future: in particular, entry to the European Economic Community means a change in the legal structure.

**The law and entry to the Common Market**
*For the first time, laws passed by a body outside Britain will become part of the law of the country; but they will hardly affect day to day living*

WITH the entry of the United Kingdom into the Common Market in January 1973 the role of Parliament as supreme law-giver is, to some extent, diminished. From that date the law governing the lives of UK citizens depends to some extent upon rules imposed by the Community, although the UK itself is represented in the law-making process in Brussels.

Common Market legislation covers only such matters as customs duties, agriculture, the free movement of labour services and capital, transport, commercial policy and competition, and the regulation of the iron and steel and nuclear industries. It can scarcely affect our criminal law, family law, the law of contract or landlord and tenant.

The Treaty of Rome, which set up the EEC in 1957, provides for three levels of Community decisions: *regulations*, which have direct effect in member states; *directives*, requiring member states to take action in any way they see fit; and *decisions*, or simple recommendations.

The actual enforcement of Community law is primarily a matter for the courts of individual member states, but in some matters the European Commission has the power to impose penalties after a hearing, subject to a right of appeal to the European Court.

Nevertheless the changes involved in the United Kingdom's entry to Europe will not alter the basic features of our way of justice: the system by which our laws are made by Parliament and by the accumulating decisions of the courts, known as 'precedents'; the system of trial in which two sides oppose one another before an impartial judge; and the method by which the law constantly renews itself so as to fit the needs of our changing society.

**Parliament: the law-giver**
*The British Constitution gives to the people, acting through their elected Parliament, the power to make and unmake the law*

DESPITE this acceptance of modification to the laws of England from an outside body, Parliament remains the principal law-giver in this country. This principle was established after the 17th-century's constitutional battles, through which Parliament forced the Monarchy to accept that the king had no power to alter the law.

The courts of the country cannot in any way challenge the lawfulness of legislation, unlike those in other countries, such as the United States. Rules made by Parliament bind everyone except Parliament itself, and what Parliament has done, it alone can undo.

Members of Parliament are, of course, free representatives of their electors and not merely delegates. But as each

Parliament has a life of only five years, they are in the end answerable for their decisions to the voters. In this way the people ultimately have the power to influence the law.

Legislation usually starts in the House of Commons and then goes on to the House of Lords, but there is no rule that it must start in the Commons, except in the case of Bills concerning taxation.

In each House the Bill is considered in three different stages, called 'readings'. The first reading is purely formal, to introduce the Bill, and there is no discussion. The second reading is usually the occasion for a debate on the broad objectives of the measure. After the second reading the Bill is examined in detail by a committee. In the House of Commons, membership of the committee reflects the current balance between the political parties. In the House of Lords the committee is the full House. The Bill is then brought to the House for the report stage when it is discussed again and can be amended. Finally, it has its third reading and, if passed, goes to the other House.

When a measure that has been started in the Commons is altered in the Lords, the amendments have to be considered by the Commons. If the amendments are accepted, the Bill is sent direct for the Royal Assent. If the House of Commons does not agree, the Bill will be altered and then sent back to the Lords. Usually the Lords accepts the Commons' viewpoint, but it can restore its amendments.

In the event of disagreement the will of the Commons prevails, but only after a year's delay—unless the measure is certified as a finance Bill, in which case it can become law without the approval of the House of Lords.

Nowadays the Royal Assent is merely a formality. In theory the Queen could still refuse her consent; but the last monarch to do so was Queen Anne who vetoed an unpopular measure, the Scottish Militia Bill, in 1707.

UNTIL this century, the development of the law was mainly the work of the courts. It is only very recently that Parliament has become the dominant partner in the law-making process. The expression 'common law' is used to describe the ancient body of laws built up from decisions made on individual cases by judges.

The majority of cases brought before the courts do not involve questions of law at all: they raise questions of fact, problems of disputed evidence, conflicts in testimony. But a minority of cases involve questions of law where the lawyers on each side try to convince the court that their client's viewpoint of the law is the correct one. The decisions of the courts, published in the Law Reports, form the raw material from which lawyers will advise future clients and judges will later determine what the law is on particular points.

A lawyer faced with the question, 'What is the law?' looks first to see whether there are statutes—laws made by

## The law made by the courts
*The decisions made by judges over many centuries form a body of precedents which bind or guide the courts of today*

Parliament—that relate to the problem. If there are not, it means that the relevant rule is one of common law—decisions of the judges on questions of law, called precedents. The value and weight of a precedent depends on a variety of factors, the most important of which is the seniority of the court which decided the case.

The hierarchy of courts and the rules of the doctrine of precedent are central to the English legal system; for the system proceeds on the basis that decisions made on questions of law by higher courts are binding on the judges in lower courts.

The decisions of the House of Lords are therefore binding on all the other courts, though since 1966 they are no longer binding on the House itself. This means that once the law lords have pronounced on a question of law the matter is settled either 'until they change their minds or until Parliament changes the law.

The decisions of the Court of Appeal are binding on all lower courts *and* are generally also binding on the Court of Appeal itself. But other courts do not bind themselves.

Being bound by a decision means that the court in the second case *must* follow the decision of the court in the first case if the material facts are substantially similar. Judges will also normally follow precedents that are not technically binding. The precedent is then said to be persuasive.

Frequently there are not one but many precedents that the court has to consider—often pointing in contradictory directions. The judge then arrives at the applicable rule of law by analysing the factual situations in the earlier cases and considering the reasoning of the earlier judges.

General principles gradually emerge. Often the build-up takes decades before a creative judge sees that the narrow rules of several individual cases can be re-stated to give expression to a general rule.

**The law in action**
*The courts administer the law by allowing parties to present their cases against one another according to the age-old rules of evidence*

FOUR of the most distinctive features of English trials are: the adversary system, which relies on both sides arguing their cases without active intervention from the judge; the burden of proof, which means that one side (in criminal cases, this is always the prosecution) has to prove its case; the rules of evidence, which seek to ensure scrupulous fairness by making certain kinds of evidence inadmissible; and the fact that both parties and all the witnesses must usually appear in person and give evidence orally in open court.

THE ADVERSARY SYSTEM The courts leave it to each party to prepare and present his own case. In civil cases, the adversaries are usually two or more private citizens; in criminal cases one of the adversaries is usually the police. The judge rarely interferes. Unlike continental trials, he does not call witnesses; even expert witnesses are called by the parties, rather than by the court. Nor does he generally question the witnesses—apart from putting questions designed to eliminate ambiguity or misunderstanding. The basic questioning of the witnesses is left to the lawyers.

The English approach relies, therefore, on the clash of opposing interests to produce the nearest approximation to the truth. One aspect of this system that has not attracted much attention is that the adversary procedure works properly only if both sides are adequately represented. This is important, since in the vast majority of both civil and criminal trials conducted in this country only one side *is* adequately represented. This is true both in the magistrates' courts and in the county courts, which conduct the bulk of the cases. It is rare, however, for parties to be unrepresented in more serious cases, heard in the higher courts.

THE BURDEN OF PROOF It is a fundamental principle that one of the parties in proceedings in the courts has to carry the burden of proof. In civil cases this is normally the claimant or plaintiff; in criminal cases it is always the prosecution. The actual standard of proof that has to be met differs in the two classes of case. In criminal cases, because of the concern that no innocent man should be convicted and that a person should not be punished by the State unless a high degree of proof has been satisfied, the prosecution must prove its case beyond reasonable doubt. The accused is regarded as innocent until he is proved guilty, and he is entitled to the benefit of any substantial or real doubt. In civil cases, by contrast, the standard is only that the case be proved on the balance of probabilities.

This difference in the standard of proof is one reason why cases arising out of the same facts may end with apparently contradictory results. For instance, a motorist may be found not guilty of dangerous driving because the prosecution cannot satisfy the severe test of proof required in criminal proceedings; but the same man could be ordered to pay civil damages to someone injured in the accident— because the injured person would need only to prove his case on the balance of probabilities.

It is also a basic principle of criminal law that normally the prosecution has to prove beyond a reasonable doubt that the accused had the necessary intent (called by lawyers *mens rea*). To be guilty of murder, for instance, a man must have intended to kill, or at least have realised that his act was likely to result in death. If this cannot be proved but it can be shown that the accused was grossly negligent, he will be liable only for manslaughter.

To be guilty of theft, it must be shown that there was a dishonest intention to deprive the owner permanently of the article. Borrowing, even without permission, is therefore not theft.

In some situations, however, Parliament has provided that the prosecution need not prove any intent. It is enough that the act was committed. For instance, a publican commits a criminal offence in selling alcohol to someone who is drunk even though he is not aware of the customer's state; and, similarly, a motorist is guilty of a criminal offence if he sells a car which is unroadworthy even though he does not know it. In this type of case, Parliament has taken the view that the person responsible should be punishable whether or not he is, in the ordinary sense, to blame.

RULES OF EVIDENCE The English system of trial is largely based on rules of evidence designed to ensure that the trial is fair. Many of the rules have the effect of excluding evidence—although it could be relevant—on the ground that it might be prejudicial in one way or another.

An example is the rule that, in a criminal case, the court is not normally permitted to hear evidence about an accused man's previous convictions until after he has been found guilty. The only exceptions are where the accused asserts that he has a good character, or where he attacks the integrity of the prosecution witnesses, or where the facts in the previous case are so strikingly similar to the facts in the case for which he is facing trial that it is unlikely to be mere coincidence.

Another rule of evidence is the one that normally prohibits hearsay evidence—evidence of what the witness heard someone else say to him. There are now a good number of exceptions to this rule: one of the most important is that admissions or confessions can be reported. If this exception did not exist, a policeman would not be able to give evidence of a confession.

Moreover, hearsay evidence is now allowed in civil courts unless it is what is known as 'hearsay upon hearsay'. A witness in a civil case can therefore tell the court what he heard Jones tell him. But he may not give evidence as to what Jones told him Smith had said.

ORAL PROCEEDINGS Evidence in an English court is normally given in open court by the witness himself. Not much use is made of written evidence, which is common in continental courts. One of the reasons for this is that we set much store by the value of cross-examination, and witnesses who are not present in court cannot be questioned.

There are few exceptions to the rule that anyone can give evidence in an English court. One exception is young children, who can give evidence in civil cases only if the judge rules that they are old enough to take the oath. In criminal cases, a child may be allowed to make an unsworn statement, but only if the judge decides that he or she is old enough to understand the duty to speak the truth.

The accused in a criminal case cannot be required to give evidence. If he remains silent, the prosecution are not allowed to comment on the fact—though the judge may do so if he thinks fit. The accused person's husband or wife cannot be required to give evidence for the prosecution except in cases where he or she has been the victim of the alleged offence. Witnesses can normally be compelled to give evidence. If they decline to come to court, they can be summonsed by subpoena; failure to obey a subpoena is contempt of court. A witness can refuse to answer a question that might incriminate himself or his spouse, but he cannot refuse to answer questions which might compromise someone else.

There is therefore no privilege for a priest protecting the secrets of the confessional, or for a doctor who keeps confidences communicated to him by his patients. There is not even a privilege to refuse to answer questions that would incriminate the witness's own child.

**The living law**
*How the law preserves its essential element of certainty while responding to the changing needs and circumstances of our society*

EVERY legal system faces the problem of the proper balance between the need for certainty and the need for flexibility. The law must be constant, so that people can arrange their affairs in reliance on it. A system of laws that is constantly changing creates confusion and bewilderment. On the other hand, there must be some way in which the system can be made responsive to the need for reform and adjustment. A legal system that was predictable but unjust would obviously not be satisfactory.

The element of certainty in the English system is secured in several ways. The doctrine of precedent is one of the most potent, since it forces judges to look back to earlier decisions, binds them to follow precedents of higher courts, and encourages them to be guided even by precedents of courts that are not binding. The continuity that results from a system based on precedent helps to create a stable legal system and enables lawyers to advise clients, on the basis of past decisions, as to what sort of judgments courts are likely to reach in future cases.

Another important force for certainty is the cumbersome nature of the law-making process, which means that once a law has been passed by Parliament it is not quickly repealed or amended.

A third pressure which helps to ensure stability is the strong conservative tradition that prevails amongst lawyers generally and judges in particular. A legal system in any country is almost inevitably a conservative element in society, if for no other reason than that it is based to such an extent on decisions taken in the past.

The main force in the direction of change and fluidity is that the system has to respond to the continually changing needs of society. A legal system that stood still would be unable to cope with the demands of modern life.

Change in the law and the legal system is the work of various agencies. The most powerful and effective is Parliament, through the ordinary processes of legislation. Law-making by Parliament is normally the prerogative of the Government of the day which dominates the process almost—but not entirely—to the exclusion of all others.

The chief exception is the work of the private Member of Parliament who carries on to the statute book some piece of legislation which he has personally promoted, normally with Government support. There have been a number of notable private Members' Bills in recent years, including those legalising homosexual relations in private between consenting adults, abolishing capital punishment, broadening the law on abortion and reforming the divorce laws.

Traditionally, English judges are shy about admitting the extent to which they are themselves responsible for the content of the law. Even today, judges will occasionally remind a barrister arguing a case that the court's task is to find what the law *is*, not what it *ought* to be. But this is largely a false contrast—for the question of what the law *is* often includes the question of what it should be.

If the precedents are clear and weighty and point to one result, most judges will feel compelled to follow previous decisions. But the issue is usually not so clear-cut. For one thing, there are normally some precedents that support each side, and the court has to decide which is more relevant.

The law is also constantly undergoing reform through the courts, though this does have distinct limitations. It is haphazard, since it depends on the accidents of litigation. Not infrequently, for instance, a crucial question of law is settled at a relatively low level of decision-making simply because the losing party lacks the funds to appeal. Or parties come to an amicable settlement that resolves their dispute but leaves the question of law open.

Also, the courts have hardly any chance of studying the non-legal considerations implicit in legal questions. In a case involving strike law, for instance, a court cannot consider evidence about the economic consequences that its ruling could have on trade union members, or employers. They are confined to arguments put by the two sides.

In addition, the course of law reform through the courts may be handicapped by the doctrine of precedent in cases where it virtually compels unsatisfactory solutions.

Moreover, a legal system based on law built up slowly from decided cases is unwieldy and costly to administer.

**Tomorrow's law**
*Codes are being drawn up which will one day bring a new degree of cohesion and simplicity to the laws of England, Wales and Scotland*

IN 1965 Parliament set up Law Commissions to plan and conduct the reform of the whole of the law: one for England and Wales and one for Scotland.

The establishment of the Law Commissions is perhaps the most important single event in the development of the legal system for well over a hundred years. The Commissions prepare reports proposing draft statutes, which are laid before Parliament and will usually become the new law.

The English Commission has undertaken the review of several massive areas of law, with a view to preparing codes. These include family law, the law of landlord and tenant, contract law, and the general principles of criminal law, and could take 10–20 years to draft.

Codes have long been a part of other legal systems. Their main feature is that they state the whole of the law on a subject, substituting a single, comprehensive measure for the thousands of judicial decisions and the accretion of innumerable statutes. If the law is largely codified, it should be simpler to understand and cheaper to apply.

# YOUR CAR

# Learning to drive

ANYONE who wants to learn to drive a car must first obtain a current provisional driving licence. This allows the holder to drive when supervised by a qualified driver in a vehicle displaying 'L' plates. Licences are issued by the taxation (or licensing) departments of borough and county councils.

### Obtaining a provisional licence
Application forms can be obtained from the council office or any post office. Send the completed form with the necessary fee to the council office. The licence must be signed in ink by the holder as soon as it is received. Failure to sign it can result in a prosecution and a fine of up to £20.

The minimum age for holding a provisional licence to drive a car is 17. Applicants have to state that they do not suffer from any physical or mental defect which could impair normal driving ability, and that no court has banned them from holding a licence or has ordered an endorsement on any licence they hold or may later hold.

If there is any doubt in answering these questions, full details must be given and further inquiries may have to be made, or a medical examination ordered, before the authority decides whether to issue a licence.

A licence is valid for one year. If the holder has not passed the Department of the Environment driving test by that time, a second licence can be obtained for a further fee.

### Rules for learner drivers
Any vehicle being driven by a learner must carry 'L' plates at the front and rear. These plates—a red 'L' 4 in. high, 3½ in. wide and 1½ in. thick on a 7 in. × 7 in. white background —can be bought from most motor-accessory shops and garages.

Driving without a licence is a serious offence and is aggravated where no licence could have been issued or where the conditions of a provisional licence are not complied with. The offender can be fined up to £50. Any other breach of the provisional-licence regulations can lead to a fine of up to £20.

In serious or persistent cases the learner can be disqualified from driving. This prohibits him from applying for a licence until the period of disqualification has expired.

Learners are not allowed to drive a vehicle towing a trailer or caravan, and are prohibited from driving on motorways.

Officially, the law demands the same standard of driving from learners as from qualified drivers, and imposes the same penalties. In practice, the police tend to use their discretion where learners are involved.

A learner can also be held liable for damages for injury to a pedestrian or a passenger. A passenger is deprived of the right to sue only if he knowingly accepts the risk of injury due to the learner's inexperience.

SUPERVISORS The learner must always be accompanied by a supervisor who holds a full driving licence entitling him to drive the type of vehicle covered by the learner's provisional licence. The holder of a licence to drive a different class of vehicle does not qualify.

For example, a driver whose full licence is limited to driving cars with automatic transmission is not permitted to supervise a learner in a car with manually operated gears.

The supervisor must ensure, as far as is reasonably possible, that the learner does not drive dangerously or carelessly or break the law in any other way. If he fails to exercise proper restraint on the learner, he may be prosecuted for aiding and abetting the offence committed by the learner and be dealt with as if he had broken the law himself.

The supervisor is regarded in law as being in charge of the vehicle—a drunken supervisor could be prosecuted.

The learner may carry additional passengers besides the qualified supervisor.

### Taking a driving test
Application forms for a driving test are available from post offices and Department of the Environment traffic area offices. A fee is charged when the application is submitted.

A learner driver should apply for a test well before he hopes to take it. Waiting lists vary in length from area to area, but tests are usually arranged not less than one month after the date of application.

As soon as a test date is fixed, it should be

checked against the expiry date of the learner's provisional licence, which may have to be renewed. The examiner will want to see the licence, and will cancel the test even if the licence is only one day out of date.

Anyone unable to keep the appointment loses his test fee unless he gives at least three days' notice of cancellation.

A learner driver can be tested at any of the Department of the Environment's 400 driving test centres—not necessarily the one nearest his home.

The test is conducted by one of the Department's driving examiners who chooses a route to provide a fair all-round test of driving competence.

The learner has to supply the car used for the test. Anyone who has been taking lessons with a driving school can usually arrange to hire a school car for the test.

If the learner driver passes the test in a car which has automatic transmission, his full licence will be limited to automatic cars. He has to take a further test in a car with hand-operated gears before he can obtain a licence to drive that type of car. But if he passes his test in a car with manual gear-change, he will be qualified to drive both types.

Before issuing a 'pass' certificate, the examiner has to be satisfied that the learner knows the Highway Code and can drive without danger to, and with due consideration for, other road users.

The examiner also makes sure that the learner can read a car number plate from 75 ft or, in the case of the new type of plate with smaller characters, 67 ft. The learner may wear spectacles.

When the learner arrives at the test centre, he is first asked to sign an appointment sheet confirming his identity and detailing the make and registration number of the car in which he intends to take the test.

The car must be taxed, insured, and carry 'L' plates. It must also be in a roadworthy condition—with a current Annual Vehicle (MoT) Test certificate if it is more than three years old, and seat belts fitted if it was registered on or after January 1, 1965.

The examiner will first check the learner's provisional licence and then carry out the eyesight test. The practical part of the test

## Learning through a driving school

THE learner is free to gain his driving experience with anyone qualified and willing to teach him; there is no stipulation that the supervisor must be a registered professional instructor.

However, the driving test contains certain technical requirements demanding not only driving proficiency but an ability to cope with everyday motoring practices and situations.

For this reason, many people learn to drive through recognised driving schools with professional instructors and in cars with dual controls, to lessen the risk of accidents.

Driving-school instructors have to be registered and approved by the Department of the Environment and must pass a special test themselves before being allowed to operate as instructors. It is an offence for anyone to claim to be an approved instructor unless he holds the official instructor's licence.

A professional driving instructor should know the finer points of driving required for the test and be able to use techniques to help the learner master the skills of motoring.

For example, many driving instructors tape a matchstick in the centre of the lower edge of the rear window to give the learner a fixed point in the centre of the car which he can line up with the kerb to keep an even course when reversing round a corner.

The instructor will advise the learner when he is competent enough to take the test and book a test for him. If required, the instructor will provide the car in which his pupil learnt to drive for the test itself.

The number of lessons required varies according to the learner's aptitude and previous driving experience, but most schools will conduct a driving assessment as a guide to the number of lessons likely to be required.

The cost of lessons varies from school to school. It is usually worked out on an hourly basis, which includes petrol and insurance. Many schools offer a reduction for a course of, say, 20 or 30 lessons, but an additional charge is often made for Sunday tuition.

The learner should try to persuade the driving school to agree to provide the same instructor for each lesson he takes, as far as is reasonably possible.

A copy of the Highway Code and one good driving manual are essential for any learner.

lasts about 30 minutes and consists of four main sections:

**1.** Comparatively easy driving to enable the learner to lose any nervousness caused by having the examiner in the car.

**2.** An emergency stop.

**3.** Specific manoeuvres including a three-point turn, reversing round a corner, and stopping and starting a car on a slope.

**4.** Driving through busier areas to cope with normal traffic situations, such as overtaking, stopping for pedestrians on a crossing, giving adequate clearance to other road users and anticipating the actions of other drivers.

When the emergency stop is tested the examiner will warn the learner that during the next few minutes he will give a signal, usually a sharp tap on the dashboard, upon which the car must be brought to a halt as quickly as possible. The examiner will make sure that there is no traffic immediately behind the learner when this is done.

The test does not include any traps or catches, such as asking a learner to stop in a no-waiting area, and the examiner may overlook a minor mistake or two if he finds the overall standard of driving satisfactory.

The final part of the test is an oral section in which the learner is asked a number of questions on the Highway Code and general points of competent, responsible driving such as parking, coping with skids, and the appropriate action to take at night or in bad weather.

### The examiner's decision

When these questions have been answered the examiner will tell the learner whether he has passed or failed. Then he fills in either a pink Certificate of Competence, which has to be signed in the examiner's presence, or a Statement of Failure detailing the aspects of driving which he considered were below the required standard. Examiners are not allowed to discuss their reasons for failing a learner.

Once a Certificate of Competence has been issued the provisional licence holder is allowed to drive unaccompanied and without 'L' plates. He is not required to apply for a full driving licence immediately, but must submit his Certificate of Competence with an application for a full licence before his provisional licence expires.

Anyone who fails the test must wait a month before taking another, but he can *apply* for another test immediately.

It is an offence, punishable by imprisonment, to attempt to bribe a driving examiner. It is also illegal to impersonate a learner and take the test for him; in this case, both learner and impersonator would be liable to a severe fine and possible imprisonment for conspiracy to defraud.

If a learner considers that he has failed because of a serious irregularity—for example, because the examiner was drunk, under the influence of drugs, acted out of malice or was dishonest—he has the right to appeal to a magistrates' court. If the court upholds the appeal, another test will be arranged free.

### Disabled drivers

Acute disabilities such as mental disorder, failure to meet the eyesight requirements and liability to sudden attacks of disabling giddiness or fainting are absolute bars to driving.

People suffering from epilepsy may be issued with a licence provided that three conditions are met. They must have had no epileptic attack while awake for at least three years before date when the licence is to have effect. If they have had epileptic attacks while asleep during that period, they must also have been subject to such attacks before the beginning of the three years. And their driving must not be a likely source of danger to the public. Sufferers from less-severe handicaps can often satisfy the law by using an invalid carriage or specially adapted car. ☐ Invalid carriages, p. 169.

The granting of a driving licence to a disabled person depends on whether his disability is likely to make his driving a danger to the public. The licensing authorities are entitled to make their own inquiries before deciding whether to grant a licence.

Disabled drivers have to undergo the same driving test as an ordinary driver, prove the same standards of competence, carry out the same manoeuvres and possess the same knowledge of the Highway Code. The examiner will pay particular attention to mechanical signals if hand signals are not possible.

If the test is taken in a specially built or adapted vehicle, the licence issued will restrict the driver to similar vehicles.

Once the licensing authority is satisfied that the driver is either an invalid or disabled, and is using an invalid carriage, an exempt excise licence is issued. It is the same as a vehicle excise licence disc issued on payment of duty, and has to be displayed in the same way. People who, because of their disabilities, can use only specially adapted motor vehicles may also be issued with an exempt excise licence. They must obtain and show to the licensing authority Form MHS 330 which is issued by the Department of Health and Social Security. ☐ Taxing and insuring a car, p. 32.

# The driving licence

*How to apply*  *Visitors to Britain*
*Renewing a licence*

ANYONE driving or accompanying a learner driver on a public road must hold a driving licence. He can be stopped by the police and must show his licence on request. The police can also demand to see the licence of any driver they have good reason to think has been involved in an accident or has committed a motoring offence.

A policeman is allowed to use the licence to establish only the name and address of the licence holder, its date of issue and licensing authority—all of which are detailed on the first page. He has no right to look through subsequent pages to see if the licence has been endorsed.

A driver is within his rights simply to show this page without handing the licence to the policeman; but this may not always be tactful if there is a chance of being let off with a warning for a minor offence.

A driver who is not carrying his licence and is asked to produce it must give the name of a police station to which he will take it for inspection within five days.

## How to apply
To qualify for a full licence, an applicant must:
1. Be at least 17 years old (16 for a licence to drive a moped with pedals up to 50 c.c.).
2. Have passed the driving test.
3. Be free of any disability that would make his or her driving a danger to the public.
4. Not be disqualified by any court from holding a driving licence.
5. Pay the prescribed fee.

Application forms for driving licences are available from post offices and local-authority licensing offices. The fee (which changes from time to time) and either a current full licence or the pink Certificate of Competence issued by the driving test examiner should be sent with the completed application form to the licensing office. The Certificate of Competence is retained by the office.

Like the provisional licence, the full driving licence must be signed in ink by the holder as soon as it is received.

It will specify, according to which test or tests have been passed, the groups of vehicles which it entitles the holder to drive. The driving licence is valid for three years from its date of issue. A licence must be renewed on or before expiry; no days of grace are allowed, and it is not a valid excuse if stopped without a licence to say that an application for a new one is in the post.

## Renewing a licence
To renew a licence, send it with a completed application form and fee to the licensing office. Usually a new licence booklet is not issued unless the old one is in a poor condition. In this case an additional fee may be charged.

A driving test does not have to be taken unless there is a lapse of more than ten years since the last licence was issued.

If a licence is lost, a duplicate (containing any unexpired endorsements on the original licence) can be obtained from the office which issued the original, for a small fee. If, after obtaining a replacement, the holder finds the original, he must return the original to the issuing office. A driver who finds his licence is in the unlawful possession of another person must take reasonable steps to recover it.

A driver may also ask for his licence to be exchanged on expiry of any endorsements on it, or if the licence is defaced, or when he changes his name or address.

## Visitors to Britain
The holder of a full driving licence issued within the last ten years in Northern Ireland, the Channel Islands or the Isle of Man is entitled to a full British driving licence without having to take a driving test. The driver can either apply in person to the local motor taxation office, or fill in Form DL1, obtainable at any post office, and send it to the office with his present licence and the fee.

Visitors from abroad who hold a foreign or international driving licence can use it to drive in Britain for one year.

If during that time a visitor becomes a British resident, or if his licence expires, he must take out a provisional licence, drive with a supervisor and go through the usual learner's procedure.

After one year a visitor or new resident must qualify for a British licence.

23

# Buying a car

NEXT to a house, a car is probably the most expensive single item the average family buys. So it pays a purchaser to choose carefully the model which is best suited to his needs, and the most economical way of raising the money if he is not buying outright for cash.

Since new cars sometimes prove to be defective, it is also necessary for the buyer to make sure that he is in as strong a position as possible to get any faults in the vehicle rectified without delay.

### Choosing the model
Individual circumstances and personal preferences usually dictate the price range and model a buyer chooses—saloon, convertible, estate or sports car.

In deciding on the model, an AA member has the advantage—in the case of most popular cars—of being able to consult the evaluation test carried out by the Association's own test drivers. He thus has an independent critical assessment of the car's performance.

In comparing the price of rival models, bear in mind that the advertised price often does not include a number of other charges which have to be paid before the car can be taken on the road. These include charges for delivery from factory to dealer, and for supplying and fitting number plates and compulsory safety belts. The buyer also has to arrange insurance and obtain an excise licence.
□ Taxing and insuring a car, p. 32.

### Deciding about finance
Only a minority of customers buying new cars pay the full cash price immediately. The most common reason is that not many people have sufficient savings to meet the considerable cost of a new car.

Apart from necessity, however, there are sound economic arguments in times of inflation for borrowing the money over a relatively long period. Because of the decline in the value of money, £1000 today may in three years' time be worth only £850 at today's values.

Again, if incomes continue to rise at their present rate—they have risen an average of 5 per cent a year over the last 20 years—it will be easier to earn and pay off a loan of £1000 in three years' time than it is to earn the same amount of cash today and avoid borrowing.

A customer who decides to borrow part of the cost of his new car often finds he is offered credit facilities by the car dealer under arrangements with a finance company. This can benefit both customer and dealer.

The customer can sign the necessary papers at the showroom and, as long as checks on his credit-worthiness are satisfactory, can pay a deposit and drive the car away. The dealer is repaid promptly by the finance company and earns a commission that he would not receive on a cash sale.

From the customer's point of view, however, there are many ways of raising a loan, and some may have advantages over facilities offered by the dealer.

In shopping around for finance, most people take into account four main points:
**1.** The amount that has to be repaid each week or month.
**2.** The interest rate.
**3.** The amount of tax relief (if any).
**4.** The customer's legal rights and responsibilities under the agreement.
INSTALMENTS The amount of each weekly or monthly instalment depends mainly on the period of the loan (and, of course, the sum borrowed). Beware of choosing a credit arrangement solely because the repayment terms are easy; low instalments sometimes mask excessive interest rates.
INTEREST RATE Not all loans or credit arrangements state the interest rate; even when they do the figure given may be misleading. Many lenders, for example, give a figure which, though they do not say so, is a flat rate of interest—a figure calculated as if none of the money borrowed were repaid until the end of the period.

The true rate of interest, calculated periodically on the amount still owing, may be twice the flat rate cited. □ Working out the true interest rate, p. 493.
TAX RELIEF If a credit arrangement qualifies for tax relief, some or all of the interest paid

by the customer is deducted from his income before tax is charged. Rules about tax relief on loans may change from Budget to Budget, or more frequently; those given here apply in the 1972–3 tax year.

LEGAL RIGHTS AND RESPONSIBILITIES The terms of the agreement under which money is borrowed may limit the customer's chance of redress if the vehicle is defective, restrict his right to sell it and lay down what happens if he has difficulty in making repayments. ☐ Re-arranging family finances, p. 544.

## Ways of raising the money

If the car dealer offers credit facilities, it will usually be in the form of a hire purchase, credit-sale or conditional-sale agreement or a personal loan.

HIRE PURCHASE Repayments under a hire-purchase agreement are usually phased over up to three years; individual repayments are average compared with other forms of lending. True interest rates are comparatively high —between 20 and 30 per cent is common— and there is no tax relief.

The agreement the customer signs may limit his rights to replacement or compensation if the car is faulty, though the law gives him more protection than other borrowers against attempts by dealers to escape their responsibility for the car's condition.

Technically, the hire-purchase customer is merely hiring the car until the last repayment is made; he therefore has to get the consent of the finance company before he can sell. If he gets into financial difficulties he is entitled to hand the car back, though he may have to make up half the total purchase price and pay any instalments outstanding.

If the customer falls behind with repayments, the finance company cannot take the car back against his will without a court order. Again, the law gives the customer valuable protection, and courts often allow customers a second chance to pay. ☐ Hire purchase, p. 498.

CREDIT SALE Repayments and interest charges under credit-sale agreements are similar to those for hire purchase.

In this case, however, the customer is entitled to claim tax relief (in the 1972–3 tax year) on all but the first £35 a year which he pays in interest. To help customers claim tax relief, the agreement usually indicates how much of each repayment consists of interest charges.

Credit-sale agreements usually limit customers' rights to redress if the car is faulty

more severely than under hire purchase. The customer becomes the owner of the vehicle as soon as the agreement is signed. He does not need the company's permission to sell, though the agreement may require him to repay all outstanding charges when he does so.

If he gets into financial difficulties, the customer has no right to return the car. If he falls behind with repayments, the finance company cannot take the car back, but must sue for debt in the same way as they would for any other debt. ☐ Credit sale, p. 503; Legal action II: suing to recover a debt, p. 725.

CONDITIONAL SALE From the customer's point of view, a conditional-sale agreement combines some of the benefits of hire purchase with some of those of credit sale. Instalments and interest rates are similar under all three.

The conditional-sale customer can claim tax relief on interest payments over £35 a year, and the amount is usually shown on the agreement or will be supplied on request by the company.

His rights to redress for a faulty vehicle are similar to those of the hire-purchase customer. Usually he becomes the owner part way through the repayment period—the agreement says when. Before that time he needs the company's consent to sell; after he becomes owner he can sell whenever he wants, though under the terms of the agreement he may be obliged to repay the balance immediately.

In cases of financial difficulty his position up to the time he becomes the legal owner is similar to that of the hire-purchase customer; after that he is in the same situation as the person who buys on credit sale.

PERSONAL LOANS If a personal loan is arranged by the car dealer with a finance company, it may be spread over up to 5 years, making individual repayments correspondingly lower. True interest rates, however, are still high—between 20 and 30 per cent.

The customer can claim tax relief on all the interest he pays over £35 a year.

The loan agreement is unlikely to deal with questions such as redress for defects or when the borrower can sell. If the customer fails to repay, the debt must be claimed in the same way as any other debt. ☐ Legal action II: suing to recover a debt, p. 725.

ARRANGING A LOAN DIRECT There is no obligation on a car buyer to arrange his finance through the car dealer; in fact there is much to be said for shopping around for the best terms. AA members, for example, may be able to get personal loans from a finance house at a preferential rate through arrangements made by the Association with a finance house.

SECOND MORTGAGES Home-owners can raise a loan on the security of their property by arranging a second mortgage with a finance company. The loan may be over five to seven years, which keeps instalments low. True interest rates are usually better than on other finance house loans—15 to 25 per cent is typical.

The borrower can claim tax relief on interest over £35 a year.

A second mortgage has no effect on the borrower's rights if his car proves to be faulty or if he wants to sell. The finance company may allow reduced payments to a borrower in financial difficulties; in the last resort, however, it can take legal action to force the sale of his house. ☐ Personal loans and second mortgages, p. 506; Re-arranging family finances, p. 544.

BORROWING FROM A BANK The cheapest way to borrow is probably to ask your bank manager for an overdraft on your current account. Interest is charged only on the amount outstanding, and the true rate is usually lower than on any other form of loan—possibly 10 per cent or less.

Different customers may be charged different rates, at the discretion of the individual bank manger, depending on their financial standing with the bank, and whether or not they have stocks and shares which can be assigned to the bank as security.

The repayment period is a matter of arrangement, but it is likely to be comparatively short—two years, perhaps. So individual repayments will be higher.

Tax relief is available on interest over £35 a year.

In theory, overdrafts can be recalled at any time. In practice, a bank is likely to do this only if the customer exceeds the overdraft limit or fails to repay at the agreed rate, or if economic circumstances force the bank seriously to curtail its lending.

In practice, banks often prefer customers seeking finance for car purchase to borrow the money through a personal loan. The period of the loan, and hence individual repayments, are similar to those on an overdraft. Interest is often quoted at a flat rate; the true rate is higher than that on overdrafts, but lower than on most other types of loan. True rates in the 12 to 15 per cent range are typical. Again, tax relief is available on interest over £35 a year.

Once granted, personal loans cannot be recalled before the agreed time.

Neither overdrafts nor bank personal loans affect the customer's rights to get recompense for a faulty car or his right to sell whenever he chooses. If the customer fails to repay, any securities he has assigned may be sold; otherwise, the bank must take action to recover the money in the same way as for any other debt. ☐ Personal loans and second mortgages, p. 506; Legal action II: suing to recover a debt, p. 725.

## Protecting the customer's rights

Despite checks made by manufacturer and dealer, it is not uncommon for a customer to find defects in his new car when he begins to use it. So he needs to ensure that the agreement he makes with the dealer leaves him in a strong position to get such defects rectified without expense.

If the customer and dealer make no special arrangements about the subject, the Sale of Goods Act 1893 ensures the customer's rights to redress for defects.

In practice, however, manufacturers prefer to deal with defects through the warranty system. The best of these systems deal free of charge with most, if not all, defects which come to light after the vehicle has been handed over. If the warranty is as good as this, it simply becomes a practical way of implementing the customer's legal rights.

Not all warranties are as good as this, however. Some merely promise to attend to minor adjustments for a limited period, and at the same time attempt to get the customer to sign away his other legal rights.

The customer, therefore, has to read carefully anything he is asked to sign—usually a retail order form and possibly the warranty as well. If these give him rights as good as, or better than, those provided by law, he should sign.

If, however, they give less, he has to decide whether to settle for restricted rights, which in practice should be relatively easy to claim, or to protect his rights in law by not signing—and face the possibility of having to take legal action to get defects rectified.

The hire-purchase customer escapes this problem. He has no option but to sign the agreement—but by law this preserves many of his more important rights.

## Reading the retail order form

Anyone who buys a new car for cash or cash and trade-in—irrespective of how he has borrowed the money—or by credit-sale agreement is almost invariably asked by the dealer to sign a retail order form.

Details of the car the customer is buying are given on the front of the form, together with any extras or special accessories, the purchase price and any trade-in allowance. On the reverse, in small print, the terms of the sale are listed.

Once the buyer signs this form, he is legally bound by the conditions printed on it.

Some order forms contain an assurance that by signing the customer is not surrendering his rights in law.

For example, the form used by Ford main dealers says: 'The seller does not derogate from or exclude any of the contractual rights of the retail customer under the Sale of Goods Act 1893 or at common law; save that it is a condition precedent of the exercise of any of the said rights that if the retail customer believes that there are any defects in the vehicle he will first give the seller every reasonable opportunity to examine and rectify such defects (if any) in accordance with (the warranty).'

The effect of such a clause is that the customer who finds a defect in his new car must first take it back to the dealer and ask for it to be put right before taking legal action. There is little reason to object to this requirement, since it will normally be in the customer's interests to first try to get work done under warranty.

The value of this clause to the customer is that—unlike clauses on many other order forms—it leaves the customer free to take legal action if he is not satisfied with the work done by the dealer under the warranty scheme.

If the order form contains a clause similar to this one, it will usually be in the customer's interests to sign, though he should check first that none of the remaining clauses restricts his rights in a way which he finds unacceptable.

Not all order forms are as good as this, however. Some attempt to restrict the buyer's legal rights in exchange for the benefits of the warranty. Such a form may include clauses such as these:

1. The seller undertakes that the vehicle and accessories will be of 'merchantable quality' (in other words, not defective).

2. The customer agrees that if any defects appear in the car itself, or in its accessories, he will give the dealer 'every reasonable opportunity' to have them put right under the terms of the manufacturer's warranty.

3. The customer also agrees to surrender all his other rights in law—what the form may call 'all conditions and warranties,

whether expressed or implied by statute, common law or otherwise'.

There is no need for such a clause unless the customer's rights under the warranty are inferior to those in law. So if the retail order form contains such a clause, the customer needs to examine closely the terms of the warranty and compare them with his rights in law before deciding whether to sign.

NEW CAR WARRANTIES Under most warranties, the manufacturer provides the new car buyer with a satisfactory method of dealing with routine repairs and minor defects—but only if the work becomes necessary within a set period, usually a year or before 12,000 miles. They often provide extra fringe benefits, such as a free 500-mile service.

Repair work under a warranty can usually be carried out by any authorised dealer in the United Kingdom, and in many cases on the Continent as well—not just by the dealer who sells the car.

Another advantage of warranties is that they do not depend on the solvency of the dealer who sells the car.

If a dealer should go out of business after supplying a new car, the manufacturers usually arrange for another dealer to carry out repair work under the warranty. They will do this unless the dealer made himself responsible for the warranty and did not simply pass it on direct from the manufacturers.

The warranty, however, may contain a number of major snags.

Not all defects may be covered, for example, even though they may be caused by faulty design or bad workmanship.

Some warranties exclude certain items not made by the manufacturer—the tyres, battery and windows, for example—although these are often guaranteed by their own makers.

If the car has not been serviced regularly, the manufacturer may be legally entitled to reject a warranty claim, even if the lack of servicing did not directly cause the failure. This might also apply if the car is serviced or repaired by an unauthorised garage.

Similarly, manufacturers sometimes refuse to carry out repairs on the grounds that the vehicle was used for an 'unsuitable purpose'—such as towing a heavy caravan, boat or trailer.

In addition, many warranties state that any claims must be made within a certain time—anything from seven to 14 days—after the defect first appears.

The buyer who accepts a limited warranty may also sign away his right to claim from the manufacturer if he suffers loss or injury as a result of negligence in the manufacture of the car.

RELYING ON RIGHTS IN LAW A buyer can retain his rights in law by not signing the order form or by striking out the clauses which would take away his common-law rights (though he must make sure that the dealer knows what he is deleting). He then retains the right under the Sale of Goods Act 1893 to claim against the dealer (not the manufacturer) if the car is defective or not fit for the purpose for which it was intended.

This means that the car must be of a reasonable standard in relation to the price which the buyer paid for it.

If the car turns out to have a major defect which makes it unusable or dangerous, the buyer is entitled to return it and claim his money back, provided he does so without delay. If other defects appear which make the car unmerchantable, the dealer is obliged to put them right without charge, or to compensate the buyer by reducing the purchase price. No parts or components are excluded from this obligation.

Damage which results directly from a defect will also be the dealer's responsibility, though his liability is reduced if he can prove contributory negligence by the buyer.

There is no automatic limit of one year or 12,000 miles to the dealer's obligations under the Sale of Goods Act, and the dealer can be held responsible for any reasonable costs incurred by the buyer while his car was off the road being repaired. This may include the cost of hiring a similar car if the customer can prove that it is impossible for him to use any other form of transport.

By not accepting a limited warranty, the buyer also preserves his right to claim against the manufacturer if negligence in manufacture causes him loss or injury.

DRAWBACKS OF REJECTING A WARRANTY A customer's legal rights are sometimes valuable, but there is one disadvantage in relying on them and rejecting a warranty. If a defect appears, the dealer may refuse to carry out work on the car or to offer compensation. If this happens, the customer may have to threaten—and perhaps take—legal action to get redress.

Most reputable dealers do not want to tarnish their good name by being involved in a court case—unless they have good grounds for resisting the claim. If, despite this, a court action is necessary, it will take time and usually proves expensive. Even if the buyer wins and the dealer is ordered to pay his costs, he will rarely receive all that

the case has cost him. Most solicitors advise clients to write off claims for sums of less than £30 as not being worth the costs involved.

Many dealers refuse to sell a car unless the buyer signs an order form and accepts a manufacturer's warranty. As a result, the buyer who decides to rely only on his legal rights may have to shop around to find a dealer who will sell on these terms.

## New cars on hire purchase

Anyone who acquires a new car on hire purchase gets the benefit of the manufacturer's warranty as well as many of the major advantages of legal protection—as long as purchase price and interest charges do not exceed £2000.

Even by accepting the manufacturer's warranty the customer does not forfeit his normal rights in law as far as the quality of the car is concerned, no matter what terms are included on the order form. The Hire Purchase Act stipulates that nothing the customer signs can take away his right to claim if the car is defective or, in law, is not of 'merchantable quality'. This applies even when the hire-purchase agreement contains clauses apparently excluding these rights. There is one exception to this, however. If the customer has examined the car, the seller will not be liable for defects which the examination could have been expected to reveal.

There are disadvantages in getting a car on hire purchase—the same disadvantages that apply to any hire-purchase transaction. ☐ Hire purchase, p. 498.

## Buying a used car

Used cars bought from dealers are covered by the Sale of Goods Act unless the buyer agrees to forfeit his legal rights.

The dealer usually deprives the buyer of these rights by insisting that he signs an order form or guarantee containing a clause relieving the dealer of any liability.

Many such guarantees issued for used cars are almost worthless. Often described as 'Our Special Warranty For Used Cars' to impress the unsuspecting buyer, they frequently last for only three months and by careful wording eliminate the claims most likely to be made by the buyer.

A used-car warranty issued by a dealer may include a clause stating that it has been issued 'in lieu of and in substitution for all or any other warranties or conditions whether express or implied'.

When the purchase is covered by the Sale of Goods Act, the dealer is under the same obligation to see that the car is reasonably fit for its purpose and of 'merchantable quality', as he is in the case of a new car.

➤ THE BARGAIN CAR THAT CRASHED *Commercial traveller George Andrews went to buy a small car and told the salesman that he was looking for a second-hand vehicle costing around £100. The salesman took him for a test drive in a 1934 saloon, about which he said: 'It's a good little bus—I would stake my life on it. You'll have no trouble with it.'*

*Mr Andrews agreed to take the car for £120, paying £50 deposit and the balance under a hire-purchase agreement.*

*Just over a week later, Mr Andrews was driving the car when it suddenly swerved and hit a lorry. He was injured and his car wrecked.*

*A motor engineer who inspected it discovered that the steering was badly worn and that various other components were either defective or missing altogether. The car had been driven only 155 miles between the time Mr Andrews took delivery of it and the accident. In 1957 Mr Andrews sued the dealer who had sold him the car.*

DECISION *Mr Andrews was awarded damages of £645. The judge found that the salesman's statement amounted to a warranty that the car was in good condition and reasonably safe for use on the road.*

*Mr Andrews had acted on this warranty in accepting the car and entering into the hire-purchase agreement and he was entitled to claim damages. (Andrews* v. *Hopkinson.)* ◄

The law relates 'merchantable quality' to the price paid for the goods. With a second-hand car this means that the vehicle should be in usable condition, not that it should be perfect. Courts take the view that anyone who buys a used car must expect defects to appear sooner or later, depending on the car's age and condition at the time it was purchased.

Sometimes when a used car is sold, certain faults are pointed out to the buyer. In this case the dealer cannot be held responsible for these defects afterwards.

## Tests by motoring organisations

A valuable service is provided by the AA for members buying used cars. On payment of an inspection fee of £7·50 the AA will arrange for one of its qualified vehicle examiners to test a car and provide the potential buyer with a written report on its condition, detailing any defects which are discovered. All AA area offices have a vehicle-inspection department which does this work.

An examination can be carried out only with the permission of the seller, so ask if he has any objection before arranging the test with a motoring organisation. If he objects, it may be an indication that the car is faulty.

## When the buyer is misled

Anyone who buys a car and finds later that it fails to live up to the promises made about it by the salesman may have grounds for two types of legal action.

**1.** If the dealer has applied a false trade description to the vehicle he will be guilty of an offence under the Trade Descriptions Act 1968. The buyer can report the facts to the local weights and measures inspector (who can be contacted at the offices of the local authority). The inspector may then decide to prosecute.

**2.** If the dealer has given deliberately misleading information about the vehicle, the buyer may be able to sue him for damages under the Misrepresentation Act 1957.

PROSECUTION If the dealer has applied a false trade description to the vehicle, whether or not he intended to mislead, he will be guilty of an offence.

In law, a trade description is any description, statement or other indication, direct or indirect, about a number of matters listed in the Trade Descriptions Act.

It is an offence, for example, to give false information about when the car was first registered or who it was made by. It is also an offence to make misleading statements about its history—to say, for example, 'little used, only one owner' when in fact the vehicle has been used extensively by a car hire firm or a motoring school.

At one time it was common practice among less scrupulous car dealers to 'turn back the clock' on used cars so that the total mileage reading was far less than the mileage the car had in fact done.

This also is an offence under the Trade Descriptions Act. The dealer can be charged even if the mileage recorder was to his knowledge tampered with by a previous owner and not by the dealer himself. Resetting the recorder completely so that it indicates zero does not infringe the Act, as long as the dealer makes it clear that he has done this. Most dealers who 'zero' the recorder meet this requirement by sticking a label over it stating that they have done so.

Alternatively, they can leave the mileage recorder as it is. A label stating that the mileage recorded cannot be relied on as indicating the true mileage the car has done will cover the dealer against being sued if someone else has tampered with the mileage recorder. If, however, it is indicated in writing on the company's official document that the mileage is a true one, the dealer will be responsible for any mistake.

There will be ground for prosecution if the dealer gives false information about any of the vehicle's physical characteristics—if, for example, he claims wrongly that it has disc brakes—or if he claims that it is in good condition when in fact it is not.

➤ THE 'BEAUTIFUL' CAR THAT WOULDN'T GO *When Mrs Elsie Walker was looking for a car to buy she read an advertisement in her local newspaper which said: 'Taxed, tested full year, beautiful car.' Mrs Walker went to see the car at the Cleveland Service Station in South Bank Road, Middlesbrough and liked what she saw: the bodywork was well polished and the chrome sparkled. She decided to buy the car.*

*Unfortunately Mrs Walker knew little about the mechanical side of cars. But it did not take her long to discover that the car was badly rusted, thoroughly unroadworthy and unfit for use. She complained to Teesside corporation's chief weights and measures inspector, who prosecuted the car dealer, Mr Pasquale Dicicco, for falsely describing the vehicle in the advertisement as a 'beautiful car'.*

*In court, Mr Dicicco's solicitor argued that since Mrs Walker found the car beautiful, the description was true. The magistrates agreed and dismissed the case. The prosecution appealed.*
DECISION *The Court of Appeal ruled in 1972 that Mr Dicicco was guilty. Lord Widgery, the Lord Chief Justice, said it was likely that anyone who heard a car described as 'beautiful' would think that, as well as looking beautiful, the car ran beautifully. If it did not, the dealer was guilty of applying a false trade description about the car's performance. (Robertson v. Dicicco.)* ◄

SUING FOR DAMAGES To recover compensation for misleading statements, the car buyer must sue for damages. He will be successful if he can show that the dealer made a false 'representation of fact' about the vehicle. The dealer must have known it was untrue, or must have made it recklessly, not caring whether it was true. He must have intended the buyer to act on it, and the buyer must have done so.

For example, if a salesman said in the presence of an independent witness, or stated in writing, that a car had previously had only one owner and later the buyer discovered from the log book that there had been three previous owners, there would be good grounds for taking action against the dealer for misrepresentation. Even if there was no witness or statement in writing an action could still be brought, but the buyer's case would then be harder to prove.

**Buying privately**
Anyone who buys a car privately may be able to save the extra 15 or 20 per cent commission which a dealer would charge. But he has to be more careful than normal in checking ownership and condition of the vehicle; he has far less protection in law than when he buys from a dealer.

CHECKING ON OWNERSHIP Many people have bought cars from private individuals and later discovered that the seller was not in fact the legal owner of the vehicle. ☐ Buying stolen goods, p. 457.

This often happens when a car has been stolen, or is being acquired under a hire-purchase agreement, and payments have not been completed. In the case of hire purchase, the buyer is usually protected as long as he bought the car in good faith and without knowledge of the hire-purchase agreement. But the innocent party must have been a private purchaser.

Ask to see the car's log book, and be wary if the book is a duplicate or if the seller says that it is at home, lost, or with the registration authority. Check engine and chassis numbers given in the log book against those on the vehicle.

Never assume that the seller owns a car simply because he holds the log book. The name and address it bears is that of the person in whose name the car is registered —who is not necessarily the owner. Log books are frequently stolen or forged.

Anyone buying a second-hand car can ask the AA (if he is a member) or his local Citizens' Advice Bureau to check with Hire Purchase Information Ltd whether the vehicle has been registered as the subject of a current hire-purchase agreement. If it has, he should not buy the car until it is proved that the debt has been cleared. Hire Purchase Information Ltd was set up to keep a register of all hire-purchase agreements.

In addition to making this check, ask the seller whether the car is on hire purchase. If the seller claims that the agreement has ended, ask for definite proof that all the instalments have been paid, including the option-to-purchase fee—usually a nominal

£2·10 to £5·25 which is paid after the final instalment, to transfer ownership.

When this has been done, most hire-purchase companies issue a final receipt or similar document stating that the agreement has been satisfactorily concluded.

CHECKING THE TEST CERTIFICATE If the car is more than three years old, ask to see the annual vehicle (MoT) test certificate, and make sure that it has not expired.

CHECKING THE CONDITION Never rely on what the seller says about the car's condition or performance. A private seller, unless he makes a habit of selling cars, is not liable to prosecution under the Trade Descriptions Act for making false statements about what he sells, and so may be less scrupulous.

Unless you are an experienced mechanic, consider getting an independent report on the vehicle's condition.

PUTTING IT IN WRITING Though there is no legal necessity, it is advisable to ask the seller for a receipt bearing his name and address, the amount paid for the car, and a statement that it is free from hire purchase.

Anyone selling a car should be prepared to do this; if they are not, it may be a sign that something is amiss.

**Making sure that the car is roadworthy**
The buyer has to take steps to see that the car is in a roadworthy condition. Once the car has been bought, responsibility rests with its new owner and driver.

In addition, anyone who sells or supplies, or even offers to sell or supply, a car which is not roadworthy is liable to be prosecuted and can be fined up to £1000. ☐ The law on car safety, p. 39.

If an unroadworthy car is sold at an auction, the owner who is selling—not the auctioneer— is open to prosecution.

This does not mean the motorist who buys an unroadworthy car is automatically entitled to return it and get his money back. Even if the dealer is convicted the buyer seeking compensation still has to establish a separate claim in the civil courts. If, however, the dealer is convicted of the criminal offence, the conviction will strengthen the buyer's claim for damages.

**Getting defects put right**
A motorist who finds a fault in the new or used car he has bought should first try to get it repaired under the terms of any warranty or guarantee from manufacturer or dealer.

Under most schemes, such work can be done only by the dealer who sold the car, or— in the case of new cars—by another dealer authorised by the manufacturer.

A buyer relying on his rights in law should take the vehicle back to the dealer who sold it. If this is not possible, arrange to collect all defective parts from the garage that does the repair, together with a detailed receipt, to present to the original dealer when a claim is made.

## A change of ownership: what the law requires

WHEN a car changes hands, there are two main legal requirements. The new owner must register the vehicle in his name as soon as possible and the seller must notify the change of ownership.

In both cases this is done through the local authority. The new owner fills in his name and address in the next blank space on the car's log book and sends it to the local authority serving the area in which he lives. The new particulars will be recorded and the log book stamped and returned to him.

Often, motorists leave this until they next call at the local authority licensing department to renew the excise licence. This is unwise, since an owner has a legal duty to register the vehicle in his name as soon as possible. He would be liable to prosecution and to a maxi- .

mum fine of £50 if, for example, he bought a car in January and did not register it in his own name until the following December.

The court would probably regard a delay of 11 months as unreasonable unless the new owner had been ill or abroad or had been unable to register the car for some other good reason.

The seller must also notify the local authority within a reasonable time of the change of ownership. He can do so by writing a letter giving his name and address, the buyer's name and address and the registration number of the car. Alternatively, he can fill in these details on a specially printed postcard (VE/70) available at all post offices. The maximum penalty for failing to notify a change of ownership is a fine of £20.

# Taxing and insuring a car

*Choosing the type of policy*  
*Choosing the company*  
*The cost of insurance*

*No-claim bonuses*  
*Renewing a policy*  
*When an insurance company collapses*

THE law requires that every driver is covered by a basic insurance policy as protection for other road users. This ensures that if an accident is caused by a driver's negligence, compensation is paid to anyone who is injured, or to the relatives of anyone killed.

The owner of a car has certain responsibilities even when he is not himself driving. It is, for example, a criminal offence to allow someone else to drive a car knowing that he is not properly insured. □ Borrowing and lending a car, p. 38.

**How insurance works**

Insurance works on the principle that in exchange for a payment (the premium) the insurance company undertakes to compensate the policy-holder for loss suffered in the circumstances detailed in the policy.

## Comparing the cover under four types of policy

**Legend:**
- ● Always covered
- ○ Usually covered
- ◎ Covered at extra premium
- ▨ Paid to a maximum

| | ROAD TRAFFIC ACT ONLY | THIRD PARTY ONLY | THIRD PARTY, FIRE AND THEFT | COMPREHENSIVE | SPECIAL COVER OBTAINABLE |
|---|---|---|---|---|---|
| **DEATH OR INJURY** | | | | | |
| Emergency medical treatment for any person injured by the insured driver | ● | ● | ● | ● | |
| Claims for injury to or death of any person (including passengers) caused by the insured driver | ● | ● | ● | ● | |
| Claims for injury to or death of any person caused by negligence of passengers getting in or out of the car | | ○ | ○ | ○ | |
| Emergency medical treatment for people injured by the insured person while driving someone else's car | ○ | ○ | ○ | ○ | |
| Claims for injury to or death of others when insured person is driving someone else's car | | ○ | ○ | ○ | |
| Emergency treatment for insured driver injured in an accident | ● | ● | ● | ● | |
| Fixed benefits for injury to or death of insured and spouse in accident | | | - | ○ | |
| Fixed benefits for injury to or death of other passengers without court action | | | | | ◎ |
| **DAMAGE TO PROPERTY** | | | | | |
| Claims for compensation for damage to other people's property (including passengers') caused by the insured driver | | ○ | ○ | ○ | |
| Claims for damage to others' property when insured person is driving someone else's car | | ○ | ○ | ○ | |
| Claim for damage to insured driver's own property in his car | | | | ○ | ◎ |
| **DAMAGE TO CAR** | | | | | |
| Claim for accidental damage caused by the insured person to his own car | | | | ○ | |

Before an insurance policy can be issued, the company asks the driver to complete a proposal form in which he gives details about himself, his driving record, the car he intends to use and other people who are likely to drive it. From this the company assesses the risk it is taking, and the premium it will charge.

Once the company has agreed to insure the driver, a temporary cover note is issued and a policy is then prepared. This is sent to the driver, with a certificate of insurance naming the policy-holder, car registration number and date on which the insurance expires.

It is the certificate, not the policy itself, which has to be produced before the car can be taxed or if a policeman asks for proof that the car is insured.

The certificate states the date and time from which cover operated, and a motorist arranging insurance by post should telephone the company before driving to confirm that it has completed a certificate or cover note for him. Simply posting a cheque and the proposal form or renewal form is not sufficient, since cover may be refused.

When the driver changes his car he may have to return the certificate and ask the company to issue another for the new vehicle. With a higher-powered or specialist-built car an additional premium may be charged.

However, some companies issue what is termed an 'open certificate' which does not restrict the driver to one particular car, but covers him for any car he owns or has permission to use, other than sports and high-performance cars. ☐ Borrowing and lending a car, p. 38.

Open certificates should always be checked,

● Always covered

O Usually covered

◎ Covered at extra premium

▩ Paid to a maximum

| | ROAD TRAFFIC ACT ONLY | THIRD PARTY ONLY | THIRD PARTY, FIRE AND THEFT | COMPREHENSIVE | SPECIAL COVER OBTAINABLE |
|---|---|---|---|---|---|
| **DAMAGE TO CAR** (Continued) | | | | | |
| Claim for damage to insured person's car when it was driven by someone else without his knowledge or consent | | | O | O | |
| Claim for damage to someone else's car when it was being driven by insured person with his own policy | | | | | ◎ |
| Claim for damage to car when left at a garage for maintenance or repair | | | | O | |
| **FIRE AND THEFT** | | | | | |
| Claim for value of a car that has been damaged by fire, or destroyed by fire | | | O | O | |
| Claim for damage to property in car, caused by fire | | | | O (paid to a maximum) | |
| Claim for value of car when it has been stolen | | | O | O | |
| Claim for loss of property stolen from car | | | | O (paid to a maximum) | |
| **OTHER CLAIMS** | | | | | |
| Claim for cost of hiring a car when insured vehicle has been damaged, destroyed or stolen | | | | | ◎ |
| Claim for cost of replacing defective parts after guarantee has expired | | | | | ◎ |
| Claim for legal costs arising out of an accident causing proceedings to be taken for manslaughter or causing death by reckless or dangerous driving | | O (paid to a maximum) | O (paid to a maximum) | O (paid to a maximum) | |
| Claim for legal costs incurred with the insurer's agreement for representation or defence following an accident covered under the insurance policy | O | O | O | O | |

and the insurance broker or company consulted, if necessary, to ensure that the policy provides the driver with the precise cover he wants. For example, a motorist with a comprehensive policy will find that, if he changes his vehicle without informing the insurance company, his open certificate provides him with only third-party cover.

If the insurance certificate is lost or accidentally destroyed, tell the company immediately and ask for a replacement.

## Choosing the type of policy

Insurance companies issue four main types of motor policy which are roughly geared to suit the different requirements of drivers.

The four policies are: Road Traffic Act; Third Party Only; Third Party, Fire and Theft; and Comprehensive.

ROAD TRAFFIC ACT As its name implies, the Road Traffic Act policy gives the minimum insurance necessary to comply with the law. The company agrees to pay anyone—including any passenger in the car—who has a legal claim for bodily injury against the driver. The main disadvantage of this type of policy is that it does not cover claims for damage to property. Any such claims must be met by the driver himself.

If paying passengers are being carried, the law insists that additional insurance cover must be taken out to meet possible claims if they are injured or killed.

For these purposes a paying passenger is not only someone who pays a fare. The person who gives a driver 'petrol money' in return for a lift to work or shares the expenses of a motoring holiday is, in law, a paying passenger who must be covered by insurance. If there is a doubt over a particular situation, consult the insurance company or broker. ☐ Pitfalls of motor insurance, p. 37.

Most drivers consider that the protection afforded by a Road Traffic Act policy, while satisfying the law, is insufficient for everyday motoring. Yet there are occasions when, as the cheapest policy available, it can be useful. For example, someone who has a car which is worth very little money and is kept only for emergency use, might require nothing more than a Road Traffic Act policy. Drivers who have a bad motoring record may have no alternative if no insurance company is prepared to give wider cover.

THIRD PARTY ONLY In addition to the basic insurance required by law, a Third Party Only policy covers claims for damage to other people's property as well as for any injury to them. Some insurance companies include fringe benefits, such as certain legal costs, in this type of policy.

Again, many car owners reject a Third Party Only policy because it leaves them to pay for any damage to their own vehicle—unless another driver is at fault and they can claim successfully from him. Where limited insurance for a comparatively small premium is required, however, this type of policy can be the best choice.

THIRD PARTY, FIRE AND THEFT The motorist who opts for a Third Party, Fire and Theft policy has all the benefits of a Third Party Only policy, and in addition he can claim compensation if his car is damaged or destroyed by fire, or is stolen. He is also entitled to compensation for damage done when the car is stolen, for example if the thief crashes it or maliciously damages it.

Although the proposal form asks the driver to state the value of his car, this does not mean that the insurance company will pay that amount if the car is lost through fire or theft. Usually the insurance company pays the market value of the car at the time of loss. If, however, the policy has a special 'agreed-value' clause written into it when the insurance is first arranged, the company pays the value agreed at the time of the most recent renewal.

A Third Party, Fire and Theft policy is generally suitable for the motorist with a lower-priced car, or for anyone motoring on a tight budget who still wants to protect himself as far as possible against losing the vehicle. He has no insurance protection, however, if the vehicle is damaged in an accident.

COMPREHENSIVE About 68 per cent of the motor policies issued in Britain today are Comprehensive—probably because finance companies safeguard themselves by insisting that a car is comprehensively insured before they advance money on hire purchase.

A Comprehensive policy gives all the benefits of Third Party, Fire and Theft insurance, but also provides cover against a wide range of other risks. Most Comprehensives include:
1. Accidental damage cover, which provides compensation for damage to the car irrespective of who is to blame for an accident. Other damage, such as a windscreen shattering or frost damage, is also covered, provided reasonable precautions were taken to prevent it. Depreciation and mechanical or electrical breakdowns are not included, however.
2. Personal accident benefit, which is paid if the policy-holder is seriously injured in an accident in which the insured car is involved, or if he is badly injured while travelling in another private car or while getting in or out

of it. Usual payments are £1000 on death, £500 for the loss of sight in both eyes or two limbs, or £250 for the loss of sight in one eye or the loss of one limb. Generally, only the policy-holder or his estate is entitled to these benefits unless the policy has been extended to cover a husband, wife or family, and the premium has been increased.

**3.** Medical expenses for each person in the car injured at the time of an accident may also be paid by the insurance company. Usually these are limited to £20–25 per person.

**4.** Rugs, clothing and personal possessions cover, which provides compensation for loss or damage to rugs, clothes or any personal property left in the car. Again, there is usually a set limit—£25 is typical—for each

incident. Trade samples, money, documents or securities are not covered.

Even the best type of Comprehensive policy is not as extensive as its name implies. It will seldom provide compensation for loss of earnings if the driver is injured and unable to work. Nor will it pay for the hire of a replacement car while the policy-holder's own car is off the road after an accident. Separate policies can be arranged to cover these circumstances.

**Choosing the company**
For most people, there are two points to consider when arranging car insurance—security and value for money. As a guide to financial soundness, deal only with a Lloyd's underwriter or a member of the British

## Taxing a car

ALMOST all mechanically propelled vehicles have to be licensed—'taxed'—before they can legally be used on any public road.

The excise licence—road-fund licence, as it is sometimes called—is obtained initially from the local authority licensing department. A licence application form, obtainable from any post office or local authority licensing department, must be completed and returned to the licensing office with the licence fee. Also needed are the vehicle log book, insurance certificate and, if the car is more than three years old, a current test certificate. These documents are checked and returned.

Vehicle excise licences are valid for four or 12 months and come into force on the day of issue. They cannot be back-dated, but the expiry date and fee are always calculated from the first day of the month during which the licence was issued. There is, contrary to common belief, no period of 14 days grace for renewal although in practice the police tend not to prosecute a motorist driving without a current excise licence if he can show that he has already applied for one.

Car excise licences can be renewed either yearly or every four months, at the local authority licensing department or at any head post office in the county or borough in which the car is registered.

The log book, insurance certificate and test certificate must be submitted with the renewal form. Post offices will not renew vehicle excise licences after 1 p.m. on Saturday.

A licence paid for by a cheque which is

subsequently dishonoured becomes void from the day on which it was issued.

It is not only an offence not to have a current excise licence; it is also against the law not to display the licence properly. It must be in a position where it can be seen from the kerb.

In law, any vehicle which is on a public road is classed as being 'used'. It does not escape legal provisions merely because it is not being driven, or is not in regular use. It does not even have to be capable of being driven, and has to be licensed even if its rear wheels and axle have been removed.

Exempt licences are issued free for invalid carriages, vehicles adapted for the disabled and agricultural or commercial vehicles which comply with certain regulations. Special applications have to be made in these cases.

A vehicle does not have to be licensed if it is on its way to, or returning from, a garage for the Annual Vehicle Test. But any other vehicle on tow must be licensed.

The registration of vehicles and issuing of vehicle excise licences and driving licences is gradually being transferred from local authorities to a central motor registration office at Swansea. When this is complete, motorists will have to apply by post to the central office, at The Motor Vehicle Licensing and Taxation Centre, Swansea, Glamorgan.

Temporary excise licences will, however, be issued on personal application to any one of 80 local authority licensing departments or head post offices.

Insurance Association (a list is available from the association at Aldermary House, Queen Street, London EC4P 4JD).

Members of Lloyd's have to submit to regular audits aimed at detecting financial weakness; and if an underwriter were to go into liquidation, policy-holders would be compensated from a central guarantee fund. The British Insurance Association ensures that a company is financially sound before admitting it to membership, but there is no provision for compensating policy-holders if a member company has to stop trading.

To get the best value for money it is better to arrange insurance through a competent insurance broker rather than to go direct to an insurance company, unless the motorist has already built up a certain amount of goodwill with a particular company.

A good broker, representing a large number of insurance companies, will advise which company offers a policy most suited to the motorist's requirements and which companies settle claims most fairly and promptly.

If a motorist is having difficulty in obtaining insurance—perhaps because he wants to drive a sports car—a good broker may be able to negotiate acceptable terms with a company specialising in 'difficult' insurance.

These services are free since the broker is paid a commission by the insurance company on every policy he sells.

Brokers also deal with claims on behalf of their clients, and in many cases their specialist knowledge can help a motorist to get the maximum benefit from his policy, but they may make a charge for handling claims.

Because anyone can set up business as an insurance broker, it is better to deal only with brokers belonging to one of the professional associations which lay down codes of conduct under which their members must operate. These associations are:

The Corporation of Insurance Brokers, 15 St Helen's Place, London EC3A 6DS.

The Association of Insurance Brokers, Craven House, 121 Kingsway, London WC2B 6PD.

Lloyd's Insurance Brokers' Association, 3/4 Lime Street, London EC3M 7HA.

Brokers should not be confused with part-time agents, garage proprietors or accountants who often act for insurance companies and earn commission on business they introduce. These people rarely have sufficiently wide knowledge of insurance to be able to find the best policy for an individual driver.

Some motorists believe they can select the best available policy by asking different insurance companies for quotations. But it is virtually impossible for anyone who does not have a specialist knowledge of insurance to evaluate fully the various policies offered.

Motoring organisations, trade unions and other bodies often offer to arrange insurance for their members at special rates. This can prove useful and save the motorist money—as long as the policy provides him with all the cover he requires.

The Automobile Association, for example, negotiates special terms for its members and also offers free, quick and impartial arbitration by the AA Committee should any dispute over a claim arise between the insurance company and one of its members.

### The cost of insurance

How much a driver will have to pay for his insurance depends on how much of a risk he is to the insurance company.

This liability is not assessed in a uniform way; different companies use different methods, so there are varying premium quotations. But all companies take into account some, or all, of the following factors when determining a premium:

The driver's age; his driving record; his job; his country of origin and familiarity with British motoring conditions (although it is illegal to charge a higher premium on the grounds of race or colour); what use the car will be put to (business or pleasure); the type of car; where it is garaged; what it is worth.

While it may seem unfair in individual cases to make some age groups pay more than others, insurance companies know from experience that the most accident-prone drivers are those aged under 25 and the safest are the middle-aged.

CUTTING THE COST If, after completing a proposal form, a driver finds that the premium he is quoted is too high for him, the insurance company will usually agree to a lower charge if the driver agrees to restrict his insurance cover. Such restrictions are calculated as a percentage off the full premium and vary from company to company.

A driver who agrees to the insurance being restricted to himself alone, for example, can usually expect a discount of between 10 and 20 per cent. Most companies will agree to a smaller discount if the insurance cover is restricted to just two drivers.

Premiums can also be reduced by the driver agreeing to pay the first part—perhaps £20 or £25—of a claim. The driver who undertakes to pay such an excess on any claim can expect a discount of between 15 and 20 per cent. An excess paid only when a claim is made for accidental damage to the driver's own car will command a lower discount.

An excess on a policy means that the insurance company will not be bothered by, or have to pay for, minor claims where the damage done in an accident amounts to less than the agreed excess.

But the company should still be informed about every accident to a car. If a claim is lodged some time after an accident of which the company knew nothing, they might be entitled in law to refuse to settle.

**No-claim bonuses**
The most effective, though not the quickest, way to reduce a premium without restricting the insurance cover is by building up a no-claim bonus.

Most insurance companies reduce premiums progressively by a discount calculated on the number of years the insurance has been in force without a claim being made either by

or against the driver. Usually a discount of 60 per cent can be expected after four or five years' claim-free motoring. Each year's discount is deducted from the original full premium, not the last premium which the driver paid.

A driver who wants to change his insurance company is usually allowed by the new company to transfer his no-claim bonus. No-claim bonus entitlements are usually recognised for up to two years if there has been a break in driving.

Typical no-claim bonuses available from most companies are:

| Claim-free years | Percentage discount | Premium of £45 reduces to |
|---|---|---|
| 1 | 30 | £31·50 |
| 2 | 40 | £27·00 |
| 3 | 50 | £22·50 |
| 4 | 60 | £18·00 |

A single claim rarely nullifies several years' no-claim bonus, but with most companies the

---

## Pitfalls of motor insurance

DO NOT give an insurance broker or agent money for a cover note and leave him to fill in the proposal form and arrange the policy. The driver may find that the premium he is asked to pay is higher than expected, or the policy provides less cover than he wants.

If he tries to withdraw and goes elsewhere for his insurance he may find that he gets only a small refund on the money he has paid, because for the short time the cover note has been in force, insurance has to be charged at high temporary rates.

If a broker is left to fill in the form, it is also possible that he may make a mistake when filling in the form, which might later enable the company to repudiate the policy. For example, if he said the car was kept in a garage when it was parked in a street, and the car was damaged in any way, the insurance company could refuse to pay.

DO NOT use the car for any purpose other than those listed in the policy. This is not always as clear-cut as it may appear. For example, the motorist who receives 'petrol money' for picking up a friend's trunk from the station is, technically, using his car for reward. If his policy is restricted to social, domestic and pleasure use, he may be uninsured and breaking the law by driving without insurance.

DO NOT rely on a reminder from the broker or insurance company to indicate when the policy is due for renewal. Most will see that this is done merely to ensure that they keep their business; but reminders can go astray in the post, or a clerical error can mean that a driver is not warned in time that his policy is about to expire.

DO be absolutely honest when completing the insurance proposal form. Insurance companies often cross-check details. Vague descriptions of employment or untruthful answers to questions about previous accidents and claims will invalidate a policy. The company must also be told immediately of any circumstances which may affect the policy —a change of occupation, for example.

DO read the policy carefully. Check with the broker or company any points which are difficult to understand and get a clear idea of what is, and is not, insured and in what circumstances the policy is invalid. For instance, private insurance policies rarely cover the loan of cars for business purposes.

DO check before taking part in any rally, trial or competition that your car is insured for such purposes. Even a car treasure-hunt can be classed as a rally and will invalidate some insurance policies.

driver is pushed back two years on the discount scale. ☐ Getting the best from a no-claim bonus, p. 120.

**Renewing a policy**
Most motor-insurance policies are annual contracts which have to be renewed, usually by paying a fresh premium, every 12 months. If the insurance company or broker has not sent a renewal notice at least two weeks before the policy expires, it is essential to remind them.

It is the motorist's responsibility to ensure that the policy is renewed. Insist on receiving the company's own printed notice. Without it, the motorist loses evidence of the no-claim bonus he has earned—which is vital if he changes companies.

**When an insurance company collapses**
A motorist whose insurance company goes out of business is taking a serious risk if he uses his car even for a few days before arranging alternative cover.

If the collapsed insurance company state

that third-party cover remains in force until it is formally cancelled by them, he is not breaking the law by continuing to use his car without new insurance. But any claim by a third party in a subsequent accident will eventually have to be met, at least in part, by the driver at fault.

In law, motor insurance is an arrangement by which an insurance company agrees to meet a motorist's obligations to anyone he injures while using his car.

If the arrangement breaks down because the insurance company goes out of business, the driver has to meet his obligations himself. Claims which are unsettled when the company goes into liquidation receive no priority, but merely take their place in the list of the company's debts.

Any motorist with a no-claim bonus whose insurance company collapses should ask for a note from them confirming his no-claim entitlement. This will avoid any delay or dispute over transferring his no-claim bonus when arranging new insurance.

## Lending and borrowing a car

ANYONE who lends or borrows a car should first check that the car will be properly insured. Failure to do so can lead to grave financial difficulties, and both borrower and lender may lay themselves open to prosecution.
LENDING A CAR Except in an emergency, never lend your car unless your insurance policy covers any driver, or the borrower is named on your certificate of insurance.

The borrower's own policy, if he has one, may cover him for driving a car which he borrows. Only in an emergency is this likely to be satisfactory. Most policies give cover in such circumstances only against claims for injury or damage made by people other than the owner and the borrower.

So lending a car to someone who will be covered only by his own insurance could lead to the embarrassment of trying to recover from him personally the cost of any damage which the vehicle suffers.

Never agree to accept payment of any kind for lending your car unless special insurance arrangements are made with either your own or the borrower's insurance company. If these arrangements are made with the borrower's company, ask to see his insurance policy and check that the cover is adequate.

Anyone who lends his car to a driver whom he knows, or ought to know, is not insured to drive it can be prosecuted for permitting the car to be driven without insurance.

He may also have to pay damages out of his own pocket if there is an accident on a journey which is partly to his benefit—if, for example, the accident happens while the borrower is running an errand for him.

The owner would be liable to anyone who was injured or whose property was damaged through the borrower's fault, except the borrower himself.
BORROWING A CAR It is unwise to borrow a car unless you are covered by the owner's insurance—either as a named driver or because the policy covers any driver.

A motorist's own policy may cover him for driving a borrowed car, but this will not cover damage to the car itself.

If you intend to pay the owner for borrowing his car, inform your insurance company and expect to pay an extra premium. Alternatively, the owner may be able to extend his policy for an additional payment.

Anyone who drives while uninsured, even though he believes himself to be covered, is liable to prosecution.

# The law on car safety

*Roadside checks*
*Inspecting the brakes*
*Maintaining the steering system*

*Standards for tyres*
*Accessories that are compulsory*
*Checking underneath the car*

ALL motor vehicles must be properly maintained and must not be allowed to deteriorate into a dangerous condition. They must comply with detailed Government standards laid down for brakes, steering, tyres, suspension, lights, seat belts and the exhaust and silencer system.

Both the driver and the owner of a vehicle who allows it to be used are responsible if any of these items are defective.

Although in some cases—for example, brakes and lights—there are well-defined standards, the law does not always make clear what might be regarded as a dangerous condition. It is left to the courts to decide.

A court is likely to consider a dented wing with a sharp exposed edge or a distorted bumper that is bent wide of the body of the car as potential dangers to other road users.

A shattered wing mirror that still contains glass could also lead to a conviction. A driver whose car is found to have defective brakes could be charged with breaking the specific Construction and Use Regulations or with using a car in a dangerous condition.

**Roadside checks**
Only uniformed policemen have the power to stop a car to check it for defects. If the car is already stationary, it can be inspected by certain policemen or by a Department of the Environment examiner.

The examiner or policeman should produce evidence of his authority if the motorist asks to see it. An ordinary police warrant card is not enough; the officer should also have a certificate which authorises him to inspect motor vehicles.

## Points the police may check

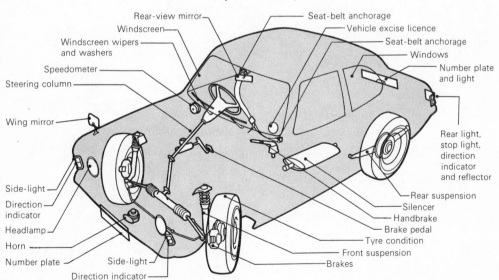

Rear-view mirror
Windscreen
Windscreen wipers and washers
Speedometer
Steering column
Wing mirror
Side-light
Direction indicator
Headlamp
Horn
Number plate
Side-light
Direction indicator

Seat-belt anchorage
Vehicle excise licence
Seat-belt anchorage
Windows
Number plate and light
Rear light, stop light, direction indicator and reflector
Rear suspension
Silencer
Handbrake
Brake pedal
Tyre condition
Front suspension
Brakes

When a uniformed policeman or examiner makes a roadside inspection of a vehicle, he may test any mechanical part or any area of bodywork that could endanger the driver, occupants or other road users. He must ensure that all compulsory lights and accessories are correctly fixed and in working order

POSTPONING THE TEST A driver is normally entitled to ask for the check to be postponed for up to 30 days and to choose where it is to be carried out. He must give the police an opportunity to inspect the car within a seven-day period before the end of the 30 days. But if the car has been in an accident or the policeman believes that it is unsafe the police can insist on a check without delay.

A car on private premises cannot be tested unless the owner of the premises gives his consent or the car owner has been given 48 hours' notice. No notice or consent is required if the police believe that the car has been in a 'reportable' accident, within the last 48 hours. ☐ At the scene of an accident, p. 106.

If the owner of premises refuses to allow the police to check a vehicle, they can apply for a magistrates' warrant. ☐ Officials' rights of entry into the home, p. 293.

When the police do conduct a check they may examine the general condition of a car as well as the specific points governed by Construction and Use Regulations. ☐ Points the police may check, p. 39.

**Inspecting the brakes**
Every car must have a braking system so designed that if there is a failure in any part of it, the driver has some other means of applying brakes to at least half the wheels to stop within a reasonable distance.

Braking efficiency is tested by specialists using an instrument called a decelerometer. If the braking system works on all wheels, it must register at least 50 per cent efficiency. If it operates in two halves, each part must be at least 25 per cent efficient.

HAND-BRAKE EFFICIENCY Cars used before January 1, 1968 must have a parking-brake

# How braking systems work

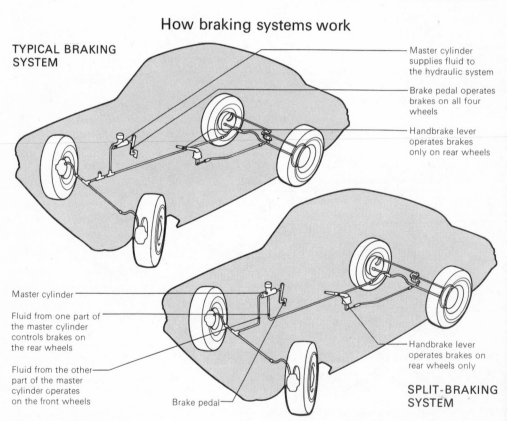

**TYPICAL BRAKING SYSTEM**

Master cylinder supplies fluid to the hydraulic system

Brake pedal operates brakes on all four wheels

Handbrake lever operates brakes only on rear wheels

Master cylinder

Fluid from one part of the master cylinder controls brakes on the rear wheels

Fluid from the other part of the master cylinder operates on the front wheels

Brake pedal

Handbrake lever operates brakes on rear wheels only

**SPLIT-BRAKING SYSTEM**

When the brake pedal operates as a single system on all four wheels, the system must have an efficiency of at least 50 per cent

When the braking system operates in two halves — part on the front wheels, part on the rear — both halves must be at least 25 per cent efficient (hand-brake) capable of preventing at least two wheels from revolving when the engine is switched off. Cars must have a parking-brake which is at least 25 per cent efficient. If the car has a split-braking system, the parking-brake must be 16 per cent efficient. ☐ How braking systems work, p. 40.

A driver can be prosecuted for failing to maintain any part of the braking system.

Never over-lubricate wheel bearings or rear axles: surplus oil and grease may leak on to the brake linings and make them ineffective.

### Maintaining the steering system

The law does not lay down specific standards for the efficiency of a car's steering system, but it states that the system should be properly adjusted and that it should be in good and efficient working order when the car is used on a public road.

The most common case for prosecution is where the police find excessive play at the steering wheel—when it takes unreasonable turning to move the car's front wheels.

### Standards for tyres

All tyres fitted to a car must be pneumatic (that is, filled with air) and be correctly inflated. Car and tyre manufacturers publish recommended air pressures.

The tyres must be in good condition. The tread pattern must be at least 1 mm deep for at least three-quarters of the tread's width all round the tyre. Tyres with superficial cuts are not illegal, but there must be no breaks or cuts more than 1 in. long or 10 per cent of the section width, whichever is the greater, penetrating down to the fabric of the tyre.

Tyres must have no lumps or bulges, and the ply or cord must not be exposed. It is

## Checking that the steering system is in order

Try to move the wheel horizontally to check steering

Try to move the wheel vertically to check bearings

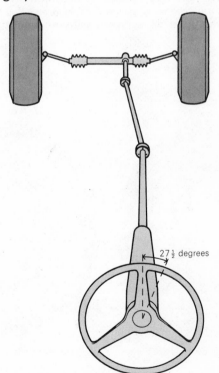

27½ degrees

Check that the steering wheel moves when the front wheel is pulled and pushed from side to side. Check there is no free play vertically

Turn the steering wheel to one side, then the other. If there is more than 27½ degrees movement before the wheels turn, the steering is worn

illegal to fit re-cut tyres—old, worn tyres with a new tread cut into their surface.

MIXING TYPES OF TYRES Three main types of tyres are commonly available: radial, cross-ply and bias-belted. It is illegal to mix any of the three types on the same axle. The only mixing permitted is cross-ply on the front wheels with radials on the rear.

Because of the difficulty of carrying a spare tyre of each type, it is better to use either radial or cross-ply on all four wheels.

All tyres have code letters and sizes imprinted on their sides. Tyres with an 'R' marking are radials. It is advisable to see that the diameter and tread pattern of a new tyre match those of the tyres already on a car.

Never fit spacers behind the wheels to widen the track of the car if there is a risk that the tyres would then rub on the body.

Do not fit oversize tyres to any wheel and never drive a car unless all the wheel nuts are tightly secured.

## Accessories that are compulsory

Every car must have an instrument, usually a horn, capable of giving audible and sufficient warning of the approach and position of the vehicle. Bells, gongs, sirens and two-tone horns are forbidden, except on public authority vehicles—for example, police cars, ambulances and fire engines.

With cars first used before August 1, 1973 the restriction applies only to horns alternating at regular intervals between two fixed notes; twin horns with different notes sounding together are legal, as are more than two horns that play a tune. With cars first used after August 1, 1973, however, the note must be continuous and uniform, and not strident.

It is illegal to sound a horn, except in an emergency, when a car is stationary or to use it between 11.30 p.m. and 7 a.m. when driving along a road that has street lamps not more than 200 yds apart or where there is a speed limit of 30 mph or less.

MIRRORS All cars must have at least one driving mirror, fitted inside or outside, to enable the driver to see traffic approaching from behind. If the mirror is fitted inside a car first used on or after April 1, 1969, it must have protective edges to prevent injury. ☐ Points the police may check, p. 39.

If a vehicle has been adapted to carry more than seven passengers—not including the

# Faults that make a tyre illegal

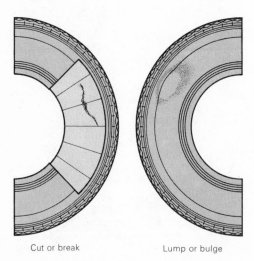
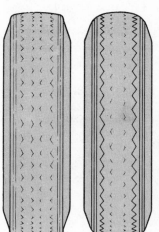

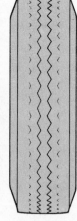

| Cut or break | Lump or bulge | Poor tread over whole width | Over-inflated (wear in centre) | Under-inflated (wear at edges) |

Car tyres must have no cut or break longer than 1 in or 10 per cent of the width. If in doubt ask a specialist to check the condition of the fabric inside. There must be no external lump or bulge

Tyres must have a tread depth of at least 1 mm across at least three-quarters of the width, around the whole circumference. They must be properly inflated. Check manufacturer's recommendations

driver—or if it is a dual-purpose vehicle, it must have at least two mirrors, one outside on the offside, the other inside or externally on the nearside.

Do not overfill a car so that the driver cannot see out of the rear mirror, unless at least one outside mirror is fitted.

NUMBER PLATES The registration numbers and letters of a car must be shown at front and back of the vehicle. They must be on a flat, unbroken surface of the car or on a flat plate, and they must be clearly visible at all times.

The numbers and letters can be white, silver or light grey on a black background; or they can be black on a white reflective plate at the front of the car and black on a yellow reflective plate at the back. Reflective plates must be stamped with the British Standards number AU145/1967. Do not paint existing number plates to make them appear reflective.

Reflective plates are compulsory on cars first registered after January 1, 1973.

Letters and numbers may measure either: $3\frac{1}{2}$ in. high, $2\frac{1}{2}$ in. wide and $\frac{5}{8}$ in. thick or $3\frac{1}{8}$ in. high, $2\frac{1}{4}$ in. wide and $\frac{9}{16}$ in. thick. The driver may choose either style, but it is illegal to mix the two.

SEAT BELTS Anchorage points and seat belts for the driver and one front passenger must be fitted to all cars first used after January 1, 1965. On cars registered since April 1, 1967, the seat belts must carry the British Standards Institution mark.

If the car has seats for more than one front passenger, a belt need be provided only for the passenger furthest from the driver.

SILENCERS AND EXHAUST Every car must have silencers maintained in efficient working order. Exhaust gases must not escape without passing through the silencing system. Never alter a silencer so that the noise caused by the escape of exhaust gases is increased.

The noise made by a car must not exceed 87 decibels (dBA), measured under certain circumstances by examiners. It is a defence to show that the excessive noise was caused accidentally, through no fault of the driver.

It is illegal to use a car that emits smoke, sparks or visible vapour that could damage property or injure other road users.

SPEEDOMETER All cars first used on or after October 1, 1937 must have a speedometer in good working order. It must be accurate to within 10 per cent when the car is driven

## How a car number plate must be fitted

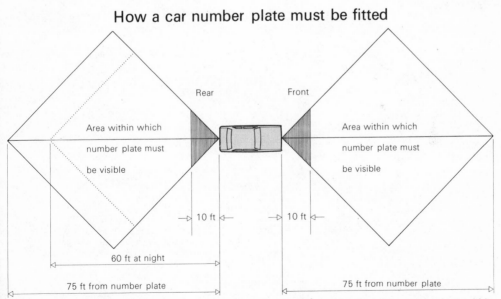

A front number plate must be visible to anyone standing on the same level as the car, anywhere within a square that has an imaginary diagonal line stretching 75 ft straight ahead from the plate. The rear plate must be visible within a similar area to the rear during the day; at night the imaginary diagonal of the square is reduced to 60 ft. The number plates, however, need not be visible to anyone standing within the triangles 10 ft from front and back of the car faster than 10 mph, and must be easily seen by the driver sitting normally at the wheel.

It is a good defence if a driver, charged with having a defective speedometer, can show that the defect occurred on the journey being made when it was tested, or that steps had been taken to have it remedied.

SUPPRESSORS All petrol-engined vehicles on public roads must have suppressors to prevent television reception interference.

WINDOWS AND WINDSCREENS All glass on the outside of a car must be 'safety glass'—laminated or specially toughened.

All windows must be kept clean so that the driver's view is in no way obscured. It would be an offence to fix stickers or pennants in a position that interfered with his view. This restriction also applies to the positioning of tax discs or an official parking permit. □ Taxing a car, p. 35; Problems of parking, p. 77.
WINDSCREEN WIPERS AND WASHERS After September 30, 1972, all cars must be fitted with windscreen wipers and washers—unless the windscreen can be opened. The wipers must be automatic: hand-operated types are not allowed. Wipers and washers must be maintained in good working order.

The wipers must operate so that the driver can see straight ahead and to both sides of the front of the car.

WINGS Every car must have wings to deflect mud or water thrown up by the wheels, unless the car's body gives adequate protection. Never alter the wheels or tyres in any way that would make the wings ineffective.

### Restrictions on other accessories

Mascots with projections that could injure other road users are forbidden on cars registered since October 1, 1937.

TELEVISION SETS It is illegal to fit a television set in a position where it can be seen either by the driver of the car or by any other driver using the road. Only the volume control and the on/off switch may be within his reach.

A separate TV licence is needed if the set is fitted permanently in the car.

### Checking underneath the car

Police and authorised examiners are entitled to check the suspension of a car stopped for a roadside check. Suitable and efficient springs must be fitted between the wheels and the frame of the vehicle. But a spring has never

## Checking a car's suspension system

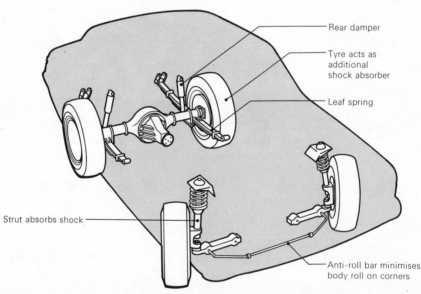

Rear damper

Tyre acts as additional shock absorber

Leaf spring

Strut absorbs shock

Anti-roll bar minimises body roll on corners

The suspension systems of modern cars are varied, and the regulations governing their construction and use are not well defined. The law states, however, that every car must have some kind of efficient system of suspension between the wheels and the frame to absorb shock from the road

been defined in law, and consequently bags of air and rubber blocks have been successfully and legally used as springs.

Springs are not needed on a car being towed to a garage for repair or breaking up. Never lower a car's suspension if it would bring the headlamps below the legal limit. ☐The lights a car must have, p. 46.

OVERHANG DISTANCE The distance from the rear axle to the rearmost part of a car, called the overhang, must not be greater than 60 per cent of the vehicle's wheelbase—the distance from the front to the rear axle.

LENGTH AND WIDTH A car must not be longer than 11 metres, measured from the foremost fixed point to the rearmost fixed point. It must not be more than 2·5 metres wide. Driving mirrors and direction indicators are not included in the measurement.

## Carrying and storing petrol

It is illegal to store more than 60 gallons of petrol outside the tank of a motor vehicle unless a special licence has been granted by the local council. Any quantity of petrol between 2 and 60 gallons that is not in a vehicle petrol tank must be in a special storage place at least 20 ft away from any building or highway. The local council must be told.

Up to 2 gallons can be kept in a metal (not plastic) container that is secure against breakage or leakage. It must bear the words 'Petroleum Spirit: Highly Inflammable'.

## Loading and general safety requirements

Loads carried in a car must never be such as to cause danger to anyone in the vehicle or on the road. Danger can be caused by the distribution of a load or the number of passengers. OPENING DOORS It is illegal to open a car door in a way that causes injury or danger to any other road user.

## Checking a car's lights

Every car must have a minimum number of lights to the front and rear, and their fitting and use must conform to government regulations. ☐ The lights a car must have, p. 46.

When a driver fits additional lights he must make sure that they comply with the regulations. It is not legal for example to use an old headlamp as a reversing lamp: the maximum rating for reversing lamps is 24 watts. ☐ Lights not required by law, p. 48.

## Lights required by law

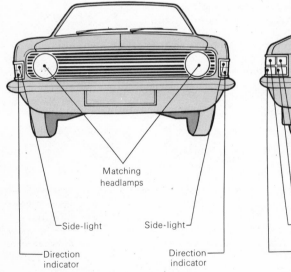
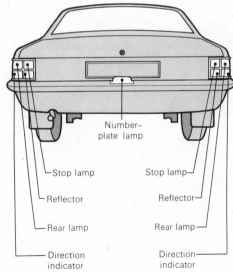

Matching headlamps

Side-light    Side-light

Direction indicator    Direction indicator

Number-plate lamp

Stop lamp    Stop lamp

Reflector    Reflector

Rear lamp    Rear lamp

Direction indicator    Direction indicator

The position of the compulsory lights at the front and back of every car is controlled by Government regulations. Additional lights may be fitted, but they must conform to similar rules. ☐ The lights a car must have, p. 46; Lights not required by law, p. 48

# The lights a car must have

| LIGHTS | NUMBER, SIZE AND WATTAGE | COLOUR |
|---|---|---|
| Side lamps | Two, at the front of the car. Maximum wattage is 7 watts. Lamps over 7 watts are classified as head-lamps. The light must be visible from a reasonable distance; it must be deflected downwards or diffused. Bulbs must be indelibly marked with their wattage | White |
| Headlamps (not required on cars registered before January 1, 1931) | Two lamps that can show a main beam and a dipped beam, or two groups of lamps so arranged that when the outermost pair are dipped, the main beams from the others go out. Each beam must come from a filament of at least 30 watts | White or yellow, but the colour must be the same for all headlamps |
| Rear lamps | Two, each at least 2 in. across if they are circular, or capable of containing a 1 in. diameter circle if not. Bulbs must not be less than 5 watts, and the light must be visible from a reasonable distance. On cars registered on or after April 1, 1959 rear lamps must conform to British Standards | Red |
| Reflectors | Two, at the rear of the car. Each must be at least $1\frac{1}{2}$ in. if circular, or able to contain a 1 in. diameter circle if not | Red |
| Direction indicators (not required on cars used before January 1, 1936) | One pair of front and one pair of rear indicators, or one pair of rear and one pair of shoulder indicators or one pair of side indicators. Must be 15–36 watts. Indicators must flash at 60–120 times a minute | Amber to front and rear |
| | Semaphore arm type | White or amber to front; red or amber to rear |
| | Roof fitting: the indicators must have an area of at least $3\frac{1}{2}$ sq. in. | White or amber to front; red or amber to rear |
| | Combined with side and rear lamps: must have an area of at least $3\frac{1}{2}$ sq. in. | White or amber to front; red or amber to rear |

| POSITION | POINTS TO NOTE |
|---|---|
| The centre of each lamp must be within 12 in. of its side of the car. They must be at equal height, no greater than 5 ft from the ground. There is no minimum height | Side lamps must be in working order even during daylight hours. They must normally be lit when the car is in use on a public road during the hours of darkness—from half-an-hour after sunset to half-an-hour before sunrise |
| At an equal height, with the centre of the lamps 24–42 in. from the ground.<br><br>    On a car used before October 1, 1969 the lamps' inner edges must be at least 350 mm apart.<br><br>    On a car first used on or after October 1, 1969 and before June 1, 1972 the inner edges of the lamps must be at least 600 mm apart.<br><br>    On cars first used on or after June 1, 1972 the illuminated area of each lamp must be no more than 400 mm from its edge of the car | Headlights must be used during the hours of darkness, except when the car is being driven on a road lit by street lamps not more than 200 yds apart.<br><br>    When it is foggy or snowing, fog lamps or a matching fog lamp and spot lamp may be used instead.<br><br>    Headlamps must be switched off when the car is stationary, except in traffic stops.<br><br>    Lamps must be able to be deflected so that their light does not dazzle someone 25 yds ahead with an eye level of 42 in. from the ground |
| Maximum height 42 in. from the ground. No minimum height on cars registered before October 1, 1954. On later cars, they must be at least 15 in. from the ground.<br><br>    On cars registered before October 1, 1954, they must be no more than 24 in. from each side of the car. On later cars the maximum is 16 in.<br><br>    Rear lamps must be no more than 30 in. from the rearmost part of the vehicle | Rear lamps must be so wired that if one fails, the other does not go out.<br>    Additional rear lamps may be fitted |
| They must be positioned as rear lamps on cars registered on or after October 1, 1954. They must be vertical and face squarely to the rear | Reflectors may be incorporated in the rear lamps |
| Minimum height: 17 in. from the ground<br>Maximum height: 90 in. from the ground | Indicators must be optically separate from any other lamp. There must be a visible or audible device inside the car to warn the driver that indicators are operating.<br><br>    All indicators on one side of a car must be operated by the same switch.<br><br>    On cars first used after July 1, 1973, indicators must have two levels of illumination so that when side and rear lamps are lit, the indicators show at a lower intensity |
| No more than 6 ft behind windscreen | Permitted only on cars used before September 1, 1965; light may be steady or flashing |
| On the side of the roof of the car | Permitted only on cars used before September 1, 1965 |
| Regulations for side and rear lamps apply | Permitted only on cars used before September 1, 1965 |

continued ▶

**The lights a car must have** continued

| LIGHTS | NUMBER, SIZE AND WATTAGE | COLOUR |
| --- | --- | --- |
| Stop lamps | On cars used before January 1, 1971: one stop lamp, at the rear of the car | Red, diffused |
| | On cars first used since January 1, 1971: two lamps. Each must have bulbs with a rating of 15–36 watts | Red, diffused |
| Rear number-plate lamp | One. Must illuminate number plate so that letters and figures are easily legible from 60 ft away. ☐ How a car number plate must be fitted, p. 43 | White |

# Lights not required by law

| LIGHTS | NUMBER, SIZE AND WATTAGE | COLOUR |
| --- | --- | --- |
| Reversing lamps | Not more than two, each with a bulb of not more than 24 watts | White |
| Indicator repeater | Rules for direction indicators apply. ☐ The lights a car must have, p. 46 | Amber |
| Additional head-lamps | Must be fitted in pairs of equal shape and size, and be wired so that when outer lamps are dipped the others go out. Must conform to the regulations for compulsory headlamps. ☐ The lights a car must have, p. 46 | Same colour as main headlamps |
| Fog or spot lamps | One | White or yellow |
| | Any number of pairs, fitted symmetrically on each side of the car | White or yellow |
| Parking lamps | Some cars have a special switch to operate only the side and rear lamps on the offside of the car. On roads where lights are required, these lamps no longer meet the legal requirements. Nor do clip-on parking lights that fit on the offside door window. ☐ Problems of parking, p. 77 | |
| Movable spot lamps | No restrictions on number, shape, size and wattage | White or yellow |

| POSITION | POINTS TO NOTE |
|---|---|
| Must be situated between the centre and offside of the car. No height regulations. Duplicate may be fitted on nearside | Any stop lamp must be wired to light when brakes are applied.<br>On cars first used on or after July 1, 1973, they must have two levels of illumination, wired in such a way that when the rear lamps are lit, the stop lamp lights at a lower intensity. The light from stop lamps must be steady, not flashing |
| Centre of the lamps must be at 400–1500 mm from the ground. Their inner edges must be at least 600 mm apart | |
| No regulations | Must be illuminated when vehicle is in use on a public road during the hours of darkness |

| POSITION | POINTS TO NOTE |
|---|---|
| No positioning regulations, but the lights must be deflected downwards so that they will not dazzle someone 25 ft away with an eye level of 42 in. from the ground | Reversing lamps must be operated by selecting reverse gear, or by a switch which serves no other purpose. If a switch is used, there must be a warning light in the car to indicate that the lamp is on. Reversing lights must be used only for reversing |
| May be positioned on sides of car | Must be operated by same switch as direction indicators |
| Must be at same height as main headlamps | |
| Centre of lamp must be 24–42 in. from the ground, with beam deflected so that it does not dazzle someone 25 ft away with an eye level of 42 in. from the ground | May be used only in addition to the car's main headlamps on a road where there is no street lighting |
| Centre of lamp must be no more than 42 in. from the ground, with beam deflected. No minimum height. On cars used before January 1, 1971, inner edges of lamps must be at least 350 mm apart.<br>On cars first used on or after January 1, 1971, centre of lamps must be not more than 400 mm from the edges of the car | If the lamps are lower than 24 in. from the ground it is illegal to use them except when it is foggy or snow is falling, but in those conditions it is unnecessary for the headlamps to be in use.<br>Fog or spot lamps which are positioned between 24–42 in. from the ground may be used only in addition to headlamps |
| May be positioned anywhere on car | Must not be used when the car is moving |

49

# The Annual Vehicle Test

A MAJOR factor in keeping potentially dangerous vehicles off the road is the Annual Vehicle Test (formerly the MoT test) which, by law, must be carried out on all cars three years after they were first used in England, Scotland or Wales (foreign cars and cars which have been used abroad and then registered in this country may be subject to the test sooner).

The official blue-and-white sign exhibited by garages authorised by the Department of the Environment to conduct vehicle tests

The purpose of the test is to find out whether certain legal requirements for brakes, steering, lights, tyres and seat belts are being complied with. The owner must have the defects repaired before the vehicle can pass the test and legally be used again.

The testing scheme is operated at authorised garages throughout the country. Some local authorities have set up testing stations and the Government also has a testing centre at Hendon, in North London.

Garages authorised to carry out the test display a triple triangle sign, and a list of authorised mechanics inside.

In general, an examiner must test a car once an appointment has been made, and he is entitled to ask for the test fee before starting work. He is, however, justified in refusing to carry out a test if:

**1.** The registration book or other evidence of the date of first registration is not produced.

**2.** A vehicle is in such a dirty condition that examining it would be unreasonably difficult.

**3.** When presented or under examination a car turns out to have insufficient petrol or oil.

**4.** A vehicle is presented for the test while loaded and the examiner considers that the load is insecure or a hindrance to the test. The driver can meet this objection by making sure that the load is properly secured or removed.

If the examiner finds that the brakes are so defective as to make the vehicle unsafe, he is entitled to refuse to complete the test.

The test is limited to certain specific parts of the car—brakes, tyres, lights, steering and seat belts. But a car may fail the test because of defects which directly affect any of these—for example, a broken suspension spring could impair braking efficiency.

If the car passes the test the examiner signs and issues a Test Certificate. If it fails, he signs and issues a Notification of Refusal, which specifies the defects.

The car can then be left at the garage for the defects to be repaired or, in the case of missing seat belts, for their installation. A Test Certificate will then be issued for a further fee. Alternatively, the car can be taken away once the Notification of Refusal has been paid for. It can be repaired independently, and submitted for re-test at the same garage or any other testing station, when the full fee is payable. If, however, the vehicle is returned to the original garage to be repaired and re-tested, the fee depends on the number of defects which have to be put right and re-tested.

A car can be tested up to one month before its current Test Certificate is due for renewal, in which case the new certificate will run from the expiry date of the old certificate.

No certificate needs to be in force if a car is being driven to or from a testing station or to a garage where an appointment has been made to rectify defects found during a test. But the driver may be prosecuted if the vehicle is in a dangerous condition or contravenes the law in any other way. A car being towed away to be broken up needs no certificate.

Keep a record of the date of the test and the serial number of the Test Certificate. Anyone who loses a Test Certificate can apply to the testing station which issued it for a duplicate, by giving the serial number of the missing certificate, and the approximate date of the test, and paying a nominal fee.

If a driver has an accident due to a fault not detected in the test, he is unlikely to be awarded substantial damages if he takes legal action against the garage or the tester. Even if a mechanic had been negligent, damages would be minimal, for the test is not an insurance against mishaps. The test simply certifies the condition of the vehicle on the date it is tested, and cannot be used as the basis for an action if something should break down later.

# Garaging a car

*Parking outside your home*   *Building a car port or garage*
*Parking in your drive*   *Renting a garage*
*Making a hard-standing*   *Using a commercial car park*

A MOTORIST seeking a permanent place to leave his car while it is not in use may have to comply with a host of legal requirements, whether he leaves the vehicle in the road outside his home, in a drive, on a hard-standing, in a car port or garage or in a commercial car park.

In the last resort, he may also need to rely on the law in settling disputes with fellow car owners, or in deciding claims for compensation for damaged vehicles.

**Parking outside your home**
Contrary to popular belief, no one is automatically entitled to park in the road outside his own home (unless it happens to be a designated parking area such as a meter bay). Property owners and tenants have no more rights over the road outside their homes than the public at large—they may use the highway for travel. ☐ Problems of parking, p. 77.

This rule also applies to any 'private' road over which there is a public right of way, despite the fact that it may be maintained by owners of adjoining property.

Obviously, anyone who stops or parks a car on the road is not automatically breaking the law—it depends on whether the car is causing a wilful, unnecessary or unreasonable obstruction. If proceedings are taken, this is a matter to be decided by the court.

In practice, the length of time a car is parked on a road, the time of day and the density of traffic tend to be the main factors on which courts decide.

It is no defence to a charge of obstruction to show that the car was parked outside the owner's home, or that it was one of a line of parked cars.

In deciding whether to park regularly outside his home, a prudent motorist should take into account the nature of the road in which he lives—whether it is quiet or busy, wide or narrow and so on. He should avoid the places described as unsuitable for parking in the Highway Code. These include:
**1.** Where there are restrictions indicated by no-parking and clearway signs, yellow lines beside the kerb or double white lines in the middle of the road.
**2.** Where parking would make it difficult for others to see clearly—at or near a junction, a bend, the brow of a hill, a hump-back bridge, or a level crossing.
**3.** Where parking would be a danger to other road users—at or near a bus stop, near a pedestrian crossing, at or near a school entrance, on a footpath, pavement or cycle path, on the right-hand side of the road at night (except in a one-way street) and where it would hide a traffic sign.
**4.** Where emergency vehicles stop, or go in and out—near hospitals, doctors' surgeries, fire stations and fire hydrants.
RESERVING A SPACE Sometimes car owners try to reserve a parking place outside their homes by placing barrels, drums or bricks in the road. Such action is highly dangerous and constitutes wilful obstruction of the highway. The person responsible is likely to be prosecuted.
RESIDENTS' PARKING PERMITS Some local authorities, particularly in the London area, operate a residents' parking permit scheme in certain residential streets.

In effect the local authority creates a no-waiting area but invites resident householders to apply for parking permits for a fee. The permit allows the resident to park in his particular road whenever and for however long he wishes. Although it does not guarantee a parking place, in practice the no-waiting order usually means that there is sufficient space for residents' cars.

A permit must be displayed on the windscreen in a place where it does not obstruct the driver's view of the road—just above the excise (road fund) licence is usually best. A permit cannot be transferred to another vehicle or person without local-authority permission.
OPPOSING PARKING RESTRICTIONS Some people find that the road in which they live is to be turned into a no-waiting area or a parking-meter zone and no special provision is to be made for local residents.

Those who object to such proposals are unlikely to be able to persuade the local authority to drop the scheme altogether. But by presenting a strong case against the proposals as soon as they are announced, and by suggesting alternatives which would create less inconvenience, householders may persuade the local authority to modify its plans. Local councillors, on whose decision the order rests, can be lobbied, and letters to local newspapers may enlist extra support.

Quick action is essential if objections are to have any chance of success. As soon as the proposals are released (local newspapers are usually the first source of such information), residents who object should form themselves into an association to fight the scheme, and should press for a meeting with the authority to present objections.

PARKING LIGHTS Anyone who parks outside his home—or on any other public road—during the hours of darkness should take care to obey the laws about compulsory lights.

If the speed limit on the road is more than 30 mph, parked vehicles must show two white side-lights to the front and two red lights to the rear.

Where the speed limit is 30 mph or less, no lights are needed on cars and motor cycles, so long as:
1. The vehicle is parked close to, and parallel with, the kerb, with its nearside to the kerb (either side in a one-way street).
2. No part of the vehicle is within 15 yds of a road junction.

Where lights are compulsory for parking, off-side lights only or clip-on parking lights do not meet the legal requirements. Anyone who wishes to use them on other roads as an additional precaution is free to do so.

## Parking in your drive

A motorist normally has a right to park in his own driveway, and to take his car on to the road and back. If the drive is shared with a neighbour, however, each householder may be entitled to use the drive only to gain access to an unshared drive, hard-standing, car port or garage.

When two properties share the same driveway each householder usually owns half, and has the right to pass over the other half.

Such a right of passage, called an easement, may be written into the deeds of the properties, may arise from long practice (at least 20 years) or may be created by direct or implied agreement. ☐ Rights and responsibilities of running a home, p. 280.

Where there is a right of passage over a neighbour's part of a shared drive, it is usually restricted to 'reasonable use'.

What constitutes reasonable use is not defined precisely, but is often a matter of common sense. In law, it would probably be regarded as unreasonable to block the driveway with a vehicle for several hours, to bring on to it heavy vehicles which could damage its surface, to leave rubbish blocking it or to start a garage business at the end of the driveway so that it was used excessively. The best way to settle disputes about shared drives is probably to discuss it with the other party and try to reach a compromise.

If this fails, you can get a solicitor to write a warning letter to the neighbour, pointing out that legal action will be taken if he persists in making unreasonable use of the driveway.

In the few cases where the nuisance continues despite such a warning, a solicitor may advise suing the neighbour for damages in the county court and/or applying for a court order called an injunction restraining him from persisting in his conduct. ☐ Three ways of settling disputes, p. 717.

Legal action should be considered only as a last resort. Any damages awarded are unlikely to exceed the legal costs involved, and legal aid is seldom available.

Instead of legal action, anyone denied access to a shared driveway may prefer to remove the obstruction himself. He is entitled to do so as long as he does not cause damage to his neighbour's half of the driveway or to the obstruction itself if it is a vehicle or anything else of value.

## Making a hard-standing

Anyone planning to construct a hard-standing should first make sure that he has the permission of anyone or any organisation with a right to be consulted.

If there is a mortgage on the property, the building society (or other lender) may have to give its consent. If in doubt, check in the mortgage deed, or with the lender. If the house is leasehold, the ground landlord usually has a right to be consulted; again, if in doubt, check the terms of the lease.

Many building developments also require the permission of the local authority. In practice this consent, commonly known as planning permission, may not be required for a car hard-standing. But an informal check with planning department officials is a wise precaution; if work requiring permission goes ahead without it, and the local authority later refuses to sanction the work, the householder can be made to restore the site to its original condition.

If planning consent is required, the householder (or his builder or architect) has to supply details of the proposed hard-standing, including its measurements and the materials to be used, on a planning application form obtainable from the local authority. A sketch plan showing the proposed hard-standing in relation to existing structures is also required. ☐ Repairs and improvements, p. 223.

The local authority may grant the application, refuse it altogether, or allow the work to go ahead only if amendments are made or conditions met. Much depends on the particular property and area where it is planned to build.

For example, permission is likely to be refused for a hard-standing which would completely replace the front garden of a house on an open-plan estate. On the other hand, a similar hard-standing in front of a terraced house in a narrow street where parked cars are a traffic hazard might be allowed.

Among the conditions local authorities sometimes impose are the following:

**1.** That it shall be used solely for residential purposes—that is, for a private car and not a delivery van or lorry.
**2.** That it shall be of hammer-head shape to allow a vehicle to turn around, so eliminating the possibility of a traffic hazard through vehicles backing from a hard-standing into a busy road.
**3.** That it shall be built only from the materials specified by the local authority.

When a hard-standing is being built it is often advisable to bring the edge of the pavement down to road level (if it has not already been lowered) to avoid having to drive up and down the kerb. Some local authorities make this compulsory. ☐ Lowering the level of the kerb, p. 55.

**Building a car port or garage**
To build a car port or garage, a householder needs to check that there are no restrictions on the use of the property which could affect

---

## What to do about vehicles blocking entry to your drive

IN built-up areas, householders sometimes find that vehicles parked in the road outside their homes make access to their drive difficult or impossible.

The best practical remedy, if the owners of offending vehicles are known, is to approach them informally and point out the nuisance they are causing.

If this fails, it is sometimes possible to persuade a local policeman to speak to the owners of the vehicles about the obstruction they are causing. In serious cases, the police may even be willing to tow or drive the vehicle away themselves.

Unofficial 'No Parking' notices on walls or fences are rarely effective since they have no legal force.

In law, there is little that can be done to prevent obstruction of a drive. The motorist affected can complain to the police, and this might result in a prosecution if the vehicle could be shown to be a wilful, unreasonable or unnecessary obstruction. But unless the vehicle is creating an obvious danger to other road users the police are often reluctant to take action—especially if they suspect that they are being involved in a dispute between neighbours.

The person whose access is blocked could attempt to bring a private prosecution for obstruction. But employing a lawyer to present the case in court is likely to be expensive, and if the case is dismissed the motorist bringing the case may be ordered to pay defence costs as well as his own.

REMOVING AN OBSTRUCTION When the owner of a vehicle obstructing a driveway cannot be found, or refuses to move it, the householder is entitled to move it himself.

If the car is unlocked, he can push or drive it out of the way. It is best not to move the vehicle any further than is necessary. Anyone moving a car should make sure he does not leave it in a dangerous position.

If the vehicle is locked, and there is no other way of getting it moved, the householder would be justified in forcing a window—a quarter-light is probably best—in order to get inside and release the handbrake.

Breaking into a vehicle to move it should always be regarded as a last resort. No more damage must be done than is absolutely necessary.

If possible, get an independent witness to watch what is happening. Take a photograph of the vehicle showing the nuisance it is causing before removing it. This will provide valuable evidence should the vehicle owner bring proceedings for criminal damage and civil trespass.

his plans; he must also take steps to obtain all the necessary consents.

CHECKING RESTRICTIONS When a house or land is sold, the seller may impose restrictions on what the purchaser may do with the property. These restrictions, known as restrictive covenants, usually become binding on later purchasers, too.

Restrictive covenants are often imposed to protect the rights of owners of property near by. They may bind the purchaser to use the property only as a private dwelling-house, for example, or prevent him adding to its height.

A common covenant is one which binds successive owners not to erect any other building on the land. This obviously poses difficulties for the owner who wishes to build a car port or garage.

To discover whether your property is covered by such a restriction, check the title deeds (if the title is unregistered), or the Land Certificate (if the title is registered). Where a property is mortgaged, these documents are usually held by the building society or other lender, which will provide information about restrictive covenants on request.

A restrictive covenant need not prevent a householder building a garage, however. It is not a criminal offence to break a covenant; but to do so may give those affected the right to take legal action to enforce the covenant.

A householder with a problem about a covenant should consult a solicitor; the action the solicitor recommends may depend on the likelihood of anyone else wanting to enforce the covenant. If a large number of local residents have themselves built garages, for example, it is less likely that they will object.

Some solicitors will advise the house-holder to go ahead despite the covenant. At the same time they will arrange for him to take out an insurance policy which will cover any loss he might suffer if he were later made to obey the covenant and pull down the car port or garage.

Alternatively, the householder's solicitor can attempt to have the covenant lifted by applying either to the person or company which created it, or to the Lands Tribunal, to have it waived.

The only ground on which an appeal to the Tribunal is likely to succeed is that the covenant has become pointless as a result of development that has gone on around the property since the covenant was created.

GETTING CONSENT As with a hard-standing, a car port or garage may need the consent of the lender (for mortgaged property) and of the landlord (for leasehold homes). The householder will have to obtain planning permission, and the local authority surveyor's department will want to check that the structure will comply with building regulations. ☐ Repairs and improvements, p. 223.

The application for planning permission must give details of construction and materials to be used, and the local authority may also want to know whether the householder intends doing the work himself or calling in a builder.

A site plan showing the proposed garage in relation to adjoining properties is also required, together with plans of the front, side and rear elevations. An architect or the builder employed to do the construction work will prepare these plans.

For a simple car port or garage, some local authorities accept plans drawn up by the householder himself, as long as they include all the relevant information. If the house-holder has recently bought a new house, he may be able to take a tracing of existing properties from the builder's or developer's site plan, and then superimpose his proposed garage or car port on it.

Before deciding whether to draw up plans himself, the householder is well advised to discuss the project with the local authority planning department and find out whether his plans are likely to be acceptable.

When submitted, the plans are first scrutinised by a planning department official. They then have to be put before the local authority planning committee, which usually meets only once a month. It is usually at least a month after submitting plans that the householder is told whether planning permission has been granted.

There are a number of circumstances in which permission will generally be refused:
1. If the garage would be near a bend in the road and obstruct the vision of passing drivers.
2. If the garage would have no forecourt turning space and, as a result, the householder would have to reverse his vehicle into a busy road.
3. If the garage would project beyond the building line of the property.
4. If the garage would interfere with the light or other amenity of a neighbour.
5. If the garage would be excessively large or ugly. Anything larger than a double garage which would spoil the appearance of an attractive residential area would be unlikely to get consent.

Planning authorities tend not to favour the 'lean-to' type of garage, preferring an independent or properly integrated structure. They try to maintain a certain amount of space between houses and garages to give a free access to the rear of the property, but in recent years this has not been so closely adhered to, especially since new houses linked by garages have been permitted.

When granting planning permission, local authorities frequently attach conditions to their consent, for example that part of a front garden must be used for a hammer-head drive which allows a car to be turned round, so avoiding reversing on to a busy road.

When planning consent is refused, or if it is granted subject to conditions which the householder is unable to accept, he is entitled to appeal within six months to the Department of the Environment. ☐ Repairs and improvements, p. 223.

Professional help from a solicitor, architect or surveyor is essential before appealing.

CHOOSING A BUILDER If the householder does not know of a reliable builder, his best course is to seek a recommendation from an architect or surveyor or from a neighbour who has had building work done recently.

At least two builders, preferably three, should be invited to quote a price for the work, based on plans drawn up by the householder, his architect, or the builder himself. ☐ Calling in a contractor, p. 471.

The contract form is usually drawn up by the builder but both sides should retain copies, together with the agreed plans.

The householder should read the terms of the contract carefully before signing. He can strike out any clause which he thinks unreasonable, but this may result in the builder refusing to accept the work. Usually, however, disagreements over a contract can be resolved by negotiation, especially if an architect or surveyor is employed. ☐ Reading the small print on a builder's estimate, p. 472.

The main points to watch out for in a contract are:

**1.** *Variation of plans* Make sure no clause gives the builder the right to vary the plans without your written consent.

**2.** *Changes in price* Ask for a fixed price contract, rather than one which allows fluctuations to cover changes in the cost of labour and materials.

**3.** *The right to sub-contract* Resist any clause which gives the builder the right to put part of the work out to sub-contractors. In some cases, poor workmanship may result and redress may be difficult.

**4.** *Unsatisfactory plans* If you are providing the plans yourself, include a clause that the builder must immediately inform the householder if the plans are in any way defective or impracticable.

**5.** *Legal liability* Avoid at all costs an exclusion clause, that is a clause excusing the builder from legal liability if the work is defective. Only a builder with doubtful standards needs to insist on being relieved of responsibility for defective workmanship. From January 1, 1974, when the Defective Premises Act 1972 comes into force, builders will not be able to escape responsibility for proper workmanship and materials in building

---

## Lowering the level of the kerb

MOTORISTS planning to keep a car on their property for the first time, whether they are constructing a hard-standing, car port or garage, may have difficulty in taking the vehicle over the kerb.

Some householders solve the problem by leaving metal or wooden ramps in the gutter to make it easier to drive a car in and out of their property.

Technically, this is an obstruction of the highway, for the householder has no legal right to place anything in the road. Such ramps may also impede the flow of rain water and hinder road sweepers, especially mechanical sweepers.

A more satisfactory solution is to drop the level of the kerb. Such an alteration requires planning permission, which can be sought at the same time as consent for constructing the hard-standing, car port or garage.

If the proposed access is to an A class trunk road, permission to lower the kerb must also be obtained from the Department of the Environment.

Most local authorities have workmen employed on kerb dropping; alternatively, the householder can employ a private builder to do the work. ☐ Calling in a contractor, p. 471.

Whichever he chooses, it is the householder, not the local authority, who pays the costs of the work since it is done for his benefit.

a dwelling house, including an integral or attached garage.

**6.** *Method of payment* Never agree to payment in advance. Bankruptcy is common in the building industry, and a system of payment for work satisfactorily completed provides a greater incentive for a quick, workmanlike job.

DEFECTIVE WORK Anyone who employs a professional builder to build a garage or car port is entitled, by law, to have the work brought up to standard if it is done badly.
☐ What to do about bad workmanship, p. 474.

INCREASED RATES Because a car port or garage increases the value of property and, accordingly its rateable value, the householder will almost certainly be liable to pay extra rates once he starts using it. ☐ Rates I: how the system works, p. 219.

A householder who is dissatisfied with the valuation officer's assessment of his property can appeal for a reduction to the local valuation panel. ☐ Rates II: how to apply for a reduction, p. 221.

## Renting a garage

Most people who rent garages do not have a written agreement. Without it, the duties and obligations of the garage owner are few. He must make the garage available, but he has no obligation to keep it repaired, or to see that it is secure against intruders.

The person renting the garage has no right to claim damages if he suffers through the owner's negligence—if he is injured tripping on an uneven floor, or if his car is damaged by a badly maintained garage door falling on it. Similarly, the landlord is not liable if a defective lock on the garage door enables a thief to break in and steal the car, or if it is damaged by fire.

The landlord merely has a duty not to deliberately injure the tenant or damage his car. He must also give proper notice of any increase in rent.

TENANT'S OBLIGATIONS For his part, the person renting the garage must pay the agreed rent at the agreed times and use the garage in a reasonable manner.

He is not liable to carry out repairs needed because of fair wear and tear. But he must pay for any deliberate or negligent damage he may cause.

If a visitor enters the garage at the invitation of the tenant and is injured, the visitor will be entitled to sue the tenant for damages if he can show that he knew and should have warned about the danger.

EVICTION If the landlord decides to evict the tenant, the notice he must give depends on the intervals at which the rent is usually paid.

If it is a weekly payment, he must give a week's notice; for a monthly rental, a month's notice. But if he charges a yearly rent he would probably be entitled to give only six months' notice.

A garage owner who tries to stop the person renting it from using it without giving proper notice can, theoretically, be sued for breach of contract even though the contract may be an unwritten, informal arrangement. But unless he is holding a large amount of rent in advance, this problem is better solved by negotiation.

WRITTEN AGREEMENT With the present demand for garages, a garage tenant is unlikely to be offered a written contract; but if he is lucky enough to negotiate one he should press for terms making the landlord responsible for ensuring that the garage is always kept in good repair.

## Using a commercial car park

Vehicles are usually parked in commercial car parks subject to conditions imposed by the owners and posted on notices.

These conditions attempt to free the owners from liability if cars are damaged or stolen, or if customers are injured on the premises. The effectiveness of such conditions depends on the type of car park and the way the customer is notified about them. ☐ When a car is stolen from a parking place, p. 65.

MUNICIPAL CAR PARKS If a local authority makes a condition that, on parking, a motorist must buy a ticket and display it on his car, a driver who fails to do so is committing an offence and may be prosecuted and fined. But he has a defence if he can show that the ticket machine was out of order or that no attendant was present to issue a ticket.

If he has bought a ticket and can produce it he is still, strictly speaking, liable to prosecution if he has not stuck it on his car.

HOTEL CAR PARKS When leaving a car in a hotel garage or hotel car park while staying overnight, it is worthwhile taking all luggage and valuables from the car into the hotel room, even if they may not be needed. This is because, under the Hotel Proprietors Act the hotel has a special obligation to look after the property of guests staying overnight. The hotelier is, in fact, liable for any property taken into the hotel which is lost, stolen or damaged, although claims are limited to £50 to any one article and £100 for any one guest.

This protection does not extend to a car or anything left in it. ☐ Arranging a holiday in Britain, p. 158.

# Getting a car repaired and serviced

*Choosing a garage*       *Trouble with a garage*
*Instructing a garage*    *Disputing the bill*
*Getting an estimate*     *Taking legal action*

WHEN he needs his car repaired or serviced, a motorist should choose a garage that is equipped to deal with his particular make of vehicle, give careful instructions about work to be done and, where appropriate, get an estimate of the cost.

These precautions should help to get the best out of any garage and give valuable protection in any dispute.

## Choosing a garage

The complexity of modern cars makes it essential that major repairs are carried out by a garage with specialist tools and equipment and a staff trained to deal with specific models. In practice, this means that the motorist should use only a garage that holds a franchise from the manufacturer of his car.

Only then can he be sure that the garage is adequately equipped and that it regularly receives up-to-date information from the car manufacturer on improvements, modifications and known faults affecting cars in his range.

Even in dealing with highly reputable garages, a dispute may arise. A garage that belongs to a scheme for settling disputes is therefore preferable to one which does not.

Look for the black-and-yellow 'spanner' signs that indicate that the garage is part of the AA's Garage Plan. □ The AA system of grading garages, below.

There are also advantages in dealing with a member of the Motor Agents' Association or, in Scotland, the Scottish Motor Trade Association. Both trade organisations try to settle disputes involving members.

INSURANCE Find out whether the garage is insured against loss or damage to vehicles in their care. If it is not, the motorist should check his own insurance policy and certificate

## The AA system of grading garages

GARAGES approved by the AA normally display a sign showing one or more black spanners on a yellow background. These signs are intended to give a broad indication of the range of services which are provided by the garage.

ONE SPANNER The garage can adjust and replace all major mechanical components for a given range of cars. At least half of its staff is qualified.

TWO SPANNERS The garage can carry out all routine service and repair jobs and undertake specialised tuning and brake testing. At least two-thirds of its staff is qualified.

THREE SPANNERS The garage can carry out inspection, servicing, diagnosis and repair. It has equipment to detect electrical and mechanical faults and it can undertake high-standard bodywork repairs. Almost all the adult staff are qualified.

BREAKDOWN TRUCK A garage which displays a yellow sign showing a black breakdown truck can recover damaged or broken-down cars and provide reliable mechanical and electrical first aid, at least until midnight. It carries a range of spares for most makes of car.

### AA code of practice

ESTIMATES When work is to cost more than £10 the garage will provide a written estimate. The AA member has 48 hours in which to tell the garage not to proceed; otherwise work may be started. The customer must pay a fair price for exploratory work.

REFUSING WORK The garage has a right to refuse complex work, particularly if it does not hold the relevant franchise. When it accepts a job it must do it quickly and efficiently.

GUARANTEES The garage guarantees repaired or renewed parts under normal operating conditions for at least three months. It undertakes to warn the AA member if a repair is not likely to be satisfactory.

DISPUTES The garage co-operates in settling disputes involving AA members.

and, if necessary, consider negotiating special terms with his insurance company. ☐ When the garage damages a car, p. 59.

Garages are normally liable to pay compensation for cars stolen or damaged while in their care, but many accept work only if they are released from this liability.

## Instructing a garage

The way in which a motorist instructs a garage can have important legal consequences if a dispute arises about what work was done or the way in which it was carried out.

BOOKING A SERVICE When a car is to be serviced, always tell the garage at the time of booking what type of service is required and make sure that any extra work is mentioned. Always ask the garage to follow the manufacturer's servicing instructions. These are usually found in the owner's handbook or in the special service voucher book.

When a garage is asked to follow the manufacturer's instructions for a given mileage or time period there is less chance that important items will be overlooked. A motorist dissatisfied with a service also has a stronger case if the garage has ignored a request to follow such instructions.

ORDERING REPAIRS When a car is faulty, always explain the symptoms. Do not try to tell the mechanic or reception clerk what *might* be the cause.

The motorist who wrongly diagnoses a fault and asks the garage to change a mechanical part which turns out not to be faulty has no ground for complaint if the garage carries out his instructions—even if the car is in no better condition as a result.

PROVIDING MATERIALS It is not advisable to buy spare parts separately and then to ask a garage to use them when repairing the car. The motorist has no chance of a successful claim for compensation against the garage if he finds that such parts are defective.

## Getting an estimate

To avoid disputes about charges, always ask for an estimate. If the garage thinks the work may cost more than £10, ask for the estimate in writing.

In some cases a garage may say that it is not possible to give a reliable estimate until the car has been dismantled to allow a proper diagnosis. In that case ask for an estimate of the cost of such exploratory work, and when that has been completed, for a separate estimate of the repair job.

When an estimate seems unreasonably high, try to find another franchised garage and ask

for an estimate there. If the first garage has carried out exploratory work, however, it is entitled to payment for that work.

When a motorist agrees an estimate with a garage, he normally cannot be asked to pay more. If the garage finds other urgent work that should be undertaken, it should not go ahead without the customer's authority.

The owner is not legally bound to pay for work that he has not authorised. But, in practice, in disputes of this kind the motorist is at a disadvantage, for his car is usually still in the possession of the garage, which may refuse to hand it over until its proper charges are paid.

Moreover, the owner is not entitled to the benefit of repairs that he is not willing to pay for. If he later refuses to pay part of the bill, the garage is entitled to undo that part of the work.

WORK WITHOUT AN ESTIMATE When no estimate is given, the garage is entitled to charge only a fair price for the work that was authorised.

ESTIMATING TIME It is always wise to ask a garage how long a job is likely to take, especially if the car is required at a specific time or on a particular day.

Although technically a garage might be sued for breach of contract if it failed to have the car ready by the time promised, in practice there is little the motorist can do to force the garage to complete the work on time. The cost of legal action in such cases is usually greater than any likely compensation.

## Inspecting the guarantee

Many garages give a guarantee when major repair work is carried out. This may provide for free replacement of defective parts used in the repair, but does not usually cover labour costs. More important, it may exclude the motorist's existing legal rights, which may be of greater value to him than the rights given by the guarantee.

The motorist should always read guarantees carefully and refuse to sign any document that contains too wide a clause excluding liability. ☐ Buying household goods, p. 448.

## Trouble with a garage

If you are not satisfied with work carried out by a garage, complain in the first place to the garage manager. There is nothing to be gained by bringing in a third party until the people involved have had a chance to put matters right.

If complaining directly to the garage does not produce results, however, an AA member should write immediately to the Automobile Association. The AA's team of engineers is often successful in sorting out difficulties and in getting a satisfactory settlement.

OTHER SOURCES OF HELP A motorist who is not a member of the AA may be able to get help from other sources. If the garage is a franchise-holder, write to the car manufacturer explaining fully—but fairly—the grounds for complaint.

When a garage belongs to the Motor Agents' Association, the motorist can write within three months to the MAA Investigation and Advisory Service, 201 Great Portland Street, London W1N 6AB. A similar scheme is operated in Scotland by the Scottish Motor Trade Association, 3 Palmerston Place, Edinburgh EH12 5AQ.

If the MAA conciliators are not able to get the garage and the motorist to agree, they try to persuade them to accept an independent arbitrator. ☐ Going to arbitration, p. 719.

The advantage of arbitration is that it is a cheaper and more informal method of reaching a settlement than suing in the courts. The motorist pays a small deposit which is returned if the arbitrator finds in his favour.

The parties are not asked to attend a hearing. They submit written evidence of their case and this is considered by the arbitrator and his panel of experts. Both sides are then informed of his verdict.

## Disputing the bill

When a motorist disputes the bill, he should take steps to reach agreement with the garage, if necessary with the aid of the AA or other outside body. It is not enough simply to refuse to pay, and take no further action.

In a dispute over a repair bill, the garage

## When the garage damages a car

MANY garages accept no responsibility for loss or damage to customers' cars. Provided that they bring this to the notice of customers before or at the time the contract is made—by posting conspicuous signs or including a clause in the order form—they are legally entitled to deny liability when a car is damaged or stolen.

They do not have this protection, however, if they send the car to another garage without the owner's consent.

Even where a garage does not try to avoid responsibility, there are occasions on which the motorist is not entitled to compensation for loss or damage.

In law, a garage must behave only as a reasonably competent garage would. If no reasonable man could be expected to foresee that a car was likely to be damaged as a result of the way in which the garage conducted its business, then the owner of a damaged car has no claim.

For example, a fire which destroys a customer's car through no fault of the garage is simply an accident, and the garage is not liable to pay compensation.

Similarly, a garage does not need to pay compensation if an outsider steals a car that it has taken reasonable precautions to keep safely. But in some cases it is liable for theft by one of its employees.

When a mechanic steals a car on which he has been instructed to work, the garage is liable—because the crime is committed in the course of his employment. If an employee steals a car on which he has not been working, however, the law does not regard the garage as liable for the loss.

Because the law gives little protection to a motorist who leaves his car at a garage, it is advisable always to check the terms of your own insurance policy.

Most policies exclude cover while a car is used 'for any purpose in connection with the motor trade'. This means that if a car is damaged while it is being road-tested by a mechanic, the motorist's own insurance company will not meet the claim. If the garage has successfully excluded its own liability by posting a notice, the customer is left to pay the cost of repairs himself.

Only by reading the small print can a motorist be sure that he is covered. Ideally, he should try to get his insurance company to provide cover while the car is being driven by a garage employee for 'overhaul, upkeep or repairing'.

When a car is damaged because a garage employee takes it out on a joy-ride without permission from his employers or from the owner of the car, a claim will be met only if the policy covers damage while the car is in the hands of someone without the owner's consent.

☐ What to do if your car is stolen, p. 64.

has a right to keep a car until its proper charges are paid. This is called in law the right of lien.

This right cannot be used to force a motorist to pay money outstanding on a hire-purchase debt, however, nor on a bill for maintenance or servicing.

The garage can exercise its right of lien for repairs at any time. This means that if the car is later taken back for servicing, the garage is entitled to keep it, even when the servicing bill is paid immediately, if it can show that there is an outstanding bill for earlier repair work on the vehicle.

When a car is subject to a hire-purchase agreement, the garage can keep it in the same way. In this case, however, their claim for the money owing is against the hire-purchase company, which, in law, is the owner of the vehicle.

STORAGE CHARGES A garage which decides to keep a car until a bill is paid cannot charge the motorist for storage. But if the bill remains unpaid at the end of 12 months the garage is entitled to sell the car and take the amount owing.

The balance, if any, must be handed over to the owner of the car, who also has the right to demand from the garage a proper record of the sale at any time within six years.

If there is still money owing after the car has been sold, the garage's only course is to take legal action to recover the balance.

**Taking legal action**

When all other efforts have failed to resolve a dispute with a garage, the only redress for the motorist who wants to pursue his complaint and try to obtain compensation is to take legal action.

He should always first take legal advice, possibly by consulting a local solicitor known to him or recommended by a friend or professional adviser. An AA member may also get advice by writing to the association's legal department, Fanum House, Leicester Square, London WC2H 7LY.

Most solicitors advise against court action unless the motorist seems to have a good case that would result in damages of more than £30. The costs even of a simple case would be too high to merit action if the dispute involved less than that amount.

GROUNDS FOR ACTION The terms on which the garage and the motorist agreed that work should be carried out may determine whether there is a good chance of winning a claim.

If a garage was instructed to do a specific job—such as replacing a worn part or fitting a

particular accessory—and then fails to do so, it is liable for breach of contract.

Similarly if it fits a second-hand part when a new part was specified by the motorist, its action amounts to breach of contract and it can be made to pay damages or to put right the defect.

In some cases the garage can be made not only to remedy the defect but also to pay the motorist for any loss he has incurred as a result of its faulty workmanship.

If the garage has been asked to provide suitable parts or materials for the motorist to fit himself, it must make sure that they are suitable for his purpose and that they are of good quality. The motorist has the same protection in such a case as in any other consumer transaction. □ Buying household goods, p. 448.

If, however, the motorist has ordered a specific product by a brand name, the garage is not responsible if that product is not suitable for the motorist's car.

Even when the parts fitted to a car are not themselves faulty, the motorist may have a claim if he can show that the workmanship was defective.

A garage has a duty to carry out work which is reasonably competent for the type of garage it claims to be. In law, this is described as the duty not to be negligent.

Negligence, however, is difficult to prove—particularly if the garage does not claim to be competent to carry out certain work. Suppose, for example, that a garage tells a customer that it has no specialist knowledge of automatic transmission, but at his request attempts a repair to an automatic gearbox. In this case the garage would probably not be liable to pay damages if the repair subsequently proved unsuccessful.

It is no defence for a garage to say that it is not responsible for defective workmanship because the fault was that of its employees. In law the garage is responsible for its workers' actions.

When the dispute is about the amount of a bill, the court will take account of the original estimate and the fairness of any increase.

If there has been a rise in the price of materials during the period in which the work was done, it is likely that the garage will be allowed to charge extra to cover its increase in costs.

When no estimate was given before the work started, the court will hear expert evidence and determine for itself what it considers to be a fair price.

# Hiring a car

*Arranging the insurance*     *The hirer's legal obligations*
*Precautions before signing*     *Long-term hire*

THE rights and responsibilities of a motorist who hires a car are usually defined in the agreement he signs with the hire firm. Most firms charge either a flat rate for daily or weekly hire, or a flat rate plus so much a mile after a stipulated mileage. Occasionally, cars are hired on a mileage basis only.

The driver who intends making a long journey will probably find it cheaper to hire through a firm which levies a fixed daily or weekly charge, rather than pay for mileage.

DEPOSIT Hire-car firms invariably ask for a deposit—usually around £15, although a young driver may be charged more—against the safe return of the vehicle.

Sometimes a hirer is asked to pay the deposit when he makes a booking. In this case, try to get the firm to agree in writing to return the deposit if the hire has to be cancelled for a good reason—illness, for example.

## Arranging the insurance

Hire firms usually arrange insurance for their clients, but the driver may find it cheaper to extend his own policy to cover the use of the hire car. Many hire firms, however, insist that insurance is taken out through them.

Generally, the hirer only is insured to drive, unless arrangements are made to insure someone else as well. Anyone who drives a hired car without insurance is committing a serious offence. If he has an accident, not only will the insurance offence come to light, but if he is to blame he will have to pay for any damage out of his own pocket.

The standard insurance arranged by hire firms should cover passengers' claims but the customer is usually responsible for paying the first £25 or £30 of any claim. For an additional charge, the whole of a claim can be met through a 'collision damage waiver'.

The waiver ensures that the driver does not suffer financially for an accident that is not his fault. Without the waiver the hirer might have to pay the first part of a claim if he left the car in a public car park and returned to find it damaged with no offending driver in sight from whom he could claim repair costs.

The customer may also have to pay an increased premium if he wants personal accident cover for himself. Any driver who extends the period of hire after taking the car should see his insurance is also extended.

Most hire companies have a group insurance policy that covers all their cars. The hirer is not given a cover note or insurance certificate, but he should be given the opportunity to consult a list of the policy provisions. If he is asked by a policeman to produce an insurance certificate he should inform the hire company immediately.

## Precautions before signing

Most hire agreements make the customer responsible for returning the car with all tyres, tools and accessories in the same condition as when received, apart from ordinary wear and tear. Examine the car carefully before taking it away. Ask the representative to note any obvious damage.

People in some jobs and professions—actors, turf accountants and scrap-metal dealers, for example—may find it difficult to

---

### Hiring a touring caravan

MANY caravan-hire firms operate on a common-law basis and are preferable to those that ask clients to enter into contracts imposing conditions which common law would otherwise provide.

Most operators insist on a deposit (usually a third of the hire charge) which is held as security for the safe return of the caravan.

If the hirer's car does not have a tow bar, he should ask the company whether it is their responsibility or his to fit one. The motorist should make sure his car is suitable for towing a caravan. If the car is new he should make certain that towing will not invalidate the maker's warranty.

The hirer should also check to see if his car-insurance policy covers a caravan—both while it is being towed and while it is not attached to the vehicle. It may be necessary to take out an additional policy.

hire a car. There is no point in anybody who falls into one of these categories trying to disguise the fact. The insurance proposal form must be completed accurately or the company is entitled to declare the insurance void in the event of a claim.

## The hirer's legal obligations

Anyone who drives a hired car must observe the law in exactly the same way as a person driving his own car. But it is possible that when certain offences have been committed by the driver—such as using a car in a dangerous condition—the hire firm may also be prosecuted for permitting the offence. But it must be proved that the firm knew the car was defective and did nothing about it.

It has, however, been held that it is the hirer who is responsible for any breach of the rules prohibiting the use of a car with worn tyres. The hire firm would be liable only for permitting or causing its use.

It is no defence for the driver of a hired car to say that the car was in a dangerous condition when he accepted it from the firm. As the driver, he is responsible for the condition of the car while it is in his charge.

Under the hire agreement, the customer undertakes not to drive the car, or allow it to be driven, by anyone 'under the influence of alcohol, hallucinatory drugs, narcotics or barbiturates'. In addition, he agrees not to use the car 'for hire or reward, pace-making, speed trials . . . or for any illegal purpose'.

If any condition is broken, and an accident results, the insurance policy is likely to be invalid. Then the customer will have to pay for repairs and meet any claims.

DEFECTS AND BREAKDOWNS Another clause usually places a duty on the customer to inform the hire firm 'of any loss of, damage to or fault in the vehicle'. He must not 'use the vehicle while it is in an unroadworthy condition or liable to cause damage to any person or property'. The hirer does not have to report minor faults at once, unless they make the vehicle unroadworthy, but he must point out the defect when he returns the car.

ACCIDENTS The hirer is responsible under most agreements for reporting any accident 'at once' to the nearest office of the firm. He also agrees to complete an accident report form within 24 hours. He must not admit liability, but must obtain the other driver's name and address, and insurance particulars if possible.

The hirer also agrees to be a party to any necessary legal proceedings against third parties brought by the hire firm 'at their request and cost'. This means that if the hire firm sues another person after an accident, the customer must allow the legal action to be taken in his name, if necessary, and must agree to give evidence at the hearing.

## Long-term hire

When a car is hired for months or years at a time, the arrangement is usually known as 'contract hire'. Again, the legal rights and responsibilities of the hire firm and the customer are likely to be defined by the agreement which they sign.

CONDITION OF THE CAR It is difficult for a customer to end a contract-hire agreement early without substantial financial loss. So it is crucial to make sure that the vehicle is in a satisfactory condition at the beginning of the hire period.

In law, the hire firm normally has an obligation to make sure that the vehicle is free from serious defects when the hire starts, and could be made to repair any serious defects which appeared soon after.

But they can escape from this responsibility by inserting a suitably worded clause in the agreement. The potential hirer should be on the lookout for any clause of this sort.

Almost as damaging to the customer's interests are clauses which put responsibility for detecting faults on the customer: 'The hirer's acceptance of delivery of the goods shall be conclusive that he has examined the goods and found them to be complete and in good order and condition and in every way satisfactory to him.'

Try to avoid an agreement with such clauses, or get the hire firm's permission to cross them out. If this is not possible, make arrangements before accepting delivery for a qualified motor mechanic—possibly from the Automobile Association—to make a detailed examination of the car, to see that it is in a satisfactory condition.

TERM OF THE HIRE The agreement usually states that the hire will continue for a fixed period at an annual rental, payable monthly in advance. Interest is charged on all amounts overdue, often at 8 per cent.

ENDING AN AGREEMENT EARLY The agreement often gives the customer the right to end the contract early, but if he does so before half the agreed period has elapsed, the cost is likely to be high.

A typical agreement says that if the hire is ended by the customer 'the hirer shall pay all rentals due or in arrear at the date of such termination. If, when he has paid those amounts, the total amount which he has paid under the agreement is less than half the total hire shown in the schedule, he must also pay enough to make up that sum'.

In addition, the customer would have to pay for any repairs other than those made necessary by fair wear and tear.

Anyone who signs a contract-hire agreement cannot hope to escape the early termination provisions, which have been held by the courts to be fair and reasonable.

SERVICING Under most contract-hire agreements, the customer pays for servicing and maintenance. He may also be responsible, in the words of one agreement, for 'making good all damage whether or not caused or occasioned by his own act or default'.

The effect of this clause is to make the customer responsible for the cost of repairing breakdowns or damage to the car which cannot be claimed against insurance.

As an alternative to this agreement, some hire firms deal with repairs and servicing themselves for a substantial extra charge. From the customer's point of view this arrangement has the advantage that his annual outlay on servicing—that is, the firm's charge—is known in advance.

There is, however, a practical disadvantage. Many agreements of this type contain a clause to the effect that 'the hirer shall not be entitled to any rebate of rental in respect of any period during which the goods are unserviceable'. Such a clause gives the hire firm no incentive to do the repair work speedily and efficiently. They know he cannot go elsewhere and they lose no rental income by giving other paying jobs priority over contract-hire work.

A hirer who stands to be seriously inconvenienced or to lose money by delays over repairs, might try to get a clause substituted in the agreement giving him the right to a replacement vehicle without extra charge while the hire car is off the road.

If this proves impossible, he would probably be better off making his own arrangements for repairs and leaving himself free to choose a repairer on whom he can bring pressure to get quick and efficient service.

## What happens if the car is faulty

A FIRM which hires out cars has an obligation in law, unless anything is agreed to the contrary, to see that a vehicle is free from serious defects when it is first handed over to the hirer. The customer who takes a car on these terms can therefore expect the hire firm to provide a vehicle which is in good, roadworthy condition and to rectify any apparent faults which are found soon after hire. A hire firm is entitled to alter these conditions by inserting a suitable clause in its hire agreement. In practice, few firms do so. It is common, however, for vehicle-hire firms to protect themselves against the *consequences* of hiring out a faulty vehicle—such as the damage it causes in an accident.

> The Lessor accepts no responsibility for delays in consequence of breakdown or other circumstances.

**Compensation for breakdowns** A car-hire firm (in law, the lessor) would normally be responsible for negligence in the maintenance of its vehicles, and for the results of that negligence—if a customer missed his car ferry through a breakdown, for example, or suffered some other loss because of delay. This clause protects the firm against such claims.

In practice, a customer who hires from one of the large groups should be able to get a replacement vehicle without difficulty; but under the terms of this clause he cannot claim if no replacement is available. However, without a further clause to the contrary, he is not liable for any hire charges while the car is unusable.

> Lessor will in no event be liable for any loss of or damage to any property left or placed by the customer or any other person in or on the vehicle or the premises of the Lessor either before, during or after the period of rental. The customer will indemnify Lessor against all claims for any such loss or damage.

**Customer's property** A defective vehicle may, in rare cases, cause damage to other property—badly maintained wiring, for example, may cause a fire in which luggage is damaged. Normally, a hirer would be able to claim compensation from the hire firm if negligence could be proved. Under this clause the customer not only forgoes his right to claim compensation himself, but undertakes to pay any compensation which the firm would normally have to make to anyone else whose property was damaged by the fire.

# What to do if your car is stolen

*Reporting to police and owner*   *If the car is found*
*Informing the insurers*   *When a thief is charged*
*When the car is not found*   *If someone else claims the car*

WHEN a driver believes that his car has been stolen, he should report its disappearance to the nearest police station immediately. He should also inform the car's owner, if it is not his own, and the owner should contact his insurance company, either directly or through his agent or broker.

## Reporting to the police
A car which has been moved from the place where the driver left it may not have been stolen, but towed or driven away for being illegally parked. If this is so, the driver will be told the car pound from which the vehicle can be recovered when he reports its disappearance to the police. □ Problems of parking, p. 77.

If hire purchase is involved, he should make sure that the vehicle has not been repossessed by agents acting for the hire-purchase company.

If the car has been stolen, the driver should give police full details—registration mark, make, year, colour, and any distinguishing characteristics—and tell them where and when it was left.

It is the motorist's duty to co-operate with the police. Later he will have to make a statement and, if requested, he must attend court to give evidence against anyone charged with taking the vehicle.

## Reporting to the owner
If the car belongs to someone else, is on hire, or subject to a hire-purchase agreement, inform its owner or the company concerned that it has been stolen.

## Informing the insurers
A motorist with a Third Party, Fire and Theft or a Comprehensive insurance policy can claim for loss when his own car is stolen, but he has no claim if he is insured under a Road Traffic Act or Third Party Only policy. He has no claim on his own policy for the theft of a borrowed car.

The owner should write to or telephone the agent, broker or insurance company, who will send him a claim form. The form must be completed carefully and fully. The

claimant should make sure that no mistakes are made when he fills in the form, as an error or omission might later be held to invalidate his claim.

When the claimant is giving details about the stolen vehicle, he should list any extras that have been fitted and give their value and the total value of the vehicle. If the policy covers personal property left in the car, this should also be listed.

Most insurance policies exclude claims for accessories and spare parts, such as spare wheels and wing mirrors, stolen from a car left parked in the street at night. But if the car itself has been stolen, the insurers will usually pay out for loss of accessories, too.

## When the car is not found
After confirming with police that the car has been reported stolen, the insurance company usually waits six or eight weeks before making payment, to allow time for the vehicle to be found.

While a driver is waiting for his car to be found or his claim to be met, he may be able to hire a car at the insurers' expense—but only if this is provided for in his policy. Always check first with the insurance company if there is any doubt about whether hiring is covered by the policy.

If the stolen car was a hired vehicle, the hire company may provide a replacement. If it does not, no further hire charges need normally be paid.

When the car is not recovered and the insurance company is satisfied that insurance and claim are in order, the company tells the policy-holder what it is prepared to pay to settle the claim. If he accepts, the owner must sign a form of discharge which transfers his rights in the car to the insurers.

In most cases the company will pay only the market value of the car at the time it was stolen, not the value stated on the proposal form (unless the policy is an agreed value policy under which insurance company and policy-holder agree the value of the vehicle each time the policy is renewed). Market value is determined by referring to specialist motor trade lists of second-hand prices, such as

*Glass's Guide* (not available to the public). The market value may be increased if the policy-holder can prove that extras were fitted to the car.

If the company's offer seems too low, the owner can refuse to accept it, and take the dispute to arbitration, which is provided for in most policies.

An advantage of being insured with a company through the Automobile Association is that in the event of a dispute a member is offered free and impartial arbitration by the Committee of the AA.

A member who is not insured through the AA can consult the Association's Legal Services Department for free advice in any dispute of this nature.

If there was a hire-purchase debt outstanding on the car when it was stolen, the insurance company will first meet the finance company's claim, and then pay the motorist the balance, if any.

**When the claim has been paid**
After the owner has been paid, the insurance company has the right to sue the thief or anyone liable for loss of the vehicle—a car-park owner, for example. ☐ When a car is stolen from a parking place, p. 65.

**If the car is found**
If a stolen vehicle is recovered after the claim has been settled, it is the property of the insurance company and is usually sold through the trade.

When a stolen car is recovered before the insurers have made payment, the owner naturally loses his right to claim for its loss.

---

## When a car is stolen from a parking place

CARS are usually stolen from the street or a private garage and in such cases the owner can claim only against his insurance company. Occasionally, however, a third party may be involved—for example, when the car is stolen from a car park.

Whether the park owners must pay compensation for vehicles stolen from their park depends on the park and method of parking.

If a car park is open-air wasteland and drivers park for a fee, they get what is known in law as a licence to park. The car-park owner is not liable if a car is stolen—even if through his or his employees' negligence.

But in the case of an enclosed park, where the driver hands over his car and ignition key to an attendant who actually parks the vehicle, the car-park owner could be liable if the vehicle is stolen.

In practice, however, car-park owners protect themselves by disclaimer notices, which state that they accept no responsibility for loss or damage to cars.

In a multi-storey or underground car park the owner has to make sure that the disclaimer is brought to the motorist's attention, because a contract is being created, and a term of the contract is binding only if both parties are aware of it in advance.

➤ THE AUTOMATIC TICKET *Freelance trumpeter Francis Thornton left his car in the Shoe Lane Parking Garage on his way to a BBC broadcast. A notice outside said: 'All cars parked at owner's risk' but there was no attendant, and he accepted a ticket from an automatic machine.*

*Three hours later he was seriously injured in an accident while collecting the car, and he sued the garage. The garage owners argued on appeal that they were not liable because the ticket drew attention to conditions exempting them from liability.*

DECISION *The garage lost, and Mr Thornton was awarded £3637 damages. The court held in 1971 that where exempting conditions were unusually broad the precise terms had to be drawn to the customer's attention. A contract was concluded when Mr Thornton accepted the ticket, and any conditions not drawn to his attention at that point were not legally binding. (Thornton v. Shoe Lane Parking Ltd.)* ◄

In some cases, a motorist might claim against a car-park attendant, if he could show that his car had been stolen as a result of the attendant's negligence.

The courts have held that no exclusion clause can protect an employee (such as the attendant) from legal action, since he is not a party to the contract.

The car-park owner might pay any damages awarded against the attendant, though he would have no legal obligation to do so. If he did not, it is unlikely that an attendant would be able to pay substantial damages.

He may, however, be able to claim for any damage caused by the thief, if this is covered by his policy.

Damage may not be obvious—for example, the car may have been driven beyond its capacity or without adequate oil in the engine. The owner should have the vehicle examined by an independent expert before agreeing any settlement with the insurers. Automobile Association engineers will give the car a thorough inspection, for a fee, and assess specified parts on a scale ranging from 'satisfactory' to dangerous'.

If the owner finds that the car has been damaged, he should immediately submit a new claim to the insurance company—for damage caused by the thief. But he can do this only if his policy covers him for damage. He cannot claim if he is covered for loss only.
THE 'BORROWER' The policy-holder may be barred from claiming if the car has been taken and later abandoned by a joy rider, or by someone who missed his last bus.

If the car is merely 'borrowed' without the owner's consent there has been no theft, and any damage to the car is probably not covered by the theft section of the policy.

Damage may not even be covered under the general loss and damage section in a comprehensive policy, because the car has been driven by someone who did not have the consent of the policy-holder and so was not permitted to drive under the policy.

The owner can claim only if a clause under the loss or damage section states that cover is provided while the car is driven by someone not included in the certificate and *without the insured person's knowledge*. Damage, as well as loss, is then covered.

**When a thief is charged**
A motorist must attend court if asked to do so when someone is charged with stealing his car. If the vehicle was recovered damaged the driver can apply to the magistrates or Crown Court for compensation. The courts have power to order the thief to pay compensation up to a maximum of £400.

There may be little financial point in making such a claim, however, if the defendant seems unlikely to have the money to pay any compensation awarded.

**If someone else claims the car**
Occasionally when a stolen vehicle is traced, the person in possession claims he came by the car honestly. He may have bought it innocently from the thief, for example.

If, in these circumstances, the police are reluctant to return the car to its original owner, he can take proceedings in a magistrates' court under the Police (Property) Act 1897 to determine ownership.

Magistrates can also order stolen property to be restored to its owner. They can order that the proceeds of the sale of stolen property must be handed to the owner, or that he must be compensated out of any money the thief had on him when arrested.

Such an order is final, but it does not bind a civil court, where ownership of a vehicle may be questioned later.

## Insurance claims for property stolen from a car

THE general loss or damage section in most insurance policies does not cover claims for the theft of property that is not an accessory or spare part. Such property must be covered in a separate section, usually called 'Rugs, coats and luggage', and the maximum that can be claimed is always limited— usually to about £20 or £25.

Cover does not normally apply to money, stamps or securities and claims for property stolen from a car parked close to the owner's home may be barred where a car is habitually parked in the open overnight.

Whether something is an accessory or is merely being carried in the car—for example, a portable radio attachable to a bracket in the car and linked with the vehicle's fixed aerial—can be difficult to decide. There is no precise distinction, but the extent to which the property is permanently fixed would be taken into account in a dispute.

The motorist's main problem is to decide whether it is worth claiming, because of the effect on his no-claim bonus. □ Getting the best from a no-claim bonus, p. 120.

Moreover, all insurance policies provide that the insured driver must take reasonable steps to safeguard his car against loss or damage. This requirement may extend to goods left in the vehicle, and if the owner has been careless his insurers could refuse to cover the loss.

# Using a car for work

*Dangers of inadequate insurance*　　　*Driving in the course of work*
*Getting the right cover*　　　　　　　*Using a car in your own business*
*Driving to and from work*　　　　　　*Driving the firm's car*

ANYONE who uses his car in the course of his work, or to drive to and from work, should make sure that he is adequately insured. Most insurance policies for private cars, even comprehensive ones, provide cover when the car is used 'for social, domestic and pleasure purposes only'. They do not include using a car for work.

Even a single exceptional journey, such as driving an injured workmate to hospital, could be classed as outside normal insurance cover.

□ Taxing and insuring a car, p. 32.

Using a car for a purpose for which it is not insured can have grave consequences. The driver can be prosecuted for driving without insurance. If there is an accident, his insurance company may be entitled to refuse to meet claims and he may be personally liable to pay enormous sums in damages to those who are injured, or whose property is damaged. And if he is using his employer's car for an unauthorised purpose, he can be dismissed without notice.

**Getting the right cover**
When arranging insurance a driver must ensure that the policy covers his car for the purpose for which he intends to use it. Policies are generally limited to a particular class or classes of use, and the driver cannot use the car in any other way without breaking the law.

The purposes for which a vehicle is insured are usually shown on the Certificate of Insurance; this should be checked against the policy itself, since this is the authoritative document.

A typical certificate contains a list of classes of use in numerical or alphabetical order, and has words such as 'limitations as to use' followed by the numbers or figures of the classes covered. Typical classes are:
1. Use for social, domestic and pleasure purposes.
2. Use by the policyholder in person in connection with his business.
3. Use in connection with the policyholder's business.
4. Use for the business of the policyholder's employer or partner.

When the cover note or certificate is issued by the company, make sure the right cover has been given. If not, have it amended.

DRIVING TO AND FROM WORK An employee who uses his car simply to get to and from work will usually be adequately covered if his policy is restricted to 'social, domestic and pleasure use only'.

Some insurers specifically ask if the car is to be used for driving to and from work and charge a slightly higher premium if it is.

Social, domestic and pleasure cover should also allow a driver to give other people a lift to and from work—as long as he is not paid for doing so, either by the people themselves or the employer. Once any sort of payment is made, even on an informal 'petrol money' basis, the car is, in insurance terms, being used 'for hire or reward'. This is outside the scope of normal insurance and arrangements must be made with the insurance company for cover to be extended. □ Pitfalls of motor insurance, p. 37.

DRIVING IN THE COURSE OF WORK An employee who uses his own car for journeys between his employer's premises and the place where he is working—for example, a carpet fitter travelling to customers' homes— should extend his policy to cover the use of his car on his employer's business.

USING A CAR IN YOUR OWN BUSINESS A self-employed person who uses his car on business trips should arrange cover for use in connection with his business. This will also cover an employee using the car with his consent, but not a business partner.

A self-employed person who is a company director requires cover for using the car on his employer's business, not his own. This is because, strictly speaking, the company director is an employee of the company, even if he virtually owns it.

DRIVING THE FIRM'S CAR An employee provided with a firm's car and allowed to use it for his own pleasure will probably find that insurance is arranged by his firm. But he should check that it covers private as well as business use. Some firms allow an employee's wife to be included; others restrict such cover to emergencies only.

# Signs, lines and signals

*Signs and their legal significance*  *Signals given by police*
*What white lines indicate*  *Signals at level crossings*
*How lights control traffic*

THE police and highway authorities (the borough, county and urban district councils) are the only bodies authorised to erect road signs or traffic lights or to paint lines on the road. Regulations by the Secretary of State for the Environment stipulate the exact size, shape and colour of road signs.

People who erect road signs outside their own property—for instance, 'No Parking', 'No Entry' or 'No Turning'—are acting unofficially. They are even liable to prosecution, though this rarely happens. In practice, unofficial signs may serve as a deterrent but they cannot be enforced by law.

### Signs and their legal significance
Official road signs are divided into two main groups—those that instruct and those that warn. A motorist can be prosecuted for

ignoring a sign in the first group, which includes such signs as 'Stop', 'Turn Left', 'No Right Turn' and 'No Entry'.

It makes no difference whether or not it was safe to ignore the sign. Motorists have been prosecuted, for instance, for not stopping at a 'Stop' sign (the word 'Stop' inside a red triangle) even though they could see that the road ahead was clear and they crossed the white lines very slowly.

But it does make a difference if the sign itself fails to conform to regulations. A motorist accused of not complying with a sign's instruction can win his case if he shows that the sign was somehow defective.

► THE CASE OF THE CRYPTIC SIGNS *Mr David James parked on the east side of Queen's Gardens, Brighton on Monday, November 15,*

## Traffic signs that must be obeyed

Traffic signs that must be obeyed are usually circular with a red border or blue with a white rim. The main exception is the compulsory 'Give Way' sign—an inverted red triangle. To disobey these signs, even when there is no danger, is an offence. Although rectangular signs give only a warning, if a motorist disobeys them and causes an accident he could be prosecuted for careless driving

Stop and give way

Give way to traffic on major road

Figures show maximum speed limit

Maximum speed limit 70 mph

Stop for accident or traffic check

Stop for children crossing

No entry (usually one-way)

Give way to oncoming vehicles

All vehicles prohibited (both ways)

No cycling or mopeds allowed

Lorries prohibited

All motor vehicles prohibited

No overtaking

No right turn (reversed for left)

*1965. Signs in the road indicated only that it was covered by an 'alternative day waiting' order. But parking was in fact forbidden on that side of the road in those weeks in which Monday fell on an odd date. Mr James was prosecuted for illegal parking.*

DECISION *He was found not guilty. The court held that he could not be convicted because the signs failed to make it clear when parking was forbidden. (James v. Cavey.)* ◄

A motorist is not expected to comply with a sign he cannot see, however—a non-reflective sign that is not lit at night or one that is obscured by an overgrown hedgerow, for instance. It is unlikely that a court would punish a motorist for not observing such a sign. But if an accident resulted because a motorist did not take the care demanded on a stretch of road, he could be prosecuted for driving without due care and attention or for dangerous driving. Whether or not the signs could be seen would be immaterial.

Road signs in the other group usually warn of a specific hazard or danger ahead. These signs are now usually in the form of a self-explanatory symbol.

Motorists cannot be prosecuted merely for ignoring warning signs. But evidence that a sign was disregarded can support a prosecution for another motoring offence.

### What white lines indicate

LINES ACROSS THE ROAD Two broken white lines at junctions indicate 'give way to traffic on the major road'. On roundabouts, a single broken white line means 'give way to traffic on (or entering) the roundabout'.

Two solid white lines accompany a 'Stop' sign, and cars must halt at the lines until it is safe to move out. A single solid white line is painted at traffic lights or police controls. Cars must halt at the line until the lights, a policeman or a traffic warden signals that they can move out.

LINES ALONG THE ROAD White lines that run along the road, dividing the traffic into lanes, are either single or double.

There are three types of single white lines:
1. Short white lines with fairly large gaps between them divide roads into driving lanes for traffic travelling in the same direction.
2. Broken white lines the same length as the gaps between them divide the road for traffic travelling in opposite directions.
3. Long lines with short gaps between them

Figures show minimum speed limit

Ahead only

Turn left ahead (reversed for right)

Turn left only (reversed for right)

Keep left (reversed for right)

No waiting and loading—times and directions

Roundabout traffic circulation

Compulsory route for cycles and mopeds

Police signs usually erected when police are directing traffic

Times of limited waiting

No stopping on days and at times shown

No U-turns

Maximum width

Maximum height

Maximum weight

No waiting

No stopping on clearway

are designed to warn drivers not to cross them without taking extreme care.

There are three kinds of double white lines:
**1.** Unbroken double white lines are normally painted on the road at hills, bends or narrow stretches when it is essential for each line of traffic to keep to its own side of the road. These lines can be crossed only to gain access to property on the other side or to make a right turn into another road. Motorists who cross or straddle them for any other reason can be prosecuted and fined.

**2.** An unbroken white line running parallel with a line of short broken white markings means that motorists must not cross if the unbroken line is on their side of the road. But drivers with the broken line on their side of the road are allowed to straddle or cross the line if it is safe to do so.

**3.** Diagonal white stripes running across part

# Markings across and along the road

## IN THE CENTRE OF THE ROAD

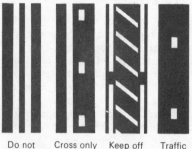

| Do not cross or straddle | Cross only if broken line nearer | Keep off marked area | Traffic lane line | Road centre line | Warning line |

## ACROSS THE ROAD

Stop before signals or police control

Stop line before a Stop sign

Give way at double line at junctions, and at single line at roundabouts

## AT THE EDGE OF THE ROAD

Lines indicating the edge of the road

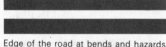

Edge of the road at bends and hazards

Road edge at junction with give way lines

Edge of road at junctions and lay-bys

Road markings indicating area around the entrance to a school. Marked area should be kept clear of stationary vehicles

## JUNCTION WARNING

Drivers must give way

## BOX JUNCTION

Do not enter the box junction unless your exit is clear

## ZIG-ZAG CROSSING

Stop at the broken line before the zebra markings if pedestrians are crossing. Do not overtake, wait or park within the zig-zag markings

of the centre of the road and bounded by unbroken double white lines mark out an area that must not be entered.

Motorists are allowed to cross the unbroken white lines and the diagonal stripes to avoid an accident or to pass a vehicle that has broken down or is parked or stationary.

White line markings that fail to comply with the regulations cannot form the basis of a successful prosecution.

➤ THE MEANINGLESS LINES *Magistrates fined Mr Davies after he had pleaded not guilty to failing to keep to the left of a continuous white line while he was overtaking a lorry. He appealed to the Divisional Court.*
DECISION *Mr Davies was able to show that the road markings he was supposed to have disobeyed consisted of two continuous white lines with another intermittent line between. This marking, he held, was not a proper road sign at all. The*

## Motorway and pelican-crossing signals

### BESIDE THE ROAD

### EARLIER-TYPE SIGNS

Signs at entrances advise maximum speed. If the flashing amber lights change to flashing red, stop at the signal

Signs on the central reservation may show maximum speed or (as here) indicate that a lane ahead is closed

Flashing amber lights show that the advised maximum speed is 30 mph and warn of dangers ahead, such as fog

### ABOVE THE LANES

This sign advises on maximum speed. If the flashing amber lights change to flashing red, motorists must stop at the sign

Motorists should move to lane on the left (reversed for move right)

Leave motorway at the first exit point that lies ahead

Restrictions at an end; lane ahead is clear (also beside road)

### PELICAN CROSSINGS

At pelican crossings, the pedestrian controls the lights by means of a push-button. The difference, compared with normal traffic lights, is that the motorist does not see a red-with-amber before the green light, but a flashing amber. This means he can proceed, but must give priority to pedestrians

Green means that drivers have priority to cross

Amber means stop, unless it is unsafe to do so

Red means stop— pedestrians have priority

Flashing amber means give way to pedestrians

*court agreed, and ruled that because the marks on the road failed to comply with regulations laid down for road signs they did not, in fact, constitute a sign. The appeal was upheld. (Davies v. Heatley.)* ◄

PEDESTRIAN CROSSINGS Black-and-white stripes painted across the road indicate pedestrian crossings, known as zebra crossings. They have orange beacons on either side of the road, and lines of studs set across the left-hand side of the road on either side of the crossing. It is an offence to park between the crossing and the studs.

Some pedestrian crossings also have zigzag markings before and after them. Drivers are not allowed to stop or park within the lines, except to let pedestrians cross. This is to eliminate dangers that might be caused by overtaking.

Pedestrians have precedence over all vehicles on zebra crossings. Motorists who fail to stop for them commit an offence.

Some pedestrian crossings are divided by a central island. In this case, the law regards the two sections as separate crossings. A motorist does not have to stop if someone appears to be waiting to use the crossing, but he must stop immediately if any pedestrian steps on to it. A motorist can be sure of not

committing an offence only if he approaches so slowly that he can stop immediately if any pedestrian suddenly decides to use it.

Signals given by a policeman or traffic warden controlling traffic take precedence over crossing regulations.

**How lights control traffic**
Traffic lights operate in the sequence: red ('stop'), red-with-amber ('wait'), green ('go'), followed by amber ('be ready to stop'), and red again.

Every vehicle must obey red and amber traffic lights. This rule includes police cars, ambulances, fire engines or even someone pushing a barrow or a bicycle in the road. Many motorists start to move forward over the white line when the traffic lights show red-with-amber. This is an offence, for a driver must not cross the white stop line at traffic lights until green shows. Some motorists also cross after the green changes to amber. In law they are obliged to stop, unless to do so would cause an accident.

The way in which the courts approach this problem is illustrated in two cases:

► GREEN DID NOT MEAN GO *Motorist Mr Kemp entered a five-way junction when lights turned green in his favour, and struck and*

## Signals at automatic rail crossings

Automatic half-barrier crossings have barriers across the left side of the road. Flashing red lights and bells warn that the barriers are about to fall. Motorists must then wait at the stop line, but if they are actually on the crossing they must keep going. They must not cross once the signals begin, or zigzag round the barriers. If the red lights continue to flash after a train has passed, another train is due

*injured a cyclist, Mr Radburn, who sued him.*
DECISION *Mr Kemp was ordered to pay damages to the cyclist. The Court of Appeal held that even though the lights were green he should not have entered the junction unless it was safe to do so. He might have avoided total responsibility if he could have shown that Mr Radburn would have seen his car, had he been keeping a proper lookout, but he had not shown this. (Radburn v. Kemp.)* ◄

► QUARREL BLOCKED JUNCTION *Mr Sudds entered a junction on a green light and ran into a car crossing on red. The second car was continuing its passage across after having to wait while another driver blocked the junction to argue with someone else. Mr Sudds sued the driver of the car he struck.*
DECISION *Mr Sudds won his case. The court held that he was in the right, although no driver should enter a junction, even on a green light, if there is an obstruction. In this case, the second driver's car was far enough back for Mr Sudds to assume that it would not move forward when the lights changed. (Sudds v. Hanscombe.)* ◄

Frequently, after collisions at traffic lights, both drivers will swear on oath in court that the lights were in their favour. Both, in fact, could be in the wrong if one started too quickly and the other tried to jump the lights.

It is difficult for courts to apportion blame in this type of accident unless there is evidence from independent witnesses. In civil cases, when one motorist claims against another in this situation, a judge may decide that the claim has not succeeded, or may decide to apportion the blame between both drivers. Courts have ruled that a driver who enters a crossing too fast as soon as the green light shows and hits another car is guilty of driving without due care and attention. The green light is not an order to proceed, as the red light is an order to stop. Motorists should go forward only if there is no danger to any road-user or pedestrian anywhere on the junction.

Traffic lights sometimes break down and keep motorists waiting against the red light. In theory, a driver should leave his car, find a policeman and ask him to control the crossing. If this is not practicable, motorists should wait until they are sure the lights are out of order and then cross cautiously.
PELICAN CROSSINGS One type of pedestrian crossing controlled by lights is the pelican crossing. The lights operate mainly in the same way as traffic lights but include a flashing amber phase. While this is operating,

motorists can go through if the crossing is clear but must give way to pedestrians.
BOX JUNCTIONS Jams frequently build up at lights. Box junctions are an attempt to reduce this congestion. They have a cross-hatch of diagonal yellow lines painted on the road junction, marking out an area that must not be entered by a driver—even if the lights are green—unless the road is clear enough for him to be able to leave the junction.
TRAFFIC CONTROL AT ROADWORKS When roadworks block one side of a road, temporary traffic lights may be set up. These lights must be obeyed in exactly the same way as ordinary traffic lights.

Sometimes the signals at the scene of roadworks are given by workmen holding up signs with the words 'Stop' on a red background on one side, and the word 'Go' on a green background on the other. To disobey a signal given by a workman is not an offence in itself. It could, however, result in a prosecution for dangerous driving or careless driving if an accident happened or was likely because a motorist ignored such a signal.

### Signals given by police
It is an offence to disobey signals by police officers, and their signals overrule all other road signals and markings. But motorists must give precedence to any pedestrians before they obey a police officer's signal.

### Signals at level crossings
The United Kingdom has three types of level crossing—open level crossings, those with gates or full barriers and the automatic half-barrier level crossing.

Some open level crossings have flashing red lights. There are also red flashing lights on level crossings with gates and barriers. Drivers must stop as soon as they start to flash.

Some unmanned crossings of this type have small green and red warning lights. The red light means stop. If the green light is showing, a driver should open both gates, drive across and close both gates quickly.

Automatic level crossings have half barriers across the left side of the road. Drivers must stop when the red flashing lights and bells warn that the barrier is about to come down. A telephone is provided to contact the nearest signal box in an emergency.

To ignore or disregard any of these signs and instructions is in itself an offence. Any driver who does so is also liable to be prosecuted for driving without due care and attention should an accident happen or be made likely to happen by his actions.

# Road safety and the law

ONE of the main purposes of motoring legislation is to make the roads safer. The criminal law attempts to reduce the dangers of motoring by setting standards of vehicle construction and maintenance, and by penalising drivers who cause or are likely to cause injury or damage.

But to what extent can the law succeed in this aim of cutting down accidents and reducing the dangers of motoring?

Scientific investigation of road accidents shows the strengths and limitations of the law in promoting road safety; it also indicates how a prudent driver can reduce the chances of becoming involved in an accident himself.

### Three causes of accidents
Traffic authorities tend to blame road accidents on the recklessness, stupidity or human error of drivers. Closer examination shows that the causes of many road accidents are more complex than this.

Driving involves three factors which interact on each other—the driver, the vehicle and the driving environment (the road, traffic volume, weather, etc.). A team of specialists from the Government's Transport and Road Research Laboratory (T.R.R.L.) conducted a detailed investigation in 1968–9 in an attempt to show the part played by these factors in 247 accidents.
*The driver's conduct* was a contributing factor in 74 per cent of the accidents.
*The vehicle's condition or design* was a contributing factor in 25 per cent.
*Driving environment* was a contributing factor in 28 per cent. (Since several factors often contribute to a single accident, percentages total more than 100 per cent.)

### Accidents due to bad driving
Accidents caused at least partly by the driver's conduct may be due to one or more of a number of factors, including lack of skill, attitude to driving, failure of concentration, tiredness and poor health.
THE DRIVER'S SKILL Research results confirm the part played in accidents by lack of skill. Without attributing blame, police reports show that over 10 per cent of accidents

causing injury in 1970 happened when vehicles were turning right or waiting to turn. Nearly 10 per cent more involved overtaking.

The law tries to set minimum standards of driving competence by laying down that no one is issued with a full driving licence until he has passed the driving test. If he commits an offence which throws serious doubt on his competence to drive, he can be disqualified.

The law further encourages good driving through the Highway Code. All changes in the Code must be approved by Parliament, but the Code does not have legal force. The Road Traffic Act 1972 says that failure to observe the Code is not a criminal offence, but can be used as evidence tending to show that a driver was legally at fault.

➤ POLICE CAR DISOBEYED HIGHWAY CODE
*In 1938 a police car overtaking two lines of traffic at a crossroads collided with a van which had gone through a red traffic light. The Highway Code of the day advised against overtaking at crossroads.*

*The police officer, Mr Stanley Reeves, suffered severe injuries. He sued for damages. The van owners, Joseph Eva Ltd, defended the action by claiming that the police car driver was at fault in disobeying the Highway Code.*
DECISION *Mr Reeves was awarded £3000 damages. The court held that he was not to blame because he complied with traffic light regulations and these took precedence over the Highway Code. (Joseph Eva Ltd v. Reeves.)* ◄

THE DRIVER'S ATTITUDE Perhaps the most important aspect of safe driving over which the law has little direct control is the driver's attitude—his restraint, and the degree of courtesy and consideration he shows to other road users.

No one knows for certain what makes a normally courteous and passive person turn into an aggressive, selfish character once he is behind the steering wheel. The T.R.R.L. describes it as the 'competitiveness' of drivers; in many cases, psychologists diagnose it as masculine assertiveness.

Psychologists also believe that isolation in a metal and glass box, with contact with the outside world only through mechanical devices such as horns, lights and indicators, may be responsible.

The aggressive driver can be identified by badly judged overtaking, often without adequate warning; driving too close to the vehicle in front; and erratic manoeuvres which force other drivers to take evasive action.

THE 'SWITCHED-OFF' DRIVER The Road Traffic Acts classify bad drivers as 'careless' and 'dangerous'. These terms, however, apply to results of driving errors, rather than causes.

The T.R.R.L. has attempted a system of classification which introduces the idea of the dissociated driver—the driver who 'switches off' to the driving environment and is unaware of, or neglects, some of the information he should take into account when driving. Relevant information is anything which may occur during a journey which should influence a driver—for example, a red traffic light or a stationary ice-cream van where children may be crossing carelessly.

The T.R.R.L. suggests four categories:
*Safe drivers* are fully aware of all the relevant information which presents itself as they drive, and do not carry out unnecessary manoeuvres or take risks.
*Injudicious drivers* are fully aware of all the relevant information but sometimes make false judgments on the basis of this information.
*Dissociated active drivers* are not completely aware of all the information or neglect some aspect of it, and take risks actively and consciously.
*Dissociated passive drivers* are again not completely aware of all the relevant information or neglect some aspect of it; through failure to respond to traffic conditions they find themselves in situations with which they cannot cope in the time and space available.

Both types of dissociated driver fail to use their mirrors enough. The main differences between them are that the dissociated active driver varies his speed unnecessarily, overtakes dangerously and is unpredictable; the dissociated passive driver drives at a consistent speed even when variation is necessary, is content to follow other drivers and is predictable.

THE YOUNG DRIVER The law sets a minimum age for driving on a public road, but imposes no further restrictions on young drivers. Yet research shows that about half of all drivers involved in accidents are under the age of 30.

Young drivers are particularly prone to the 'single vehicle' accident in which the car runs out of control—because a bend was taken too fast, for example.

Speeding was, in fact, a significant factor in almost half of the accidents involving young drivers investigated by the T.R.R.L. Their speed tended to be too fast in relation to road structure and layout.

The faults of young drivers tend to be either psychological—impatient or frustrated driving—or the result of inexperience when faced with unexpected situations.

THE TIRED DRIVER Medical researchers have found that fatigue plays an important part in reducing a driver's safety range.

Fatigue can occur in two forms—physical tiredness from the strain of driving, and psychological lethargy resulting from long, monotonous journeys and mechanical repetition of driving actions.

Physical tiredness is easy to detect and relatively easy to guard against. A driver who feels so tired that he becomes unsure about his driving should stop and take a rest. (On a motorway, he should turn into a side road or service area—stopping on the hard shoulder to rest is illegal.)

The psychological lethargy produced by monotonous or lonely driving is harder to detect and guard against.

The Medical Commission on Accident Prevention, a body composed of eminent doctors and scientists, says it is particularly likely to occur in the 'relatively unchanging conditions experienced when driving for long periods in low density traffic, in fog, at night, or on a motorway'.

In the United States wide-ranging research into road accidents has produced evidence that as traffic on some roads increases in density, the accident and road fatality rate decreases. It is on the long, lonely stretches of highway that the majority of accidents occur.

The best way of avoiding psychological lethargy depends on the individual. Some drivers can train themselves to detect a 'hypnotic' element in their driving and stop for a rest. For others, a car radio can keep the mind occupied.

THE DRIVER IN POOR HEALTH A driver who is ill is obviously unable to exercise the degree of continual mental alertness and concentration that is essential to safe driving.

Drugs and medicines prescribed by doctors were found by the Medical Commission to play a part in driving accidents. Patients are not always warned by doctors of the driving hazard of medicines or drugs.

An AA survey revealed that out of a sample 945 drivers, 53 had taken medicinal drugs on prescription in the previous 24 hours. Of these, only five had been warned of the potential danger in driving a car during their treatment.

The law makes it an offence to drive under the influence of drugs, but the effects must usually be pronounced to secure conviction. A warning on the label of drugs or medicines might do much to make the public aware of the dangers; a patient can also make a point of asking his doctor.

People suffering from various illnesses and disabilities (for example, impaired sight or hearing) may find that they are refused a driving licence. Regulations made in 1971, when brought into force, give the authorities the right to withdraw a licence if it comes to their notice that a driver is suffering from a condition that makes driving inadvisable.

**Accidents due to defective vehicles**
Probably no section of English law is more detailed than the regulations governing the construction and maintenance of motor vehicles. ☐ The law on car safety, p. 39.

In addition, the Annual Vehicle (MoT) Test and the powers to examine vehicles at the roadside play a major part in keeping defective vehicles off the road. Accident prevention research, still incomplete, suggests the most serious hazards are poor tyres and inefficient brakes. Defective tyres accounted for 18 per cent of the defects and suspected defects in vehicles which were involved in accidents in 1970, for example. Another 15 per cent were faults in brakes.
TYRES Worn tyres are an obvious risk, especially on wet roads. Tyre bursts and unequal tyre pressures also take their toll.
BRAKES By law, brakes must be kept in an efficient working condition, and it is wise to check them at the first sign of deterioration. Women drivers who find braking tiring may find a power unit reduces fatigue.
MIRRORS A frequent cause of road accidents is insufficient use of the rear-view mirror, especially before overtaking. Wing mirrors can compensate for the narrow corridor of vision provided by an internal rear-view mirror. But because wing mirrors are positioned several feet from the driver's eye they can sometimes create hazards by making vehicles approaching from behind appear further away than they really are.
SEAT BELTS Cars registered since January 1, 1965 must be fitted with seat belts for the front seats. Their purpose is to prevent injuries sustained by violent impact with the car's interior.

Use of seat belts might have prevented 15,000 (or 40 per cent) of the 37,500 fatal and serious casualties in 1970, according to Department of the Environment estimates. Yet seat belts have been slow to gain acceptance. Surveys suggest that only 32 per cent of front-seat occupants use belts on motorways, 23 per cent on A class roads and 8 per cent on town roads.

New laws may make the wearing of seat belts compulsory, but enforcement will be difficult, especially at night.

**Accidents due to road hazards**
Most drivers feel that they are entitled to expect that the roads which they use will not expose them to traps and unnecessary hazards. More cautiously, Government investigators say in one T.R.R.L. report that they 'have tried to take the view that an appropriate road layout needs to be provided which the inadequate and less able driver can use safely'.

The most serious road hazards are seldom the obvious ones. A sharp bend, visible from a distance, is not usually as dangerous as a subtle optical effect which misleads drivers about distance or a dip in a straight road which, for a few vital seconds, obscures oncoming traffic.
ROAD SURFACING Poor drainage, the constant pounding of the surface by heavy traffic and a lack of proper maintenance can make a road a hazard in itself, particularly in wet weather.
ROAD JUNCTION DESIGN Badly designed road junctions are another potential danger. Some 136 of the 247 accidents investigated by the T.R.R.L. involved turning at junctions or entrances—62 of them T junctions.
WARNING SIGNS Most drivers rely on warning signs to alert them to dangers, but badly positioned or unlit signs are not always effective and confusion can be caused by a multiplicity of signs.
LIGHT AND VISIBILITY The accident rate in darkness is about twice that in daylight. Contributory factors are alcohol, different traffic composition and speed, with drivers travelling too fast for the range of vision allowed by their headlights.

**Towards safer motoring**
Research into the part played in accidents by defective vehicles and badly constructed roads may eventually produce better traffic laws and safer motoring conditions. But research also shows that human factors contribute to nearly three-quarters of the accidents investigated. It is also the driver who bears much of the responsibility for the safety of himself, his passengers and the pedestrians he encounters.

# Problems of parking

*Illegal parking*
*The parking-meter system*
*How disc parking works*

*Traffic wardens and parking*
*When vehicles can be removed*
*Parking at night*

THE motorist has no automatic right to park his car on the highway. Under common law, roads are for general public use 'for the purpose of passage'. Anyone who obstructs this passage may commit one of a number of offences.

There are only two means of parking and keeping within the law. The first is to use an authorised parking place—such as a meter bay—where the motorist has the right to park, provided he observes the regulations.

The second is to park with the consent of a policeman or traffic warden. If a motorist obtains explicit permission from a policeman in uniform or from a traffic warden, and preferably has independent witnesses to support him, he should have a complete answer to a prosecution.

Waiting restrictions do not create any right to park during periods when the restrictions are lifted. But in practice, a motorist who takes advantage of such controls need not fear action by the police.

In all other circumstances, a motorist who parks on the road does so at his own risk.

## Illegal parking

A variety of offences can be committed by a motorist who parks his vehicle in an unauthorised place.

OBSTRUCTION Every car parked on a public road forms an obstruction. It can be an unreasonable use of the road—even if no other road-user is obstructed. The time for which a car is parked is the deciding factor.

A driver is not guilty of an offence, however, if he can show that the obstruction was not unreasonable. If he is prosecuted after leaving his car for a reasonable time in a street where there are no parking restrictions, he may be able to persuade the magistrates on the facts of the case that the obstruction was not what the law calls 'unnecessary'.

➤WHEN OBSTRUCTION IS NOT UNNECESSARY *Dentist Mr David Barker left his car for 75 minutes on a road in Oswestry, Shropshire on market day in October 1971. He was charged with obstruction along with three other motorists who parked in the same road.*

*The three other motorists pleaded guilty, but Mr Barker denied the charge. The evidence showed that there were no yellow lines on the road to indicate parking restrictions and there was 20 ft clearance between the offside of his car and the other side of the road.*
DECISION *Mr Barker was found not guilty. The magistrates decided that no evidence had been produced that the obstruction was unnecessary. The Court of Appeal upheld their decision. (Evans v. Barker.)*◄

A traffic warden may report an alleged obstruction and can have a car towed away. But he cannot issue a fixed-penalty ticket, and all prosecutions for obstruction must be tried by the courts.

Wilful obstruction of the highway is a more serious offence, for which a driver can be arrested. There are also local bye-laws which enable police to prosecute anyone causing obstruction in the street.

DANGEROUS PARKING It is an offence to park a vehicle 'in such a position or in such a condition or in such circumstances as to be likely to cause danger to other persons using the road'. This wide regulation covers every case of dangerous parking. There is no parking code of dangerous places where it is an offence to park; but examples are listed in the Highway Code, which the law says can be used in evidence to support a charge. The examples include parking at or near a road junction or bend, or parking a car on the wrong side of the road at night.

The test of dangerous parking is always the likelihood of danger—there does not have to be an accident before a prosecution can be brought against the driver.

When a parked vehicle does cause an accident, anyone who is injured may be able to claim damages. Whether the driver who parked the car is liable depends on whether he was negligent; but if he parked reasonably he will not be held responsible.

➤THE DAZZLED DRIVER *Mr Heslop parked his car on a busy, narrow main road at night. Another driver, Mr Watson, dazzled by the lights of an oncoming car, ran into the parked vehicle and was injured. He claimed damages from Mr Heslop.*

DECISION *Mr Heslop, the driver of the parked car, was held to be 70 per cent responsible for the accident. Mr Watson was 30 per cent responsible; he would have seen the parked car before being dazzled if he had been keeping a proper look-out. (Watson v. Heslop.)◄*

PARKING NEAR A ZEBRA CROSSING It is an offence to leave a car within the approach to a zebra (pedestrian) crossing and, in some cases, beyond the crossing.

The prohibited area, in the first instance, is marked by a double line of studs in the roadway 15 yds from the crossing. This may be extended to 25 yds where the speed limit is higher than 30 mph. No part of the vehicle may be over the line of studs, and it is no defence to prove that the studs were indistinct or obscured.

In the case of crossings marked by broken, zig-zag lines for 25 yds on either side, motorists are not allowed to overtake or park within the area marked.

PARKING ON A CLEARWAY Urban clearways, marked by yellow lines at the edge of the road-way, indicate that no parking is permitted during peak traffic hours, and waiting outside those hours is limited. On rural clearways parking is prohibited at all times, though lay bys are provided.

PARKING ON A MOTORWAY Drivers are not allowed to stop or park on motorways except in emergencies, and then only on the hard shoulder. In these circumstances, a driver must see that his car is removed as soon as possible from the roadside.

The courts have ruled that to be in need of sleep is not an emergency which permits a motorist to stop.

►THE DRIVER WHO FELT DROWSY *One afternoon in April 1971 the police found a Ford Escort car stopped on the verge of a slip road leading to the M62 motorway in Lancashire. The driver, Mr Arthur Bernard of Bingley, was sitting in the car.*

*When Mr Bernard explained that he had stopped for a rest, police pointed out that he could have stopped a quarter of a mile back, before he turned on to the motorway slip road.*

*Mr Bernard said: 'I didn't feel too bad*

# How road markings regulate parking

The warning sign of a no-waiting restriction—except for loading and unloading—is a yellow line painted on the roadway running parallel to the kerb. The exact no-waiting times are specified on a nearby plate and should always be checked, since road markings are only a general indication of what is permitted. Parking is also prohibited at zig-zag zebra crossings. ☐ Signs, lines and signals, p. 68

Loading and unloading restrictions are indicated by short yellow markings painted on the kerb. Check the exact times that the restrictions are enforced on the nearby plate since they may be varied outside the broad categories indicated by the road markings, to suit local traffic conditions

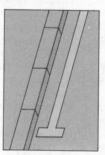

A single line restricts waiting during the working day

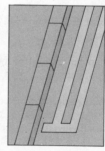

Double lines restrict waiting for more than the working day

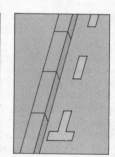

A broken line allows waiting during the working day for limited periods

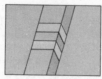

Two lines painted on the kerb indicate no loading is permitted during the working day

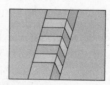

Three lines on the kerb indicate no loading allowed during the working day or at times shown on plate

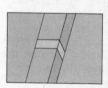

One line shows that loading is allowed for limited periods during the working day

*then. I appreciate it is not an emergency, but I felt I had to have a rest.'* He said he had been feeling extremely drowsy over the last mile.

Mr Bernard was charged with stopping his car illegally on the verge of a motorway.
DECISION *He was found guilty. The High Court ruled that since stopping on a motorway verge was permitted only in an emergency, a defendant had to show that something happened after he entered the motorway to make it unsafe for him to proceed. Mr Bernard, however, realised before he went on to the motorway that he was feeling drowsy.* (Higgins v. Bernard.)◄

PARKING BY DOUBLE WHITE LINES It is an offence to cross or straddle double white lines down the centre of a road, or to park on either side of a road with these markings.
PARKING OFF THE ROAD The grass verge has been held to be part of the road, and the drivers of cars parked on grass verges risk prosecution for causing unnecessary obstruction. Parking on common land more than 15 yds from a highway is also an offence.

## When parking is controlled
Local authorities are permitted by Parliament to devise their own individual systems of traffic control.

Some local authorities follow the example of London and use parking meters. Others, such as Leicester, rely on conventional waiting and loading restrictions. A few have adopted the continental disc system. There are also places with ticket-issuing machines or attendants to collect parking charges.

All use the yellow line to draw attention to the general rule that parking in controlled zones within the prescribed hours is limited to designated parking places. These places are shown by a P sign, the presence of parking meters, or by a sign stipulating at what time parking is allowed.
'NO WAITING' ORDERS The period of the day during which waiting is not permitted varies from place to place. 'Waiting', which includes any stopping except to pick up or set down a passenger or to load or unload, is normally prohibited on all main thoroughfares during the working day. The restrictions are less severe on roads where parked cars are less likely to interrupt the flow of traffic.

In some places, the restrictions set a limited period for waiting—say 20 minutes in the hour. Others allow parking on alternate sides of the road on alternate days.

All waiting restrictions must be clearly indicated by traffic signs. The warning sign of a restriction is a yellow line painted on the roadway alongside the kerb. The times during which the restriction is in force must be shown on a plate displayed near by.

There can be no conviction in the absence of either the yellow line or the plate, except that in Controlled Parking Zones the yellow line alone speaks for itself. A single yellow line means that no waiting is allowed during the working day. Double yellow lines mean no waiting for more than the working day. A broken yellow line means no waiting for shorter periods. The exact times are shown on the nearby time plate. Check to see whether the restriction applies on Sundays.
LOADING AND UNLOADING RESTRICTIONS A motorist's right to stop for a reasonable time and without causing undue obstruction to load or unload his vehicle has always been recognised by the law. But it is a right normally confined to goods vehicles or to private cars adapted to carry goods.

Local traffic orders generally recognise the right to load and unload goods, but this is only an exemption from the 'no waiting' restrictions. The burden of proof that the vehicle was being used throughout to load or unload goods lies with the motorist.

There is no precise guide as to what may constitute 'goods'. The test may be whether the use of the car is essential or merely convenient. Normal household shopping may not qualify for exemption.

In the absence of kerb markings, a private motorist may park for a limited time—usually 20 minutes—to load or unload.

Local orders require also that a vehicle used for loading or unloading must be parked near the premises where loading or unloading is taking place.

Yellow marks at right angles to the kerb restrict or prevent unloading during certain times. A nearby plate specifies the times.

## The parking-meter system
The boundaries of parking-meter zones are indicated by signs saying 'Meter Zone' and 'Zone Ends'.

During the hours shown on the parking meter (for example, 8 a.m. to 6.30 p.m. excluding Sundays, Good Friday, Christmas Day and Bank Holidays) motorist may leave their cars only in marked-out parking places.

A parking place is the whole length of the road between the double white lines, divided into a number of meter bays by single white lines. Once they leave a bay, motorists are not allowed to park again in the same parking place, even at a different meter, before one hour has elapsed.

Outside the prescribed hours, parking is free everywhere unless indicated by double yellow lines or special signs restricting parking.

Cars must be parked at the nearside kerb, except in a one-way street, and within 12 in. of the kerb, with no overhang over the footway. In some places, especially where parking bays are at an angle to the road, parking with part of the car over the footway has become common practice. Motorists who do this are technically liable to be prosecuted for obstructing the pavement. The whole of the vehicle must be within the white lines.

Solo motor cycles and scooters may be parked free in motor-cycle parking places. Riders of motor-cycle combinations must use the normal meters provided.

Payment must be made immediately on leaving the vehicle in the meter bay—the motorist who leaves his car to go into a shop for small change to put in the meter is technically open to prosecution. No payment is required if the meter is showing unexpired time; but if further time is required beyond the unexpired time, payment must be made on parking. It is an offence for a motorist to 'feed' a meter by inserting additional coins after he has been parked for some time.

WHEN A METER IS NOT IN USE Motorists are entitled to park at a meter which is covered by a hood bearing the words 'Out of Order', and parking is free. But when the meter is put in order, it will be set to give the appropriate maximum time.

If the motorist does not remove his car before this time expires, he must pay the excess charge.

No parking is allowed at a temporarily suspended meter. Normally this is marked by a red hood, with the words 'bay suspended'.

Gaps between meters are marked with a yellow line and are an indication that loading or unloading is permitted, usually for up to 20 minutes. Private cars left in loading gaps are usually 'booked' by wardens, and unless there is evidence of actual loading or unloading, a ticket may be issued for parking 'elsewhere than in a parking bay'.

If a meter fails to work correctly, it is usually due to the mechanism having been jammed by the insertion of a 'foreign object'. It is the traffic warden's duty to place a bag or hood over any meter reported as out of order, and to have it investigated.

OVERSTAYING THE TIME Three minutes after the time paid for on a meter has expired, a yellow excess flag shows on the meter. It is not in itself an offence to run into excess time on a meter; but if an excess charge becomes due, it is the duty of a warden to issue an excess ticket.

If the car remains at the meter after the excess time expires, a red penalty flag appears and an offence *has* been committed. A fixed penalty ticket may be issued, and the vehicle is liable to be towed away.

Excess charges, which vary from area to area, must be paid to the local authority within seven days. It is an offence not to pay within this time, and late payment will not always be accepted.

Any motorist who disputes the excess, or considers that he has been wrongly penalised in the circumstances, is entitled to have his case heard, in the same way as a normal parking offence.

### How disc parking works

Disc parking was first introduced in Cheltenham in 1965 and similar schemes operate in Harrogate, Devizes, Ripon, Birkenhead and Oxford. The disc, of double-thickness cardboard, has windows on each side and a rotating dial. Discs are available free from parking attendants, local garages and shops.

When the motorist arrives at the parking place, he sets the dial to indicate the arrival time, and this automatically shows the prescribed departure time—one or one-and-a-half hours after arrival—in the appropriate window. No parking is allowed in the same parking place within an hour of leaving. The disc must be displayed on the nearside of the front windscreen and it is an offence to park within the disc parking area without displaying a disc properly, or to advance the dial to gain extra parking time.

### Traffic wardens and parking

Traffic wardens act under the direction of the police and are employed by the local police authority. They were first appointed in 1960 when their sole function was the enforcement of parking law. Their functions have since been extended to the control and regulation of traffic generally. However, their powers of law enforcement are still limited. ☐ Powers of the police and traffic wardens, p. 82.

As far as parking offences are concerned, traffic wardens have the same powers as the police. A warden can require a motorist to give his name and address and can issue penalty tickets for all parking offences other than alleged wilful or unnecessary obstruction.

The United Kingdom parking-ticket system, unlike those systems used in other countries, is not a fine on the spot, nor is it a summons. It merely notifies the alleged offender that he has the opportunity to settle liability by paying a fixed amount.

If the motorist pays within 21 days, no conviction is recorded against him. If he fails to pay, he will be prosecuted, with the risk of a higher court fine and costs if he is convicted of the offence.

Payment on a parking ticket must be accepted by the authorities at any time before proceedings have actually started. But it is too late for a motorist to offer the penalty once a summons has been issued.

Parking tickets in the London area cover any of the following offences:
1. Waiting in a restricted street.
2. Waiting on a clearway.
3. Failure to pay a meter charge.
4. Exceeding the meter excess period.
5. Leaving a vehicle elsewhere than in a parking bay—for example, in a loading gap.
6. Leaving a vehicle at a suspended bay.
7. Leaving a vehicle where a traffic sign indicates No Parking.
8. Leaving a vehicle on a cab rank.
9. Leaving a vehicle on a Residents' Parking Place without a permit or a ticket.
10. Leaving a vehicle without lights.

Traffic wardens are also employed to trace drivers who have failed to pay parking tickets, and it is an offence for a driver not to disclose his identity to a traffic warden when asked to do so.

## When vehicles can be removed

Police have the right to remove a vehicle for any parking offence. The majority of cases in which they use this right involve cars which are waiting on double yellow lines, waiting over the excess period at a parking meter, or causing an obstruction.

The removal may be 'by towing or driving the vehicle or in such other manner as the police constable may think necessary'. The police officer is allowed to take whatever measures he thinks necessary to remove the car. In practice, he normally uses a car key and drives it away. If the policeman damages the car through negligence, the owner can seek compensation from the police authority. If no negligence is involved, however, the car owner has no remedy.

Cars which are removed are taken to a car pound to await collection by their owners. A charge of £4—in London and Birmingham £4·50—is made for removal, and 50p a day for storage. The police are not entitled to retain the vehicle until this is paid; if the driver does not pay after collection, proceedings to recover removal charges can be taken in the magistrates' courts.

## People with special privileges

Residents have no special privileges beyond the common-law right of free access to their own premises. In some London boroughs, permits give residents parking priority.

Traffic wardens exercise discretion when cars show the British Medical Association badge and a notice that the doctor is visiting.

Police, as long as they are on duty, have special privileges in no-waiting areas, even if they are using a private car.

▶THE POLICEMAN WHO GOT A TICKET
*A detective sergeant was instructed by his superior officer to interview a suspect and then report back. He drove his own car, as he was entitled to do under a local police scheme. On his return, he parked in a no-waiting area and was then told to assist in making an arrest.*

*He returned to find that a traffic warden had put a parking ticket on his car. He was convicted of causing the car to wait in contravention of a No-Waiting Order. He appealed to the Divisional Court.*

DECISION *His appeal was allowed. At the material time the vehicle was in the service of the police force, under the authority of the chief constable for police duties. (Webb v. Furber.)*◀

Commercial travellers get no special concessions beyond the normal allowances for collecting or delivering goods.

Foreign visitors get no exemption from parking regulations, but traffic wardens will not normally penalise a car with a foreign registration, since the ticket may be unenforceable. Foreign cars are, however, liable to be towed away, as also are the cars of those who claim diplomatic privilege.

## Parking at night

No lights are needed on cars and motor cycles parked at night on roads (including bus routes) which are subject to a speed limit of 30 miles per hour or less. Vehicles must be parked close to, and parallel with, the kerb. Vehicles must be parked with their near side to the kerb (either side in a one-way street), and no part must be within 15 yards of a road junction.

On all other roads vehicles parked during the hours of darkness must show two white lights to the front and two red lights to the rear. A single parking lamp does not meet the legal requirements.

# Powers of the police and traffic wardens

*How traffic is regulated*  
*When a car may be removed*  
*When a motorist can be stopped*

*Questions a motorist must answer*  
*When police can search a vehicle*  
*When a motorist can be arrested*

TRAFFIC on Britain's roads may be controlled by uniformed policemen (including special constables), traffic wardens and school-crossing patrolmen. Directions and signals given by them must be obeyed, even when such directions conflict with fixed signs and signals on the road.

The law gives the police specific rights to deal with vehicles and traffic. These are in addition to their general powers. ☐ The police and the public, p. 736.

### How traffic is regulated

The police and traffic wardens have full power to divert or direct traffic for any reason connected with the regulation of traffic. Anyone who refuses to obey a direction—for example, to turn off a main road or take a particular lane—commits an offence. ☐ Penalties for motoring offenders, p. 173.

When a motorist ignores the directions of a traffic warden employed on traffic control, the warden has the right to demand the motorist's name and address. It is an offence to refuse to stop and give this information. But in this case a warden, unlike a policeman, has no power to demand that a motorist produces his driving documents.

When a motorist is directed to proceed against a red light or to drive the wrong way up a one-way street, he must do so—unless there is an obvious danger that the policeman or traffic warden has not seen. The motorist runs no risk of prosecution, for an instruction from a police officer or traffic warden takes precedence over traffic signs and signals.

A motorist's right to use the highway is basically for travel, but he is entitled to stop to pick up and set down passengers and to load or unload. In some towns he must find authorised loading or parking areas if he wants to wait for more than a few minutes. ☐ Problems of parking, p. 77.

When a motorist wants to park in an area where restrictions forbid waiting, he should ask a policeman or traffic warden for permission. If granted, this overrides the restrictions; but permission can be withdrawn at any time and the motorist may be told to move on.

If he is in the car, he must drive off or risk prosecution for obstructing the highway, obstructing traffic or obstructing a police officer in the execution of his duty.

Traffic wardens are also responsible for administering parking regulations in many towns and cities. They may issue fixed-penalty tickets or report offenders. ☐ Problems of parking, p. 77.

### When a car may be removed

When a motorist leaves his car unattended and a police officer or traffic warden believes it to be causing a serious obstruction, or when a motorist ignores restrictions in a meter zone, the vehicle may be removed to another street or an official car pound.

Removals are usually carried out by specially trained police officers or by civilian employees. The police are also entitled to subcontract removal work to a local garage. ☐ Problems of parking, p. 77.

### When a motorist can be stopped

A uniformed policeman can stop any vehicle for any reason at any time. A traffic warden can stop a moving vehicle only if he is actually regulating traffic on the road at the time.

By law, the stop signal shown by school-crossing patrolmen must also be obeyed between 8 a.m. and 5.30 p.m. In rare cases a motorist prosecuted for failing to obey such a sign might have a defence if he could show that the patrolman was exceeding his authority —perhaps by stopping traffic only to allow adults to cross.

In all cases, when a motorist has been stopped he must not drive on until he has been given permission or received a signal indicating that he can proceed.

### Questions a motorist must answer

When he is stopped by the police, a motorist must give on demand his name, address and date of birth and the name and address of the owner of the vehicle.

The police also have a right to ask for the name and address of the person driving the car on a previous occasion when it was involved in an accident or when an offence is alleged to have been committed.

A traffic warden has a right to ask for name and address if he believes a motorist or pedestrian has failed to observe a traffic sign or direction. He may also do so if he thinks a motorist is in charge of a car without an excise (road fund) licence or has left a car without proper lights and reflectors at night. ☐ The law on car safety, p. 39.

Traffic wardens also have powers to issue £2 penalty tickets against vehicles not displaying current excise licences.

PRODUCING A DRIVING LICENCE A driving licence must be produced at the request of a uniformed policeman. He is entitled to examine it to find the driver's name and address, the date of issue and the name of the local authority issuing the licence.

When a driver is not carrying his driving licence he must take it to a police station which he specifies within five days.

A traffic warden has no general right to see a motorist's driving licence or to ask his age. He may do so, however, if he has been authorised by the local chief constable, or if he works at a car pound and the motorist is reclaiming his vehicle. In this case he can also ask a motorist's name and address.

Where a warden is entitled to ask a motorist's name and address, the warden probably does no wrong if he also asks to see a driving licence to confirm that he has been given the right name.

There is no offence of obstructing a warden, but a motorist should be cautious about declining to co-operate unless he is sure of his position.

INSURANCE AND TEST CERTIFICATES A driver should produce an insurance certificate and the annual vehicle (MoT) test certificate on request. He may, however, arrange to take it or to have it taken to a police station he specifies within five days.

OWNER'S OBLIGATIONS The owner of any vehicle also has a responsibility to help the police in certain circumstances. He must give any information required to enable the police to discover whether the vehicle is insured.

If the police believe that someone driving the vehicle has committed an offence, its owner must give any information that would help them identify the driver.

## When police can search a vehicle

A police officer may search any vehicle without a warrant if he has reasonable cause to suspect that the driver is carrying a firearm or game that has been poached or wild birds that have been unlawfully seized or killed. ☐ Hunting, shooting and fishing, p. 137.

The police also have powers to search without a warrant if they believe that certain drugs are being carried. And in some areas—for example, London—they may also search where it is reasonably suspected that the driver is in possession of stolen goods.

VEHICLE EXAMINATION When a car has been stopped on the road, the police may decide to carry out a roadside examination. The motorist is entitled to satisfy himself that a uniformed police officer has a special authorisation card in addition to his ordinary warrant card. ☐ The law on car safety, p. 39.

Normally a motorist is within his rights to stay in his car. But if he is asked to step out into the road he is usually better advised to do so. Failure to do so—for example if the police want to administer a breath test—could lead to a charge of obstructing the police.

## When a motorist can be arrested

Police have powers in motoring cases to arrest without warrant any driver who:

**1.** Is believed to be unfit to drive through drink or drugs.

**2.** Refuses to give his name and address after he has been seen driving recklessly, dangerously or carelessly.

**3.** Refuses to take a breath test, when the police have reasonable grounds for believing that there is alcohol in his body.

**4.** Takes a breath test which shows positive (though a driver cannot be arrested if he is already in hospital).

**5.** Wilfully obstructs the free passage of the highway.

**6.** Is suspected of driving while disqualified.

**7.** Is suspected of taking the vehicle unlawfully or driving it knowing that it has been stolen. A passenger can also be arrested if he knows that it was taken unlawfully.

In many cases, a motorist can be arrested even if he is not actually driving. It is enough that he may be about to attempt to drive or that he is in charge of the vehicle. ☐ Drink and driving I: the breathalyser law, p. 87.

Where the police believe that a car may have been stolen—perhaps because the driver cannot remember the registration number or cannot prove that it is hired or borrowed—they may ask him to go to the police station. He is not obliged to do so unless he is arrested.

Failure to help the police, however, may complicate the situation and antagonise the officers involved. A person who has an innocent explanation is usually best advised to co-operate.

# Speeding

No offence on the statute book brings more motorists into court—and more fines into State coffers—than speeding. Recently nearly 250,000 private motorists were convicted for speeding in a single year, and over 3000 of them were disqualified from driving for various periods. Speeding fines that year totalled more than £1,800,000—an average of £7 per driver.

The basic rule, to avoid prosecution and accidents, is always to drive at a speed which is reasonable in the circumstances. A safe speed will be dictated by three factors:
1. The condition of the road—whether it is wet, icy, holed, or under repair, and so on.
2. The visibility—this depends on the weather conditions at the time.
3. The flow and nature of other traffic.

In addition to these common-sense restraints on speed, the law imposes speed limits (not always indicated by signs) on particular kinds of road or stretches of road. It is an offence to exceed the limit for only a short distance—when overtaking, for example.

A motorist who is convicted of speeding has his licence endorsed automatically and can be disqualified, as well as fined, even for a first offence.

Speeding can also result in more serious charges, such as dangerous driving or failing to stop at traffic lights or a pedestrian crossing.

## The speed limits
Although speed limits vary according to the type of road to which they apply, there is an upper limit of 70 mph on *all* roads in Britain, including motorways. Motorists are expected to know and observe this 70 mph limit, even if there are no speed-limit signs to remind them.

In built-up or densely populated areas, it is an offence to drive at more than 30 mph, even though there may be no speed-limit signs. Streets and roads in these areas are called 'restricted roads'. The law defines them as roads in which the street lamps are situated not more than 200 yds apart.

A road does not cease to be restricted simply because one or more lamps are temporarily missing or out of order. What matters in law is not whether the lamps are working at a given moment, but whether they exist as part of a regular lighting system.

Even when this regular system exists, there are occasions when the 30 mph limit may not apply. In these cases, special signs indicate that the limit has been lowered or increased—the 70 mph sign on de-restricted roads, for example.

Trunk roads and classified roads (which have the letter 'A' or 'B' before the number) often have lights every 200 yds or less; yet they are not always subject to the 30 mph limit. This is because a restriction on such roads depends on when the street lighting was installed. If it was there before July 1, 1957, the road is restricted and the 30 mph limit applies. If the lights were erected after that date, the road is not restricted.

A driver charged with speeding on a trunk or classified road which has no speed-limit signs can check with the local town hall when the lighting was installed.

## Special speed limits
Watch out for signs imposing special speed limits. To drive at a speed greater than the limit is an offence in itself, and it may count as evidence of a more serious charge—careless or dangerous driving, for example.

UNRESTRICTED TRUNK ROADS The most common 'special' limit on trunk roads not subject to the 30 mph limit is 40 mph. There are also roads with a 50 mph limit.

ROADWORKS Two kinds of speed limits are set at roadworks: advisory (black-and-white signs laying down recommended top speeds) which can be disregarded without committing an offence; and mandatory (the usual speed-limit signs), which carry the normal criminal consequences if they are not obeyed. These speed limits, which depend on the position of the roadworks, vary from 20 to 50 mph.
☐ Signs, lines and signals, p. 68.

HOSPITAL GROUNDS AND CAR PARKS The stated limits are those advised by the hospital or local authority, and have no legal force beyond a warning that special hazards are involved. Drivers exceeding the limits could be prosecuted for dangerous driving or for some other offence—not for speeding.

ROYAL PARKS Each Royal park has its own speed limit so, again, watch out for the signs. There is a 30 mph limit in Richmond Park, Surrey, for example. It is an offence to break these special limits.

**Minimum limits**

Regulations which make it an offence to drive below a stated speed limit are not common at present, although the Department of the Environment intends to make more use of them because they help to keep traffic moving.

The sign (the limit figure on a blue background with a white border) is mainly used in tunnels, on long bridges and at the approaches to airports.

**Special limits for certain vehicles**

All general speed limits apply only to ordinary motor cars, motor cycles and to dual-purpose vehicles such as estate cars, shooting brakes and Land Rovers. The ordinary motor car is defined for the purpose of the speed regulations as a passenger-carrying vehicle weighing not more than 3 tons unladen and designed to carry not more than seven passengers, not counting the driver.

The driver of a motor car or dual-purpose vehicle drawing a trailer or caravan faces a further restriction. The maximum speed at which he may drive is 40 mph, no matter what traffic signs say. However, a motorised caravan, such as a Dormobile, is not subject to special speed limits if it has side windows.

Tractors, goods vehicles, public-transport vehicles and many others are subject to special, lower speed limits. For details, consult the Road Transport Regulations Act 1967, Schedule 5 (No. 1967/c.76), which can be bought at any bookshop of H.M. Stationery Office. Alternatively, ask the police or a motoring organisation if you are uncertain whether a special limit applies to your vehicle.

**How the police catch speeding drivers**

The two main methods used by the police to catch speeding motorists are the radar trap and pursuit by police car or motor cycle. These methods have largely superseded the method of timing vehicles by stop-watch over a measured distance.

THE RADAR TRAP Police can catch speeding motorists with a radar device which 'bounces' a beam of very-high-frequency radio waves off a moving car and records the mph on a meter.

The principle is that if radiated energy is reflected by a moving object, the wavelength frequency of the energy is changed, and the amount of change depends on the speed of the moving object. This is called the Doppler effect.

It is because of the Doppler effect that the pitch of a train's whistle changes more noticeably the higher the speed at which the train approaches and recedes.

Police use an instrument called PETA—portable electronic traffic analyser—which radiates energy in the form of radio waves. The moving objects which reflect the energy are cars. The instrument is set up in a concealed position at the roadside, pointing across the road at an angle of 20 degrees. The beam

## Setting the radar speed trap

The police radar device is often concealed in the open boot of a police car. The beam of radio waves is directed along the road at an angle of 20 degrees, and accurately controlled within an arc of 4 degrees. When a car travels through the beam, signals are reflected back to the radar instrument, which converts them into an mph reading on a meter. The device should be set up so that there is no interference from other reflecting objects when cars are under scrutiny

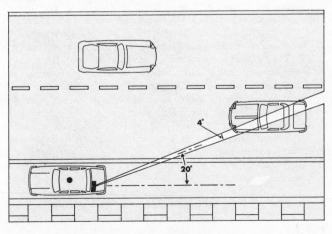

of high-frequency radio waves has a working range of 150 ft.

When a car passes through the beam, it reflects signals back to the PETA, which shows the mph on a meter. This reading is held for approximately 1½ seconds. The margin of error at all speeds is plus or minus 2 per cent, which is 1 mile an hour at 50 mph.

Experts do not discount the possibility of interference. For example, roadside reflectors or another vehicle which may be going in the opposite direction may cause a double reflection of the beam and interfere with the meter reading.

But in most cases the police will claim that the instrument was set up to avoid any possibility of error.

A radar expert could be called to support the possibility of error, but the motorist must remember that courts are not always impressed by scientific arguments.

Radar speed checking is called a 'trap' because the device is usually concealed. Often the first knowledge a motorist has of a radar trap is when a policeman to whom his speed has been signalled waves him to a halt.

THE POLICE-CAR TRAP Besides the radar trap, the speeding motorist may be caught by a police car or solo motor cyclist in pursuit. The police follow at an even distance and check his speed, usually for three-tenths of a mile.

The solo police motor cyclist can easily tail a car in a 'blind-spot' position and avoid detection by the driver.

THE STOP-WATCH TRAP The accuracy of the old-fashioned speed trap, with two policemen timing a motorist over a measured distance, depends on human reactions. For example, over a furlong, if the two watches synchronise at less than 15 seconds' difference, then the car's speed is more than 30 mph.

## Corroboration

While the law says that no. one may be convicted of speeding on the opinion of a single witness, this does not mean that a speeding charge requires two police witnesses. It has been held that the evidence of a police speedometer provides corroboration, and this applies equally to radar.

Similarly, the motorist does not need a witness to corroborate his own evidence, though in practice the evidence of a passenger, even if it is his wife or member of the family, can provide useful support.

## Warning speeding motorists

It is illegal to do anything which might alert motorists to a police speed trap. Anyone who attempts to give such a warning—by putting up a sign, for example, or flashing his headlights—runs the risk of prosecution for obstructing the police in the execution of their duty.

## What to do when stopped for speeding

A MOTORIST stopped for speeding may be cautioned or told that he will be reported 'for the question to be considered of prosecuting for exceeding the speed limit'.

If the alleged speed was less than 5 mph over the limit, the police may caution the motorist on the spot or send a written caution.

The law does not require the motorist to be told his exact speed at the time. He should, however, always ask what speed is alleged.

If he disputes the speed, he should say so at once. Even if the police allegation is exaggerated, the motorist will still have committed an offence if he has to admit that his speed was, in fact, excessive.

A motorist who intends to plead not guilty on the ground that he was not exceeding the speed limit should immediately take the precaution of having his speedometer tested. He should not wait until he receives the summons.

The AA does not test speedometers, but will recommend where arrangements can be made for this to be done.

The tester should provide a statement which can be submitted as written evidence, and should be prepared to attend court if his statement is challenged.

Being stopped for speeding usually means a summons within a month, though the police have up to six months in which they may start proceedings.

Speeding charges are among the most difficult to defend successfully. Motorists who seriously consider disputing the case, especially when conviction can involve disqualification, should always be legally represented.

A solicitor, or the legal department of the AA, will require full information about the circumstances of the alleged offence, including the road concerned.

# Drink and driving I : the breathalyser law

*The two drink-driving laws*
*Why the breathalyser is used*
*The correct procedure for a breath test*

*What happens if the test is positive*
*Compulsory blood or urine tests*
*Results of the test*

THE motorist who drives while affected by alcohol does so at his peril. He faces an increased risk of damaging his car and injuring or killing himself, his passengers or other road users. The man who drives soon after drinking three double whiskies or their equivalent is four times more likely to have a serious accident than the sober driver.

In addition, the drinking driver risks a whole series of legal consequences and penalties. If he is sued for damages, he stands little chance of successfully defending the action. Even though the damages may be covered by insurance, he will afterwards pay a loaded premium and perhaps get only limited insurance cover.

If he is prosecuted, the drink-driving offender faces a stiff fine, possible imprisonment, and almost certain disqualification for at least a year. No notice is taken of personal excuses or tales of hardship.

**The two drink-driving laws**
The drink-driving laws are contained in two sections of the Road Traffic Act 1972. Section 5 deals with the 'impairment' law (previously covered by the Road Traffic Act 1960), and Section 6 with the 'breathalyser' law (previously the Road Safety Act 1967).

The 'impairment' law makes it an offence to drive, attempt to drive, or be in charge of a motor vehicle when unfit through drink or drugs. The 'breathalyser' law makes it an offence to drive, attempt to drive, or be in charge of a motor vehicle when the proportion of alcohol in the blood, as proved by laboratory tests, is above the legal level of 80 mg (milligrammes) of alcohol in 100 ml (millilitres) of blood.

Most drink-driving prosecutions are now brought under the 'breathalyser' law. This is because, despite the legal technicalities, the police find it simpler than prosecuting under the 'impairment' law.

The merits of the 'breathalyser' law are two-fold. By using the breathalyser, the police can get a preliminary indication of whether a motorist has excess alcohol in his bloodstream. Those who have been drinking in legal moderation, or not at all, are not then required to undergo further tests. Secondly, it provides a standard test—the scientific measurement of the alcohol concentration in the blood. This eliminates the guesswork and conflict of medical opinions that occur in cases brought under the 'impairment' law.

Many drivers convicted under the 'breathalyser' law complain that they were driving safely when stopped. But the use of a scientific yardstick makes the defendant's driving ability irrelevant.

Some drivers will be sober with an alcohol level over 80 mg in 100 ml of blood (expressed as 80 mg per cent). But the level was fixed at that figure because extensive research proved it was the point at which most drivers became unmistakably accident-prone through drink.

Similarly, some people are more susceptible to the effects of alcohol because of age, sex or physical characteristics, or because, perhaps unwittingly, they have taken medicines or inhaled industrial gases that produce an abnormal reaction to alcohol. The 'breathalyser' law makes no exception for these cases. HOW THE TESTS WORK The familiar effects of drinking are due to the action of alcohol on the brain, where it cannot be measured. The tests under the drink-driving laws depend on the fact that, once absorbed into the system, alcohol is distributed throughout the body in uniform proportions.

This is because the body is made up predominantly of water: the effect of drinking alcohol is like that of adding flavouring to soup—it soon diffuses throughout the liquid. Alcohol passes through the stomach walls into the bloodstream, which carries it to the various organs—the liver, lungs, bladder and brain. It can therefore be measured by testing body fluids at various points.

Three kinds of tests are carried out under the drink-driving laws—breath tests, blood tests and urine tests. Since the blood uniformly dilutes the alcohol that has been taken by the drinker, it is an easy matter to measure the proportion of alcohol in it by breaking down and analysing the contents of a drop of blood taken from the body.

For this reason, the standard measure of alcohol in the body is the blood-alcohol level. The level of alcohol in other body fluids, for example urine, is converted to milli-grammes of alcohol per millilitre of blood.

**Why the breathalyser is used**
The most reliable tests of the proportion of alcohol in the blood are tests on blood itself, and to a lesser extent on urine. However, to avoid giving one of these tests to every motorist suspected of driving with excess alcohol, suspects are first required to take a breath test. In this, a motorist blows air from his lungs into an instrument called the Alcotest ® 80—popularly known as the breathalyser.

The breath test gives only a positive or a negative indication of whether a driver has

alcohol in excess of the prescribed level: it does not measure the excess. People whose test results are negative are allowed to go (unless they are to be charged with another offence); those who give a positive result are arrested and taken to a police station for a blood or urine test.

Just because a driver gives a positive breath test does not mean that he is guilty. A conviction depends on the blood or urine test.

REFUSING TO GIVE A BREATH TEST It is an offence to fail, without a reasonable excuse (such as illness or injury), to give a breath test when properly required to do so.

Anyone who does not give a test, even if he has a reasonable excuse for not doing so, can

## Taking a breathalyser test

A driver's conduct if he is asked to take a breath test can dictate whether or not he is subsequently prosecuted. It is therefore advisable to follow a few simple rules.
**1.** If you have not been drinking or think you have had less than the legal maximum, do not refuse the breath test. It is intended to avoid inconvenience to innocent people.
**2.** If you have been stopped for a breath test, ask the policeman to tell you his grounds for making the request. He can give a breath test only if he reasonably suspects that you have alcohol in your body, or that you have committed a traffic offence or have been in an accident while driving.

Make a note of what he says, and press for details of places, times and any other information that seems relevant. Be firm but polite. Avoid giving the impression that you are attempting to stall. (Creating delay or making difficulties can be taken as a refusal to take the test.)
**3.** If you have not been stopped, but are in a stationary car, or have recently left it, ask the policeman what facts have led him to think that you are 'driving'. Once again note what he says. The information may help your solicitor later if he pleads that the policeman was not within his rights in demanding a test. A motorist suspected of breaking a drink-driving law is not obliged to give the police any explanation of why he stopped or happened to be at a particular place.
**4.** The policeman might ask when you had your last drink, because the breathalyser test may only be applied 20 minutes or more after a driver has last taken an alcoholic drink.

If you have been drinking within the previous 20 minutes tell the policeman. A breath test taken

too early measures alcohol in the saliva, which could give an abnormally high reaction.

If you fail to tell him, you will not be able to rely on the fact that he did not follow the test instructions requiring a delay of 20 minutes after drinking.

If a person takes a drink after being stopped this invalidates the test, but if he does so for that purpose he is guilty of obstructing the police.
**5.** Make sure that the crystals in the tube are a clear yellow colour, that the seals at each end are broken in your presence, and that the equipment is properly assembled.
**6.** Wipe your lips before taking the test. Alcohol adheres to the lips for a while after drinking.
**7.** To comply with the instructions, you should fill the bag in one breath. If you take more you would not necessarily be refusing the test. If, however, you are asked to try again with one breath, it would probably amount to a refusal or failure to take the test if without an excuse, such as illness, you failed to comply.
**8.** If you have recently been smoking, mention this fact, since it can turn the crystals brown.
**9.** If you are told that the test is positive ask to see the tube. Make sure that it is studied in a proper light—either the light of a torch or of vehicle headlamps, and not street lighting. If the result of the test is doubtful, because the colour change has not clearly exceeded the mark, ask that the point of the colour-change be marked on the tube (it will take pencil or ball-point pen) and ask the policeman to preserve the tube as evidence.
**10.** If you are arrested, ask under which section of the Act you are being arrested and on what grounds, and note the policeman's answer.

be arrested and taken to a police station for further tests. This does not apply, however, if the suspect is a patient in a hospital, since no tests can be carried out on a hospital patient without the permission of the doctor in charge of the case.

The only lawful reasons for failing to take a breath test are:

**1.** That the motorist is injured or suffering from an illness which makes it impossible for him to take the test.

**2.** That the correct legal procedure for requiring the test has not been followed.

Obstructive behaviour, excuses or delays on the part of the motorist may sometimes be regarded in law as a refusal to take a breathalyser test. Among excuses rejected by the courts are wanting to make a phone call and asking for a solicitor to be present.

Alternatively, such behaviour may constitute the separate offence of obstructing the police. A driver who took a drink of whisky after being stopped, preventing the breath test from being legally administered for a further 20 minutes, was convicted of obstruction.

**The correct procedure for a breath test**
The courts expect the police to keep strictly within powers allowed by the Road Traffic Act 1972. They will acquit a driver who was driving with excessive alcohol in his blood if

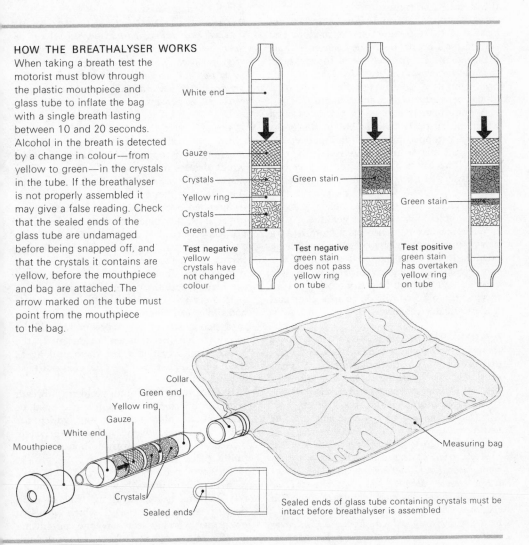

## HOW THE BREATHALYSER WORKS

When taking a breath test the motorist must blow through the plastic mouthpiece and glass tube to inflate the bag with a single breath lasting between 10 and 20 seconds. Alcohol in the breath is detected by a change in colour—from yellow to green—in the crystals in the tube. If the breathalyser is not properly assembled it may give a false reading. Check that the sealed ends of the glass tube are undamaged before being snapped off, and that the crystals it contains are yellow, before the mouthpiece and bag are attached. The arrow marked on the tube must point from the mouthpiece to the bag.

White end

Gauze

Crystals

Yellow ring

Crystals

Green end

Green stain

Green stain

**Test negative**
yellow crystals have not changed colour

**Test negative**
green stain does not pass yellow ring on tube

**Test positive**
green stain has overtaken yellow ring on tube

Collar
Green end
Yellow ring
Gauze
White end
Mouthpiece

Measuring bag

Crystals

Sealed ends

Sealed ends of glass tube containing crystals must be intact before breathalyser is assembled

89

the carefully defined procedure has not been observed by the police. But the onus of proof is on the accused.

In the case of the breath test, the courts have rules about who can require a test, the circumstances in which it can be applied, and the way it is applied.

Anyone who believes the police are not within their rights in asking him to take a test is usually best advised to comply, and to point out the apparent irregularities to his solicitor later.

WHO CAN ADMINISTER THE TEST Only a policeman in uniform—not, for example, a plain-clothes detective—is entitled to stop a motorist and require him to take a breath test. The uniform does not have to be complete— a missing helmet, for example, does not give the motorist the right to refuse.

GROUNDS FOR THE TEST The police are not permitted to stop motorists at random and administer a breath test. They can do so only if they genuinely suspect one of three things: that the motorist has been drinking; that he has committed a driving offence; or that he has been involved in an accident.

A policeman is entitled to test a motorist whom he suspects has alcohol in his body, even if he stopped him for a different reason. It does not matter how he arrived at the suspicion. The constable need not suspect that the driver was intoxicated or had alcohol in excess of the limit. It would not matter that the driver had not taken alcohol, as long as the constable's suspicion was genuine.

When a policeman suspects a motorist of a driving infringement, this covers any motoring offence. It does not matter if in fact no law was broken, as long as the suspicion was genuine. When requiring a motorist to take the test the officer must do so in a clear and understandable manner.

➤ WHEN SUSPICIONS WERE ENOUGH *Police stopped Mr Downey because of the way he was driving, and they noticed that his breath smelt of alcohol. The police said that they suspected that Mr Downey had committed a moving-traffic offence, and asked him to take a breath test. Mr Downey refused the test, claiming that he had committed no offence. He was arrested, and continued to refuse to produce a specimen.*

*At his trial, he argued that the reason for his refusal was that he had not committed a moving-traffic offence. However, he was convicted for failing, without reasonable excuse, to provide a specimen. Mr Downey appealed.*
DECISION *His appeal was dismissed. The court said it was not necessary for the police to prove*
*that an offence had been committed by the motorist—only that they had reasonable cause to suspect it. (R. v. Downey.)* ◄

Suspicion that a driver has been in an accident is not sufficient to warrant a breath test. Police must have proof of an accident.

➤ THE ACCIDENT WAS NOT PROVED *Police patrolling on the Winchester by-pass found a car on the verge of the road with its wheels in what was described as a ditch. Believing that there had been an accident, they found the driver, Mr Seward, who was walking home along the road, and asked him to take a breath test. He complied, and since his subsequent blood test was positive, the court convicted him of driving with a blood-alcohol level above the permitted limit. Mr Seward appealed.*
DECISION *The court quashed the verdict. Mr Seward had claimed he had parked his car on the verge, and the court ruled that in the absence of proper proof of the alleged accident, there was no reason for demanding a breath test, or for arresting Mr Seward and giving him the other tests. (R. v. Seward.)* ◄

In such cases the word 'accident' must be given an ordinary rather than technical meaning. It is not limited to accidents after which drivers must stop and exchange information. The Lord Chief Justice has stated that in this context 'accident' means any unintended occurrence which has an adverse physical result, unless this was so trivial as not to be worth bothering about.

PLACE FOR THE TEST Since the first breath test is meant to be a roadside screening test, it must normally be carried out at or 'near by' the place where the driver is stopped.

If there has been an accident, however, a constable can require the motorist to go to a police station for a breath test; if the motorist has been taken to hospital, the police can carry out a test there as long as the doctor in charge of the case does not raise any objection.

Except in the case of an accident, a breath test can be carried out only on a road or other public place—that is, one which the public freely use, whether or not it is privately owned. The drive of a private house is not a public place in this sense.

The test need not be carried out on a road or public place, however, if the police rely on what is known as the 'rule of fresh pursuit'—a legal concept which gives a policeman who has seen someone committing an offence the right to follow and arrest him.

For example, a policeman who sees a driver commit a moving-traffic offence on a road is entitled to follow him on to private property and ask him to take a breath test there.

For a policeman to be able to rely on the rule of fresh pursuit, there must be no interruption in the chain of events between witnessing the offence and the arrest. If, for example, he loses track of a suspect and only finds him later in the drive of his house, the policeman would not be entitled to demand the breath test or arrest him for refusing.

WHO CAN BE TESTED The Road Traffic Act 1972 says that, where there are grounds, a breath test can be required only of any person 'driving or attempting to drive'—it does not say 'any driver'.

A motorist at the wheel of a car in motion is obviously driving, and can be stopped for a breath test. Even if he stops—to read a map, perhaps, or to mend a puncture or clean the windscreen—he can still, in law, be regarded as driving.

A motorist who happened to be held up in a traffic jam and dashed out of his car to buy a newspaper would be 'driving'. But one who parked his car to go shopping would not be, and the police would have no right to follow him into the supermarket to demand a breath test (except the right of fresh pursuit if he had been seen committing a driving offence). Nor would a motorist be 'driving' if he were waiting in a parked car for his wife.

A person has been held to be 'driving' when his engine-less car was being pushed and he was walking beside it, steering through the open window.

The expression 'attempting to drive' could include a driver trying to open the door of his car or trying to get the car started. It *might* also cover a driver asleep at the wheel of a stationary car.

MOTORIST 'IN CHARGE' No breath test can be given to a motorist who is merely 'in charge' of a vehicle—that is, a motorist who, though not actually driving, retains the means to drive. It is nevertheless an offence if he remains in charge of the vehicle while he has excess alcohol in his blood.

Though the police cannot arrest him under Section 6 (the 'breathalyser' law), they are entitled to arrest him under Section 5 (the 'impairment' law), and take him to a police station for a blood or urine test.

In road-traffic law, the term 'in charge' means something less than driving. As explained by a judge, 'the words "in charge" mean being responsible for the control or driving of the car . . . the person who is for the time being in control of the vehicle'. This means that somebody can be 'in charge' of a car even though it is parked, with the engine switched off.

Generally speaking, a person who has possession of the ignition key and who is in the car or in the near vicinity, is in charge of it. It is, however, a defence to prove that there was no likelihood of driving while the motorist's driving ability was impaired.

To establish this defence, he must do more than assure the court that he would never have considered driving in that state. The burden of proof is on him to satisfy the court that the *circumstances* were such that there was no likelihood of driving.

The best advice to a driver who feels that he has drunk too much is to give the keys to somebody else, or to put them away, in circumstances that ensure that he will not get them back until he has recovered.

## What happens if the test is positive

If the breath test is positive—that is, if the crystals turn green beyond the yellow ring on the breathalyser tube—the policeman has the right to arrest the driver and take him to a police station for further tests. A driver who is unable or unwilling to take the breath test can be arrested in the same way.

The arrest, and anything that follows it, has no legal effect if the breath test has not been properly conducted. This is why some motorists have been acquitted despite blood or urine tests which have shown that they were driving with an excess amount of alcohol in the blood.

In one case a motorist was told he was being arrested because of a positive result with a bag that had a hole. This was held not to be a valid arrest, and his conviction was quashed. He could have been arrested for refusing to take a second test, but this was not done.

The arrest must be clear and unambiguous. It must be made by words or actions that leave no doubt that the suspected driver has been placed under restraint, and is not free to leave at will. A polite request to accompany the constable to the police station has been held not to be an arrest.

The suspected driver must also be told, in general terms, the grounds on which the arrest is being made. It is not lawful for a motorist to be arrested for dangerous driving without any mention of drink, and then made to undergo blood or urine tests for alcohol in the police station. The prosecution must prove there was a valid arrest.

In some circumstances, however, he can be arrested under one of the drink-driving laws, given a blood or urine test, and prosecuted under the other drink-driving law.

To cut down the chance of this happening, a motorist being arrested after a breath test should ask the grounds of his arrest and, if possible, write down what he is told.

Suppose, for example, that a motorist is breathalysed under Section 6 of the Act, arrested and given further tests at a police station. Suppose, too, that the police then decide that the evidence appears more likely to secure a conviction under Section 5 (the 'impairment' law). If notes taken by the motorist at the time of his arrest show no mention was made of Section 5, and no evidence is produced that there were grounds for arrest under Section 5, this might cast doubt on the prosecution's case.

The police may overcome this difficulty, however, by telling a driver he is arrested under *both* drink-driving laws.

AT THE POLICE STATION A driver arrested under either of the drink-driving laws is offered the chance of a breath test at the police station, whether or not he has had a roadside test.

When the arrest has been made under the 'breathalyser' law this will be his second breath test which acts as a check on the first. It is carried out in the presence of a different and perhaps senior police officer, so that there is no possibility of a motorist having to undergo blood or urine tests if the first breathalyser test was wrong.

Everyone is entitled to refuse to undergo the blood or urine test until he has been offered this breath test in the police station.

## Compulsory blood or urine tests

If the breath test in the police station is positive (or if the motorist refuses it), the police can move on to the next stage. This is to ask the driver to undergo a blood or urine test.

The driver must be warned that refusal to provide a specimen of blood or urine will make him liable to imprisonment, a fine and disqualification. If this warning is not given, a driver who refuses to take the test should be acquitted in any later criminal proceedings. Should he agree, however, in spite of not being warned, the court would probably disregard the omission.

If a specimen is taken from a hospital patient the doctor must be asked whether it is all right for the warning to be given.

In requesting the test, the police must follow the correct procedure:

**1.** The arrested person must first be asked to provide a specimen of blood.
**2.** If he refuses, he is asked to provide two specimens of urine within the hour.
**3.** If he fails or refuses, he must be asked again to provide a specimen of blood.

If he continues to refuse, and there is no reasonable excuse for his refusal—such as ill-health—he is treated as if he had provided a specimen which proved positive, and is liable to be prosecuted and punished accordingly.

DECIDING WHICH TEST TO CHOOSE Nearly all doctors who have experience of the drink-driving laws prefer the blood test, because it gives a more reliable reading of the proportion of alcohol in the blood. The urine test can give a reading higher or lower than a blood test taken at the same time.

## The blood test

Specimens of blood are taken by a doctor, usually a police surgeon. The courts have ruled that a refusal to let the doctor draw blood from the place he considers suitable amounts to refusal to provide a specimen.

Usually, the blood is taken in a room set aside for the purpose, Many doctors carry out a medical examination before taking blood—both to find out if the driver needs attention, perhaps for an undetected injury after an accident, and also to make sure that the apparent symptoms of drunkenness are not due to illness.

The doctor will usually explain the difference between the blood and urine tests. If the suspect chooses to provide a blood specimen, the doctor will then ask him for permission to proceed.

The motorist is entitled to have his own doctor and solicitor present at any examination, provided they come without undue delay. Delay can obviously defeat the object of the tests and a court has held that a driver who delayed taking tests for an unreasonable time while awaiting the arrival of his doctor and solicitor had refused the test.

The police surgeon will normally say where he is going to take the blood from and indicate the method he will use—taking blood from capillaries or from a vein.

If capillary blood is taken, the method used is 'stabbing'—with a small, shovel-like instrument—which can be slightly unpleasant. Capillary blood is taken from a skin puncture, most commonly of the finger, or perhaps the ear lobe.

The operation must be performed so as to produce enough blood for testing without squeezing the skin, since this results in the specimen being contaminated with plasma, which has a higher alcohol content than the blood itself. In addition, the sample must not be contaminated by an alcohol-based disinfectant used to clean the skin before the incision is made.

Most police surgeons use a syringe to extract blood from a vein, usually in the arm. This is painless, simple and quick, and there is a minimum risk of a misleadingly high reading through contamination. A motorist would have every right to ask the doctor to extract blood from a vein.

Sufficient blood must be taken both to carry out tests and to provide the arrested driver with a sample for independent testing. This means not fewer than nine drops, which are collected with as little delay as possible, and put into three cups, which are numbered 1, 2 and 3.

The cups, which contain an anti-coagulant substance to prevent the blood from clotting, are sealed and labelled in the presence of the suspect. Cups 1 and 2 are then placed in a special tin container, which is itself sealed, and the label is signed by the police officer in charge. These samples are handed to the police officer, in the presence of the suspect, to be forwarded to the laboratory for testing.

Cup 3 is also placed in a sealed tin—to prevent interference with the contents—and signed by the police officer. The suspect should be told that this sample will, on his release, be handed to him for independent analysis if he wishes it. If a suspect asks for a sample but is not given one, no evidence of the result of the laboratory test on the specimen will be admissible in court.

The request can be made days after release from the police station, provided the delay is not unreasonable.

### The urine test

If the motorist chooses the urine test, a doctor is not called unless there are special circumstances, such as suspicion of injury from an accident. The police, as far as possible, respect the driver's feelings of modesty when he is asked to provide urine. Nevertheless they keep a discreet watch, to ensure that the specimen is not diluted or tampered with by the driver.

Although the arrested driver is given a free choice between a blood test and a urine test, the urine test is, in many ways, less satisfactory than the blood test.

Since the walls of the bladder are poorly provided with blood vessels, alcohol in the body takes longer to permeate into the urine.

For the same reason, once in the urine, it takes longer to be eliminated.

This means that there is always a time-lag between the alcohol levels in the blood and urine. In the early stages of drinking, or soon afterwards, there is a lower level in the urine than in the blood; in the later stages, there is a higher level in the urine than in the blood.

Furthermore, when drinking commences, alcohol is diluted by the alcohol-free urine already contained in the bladder. This gives a completely false reflection of the alcohol content of the body as a whole—at least until the drinker passes water.

To try to equalise all these factors, the suspect is required to provide *two* samples of urine—the first to be disregarded, the second to be provided within one hour. This is a way of getting the suspect to empty his bladder before giving the test specimen.

The Act also states that the alcohol level in the urine is to be multiplied by a factor of 107/80. This is to convert it to the blood-alcohol level reading.

MARGINS OF ERROR The method used for measuring the proportion of alcohol in the blood or urine—the gas chromatography test—is considered accurate to within 2 per cent. Since it might be unsafe to convict a driver on a test result that showed an alcohol level of 80 mg per cent or marginally above it, the police do not normally prosecute unless the level is more than 86 mg per cent.

### Results of the test

Once the test or tests have been completed, the motorist will be allowed to go—usually after yet another breath test to show that he is sober enough to drive his vehicle.

Alternatively, the motorist can use public transport or may be taken home in a police car.

The result of blood or urine tests is not known for some time—usually about three weeks. If the test is positive, the motorist receives a summons, together with a copy of the laboratory analyst's report. The report must be sent to the motorist at least seven days before the trial. If it is not he is entitled to object to its admissibility before the close of the prosecution's case.

If the test is negative, the motorist is usually informed—though there is no legal obligation on the police to let him know.

There is no time limit within which a summons must be issued after a breath test; but if an unreasonable delay occurred, the case might be dismissed on the ground that the defence had been hampered by the delay.
□ Penalties for motoring offenders, p. 173.

# How much can you drink—and drive?

THE blood-alcohol level above which a motorist can be prosecuted under the 'breathalyser' law was fixed at 80 mg per 100 ml of blood, because at this point the driving ability of most motorists will be impaired. But there is no way of measuring how dangerous or incompetent a driver will be at this point—indeed, some will still be able to drive safely and competently.

Nor can it be accurately stated how much drink will have to be consumed to reach 80 mg per cent. This depends on many factors—the form in which alcohol is taken, and the rate at which it is absorbed by the bloodstream; the physique and general condition of the drinker; the time taken for drinking; and whether the drink was taken with a meal or on an empty stomach.

DIFFERENT FORMS OF ALCOHOL There is a constant process of destruction of alcohol by the liver. It can break down the equivalent of a single whisky in about an hour, and so cope with moderate amounts of alcohol if they are in a form which is absorbed slowly. But forms of alcohol which are absorbed quickly soon overtake the destruction rate, and give rise to a building-up of the blood-alcohol level.

*Wine* is absorbed slowly, because of its sugar content.

*Beer* is a diluted form of alcohol because of its high content of soluble nutrients, and is absorbed slowly. Doctors assume that the blood-alcohol level after drinking beer will be as little as one-third of that when the same amount of alcohol is drunk as hard spirits.

*Spirits* are absorbed rapidly when taken neat or diluted, because the process is not slowed down by a sugar or nutrient content. They are absorbed even more quickly when taken with soda, because the aeration keeps the alcohol circulating in the digestive system.

THE DRIVER'S PHYSIQUE The blood-alcohol level after consuming a fixed amount of alcohol will also vary according to the body-weight of the drinker.

What the blood test measures is the concentration of alcohol in the body fluids, and hence the amount that can affect the brain. A small person, taking the same amount of alcohol as a larger person, has less body fluids to dilute it, and so will have a higher blood-alcohol level. One important result of this is that 80 mg per cent is reached in the average woman with about two-thirds of the alcohol required to reach the same level in the average man.

People who are overweight will also have a higher blood-alcohol level for a given amount of alcohol, because fat absorbs alcohol slowly, and by not taking its share of the absorption, leaves a higher proportion of alcohol in the blood and other body tissues.

Heavy drinkers absorb alcohol more quickly than others, because there is less delay in the alcohol passing into the intestines, from which it passes rapidly into the bloodstream.

The same amount of alcohol might at different times produce different blood-alcohol levels in the same person. This would depend on his state of health, fatigue, and on the possible effect of medicines or other drugs that he may have in his system.

THE TIME TAKEN FOR DRINKING When drink is taken over a period, and in moderation, absorption will act as the driver's protection. Drinks taken socially with food and at leisure, result in considerably lower blood-alcohol concentrations than solitary drinking in unconvivial circumstances.

THE EFFECT OF A MEAL Most of all, the rate of absorption of alcohol depends on whether the drinker has food in his stomach before drinking. Foods such as mashed potatoes, gravy, milk and oils insulate the stomach walls from alcohol, and so decrease both the risk of drunkenness and the blood-alcohol level. A meal taken with drink has some effect on reducing the blood-alcohol level, but it does not help to eat *after* drinking.

HOW MUCH IS IT SAFE TO DRINK? Because the same amount of alcohol can produce widely differing blood-alcohol levels in different people—or even in the same person at different times and under different circumstances—medical authorities are unanimous in the belief that no reliable guide can be given as to how much a driver can drink without the danger of exceeding the limit.

Indeed, such a guide can be positively harmful if it encourages a motorist to believe that he can 'safely' drink a given amount. For if that amount, however small, impairs his driving ability, he is liable to be prosecuted for driving, attempting to drive or being in charge of a car when unfit through drink or drugs. Such a charge can be brought irrespective of a motorist's blood-alcohol level.

# Drink and driving II : the 'impairment' law

*What 'impairment' means*
*The right to refuse a test*

A MOTORIST whose ability to drive is impaired by drink or drugs can be prosecuted without a breath test, or even if his breath test proves negative. The prosecution will be under Section 5 of the Road Traffic Act 1972 (the 'impairment' law) which makes it an offence to drive, attempt to drive, or be in charge of a motor vehicle on a road or any public place when unfit through drink or drugs. It defines 'unfitness to drive' as meaning that 'the ability to drive properly is for the time being impaired'.

'Drugs' include any medicinal substance—even one which has no effect on driving ability by itself, but is harmful with alcohol.

The 'impairment' law covers a variety of situations in which the motorist's conduct does not warrant prosecution under Section 6 of the Act (the 'breathalyser' law), or in which Section 6 is difficult to apply for practical reasons.

One such situation is the case of the driver who has less than the prescribed level of alcohol in his bloodstream, but has consumed enough to make his driving a danger.

It is used, too, by the policemen on the beat. Since the breathalyser equipment is not suitable for carrying in the pocket, it is not issued to them, but they can make an arrest under the 'impairment' law (which does not require a breath test), and take the suspect to a police station for a blood or urine test.

## What 'impairment' means
In theory, the slightest impairment of driving ability through drink or drugs is enough to infringe the law. In practice, it has not worked out like that.

An experienced driver, slightly impaired by drink, may still be a safer and better driver than a learner who has had no drink.

Again, impairment is a matter of opinion and of degree. There is no way of measuring it accurately.

For these reasons, a conviction will result only when there has been a clear case of a driver being intoxicated.

Three main types of evidence are accepted by the courts to show that a motorist's driving is impaired: the observations of witnesses, medical examinations by doctors, and the results of blood or urine tests.

OBSERVATIONS OF WITNESSES Evidence of the way the defendant was driving, or of his behaviour soon afterwards, may be given by witnesses.

Evidence is often given of the defendant's erratic driving—or of over-cautious driving, which is a well-known characteristic of the inebriated driver.

MEDICAL EVIDENCE Abnormal driving (including driving which causes an accident) can be the result of causes other than alcohol—illness or injury sustained in a previous accident, for example. For this reason, a medical certificate from a doctor who examined the driver in the police station is a condition for any proceedings under the 'impairment' law.

Medical evidence cannot be used unless the driver agrees to the examination. If he agrees, under a misapprehension that the examination was solely to find out if he had been injured in a crash, the courts have held that the doctor's evidence or a medical report *cannot* be used in an attempt to prove intoxication.

TEST RESULTS The results of blood and urine tests have been standard evidence in drink-driving cases since 1962. Although there is no set limit of alcohol intake in 'impairment' cases, doctors and the courts have accepted that the driving ability of anybody who drinks a large quantity of alcohol is likely to be impaired.

## The right to refuse a test
Under the 'impairment' law, a driver has to consent before a blood or urine test can be carried out. He will be committing no offence if he refuses, but the fact that he has refused can be pointed out to the court or jury.

On the other hand, under the 'breathalyser' law, a driver who refuses to provide a blood or urine sample is treated as if the test were positive. □ The breathalyser law, p. 87.

A driver should try to find out, and write down at the time of his arrest, under which section of the Road Traffic Act 1972 he is being arrested—Section 5 (the 'impairment' law) or Section 6 (the 'breathalyser' law). □ Penalties for motoring offenders, p. 173.

# Dealing with bad driving

*Reckless or dangerous driving*
*Defences against dangerous driving*

*Careless or inconsiderate driving*

**B**AD driving is divided by law into two broad offences—reckless or dangerous driving and careless or inconsiderate driving. They are vaguely defined offences which often overlap with one another and with other minor offences. Driving without lights at night, for instance, speeding, or driving with excess alcohol in the blood, besides being offences in themselves, might also amount to dangerous or careless driving. Whether they do or not depends on the risks created for other road users.

The two offences have been phrased vaguely to allow flexibility in their application, since their primary purpose is to enforce safe driving standards.

Reckless or dangerous driving is considered more serious than careless or inconsiderate driving and the maximum penalties are higher. It is a charge aimed at drivers who are gravely irresponsible, and has been defined by one judge as the deliberate choice by a driver of a course of conduct that created danger.

Careless or inconsiderate driving is a charge designed to deal with the foolish, inattentive or thoughtless driver.

The distinction, however, is largely theoretical. In practice, the more serious charge of reckless or dangerous driving is usually brought against the motorist who, in the opinion of the police, has caused an accident. Conversely, since it is difficult to prove dangerous or reckless driving in the abstract, the erring motorist who has not actually caused an accident is usually charged with careless driving. Thus a motorist is liable to more severe punishment for a minor driving lapse that causes an accident, than for really bad driving that harms no one.

## Reckless or dangerous driving

In effect, the offence of reckless or dangerous driving amounts to three separate offences: reckless driving; driving at a dangerous speed; and driving in a dangerous manner.

RECKLESS DRIVING The courts interpret reckless driving as taking risks with gross indifference to the safety of others. It contains an element of wilfully aggressive driving which does not necessarily have to be present

for charges of driving at a dangerous speed or in a dangerous manner to be brought, and is usually punished more severely.

An example would be a driver who speeds along a street crowded with children leaving school, expecting them to flee for safety.

Anyone can note such a driver's registration number and report him to the police. The more evidence there is from other witnesses, the more likely the police are to take action against the driver.

DRIVING AT A DANGEROUS SPEED Whether speeding amounts to dangerous driving depends not only on traffic on the road but also on potential traffic.

Speed must be related to other factors to decide whether it amounts to dangerous driving. For example, a motorist travelling at 65 mph on a straight, unrestricted road would not normally be guilty of driving at a dangerous speed. But if he accelerated to 65 mph to overtake another car which was itself overtaking a bus he almost certainly would be guilty, since the whole manoeuvre would be considered dangerous.

Exceeding the speed limit is not the same as driving at a dangerous speed. It might not be dangerous to drive at, say, 35 mph on a restricted road, even though this would be a speeding offence.

Speeding is made dangerous by weather conditions (say, ice or fog), the road surface or the presence of other traffic, and similar circumstances. ☐ Speeding, p. 84.

➤FAST, BUT NOT DANGEROUS *A motor cyclist riding on a main road in 1959 (before the maximum 70 mph limit was imposed) passed a minor road junction at 85–90 mph. The minor road was controlled by a 'Slow—major road ahead' sign, and the motor cyclist had a clear view along both the major and minor roads before and during his crossing of the junction. However, he was charged with dangerous driving and also with driving without due care and attention.*
DECISION *Although his speed had been excessive, there were no circumstances to show that it was dangerous. He was found not guilty on both charges. (Johnstone* v. *Hawkins.)*◄

DRIVING IN A DANGEROUS MANNER A large number of driving errors are covered by the offence of driving in a dangerous manner—for instance, failing to stop at a traffic light; driving too fast in fog; swerving in front of other traffic; and driving with faulty brakes. In fact, any lapse from 'reasonable' standards can amount to dangerous driving.

The standard of care which the law demands from all drivers has been summed up by a judge in this way: 'It is clear . . . that if a driver adopts a manner of driving which the jury thinks was dangerous to other road users in all the circumstances, then on the issue of guilt it matters not whether he was deliberately reckless, careless, momentarily inattentive or even doing his incompetent best.'

So, although this is one of the most serious driving offences, it can be committed by the slightest miscalculation or inattention.

A charge of dangerous driving can result from driving a car in a defective condition.

When it appears that an accident was caused by a sudden mechanical fault, it is usual for a police mechanic to inspect the vehicle to see whether a prudent motorist could reasonably have suspected or have known about the defect, or whether it was caused by inadequate maintenance. Such evidence would be produced to support a charge of dangerous driving.

The courts have held that, when an unforeseeable mechanical defect in the vehicle causes an accident, the driver is not guilty of dangerous driving.

**Defences against dangerous driving**
At one time a motorist was held to be guilty of dangerous driving if he created a dangerous situation, irrespective of whether he thought he was doing the right or safe thing.

In 1972, however, the Appeal Court ruled that a driver who does everything possible to avoid causing a dangerous situation is not guilty of the offence.

➤ THE WRONG-WAY DRIVER *Mrs Doreen Rose Gosney drove the wrong way down a dual carriageway. She was charged with dangerous driving. The court refused to hear her explanation—that she had turned into the road and there was nothing to suggest that a right turn was prohibited or that it led her to go the wrong direction down a dual carriageway. The court held that such evidence was irrelevant since the offence was committed whether or not she was to blame. She appealed.*
DECISION *The Court of Appeal quashed her conviction. It ruled that before a driver could be guilty of the offence, it must be shown that he was in some way to blame.*

*This did not mean that he must have been deliberately reckless or careless: a slight or momentary lapse would be enough. A poor or inexperienced driver would be guilty if he fell below the standard of a competent driver even though he was genuinely doing his best.*

*The court added that it need not be shown that the fault was the sole cause of the dangerous situation—it was enough if it was a cause. But if the driver could show that he was not to blame at all he should be acquitted. (R. v. Gosney.)* ◄

The courts recognise a defence known as 'automatism'. When a driver has lost physical control over his actions through no fault of his own, he is regarded in law as not driving at all.

So the driver who is stung by a swarm of bees, stunned by a stone thrown up through an open window or who suffers an unexpected blackout and loses control of his car is not guilty of dangerous driving. A defence of automatism rarely succeeds.

A sudden unexpected emergency can sometimes be a defence—swerving into another car to avoid hitting a child, for example, or a sudden shattering of the windscreen. But the emergency must not have been created by the driver's own actions.

The driver who felt giddy and lost control of his car ten minutes after being hit by a stone would have no defence if it could be proved that he could have pulled up to recover in the meantime.

PROCEDURE A prosecution for one of these offences will fail unless the police warn the defendant at the time of the offence that he will be reported with a view to prosecution, or the police send a written notice of intended prosecution or summons in the prescribed manner. ☐ What happens if you are prosecuted, p. 100.

The written notice will normally be for three offences—dangerous or reckless driving, careless driving and driving without reasonable consideration. Until he receives the summons, the motorist will not know which charge is to be proceeded with.

Motorists who are charged with dangerous driving have a choice of being tried either in a magistrates' court or by a jury at a Crown Court.

The motorist who considers he might stand a better chance of being acquitted by a jury should, however, bear in mind that if there is any alternative summons for careless driving, this will be adjourned and he may still have to face this summons even if acquitted on the charge of dangerous driving.

Anyone charged with both dangerous and careless driving may hope that, if he pleads guilty to the lesser charge, no evidence will be offered on the more serious offence. However, courts usually insist on hearing the evidence before permitting a charge of dangerous driving to be withdrawn.

## Careless or inconsiderate driving

Driving without due care and attention, and driving without reasonable consideration for other people using the road, are two separate offences. The prosecution must take action for one offence or the other, and an accused driver is entitled to know which of the two offences he is accused of committing.

The offences are vaguely defined, to deal with a wide range of driving misbehaviour. The test is whether the motorist was exercising the degree of care and attention or consideration for other road users that a prudent driver would have used in the same circumstances.

In many cases, evidence that the accused motorist failed to comply with the Highway Code is given in support of a prosecution.

CARE AND ATTENTION Motorists have been found guilty of driving without due care and attention for:

Signalling a turn to the right and then turning left.

Overtaking on a curve, in the mistaken belief that the car ahead was signalling that it was safe to pass.

Edging on to a road, when the view of the road was obstructed by other vehicles.

Driving at 25 mph past an obscured halt sign, although the white line was visible, and colliding with a car on the main road.

Reading a newspaper while driving.

Skidding on to the pavement and hitting a telegraph pole 3 ft from the road in normal weather conditions.

REASONABLE CONSIDERATION Motorists have been convicted of driving without reasonable consideration for:

Failing to dip main beam headlights for oncoming traffic.

Driving quickly through a puddle and drenching pedestrians.

Driving a bus in such a way as to frighten passengers and people on the road.

PROCEDURE Careless or inconsiderate driving cases are heard only by magistrates.

☐ Penalties for motoring offenders, p. 173.

---

## What happens if the motorist is ill or tired

IF a motorist loses control of his car as a result of a sudden attack of illness—and thereby endangers others—he is guilty of dangerous driving if he could have known that an attack would occur.

People taking drugs are expected to seek medical advice on whether their driving is likely to be impaired, and if necessary to abstain from driving until the course of treatment has ended.

Any driver with a history of blackouts or a recurring illness runs the risk of committing the offence.

➤THE MOTORIST WHO BLACKED OUT *Mr Sibbles, who suffered from high blood pressure and dizzy spells, had a drink before starting a journey. During the drive, his car swerved from side to side and collided with an oncoming car, killing a passenger. He was charged with driving in a dangerous manner.*

*Mr Sibbles claimed he had no recollection of the accident; he said that all he remembered was feeling unwell just before the accident occurred* *and banging his head on the windscreen.*
DECISION *Mr Sibbles was convicted. The court said that a person who knows he is prone to dizzy spells or blackouts could not use this as a defence against a charge of dangerous driving. (R. v. Sibbles.)* ◄

Falling asleep or driving while in a state of drowsiness can amount to dangerous driving. In one case it was argued that a driver who fell asleep at the wheel was in the same position as one overcome by a sudden coma—he had no control over his actions and therefore, from a legal point of view, he could not be guilty because he was not driving at all—a defence known as automatism.

The courts rejected this argument, stating that a driver must stop when he feels drowsiness coming on. But if he is on a motorway, he must continue until the next exit or service area—since not even drowsiness is an excuse for stopping on the hard shoulder. Any person who stops on the hard shoulder of a motorway because of tiredness can be prosecuted.

# Causing death on the road

*Manslaughter*
*Death by dangerous driving*

A MOTORIST who kills somebody by bad driving may be guilty either of manslaughter, or of causing death by reckless or dangerous driving. Most prosecutions which follow a road death are for causing death by dangerous driving.

## Manslaughter
Killing by motor vehicle is only one of the methods of killing dealt with under the heading of manslaughter. A driver can be convicted only if the death resulted from particularly ruthless or callous driving. Death must be proved to be the result of the criminal manner of driving. But it is no defence in a manslaughter case to show that the dead person was partly to blame through his own negligence, or that he died because he did not get prompt or adequate medical attention.

A manslaughter charge can be brought only if the death occurred within a year and a day of the road accident.

PROCEDURE Manslaughter cases can be tried only by a Crown Court. It is *not* necessary for a motorist to be served with a notice of intended prosecution.

## Death by dangerous driving
The offence of causing death by dangerous driving was created because juries were thought to be over-sympathetic to motorists charged with manslaughter, and tended to acquit many killer-drivers.

If the death of a person—another driver, perhaps, a pedestrian, or a passenger in the defendant's car—is caused wholly or partly by driving recklessly, dangerously or at a dangerous speed, the offence of causing death by dangerous driving has been committed. The slightest lapse from reasonable driving standards, and sometimes even blameless driving that creates a road danger, is sufficient for a motorist to be convicted. ☐ Dealing with bad driving, p. 96.

It is no defence for a driver to say that the accident was the result of a minor mistake or miscalculation on his part if his driving error resulted in the dangerous situation that caused the death.

Causing death by dangerous driving is an offence of strict liability. The same standard of driving is expected of everyone—the court looks at the results, not the driver.

> ➤ HALF A DUAL CARRIAGEWAY *Mr Johnson was driving at night on a road where a flyover was under construction. One side of the road was closed, so that traffic going in both directions had to use the same half of the road. He pulled out to overtake and came into head-on collision with another car, the driver of which was killed.*
> *Mr Johnson was charged with causing death by dangerous driving. He claimed that he was innocent because he reasonably thought that he was driving along a dual carriageway and that any oncoming traffic would be on the other part of the road.*
> DECISION *The court ruled that the intention of the driver as to the way in which he was driving was immaterial to the charge. A mistaken belief that he was on a dual carriageway was an explanation of dangerous driving, but it was no answer to the charge. Mr Johnson was convicted, fined £75 and disqualified from driving for three years. (R. v. Johnson.)*◄

Once the jury is satisfied that the defendant drove recklessly or dangerously, it must then decide whether this driving caused the death. This can often be a difficult problem, for it is not uncommon, after an accident, to find that more than one person is to blame.

If the dangerous driving was a substantial cause of death, the driver is guilty—and what the court considers 'substantial' depends on the facts. Usually if other drivers are chiefly to blame and the defendant's contribution is very slight, he will be acquitted.

If a number of people are jointly responsible for a death in a road accident, this will not exonerate any one of them who is subsequently charged with causing the death by reckless or dangerous driving.

PROCEDURE Causing death by reckless or dangerous driving can be tried only by a Crown Court.

A prison sentence can be imposed even for a first offence, especially if the motorist failed to stop after the accident. ☐ Penalties for motoring offenders, p. 173.

# What happens if you are prosecuted

*Receiving a warning*  *Deciding how to plead*
*Getting legal advice*  *Preparing the case*
*Receiving the summons*  *What happens in court*

THE sooner a driver hears that he may face prosecution for a motoring offence, the sooner he can begin collecting evidence and preparing his defence. Too long a delay may seriously hamper attempts to prove his innocence.

The law therefore aims to ensure that, as soon as the police have grounds to believe that a motorist has committed an offence, he is informed that he may be prosecuted.

In some cases a motorist may be seen by the police at the scene of an incident and told that he will be reported 'with a view to prosecution'; in others, he may be notified by post. In the most serious cases he may be arrested and taken to a police station to be charged there. ☐ How defendants are brought to court, p. 741.

### Receiving a warning

There are a number of offences for which a motorist cannot be prosecuted successfully unless he is notified promptly that proceedings may be taken.

These offences are:

**1.** Failing to comply with traffic signals or police directions.

**2.** Leaving a car or other vehicle in a dangerous position.

**3.** Speeding.

**4.** Careless, dangerous or reckless driving (or cycling).

A prosecution for any of these offences will not succeed unless the motorist is warned at the time of the incident that he may be prosecuted, or the police can show that a summons or a document called a notice of intended prosecution was delivered to him within 14 days of the alleged offence.

A summons is an order to appear in court; a notice of intended prosecution is a document setting out the offence for which the police intend to prosecute.

A notice of intended prosecution for careless or dangerous driving must be addressed to the motorist who is to be charged.

A notice for any other offence may be addressed either to the motorist to be charged or to the registered owner of the vehicle. To be valid, it must be posted in time for it to be delivered within 14 days of the alleged offence.

If the notice fails to arrive within 14 days of the alleged offence for reasons other than late posting—for example, because of the inefficiency of the Post Office—it is still valid in law.

### Getting legal advice

When a motorist learns that he may be prosecuted, he should take steps as soon as possible to obtain legal advice.

He may decide to use a solicitor who has acted for him before or he may choose to find someone who deals specifically with motoring offences. The advice of a professional friend or someone who has had experience of a motoring charge may help him to choose.

If help is needed with fees, he should inform the solicitor at the outset. ☐ Legal aid I: help with fees and costs, p. 710.

THE AA SCHEME Members of motoring organisations can usually obtain legal advice and often representation in court when they are charged with an offence involving a vehicle. The Automobile Association, for example, offers free legal advice and representation for cases heard in a magistrates' court, and may also provide free legal help when a member is charged with manslaughter or with causing death by dangerous driving.

A motorist who wants to make use of this service should send the notice of intended prosecution (or summons) to the AA's legal department as soon as it is received. Write to the nearest AA regional office, giving a full, clear account of what happened.

The AA, either directly or through solicitors working for it in towns throughout Britain, then acts on behalf of the member.

He will be informed of the solicitor handling his case and it will be necessary for him to visit the solicitor's office—possibly more than once—in order to arrange the preparation of his defence.

PRESENTING HIS OWN CASE Where a serious offence is involved, the motorist should always seek legal advice, but in minor matters he may decide to present his own case or to appear in court with the help of a friend who is not a lawyer. It is important for him to remember, however, that when he does so he may be at a disadvantage because of his lack of legal knowledge.

His first line of defence is to make sure that he has been properly charged. If there are mistakes in the charge or in the procedure in presenting it, he may be able to get it dropped on technical grounds. Even when this happens, however, the police may still be able to charge him again correctly—within certain time limits.

WHERE TO CHECK A defendant can check the legal implications of a charge in reference books. All offences that can be tried in a magistrates' court are listed in *Stone's Justices' Manual* (Butterworth). A comprehensive guide to the law is provided by *Halsbury's Laws of England* (Butterworth).

Someone without legal training may find it easier to understand a textbook which deals not only with the law itself but also includes an interpretation of it. The one used by lawyers is Archbold, *Criminal Pleading, Evidence and Practice* (Sweet and Maxwell).

A detailed account of motoring law is given in *Road Traffic Offences* by G. S. Wilkinson (Oyez Publications), which covers Acts of Parliament and cases showing how these are interpreted by the courts.

If the offence with which he is charged is covered by an Act of Parliament, the motorist can buy a copy at Her Majesty's Stationery Office or a bookshop that sells HMSO publications. If a local bye-law is involved, he should get a copy from the offices of the local authority.

## Receiving the summons

The notice of intended prosecution is not itself an order for the defendant to appear in court. He is not obliged to answer any charge until he has received a summons, giving his name, address, the charge against him, and the time and place of the hearing.

He is entitled to reasonable notice of the hearing and if he feels that he cannot adequately prepare his defence in the time allowed, he or his solicitor should write to the clerk of the court immediately he receives notification of the date and ask for an adjournment.

An application can also be made on the day of the hearing, but if it is not granted, the accused has no alternative but to proceed with his defence as best he can, even if his case is not complete.

FAILING TO ANSWER A SUMMONS A defendant should never ignore a summons. In most cases if he does not appear in court when the case is called, the magistrate is entitled to issue a warrant for his arrest. □ How defendants are brought to court, p. 741.

## Deciding how to plead

The most important decision a defendant has to take is what answer he intends to give to the charge against him. When a serious offence is involved he should take legal advice before making his decision. Even on minor matters he should not plead guilty if he believes that he is innocent of the offence.

Some people plead guilty because they think it is not worth contesting the word of a police officer, or because they do not want to spare the time to attend the hearing.

Yet except in limited cases, involving offences for which there are fixed penalties, when a defendant pleads guilty he has a conviction recorded against him. □ Powers of police and traffic wardens, p. 82.

PLEADING GUILTY BY POST If the offence is one which can be tried only at a magistrates' court or which cannot be punished with more than three months' imprisonment, the defendant may, if he wishes, plead guilty by post. He does not then have to appear personally at the hearing. □ Penalties for motoring offenders, p. 173.

The summons is accompanied by a form which must be completed by anyone who wants to plead guilty by post. The form also has a section in which the defendant can give any extenuating circumstances that he thinks the magistrates should take into consideration when deciding what penalty to impose.

In general, however, it is advisable for a defendant who believes there are special reasons why he should be treated leniently to attend court in person.

A defendant who pleads guilty by post can decide at any time before the hearing that he wants to attend and he can even change his plea to one of 'not guilty'.

In such circumstances, he should inform the clerk of the court in good time so that the police may ensure that their witnesses can appear if necessary.

CHOOSING THE COURT Most of the motoring charges heard in England and Wales are dealt with in magistrates' courts. But in some circumstances the defendant—or the police—can choose to have the case tried by a judge sitting with a jury, instead of having it heard by the magistrates.

Motoring cases which can be heard by a jury are:

**1.** Dangerous driving.

**2.** Drink and driving charges.

**3.** Taking away a motor vehicle without the owner's consent.

**4.** Driving while disqualified.

**5.** Offences involving false declarations and fraudulent use of excise licences.

Before deciding to ask for trial by jury, the defendant should take legal advice. Although there may be advantages in having his case decided by the ordinary members of the public who make up a jury, on the other hand the penalties that can be imposed in a higher court are more severe. In addition, AA free legal services are not available. ☐ Penalties for motoring offenders, p. 173; How defendants are brought to court, p. 741.

WHEN THE ACCUSED HAS NO CHOICE A motorist who is accused of motor manslaughter or causing death by dangerous driving can be tried only at a Crown Court. He must usually appear before magistrates for committal to the higher court.

### Preparing the case

When a defendant has a solicitor acting on his behalf, the preparation of the case may be left to his lawyer. The motorist who decides to represent himself in court must obtain as much supporting evidence as possible.

WITNESSES' STATEMENTS When he intends to call witnesses in court, a defendant should prepare a written or typed statement of the evidence they will give. Each statement should have the name, address and occupation of the witness at the top of the page. Underneath should be a summary of the evidence the witness intends to give in court, in the order that the events happened.

Witnesses are not allowed to read their statements in court, but the defendant can use the statements as a guide for his questioning, and they will also help him in the preparation of his defence.

A witness can give evidence only about matters within his personal knowledge. Anything that he has heard from other people and of which he has no direct knowledge is 'hearsay' evidence and is not normally allowed in English law.

ISSUING A SUBPOENA No witness is under an automatic legal obligation to give evidence. But if he refuses, the defendant can apply for a witness summons or subpoena to compel his attendance.

It is advisable, however, to think carefully before compelling a reluctant witness to appear on your behalf. Such evidence can often add to a defendant's difficulties.

When a defendant decides nevertheless to subpoena a reluctant witness he must apply

to the court in which the case is to be heard. If the order is granted, it is served on the witness by the police.

It is important that a defendant should know the proper name and address of any witness he intends to subpoena, to help police to serve the summons.

If a subpoena or witness summons has to be issued, the court must be given reasonable time in which to serve it. At the same time, what is called 'conduct money' must be paid or offered to the witness. This is a sum of money to cover the cost of the witness's travelling to and from court, plus compensation for his loss of time. These amounts are calculated according to a scale depending on the distance to be travelled and the witness's occupation.

ATTENDANCE BY WITNESSES It is the defendant's responsibility to ensure that his witnesses attend the court at the time of the hearing and he should issue a subpoena if he thinks it doubtful whether they may attend.

In the case of expert witnesses such as doctors or engineers who are required to give professional advice, a fee must be paid, agreed by arrangement and probably paid before they attend the hearing.

WHEN WITNESSES NEED NOT ATTEND When a witness's evidence is formal or not contested by the police, it may be unnecessary for him to be present at the hearing.

When a defendant wants to make an arrangement of this kind, he must follow the procedure laid down by Section 10 of the Criminal Justice Act 1967. He must ensure that the witness writes on each page of his statement of evidence: 'The contents of this page are true to the best of my knowledge and belief and I know that I am liable to prosecution if they are false or known to be untrue.' He must also sign each individual page of the statement separately.

One copy of the evidence must then be delivered to the police and a copy to the clerk of the court.

If the prosecution chooses, it can insist that any witness should appear at the court hearing to answer questions under cross-examination. The magistrates themselves may also decide that a witness should attend the hearing to explain his evidence.

### Attending the hearing

On the day of the trial, a defendant and his witnesses should arrive at the magistrates' court named in the summons well before the session is due to begin. The time the court starts is given in the summons. Although the time stated is often 10 or 10.30 in the morning, the case may not in fact be called until late in the afternoon.

On arriving at the court, the defendant should check the list of cases to be heard that day or ask at the court office to find out in which court his case is to be heard.

It is also useful for him or his solicitor to contact the police or the prosecution's solicitor to find out if it is likely that the case will not be reached. At such times, it may be possible to release witnesses, although the defendant will have to remain in the court in case the magistrates are ready to begin the hearing.

The defendant should take with him all the relevant and original documents that concern his case, including letters and receipts. For example, a motorist accused of driving a faulty vehicle might well produce garage bills and receipts showing that the faulty parts had been checked or repaired shortly before the alleged offence.

If a driver was involved in an accident, he should draw a map, and bring it to court. □ Making a plan of the accident, p. 108.

TAKING NOTES IN COURT A defendant, even

## Who's who in a magistrates' court

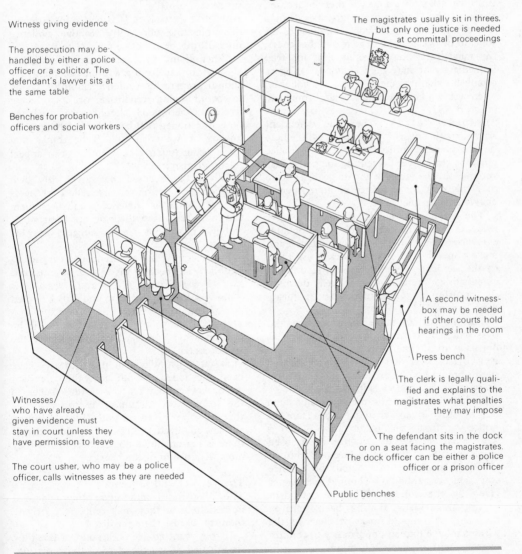

Witness giving evidence

The prosecution may be handled by either a police officer or a solicitor. The defendant's lawyer sits at the same table

Benches for probation officers and social workers

The magistrates usually sit in threes, but only one justice is needed at committal proceedings

A second witness-box may be needed if other courts hold hearings in the room

Press bench

The clerk is legally qualified and explains to the magistrates what penalties they may impose

Witnesses who have already given evidence must stay in court unless they have permission to leave

The court usher, who may be a police officer, calls witnesses as they are needed

The defendant sits in the dock or on a seat facing the magistrates. The dock officer can be either a police officer or a prison officer

Public benches

if he is legally represented, should have with him a notepad and pencil with which to take note of any points that arise during the hearing. If the defendant is conducting his own case, he should have prepared a list of questions that he wants his own witnesses or the police to answer.

## What happens in court

When a case is reached, the name of the accused person is called out by a court official or police officer on duty. He is taken into the courtroom, where he stands in front of the magistrates while the clerk of the court reads the charge and asks him whether he pleads guilty or not guilty.

In certain circumstances, the clerk of the court will ask at this stage whether the accused chooses to be tried by the magistrates or by a jury at a higher court. If on the advice of his solicitor he has decided to go to a higher court, the magistrates may commit him for trial immediately or may hold a short hearing to establish whether there is a case for him to answer. ☐ How defendants are brought to court, p. 741.

PLEADING GUILTY When the defendant answers with a plea of guilty (or in cases where he has pleaded guilty by post), the police officer or the lawyer presenting the police case summarises the facts for the magistrates, who may then ask for evidence of any previous convictions he may have.

The defendant can call witnesses to give evidence about his character, before or after evidence of any previous convictions, and make a speech to the magistrates to ask them to be lenient—giving any mitigating or extenuating circumstances—when deciding the punishment. ☐ Penalties for motoring offenders, p. 173.

The magistrates make their decision and pass sentence. If he is fined, the motorist is normally given time to pay.

PLEADING NOT GUILTY If the accused pleads not guilty, the prosecution gives a summary of its case and calls its witnesses.

Each witness goes into the witness box and tells his story in answer to questions from the police or from the magistrates. When a witness has finished his evidence, the accused or his solicitor is entitled to question him.

This is not the time to tell the defence story. Questions should be limited to evidence given by the witness. When a defendant contests the evidence that has been heard by the court, he should make it clear to the witness to give him an opportunity to confirm his statement or change his mind.

When he wishes to imply that the witness is not telling the truth he should do so without becoming angry or rude. He should not say: 'You are lying.' It is better to put it: 'Is it not true, on the contrary, that . . .'

### Replying to the charge

When all the prosecution witnesses have given evidence, the accused or his solicitor are entitled to try to stop the trial by suggesting that there is no case to answer.

If the magistrates agree, the accused is acquitted and is discharged immediately.

If the submission is rejected, however, this does not mean that the magistrates have already made up their minds that the accused is guilty. If they are in any doubt, the case proceeds normally.

DEFENCE EVIDENCE It is better for a defendant pleading not guilty to give evidence himself, but he is not compelled to do so.

When giving evidence the defendant is not allowed to read from a written statement. He should prepare his evidence carefully, trying to avoid being repetitive or introducing irrelevant matters. He should make sure when he is questioned that he is allowed to give the answer he wants in full. If he thinks that he is being unfairly cut short he can appeal to the magistrates.

When the accused has given his own evidence, his witnesses are called. If he is conducting his own defence he must ask them the questions that will bring out their story, but he must not try to suggest answers to them.

For example, if the defendant is trying to establish the speed of his vehicle he must not say: 'I was driving at 25 mph, wasn't I?' This is a leading question and will be ruled out by the magistrates.

Instead he should ask his witness if he noticed what speed was registered on the speedometer.

SUMMING UP When all the witnesses have been questioned by both sides, the defendant or his lawyer may make a closing speech to the magistrates, summing up the evidence that has been given on both sides, outlining any law involved and reminding them that if there is reasonable doubt in their minds they must acquit him of the charge.

### The verdict and sentence

The magistrates may make their decision immediately or they may retire to a private room to discuss their verdict.

If they want advice on a point of law they are entitled to call the clerk of the court into their room, but he should leave before they come to their decision. They then return to the courtroom and give their verdict. A defendant found not guilty is discharged and may leave the court.

If the defendant is found guilty, the magistrates ask the police for evidence of previous convictions and the accused or his solicitor are entitled to make a plea for leniency. The court should not be told of previous convictions until the magistrates are ready to pass sentence—unless the defence has decided to introduce evidence of convictions in the course of its presentation of the accused's case.

Maximum sentences for many offences are laid down by Act of Parliament and there are limits on the penalties that magistrates can impose. In practice the magistrates usually impose a sentence below the maximum allowable except where they think the offence particularly serious. ☐ Penalties for motoring offenders, p. 173.

If he is fined, the motorist is normally given time to pay.

PAYING THE COSTS When a defendant is found not guilty, he or his solicitor may apply to the magistrates for costs against the prosecution. If he has not been represented by a lawyer the amount is likely to be small.

If he is found guilty, the magistrates may decide that he should pay all, or part, of the prosecution costs.

When a defendant is receiving legal aid under the State scheme, he may have to make some contribution towards the costs whether he is acquitted or convicted. ☐ Legal aid I: help with fees and costs, p. 710.

## The odds against escaping conviction

A DRIVER who is reported for one of the 1¾ million motoring offences which the police believe are committed in England and Wales every year has only a one-in-five chance of escaping conviction, according to Home Office statistics.

His best hope may be to look contrite and hope to be warned and let off. In 13 per cent of the 1970 cases police sent a written warning; in many others, one was given verbally by an officer on the spot and the alleged offence went unrecorded.

Once the police decide to prosecute, the chances of getting off diminish further. More than 1½ million charges were brought in 1970, and in less than one in ten was the motorist found not guilty.

Overall figures for all reported offences were: warnings, 13 per cent; convictions, 80 per cent; acquittals, 7 per cent.

The convicted motorist's chances of having his driving licence endorsed are about even —endorsements were ordered in about 55 per cent of 1970 convictions. But in only one case in 20 was the motorist disqualified.

Two-thirds of the 1000 drivers who applied had their disqualifications lifted.

The most common penalty, of course, was the fine. Nearly a million motorists were fined, and the total amount they had to pay was £9½m. Fines ranged from £2 paid by one of the only two motorists in England and Wales to be found guilty of exceeding the permitted sound level (the other was given an absolute discharge), to a total of £1,579,091 collected from the 120,908 motorists convicted of careless driving.

Nearly 6000 people on motoring charges were sent to prison for up to six months, without option of a fine, and about the same number were given suspended sentences.

The most common offence was speeding, which accounted for 17 per cent of all motoring convictions. Next came obstruction, waiting and parking (12 per cent); dangerous and defective vehicles (11 per cent); and careless driving (8½ per cent).

Drink-and-driving offences, despite the prominence they receive in newspaper reports, were only a fraction of total motoring convictions—less than 2 per cent.

Statistics about prosecutions under the 'breathalyser law' show that—in 1970 at least —most prosecutions were against motorists whose blood-alcohol level was well over the legal limit of 80 ml per cent. Over 18,000 of the motorists prosecuted had a rating of 121 ml or more, compared with less than 7000 between 81 and 120 ml.

The overwhelming majority of motoring cases were dealt with in magistrates' courts— 99 out of every 100, in fact.

Statistics about motoring offences are issued each year by the Home Office in a report called *Offences relating to motor vehicles* (published by HMSO).

# At the scene of an accident

*Stopping after an accident*  *Exchanging particulars*
*Summoning assistance*  *Making statements*
*Clearing the road*  *Collecting and recording evidence*

THE very nature of driving—propelling a fast machine along a narrow tarmac strip crowded with similar machines— makes it inherently dangerous to careful and careless drivers alike. A motorist can be the innocent victim of another's bad driving. Freak road situations can create sudden emergencies. A moment's inattention or a minor miscalculation—to which everyone is prone—can lead to disaster.

An accident can have legal consequences lasting years. First, there are the immediate formalities—informing the police and exchanging names and addresses. Then a driver or drivers may be prosecuted. People involved may make claims against their own or other people's insurance companies. Finally, a court may be asked to apportion blame and decide to what damages injured parties are entitled.

Many of these processes are complicated by the fact that most motorists are often too bewildered or unprepared to deal with an accident when it occurs.

A prudent motorist accepts that he may one day be involved in an accident, and is equipped to cope with it. Ideally, he should carry in his car:
1. A notebook and pencil.
2. An insurance claim form.
3. A steel tape.
4. Chalk.
5. A red warning triangle.
6. A flashing torch.
7. A loaded camera.
8. First-aid kit.

## Stopping after an accident
A motorist involved in an accident is obliged by law to stop at the scene if:
1. Anybody outside or inside his car, apart from himself, has been injured.
2. Any vehicle, apart from his own, has been damaged (but not other property).
3. Any horse, cattle, ass, mule, sheep, pig, dog or goat (outside his vehicle) has been injured.

A motorist does not have to stop, therefore, if he damages only his own car, or hits a brick wall, or runs over a cat or a tortoise.

The driver who fails to stop when he is required to do so by law is liable to be prosecuted and sent to prison for up to three months, or fined up to £50, or both.

The driver himself must remain at the scene of the accident, not merely leave his vehicle there. If a driver is unaware of an accident, he does not commit an offence by failing to stop. A lorry driver satisfied a court that he did not know that the trailer he was towing had hit and damaged a stationary vehicle. He was reported by onlookers. The court accepted that ignorance of the accident was a good defence, and the driver was acquitted of failing to stop.

The courts, however, are wary of such an excuse. If the prosecution proves that someone was injured or a vehicle damaged, it will need strong evidence to convince a court that the driver did not suspect that he had been involved in an accident.

The driver must stop for a reasonable period—long enough to supply other people involved with the information to which they are legally entitled. The law does not require that a motorist should wait until the police arrive, although it is often in his own interests to do so.

## Summoning assistance
It may be necessary to call an ambulance, the police or even the fire brigade. But first ensure that no danger is created for other road-users. The best way of doing this is to set a red warning triangle in the road at an appropriate distance behind the scene of the crash.

AMBULANCE Call an ambulance if anyone has been injured—or appears to be—or if anyone seems to be suffering from shock. Ignore protests from anyone who does not want an ambulance; injuries are not always evident, and severe shock needs medical attention.

FIRE SERVICE If anyone is trapped, call the fire service to free them. If petrol has been spilt on the road in any great quantity, the fire service should be called to wash it away.

POLICE No law says that the police must be called to the scene of an accident. In all but minor accidents, however, it is to the advantage of drivers concerned to have an independent police record of what has happened, although the police cannot be made to attend.

There are some situations in which it makes sense to call the police:

1. If the other driver appears to have been guilty of a traffic offence. Any conviction which results from the police being called will strengthen a damages claim against him.

2. If working out who is responsible for the accident is likely to involve making a record of vehicle positions, skid marks and other road features. This is a job at which the police are expert, although they are under no obligation to do so unless they suspect that an offence has been committed.

### Clearing the road

When anyone injured in a road crash has been taken to hospital, or is being properly attended to, the drivers—provided they are not injured too—can turn their attention to dealing with the damaged vehicles.

It is generally unwise to move any vehicle unless it is obviously causing a danger or serious obstruction to other traffic. If necessary, operate a temporary one-way system by directing traffic until the police arrive, rather than attempt to move vehicles. This is especially important when the position of the vehicles gives a clear indication of who was to blame for the accident.

If a vehicle must be moved before police arrive, first mark its position with chalk, indicating the corners of the car and the position of its wheels. If possible, get the other driver or an independent person to confirm in writing the accuracy of the marks.

It is always in a driver's interests to wait until the police have arrived, even when he considers himself to be completely blameless. The driver who leaves the scene before the arrival of the police may find later that they have been given a one-sided account of what happened. This may show him in an unfavourable light, and may be difficult to refute.

In addition, a driver will usually want to bring details to the notice of the police and ensure that the police report is accurate.

### Exchanging particulars

Every driver involved in an accident is under an obligation to give his name, address, the registration number of his car (and, if he is not the owner, the owner's name and address) to anyone who has reasonable grounds for wanting them. This means, in effect, to anyone directly or indirectly involved or affected by the accident.

If someone is injured, a driver involved must, if requested, produce his insurance certificate to anyone who is entitled to see it.

INFORMING THE POLICE An accident need *not* be reported to the police if names and addresses have been exchanged and—where someone is injured—insurance certificates have been produced.

Sometimes a motorist cannot comply with the law's requirements immediately. He may have hit a parked vehicle whose owner is not around at the time; or have run into a cyclist who is taken straight to hospital; or have run over a dog on a lonely road. In situations like these—or if no one has asked for particulars—the accident must be reported to a police officer within 24 hours.

If anyone has been injured and a motorist does not produce his insurance certificate at the scene of the accident, it must be produced to the police within 24 hours. Where this is impossible, the insurance certificate may be produced within five days at any police station, as long as this is arranged with the police within 24 hours of the accident.

These requirements must be complied with, no matter who was to blame for the accident, and a motorist who fails to do so is liable to prosecution. The penalties are imprisonment for up to three months, or a fine of up to £50.

### Making statements

Avoid getting involved in discussions about the cause of an accident. Never admit blame for an accident, even when it seems clear who was at fault. Generally, the less said at the scene of an accident, the better. A seemingly innocent remark can subsequently be given a sinister twist during cross-examination, or

## Using notes in court

A MOTORIST who has the presence of mind to collect and record evidence at the scene of an accident benefits if he has to appear in court later.

If he is precise in his observations, definite in his measurements and relates his recollections to identifiable objects, his testimony will carry more weight.

When the driver has made notes and plans on the spot, he is entitled to refer to them while giving evidence, to 'refresh his memory'. This will give clarity and credibility to what he says in court.

Notes which are made later some way from the scene of the accident cannot usually be referred to in court.

could even be construed later as an admission of liability by the motorist.

In addition, insurance companies invariably have the right to refuse to consider a claim if their policy-holder has admitted liability. ☐ Making an insurance claim, p. 112.

Never offer money to an injured person. If a motorist collides with a cyclist and later pays for the repair of the machine, it could easily be interpreted as an admission of liability.

In any case, immediately after an accident has happened is probably the worst time to try to evaluate the situation. No one can be sure of the extent of damage or injuries, and anyone who admits liability, or even appears to, could be taking on an obligation without realising its size or consequences.

People involved in an accident are often asked by the police to make a written statement. But it is not always wise to do so, especially if the accident is serious or if someone has been injured.

The law recognises that a motorist could incriminate himself by making a statement to the police, and allows him to decline if he wishes to do so. There are no exceptions to this rule—it applies equally at the scene of an accident or at a police station. Any motorist is within his rights in declining to discuss an accident with a police officer.

Be firm, but polite. Say something like 'I don't wish to say anything at this stage. This is my legal right, as you must know'. Give your name and address and supply all the

# Making a plan of the accident

Draw a sketch map of the scene of the accident. If possible, use squared paper to make the map to scale, and enter any details which may later help to show how the accident occurred.

LAYOUT OF THE ROAD  Draw the road or roads as accurately as possible, and note whether they are trunk roads or dual carriageways. Write in the names and widths, and show clearly the positions and types of any traffic signs, traffic lights or road markings. Indicate the position of zebra crossings and bus stops. Note any gradients, and say whether they created special traps, such as making it impossible to see a car coming out of a dip in the road until the last moment.

Examine the road surface. Many accidents happen through slippery or greasy roads, and driving conditions are always made worse by misty or foggy weather.

Plot on the sketch plan any features which might have contributed towards the accident—a wall which obscured the view of traffic coming over a crossroads, for example. If trees or bushes are involved, note whether they are in foliage or not.

Make a note if a bollard, lamp post, wall or other property is damaged.

DIRECTION OF TRAVEL  Try to show the direction of travel of vehicles involved in the accident immediately before the impact.

POINTS OF IMPACT  Look for evidence which may show where the vehicles met—a deposit of mud shaken on to the road from the inside of mudguards, perhaps, or broken glass.

Sometimes the point of impact can be identified by a scoring of the road, which frequently happens when the accident has caused tyres to burst.

SKID MARKS  Measure the length of skid marks and try with reasonable accuracy to plot their direction on the map. Skid marks indicate a number of things—the speed of the vehicle, its direction and, often, the point at which it came into collision with the other car.

RESTING POINT  Mark with chalk the four corners of each vehicle at the point where each came to rest on the road after the accident, and copy them accurately on to the sketch plan.

Note if the vehicles remained upright, or turned over or collapsed, and if tyres were punctured. Where the vehicles land up and the direction in which they are pointing can tell a great deal about their movements immediately before and after the moment of impact.

If possible, relate these measurements to physical features at the spot. For instance, say 'the front left wheel was resting against the fifth kerbstone from the corner'. Or, 'the lorry was facing directly towards the centre of the bollard'.

POINTS OF THE COMPASS  North should be shown on the sketch plan by drawing an arrow pointing north with the letter N against it. In any subsequent legal action, much of the evidence prepared by police officers will refer to compass points, and is impossible to follow unless the direction of north is plotted on the accident map.

The important thing in collecting this information is *speed*. People may move away, cars will be removed, marks on the road will fade or be erased by other traffic or the weather.

Evidence vital to the outcome of criminal or civil proceedings and the awarding of damages must be gathered before it disappears.

necessary documents, but restrict your remarks to neutral information such as where you were going and the names of your passengers.

When another driver is clearly at fault, the motorist may decide to make a statement to the police—to exonerate himself, perhaps, or to provide evidence on which the police could base a prosecution against the other driver.

He should insist that he writes the statement himself, using his own words and giving an accurate account of what happened. Avoid vague or ambiguous phrases which could later be misinterpreted or misconstrued.

This may sound elementary, but some policemen give the person from whom they are taking a statement the impression that the procedure is for the police officer to write it at the motorist's dictation. Unfortunately, many police officers do not immediately write down the exact words spoken, and sometimes the statement tends to become a summary of how the police, not the motorist, believe the accident happened.

When the statement has been completed, the police officer will read it out, or ask the motorist to read it, and then sign it. At this stage, alterations or deletions can be made or additional explanations inserted, but each one must be initialled by the motorist. The driver should take great care not to sign the statement until he is satisfied that it is accurate and gives a complete account of how the accident occurred.

The police have the right, in certain

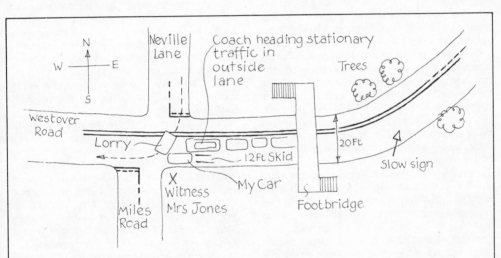

I was driving home westwards along the inside lane of the Westover Road on Tuesday, May 4th 1972 at 5pm in a light drizzle. I was slowing down to just under 30 m.p.h. on the newly surfaced stretch of the road in my car Reg DPG 44 B. A lorry turning west into Westover Road swerved across from Neville Lane junction, on the north side of Westover Road. Stationary traffic in the outside lane stretching from the junction to the footbridge, headed by a tours coach, obscured the lorry until it was on the inside lane. I braked, the skid measured 12 feet, and stopped two yards east of Miles Road junction, on the south side of Westover Road which was the point of impact. My offside front tyre was burst by the lorry's nearside metal hub cap which badly damaged my bumper, and my windscreen was shattered. There were no injuries. A pedestrian, Mrs Anne Jones, of 101 Beaulieu Gardens, Westover, witnessed the incident ten yards from the impact as she approached Westover Road from Miles Road.

circumstances, to arrest a motorist at the scene of an accident. Anyone who refuses to take a breathalyser test, or who takes one which proves positive, can be arrested. So, too, can anyone suspected of dangerous or careless driving, unless the motorist who is under suspicion gives his name and address and produces his driving licence.

### Collecting and recording evidence

When deciding on compensation or damages after a road accident, a court or an insurance company attempts to piece together a picture of what happened from a number of sources. Witnesses may give conflicting accounts of how the accident happened; there may be facts to be gleaned from skid marks, vehicle damage, glass on the road, or similar evidence; and there will probably be reports by the police and engineering experts.

The most important witnesses of a road accident are the drivers involved. Every driver who has an accident should record the salient points on which may depend his claim for compensation or his defence in a prosecution.

If a motorist carries with him an insurance-company claim form, he can complete the form on the spot. This ensures that all the information the company is likely to require is collected at the best time. Additional information—such as statements of admission by the other driver—should be noted separately.

NAMES AND ADDRESSES Make a careful note of the names and addresses of other people involved in the accident. Remember that other drivers concerned are obliged by law to provide this information, and check the registration number the other driver gives with that on his vehicle. Where there has been physical injury, drivers must also produce their insurance certificates. Take down the name and address of the insurance company on the certificate, the number of the certificate and the name of the person insured.

Make a note of the registration numbers of other vehicles at the scene if it seems likely that their drivers could be useful witnesses. Even if such a driver leaves before his name can be noted, or refuses to give his name and address, he can often be traced through the number of his vehicle.

The licensing authority which issued the registration number, or the authority with which the vehicle is registered, can be identified from the number through one of the motoring organisations. Licensing authorities will usually supply the name and address of an owner to someone with a valid interest on payment of a small fee. The driver can then be contacted and asked to give evidence. If he refuses, and you consider his evidence vital to a court case, he may change his mind if you explain how necessary his evidence is, or if you tell him that you are considering applying for a witness summons to ensure that the court hears his account of the accident.

Ask people who saw the accident for their names and addresses, if they will give them. Do not spend time taking detailed statements at this stage. Instead, compile a list of names and addresses of *all* potential witnesses and decide which are most useful afterwards. Pedestrians who had a clear view of the road at the time, and 'professionals'—bus, taxi or lorry drivers who drive for a living—are particularly useful witnesses.

A list of possible witnesses is often the most useful information that a driver can give his insurance company or solicitor. So noting names, addresses and registration numbers should always be given priority once the injured have been attended to. Beware of doing anything which might be construed as trying to bribe witnesses—for example offering to pay any expense they may be put to if they are required to give evidence.

TRAFFIC Make a note of the state of the traffic: if it is fast-moving, if the road was busy, and so on.

WEATHER CONDITIONS Make a note of the time of day and whether visibility was good or bad. Record if there was a lamp near by which lit up the road. Make a note if it was raining, foggy or if the conditions were icy.

VEHICLES Make a detailed note of damage to all the vehicles involved. This can indicate how the accident happened and will be useful when the cost of repairs is calculated later.

TAKING PHOTOGRAPHS If possible, take photographs as evidence. In particular, take pictures of the vehicles—making sure to get a number of shots from several angles showing where they came to rest after the collision and the extent of the damage. Use photographs to show the scene of the accident and take individual shots of any features such as concealed entrances or obscured road signs which may be relevant.

If for any reason photographs are not taken at the time of the accident, return to take pictures as soon as possible—the same day or the next. Even though vehicles will have been moved, it may still be useful to have pictures of features of the road, such as obscured signs or hazards. If necessary, employ a professional photographer, but check that he is willing to attend court and give evidence of taking the pictures before employing him.

# Criminal proceedings following an accident

*How a prosecution is brought*     *How the result affects damages claims*
*Preparing the defence*

CAUSING a road accident is not, in itself, an offence. But motorists involved in accidents frequently find themselves prosecuted for any offence or offences which led up to the accident. □ Dealing with bad driving, p. 96.

If there is to be a police prosecution arising from an accident, it will invariably take place before any civil action for damages. A claim for damages against a motorist does not succeed automatically just because the motorist has been convicted of a motoring offence. But the criminal hearing gives people involved in civil cases a good chance to assess their prospects in a damages action.

## How a prosecution is brought
The police officer investigating an accident usually issues a Notice of Intended Prosecution to any driver he considers guilty of an offence. He then submits a report to a police superintendent or chief inspector.

If the police decide that proceedings should be taken, a summons is applied for and served on the motorist. It details the alleged offence and informs him when and where the case is being heard.

The police are entitled to use their discretion in deciding whether to bring criminal proceedings. So if there are circumstances which appear to make the offence less serious, inform the officer making the report. The police must be made aware of any mitigating circumstances immediately, as they are unlikely to drop proceedings once a summons has been issued.

In theory, the seriousness of an accident should not determine the seriousness of the offence with which a motorist is charged. However, police often judge by results, so it is essential that anyone in danger of being prosecuted obtains proper legal advice.

## Preparing the defence
Insurance companies usually have a stake in criminal proceedings, because their liability to pay damages to a third party is often affected by the result.

Consequently, they usually offer to provide lawyers for the defence. Obviously a motorist should take full advantage of the legal services provided by his insurers.

If the driver has made notes at the scene of the accident, he will be able to use them in court. □ Using notes in court, p. 107.

## How the result affects damages claims
If a motorist is convicted on a charge arising from an accident, this generally puts him at a disadvantage in any later proceedings or negotiations for damages. But a verdict of guilty does not necessarily mean that the defendant or his insurance company is automatically liable to pay the damages of injured parties.

At the civil hearing, the court will take into account the relative responsibility for the accident of the drivers involved, and apportion damages accordingly. Parties suing for damages who were not drivers—pedestrians or passengers—may be entitled to receive damages from each driver involved if no one was wholly to blame.

There is also a different burden of proof in a civil court. In a criminal case the prosecution must prove guilt beyond reasonable doubt. But in a civil case it is usually up to the plaintiff to show that, on the balance of probabilities, he was in the right.

Proof that the defendant broke the law does not by itself mean that he was responsible for the accident. When damages are claimed, it must be shown that the breach of law was the cause of the accident.

However, if the verdict of guilty involves a finding that the defendant was negligent—if, for example, he is convicted of careless driving—then that fact will be taken as proved in the civil case though it can be challenged by the defendant in the course of the case.

WATCHING BRIEF If an accident is serious and there are likely to be claims for substantial damages, it is usual for a solicitor to attend the criminal hearing as an observer, on behalf of people who may be concerned in a later civil case. The solicitor does not participate in the proceedings. But he can see the witnesses and review the evidence before advising his client about the chances of success in subsequent proceedings for damages.

# Making an insurance claim

*Reporting to the company*　　*When a car is written off*
*Filling in the claim form*　　*Other comprehensive policy claims*
*Repairing the car*　　　　　*Writs, claims and summonses*

A DRIVER involved in an accident may find that he can make two types of claim against his insurance company. Firstly, he can demand the indemnity provided by his policy against claims made by anyone else involved, passing over to his insurance company any claims against him for damages. ☐ Taxing and insuring a car, p. 32.

In addition, if the terms of his policy allow, the driver may be able to claim against his insurance company for any damage caused to his own vehicle.

In practice, the two types of claim are usually made at the same time by completing a single claim form. And both can be made whether or not the policy-holder is to blame.

If a driver does not wish to claim against his insurance company for some reason—such as to preserve his no-claim bonus—he can settle the claim privately with the other driver or the other driver's insurance company, although he must still keep his own insurance company fully informed. ☐ Making and settling a claim privately, p. 115.

### Reporting to the company
A motorist involved in an accident should inform his insurance company or broker as soon as possible—within a week at the outside. Make the first report by telephone, and follow this up immediately with a letter of confirmation, taking care to keep a copy. If a motorist cannot report an accident personally, a friend or relative must do it for him.

There is no need, in the initial report, to give a detailed account of what happened. Full details will need to be given on the insurance claim form, which can be obtained from the company or from their agents or brokers. Some motorists carry a blank claim form in their car, so that if they have an accident, they can answer the questions on the spot while their memories are fresh.

### Filling in the claim form
Answer all questions on the form honestly and accurately. Where it is not possible to give an answer, say so clearly on the form or in a covering letter. False or misleading information may give the insurance company the right to refuse a claim. Do not leave blank spaces, even if making an entry means repeating information already on the form.

Answer all questions about the vehicles involved, even if your policy does not allow you to claim for damage to your own car. The insurers may wish to inspect the vehicle to see whether policy conditions have been complied with, or whether the damage will help them in arguing against a claim by somebody else.

Give the date, place and time of the accident, the speeds of the vehicles involved, the road conditions and visibility. Describe the accident fully, and include events leading up to the collision, such as whether the driver or drivers gave signals, braked, changed gear or swerved. If there is not enough room on the form, continue the description on a separate sheet of paper.

Be sure to include a copy of any sketch map made at the crash scene. ☐ At the scene of the accident, p. 106.

Give the names and addresses of passengers and independent witnesses, and state whether the police were called.

### Repairing the car
The holder of a comprehensive policy is entitled to claim for damage to his own vehicle. To do so, he must obtain from a garage a detailed written estimate of the cost of repairing his vehicle. The policy-holder may choose the garage himself.

If the car is badly damaged, it will already have been towed to a garage. If this garage cannot carry out the repairs, most policies cover the cost of towing to the nearest competent repairer. If the policy-holder wants his car taken further—to his regular garage, for instance—he may have to pay for the additional towing.

If possible, the repair estimate should be sent to the insurance company at the same time as the claim form.

The policy-holder may be able to instruct the garage to start repairs at this stage. Most policies allow this, as long as an estimate is in the post to the insurance company and no new parts are fitted to the vehicle before a company engineer inspects it. Some policies allow the policy-holder to instruct the garage only if the repairs will not exceed a certain amount. Read the policy carefully and, if there is any doubt, check with the insurers before work starts.

After receiving the claim form and estimate the insurance company may arrange for an engineer to inspect the damage and discuss the cost of repairs with the garage. The engineer may be able to instruct the garage to start work straight away. Usually, however, he has to report to the insurance company, who will then decide whether to give the go-ahead on repair work.

If the engineer feels the estimate is unreasonable, he will try to negotiate a reduction with the garage. If this fails, the policy-holder may be asked to obtain a new estimate from another garage.

Once a garage has been asked to start work, the policy-holder should keep a careful eye on progress. If there seems to be an unreasonable delay, tell the insurance company—particularly if a claim is being made against the other driver for the cost of hiring a substitute vehicle while repairs are being carried out.

When repairs are finished, the policy-holder is usually asked to sign a satisfaction note, and to pay any part of the costs he is liable for (a £15 or £25 excess, perhaps). Before signing, inspect the vehicle carefully and, if possible, take it for a test drive.

The insurance company's engineer does not normally inspect the vehicle again at this stage. But an independent engineer should be engaged to check repairs if the car's chassis, steering or suspension was damaged.

An independent check can be arranged through the Automobile Association, or by writing for a list of members to the Institute of Automobile Assessors, 17 Pudding Lane, London EC3R 8AE. The cost will not be paid by the insurance company, but it will be money well spent.

If the repairs are not satisfactory, refuse to sign the note, and inform the insurance company at once. Arrangements will then be made to correct the faults at the insurance company's expense.

## When a car is written off

A car is written off if the insurance company's engineer reports that the cost of repairing it is more than its market value (or more than the amount for which it is insured). In this case the company is entitled, under a comprehensive policy, to offer a lump-sum payment, instead of paying for repairs.

But there is often misunderstanding over the amount the policy-holder is entitled to if his car is written off.

In the vast majority of cases, the policy-holder is entitled to the market value of his car immediately before the accident. Only in two circumstances does he get more or less than this:

1. He receives the sum the car is insured for if this is less than the market value.

2. If he has one of the less-common policies with an 'agreed value' clause, he is entitled to the sum agreed with the insurance company when the policy was last renewed. ☐ Taxing and insuring a car, p. 32.

When a vehicle is to be written off, the policy-holder receives an offer in writing from the company. If he accepts the offer, he has to return his certificate of insurance and hand over the registration book of the vehicle. The company is then entitled to take what is left of the vehicle and sell it as scrap.

SETTLING A HIRE-PURCHASE AGREEMENT If the vehicle is still covered by a hire-purchase agreement, remind the insurance company, as they will need the finance company's consent before selling the car as scrap.

If a hire-purchase agreement is still in force when the vehicle is written off, the insurance company pays the finance company any instalments outstanding. The policy-holder then recovers the balance, if any.

If a new or nearly new car on hire purchase is written off, the policy-holder can suffer financially. If the car is written off during the first 12 months, the sum paid by the insurance company may only just cover the amount still due under the agreement.

DISPUTES OVER VALUATION The market price of a vehicle is usually taken from the motor trade's second-hand price guide. This guide is not available to the public, but the insurance company's figure can be checked against prices for similar models in newspaper advertisements, or by asking local dealers or one of the motoring organisations.

If the policy-holder and insurance company cannot agree on the market value, the dispute can be referred to an independent arbitrator, or to court. Either of these courses is expensive, and the policy-holder should ask a solicitor if it is likely to be worth while.

If the vehicle is old, the market value will be low, and even comparatively minor damage may make it a write-off. If the policy-holder prefers to keep the vehicle, he can ask the company to pay the market value, less its value on the scrap-market.

END OF POLICY When a vehicle is written off, the insurance policy, strictly speaking, comes to an end. If this happens shortly after the policy has been taken out or renewed, the policy-holder may have paid a premium for a whole year's insurance, but he will have had the benefit of the policy only for the short period leading up to the accident.

Under some insurance policies, the cover can be transferred to a replacement vehicle, or the balance of the premium can be deducted from the cost of a new policy on another vehicle. If the policy does not mention this point, the policy-holder is probably not entitled to a refund.

**Other comprehensive policy claims**
After an accident, study the insurance policy carefully to ensure that you claim all the benefits to which you are entitled.
LUGGAGE AND BELONGINGS Personal effects and luggage may be covered under a 'rugs, coats and luggage' section, up to a fixed—and usually small—amount. Send the company a full list of items damaged or lost, together with any receipts. Keep any damaged items, in case the company wishes to examine them.
PERSONAL INJURIES The policy may give cover for personal injuries, disablement or death suffered by the policy-holder and, sometimes, the wife or husband. These claims can be made in addition to claims for damages for the same injuries which are made against the driver whose negligence caused them. The

two claims are entirely separate. ☐ Grounds for claiming damages, p. 121.

Claims under the personal-accident section must be accompanied by medical certificates.
MEDICAL EXPENSES The cost of obtaining private medical treatment after an accident may be covered, but the amount that can be claimed by an injured person is small.

**Writs, claims and summonses**
A policy-holder has an obligation in law to keep his insurance company informed of developments arising out of an accident.

If another driver involved in the accident makes a claim—in writing, by telephone or in person—report it to the company at once. Send on letters unanswered.

If you are notified that a claim for damages is being made against you, send the document to your insurance company on the day it arrives, or at the very latest on the following day. The insurance company must be able to act without delay if it is to defend a writ or county-court summons.

If a notice of intended prosecution or a summons is received from the police, send it to the company. Not only is the policy-holder obliged to do so under the terms of his policy, but he may be entitled to have his defence arranged and paid for by the insurance company. ☐ Criminal proceedings following an accident, p. 111.

---

## When passengers should claim

A PASSENGER injured in a collision between two vehicles may be able to claim damages against his own driver, against the other driver, or against both of them.

By law, all drivers must have insurance which covers them against claims for personal injury made by passengers in other vehicles. Since 1971, when the Motor Vehicles (Passenger Insurance) Act became law, it has also been compulsory for drivers to be insured for similar claims from their own passengers.

The passenger has to show that the driver against whom he claims was negligent. His claim will succeed in full if he can show that the driver against whom he claims was only *partly* to blame. A driver faced with a passenger claim can therefore escape paying the claim only by showing that the other driver was *wholly* to blame.

Since a driver is insured against claims by

passengers, his passengers need not feel any embarrassment about claiming against him, even if they are close friends or members of his family. The claim will be paid by the insurance company, not the driver, although his insurance premium is likely to be increased.

There is no reason why passengers should abandon their claims simply because their driver was to blame for the accident and cannot make a claim himself.

Suppose, for example, that a young child travelling in his or her father's car is seriously injured in an accident which is wholly the father's fault. The child is legally entitled to make a claim—through an adult known in law as a 'next friend'—against the father. If the father is insured, the damages paid by his insurance company will help to alleviate some of the hardship caused to the parents as well as to the child by the accident.

# Making and settling a claim privately

*Making your own claim*    *Settling a claim*
*If the offer is too small*    *Pitfalls of 'on-the-spot' settlements*

WHEN a motorist has been in an accident, he may not always wish to involve his insurance company in any claim made by or against him. For if he does so, he may risk losing his no-claim bonus or having it reduced, even if he was not to blame for the accident. ☐ Getting the best from a no-claim bonus, p. 120.

If the bonus, or the percentage of it which the motorist would lose, is worth more than his own claim and the claim against him, it will pay him to handle the claim privately.

In addition, there are two situations in which there is no choice but to handle a claim privately, if it is to be pursued at all.

Firstly, many drivers have an 'accidental damages excess' clause written into their comprehensive insurance policies. This means that, usually in return for a reduced premium, they have undertaken to pay the first part (say £15 or £25) of any claim for accidental damage to their cars, called the excess.

If the cost of damage to a driver's own car is less than this initial amount he has agreed to pay, there is no point in making a claim on his own insurance company. Even where the cost is more, the motorist may wish to claim privately the excess which cannot be re-covered under his own policy.

Secondly, some drivers have only Third Party or Road Traffic Act insurance, which does not give cover for damage to the driver's own car. Again, such a driver would have to make his own claim for damage to his car.

If there is a choice, the motorist should consider dealing with a claim himself only if the sum of money involved is comparatively small, and responsibility for the accident is clear-cut and indisputable. Motoring law is extremely complex and a layman can easily find himself in great difficulty if he tries to deal personally with anything other than a simple repairs claim.

Even when a motorist intends to make or deal with a claim himself, he must always report the accident to his insurance company. Not only is he legally obliged to do so, but it also provides him with valuable protection if anything goes wrong. He should give the company brief details of the accident, and add that he does not intend to claim at present. This leaves him free to claim on the insurance later if the damage turns out to be more costly than anticipated, or if he fails to negotiate a satisfactory settlement with the other driver involved in the accident.

## Making your own claim

The first step for a motorist who wants to claim the cost of repairing his damaged vehicle from another driver is to obtain an estimate from a garage.

Next, write to the other driver, or prefer-ably his insurance company, with a copy of the estimate and details of other claims to be made—for example, the cost of hiring a replacement vehicle. Make it clear that the other driver is being held responsible for the accident, and ask for confirmation that the claim will be met. Keep a copy of this letter, and any subsequent correspondence.

The other driver or his insurance company may offer to settle the claim immediately by paying the estimated cost of repairs. If the garage has agreed a fixed price, the claimant will be safe accepting the offer. This may prevent him claiming for other losses which arise while the repairs are being done—hire charges or fares, for example—but these are not likely to be substantial if the claim itself is a small one.

PAYING FIRST AND CLAIMING LATER The garage may refuse to commit itself to a firm quotation; or, more likely, the insurance company may demand that the repairs are carried out and a final account produced before they settle the claim.

Problems can arise at this point. The motorist may have to instruct the garage to do the repairs before the other driver's insurance company will consider the claim, and without any clear indication that they will pay up when work is completed.

Until the garage is paid, it is entitled in law to refuse to release the motorist's vehicle. And if the repairs are going to be costly, the garage may even refuse to start work without confirmation from the insurance company that a settlement will be made.

In these situations, the motorist should put

his claim in the hands of his own insurance company as soon as possible, or seek the help of a solicitor or the legal department of the Automobile Association.

Sometimes, an engineer from the other driver's insurance company may inspect the damage. If he thinks the estimate is too high, the motorist making the claim may be asked to obtain one or more competitive estimates from other garages.

The insurance company will usually be prepared to accept the lowest of these. But before he agrees to settle, the motorist should make certain that the garage which prepared this estimate will do the work properly.

WHAT CAN BE CLAIMED If the other driver's insurance company accepts an estimate, and repairs are paid for by the motorist whose car was damaged, he should write to the company setting out the final details of his claim. Only a solicitor can tell precisely what he can claim in an individual situation, but usually it will include some or all of the following:

1. The cost of repairing his car.
2. The cost of towing the vehicle to a garage, if this is necessary.
3. The cost of hiring alternative transport, or the cost of fares on public transport while the vehicle is being repaired.

Claims for hire must not include petrol used in the hired car, and claims for fares must make allowance for the petrol which would have been used had the same distance been covered in the car being repaired.

If the motorist has any doubt at all about his right to make any further claim or claims, he should seek legal advice.

If the insurance company accepts the claim, it will send a cheque in settlement.

DEALING WITH DELAY Most insurance companies settle this type of small claim quickly, to save themselves becoming involved in legal costs. There may, however, be delays while they complete investigations into the circumstances of the accident or wait for information from their own policy-holder.

The motorist making the claim should be ready to deal with any delays that arise. Do not wait longer than a week for a reply to your first letter making the claim, or more than two for a reply to the letter setting out the full details of your claim, unless you know of some good reason for such delays.

If there is a delay, send the insurance

## Claiming the cost of repairs

A motorist claiming the cost of repairing his car from another driver or the other driver's insurance company should start negotiations as soon as possible after the accident. From the outset, he should make it clear that he is holding the other driver responsible for the damage.

The motorist who is claiming for repairs—and perhaps other expenses incurred as a result of the accident—should keep all bills and receipts relating to his claim. It is also important to keep copies of all relevant correspondence.

Although it is often possible to make a satisfactory settlement by dealing direct with the other driver, it is generally preferable to negotiate with his insurance company. Most companies settle claims promptly, to avoid legal expenses.

But if the other driver or his insurance company delay matters unreasonably, the claimant should either ask his own insurance company whether it will take over the claim, or consult a solicitor or the legal department of his motoring organisation.

When the final account is sent to the other driver or his insurers, the claimant should ask for settlement within a specific time—seven days would probably be a reasonable limit

27 Beeding Way, Belvedere, Warwickshire. 1/6/72

Dear Sir,
I am holding you responsible for the accident in which we were involved on May 22nd, 1972, in Harcourt Street, Richmond, Birmingham. I shall be claiming the cost of repairing my car in accordance with the enclosed estimate, and for any other losses which may arise.
Please put me in touch with your insurance company or confirm that you will pay my claim yourself.
Yours faithfully,
J. G. N. Browne

A copy of the repair estimate should be sent with a motorist's initial letter of claim to the other driver. If he agrees to pay, the claimant can settle immediately or wait until repairs are complete and send a final account. If he refuses to pay, or fails to reply, write to his insurance company, or seek legal advice

company a strong reminder, threatening to take legal action. If this does not produce a satisfactory reply within a week, ask your insurance company whether it will handle the claim, or seek legal advice.

Sometimes a telephone call or a visit to the insurance company's offices will be more effective than writing letters. Any promise or agreement given by an official of the insurance company should be recorded by writing a letter confirming the promise or agreement. Send the letter to the insurance company as soon as possible after the interview.

### If the offer is too small
Insurance companies often start by offering less than the amount claimed, and it is therefore perfectly proper to reject the offer and ask for more.

If the insurance company refuses to make a reasonable increase in its original offer without delay, do not indulge in lengthy bargaining but seek legal advice.

When an acceptable offer is made, write confirming acceptance. If you are to be paid a reduced amount because the company claims you were partly to blame for the accident, the letter should make it clear that, although you accept the offer, this is without admitting liability.

Whenever an insurance company settles a claim, the claimant is asked to sign a discharge, which releases their policy-holder from any further liability. If the claimant is sure that everything he is entitled to claim is included in the settlement, there is no reason why he should not sign.

The discharge may take the form of an agreement to be signed before the claim is paid, a receipt to be signed when the claim is paid, or an endorsement on the back of the insurance company's settlement cheque which has to be signed when the motorist pays it into his bank.

A motorist cannot make a further claim once the discharge is signed. This rule applies even if he did not claim all the damages to which he was entitled, or did not know of a particular loss at the time he settled.

### Settling a claim
Before deciding to deal personally with a claim made against him by another driver, a motorist must be certain that he is not laying

---

27 Beeding Way, Belvedere, Warwickshire. 10/7/72

Dear Sirs,
On May 22nd, 1972, in Harcourt Street, Richmond, Birmingham, I was involved in a motor accident for which I hold responsible your insured, Mr D.W. Steel, of 79 Salisbury Place, Hampton, Birmingham, whose insurance certificate number is IVC/17493/63R.
I shall be claiming for the cost of repairing my car, and any other losses which may arise. I enclose a repairs estimate. Please let me know whether you wish to inspect the damage. Please also confirm that you will pay my claim in due course.
Yours faithfully,
J.G.N. Browne

---

27 Beeding Way, Belvedere, Warwickshire. 27/8/72

Dear Sirs,
                    Without prejudice
I can now give you details of my claim as follows:
1. Cost of repairing my car:                    £15
2. Cost of towing it to the garage:             £ 5
3. Cost of hiring alternative transport:        £10
4. Train fare from Birmingham to London:        £ 1.90
                                                £31.90

I enclose bills for the repairs, towing and hire. Please let me have your cheque for £31.90 within the next seven days.
Yours faithfully,
J.G.N. Browne

---

When the claim is against the other driver's insurance company, write to the company outlining the claim and enclose a copy of the estimate. Allow time, at least a week, for a reply before starting work on repairs, as the company will probably want its engineer to inspect the damage

If the claim was not settled on the basis of the estimate, the insurance company or the other driver should be given a final account, listing details of the claim. Bills should be enclosed. Head the letter 'Without prejudice' to prevent it being used in court without your consent

himself open to a far greater financial liability than at first seems likely.

Even a minor collision can bring a large claim. Repair costs, even for what seems superficial damage, can be far higher than would seem possible. A simple nose-to-tail collision at low speed may lead to further consequences—for example, a neck injury to the driver of the car in front which could result in a claim for thousands of pounds.

In cases where the damage to the other vehicle is quite clearly going to be less expensive than the loss or reduction of a no-claim bonus, the motorist is fairly safe in dealing with the claim himself. He should inform his own insurance company of the accident and make it clear that he does not wish to claim from them at this stage.

Ask the other driver to supply an estimate for repairing his vehicle. If this is far more than was expected, pass the claim to your insurance company. If the estimate is less than you stand to lose from your no-claim bonus, it is probably safe to continue to deal with the claim personally.

If the price quoted seems reasonable for the amount of damage done, try to settle the claim immediately. Make it clear that any payment is in 'full and final' settlement, and is made without admission of liability.

IF THE ESTIMATE IS TOO HIGH If the estimate seems excessive for the damage done, or appears to include damage which was not caused in the accident, take the matter up with the other driver. If he is not prepared to have it reduced, ask an experienced motor mechanic or, preferably, a qualified motor engineer, to inspect the damage and provide an independent report.

It is worth going to these lengths only if the amount at issue is quite large, because the engineer's fees will have to be paid.

If the engineer confirms that the estimate is too high, the driver making the claim may agree to reduce it. If he insists on claiming the full estimated cost or refuses to allow an inspection at all, ask him to obtain a competitive estimate.

Where a driver making a claim refuses to co-operate at all, write to him making a firm offer of what seems a fair amount, and record in the letter the fact that he has refused to allow an inspection, to obtain a competitive estimate or to listen to the engineer's views.

## Paying another driver's claim

When a motorist offers to settle a claim, or makes an actual settlement, he should do so in writing. He should keep a copy of all letters.

Put a time limit on accepting any offer—seven days is common—and make it clear that any money paid is without admission of liability and is in 'full and final' settlement of the claim.

This should be enough to prevent the other driver re-opening his claim after settlement, or trying to bring new claims.

As an added precaution, he can be asked to sign a discharge similar to that used by insurance companies. Such a discharge can be prepared by adding suitable words to a receipt, above the space for the signature.

For instance, in signing the receipt the other motorist should be asked to re-affirm that he is accepting the payment 'as full and final settlement of all claims of whatsoever nature now or hereafter manifest arising out of the motor accident'. The date and place of the accident should be specified and the claimant should be asked to acknowledge that the payment does not signify any admission of liability on the part of the driver who is making the settlement

> 15 Walton Road,
> Berkeley,
> Sussex.
> September 12, 1972.
>
> Dear Sir,
> I am, without admitting liability, enclosing £23.17 in full and final settlement of your claim against me arising out of the accident in which we were involved on June 17, 1972, in Main Road, Berkeley, Sussex. Please acknowledge safe receipt.
>
> Yours faithfully
> C. F. Keen

If the driver making a claim submits an estimate that seems reasonable, send the money as soon as possible, with a covering letter stating it is a full and final settlement. If the driver accepts—by banking the cheque, for example—he will usually be barred from making any further claim, even if the repairs eventually cost more than expected

If the offer is rejected, refer the claim to your insurance company or seek legal advice. Alternatively, if the amount being disputed is only a few pounds, it might be better to pay up rather than incur legal costs or lose a no-claim bonus.

The other driver may decide that he would rather have the repairs carried out before settling. If so, ask him to produce the final account as well as the estimate. Check the two documents against one another and ask for an explanation of any discrepancy.

If the other driver claims the cost of hiring alternative transport while the repairs are carried out, make sure that he produces an account, and study it carefully.

Check that the hiring did not extend beyond the time his vehicle was being repaired, that the vehicle he hired was not a more expensive model than his own vehicle, and that the account does not include petrol used in the hired car.

DECIDING WHETHER TO PAY IN FULL Once he receives final details of the other driver's claims, the motorist has to decide whether or not to pay the full amount.

There may be valid reasons for reducing the claim if the other driver was partly responsible for the accident. But it is not worth arguing at length about liability. The essence of settling a claim without involving insurance companies is to do so quickly and with the minimum expense to both parties.

**Pitfalls of 'on-the-spot' settlements**
A driver who causes an accident may occasionally offer the other a few pounds on the spot to settle the matter. Such an offer may be tempting if the damage to the vehicle seems limited—if it just appears to be dented, for instance—but it should be refused until a garage can prepare a proper estimate of what the vehicle will cost to repair.

Again, a driver who is at fault may suggest that his garage should carry out the repairs at his expense. This offer, too, should be refused. There is no control over the time taken for the repairs or the standard of workmanship in this type of case.

Any agreement to settle a claim without involving insurance companies should be on the basis that settlement must be made within a specified time and for the full amount of the damage caused.

---

June 10, 1972.

The Spinney,
Copse Lane,
Bloomsgate,
Devon.

Dear Sir,
I am, without admitting liability, prepared to pay £27.98 in full and final settlement of your claim against me arising out of the motor accident in which we were involved on May 9, 1972, at Dankwater Road, Bloomsgate, Devon.

My offer will remain open for seven days. Please confirm that it is accepted.

Yours faithfully,

H.A. Charles

---

July 5, 1972,

The Spinney
Copse Lane,
Bloomsgate,
Devon.

Dear Sir,
You have agreed to accept my offer of £27.98 in settlement of your claim. I enclose this amount, without admission of liability. This payment is in full and final settlement of your claim against me arising out of the motor accident in which we were involved on May 9, 1972, at Dankwater Road, Bloomsgate, Devon. Please acknowledge safe receipt.

Yours faithfully,

H.A. Charles

---

If the other driver sends a detailed bill after repairs have been completed, check it carefully before making him a settlement offer. It may be necessary to reduce the figure if he has claimed for petrol used in a hired car, for example, if the car is a more expensive model than his own, or if he was partly to blame for the accident

When a price is agreed, send a letter with the cheque, noting that the other driver has stated his willingness to accept the amount. Although this payment will finally resolve the dispute, it is as well to state once again that it does not signify an admission of liability and that it is a full and final settlement. Keep a copy of this letter

# Getting the best from a no-claim bonus

THE motorist who has driven for several years without making a claim on his insurance may be entitled to a fairly substantial no-claim bonus (sometimes called a no-claim discount). A motorist who plans carefully can retain his bonus even if he is involved in a few minor accidents.

A typical no-claim bonus amounts to a 30 per cent discount on the original premium after one claim-free year, a 40 per cent discount after two years, 50 per cent after three years, and a maximum of 60 per cent after four years. In each case the discount is deducted from the original premium, not from that paid in the preceding year.

Therefore a driver getting the maximum 60 per cent bonus after four years of accident-free driving will have an original premium of, say, £45 reduced to £18.

A motorist stands to lose part or all of his discount if he makes a claim for injury or damage for which he was partly or wholly to blame, or for which no one was to blame.

Many people feel unfairly treated when they discover that their insurance company intends to reduce a no-claim bonus after a claim for damages caused by an accident which was no one's fault. The company, however, is entitled to take this action.

Insurance companies point out that it is a no-*claim* bonus, not a no-*blame* bonus. So a company feels justified in reducing the bonus if it loses money in paying out a claim against a motorist's policy, irrespective of whether or not he was at fault.

## How a claim affects the bonus

A claim does not usually cancel all the discount; with most companies, the policyholder who makes a claim drops back two steps on the discount scale. So the driver with four years' claim-free motoring who makes a claim will have his next premium increased so that it is only 40 per cent off the original, instead of 60 per cent.

## Deciding whether to claim

If a motorist has an accident and is faced with a repair bill, either for his own car or for the car of another motorist who was not to blame, he will have to work out whether it will benefit him to make a claim or to pay the bill himself.

If the bill amounts to £10, the difference will be as follows (percentages refer to the discount on the original premium of £45):

| | If he makes a claim | If he pays for repairs himself |
|---|---|---|
| Cost of repairs | nil | £10 |
| Premium next year | £27 (40%) | £18 (60%) |
| Premium year after | £22·50 (50%) | £18 (60%) |
| Total | £49·50 | £46 |

In this case, the motorist can reasonably expect to save £3·50 over the next two years by paying for the repairs himself. However, this calculation is based on the assumption that he will not be involved in another accident during this period. A motorist who is obliged to make a claim following a second accident (perhaps because the repair bill is much greater) loses the benefit of not claiming after the first accident.

Even if the motorist has decided to preserve his no-claim bonus by paying for repairs himself, he must still inform the company promptly, saying that he does not intend to claim 'at this stage'. This leaves him free to claim later if the cost of repairs is excessive.

## 'Knock-for-knock' agreements

When another driver is to blame for an accident, a claim should not result in the loss of the innocent driver's bonus. The insurance company should be able to recover their costs from the other driver's insurers.

This does not always work in practice, however, because many companies have a 'knock-for-knock' agreement whereby each pays the cost of repairs to the car it insures, irrespective of who is to blame for an accident. This avoids expensive court cases to apportion blame, but as a result both drivers may lose their no-claim bonuses.

A motorist who finds that he is to have his bonus reduced unjustly because of this system should try to convince the company that they could have recovered the money from the other driver's insurers.

The most effective way of doing this is to try to recover any uninsured losses (such as an excess) from the other driver's insurance company. If the company pays in full, your own insurers should not reduce your bonus.

# Grounds for claiming damages

*The meaning of negligence*     *When a motorist breaks the law*
*Who is entitled to claim*     *Health and medical treatment*
*Who to claim against*     *Accepting the risk*

CLAIMS for damages after a road accident are most often settled by the insurance companies of the people involved. Occasionally claims are settled by private agreement between the parties or their solicitors. Where the people involved cannot agree on who is responsible for an accident, how responsibility should be shared or how much money should be paid, one or more of them may sue for damages.

Such claims for damages are decided as if the motorist is paying any compensation awarded out of his own pocket. The fact that it is usually an insurance company which pays any damages is ignored by the courts.

## The meaning of negligence

Actions for damages following a road accident —and private settlements, which are based on the same principles—depend on the law of negligence. There are no special rules covering liability in road accidents; the law of negligence applies equally to all types of accidents, wherever they occur.

The law of negligence as it applies to motoring is based on the principle that every road-user has a legal obligation to drive carefully at all times, and to exercise proper care to all those whom he could reasonably foresee might be injured by his driving. Thus, for legal purposes, negligence can be defined as a failure to take reasonable care which causes injury or damage to someone else.

A claim is not barred even when the injured person was himself partly to blame for the accident. If any negligence can be attributed to someone else there is basis for a claim against him.

## Who is entitled to claim

Not everyone who is injured or suffers damage through negligent driving has a right to claim compensation from the person responsible.

This is because the duty of care imposed on a motorist is limited only to such people as could reasonably be expected to be harmed by his careless driving.

Suppose a motorist is driving with his wife in the front passenger seat and in the back seat is a hitch-hiker they picked up five minutes earlier. Through inattention on the driver's part, the car runs off the road and crashes into an electricity transformer. A pedestrian standing on the pavement is killed, the driver's wife suffers broken ribs, the hitch-hiker's leg is broken, and damage to the transformer causes a power failure.

Many people involved in the crash are entitled to claim damages. The hitch-hiker can claim because the driver owed him a duty of care—he must have been aware that if he drove carelessly he would put passengers at risk.

Similarly, the driver's wife can make a claim against her husband. The fact that they are married makes no difference to her right to claim. If the insurance company contests the claim, the action goes to court and the wife will be suing her husband. But in fact his insurance company will have to pay if she is successful.

Dependants of the pedestrian who was killed can also claim damages. Relations whom he was wholly or partially supporting, usually a wife and children and in some cases an aged parent, will probably have a claim for a large sum. A small claim could also be made by the pedestrian's estate for compensation for loss of expectation of life. Any money awarded would go to the dead man's heirs.

If, however, a photographic studio has a power cut as a result of the damage to the transformer, and is forced to suspend business for two days, the owners cannot recover damages from the motorist. Courts have ruled that a driver owes no duty of care to people who might suffer in such a remote way.

A motorist is responsible for the foreseeable consequences of his negligence—which may include, in some cases, causing accidents in which he is not personally involved.

A motorist, for instance, drives carelessly and causes his car to mount a pavement near a bus stop. A student, waiting for a bus, jumps into the road to avoid being hurt, and is struck by another vehicle.

The student can recover damages from the driver because his injury is a direct and foreseeable result of the driver's negligence.

CLAIMS BY ONLOOKERS Sometimes an onlooker suffers nervous shock as a result of merely witnessing an accident. The law recognises nervous shock as a form of personal injury, and in certain circumstances the onlooker who suffers shock has grounds to claim. For the claim to be successful, the shock must have been foreseeable to the motorist—a difficult test for a court to apply.

Suppose, for example, that a mother sees a lorry with no driver running down a hill towards a spot where her children are playing, and it turns out that the lorry was negligently parked by its driver. Although the children escape unhurt, the mother is so frightened and shocked by the danger which threatens them that she collapses and becomes seriously ill. In this case, the mother could probably recover damages.

A slightly different case is that of the motor cyclist who swerves dangerously on a sharp bend, collides with a lorry and is killed. A pregnant housewife sees the motor cyclist a second before the impact, hears the crash and sees blood at the scene. She is badly shocked and has a miscarriage.

In this instance, the housewife probably cannot recover damages from the motor cyclist's estate. The courts ruled in a similar case that the motor cyclist could not have foreseen that he would harm someone in the position of the pregnant housewife. Thus he owed her no duty of care.

**Who to claim against**
Where an accident is the fault of more than one driver, anyone who is injured may be able to claim compensation from a number of people. A court—or the parties themselves, in a private negotiation—then decides on the degree of negligence of each driver involved.

Take the case of the motorist who is driving his sports car with his fiancée as a passenger. He takes a wrong turning and then reverses into the main road which he had just left. This dangerous manoeuvre leads to a collision with a lorry. The lorry driver was taking a short cut to return the lorry to his employer's depot and was travelling at 50 mph on a road with a 40 mph speed limit. In addition, at the moment of impact he was trying to read a map, and was therefore not keeping a proper look-out for other road-users.

If the fiancée is injured, she can recover damages from both drivers, since both were negligent. In addition, the lorry owners would have to pay her damages, since employers are liable for harm negligently inflicted on others by their employees while acting within the scope of their employment.

The drivers may also have claims against

one another. Assuming that the accident was 30 per cent due to the negligence of the sports-car driver and 70 per cent due to the lorry driver's negligence, the sports-car driver can recover 70 per cent of his damages. The lorry driver and, through him, his employers are liable for this amount. In turn, they can recover 30 per cent of their claim or claims from the sports-car driver.

A vehicle owner can be held responsible when neither driving nor in charge of a vehicle in only two circumstances.
**1.** Where he employs the driver, and the vehicle is being used on the firm's business. ☐ Using a car for work, p. 67.
**2.** Where the driver is acting on the owner's behalf as his agent—that is, using the vehicle expressly at the owner's request. ☐ Lending and borrowing a car, p. 38.

The fact that a driver is using a car with the owner's permission does not make the owner liable if an accident occurs. So the owner of a family car is not responsible if the marriage partner causes an accident.

ACCIDENTS CAUSED BY CHILDREN When a child causes an accident, claims may be made against the person or organisation responsible for the child at the time—usually the parents—if that person exercised inadequate control in relation to a child of that age. ☐ Looking after children, p. 342.

Sometimes, people other than the parents are in control of a child—for example, teachers and, through them, school authorities. So if a motorist is injured while trying to avoid a child who runs from a school into the street, he may be able to claim against the school authorities if it can be shown that they were negligent in leaving a gate unlocked which gave direct access to the street. He can also claim against the child's schoolteacher, and her employers, if he is able to prove negligence on the teacher's part in allowing the child to stray.

CLAIMS AGAINST THE LOCAL COUNCIL If the accident was wholly or partly caused by the condition of the road there may be the basis of an action against the local authority for negligent failure to maintain the roadway.

The authority could also be liable to pay damages for an accident caused by the negligence of its employees—if, for instance, the accident was due to the carelessness of a school crossing patrolman.

**When a motorist breaks the law**
The fact that a motorist is breaking the law at the time he is injured does not automatically make his damages claim invalid. If a motorist, driving at night at 45 mph on a

clearway with a 40 mph restriction, crashes into a car parked without lights at the roadside, he may be able to claim against the person in charge of the parked vehicle.

It might be that his breaking the speed limit had nothing to do with the accident. Should the court find that the accident could have occurred even if the motorist had been travelling at 39 mph, he would get his full damages. Otherwise he would be awarded a proportional amount.

Similarly, anyone injured in a road accident will not automatically get damages just because he can show that the other driver failed to observe the statutory safety regulations—by driving a car in a dangerous condition, for example.

Breach of a statutory duty does not, in a motoring case, automatically give grounds for a claim. Negligence must be proved. Breach of a regulation might, however, be *evidence* of negligence.

Some breaches of the law need have no effect on the question of liability. Take the case of the 17-year-old unqualified driver who takes his father's car without permission. While driving in town, he runs into a pedestrian who has darted in front of the car.

Is the unqualified driver liable? Not necessarily. If it could be shown that the accident would have happened even if he had been a qualified driver, he would not be held liable.

## Health and medical treatment

Identical injuries can have different effects on victims in different states of health. A healthy young man, for example, might recover relatively quickly from injuries which could kill an older man with a weak heart. The law, however, requires that a motorist, or anyone else, must take the victim of his actions as he finds him.

If the victim happens to have an 'eggshell skull' or a weak spine, or to be a haemophiliac, this provides no defence for the motorist who injures him in an accident. But the fact that the victim had a weak heart would be taken into account, and damages would be assessed on a shortened expectation of life.

FAULTY MEDICAL TREATMENT The courts sometimes have to deal with cases where someone injured in an accident subsequently receives faulty medical treatment. A cyclist, for example, might be injured by a motorist ignoring a red traffic light. The cyclist is taken to hospital and given faulty treatment, after which he dies.

Is the motorist liable for damages resulting from the cyclist's death? There is no definite answer. If the cyclist was badly injured, and was likely to die anyway, the courts would probably hold the motorist liable.

Where the death is accelerated by some clear act of negligence by the hospital—for example, giving a transfusion of blood of the wrong group—the tendency of the courts is not to hold the motorist liable for the further consequences, and to reduce any damages awarded against him for the injury he originally caused. The hospital would then be liable for its share of the damages.

## Accepting the risk

A person who voluntarily exposes himself to danger cannot usually claim damages if he is injured as a result.

A man who accepts a lift from a neighbour, and notices that the neighbour smells strongly of drink, may therefore not be able to claim damages if he is injured in an accident caused by the neighbour driving under the influence of drink. The court might hold that he has 'assumed' the risk by willingly exposing himself to the danger.

In this case, it would depend on how obvious was the state of the neighbour's drunkenness and whether the man who accepted the lift had any opportunity to get out of the car when he discovered it.

RIGHTS OF THE RESCUER The rule that anyone who deliberately exposes himself to danger has no grounds to claim damages does not apply to injuries which result from a rescue attempt. So people who are injured while attempting a rescue can recover damages from whoever is responsible for the accident. As one judge put it: 'Danger invites rescue.'

Those responsible for causing an accident must foresee that there might be rescue operations as a result of which people are injured. If a person who is rescued from a car dies, a claim can be made against his estate—though, once again, the insurance company would pay. If two drivers are responsible for an accident, the rescuer injured trying to save one of them is entitled to claim damages against both.

## Liability of emergency services

Fire engines, police cars and ambulances have to observe the same duty of care as anyone else—even though, in some circumstances, they may exceed the speed limit. If they injure others while answering an emergency call, they can be sued for damages. Only in very rare cases—for example, while using unfamiliar vehicles in time of war—can the court hold that the emergency excuses the duty of care.

# How a damages claim is decided

*Engaging a solicitor*　　*Taking a claim to court*
*Gathering evidence*　　*The court hearing*
*Negotiating a settlement*　　*Damages for personal injury*

ANYONE injured in an accident may be able to recover damages from the person whose negligence caused or contributed to his injuries. But before an injured person makes a claim he must be sure that he has good legal grounds—a claim that fails can cost a considerable amount in legal fees.

Grounds for claiming damages for injury are set out on the following pages, according to the individual or organisation against which a claim can be made:

Grounds on which dependants can claim damages for fatal injuries are given on p. 417.

It is important to assess whether the person to be sued can afford to pay any damages awarded. In most cases this means finding out whether he is insured against such claims.

## Engaging a solicitor

It is not advisable to pursue or defend an action for damages without the help of a solicitor. Claims often fail for lack of expert help, and a claimant who is unrepresented may agree to accept less damages than he is really entitled to. □ Getting advice on a legal problem, p. 708.

The claimant should give his solicitor full details of the accident, his injury and his personal circumstances.

The solicitor's first action, if he is satisfied that his client has grounds for a claim, is to write to the person he believes to be responsible, saying that a claim is being made. When he receives this notification the defendant should inform his own solicitor or insurance company immediately. If he intends to contest the action, he must get statements from witnesses and prepare his defence quickly.

## Gathering evidence

MEDICAL EXAMINATIONS The claimant's solicitor and the defendant's insurance company (if he is insured) will both want medical evidence of the injury. This usually means two private medical examinations—one, if possible, by the doctor who first treated the claimant in hospital; and the other by the insurance company's doctor.

ASSESSING THE LOSS The solicitor now tries to assess the financial loss caused to the claimant by the accident. If the claimant has recovered and returned to his normal work, the loss can be worked out easily, but in many serious cases the calculation has to wait until it is possible to judge what effect the accident will have on the claimant's earning capacity.

## Negotiating a settlement

Nearly all claims, even those that eventually go to court, start with negotiations. When both sides have gathered information, a meeting is arranged. This seldom takes place less than four months after the letter of claim.

If the insurance representative or the defendant has decided that the claimant is likely to win his case if it goes to court, he may say at the first meeting that he is not disputing liability. He usually makes it clear, however, that he does so 'without prejudice'. This means that, if he later wishes to change his mind and deny liability, his earlier admission cannot be used against him in court.

When the defendant denies liability from the outset, the claimant has to prove he was to blame. Often an insurance company accepts that some liability rests on the defendant but considers the claimant partly to blame.

There may be a succession of meetings spread over several months before a possible agreement is in sight. If the defendant is prepared to settle, the negotiators will try to agree on the amount of damages that would be awarded in a successful court action. The decision on whether to accept the defendant's offer has to be taken by the claimant.

In a negotiated settlement, the claimant can usually recover his costs from the defendant. This should be agreed before the settlement is made binding. Where a child is involved, any agreement reached has to be approved by the High Court before it becomes binding.

PAYMENT INTO COURT At some stage in the negotiations, a defendant often makes a payment into court. This means that he offers the claimant that sum in full settlement of his claim. If the claimant accepts, that is the end of the action. If he does not, negotiations (and possible court action) continue as before.

If the damages eventually awarded are less than the amount offered by the payment into the court, the claimant has to pay the costs of the losing defendant from the time of the payment into court. Whether or not to accept such an offer is therefore critical.

## Taking a claim to court

If negotiations fail, a personal-injury claim may be pursued either in a county court, where the limit on damages is £750, or in the High Court, where there is no limit. If it is contested, the county court will hear the claim within eight to ten weeks. For a High Court hearing, it may be necessary to wait between a year and 18 months.

Proceedings in a county court are simpler and cheaper; a claimant determined to conduct his own case might be able to do so with the guidance of court officials. ☐ Legal action II: suing to recover a debt, p. 725; Legal aid I: help with fees and costs, p. 710.

THE FIRST STEPS A High Court action is started by the person who is making the claim —called the plaintiff—issuing to the defendant a document called a writ of summons. The writ states that an action is to be brought, and gives brief details of the reasons.

Alternatively, the plaintiff can choose to include in the writ full details of his claim instead of a summary, so that at a later stage the case can be settled quickly.

Two copies of the writ must be taken or sent to the Action Department of the Central Office of the Supreme Court, Royal Courts of Justice, Strand, London WC2A 2LL, or to one of the district registries of the High Court in the larger cities and towns. One copy is stamped and filed by the court and the other is returned to the plaintiff, who serves it on the defendant.

Within eight days of receiving the writ, the defendant must give notice that he intends to contest the action. This can be done only on a form obtainable from either the Central Office of the Supreme Court in London or from a district registry.

He must take or send two copies of the completed form to the Central Office. One copy is filed and the other is returned to the defendant, who sends it to the plaintiff. This process is known as entering an appearance.

If the defendant fails to enter an appearance, the case may be heard in his absence: the action then comes before an officer of the Queen's Bench Division of the High Court called a master, who gives a judgment on the evidence presented by the plaintiff.

EXCHANGING DOCUMENTS Documents containing statements of the issues on which the action is based are then sent to the defendant by the plaintiff. The first to be delivered— unless it has been included on the writ of summons—is the statement of claim, giving details of the facts in support of the plaintiff's case. It is usually sent within ten days.

In turn, the defendant should send his defence to the claim within 14 days of receiving the statement of claim or of entering an appearance, whichever is later. He can admit or deny the allegations, or produce additional facts to show that other factors were involved.

The plaintiff can make a reply to the defence within seven days, and must do so if the defendant has made a counter-claim. All these documents are known as pleadings.

## Settling the case quickly

If the plaintiff believes that the defendant has no case, he is entitled, in some instances, to ask the master to give a judgment without hearing the defence. (This course, incidentally, cannot be taken where the action is for libel, slander, malicious prosecution, false imprisonment or fraud.)

The defendant can take the same course if he has made a counter-claim to which he believes the plaintiff has no answer.

The party asking for judgment has to make a sworn, written statement—called an affidavit —giving the reason for the action, the amount he is claiming, and stating that he believes there is no defence to the claim.

He takes out a summons at the Action Department of the Central Office asking for a speedy judgment to be made. The summons is served on the defendant, who can, if he wishes, also swear an affidavit giving details of his defence and asking for permission to present it to the court.

A date is fixed for a hearing, and the

master, or the district registrar if the action is brought outside London, reads the affidavits and hears any arguments from the two sides.

He then either gives a judgment or orders that the action must go for trial, and says where it is to be heard and whether it is to be before a jury.

**Arranging the trial**

If there is no application for judgment, the plaintiff must ask the master or district registrar for an order fixing where the trial is to be held. This should be done not later than a month after the end of the pleadings.

To get the order, the plaintiff must take out a summons on a special form at the Action Department of the Central Office or the district registry. This is known as a summons for directions.

He serves the summons on the defendant, and a hearing is held at the offices of the master or the district registrar. If the plaintiff fails to issue a summons for directions, the defendant may apply for one, or he may ask for an order dismissing the action.

If he is asked to by the plaintiff or the defendant, the master can order either side to answer on oath written questions, called interrogatories, submitted by the other side. He can also make an order forcing each side to allow the other to inspect documents.

Once the master or district registrar has made his decision on these matters, the plaintiff can make an application in writing to the Crown Office and Associates' Department, Room 478, Royal Courts of Justice, Strand, London WC2A 2LL—or to the district registrar, if the case is being held outside London—for the action to be entered in the list specified by the master. This is called setting down for trial.

If the defendant took out the summons for directions, he is entitled to set down the action for trial. The side which asks for the action to be entered in the list must inform the opposition within 24 hours that this has been done. The action then takes its place in the list of cases waiting for trial. If an action is set down for trial without a jury in London, either the plaintiff or the defendant can write to the Clerk of the Lists, Queen's Bench Division, Room 419, Royal Courts of Justice, Strand, London WC2A 2LL, asking for a date to be fixed for a hearing.

**The court hearing**

When the action is heard in the High Court, either party can appear on his own behalf—which is very rare—or he can be represented by a barrister, often referred to as a counsel.

Counsel for the plaintiff opens the trial by outlining the facts of the case and the issues which are disputed.

Each witness, after being questioned by the plaintiff's counsel, can be cross-examined by the defence. The plaintiff may then ask further questions, to re-establish any points weakened by the defence questioning.

When all the witnesses for the plaintiff have been heard, counsel for the defendant usually opens his case with an outline of the facts, and then examines the defence witnesses one by one. Their evidence can be tested by questioning in the same way as the plaintiff's witnesses.

Finally, counsel for the defendant makes a closing speech, followed by counsel for the plaintiff. If there is no jury, the judge gives his judgment; otherwise, the judge sums up and the jury gives its verdict.

Where the case is being heard by a jury, it is the jury that decides on the amount of damages the plaintiff is to receive; if there is no jury, the judge decides.

The judge always decides whether to order one side to pay the costs of the other. Normally, the loser is ordered to pay the costs of the winner. If no order is made each side pays its own costs.

If there is an appeal against a High Court or county court decision it will go to the Court of Appeal, which can vary the court's decision, reduce the damages or order a retrial. If damages have been awarded by a jury in the High Court, they can be varied only if both parties give their consent. If either refuses there must be a retrial. The Court of Appeal is reluctant to interfere with a jury's award of damages, but it will alter a judge's decision on damages if it thinks it wrong.

If the case involves points of law of public importance, either party may be able to appeal to the House of Lords if permission is obtained from the Court of Appeal or the House of Lords itself.

**Damages for personal injury**

In trying to reach a settlement on damages for personal injury, the aim is to restore the plaintiff to the financial position he would have been in had the accident not occurred.

Three main factors are considered—the direct financial loss incurred by the claimant between the accident and the trial; the probable future loss; and the pain, disability and inconvenience which the claimant has suffered and will suffer in the future.

The sum awarded for direct financial loss is

known as 'special damages'; compensation for the other two is called 'general damages'.

DIRECT FINANCIAL LOSS The amount of earnings lost through an accident is calculated between the dates of the accident and the court hearing—often two years or more. The award also includes loss of possible future earnings. Compensation is paid only for legitimate absence from work, approved by a doctor.

SALARY OR WAGES If the claimant's earnings are fixed and paid regularly, the total earnings lost—after tax, but not including graduated pension contributions—are easily calculated. Any sick pay from an employer is deducted.

Compensation is increased if the weekly wage or overtime rate for the claimant's job has risen since his accident; and it is reduced if his job would have ended through 'natural causes', such as redundancy—although the court has to consider whether he might have found another job. Compensation is also reduced if the claimant would have retired. A claim for lost earnings is limited to the period he is likely to have continued working.

Savings resulting from not working—for example, a cut in travelling expenses—may reduce the damages. But a loss of privileges—of cheap meals, for instance—increases them.

If a claimant returns to work for a period before the trial, but loses earnings because his disability prevents him from doing the job he held previously, he can also be compensated for the drop in pay—plus, of course, the full wage he lost while off work.

SELF-EMPLOYED If the claimant is self-employed, a partner in a firm or a working director of a company, he has to show that the probable profits of the firm or company have been reduced because of his inability to work and, as a result, that he himself has lost money. This figure varies according to the number of partners or directors and the wealth of the firm or company.

DEDUCTIONS Half of all State-sickness, in-dustrial-injury or disablement benefits likely to be received over the five years after the accident is deducted from the compensation.

If disablement benefit is paid in a lump sum, it is averaged over the claimant's probable life to find an annual sum. This yearly figure is then calculated for the period before the award and the five years after it, and half the total is deducted from the claim. Any benefit the claimant may receive from an insurance policy for which he himself pays all or part of the premium is disregarded. If, however, the person sued has contributed to the premium, the policy benefits are included.

INCOME TAX ON DAMAGES If the damages are to compensate for the loss of income on which the claimant would otherwise have had to pay tax, the courts make a deduction for this tax liability. Damages for loss of earnings, for example, are calculated on what the claimant would have earned after tax. No deduction for tax is made from damages for factors such as pain, suffering, loss of enjoy-ment of life or loss of expectation of life. Nor is any deduction made if the item in the award is itself taxable—as, for instance, is the case with interest on damages.

Damages for wrongful dismissal or 'golden handshakes' to former employees are tax-free up to £5000, and taxable over £5000. The courts, therefore, deduct tax for the amount under £5000, but not for the excess.

ADDITIONAL EXPENSES The injured party can claim the cost of visits to hospital by a wife or children, if they can reasonably be regarded as likely to help his recovery. The cost of visits by a parent to an injured child under the age of 18 can be recovered only if the child nor-mally lives at home and the parent is a party to any court proceedings in his own right.

If the wife or a relative of the injured person gives up work to look after him, or a husband stays away from work to look after the children during his wife's incapacity, the loss of earnings will be allowed only if this was the cheapest means of providing the service.

The cost of private treatment, prescriptions, nursing homes, convalescent homes or holi-days can be claimed if they are undertaken on competent medical advice.

The full cost of convalescent holidays is rarely allowed. Only the claimant's own expenses can normally be recovered, unless he can show that it was necessary to have some other person with him.

The standard of accommodation should be no higher than the claimant would normally use, unless his state of health makes greater luxury reasonably necessary.

## Future financial loss

In heavy awards of damages, it is usually the future financial loss and expense which is the most important element.

In serious cases, the claim is not usually settled or tried for at least two years after the accident—often much later. So by the time damages for future loss and expense come to be assessed, it is possible to form an estimate of the cost from the amount already lost.

If the claimant has had to take a job at a lower wage, he can claim compensation for the estimated future loss in earnings. Probable future medical expenses, which may be attributed to the accident, can also be added.

If the claimant is under the age of 30, the damages will probably be calculated over 15 years; but if he is 60 or more, they may be calculated over only four years or so.

The reason for these limits is that the court calculates the amount needed to buy an annuity that would provide an equivalent income until retirement age.

A period of more than 15 years may be used if it is thought that the claimant's earnings would have continued to increase. Similarly, the period is increased if the claimant is likely to require nursing for the rest of his life.

### Compensation for pain and disability

A court calculating damages for pain and disability has to consider the extent to which an injury is likely to handicap the claimant in his enjoyment of life; the pain and discomfort involved; any reduction in his normal expectation of life; and the extent to which his leisure pursuits are disrupted.

In cases where there is a lasting disability, damages for pain and discomfort caused by the accident may be included in the figure awarded for the disability, though a man whose arm is amputated after a long period of unsuccessful treatment will receive heavier damages than one whose arm is amputated immediately and makes a quick recovery.

In minor cases, where the accident causes a few weeks' absence from work, damages tend to be at the rate of about £8–£10 per week for the period of total disability, tapering to nothing after he returns to work and makes a full recovery. Figures are rounded up to the nearest multiple of £25.

## Estimating compensation for injury and pain

Damages for injury and pain are difficult to assess. But by studying similar cases, some estimate of the probable award can be made. Newspaper reports are not a good guide because usually they publish only the total damages, including the actual financial loss already incurred, known as 'special damages'. *The Current Law Year Book*—which is available at many major public libraries—contains a summary of all cases which have been reported during the year. They are listed under 'Damages for personal injury'—with particular types of injuries grouped together. The figures given do not include special damages for financial loss.

| | |
|---|---|
| Multiple injuries | Boy, 16, four limbs crippled, awarded £62,000<br>Woman, 44, similarly disabled, £35,000 |
| Brain and skull injuries | Man, 36, fits and loss of memory, £45,750<br>Girl, 9, personality change, fits, £12,000 |
| Face | Woman, 18, needed 22 stitches, £910 |
| Burns and scars | Man, 49, legs scalded, £1658 |
| Eye injuries | Man, 39, with one eye blinded, £6640 |
| Spinal injuries | Man, 63, injury impaired sex activity, limbs spastic, gangrene, loss of leg, £20,000<br>Woman, 38, strained back prevented sport or housework, £2250 |
| Body injuries | Man, 36, broken pelvis, £3150 |
| Arms | Man, 43, use of arm limited, £12,000<br>Woman, 58, fractured arm shortened, £500 |
| Hand | Man, 23, nerve and tendons damaged, £10,500<br>Woman, 56, finger amputated, £1182 |
| Leg | Man, 46, knee damaged, £12,000 |
| Feet | Man, 22, feet amputated, £10,000 |
| Neurosis | Man, 38, personality change, £5000<br>Woman, 32, depression after injury, £4500 |
| Minor injuries | Man, 39, severe blow to head, £250 |

# Car sports

*Treasure hunts and rallies*
*Off-the-road events*
*Travelling to and from the course*

*Unlicensed events*
*Compensation for the injured*

THE use of public roads in Britain for motor sports such as treasure hunts and rallies is strictly controlled by law. The aim is to ensure that these events do not cause annoyance to people living along the route, or increase congestion or the risk of accidents on the road.

Competitors taking part in off-the-road events such as racing and hill-climbs are subject to the organisers' rules, and must observe the laws about construction and maintenance of vehicles when taking their cars to and from the sports venue.

## Treasure hunts and rallies

There are few formalities involved in organising or taking part in small treasure hunts and rallies—those limited to 12 or fewer cars, with a total route of less than 100 miles and no time-keeping involved.

Competitors should check that their insurance covers them while taking part in such events—many domestic policies exclude cover for any form of 'motor competition' or reduce it to liability under the Road Traffic Acts (so that no claim can be made for damage to the policy-holder's vehicle, for example).

Where a policy provides no cover for rallies and treasure hunts, it is essential to extend it before taking part. Failure to do so could lead to prosecution for driving while uninsured, as well as invalidating claims under the policy.

Organisers must discuss their route with the local police well in advance. Police forces keep a note of areas in which a procession of cars will not be welcome—usually places where landowners, particularly farmers, have complained in the past.

Similarly the police will want to keep treasure hunts away from accident black spots, narrow roads or routes to beauty spots where additional vehicles could cause congestion or hazards.

Organisers should avoid leaving clues or articles that have to be collected in any place that might lead a competitor to trespass on private land, unless special permission has been obtained from the landowner. Other-

wise the competitor and organisers could be sued for damages by the landowner. ☐ The law on trespassing, p. 133.

LARGER RALLIES Stricter controls are placed on rallies in which more than 12 cars take part, or where the route is 100 miles or more, or where time-keeping is involved (that is, where competitors are required to follow an exact route laid down by the organisers at a specific average speed).

The Department of the Environment has powers to control such events under the Motor Vehicles (Competitions and Trials) Regulations 1965. These powers are delegated to the Royal Automobile Club (and through them, for motor-cycle events, to the Auto-Cycle Union).

Rallies can be run only by clubs approved by the RAC and organisers must submit proposed routes and timetables three months in advance. These should be sent to the RAC's Motor Sport Division, 31 Belgrave Square, London SW1X 8QH.

The RAC checks that the route does not cover roads where there have been frequent complaints about traffic dangers. Officials also ensure that no road is used for rallying more than once in any month.

In addition, the RAC may insist that some sections of the proposed route—through villages, for example—should be negotiated at low average speeds, and may demand that checks be made on vehicle noise.

All rally cars are driven on public roads and must, therefore, comply with legal requirements. In particular, competitors who tune their car engines should ensure that the noise level does not exceed the permitted maximum of 84 decibels (dBA).

Most competitors fit extra lights to their cars. Spot lights and fog lights must be fitted so that they cannot swing round and dazzle other road users. They must also be wired so that they extinguish automatically when headlights are dipped. ☐ Lights not required by law, p. 48.

Extra reversing lights must be wired to light up only when the car is in reverse gear or, if they are manually operated, a visual warning must be installed. Rally drivers should also make sure that all their wheels and the exhaust system are covered by the car's bodywork.

## Off-the-road events

Most motor sports are organised under licence from the RAC (or, in the case of motor-cycles, the Auto-Cycle Union). Strict regulations cover the safety of spectators and competitors at these licensed events:

1. Race meetings at permanent circuits.
2. Autocross (a speed event on grass or other unsealed surface).
3. Drag racing (a race or speed event over a flat, straight, 440-yd course).
4. Rallycross (a race or speed event over both sealed and unsealed surfaces).
5. Hill-climbs (an uphill speed event on a sealed surface).
6. Sprints (a speed event on a sealed surface, usually run on a race circuit).

USING THE FAMILY CAR Most vehicles used in motor sport are unsuitable for the roads. But anyone who wishes to use the family car should make sure that he is covered by insurance, as most policies exclude racing or pace-making.

Not only will the driver be without cover while participating, but any damage to the vehicle during the event that could later be held to have contributed towards an accident on a public road may give an insurance company grounds for refusing a claim.

RISK OF ACCIDENTS Anyone attending a properly organised event on private land will find conditions of admission displayed on tickets and posters. These absolve everyone connected with the organisation and conduct of the event—including competitors—from liability for injury to spectators and damage to their property.

Competitors sign a declaration indemnifying the RAC and its officials against claims for injury and loss or damage to property. These disclaimers do not protect a competitor judged guilty of reckless driving under the organising body's competition rules.

At most stadiums, safety precautions are strict, but people attending other forms of motor sports should examine the course for safety fences, barriers and run-off areas that prevent cars out of control from reaching spectators. If a position looks at all dangerous, stand elsewhere.

## Travelling to and from the course

A driver using his own car in a motor sports event should not remove anything from the bodywork, such as bumpers, until he has reached the private land on which the event is being held. These parts should be replaced before leaving the site. Any mud adhering to the car should also be removed as local bye-laws often make it an offence to deposit excessive mud on the road.

After the event, check that lights and indicators are in working order. Electrical connections can be shaken loose on rough ground and bulb failure is common.

Make sure that all wheels and the exhaust system are covered by the bodywork, and that the exhaust system has sustained no damage. Examine the car carefully for any sharp or jagged edges on the bodywork.

If the vehicle has been damaged, it is wiser to have it towed away than attempt to drive it, for a motorist may be breaking the law if it is in poor condition. □ The law on car safety, p. 39.

TRAILERS Most competitors take cars to meetings on trailers. These must conform to the regulations governing trailers. □ Caravans and trailers, p. 166.

A trailer must not be towed at more than 40 mph, even on a motorway. The driver must make sure that the vehicle being carried is secure and does not protrude over the ends of the trailer.

## Unlicensed events

Competitors and spectators at events not licensed by the RAC—including stock-car and midget-car racing, figure-of-eight racing and most grass-track racing—do not have the protection of the RAC's stringent safety regulations.

Spectators should take care to watch from places which are safe from cars running out of control. Before taking part, competitors should check that they are insured by the organisers against claims for personal injury or damage which might be brought by spectators or other competitors.

## Compensation for the injured

Whether someone injured in an accident at a motor sports event can successfully claim compensation will depend on the conditions of admission and the cause of the accident. □ Accidents at sporting events, p. 131.

If a claim is successful, anyone injured at an event licensed by the RAC should be sure of receiving the sum awarded, since all RAC-licensed events are covered by insurance to meet such claims.

At other events, the chances of getting paid would depend on insurance arrangements (if any) made by the organisers.

# Accidents at sporting events

*Injuries caused by negligence*
*Precautions against accidents*

MANY sports can be dangerous, and often players and spectators risk being injured or even killed. Because of these risks, the law gives people causing accidents in sport a little more protection against claims for damages than it gives to people who are responsible for other kinds of accidents in everyday life.

Damages will not be awarded simply because a spectator or player has been injured and the injury has been caused by someone's carelessness. The law also takes into account that certain types of accident are foreseeable in sport and that, by participating or watching, the person injured has to some degree accepted the risk of injury.

But players and spectators alike are assumed in law to have accepted the risks of a sport only when it is played in the normal way. If an injury results from play wholly outside the rules of the game, there are normally grounds for claiming damages.

For example, a footballer risks injury from being tripped by a foul, and he would not usually be able to claim for damages, no matter how serious the injury. But if the injury were caused by an unusually vicious and deliberate foul, he could have a good case for suing the other player.

▶ A DELIBERATE KICK *In 1967, in a match between Eastbourne Olympics and Hotchkiss, Roger Brookshaw played outside-right for the Olympics, and Alan Lewis was centre-forward for Hotchkiss. After a tackle, Brookshaw kicked Lewis, breaking his right leg. Lewis had to be carried from the field and was unable to play football again. He claimed damages.*
DECISION *The court found that Brookshaw had deliberately fouled his opponent. He was ordered to pay £5400 damages. (Lewis v. Brookshaw.)* ◀

A deliberate and serious foul might even lead to a criminal prosecution—for instance, a charge of causing grievous bodily harm.

## Injuries caused by negligence
An injured player or spectator will be entitled to damages if he can show that his injury resulted from another person's negligence

beyond what could reasonably be foreseen as part of the game. For example, if a tennis player, in a show of temperament, hurled his racquet into the crowd, injuring a spectator, he could be made to pay damages.

## Precautions against accidents
The success or failure of an action for damages —particularly against the organisers of sporting events, or the owners of the premises— usually depends on whether or not the accident could have been foreseen and how clearly people were warned about the risks involved.

For example, the owners of a motor-racing track would be liable if a car careered into the crowd, unless they could show they had taken all reasonable precautions.

WARNING NOTICES A notice saying 'Spectators admitted at their own risk' or similar warnings printed on tickets and in programmes may not rule out the possibility of claiming damages for an injury. But if the person injured could not help being aware of the warnings, he is unlikely to be successful. ☐ Car sports, p. 129.

▶ THE JALOPY RACER *Mr Graham White, a plumber who enjoyed jalopy racing, competed at an RAF charity meeting on Battle of Britain Day and stayed to watch other events. He was resting at a post holding the safety rope when a car struck the rope a third of a mile away. Mr White was jerked into the air and injured. He died, and his widow sued the organisers. Her claim was rejected and she appealed.*
DECISION *Mrs White lost. The Appeal Court ruled by a two-to-one majority that warning notices were sufficiently obvious, and that Mr White, even in his capacity as a spectator, was well aware of the risks. (White v. Blackmore and others.)* ◀

INSURANCE Organisers of sporting events attended by large crowds should insure against claims for injury damages from spectators.

Sportsmen facing a clear risk of serious injury—motor rally drivers or footballers, for example—should also take out insurance cover. ☐ Life assurance, p. 518.

# Access to the countryside

Problems for motorists    National parks and open countryside
Public footpaths         Commons and village greens
Hazards on footpaths     Cycling, horse-riding and camping

THE public's right of access to, and use of, the countryside, commons and foot-paths is controlled by law. Every square mile in Britain, including the foreshore, has a legal owner—whether an individual, a commercial concern, a statutory body such as a local authority, or the Crown.

About 1·25 million acres of land, however, are specifically set aside by Act of Parliament for leisure pursuits such as rambling, riding, motoring, picnicking or camping.

But the public has no right to enter land where there is no public right of way.

## Problems for motorists

The driver who takes his car out into the country has two main problems: where he can go without causing offence, and where he may park the vehicle.

PRIVATE LAND The motorist must always have permission from the landowner before he drives across private land. Otherwise, he is trespassing.

But signs saying 'Private road' are illegal where a public right of way exists, such as a highway. These public rights of way are marked on Ordnance Survey maps. A land-owner who erects such a misleading sign can be prosecuted by the local authority.

PARKING When cars converge on beauty spots or at the seaside, parking is often difficult. If there are no restriction signs the general law applies that it is an offence to park if it causes 'unnecessary obstruction'. Offenders can be fined up to £50. □ Problems of parking, p. 77.

OFF THE ROAD Drivers who park their cars on grass verges are also liable to prosecution for obstruction, and it is an offence to park on common land within 15 yards of a highway.

Motorists who park on common land in towns or urban areas commit an offence under the Law of Property Act 1925.

## Public footpaths

Before a motorist can take his car along any public right of way, such as a footpath or bridleway (where a member of the public can lead or ride a horse) that crosses private land, he must first have the permission of the land-owner. A driver using such a right of way without permission may be taken to court, and faces a fine of up to £10.

RULES FOR WALKERS In law, a walker may use a public footpath to 'pass and repass' from one point to another, but he must not obstruct the path in any way, or damage it—for instance, by riding a horse on it. If the path is already obstructed, say by machinery or an unauthorised fence, he can remove the obstruction—but no more than necessary to get past.

He must not cause any damage by moving the obstacle and must be able to prove, if necessary, that the obstacle had to be removed before he could continue.

If the path is blocked by a more bulky obstruction, such as a tree, he may go round it, across adjoining land, even if the land is private or has crops growing on it. But his detour must be no more than is necessary to avoid the obstacle.

If a landowner allows the path to become impassable, he must tolerate walkers crossing his land to get round an obstruction.

If the path has been blocked deliberately by the landowner—for instance, with barbed wire—the walker can remove the obstacle and should then report the matter to the local-authority highways department. It is a criminal offence to block a path without a legal right to do so, and the council can prosecute the person responsible. A fine of up to £50 can be imposed on conviction.

The landowner does not have to carry out repairs to the surface of the footpath; that is the responsibility of the highway authority —the county, borough or district council. But the landowner must repair stiles and gates.

PLOUGHED-UP PATHS A farmer who ploughs up a path illegally is similarly liable to prose-cution. It can be a defence in any court proceedings for the farmer to show that the path had been ploughed for many years.

A footpath may have been dedicated to the public as a right of way across a field only on condition that the owner of the field may plough up the path and temporarily destroy all trace of it, though the public can still use it.

A farmer who has a common-law right to

plough up a path need not restore the surface. But if the path comes under the Highways Act 1959 (the local council will have a list of these footpaths) he must 'make it reasonably convenient for the exercise of the public right of way'.

### Hazards on footpaths
Barbed wire by the side of a path can be a hazard to walkers. If the highway authority believes that the barbed wire is a danger to passers-by, it can serve the landowner with a notice requiring him to put an end to the nuisance—to 'abate' it within a certain time.

If the owner does not remove the barbed wire, the highway authority may apply to a magistrates' court for an abatement order and may then carry out the removal itself, recovering the expense from the owner.

If a walker has his clothing damaged or is himself hurt by the barbed wire, he can claim damages from the owner.

A walker who is injured because a path has been allowed to fall into disrepair can sue the highway authority for damages.

The damages will be reduced—or may be refused altogether—if the authority can show that the walker was behaving unreasonably or was being careless when the accident occurred, or that it took reasonable care to check for dangers on the footpath.

### Commons and village greens
Common land is an area where some people other than the owner have the right to share natural produce—grass, firewood, peat and perhaps stone or sand. Those who have these rights are called 'commoners' and normally live in adjoining property. They have what is known as 'right of common'. Common-land rights are not held by the general public. They may have a right to use a common, however.

VILLAGE GREENS The village green is defined in law as land allotted for the exercise or recreation of local inhabitants, or where they have a customary right to indulge in 'sports and pastimes'.

On both greens and commons, the only real restrictions on the public may be those laid down by local bye-laws.

### Cycling and horse-riding
Pedal cycles (but not motorised bicycles) may be ridden on footpaths and bridleways. They may also be allowed in parks, subject to local authority bye-laws.

---

## The law on trespassing

IT IS not a crime to trespass, and trespassers cannot be prosecuted. Trespass is a civil wrong, or 'tort', which gives a landowner the right to order a trespasser to leave his property at once, even to use a certain amount of reasonable force to make sure that he does so.
☐ Rights and responsibilities of running a home, p. 280.

He can also get an injunction (a court order) to prevent the intruder repeating the action and can sue for trespass itself, and for any damage the trespasser may have caused.
THE MOTORIST If a driver parks his car on private land he is trespassing, even if he has done no damage. The owner of the land can order him to drive off, and may even move the vehicle himself. He can also sue the driver for damages.
THE WALKER It is trespass to walk on private land unless the owner has given permission or there is a public right of way—such as a highway, footpath or a bridleway. These are clearly marked on Ordnance Survey maps.

Sometimes a walker who has the right to make a necessary detour from the right of way in order to avoid an obstacle may find it more sensible to go round the edge of a field, rather than through crops adjoining the path. Strictly speaking, this would be trespassing, because he is going further out of his way than is necessary.
THE CAMPER Anyone who camps on private or public land without permission is trespassing and can be ordered off and sued for any damage he may have done.
CAUSING DAMAGE A trespasser who picks mushrooms growing wild, or who picks flowers, fruit or foliage from wild plants, shrubs and trees, may be sued for damages.

But he is not guilty of stealing, no matter whose land he is on, unless he has taken the plants for reward or sale or for some other commercial purpose.

If the trespasser picks cultivated flowers, fruit or foliage, it is theft—unless he can prove that he thought he was entitled to pick them.

Bridleways are available for horse-riders. The law on bridleways is similar to that for footpaths, except that certain features—such as stiles—are forbidden.

## Camping

A landowner may allow camping on his land for a fee, but it is an offence for him to set up a camping site without first obtaining planning permission and a site licence from the local authority.

Details of official camping sites can be obtained from motoring organisations such as the Automobile Association, Fanum House, Leicester Square, London WC2H 7LY; the Caravan Club, 65 South Molton Street, London W1Y 2AB, the Youth Hostels' Association, 29 John Adam Street, London WC2N 6JE; and other similar bodies.

A camper is not allowed to pitch his tent wherever he likes in a national park. But there are adequate official sites provided.

## National parks and open countryside

Many areas of mountains, moors, heaths, cliffs and sand dunes are specially protected for public enjoyment, such as Britain's ten national parks: Dartmoor, Exmoor, the Brecon Beacons, the Pembrokeshire Coast, Snowdonia, Northumberland, the Lake Dis-

trict, the North Yorkshire Moors, the Yorkshire Dales and the Peak District.

Much of the land is privately owned in national parks, so that rights of access are the same as in other parts of the countryside.

In addition to the national parks, other districts have been designated areas of outstanding natural beauty.

The public can also make use of (within the local bye-laws) country parks, nature reserves, picnic sites and any stretch of open country belonging to a local authority.

Open country is defined, in the National Parks and Access to the Countryside Act 1949, as consisting 'wholly or predominantly of mountain, moor, heath, down, cliff or foreshore'. The definition was extended in 1968 to cover areas of woodland and most rivers and canals.

There are no special statutory laws limiting the public's right to move at will round these areas; but local authorities may lay down bye-laws. They can enforce these bye-laws by prosecution through the courts.

On nature reserves, the Nature Conservancy can create bye-laws—for instance, banning the destruction or disturbance of all birds' nests (not only those protected by law); the shooting of birds or other animals; or the lighting of fires.

## On the beach

MOST beaches that are normally used by the public—such as those at holiday resorts—are administered by local authorities, and there is never difficulty about using them. But a number of large stretches of the seashore are privately owned.

A notice saying 'Private beach—keep off' need not, however, be taken too literally. The ownership extends, in most cases, only to the beach as far as the high-water mark. The foreshore—that is, the area between high and low tides—technically belongs to the Crown. The exceptions are the few cases, mainly in Cornwall, where the foreshore has been sold by the Crown to a specific public or private concern, perhaps a holiday-camp company.

Generally, anyone is entitled to use the foreshore. The adjacent landowner can exercise no rights over it.

GETTING TO THE FORESHORE The landowner who does not own the foreshore can effectively preserve his privacy by blocking

access to it. He is entitled to order any trespassers off his land or remove them, with no more than reasonable force, if they refuse.

His privacy is at risk from the landward approach only if there is a public right of way to the foreshore. But he has no way of preventing a 'landing' from the sea. The landowner cannot stop people from stepping ashore from a boat and using the foreshore. All he can do is to order back anyone who strays past the high-water mark on to his land.

WALKING INTO DANGER Sometimes a stretch of beach may be used by a Government department—for example, a Ministry of Defence gunnery range.

Warning notices are usually displayed, advising people to keep clear. Any subsequent claim for damages by anyone deliberately or carelessly ignoring warnings would have little chance of success. A watch should also be kept for warnings about the possibility of undetected wartime mines.

# Boating and the right of navigation

A MOTORIST who wants to transport a boat by car must ensure that it is secure and does not cause danger. He must also comply with regulations covering carrying boats on roof racks and trailers.

ROOF RACK On the average family car, a roof rack can carry a load of up to 100 lb. It is dangerous to exceed this weight.

If the boat projects 3 ft 6 in. or more beyond the rearmost point of the vehicle, the driver must make the end of the boat clearly visible to other road users—by attaching a piece of cloth, for example.

If the boat projects 6 ft or more at front or rear, red-and-white triangular marker boards must be fitted at sides and rear, instead of the cloth. If the projection is to the front, a second person must be carried in the towing vehicle to help the driver when necessary. The marker board and second person regulations do not apply to carrying racing boats which are propelled by oars.

Anyone planning to carry a boat which projects more than 10 ft front or rear must obtain police approval of the route and time of his journey at least two days in advance.

If the boat projects 3 ft 6 in. or more beyond the towing vehicle's rear lights, an additional rear light must be fitted so that no part of the boat projects more than 3 ft 6 in. from that additional light.

TRAILERS Any trailer used in towing a boat must comply with regulations about brakes, lighting, registration mark and so on. ☐ Caravans and trailers, p. 166.

Always make sure that the boat is secure on the trailer, including the mast in the case of a sailing boat. Check periodically that the wheels of the trailer are safe—these are often immersed in water when a boat is launched and the wheel bearings can corrode and make the trailer dangerous.

## The right to sail
The common-law right to use a boat at sea or on tidal stretches of any river does not extend to inland waterways such as canals, lakes and non-tidal rivers. Here permission must be sought from the owners of the waterway, unless the right to use the water for boating has been established by custom.

ANCHORING Boats can anchor for a reasonable time, perhaps to wait for favourable weather or to carry out repairs.

MOORING There is no automatic right to moor a boat. To do this without permission involves trespassing. ☐ The law on trespassing, p. 133.

In harbours and rivers, mooring is closely controlled by local regulations.

DISEMBARKING A boat can be brought alongside the bank without permission only when there is a towpath, public landing stage or road there. Otherwise, permission is needed, except in emergencies.

BOATING AND FISHING Right of navigation takes precedence over the right to fish, but boats must not unreasonably interfere with fishing, and the right to navigate does not include the right to fish.

AT A RESORT The right to sail at sea may be restricted at the seaside by local bye-laws. Check with the local authority or river and harbour authorities. Pleasure boats may be restricted under the Public Health Act 1961, to prevent danger, obstruction or annoyance to bathers. Bye-laws may also require silencers on power-driven boats.

## Insuring a boat
There is no legal obligation for a private pleasure vessel to be insured, but it is a wise precaution. Take care to give all the relevant information, as failure to do so may give the insurers the right to refuse a claim.

Separate policies are available for yachts, motorboats, speedboats and dinghies. Most policies give cover for damage to the policyholder's vessel caused by fire and a variety of other accidents; for theft of the vessel; and, in some circumstances, for theft of machinery or equipment. Injury to other people, and damage to their property, is also included.

In all cases it is wise to make sure—if necessary with the advice of the insurer or a broker—that the cover is sufficient. Extensions can usually be arranged on request.

Check, in particular, the maximum that can be claimed for injury or damage to third parties—sometimes the total amount payable on any claim is limited to the insured value of the policy-holder's own vessel, unless an extension is arranged.

## Responsibilities of boating

Anyone in charge of a boat has a duty to take reasonable care in his handling of the craft so that he does not cause injury or damage. If, by failing to do so, he injures a swimmer, for example, or damages a landing-stage or fishing tackle, he will be liable to pay compensation and can be sued for damages.

He must also observe the International Regulations for Preventing Collisions at Sea, which came into operation in 1965. If the person in charge of a boat ignores these rules and a collision results, he may again be liable for damages.

## The rules of navigation

The rule for sailing vessels is that a boat with the wind on its right-hand (starboard) side or quarter has priority and a boat with the wind on the left-hand side (port) must keep out of its way. When both vessels have the wind on the same side, the craft which is to windward (that is, on the side from which the wind is blowing) must keep out of the way of the leeward vessel.

Power-driven craft usually give way to sail, but if there is a risk involved—say of a larger vessel running aground by changing course—the sailing craft should give way.

In narrow channels, power-driven craft should keep to the right.

At night, navigation lights must be carried; a red light on the port side and a green light on the starboard side. Certain power-driven vessels must also carry a white light on the masthead.

## Hiring boats

The conditions under which boats are hired are fairly standard in Britain and abroad. But there is often a variation in the amount of the deposit required, the sum which has to be paid in case of cancellation, and the degree of liability accepted by the owner of the boat in the event of damage.

DEPOSIT The amount of deposit to be paid when booking is usually a percentage of the hiring fee and is often one-third of the full cost. Some companies ask for a deposit of a set figure for each person.

CANCELLATION Most hiring companies insert a cancellation clause in their booking conditions to protect them from any change in the hirer's plans. It is often a condition of hiring that the hirer must pay the whole fee if

he cancels and the company is unable to re-let the boat. It is best, in such cases, to insure against cancellation through illness or other unforeseen causes. Some boat-hire companies can arrange such cover for a small fee—usually £1·50 for a fortnight—while others leave it to the hirer to arrange his own insurance. Check if insurance is included when the booking is made.

OWNER'S LIABILITY Booking conditions always limit the owner's liability in some way, and usually rule out any responsibility by the owner and his employees if anything is wrong with the boat.

The conditions usually make the hirer responsible for the 'safe navigation of the craft', but sometimes also make the hirer responsible for all damage 'howsoever caused'. The hirer should make sure that he is insured against such losses.

Some companies ask for an additional 'security deposit' when the boat is taken over, to be held by the company against loss or damage during the time the boat is hired.

Under the booking conditions, the owner will often refuse to accept any responsibility for time lost or expense caused by breakdown or other defects. Usually the owner undertakes to 'issue the necessary instructions' about repairs, or states that 'immediate steps will be taken to repair'. Conditions of this sort prevent the hirer from claiming anything from the owner for any loss.

## Foreign cruising

All hired craft with a registered weight of under 40 tons which are going further than 12 nautical miles from the coast between North Foreland and Beachy Head, or 36 miles seawards from any other part of the coast, must have a licence from the Customs authority. If a licence is not obtained or kept on board when outside these limits, the craft is liable to be forfeited.

The port Customs officer should always be notified a few days before a boat leaves if a voyage outside the limit is planned.

Certain countries require a Maritime Health Declaration before a boat is cleared for entry. This can be obtained from the medical officer at the port of departure.

All private craft arriving from abroad are subject to Customs, Home Office and health authority regulations. Craft entering a home port from abroad should hoist the international code flag 'Q' and wait until the Customs officer clears the boat. Until this is done, no one except a medical or immigration officer should be allowed to board.

# Hunting, shooting and fishing

*Hunting foxes and deer*
*Shooting and trapping game*
*Certificates for shotguns and firearms*

*Traps and snares*
*When anglers need permission*
*Poaching and illegal fishing*

SEVERAL types of legal restriction are placed on the fox or deer hunter, the shooter and the angler. He may need a fishing or game licence; there may be a 'closed season' for his activities; his weapons may have to be licensed; and he usually must seek the consent of the occupier of land or the person who owns the sporting rights.

**Hunting foxes and deer**
The only consent required for hunting foxes or deer with hounds is the consent of the occupier of the land over which the hunt passes. No official licence is necessary for this kind of hunting.

An occupier may give his consent in writing or by word of mouth, or it may be implied from his habitual acquiescence. He can, however, withdraw express or implied permission at any time he chooses.

If a hunt enters land without permission, the occupier can claim compensation for trespass, and for any injury or damage done. If employees of the hunt—that is, the professional huntsmen—are to blame, the occupier of the land can sue the Master of the Hunt as their employer.

The Master can also be held liable for trespass and damage which is caused by people following the hunt, unless he can show that he instructed them not to go on the land in question. Any identified member of the hunt who trespasses can also be sued.

➤WHEN THE HOUNDS KILLED A CAT *In September 1969, the hounds of Hambledon Hunt, Hampshire, entered gardens in the village of Curdridge and roamed about for ten minutes. An 18-month-old boy was said to have been terrified and a cat was killed. Mr and Mrs David Pearce, of Gordon Road, Curdridge, sued Lieutenant-Colonel Frank Mitchell, the Master of the Hunt, at Southampton County Court for trespass and the loss of the cat. They also sought an injunction restraining the hunt from trespassing in gardens in Curdridge. Their neighbours, Mr and Mrs Christopher Chapman, also sued for trespass.*
DECISION *The judge awarded Mr and Mrs Pearce £5 for trespass and £7 for the loss of the*
*cat. Mr and Mrs Chapman were awarded 1s. for trespass. The judge, however, refused the injunction. 'No injunction will be granted and I hope no application for an injunction will ever again be brought against the hunt, which has known how to behave for 170 years,' he said. (Pearce v. Mitchell.)*◄

Members of a hunt can also be prosecuted if they cause unnecessary suffering to their horses or hounds or to the animal being pursued. ☐ Cruelty to animals, p. 288.

**Shooting and trapping game**
In general, people who set out after game need a game licence and the permission of the owner of the gaming rights over the land on which they intend to pursue their sport.

A game licence must be obtained (from a post office or local authority) by anyone who wants to shoot pheasants, partridges, grouse, heath or moor game, black game, woodcock, snipe, hares, rabbits and deer. Licences are issued for a year or shorter periods. There are three main types: Red licence—for a year to July 31. Green licence—from August 1 to October 31. Blue licence—from November 1 to July 31.

It is also possible to take out a licence for any period of 14 days. A special licence, valid for a year, is available for gamekeepers.

It is an offence to pursue game without a game licence, and anyone who does so is liable to a fine of up to £20.

A motorist who accidentally kills game by running into it in his car may break the law if he takes the bird or animal away with him. He is entitled to do so only if he has a game licence and the permission of the landowner.

Anyone who takes a gun or dog on land where there is game can be required to produce a game licence by an authorised officer of the local authority, the owner or occupier of the land, a gamekeeper, a person who himself has a licence, or a police officer.

If he does not have the licence with him, he can give his name and address and the place where the licence was taken out. Anyone who, in those circumstances, refuses to produce a licence or gives false information, is liable to prosecution and a fine of up to £20. Owners or occupiers of land do not need a licence to shoot rabbits or hares or to hunt them with beagles or hounds on their own land.

**Getting permission**

In addition to having the necessary licences or certificates, anyone wishing to shoot or trap game must get permission from the person who holds the game rights to the land.

The right to kill game birds belongs to the owner of the land on which they are found, unless these rights have been disposed of, or there is an agreement to the contrary. When an owner lets his land, the sporting rights are, in law, presumed to be let to the tenant also, unless they are reserved by the landlord in the tenancy agreement.

The landowner cannot legally deprive his tenant of the right to kill hares and rabbits, known as 'ground game'. But he can share the right with the tenant. The tenant is entitled to authorise one other person—a family member or employee—to kill ground game.

POACHING Game in the wild does not belong to anyone, not even the landowner, until it has been killed or captured. A poacher who kills a rabbit and takes it away cannot be prosecuted for theft because, at the time he killed it, the rabbit did not, legally, belong to anyone. But he can be prosecuted for entering land in search of game without permission.

A trespasser who is caught pursuing game by day and refuses to give his name and address, or who gives false particulars, can be prosecuted and fined up to £5. Anyone who pursues game at night without permission risks imprisonment. The poacher does not have to succeed in killing game—the offence is committed when he enters property in pursuit of game.

GAME OVER A NEIGHBOUR'S LAND The sportsman is entitled to any game he kills on his own land. If he shoots a bird over his own land but it falls on a neighbour's land, the bird belongs to him.

The hunter is trespassing, however, if he goes to get it. Strictly speaking, all he can do is to ask permission to retrieve it. If the neighbour refuses and will not hand over the game, nothing can be done. But the neighbour has no right to the bird himself.

POWERS OF ARREST The occupying tenant, anyone else who has the right to kill game, and the employees of either of them, can arrest a trespasser pursuing game who refuses to leave the land or to give his true name and address. A policeman also has the power to arrest a trespasser in these circumstances.

The police are allowed to stop on the road anyone they reasonably suspect to have been poaching. They can search a suspect and any vehicle in which he may be travelling. If the police find any game or poaching equipment, they can seize it and charge the suspect, but they cannot arrest him for this reason alone. He can be arrested, however, if he is found poaching on someone else's land at night.

SELLING GAME Only the holder of a full year's licence can sell game, and then he must sell it only to a licensed game dealer.

**Certificates for shotguns and firearms**

With a few rare exceptions, anyone who possesses a shotgun or any other firearm must obtain a certificate from the local police, even if he already holds a game licence.

SHOTGUNS Certificates, which are valid for three years, are required for almost any shotgun. People who are exempt include:
1. People shooting at artificial targets at a time and place approved by the police.
2. Visitors to Britain for a brief period, if they have not stayed in this country for more than 30 days in the preceding 12 months.
3. People who borrow guns from the occupier of land and use them in his presence.
4. People who carry shotguns for the use of a certificate-holder and under his instructions. In this case, the person without a certificate must not fire the gun.

FIREARMS If a hunter or marksman wishes to own a firearm other than a shotgun he must obtain a firearms certificate from the police.

The police must refuse certificates to anyone under 14. They will also refuse certificates to anyone who appears to them to be unfitted to be entrusted with a firearm. An appeal against the police's refusal to issue a certificate can be made to the Crown Court.

Any false statement made knowingly in an application for a firearms certificate can lead to a fine of up to £200 or six months' imprisonment, or both.

A certificate is required for some very high-powered airguns but not for the more usual low-powered weapons. No certificate is needed for an antique gun which is kept as an ornament or curiosity.

A firearms certificate is valid for three years, and can be renewed. The certificate specifies the number and kind of firearms and ammunition which may be owned.

PERMITS In certain cases it is not necessary to take out a certificate. It is possible to ask merely for a police permit, for which there is no fee. This is usually given only in special circumstances and for short periods—for instance, to authorise the executors of an estate to retain a gun until they dispose of it. SAFEKEEPING Firearms and shotguns covered by certificates have to be kept in a safe place. The loss of such a gun should be reported immediately to the chief of police by whom the certificate was issued, who must also be told if the certificate holder changes his address.

Anyone holding a firearm or shotgun certificate may sell, give, lend or hire his gun only to a registered firearms dealer, or to someone who has a relevant certificate or can show he needs none. The police chief who issued the certificate must be told of a firearm's disposal within 48 hours.

**Firearms offences**
Anyone who has a loaded shotgun, air weapon or any other firearm in a public place without lawful authority or a valid reason is committing

## When birds and game must not be killed

As a general rule, it is an offence to kill, injure or take most wild birds or to take or destroy their nests or eggs at any time. The penalty for an offence, under the Protection of Birds Act 1954, is a fine of up to £5.

For some birds there is a special penalty of £25 or one month's imprisonment, or both, for a first offence, and £25 or three months' imprisonment, or both, for second or subsequent offences.

Never photograph wild birds at or near their nests, as this may cause them to desert. In many cases it is also an offence.

Certain birds may, however, legally be killed with the permission of the owner of the relevant sporting rights (though in some counties not on Sundays or Christmas Day). The following lists refer only to England and Wales; there are some differences in Scotland and Northern Ireland.

The owner or occupier of land, or someone with his permission, can kill the following birds at any time of year. (Alternatively, certain bodies, such as local authorities and the Nature Conservancy, may authorise the killing of these birds, though the owner's permission is also needed before entering private land.)

| | |
|---|---|
| bullfinch (in some areas only) | jackdaw |
| black-backed gull | magpie |
| (greater and lesser) | oyster-catcher |
| carrion crow | (in some areas only) |
| cormorant | rook |
| domestic pigeon (turned wild) | shag |
| herring gull | starling |
| hooded crow | stock dove |
| house sparrow | wood-pigeon |

The following birds may be killed except from February 1 to August 31:

| | |
|---|---|
| bar-tailed godwit | golden plover |
| common redshank | grey plover |
| coot | moorhen |
| curlew (except stone curlew) | whimbrel |

The following may be killed except from February 1 to August 31 inland, and from February 21 to August 31 on the foreshore:

| | |
|---|---|
| bean goose | pintail |
| Canada goose | pochard |
| common scoter | scaup |
| gadwall | shoveler |
| garganey | teal |
| goldeneye | tufted duck |
| greylag goose | velvet scoter |
| long-tailed duck | white-fronted goose |
| mallard | wigeon |
| pink-footed goose | |

The following may be killed, except between 1 hour after sunset and 1 hour before sunrise, and between the following dates:

| | |
|---|---|
| blackgame | December 11 to August 11 |
| capercaillie | February 1 to September 30 |
| partridge | February 2 to August 31 |
| pheasant | February 2 to September 30 |
| red grouse | December 11 to August 11 |
| snipe and jack snipe | February 1 to August 11 |
| woodcock | February 1 to September 30 |

PROTECTED BIRDS It is generally illegal to kill any bird except those listed.

BIRDS CAUSING DAMAGE It is, however, a defence to a charge of killing *some* wild birds to show the killing was necessary to prevent serious damage to one's crops, fisheries, or other property.

INJURED BIRDS It is legal to keep a sick or injured bird in captivity as long as it is released when it can fend for itself.

GROUND GAME The occupier of enclosed arable land may kill rabbits and hares at any time of year. The occupier of moorland or unenclosed arable land may not kill them by any means from April 1 to August 31, nor shoot them from September 1 to December 10.

Rabbits and hares must not be killed at night; hares may not be killed on Sundays or Christmas Day, nor sold between March 1 and July 31.

an offence. If the weapon is unloaded and the person carrying it has ammunition for it with him, he is still liable to prosecution. The penalty is a maximum of six years' imprisonment or an unlimited fine, or both, unless the weapon is an air weapon, in which case the maximum is six months' imprisonment or a fine of £200, or both.

POWERS OF SEARCH AND ARREST The police do not always need a warrant to search for firearms and they also have special powers of arrest. In certain circumstances they can make an arrest without a warrant.

ALTERATIONS It is a criminal offence for anyone other than a registered firearms dealer to shorten the barrel of a shotgun to less than 24 inches. A firearms dealer may do so only to replace a defective part.

## Traps and snares
In general, it is illegal to trap or snare game or to stupefy game, for example by using gas. Spring traps can, however, be used to catch vermin, and this includes rabbits and hares.

Under the Pests Act 1954, the trap must be of a design approved by the Ministry of Agriculture. The use of a trap or snare which has not been approved is punishable by a fine of up to £20 for a first offence and up to £50 for subsequent offences.

Another Act, the Prevention of Damage by Rabbits Act 1939, states that the traps can be laid only in rabbit holes and must be inspected at least once a day between sunrise and sunset. Offences are punishable by fines of up to £5.

Anyone setting illegal traps or snares on farmland could also be prosecuted under the Criminal Damage Act 1971, if farm animals are injured by the trap. Under the Act, deliberate and unauthorised killing, maiming or wounding of cattle or domestic animals is punishable by imprisonment for up to ten years. The person convicted may also be ordered to pay compensation.

## Fishing
The public has the right to fish in the sea and in most tidal waters, but no one is entitled to fish in any non-tidal river or stream without first obtaining permission.

The landowners adjacent to the water, known as the 'riparian owners', have the fishing rights, unless they or their predecessors have disposed of them. The owner of the bank beside the non-tidal part of a river also owns the river bed up to the middle of the stream and has a right to stop people fishing there, for example, from boats.

Tidal waters end at the point where salt water gives way to fresh water, or where ordinary sea tides no longer move the water.

The public right to fish in tidal waters extends to the foreshore between the high and low water marks. This right includes the taking of shell fish. But it does not include any right to take seaweed from the beach and probably does not include the right to take empty shells. In non-tidal waters there is no public right to fish even in places where people have fished for many years.

➤ FORTY YEARS OF FISHING *In 1964, Frank Wells, the assistant secretary of the Fulham Angling Club, was charged with trespassing by fishing in the Thames at Taplow, Buckinghamshire, without the permission of the adjoining landowner, Stanley Hobson Hardy. The evidence showed that the public had fished there regularly for more than 40 years. Mr Wells was not even keeping the fish he caught—he put them back at the end of the day after keeping them in a net in the water.*
DECISION *Mr Wells was found guilty and fined 5s. (Hardy v. Wells.)* ◄

The owner's permission can be given orally or in writing. One way of getting permission is to join an angling club or buy a 'day ticket' from the person or organisation which holds the fishing rights.

FISHING OFF THE PIER Angling is commonly allowed from piers at the discretion of the owner of the pier, normally the local authority. The rules for such fishing may be found in local bye-laws or obtained from the pier staff.

## When a licence is needed for fishing
In addition to having the permission of whoever has the fishing rights, anglers need a licence to fish for salmon or trout. This can be obtained from the fisheries officer at the river-authority offices or from some post offices, fishing-tackle shops or angling clubs. The fee varies in different parts of the country. Anyone who has a licence for trout or salmon is automatically covered to fish for most other freshwater fish as well.

A licence is needed for other freshwater fish in all areas except Cornwall, Cumberland, Devon, Gwynedd, Hampshire, Mersey and Weaver, South-west Wales and Usk, the area of the Dee and Clwyd river authority other than the Dee itself and the Shropshire Union Canal, and the area of the Hertfordshire Lee.

A licence can be used only by the person named on it and usually allows the use of only one rod. But any person or association with the exclusive right to fish a stretch of water can get a licence which covers someone else authorised in writing by the licence-holder.

Fishing without a licence when one is needed is an offence. But an angler trying to catch fish for which a licence is not required does not commit an offence if he happens to hook a fish for which a licence is required and returns it to the water.

**Taking fish without permission**
Anyone who takes fish without the permission of the person who holds the fishing rights is poaching. The penalty for poaching by night is a maximum fine of £50 for the first offence. For the second or subsequent offences a maximum fine of £100 and/or three months' imprisonment can be imposed.

The penalty for poaching by day is a maximum fine of £20. The penalty for poaching fish by day other than by angling—for example, by using explosives—is the same as for poaching by night.

**When fish are protected**
There is no close season for sea fishing, but Parliament has established close seasons when it is forbidden to fish for freshwater fish,

salmon and trout. The close season, which allows the fish to spawn in safety, varies from place to place and from fish to fish.

For coarse fish it is March 14 to June 16, unless local bye-laws have laid down any other period. For salmon the standard close season for fishing by rod and line is October 31 to February 1, and for trout it is September 30 to March 1. These standard close seasons are frequently varied.

If the local bye-laws are not displayed beside the river, check with the river authority for any variations in the close season.

**Illegal methods of fishing**
It is illegal to fish with explosives, poisons or electrical devices either inland or at sea within the territorial limits of the British Isles. It is also an offence to use a light for taking fish, but it is thought that this does not prevent the practice of shining a light on a float to see when the fish are biting.

It is illegal to use fish roe of any kind for fish bait. There are also rules preventing the use of a variety of instruments for what is called 'foul hooking'—hooking the fish other than by the mouth.

# Children and firearms

A CHILD under 14 is not allowed to own an airgun, but he can lawfully fire one at a shooting gallery or rifle range, or on land or premises when the pellets will not go off the property. In this case, however, he must be under the supervision of someone who is aged 21 or over.

A person aged 14 or over but under 17 may carry an airgun in a public place, provided it is securely fastened in a gun cover so that it cannot be fired. He may not possess an air pistol in a public place in any circumstances.

The penalty for giving an airgun to a child under 14 is a maximum fine of £50. The child can be fined the same amount.
SHOTGUNS A child under 15 may not possess an assembled shotgun unless he is either under the supervision of a person over 21, or the shotgun is in a securely fastened gun case or cover so that it cannot be fired.

Any child under 15 who has a shotgun illegally can be fined up to £50, and so can the person who gave it to him.

A child, like an adult, usually needs to have a shotgun certificate.

OTHER FIREARMS A child under 14 is not normally allowed to possess or to use any other kind of firearm or ammunition. There are three exceptions:
1. He may carry firearms under instructions from a person who has a firearms certificate and who is using them for sporting purposes.
2. He may use them as a member of a rifle club or cadet corps.
3. He may use them at a shooting gallery.

The penalty for giving or lending a firearm other than an airgun or shotgun to someone under 14 is a maximum of six months' imprisonment or a fine of up to £200, or both. The penalty for the child for possessing the firearm is the same.

Young people aged 14 and over but under 17 can be given or lent other firearms, subject to the rules that apply to adults. But no one under the age of 17 is allowed to buy or hire any other firearm or ammunition. It is an offence to sell or hire a firearm or ammunition to anyone under 17. The penalty for both child and seller is the same; up to six months' imprisonment or a fine of up to £200, or both.

# Booking a foreign holiday

*Choosing the operator*  
*Making a booking*  
*Taking out holiday insurance*

*What happens if you cancel*  
*What to do if things go wrong*

A MOTORIST wishing to take his car when he goes touring abroad can make his own arrangements—working out mileages, booking hotels and making sure that he is covered against all possible risks before setting out. ☐ Taking a car abroad, p. 147.

Alternatively, a driver can take advantage of the package tours specially arranged for people seeking a motoring holiday abroad, in which an all-in price is charged for hotel and travel.

If the motorist prefers not to take his own vehicle, he can arrange to have a car waiting for him on the Continent by joining a 'fly and drive' scheme such as one open to members of the Automobile Association.

A driver choosing a package tour should compare not only price but conditions of booking and the guarantees which each company offers. In some cases even an unavoidable cancellation—say through illness—could cost a holidaymaker the entire price of his trip.

The Automobile Association scheme, on the other hand, gives a firm guarantee of protection to any motorist who selects one of its sponsored package motoring holidays.

Anyone booking a package holiday abroad can, in theory, claim the same legal protection as anyone else who pays money for goods and services. The peculiar difficulty about a package holiday, however, is that the customer has little opportunity to 'examine' what he is paying for before he hands over his money.

All he can do is to try to ensure that he does not sign away his right to compensation if the holiday does not live up to the operator's description, or if there are difficulties such as cancellation or double-booking.

## Choosing the operator

Different tour operators often offer what appear to be identical holidays, visiting the same resort and even using the same hotel; yet one may cost more than the other.

There are several possible reasons for this. First, the cheaper holiday may provide flights at less convenient times—mid-week instead of weekends, for example, and at night rather than during the day. The standard and type of accommodation available within the same

hotel can also make a substantial difference.

In addition, the dearer holiday may include additional features which are charged as extras by the firm offering the cheaper holiday or simply not included at all.

## Making a booking

Package holidays can be booked either with the tour operator direct or through a firm of travel agents.

A firm acting as a travel agent is regarded in law simply as the tour operator's agent who brings together the client and the tour operator and arranges a contract between them.

If the holiday is booked through an agent and something goes wrong, he cannot be sued for damages unless he has failed to carry out the client's instructions—for example if he has made a mistake over the resort or the holiday dates. As an agent, he is not responsible for the service provided by the tour operators, hotels or airlines he represents.

THE BOOKING FORM Almost all travel agents and tour operators require their customers to sign a booking form which has the tour operator's conditions printed on the back, or contains a clause stating that the booking is subject to conditions which appear in the operator's brochure.

These conditions invariably limit the customer's legal rights. They may give the operator the right to raise the price of the holiday without notice; to switch to alternative (and possibly inferior) accommodation without adjusting the price; or to cancel the holiday without compensation.

In theory, there are several possible ways in which the customer may be able to avoid binding himself to conditions such as these. He can alter the form by looking for the conditions he considers unfair, and crossing them out before signing. Or he can cross out the sentence on the form that states something to the effect: 'I agree to accept the company's current booking conditions.' But in either case the operator will probably refuse to accept the booking.

The other way of trying to avoid unfair conditions is to write the operator a letter booking the holiday, giving all the information he usually requires on his booking form, and enclosing a deposit. If a booking is accepted on these terms, the customer will have preserved his legal rights.

►THE TOURIST SENT TO AN ANNEXE *Mr Trackman booked a hotel by letter with a tour operator, New Vistas Ltd, in 1959 at the Hotel Mañana, Lloret de Mar, Spain, and the operator agreed the type of accommodation to be provided. When he arrived at the hotel Mr Trackman and his family were asked to take a room in an annexe about 200 yds away. He refused, found alternative accommodation himself, and on his return sued New Vistas Ltd for breach of contract.*
DECISION *Mr Trackman won his case and was awarded damages to compensate for the additional expense to which he was put. Since his arrangement with New Vistas Ltd was made by an exchange of letters, their liability towards him was not limited by any booking-form conditions or clauses. (Trackman v. New Vistas Ltd.)* ◄

## Taking out holiday insurance
Even the most carefully planned holiday can lead to unexpected financial difficulties through illness, injury or theft. The tourist can protect himself against such difficulties by taking out holiday insurance.

All the tour operators and travel agencies advise holidaymakers to insure, and many provide insurance for customers automatically.

The package policy usually provides cover under four headings: medical expenses; luggage and personal money; cancellation charges; and injury and death.
MEDICAL EXPENSES Holidaymakers taken ill can claim the cost of treatment and additional hotel and travel expenses resulting from illness or accident. There is a fixed limit—the more the customer pays, the higher the limit. A minimum cover of not less than £250 a person is advisable.
LUGGAGE AND PERSONAL MONEY Compensation is provided for personal money lost, usually up to a fixed limit of £50. It is usual for the first £2·50 or £5 to be excluded, and in addition the loss must be reported to the local police within 24 hours.

Baggage and personal effects are also covered, again up to a fixed limit, which is normally £150. The cover normally extends to loss *or* damage.
CANCELLATION CHARGES The tourist who takes out a package insurance policy can

## Charter flights for club members

MANY people taking a foreign holiday or visiting relations overseas travel at greatly reduced fares through a club chartering an aircraft—technically known as an 'affinity' group charter flight.

But there can be drawbacks to this type of cheap air travel. If a flight does not comply with the provisions of the Civil Aviation (Licensing) Act 1960, it is likely to be investigated by the Department of Trade and Industry and may be cancelled by the airline concerned. The passengers involved are not penalised, but are inconvenienced by being unable to take the holiday they had arranged. In addition they may have to take legal action to recover any fare they have paid.

'Affinity' group charter flights are controlled by a number of restrictions.
1. Each member going on the flight must have belonged to the club for at least six months and attended six meetings. (The rules do, however, allow members to take with them any of their immediate relatives—husband or wife, children, and parents living in the same household.)

2. Normally the club must not have more than 20,000 members, although there are certain exceptions. This may rule out such groups as political parties or the national motoring organisations. But it is possible that smaller, individual, regional branches of a major national organisation could be allowed to organise charter flights.
3. The club must not have been formed with travel as its main objective.
4. The club must not advertise its flight outside its membership.

There is no penalty under the Civil Aviation (Licensing) Act 1960 for passengers who break any of these rules, but airlines and tour operators who agree to fly illegal groups can be fined and their executives jailed.
HOW TO CHECK The traveller who is in doubt about the legality of a charter flight on which he has booked should check that the club is genuine and not breaking the rules. He can then ask the Department of Trade and Industry to investigate if he has evidence that any of the rules have been broken.

usually claim for payments lost as a result of cancellation caused by accident or illness to himself or any member of his family. This is up to a fixed limit. Check that the maximum amount of money that could be lost is below the fixed limit.

ACCIDENT AND DEATH The cover is normally for a lump sum of £1000 on death or permanent disablement, together with weekly benefits for a limited period if the holidaymaker is temporarily incapacitated.

Package policies arranged through tour operators are not adequate for everyone, however. For example, a holidaymaker may have a valuable camera which would not be covered by a package policy; or he may be outside the normal age limits for insurance for medical expenses. (Children under two and people over 75 are normally excluded.)

In this case, the holidaymaker should see his own insurance company or a broker and arrange a policy tailor-made for his needs.

**What happens if you cancel**
The amount a customer has to pay if he is forced to cancel a package holiday depends on the terms he has agreed with the tour operator, and the notice he is able to give.

Most operators adopt the rule that if the holiday is cancelled by the client before the date when the balance of the cost is due—usually six weeks before departure date—the client forfeits his deposit. If he cancels after this period he may also have to forfeit a percentage of the total cost of the holiday. The Association of British Travel Agents, recommends the following scale of cancellation charges: cancellation more than six weeks

## How a holidaymaker can lose his rights

Booking conditions vary from operator to operator. They usually deprive the holidaymaker of his legal right to claim compensation from the operator if the holiday proves inferior to the accommodation and facilities he has booked and paid for. Frequently, a tour operator's conditions do not appear on the booking form but are printed elsewhere in his brochure. They are made binding by a clause on the form stating that the client accepts the booking conditions

All arrangements for accommodation, travel and services are made on the express understanding that the company does not accept any responsibility for any default, whether negligent or otherwise, on the part of themselves, their employees and agents, and any services or hotels with which bookings are made. The company will not be responsible for any loss or additional expense occasioned by delay, alterations in airline or other travel services, sickness, injuries, weather, avalanches, strikes, civil disturbance, quarantine, floods, war or any other circumstance whatsoever.

The tour operator who includes this condition is attempting to exempt himself from almost every liability. Even if the operator, his employees, the hotel or airline or other travel service employees are negligent, the client has no grounds on which he can claim compensation.

Without this clause, the operator would be liable to pay compensation for any injury or loss caused by his own negligence, or that of his employees, and for any failure to provide the accommodation and services he has agreed to provide

To the best of the company's knowledge and belief the representations made regarding travel and hotel facilities are true, but the company does not warrant the same and the client acknowledges that the company had reasonable grounds to believe and did believe up to the time of the client's booking that the facts and descriptions relating to the travel and hotel facilities were true.

The client who is provided with hotel or travel facilities which are inferior to those he booked, normally has a right to claim compensation. This could be the case if he had been offered a bathroom to himself, for example, or if he had been offered a room with a view of the sea, but these facilities were not eventually provided. But if the client accepts a clause like this, all such claims are barred, unless a court rules otherwise. This clause would not, however, rule out proceedings against the operator if it were found that the accommodation he offered had never existed

before departure—deposit only. Less than six, but more than four weeks before departure—30 per cent of the holiday price. Less than four but more than two weeks before departure—45 per cent of the price. And two weeks or less before departure—60 per cent.

In practice, some firms charge less if they are able to get a substitute booking.

Where the customer books by letter, without accepting the operator's standard conditions, the common-law rule is that he must pay compensation for the operator's genuine expenses and loss of profit. If the operator is able to re-book, his loss may well be minimal.

## What to do if things go wrong

A package holiday can turn out to be unsatisfactory for a variety of reasons. The hotel, or some of its basic amenities (such as a swimming pool), may be still under construction; accommodation provided may not be what was booked; or the tour operator's brochure may have given a false idea of the holiday.

In each case, a dissatisfied holidaymaker should take up this complaint immediately on the spot—either with the hotel proprietor or with the tour operator's representative, or both. If this fails, four types of remedy may be theoretically available: prosecuting the operator, claiming compensation, going to arbitration and appealing to the Association of British Travel Agents.

PROSECUTING THE OPERATOR The Trade Descriptions Act 1968 makes it an offence to give any misleading information regarding holiday facilities. The holidaymaker must persuade the local weights and measures

The company offers a number of holidays in this brochure based on accommodation at hotels still under construction. Bookings for these holidays are accepted only on the express understanding that if the hotel should not be completed by the advertised holiday date, whether through building delays or for any other reason, the client agrees to accept such alternative accommodation as the company is able to offer.

The client who arrives at his holiday resort and finds that the first-class hotel in which he was booked is still being built will, under this clause, be automatically bound to accept whatever alternative accommodation the tour operator offers him—even if it is inferior. Without this clause, the client is entitled to demand accommodation of the standard he booked. If the tour operator fails to provide this type of accommodation, the holidaymaker can find himself suitable accommodation in a first-class hotel—and sue for the extra cost. This would also include any extra expenses in finding another hotel, such as fares and telephone calls

### DEPOSITS AND CANCELLATION

8. A deposit of £6 per person is payable on the making of a booking and the balance is due six weeks before the quoted date of departure. Should the balance not have been paid in full six weeks before the departure date the company will be entitled to cancel the booking without being liable to refund the deposit or to pay any other claim whatsoever arising out of the cancellation.

9. The company reserves the right to withdraw any booking application or cancel any bookings made for the client at any time in which circumstances no liability whatsoever in respect of such cancellation or withdrawal shall fall upon the company except that any money paid by the client in respect of bookings so cancelled or applications so withdrawn shall be refunded.

Deposits are forfeited if the client cancels the booking, or if he fails to pay the balance of the cost of the holiday six weeks before it is due to start. The booking will be cancelled and no claims of any sort can be made on the operator. But the operator reserves the right to cancel the holiday at any time, when the client's only right is a refund of the money he has already paid with nothing extra for any expense or loss he may suffer—possibly in having to book a more expensive, alternative holiday at the last minute. Without such a clause, either the holidaymaker or the operator would be liable in law to compensation for the actual loss caused by a cancellation.

inspector to prosecute the tour operator.

Though a successful prosecution may give the holidaymaker satisfaction, it does not provide him with compensation. Moreover, the travel agency or operator may have a defence if he can show that he took reasonable precautions to see that the information he was providing was accurate, and that the fault was due to another person.

CLAIMING COMPENSATION If the operator fails to keep his part of the bargain in providing the holiday he promised, the holidaymaker may be entitled to claim compensation, as long as this is not ruled out by the conditions he accepted when he booked. There may also be a case for compensation if the holidaymaker can prove that he chose the holiday on the basis of a misleading statement by the operator.

If in either of these cases the operator refuses to meet a claim, the holidaymaker has the alternatives of taking legal action or dropping the matter. Only if there is a substantial sum of money involved—£30 at least—is legal action financially worth while.

The conditions laid down by operators usually attempt to bar almost every claim the holidaymaker might make. Faced with such conditions, a determined holidaymaker *might* be successful in a legal action against an operator, if the holiday went seriously wrong.

In recent years, the courts have developed a doctrine that no clause in a contract can exempt a person from liability for breach of the contract, if the breach strikes at the fundamental basis of the agreement.

Under this doctrine, if the defendant is guilty of such a fundamental breach of contract that the contract is, in fact, at an end, he cannot rely on an exemption clause when sued for breach of contract.

Fighting an action on this basis would be bound to be costly for a holidaymaker. The money the holidaymaker would have to pay in legal expenses, even if he was successful, would probably be more than he might win.

GOING TO ARBITRATION Another method of settling a dispute with a tour operator is arbitration. There may be provision for arbitration in the conditions on the booking form, or the operator or holidaymaker may suggest it when a dispute arises.

Arbitration provides a useful method of resolving disputes: the arbitrator is a qualified, impartial third party who will investigate and decide the issue. Often arbitration is cheaper and simpler than going to court, but the parties must decide beforehand who is going to pay the costs. Usually, the loser pays all. ☐ Going to arbitration, p. 719.

APPEALING TO ABTA The majority of the tour firms belong to the Association of British Travel Agents, 50–57 Newman Street, London W1P 4AH. If a holidaymaker has a complaint about a member firm, and the firm itself will not give satisfaction, the holidaymaker can complain to ABTA.

If there has been a breach of its code, ABTA may discipline a member and bring pressure on him to compensate the holidaymaker. There is no guarantee, however, that this will give the holidaymaker any financial compensation. ☐ Complaints: how to bring pressure, p. 478.

The Association may also offer replacement holidays to people whose holidays are cancelled because an ABTA firm collapses.

## Help for the traveller in trouble

A TRAVELLER abroad who is accused of a criminal offence has the same rights as a citizen of the country in which he happens to be. In most European countries the local British consul gives the accused advice and help and, if necessary, intervenes on his behalf. The consul is entitled to see the accused if he is detained in prison.

If the accused traveller wishes members of his family to be told that he has been arrested, he can ask the consul to notify them. The consul tells the family where the accused is being detained and explains the procedure for getting in touch with him. In some cases,

the family have to send their letters to the governor of the prison who will then hand them over to the detainee.

If proceedings are brought against a Briton abroad, the consul advises the family about which local lawyer to choose. However, the family themselves must pay any legal expenses that may be incurred during the trial. If the traveller is found guilty and sent to prison, the consul tries to see that he receives proper treatment. The consul can insist that the standard of treatment should not be less than that received by a citizen of the country in which he is being detained.

# Taking a car abroad

*Arranging insurance*  *Restrictions on parking and speed*
*Preparing for the trip*  *Dealing with motoring offenders*
*Continental traffic laws*  *What to do in an accident*

ANYONE driving abroad is confronted with different traffic laws and different insurance requirements from those at home. The way to ensure trouble-free motoring is to attend to the formalities and learn in advance about the regulations of the countries you intend to visit.

First, make sure that everyone in the party who intends to drive possesses a full driving licence valid at the time of going abroad. A provisional licence is not sufficient.

In addition, each driver must be at least 18 years of age, except in Sweden, where the minimum age is 17.

## Arranging insurance

Arrange insurance cover at least a month before the trip. Three types may be needed:
**1.** The minimum insurance required by the laws of the countries to be visited. For this, the insurance company supplies an International Motor Insurance Card, known as the 'green card'. Terms differ from country to country, but the green card may cover only claims for injury to people other than the motorist and for damage to other people's property.

When applying for the green card, tell the insurers the dates of the trip, and the countries to be visited, or that may have to be crossed in an emergency. The company supplies a list of agencies abroad that will help a motorist in case of trouble.
*Belgium* Green card must also be valid for Netherlands and Luxembourg.
*Denmark* Green card must also be valid for Finland, Sweden and Norway.
*Switzerland* Take a duplicate green card, obtainable from your insurers.
**2.** For an extra premium, motorists can arrange an extension of their British policy to give some or all of the cover that applies in Britain, such as compensation for damage to the motorist's own vehicle, or for injury to his passengers or himself.
**3.** In addition, the motorist may take out a package-deal policy to give special protection against additional hazards abroad. The Automobile Association's 5-Star Travel Service provides a range of benefits if the policy-holder's car breaks down, or is damaged or stolen abroad, or if the motorist becomes medically unfit to drive. The policy may pay legal costs (up to a maximum), travel expenses, hotel bills and the cost of bringing a vehicle home to be repaired.
CARAVAN INSURANCE If a trailer caravan is taken abroad, check the caravan policy and, if necessary, arrange for an extension. Ask the car insurers to include a description of the caravan on the green card.
FRONTIER INSURANCE A motorist who arrives at a frontier without the necessary insurance cover—perhaps as a result of making a sudden detour—can take out 'frontier insurance'. This usually provides third party cover only. The cost and period of validity varies from country to country.
*Yugoslavia* Frontier insurance is expensive, because of a 40 per cent tax on premiums.

## Preparing for the trip

Drivers preparing for a motoring holiday abroad must make sure they have the necessary documents and accessories.
ESSENTIAL DOCUMENTS As well as driving licences and green card insurance, take the vehicle's log book and valid passports.

Campers not using official camping sites should take an International Camping Carnet, available from the AA or from the Camping Club of Great Britain, 11 Lower Grosvenor Place, London SW1W 0EY.
*Italy* Take an official translation of each driver's licence, obtainable from the AA. The translated licence should be completed by the driver before entering Italy.
*Spain* Take an International Driving Permit, obtainable from the AA, or a translation of the driving licence stamped by the Spanish Consulate. Ask your insurance company for a 'bail bond'—a guarantee that cash will be paid by the insurance company to a Spanish court as surety for bail or security for a fine if the driver is prosecuted.
*Yugoslavia* Declare any vehicle damage to frontier police and get a certificate. If your car is damaged while in the country, police issue a certificate that must be produced on leaving. If the certificate is not produced and

147

the car shows damage, it may be held while an inquiry is made.

NATIONALITY PLATE Fit a 'GB' plate of the official size and design, obtainable from the AA, to the left of the rear number plate of cars, caravans and trailers.

SPEEDOMETER Continental speed limits are expressed in kilometres per hour (kph). Motorists can mark their speedometer glass with the equivalent speeds in kilometres, or stick a transparent cut-out (obtainable from motor-accessory shops) over the glass, showing the main speed limits:

| kph | 40 | 50 | 60 | 70 | 80 | 90 | 100 | 110 |
|-----|------|------|------|------|------|------|------|------|
| mph | 24.9 | 31.1 | 37.3 | 43.5 | 49.7 | 55.9 | 62.1 | 68.3 |

WARNING TRIANGLE Take a red warning triangle (available from motor-accessory shops) to place about 50–100 yds behind your car when it is stopped in poor visibility, broken down or has been in an accident.

FIRST-AID KITS A first-aid kit is compulsory in Austria, and recommended elsewhere.

SPARE PARTS Take spares, as they are often difficult to obtain abroad. Spare light bulbs are compulsory in Spain. In winter months, chains must be fitted to tyres on some Swiss mountain roads.

ADJUSTING HEADLAMPS Headlamps on British cars dip to the left. For driving on the right, they must be made to dip to the right by fitting clip-on shades that alter the angle of the beam, or by changing bulbs. Make any change shortly before embarking, as it is an offence to drive on British roads with lamps dipping to the right.

Headlamps that dip to the right are compulsory in Germany, Sweden and Denmark.

In France, amber lamps are preferred by the authorities, though not compulsory.

## Continental traffic laws

Each country has its own traffic laws, but the general principles are the same in almost every continental country.

DRIVING ON THE RIGHT Nearly all visitors to the Continent adapt quickly to driving on the right. But guard against the tendency to stray to the left, particularly after stopping or turning left, or on roundabouts.

Give way to vehicles entering your road from the right, unless signs give you priority.
□ International road signs, p. 150.

At junctions, cars approaching from opposite directions to turn across each other's path pass in front of each other—not behind as in Britain.

Give priority to trams and their passengers, emergency service vehicles, military columns, funeral processions and, on mountain roads, to vehicles travelling uphill. Give way to pedestrians crossing roads into which you are turning.

*France* Cleaning vehicles have priority.

*Germany* Do not overtake school buses flashing lights at all four corners—children are boarding or dismounting.

*Netherlands* Give way to cyclists and—at junctions where both roads are of equal importance—to trams.

*Switzerland* Give priority to postal buses.

ROAD MARKINGS It is an offence to straddle a single, unbroken yellow or white line down the centre of the road. Other markings are similar to those in Britain.

*Netherlands* An unbroken white line at the side of the road indicates a cycling lane.

TRAFFIC LIGHTS Continental countries use the three-colour system of traffic lights. A flashing amber light, which is used outside busy hours, means proceed with caution. Other flashing signals indicate danger or warnings.

*Austria* A flashing green light means prepare to stop, lights are changing to red.

*France* Flashing red lights mark obstacles or indicate No Entry.

*Italy* Drivers in filter lanes shown by a green arrow must follow the arrow.

*Netherlands* Green arrow over the motorway shows lane to be taken. Lights forming a red cross mean lane closed. Twin flashing red lights at crossings with half barriers mean train is approaching. White light at open crossing means all clear

ROUNDABOUTS In all continental countries, except Greece and Yugoslavia, traffic on a roundabout must give way to traffic entering. In Greece and Yugoslavia, traffic on the roundabout has right of way.

OVERTAKING Overtaking is prohibited at crossings, on bends, in tunnels, at crossroads and junctions, or on hills and narrow roads. Otherwise, overtaking is normally permitted only on the left.

Trams in motion may often be overtaken on the right. Normally they must not be overtaken when picking up or setting down passengers.

*Denmark* Overtake trams on the right only.

*France* Overtake trams on the right, or in one-way streets on the left if there is insufficient space on the right.

*Germany* Cars may overtake stationary or moving trams, but not stationary school buses.

*Italy* Overtake moving trams only on the right. Do not overtake stationary trams unless at a loading island for passengers.

*Netherlands* Overtake moving trams on the right, or the left if space on the right is

restricted. Never overtake stationary trams.
*Spain* Overtake moving trams on the right, or on the left if space on the right is insufficient; never overtake trams picking up or setting down passengers. Flash right-hand indicators when the road is clear for a following vehicle to overtake. Heavy lorries show a flashing green light at the back when driver understands you wish to overtake, and flash right-hand indicators when the road is clear for overtaking.
*Switzerland* Overtake trains and trams on the right—either side in one-way streets when trams are moving. Never overtake a stationary tram unless at a passenger island.
LIGHTS AND HORNS Dipped headlights must be used in built-up areas. Headlights may be flashed to warn of overtaking. Most countries permit foglights in pairs with sidelights (in Yugoslavia, one or two foglights).

Horns should be low-toned and used only in emergency. In open country they can be used to indicate that you wish to overtake.
*Belgium* Always use headlights at night. Foglights may be used without sidelights when less than 16 in. from edge of vehicle.
*Denmark* Alpine and multi-toned horns are prohibited.
*Spain* Use dipped headlights at night on motorways and fast dual carriageways, even if well lit.
*Switzerland* Lights must be used in tunnels. For night parking, use side and rear lights (or parking lights in built-up areas). No lights are needed on vehicles near a street lamp or in a special parking area.
TOLLS Motorways and tunnels in France, Italy and Switzerland are subject to tolls.
CHILDREN IN CARS Children should not be carried on front seats. In Austria it is an

## Driving on the right

Motorists in Europe must give way to traffic approaching from their right (even vehicles entering from a side road) unless there are special signs giving them priority. But no motorist should ever drive on the assumption that he has automatic right of way, since European road rules vary considerably from those in the United Kingdom.

If a motorist stops, it is reasonable for other drivers to assume that he has forfeited his right of way. It is far safer, however, for the stationary motorist to give a clear hand signal to other drivers to indicate that they have been given priority.

Except in Greece and Yugoslavia, the 'priority to the right' rule also applies on roundabouts, where traffic entering from the junctions has the right of way over traffic on the roundabout. In Greece and Yugoslavia traffic already on the roundabout has priority over vehicles entering.

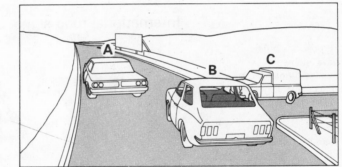

The driver of car B must give way to van C, because it is approaching from his right. But car B has priority over car A, which is waiting to turn across car B's path into the side road

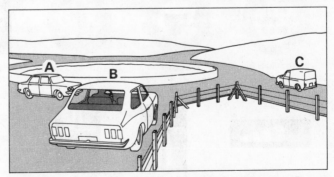

The driver of car B, entering the roundabout, has priority over car A on the roundabout. Once on the roundabout car B must give way to van C, which is entering from car B's right

offence for a child under 12 to occupy a front seat.

DRINK AND DRIVING Laws against drinking and driving are strict. A conviction may mean jail and suspension of the driver's licence—making it illegal for him to drive his car out of the country where he was convicted.

## Restrictions on speed

Speed limits are clearly indicated. In built-up areas the general limit is 50–60 kph. On open country roads the maximum (if any) is usually 110 kph. Vehicles towing trailers are restricted to 70–80 kph, or less. There is often a minimum speed restriction on motorways.

*Austria* Temporary limits may be imposed at weekends or public holidays. Caravans and trailers are limited to 60 kph maximum, even on motorways. Vehicles using studded tyres are restricted to 90 kph and must carry a '90' plate on the back.

*Belgium* Minimum is 60 kph on straight level stretches of road, with no maximum on motorways. On other roads, maximum is 90 kph. Built-up areas limit is 60 kph, but sometimes higher.

*Denmark* Trailers are limited to 70 kph.

*France* Drivers qualified for less than a year are restricted to 90 kph.

*Germany* Signs with two numbers—for example, '70–100'—show minimum and maximum speeds.

*Greece* Limits are usually 50 kph in built-up areas and 110 kph on open roads. Only exceptions are signposted.

*Italy* Minimum speed limits may be signposted on motorways (autostradas).

*Netherlands* Cars with trailers are restricted to 80 kph maximum. Built-up area maximum is 50 kph, sometimes 70 kph.

*Spain* Cars with trailers are limited to 80 kph. The maximum in built-up areas is 40 kph or 50 kph.

*Switzerland* Limit in built-up areas and country villages is 60 kph maximum. Vehicles

# International road signs

European countries have adopted a number of road signs that are internationally recognised on the Continent. Many of them are similar to signs in Britain.
☐ Signs, lines and signals, p. 68

Stop at intersection

Priority road ahead

Intersection with a non-priority road

Stop at Customs post

Speed limits for light and heavy motor vehicles

Road closed to vehicles towing heavy trailers

No parking—on left on odd dates; on right on even dates

Road reserved for motor traffic

End of two-way traffic

Danger from cross-winds

Motorway ahead

End of the motorway

Priority road

End of priority road

incapable of more than 60 kph are banned from semi-motorways. Overall speed limit is 100 kph on all roads except motorways. There are no official limits on motorways, but recommended maximum speeds are signposted.

### Restrictions on parking

Systems of parking control include disc and meter parking and traffic-free 'Blue Zones', where short-term parking is allowed using discs from shops, motoring organisations, tourist offices and police.

Motorists must not park facing oncoming traffic. At night, side and rear lamps must be used, except where street lighting makes vehicles easily visible.

*Austria* Blue Zones display No Parking signs with the word 'Zone' on them—or 'Kurzparkzone' for short waiting periods—and blue marks on roads. Blue Zone discs allow up to 90 minutes free parking. Waiting elsewhere is allowed for up to ten minutes. No parking is allowed at entrances to houses, public buildings, petrol stations, or in narrow streets. No parking *or* waiting is permitted near zebra crossings, bus and tram stops, and level crossings. Yellow crosses on the road prohibit parking.

*Belgium* Meters take tokens. Red meters allow parking for 30 minutes, grey up to two hours, blue up to 24 hours. Two days are allowed to pay fines by buying special stamps at post offices; otherwise prosecution follows.

*France* Red kerb markings prohibit parking. Discs are not needed on Sundays and public holidays. The Blue Zone in Paris—shown by blue bands on lamp posts—is closed to trailers and caravans from 2 p.m. to 8.30 p.m. on weekdays.

*Germany* Signs indicating 'Limited Waiting' allow drivers to pick up or unload. Meters are used in business areas. Parking permits are sometimes issued.

*Greece* No parking on steep slopes or close to traffic lights and fire hydrants. Parking limited to 30 minutes or two hours at meters.

---

## Road signs of individual European countries

Many continental countries use their own national road signs, as well as the agreed international symbols, and some of these may be misunderstood, especially when they are worded in the local language. Motorists going abroad should make themselves familiar with the country's national signs before they leave Britain

### AUSTRIA

### BELGIUM

No stopping—on left on odd dates; on right on even dates

Blue Zone parking (French plate)

Blue Zone parking (Flemish plate)

Federal highway with priority

Federal highway without priority

End of the Blue Zone parking area

Priority road bears right

Traffic must move in parallel lanes

Diversion—in the direction indicated by the arrow

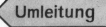

One-way street, with traffic flow following the arrow

Traffic restricted by snow barriers alongside road

Diversion—in direction indicated by the arrow

Gent 47

Direction to town shown and distance in kilometres

continued ▶

Unexpired time on meters may not be used.
*Italy* Restrictions usually apply between 8 a.m.
and 8 p.m., but times differ in major cities
and cars may be towed away. Parking discs
permit one hour's parking.

*Netherlands* Vehicle poorly lit at night must
display red warning triangle. Cities have
meters and Blue Zones using discs.

*Spain* No parking opposite theatres, cinemas
and public buildings. Blue Zone disc parking
for up to 90 minutes.

*Switzerland* Vehicles left on slopes must be
in gear, with wheels turned in to the kerb.
On steep hills, wheels must also be chocked.
Meters allow parking for 15–30 minutes;
unexpired time may not be used. There is
disc parking in Blue Zones.

*Yugoslavia* Up to 90 minutes parking allowed
at meters on weekdays, 8 a.m. to 7 p.m. At
other times, parking is free.

### Caravans and camping

Most countries have strict regulations about
the maximum weights and sizes of caravans
and trailers. Particulars can be obtained from
the AA. Overnight stops are allowed only on
authorised sites or, with the owner's permission, on private land. Sleeping overnight
in laybys is illegal.

*Spain* Tents may be pitched and caravans
parked on official sites, which are well
signposted. They may be left for up to three
days on private land if the owner gives his
permission.

*Switzerland* Some mountain roads are closed
to caravans and trailers.

*Yugoslavia* Official camp sites must be used.

### Dealing with motoring offenders

For minor traffic offences, drivers may be
fined on the spot by police. Serious offences
are dealt with by the courts. A motorist
charged with a serious offence should ask
to see the British consul before making a
statement.

A prosecution can take place in a foreign
country after the motorist has returned home.
Normally, the motorist cannot be made to go
back to the country to face trial, and any
fines imposed may be difficult to collect.

## Road signs of individual European countries continued

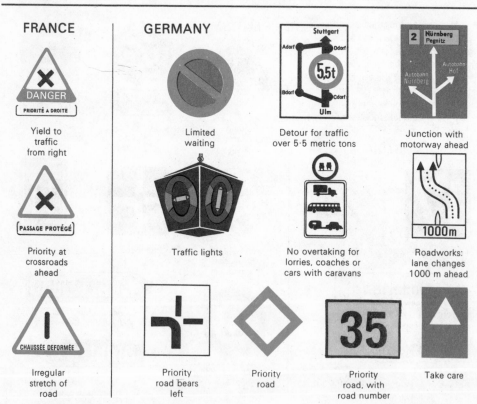

FRANCE

**Yield to traffic from right**

**Priority at crossroads ahead**

**Irregular stretch of road**

GERMANY

**Limited waiting**

**Traffic lights**

**Priority road bears left**

**Detour for traffic over 5·5 metric tons**

**No overtaking for lorries, coaches or cars with caravans**

**Priority road**

**Junction with motorway ahead**

**Roadworks: lane changes 1000 m ahead**

**Priority road, with road number**

**Take care**

But conviction could cause problems if the motorist wanted to return to the country.

Motorists asked to make a statement or swear an affirmation after returning to Britain should consult a solicitor or, if members, the AA legal department.

In cases of drinking and driving, penalties can be severe. A driving ban is effective only in the country concerned.

*Austria* For driving under influence of drink or drugs a driver can be fined or imprisoned for a week.

*Belgium* If a breath test shows more than 80 mg alcohol per ml of blood, driver will be banned from driving for 12 hours—longer for higher amounts.

*Denmark* If a breath test registers 50 mg per ml of blood or more, a driver must take a blood test. More than 100 mg of alcohol per ml brings automatic 20-day prison sentence and 18 months' suspension; 200 mg means imprisonment for 30 days to a year and a driving ban for at least two years. There are no on-the-spot fines.

*France* Vehicles illegally parked may be towed away. At holiday times, many offences are dealt with by roadside courts.

*Germany* Police can impose on-the-spot fines for parking offences. Drink-and-driving offenders may be banned for at least six months and their licences endorsed.

*Greece* Severe penalties are imposed on drivers with more than 50 mg of alcohol per ml of blood.

*Italy* On-the-spot fines are imposed.

*Netherlands* Penalty for drink-driving offences is up to three months in prison and ban of up to five years.

*Switzerland* Blood tests may be carried out, whether driver consents or not, if motorist is suspected of drink-driving offence.

*Yugoslavia* Employees of Department of Internal Affairs impose on-the-spot fines. Heavy fines or up to two months in prison for drink-driving offences.

### What to do in an accident

If there is an accident, place a warning triangle in the road 50–100 yds behind the vehicle involved. Get help for the injured

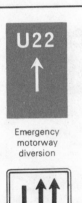

Emergency motorway diversion

Oncoming traffic on one lane

School crossing patrol

## ITALY

Obligatory lane for special use of slow commercial vehicles

## NETHERLANDS

Beginning of Blue Zone parking

End of Blue Zone parking

Lane indications (left to right) for overtaking, straight on, emergencies

Chains or studded or snow tyres needed 174 km ahead

Cycle crossings

No overtaking for vehicles towing trailers

End of trailer restrictions

Traffic pillar: cars either side, cyclists on right

continued ▶

(in some countries it is an offence not to do so) and exchange particulars. Call the police if:
**1.** There has been death or injury.
**2.** There is no one present to represent the party whose property is damaged.
**3.** Damage is serious.

Do not move vehicles unless they are causing an obstruction, in which case they should be moved only after marking their positions on the road and getting them confirmed by an independent witness.

Send details to the insurance company promptly, and notify the local agent.

*Belgium* Move vehicles as soon as possible after an accident, except in cases where someone has been injured.

*France* Get an immediate written report *(process verbal)* from a bailiff *(huissier)*— if possible, before the vehicle is moved. This helps establish responsibility in the event of a damages claim. Drivers may have to deposit money with police to cover court costs or fines.

*Italy* Report accident to insurance company and agents within three days.

*Switzerland* Duplicate green cards must be handed to police after an accident.

*Yugoslavia* Report any accident to the police and get a certificate giving details. This must be given up on leaving.

CLAIMING DAMAGES The cost of claiming damages abroad for accident injury or damage is often high. Even if a claim succeeds, it may be difficult to collect any money awarded by a foreign court.

Most standard insurance policies do not cover costs of claiming compensation for personal injury abroad. Where an injured motorist has little option but to sue abroad— for example, if he is seriously injured or disabled—he should consult a British solicitor, who may employ a foreign colleague to pursue the case.

**Changes in the law**
Continental traffic laws, like those in Britain, are subject to change. Motorists going abroad should check the latest regulations with the AA (if members) or the tourist offices of the countries concerned.

**Roadsigns of individual European countries** continued

## SPAIN

Take care
(yellow or
white triangle)

Turning
permitted
300 m ahead

No entry

## SWITZERLAND

Mountain road
used by
postal buses

End of
mountain
postal road

Prohibition sign,
showing
exceptions

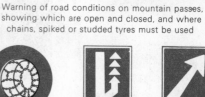

Warning of road conditions on mountain passes,
showing which are open and closed, and where
chains, spiked or studded tyres must be used

Wheel chains
compulsory

Parking
disc
compulsory

Slow lane

Semi-
motorway

Exit road

End of
semi-
motorway

# Passports and visas

*Applying for a British passport*     *When a passport will not be granted*
*Passports for wives and children*

To move between countries, a passport is needed as evidence of identity and national status. In addition, to gain entry to certain countries or to stay for any length of time, a visitor also needs a special entry permit called a visa. A list of countries requiring visas is given in the current official leaflet, *Essential Information*, which may be obtained from the nearest passport office.

### Applying for a British passport
Any citizen of the United Kingdom and colonies, British subjects without citizenship and British-protected persons, can apply for a British passport.

Application forms may be obtained from any office of the Department of Employment, from most travel agents or from one of six regional passport offices. Birth and marriage certificates are required. The form must be countersigned by a qualified teacher, chemist, nurse, doctor, accountant, lawyer, police officer, M.P., clergyman, J.P., or anyone with a British professional qualification who has known the applicant for at least two years.

Two passport photographs (one certified as a true likeness by the person who countersigned the application) must be produced. These should be head-and-shoulder photographs (without hat) measuring not more than $2\frac{1}{2}$ in. $\times$ 2 in. and not less than 2 in. $\times 1\frac{1}{2}$ in.

The completed application form should be taken with any necessary documents and the signed photographs to an employment exchange or posted to a passport office.

There are three types of British passports: a standard passport, a British visitor's passport and a collective passport.
STANDARD PASSPORT Most people obtain the standard passport which is valid for travel anywhere in the world as long as visas are arranged for the countries which require them. The standard passport is valid for ten years and in 1972 cost £5.
BRITISH VISITOR'S PASSPORT A simplified form of U.K. passport is available for citizens of the U.K. and colonies.

It is valid for one year only, costs £1·50 and can be used for a visit of up to three months to the following countries: Andorra, Austria, Belgium, France, Gibraltar, Greece (but only for journeys not using the land route through Yugoslavia), Italy, Liechtenstein, Luxembourg, Malta, Monaco, the Netherlands, Portugal (including Madeira and the Azores), San Marino, Spain (including the Balearic and Canary Islands), Switzerland, Turkey and West Berlin (but only if flying there; it is not valid for travel through East Germany or East Berlin).

In Denmark, Finland, Federal Republic of Germany, Iceland, Norway and Sweden it is valid for a total of three months in any year. In Canada, the British visitor's passport must be valid for three months after the date when the visitor is due to return home.
COLLECTIVE PASSPORT Groups of British students and people aged under 18 in the care of a responsible adult can go abroad on a collective passport, which costs £5.

### Passports for wives and children
After marriage, a woman can have a new passport in her married name. Alternatively her married name can be added to her existing passport, or she may continue using her passport in her maiden name until it expires. It is also possible for a wife to be included on a joint passport with her husband.

A bride-to-be planning a foreign honeymoon may apply for a passport in her married name before the wedding. She is not allowed to use it before the wedding, and must agree to surrender it if there is no marriage.
CHILDREN Separate passports can be issued to children of any age.

Children can also be included on their parents' passports. British visitor's passports are available for children over eight.

### When a passport will not be granted
Certain people may be refused a passport. These include people under 18 travelling against the wishes of their guardians; people for whom a British arrest warrant has been issued; repatriated U.K. nationals who have not repaid their fares; U.K. nationals who have aided, or are likely to aid, Rhodesia; and in rare cases, people to whom granting a passport would be against the public interest.

# Going through Customs

*Going abroad*      *Procedure at Customs posts*
*Coming home*      *Paying the duty*
*Duty-free allowances*      *Penalties for smuggling offences*

A NY item imported into Britain may be liable to Customs duty. The amount payable depends on the article and the price it would be sold for in Britain. The duty ensures that any item bought cheaply abroad eventually costs the buyer as much as if he had bought it in a British shop. In this way, British industries and prices are protected.

The tax is collected at seaports and airports by Customs and Excise officers. A returning traveller must declare for tax anything bought, given or acquired that is not covered by the duty-free allowances. Limited amounts of cigarettes, spirits, perfumes and gifts up to the value of £10 are allowed in free.

A husband and wife passing through Customs can combine their allowances. For instance, apart from their joint tobacco and spirits allowance, the wife may have a dress that cost £17 and the husband may have gramophone records worth £2·50. The joint total is £19·50, so they have no need to declare their items.

Visitors to Britain must declare anything over £10 that they intend to give away or sell.

## Going abroad

To prevent difficulties which could arise when returning through Customs, take receipts for any foreign-made articles—perhaps a camera or watch which you bought in Britain or brought through the Customs on an earlier trip. These receipts prove that articles have not been purchased on the trip and can save any argument with the Customs officer.

## Coming home

Anything in excess of the duty-free allowances, whether bought for personal use or as a gift, must be declared. This includes alterations or additions to a car.

Some goods are prohibited, or there are restrictions on their import. They include: drugs such as opium, heroin, morphine, cocaine, cannabis, amphetamines (including benzedrine) and LSD; counterfeit coins; firearms, ammunition and flick knives. Plants, bulbs, and certain vegetables and fruits, radio transmitters (including 'walkie-talkies'), meat and poultry (unless fully cooked) cannot be imported without a special licence. Indecent or obscene literature and articles and horror comics are also prohibited. Any such items are liable to be seized by the Customs, but the owner can apply to have a court decide whether the items are prohibited or not.

Regulations also restrict the importation of domestic dogs and cats, which must spend six months in quarantine before being allowed into the country. The Ministry of Agriculture will advise whether a licence is required before an uncommon bird or animal can be imported.

## Duty-free allowances

Apart from items taken out with him, the returning resident is allowed to bring in certain articles without paying duty. These allowances vary from time to time; but in 1972, each person returning to or visiting the United Kingdom could bring in, duty free:

One bottle of spirits (0·75 litre)
One bottle of wine (0·75 litre)
Perfume and toilet water (a total of 0·30 litre, but not more than 0·15 litre of perfume)
One cigarette lighter
Tobacco (250 grams—or 500 grams if resident outside Europe)

| Cigarettes | Number |
| --- | --- |
| Small-size plain | 310 |
| Small-size filter-tip | 370 |
| Normal plain | 230 |
| Normal filter-tip | 290 |
| King-size plain | 210 |
| King-size filter-tip | 260 |
| Super king-size (filter-tip only) | 210 |

The spirits, wine and tobacco allowances apply only to people aged 17 or over.

There are no allowances for day trippers—anyone who leaves the United Kingdom and returns within 24 hours.

Duty is paid on all amounts of the commodities which exceed the allowances. This brings the price up to what would be paid for them in Britain.

PETROL There is no restriction on the amount which can be imported in the tank of a car.

OTHER GOODS There is a general duty-free allowance, to a total value of £10, on most other goods brought into Britain.

ANTIQUES There is no duty or purchase tax on articles over 100 years old—but the Customs may require proof of their age.

## Procedure at Customs posts

Because of the increasing number of travellers passing through the Customs, the 'declaration' system has been simplified. People who have kept within the duty-free allowances and have nothing to declare may pass through the 'green channel'. This allows them to go through without formalities—though there are occasional spot checks. Motorists who want to go through the green channel should display a green sticker—available on the ship or air ferry—which states 'Nothing to declare'.

Travellers who do have items to declare should go through the 'red channel', where a Customs officer will inspect their baggage and assess the duty to be paid. Drivers with articles to declare should display a red 'Goods to declare' sticker on the windscreen.

## Paying the duty

Normally, duty or purchase tax is paid before the traveller leaves the Customs hall. The traveller should keep the receipt issued by the Customs officer as proof that duty has been paid, in case he takes the item abroad later.

The rates for duty and tax change, but there are two main principles:
1. Spirits, wine, tobacco, lighters and perfume are charged according to type and quantity.

## Stickers for cars

Car stickers which enable motorists to pass more quickly through Customs are available on ships and ferries. The motorist who is bringing into the country no more than the duty-free allowances, and gifts worth not more than £10, attaches the green 'Nothing to declare' sticker to the windscreen of his car. Others must use the red 'Goods to declare' label. Cars displaying green stickers go through Customs without formalities, though spot checks may be made

The duty is likely to be more than the price paid abroad, but it is charged only on the excess over the duty-free allowances.
2. Other goods worth more than £10—up to a maximum of £35—are charged, with certain exceptions, at a flat rate of 33⅓ per cent of what they would cost in Britain. This covers both duty and purchase tax. (On goods subject to purchase tax only, or those from Commonwealth and European Free Trade Association (EFTA) countries, the charge is 16⅔ per cent.) Goods worth more than £35 are charged at the normal import rate. The amount depends on the kind of goods.

Duty and tax at the ordinary rate must be paid, however, on any cameras and lenses, projectors, watches and radios which do not come within the £10 allowance, and on any article worth more than £25.

## Penalties for smuggling offences

A traveller caught trying to bring an article through the Customs without declaring it, or bringing through more than he has actually declared, risks having the goods confiscated. He may also be fined up to £100 or three times the value of the goods, whichever is greater, and be jailed for up to two years.

If the traveller has committed a major smuggling offence, such as concealing drugs, he will be arrested. For lesser offences, the traveller may be charged extra duty, if the Customs officer thinks there has been a genuine error although he can be summonsed to appear in court.

A traveller is entitled to a receipt for any goods confiscated. If he is in any doubt about the regulations or disagrees with the assessment of duty or tax, he should ask to see the senior duty officer.

Anyone who attempts to bribe a Customs officer can be fined up to £500. The penalty for obstructing an officer—for example, by destroying articles he is trying to seize—is up to two years' imprisonment.

Customs and Excise officers can board and search any ships within the territorial 3-mile limit, and are entitled to land their vessels on any part of the coast, or on the banks of any river. They may patrol any shore, river or creek; they can go across any railway or airfield, or across land adjoining an airfield. But they need a warrant to enter private property. ☐ Officials' rights of entry into the home, p. 293.

It is an offence to sell smuggled goods, whether the articles are liable to duty or not. The penalty is three times the value of the article or £100, whichever is the greater.

# Arranging a holiday in Britain

*Booking a hotel*
*The right to accommodation*
*Mix-ups over booking*

*Lost property and complaints*
*Payments for cancellation*
*Holiday camps and caravan sites*

MOST people who take their holidays in Britain make their own arrangements for accommodation and travel. In many cases they therefore qualify for greater legal protection than someone who books a package holiday in which the operator attempts to avoid liability for many of his legal obligations.

A family holidaying by car who have several hundred miles to travel to their holiday centre can avoid a long, tiring journey by arranging to have the vehicle transported there by rail.

British Railways' 'Motorail' services cover a large number of long-distance routes, and cater for vehicles up to 6 ft 6 in. high, including roof racks. Boats and trailers may also be carried. Bookings must be made well in advance.

CANCELLATIONS No refund is made unless the booking is cancelled at least eight clear days before the date of intended departure.

INSURANCE Most comprehensive policies provide cover against damage caused to the vehicle while it is in transit. Additional insurance can be arranged at the time of booking to cover loading and unloading of the car, personal accident cover and cover against cancellation of the booking, the theft of luggage from a locked car, and forfeiture of a no-claim bonus.

Information about Motorail services can be obtained from any large station or from the British Railways Board, Melbury House, Melbury Terrace, London NW1 6JU.

## Booking a hotel

When first contacting a hotel, the holiday-maker should mention any special requirements before agreeing to take the accommodation. Confirm a booking in writing and ask the hotel to acknowledge it. Bookings normally run from noon on the day of arrival to noon on the day of departure.

Charges should also be agreed when booking. Hotels may ask for a deposit, which is forfeited if the booking is cancelled.

When he arrives at a hotel, the guest should ask to see the room before signing the register. If it is not satisfactory, the person who has paid a deposit is obviously not in such a good bargaining position as the person who has parted with no money.

## The right to accommodation

The traveller who arrives at a hotel even without a booking must usually be given accommodation if there is any available. A hotelier (in law, an 'innkeeper') cannot pick and choose his guests. He can refuse to serve or accommodate a customer only if the customer is in a disreputable condition or if the hotelier has reasonable cause to think that he would be unable to pay the bill.

At the same time, the hotelier can be expected to provide only accommodation and facilities which are reasonable. If the hotel is already full, or if he is knocked up by a would-be guest in the middle of the night, the hotelier is justified in refusing to provide accommodation.

A hotelier is legally obliged to provide a meal at any reasonable time—but if his dining-room is full, even if a number of reserved tables have not yet been taken, he is entitled to refuse anyone else. He is also entitled to keep food in reserve for guests he is expecting later, for his family or staff, or for breakfast the following morning.

The customer has a right to accommodation and food only in a genuine hotel. The Hotel Proprietors Act 1956, which sets out a hotelier's legal liabilities, defines a hotel as 'an establishment held out by the proprietor as offering food, drink and, if required, sleeping accommodation without special contract to any traveller presenting himself who appears able and willing to pay a reasonable sum for the services and facilities provided and who is in a fit state to be received'.

Many public houses, although they include the word 'hotel' in their name, are not hotels in the legal sense if they sell only drinks and snacks and do not provide accommodation. Nor are many lodging houses, boarding houses and 'private' hotels which may have a drinks licence but accept their guests only by prior arrangement.

The visitor or guest in these premises has no protection other than his ordinary, common-law rights; the proprietor's legal liability towards him goes no further than an ordinary duty of care.

## Mix-ups over booking

Anyone whose booking has been accepted by a hotel, boarding house, guest house, 'private' hotel, or any other establishment has a right to expect the accommodation specified to be provided when he arrives. If it is not, or if it differs considerably from the accommodation he was offered, the holidaymaker is entitled to compensation. But he will have to show that his booking had been accepted—that a contract had been made between himself and the hotel or boarding house.

If the accommodation offered is different from that booked the holidaymaker is entitled to refuse to stay at the hotel. He can then find suitable alternative accommodation and claim a refund of any deposit paid and compensation for any extra expense or inconvenience. This could include money spent on petrol and telephone calls to find a second hotel and any difference between the price of the accommodation he had booked and the cost of alternative accommodation. But he must act reasonably and not use a much more expensive hotel unless it is the only one available.

If a hotel refuses to pay such a claim, a solicitor will advise on how far it is worth pursuing. This will depend on the amount of money involved and the chances of proving what accommodation the hotel agreed to supply when the booking was made.

## What happens about lost property

Any personal property or belongings which an overnight guest takes into a hotel (but not a boarding house or 'private' hotel) are also protected by the Hotel Proprietors Act. This protection does not extend to a motor vehicle or to any items left in it.

The hotelier is liable for any property taken into the hotel which is lost, stolen or damaged. But claims are limited to £50 for any one article and to £100 for any one guest.

Only guests who have booked overnight accommodation qualify for this protection. The loss or damage must have occurred between the midnight immediately before and the midnight immediately after the period for which the accommodation was booked. It makes no difference whether or not the hotel or its staff were negligent, though the hotel is not liable for damage caused by the guest or a member of his party.

A notice in a hotel stating that the hotelier is not responsible for his guests' personal property does not absolve him from liability.

But in a guest house, 'private' hotel, public house or similar premises, which are not hotels in a legal sense, such a notice reduces the proprietor's responsibility if it is prominently displayed in a position where it can be seen *before* any contract is made—say, at a reception desk, or in a brochure or tariff.

Hotels of all kinds have an unlimited liability for anything deposited with them. It is advisable to ask for a receipt when handing over the item to their care.

## Complaints over the bill

Any complaints about service or facilities should be made to the hotelier as soon as possible. It would be unrealistic to expect a reduction in the bill because of a shortcoming which had not been mentioned until the day before departure.

A hotel guest who finds that unsatisfactory conditions are not remedied after complaining to the management is legally entitled to deduct a reasonable sum from the bill as compensation for the inconvenience. If the hotelier protests, the guest can always invite him to sue for the unpaid amount of his bill.

Hotels have a right to withhold a guest's luggage or belongings until his bill has been settled. In law, this is called taking a lien on his possessions. So any guest who intends disputing the bill will find it best first to make sure his luggage is in his possession, preferably inside his car.

Disputes with hotels often arise over a 10 per cent service charge added to the bill. The hotelier is allowed to make this charge only if his brochure or tariff states that a service charge is payable. If it does, the guest cannot ask for the charge to be deleted from the bill on the grounds that he has already given a gratuity to particular hotel staff.

## Payments for cancellation

If accommodation that has been booked has to be cancelled, the hotel is generally entitled to keep any booking deposit. Some hotels also send a bill for 'cancellation charges', but these extra charges can only be enforced legally to the extent that the hotel can show that the expense incurred exceeds the deposit.

If no deposit has been paid, the hotel's brochure or notepaper may contain clauses outlining the holidaymaker's obligations and charges payable on cancellation.

Some hotels omit any cancellation procedure from their brochures or other publicity material and instead try to impose a cancellation charge of two-thirds of the total cost of the booking. Again, the charge is not legally enforceable unless the hotel can show that this was the actual amount of its loss.

If, after cancellation, a hotel re-lets the room to another client, the person who cancelled can be charged only a nominal sum to cover administration expenses. If the hotel is unable to re-let the room, a charge may be made for loss of profit and overheads.

Always ask for a cancellation charge to be itemised before paying it, and query any charge that appears unjustified or excessive.

It may be difficult to establish whether a hotel was able to re-let cancelled accommodation, although the length of time between cancellation and the date for which the accommodation was booked would probably be taken into account in any dispute.

Generally, the law regards cancellation charges as a means to compensate the hotelier for his loss; they must not be used to make money out of a holidaymaker's misfortune.

### Staying at a holiday camp

Anyone wishing to book accommodation at a holiday camp finds that the owners, like the suppliers of other types of holidays, often include conditions on their booking forms which give the holidaymaker less protection than that otherwise given by the law. The conditions found on most booking forms seek to absolve the owner from some or all of his normal legal responsibilities. The holidaymaker may be able to protect his rights by striking out objectionable clauses or crossing out the sentence which says that he accepts the owner's terms.

Most owners, however, will probably refuse to accept a booking if this is done. Alternatively, the holidaymaker can make a booking by letter, giving all the information normally required on the booking form and enclosing payment of the deposit. If the deposit is accepted, the booking is legally enforceable under common-law terms.

When the customer books a holiday, he has to send a deposit—usually £2 for an adult and £1 for each child for every week of the proposed stay.

The balance of the fee normally has to be paid seven days before the holiday is due to start or when the holidaymaker arrives.

The deposit is usually regarded as a booking fee. If the holiday is cancelled for any reason by the holidaymaker the deposit is forfeited automatically, though in some cases the camp will give credit for half the fee if notice of cancellation is given in writing at least 21 days before the holiday was due to start, or if the

camper produces a doctor's certificate saying illness caused him to cancel the holiday.

When he arrives, the camper is usually not entitled to move into his chalet until midday or later. When he leaves, he may have to vacate the chalet by 10.30 a.m. on the day of departure. However, his rights to meals in the camp restaurants and his use of camp facilities on the day of arrival and departure are not affected by this rule.

If the holidaymaker finds on arrival that the camp does not match up to its advertised claims, he may be able to persuade the local weights and measures inspector to prosecute the camp operator under the Trade Descriptions Act 1968. Though such a prosecution may result in the camp owner being fined, it provides no financial compensation for the disappointed holidaymaker.

### Hiring a site caravan

Caravan-site operators frequently impose booking conditions similar to those used by holiday-camp operators, and normally there are additional site regulations controlling, say, the admittance of pets and rubbish disposal.

The terms of letting often absolve the owners from having to pay compensation for damage to persons or property and make the hirer responsible for the cost of any damage done to the caravan, its fixtures or fittings.

Again, the owners often refuse to take responsibility if the caravans are dirty or badly equipped, and reserve the right to change the booking if special circumstances— the sale of or damage to the caravan, for example—make this necessary.

The whole of the letting charge usually has to be paid on the day of arrival, otherwise the caravan may be re-let.

Private caravan owners who have leased a position on a site often hire their caravan out for the weeks during the summer when they are not using it themselves. Frequently they advertise their caravan and the dates on which it is vacant in local newspapers. Letting arrangements are made by an exchange of letters and sometimes by a personal visit. Such an arrangement deprives the holidaymaker of none of his common-law rights.

It is always advisable to ask for an inventory of the contents of the caravan before moving in. This will eliminate the possibility of a claim being made for items which may have disappeared before the holidaymaker arrived. It also serves to establish exactly what cutlery, crockery and bed linen is provided. Charges for heat, light, cooking and other services should also be agreed beforehand.

# Rights of the traveller

*Travelling by rail*
*Bus and coach travel*
*Travelling by sea*

*Travelling by air*
*When luggage is lost or damaged*
*Travelling with pets*

ANYONE who pays to travel by bus, train, sea or air makes a contract with the transport operator involved. The rights of the traveller are controlled by Act of Parliament and by the rules of the bus company, railways board, shipping line or airline.

These regulations, which are made conditions of the contract, are printed on posters and displayed at stations or in company timetables. Sometimes extracts from the conditions appear on the backs of tickets.

Transport operators, like private individuals, are obliged under common law to take care not to do anything which causes injury or death to their fare-paying passengers. They cannot rely on their own regulations to absolve them from this duty. If they neglect their duty and a passenger is injured as a result, he may be entitled to claim damages from the operator. If he is killed on a journey, his dependants may claim. ☐ How a damages claim is decided, p. 124; Claiming damages for fatal accidents, p. 417.

A traveller who books his ticket through a travel agent cannot claim from the agent if he is injured in a vehicle belonging to the transport operator. Instead he must sue the operator in the same way as if he had bought the ticket direct from him.

## Travelling by rail
A rail ticket entitles a passenger to be taken to the destination stated on it in a reasonable time, but it does not guarantee him a seat. On trains other than commuter services, seats can be reserved by paying an additional fee.

It is against the law to travel by train with the intention of not paying the fare.

A passenger does not commit an offence if he boards a train without a ticket, provided he can show that he intends to pay either when asked for his fare or at the other end. But a ticket collector is entitled to stop anyone without a ticket from going on to the platform.

A passenger who lied about the point at which he boarded the train in order to avoid paying the correct fare would be guilty of intending to defraud the British Railways Board. The maximum penalty on first conviction is a fine of £50. For a subsequent offence, an offender can be sent to prison for up to three months and fined up to £100.

Passengers must show their tickets when asked to do so by a ticket collector, inspector or guard. If a passenger loses his ticket he must pay again or give his name and address and provide proof of his identity so that the bill for the fare can be sent to him. But he will not have to pay twice if he can prove that he bought a ticket—for example by producing a travel-agent's receipt.

Anyone who fails to produce a ticket and refuses to pay or to give his name and address can be detained by railway staff and handed over to the police. A traveller without a ticket who tries to pass the ticket barrier without paying may be arrested and charged with attempting to defraud the railways.

A passenger with a second-class ticket who travels in a first-class seat must pay the difference in fare, even if all the second-class seats are taken. The holder of a second-class *season* ticket who travels first class must pay the full first-class fare.

If a guard decides to allow second-class passengers to travel in a first-class compartment, with or without paying the extra fare, he does not have to seek the agreement of first-class passengers. No refunds are paid in these circumstances to first-class passengers.

Passengers cannot legally reserve a seat on a train by putting a newspaper or suitcase on it—even if they are away for only a few minutes to go to the buffet car or lavatory. In law, once a seat has been vacated any other passenger is entitled to use it.

It is an offence to smoke in a no-smoking compartment, even if other passengers do not object; to sing; to play a musical instrument; or to use a record player or transistor radio if it annoys anyone else.

It is also an offence to pull the communication cord, or to use any other emergency device, unless there is a genuine emergency. The maximum penalty is £25. A passenger is not justified in trying to stop the train if he misses his station.

RAILWAY ACCIDENTS Anyone injured on a train or on railway property should report the accident as soon as possible to a railway official.

161

If there are any witnesses, take their names and addresses and get statements from them.

The injured person should also be examined by his family doctor without delay, and should ask for a written medical report. He should also consult a solicitor, to ensure that the claim is pursued most effectively.

Once British Railways have investigated a claim and accepted responsibility for the accident, a settlement offer will be made.

If British Railways deny liability or if an injured person is dissatisfied with the amount offered, a solicitor may advise taking action for damages in a civil court. But generally, most claims are settled out of court.

Private insurance against personal injury is available at railway booking offices for 5p or 10p.

If a traveller dies in a railway accident, his dependants should seek the advice of a solicitor immediately.

RAIL TRAVEL ON THE CONTINENT Most European countries have signed an agreement called the International Convention Concerning the Carriage of Passengers and Luggage by Rail under which compensation claims are settled according to the laws of the country in which the accident occurred.

This means that if a traveller is injured on a ferry operated by British Railways, he can claim in the same way as if he were injured on a train in England. But a passenger travelling by train from, say, London to Paris, must claim from the French authorities if he is injured in France—even though he may have bought the train ticket from British Railways. He should consult his solicitor for advice on how his claim can be brought.

## Bus and coach travel

A bus conductor or driver is entitled, under the statutory public-service vehicle regulations, to turn a passenger off a bus, or stop him boarding it, in many circumstances. These include:

**1.** When the bus is already carrying the total number of passengers allowed, or if the passenger is trying to get on at a point other than an official bus stop for the bus's particular route. For example, a passenger going only a short distance may not be entitled to board a long-distance bus even though his destination is on its route.

**2.** If a passenger smokes, or carries a lighted cigarette, cigar or pipe, in a section of the bus where smoking is prohibited.

**3.** If he tries to travel on the upper deck of a bus when all the seats on the upper deck are already occupied by passengers.

**4.** If he tries to distribute printed or similar material, or advertising leaflets.

**5.** If he gives a signal which might be taken by the driver as a signal from the conductor to start the bus.

**6.** If he uses obscene or offensive language or is riotous or disorderly.

A passenger can also be put off a bus, or stopped from boarding it, if he is likely to offend other passengers or if his clothing may make the seats dirty. Anyone made to get off a bus in such circumstances is entitled to a refund of his fare.

Loaded firearms and other dangerous or offensive articles are not allowed on buses. Nor is bulky or cumbersome luggage unless the conductor gives his permission. If he does allow them on the bus, the conductor is entitled to stipulate where such inconvenient articles are to be placed.

It is an offence to try to leave a bus without paying the fare and with intent to avoid paying. Tickets must be handed in at the end of a journey if asked for, and season tickets surrendered at the end of the period for which they were issued.

A passenger who breaks any of the regulations may be removed from the bus by the conductor, driver or a policeman.

BUS AND COACH ACCIDENTS Bus and coach operators must, by law, be insured against claims by passengers or their relatives for damages for injury or death. Nothing in their regulations can be used to absolve them of liability to fare-paying passengers during the time they are on the bus, and when they board and leave it.

Bus operators may, however, attempt to escape their liability to passengers who do not pay fares (pensioners with free passes, for example), and to fare-paying passengers at other times—when they are waiting at a bus stop, for example.

But anyone who is injured is still entitled to sue a negligent bus-company employee, and through him the bus operator, since employers are responsible for the actions of employees during the course of their work.

FOREIGN COACH TOURS There is no international agreement covering coach tours. Most British operators arrange unlimited-liability insurance cover for passengers while abroad, in the same way as if they were touring at home. If a traveller is injured, his solicitor writes to the coach operators and the claim is usually then passed to their insurers, who assess any damages that are to be paid.

If there is any dispute over a claim arising from an injury which occurred overseas, the injured passenger usually has to take action in the country where his injury occurred. In such a case, damages, if any, would be determined under the laws of that particular country. But if both the injured passenger and the person or company responsible for the accident are resident in Britain, any legal action would be in Britain.

## Travelling by sea
Most shipping companies attempt to limit their liability to passengers by extensive conditions, usually printed on the ticket.

The conditions may, for example, say: 'The carrier shall not be liable to the passenger in any capacity for any claim arising from injury, death or delay . . . or for any other claim whatsoever. In all circumstances where it may be possible to contract against the consequence of negligence, the carrier, although negligent, shall not be under any liability; the burden of proving negligence shall be on the party asserting it, and it is agreed that there shall not be any presumption or inference of negligence because of the occurrence of the facts out of which any claim may arise.'

Although these conditions appear to exempt the company from any liability whatsoever, its employees are not exempt. A passenger may therefore sue any company employee who is negligent and the employer will have to meet any damages awarded.

Nor can the company extend its exemption from liability to its agents or employees because such people are not parties to the contract which is made between the company and the passenger.

➤ THE CLAUSE THAT WAS TOO WIDE *In 1952 Mrs Adler was a first-class passenger on the P & O line ship* Himalaya. *As she climbed the gang-plank of the ship, it moved and fell. Mrs Adler dropped 16 ft to the wharf, and was severely injured. She brought an action against the master of the* Himalaya *Captain Dickson, and the ship's boatswain.*

*P & O had exempted itself from liability, and had tried to extend this exemption to its agents and servants.*

*Part of the exemption clause read: 'The company will not be responsible for, and shall be exempt from, liability in respect of, any . . . injury whatsoever.' It said the exemption would apply in the case of any 'acts, defaults or negligence of the . . . master, mariners . . . company's agents or servants of any kind under any circumstances whatsoever'.*

DECISION *Mrs Adler won her case. The Court of Appeal held that the clause did not protect the* master and boatswain from liability. They were not parties to the contract, and could not shelter behind the protection afforded to the company by the clause. (Adler v. Dickson and others.)*◄

## Travelling by air
An airline, like a railway or bus company, makes a contract with a passenger once he buys a ticket. But it is only when the passenger has had his ticket 'validated'—that is, when he has checked in, had his baggage weighed and collected his ticket coupon—that the airline has a legal responsibility to carry him on a particular flight.

A passenger can still be refused permission to board the aircraft, however, if he is unfit to travel—for example, if he is drunk, under the influence of drugs, or ill.

If a passenger finds that his flight has been overbooked, he is entitled to insist that passengers are offloaded in reverse order to the time that they checked in and had their tickets validated—not in the order that the tickets were bought.

It is the airline's responsibility to see that any offloaded passengers are taken on the next free reservation, even if the flight is operated by another airline. If, as a result of offloading, a first-class passenger finds he has to travel ordinary or tourist class, he is entitled to a refund of the difference in fares.

An airline's liability to its passengers does not extend to meeting any expenses incurred because of a delay, however. It may provide meals and accommodation, but is not legally obliged to do so.

A passenger is not entitled to any particular seat on an aircraft unless seat numbers are stipulated on tickets or boarding passes. The general practice, especially on short flights, is that those first aboard have first choice.

Sometimes, especially during busy holiday periods when flights are fully booked well in advance, passengers may be offered what are termed 'stand-by' tickets. These tickets do not guarantee a passenger a reservation. Instead, his name is put on the airline's stand-by list.

Any seats still vacant on the flight after ordinary passengers have been called are then given, in strict order of validation, to stand-by passengers.

PLANE CRASHES Air travellers may get compensation for injury or, in the case of death, their next-of-kin can claim compensation from the airline company under various domestic and international agreements.

The rules governing compensation, and the agreements under which the compensation is payable, are complex. Domestic flights, which include flights to British colonies, are covered by English statutes which fix a ceiling of about £24,185 payable to next-of-kin for injury to or death of a passenger.

International flights are usually covered either by the Hague Convention, which sets a limit of about £6910 payable for injury or death, or the Warsaw Convention, which has a limit of about £3455. There are other agreements between the United States and the United Kingdom which set liability at about the British domestic level.

A passenger may ask the airline company which international agreement will cover him. He may, for example, wish to take out a certain amount of personal life assurance to provide extra cover for death or injury in addition to the amount his family could expect to get under an international agreement.

The international agreement that applies to a traveller depends on the countries he flies to and the route taken.

If, for example, he flies on a single journey to Turkey, he is treated as though he were on a domestic flight, and liability is fixed at the English domestic level because Turkey is not a party to international flight agreements.

However, if he flies from London to Turkey on a return ticket, he will be covered by the terms of the Hague Convention because the United Kingdom is a signatory to the Convention, and his flight takes off from a Convention country and returns to it.

## When luggage is lost or damaged

In common law, any travel operator has a duty to take reasonable care of a passenger's property. If a firm neglects this duty, the passenger may be able to claim compensation. But most travel operators limit their liability for compensating the owner of lost or damaged luggage, or exempt themselves for responsibility altogether.

British Railways limit their liability for luggage sent in advance at the railways' risk to a maximum of £800 a ton, about 36p a lb. The actual loss to the passenger could therefore be far more than the compensation he will usually get.

If luggage is lost through a traveller's own carelessness (for example, if he leaves a case in a compartment while he goes to the buffet car) he will have no claim against the railways. But if the luggage is lost or damaged in the guard's van, then the railways must show they were not negligent.

Where there is no exemption clause, a travel operator can be sued for negligence under common law. If there is an exemption clause, it may have no effect if an employee of the travel operator can be shown to have mishandled the passenger's goods.

➤ THE MISSING CASES *Mr and Mrs Houghland, two pensioners, went to Jersey in 1960. On the return trip, they travelled by coach from Southampton to Cheshire. Before reaching Cheshire, however, their coach broke down. Luggage was transferred to the relief coach by the passengers, but no one supervised the removal. Several stops were made on the way to Cheshire, to let passengers off, and each time the boot was unlocked so that cases could be unloaded. When Mr and Mrs Houghland finally arrived in Cheshire, their suitcases were missing. They later sued the coach proprietors.*

DECISION *The Court of Appeal said that a coach proprietor was under a duty to take reasonable care for the safety of passengers' luggage throughout the journey. The driver was negligent in leaving the coach unattended and in failing to supervise the unloading. Mr and Mrs Houghland had only to prove that the suitcases had been lost, and it was up to the proprietors of the coach to show they were not negligent. Mr and Mrs Houghland recovered the value of the suitcases and contents. (Houghland v. R. R. Low, Luxury Coaches Ltd.)* ◄

Most airline companies have insurance policies covering loss or damage to passenger luggage, and the amount recoverable is usually subject to negotiation.

## Travelling with pets

Most transport operators reserve the right to refuse to carry a pet if it is felt the animal would annoy other passengers or cause damage. For example, dogs may travel by rail only if other passengers do not object.

A charge can be made when pets are carried. For example, British Railways charge a half fare for dogs and cats, with a maximum charge of £1·75 single fare, and £3·50 return. However, small animals and birds can travel free provided their container has no side larger than 18 in.

In London, a fare has to be paid to take a dog on the Underground. Animals carried in baskets or other containers on the Underground travel free. Pets can be taken on London buses as long as the conductor agrees, and they are not charged fares. Whether or not an animal is allowed is entirely at the conductor's discretion (or driver's discretion if it is a one-man bus). If there is one dog on the bus, the conductor is unlikely to allow another to be carried.

# Motor and pedal cycles

*Regulations on motor cycles*  *Other restrictions*
*Learning to drive*  *The law and pedal cycles*

THE construction of motor cycles, mopeds, motor scooters and pedal cycles is governed by specific regulations, but laws concerning their use on the road are similar to those for the car. ☐ The law on car safety, p. 39.

They must be properly maintained, and drivers must obey the usual road traffic regulations. ☐ Signs, lines and signals, p. 68.

## Regulations on motor cycles

CONSTRUCTION A motor cycle must have two independently operated brakes. The front brake, operated by hand control, should have a minimum efficiency of 30 per cent. The back brake, operated usually by a foot pedal, or by back-pedalling on a moped, must be at least 25 per cent efficient.

A solo machine must have lights front and back, and a red rear reflector. No parking light is needed, but a stop light is compulsory. A moped used before January 1972 may have a headlight with a permanently dipped beam. Both wheels must have mudguards.

NOISE Motor cycles under 50 cc are restricted to a maximum noise level of 80 decibels; for 50 cc and over but less than 125 cc, the limit is 85 decibels; and for 125 cc and over, it is 89 decibels. Motor cyclists can be prosecuted for exceeding the limits.

ROADWORTHINESS Motor cycles more than three years old must, like cars, have annual tests. ☐ The annual vehicle test, p. 50.

MOTOR CYCLE COMBINATIONS A motor cycle and sidecar combination is subject to most motor cycle rules. It must have one headlamp, two rear reflectors (which must be on the same level), and two front side-lights and two red rear lights (not necessarily on the same level). It may pull a trailer up to 5 cwt unladen and 5 ft wide.

## Learning to drive

A learner may ride a moped up to 50 cc at 16. The minimum age at which he is permitted to ride a motor cycle (or moped over 50 cc) is 17.

A learner is allowed to ride a motor cycle of 250 cc or less, but must not ride a larger one until he has passed his driving test. A learner

can ride a motor cycle of any capacity if it has a sidecar attached.

He may also carry a passenger if his machine is equipped with a pillion (which must be a proper seat securely attached behind the driver) and foot rests, but only if the passenger is qualified. He may carry an unqualified passenger in a sidecar.

No passenger may sit side-saddle. It is an offence for a motor cyclist to carry passengers other than on the pillion.

## Other restrictions

Motor cycles of less than 50 cc are not allowed on motorways, and in parking meter areas motor cycles must use the free bays.

The use of crash helmets is not compulsory, but any helmets sold must conform to British Standards specifications.

## The law and pedal cycles

CONSTRUCTION A pedal cycle with wheels bigger than 18 in. in diameter and a free wheel must have two brakes (other cycles need only one). It must have a white light in front and a red one at the back. It must also have a red rear reflector and, if it has a sidecar, must carry two front lights. Lights and reflectors are obligatory, whether or not the cycle is used at night.

ROAD OFFENCES Anyone riding a pedal cycle recklessly, dangerously, without care and attention, or reasonable consideration for other road users, can be prosecuted.

These offences cover a number of situations, such as riding at a dangerous speed, turning without giving signals or taking hold of another vehicle for a tow. Cycling on the footpath is illegal, and if a passenger is carried on a single machine both riders can be prosecuted.

A cyclist can be prosecuted for riding while under the influence of drink or drugs—but he cannot be made to take a breathalyser test. Anyone leaving a cycle where it could be a danger to other road users is also liable to prosecution.

The Highway Code advises cyclists not to ride more than two abreast, and to ride in single file on busy or narrow roads.

# Caravans and trailers

*Motorised caravans*    *Where to park*
*Trailer regulations*    *Insuring a caravan*
*Waste disposal*    *Going abroad*

THERE are two types of caravan—the motorised, self-contained single unit, and the trailer. Regulations controlling their size and weight, loads, speeds, brakes and lights are designed to give the maximum protection to other road users.

### Motorised caravans
The advantage of the motorised caravan is that it can be used throughout the year as a private vehicle, in the same way as a car, and as a home from home at holiday time.

Motorised caravans are subject to the same laws governing construction and use as apply to cars. In addition, there are regulations governing waste disposal. ☐ The law on car safety, p. 39.

Unlike trailers, motorised caravans must be tested every year after they have been on the road three years, and must have excise licences, just like private cars. ☐ Taxing a car, p. 37.

Anyone converting a goods vehicle to a motor caravan may have to pay purchase tax (VAT after April 1, 1973) if the vehicle fails to comply with the motor caravan specification, obtainable from Customs and Excise offices. When the conversion is completed, inform the motor taxation authority, which may require to test it.

### Trailer regulations
Special rules for trailer caravans deal with construction and use both on the road and at a caravan site.

SIZE Two-wheeled trailers and those drawn by light cars are limited to 7 metres (22 ft 11½ in.) in length. Four-wheeled trailers

## The lights a caravan must have

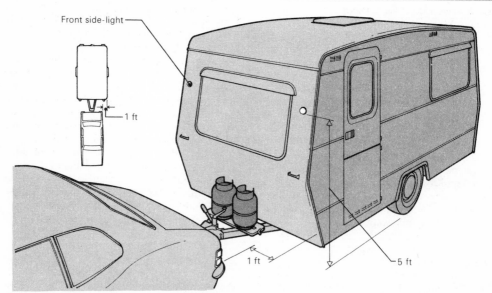

Front side-light

1 ft

1 ft    5 ft

The lights on a trailer caravan should generally be the same as those on the towing vehicle. Front headlights are not needed, but where a trailer juts out more than 1 ft beyond the towing car's side-lights it must have front side-lights fitted not more than 5 ft from the ground

drawn by a vehicle of at least 2 tons may be as long as 12 metres (39 ft 4¼ in.).

The overall width of either type must be no more than 7 ft 6 in., but this may be increased if it is drawn by a vehicle with an unladen weight of more than 3 tons. This means that many of the larger trailers have to be towed by lorries.

BRAKES If a trailer weighs less than 2 cwt—the sort of vehicle used for carrying camping equipment or moving extra luggage—no brakes are needed. But trailers over that weight and manufactured after January 1, 1968 must have brakes on at least half its wheels and on at least four wheels if the trailer has more than four.

Any trailer made after January 1, 1968 must have its braking system constructed so that in the event of failure brakes can still be applied to at least two of the wheels (or to one of the wheels in the case of the two-wheeled trailer).

A parking brake is also required on any trailer over 2 cwt. It must be positioned so that it can be operated by a person standing on the ground.

The parking brake must be set as soon as a trailer is parted from its tow. Where there is no parking brake—as on a small trailer—it must be secured by chaining a wheel to the axle or mudguard stay.

LIGHTS Front side-lights must be fitted to a trailer caravan in any of three circumstances:
**1.** If the trailer is 5 ft or more from the towing vehicle. This measurement includes the length of the tow bar.
**2.** If the trailer juts out 1 ft or more beyond the towing vehicle's side-lights.
**3.** If the total overall length of car plus trailer exceeds 40 ft.

If it is any longer, or if it is towed by a goods vehicle, front corner lights must be fitted not more than 5 ft high.

Rear lights, two triangular reflectors, stop lights and flashing direction indicators are compulsory and must be in good order.

The triangular reflectors must conform to British Standards, with sides 150–200 mm long. If the centre is non-reflecting, the width of the sides must be one-fifth their length. They must be fitted at least 21 in. apart, not more than 30 in. from the rearmost point of the trailer and 15–42 in. from the ground. The only exception is a boat trailer, where the height should be 15–54 in.

From January 1, 1973, stop lights and

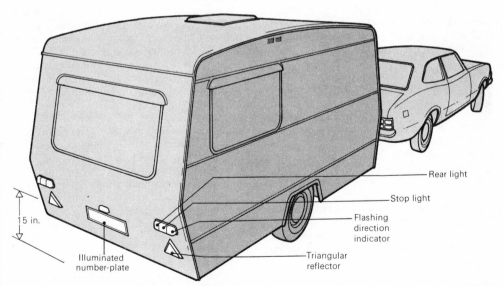

Rear light
Stop light
Flashing direction indicator
Triangular reflector
Illuminated number-plate
15 in.

Rear lights, reflectors, direction indicators, stop lights and illuminated number plates are compulsory fittings on caravans, but triangular trailer plates are compulsory only on trailers being towed by goods vehicles or vehicles that can carry more than seven passengers flashing indicators must provide two levels of light intensity on all new trailers. This regulation ensures that lights are brighter by day and dimmer at night, reducing dazzle.

SIDE MARKER LIGHTS Any trailer more than 30 ft long must be fitted with side marker lights within 5 ft of the halfway point between front and rear.

RESTRICTIONS ON LOADS The maximum permitted laden weight of a trailer is 14 tons per axle—or 9 tons per axle if the trailer has more than four wheels.

Pack caravan and trailer loads carefully. Heavy cases and equipment should be made fast, so that they cannot fall and unbalance the vehicle. Doors should be locked.

Passengers must not be carried in a caravan with fewer than four wheels, or in one with close-coupled wheels (unless it is in the process of being tested by the manufacturer or repairer).

SPEED LIMITS A trailer caravan is limited to a speed of 40 mph—or 30 mph if it is towed by a goods vehicle. On some roads, lower limits may be indicated.

On a motorway the limit is 40 mph if the trailer has two wheels and 70 mph if it has four or more. But if it is being towed by a goods vehicle heavier than 3 tons the limit is 60 mph.

ATTENDANTS Bigger trailers should have an attendant on the drawing vehicle or the trailer, as well as the driver. This regulation does not apply to two-wheeled trailers or four-wheelers where the wheels are close-coupled (that is, they are not steerable and the wheels on the same side are less than 33 in. apart).

Trailers with over-run brakes (which operate independently as the drawing vehicle halts) are also exempt.

OTHER REGULATIONS The driver of the towing vehicle must be able to see the road behind, so a periscope rear-view mirror or suitably extended wing mirrors should be fitted to ensure this.

Every trailer should carry the registration number plate at the rear, and this should be illuminated at night.

It must carry the same number as the towing vehicle, but there are two exceptions: trailers used with a number of works trucks, and a farmer's towed equipment, which may be hauled by different tractors.

**Waste disposal**
Closets, urinals, sinks or basins must not empty or leak on to the road. They must be fitted either with tanks ventilated by a pipe with an external outlet or must contain an efficient deodorant and germicidal chemical.

Sinks and washbasins must not empty into the same tank as closets and urinals.

**Where to park**
A caravan used as a permanent home must be parked on a site approved by a local authority.

When a touring caravan is not being used, it may be parked on the owner's property, provided that it is not obtrusive and does not obstruct motorists' view of the road.

If a parked caravan annoys neighbours they may complain to the police, and a prosecution may be possible under local bye-laws.

On tour, a caravan or trailer may be parked on temporary unlicensed sites, such as a farmer's field, as long as the landowner gives his consent. There should be no more than three caravans parked at any one time on such a site, and they may stay there only up to a maximum 28 days.

Caravans can be parked without restriction on approved sites—that is, those that have been licensed by the local authority. The authority must be satisfied that sanitary arrangements are adequate.

Probably the easiest way to find sites is to join the Caravan Club, 65 South Molton Street, London W1Y 2AB. The club provides its members with an up-to-date list of approved sites for caravan parking.

**Insuring a caravan**
A car owner who buys a caravan cannot usually extend his car insurance policy to cover his new purchase. He must obtain separate cover for the caravan.

He should, in any case, let his car insurance company know that he intends to tow a trailer, as this could affect the terms of his car insurance policy.

A normal policy for a caravan will cover construction and contents and give cover against liability in the event of an accident— for example, should the trailer break away from its tow and crash.

The insurers should also be informed if the trailer is parked on a permanent site, and not at the owner's home. If it is on a site, there is obviously a greater risk of fire and theft.

**Going abroad**
Most of the laws and regulations concerning caravans and trailers going abroad are the same as those applying to cars. The Automobile Association helps members planning holidays abroad by advising them on regulations in countries they intend to visit.
☐ Taking a car abroad, p. 147.

# Three-wheelers

*Taxing and insuring a three-wheeler*
*Construction and use*

MOST three-wheeled vehicles are manufactured so that they weigh less than 8 cwt, which means that in law they can be classified as motor cycles.

The immediate advantage is that the owner has a vehicle that gives some of the comforts of a motor car while he has to pay only the reduced motor-cycle excise licence. ☐ Taxing a car, p. 35; Motor and pedal cycles, p. 165.

The premiums for three-wheeler insurance cover are also lower than those for comparable motor car policies.

### Construction and use
In general a three-wheeler must comply with the regulations governing the construction and use of motor cars. ☐ The law on car safety, p. 39.

It must have two separate braking systems, one of which can be a hand-operated parking brake. If the main braking system operates on all three wheels, it must register at least 40 per cent efficiency when measured on a decelerometer; if it operates on only two wheels, then at least 30 per cent efficiency is required. A parking brake must be at least 25 per cent efficient. ☐ How braking systems work, p. 40.

A three-wheeler must have two sidelamps complying with car lights rules. If it weighs over 400 kg (7·9 cwt) or is wider than 1·3 m (3 ft 4½ in.), it must have two headlamps. But a three-wheeler used before January 1, 1972 needs only one headlamp.

All three-wheelers must have two rear lights, reflectors, stop lamps and flashing indicators.

The regulations governing the position of headlamps and any additional lights are the same as for a car. ☐ Lights a car must have, p. 46; Lights not required by law, p. 48.

Seat belts are compulsory if the vehicle weighs more than 5 cwt and was first used after September 1, 1970.

Unlike a four-wheeled car, there is no regulation requiring a three-wheeler to have springs, although in practice most manufacturers provide a suspension system for comfort.

TRAILERS A three-wheeler must not be used to tow a trailer that weighs more than 5 cwt unladen or that is more than 5 ft wide.

## Invalid carriages

THREE-WHEELED invalid carriages are exempt from road tax, and this exemption is extended to four-wheeled cars that have been converted for the use of an invalid, provided that the unladen weight does not exceed 8 cwt.

Small invalid carriages, specially built for handicapped people and weighing less than 5 cwt, are also exempt from the law requiring insurance cover, but this is usually provided by the Department of Health and Social Security.

These vehicles are provided free by the Department, which also pays for maintenance and contributes £5 a year towards petrol costs. In some cases the disabled driver may also claim towards the cost of a garage and the local authority can help to provide access for the vehicle, which is the Department's property.

If the owner of a private car wishes it to be converted for invalid use, the Department will usually contribute up to £90 towards the cost. Additional grants may be made at intervals of five years, but running costs must be met by the owner.

When the Department supplies an invalid carriage, it also pays for driving lessons given by a specialist instructor at one of the disability training centres run by the British School of Motoring. Owners of cars that have been converted must pay for their own lessons, but discounts may be avilable to motoring-organisation members.

# Putting a vehicle up for sale

*Preparing for the sale*  *Selling by auction*
*Selling privately*  *Notifying change of ownership*
*Selling to a garage*

THERE are four main ways in which an owner can sell a vehicle: he can make a private sale, trade it in as part of the price of a new vehicle, sell to a garage for cash or put it up for auction.

An owner with the necessary time who knows how much to ask often gets the best price by selling privately. If his particular model is in demand, trade-in may also provide a good bargain, though in making an offer the dealer has to allow for his own profit. The price obtainable by selling by auction or to a garage for cash depends on demand and circumstances.

## Preparing for the sale
There are a number of formalities an owner has to attend to before he can put his vehicle on the market.

ENDING A CREDIT AGREEMENT If the vehicle was originally acquired on deferred terms or with the help of a loan, and the final payment has not been made, it may be necessary to inform the organisation providing finance and even to obtain its consent.

Read the terms of the agreement, and if in doubt check with the organisation concerned.

If the loan was provided by a clearing bank, it may be possible to go ahead with the sale and continue repaying the loan at the same rate. Anyone with a personal loan from a finance house, on the other hand, may have to inform the company of his intention to sell, and then repay the balance of the loan and any other charges as soon as the sale is completed.

If the dealer who sold the vehicle arranged deferred payments, this will usually have been in the form of a credit sale or hire-purchase agreement.

With credit sale, the owner does not require permission to sell but may have to repay the loan when the sale goes through.

A car on hire purchase, however, does not become the property of the customer until he has paid all the instalments and a nominal 50p or £1 option-to-purchase fee.

Until that time, he is not entitled to sell without the written permission of the finance company. If he tries to do so he may be sued

for damages and—if dishonesty is involved—prosecuted for theft.

If the customer has the cash available, he can settle all outstanding hire-purchase payments in a lump sum. He is then entitled to sell the vehicle whenever he wants without the need for finance company consent. A garage buying a second-hand car from a customer will usually arrange to end the hire-purchase agreement in this way.

If the customer does not have the ready cash to repay before the sale, the finance company may agree to let him sell the vehicle on condition that the purchaser pays the amount outstanding direct to the company. Finance companies are often reluctant to allow this, however.

Alternatively, the finance company may agree that the new purchaser should take over the hire-purchase agreement and continue making payments on it. If the company agrees to this—and, again, many are reluctant to do so—it may require the person handing over the vehicle to guarantee the loan in case the new purchaser falls down on the payments.

This is a serious responsibility, and can involve heavy financial penalties. □ Guaranteeing a credit agreement, p. 505.

TAXING THE CAR If the car has been laid up before the sale, it may not have a current excise (road fund) licence. It is illegal to drive the car on a public road without renewing the licence, even for a short demonstration drive. □ Taxing a car, p. 35.

CHECKING INSURANCE Make sure the car is properly insured for a test drive. If your own policy is for named drivers only or for the policyholder only, it will not cover prospective purchasers when they are driving.

In these circumstances, the best course is to ask your insurance company to extend the policy to any driver for a limited period. Though this will cost money, it is a wise safeguard.

The alternative—to rely on the insurance of prospective purchasers—is unsatisfactory. Such insurance is likely to provide only third-party cover, with no compensation if the car is damaged. In addition the seller cannot be sure that prospective purchasers have the insurance they claim to have; and if he allows his car to be driven by someone who he knows or ought to know is uninsured, he can be prosecuted.

ANNUAL VEHICLE TEST If you are selling a car more than three years old which has been laid up for some time, make sure that the Annual Vehicle (MoT) Test certificate has not expired. It is an offence to take the car on the road, or allow it to be taken on to the road, without a certificate, except to drive it to a garage where an appointment has been made for a test. ☐ The Annual Vehicle Test, p. 50.

CHECKING ROADWORTHINESS Before selling, check that brakes, steering and tyres are in good order and that the compulsory lights and other equipment required by law are fitted and properly maintained. ☐ The law on car safety, p. 39.

It is an offence to put a car up for sale in an unroadworthy condition. If the car is defective, the owner is guilty whether or not he knew of the defect; and a current Annual Vehicle Test certificate is no automatic defence. Even someone who sells a car a few days after he bought it can be convicted if the car is defective.

The only general defence is that the seller believed that the car was going to be taken abroad (which is unlikely in the case of a second-hand car). A seller charged with trying to sell a car with defective lights has a defence if he can show that he believed the buyer was going to put the defects right before putting the car on the road.

If an unroadworthy car is sold by auction, it is the owner—not the auctioneer acting on his behalf—who is guilty of an offence.

## Selling privately

A private seller who advertises in a shop window, a local newspaper or the trade Press must take care to describe the car accurately. He has no obligation to point out its defects, but any statements he makes must be truthful and not misleading.

A misleading statement may give the buyer the right to sue for damages under the Misrepresentation Act 1967. If the seller makes a habit of selling cars, any false information he gives about the car may lead to prosecution under the Trade Descriptions Act 1968 (which covers mainly trade sales). ☐ Recouping money lost through fraud, p. 548; What to do about faulty goods, p. 460.

DECIDING THE PRICE Anyone selling privately may be able to get an idea of the price to ask by checking how much local dealers charge for cars of the same model and year which are in a similar condition. He can also check in the monthly *Motorists' Guide to New and Used Car Prices*.

RECEIVING PAYMENT When a buyer has been found, discuss the best method of payment. If the buyer wants to pay by cheque, insist that he should not take possession of the car until the cheque has been cleared—that is, until your own bank has been able to confirm that the cheque will be paid. For a small fee, most banks can arrange to provide this information within a day. ☐ Using a bank, p. 434.

Beware of parting with the car before payment is confirmed, no matter how genuine the buyer appears to be or how plausible are his reasons for needing the vehicle quickly. There have been many cases of rogues with stolen evidence of identity who have bought a car with a dud cheque, sold it immediately for cash and then disappeared, leaving seller and buyer to fight it out. The courts usually decide in such cases that the car should remain with the buyer.

A banker's card or credit card should not be regarded as authenticating a cheque for a substantial sum. Most credit cards do not guarantee cheques; banker's cards usually guarantee payment only up to a relatively small amount (usually £25 or £30). A banker's draft, on the other hand, or an authenticated undertaking from a solicitor that a cheque will be met, can always be accepted.

CLINCHING THE DEAL When the car is handed over, there is no requirement in law that the sale should be recorded in writing. Nor does the seller gain any advantage from doing so.

## Selling to a garage

A car owner selling to a garage has the same obligations as when he sells privately—he must give accurate information about the vehicle, and make sure that it is roadworthy. If he takes the car on the road, he must make sure it is taxed, insured and where applicable has a current Annual Vehicle Test certificate.

If he is trading his car in, he should shop around for the best deal among dealers in the type of vehicle he wishes to buy. Compare not only trade-in allowances but also the price on the road of the new car.

A monthly publication, *Parker's New, Used and Trade Car Price Guide*, gives a list of current trade-in prices.

Anyone selling to a garage for cash should

again shop around, and deal only with a dealer whose reputation is sufficient guarantee that his cheque will be honoured.

### Selling by auction

Car auctions are advertised in local newspapers and the trade Press. Sellers usually complete a form which describes the car and its condition in general terms. Once the car has been entered for an auction it can be withdrawn only after paying a fee.

Before entering a car for an auction, find out what the auctioneer's charge will be—including what fee (if any) he will expect if the vehicle is not sold.

Auctioneers may charge a fixed fee, or one based on the price the car fetches, or a combination of both. Typical charges are a £1 entry fee, with 5 per cent of the selling price up to £300 and 1 per cent commission on the remainder.

Find out whether there are any charges in addition to commission—for handling or storage, for example.

Most auctions allow the seller to name a reserve price—that is, a price below which the car will not be sold. If a reserve price is put on the vehicle, the fact must be announced at the sale, though the amount will not usually be disclosed.

A reserve price is a useful safeguard against the car being sold for a pittance. But be realistic in setting a price; there is no point in ending up with an unsold car and possible auctioneer's charges because the reserve price is over-optimistic.

Make sure any reserve price is recorded in writing. If the auctioneer sells at below the agreed reserve, the seller is entitled in law to recover the car from the buyer. In practice this is difficult, and the seller may have to sue the auctioneer for breach of contract.

If a seller wants to bid at the auction to force the price up, he must agree this in advance with the auctioneer and the fact that the seller reserves the right to bid must be announced in advance at the auction. Then bids may be made by only one person representing the seller—the seller himself or someone acting for him, but not both. Bidding by the seller may make potential buyers reluctant to bid.

If no announcement is made, it is illegal for the seller (or anyone acting on his behalf) to bid, and for the auctioneer to accept bids from him.

In law, the auctioneer is the agent of the seller. If the auctioneer makes false statements about the vehicle, a buyer may be able to sue both seller and auctioneer. The seller will be able to defend the action if he can show that the auctioneer made the statement without authority.

### Notifying change of ownership

Once the car has been sold, the seller must notify change of ownership to the licensing department of the local authority with which the car is registered. He can do so on a special postcard available at post offices.

Alternatively he can write to the authority giving his own name and address, the name and address of the new owner, and the registration mark of the car.

Failure to notify the local authority is punishable with a fine of up to £20.

---

## Disposing of a worn-out vehicle

ANYONE who wants to dispose of a car which is too old and worn-out to be saleable can take it to the local authority refuse dump designated for this purpose, where it will be accepted free of charge.

If it is not possible to drive the car to the dump, the local authority engineer's department will collect it for a fee.

Disposing of an unwanted vehicle, or any part of it, by simply leaving it on the road, at the side of the road or on open land is an offence. Penalties, which vary according to where the car is left, include fines of up to £100 for a first offence; for later offences, maximum penalties are up to three months' imprisonment, and a fine of up to £100, or both.

If a car is left on a public road and appears to have been abandoned—because the tyres are deflated or it displays no current excise licence, for example—the local authority may attach a notice warning that the vehicle will be disposed of after a stated period unless it is removed.

If the car is still there at the end of the period, it is removed by the council, and the owner—if he can be traced—has to pay the cost of removing and disposing of it.

# Penalties for motoring offenders

*Disqualification*    *'Mitigating grounds'*
*Endorsement*    *'Special reasons'*

A DRIVER found guilty of a motoring offence faces a fine or, for the more serious offences, a prison sentence. In addition, there are some offences for which a motorist may be banned from driving; or details of his offence may be endorsed (written) on his licence as a first step to a ban.

All motoring offences are first heard in a magistrates' court. After a preliminary hearing, the most serious may be transferred to a Crown Court. In a higher court a charge is heard 'on indictment', that is, in answer to a written statement of the alleged offence.

## Disqualification

The threat of losing his licence is what most effectively deters a motorist from breaking the law. There are two kinds of disqualification:

COMPULSORY DISQUALIFICATION A driver convicted of any of the more serious motoring offences must be disqualified for at least a year—unless there are 'special reasons' for not doing so. 'Special reasons' is a legal term that limits a court's right to act leniently.

Any driver convicted of certain drink-driving offences for a second time within ten years must be disqualified for at least three years unless there are 'special reasons' for not doing so. These offences are driving or attempting to drive when unfit through drink or drugs, driving with excess alcohol in the blood, or refusing to give a specimen of blood or urine after driving or attempting to drive.

DISCRETIONARY DISQUALIFICATION For certain lesser offences a court can disqualify or not, as it thinks fit.

Disqualification bars a driver from holding any type of driving licence. The courts have no hesitation in jailing anyone who drives while disqualified.

A disqualification comes into force the moment it is ordered by the court. A person who drives after the date on which he has been disqualified commits an offence even although he has not received notification.

The court takes possession of the offender's driving licence, and sends it to the licensing authority to be kept for the period of the disqualification.

Where a lengthy disqualification has been imposed, a motorist is sometimes entitled to apply to the court to have the disqualification lifted early. The motorist must have been disqualified for two years or more, and at least half of the period must have elapsed. No application can be made for at least two years.

## Endorsement

When convicting for any of the offences where disqualification is possible, a court must order the details of the conviction and sentence to be endorsed on the defendant's licence, unless there are 'special reasons'. Here, 'special reasons' are the same as for disqualification.

If three endorsements are entered on a licence within three years (from the date of the first conviction to the date of the third offence), the court must disqualify the holder for at least six months, unless there are 'mitigating grounds' for doing otherwise.

The phrase 'mitigating grounds', which was deliberately chosen to differ from 'special reasons', gives the court greater flexibility.

## 'Mitigating grounds' and 'special reasons'

No Act of Parliament defines either 'mitigating grounds' or 'special reasons'. It is left to the courts to decide when they apply.

MITIGATING GROUNDS A court can decide not to disqualify a driver whose licence has been endorsed three times within three years if anything about the offence or the offender himself makes this desirable.

Thus a motorist might escape disqualification if a court regarded the circumstances of his offence as meriting leniency, or if there are personal reasons why he might suffer undue hardship—because he drives for a living, for example, or because he is an invalid.

SPECIAL REASONS A court has the right to depart from the strict requirements for compulsory disqualification or for endorsing licences if there are special reasons. Unlike mitigating grounds, special reasons relate only to the circumstances of the *offence*, not to the particular circumstances of the *driver*.

Motorists who have successfully claimed that special reasons applied to them include: A driver to whom a drug had been administered without his knowledge; one whose drink had been laced without his knowledge; a driver convicted of driving while unfit through drink or drugs who drank a small amount of beer while unaware that he was suffering from diabetes; a disqualified motorist who moved a car a few yards when ordered to do so by a policeman, because the chauffeur normally

provided by his firm was not available at that time to drive it.

The following motorists have been ruled *not* to have special reasons for disqualification or endorsement: a motorist whose licence was essential for his livelihood; a motorist who drove with blood alcohol only a fraction above

## How motoring offences are punished

| OFFENCE | MAXIMUM PENALTY | USUAL PENALTY | WILL THE LICENCE BE ENDORSED? | CAN THE OFFENDER BE DISQUALIFIED? |
|---|---|---|---|---|
| **LICENCE** | | | | |
| Driving without a current licence | £50 | £2–£5 | Only if driver has not passed test and breaks provisional licence regulations or drives vehicle barred to him | Yes (at court's discretion) provided the offence is one for which endorsement is possible |
| Failing to sign driving licence | £20 | 50p–£2 | No | No |
| Driving while under age | £50 | Depends on age and circumstances | Yes | Yes (at the court's discretion) |
| Driving with uncorrected eyesight | £50 or 3 months' jail | £2–£10 | Yes | Yes (discretionary, although licence may be revoked) |
| Refusing to submit to eyesight test | £50 | £2–£10 | Yes | Yes (discretionary, although licence may be revoked) |
| Driving while disqualified | £50 and/or six months' jail (on indictment £100 and/or 12 months' jail) | Anything from a £10 fine to imprisonment | Yes | Yes (at the court's discretion) |
| Obtaining a licence when disqualified | £50 and/or six months' jail | Anything from a £10 fine to imprisonment | No | No |
| Making false statement to obtain a driving licence | £100 and/or four months' jail | Anything from a £10 fine to imprisonment | No | No |
| Failing to produce licence to police or traffic warden | £50 | 50p–£2 | No | No |

the limit; a motorist whose driving did not cause the accident in which he was involved; a man who was convicted for driving while uninsured and who said he was wealthy enough to meet any possible claims; a motorist whose driving ability was not impaired, even though he was driving with excess alcohol in the blood; a disabled driver who claimed that he would be stranded if he was banned from driving.

Sometimes, when convicting a motorist and imposing a penalty, a court will, in addition, order a motorist's licence to be suspended until he passes a fresh driving test.

| OFFENCE | MAXIMUM PENALTY | USUAL PENALTY | WILL THE LICENCE BE ENDORSED? | CAN THE OFFENDER BE DISQUALIFIED? |
|---|---|---|---|---|
| Failing to produce licence to court | £50 | £2–£5 | No—but once the court has ordered a driver to produce his licence it is suspended until he does so | |
| Forging driving licence | £100 and/or four months' jail (on indictment up to two years) | Anything from a £10 fine to imprisonment | No | No |
| Using a driving licence with intent to deceive | £100 and/or four months' jail (on indictment up to two years) | Anything from a £10 fine to imprisonment | No | No |
| **PROVISIONAL LICENCE** Provisional licence-holder not accompanied by qualified driver | £50 | £5–£10 | Yes | Yes (at the court's discretion) |
| Provisional licence-holder driving without L plates | £50 | £3–£8 | Yes | Yes (at the court's discretion) |
| Provisional licence-holder towing caravan or trailer | £50 | £5–£10 | Yes | Yes (at the court's discretion) |
| Provisional motor-cycle licence-holder carrying an unauthorised passenger | £50 | £5–£10 | Yes | Yes (at the court's discretion) |
| Provisional licence-holder driving on motorway | £50 | £5–£10 | Yes | Yes (at the court's discretion) |
| Attempting to bribe driving-test examiner | £200 and/or four months' jail (two years on indictment) | Anything from a fine to imprisonment | No | No |

continued▶

## How motoring offences are punished continued

| OFFENCE | MAXIMUM PENALTY | USUAL PENALTY | WILL THE LICENCE BE ENDORSED? | CAN THE OFFENDER BE DISQUALIFIED? |
|---|---|---|---|---|
| **CONDITION OF VEHICLE** | | | | |
| Using motor vehicle in a dangerous condition | £50 (£200 if goods vehicle) | £5–£20 | Yes | Yes (at the court's discretion). Not if offender proves he neither knew nor ought to have known that the offence would be committed |
| Using motor vehicle with defective steering gear, brakes or tyre | £50 (£200 if goods vehicle) | £5–£20 | Yes | |
| Using motor vehicle with dangerously insecure load | £50 | £5–£20 | No | No |
| Using motor vehicle with defective silencer | £50 | £2–£10 | No | No |
| Using motor vehicle without lights (or any other breach of lighting regulations) | £50 | 50p–£10 | No | No |
| Any breach of Construction and Use Regulations. □ Law on car safety, p. 39 | £50 | 50p–£5 | No | No |
| Using vehicle without current test certificate | £50 | £2–£5 | No | No |
| **DRIVING** | | | | |
| Driving motor vehicle without having proper control | £50 | £2–£5 | No | No |
| Dangerous or reckless driving | £100 and/or four months' jail (on indictment two years) | £15–£50 | Yes | Yes (compulsory only if convicted of dangerous or reckless driving or causing death by dangerous driving in previous three years) |
| Causing death by dangerous or reckless driving | Five years' jail | Depends entirely on circumstances of the case | Yes | Yes (compulsory disqualification for at least 12 months unless there are 'special reasons') |
| Manslaughter by the driver of a motor vehicle | Life imprisonment | Depends entirely on circumstances of the case | Yes | Yes (compulsory disqualification for at least 12 months unless there are 'special reasons') |

| OFFENCE | MAXIMUM PENALTY | USUAL PENALTY | WILL THE LICENCE BE ENDORSED? | CAN THE OFFENDER BE DISQUALIFIED? |
|---|---|---|---|---|
| Driving without due care and attention | £100 (for subsequent offence and/or three months' jail) | £5–£30 | Yes | Yes (at the court's discretion) |
| Driving without reasonable consideration for other road users | £100 (for subsequent offence and/or three months' jail) | £5–£30 | Yes | Yes (at the court's discretion) |
| Reversing vehicle for unreasonable distance | £50 | £2–£5 | No | No |
| Sounding motor-vehicle horn during prohibited hours, or while vehicle is stationary | £50 | £2–£5 | No | No |
| Failing to stop after an accident. Failing to report an accident | £50 and/or three months' jail | £5–£20 | Yes | Yes (at the court's discretion) |
| Alleged careless or dangerous driver failing to give name and address to others involved | £20 (subsequent offence £50 or three months' jail) | £2–£5 | No | No |
| Failing to observe a maximum speed limit | £50 | £5–£15 (many courts fine 50p for each mph above the limit) | Yes | Yes (at the court's discretion) |
| Failing to observe a minimum speed limit | £50 | * | No | No |
| Failing to obey signal by police officer or traffic warden | £50 | £5–£20 | Yes | Yes (at the court's discretion) |
| Failing to comply with traffic light signals, a stop sign or double white lines | £50 | £5–£20 | Yes | Yes (at the court's discretion) |
| Failing to stop at pedestrian crossing or school crossing | £50 | £5–£20 | Yes | Yes (at the court's discretion) |

* Prosecutions are brought so rarely that no 'usual penalty' can be given.

continued ▶

## How motoring offences are punished continued

| OFFENCE | MAXIMUM PENALTY | USUAL PENALTY | WILL THE LICENCE BE ENDORSED? | CAN THE OFFENDER BE DISQUALIFIED? |
|---|---|---|---|---|
| Driving a prohibited vehicle on motorway | £50 | £5–£20 | Yes | Yes (at the court's discretion) |
| Opening door of motor vehicle, causing danger or injury to other road users | £50 | £5–£20 | No | No |
| **DRINK AND DRUGS** | | | | |
| Driving or attempting to drive a motor vehicle while unfit through drink or drugs | £100 and/or four months' jail (two years on indictment) | £15–£50 | Yes | Yes (compulsory) |
| Being in charge of motor vehicle while unfit through drink or drugs | £100 and/or four months' jail (12 months on indictment) | £10–£30 | Yes | Yes (at the court's discretion) |
| Driving or attempting to drive a motor vehicle with excessive alcohol in the blood | £100 and/or four months' jail (two years on indictment) | £15–£50 | Yes | Yes (compulsory) |
| Being in charge of motor vehicle with excessive alcohol in the blood | £100 and/or four months' jail (12 months on indictment) | £10–£30 | Yes | Yes (at the court's discretion) |
| Failing to provide a specimen for the police laboratory test after driving or attempting to drive motor vehicle | £100 and/or four months' jail (two years on indictment) | £15–£50 | Yes | Yes (compulsory) |
| Failing to provide a specimen for test after being in charge of a motor vehicle | £100 and/or four months' jail (12 months on indictment) | £10–£30 | Yes | Yes (at the court's discretion) |
| Refusing to take a breathalyser test | £50 | £2–£5 | †No | †No |

†Although a driver cannot have his licence endorsed or be disqualified for refusing to take a breathalyser test, the police have powers to arrest without warrant any driver, person attempting to drive, or person in charge of a motor vehicle, whom they suspect of having alcohol in his body, and take him to a police station.

There he must be offered another breath test and, if it proves positive, he must provide samples of blood or urine. Anyone who, in these circumstances, fails to provide a blood or urine sample without valid reason is committing the offence of refusing to provide a sample for laboratory analysis, for which he is likely to be disqualified. ☐ Compulsory and discretionary disqualification, p. 173.

| OFFENCE | MAXIMUM PENALTY | USUAL PENALTY | WILL THE LICENCE BE ENDORSED? | CAN THE OFFENDER BE DISQUALIFIED? |
|---|---|---|---|---|
| **INSURANCE** Using motor vehicle with no third-party insurance | £50 and/or three months' jail | £5–£20 | Yes | Yes (at the court's discretion) |
| Failing to produce a certificate of insurance | £50 | 50p–£3 | No | No |
| Making a false statement to obtain an insurance certificate | £100 and/or four months' jail | From £10 to a term of imprisonment | No | No |
| Forging, altering or using a certificate of insurance with intent to deceive | £100 and/or four months' jail (two years on indictment) | From £10 to a term of imprisonment | No | No |
| **TAXATION AND REGISTRATION** Using vehicle without current excise licence | £50 or five times the annual rate of duty, whichever is the greater | £5–£20 plus any duty lost | No | No |
| Using vehicle not exhibiting excise licence in the correct position | £20 | 50p–£5 | No | No |
| Making a false statement to obtain an excise licence | £200 (on indictment two years' jail) | £10–£30 | No | No |
| Fraudulently using an excise licence | £200 (on indictment two years' jail) | £10–£30 | No | No |
| Using motor vehicle not displaying registration mark or with obscured registration mark | £20 (£50 for a subsequent offence) | 50p–£5 | No | No |
| Failing to register a motor vehicle | £50 | * | No | No |
| Failing to notify change of ownership or change in construction of motor vehicle | £50 | 50p–£5 | No | No |

*Prosecutions are brought so rarely that no 'usual penalty' can be given.

continued ▶

## How motoring offences are punished continued

| OFFENCE | MAXIMUM PENALTY | USUAL PENALTY | WILL THE LICENCE BE ENDORSED? | CAN THE OFFENDER BE DISQUALIFIED? |
|---|---|---|---|---|
| **PARKING** Causing wilful or unnecessary obstruction with a motor vehicle | £50 | 50p–£5 | No | No |
| Leaving motor vehicle in a dangerous position | £50 | £5–£20 | Yes | Yes (at the court's discretion) |
| Leaving motor vehicle without applying handbrake or with engine running | £50 | 50p–£5 | No | No |
| Stopping on approach to a zebra crossing | £50 | £2–£10 | Yes | Yes (at the court's discretion) |
| Parking on offside of road at night | £50 | 50p–£5 | No | No |
| Waiting in a prohibited area | £20 | £2–£5 | No | No |
| Failing to comply with parking-meter regulations | £5 (£10 for subsequent offence) | £2–£5 | No | No |
| Failing to pay an excess parking charge | £5 (£10 for subsequent offence) | £2–£5 | No | No |
| Failing to comply with waiting or loading regulations | £20 | £2–£5 | No | No |
| Stopping motor vehicle on motorway hard shoulder other than in an emergency | £20 | £2–£5 | No | No |
| **OTHER OFFENCES** Selling, supplying or offering for sale an unroadworthy motor vehicle | £100 | £2–£100 | No | No |
| Giving driving instruction for payment when not a registered driving instructor | £100 and/or four months' jail | * | No | No |

*Prosecutions are brought so rarely that no 'usual penalty' can be given.

# YOUR HOME

# Deciding what you can afford

*The size of the loan*
*The amount of ready cash*
*Lender's valuation*

*Selling and buying*
*Bridging loans*

THE potential home-buyer, before he decides what price and type of house he can afford, has first to consider his financial position and calculate:

How much can he hope to borrow?

What can he afford in weekly, monthly or quarterly mortgage repayments?

How much can he hope to have in ready cash, either from savings, or from the sale of his present property?

How much of this ready cash will be needed for legal fees, moving expenses and so on?

How much money will that leave for a deposit on the new property?

## The size of the loan

Few people have enough capital to be able to pay for a house outright; and probably many who could afford it prefer to put their money into a more profitable investment, buying their home with a loan or a mortgage.

The size and availability of mortgages are major factors in determining what the house-buyer can afford.

There is no hard-and-fast rule about how much an individual will be allowed to borrow. It depends partly on income, and partly on the age and type of house.

First, to be eligible for any mortgage at all, the buyer must have a regular source of income. He will be asked to give the name of someone—usually his employer—who will vouch for this. If the potential home-buyer is self-employed or works freelance, the lender may accept evidence of regular income from his accountant, his bank manager or the firm for which he does most work. Occasionally they may accept his own accounts.

The borrower must also have a good credit record. No building society, local authority or insurance company will risk its money on a man with a long history of county court judgments against him for debt.

When it comes to deciding the size of the loan, the main consideration which lenders take into account is the applicant's earning power; as a rule of thumb, the maximum loan over 25 years will be somewhere between two-and-a-half and three times the borrower's annual gross income. Overtime earnings and

any income the borrower's wife earns are not usually included by most lenders.

There may be special cases where a woman is granted a mortgage or a wife's salary can be taken into account, but in general it is considered that a woman's income is always liable to fluctuate as she may need to spend more of her time at home with her family.

A lender will also want to be sure that the borrower can make regular repayments. For this reason they will normally insist that he should have to repay in a month no more than his earnings for a week after deducting income tax, National Insurance and pension contributions.

## The amount of ready cash

The buyer will, of course, need to have ready cash available to make up the difference between the loan and the purchase price of his home. He will also need money to pay legal and other fees, and to cover the expense of moving house and the cost of any new curtains, carpets or furniture needed in the new home.

Any organisation that lends money for house-buying will lay down not only the maximum loan it will make to any particular borrower, but also the maximum it will lend on any particular property.

To do this, it arranges for a professional valuer to inspect the property. His job is to decide how much money it could be sold for if the borrower failed to keep up the mortgage repayments. Naturally his valuation will be a cautious one, often less than the price the buyer is paying.

The maximum loan possible on the property is then given as a percentage of this valuation —say 80 per cent or 90 per cent. In rare cases where the purchase price is lower than this valuation, the percentage of the loan is based on the purchase price.

Some lenders issue guide-lines on the percentage loans for which different ages and types of property may qualify. Generally the highest percentages are for newer properties built on conventional lines, with lower amounts for houses built before the First World War.

The home-buyer with only a small amount

of ready cash may be able to get a 95 per cent advance if he chooses a type favoured by lenders—modern and of conventional design.

It would be unwise to base home-buying plans on hopes of getting a 100 per cent loan. Though such loans are made occasionally, they are uncommon for a number of reasons, not least because many lenders—among them building societies—prefer the borrower to have a personal stake in his home from the start.

### Lender's valuation
Even where the buyer obtains a 95 per cent loan, this will not necessarily mean that he has to find only 5 per cent of the price. Where the lender has valued the property at less than the purchase price, the borrower will also have to make up the difference.

The calculation might be like this:

| | |
|---|---|
| Purchase price | £6500 |
| Lender's valuation: £6000 Advance: 95 per cent of £6000 | £5700 |
| Buyer must find balance of | £800 |

There is no way of telling in advance whether a lender will value a house at much less than the purchase price. The buyer can only apply for a mortgage and wait to see what size of loan he is offered. If this proves less than he needs to go through with the purchase, he should be able to withdraw.

Alternatively, he may try to borrow the balance elsewhere, though this will be difficult. If the home-buyer's income is sufficient, his bank may agree to a short-term loan. If his employer values his services highly, the firm may be willing to help. Some people may be able to make private arrangements with a relative or friend.

Perhaps the most common source of a loan would be a finance company, which may be willing to lend on a second mortgage. But there are serious disadvantages in borrowing in this way. Charges and rates of interest on such loans are high (over 20 per cent is usual), and terms are often bad.

There is also the likelihood that the lender providing the first mortgage will withdraw its offer if a second mortgage is involved. Many building societies and insurance companies take the view that the heavy repayments required by a second mortgage are likely to place too great a strain on the buyer's resources. ☐ Personal loans and second mortgages, p. 506.

In addition to the cost of the land, bricks and mortar, there are other expenses which have to be met when any property is bought: legal fees, the cost of having the property surveyed, the lender's valuation fee, and compulsory government duty on the transaction.

These vary considerably from one property to another and are normally based on the purchase price of the house or flat, and the amount of the mortgage. They may amount to between 3 and 5 per cent of the purchase price. As soon as he moves in, the new owner may have to find money for rates and insurance premiums. ☐ Counting the cost, p. 213.

In total, therefore, the buyer can expect to have to find in cash the equivalent of at least 8–10 per cent of the agreed price.

### Selling and buying
Anybody with a house to sell may not need such substantial savings; he will have the proceeds from the sale of his present property after paying off his mortgage. He should bear in mind, however, that the legal expenses of the move will be higher.

In addition to the costs of house purchase, there will be solicitor's and estate agent's fees for selling the present house; these could amount to some 4 or 5 per cent of the selling price. There will also be expenses and fees for paying off the existing mortgage. These costs will depend on the lender's rules and on how long the mortgage has to run.

In general the newer the mortgage is, the more expensive it will be to terminate, for the lender will make some charge to compensate for the interest which would have been payable if the loan had run its course.

The difficulty in buying and selling at the same time is getting money from the sale of the house in time to meet the expenses of buying. Ten per cent of the purchase price has to be handed over at exchange of contracts—even before the purchase has been completed—and the buyer has to provide some or all of this, depending on the size of his mortgage. ☐ Exchanging contracts, p. 205.

### Bridging loans
A bank may be able to help by providing a bridging loan to cover the time when the money is needed but has not yet been handed over. This is a matter of individual negotiation with the bank manager.

Occasionally it happens the other way round; the sale of the present home is agreed, but the purchase of the new one falls through. In such cases a solicitor may be able to delay completing the sale while his client finds another property. When this is not possible, the seller may be obliged to move out and incur the expense of temporary accommodation while the search for a new home goes on.

# Looking for a home to buy

*Getting to know the district*  
*Choosing between freehold and leasehold*  
*Special kinds of property*

*New houses*  
*Estate agents*

HOUSE-HUNTING can be a long and arduous process. But the buyer can save time and effort in the long run by starting with a number of general inquiries about the district of his choice, finding out about its amenities, its possible disadvantages and the types of housing available.

**Getting to know the district**  
Drive, cycle or walk around an area that is new to you, to get the feel of the community. Make several visits, at different times of the day and week. Do not assume that streets which are quiet on a Sunday afternoon remain so for the rest of the week.

This groundwork will show the kind of property available. Back this up by studying estate agents' windows, to get an idea of the price range of local houses and flats.

CHECKING DEVELOPMENT PLANS Telephone the nearest council offices and ask which authority is responsible for planning; usually it is a borough or a county council. Then go to this planning department and

## Differences between freehold and leasehold property

|  | FREEHOLD | LEASEHOLD |
|---|---|---|
| Price | Older properties are generally more expensive; new freehold properties are likely to be similar in price to new properties with a lease of 99 or 999 years. | Likely to be cheaper than similar freehold property—how much cheaper depends on how long the lease has still to run. |
| Mortgage | Mortgages on houses are usually easier to obtain. Mortgages on flats and maisonettes may be more difficult to obtain because there is no landlord responsible for maintenance of common parts: for example, stairs and corridors. | Building societies often refuse loans unless the lease will have at least 40 years to run *after* the loan has been paid off. High-percentage loans may not be granted unless special insurance arrangements are made. □ Applying for a mortgage, p. 194. |
| Rent | Nothing to pay. But freehold properties are sometimes subject to a charge on the land, known as a 'rent charge'. This is particularly common in Bristol, Teesside and Manchester. | Occupier has to pay annual ground rent—£5 to £50 is common. |
| Security | The occupier can be evicted only if: **1.** He fails to keep up with his mortgage repayments. **2.** The property is compulsorily purchased by the Government or the local or other authority. □ Threats to the home, p. 300. | The occupier can be evicted if: **1.** He fails to keep up with his mortgage repayments. **2.** The property is compulsorily purchased by the Government or the local authority or other authority. **3.** He fails to pay the ground rent. **4.** He breaks any other term of the lease. **5.** The lease expires. Alternatively he may be entitled, under the Leasehold Reform Act 1967, to buy the freehold before or when the lease expires, even if the owner does not want to sell; or he may be entitled to have the lease extended at a low ground rent. Buyers interested in a leasehold property should ask their solicitor whether it will eventually qualify under the Act. □ Security for leaseholders, p. 232. |

inquire about major development schemes outlined either in the authority's Structure Plan or in its Development Plan.

Changes may be imminent which could affect the whole appearance of the district and make it a very different place to live in. There may be plans for a new motorway or other road scheme, town centre redevelopment, new estates and so on.

Do not be concerned at this stage about detailed changes which might affect particular streets or houses; there will be time enough later to check on what will happen to any particular property. Concentrate on getting the overall picture, and deciding whether any likely changes make it necessary to rule out the area, or parts of it, as a place to live.

TRANSPORT Find out what form of transport members of the family will have to use to get to work or school. Check the frequency of the public services, and the times of first and last buses and trains. How much will fares cost? Is it possible to get a season ticket?

A journey on the bus or train during the rush hour will show how long it takes, and how convenient the service is. If members of the family intend to travel to work by car, drive over the route—again preferably during the rush hour.

EDUCATION The accessibility of schools of the right type and the quality of education in them can be major factors for many families in choosing a place to live.

The local council office will be able to supply the basic information about where the schools are and what system of secondary education is in force. But they are not likely to pass on information about the reputation of a school. One way to discover this is to ask prospective neighbours. Another is to visit the school and talk to the headmaster or headmistress.

Parents with very young children should be

| | FREEHOLD | LEASEHOLD |
|---|---|---|
| Repairs | The occupier may be obliged to do certain repairs and maintenance under the terms of his mortgage. Otherwise he can carry out repairs and maintenance or do none, as he pleases. | The occupier is normally obliged to keep the property in a good state of repair, and sometimes to repaint at specified intervals. At the end of the lease, the property may have to be handed back to the ground landlord in a good state of repair. |
| Alterations | The occupier is free to make any alterations he wishes, provided consent is obtained from the local authority where this is necessary. ☐ Repairs and improvements, p. 223. | The occupier's right to make alterations may be limited by: **1.** The need to obtain consent of the ground landlord; **2.** The need to obtain consent from the appropriate local authority. ☐ Repairs and improvements, p. 223. |
| Use | In general, property can be used for any purpose—as a home, an office, a boarding-house, even a factory. This right can be limited only by: **1.** The need to get planning permission if the use of the premises is changed, say from a private home to an office. ☐ Repairs and improvements, p. 223. **2.** Any restrictions inherited from previous owners of the property in the form of restrictive covenants. | Property can be used only for purposes stated in the lease—usually as a 'private dwelling-house'. |
| Investment | Property frequently increases in value. | Capital value may increase in rapidly improving areas, or if there is more than 40 years to run; value may tend to diminish when the lease has less than 40 years unexpired, and is lost completely when the lease expires, unless the leaseholder qualifies to buy the freehold under the Leasehold Reform Act 1967. ☐ Security for leaseholders, p. 232. |

able to get information about nursery schools from the council's education department. Details of local playgroups may be available from the council's social services department, which is responsible for registering them. Failing that, write to the Pre-School Playgroups Association, Alford House, Aveline Street, London SE11 5DQ.

THE RISK OF FLOODING Property on low-lying ground, especially near a river or the sea, may be liable to damage from flooding. To find out if there is recurrent danger, contact the council surveyor's or engineer's department. They are responsible for flood prevention and rescue; they will know if flooding occurs and may have maps showing the extent of previous flooding.

AMENITIES An hour spent browsing through back copies of the local newspaper will yield useful information about amenities, such as places of entertainment and social, political and religious organisations.

### Choosing between freehold and leasehold

At some stage the home-buyer has to choose between the two main classes of property, freehold and leasehold. Most houses are freehold; most flats and maisonettes are leasehold.

Where property is freehold, there is no time-limit on the owner's possession. Where property is leasehold, the occupier of the property merely leases it for a set period—usually 99 or 999 years in the case of a new house, but often a shorter period in the case of an older building. He pays an annual sum, known as the 'ground rent', to the freehold owner of the land, who is sometimes called the ground landlord. A ground rent of between £5 and £50 is common. ☐ Differences between freehold and leasehold property, p. 184.

### Special kinds of property

It is sometimes difficult to obtain a mortgage on certain types of property—period houses and cottages, heavily timbered houses and properties with an unusual design. This is because building societies and other lenders know from experience that should they have to call in a mortgage they may have difficulty in re-selling such houses. If you are considering buying an unconventional house, bear this problem in mind.

### New houses

The buyer looking for a new house may have to commit himself before the property is built. There are, however, a number of ways of ensuring that he does not suffer because of bad workmanship on the part of the firm which is building the house. Inspecting other houses the builder has erected is one way of checking what kind of quality to expect. Similarly, talking to people who already have houses put up by the builder may give a good idea of any problems involved.

The best safeguard is to deal with a builder registered with the National House-Builders' Registration Council. A list is kept by libraries, Citizens' Advice Bureaux and building society offices. Anyone buying a house from a registered builder has a guarantee that serious defects will be put right. ☐ The guarantee with a new house, p. 187.

As the list is revised every six months, it is possible for the name of a builder who has been expelled to appear on the current register. So ask the builder whether he will guarantee the house under the N.H.B.R.C. scheme. Only a small number of houses are currently built without the guarantee, which is often a condition of granting a mortgage.

A house built by a registered N.H.B.R.C. firm can still be refused a guarantee certificate if it fails to come up to standard. To protect himself the home-buyer should ensure, preferably through his solicitor, that any contract he signs gives him the right to withdraw, and have his deposit returned in full, if the house is refused a certificate. The contract should give him a similar right if the price rises unreasonably during building.

### Estate agents

Most of the property for sale in the district will be in the hands of local estate agents, who will be happy to supply details free of charge. Let them know the type of property wanted—house, flat or maisonette—the price range, number of bedrooms and any special requirements, such as a garage, large garden or central heating.

A maisonette usually offers less privacy than a house, because the garden and other facilities may have to be shared. People who move into flats have still less privacy.

Although completely self-contained and usually with its own front door, a flat will almost certainly have a lift or staircase which is shared, and possibly common gardens and garage space.

In some cases, central heating may be provided on a shared basis, and there may be a service charge for caretakers, porters, and so on. Flat-dwellers have to be much more prepared to co-operate with neighbours—especially over such matters as common television aerials and passageway decoration.

Most agents compile a list or register of

properties for sale and send out details to interested buyers daily or weekly.

Remember, though, that an estate agent is a salesman employed and paid by the seller. His advice should be regarded in this light.

The estate agent is under no obligation to provide *all* the information about a house. Unless he is asked, he need not mention that it has dry rot or that it is opposite a noisy club.

He must, however, take pains to see that the information he provides is accurate, and he must answer questions truthfully. Anyone who buys a property on the basis of false information provided verbally or in writing by an estate agent—or by the seller or his solicitor—would have grounds for legal action under the Misrepresentation Act 1967.

Even reputable agents try to protect themselves by including in their written particulars a disclaimer saying that the accuracy of the information is not guaranteed. Though it has not been tested in the courts since the Misrepresentation Act was passed, this disclaimer may give them a safeguard against legal action.

It means, too, that the buyer should regard agents' particulars as no more than a useful guide, and should check their accuracy.

When agents are used in this way, it costs the buyer nothing; it is the seller who is responsible for paying the agent.

It is possible, however, for a buyer to engage an agent to find him a house. In such a case, the buyer pays the agent a fee based on the value of the house. On a £6500 house it will be about £150; on a £10,000 home, £200.

Although this method of finding a house is apparently expensive, it can result in savings. It is used most often by buyers who know the type of house they want, usually a property in the high price range. After finding a suitable house, the agent may be able to negotiate a price reduction, saving the buyer much more than the amount of his own fee.

There are other ways of finding properties for sale, apart from going directly to an agent. Some houses display a 'For Sale' notice in the garden; and many private sellers, as well as agents, advertise property in newspapers. If a house is sold privately, no estate agent's fee is normally due, so the price may be lower.

## The guarantee with a new house

THE certificate of the National House-Builders' Registration Council is normally issued as soon as the house has been completed and inspected. It provides a guarantee for two years against such minor faults as poor decoration, badly fitting doors, rusty gutters and faulty plumbing. Normal wear and tear and shrinkage are excluded, and central-heating systems are normally guaranteed for only one year.

The owner is also protected for ten years from the time the house is completed against any major defect—up to a value of £5000. This covers subsidence, dry rot, collapse or serious distortion, and chemical failure of any materials used.

The scheme is designed to protect the house-owner against faulty building without relieving him of the normal obligation of maintenance and keeping his home in good repair. The scheme does not pay for repairs to damage caused by the weather, or accidents which are usually covered under a normal insurance policy.

After six years the owner has to meet the first £15 of any claim that is accepted by the N.H.B.R.C. He also has to pay for any inspec-

Builders offering homes with a ten-year guarantee display the symbol of the National House-Builders' Registration Council

**REGISTERED HOUSE-BUILDER**

tion by an N.H.B.R.C. surveyor, though this survey fee is returned if the council thinks the claim reasonable.

Where a dispute between a builder and a purchaser cannot be resolved, it is submitted to arbitration by an independent professional expert. His decision is final.

If a builder should become bankrupt or go out of business during the ten-year guarantee period, or if he should refuse to abide by the arbitrator's decision, the council will honour any award that has been made to the house-owner. But the council will only be liable for up to £5000 on any one house, with a total limit of £250,000 for all claims against a single builder in a year.

The rights of the guarantee are passed to any owner who takes over the house any time within the ten-year period.

# Choosing a solicitor

*Do-it-yourself home-buying*　　*The seller's solicitor*
*Other help*　　　　　　　　　*The lender's solicitor*
*How to find a solicitor*　　　 *Discussing the solicitor's fee*

As soon as a home-buyer begins house-hunting in earnest, he should consider making contact with a solicitor who can handle the legal side of the deal for him and can give professional advice on all aspects of the transaction—how and where to get a mortgage, which surveyor to employ, how and when to insure and so on.

It is possible, however, to buy a house without the help of a solicitor. In some cases a house buyer can do the work himself and save legal fees.

### Do-it-yourself home-buying
The legal work involved in transferring the house is complex, time-consuming and usually handled by solicitors. But it is not necessarily beyond the ability of the intelligent layman. By law, only solicitors can do this work 'for gain', but a purchaser is entitled to do his own conveyancing. By doing so, he stands to save a substantial sum of money in fees—probably about £80 on a £6500 house bought with a 95 per cent mortgage. □ Counting the cost, p. 213.

He has to be aware, however, of the risks. He may find the work so complicated that he gets into a muddle from which only a solicitor can rescue him. He could then end up paying more in legal fees than he would if he had gone to a solicitor in the first place.

Again, there may be rival buyers to consider. It is quite legal for a seller to accept offers subject to contract from more than one buyer, although this practice is discouraged by many solicitors and estate agents.

This means that the house may go to the buyer who is quickest with the legal work. The individual who tries to do his own conveyancing will inevitably be at a disadvantage in any race with a solicitor acting for a rival buyer.

Before he finally makes up his mind whether to do the job on his own, the purchaser will need to know whether the land on which the house stands is registered or unregistered. The seller's solicitors will know the answer to this question if the seller himself cannot help.

If the house is on registered land, many of the details about it will be on file at the appropriate District Land Registry. These Registries are at Croydon, Harrow, Nottingham, Tunbridge Wells, Gloucester, Lytham St Annes, Stevenage, Durham and Plymouth. It should not be too difficult even for an inexperienced person to establish that the property on registered land really belongs to the person who is trying to sell it. All he has to do is to complete certain forms and send them to the District Land Registry.

Once this initial problem of legal ownership has been cleared up, the buyer may be able to do the legal work of conveyancing himself if he has the time and perseverance. The Consumers' Association (14 Buckingham Street, London WC2N 6DS) publishes a step-by-step guide to conveyancing.

If, on the other hand, the house is unregistered, its history has to be checked afresh every time it is sold. This will involve reading and interpreting complex documents and it is likely to prove beyond the capacity of anyone without the necessary legal training.

### Other help
There is a third course open to the buyer, apart from doing the conveyancing himself or employing a solicitor—that is to join an organisation which has been established to do this work on behalf of its members.

Such groups—the best known is probably the National House Owners' Society, of 19 Sheepcote Road, Harrow, Middlesex HA1 2JL—undertake all the conveyancing work as a service to their members. The cost is normally considerably lower than that of employing a solicitor.

The National House Owners' Society has carried out 12,500 house transactions in nine years on behalf of members, but this conveyancing is not supervised by qualified solicitors and the work usually takes longer than conveyancing carried out by a solicitor.

### How to find a solicitor
Lawyers—like doctors and dentists—are not allowed by their professional bodies to advertise their services.

Solicitors are, however, listed in the classified telephone directory, and local offices of the Citizens' Advice Bureau can provide the names of solicitors' firms practising locally.

Neither of these sources can recommend which solicitor to choose, or state whether a particular solicitor specialises in criminal cases, divorce or conveyancing.

One of the soundest ways of making this individual choice is to rely on the advice of a friend who has recently bought a property with the help of a local solicitor. The buyer's bank manager may also be able to suggest a suitable name.

In approaching a firm of solicitors for the first time, ask if they specialise in the kind of work to be undertaken. If for some reason a solicitor does not want to handle the job, he will normally suggest another firm, and he will not make a charge for giving this advice.

**The seller's solicitor**
It is never wise for the purchaser to use the same solicitor as the seller, even though it may be claimed that this speeds up the transaction.

The interests of the buyer and seller of a house sometimes conflict and the solicitor would be in a difficult professional position if he had to mediate between two of his own clients. For this reason, the Law Society discourages solicitors from acting for both parties.

**The lender's solicitor**
It is possible, however, to save on costs in some cases by using the same solicitor as the organisation which grants the mortgage to buy the house. In such a case there is unlikely to be any conflict of interests: both parties want to ensure that the house can legitimately be sold by the seller and that there are no legal drawbacks.

Most solicitors are on the panels of a number of building societies and insurance companies, so that they will be allowed to do the lender's legal work in addition to the buyer's. Some societies do not have panels but normally use the buyer's solicitor.

Other building societies insist on using an independent solicitor, and in such cases the buyer has no alternative but to pay the charges for both. This consideration may, however, influence his choice of lender.

**Discussing the solicitor's fee**
In choosing a solicitor, the home-buyer may also wish to take into account the fee he will charge. In any case, the fee should be discussed by solicitor and client at the outset.

From late 1972, a solicitor's fee for handling the legal side of buying or selling a house is usually based on the amount of work involved. Before that date, the fee was based on the price of the property and calculated on a scale laid down by law.

When the scale was abolished, the Lord Chancellor expressed the hope that abolition would lead to a stabilisation of fees, and in some cases reductions.

In negotiating a fee, the home-buyer can use the old scale as a guide. □ Counting the cost, p. 213.

In most cases he should regard this as a *maximum*. The now-defunct National Board for Prices and Incomes, which reported on the earnings of solicitors in 1968, concluded that charges on this scale were very profitable. A survey conducted for the board showed that the cost to the solicitor in the average conveyancing transaction—after allowing not only for overheads, but also for his ordinary profit—was only 55 per cent of the charge to the client.

A client should therefore think twice about agreeing to pay more than the old scale fee except in two circumstances:
**1.** Where the solicitor can show that an exceptionally large amount of work will have to be done.
**2.** Where the price of the house is unusually low. The PIB report suggested that a scale charge provided the solicitor with an inadequate income on properties costing up to £2500.

A client who is eventually asked to pay a higher charge than seems reasonable can ask to have the bill reviewed by the Law Society, or by a High Court official called a taxing master. He can ask for a review even if he has earlier agreed to the charge. □ Complaining about the bill, p. 753.

---

## How long will it take?

FROM the time the buyer first makes an offer for a house to the time when he can move in may take two or three months or even longer. During this period a lot has to be done—establishing the house's soundness and value, exchanging contracts, making sure that the property can be legally sold, arranging the mortgage, and handing over the deeds.

If the buyer is in a hurry, his solicitor may be able to speed things up. But if the seller has not yet found a new home, there is nothing to prevent his instructing his solicitor to delay matters.

# Making an offer

*Fixing the price*　　　　　　　*The preliminary deposit*
*Gazumping and price changes*　*'Do-it-yourself' contracts*
*Furniture and furnishings*　　 *Buying by auction and tender*

THE house-hunter who finds the home he wants must act quickly to prevent someone else buying it before him. Yet any hasty or ill-considered action can have unfortunate consequences. He must avoid committing himself to purchasing the property until his surveyor and solicitor have had a chance to investigate it; but at the same time he needs to convince the seller that he intends to complete the transaction unless a serious drawback is uncovered.

This means making an offer, and perhaps backing it up by the payment of a preliminary deposit as proof of good faith.

### Fixing the price

Many sellers deliberately set a high figure, to allow a margin for bargaining. The would-be purchaser may then offer a figure slightly below what he expects to pay, and eventually the two come to a compromise.

In this way, the buyer may save himself a substantial sum—though, of course, he risks losing the house if another purchaser offers the full price.

There is no easy way to work out how much to offer. In practice, the buyer will often be able to develop a shrewd idea of property values in the neighbourhood by inspecting a number of houses or flats.

It is possible, however, to get professional advice. If the house is an unusual one—a large period property, say—it may be useful to obtain a valuation from a qualified valuer before making an offer. Fees for valuations of freehold properties are on a fixed scale and work out at about £31 for a £5000 house, £49 for an £8000 one and £57 for a £10,000 house.

In some cases it may be worth paying an estate agent to negotiate the price—if, for example, the property has been on the market for some time, and there seems little danger of a rival buyer. Estate agents' fees for this service are rather high—£105 on a £7000 house, £275 on a £20,000 property, for instance—but the agent may be able to get a reduction in the purchase price which is larger than his fee.

Any offer at this stage must always be provisional; it should be made 'subject to contract and subject to survey'. This means that if further investigation reveals defects in the property or drawbacks—such as new roads to be built near by—or if the purchaser changes his mind for any other reason, he is free to back out at any time up to exchange of contracts.

### Gazumping and price changes

In times of acute property shortage and rapidly rising prices, a prospective purchaser may agree a price for a home or flat and later find the seller refuses to go ahead with the transaction unless the price is increased.

This practice of increasing a price after it has been agreed—sometimes called gazumping—can be a source of much ill-feeling between buyers and sellers. But until contracts are exchanged, the seller is within his rights in raising the price. The prospective purchaser need not accept; he can carry on bargaining, or simply withdraw.

Unhappily, there is little a prospective purchaser can do to avoid the danger of price rises. His best protection is to ensure that, between the original agreement and exchange of contracts, there is no unnecessary delay which might give the seller a pretext to ask a higher price.

In times when property is plentiful and there is a shortage of purchasers, the situation may be reversed—prospective purchasers may be able to demand a price *reduction* after the initial agreement.

### Furniture and furnishings

During negotiations over the purchase price, the seller or the seller's agent may suggest that furniture and furnishings be included in the price of the house. These can include carpets, linoleum and curtains which have been made to fit the house and would not be suitable for the seller's new property.

If possible, try to persuade the seller to agree to a separate price for the furnishings, rather than an 'all-in' figure. Such an arrangement has no effect on the mortgage advance—since this can never cover furnishings—but it does save stamp duties and Land Registry fees, which are based on the total purchase price.

It may also reduce the solicitor's fees, though since late-1972 these are normally based on work involved, not purchase price.

If furnishings are paid for separately, they need not be mentioned in the house-sale contract. An exchange of letters between the solicitors for each side will be enough to confirm the agreement.

If a separate deal is not possible, make sure, when applying for a mortgage, to tell the lender that the purchase price includes furnishings. In cases where the mortgage advance is based on a percentage of the purchase price, the value of any furnishings is usually deducted before the percentage calculation is made.

If the purchaser fails to inform the lender that furnishings are included, the original mortgage offer is likely to be scaled down later—and as a result, the purchaser may find himself unexpectedly short of funds.

The same difficulty can affect mortgage arrangements for new houses if they include cookers, refrigerators, carpets or curtains. The lender's surveyor is unlikely to take these items into account in making his valuation; and even if the mortgage is based on the purchase price, rather than the valuation, the cost of the kitchen equipment and furnishings will probably be deducted before the final calculation is made.

Where an 'all-in' price is paid for the house and furnishings, it is essential that a list of furnishings should be referred to in the house-sale contract and attached to it.

### The preliminary deposit

As soon as an offer has been made and accepted, the seller or his estate agent will probably ask for a preliminary deposit. This can range from £5 to £100, depending on the price of the property.

This deposit is not essential to the house-buying transaction, and has no significance in law. If it is made correctly, it will not bind either party to complete the transaction; the seller remains free to consider offers from other people, just as the buyer remains free to consider other properties.

The real purpose is psychological—the deposit assures the seller that the buyer is seriously interested in the property.

In paying it, the buyer must make certain that the money will be repaid in full if for any reason he decides not to buy the property.

The best safeguard is for the buyer to pay the deposit through his solicitor to the seller's solicitor who will be stakeholder.

However, this process will involve a few days' delay, and the purchaser may want to

pay immediately, in the hope of persuading the seller not to accept another offer.

In such cases he can make the payment himself. The words 'paid subject to contract and survey and to be held as stakeholder' should be written on the cheque, and repeated in any accompanying letter.

This procedure gives a great deal of protection to the buyer. Anyone who holds money 'as stakeholder' is obliged by law to look after it, not to use it for his own purposes, and not to pay it to anyone else without the written permission of the buyer. He will also be obliged to pay it back if the buyer decides not to go ahead with the transaction—for whatever reason. The cheque should be made payable to the seller's solicitor, or in some cases to the estate agent, rather than to the seller himself.

In the rare event of a solicitor going bankrupt or using a deposit he is holding dishonestly, the Compensation Fund of the solicitors' professional body, the Law Society, will normally refund the money.

A similar indemnity scheme covers deposits which are paid to estate agents where one or more of the partners is a member of the Royal Institution of Chartered Surveyors (F.R.I.C.S. and A.R.I.C.S.) or a member of the Incorporated Society of Valuers and Auctioneers (F.S.V.A. and A.S.V.A.).

Where the purchaser is buying a house which is not yet built, the developer will ask for a similar preliminary deposit—usually £50. This should be paid 'subject to contract', and it is important not to enter into any binding agreement at this stage. After making his offer, the purchaser should immediately contact his solicitor.

### 'Do-it-yourself' contracts

It sometimes happens that both the buyer and the seller are anxious to proceed with the purchase without any delay, and each may imagine that it is in his interests to 'tie-up' the other so that the transaction cannot possibly fall through.

In such circumstances they may be tempted to write out a home-made contract and both sign it, or they may ask the estate agent to arrange a contract between them.

Both these types of contract, however rough-and-ready, are likely to be legally enforceable; and both are dangerous, mainly because they commit the buyer to go through with the purchase before he is really in a position to commit himself.

The normal legal procedure allows time for the buyer to find out whether he can raise a mortgage. A do-it-yourself contract may bind him to go ahead even if his mortgage application is turned down.

Again, the house may turn out to have serious structural defects; it may be scheduled to be knocked down as part of a development scheme; the seller may have made an extension without the necessary planning permission; or there may be a restrictive covenant which will prevent the buyer from carrying out his business in part of the house, for example, or prevent him building a garage.

Any of these matters might well have deterred the buyer from proceeding to purchase if he had known about them from his surveyor or solicitor before committing himself. If you sign a do-it-yourself contract without legal advice, you can easily forfeit your right to withdraw without penalty.

The buyer of a new house faces a similar danger. He may be pressed by the builder to sign an agreement to secure the house, but he would be unwise to do so without legal advice.

Such agreements may appear to the buyer to offer a useful guarantee; in fact, they sometimes deprive him of his legal rights.

The agreement may state, for example, that major defects will be put right at the builder's expense for two years after the house is completed. This may seem at first a reasonable guarantee. But in law the builder will be responsible for many defects for much longer than two years. By signing such an agreement, the buyer is giving up this protection.

## Buying at an auction

Larger and more unusual homes, particularly period properties and country houses, are sometimes sold by auction.

The person who makes the last bid before the fall of the auctioneer's hammer is committed to the purchase of the property. This

---

# Which fixtures and fittings go with the house?

THE question of what fixtures and fittings automatically 'go with the house' is the most frequent cause of disputes and misunderstandings between purchasers and sellers.

The law leaves buyer and seller free to make whatever arrangements they want. There is nothing to stop them agreeing, for example, that the seller should take away the bath.

Where no agreement is made, however, the law assumes that certain things—such as electrical wiring and plumbing—are handed over with the house when the sale is completed, and that others—like cookers and refrigerators—are removed by the seller.

Unfortunately, there are a number of fixtures and fittings on which the law is uncertain. If there are any of these in the house, the purchaser should mention them specifically at the time of making his offer, and agree with the seller whether or not they are regarded as part of the property. This agreement will then be included in the written contract.

### Removable

Free-standing kitchen appliances: gas or electric cookers, refrigerators, washing machines and dishwashers.

Free-standing kitchen units which are lightly attached to the walls.

Hanging light fittings, and all electrical fittings which are plugged in.

Gas and electric fires which cannot reasonably be described as 'built-in'.

Fitted wardrobes and cupboards which, though often described as 'built-in', are in fact designed to be easily removed.

Carpets and linoleum of all types, including fitted carpets.

Most garden furniture and garden ornaments, such as statues.

### Permanent fixtures

Built-in extractor fans, wiring, plumbing, switches and plug sockets; any part of the bathroom suite. Any part of a central-heating system (with the possible exception of plug-in electric radiators).

Built-in kitchen units and cupboards, and wardrobes which have been 'purpose-made'.

Any outbuildings with foundations, and any plants, trees or shrubs in the garden.

### Uncertain

Fitted curtain rails and tracks designed to a particular shape.

Fitted bookshelves and fixed decorative wall mirrors.

Built-in gas and electric fires, and built-in kitchen appliances, including plumbed-in water softeners.

Structures in the garden without proper foundations.

means that the whole process of finding out whether the buyer can raise the money, and whether there are any hidden drawbacks about the property, has to be satisfactorily concluded *before* the auction.

The potential buyer must therefore spend money on a private survey, and pay a fee for a mortgage valuation, on a property which may easily pass to another bidder at the auction.

There is also the risk that the house may be sold to another purchaser before the sale takes place. Many estate agents state in their advertisements that the property will be put up for sale 'unless sold prior to auction'.

For these reasons, bidding at an auction is not a good method of purchase for a house-hunter who needs to borrow a substantial part of the price, particularly if he cannot afford to risk fees on homes he may not be able to buy.

If a buyer decides to bid for a house at an auction, he should have obtained from the auctioneers the printed particulars of the property. These usually contain a description of the house, together with the conditions of sale and a Memorandum of Agreement—which is really a contract to be used by the eventual purchaser.

Do not bid at the auction without a letter of offer from a building society or other lender if you need a mortgage, and without establishing the maximum figure you can afford to pay for the property. Whatever happens, stick to this figure and refuse the temptation to bid beyond your resources.

After the hammer has fallen, the purchaser will be asked to sign the Memorandum and pay a cheque for 10 per cent of the figure he has bid for the property.

The date for completing the whole transaction is given in the conditions of sale. It is usually one month after the auction.

In London and most other parts of Britain the auctioneer's commission and expenses are paid by the seller; but in some districts the purchaser pays a proportion of these costs. The purchaser meets his own solicitor's fees, search fees and stamp duties as normal.

## Buying by tender

A method of buying and selling property, which is similar to an auction but less expensive for the seller, is sale by tender.

It is sometimes used by public bodies as a fair and relatively cheap way to dispose of surplus property, such as disused railway buildings or derelict cottages on Forestry Commission land.

The properties are advertised in the Press with the words 'for sale by tender'. Interested applicants are sent particulars with a form of tender on which to make an offer.

A prospective purchaser will frequently need professional advice about how much to offer; and if he hopes to raise a mortgage, or have the property surveyed, he will need to do so before the specified date for the return of the tender—usually six to eight weeks after the first advertisement.

All the tenders submitted are opened on the same day, and the property goes to the person who has submitted the highest tender. He is then legally committed to buying at that price.

The purchaser will be asked to pay 10 per cent of the price immediately, and the time allowed to complete the legal formalities is usually 28 days.

As with auctions, sales by tender may be too uncertain for the house-hunter who needs to borrow a substantial part of the purchase price and cannot afford to spend survey fees on properties he may not succeed in buying.

Estate agents handling these sales are able to give only very broad guide-lines as to the likely price at which the property will be sold. A would-be purchaser can easily miss the property by a narrow margin of, say, £25—a figure which he might well have been prepared to add to his bid if he had known that it would win him the house.

Alternatively, a purchaser who is determined to secure the property may offer a figure which turns out to be far higher than any other tender—and considerably more than the property would have fetched at auction or in a normal private-treaty sale.

## Can a seller pick and choose?

If a house-hunter feels that his offer has been refused because of his race or colour, he can complain to the Race Relations Board at 5 Lower Belgrave Street, London SW1W 0MR, or to the local conciliation committee which can be contacted through the nearest local authority office.

Only if the seller keeps the sale completely private—if he just asks friends to keep a look out for anyone interested—is he entitled to practise discrimination.

If the seller advertises his home, or uses an estate agent, a would-be buyer who feels he is a victim of discrimination on grounds of colour, race, or ethnic or national origin, can complain to the Board. If, after investigating, the Board finds the complaint to be well-founded, it will try to reach an agreed solution. If this fails, the Board can take the seller to court and seek damages or get an injunction to prevent discrimination.

# Applying for a mortgage

*Capital repayment mortgage*　*Cheaper mortgages for the lower-paid*
*Endowment mortgage*　*Sources of mortgages*
*How borrowers pay less tax*　*Making an application*

**M**OST homes in Britain are bought with the help of a mortgage—a loan which the buyer obtains by giving the lender the deeds of the house as security. Even when the buyer can pay for the house outright, he may find that it is more profitable to borrow part of the purchase price on mortgage and invest any money left in some other way.

There are two main types of loan for buying a house or flat: capital repayment mortgage and endowment mortgage.

## Capital repayment mortgage
The most common mortgage is the capital repayment type, under which the borrower repays part of the loan, plus interest on it, at intervals for the entire period of the mortgage.

Building societies and local authorities, which provide such mortgages, issue tables showing how much the borrower has to repay each week or month.

The monthly payment is known as the subscription, and the loan is the principal.

Under the capital repayment scheme, interest is paid year by year along with a repayment of part of the original loan. So in the early part the borrower is repaying mainly interest, without greatly reducing the sum borrowed.

Take the case of a £5000 loan at 8½ per cent over 25 years. The position in the first year would be calculated like this:

| | |
|---|---|
| Year's total repayments | £40·75×12=£489 |
| Interest due on £5000 loan at 8½ per cent | $£5000 \times \frac{8\frac{1}{2}}{100} = £425$ |
| Balance paid off loan | £64 |

Thus, despite the fact that the borrower has paid £489 during the year, his debt has been reduced by only £64.

The position in the second year is slightly better:

| | |
|---|---|
| Year's total repayments | £40·75×12=£489 |
| Interest due on loan of £4936 (£5000—£64) at 8½ per cent | $£4936 \times \frac{8\frac{1}{2}}{100} = £419·56$ |
| Balance paid off loan | £69·44 |

As time progresses the repayments go more towards reducing the principal. The house-owner who decides to sell his house after five years and pay off his £5000 mortgage has paid the lender 5 × £489, that is £2445. But the loan outstanding is more than £4620.

## Endowment mortgage
The other main type of mortgage is one under which the borrower pays interest on the loan, together with premiums on an endowment assurance policy, at regular intervals. The loan itself is not repaid until the assurance policy matures, or the mortgage is ended, or the holder dies before the policy matures.

The repayment system is entirely different from that of the capital repayment scheme. None of the principal is paid off during the period of the loan. Instead, the endowment policy matures at the end of the period and the loan is repaid in a lump sum. If the borrower dies before the end of the period, the policy becomes payable and the mortgage debt is similarly paid off.

The borrower therefore has to make two sets of periodic payments—one to cover the interest on the total sum borrowed, and another a premium on his endowment policy.

The size of the premium is fixed when the policy is taken out at the start of the mortgage and does not change. It depends on the amount of the loan and the borrower's age, occupation and state of health.

The amount of interest payable to the lender will vary only if the mortgage interest rate changes. It is based not—as in the case of capital repayment mortgages—on a gradually decreasing principal, but on the full amount of the original loan.

An advantage of the endowment mortgage is that it has built-in protection against the death of the borrower. In the event of death, the insurance policy pays off the whole of the mortgage debt.

With a capital repayment mortgage, the borrower has to take out a separate mortgage protection policy to ensure that, should he die, his dependants will not be left to pay off a mortgage. ☐ Insuring the home, p. 216.

On the debit side of endowment mortgages, however, is the fact that some lenders add ¼ per cent (£12·50 per year on £5000) to their current rate of interest to compensate for the fact that they get none of their principal returned until the end of the loan period.

Moreover, the endowment mortgage is less useful for the buyer who, some years after taking out his original mortgage, wants to move to a more expensive house.

If he has a capital repayment mortgage, the borrower can sell his house and pay off what remains of the loan. As long as the property has not lost value he should now have a substantial sum of money left over from the sale to put down as a deposit on his new property.

The borrower who has an endowment mortgage can also sell his home and pay off the loan. But since this loan is the same as it was when he first took out the mortgage, he will have no extra money in hand as a new deposit, apart from any profit he has made on the sale. He will, of course, have a valuable endowment policy which it may be possible to use as security for a further endowment mortgage over the term of the original policy.

### Endowment mortgage with profits

A modification of the ordinary endowment mortgage is one in which the borrower pays a higher premium, and has part of the money invested by the insurance company.

When the policy matures, the home-buyer's mortgage is paid off in full in the normal way, but in addition he is given the profits of that investment. Similarly, if he dies before the policy matures, his wife or family receive any profits that have built up.

House-purchasers considering endowment mortgages may find a 'with-profits' policy a useful form of saving, but only if they choose to pay the higher premiums.

### The standing mortgage

The endowment mortgage is basically one form of standing mortgage—that is, a mortgage where the borrower pays only interest on the sum borrowed during the term of the loan. The principal is repaid in full at the end.

Standing mortgages are not usually used for private house purchase unless linked to an endowment assurance policy.

### How borrowers pay less tax

Most people pay less tax as a result of taking out a mortgage. How much less depends on the rate at which the borrower pays tax, the amount he borrows and the type of mortgage.

In general, the borrower is not taxed on any money used to pay interest on a mortgage loan. So if he makes mortgage repayments of £490 in a year, and £425 of that is interest, the whole of the £425 is deducted from his income before tax is charged.

This amounts to a substantial Government 'subsidy' on the expense of buying a house.

## How a capital repayment mortgage works

The home-buyer with a capital repayment mortgage—the type most commonly granted by building societies—usually pays the same amount each month throughout the entire life of the mortgage, provided the rate of interest does not change. Each payment is made up of two parts: interest on the outstanding loan, and repayment of the money borrowed. The proportions of these two items change from year to year. In the first few years payments are used up mainly in paying off interest. Later a larger proportion goes to repaying the loan. For example, the home-buyer who borrows £5000 over 25 years at 8½ per cent pays £489 each year, but in the first year he reduces the outstanding loan by only £64—less than 14 per cent of the annual repayment. In the tenth year, repayment of capital accounts for £133·40 (£133 8s.) or 27·3 per cent of the total. The proportion of the monthly payment which goes to pay off the loan rises to 85·5 per cent in the 24th year.

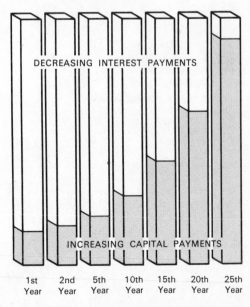

DECREASING INTEREST PAYMENTS

INCREASING CAPITAL PAYMENTS

| 1st Year | 2nd Year | 5th Year | 10th Year | 15th Year | 20th Year | 25th Year |

For the borrower paying £425 a year in interest, for example, the tax-saving is at least £127 (assuming an effective rate of tax of 30 per cent). ☐ How the income-tax system works, p. 556.

Tax relief on mortgage payments benefits only people normally liable to pay tax on a substantial part of their income.

Tax relief on a capital repayment mortgage gradually decreases year by year as the amount of the borrower's loan—and therefore the amount of interest he has to pay—is reduced.

On an endowment mortgage, however, it remains constant, since no part of the loan is repaid until the mortgage ends.

Holders of endowment mortgages can usually claim further tax relief. They may escape paying tax on part of the insurance policy premiums, subject to two restrictions.

The first, which may affect borrowers who already hold a large amount of life assurance, is that any premiums in one year over one-sixth of total income for that year do *not* qualify for relief. The second restriction is that, to qualify for any relief at all, the annual premiums on the policy must not amount to more than 7 per cent of the sum borrowed. ☐ Life assurance, p. 518.

**Cheaper mortgages for the lower-paid**
To help house-buyers in the lower income ranges, the Option Mortgage Scheme gives the choice of foregoing tax relief in return for a Government subsidy which reduces the interest on the mortgage.

The reduction depends on the rate of interest being charged by the lender.

| Lender's interest rate Per cent | Percentage reduction on Option Mortgage | |
|---|---|---|
| | Capital Repayment | Endowment |
| 6–7 | 2 | $1\frac{3}{4}$ |
| $7\frac{1}{8}$–$7\frac{7}{8}$ | $2\frac{1}{4}$ | 2 |
| 8–$8\frac{3}{4}$ | $2\frac{1}{2}$ | $2\frac{1}{4}$ |
| $8\frac{7}{8}$–$9\frac{5}{8}$ | $2\frac{3}{4}$ | $2\frac{1}{2}$ |
| over $9\frac{5}{8}$ | 3 | $2\frac{3}{4}$ |

When the scheme is linked to an endowment mortgage the subsidy is paid only for the mortgage interest, not for the insurance

# Three types of mortgage, and how they are made up

Different types of mortgage are repaid in different ways. Some are geared to reduce the loan throughout the life of the mortgage; others provide for one lump-sum repayment at the end.
CAPITAL REPAYMENT MORTGAGE The longer the mortgage runs the greater the proportion of the monthly repayment which goes to reducing the loan and the smaller the interest payment. Consequently, tax relief on interest payments decreases throughout the life of the mortgage.
OPTION MORTGAGE (CAPITAL REPAYMENT) No tax relief is allowed on interest paid on an option mortgage. Instead, a Government subsidy is paid direct to the lender reducing the interest rate for the home-buyer.
ENDOWMENT MORTGAGE Two payments are made regularly—assurance premiums and interest on the loan—and the borrower may be eligible for tax relief on both. When the policy matures the loan is repaid in one lump-sum— and in the case of a 'with profits' policy the home-buyer also receives a share of the company's investment profits. The Government Option Mortgage Scheme can also be linked to an endowment mortgage, with a subsidy reducing the interest payment while tax relief is still allowed on the assurance premium.

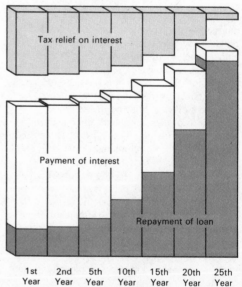

CAPITAL REPAYMENT MORTGAGE

Tax relief on interest

Payment of interest

Repayment of loan

| 1st Year | 2nd Year | 5th Year | 10th Year | 15th Year | 20th Year | 25th Year |

premiums. But the borrower can claim tax relief in the normal way on these premiums.

Borrowers who make use of the Option Mortgage Scheme can sometimes secure a 100 per cent loan even when their building society will advance only 80 or 90 per cent of the full purchase price of a property.

The additional advance required is guaranteed by an insurance policy, with the Government sharing the risk equally with the insurance company. As a result the borrower pays a reduced premium.

A borrower can choose the subsidy scheme and change to tax relief after a minimum of four years. It is also possible in cases of hardship to change from tax relief to subsidy.

### Sources of mortgages
The main organisations providing mortgages for home-buyers are building societies, local authorities and assurance companies.

BUILDING SOCIETIES The amount of money a building society is prepared to lend depends on the prospective borrower's age and income, the age and type of the property, and its value or purchase price. □ Deciding what you can afford, p. 182.

Building societies usually limit their advance to 80 per cent of the valuation of a modern, freehold house. But if the buyer's income merits it, a society may increase its advance to 95 per cent on the added security of a mortgage guarantee insurance policy. Premiums vary between £4 and £7.50 for every £100 covered.

LOCAL AUTHORITIES Councils sometimes advance as much as 100 per cent of the valuation of the property, with repayments spread over as many as 35 years. Local authorities also lend money for pre-1920 houses on which other lenders may be unwilling to make substantial advances.

The time taken for a mortgage application to be agreed by a local authority, however, is often far longer than with other lenders. Moreover, interest rates are normally higher than charged by building societies.

LIFE ASSURANCE COMPANIES People with an endowment assurance policy can sometimes get a mortgage from their assurance

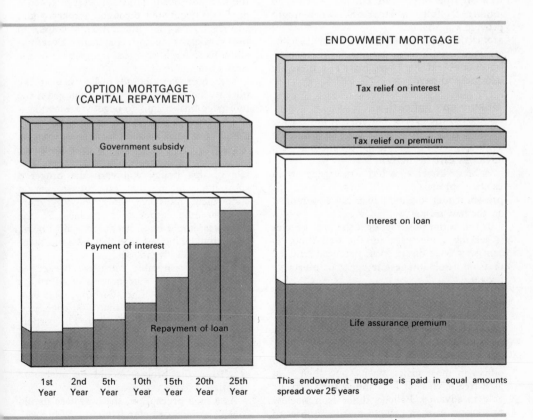

OPTION MORTGAGE
(CAPITAL REPAYMENT)

Government subsidy

Payment of interest

Repayment of loan

1st Year  2nd Year  5th Year  10th Year  15th Year  20th Year  25th Year

ENDOWMENT MORTGAGE

Tax relief on interest

Tax relief on premium

Interest on loan

Life assurance premium

This endowment mortgage is paid in equal amounts spread over 25 years

company. Interest rates often exceed those of building societies, but insurance companies lend money on higher-priced and older houses, and on properties which are to be partly let.

BANKS When Government lending restrictions permit, banks may agree to advance a small proportion of the purchase price (say 20 per cent) over three to five years to a well-established customer who can find the balance. The bank holds the title deeds and may require a formal mortgage deed to be executed. This document covers all sums owed to the bank, and even after the house-purchase loan is repaid, the bank is entitled to retain the deeds if the customer has an overdraft on his current account.

PRIVATE MORTGAGES A home-buyer with an interest under a private trust may find that trustees, approached through a solicitor, will agree to provide a mortgage.

Private mortgages are sometimes granted by employers to key staff, often on favourable terms. However, if the employee wants to leave the firm he usually has to negotiate a mortgage from another lender.

If the seller of the property appears to be well off, the buyer can ask his solicitor to inquire tactfully whether the seller might provide a mortgage.

FINANCE COMPANIES House-purchase loans are occasionally made by finance companies, but interest rates are very high, and there are extra fees to pay.

## Making an application

As most of the delays that arise in purchasing a house spring from difficulties in arranging a mortgage, the buyer should set about getting advice as early as he can.

A home-buyer who has a mortgage on an existing property should first contact his present lender to see if a loan can be arranged on the new property.

If this is not possible, or if the home-buyer is seeking a mortgage for the first time, he can get advice direct from potential lenders, or from a solicitor, estate agent or mortgage broker.

GETTING ADVICE DIRECT When money for loans is plentiful, and the home-buyer is seeking an advance on a conventional post-1920 house, the simplest course is to seek advice direct from potential lenders.

Larger building societies have branch offices in most major towns, and their staff give free advice on how much they may be able to advance. Policies differ from society to society; it often pays to make enquiries of

a number of societies before deciding where to submit a formal application.

Local authorities can be approached through the housing department, either in the area in which the inquirer is living or in the place where he intends to buy a house.

AN ESTATE AGENT Many estate agents are also agents for a building society or insurance company. Since they earn their commission (from the seller) only when a house is sold, it is to their advantage to help a buyer to secure a mortgage. Estate agents are also likely to know about the lending policy of the local authority. Their advice is usually free.

A SOLICITOR From calculations based on the buyer's income and financial commitments, a solicitor will be able to estimate the maximum amount likely to be advanced. He may suggest particular lenders, or he may refer the buyer to a mortgage broker. Solicitors rarely charge for this preliminary advice.

A MORTGAGE BROKER The middle man of the mortgage world is the mortgage broker. It is his business to know who is most likely to advance money, and what the terms will be.

The broker sells his specialist knowledge for a 'procuration fee', usually 2 per cent of the loan advanced. Thus a mortgage advance of £4000 negotiated through a broker would cost the buyer £80—in addition, of course, to the usual legal costs and repayments. Occasionally a fixed fee is charged, irrespective of the amount of the loan.

The borrower should make sure at the outset what fees, if any, will be charged if the mortgage broker fails to negotiate a loan.

The broker may offer an endowment mortgage, under which the borrower takes out an endowment assurance policy with an insurance company which the broker represents. The sale of this policy will earn the broker a substantial commission. The repayments on endowment mortgages are invariably more than on other types of mortgages. So the borrower should be on his guard against being talked into taking out an endowment mortgage unless he really wants one.

A list of reputable mortgage brokers is available from the Corporation of Mortgage Brokers Ltd, 6a The Forbury, Reading, Berks, which has more than 200 members, mainly in the south of England. The corporation's code of conduct stipulates a fee of up to 2 per cent of the loan obtained or 30 guineas, whichever is the higher, and a maximum fee of £10 if the broker should be unable to negotiate a loan.

As a final precaution, the borrower should consult a solicitor before committing himself.

# Engaging a surveyor

*When to have a survey done*
*How to find a surveyor*
*Deciding what should be included*

*The cost*
*Discussing the report*
*Complaints against a surveyor*

ANY offer for a house or flat which is made 'subject to contract and subject to survey' gives the prospective buyer the right to withdraw from the deal before contracts are signed and have his preliminary deposit returned without penalty—for example, if a structural defect is found in the house.

A building society (or other lender) which is to provide a mortgage will usually have the house valued—building societies, indeed, are obliged by law to do so. But the valuation carried out on their behalf is confidential, and therefore is not available to the buyer.

Its purpose, in any case, is different. The lender has a valuation survey to estimate what the house is worth. The buyer has a structural survey to ensure that the house is sound, and to find out whether repairs or alterations will be needed when he moves in.

So although the house is valued by the lender, the buyer is well advised to arrange for an independent structural survey.

## When to have a survey done
The buyer will obviously want to see the results of the survey before he commits himself irrevocably to continuing with the deal: that is, before he signs a contract to buy. The exact timing, however, depends on individual circumstances.

If the buyer is in any doubt about his ability to raise the money required, he can afford to wait until he knows the result of his mortgage application. If the offer is inadequate, he will at least have saved the expense of a survey.

If, on the other hand, there is competition for the house, the buyer will want to complete the formalities as quickly as possible. This means that the survey will have to be carried out immediately after an offer is made.

## How to find a surveyor
A buyer who wants his own survey undertaken before learning the result of the mortgage application can ask the building society or insurance company to allow him to use the same surveyor as it uses for valuation. This usually means a reduction in fees.

Normally, the borrower then pays a valuation fee to the lender at the time he submits

---

## Finding a qualified surveyor

THE two largest professional bodies of surveyors are the Royal Institution of Chartered Surveyors, 12 Great George Street, London SW1P 3AD, and the Incorporated Society of Valuers and Auctioneers, 3 Cadogan Gate, London SW1X 0AS.

If there is any difficulty in finding a suitable surveyor, either organisation will give the names of members acting as general-practice surveyors in the buyer's area. Members of these bodies, when qualified, are called associates, and have the letters A.R.I.C.S. or A.S.V.A. after their names. If they have been in practice for many years, they may have become fellows of the Institution or Society (F.R.I.C.S. or F.S.V.A.).

---

his mortgage application, and a reduced fee to the surveyor when his own private survey report is completed.

Some lenders, however, may even allow the borrower to agree a single fee covering both valuation and survey direct with the surveyor. This is likely to mean a further financial saving.

The buyer who prefers to delay commissioning his own survey until he receives an offer of advance from the lender can still ask to use the same surveyor. In this case, however, his saving in fees is likely to be less, since the surveyor will have to make a second visit to the property.

If the lender is not prepared to share a surveyor, the buyer will have to find one himself. His best course is to ask the advice of his solicitor or bank manager. If, however, he has decided not to buy through a solicitor he may encounter difficulties in obtaining a professional recommendation.

Then he will need to consult friends, local advertisements or the local classified telephone directory. Since anyone may call himself a surveyor, it is advisable to choose only one who is a member of a professional organisation with established standards and a code of conduct.

There are at least a dozen different branches of survey work, and it is general-practice surveyors who specialise in surveying houses and flats. Many of them are also estate agents, so check that the surveyor chosen is not also acting as an agent for the seller of the house. There would inevitably be a conflict of interest between his duty to sell the house for one client and his duty to give a full—and possibly damaging—report to the other.

If possible use a local surveyor, for he is much more likely to have specialist knowledge of the area and any particular problems, such as subsidence, underground tunnels or infestation by woodworm.

**Deciding what should be included**

There is no such thing as a standard survey. The surveyor will report only on what he is asked to inspect, so the buyer must decide what he wants included and make his instructions clear.

The best course is to ask for a full structural survey, and make it clear that this covers the structure, timbers and main fittings in the house, the cost of any repairs which are necessary and an assessment of the running costs of the house. Several important features of the house will not be included unless the buyer asks for a report on them.

DRAINS If there is any system of drainage other than mains drainage—such as a septic tank—it is wise to have the system tested. The surveyor will usually have to call in a specialist for this type of examination.

ELECTRIC WIRING AND GAS FITTINGS In older properties power systems may be inefficient or even dangerous. If there are raised metal-covered light switches, the wiring will probably be old enough to require testing by a qualified electrician. Where gas piping seems to have been installed some time ago, get a specialist opinion on how soon it will need renewing. The surveyor will be able to arrange these tests, or the local gas or electricity boards can be employed.

WOODWORM AND DRY AND WET ROT If the house is still occupied and furnished, the surveyor may be unable to get into the loft to inspect the roof timbers or lift carpets to look at the floors.

As a result, surveyors' reports often contain such phrases as 'the joists *seem* to be sound as far as we could see' or 'the woodwork is *fairly* free of woodworm'.

To avoid this, ask the seller to see that the surveyor is able to get into the loft. If

the carpets are fitted, and the seller agrees, get a skilled carpet-layer to take them up while the survey is done and then to replace them. The extra expense will be well worth while if serious dry rot, wet rot or woodworm is discovered.

When timber defects are detected it is advisable, again with the permission of the seller, to call in a specialist firm, who will give a free estimate of remedial costs.

FOUNDATIONS The surveyor will be on the lookout for signs of defective foundations such as settlement. A full-scale survey is normally impossible without digging holes in the garden and, apart from expense, the seller may not be willing to give permission.

CENTRAL HEATING If requested, the surveyor will get a heating consultant to examine and report on whether the central-heating system functions efficiently and gives the required temperatures in all parts of the house.

VALUATION For an additional fee the surveyor will give a valuation of the property, taking into account its general condition and upkeep, including interior and exterior decoration, its location and the state of the local property market at the time.

Valuations are expensive, but the expense may be justified where there is any chance of persuading the seller to accept a lower price—where, for example, the property is old or unconventional in design and has been on the market for some time, or where the price is high and no rival buyers are in sight.

There are times, however, where the extra cost of a valuation may be fairly safely avoided. If a lender has already agreed to advance a substantial proportion of the price—say 90 per cent—it is a fair indication that the price is not greatly excessive.

Again, where the seller's solicitor has already sent contracts to more than one buyer, there is obviously little prospect of negotiating a reduction in price, and a valuation may then be superfluous.

In some parts of the country the surveyor is often told the purchase price of the house and, without making a precise valuation or charging extra, he states at the end of his report whether or not he regards the purchase price as reasonable.

Even where the surveyor is asked to do no more than a basic structural survey, it is a useful precaution to ask whether, after looking at the property, he advises more detailed examinations of drains, power fittings, timber, foundations or central heating. In this way the buyer will have an opportunity to consider whether he wants the extra information before committing himself to paying further fees. Finally, agree a date with the surveyor by which his report is to be submitted.

## The cost

Fees for survey work vary greatly, and the buyer should agree a price with the surveyor before the work is commissioned.

Generally, a survey on a normal family house would cost between £20 and £30. However, the fee may vary according to the amount of work done, the travel undertaken by the surveyor and the number of visits.

If extra tests have to be made, on the drains or electrical system for example, and the surveyor has to call in and pay a builder or electrician, expect to pay up to £6 extra for each professional visit.

An extra fee is charged for a formal valuation. For this, some surveyors use a scale based on a percentage of the final valuation:

| | |
|---|---|
| For the first £1000 | £1·05 per £100 |
| For the next £9000 | 52½p per £100 |
| For the remainder | 26p per £100 |

Other surveyors have two valuation fees, again related to the value of the property:

| | |
|---|---|
| Up to £5000 | £31·50 |
| £5000 to £10,000 | £57·75 |

Sometimes additional fees are charged for leasehold properties.

Find out before the valuation is done which scale the surveyor uses, for it can make a considerable difference. On the first scale, valuation of a £6000 house would cost £36·75; the same house on the second scale would cost £57·75 to value.

## Discussing the report

Most surveyors prefer the buyer not to accompany them during the inspection, but it should be possible, if the property is empty, for buyer and surveyor to go over it later so that the buyer can have any complicated or technical points in the report explained.

Where this cannot be done, arrange to meet the surveyor to discuss the report. A surveyor will naturally be careful not to put anything in writing which could possibly be held against him later. His remarks in conversation, however, will often turn out to be more helpful. □ Exchange contracts, p. 205.

## Complaints against a surveyor

A surveyor's report cannot be regarded as a guarantee of the condition of the property. Surveyors, like everyone else, can make mistakes, be misled or overlook things. It is only if the surveyor is negligent that the buyer has grounds for legal action—if, for example, he misses something which a competent and qualified man ought to have seen.

A house purchaser who feels dissatisfied with the work of the surveyor may complain to the surveyor's professional body. These bodies are not independent, of course, but one of their principal functions is to maintain professional standards. □ Finding a qualified surveyor, p. 199.

Where there appears to have been negligence, the purchaser should seek his solicitor's advice on whether to claim damages against the surveyor. For an action to be successful, the householder would have to prove that:

**1.** The surveyor's report was incorrect in an important respect.

**2.** This inaccuracy was caused by the surveyor's negligence.

**3.** The householder had lost money as a result of the error.

It is unlikely that the surveyor would meet the claim without at least the threat of legal action. Here the advice of a solicitor is indispensable. For a small fee, the solicitor should be able to help his client judge whether he has grounds for legal action and whether it would be financially worth while.

▶ THE CARE A SURVEYOR MUST EXERCISE *A firm of estate agents and valuers, was employed by a lender to value a property at Maidenhead. They failed to inquire locally about the market value of the property, and valued it at £1800 though it had been purchased for only £600. The highest price for which it had changed hands in recent years was less than £850.*

*The valuers advised the lender to advance £1200 on the first mortgage and £150 on a second mortgage. When later it became necessary to foreclose on the mortgage, the lender's solicitor discovered that the property had been overvalued and the lender sued the valuers for damages.*

DECISION *The property had been overvalued and the defendant had failed to exercise the amount of care an expert should bring to his work. The lender received damages for the total loss he had sustained. (Baxter v. F. W. Gapp & Co. Ltd.)* ◀

Most complaints about inaccurate valuations are settled privately between solicitors acting for the dissatisfied client and the valuer.

If a case should come to court, damages are normally based on the cost of making good the property at the time the survey was carried out—even though the cost of labour and materials may have risen since then.

# Drawing up the contract

*Checking the contract*  
*What happens in a 'contract race'*  
*Proving title or ownership*

*Rights over property*  
*Information from the local authority*

BEFORE a house or flat can be transferred from one owner to another, contracts must be signed and exchanged. Two copies of the contract are drawn up by the seller's solicitor and checked by the buyer's solicitor. Then buyer and seller each sign a copy and exchange them. At this stage they become legally committed to going ahead.

Since many of the seller's and buyer's rights and duties are common to all house-buying, standard sets of contract conditions have been drawn up. Two main types are used: the National Conditions of Sale, printed as a set of standard clauses on the back of one type of contract form, and the Law Society Conditions, which are not printed on the contract form itself, but are published separately in a booklet, *The Law Society's Conditions of Sale*.

## Checking the contract

The contract states which set applies to the transaction, but they are in any case very similar in the points they cover.

RATES AND GROUND RENT The seller may have paid ground rent, and general and water rates until the end of the year, or half year, but the house may change hands earlier. The contract stipulates that the buyer makes a payment to the seller to cover the portion he owes.

WHEN THE BUYER MAY MOVE IN The contract lays down when the buyer may move into the house. Normally this is not possible before the deal is completed.

If, however, the buyer wants to move in earlier—perhaps because he has sold his own home and wants to reduce the cost of keeping his furniture in store—the seller may occasionally agree. The standard conditions state the terms for earlier possession.

If the buyer or the seller wants to make some amendment to the standard conditions, he must insert a clause in the Special Conditions section of the contract.

The Standard Conditions, for example, say that the buyer should pay the seller interest on the purchase price if the sale is not completed on the date agreed. The Standard Condition in the National Conditions of Sale stipulates that the interest rate will be 1 per cent above Bank Rate. But most solicitors acting for the seller amend this to 2 per cent above Bank Rate.

The three most common Special Conditions are those which deal with the way in which the seller proves that he is legally able to sell the house; those which give a detailed list of any fixtures and fittings being sold with the house; and any special restrictions (called 'restrictive covenants') on how the house can be used.

## What happens in a 'contract race'

The work of checking the contract must sometimes be done quickly, for it occasionally happens that the seller's solicitor gives draft contracts to several prospective buyers at the same time.

This practice is perfectly in order. It gives valuable protection to the seller, who might otherwise find, after turning prospective buyers away, that the one who made the first offer had changed his mind.

The solicitor's ethical code requires that each prospective buyer who receives a draft contract should be informed if a contract for the property has been sent to anyone else.

Where more than one contract has been sent out, the legal work becomes a race between solicitors for the rival buyers—indeed, solicitors call it a 'contract race'. The first buyer to sign and exchange contracts will secure the property.

## Proving title or ownership

When ownership of the property is registered at the Land Registry, the seller will have little difficulty in proving that he is the owner—in legal language that he has the title to it. He simply gives the buyer's solicitor authority to inspect the relevant entry on the register.

Where the house is not registered, however, he must prove ownership by producing an abstract or summary for a given number of years of all the transactions when the house has changed hands. In the Special Conditions, the seller may try to limit how far back he has to go to prove ownership. A minimum of 15 years is considered reasonable in most cases.

The contract may have a Special Condition stating that the house is being sold 'subject to covenants'—which means that there are restrictions on what the buyer can use the house for, or how he may alter the property. The buyer's solicitor will find out what these restrictions are. They will form part of the information which the prospective buyer needs when it comes to making a decision about whether or not to complete the purchase. ☐ Exchanging contracts, p. 205.

### Rights over property
Similar information will be sought by the buyer's solicitor about whether, for example, neighbours have a right to enter or cross the property. Such rights are called easements.

The buyer, on the other hand, may gain easements over a neighbour's property, and this is another matter which must be checked.

The seller's solicitor must give accurate information about the buyer's rights and

obligations. This information usually becomes a binding condition of the contract and, if it later proves to be incorrect, the buyer could possibly sue the seller for damages.

### Information from the local authority
Before deciding whether to advise his client to proceed to bind himself to the transaction, the buyer's solicitor will also seek information from the local authority, which keeps a record of matters affecting all property in its area. The record includes details which might affect the usefulness and comfort of a property and is known as the 'local land charges register'.

The 'charges' do not relate to money, but show, for example, whether a notice has been sent to a previous owner because he was breaking building regulations. It may also

## Details of ownership on the contract

**CONTRACT** by reference to the Eighteenth Edition of
**The National Conditions of Sale**

Vendor  ANDREW NEIL CAMERON
1 Blue Road,
Redberry,
Herts.

Purchaser  WILLIAM ARTHUR BROWN
247 Red Lane,
Woodstock,
Essex.

**(1)** Vendor sells as
Beneficial Owner

Purchase price
Five thousand, six hundred pounds

Completion date
25th September, 1972

10% deposit to BERNARD SLOUGH & CO.
14 Red Lane,
Woodstock, Essex.
as Stakeholders

Property and interest therein sold

Number 24 Burnt Lane,
Wood Green in the London
Borough of Haringey.

H.M. Land Registry
County, county borough or London borough
Haringey
Title No. MX 12345

**(2)** Registered at H.M. Land Registry with Title Absolute. **(3)**

**1. Seller's status** A seller who owns the house outright is called the 'beneficial owner'. Executors are named as the 'personal representatives' and joint owners 'trustees for sale'

**2. Registered land** A home on the register at the Land Registry is normally quicker and cheaper to transfer. If the land is unregistered, a full description of it has to be given here

**3. Ownership** If the seller has 'title absolute', ownership is guaranteed by the Land Registry. If he has 'possessory title' only his present right to occupy has been established

record restrictions on the use of the property, and certain types of planning proposals which directly affect the house.

By submitting the appropriate forms, the buyer's solicitor can have the register searched and make other inquiries about the property. This usually takes about two weeks.

It is also possible that searches may not reveal all plans likely to affect a buyer's

decision because a local authority will not give details of proposed developments which are in an insufficiently advanced stage. If a sky-scraper block of flats is to be built near by, but the scheme has not been formally approved, the buyer's solicitor will not be told about it.

There is virtually nothing which can be done to guard against this type of problem.

## Special conditions which cover the sale

CAMERON ..........................to.. BROWN

VENDOR'S SOLICITORS *BERNARD SLOUGH & CO.*

*14 Red Lane,*
*Woodstock, Essex.*

PURCHASER'S SOLICITORS *J. R. PRINCE & CO.*

*248 High Street,*
*Brighton.*

LOCAL AUTHORITIES liable to register Local Land Charges
*London Borough of Haringey, Town Hall, High Road, Wood Green, N. 22.*

**1**

HIGHWAY AUTHORITY
*London Borough of Haringey*

PLANNING AUTHORITY
*London Borough of Haringey*

COUNTY AGRICULTURAL EXECUTIVE COMMITTEE

ADDRESS OF LAND REGISTRY
*Harrow District Land Registry*

SPECIAL CONDITIONS OF SALE:

A. *The rate of interest specified in General Condition 1 (4) shall be 2 per cent above Bank Rate in lieu of 1 per cent.*

B. *Title shall be deduced in accordance with Sec. 110 of the Land Registration Act, 1925.*

C. *The sale includes the chattels, fittings and separate items specified in the inventory annexed which are to be taken by the Purchaser for the sum of £250.*

D. *The property is sold subject to the restrictions and stipulations set out in the Charges Register of the said title. A copy of the said Charges Register having been supplied to the Purchaser or to his Solicitor, he shall be deemed to purchase with full knowledge thereof and shall raise no objection or requisition thereon.*

**2**

**1. Where to check** The buyer's solicitor checks in the local land charges register that there are no plans or restrictions registered by the local authority which affect the property. He

gets details of possible future developments from the highway authority and planning committee. At the Land Registry he may be able to check on the history of ownership

**2. Special conditions** The value of any furnishings and fittings being sold with the house should be given, and also any restrictions concerning the use of the property

# Exchanging contracts

*Mortgage offer*           *Local authority inquiries*
*Extra money*              *Surveyor's report*
*The solicitor's inquiries*  *The exchange*

THREE things will usually determine whether someone who has made an offer for a property decides to go ahead with the purchase: the result of his mortgage application, the surveyor's report on the condition of the property, and the result of searches and inquiries made by his solicitor into anything that may affect the future value of the property or an owner's enjoyment of it —restrictions on its use, for example, or new roads or other developments in the vicinity.

By stating that his offer is 'subject to contract', the prospective buyer has left himself free to cancel the purchase if either the condition of the property or his financial position make it necessary or if, for any other reason, he decides not to buy. Alternatively, he may wish, in the light of the new information, to make a lower offer.

## Mortgage offer
The offer of a mortgage is usually made on a special Offer of Advance form which the borrower receives by post from the lender. The offer is not binding on either side, but sets out the amount of money the lender is prepared to advance, the interest rate and the number of years over which the loan has to be repaid (20, 25 or 30 years are the most common periods).

The form also names the lender's solicitors and gives details of any special restrictions—a ban on sub-letting for example—which the lender intends making.

If, after checking the figures and noting any special terms, the applicant wants to take up a mortgage on these terms, he must usually sign an acceptance form and return it to the lender. Proposal forms for any insurance required as security for the mortgage are sometimes sent to the borrower by the building society (or other lender) at the same time.

Before returning the acceptance form, the buyer should send it to his solicitor who may possibly persuade the lender to modify or delete any conditions which the buyer may want to avoid. When the house is still being built and the contract with the builder provides for payments at several stages before it is finished, the solicitor will see that the

lender is prepared to release the money at the different stages.

A time limit, usually three months, is set on the offer. This does not mean that, if the applicant decides not to buy the present property, the lender will not consider granting a mortgage again on another property. When mortgages are scarce, it is possible, however, that a buyer who simply allows the Offer of Advance to expire without informing the lenders will find that they are not prepared to consider another application for some time.

## Extra money
If the mortgage offered is slightly less than the loan required, the buyer may first try to borrow the balance from his bank, employer, family or friends. If that is unsuccessful a second mortgage from a finance company may be the only solution.

Most building societies insist that the buyer uses his own money for the balance of the purchase price, but if the amount needed is comparatively small they may be persuaded to allow a second mortgage.

Before accepting a second mortgage, the buyer should make sure that he can afford the repayments on top of all his other outgoings—first mortgage repayment, rates, ground rent (if any), and maintenance and decoration. But there may be disadvantages in borrowing in this way. □ Personal loans and second mortgages, p. 506.

## The solicitor's inquiries
Much of the solicitor's work in the early stages of house-purchase consists in finding out whether there is anything about the house which could affect its future value or the comfort of its new owner.

There may be restrictions on what the buyer can use the house or land for and how he can alter it; other people may have rights over the land; and there may be plans for developments in the district which could affect it. Any of these might influence the prospective buyer's decision on whether to go ahead with the transaction.

RESTRICTIONS It is common for a builder selling a new house to get the buyer to agree to restrictions on what the house can be used for and how it can be altered.

These restrictions, called 'restrictive covenants', may be imposed in order to preserve the appearance of the whole estate or to prevent the view from one house being spoiled by alterations to another. Similar restrictive covenants may be created by the seller of the land.

Every time the land or property is sold, the covenants become binding on the new owner. The buyer has therefore to make sure that they are acceptable; for if he buys the property he is taken to have read, understood and agreed to abide by them.

Typical covenants might bind the owner:
1. Not to erect any other building on the land. This restriction might pose a problem for anyone who planned to have a garage built.
2. To make use of the property only as a private dwelling house. This could prevent a doctor from holding his surgery in the property, for example, or make it impossible for a minicab driver to run his business from home.
3. Not to add anything that would alter the height of the house. Such a covenant might hamper the development and improvement of the property.

Where restrictive covenants such as these prove an obstacle to the sale, the seller's solicitor can attempt to have the covenant lifted by applying either to the person or company which created it—or, if it is a very old restriction, by applying to the Lands Tribunal to have it waived.

The only ground, however, on which an appeal of this kind is likely to succeed is if the seller can show that the covenant has become pointless and obsolete as a result of development that has gone on around the property in the meantime.

Covenants are intended to protect and be of benefit to someone—usually other residents. If all the other residents have meanwhile built garages, a covenant against a garage at one house might be ruled obsolete.

The older the covenant, the more likely a buyer is to be able to break it without opposition. But the buyer must always assume for his own protection that it could be enforced.

Some solicitors will advise a householder to ignore the covenant and carry out any development he wants to make. At the same time they will arrange for him to take out an insurance policy which will cover any loss he might suffer if he were later made to obey the covenant and pull down what has been built.

The buyer's solicitor will have to check that no covenant has been broken in the past—that no garage has been built, for example, where a covenant forbids it.

Where a covenant has been broken, steps may again have to be taken to get it lifted, or at least to check whether anyone is likely to raise objections.

OTHER PEOPLE'S RIGHTS The prospective buyer may find, as a result of his solicitor's inquiries, that other people have rights, known in law as easements, over the property.

He might, for example, have to allow people to cross his property where there is a right of way. Water pipes, drains or electric cables serving adjoining property may run across his property. Or a neighbour may have a right to draw water from a common stream.

## Local authority inquiries

Information requested from the local authority by the prospective buyer's solicitor can also affect his decision about whether to go ahead with the purchase.
1. There may be plans—for the construction of a motorway, for example—which could affect the house. The road outside the house might be due to be widened, possibly taking away part of the garden.
2. The house may come under a Smoke Control Order, compelling the owner to use only more expensive smokeless fuel. This is probably not a reason to withdraw, but it is worth knowing about.
3. Some development of the property may have been refused. Planning permission is often required before any major alterations or additions can be made to a house (even the building of a garage), or before it can be used for any purpose other than as a 'dwelling house'—as an office or shop, for example.

The buyer may find it very difficult to get permission to make a similar development, especially if the refusal is recent. His solicitor or a surveyor will advise whether it is worth re-applying for planning permission.
4. The local council may have served a 'notice' on the property because the owner had broken building or health regulations. Typical cases would be where the owner had built a garage without the necessary permission, or where a public health inspector considers the drains to be insanitary.

The notice is an order to the occupier of the house to put the matter right—to obtain permission for the garage or remove it, or to repair the drains. If the notice has still not been obeyed when the transaction is completed, the buyer will become responsible and will have to pay for the work out of his own pocket. So his solicitor will make sure either that it has been obeyed or that it will be before the transaction is completed.

Other such notices could cover over-crowding or dangerous premises, or even a compulsory purchase of the house (in which case the buyer would almost certainly want to withdraw from the transaction).

**5.** The road outside the house may be a private one, in which case the buyer would have to contribute to its upkeep.

**6.** Trees on the property may be subject to a preservation order, preventing any owner from topping them or cutting them down.

### Surveyor's report
Very few buyers find their surveyor's report completely reassuring; it is, after all, the surveyor's job to seek out defects.

But many of the minor faults likely to be listed (a missing tile or slate, or a broken gutter for instance) can be disregarded as no better and no worse than in the average house.

Again, many people buy houses in a poor state of repair because they can get them more cheaply and are prepared to spend time and money on having them modernised. Government grants are now available for improvements and the surveyor is normally able to advise whether the property will qualify.

A buyer with this in mind might therefore not be deterred by such things as broken rain-water pipes, minor plaster defects or damp spots caused by blocked wall cavities. But serious defects in a house which the surveyor considers expensive to remedy may make a prospective buyer consider whether it may be advisable to call off the deal.

### The exchange
When the buyer is satisfied—from his surveyor's report—that the house is worth buying; when he has obtained any loan he needs; and when his solicitor advises him that all inquiries have been answered satisfactorily, he can decide whether to proceed.

At this stage, both the buyer and seller receive from their solicitors the contract as it has finally been agreed. The buyer must sign it, but not date it. He sends or takes it to his own solicitor, who in turn sends it back to the seller's solicitor together with the agreed deposit—usually 10 per cent of the purchase price minus any preliminary deposit already paid.

When the seller has signed his identical part of the contract, he also returns it to his solicitor who dates both copies, adds the date by which the sale is to be completed, and posts the seller's signed part to the buyer's solicitor.

It is at the time the seller's copy is posted that contracts are said to have been exchanged —and both parties become firmly committed to going ahead with the sale.

Even if one or both of them dies before the sale is actually completed, the deal will have to be completed by their representatives.

## What happens if a local council makes a mistake

AN ESSENTIAL precaution which a solicitor takes on behalf of a client buying a house is to find out from local councils about development plans affecting the property. If a council gives incorrect information, the buyer may have grounds for claiming damages for breach of contract to supply correct information, or for negligence in supplying it, or sometimes for both.

➤ THE SHOP-OWNER WHO WAS MISLED *A retail firm planning to buy a shop asked Birmingham Corporation whether plans had been approved for a subway or underpass in the road opposite. In reply, a clerk sent a form saying that no such plans had been approved. The form added that the council, its officers and employees were not legally responsible for the accuracy of replies. Thus reassured, the firm bought the shop. It later* discovered that, at the time the inquiry was made, plans had already been approved for a pedestrian subway outside the shop. When work started on the subway, the company suffered loss. It sued the Corporation for damages.

DECISION *In 1971 the Corporation was ordered to pay. It could not escape liability for negligence, because the exclusion clause made no mention of negligence.*

*In addition, no exclusion clause could exclude the council from liability for so fundamental a breach of contract. (Coats Patons Retail Ltd., v. Birmingham Corporation.)* ◄

As a result of this decision, many local authorities redrafted the exclusion clause to exclude liability for negligence. But no re-drafting can enable a council to escape liability for a fundamental breach of contract.

# Completing the purchase

*All about insurance*
*Proving ownership*
*Transfer documents and Stamp Duty*

*Final checks before transfer*
*Bridging loans*
*Completion and moving in*

BETWEEN the time that contracts are exchanged and the purchase is completed, the buyer's solicitor must make sure that the seller really owns the property, and he must complete arrangements for his client's mortgage.

The first step for the buyer, however—and it may be a condition of a mortgage—is to insure the house.

The seller is responsible for protecting the property from serious deterioration. For instance, if a leak developed in the roof he would be under a duty to repair it.

The buyer, however, has committed himself to completing the purchase, and must pay for the house no matter what happens to it—even if it burns down. He therefore has an interest in insuring it as soon as possible.

The seller, of course, may have his own insurance, but he is not required by law to maintain it. In any case, it is probable that the amount insured is not the amount the buyer is paying for the house.

### How to insure
The buyer may be able to choose his own insurance company—or he may be able to take over the seller's policy if it is suitable. But it is more likely that the building society (or other lender) will select the insurance company and send an insurance proposal form when it agrees to make a loan.

When this happens, the insurance premium will be collected by the lender. This policy generally covers only the building itself. The contents can later be insured separately.
☐ Insuring the home, p. 216.

### How much to insure for
In most cases, the lender will specify how much the property should be insured for. Some lenders are satisfied as long as insurance covers the amount of money they are advancing on mortgage.

Yet if anything happened to the house, the buyer would still have to pay the full purchase price. If it burned down, his only remaining asset would be the site itself.

The buyer therefore needs to make sure that if the property is completely destroyed,

either before or after he moves in, his insurance will provide enough money to rebuild the property. This may be more or less than the purchase price, depending on the type of property concerned.

NEW HOUSE In theory, the cost of rebuilding a new house which is destroyed on the day it is completed should be the purchase price *minus* the value of the site (which will, of course, still be left for building on).

In practice, the cost of labour and materials may have gone up since the house was built, and there could be additional charges for clearing the site. If the buyer insures for the purchase price without deducting the value of the site, he will be protecting himself against this increase in costs, though in the early years he will probably be over-insured—and consequently be paying more than is strictly necessary in premiums.

An alternative is to get an estimate of the value of the site—from a surveyor or perhaps a solicitor—and insure for the purchase price minus *half* the site value. This should provide an adequate margin against increased costs of labour and materials.

If the property is a suburban, three-bedroomed house, costing £5000, with a site worth about £1000, the owner should be safe in insuring it for the cost less half the site value—that is £5000 less £500 which makes a balance of £4500.

If anything happened to the house, the buyer would be entitled to claim up to £4500 from the insurance company and still be able to sell the site for £1000—a total of up to £5500. On the other hand, if he decided to rebuild on the site—or if the lender insisted that the property be rebuilt—he would have up to £4500 available to do so.

Whether or not it is worth going to the trouble and expense of valuing the site will depend on the individual property. In general, the more expensive the site is likely to be, the more worthwhile it is to have it valued professionally before arranging insurance.

OLD HOUSE The purchaser of an old property should always insure for at least the full purchase price, to allow for increasing costs. Better still, add a percentage—say 15 per cent—to allow for site-clearing and surveyor's and architect's fees involved in any rebuilding.

It might be particularly costly to rebuild a property on a very difficult town-centre site. Again large properties bought relatively cheaply because they are in remote parts of the country could cost much more than their purchase price to rebuild.

An insurance company would agree to insure for £7000 a house which cost only £5000 to buy if the owner could show that the larger sum would be needed to rebuild a similar house on the same site.

### The danger of under-insuring
Many insurance companies require the house-owner to sign a declaration on the proposal form that the house is being insured for its full value. It is never in the buyer's interest—for the sake of a few pounds or shillings saved on the premiums—to try to insure for less.

If a claim is made on a property that is not insured for its full value, the insurance company could, theoretically, refuse to pay anything at all. In practice, it is likely to pay compensation in proportion to the sum insured, not the actual value of the property.

### What the insurance covers
Most household insurance policies give cover against fire, earthquakes, riots, and damage done by burglars to the building itself (but not to furniture and other contents). They insure the householder against leakage from the central-heating system, damage to underground pipes and cables and damage caused by things being dropped from aircraft, though some items may be excluded from the cover given in the policy if the house is unoccupied or unfurnished.

The householder is usually required to pay the first £15 of the cost of repairing storm damage or damage caused by burst pipes (unless he pays a slightly higher premium to cover this cost).

The policy will normally meet any claims up to £100,000, for injury to passers-by or for accidental damage caused by the owner to his neighbour's property.

A policy of this type is described as a House-holder's or House-owner's. Check, before applying, just what it does cover, and make certain that no important item is excluded.

### Insuring leasehold property
Insuring leasehold property is sometimes more complicated. Leases of more than 21 years—under which many houses, flats and maisonettes are held—usually require the property to be insured through the ground landlord and with a company chosen or approved by him.

This, however, may conflict with the wishes of the lender, who may also want to control the insurance arrangements himself.

It is frequently convenient for landlords of blocks of flats and maisonettes to insure them all under one 'block' policy. In this way the premium for the whole estate is shared among all the leaseholders; so is the amount for which the properties are insured. For example, an estate of 20 flats and maisonettes might be insured for £100,000. But this system cannot take into account the increased values of individual flats or maisonettes due to redecoration and improvements.

If his property is not adequately protected, and the landlord is not prepared to adjust the cover under the block insurance, a buyer would be wise to arrange an additional policy to cover the difference between the amount allowed for by the landlord and the full value of the property. A lender is almost certain to insist on this being done.

### Proving ownership
The contracts exchanged between buyer and seller usually include a clause stipulating a time limit—normally 14 days—within which the seller's solicitor must provide the buyer's solicitor with the documents that prove who owns the house.

REGISTERED LAND When the land is registered, all the details concerning its ownership are recorded at the Land Registry.

This covers the title number of the piece of land on which the house stands, so avoiding the need for a very full description of the property; any special details of mortgages or restrictions affecting the house; and the name of the owner.

The buyer's solicitor receives a copy of these entries, together with a signed authority for him to inspect the register, and a copy of the filed plan. No one is allowed to inspect the register without the permission of the owner or his solicitor.

UNREGISTERED LAND When the land has not been registered, however, there is no simple central record of details. This means that the seller must prove that he owns the house by referring to the deeds and documents covering transactions since the date stipulated in the contract, usually going back at least 15 years.

The summary of this information—called the Abstract of Title—is sent to the buyer's solicitor, whose job it then is to check each original deed mentioned against the summary, to ensure that there is an unbroken chain of ownership, finishing with the seller.

Obviously, this usually involves more work than the comparatively simple check with the Land Registry. For this reason, solicitors' charges are higher for arranging the transfer of an unregistered house. Even if the work actually involved proves to be very slight, a solicitor is still entitled to charge his full fee. ☐ Counting the cost, p. 213.

## The transfer documents

Once the buyer and his solicitor are satisfied that the seller does own the house and that no one else has any claim to it, the buyer's solicitor draws up the legal documents needed to transfer ownership of the property.

REGISTERED LAND The solicitor prepares the transfer—usually a fairly simple document giving the registry title number of the property, its address, the names of the seller and the buyer, and the price being paid.

UNREGISTERED LAND The document for the transfer of freehold unregistered property is called the conveyance—from which the whole legal process of 'conveyancing' gets its name. If the land is leasehold, the document is called an assignment.

The conveyance or assignment, like the transfer, contains the essential details about buyer and seller, but it must also include a much fuller description of the land—if necessary with a plan.

This document then becomes part of the title of the house, which will be examined when the ownership of the house is next transferred to a new owner.

If only part of an unregistered property is being sold—for example, a house may have been divided, and sold to two separate buyers —the deeds of the property will not be available for both buyers. The conveyance will, in that case, contain a promise by the seller that the deeds will be kept safely.

## Duty on the transfer

In any land transaction—registered or un-registered—a form of tax called stamp duty is payable on the deed, but only if the selling price, or value of the property transferred, is more than £10,000. A reduced levy is charged on sums between £10,000 and £15,000 but, above £15,000, the full rate of duty—1 per cent of the purchase price—is payable.

To ensure that a buyer and seller do not conspire to evade this tax, the law requires a signed statement when the price is £15,000 or less. This certifies that the price shown is the true price and that it is not part of a larger deal which would be liable to stamp duty. This statement is the Certificate of Value, and is usually the last clause in the transfer document where the property being transferred costs £15,000 or less.

The buyer's solicitor sends the draft transfer document to the seller's solicitor for approval. When both buyer and seller, through their solicitors, have agreed on the contents of the document, the buyer's solicitor prepares the final copy of the document for the seller's signature. The seller signs his normal signature, in the presence of a witness (not a husband or wife), to the left of a small red seal attached to the document. This is known as the execution of the deed.

If the house is being bought on mortgage, and the buyer's solicitor is not also acting for the lender, the buyer's solicitor will send the contract, and the results of all his searches and inquiries, together with the abstract of title or copy entries and any other documents which may be requested, to the lender's solicitor. This is done immediately the contracts have been signed and exchanged.

Even at this stage, the lender may, through his solicitor, raise queries on the ownership of the property and other matters which will have to be answered by the buyer's solicitor, who passes them on to the seller's solicitor. When the lender's solicitor has satisfied himself that the seller is the true owner of the property and that appropriate arrangements have been made to meet the lender's requirements, he will prepare the mortgage deed and send it to the buyer's solicitor.

Included in the mortgage deed (the legal agreement between the borrower and the lender) will be the names of the parties, the amount of the loan, the rate of interest, the period and amount of repayments and a description of the property.

Most mortgage deeds contain clauses permitting the lender to raise the interest rate, and setting out the terms on which repayment will be accepted, should the borrower repay before the mortgage has run its full term. Alternatively, the terms will be found in the lender's rules for borrowers.

Check these terms carefully before signing, and ask your solicitor for advice if necessary. Check particularly what happens if the mortgage is ended early. Here arrangements vary substantially, but usually interest is charged only up to the date of repayment—provided the mortgage has run for a minimum number of years, often five. In rare cases, the mortgage deed contains a clause which provides for the lender to receive *all* the interest which would have been due had the mortgage run its full term. The borrower should certainly beware of borrowing money on these terms.

Mortgage deeds usually stipulate that the borrower must keep the property in good repair and adequately insured, and must not carry out any major alterations, or let the property, without consent.

### Final checks before transfer

Completion takes place when the deeds of the property are handed over in exchange for the balance of the purchase money, making the buyer the new owner of the property. Before this, however, the buyer's solicitor makes a final check, to ensure that nothing has happened within the previous few days to affect the transaction.

REGISTERED LAND The buyer's solicitor asks the Land Registry to make a final search, to check that the house has not been sold or mortgaged by the seller since the register was last examined or since the date on which the copy entries sent from the Registry to the buyer's solicitor were prepared.

This final search is valid for 15 working days—which means that no other deal involving the property can effectively take place during that time. It is essential, therefore, for the buyer to see that the purchase is completed before this time limit expires, or for the final search to be renewed.

UNREGISTERED LAND The buyer's solicitor will have a search made at the Land Charges Registry (a separate department of the Land Registry) to ensure that there are no outstanding matters—for example a bankruptcy order —against the seller or claims against the property. This search at the Land Charges Registry gives the buyer 14 working days' priority over any later transactions.

### The completion statement

Shortly before the date agreed for completing the purchase, the seller's solicitor sends the buyer's solicitor a statement showing how much has to be paid on completion. This document includes the balance of the purchase price and any interest due because of a delay in completion. It also sets out the amount the buyer has to contribute towards general outgoings already paid by the seller— general rates, water rates, ground rent (in the case of leasehold property) and sometimes insurance premiums, if the buyer is taking over the seller's policy. Lawyers call these items 'apportionments'.

If, for example, the seller has paid his general and water rates up to September 30 and completion takes place on August 1, he will be able to claim the amount for the outstanding two months from the buyer.

Other outgoings—such as electricity, gas and telephone bills—are not normally dealt with by solicitors. The buyer should see that the meters are read on completion, and that the gas and electricity boards and Post Office (if there is a telephone) are informed of the change of ownership.

The completion statement is sent to the buyer by his solicitor, together with a request for the appropriate payment, which is usually made by banker's draft.

At about the same time, the buyer will also receive from his solicitor the bills for his own costs and, if separately represented, those of the lender's solicitor. These bills are usually paid before completion.

### Bridging loans

When a householder sells his existing property to buy a new house, he may find that the two transactions do not coincide.

For example, he may have arranged to complete the purchase of his new house on, say, August 1, while the person to whom he is selling his existing house may not want to complete the deal before September 28.

The householder therefore has to find enough money to complete his own purchase on August 1. He needs it for only two months —until he sells his own property. With luck, the householder's bank will provide him with a loan to bridge those two months.

The bank will require a solicitor's letter giving the relevant facts and figures of the sale and purchase. They will also want to see the contract. If the owner's existing house is free from mortgage, the bank will probably ask for the deeds to be deposited with them as security. If the previous mortgage has not been paid off, the bank may be prepared to lend, through the solicitor, just enough to pay off the old mortgage, and will then hold the deeds of the old property as security.

Interest on a bridging loan is normally 2 per cent above the bank's base rate—the rate used as a basis for calculating interest on various types of loan—and the borrower will probably have to pay an additional 'commitment fee'. Security for a bridging loan—in addition to depositing the deeds of the property with the bank—varies considerably. Sometimes a solicitor's written undertaking is acceptable to the bank; in other cases a formal mortgage deed may have to be drawn up.

But an owner should always insist, whatever the circumstances, that his solicitor does not commit him to completing the purchase of the new house before the date fixed for the sale of his present property—unless the bank has already agreed, in writing, to provide a bridging loan.

## Completion

Neither the buyer nor the seller need attend the actual completion when the solicitors exchange the balance of the purchase money for the title deeds.

If the house is being bought on mortgage and the buyer's solicitor is not also acting for the lender, the lender's solicitor will have to attend, to pay the loan.

In this case, after the deeds have been inspected by the buyer's solicitor they are handed over to the lender's solicitor or the lender as security, and will be returned to the buyer when the loan has been repaid.

Before handing over the money, the buyer's solicitor will inspect the last receipts for outgoings, to ensure that the figures on the completion statement are correct.

If the deposit was paid to an agent as stakeholder, the buyer's solicitor will have to give his authority for the money to be released and paid to the seller.

Sometimes the keys of the house are handed over on completion. Alternatively, a written authorisation is given to the buyer or his solicitor to collect them, often from a neighbour or estate agent. More often than not, the buyer and seller make arrangements together about handing over the keys.

After completion, the lender's solicitor (or the buyer's, if there is no mortgage) will pay the appropriate stamp duty and the deeds will be stamped accordingly. If the property is registered, the deeds must be lodged with the Land Registry for the change of ownership to be recorded. Where the lender holds the deeds, this will be done by his solicitor.

## Moving in

Once contracts are exchanged the seller must not allow the property to deteriorate seriously, even if this means carrying out repairs. If the house is damaged in any way before the buyer takes possession, he is entitled to insist on a reduction in price as compensation.

Unless special arrangements have been written into the contract, the seller must move out on or before the day of completion, when the buyer is entitled to take possession.

Occasionally a buyer may ask to move in before this date, but the seller's solicitor usually advises against such a step.

The seller, however, cannot stay on in the property after completion without the purchaser's consent. If he does so, he is then in the position of a squatter and the purchaser can take legal action to evict him. But this rarely happens, as such legal cases are costly and slow. ☐ Rights and responsibilities of running a home, p. 280.

---

## What to do if completion is delayed

ANY delay at this stage can have far-reaching consequences, particularly if one house is being bought while another is being sold. But if one party is late in completing, this does not necessarily allow the other to withdraw from the transaction.

If the buyer fails to complete the transaction by the agreed date, the seller can, for the period of the delay, charge interest on the balance of the purchase price which is still to be paid. The rate of interest would be that specified in the contract.

If the seller's solicitor suspects that the delay is likely to be more than just a few days, or that the buyer is unlikely to complete unless he is forced to, he can serve a 'notice to complete' on the buyer.

This is a formal notice requiring the buyer to complete within a specified time, usually 28 days. If he does not, the seller has three courses open to him:

**1.** He can keep the deposit paid by the buyer *and*, once the buyer's solicitor has been informed, offer the house for sale elsewhere.

**2.** He can start legal proceedings, asking for a court order forcing the buyer to complete.

**3.** He can sue the buyer for damages for breach of contract.

If it is the seller who is causing the delay, the buyer's position is not as strong. His solicitor can serve on the seller a notice to complete. If the seller does not complete within the time limit, the buyer may refuse to go any further with the transaction and may sue for damages.

Alternatively, the buyer may start legal proceedings to force the seller to complete the sale according to the contract.

# Counting the cost

*Surveyor's fees*     *Land registry fees*
*Solicitor's fees*     *Stamp duties*

IT is not usually possible to buy a flat or house without a substantial amount of ready cash. When he first makes an offer, the buyer may have to put down a small preliminary deposit. This is usually between £5 and £100. Then there will be fees for the lender's valuation and any survey which the buyer has commissioned. When contracts are exchanged, the prospective buyer has to make up the deposit to an agreed proportion of the purchase price, usually 10 per cent. Finally, usually just before completion of the transaction, the buyer has to pay solicitor's fees and any Land Registry fees and stamp duty.

## The solicitor's account for buying a house

The amount of work a solicitor does in handling the legal side of buying a house or flat now governs the fee he charges. Fixed fees on a scale related to the purchase price were abolished in late 1972. Extra charges are made for dealing with a mortgage, and for expenses such as search fees. The buyer also has to pay a tax called stamp duty if the house costs more than £10,000

The solicitor's conveyancing charge is based on the time and work involved. The fee is generally higher for unregistered property

Mortgage fees, based on the amount of the loan, are calculated on a scale agreed by the Law Society and the Building Societies' Association

The Land Registry keeps a record of both the transfer of house-ownership and of any mortgage on the property. The fees, paid on the buyer's behalf by his solicitor, are on a scale based on the purchase price

## J.R. Prince & Company (solicitors)

243 High Street Brighton Sussex
Telephone Brighton 8780

W. A. Brown, Esq.,
247 Red Lane,
Woodstock,
Essex

25th September 1972

24 Burnt Lane, Wood Green, Haringey, London, N 22

| 1972 25 July to 25 September | To professional charges in connection with your purchase of the above registered freehold property for £5600 | | £46.00 |
|---|---|---|---|
| | The like in connection with a mortgage from the Mentor Building Society for £4000 | | |
| | Building Societies' Scale Charge | | £20.00 |
| | Disbursements | | |
| | Land Registry fees on Transfer | 15.20 | |
| | Land Registry fees on Mortgage | 5.20 | |
| | Local Search fees | 1.60 | |
| | Petty disbursements | 3.15 | £25.15 |
| | | | £91.15 |

## SURVEYORS' FEES

Most lenders value the property, at the applicant's expense, to ensure that it is adequate security for the money they are advancing.

The valuer's charges are based on the valuation of the house, if he represents a building society, and are payable whether a loan is subsequently offered or not. Most lenders use the Building Societies Association scale of survey fees. However, local authority fees may be lower.

If the buyer orders a structural survey, it will probably cost £20 to £30.

Inspection of drains or wiring is charged separately and may cost £5 to £15.

If the buyer requires a formal valuation, the fee will usually be based on the Royal Institute of Chartered Surveyors' scale. If the same surveyor does a structural survey *and* a valuation, it may be less.

## BUILDING SOCIETIES ASSOCIATION SURVEY SCALE FEES

| Purchase price £ | Fee £ |
|---|---|
| 2000 | 5 |
| 3000 | 7 |
| 4000 | 9 |
| 5000 | 11 |
| 6000 | 13 |
| 7000 | 15 |
| 8000 | 17 |
| 9000 | 19 |
| 10,000 | 21 |

Units of £500 are charged at £1 per unit. Travelling expenses may be payable in addition. A fee is negotiated for properties selling at above £10,000

## SURVEYOR'S VALUATION FEE

| Valuation £ | Fee £ |
|---|---|
| 3000 | 21·00 |
| 4000 | 26·25 |
| 5000 | 31·50 |
| 6000 | 36·75 |
| 7500 | 44·63 |
| 9000 | 52·50 |
| 10,000 | 57·75 |
| 12,000 | 63·00 |

There is a minimum fee of £7·53

## SOLICITORS' FEES

Charges for conveyancing are based on the nature of the work and the time taken. Property which is unregistered usually requires more work, and fees are therefore higher.

Before late-1972, fees were calculated on the scale printed below. House-buyers are now free to negotiate the fee; in all but exceptional cases, it should be lower than that on the old scale. ☐ Choosing a solicitor, p. 188.

A solicitor may also charge for out-of-pocket expenses, such as travelling and postage.

## GUIDE TO MAXIMUM SOLICITORS' FEES
(Scale abolished late-1972)

| Purchase or sale price £ | Registered land £ | Unregistered land £ |
|---|---|---|
| 1000 | 22·50 | 30·00 |
| 1500 | 27·50 | 37·50 |
| 2000 | 30·00 | 45·00 |
| 2500 | 32·50 | 48·75 |
| 3000 | 35·00 | 52·50 |
| 3500 | 37·50 | 56·25 |
| 4000 | 40·00 | 60·00 |
| 4500 | 41·87½ | 63·75 |
| 5000 | 43·75 | 67·50 |
| 5500 | 45·62½ | 71·25 |
| 6000 | 47·50 | 75·00 |
| 6500 | 49·37½ | 78·75 |
| 7000 | 51·25 | 82·50 |
| 7500 | 53·12½ | 86·25 |
| 8000 | 55·00 | 90·00 |
| 8500 | 56·87½ | 93·75 |
| 9000 | 58·75 | 97·50 |
| 9500 | 60·62½ | 101·25 |
| 10,000 | 62·50 | 105·00 |
| 10,500 | 64·37½ | 107·50 |
| 11,000 | 66·25 | 110·00 |
| 11,500 | 68·12½ | 112·50 |
| 12,000 | *70·00 | †115·00 |

*Then add 37½p for every £100 up to £13,000, 25p per £100 to £17,000, and 20p per £100 thereafter
†Then add 25p for every £50 or part of £50—i.e. 50p per £100 or £5 per £1000
Intermediate values are calculated in multiples of £100

## MORTGAGE FEES

Fees for dealing with a mortgage are extra. They may have to be paid twice—to the lender's solicitor and to the buyer's. They are based on the loan (*not* the purchase price) and are usually calculated according to a scale agreed between the Law Society and the Building Societies Association.

Building societies often share a solicitor with the person buying the house. In that case the buyer pays one mortgage fee only.

On unregistered property it is calculated on the Law Society/Building Societies Association scale. On registered property it is not more than half the registered scale fee shown in the table on the left, substituting the amount of the mortgage for the purchase price.

In the case of mortgages other than from building societies, the lender's solicitor may charge twice the appropriate full-scale fee set out in the table below, except that the amount of the loan will, again, replace the purchase price for calculating the charge.

## SOLICITORS CHARGES FOR DEALING WITH A MORTGAGE

Law Society/Building Societies Association scale

| Amount of loan £ | Charge £ |
|---|---|
| 1000 | 10·00 |
| 1500 | 11·50 |
| 2000 | 14·00 |
| 2500 | 16·50 |
| 3000 | 19·00 |
| 3500 | 21·50 |
| 4000 | 24·00 |
| 4500 | 26·50 |
| 5000 | 29·00 |
| 5500 | 31·50 |
| 6000 | 34·00 |
| 6500 | 36·50 |
| *7000 | 39·00 |

* Over £7000, fee by arrangement

Fees are calculated for each £50 increase in the amount of the loan

## LAND REGISTRY FEES

Where land is unregistered in a compulsory registration area, it must be registered when the house changes hands. The fee depends on the purchase price. A different scale is used for recording the transfer of registered property.

Compulsory registration areas now include most of the Home Counties and the major county boroughs throughout the country. The aim of the Land Registry Office is to have all built-up areas, with populations of 10,000 or more, made compulsory registration areas by 1973.

Sometimes land outside a compulsory registration area may be registered, for example a large rural housing estate.

There are additional fees for mortgages on registered land, based on the amount of the loan. When a transfer and a mortgage are registered at the same time, the mortgage fee is halved. No separate mortgage fee is paid when the property is first registered.

There are no fees on unregistered property which does not qualify for registration.

### LAND REGISTRY SCALE FEES

| Purchase price or amount of mortgage £ | *First regis-tration £ | †Land already regis-tered £ |
|---|---|---|
| 1000 | 1·80 | 2·60 |
| 2000 | 3·60 | 5·20 |
| 3000 | 5·40 | 7·80 |
| 4000 | 7·20 | 10·40 |
| 5000 | 9·00 | 13·00 |
| 6000 | 10·40 | 15·20 |
| 7000 | 11·80 | 17·40 |
| 8000 | 13·20 | 19·60 |
| 9000 | 14·60 | 21·80 |
| 10,000 | 16·00 | 24·00 |

*For £5000 and below add 90p for every £500 or part of £500. Above £5000 add 70p for every £500 or part of £500
†For £5000 and below add £1·30 for every £500 or part of £500. Above £5000 add £1·10 for every £500 or part of £500

## STAMP DUTIES

Documents transferring land and property together worth more than £10,000 must have an Inland Revenue stamp impressed. Land transfer documents on properties of less than £10,000 are exempt, provided that the transfer document contains a certificate of value stating that the price given is the true one. This certificate is required for all sales under £15,000 and is usually the last clause in the transfer document.

The amount of duty payable depends on the purchase price of the property.

If a house is sold with carpets, curtains, or other 'extras' which are not permanent fixtures, a realistic part of the price can be allotted to them. This may reduce the price of the property to a figure below £10,000 and, as a result, exempt the transfer from stamp duty.

Purchase duty is paid by the buyer on completion of the sale of the property.

### STAMP DUTIES

| Purchase price of property £ | Purchase deed stamp £ |
|---|---|
| under 10,000 | — |
| 10,000 | — |
| 10,500 | 52·50 |
| 11,000 | 55·00 |
| 11,500 | 57·50 |
| 12,000 | 60·00 |
| 12,500 | 62·50 |
| 13,000 | 65·00 |
| 13,500 | 67·50 |
| 14,000 | 70·00 |
| 14,500 | 72·50 |
| 15,000 | 75·00 |
| 15,500 | 155·00 |
| 16,000 | 160·00 |
| 17,000 | 170·00 |
| 18,000 | 180·00 |
| 19,000 | 190·00 |
| 20,000 | 200·00 |

For prices between £10,050 and £15,000 add 25p for every £50 or part of £50 (50p per £100). For prices over £15,000, add 50p for every £50 or part of £50 (£1 per £100).

## OTHER EXPENSES

### Rates, water rates, ground rent

If the seller has paid general rates, water rates, ground rent and sometimes insurance up to a date after the completion date. he will, on the completion statement, recover a proportion from the buyer. The buyer must therefore take this added expense into account in his calculations. For general rates, it is simpler for the seller to get a refund if he has paid in advance.

### Estate agent's commission

Estate agents do not usually charge ordinary house buyers a fee. But a charge is made if an estate agent is instructed to seek and arrange the purchase of a house (perhaps $2\frac{1}{2}$ per cent on the first £5000, $1\frac{1}{2}$ per cent on the next £10,000 and 1 per cent on the rest) or if he negotiates the purchase of a house found by the purchaser (perhaps $1\frac{1}{2}$ per cent on the first £15,000 and 1 per cent on the rest).

### Bridging loans

Some banks may charge a 'bridging loan fee' as well as loan interest.

### Other charges

When an insurance policy is used to secure a mortgage and is assigned to the lender, the solicitor will usually charge under £10.

For preparing and filing Finance Act forms, his fee is about £3.

If a second mortgage is arranged, his charge will depend upon the amount of the loan and the work involved.

If planning applications or appeals against planning decisions are made the solicitor should be asked for an estimate at the outset since the costs of such action could be substantial.

# Insuring the home

*Mortgage protection policy*     *Moving house*
*Insuring the contents*     *Making a claim*
*All-risks policy*

WHEN a home is bought on mortgage, the lender usually insists on a suitable household insurance to cover the loan. The house-buyer has to take out a policy before arrangements for his mortgage are completed—usually as soon as contracts have been exchanged. ☐ Completing the purchase, p. 208.

Even when no mortgage is involved, however, insurance of the house, fences and any outbuildings is essential if the owner is not to risk losing a considerable asset.

In later years, when perhaps a substantial amount has been paid off the mortgage, it is just as important to keep the home adequately insured. Values of land and property generally increase with time, and the house-owner has to keep his insurance continually under review. It should also be brought up to date if any improvement or addition is made to the house.

With many insurance policies, the home-owner has to declare that the property is being insured for its full value. There is also an obligation to keep the insurance company informed of any changes affecting the property.

If the property is insured through a Lloyd's underwriter, and no increase in value is allowed for, the amount of any settlement for a claim will be reduced by however much the property was under-insured. Thus, a house which has risen in value from £5000 to £10,000 without the insurance cover being adjusted will be considered by the underwriter to be 50 per cent under-insured. If £2000 worth of damage is done, the company will pay no more than 50 per cent of the claim, or £1000. If the house is totally destroyed, the most the policy-holder could claim would be £5000.

Although insurance companies are not legally bound to pay anything at all on claims where the property is found to be under-insured, most follow the Lloyd's procedure of settling for a proportionally reduced figure.

Householders with insurance arranged by their building societies will usually find they are covered by what is conveniently known as a Householder's or Home-owner's policy.

The risks covered are only those detailed in the policy, and although it normally covers a wide range—for example, fire, explosion, storm, earthquake, riot, burst pipes, burglars, or even an aircraft crashing or dropping something on the house—there are gaps.

Though damage caused by burst water pipes is covered, other damage caused by frost is not. Nor is normal wear and tear, or damage through neglect. No policy provides for damage by radioactive contamination, nuclear explosion or any form of warfare.

## Mortgage protection policy

When a house is bought with an endowment mortgage, the entire mortgage debt is paid by the insurance company if the house-owner dies. A householder with a capital repayment mortgage does not automatically have this protection. But he can ensure that his widow is not left with a mortgage to pay off by taking out a mortgage protection policy—which is a form of life assurance.

The premium for this policy will be low, for as more and more of the mortgage debt is repaid, so the amount the insurance company would have to pay is reduced. If a policy-holder lives to pay off the mortgage completely, the company pays nothing at all.

Premiums on the policy are usually paid monthly or yearly. They depend on the age and health of the policy-holder, the amount and interest rate of the mortgage and the number of years the mortgage has to run when the policy is taken out. A certificate of health from the prospective policy-holder's doctor, or a medical examination may be required before a policy is issued.

In some cases it may be possible to take out a protection policy by paying a single lump-sum premium, which can be included in the mortgage advance.

If a householder sells his home, pays off his mortgage and buys another house or flat on another mortgage, most insurance companies will allow him to transfer his existing mortgage protection policy to cover the new mortgage.

There will, of course, be amendments to fit the policy to the new circumstances. But in most cases the householder who has already undergone a medical examination will not need to be examined again.

In the same way a householder can have the

policy changed to meet any new situation—for example, if he has the period of his mortgage extended because of increases in the rate of interest, or if he gets a further loan to pay for improvements to the house.

Although most protection policies yield nothing to the householder if he lives until his mortgage is repaid, it is possible, for a slightly higher premium, to take out a similar policy with a 'survival benefit'—which would be paid at the end of the policy term.

Some insurance agents are more enthusiastic about this type of policy, not least because it pays them a higher rate of commission. But the extra premium required is often better invested in, or put towards the cost of, a normal life policy or an endowment policy.

### Insuring the contents

Most home-owners choose to insure not only the bricks and mortar of the property, but also its contents—furniture, equipment and personal belongings.

Home-owners with insurance company mortgages may find that the company also insists on controlling their contents insurance.

Where the householder has a choice of insurance companies, there are advantages in choosing the same company for insuring both the house and its contents. If, for example, both the house and contents are damaged by fire or flooding, the householder will have to deal with only one set of claim forms and only one company. This will help to speed up settlement of the claims.

When a contents insurance policy is taken out, the total value of the contents of the home must be given. The best way to arrive at this figure is to make a room-by-room list of furniture, carpets, curtains and all other possessions, assessing their *current* value. The insurance company will pay only the current value in the event of a claim, not what an item cost to buy new. Make sure, therefore, that the insurance is constantly reviewed—giving the up-to-date values—and inform the insurance company whenever a costly item of equipment or furniture is bought.

Insurance companies often make restrictions on what can be covered under a contents policy. They may increase the premium rate if the total value of any jewellery, furs or precious metals exceeds one-third of the total sum insured, or if any single item is worth more than 5 per cent of the total insurance.

A house contents policy usually provides some cover for a householder's legal liability for accidents to members of the public, other than his family, caused by the property—for instance, a chair collapsing under a visitor or a guest tripping on a carpet. The maximum a policy will pay out to a victim is usually

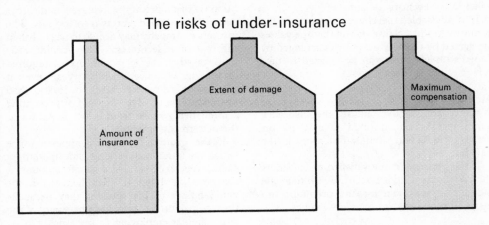

## The risks of under-insurance

Amount of insurance

Extent of damage

Maximum compensation

It is dangerous to under-insure a home, for insurance companies are entitled to reject a claim if the house is not adequately covered. In practice, most companies meet only part of a claim on under-insured properties. If, for example, a claim of £1000 is made for damage to a house worth £5000 but insured for only £2500, the insurance company is likely to pay not more than half the claim—£500. The maximum it would pay if the house were totally destroyed would be the amount insured, £2500. This is known as the 'principle of average'. With rapidly rising prices a home can soon become under-insured unless the owner increases the cover from time to time

£100,000, plus legal costs. In addition, the basic householder's policy can be extended to cover personal liability for all the family.

## All-risks policy

If the valuables in the house are over the limit of a contents insurance policy, they will have to be insured separately, usually under an 'all-risks' policy. Whereas building or contents policies cover only the risks stated in the policies—loss through fire, storm, explosion, flood, theft, and so on—an all-risks policy covers loss or damage no matter how it is caused *unless the risk is specifically excluded*.

These policies are frequently full of 'ifs' and 'buts'.

Wear and tear, breakage of extremely brittle articles, and loss through riot or civil commotion in Northern Ireland are all likely to be excluded. So a home-owner should seek advice from the insurance company or an insurance broker about exactly what is covered, and in what circumstances a claim may or may not be made.

The insurance company will often require proof of the value of the items insured, and original receipts will have to be provided or an expert valuation can be made at the policy-holder's expense.

Under the terms of many policies, the fact that the insurers accept the policy-holder's valuation at the time the policy is taken out does not prevent them from disputing the value in the event of a claim.

It is advisable, therefore, to persuade the company to add a clause stating that the values are agreed by them. Most policies arranged by Lloyd's underwriters can be worded to take this requirement into account.

## Moving house

When a family moves house, the insurance company must be informed. It may ask for details of locks and window-fastenings in the new house.

If the company is not satisfied or considers the new house a higher security risk than the old one, it may increase the premium and insist on new locks and window-latches.

## Making a claim

If insured property is damaged, inform the insurance company immediately. The appropriate claim form will be supplied by the company and the householder should complete it as promptly as possible.

Before deciding to claim for a small amount of damage, however, consider whether it might be cheaper in the long run to bear the loss yourself. A policy-holder who makes a number of claims may find that the insurance company considers him a bad risk, and his premium may be increased accordingly.

The claim form asks for details of how the damage occurred and the value of the damaged property. Because the insurers require this information quickly, there may not be time to assess all the damage when several items are involved: state in writing, therefore, that the claim may not be complete. This reserves the right to amend it later, if necessary.

When the insurance company receives the claim, a representative will normally be sent to inspect the damage if the claim is for more than £200. Where the company disputes the value of the damaged property, it may be worth while engaging an independent assessor.

The assessor is likely to charge between 10 and 15 per cent of the total eventually paid by the insurance company; but this may be money well spent if he can settle a claim more quickly than the policy-holder himself, and also on better terms.

Sometimes, after a house has been damaged by fire, an assessor may call and offer his services. If this happens, try to check with neighbours or tradesmen who might have an idea of his reputation, and beware of signing any agreement which would give the assessor an exorbitant percentage of the claim as fee.

An insurance company can refuse to pay the full cost of repairing damaged property. Suppose that a fire in the living-room destroys decorations carried out two years ago. The insurance company may decide to pay only half the cost of redecoration. They could argue that as the room would have required decorating within another two years even if there had been no fire, the old decoration had lost half its value. This method of preventing a profit being made from a loss is known as the betterment principle.

If the insurance company appears to be taking an unreasonably long time to settle a claim, especially where a small amount is concerned, a letter of complaint from the policy-holder or his solicitor may persuade them to pay up and avoid the necessity of the policy-holder employing an assessor.

When the cheque for the damage is received, the policy-holder will invariably be expected to sign and return a receipt which states that the payment has been made 'in full and final settlement' of the claim. Check that all the damage has been accounted for in this payment, as no further claim will be accepted by the insurance company once the receipt has been signed and returned to them.

# Rates I : how the system works

OCCUPIERS or owners of property have to pay rates—a yearly charge calculated according to the value of the property—to their local council. The money raised pays for such things as street cleaning, sewerage, refuse collection, town and country planning, education and welfare services.

A tenant is liable for rates if his rent is 'exclusive of rates'. For council tenants, and some other tenants, rates are included in the weekly rent payment. A tenant can discover whether his rates are inclusive or exclusive from his rent book or his copy of any lease which he signed when taking over.

When a house is left vacant and without furniture, no rates will be payable unless the council goes through the proper procedure to enable it to charge a 50 per cent rate on unoccupied buildings. Anyone planning to leave his home unoccupied should check the practice of his local authority rating department.

## How the charge is levied

The amount of money to be paid in rates depends on two factors. The first is the figure calculated by the Inland Revenue Valuation Office from full information on the property, and called 'rateable value'.

The second is the proportion of the rateable value that is levied as rates by the local council. This is called the 'rate in the £'.

Only city, borough, urban and rural councils can levy and collect rates. The Greater London Council, county councils and parish councils get their money by issuing a demand—called a 'precept'—on the rate-collection councils or, as they are known, rating authorities.

## Rateable value

In order to assess the rateable value of a property, the Inland Revenue sends a questionnaire to the occupier. This must be answered and returned within 21 days. From this, and other information obtained from a survey and measurement of the building, the Inland Revenue valuation officer calculates the yearly rent at which the property might be let in current market conditions.

The calculation assumes that the tenant pays the usual rates and taxes and the landlord pays for repairs, insurance and other expenses necessary to keep the property in good order. It also takes into consideration—especially for new houses and shops—the current values of similar property in the area.

This figure is called the 'gross value'. From the gross value, a prescribed percentage is deducted to cover repairs, insurance and normal expenses necessary to maintain the property in a condition that would command the rent which has been assessed.

The amount left after these deductions is the rateable value of the property. Deductions from gross value are calculated as follows:

| DEDUCTIONS FROM GROSS VALUE | |
|---|---|
| Gross value | *Deductions* |
| Up to £55 | 45 per cent of the gross value |
| £56–430 | £25 plus one-fifth of the amount by which the gross value exceeds £55 |
| Over £430 | £100 plus one-sixth of the amount by which the gross value exceeds £430 |

| To calculate the rateable value of a house with a gross value of £200: | |
|---|---|
| Take the gross value | £200 |
| *Deduct* £25+one-fifth (£200−£55) that is, £25+one-fifth of £145 or £25+£29 equals | £54 |
| Rateable value | £146 |

## Publication of assessment

A list of the rateable values of every property in a rating authority's area, known as the valuation list, can be inspected at the local council's offices. Copies or extracts can be taken at any time free of charge, but often it is possible to obtain a rateable value figure by telephoning the council.

New properties are usually added to the current list as they are completed. In areas where a large number of houses is being built, an estimated assessment is made until the valuation officer has inspected a property, and made a precise calculation.

Lists that came into force in April 1963 are to be replaced by new ones based on a 1970 valuation which should come into force on April 1, 1973.

When they are ready, each council will advertise that its local list is available for inspection. Councils also have an obligation to tell ratepayers of their rights to lodge an objection to a rateable value assessment.

### Improvements to property

Improvements, for example the building of a garage or extension, usually mean that a property's rateable value is increased.

The local council informs the valuation officer when planning permission for an improvement is granted, and later the property and the improvement may be inspected and a new assessment made.

If the valuation officer has given at least 24 hours' notice of his intention to inspect a property, it is an offence to prevent him or the inspector representing him from entering. The maximum fine is £5. Where an improvement is made which does not require planning consent, such as the installation of central heating, the householder is under no obligation to inform the valuation officer unless a questionnaire form is sent to him.

The valuation officer is constantly valuing and revaluing property. He makes regular inspections of property, usually at five-yearly intervals. But apart from these, anyone can make a proposal to have property revalued, even though he himself may not have any legal interest in the property.

The valuation officer values the total property each time, taking into account additions such as central heating, for which no planning permission is required. But the addition of central heating does not mean that the valuation automatically rises, as other parts of the property may have depreciated.

### Rate in the £

Ratepayers do not pay an amount equal to the full rateable value of their property each year. They pay a proportion of it—the rate in the £. If, for example, a house has a rateable value of £100 and the rate is 60p in the £, the householder will pay £60 a year in rates.

The rate in the £ applies to all properties in the area, though commercial premises are charged a higher rate than domestic properties. The rate is fixed for each financial year, or half year, by the council after estimating the total expenditure it faces and the Government grants it will receive.

Ratepayers receive demand notes—bills for the amount of rates due—setting out what they must pay.

This money is officially payable in advance on April 1 each year; but it may be paid by two instalments, or a householder may be able to make arrangements in advance to pay by ten monthly instalments. Councils may also agree to other instalment arrangements. Any under or over-payment made during a period of estimated assessment should be accounted for in the first demand after a proper valuation.

### Non-payment of rates

If a ratepayer does not pay the demand seven days after it is issued, the council is entitled to take action through a magistrates' court. In practice, a longer period normally elapses and warning letters are sent. If rates are not paid, a council can apply for a summons to bring the ratepayer before a magistrates' court.

If no valid legal objection to payment is made in court—and if there is no offer to pay —the court issues a distress warrant, which gives authority to a bailiff or other responsible official to seize goods worth the unpaid rates.

The ratepayer is given at least five more days in which he can decide to pay and recover his property. If he still fails to do so, the seized goods can be sold. In cases where a bailiff is unable to gain access to a defaulter's goods, or there are not sufficient goods to cover the outstanding amount, or there is a wilful refusal to pay, a court has power to impose a prison sentence of up to three months.

### Water rates

A charge is made for water supplied to domestic premises by the local council or the water supply authority for the area. This is levied each year either as a percentage of the rateable value of the property or as a rate in the £. Water rates are normally paid by half-yearly or quarterly instalments in advance.

Although water rates do not usually depend on the quantity used, there may be an extra charge for using a hose or sprinkler.

If the quantity of water used is more than is normal for domestic purposes, the water boards will normally arrange with the occupier for a meter to be placed in the property, so that the amount of water used can be measured and then charged.

The water supply can be cut off if the rate is not paid. To have it restored, the occupier must pay the cost of cutting off and restoring the supply, as well as any rate arrears. If the rate is not paid, action can be taken to recover the money in a court.

### Other rates

Occupiers of property near common land may be charged a commons rate. This is used to maintain the common.

People in an area of special drainage works can be charged a drainage rate.

# Rates II : how to apply for a reduction

*Challenging rateable value*          *Appealing to the Lands Tribunal*
*Appealing to the valuation panel*    *Applying for a rate rebate*

THERE are two ways in which a ratepayer may be able to pay less rates. He can claim that the assessment of rateable value is unfair and try to get the valuation reduced. Or he may claim that he cannot afford to pay the rates, and apply for a rebate.

### Challenging rateable value
A ratepayer can appeal against the assessment of the rateable value of his property as soon as the valuation list comes into effect or, in the case of a new property, as soon as he is informed of the assessment.

The first stage is to make the objection in writing on a form called 'Proposal for Alteration of the Valuation List'. This form is obtained from the local valuation officer and returned to him when completed. His address will be supplied by the local council.

The proposal must specify the grounds on which it is being made, but the ratepayer does not have to state what he thinks the valuation should be. It is normally enough to say that he believes the valuation officer's assessment is 'incorrect' or 'excessive'.

The ratepayer may argue that the property could not be let at the figure suggested by the valuation officer; and to support his case he could compare the assessment with those of neighbouring properties, which can be checked in the valuation list on view at the local council offices.

The ratepayer could also feel that the property has a disadvantage, not taken into account by the valuation officer, that would affect the rent at which it could be let. The valuation officer will consider the proposal, and may inspect the property and discuss the proposal with the ratepayer.

The valuation officer may decide that the ratepayer has a case and suggest a new figure. If the ratepayer accepts the proposed alteration, the valuation list will be amended.

On the other hand, the valuation officer may refuse to make an alteration to the list. The ratepayer then has 14 days in which to decide whether to continue with his objection. If he wishes to continue, or if the officer suggests an amended value which is unacceptable, the ratepayer's appeal is heard by the local valuation panel. The valuation officer informs the clerk of the panel, and a date for a hearing is arranged.

### Appealing to the valuation panel
The local valuation court must be held as frequently as necessary, and it sits in public unless it is ruled that this would be prejudicial to one of the parties involved. Evidence can be taken on oath.

The ratepayer who appeals can appear, call witnesses and produce any documents. Other parties to the appeal can also produce documents and call witnesses, who can be questioned by the ratepayer.

The court has a chairman and two other members who are often councillors. Their decision on how a property is to be valued need not be unanimous.

Although not legally necessary, it is advisable for a householder to engage a valuer, surveyor or perhaps a solicitor to prepare a case and represent him. The council, the officers of the valuation panel and the valuation officer will all give advice on procedure and other points, but it is possible that there could be a conflict of interests.

Where a case involves large or commercial and industrial premises, a ratepayer may have to argue against solicitors representing the valuation officer and sometimes the council.

It costs a ratepayer nothing to appeal before a valuation court apart from a representative's fee if he employs one. When people are occupying a new estate it may often be worth while for a group of neighbours to band together and share the cost of a professional representative to challenge their rating assessment. If only one person makes an objection on a ground which applies equally to other properties, a valuation court might reject the case on the assumption that the majority of householders regard the assessment as fair.

### Appealing to the Lands Tribunal
If the ratepayer, the council or the valuation officer is dissatisfied with the valuation panel's decision, either side can appeal to the Lands Tribunal within 28 days. The notice of appeal should be made on a form supplied by the

221

registrar of the tribunal and returned with a copy of the valuation panel's decision.

The tribunal is made up of lawyers and surveyors appointed by the Lord Chancellor. The procedure is substantially the same as in the valuation court and the only cost to the ratepayer is for representation.

The tribunal's decision on the facts is final, but a further appeal can be made to the Court of Appeal on a point of law. If such an appeal is considered, a solicitor's advice is essential.

### Applying for a rate rebate

Tenants and owner-occupiers with low incomes can claim a rate rebate, provided that their rates are not already fully covered by a supplementary benefits payment.

People who do not make a separate payment for rates, but pay an inclusive rent to a council or to a private landlord, can also qualify for a rate rebate. A private landlord will not be concerned in any rebate application, and the council will make a cash payment to the tenant if the application succeeds.

Ratepayers who qualify for rebates are single, widowed, separated or divorced people earning less than a minimum figure—in 1972 £12 a week; and couples with a joint income of less than £14·75 a week.

An extra £2·50 a week is allowed for each dependent child.

Rebates are calculated six-monthly. Ratepayers granted maximum rebates must pay the first £3·75 of the half-yearly instalment and one-third of the balance.

The ratepayer's total income before tax or other deductions (and his wife's income except if she is not living with him) is taken into account. Pensions from all sources and disability payments are also included. So too are any regular payments which the ratepayer receives from relatives who do not live with him—for example, a weekly sum which a son pays his elderly father or mother as a dependent relative.

Where income is above the qualifying limit, the rebate is reduced by 25p for each excess £1 until it ceases to apply.

The incomes of earning children, lodgers or other people with separate incomes are not included, but they would be assumed to be paying a share of the rates.

Because of this, a ratepayer who has any of these people living with him as a tenant of part of the property would normally be granted a rebate only on the section which he occupies himself.

Other adults in the household who are not tenants, apart from one relative if there is no wife or husband, are also assumed to be helping with the payment of the rates and any rebate would be reduced according to the number of adults living in the home.

Applications for rebates for the period April to September should be made between February 1 and April 30, and for rebates for October to March between August 1 and October 31. Late applications may result in rebates being reduced.

Any ratepayer who has any doubts about whether he qualifies for a rebate can get advice in confidence from the rating department of his local council or from his local Citizens' Advice Bureau.

## Reasons for changing the rateable value

RATEABLE value can be reduced if property is adversely affected by any factor, such as an unsightly rubbish dump near by. But it must be proved that this factor was not considered when the property was assessed.

Reductions in rateable value have been granted to people whose homes were affected by the following factors:

Noise from a nearby Scout troop

A new council estate overlooking the garden

A sewer laid across the back garden

An underground watercourse which caused the foundations of two bungalows to sink and made the properties cold and damp

Noise from building and construction operations which reverberated in the confined space in front of a flat

Lack of gas, electricity and main water supplies in an exposed house close to derelict properties

Reduced privacy caused by a thick hedge being removed for development work.

Unsuccessful appeals for reductions of rateable value have been made by occupants who claimed their properties were affected by:

Aircraft noise near Heathrow Airport, London

Lack of main drainage

An untidy grass verge and a bus shelter placed in front of the property

The building of a house on an adjoining plot.

# Repairs and improvements

HOME-OWNERS keen to improve or extend their property face two immediate problems: raising the money and getting the necessary permission. Many improvements—unlike routine repairs and maintenance—qualify for loans and grants from local authorities, and there are a number of other sources from which the necessary money can be borrowed.

Again, most structural alterations require the consent of the local authority, and sometimes that of neighbours, the ground landlord (if the property is leasehold) and the building society or other lender (if there is a mortgage).

How the home-owner goes about raising the money and applying for permission depends on who does the building work. There are four possibilities:

**1.** The householder can do it himself.

**2.** If he is proposing to enlarge the property, he can get a 'package' extension from a specialist firm of builders.

**3.** He can call in a small builder.

**4.** If the alterations are substantial, he can get an architect to supervise the work.

DO-IT-YOURSELF The man who does all the building and alteration work himself will still need to apply for consent from the local authority and possibly other people as well. For this, he will probably need to commission an architect or surveyor to draw up plans. If the consent of the ground landlord is needed, he may also have to employ a solicitor.

'PACKAGE' EXTENSION FIRMS Many organisations will undertake to deal with all aspects of home extensions—legal formalities, drawing up plans, arranging credit, applying for planning permission, and the construction work itself. This is often an inexpensive method, but it has drawbacks.

The extensions available may not be quite what the householder wants and the basic design often cannot be varied much. The credit terms offered by the 'package' firms need to be studied closely—the home-owner may be able to borrow money more cheaply by making his own arrangements. □ Choosing the type of credit, p. 490.

SMALL BUILDER Unless he is sure of being given the building work, the small builder may be reluctant to prepare drawings to submit with his estimate for home improvements. If he has been asked to carry out the alteration, he will go ahead with preparing plans, both for the client and for the planning-permission application to the local council.

If the builder is unable to do this personally, he will pay an architect to do it for him. In this case, the architect's duty is to the builder rather than the house-owner.

ARCHITECT The householder can commission an architect to design an extension, obtain the necessary permission and supervise the building.

This may be more expensive. An architect charges from 12 to 20 per cent of the cost of the alterations, according to how busy or well-established he is and how big the job is. The bigger the job, the smaller the percentage. The cost may be more than offset by the money saved by using the architect's experience and knowledge. He will get competitive tenders for building materials and labour, and will keep an independent check on the quality of the work at all stages.

The Clients' Advisory Service of the Royal Institute of British Architects, 66 Portland Place, London W1N 4AB, will supply a list of members in any area who will undertake this sort of project.

## Raising the money

Money for home improvements is required in stages—not in a single lump sum when the work is completed. The architect, for instance, is paid in instalments at various stages of his work, by agreement with his client.

Each month the builder is paid 90 per cent of the architect's valuation of the work done up to that time. Five per cent of the total cost is normally withheld by the householder for three months after the job is completed, during which time the builder must put right any work not done properly.

If the property is leasehold, the occupier may have to pay a fee to the ground landlord for permission to carry out the work.

Money for improvements is available from several sources. A building society or insurance company may lend the money—even if mortgage repayments have not significantly reduced the original sum borrowed. Loans for improvements are given as an additional advance at the same interest-rate as the original mortgage, with repayments spread over the outstanding period of the mortgage.

The effect of carrying a comparatively small loan over such a long period is to make the total cost of borrowing high. For instance, a loan of £500 repaid over 25 years by monthly instalments at 8½ per cent will finally cost £1225 at £49 a year. However, this will be partly offset if tax relief can be claimed on the interest. Over the full 25-year period, the tax saving on a £500 loan would be £225·25

if the borrower pays tax at an effective rate of 30 per cent. This would bring the net cost down to just under £1000. Subject to current tax legislation, tax relief may be allowable on the money borrowed for many home improvements.

Not every borrower will pay this amount of interest. Building society loans, unlike those from some other sources, can be repaid early, and the borrower will have to pay only the interest due to date.

Banks may also advance money for home improvements—either by an overdraft or by a personal loan. The money might be used either to finance the entire operation, or to pay

## When things go wrong with a new house

A NEWLY built house is rarely perfect. Like a new car, it needs careful treatment and use in the early months after it has been built if major problems are to be avoided.

The timber, brickwork and tiles of an average three-bedroomed semi-detached house contain more than 1500 gallons of water. As some of this moisture in the house gradually dries out, there will be some shrinkage. Defects are likely to appear after about six to nine months.

Damage, such as cracked wood or plaster, is usually caused by materials drying out too quickly, so if central heating is installed, do not let the temperature rise above 18·3°C (65°F) in the first few months.

When anything that seems to be a defect does appear, report it to the builder in writing, immediately, and ask him to put it right.

If the house has a guarantee provided by the National House-Builders' Registration Council, the council will ensure that all defects caused by the builder failing to comply with its standards of construction are corrected.

These standards cover the structure of a new house from the foundations to the roof, and include electrical, gas and plumbing installations, and paths, drives and garages.

If an N.H.B.R.C. inspection shows constructional defects, the council will order the builder to carry out repairs free, and usually within 30 days. If the repairs are needed because of normal wear or shrinkage, the owner will have to pay.

Should either party reject the N.H.B.R.C. inspector's decision, the dispute will be referred to an independent arbitrator nominated by the chairman of the N.H.B.R.C.

The arbitrator can award the costs of a hearing against either party, just as a court can. He may order the house-buyer to pay if what he considers to be a reasonable offer by the builder has already been rejected by the buyer. But he can also award expenses to a house-buyer who has to find other accommodation while repair work is carried out.

Where a builder refuses to carry out work recommended by the arbitrator, or if he goes bankrupt, the N.H.B.R.C. will pay for the cost of repairs.

In the first two years after the house is completed, the council will pay up to £5000 per house to put right any defects caused, in the view of the arbitrator, by the builder's failure to comply with the council's standards. From the third to the tenth year, only major structural defects are covered, again up to a maximum of £5000 per house.

If the house does *not* have a guarantee from the N.H.B.R.C., the householder should still ask the builder to remedy any defects; but if the builder refuses, it will be more difficult to force him to act.

In law, the builder will be responsible for any repairs made necessary by his bad workmanship, unless the buyer has signed an agreement curtailing this responsibility.

The house-buyer can claim the cost of repairs from the builder, or get a solicitor to do so for him. It may be necessary, however, to threaten legal action or take the builder to court in order to recover the money. A solicitor will advise whether the prospects of success justify the cost of going to court. □ Getting advice on a legal problem, p. 708.

the builder and architect in the early stages, before a loan from a building society or other lender is received.

Interest on overdrafts is charged at 2 per cent above 'base rate'—the rate used by the bank as a basis for calculating interest on various types of loan. It is paid only on the amount outstanding, so the interest payments decrease as the overdraft is paid off.

Most banks limit the amount of a personal loan to £500, and the repayment period is usually not more than two or three years. Interest on personal loans is fixed at 1 or 2 per cent above base rate, but it is non-reducing and will cost more than an overdraft.

Banks require some form of security for an overdraft, such as a life assurance policy. This is not normally demanded in the case of a personal loan.

Where a bank manager is unable to offer a personal loan or an overdraft, he may advise the householder to apply to a finance house—and in some instances may recommend a subsidiary of the bank itself.

## Council grants

For some improvements it may be possible to get a loan or grant from the local council—which in many cases has a duty to help with projects that will keep houses in its area in good repair, or even improve them.

The council can give grants of up to half the cost of some types of improvement, and it may make a loan or grant a second mortgage for the other half.

If the council does provide a loan, it will lay down certain conditions—for example, that the council is given first priority in reclaiming its money if the owner runs into financial trouble and the property has to be sold.

In some cases, the council will advance money as the work goes on, so that a short-term bridging loan from a bank is not necessary. The council may fix a maximum amount which can be advanced on one property, in which case a supplement may have to be found elsewhere.

A council grant does not have to be repaid, and there are few strings attached. There are no restrictions on selling the home after it has been improved with the help of a grant.

Moreover, the house which is modernised, converted or improved need not be the owner's main or only home. Grants can be obtained for improving weekend cottages, provided they are used as a home at some time.

There are three types of grant:

STANDARD GRANT To qualify, a house must have been built before October 3, 1961, and the council must be satisfied that it is in a reasonable state of repair and that after the proposed improvements it will be fit to live in for at least 15 years. If it is in poor repair, the council may lend money for repairs which will make it eligible for a standard grant.

The standard grant—which the council has a legal obligation to give if the conditions are met—is made so that the householder can provide his home with the 'standard amenities'. This means a fixed bath or shower, a wash basin, a sink, an inside lavatory and a hot-and-cold water supply.

Normally the grant is given so that all five basic amenities are installed. But if the householder shows that he cannot afford to put in all five, he can still get a grant to provide his home with at least a sink that has hot and cold water and with a lavatory.

The maximum standard grant normally available is half the cost of the work up to a total grant of £200. Each improvement done separately qualifies for a maximum amount.

| Bath or shower | £30 |
| Wash basin | £10 |
| Sink | £15 |
| Lavatory | £50 |
| Hot and cold water at: | |
| Wash basin | £20 |
| Sink | £30 |
| Bath or shower | £45 |

Only where extra work is involved—for example, where a water main has to be connected—will more than £200 be given. But there is an overall maximum of £450, whatever the circumstances.

DISCRETIONARY GRANT The purpose of this grant is to bring old houses up to modern standards, to enlarge small houses, or to convert non-residential buildings into homes. A grant can be given to a householder to convert a small room into a bathroom or to convert a large house into several self-contained flats.

Before agreeing to such a grant, the council must make sure that the work proposed will bring the property up to certain minimum standards of repair: that it will be free from damp; that it will have good light and ventilation in each room; that there will be hot and cold water, and a bathroom and lavatory; and that there will be an adequate kitchen, adequate storage and efficient drainage.

A discretionary grant can be given only for a house that will have a useful life of at least another 30 years.

If the owner intends to make any of these improvements to his house, or to convert it into flats, the local authority can grant up to half the cost, subject to a maximum of £1000. Where a property of three or more storeys is converted into flats, the maximum is £1200 for each flat. Normally a discretionary grant is not given for work of less than £100.

SPECIAL GRANT Local authorities have discretion to give special grants to improve shared houses where the owners let several rooms to tenants, but not houses converted into separate self-contained flats. To qualify, a house must be lived in by several people who do not form a single household.

It is not essential that all the standard amenities are provided, and more than one amenity of the same kind may be approved. Special grants cover up to a maximum of half the cost of improvements.

Maximum standard, discretionary and special grants are increased by 50 per cent in development and intermediate areas, provided the work is started on or after June 23, 1971 and completed within two years of that date. To find whether these arrangements apply in your area, contact the local authority.

**Payment of grants**

All grants are normally paid only when improvements have been completed to the satisfaction of the council's surveyor. But the council may pay the builder or architect direct. It may even pay by instalments during the course of the work. Councils usually impose a year's time limit on any improvement work—but this can, in some cases, be extended.

The first step towards obtaining a grant is to get an application form from the council. No improvement work should start until the householder has received grant approval.

There are several other ways in which a council can provide financial help. It can grant substantial loans to cover renovations and may lend money to ensure that grant-aided improvement work is effective by providing for essential structural repairs.

If sufficient money cannot be borrowed from a council, building society or bank, the householder may wish to apply for a second mortgage. There are serious disadvantages to borrowing in this way, however. □ Personal loans and second mortgages, p. 506.

**Getting permission**

Once a householder has established that money is available for the improvements, the next step is to seek the necessary permission.

PLANNING PERMISSION Application is made on a form provided by the local authority. The form requires full details of the proposed work, together with plans and measurements.

If the householder does not wish to spend money on detailed plans, he can submit brief details and ask for approval in principle. If

## Whose consent for alterations to the home?

| Change or alteration | Planning consent | Building regul clearance (outside Lond |
|---|---|---|
| **ALTERATIONS OUTSIDE THE HOME** | | |
| Putting up a gate, fence, wall, etc. | If the fence, etc., faces a road, consent is required if it is over 4 ft high. If it does not face a road, consent is required if it is over 7 ft high | Yes in certain circumstances if it is near a h |
| Planting or felling trees | Not unless tree to be felled, lopped or topped is protected by preservation order | No |
| Adding a front porch | Probably, because in most cases it would mean building in front of the building line | Yes |
| Putting in new exterior doors | Not unless it is part of a porch which extends beyond the building line | No |
| Putting in windows | Yes, if they extend the building or are installed where there were no windows before | Yes |

* In inner London, building regulations may be slightly different

this outline permission is granted, it will justify expenditure on more detailed plans.

If planning consent is refused, or granted subject to conditions which the householder finds unacceptable, he has the right to appeal within six months to the Department of the Environment. A solicitor, surveyor or architect will be able to advise whether or not there are grounds for an appeal.

NEIGHBOURS' CONSENT Discuss any proposed alteration with immediate neighbours at an early stage. They will be less likely to complain about noise or rubble later on.

In addition, neighbours may have rights over the property. The deeds of the house, for example, may prohibit the building of a garage; only with the consent of neighbours will it be safe to ignore this restrictive covenant.

Many alterations cannot be carried out without entering a neighbour's property; this again needs permission. Even if the title deeds give the right to enter to carry out repairs—to a common wall or fence, for example—a convenient time has to be arranged.

In many cases, it will be enough to get the neighbour's verbal agreement; but if there is a restrictive covenant which would be broken if the work went ahead, get a solicitor to ask for the neighbour's written agreement.

GROUND LANDLORD'S CONSENT A solicitor will be able to tell from the lease of a leasehold property whether permission is needed from the ground landlord. If so, his consent should be obtained in writing.

The landlord will usually ask for plans, and may want his surveyor to advise whether or not consent should be given. The tenant then has to pay the landlord's costs.

In law, the landlord is not entitled to refuse permission unreasonably if the work will improve the property. If he persists in objecting, the leaseholder can either go ahead without permission and let the landlord take legal steps to stop the work, or he can seek a High Court declaration that the work may be done.

LENDER'S CONSENT The mortgage deeds should make it clear whether the lender's permission is needed before work is done. Apply in writing to the lender, quoting the mortgage number. Give full details of the proposals and, if structural alterations are involved, enclose a copy of the architect's plans.

BUILDING REGULATION CLEARANCE Contact the surveyor's department of the local authority to see whether it wants to check that the work will comply with building regulations. The regulations lay down standards for all building work, and failure to comply with them could result in the work having to be redone.

INSURANCE COMPANY Inform the insurers of the building, or the policy may be invalidated. It may be necessary to insure the work.

| Neighbour's consent | Lender's consent (check mortgage deed) | Ground landlord's consent (check lease) |
| --- | --- | --- |
| Not normally | Not normally | Usually yes |
| Yes if it would infringe neighbour's right of light | Not normally | Possibly |
| Not normally | Possibly | Usually yes |
| No | Possibly | Usually yes |
| Not unless they would infringe neighbour's right of light | Possibly | Usually yes |

continued ▶

## Whose consent for alterations to the home? continued

| Change or alteration | Planning consent | Building regul clearance (outside Lond |
|---|---|---|
| Installing a pond or swimming pool | No | Yes, if drainag works are inv |
| Making a car hard-standing | In practice, no | No |
| Erecting a carport or garage | Yes in some cases | Yes |
| Providing new access/enlarging existing access to a road | Yes | No |
| Building a garden shed or greenhouse | Only if it is over 12 ft high with a ridged roof; or over 10 ft high with any other roof | Possibly |
| Adding an extension to the house | Yes if the extension projects in front of the original building line of the house. Consent is not required for other extensions unless they are greater than 1750 cu. ft or one-tenth of the original house (up to 4000 cu. ft) | Yes |
| Demolishing outbuildings | No | No |
| **ALTERATIONS INSIDE THE HOME** | | |
| Installing a wash-hand basin or shower | No | Possibly |
| Installing a bathroom or lavatory: Converting existing room | Not unless the house is being converted into flats | Yes |
| Building extra room | Treated as extension | Yes |
| Erecting partition wall | Not unless property is being converted into flats | Yes |
| Knocking down interior walls | Not unless use of property is changed, or it is converted into more than one separate dwelling | Yes |
| Converting loft into bedroom | Not unless the house is being converted into flats | Yes |
| **CHANGING THE USE OF A HOME** | | |
| Using part of the house as an office | Yes (but consent is not required for a study) | Yes |
| Converting a private house to multiple occupation | Yes | Yes |
| Turning a house into a guest house or hotel | Yes | Yes |

*In inner London, building regulations may be slightly different

| Neighbour's consent | Lender's consent (check mortgage deed) | Ground landlord's consent (check lease) |
| --- | --- | --- |
| Not normally | Not normally | Usually yes |
| No | Not normally | Usually yes |
| Not unless covered by restrictive covenant or right of light | Usually yes | Usually yes |
| No | Usually yes | Usually yes |
| Not unless covered by restrictive covenant or right of light | Not normally | Usually yes |
| Not unless covered by restrictive covenant or right of light | Usually yes | Usually yes |
| No | Usually yes | Usually yes |
| No | Not normally | Possibly |
| Not unless use of property is changed, and there is a restrictive covenant | Possibly | Usually yes |
| Not unless affected by restrictive covenant or right of light | Usually yes | Usually yes |
| No | Not normally | Usually yes |
| Not unless use of property is changed and there is a restrictive covenant | Possibly | Usually yes |
| Not unless use of property is changed and there is a restrictive covenant | Possibly | Usually yes |
| Not unless covered by restrictive covenant | Usually yes | Usually yes |
| Not unless covered by restrictive covenant | Usually yes | Usually yes |
| Not unless covered by restrictive covenant | Usually yes | Usually yes |

# Problems of living on a private road

*Inviting the council to do the work*  
*When residents do not agree*  
*How to object*

*Payment*  
*Objecting to the final apportionment*

T HE majority of roads in Britain are public highways, the responsibility of either the local council or the Department of the Environment. One of these bodies carries out repairs and maintenance, and the people who use the road or live alongside it do not have to pay directly for its upkeep; the money comes out of rates and taxes.

The position is different, however, with private roads, which have to be maintained—if they are maintained at all—by the people who own a home or property alongside the road, and who are known as the 'frontagers'. Though private roads may be quieter and more secluded than public ones, the difficulties of organising repairs and getting all the property-owners to pay their share of the cost may mean that in practice the roads fall into a state of disrepair.

For this reason residents sometimes prefer to have the roads taken over or 'adopted' by the local council, which then becomes responsible for maintaining them.

It is not often possible to transfer the road without expense. Highway authorities will accept and adopt only roads that comply with their standards. People living on a private road who want it taken over sometimes club together to get it made up satisfactorily and then 'dedicated' as a public highway. It is more usual, however, for the council to bring the road up to standard before adoption.

### Inviting the council to do the work
The procedure followed by the local authority depends on whether it operates under a law called the Code of 1875, or that of 1892.

Under the Code of 1875, the council—on its own initiative or at the request of a majority of frontagers—serves a notice on all the residents requiring them to carry out the work within a particular time.

In practice the council does not expect them to do so and when the time limit expires the authority carries out the work and serves each frontager with a bill—the apportionment for his share of the job. This is based on the length of his property lying next to the road.

Under the 1892 procedure, the authority has to pass a resolution and then serve each

of the residents with a notice stating its intention to make up the road. A provisional apportionment of how much they may have to pay is given at the same time.

Under this code, the share of the costs an owner has to bear can be based on the benefit he will receive if the road is made up—so that someone who has no frontage, but access through a court or passage, may also have to pay a contribution.

The council must advertise its plans locally, and full estimates, specifications and provisional apportionments must be made available for inspection.

### When residents do not agree
Some residents may not want to see their private road taken over by the council because they do not wish or cannot afford to pay their share of the cost. This reason will not be accepted as a valid objection.

Similarly, a group of residents cannot prevent the council stepping in simply because they value the privacy of an unadopted road.

There are cases, however, where the residents believe themselves to be already living on a public road and consequently object to paying for it to be made up. They may argue that repairs have been carried out by the council in the past and that this amounts to unofficial recognition of the road as a highway. However, councils have the power to make emergency repairs to any highway without affecting the ownership of a private road.

On the other hand, if the road was in existence on August 31, 1835, it will be classed as a public highway, for all existing roads became public on that date.

Other grounds for objection are largely technical, relating to the way in which the council acts. It could be claimed:

**1.** That the council has not followed the correct legal procedure.

**2.** That the proposed works are insufficient or unreasonable.

**3.** That the estimated cost is excessive.

**4.** That the provisional apportionment is unfair because certain properties have been wrongly included or excluded.

**5.** That the apportionment of costs is incorrect

on some specific matter, such as the name of one of the house-owners or the extent of a property frontage.

Such objections, however, are likely only to delay the road scheme, for the council can correct any error and proceed again.

### How to object

Residents have one month from the time the council publishes a road adoption plan to make any objection. They will usually need the advice of a solicitor in order to be able to do so effectively. The authority can then either amend its assessment or refer the case to the local magistrates' court.

The residents must receive individual notices which should include the period within which they can appeal to the court.

The hearing takes the form of an application by the authority for consent to proceed. All objectors are entitled to be heard.

As a result of the magistrates' decisions, the authority may have to abandon its plans altogether; or it may again serve its notices with a correction or alter the apportionment among the residents. Alternatively, of course, the council may be allowed to proceed as it intended. Costs may be awarded to either side.

Either side may appeal against the magistrates' decision to a Crown Court. If that is unsuccessful, an appeal—but only on a point of law—may be made to the High Court.

### Payment

Where there is no objection, or the council is allowed to proceed after a court hearing, the residents receive a final bill—called the final apportionment—when the work is done. Most authorities allow 28 days after sending a demand for payment of the final apportionment. After this, they begin to charge interest on the amount outstanding at 7 per cent a year.

Until the charge is paid it is like a mortgage on the house, and the authority has the power to sell the property or appoint a receiver if the owner fails to pay.

Most local authorities accept payment by instalments. Once they have made such an arrangement, they cannot demand payment of the whole sum even if one instalment falls into arrears. They can take steps to recover individual instalments in a magistrates' court, or in the local county court. The period of repayment must not be more than 30 years and the interest rate is fixed at 7 per cent.

### Objecting to the final apportionment

Any resident who believes his bill is unfair can object to the council within one month from the date on which the bill is served on him.

The only grounds for an objection at this stage are that the actual cost exceeds the original estimate by more than 15 per cent, that there has been an unreasonable departure from the original plans and specifications or that the final apportionment has not been made in the same way as the provisional apportionment.

The case is heard by the magistrates, and further appeals or objections may be made—again, only on a point of law—to a Crown Court or to the High Court.

In some cases, instead of court action, it may be possible to appeal to the Secretary of State for the Environment, who may decide to hold a hearing.

## Keeping the road private

RESIDENTS who decide to keep their road private—because it is more pleasant, safer or quieter—normally form themselves into a road management committee or sometimes a limited company.

The committee or company is open to all frontagers (people who own property alongside the road) simply by buying a voting share, but there is no means by which any resident on the street can be forced to take part.

The total costs of keeping the road in good repair or of making it up to a good standard have therefore to be paid by those frontagers who are prepared to make a contribution.

When the committee or company is formed it normally gets professional advice from a surveyor or road-building expert on the cost of managing the road. It will then make an apportionment of the cost, setting out how much each member should contribute.

This sum is paid in advance every year by all members of the committee or company until they leave the street. Even then, it is normal for there to be a condition that they remain liable until they have formally handed over their interest to the person buying their house. This transfer has to be legalised by a transfer deed.

# Security for leaseholders

*Those who qualify*    *Seeking advice*
*What it costs*        *Fees and expenses*
*Raising the money*

MANY people who have lived in lease-hold property for at least five years are entitled to buy the freehold of their homes at prices which may be well below the market value. Tenants who do not want to pay the price of a freehold are given the alternative right to a new 50-year lease at a low ground rent. Powers to force an unwilling landlord to comply are provided under the Leasehold Reform Act 1967.

## Those who qualify

The Leasehold Reform Act applies only to homes which had a rateable value of less than £200 on March 23, 1965. In Greater London this limiting figure is £400. Householders can find out what the rateable value of their property was on this date—it may since have been changed—by inquiring at the rating department of their local authority.

In the case of a home built or converted after March 23, 1965, the deciding factor will be the rateable value first entered on the local valuation list.

To qualify, the property must be either a whole house or in a building that has been wholly divided from top to bottom to form self-contained maisonettes—not horizontally as flats. Buildings which have lost their character as private houses because they are used mainly for non-residential purposes are also excluded.

The tenant's original lease must have been for more than 21 years, and the house must be his main residence. The ground rent must be less than two-thirds of the rateable value on March 23, 1965 (or on the date on which the lease began, if that is later).

Before he can claim the right to buy the freehold, the leaseholder must have lived in the house for at least five years—either as the tenant or as a relative of the tenant.

A leaseholder who is given valid notice to quit—because his lease is at an end or, perhaps, because he has infringed its terms—must take action within two months if he wishes to purchase the freehold of the property; after this period, his rights under the Leasehold Reform Act lapse entirely.

The tenant also loses his rights if at any time he agrees to surrender his lease to his landlord. For this reason, be wary of any deal under which the tenant agrees to move out before the expiry of the lease on condition that he is not held responsible for the repairs due under the terms of his lease.

If a tenant changes his mind and withdraws his application for a freehold or for an extension of the lease, he cannot apply again for at least five years.

A tenant who qualifies has the right to make what amounts to a compulsory purchase of his own home; but there are two circumstances in which he may not have this right:

1. A private landlord can resist the tenant's application by proving that he has even greater need of the property, either for his own use or for a member of his family.
2. Public authorities—including local councils, development corporations, hospital boards and nationalised industries—are entitled under the Act to refuse to sell the freeholds of their properties on the grounds that the land is needed for redevelopment.

In both these cases, the leasehold tenant who is refused his right to purchase is entitled to compensation. The amount of compensation would normally be agreed between the landlord and tenant, on a valuer's advice. If there is a dispute, the figure can be fixed by the Lands Tribunal—an informal court, composed of barristers and chartered surveyors, which deals with valuation.

The Crown is exempt from the 1967 Act, which means that tenants with leases from the Crown Estate, the Duchy of Lancaster, the Duchy of Cornwall or a government department have no right to the freehold of their homes or to compensation.

## What it costs

THE PRICE OF A FREEHOLD The price the leaseholder will have to pay for the freehold of his home bears little resemblance to the market value of the property with vacant possession. The figure is based on the price that someone else would be willing to pay for the house on the open market—assuming that the leaseholder is in occupation with at least a 50-year lease (that is, 50 years plus any years remaining on his existing lease) at a low ground rent. Naturally, that price is low because the purchaser could not expect to get possession for at least 50 years, and in the meantime he would receive only the low ground rent as a return on his capital investment. For instance, a freehold worth £3500 if the house were sold to someone who could move in immediately might be available to the resident leaseholder for less than £1000.

If the landlord and leaseholder cannot agree on a price, the case will then be decided by the Lands Tribunal.

In practice, houses with long leases are often on large estates in which there are many properties of similar size and plan and of approximately similar value. In such cases, valuers are usually employed by the landlord and by the first leaseholder who applies for a freehold. The figure they eventually agree upon becomes the precedent for neighbours.

If the landlord has a large number of houses in the area, he stands to gain or lose a great deal by a difference of perhaps £100 in the price of this first 'test case' property. For this reason, disagreement over the price is likely and it will probably result in an appeal to the Lands Tribunal.

THE RENT FOR AN EXTENDED LEASE The terms on which a qualified leaseholder can gain a 50-year extension of the lease on his property are also favourable.

There is no premium or lump-sum downpayment; and the new lease, which takes effect when the old one expires, carries a rent based on the letting value of the site alone—taking no account of the house itself.

Even if the site is large enough to accommodate a hotel or a block of flats, the rent will be based on its annual value as a site for a building of the kind occupied by the leaseholder. This rent, known as a 'modern ground rent', is unlikely to be more than £100 a year. The landlord can, however, insist on having it reviewed after 25 years.

In deciding whether to choose to extend his lease, the tenant should bear in mind the major disadvantage that it deprives him of his right to buy the freehold at a later date. Probably for this reason, most leaseholders choose to buy the freeholds of their homes rather than extend the lease.

## Raising the money
A leaseholder with a mortgage should first approach the lender if he needs a further advance to buy the freehold. In most cases, building societies, insurance companies and local authorities will give this additional advance because it considerably increases the value of their security—the house. They may even lend enough to cover costs and expenses.

However, a tenant who bought his leasehold home with an endowment mortgage when he was younger and healthier could find it expensive to take out a new policy with a premium based on his present age and state of health. He might do better to seek a new capital repayment mortgage.

A leaseholder who has paid off his mortgage, or who has not had one, is less likely to be able to borrow the freehold price from a building society or an insurance company. But his bank may be able to help with a five-year loan at approximately 2 per cent above the bank's base rate—the rate used as a basis for calculating interest on various types of loan.

The advantage of owning a freehold are so considerable that a leaseholder who cannot raise the money from other sources may decide to approach a finance house. However, he should see his solicitor before committing himself to a loan of this kind. ☐ Personal loans and second mortgages, p. 506.

## Seeking advice
The rights of a leaseholder who can buy his freehold are valuable. Even if he does not wish to go on living in the house, he may be able to make a considerable profit by buying the freehold and then selling the property with full vacant possession.

The leaseholder can, however, forfeit his rights by making a false move. It is therefore essential to consult a solicitor.

If the solicitor agrees that the lease qualifies under the Leasehold Reform Act, he will advise whether to apply for the freehold or for a 50-year extension. He will then suggest a surveyor or valuer to advise on a fair price for the freehold or an appropriate ground rent for the extended lease.

As soon as the surveyor has suggested a price, negotiations with the landlord begin. The negotiations will be conducted by the surveyor, and could possibly be settled within a few months.

## Fees and expenses
The leaseholder who buys his freehold or extends his lease has to pay the landlord's legal and valuation costs as well as his own.

The largest item is likely to be the fees charged by the landlord's and leaseholder's surveyors. These tend to be similar from one surveyor to another, but there is no longer any national scale; fees may be reduced if the surveyors are involved in negotiations on other properties on the same estate.

# Mortgages: a change in the rate of interest

*Capital repayment mortgages*     *Local authority mortgages*
*Endowment mortgages*

BUILDING societies, insurance companies and local authorities raise or lower the rate of interest they charge on mortgages from time to time, depending on the general level of interest rates and the supply of money. When rival financial institutions start paying a higher rate of interest to depositors, the building societies may have to increase their interest rates to investors in order to attract money. This increase is passed on to the home-buyers who are borrowing from them.

**Capital repayment mortgages**
Even a small change in the rate can make a considerable difference to the house-buyer's mortgage repayments.

For instance, if the rate goes up 1 per cent in the first year of a 20-year capital repayment mortgage loan of £6000 at 7 per cent this will add £900 to the total repayments.

| | |
|---|---|
| Monthly repayments at 7 per cent | £47·22 |
| Monthly repayments at 8 per cent | £50·94 |
| Difference a month | £3·72 |

Total difference over 20 years: about £900

If the rate fell from 8 per cent to 7 per cent, there would be a corresponding saving.

If the interest rate rises, a building society will normally send the borrower a letter giving notice of when the repayments are to be increased.

Alternatively, the society may agree to extend the period of the loan, and allow the borrower to continue paying at the old rate, or at a less sharply increased rate.

Such an extension is a useful alternative for families who would find it difficult to increase their repayments. But it is less advantageous in the long term than paying the higher monthly rate.

Between 1960 and 1970, for example, mortgage interest rates rose from 5½ per cent to 8½ per cent. This meant that a house-owner with a 20-year mortgage taken out in 1960 who chose at each increase to extend his mortgage and continue to repay at the same rate would have added 15 years to his loan

period by 1970. His repayments would then not be completed until 1995, whereas under the original arrangements the property would have been free of mortgage by 1980. When the interest rate falls—as it did in 1971—the house-owner can choose to continue paying the higher rate and so reduce the mortgage period. This is particularly useful if repayments would otherwise still be due beyond retirement age.

Extending a mortgage also increases the overall cost of house-purchase. Take the case of the £6000 mortgage over 20 years. If, when the interest rate rises from 7 per cent to 8 per cent, a borrower is allowed to go on paying at the old monthly rate of £47·22 instead of the new rate of £50·94, the loan period would have to be extended by about 4½ years.

This extra 4½ years' repayment (at £47·22 a month) would add about £2500 to the total mortgage debt, compared with £900 if the higher interest rate is paid. However this difference is likely to be offset to some extent by the decrease in the value of money.

If the borrower does decide to extend the period of the loan, the terms of his mortgage protection policy must be changed. The insurance company may increase the premiums slightly.

**Endowment mortgages**
A change in the interest rate charged by building societies will mean higher repayments on those endowment mortgages that are provided jointly by a building society, which lends the money, and an insurance company, which provides the endowment protection. But in this case the borrower does not have the choice of asking for an extension.

The premiums on the endowment policy will not change, but the borrower will have to pay the increased rate of interest every month. The period of the loan cannot be extended, for if payment of interest were continued at the old rate, the actual debt owing to the building society would go up and the endowment policy would no longer be enough to cover the borrower's increased debt.

Some endowment mortgages are arranged solely by insurance companies, which both lend the money and provide the endowment policy. The insurance companies change their mortgage interest rates from time to time, usually to correspond with a change in the rate charged by building societies, but not all of them apply this change to mortgages already in existence.

Check in the mortgage deed whether the interest rate on the loan is liable to change, or if the loan is at a 'guaranteed' rate of interest.

If it is liable to fluctuate, the borrower must be prepared to pay an increased (or, possibly, decreased) rate at some time during the period of the loan, in the same way as he would for a building society mortgage. But if the loan is at a 'guaranteed' rate, he will always pay at the rate charged when the loan was granted. If the rate rises he benefits by paying less than other borrowers; if it falls he will pay more because of the fixed rate of interest.

### Local authority mortgages

Local authorities also change the rate of interest on their mortgages, especially when the rate at which they borrow the money in the first place changes.

But, as with insurance companies, most local authorities grant loans to home-buyers at a guaranteed rate of interest, so that a change has no effect on existing loans.

## Two ways of repaying when the interest rate rises

When the interest rate rises on a capital repayment mortgage, either the borrower's monthly repayment increases or he has to pay at the old rate over a longer period. How much extra he pays depends on the method he chooses—if the interest on a £5000 loan over 25 years increases from 8 to 8½ per cent at the end of the fifth year, the difference between the two methods is as much as £612

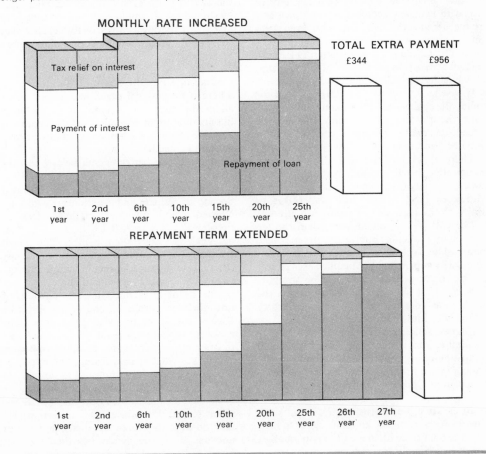

MONTHLY RATE INCREASED

Tax relief on interest

Payment of interest

Repayment of loan

TOTAL EXTRA PAYMENT
£344     £956

| 1st year | 2nd year | 6th year | 10th year | 15th year | 20th year | 25th year |

REPAYMENT TERM EXTENDED

| 1st year | 2nd year | 6th year | 10th year | 15th year | 20th year | 25th year | 26th year | 27th year |

# Selling a house or flat

*Solicitors and estate agents*    *Survey and legal work*
*Fixing the asking price*       *When to move out*
*Negotiating with buyers*     *What it will cost*

SELLING the home, like buying it, can be lengthy, complicated and expensive. The seller needs to decide from the start whether time or money is more important to him. He can save time and trouble by entrusting most of the work to a solicitor and an estate agent. Or he may be able to save money by doing some or all of the work himself.

## Is a solicitor necessary?

Anyone selling his home is free to do the legal work himself—if he can. By doing so, he stands to save a substantial fee—for example, £50–75 on a £6500 house.

In practice, however, the job is so complex that no one without legal training can hope to deal with it unless details about the property are registered at the Land Registry. Even then, only the most dogged layman is likely to succeed. The Consumers' Association (14 Buckingham Street, London WC2N 6DS) publishes a book on how to sell without using a solicitor.

If a seller trying to do without a solicitor comes up against an unforeseen difficulty or finds the process too complex, he will be forced, belatedly, to enlist the help of a solicitor—and may end up by paying more.

There is a third possibility—to join an organisation such as the National House Owners Society (19 Sheepcote Road, Harrow, Middlesex HA1 2JL), which undertakes to deal with the legal side of selling a house.

The cost will be much lower than the fee charged by a solicitor, but the process may take longer. The work of such organisations is not necessarily supervised by qualified solicitors.

The choice of a solicitor may be straightforward. If a solicitor was used when the house was bought and gave satisfactory service, use him again to sell.

If a new solicitor is required, seek a recommendation from a friend or from a professional acquaintance—a bank manager, for example. Failing this, a list of local solicitors can be obtained from Citizens' Advice Bureau offices.

## Is an estate agent necessary?

The decision to engage an estate agent to help sell the house will depend upon market factors, such as how many people are trying to sell houses in the area and how many buyers there are; and on personal factors, such as how important it is to sell quickly and how much time the seller can spare.

Estate agents charge the seller for their services. Their fees vary from area to area and are often dependent upon local competition. No national scale of recommended fees is published, but it is likely that a good local solicitor will be able to advise a house seller on the agents available who charge the most reasonable fees. It may be necessary to 'shop around' to find the best bargain.

Although the seller may save money by advertising the house himself, he will not have the benefit of the agent's advice on what price he should ask. It would be foolish to save a fee of £100 if there was a reasonable chance that the agent's efforts would secure £200 more on the sale price.

## Choosing an estate agent

There is no national organisation controlling all estate agents in Britain. It is therefore possible for anyone—honest or unscrupulous, knowledgeable or completely uninformed—to open an agency.

Many of the better agents belong to professional bodies—such as the Royal Institution of Chartered Surveyors, or the Incorporated Society of Valuers and Auctioneers—and are allowed to use the letters of these organisations (F.R.I.C.S. or A.R.I.C.S., and F.S.V.A. or A.S.V.A.) after their names. The Royal Institution of Chartered Surveyors will supply the names of general-practice chartered surveyors and estate agents in the area.

The agent is retained for the purpose of introducing a purchaser, and at the outset he advises the seller on what price should be asked for the house. He should visit the house to draw up particulars for prospective buyers and to see what special features he might be able to mention. Have nothing to do with an agent who refuses to look at the house.

In some instances the agent may advise the seller to put his house up for auction. He may do so if the house is expensive, large or unusual, or if the owner has died and the house is being sold by his executors. But an auction is unusual for the sale of a private house, when it is more likely that a buyer can be found either by the seller or by his agent. This is known as selling by private treaty.

### The estate agent's authority

The agent will usually ask for written authority to handle the sale of the property. This is usually in the form of a simple letter prepared by the agent and signed by the seller.

A seller confronted with any other form of contract should read its terms carefully and seek the advice of a solicitor if there is anything he does not understand. Make sure that the agent's letter of authority does not involve unnecessary additional expense.

The letter should make it clear, for example, that the agent is entitled to his commission only if the house is sold through his efforts. Beware, particularly, of giving an agent what are called 'sole selling rights'. Such an agreement would entitle him to full commission even if the seller found a buyer entirely by his own efforts. If the seller finds a buyer himself, the agent should have no right to claim a fee, except if one has been agreed for advertising.

In most parts of England and Wales, the estate agent's overall fee will include advertising. Since local custom varies, however, it is sensible to make inquiries first.

The seller can protect himself by agreeing a limit on the amount the agent may spend on advertising, and this should be stated in the letter of authority.

If the agent employs other agents on his own initiative, he has to pay them commission from the fee he gets from the seller. But if he approaches another agent on the seller's instructions, on the basis that there is to be a joint agency, additional commission—often 50 per cent more—will have to be paid by the seller. The occasions when this is necessary or desirable are comparatively rare.

The seller should also make sure that after a given period—say, a month—he will be free to ask a rival agent to find a buyer. When this happens, only one commission is paid—to whichever agent sells the house.

In the Midlands and the North of England, it is customary for the seller to agree in his letter of authority to the first agent not to approach a second agent for a stated period—a month, say. This is called 'giving a sole agency' for that period—not to be confused with 'sole selling rights'—and its advantage is that the agent who knows he has no fear of competition for a time, may work harder to sell the house quickly.

In the South of England there is usually no restriction on the number of agents to whom

---

## Selling by auction

THE seller who decides to dispose of his home at a public auction should first check with an auctioneer how much it will cost. In a private-treaty sale, the seller need normally pay nothing to an estate agent if the house is not sold. But most auction sales involve some expense, even if the property is not sold.

Before the auction, the seller and the auctioneer usually agree on a reserve price for the house—that is, the price below which it will not be sold.

It is an advantage for the seller to attend the auction himself or to have a representative there—preferably a solicitor—in case bidding stops just below the reserve price. A potential buyer is likely to approach the auctioneer to find out if it is possible to settle for about the reserve price, and the seller, or his authorised representative, may be able to reach an agreement with the buyer. It oftens pays to sell at just below the reserve price rather than go to the expense of re-advertising the house.

There are usually strict rules and penalties that prevent a seller from bidding in an auction of his own house. Check with the auctioneer or solicitor as early as possible before the sale if you want either to bid in person or to get someone else to bid for you in order to force the price of the house higher.

It is legal for a seller to bid only where the auctioneer states in his particulars of sale that the seller, or someone acting for him, may do so. Otherwise, under the Sale of Land by Auction Act 1867, it is a criminal offence. The buyer can withdraw from the sale, possibly also claiming damages, and the seller can be prosecuted.

Even where the rules do allow the seller to bid, however, it is better to engage someone else—possibly the auctioneer himself, or a member of his staff—to do so. It is all too easy for a seller to forget, in the excitement of the bidding, that he is not actually trying to buy the house himself.

a seller may go. This is called multiple agency. But sellers are not advised to go to more than, say, three agents, since confusion can arise.

## Fixing the asking price

The owner selling without the aid of an estate agent usually has to decide on the asking price himself. Alternatively he may feel that the cost of a valuation—£40 on a £6500 house—is justified.

Four factors may be relevant in coming to a decision about the asking price:
1. How much the owner paid for the house.
2. How much property has increased in value.
3. How much he has spent on improvements.
4. What price similar properties have sold for in the same locality.

When a seller has arrived at a figure, it is normal to add a sum for bargaining with potential buyers—say, 5 per cent—and this will give him the asking price.

If an estate agent is employed, he will advise the owner about the asking price.

It is unlikely that any agent would advise selling for substantially below the house's real worth. The seller should be on his guard against agreeing to an asking price which seems too low. Estate agents' fees are usually so calculated that if the house sells for £200 or £300 less than the seller hoped, the agent loses comparatively little in commission. For this reason less scrupulous agents may press for a quick sale at below the market price.

## Advertising the home

The main problem for a seller not employing an estate agent is to get information to potential buyers. The most effective means is a newspaper advertisement. Choose papers most likely to be read by buyers looking for the type of property to be sold—usually local evening or weekly papers—and if the house looks particularly attractive, include a photograph.

Take care to see that all advertisements are accurate. A buyer who could show that he took the house on the basis of false statements made by the seller or his agent might be able to claim damages under the Misrepresentation Act 1967 or withdraw from the purchase.

## Dealing with prospective buyers

Give potential buyers an opportunity to inspect the house and try to provide any additional information they require. People concerned about the cost of central heating, for example, will welcome the chance to see the fuel bills for previous years.

If someone expresses serious interest in the property, many sellers ask for a preliminary or holding deposit—usually between £5 and £100. This deposit has no legal significance, and gives no guarantee that the buyer will not withdraw later.

It may have its value, however, as a means of eliminating people who are too shy to admit that they think the property unsuitable.

This deposit should be paid to the seller's estate agent or solicitor.

The seller must decide, usually after discussion with his solicitor, whether to accept deposits from more than one potential buyer. There is no legal obstacle to doing so, though many solicitors dislike the practice.

When the seller accepts more than one preliminary deposit, his solicitor sends contracts to each potential buyer's solicitor, informing him that he has sent out other contracts for the sale of the property.

The sale then becomes a race between the solicitors to secure the property for their own client. Solicitors call it a 'contract race'.

From the seller's point of view, a contract race has two main advantages. Because of the element of competition, solicitors for rival buyers will be pressed to try to complete the legal work quickly; and if one prospective buyer drops out—perhaps because of failure to raise a mortgage—there will be others at an advanced stage of negotiation. In the same position, a seller who has agreed to deal only with one person would be left without a buyer, and would have to start again almost from scratch.

Despite such advantages, a seller who starts a contract race should bear in mind that it may involve a number of potential buyers in the expense of surveys and building-society valuations—all but one of them fruitlessly.

## Can the seller turn away buyers?

There is one important exception to the general rule that a house-owner has freedom to sell his house to anyone he chooses. He is not allowed to discriminate on grounds of colour, race, or ethnic or national origins. This means that an offer from a coloured person, for instance, must not be refused on the ground that a coloured person would not be welcomed in the neighbourhood.

The only case when colour or race discrimination is not unlawful is when the sale is completely private, in the sense that no estate agent or any other kind of advertising is used. If the seller simply asks his friends to keep a lookout for anyone interested, he would be entitled to refuse a coloured buyer.

A person who feels himself to be the victim of unlawful discrimination can complain to the Race Relations Board (5 Lower Belgrave Street, London SW1W 0MR). Or a complaint can be made to the nearest conciliation committee, whose address is obtainable from the town hall.

If the complaint is upheld, an attempt will be made to reach an agreed solution. If this fails, the house-owner may be taken to court and a damages claim made against him or an injunction sought to prevent a refusal.

## Furniture, fixtures and fittings

The law regards some fixtures and fittings as part of the house which can be removed only with the agreement of the buyer.

The seller may agree to sell items of furniture and removable fittings with the house, and these may either be included in the selling price or paid for separately.

Take care, however, that any separate agreement about fixtures and fittings makes clear that they will be sold only if the sale of the house goes through.

In one case, an antique dealer pretended he was interested in buying a house when he really wanted only some valuable furniture in it. He persuaded the seller to sign a letter agreeing to sell him the furniture at a modest price, but the letter made no mention of the sale of the house.

The negotiations for the house sale did not proceed, but the dealer insisted on his right to buy the furniture. The argument was eventually settled out of court, but the affair was costly to the seller. ☐ Which fixtures and fittings go with the house, p. 192.

## The survey

When the seller has accepted a buyer's provisional offer, he must be prepared to have his home inspected again. This time the inspection will be made by a surveyor.

In fact there may be two surveyors—one making a structural report for the buyer himself, and one making a valuation for the building society (or other lender) which has been asked to provide a mortgage.

A surveyor may be content to inspect the house without disturbing furniture and furnishings. In some cases, however, he may have been asked by the buyer for a survey which cannot be carried out without disturbing the contents of the house—taking up fitted carpets, for example.

The seller is free to refuse to allow any part of the survey to be carried out, though by doing so he naturally runs the risk of driving away a potential buyer. It may be better to ask the buyer to pay for the carpets

to be taken up and relaid by experts. Alternatively, the buyer can be asked, through his solicitor, to pay this fee only if the sale does not go through.

## Transferring ownership

As soon as it seems likely that the potential buyer will proceed, and after any initial deposit has been paid, the seller instructs his solicitor to begin the legal process of transferring the ownership of the property. ☐ Exchanging contracts, p. 205.

## Seller's duties

The seller has the right to stay in the house until the sale is finally completed, but once contracts are exchanged, his rights are restricted and he has obligations to the buyer.

The seller must make any repairs necessary to keep the property safe from serious deterioration but he has no obligation to improve it. He must not do anything that might damage the house. If damage is done, the buyer is entitled to a reduction in the purchase price as compensation.

Make certain that full insurance cover is maintained until the date of completion, for the seller may be liable for any damage to the house up to that date.

## When to move out

When they exchange contracts, the solicitors acting for the parties agree upon a date when the sale is to be concluded. This final step sets the 'completion date', when the keys are handed over by the seller's solicitor in exchange for the balance of the purchase money. It is often four weeks from the exchange of contracts.

Normally the seller is entitled to continue living in the property until completion takes place, but in some cases the buyer may ask to move in before completion.

The seller's solicitor will usually advise that this request be refused. There are two reasons.

Firstly, a buyer already living in the property may be less anxious to complete the transaction than one waiting to move in.

Secondly, if a last-minute difficulty arises and the buyer is unable to go through with the purchase—because he cannot raise the money, perhaps—the seller may be open to all the expense and inconvenience of legal action to regain possession of his own property.

If the seller stays beyond completion date without authorisation, the buyer can, in theory, take legal action to get him evicted. This rarely happens in practice, as the procedure is both costly and slow. Legally the buyer would be in a similar position to that of a man finding his home taken over by squatters. ☐ Rights and responsibilities of running a home, p. 280.

**What it will cost**

ESTATE AGENTS The seller who has employed an estate agent has to pay a commission that is usually based on the price for which the house is sold.

He may also have to pay the whole or part of the agent's advertising costs. This is less common in the South of England than in the Midlands and the North—where, however, the additional costs for advertising are often offset by a slightly lower charge.

SOLICITORS The seller has to pay exactly the same fee as the buyer, based on the purchase price. ☐ Counting the cost, p. 213.

In addition, the solicitor will charge a separate fee for any work he has done to pay off an existing mortgage, and for his out-of-pocket expenses, called 'disbursements', such as fares and postage. But he will not charge for things such as stationery, which form part of his overhead expenses. The solicitor may charge an additional fee for arranging the sale of furnishings and fittings.

VALUE ADDED TAX After April 1973 solicitors' and estate agents' bills will include an extra charge—value added tax. ☐ Dealing with value added tax, p. 693.

# The solicitor's account for selling a house

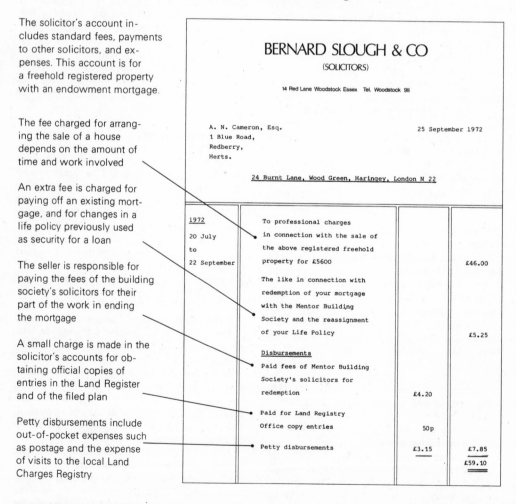

The solicitor's account includes standard fees, payments to other solicitors, and expenses. This account is for a freehold registered property with an endowment mortgage.

The fee charged for arranging the sale of a house depends on the amount of time and work involved

An extra fee is charged for paying off an existing mortgage, and for changes in a life policy previously used as security for a loan

The seller is responsible for paying the fees of the building society's solicitors for their part of the work in ending the mortgage

A small charge is made in the solicitor's accounts for obtaining official copies of entries in the Land Register and of the filed plan

Petty disbursements include out-of-pocket expenses such as postage and the expense of visits to the local Land Charges Registry

## BERNARD SLOUGH & CO
### (SOLICITORS)

14 Red Lane Woodstock Essex Tel. Woodstock 911

A. N. Cameron, Esq.                          25 September 1972
1 Blue Road,
Redberry,
Herts.

24 Burnt Lane, Wood Green, Haringey, London N 22

| 1972 | | | |
|---|---|---|---|
| 20 July | To professional charges in connection with the sale of the above registered freehold property for £5600 | | £46.00 |
| to 22 September | The like in connection with redemption of your mortgage with the Mentor Building Society and the reassignment of your Life Policy | | £5.25 |
| | Disbursements | | |
| | Paid fees of Mentor Building Society's solicitors for redemption | £4.20 | |
| | Paid for Land Registry Office copy entries | 50p | |
| | Petty disbursements | £3.15 | £7.85 |
| | | | £59.10 |

# Tax on the sale of property

ANYONE who owns land or property may have to pay capital gains tax if he sells or leases it. Should the owner die, the person to whom the land or property is left may become liable to pay tax on it if he sells.

## WHEN THE PROFIT IS TAXED

| | |
|---|---|
| **Own home** | |
| Used as residence only | No |
| Used partly for business | Yes |
| | on business part |
| Partly let | Yes, on part let |
| **Second home** | |
| Used by owner | Yes |
| Let for rent | Yes |
| Occupied by dependent | No |
| **Any other property** | Yes |
| **A vacant site** | Yes |

In general, an owner must pay capital gains tax on any profit which he makes by selling his property—except his home.

But the tax has to be paid if an owner-occupier uses part of his home for business purposes—a room as an office, or a garage as a business store room, for example. In such cases, capital gains tax is charged on the business part of the property.

If the property is rated in two parts—for example, £60 a year for the living quarters and £30 a year for the business or work part—the capital gains tax is split: two-thirds of the profit is free from tax and one-third is taxable.

In cases where there has been no separate rating, however, the owner has to come to an agreement with the Inspector of Taxes on how much the business part of the house is worth, in relation to the whole building.

A home-owner who buys a second property —a weekend cottage, for example—will have to pay capital gains tax on any profit he makes when he sells it. If the property is used as a home for a dependent relative of his own or of his wife, however, no tax will be payable. If a home-owner has two or more houses and lives in each of them intermittently, he may choose which shall be exempt from capital gains tax when he decides to sell one of them.

If the seller of property or land liable for capital gains tax makes a profit of more than £5000 in a tax year, he must pay tax at the rate of 30 per cent.

If the profit is under £5000 the seller may either pay 30 per cent tax on the whole gain or, if it is more favourable to him, add *half* the gain to his income and pay income tax and (if applicable) surtax on it.

The profit on inherited property is assessed as the difference between the probate value and the sale price. ☐ Working out the value of an estate, p. 423.

Generally speaking, a loss may be set off against a profit on any property sales made in the same tax year. Expenses incurred in buying and selling are also allowed.

These include fees to professional advisors, solicitors, surveyors, valuers and agents, advertising costs and stamp duty.

Allowable expenses might also include court costs which result from legal action taken to establish ownership of the property.

## Tax on leasehold property

Special rules are applied to most leasehold property with less than 50 years to run. Such property is treated as a wasting asset, whose cost is extinguished at an increasing rate over its unexpired life. The gain is taken as the difference between the sale price and a percentage of the cost. The percentages to be used are given in Schedule 8 of the Finance Act 1965 (available in public libraries or from H.M.S.O.).

Take, for example, a 49-year lease bought for £7000 and sold seven years later for £8000. To calculate the capital gain:

**1.** Multiply the actual cost by the percentage for the year of sale as given in the Finance Act (42 years unexpired = 96·593 per cent).
**2.** Divide the result by the percentage for the year of purchase (49 years = 99·657 per cent).
**3.** Subtract this figure (£215) from actual cost to get cost for tax purposes (£6875).
**4.** Deduct the result from the sale price. This is the capital gain (£1215).

The only exception to these special rules is where there is a sitting sub-tenant who is paying less than a market rent; the rules then apply from the expiry of the sub-tenancy.

## How the tax is collected

The Inland Revenue asks for details of capital gains on your Tax Return. The tax payable is then assessed by the Inspector of Taxes and is payable on January 1 following the end of the tax year in which the gain was made. ☐ Capital gains tax, p. 574.

# Choosing the type of home to rent

*Unfurnished and furnished*　　*A home with the job*
*Council tenants*　　　　　　　*Special landlords*
*Lodgers*　　　　　　　　　　*Long leases*

RENTING has a number of advantages over home-ownership: legal fees, if any, will be fairly small; the tenant does not have to put down a large sum at the outset; and he can leave more easily and cheaply.

There are drawbacks, though. Most tenants are less secure than owner-occupiers; they face a much greater risk of being made to leave their homes; the rent may be high, and subject to increases; and they may have difficulty in having repairs carried out.

Landlords, for their part, face rising rates and repair and maintenance costs. The result can be either rising rents or property which is allowed to fall into disrepair.

In this situation the law attempts to keep a balance between the interests of landlord and tenant. In most cases it recognises the right of the landlord to a fair rent and, except in areas of extreme housing shortage where all rents are high, a landlord who keeps his property in good condition can often expect a higher rent than the one who fails to carry out repairs.

The tenant, in return, is protected against the worst types of exploitation. Tenants of all except luxury property cannot be forced to leave without good reason, and there is a degree of protection against excessive rents.

The extent to which the tenant can rely upon the law may be limited in practice by the housing shortage.

A right which can be exercised only at the expense of being made homeless is a right which few tenants can afford. Yet all but the most unscrupulous landlord will treat with respect the tenant who knows his legal rights.

The degree of legal protection a tenant receives varies with the type of property.

## Three types of rented home

| | UNFURNISHED | FURNISHED | COUNCIL |
|---|---|---|---|
| **Availability**<br>☐ Finding a rented house or flat, p. 245 | Through accommodation bureaux, estate agents, and advertisements in shop windows and newspapers | Through accommodation bureaux, estate agents, and advertisements in shop windows and newspapers | By going on a council housing list—or through council rehousing powers |
| **Premiums and 'key money'**<br>☐ Finding a rented house or flat, p. 245 | Premiums are illegal in most cases. Excessive charges for furniture and fittings may also be illegal | Premiums are generally legal except in certain cases | Premiums not generally charged |
| **Rent** | Most properties are protected against arbitrary rent increases. In the majority of cases, rent can be fixed by a rent officer. ☐ Unfurnished property, p. 252; Controlled tenancies, p. 256 | Most properties have a limited protection against rent increases. Rent can be fixed by a rent tribunal. ☐ Furnished property, p. 259 | Tenants have no protection against arbitrary rent increases on paper. But public opinion or Government policy may restrict councils. ☐ Council houses and flats, p. 262 |
| **Peace and quiet** | All tenants have similar rights to peace and quiet and freedom from harassment by the landlord. ☐ The right to privacy, peace and quiet, p. 266 | | |

Tenants of luxury houses and flats—that is, properties which had a rateable value of £200 (in London £400) or more on March 23, 1965 —have very little protection. But since such tenants pay a high rent, they may be in a better position to negotiate with their landlord and obtain safeguards.

### Unfurnished houses and flats
People who rent unfurnished property receive more protection from the law than any other group of tenants. There is machinery to prevent unfair rent increases, and sometimes to enable them to have their rents reduced.

They should have no need to fear arbitrary eviction. Someone with an unfurnished tenancy cannot be made to leave his home until a court has examined his circumstances and those of his landlord. Even then, a tenant who has paid his rent and kept the terms of his agreement can be evicted only if his landlord has greater need of the property.

### Furnished property
The law gives less security to tenants of furnished houses or flats.

If the tenant knows how long he wants to stay, his best protection is a watertight agreement for a stated period. When the agreement ends, however, the tenant can stay only on the landlord's terms—if at all. Until he negotiates an entirely new agreement, he has no legal protection.

Faced with a landlord seeking his eviction, the tenant with no agreement can usually hope for no more than a breathing-space—usually six months, but possibly nine months or even a year. To get even this, though, he must expect a legal tussle with his landlord and it can never be certain that he can win his case.

Again, there is machinery for challenging excessive rent increases, or even for getting an existing rent lowered. But the comparative lack of security of a furnished tenancy makes this a dubious asset; an application for decreasing the rent could so antagonise the landlord that he starts legal action to get possession of his property.

### Council tenants
On paper, the council tenant seems to be worst off of all. No Act of Parliament defines when he may or may not be turned out of his home; and he has little opportunity to challenge an increase in rent.

Eviction, when it takes place, is likely to

|  | UNFURNISHED | FURNISHED | COUNCIL |
|---|---|---|---|
| **Repairs and maintenance** □ Repairs: Whose responsibility?, p. 268 | Landlords are generally responsible for repairs to the structure and the exterior. But tenants are bound by any agreement on repairs they may have signed | Landlords must ensure that the property is fit for a new tenant to live in | Councils are generally responsible for repairs to the structure and the exterior |
| **Leaving voluntarily** □ Leaving a rented home, p. 272 | Tenants must give landlords four weeks' notice in writing unless there is a lease for a fixed period | Tenants must give landlords four weeks' notice in writing unless there is a lease for a fixed period | Tenants must generally give council notice in writing |
| **Eviction** □ Leaving a rented home, p. 272 | No tenant can be evicted without a court order | | |
| | Tenant has a high degree of protection from the court | Tenant has little real protection as court order is generally just a formality | There is no protection against arbitrary eviction on paper—but in practice councils are unlikely to make their tenants homeless |

mean that the family will be moved into a cheaper or older council house or flat. Since the council is also the welfare authority, evictions which leave the family homeless are almost unheard of.

## Lodgers

A number of people who pay rent for their accommodation fall outside the framework of legal control and protection. They include anyone who occupies a house or flat through an act of friendship or charity—such as a housekeeper who, though not entitled, is allowed to stay on when her employer dies; or a family who are given temporary accommodation by neighbours after their home has been burnt down.

Lodgers are borderline cases. The rent they pay usually covers board as well as accommodation. In law, they do not normally have the exclusive right of occupation—they cannot exclude other people from the part they occupy. Most lodgers can be made to leave whenever the landlord chooses.

The rent they pay is subject only to the laws of supply and demand and if they object to an increase they have no legal redress. Their only alternative may be to look elsewhere.

Where fewer facilities are provided, the lodger may qualify for the same protection as a tenant of furnished property. It depends on whether payment for accommodation makes up a substantial part of his rent. If it does, he may be able to take legal action if his rent is increased or his security threatened.

➤ THE LODGER ENTITLED TO PROTECTION
*Mr Kasozi Luganda, a Ugandan law student, occupied room No. 53 of the Queensborough Court Hotel in London. Mr Luganda had a Yale key to his room—a bed-sitter with a double gas ring. He prepared his own meals and provided his own towels and soap. The hotel supplied the bedding, cleaned the room and changed the linen. There was a communal lavatory and bathroom, the services of a porter, and a receptionist who took telephone messages.*

*In 1959 the management decorated his room and tried to put his rent up from £4 18s. to £5 19s. Mr Luganda refused to pay the increase and took his case to the Rent Tribunal. He informed the hotel management that he was taking legal advice but would continue to pay the old rent.*

*He was given two days' notice to quit, which he ignored. Then one day he returned from work to find that the lock on his door had been changed. Later the room was re-let. Mr Luganda sought a court injunction to allow him to use the*

*room again, and this was granted. The hotel management appealed.*

DECISION *The Court of Appeal concluded that Mr Luganda, though not strictly a tenant, was protected by the Rent Acts and that his rent could not be increased. He should be allowed to return to room No. 53, and the tenant to whom it had since been let should find another room. (Luganda v. Service Hotels Ltd.)* ◄

Students in 'digs', or in university hostels, are unlikely to qualify for such protection because the value of the board forms a substantial proportion of their whole rent. Similarly, old people living in hotels and taking meals in the hotel dining-room cannot be considered tenants.

Anyone who takes rooms in a house for a holiday does not qualify for protection as a tenant of furnished property.

## A home with the job

Some people have a home provided by their employer because they could not do their job properly without it—the caretaker of a block of flats, for example, or the house master in a boarding school.

In law, such people are not tenants. Generally they are entitled to the accommodation only as long as the job lasts. The rent they pay, if any, is negotiated between them and their employer, and if they cannot agree, the law will not usually intervene.

If, however, the employer provides housing merely as an extra benefit for his employees, without its being essential for their jobs, the employees qualify for the legal protection.

## Special landlords

Homes let by the Crown or by Government bodies are not covered by the protection of the law. Nor are properties which belong to housing societies or charitable trusts.

## Long leases

When a property is let on a long lease at a low rent, the occupier is more like an owner than a tenant. He pays a lump sum for the lease and can sell it again later if he decides to move.

Such a person—technically, the qualifications are that his lease was originally for more than 21 years at an annual rent of less than two-thirds of the rateable value—is protected by completely different legislation. He may be entitled to buy the freehold of the property, even if the landlord does not wish to sell, or to have a new lease automatically when his present one expires. ☐ Security for lease-holders, p. 232.

# Finding a rented house or flat

*Accommodation bureaux*      *When a premium is illegal*
*Furnished or unfurnished*      *Furniture, fixtures and fittings*
*Part-furnished*      *Council waiting lists*

THERE are many ways of finding private property to rent—through advertisements in shop windows or the local newspaper, for instance, or through an accommodation bureau or estate agent.

Council houses or flats may be more difficult to obtain. The prospective tenant usually has to put his name down on a council waiting list and normally cannot expect a home for several years. Only someone in a desperate situation can jump the queue—for example, someone whose present home is on the point of being demolished.

Sometimes council tenants swap accommodation with other council tenants. Such exchanges must be approved by the council.

Many people with housing problems solve them by moving to a new town, where it is generally easier to find a home. Local councils can supply information about new towns, and the ways in which people moving to them can be helped to find jobs.

### Accommodation bureaux

Estate agents and accommodation bureaux provide lists of houses and flats available to rent. It is illegal for any agent or bureau to demand or accept money for simply informing a prospective tenant of homes available.

➤ COMMISSION TO FIND FLAT WAS ILLEGAL *A London barrister, Mr Vishin Tahil Haridas, obtained the tenancy of a flat through a firm of accommodation agents. They charged 10 per cent of the annual rent—a fee of £95.*

*When Mr Haridas did not pay, the company sued and were granted an order for payment. Mr Haridas appealed.*
DECISION *The Court of Appeal held that Mr Haridas did not have to pay because it was illegal under the Accommodation Agencies Act 1953 to charge a fee for registering a prospective tenant, or for giving him details of houses available. (Crouch and Lees v. Haridas.)* ◄

That Court of Appeal decision in 1971 puts in question all fees charged to prospective tenants and makes unclear what fees, if any, estate agents or accommodation bureaux are entitled to charge.

A tenant who believes that he has been asked to pay a fee illegally may have no alternative but to pay the charge if he is to obtain the tenancy he wants. It is then open

---

## Racial discrimination

MOST landlords are not allowed by law to discriminate in the letting of living accommodation on the grounds of colour, race, ethnic or national origin. There are only two exceptions.

A landlord may discriminate if he or his family live on the premises and share accommodation with the tenants, and
1. The property contains only one or two separate tenancies in addition to his own, or
2. The property is a boarding house with up to six lodgers.

It is unlawful—even for landlords who live in houses where they are allowed to discriminate—to advertise for tenants using discriminatory terms, such as 'Sorry, no coloureds' or 'Europeans only' or even 'West Indians only'.

Local authorities and estate agents are not allowed to discriminate in the way they choose tenants. It is unlawful to charge higher rents on the grounds of race or colour.

If a prospective tenant thinks he has suffered discrimination, he can complain to the Race Relations Board at 5 Lower Belgrave Street, SW1W 0MR. It is, however, unlikely that the prospective tenant will derive much benefit from this, because he will still be looking for somewhere to live. In an exceptional case he might obtain damages; but the law is intended more to provide a climate of racial tolerance than to give a legal remedy to individuals who experience discrimination.

to him to seek the advice of a solicitor about trying to recover the money by legal action. ☐ Getting advice on a legal problem, p. 708.

### Furnished or unfurnished

An unfurnished home which qualifies for legal protection gives more security to the tenant than one which is furnished. This is so even where there is a furnished-tenancy agreement.

The tenant of a furnished property whose lease or agreement expires can be made to leave almost at once, while an unfurnished tenant in the same position has security.

If someone looking for a home to rent wants the greater security of an unfurnished property, he should resist attempts to persuade him to take furnished or part-furnished accommodation unless he is desperate. He also needs to beware of any attempt by the landlord to try to get round the law.

The landlord may provide a few sticks of furniture in an attempt to give the property the appearance of being furnished; but he will not succeed in creating what the law regards as a furnished tenancy unless the part of the rent paid for the furniture or services forms a substantial proportion of the whole rent.

If a court is asked to decide, it may consider a particular tenant's need for furniture, and the value to him of what is supplied.

### Part-furnished

Anyone who chooses to rent a part-furnished house or flat, or who has no alternative because of the shortage of accommodation, may still qualify for the greater protection of unfurnished premises.

There is one pitfall he should be on the watch for—an inventory with prices against the items of furniture.

Where a landlord is letting a flat which contains furniture, it is reasonable that he should make a list for the incoming tenant to sign. It can be in the tenant's interests, too, for a tenant with a copy of an agreed inventory cannot be accused of removing furniture that was never there in the first place.

It is when the landlord presents an inven-

## Furnished or unfurnished: how the law decides

DISPUTES between landlord and tenant over whether property is furnished or unfurnished may eventually have to be settled by a county court. The tenant who wants the greater legal protection of an unfurnished tenancy may have to convince the court that, despite the furniture provided by the landlord, it is still not a furnished tenancy.

In a furnished tenancy the accommodation must include a substantial amount of furniture, and the hire of the furniture must be worth a substantial proportion of the weekly or monthly rent.

The court might consider, for example, that a bedroom is not furnished unless it has a bed, wardrobe, dressing-table, bedside table and curtains. Similarly, a sitting-room might not be considered furnished without three or four easy chairs, curtains and possibly a table.

Sometimes a formula is used to work out the value of the furniture as a proportion of the rent. Above a certain proportion, the home will be considered furnished; below that proportion, unfurnished. For example, a court might consider that if the 'hire' of the furniture is worth less than 10 per cent of the rent, the tenancy is not furnished. If it is worth more than 20 per cent it will probably be considered furnished. Between 10 and 20 per cent would be a border-line case in which other factors would have to be taken into account by the court.

A court will consider the actual value of the furniture to the tenant; it is more valuable, for example, to a tenant who has no furniture of his own and wants a home for only a few months than it is to one who has the property on a lease and has his own furniture in store.

Similarly, the tenant may have a greater need for a bed than for a Chippendale chair—although the monetary value of the Chippendale would be much higher.

A court might also consider whether, before the case, the tenant has considered his home furnished or unfurnished.

The rent book, if there is one, will be examined to see if it is headed 'furnished tenancy' or 'regulated tenancy' (the most common type of unfurnished agreement).

The effect of all these considerations is that the furnished or unfurnished status of a property may be determined by reference to the personal circumstances of the tenant. This means that the same home with the same furniture could be ruled to be furnished for one occupier and unfurnished for another.

tory with prices attached that the prospective tenant needs to beware—especially if the prices are vastly inflated. The landlord's reason for doing this will usually be to prove that the tenant is paying a substantial proportion of his rent for furniture—and therefore has a furnished tenancy.

An honest landlord has no reason to put the value of the furniture on the inventory, so in most cases the tenant's best policy is to cross out all the valuation figures before he signs.

The result may be, of course, that the landlord refuses to let the property; but the home-hunter, unless he is desperate, will be better off looking elsewhere.

A prospective tenant who is keen to receive the protection of unfurnished premises should check, finally, whether he will have to share any facilities with the landlord. People who share 'essential living-rooms' are treated as having a furnished tenancy, whether or not their accommodation includes the landlord's furniture. For this purpose, 'essential living-rooms' include a kitchen or sitting-room, but not a bathroom or lavatory.

Merely sharing with other tenants, as opposed to the landlord, makes no difference to a tenant's legal status.

## When a premium is illegal

A prospective tenant needs to find out from the outset what extra charges—if any—he will be expected to pay.

Some landlords ask the tenant to pay a lump sum, in addition to the rent, before he moves in. An outgoing tenant may demand a similar payment in return for assigning the remainder of a lease to a new tenant. Such a payment may be known as a 'premium' or as 'key money'—literally, a payment for the key to the house or flat. It may be an outright payment, or it may be in the form of a loan.

A tenant whose lease expires may also be expected to pay a premium before the lease is renewed.

In many circumstances it is against the law to ask for a premium. It is illegal in all unfurnished tenancies which qualify for Rent Acts protection—that is, all those with a rateable value on March 23, 1965 of £200 or under (£400 in London). In effect, this means most unfurnished homes.

In furnished property, a premium is illegal if any previous tenant living in the property has at some time made use of the legal machinery for getting his rent reduced. Anyone can find out whether this has happened by asking at the town hall whether the rent has been registered at any time.

In all other cases, a landlord will not be breaking the law by asking for a premium for furnished accommodation.

Where accommodation is scarce, a tenant may be loath to refuse to pay an illegal premium if this will mean losing the property altogether. If the demand for a premium is made by a landlord, there is an alternative—to pay and try to recover the money later.

Great care has to be taken over each step in the process of recovering such a payment.

STEP ONE The tenant needs evidence which would stand up in court that he has paid money and that the money is a premium. So, if possible, pay by cheque and write on the back 'paid as premium on —', adding the full address of the property. Anyone without a bank account has a right to demand a receipt before handing over the money.

STEP TWO The tenant who pays by cheque should send it to the landlord with a covering letter, mentioning that the cheque is a premium. Anyone who pays cash and gets a receipt can send a similar letter, thanking the landlord for the receipt—again mentioning that the money was paid as a premium. Be sure to keep a copy of all letters.

STEP THREE When the tenant has moved in and paid his rent (again making sure to keep a record of it) he can take steps to recover the illegal premium. First make sure that the tenancy is, in fact, one for which a premium would be illegal. Get independent advice from the rent officer (for unfurnished property) or the clerk of the Rent Tribunal (for furnished houses and flats). Their addresses will be available from the local council offices.

STEP FOUR If it seems that the premium is illegal, write to the landlord, pointing out that the premium appears to have been paid contrary to the Rent Act 1968, and asking for it to be refunded.

STEP FIVE If the landlord refuses, or simply fails to answer, write again a fortnight later, repeating the information about the premium, and say that the sum he has received illegally will be deducted from future rent payments. Reduce the amount of future rent payments until the premium is recovered in full.

Should the landlord subsequently take action to recover what he considers to be arrears of rent, take legal advice. A solicitor may arrange for the tenant to counter-claim for the money paid as an illegal premium.

An alternative method of reclaiming an illegal premium is to ask the legal department of the local council to prosecute the person who charged it. The penalty for breaking the law on premiums is a fine of up to £100. The case is heard in a magistrates' court and the tenant may have to give evidence. The court can order the premium to be refunded.

It is also open to the tenant to reclaim an illegal premium by suing the landlord (or outgoing tenant, if the premium was charged by him). A solicitor will advise whether such an action is likely to be worth while. The costs are likely to make it a poor financial proposition unless the premium was more than £30.

There are many attempts by landlords to get round the law on premiums, and the tenant has to be on his guard against them.

➤ THE CASE OF THE DISGUISED PREMIUM
*William White and his wife decided they must sell their home at Harrow, Middlesex, because they were in arrears with their mortgage repayments. While searching for somewhere to live, they saw a self-contained flat advertised in the estate agents' office of Clifford and Clifford Ltd.*

*The estate agent told them they could have the flat only if they sold their own house at £500 less than market value. The Whites felt that they had no alternative, and agreed to sell the house to Pegasus Training Estates Ltd for £1800,*

*although the market value was around £2300.*

*The flat tenancy was given by Elmdene Estates, which was closely associated by shareholders and directors to Clifford and Clifford Ltd, the estate agents, and to Pegasus Training Estates Ltd, the buyers. Later, Mr White sued for £500, saying that Elmdene Estates had charged him an illegal premium for the tenancy.*
DECISION *The House of Lords found that Elmdene Estates had demanded a premium, and that Mr White was entitled to a refund of his £500. (Elmdene Estates v. White.)* ◄

A more common form of premium is a demand for money as security against the non-payment of rent or against damage to the premises by the tenant. If a premium would be illegal for the tenancy, the landlord is breaking the law in asking for an additional payment of this type, and the tenant is entitled to the immediate return of his money.

**Furniture, fixtures and fittings**
Anyone who rents a house or flat may buy furniture, fixtures and fittings from the landlord or from another tenant who is transferring

# Finding out about the property

The law gives many tenants protection against excessive rent rises and arbitrary eviction. So as soon as he finds a suitable house or flat, the prospective tenant can check whether it qualifies for protection.

| | |
|---|---|
| **Check what the rateable value of the property was on March 23, 1965** | This can be found in the valuation list at the local council office. The property qualifies for protection if its rateable value was £200 or under (in London £400) on March 23, 1965. <br><br> The rateable value given in the valuation list may be that for the whole building. If a flat consists of one floor of a four-storey building, the tenant can work out its approximate rateable value by dividing the rateable value of the whole building by four. A couple of rooms on one floor are almost certain to come within the limit. <br><br> If a court is asked to settle the exact proportion of the total rateable value, it will calculate the number of sq. ft of floor-space occupied by the tenant and divide this into the total area of floor-space in the house |
| **Check whether the house or flat is provided because it is necessary in order for an employee to do his job** | If it is, there is no protection against eviction. Anyone offered a low-rent flat in return for caretaking duties can usually be made to leave if the landlord wants someone else to do the job. ☐ Rent: cases of limited protection, p. 264 |
| **Check whether the house is being let temporarily, while the owner is away** | If the landlord gives the tenant a notice specifying that the landlord is the owner-occupier, the tenant may have to move out of the property whenever the owner wants it back |

his lease. He may be forced to buy as a condition of being allowed to rent.

The tenant of an unfurnished house or flat will not lose the protection of an unfurnished tenancy simply because he buys furniture.

It is not illegal to make the granting of a tenancy of a house or flat conditional on the tenant's buying items of furniture, even if he does not want them. If, however, an inflated price is asked, the excess over the furniture's real value will be regarded as a premium.

A tenant asked to pay an excessive price for furniture in a property where a premium would be illegal should first ask for a detailed inventory, with prices against each item. Then he should work out its true value, possibly by checking the prices of similar items in a second-hand furniture shop. Finally, he can offer to pay a fair price for the furniture, pointing out that he regards the excess as an illegal premium. He may also report the matter to the local council office.

Again, a tenant who takes this course may lose the property altogether. The only alternative is to pay the inflated price and try to recover that part which represents a premium. Here the process will be even more difficult, because of the need to prove that the furniture prices were inflated.

### Rent in advance
The law usually prohibits the landlord from insisting on rent in advance for unfurnished property with a rateable value of £200 or less (in London £400).

In the case of tenants who make rent payments for more than six months at one time, the rent may be paid up to six months before the start of the period it covers.

### What the rent includes
The prospective tenant should find out what the rent being asked will cover. It may be purely for the use of the home, and he may have to pay extra for rates and such services as a caretaker or for a garage or pram shed—in addition to paying for gas or electricity.

### Paying for gas and electricity
In many rented flats and houses, gas and electricity are supplied through pre-payment meters installed and emptied by the landlord.

| | |
|---|---|
| Try to find out who owns the property | If it belongs to a charitable trust or registered housing association there is, strictly speaking, no legal protection. This does not necessarily mean that the tenant will be any less secure in practice. To ascertain his position, he will have to check the rules of the trust or association |
| Try to find out if you will be a sub-tenant | The only way to do this is to ask the prospective landlord whether he owns the property and, if not, whether he has the owner's consent to sub-let. Anyone who rents a home from someone who is not allowed to sub-let has no protection against eviction if his immediate landlord defaults in his obligations to the main landlord |
| Check that the property will not be overcrowded | It is a criminal offence if there are too many people sleeping in one room or too many for the number or size of the rooms. ☐ How to work out if a home is overcrowded, p. 250 |
| Try to find out whether the landlord has a mortgage on the property, and if so whether it allows him to let | There is no way of making an independent check on this and the prospective tenant will have to take the landlord's word for it, or ask to look at the mortgage deed or lease.  If there is a mortgage on the property and it is let without the lender's consent, the tenant will have little or no protection if the landlord defaults in his obligations under the mortgage. The tenant could throw himself on the mercy of a county court, but it is doubtful whether the court would prevent his eviction. He has no protection under the Rent Acts |

Each area gas and electricity board publishes the maximum amounts it recommends that landlords should charge in addition to the basic rate. Tenants can check the amount they have to pay on their pre-payment meter and compare it with the official figures, available from local showrooms.

If a tenant feels that he is being overcharged, he should bring the matter to the landlord's attention, pointing out the official rates. Although it is not a criminal offence to charge more than the recommended maximum, the landlord can be sued in the county court for the excess he is charging over and above these rates. ☐ Getting advice on a legal problem, p. 708.

## Council waiting lists

People who want to rent a council house or flat should put their names down on a waiting list as soon as possible. Different councils operate different schemes of selecting tenants, and it is difficult for a would-be tenant to

find out how long it will be before he is allotted a home. The process of selection is normally kept secret.

The simplest method of selection is one which re-houses people in the order in which they applied. These are known as date-order schemes and operate only in areas where there is surplus council housing.

A second method is the points system. Priority points may be given to applicants on such grounds as ill-health, or overcrowding in their present homes; sometimes even their war records may be considered.

A third scheme is based, rather arbitrarily, on merit, or on the importance of the applicant's job.

Councils will often give priority to tenants in private rented accommodation who are made homeless when their present home is compulsorily purchased. Tenants of private landlords whose homes are demolished in slum-clearance projects are most likely to be rehoused. ☐ Threats to the home, p. 300.

## How to work out if a home is overcrowded

ANYONE who is looking for a home to rent should make sure that it will not be considered in law as 'overcrowded' when his family moves in. Although a landlord can be prosecuted for allowing overcrowding he can also find it easier to evict a family from overcrowded premises.

There are three tests:

First, if two or more people of opposite sexes over ten years of age—apart from a couple living as husband and wife—have to share a bedroom, they are overcrowded.

Second, the law lays down a minimum number of rooms for each family, according to size. This includes the kitchen and bathroom.

| Number of rooms | 1 | 2 | 3 | 4 | 5 | 6 | 7 | 8 |
|---|---|---|---|---|---|---|---|---|
| Number of people allowed | 2 | 3 | 5 | 7½ | 10 | 12 | 14 | 16 |

Children under the age of 10 count, in this calculation, as half a person. Babies under one year old do not count at all

Third, even if both these conditions are met the home will still be, legally, overcrowded if the rooms in the house are too small.

To check, first work out the area of each room. Next, work out how many people are allowed in the home by totalling the number

allowed for each room. In this calculation, a room under 50 sq. ft does not count at all.

| Size (sq. ft) | 50–70 | 70–90 | 90–110 | Over 110 |
|---|---|---|---|---|
| People | ½ | 1 | 1½ | 2 |

As before, children under the age of 10 count, in this calculation, as half a person, and babies under one do not count at all

A family of husband, wife and two sons over 10 (four people) are not overcrowded, therefore, in three rooms—as long as there is one room over 110 sq. ft and the other two are more than 70 sq. ft, or there are two rooms over 90 sq. ft, and one over 70 sq. ft.

In exceptional circumstances, such as a seasonal increase in population in their district, the council may—if it is unable to find alternative accommodation—licence the overcrowding for a time. They may also take into account any special hardship that would be caused to a family if it had to find alternative accommodation. In most cases, however, a landlord who wants to evict tenants in these circumstances will be able to do so without difficulty.

Local authorities can also stop the owner of overcrowded property from re-letting rooms when tenants move out.

# Agreement and rent book

*Rent books*
*Tenants without rent books*
*Council tenants*

BEFORE a tenant first moves into a rented house or flat he may be asked to sign an agreement, though the tenancy will be legal without one. The agreement usually sets out where the landlord's responsibilities end and the tenant's begin. This may help to remove grounds for disputes over who pays the rates or who is responsible for repairs.

There are, however, disadvantages in a written agreement. Most agreements protect the landlord's rights more than the tenant's, and the tenant usually has to pay legal costs (usually between £5 and £15) and stamp duty (if any) which varies with the amount of rent and length of the tenancy.

If the property is furnished, the tenant with a written agreement may find, once the agreement runs out, that he has less security than the man with nothing in writing.

There is no legal machinery which gives him the right to appeal for an extension. A tenant without an agreement, however, can apply to a Rent Tribunal for an order allowing him to stay on for a period.

Agreements are frequently written in obscure legal language and may include a number of clauses which no longer have any force in law or which are to the tenant's disadvantage in some other way. Before signing, the tenant should read the agreement carefully or get a solicitor's advice.

## Rent books
Written agreements are normally given only to tenants who agree to stay for more than six months. Anyone else is likely to receive nothing more than a rent book, listing the main details of the tenancy and the tenant's principal rights in law.

Everyone who pays rent weekly is entitled to a rent book. If the landlord refuses to provide a book, the tenant can report him to the local council.

A tenant moving into an unfurnished or part-furnished property should make sure that he receives the correct rent book—it should be headed 'regulated tenancy'—to confirm that the tenant has the greater protection given by law to people in such property.

Some landlords put a small amount of furniture into an unfurnished house or flat and claim that it is furnished. If the tenant accepts a rent book headed 'furnished tenancy', he will be helping the landlord to evade the law and might be making it easier for the landlord to evict him. The rent book must contain:
1. The address of the premises.
2. The name and address of the landlord.
3. The name and address of the agent (if any).
4. The amount of rent (stating whether it is inclusive or exclusive of rates on the property).
5. The amount of rates payable.
6. A statement about whether the rent has been fixed by law.
7. Particulars of the local council's rent allowance scheme to help private tenants who cannot afford their rent. ☐ How rent rebates and allowances are calculated, p. 263.

For failing to provide current details in a rent book, or failing to provide a rent book at all, the landlord can be fined up to £50 on a first conviction and up to £100 on subsequent convictions. However, a tenant whose landlord fails to provide him with a proper rent book does not escape having to pay rent.

## Tenants without rent books
A tenant who pays rent at longer periods than weekly need not be given a rent book, though he should try to obtain one if possible. In a dispute, it may be difficult without a rent book to prove that he is the legal tenant or that he is not behind with the rent.

Payments by cheque or banker's order give adequate proof of payment. The tenant without a bank account should ask for a receipt. If the sum is over £2 the landlord has a legal obligation to provide one if asked to do so.

## Council tenants
Council tenants who pay rent weekly must be provided with a rent book or card, giving the terms of the tenancy. In practice, the rent book is the only document given to a council tenant which states the conditions of tenancy.

Nearly all councils reserve the right to increase the rent or alter the conditions of the tenancy. In a few cases, councils give three or five-year agreements. These are almost always confined to higher-priced homes.

# Rent and security: unfurnished property

Regulated rent

Applying for a rent reduction

How the rent officer decides

When the new rent is payable

Making an appeal

The tenant's security

MOST people who rent unfurnished and partly furnished property from private landlords have what is known as a 'regulated tenancy'. They have legal protection against eviction and excessive rent increases. People renting the same unfurnished or partly furnished home since before July 6, 1957, may not come into this category; they may have 'controlled tenancies'. ☐ How the law defines a controlled tenancy, p. 256.

Anyone with a regulated tenancy, or his landlord, can ask for a 'fair rent' to be fixed by the rent officer, who can be contacted through the local council offices. Once this has been done, the rent cannot be increased without the rent officer's consent, unless there is an increase in the rates or, in some cases, an increase in the cost of services to the tenant.

If the rent for a regulated tenancy has already been fixed, the figure will be shown in the rent register kept by the rent officer. A tenant moving into unfurnished or partly furnished property can check the register to ensure that he is not being asked to pay more than the landlord is legally allowed to charge.

## Regulated rent

If it is not registered, the rent a landlord may charge is still limited, normally to whatever was the rent on December 8, 1965, when the fair rent system was introduced. A rent limited in this way is called a 'regulated rent'.

If the property was occupied by a tenant on that date, the rent is fixed. Even if a new tenant moves in, the landlord cannot charge him a higher rent.

However, if there has been no regulated tenancy of the property in the previous three years—if, for example, it has been let furnished, or been vacant—the rent will not be fixed at that of December 8, 1965.

The landlord and tenant may then agree on any rent, but once an amount is set, it becomes the limit that later tenants can be charged.

## Changes in regulated rent

From January 1, 1973 the system of rent regulation changes. As from that date, a regulated rent can be replaced by one agreed by the landlord and tenant.

---

### How the law defines a regulated tenancy

PEOPLE who rent unfurnished and partly furnished property will have a regulated tenancy if all the following conditions apply to the property:

**1.** The property had a rateable value on March 23, 1965 of £200 or less (in London £400).

**2.** The rent is more than two-thirds of the rateable value on March 23, 1965.

**3.** The tenant does not share with the landlord 'essential living accommodation' such as a kitchen. Sharing a bathroom with the landlord, or any accommodation with other tenants, will not disqualify him.

**4.** No part of the property is used for business or the sale of drink.

**5.** The landlord is not the Crown, a local authority, the Government, a housing trust or a charitable housing association.

**6.** The 'hire' of any furniture does not form a substantial proportion of the rent.

---

EXISTING TENANCIES When a tenancy started before January 1, 1973, a landlord can charge more than the regulated rent only if he and the tenant enter into a written rent agreement. That agreement, which must contain a conspicuous warning that the tenant's security of tenure is not affected if he refuses, must be signed by both landlord and tenant.

A tenant should consult the rent officer before agreeing to the landlord's proposals, or he may sign away his right to a lower rent.

NEW TENANCIES When a regulated tenancy starts after January 1, 1973, the rent may be negotiated between the landlord and tenant or it may be fixed by the rent officer.

If the rent for the property has previously been fixed and registered by the rent officer it cannot be altered for about three years from the date of registration. After that time, the landlord can apply to have a new rent fixed, or he and the tenant can jointly apply for the cancellation of the existing registered rent.

The rent officer will cancel a registration only if the tenancy has at least 12 months to run and if he is satisfied that the proposed new rent is fair and that any charges for services provided by the landlord are reasonable.

It is advantageous for a landlord to have a rent registration cancelled. Instead of having to wait for up to three years, he can charge the highest rent obtainable if the house or flat becomes vacant.

## Applying for a rent reduction

A tenant can apply to the rent officer to have his rent reduced provided he has not signed a written rent agreement with the landlord and provided the rent has not been fixed by the rent officer in the last three years.

Before applying, however, the tenant will need to be reasonably sure that his rent is not going to be increased as a result of his application. Rent officers can increase rents, as well as reduce them, unless the tenancy has been granted for a fixed term.

The tenant can get an idea of whether it is in his interest to apply by checking in the register the rents fixed for similar properties in the area, and by talking to neighbours. The rent officer may also give advice.

To have his rent fixed, the tenant has to complete an application form from his local council office, and give details of the rateable value of the property and the rent he thinks should be paid.

The rateable value of each property is given in the local valuation list at council offices. If the list does not give figures for individual flats in the same house, the tenant need write only 'below £200' on his form ('below £400' in London).

The rent officer will eventually fix a fair rent irrespective of the amount suggested by either landlord or tenant, but failure to give a figure will cause the application to be rejected.

The tenant must then send the application form to the rent officer, who has to notify the landlord that the application has been made. This gives the landlord a chance to give his side of the case. Similarly, if the landlord has made the application, the tenant is informed.

The rent officer then inspects the property and asks the landlord and tenant what they think is a fair rent. Such meetings are informal, but either party may be represented.

COUNCIL INTERVENTION After 1973, local councils have power to intervene where they think excessively high rents are being charged in private unfurnished property. They can apply to the rent officer—without the tenant's

agreement—to have any rent fixed. The officer can reduce the rent, if he accepts the council's application: he cannot increase it.

## How the rent officer decides

Rent officers must take into account everything except a housing shortage and the personal circumstances of landlord and tenant. A shortage of a particular type of home in the area will not influence the rent officer's decision—although on the open market such a shortage would increase the rent.

The facts that a tenant cannot afford the rent or that the landlord will make a loss if a lower rent is fixed must also be disregarded.

Rent officers take note of the age and character of the property and will fix a lower rent for a flat in an old tenement block than, for example, for a new maisonette. Locality, too, is important. A house in a good residential area or close to buses and shops or a park is worth more than one without such advantages.

A major factor is the property's state of repair, but the rent will not be reduced if the tenant has failed to carry out repairs. Similarly, a rent will not be increased if the tenant has improved the property at his own expense.

The rent officer's most common practice is to note the average rents of similar accommodation in the area. If most rents have not been officially fixed, he will deduct from the average an amount he estimates as the 'scarcity factor'. A rent calculated by this method is said to be arrived at 'on comparables'.

For a four-bedroom, self-contained flat the calculation might be:

| | |
|---|---|
| Comparable rents of six similar flats in the area £600–£715 a year | |
| Full scarcity rent (average of six) | £650 |
| Deduct, say, 10 per cent for scarcity factor | £65 |
| Fair rent a year | £585 |

For easier comparison, rent is sometimes expressed as 'so much a square foot'. The fair rent for a flat of two rooms, kitchen and bathroom, a total of 800 sq. ft, in a three-storey terraced house might be calculated like this:

| | | |
|---|---|---|
| Registered rents in 12 terraced houses in the area 20p to 30p a square foot | | |
| Fair rent per sq. ft | | 28p |
| Fair rent per year for a 800 sq. ft flat at 28p | 800×28p | £224 |

## Cost of landlord's services

When a rent officer fixes a rent he should include any money payable by the tenant for the use of furniture or for services such as porterage, hot water or cleaning. The Rent Act allows even a fixed rent to be altered, either with the rent officer's permission or in accordance with rules which he has approved, if the costs of such services rises.

When the rent officer fixes the rent, he enters it in the register and tells the landlord and the tenant. The new rent must also be entered in the rent book, if there is one. The rent fixed is known as the 'registered rent'.

Once a rent is registered, the landlord cannot charge the tenant more than this figure without the rent officer's consent. If he tries to do so and deliberately marks the rent book in arrears, he is liable to be prosecuted and fined up to £50.

**When the new rent is payable**
The tenant and landlord have the right of appeal against the rent officer's decision to the local rent assessment committee. The tenant has to pay the new rent until the committee gives its decision.

If the rent is reduced, the new rent applies from the date of the application to fix the rent, and the landlord may owe the tenant money for the over-payment of rent. The best way to recover this is to pay a further reduced rent, or no rent at all, until the debt is cleared.

If the rent is increased, the new rent may also have to be paid from the date of the application, though the rent officer has power to fix a later date. In addition, the landlord is entitled to the new rent only if he has served the tenant with a formal document called a 'notice of increase'.

A rent increased to cover higher rates is payable from the date the rates went up—and no notice of increase is required.

If the rent has not been registered, the landlord must serve a notice of increase within six weeks of the rates change.

**Making an appeal**
The landlord or the tenant may appeal against the rent fixed by the rent officer and ask him to refer the case to the rent assessment committee. The objection must be made in writing to the rent officer within 28 days.

The rent assessment committee will ask for a written statement of objections, and may give the objector a personal hearing.

The committee consists of a chairman, usually a lawyer, and two other members. At the hearings, either party may be represented by a lawyer, a surveyor or a friend, and may call witnesses.

The committee can confirm the rent officer's decision, or alter the rent he has fixed. A

further appeal, to the High Court, against the committee's decision is possible only on a point of law—on the grounds that the committee is thought to have got the law wrong or applied the rules wrongly.

If a tenant cannot afford the increased rent, he may be able to get a council allowance. ☐ How rent rebates and allowances are calculated, p. 263.

**Further applications**
Three years after an application to the rent officer, the landlord or tenant can apply for a new rent to be fixed.

The rent officer can re-examine a case before the three years are up, if tenant and landlord make a joint application.

If only one party applies within the three-year period, the rent officer has powers to alter the rent only if circumstances have changed—for example, if the property has either been improved or has deteriorated.

**Paying the rent**
Tenants have a legal obligation to pay their rent promptly and in full. Unless there is an agreement to the contrary, it is up to the tenant to find the landlord and pay him. Failure to pay rent will almost always give the landlord just cause to evict the tenant.

The tenant should have the payment recorded in his rent book if he has one. If he has no rent book and pays in cash he should ask for a receipt, which must be supplied on demand for sums of £2 and over.

A bad landlord may refuse to collect the rent, hoping that the tenant will spend the money and fall into arrears, giving grounds for eviction. The tenant should continue to offer the rent and write to the landlord confirming that he has refused to accept it.

Keep a copy of the letter, and put the money into a safe place, such as a bank account.

A private tenant may, in rare cases, be required to pay his rent to the local council. This can happen when the landlord fails to pay rates for which he is responsible.

The tenant pays the council at the time he would have paid his landlord, and is given a receipt. He does not have to pay the landlord as well and the landlord will not be able to get the tenant evicted on the grounds that the rent has not been paid to him.

If a tenant falls into serious arrears, the landlord will usually apply to the county court to repossess the property. The court will order the tenant to pay off the arrears—as well as the current rent—at so much a week. If he fails to pay, an eviction order can be issued.

A landlord can also ask the county court for a Warrant of Distress, under which he can send bailiffs to seize furniture and goods to the value of the rent owing.

In rare cases the landlord can ask the court for a Levy of Execution, which gives similar powers. He may do this if the rent owing is considerable and he believes the tenant owns valuable items such as antique furniture or rare pictures.

## The tenant's security

The tenant of a regulated flat or house is more secure than most other tenants. He can be evicted only if the court is satisfied that one of the following grounds for eviction exists:

**1.** The landlord can provide the tenant with a suitable alternative home.

**2.** The tenant is in arrears with rent.

**3.** The tenant has broken a condition of his tenancy agreement.

**4.** The tenant or his lodger has been a nuisance or annoyed neighbours.

**5.** The tenant or his lodger has been convicted of using the house or flat for an immoral or illegal purpose.

**6.** The tenant or his lodger has damaged the property.

**7.** The tenant has sub-let without the landlord's consent.

**8.** The tenant has a lawful sub-tenant, but has charged him too much rent.

**9.** The landlord requires the home for a full-time employee and the tenant was let the home when he was an employee.

**10.** The landlord needs the home for himself or a member of his family and can prove that his hardship at being deprived of the home is greater than the tenant's.

**11.** The tenant is living in overcrowded property. This will not be a ground for eviction if the overcrowding has been licensed by the local authority. ☐ How to work out if a home is overcrowded, p. 250.

**12.** The landlord once used the house or flat as his own home, and warned a tenant moving in that the tenancy was temporary. This applies only to accommodation which was let after December 8, 1965.

**13.** The home is normally occupied by a minister of religion and the tenant was warned when he moved in that the home might be needed for such a minister.

Similar rules apply when a farmer lets a farm cottage to someone who is not an employee of his, and subsequently needs it for a farm worker.

**14.** A demolition or closing order has been made under the Housing Act 1957, because the premises are not fit to be lived in.

## Help with a surveyor's fees

TENANTS who appeal against the rent officer's decision to the rent assessment committee are not eligible for legal aid even if they choose to have their case put to the committee by an expert—sometimes a solicitor, but more usually a surveyor.

In Greater London, however, there is a Surveyors' Aid Scheme, operated by the surveyors' professional organisations on similar lines to the legal aid system, through which tenants on low incomes may obtain some help with fees. Applicants are required to give details of all their income, including any contributions from children who are working.

Anyone with savings of more than £500 is not eligible for benefit.

The tenant must tell the surveyor at the outset that he wants advice under the aid scheme. He then pays a standard fee of 50p. How much more he will have to pay depends on his net income after deduction of tax, insurance, and £1 for each child not at work—

family allowances are not included in the tenant's net income.

| Net Weekly Income £ | Total Fee £ |
|---|---|
| 10 or less | 0·50 |
| 10·05 to 11 | 1·00 |
| 11·05 to 12 | 2·00 |
| 12·05 to 13 | 3·00 |
| 13·05 to 14 | 4·00 |
| 14·05 to 15 | 5·00 |
| 15·05 to 16 | 7·00 |
| 16·05 to 17 | 9·00 |
| 17·05 to 18 | 11·00 |
| 18·05 to 19 | 13·00 |
| 19·05 to 20 | 15·00 |

If the surveyor is asked only to give advice and is not required to appear at the hearing, he can charge only one-third of the scale fees. Information about where to get advice and representation under this scheme can be obtained from the local Citizens' Advice Bureau.

# Rent and security: controlled tenancies

*Controlled rents*　　　*Converting to a regulated tenancy*
*Paying the rent*　　　*Objections by the tenant*
*The tenant's security*　*Paying the new rent*

PEOPLE who have lived in the same un-furnished or partly furnished house or flat since 1957 may have a special highly protected, or 'controlled', tenancy. Such people pay rents which are low and rigidly controlled by law, and they cannot normally be forced to leave their home as long as they fulfil the usual obligations of a tenant.

### Controlled rents

Annual rents for most controlled tenancies amount to twice the gross rateable value on November 7, 1956, plus rates.

The landlord may charge extra for the use of furniture or for services such as hot water, porterage or cleaning. If there is a dispute about the value of the services, the county court will decide.

The landlord can increase the rent if he carries out improvements to the property. Usually he is permitted to add 12½ per cent of the cost of the improvements to the annual rent.

A controlled rent will include the tenant's share of the general rates and water rate. If rates go up, the rent can be increased by the same amount. The landlord serves on the tenant an official 'notice of increase', which can be backdated for up to six weeks. If the landlord deliberately makes a false statement in the notice, he can be fined up to £50.

If the landlord overcharges the tenant, the tenant can deduct the overpayment from current rent, or sue the landlord for the excess in the county court. Any court action must be taken within two years.

### Paying the rent

Tenants have a legal obligation to pay their rent promptly and in full. The only exception to this rule is where a county court has ruled that rent may be withheld because the landlord has overcharged. The tenant should have the payments recorded in his rent book if he has one. If he has no rent book and pays in cash, he should ask for a receipt, which must be supplied on demand for sums of £2 and over.

A bad landlord may refuse to collect the rent, hoping that the tenant will spend the money and fall into arrears, giving grounds for eviction. The tenant should continue to offer

---

> ## How the law defines a controlled tenancy
>
> A CONTROLLED tenancy is one that:
> **1.** Was created before July 6, 1957, or has been renewed on the same terms since 1957, or has been inherited since then.
> **2.** Is let as a separate home, with no part being shared with the landlord (the tenant may, however, share some room or rooms with other tenants).
> **3.** Has a lease for less than 21 years.
> **4.** Is not a furnished tenancy and does not belong to the Crown, the Government, a local authority, a housing trust or a charitable housing association.
> **5.** Covers a property built or converted before August 29, 1954.

---

the rent and write to the landlord confirming that he has refused to accept it. Keep a copy of the letter and put the money into a safe place such as a bank account.

If a tenant falls into serious arrears with his rent the landlord will usually apply to the county court to repossess the property. ☐ Leaving a rented home, p. 272.

A landlord can also ask the county court for a Warrant of Distress which will allow him to send bailiffs to seize furniture and goods to the value of the rent owing.

A private tenant may occasionally be required to pay his rent to the local council. This can happen when the landlord is responsible for rates and fails to pay.

The tenant does *not* have to pay the landlord as well, and the landlord will not be able to get the tenant evicted because the rent has not been paid direct to him.

### The tenant's security

People with controlled tenancies are the most secure of all tenants. They can be made to leave only if there is a serious breach of the tenancy agreement—if the tenant falls badly into arrears with his rent, for example, or if he overcrowds the premises or uses them for an illegal purpose.

When the holder of a controlled tenancy dies, his wife or any child who has been living with him will usually have the automatic right to stay on under the same terms.

### Converting to a regulated tenancy
A controlled tenancy can be passed on within a family only once, however. So if someone who has inherited a controlled tenancy dies, a member of the family may take over, but this time the tenancy will be converted into a regulated tenancy.

If the holder of a controlled tenancy leaves, the house or flat will not be let again under a controlled tenancy. The new tenancy will be either regulated or furnished, depending on how much furniture is provided, if any.
☐ Rent and security: unfurnished property, p. 252; Furnished property, p. 259.
GENERAL DE-CONTROL A general programme of conversion, set out in the Housing Finance Act 1972, starts on January 1, 1973. Homes with the highest rateable value are due to be converted first, and the full conversion programme is expected to be completed by the end of 1975. ☐ When tenancies become de-controlled, p. 257.

The only houses excluded from that general de-control are those declared to be unfit for human habitation.

### Improving the house or flat
A tenancy may be de-controlled earlier than the date intended in the 1972 Act, if the landlord can show that the standard amenities—bath, basin, sink, hot and cold water and w.c. are already provided.

To convert a controlled tenancy in this way, the landlord must apply to the local council for a 'qualification certificate'. This confirms that the house has all the standard amenities—for the exclusive use of the tenant's family —that it is in good repair and is fit to live in. The tenant is told when a certificate is to be issued, and he can object within 28 days if he disagrees with the council's decision.

If the property does not have the standard amenities necessary for a qualification certificate, the landlord can decide to provide them. He must submit plans to the local council for provisional approval, and the council tells the tenant of the plans.

The tenant should then seek legal advice to decide whether he wants to object to the conversion. He may want to object if the landlord decides to spend a large sum on an old property, and the tenant realises that it will command a higher rent than he can afford.

If the landlord satisfies the council that the tenant's home will be provided with all the standard amenities for his exclusive use, will be in good repair, and fit for human habitation, the council will issue a 'certificate of provisional approval'.

The landlord must then ask the rent officer what the rent of the home will be once the improvements have been finished. The idea of fixing a fair rent at this stage is to give the landlord and the tenant a clear idea of what the rent will be if the work is done. When the rent officer has worked out a rent, he issues a 'fair rent certificate'.

The landlord must then obtain the tenant's consent before beginning the conversion.

### Objections by the tenant
If the tenant refuses to give his consent, the landlord can ask the county court to issue an order for the work to be done. The tenant, however, has the right to state his objections at the court hearing.

The court can refuse the landlord permission to go ahead with improvements because of inconvenience to the tenant. It is more likely, however, that it would give permission, but impose conditions such as fixing a time limit. It can also make the landlord provide alternative accommodation for the tenant and his household while the work is done.

Once the work is finished, the home must have all the standard amenities for the exclusive use of the occupants and the home must be in good repair and fit to live in.

If it fulfils all these conditions, the council will give the landlord a third certificate—his 'qualification certificate'.

Where a qualification certificate is wrongly issued or is defective, the tenant can apply to the county court to have it quashed.

The landlord then applies to the rent officer to fix a fair rent. This will normally be little more than a formality because the rent officer has already issued a certificate of fair rent. This is likely to be changed only if the work is not done according to the plans originally submitted for provisional approval.

It is possible that negotiations and objections to any improvement scheme could take so long that the house or flat becomes liable to de-control under the Housing Finance Act's general programme of conversion. When this happens the tenancy changes from controlled to regulated automatically—and this happens even if the property does not yet have all the 'standard amenities'.

A tenant who believes that his home may be liable for conversion should check its rateable value at the local council offices. The table below gives the dates on which homes will automatically be converted.

It is advisable to seek professional advice as early as possible. Consult the rent officer at the local council or ask for advice from the Citizens' Advice Bureau or a solicitor.

**Paying the new rent**
For most people with a controlled tenancy, conversion to a regulated tenancy will mean rent increases—sometimes as much as 400 per cent, from £1 a week to £5 or more. This increase, however, can be phased, if the tenant finds it impossible to pay. Tenants on low incomes may qualify for the rent allowances which come into effect on January 1, 1973.
☐ How rent rebates and allowances are calculated, p. 263.

The rent can be increased above the level of the former controlled rent only if the rent officer fixes a new figure or if the landlord and tenant sign a rent agreement and send details of it to the rent officer. Until then the tenant need pay only the old controlled rent.

The landlord, however, is entitled to apply to the rent officer for a new rent three months before the tenancy is to be de-controlled under the Housing Finance Act. This enables him to charge the new rent as soon as the tenancy is converted.

In most cases the rent officer will stipulate that the landlord can recover the increased rent in three stages:
**1.** On the date the new rent is registered, he can charge one-third of the increase or 50p more, whichever is greater.

**2.** After a year he can charge a further one-third or 50p, whichever is greater.
**3.** Two years after the date of registration of the new rent he can charge the balance of the increase.

If a controlled rent of £1 is increased to fair rent of £5, with effect from January 1, 1973, the tenant pays:

| Jan. 1, 1973 | Jan. 1, 1974 | Jan. 1, 1975 |
|---|---|---|
| £2·33 | £3·66 | £5 |

If a controlled rent of £2 is increased to a fair rent of £3·25 with effect from January 1, 1973, the tenant pays:

| Jan. 1, 1973 | Jan. 1, 1974 | Jan. 1, 1975 |
|---|---|---|
| £2·50 | £3·00 | £3·25 |

The rent officer will advise any tenant on how his increase should be paid.
AGREEMENT WITH LANDLORD Where a landlord and tenant have sent details of their private agreement on what increase is to be paid to the rent officer, the council must acknowledge receipt within 21 days. The new rent is payable after the 21 days, and the document setting out the agreement is open to public inspection at the council offices for at least three years.

A rent agreement is invalid if it does not warn the tenant that his security of tenure is not affected if he refuses to sign. It must also point out that he or the landlord still have the right to ask the rent officer to fix a fair rent for the property.

Even after such an agreement has been reached, a tenant who wants to have the increase in his rent phased over three years is entitled to apply to the rent officer to arrange this under the normal 'fair rent' procedure.

## When tenancies become de-controlled

All controlled tenancies become regulated tenancies by the end of 1975. The date of the change depends on the rateable value of the property. Only houses unfit for human habitation are excluded.

| House or flat in Greater London with a rateable value of | House or flat elsewhere in England and Wales with a rateable value of | Date of conversion |
|---|---|---|
| £95 or more | £60 or more | January 1, 1973 |
| £80 or more, but less than £95 | £45 or more, but less than £60 | July 1, 1973 |
| £70 or more, but less than £80 | £35 or more, but less than £45 | January 1, 1974 |
| £60 or more, but less than £70 | £25 or more, but less than £35 | July 1, 1974 |
| £50 or more, but less than £60 | £20 or more, but less than £25 | January 1, 1975 |
| Less than £50 | Less than £20 | July 1, 1975 |

# Rent and security: furnished property

*Applying for a rent reduction*  *Paying the rent*
*Effect of registration*  *The tenant's security*

TENANTS of furnished accommodation have limited protection against rent increases and arbitrary eviction if the rateable value of their home is £200 or less (in London £400). The tenant can apply to a rent tribunal for a rent reduction or for protection from eviction. Once the tribunal has fixed a rent, a landlord cannot lawfully ask for more without the tribunal's consent.

A tenant moving into furnished accommodation can check in the local authority rent register whether the rent for the property has been fixed. If the rent has not been fixed and the tenant thinks it is too high, he can apply to the tribunal for a reduction.

### Applying for a rent reduction
To have the rent of a furnished property fixed, the tenant applies to the rent tribunal in his area. The address will be in the local telephone directory. He is asked to fill in a form giving the address of his premises, his name, and the landlord's name and address.

If he does not know who the landlord is, he should give the name on the front of the rent book or the name and address of the person who collects the rent. A member of the tribunal's staff will give advice on how to complete the form.

Although most applications are made by tenants, the landlord or the local authority can also apply to the tribunal.

After the form-filling, known officially as 'making a reference', the tribunal asks the landlord about the accommodation. It will want to know the extent of shared accommodation (if any); to have an inventory of his furniture in the premises; and to be told of any services he provides and whether the rent includes board.

He must also give details of the rates and, if he leases the property, what rent he pays to *his* landlord.

The tenant is allowed to check this information, and should contest any incorrect items on the inventory. Landlords have been known to include furniture owned or being bought by the tenant, for the more furniture the landlord can claim to provide, the higher the rent he is likely to be allowed to charge.

> ## How the law defines a furnished tenancy
>
> A FURNISHED tenancy is one in which the landlord lets accommodation which includes substantial furniture or services and has a rateable value of £200 or less (in London £400).
>
> Generally, the 'hire' of the furniture must be worth a 'substantial proportion' of the rent paid each week or month. Where the amount of furniture is small, the tenancy may be regulated. □ Furnished or unfurnished: how the law decides, p. 246.
>
> People who live in private hotels may occasionally have the status of furnished-tenancy holders if they do not pay a substantial proportion of rent for food, lighting, heating and laundry.

Landlord and tenant can conduct the case by letter; but it is better for the tenant to choose a hearing, which gives him a chance to challenge his landlord's statements directly. Usually members of the tribunal visit the property before the hearing.

At the hearing, both sides are free to employ a lawyer, but few tenants, and not many landlords, do so. If the tenant finds that his landlord intends to be represented, he may feel that he should do the same. But he cannot obtain legal aid for a rent tribunal hearing.

### The decision
The tribunal's decision may be announced at the hearing or later. Both parties will receive a copy of the decision.

The tribunal can approve the present rent, reduce the rent, or dismiss the case.

The tribunal dismisses the case when it thinks a higher rent should be paid. On a first application it cannot increase the rent.

If there are any changes in the property after the rent is fixed, either tenant or landlord may apply again, and the tribunal then has power to increase the rent if it thinks fit. For example, if the landlord installs a hot-water system, he can ask the tribunal to raise the rent he is allowed to charge. On the other hand, the tenant who claims that the property has deteriorated can ask for a reduction.

### Effect of registration

Once the rent fixed by the tribunal is entered in the local authority's rents register, it is an offence for the landlord to charge more. The local council can prosecute, and if the landlord is convicted, he may be fined up to £100 or be sent to prison for up to six months. In addition, he may be ordered by the court to repay the amount the tenant has overpaid.

If the local authority decides not to prosecute the landlord—perhaps because it succeeds in stopping him from charging an illegal rent—the tenant who has overpaid can himself take action to get back the excess.

One disadvantage of applying to the tribunal for a rent reduction is that the landlord may retaliate by trying to evict the tenant.

He will not be able to do so immediately. If the tenant has a written fixed-term agreement he is entitled to stay until that period expires—provided that he keeps to its terms.

The tenant with no agreement—or who has an agreement for an indefinite period—is automatically given six months' security when he applies for a rent reduction, unless he has been a bad tenant, in which case it will be less than six months. This security can be extended for further periods at the tribunal's discretion.

### Paying the rent

The tenant has a legal obligation to pay his rent promptly and in full. If he fails to do so, the landlord can take legal action to evict him and recover the rent owed.

The tenant should have the payments recorded in his rent book if he has one. If he has no rent book and pays in cash, he should ask for a receipt, which must be supplied on demand for sums of £2 and over.

An unscrupulous landlord may refuse to collect the rent, hoping that the tenant will spend the money and fall into arrears, giving grounds for eviction. The tenant should continue to offer the rent and write to the landlord confirming that acceptance has been refused. Keep a copy of the letter and put the money in a safe place, such as a National Savings or clearing bank account.

A private tenant may, in rare cases, be required to pay his rent to the local council. This can happen when the landlord fails to pay rates for which he is responsible. The tenant simply pays the council at the same time as he would have paid his landlord. He does *not* have to pay the landlord as well.

### The tenant's security

In general, people who rent furnished accommodation have little protection against eviction.

A tenant in furnished property who does not have a written fixed-term agreement may be served with a notice to quit, requiring him to leave within a stated period, which must be not less than 28 days. However, if he has already applied to the rent tribunal for a rent reduction, he is automatically entitled to a period of security. The notice to quit will run from the end of that period.

If the period granted is six months, the tenant can re-apply for further security before the notice to quit expires. If it is less than six months, he cannot re-apply.

A tenant who has not already applied for a rent reduction can apply for security at any time before the notice to quit expires.

The tribunal can suspend the notice to quit for up to six months. Towards the end of that time the tenant may re-apply, and the tribunal can grant further security.

In practice, tribunals do not like to give repeated extensions, and once the period of security granted falls below six months the tenant will know that the next application will probably be refused.

If an application for a second or subsequent extension is refused, the notice to quit takes effect after seven days. The landlord can then apply for eviction through the county court.

The rent tribunal is not bound by a set of rules, and has no need to state its reasons for a decision, unless requested to do so by one of the parties involved. Some tribunals say that they apply to furnished tenancies the rules that cover controlled and regulated tenancies. This suggests that a tribunal will reduce the security of tenure of a tenant who is a bad rent-payer, or who breaks tenancy conditions, or if the landlord would suffer greater hardship by not getting possession of the premises.

Tribunals are also more ready to reduce security if there is a bad feeling between a landlord and tenant living in the same house, if the landlord wishes to sell the house with vacant possession, or if he wants to carry out structural alterations.

The tenant with a written agreement for a definite period cannot be forced to leave until the end of that period unless he breaks a term of his agreement. Once the period is up he has no protection against eviction. No legal body can grant him the right to stay.

# When a tenant of furnished property can be made to leave

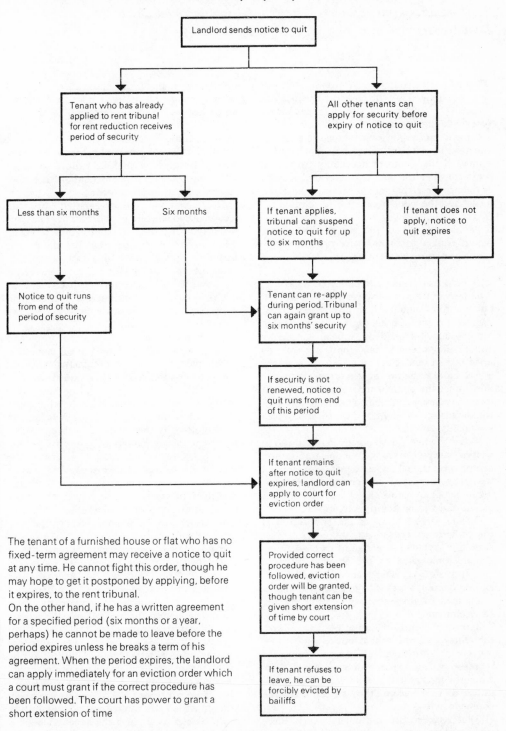

Landlord sends notice to quit

Tenant who has already applied to rent tribunal for rent reduction receives period of security

All other tenants can apply for security before expiry of notice to quit

Less than six months

Six months

If tenant applies, tribunal can suspend notice to quit for up to six months

If tenant does not apply, notice to quit expires

Notice to quit runs from end of the period of security

Tenant can re-apply during period. Tribunal can again grant up to six months' security

If security is not renewed, notice to quit runs from end of this period

If tenant remains after notice to quit expires, landlord can apply to court for eviction order

Provided correct procedure has been followed, eviction order will be granted, though tenant can be given short extension of time by court

If tenant refuses to leave, he can be forcibly evicted by bailiffs

The tenant of a furnished house or flat who has no fixed-term agreement may receive a notice to quit at any time. He cannot fight this order, though he may hope to get it postponed by applying, before it expires, to the rent tribunal.

On the other hand, if he has a written agreement for a specified period (six months or a year, perhaps) he cannot be made to leave before the period expires unless he breaks a term of his agreement. When the period expires, the landlord can apply immediately for an eviction order which a court must grant if the correct procedure has been followed. The court has power to grant a short extension of time

261

# Rent and security: council houses and flats

*The rent assessment procedure*  *Rent rebates and allowances*
*Rent arrears*  *Security*

LOCAL councils and new town corporations are obliged, by the Housing Finance Act 1972, to charge their tenants 'fair rents'. In calculating the rent of any house or flat, a council must ignore any housing shortage and take no account of the personal circumstances of the tenant or his family. Instead it must consider the age, character and locality of the property, the state of repair of the house or flat and the value of any furniture provided by the council.

A major factor is the return the council would expect to make if its property were treated as an investment.

### The rent assessment procedure
The fair rent for each house or flat is worked out by the council on a provisional basis, usually in consultation with the local rent officer—an independent official originally appointed to assess fair rents for private unfurnished tenancies.

Six months before new rents are to come into force, the council must publish a list of its provisional assessments and make sure that the details are brought to the attention of all its tenants.

Tenants who wish to object should do so in writing within one month of the publication of the provisional assessment. The council may then reconsider and change the rent, or it can decide to ignore the objection. A tenant has no right to be heard or to appeal.

Within three months of the publication of the provisional assessment, the council must submit it to the local rent scrutiny committee, a body established by the Housing Finance Act. It consists of a chairman, usually a lawyer, and six members drawn from a panel of people nominated by the Secretary of State for the Environment.

The rent scrutiny committee can confirm the rents assessed by the council or substitute other rents for them. It has the power to increase or lower the proposed rents. Only when the figures have been fixed by the committee do they become the 'fair rents' for the council's houses and flats.

Rent assessments are made every three years, unless in the case of a particular house or flat the council can show that there has been a change of circumstances that justifies an earlier review of the rent.

### Rent arrears
All tenants have a legal obligation to pay their rent promptly and in full. Failure to do so will almost always give the landlord the right to apply for an eviction order.

If a tenant falls into arrears with his rent, a council can sue him in court for debt or issue a Warrant of Distress without going to court. The warrant allows the court bailiffs to seize furniture and goods which can be sold to raise the amount of rent which is owing. If the tenant's goods are not worth enough, the council can evict him; but not without first going to court for a possession order. ☐ Leaving a rented home, p. 272.

Often the council will hold the threat of eviction over a tenant's head in the hope that he will pay off the arrears; but actual evictions are not common, since the council are also the welfare authority and, as such, are bound to see that the evicted family is rehoused. Evictions, when they do occur, are usually used by the council to move a tenant to cheaper accommodation.

### Rent rebates and allowances
Councils have the power to charge a smaller rent than the one fixed for any property if they agree that a tenant cannot afford the 'fair rent' which has been approved by the rent scrutiny committee.

To apply for a rent rebate, a tenant must give details of his own income, and his wife's, on a form provided by the council. The council will subsequently get in touch with the couple's employers in order to check these details with them. ☐ How rent rebates and allowances are calculated, p. 263.

Normally a rent rebate is given for six months, after which the tenant must re-apply. If the tenant's income changes during the six months—for example, if he gets a pay rise, or does more overtime, or if his wife takes a job—he must tell the council at once. Failure to do so could mean that the tenant loses his rebate, and he could be ordered to repay the amount of rebate that was allowed before the increase in income came to the council's notice (or before the delayed disclosure was made). He could also be liable to prosecution under the provisions of the Theft Act 1968, for having made money by deceit. ☐ ABC of crime and punishment, p. 758.

## Security

Council tenants do not have the protection of the Rent Acts, and lack the security enjoyed by the tenants of private landlords. Letting agreements for council houses and flats vary from one local authority to another, as also

do the rules which different authorities impose on their tenants.

Some allow tenants to keep pets, provided they seek permission to do so. Others, however, place a total ban on animals. Similarly, some allow television aerials to be attached to the roof, while others insist that television be 'piped' from a common master aerial.

It is always wise to give careful attention to the terms of tenancy imposed by individual councils. In law, councils are nearly always proved right and can, as a general rule, get rid of tenants who break the terms of the tenancy without much difficulty.

## How rent rebates and allowances are calculated

FROM October 1, 1972 every local council must operate a rent rebate scheme for its own tenants, and by January 1, 1973 a rent allowance scheme for tenants of private unfurnished homes.

Applicants must be able to give proof of their rent and give details of their total income. A rebate or allowance is granted for six months, after which a tenant must re-apply. The council

must be informed of any change in income during the six months.

Where the tenant is not the chief earner in the household, the allowance or rebate may be related instead to someone else's income—for example, the wage of a son who earns more than his father.

An allowance or rebate may be withdrawn if the tenant falls badly into arrears with his rent.

### HOW TO WORK OUT WHETHER YOU ARE ELIGIBLE

| | | | |
|---|---|---|---|
| Give earnings before deduction of tax, insurance and graduated pension contributions. Include incomes of husband and wife but disregard the first £2·50 of a wife's income. Weekly paid workers must take the average earned over the last five weeks. Monthly paid workers should take the average of the last two months | Weekly rent | | £7·00 |
| | Weekly earnings | £34·00 | |
| If a tenant and his wife have cash savings of more than £300, the council adds 0·1 per cent of the amount over £300 | Take your cash savings | £500 | |
| | Deduct £300 | £300 | |
| | Balance | £200 | |
| | Take 1p for each £10 of the balance | £00·20 | |
| | Add that figure to weekly earnings to get gross weekly income | £34·20 | |
| Each applicant is entitled to certain basic 'needs allowances', depending on his number of children. A leaflet giving the current rates is obtainable from council offices | Work out your 'needs allowance' (Example shows 1972 rates for a married couple with two children under 16) | £18·50 | |
| | Subtract the needs allowance from your gross weekly income | £15·70 | |
| If a tenant's gross weekly income is less than his 'needs allowance', the minimum rent is reduced to nil | Take 17 per cent of that figure (multiply by 17 and divide by 100) | | £2·67 |
| | Add 40 per cent of the rent you pay (or £1 if that is greater) to find your 'minimum weekly rent' | | £2·75 |
| | Deduct total from the rent you pay | | £5·42 |
| | **Allowance to which you are entitled** | | **£1·58** |

The following are disregarded: any payment from any other member of the family; any money paid by a sub-tenant for rent or rates; any attendance allowance; sums payable to holders of the George Cross or Victoria Cross; Social Security benefits; £2 of any disablement benefit or of any widow's pension; £1 of any charitable payment

# Rent: cases of limited protection

*Hotel guests and lodgers*　　*Luxury homes*
*A house with the job*　　　 *Farmers*
*Official landlords*　　　　　*Long tenancies at low rents*

A NUMBER of people who pay rent or a similar charge for their accommodation have strictly limited protection against eviction and rent increases. They include:
**1.** Lodgers and hotel guests.
**2.** People who are provided with accommodation by their employers, to enable them to carry out their jobs.
**3.** Farm workers in tied cottages.
**4.** Tenants whose homes have a rateable value of over £200 (in London £400).
**5.** Tenants of certain official landlords such as the Crown, public authorities, housing trusts and registered housing associations.

In addition, there are special legal provisions for tenants with leases originally granted for more than 21 years at low rents.

### Hotel guests and lodgers
The protection of the Rent Acts is given only to those who are tenants. A person who books into a hotel or lodging house does not become a tenant and cannot stay if required to leave. At law he is called a licensee. If he has booked for a particular period, however, he can bring an action for damages if asked to leave sooner.

The difference between a tenant and a licensee is not always easy to define. One indication usually is that a tenant has exclusive right of occupation whereas a licensee does not. This means he has a key to his own premises and can prevent anyone else from using it.

Another important indication of whether a tenancy has been created is the intention of the parties involved. But the courts are reluctant to accept any renting arrangement as a mere licence if the owner intended to avoid the Rent Acts.

Lodgers in private houses are licensees if any part of the rent includes payment for board. A bed-and-breakfast guest is therefore a lodger with no security of tenure. ☐ Choosing the type of home to rent, p. 244.

The only occasions when the courts are likely to classify someone in exclusive possession of property as a licensee is when that person lives there as a result of some family arrangement, or through an act of friendship or charity, or because of employment.

If a tenant, or the housekeeper of a tenant who has died, is allowed to stay on temporarily as an act of indulgence by the landlord, such people are also treated as licensees, although they are in exclusive possession.

### A house with the job
People who are given living accommodation to enable them to do their jobs—domestic servants, caretakers, house surgeons, and so on—usually have none of the rights which a tenant enjoys.

The law provides no legal machinery that they can use to get a reduction in rent (if they pay any); and when the job comes to an end, they have to leave the flat or house that goes with it—though they cannot be evicted without a court order.

The most obvious example of this is the Prime Minister's tenancy of No. 10 Downing Street. Even if he is not always thought of as a servant, he is treated as one when it comes to his home. As soon as he loses his job, he has to move out and make way for his successor.

The same is true of the caretaker at a block of flats, or the house surgeon at a hospital.

Not everyone supplied with living accommodation by his employer forfeits legal protection. This happens only if the accommodation is provided for him to carry out his duties more conveniently or more efficiently.

When the employer provides housing as a fringe benefit, without its making any difference to the way the job is carried out, the employee can still qualify for legal protection. The tenancy may be regulated, furnished or, occasionally, controlled. ☐ Rent and security: unfurnished property, p. 252; controlled tenancies, p. 256; furnished property, p. 259.

In such cases, the employee-tenant has all the usual legal protection against rent increases and eviction. But he is nevertheless in a position of greater risk than the normal regulated or controlled tenant.

This is because the law provides specifically for the case of employee tenants who leave their employment. If a house or flat is let to an employee in consequence of his employment, and he leaves that employment, the landlord can obtain possession on two grounds,

provided that the judge thinks it reasonable:
1. If the landlord wants the property for one of his own employees.
2. If he wants it for somebody employed by another of his tenants.

A further problem can arise where a house or flat goes with the job and the employer deducts the equivalent of rent from wages, or even allows his workman to live rent-free in return for a lower wage.

Unless the tenant expressly agrees to have his rent deducted from his wages each week or month, the employer is likely to be infringing the Truck Acts. These generally forbid the payment of wages in anything other than cash unless the employee consents—but they apply principally to manual workers. ☐ How wages are protected, p. 598.

FARM WORKERS Agricultural workers living in farm cottages are seldom eligible for full legal protection. It depends on why they have the accommodation.

If, for example, a farm worker is obliged by the nature of his work to live in accommodation provided by his employer, then he will not be protected. His cottage will be a tied cottage and if he loses his job, he must generally go.

Normally, his former employer would take him to the county court for possession. The court has to grant this order. But it can postpone eviction more or less indefinitely on any one of three grounds:
1. If the farm worker cannot find anywhere else to live.
2. If the efficient management of the farm will not be interfered with.
3. If it would be a greater hardship to the tenant to evict him than it would be to the farmer to let him stay.

Where the farm cottage or house is not essential to his job, the farm worker will probably have a regulated tenancy, though if he leaves his job his protection from eviction will be less than usual. His landlord, the farmer, may be able to obtain an eviction order if he needs the accommodation for another employee. Tenants of farm houses who are not actually farm workers can also be evicted to make way for farm workers, provided that they have been given adequate warning of the position by their landlord at the time they moved in.

SPECIAL CASES People who are provided with homes by their employers can lose their legal protection in other ways. Government employees, for example, do not qualify for protection, nor do Crown employees, local authority workers and policemen.

Again, a private employer can form a housing trust or register a housing association to run the company's houses. In this case, tenants would probably not be fully protected.

### Official landlords

Even ordinary tenants of homes let by the Crown estates, public authorities or charitable trusts are not protected by the Rent Acts. Tenants of registered housing associations have some legal protection against unfair rent increases, but their security of tenure depends only on the rules of the association. ☐ Rent and security: unfurnished property, p. 252.

### Luxury homes

Tenants of homes with a rateable value of more than £200 (in London £400) normally have no legal protection against eviction and rent increases. The rateable value for this purpose is the one which applied on March 23, 1965 or—for homes built since then—the first registered rateable value. A home with a rateable value above the limit on the qualifying date cannot qualify for protection, even if the rateable value later fell below the limit.

The only protection such tenants have is the right to the 'quiet enjoyment' of their homes and to a court hearing before eviction.

### Farmers

A farmer who rents his farm is not protected by the Rent Acts but by the code governing agricultural holdings. The same applies to market gardeners.

However, a tenant of a property used for agriculture or market gardening is entitled to have his rent fixed by an arbitrator. This would be based on what rent the holding would be likely to fetch if it came up in the open market.

### Long tenancies at low rents

A tenancy with a lease of more than 21 years and with a rent that is less than two-thirds of the rateable value of the property is neither controlled nor regulated, even if the house or flat rented is within the rate limits set for controlled or regulated tenancies.

Nevertheless, such a tenant still enjoys a considerable degree of security. Provided that the rateable value of his home is not more than £200 (in London £400), he can generally stay on when his lease runs out.

If he has a house (not a flat) within the same rate limit, he may have the chance to buy the freehold of his home or have his lease extended for another 50 years. ☐ Security for leaseholders, p. 232.

# The right to privacy, peace and quiet

*Nuisance and annoyance*      *Rights of officials*
*Illegal harassment*

THE tenant of a flat or house, or even the person who rents a couple of rooms, has almost as much right to say who can enter his home as an owner-occupier. The landlord is not entitled to come and go as he pleases. As a rule, he must get the tenant's permission to enter the house or flat and he has no right to keep a duplicate key.

He can enter only if he has authority under the agreement or lease, or by the landlord's rights in one of the Housing or Rent Acts. Even then, this authority is subject to the convenience of the tenant.

For example, the landlord of a home leased for less than seven years has the right under the Housing Act 1961 to inspect his property at any reasonable time—but he must give 24 hours' *written* notice to the tenant.

A landlord also has the right, under the Rent Act 1968, to be given access and facilities to carry out repairs for which he is responsible —but he must choose a *reasonable* time to do so.

Again, if the tenant has a written agreement it will probably contain a clause allowing the landlord to inspect the property at *reasonable* and *convenient* times. This means that the landlord must give the tenant warning.

In one case, a landlord demanded entry unexpectedly and the tenant refused to let him into all the rooms. A court ruled that the tenant had not broken a term of his lease.

A landlord who enters his tenant's accommodation without authority or permission may be trespassing. ☐ Rights and responsibilities of running a home, p. 280.

The landlord also has rights. Tenants with a lease of less than seven years on an unfurnished home—either a controlled or a regulated tenancy—must allow the landlord 'reasonable facilities' to make repairs, if 24 hours' notice has been given.

Under the 1961 Act the tenant can demand that the landlord make structural and other repairs. The landlord must be allowed to have the work done during *reasonable* hours.

Landlords of houses let at very low rents have a similar right, as they are bound by law to keep the houses fit for people to live in.

Council officials can also inspect council houses, but again the tenant must be given 24 hours' notice, and the officials must produce written authorisation from the council. The inspection must take place at a reasonable time —not, for instance, late at night.

## Nuisance and annoyance

A tenant has a right to live in peace and comfort. If his neighbours make too much noise or cause a nuisance in any other way, the tenant may be able to sue for damages, or ask a court to order his neighbours to stop annoying him. Such an order is called an injunction. If the neighbour disobeys it, he can be jailed for contempt of court. If, for example, somebody lives next to a member of an orchestra, he could stop him practising at 3 a.m. ☐ Disputes with neighbours, p. 283.

The tenant has a similar right to prevent other people trespassing on or wilfully damaging the property he is renting. He should remember, however, that he is also open to action by his neighbour if he does any of these things himself.

A tenant annoying his neighbours faces a further risk—if his tenancy is regulated or controlled, the nuisance he causes may give his landlord grounds for an eviction order. ☐ Grounds for eviction, p. 274.

## Illegal harassment

Landlords who cannot evict their tenants legally sometimes try to frighten them into leaving the premises.

The law protects the tenant against this sort of harassment, as it is called. A landlord, or anybody else, who tries to get a tenant out by interfering with his or her enjoyment of the home or personal possessions is committing a criminal offence.

➤ SENT TO JAIL FOR INTIMIDATION *A mother of three children took a room in North London for which she was charged £3 10s. a week in rent.*

*The landlord's brother, a student, wanted the room. When the tenant said she had nowhere to go, he smashed the lock on the door. After complaints, the council warned the student about prosecution and the penalties for harassment of tenants. But he later went into the room, threw her belongings on to the floor and smashed several windows.*

*About two weeks later, the student insisted that the woman must leave. He pulled the light from the ceiling, smashed another window and swept the contents of her dressing table on to the floor. Later that day, the student came back, banged on the door and shouted that he was going to kill the tenant.*

*It was stated that he chopped the door down with an axe. Police were called and the student was arrested, prosecuted for having the axe as an offensive weapon, and fined £20. The local authority then prosecuted him for harassment.*
DECISION *The student was jailed for four months and ordered to pay £52 10s. costs. The magistrate told him: 'This sort of intimidation of persons by someone of your kind is just bullying and it will not be tolerated.'* ◄

It is also a crime for the landlord to cut off essential services—gas, electricity or water.

The term 'harassment' also covers attempts by the landlord to stop the tenant going to the rent officer or rent tribunal to try to get his rent reduced, or to stop him going to the local council offices to complain about not having a rent book.

If a tenant thinks he is being harassed, he should tell the legal department of the local council, which has the responsibility for prosecuting in such cases.

Harassment is a difficult offence to prove, however. The tenant can help the authorities by keeping a log of any incidents in which he thinks the landlord has behaved badly, making a particular note of the time and of any witnesses present.

► THE TENANT WHO WAS LOCKED OUT
*The landlord of a house in South London wanted his tenant—a married woman—to leave. He said that she was a sitting tenant when he bought the house and that she had agreed to find somewhere else to live.*

*The evidence was that twice the landlord locked his tenant out of the house and that he swore at her and kicked and punched her. She called the police after being locked out of the house late at night, and the landlord was prosecuted for harassment.*
DECISION *The magistrates' court found him guilty of denying the tenant her right of entry to the house and of 'interfering with her peace and comfort with the intention of making her leave the house'. He was fined £45.* ◄

The maximum penalties for illegal harassment are a fine of £400 in a magistrates'

court or an unlimited fine or two years' imprisonment in a Crown Court.

The tenant can also take action himself against the landlord, especially if the local authority seems to be taking too long to act. The law protects his right to live quietly in his house or flat—what lawyers call the right of 'quiet enjoyment'. If the landlord interferes with this right, the tenant can sue for damages or ask a court for an injunction.

► THE OWNER WHO MADE EERIE NOISES *A bus conductress rented three rooms in a house in North London. But her landlord wanted her to move. The evidence was that he removed a light bulb from the passage and made eerie noises at her from behind a curtain. He also banged on her walls late at night.*

*On one occasion, the landlord came into the woman's room while she was in bed and said he wanted to talk to her. He then assaulted her by grabbing her wrists.*

*As a result of this, the conductress moved out. But she continued to pay rent on the rooms, although she was living elsewhere. While she was away, the landlord changed the lock on the door and put putty in the keyhole. The tenant applied to the county court for an injunction.*
DECISION *She was granted an injunction restraining the landlord from trespassing in her rooms or assaulting her. The judge said that by entering the tenant's room, the landlord had committed a trespass. He awarded £5 damages for trespass committed when the landlord broke into the room, and a further £5 damages for trespass when he changed the lock.*

*Finally the landlord was ordered to pay the tenant £177 7s. 6d.—a proportion of the rent of the new property she was forced to move into for 129 weeks. The judge dismissed a claim by the landlord that the tenant had abandoned the premises.* ◄

Usually the tenant claims damages for what he has already had to put up with, and seeks an injunction to stop it recurring. Again, it is difficult to establish a satisfactory case; a solicitor will advise on the likely chances of success. If a tenant is put out in the street without a court order, he can obtain an order restoring his home to him. The landlord may be jailed if he refuses to take the tenant back. ☐ Grounds for eviction, p. 274.

**Rights of officials**
There are many occasions when tenants, just like owner-occupiers, are obliged to let officials into their homes for certain strictly defined purposes. ☐ Officials' right of entry, p. 294.

# Repairs: whose responsibility?

*Duties of the landlord*     *Standards of work*
*Duties of the tenant*

W HEN a rented house or flat needs repairs, the first task is to find out whose responsibility they are. Usually the solution will be given in the lease or tenancy agreement, if there is one, or perhaps in an Act of Parliament.

### Duties of the landlord

Where there is no agreement for repairs between landlord and tenant, then the Housing Act 1961 will often provide an answer to any problems that arise.

Under the 1961 Act, leases of less than seven years made after October 24, 1961, make the landlord responsible for repairs to the structure and exterior of a property—including walls, roof, drains, gutters and pipes. He must also repair plumbing and keep gas pipes and electric wiring, sockets and switches in working order. No landlord can contract out of these responsibilities, but he need not maintain fixtures and fittings such as cookers.

Property let before October 24, 1961 is a different matter. A landlord is not generally bound to carry out repairs to unfurnished premises. He does not even have to guarantee they are fit to live in, nor is he liable if a tenant is injured because the property which he occupies is in a poor state of repair.

➤ NO DUTY TO REPAIR A COUNCIL FLAT *Mr Albert Sleafer, a tenant in a block of flats owned by the London Borough of Lambeth, found that his front door did not fit properly and jammed. He complained to the council several times, but the council failed to repair it.*

*One day in November 1955, the door knocker came away in his hand as he tried to pull the door closed. Mr Sleafer fell backwards and injured himself against a balcony. He later sued Lambeth Council for damages.*

DECISION *Mr Sleafer lost his case. The court ruled that, although his landlords normally did repairs, they were not bound by law to do so. (Sleafer v. Lambeth Borough Council.)* ◄

Landlords of property let before October 1961 are also free from liability for the death or injury of lodgers or sub-tenants as a consequence of defects in the property. Once

again, the landlord cannot be held liable, even if he normally carries out repairs and has been notified of the dangerous defect.

➤ NO LIABILITY FOR A LODGER *Mr Richard Travers was a lodger in a council house at Malmesbury Road, Gloucester. While taking a bath one morning in March 1942, he was killed by fumes from a defective geyser. His mother sued the council, the gas company and the builder for damages.*

*Some time earlier, the tenant had reported that the geyser appeared dangerous. The gas company informed the council about defects in the installation.*

DECISION *The court ruled that the council had no legal duty to the lodger to take care in the provision of the geyser. (Travers v. Gloucester Corporation.)* ◄

There are, however, liabilities from which the landlord cannot escape. Where he retains possession of the roof or a common staircase, he must carry out proper repairs. A staircase must be safe and a roof must not be allowed to fall into disrepair so that the tenant's premises underneath may be damaged. Additionally, under the Occupiers' Liability Act 1957, the landlord who neglects the upkeep of a common staircase, roof, or other part of a property he retains can be sued for damages if injury is caused.

### Duties of the tenant

The tenant must look after the property he rents. This includes small repairs such as thawing frozen water pipes, replacing window latches, unblocking kitchen sinks, and having chimneys cleaned. The landlord can ask the tenant to do jobs of this kind and, if he refuses, the landlord can apply for an eviction order.

A clause called a 'repairing covenant' found in most agreements and leases deals with the tenant's responsibility for repairs.

Covenants usually require a person either to 'keep in repair' or to 'leave in repair' the property he rents. The distinctions are crucial.

A tenant who agrees to 'keep in repair' may have to repair any defects when he moves in and then must keep the property in repair *at all times* during the tenancy. But a covenant to 'leave in repair' allows a tenant to avoid doing repairs *until the tenancy ends*.

In one case, however, a tenant who had agreed to leave a property in good repair had to pay for repairs to be carried out when he left, even though the house had not been in a satisfactory condition when he moved in.

### Standards of work

A covenant simply 'to keep in repair' means that the property must be maintained in approximately the same condition as it was in at the start of the tenancy.

The natural effects of time are taken into account. A tenant who has taken a lease on an old house is not obliged, by his repairing covenant, to hand back a completely renovated home when he goes.

The duty under a covenant to repair a property is quite distinct from an obligation to improve it. If, for example, there is dry rot, the tenant may be expected under a covenant to replace the rotting wood. But he would not be under any obligation to get rid of the *cause* of the rot—possibly poor ventilation.

A tenant will not usually have to renew or rebuild the property under a repairing covenant if it is damaged or destroyed by fire, storm, earthquake, bombing 'or like calamity'.

But he would have to rebuild if he deliberately damaged or destroyed it, or if it suffered through his negligence—for instance, if he left a fire unguarded and the house burnt down as a result.

Covenants often exclude tenants from having to repair defects caused by 'fair wear and tear'—the normal defects caused by time and the elements—but this does not absolve them from all responsibility. A tenant who left a leaking water pipe unmended would be liable for damage caused by his neglect.

---

## Repairs to controlled, furnished and low-rent property

THE law lays down special provisions about repairs to controlled, furnished and low-rent properties. ☐ How the law defines a controlled tenancy, p. 256. How the law defines a furnished tenancy, p. 259.

### Controlled tenancies

The amount of rent paid under a controlled tenancy is usually the best guide to who is responsible for repairs. In most controlled tenancies, rents are twice the gross rateable value of the property as it appeared in the 1956 valuation list—in which case the landlord is responsible for repairs, but not decoration.

But if the rent is only $1\frac{1}{3}$ times the gross rateable value, the tenant is liable. Where rents lie in between these figures, it usually means that the responsibility for repairs is split between landlord and the tenant—and it may take a court case to find out exactly how.

Tenants of controlled property have the right to apply to the local council for a certificate of disrepair. If the certificate is granted this reduces their rent to $1\frac{1}{3}$ times the gross rateable value until the landlord carries out the repairs for which he is responsible.

### Furnished premises

Furnished houses are controlled by much stricter regulations than unfurnished property. A landlord must ensure that the property is fit for the tenant to live in at the start of the tenancy—and courts have ruled that defective drains or even infestation by bed-bugs have made furnished homes unfit.

In one case, a tenant found that the house he was renting had been infected by measles shortly before he moved in. A county court judge ruled that, because of the infection, the tenant was entitled to leave immediately—and exempted him from paying any rent.

### Low-rent homes

By law, homes commanding very low rents must be fit to live in, whatever the landlord may say to the contrary. This ruling applies to homes let before July 6, 1957, at a rent of £26 a year or less—50p a week; or in London, £40 a year—80p a week. Where the house was let after July 6, 1957, the rent must be £52 a year or less—£1 a week; or in London, £80 a year—£1·60 a week.

Standards of fitness are not, however, high. Defects must be so serious that no one could reasonably be expected to live in the house in its present condition.

Under the Occupiers' Liability Act 1957, the landlord is responsible for carrying out repairs to a common staircase, roof or guttering, or other part of the property in his possession. If he fails to do so, he is responsible for any injury caused by the defects.

# Repairs: forcing the landlord to act

ONCE a tenant has established that a repair is the landlord's responsibility he should ensure that the landlord, or rent-collector, is aware that the defect needs attention. Otherwise the landlord, in law, does not have to get the repairs done—unless he has reason to know of the defect from some other source.

If the landlord consistently refuses to carry out repairs, the tenant may do them himself and send the bill to the landlord. If the landlord refuses to pay, the tenant can sue. But a more convenient way of recovering the money is to deduct the cost of repairs from the rent.

If the landlord refuses to carry out repairs and the tenant does not choose to do them himself, the local authority housing and public health departments may be able to help.

## Abatement notices

The tenant can first ask a local council public health official to inspect the property to see if it can be classed as prejudicial to health, or a nuisance.

A blocked drain or lavatory, a leaking roof, or infestation by bed-bugs can be public-health nuisances; but mere lack of redecoration would not be.

If the official agrees that there is a public-health nuisance, and that the tenant is not responsible, he will ask the council to serve an abatement notice on the landlord—a printed form detailing the defects and instructing the landlord to carry out repairs within a specified time, which varies according to the type of repair. It would not take a month to unblock a drain, but it might to replaster a kitchen wall.

If the landlord has not completed repairs by the end of the specified time, the council can apply to the local magistrates' court for a nuisance order. The landlord will then risk being fined if the repairs are not carried out. If he still refuses to do the work, the council can send its own workmen in, and recover its costs from the landlord.

Unfortunately, this could result in the tenant's having to wait up to three months for a fairly simple repair to be carried out.

There is another, quicker method. If the tenant can show that there is likely to be unreasonable delay in getting repairs done, the council may be persuaded to serve the landlord with a notice giving him seven days in which to let it know whether he intends to do the repairs.

If after nine days the council has had no reply, it may send in its own workmen and recover its costs from the landlord. But if the landlord agrees to do the repairs, the council must give him reasonable time to make a start—which brings the tenant back to relying on the normal nuisance-abatement procedure if he delays.

When the property is council-owned there is, obviously, little chance of the public health department's taking action against its own housing department. But if the local authority itself has caused the nuisance by failing to do repairs, the tenant can make a private application to the magistrates' court for a summons with a view to having a nuisance order made against the council. This course of action may produce the desired results before the case is due to be heard.

## Demolition and closing orders

Occasionally, after the tenant calls in the public health department, the official inspecting the premises decides that the house cannot be made fit to live in at a reasonable cost. The council will then make an order for the demolition of the house or, if only part of it is unfit, a closing order on the unfit part, making it illegal for the landlord to let it again.

Once either of these orders has been made, the tenant loses any protection against eviction he may have under the Rents Acts—but the council has an obligation to rehouse him. If two or more adjoining houses are involved, the council may decide to buy them under a compulsory purchase order. □ Threats to the home, p. 300.

In these circumstances any tenant who, over a number of years, has consistently spent money to keep the house well-maintained can apply to the Department of the Environment for compensation. Compensation for keeping a house well-maintained will also be paid when the council acquires the whole area for slum clearance and redevelopment. The tenant, however, should lodge a claim for compensation immediately he hears that a compulsory purchase order is likely to be made.

## Management and control orders

A tenant living in a tenement block, or a house in multiple occupation, can press the local authority to make a management order persuading the landlord to carry out repairs in line with the Department of the Environment's code of management for such premises.

This covers repair, maintenance, cleaning, water supply, drainage and disposal of refuse and litter; but the extent of repairs will usually be decided in the light of the number of people living in the house.

Boiling a kettle may be considered a suitable way of providing hot water in a bachelor bed-sitting room, but not in a flat occupied by a family with young children.

If the landlord refuses to carry out the repairs, the council can send in its own workmen—and charge the landlord. If the landlord is incapable of managing the premises properly, the council may make a control order. It then manages the property—or it may compulsorily purchase it. ·

## Certificates of disrepair

As an extra lever, anyone with a controlled tenancy can obtain a 'certificate of disrepair' from the local authority. This authorises a reduction in rent until the landlord carries out repairs which the public health department consider necessary.

To obtain a certificate of disrepair, the tenant must first fill in a form of notice to the landlord (Form G), obtainable from the local authority housing department. The tenant himself must serve the original form on the landlord or rent collector, and retain an identical copy to send to the local council. He should also take a further copy for himself.

The form requests the landlord to remedy defects classified under six headings: external structure, internal structure, external decoration, internal decoration, fixtures and fittings and other defects of repair.

If the landlord agrees to carry out the work, or to remedy some of the defects, the tenant should receive a written undertaking, signed and dated by the landlord, specifying exactly what will be done. This is as valuable to the tenant as a certificate of disrepair, for the tenant will be entitled to a reduced rent from the date the landlord agreed to do the repairs until they are completed.

If the landlord refuses to carry out the repairs, or simply ignores the form, the tenant should apply on Form I to the local authority for a certificate of disrepair. Six weeks must elapse between giving the landlord Form G and applying for the certificate.

When this form is completed and returned to the local authority, it must be accompanied by a copy of Form G served on the landlord, and a fee of $12\frac{1}{2}$p. (This can be deducted from the rent when a certificate has been granted.)

The council must give the landlord three weeks' notice before issuing a certificate.

If, during this time, the landlord promises to carry out repairs but does not complete them within six months, the tenant is, once again, entitled to a reduction in his rent from the date of his application on Form I.

Should the landlord fail to agree to carry out the repairs or ignore the notice given to him, a certificate will be granted (Form L) and the tenant's rent will be automatically reduced.

A landlord who considers that the repairs which have been listed are unnecessary, or that the tenant is responsible for any of them, can ask the county court to cancel the certificate. Otherwise he must be satisfied with the reduced rent until the defects listed are remedied, the work inspected by the local authority and the certificate cancelled.

## How reduced rent is calculated

For most controlled tenancies, the part of the rent assessed from gross rateable value is twice the gross value of the dwelling which appears in the 1956 valuation list; but it may be slightly below twice the gross value or, if the landlord is also responsible for internal decorative repairs, as high as $2\frac{1}{3}$ times. □ How the law defines a controlled tenancy, p. 256.

If a certificate of disrepair is granted, the figure is, in every case, reduced to $1\frac{1}{3}$ times the gross value. So the landlord gets a far lower rent—and while the certificate is in force he can increase the rent only to match improvements which he has carried out, or to meet increases in rates.

A certificate of disrepair cancels any notices of rent increases (other than for rates or improvements) which the landlord may have served on the tenant during the six months before the tenant applied for a certificate.

The tenant of controlled property is also entitled to a reduction in rent *from the time that he applied for his certificate*. He will therefore be entitled to a refund of the excess rent paid between the time he applied for a certificate and the time it was granted. If necessary, he can recoup this over-payment by making a further reduction in his rent.

271

# Leaving a rented home

A TENANT may leave a rented home by choice or because the landlord forces him to go. In the first case, the law protects the landlord against a tenant's leaving unexpectedly. In the second, it safeguards the tenant against arbitrary eviction.

### Giving notice

A tenant is obliged under the Rent Act 1957 to give the landlord at least four weeks' notice in writing of his intention to leave. This minimum period of notice applies to weekly, monthly or other periodic tenancies, but it does not apply in cases where the tenant has a lease for a fixed period.

If a tenant wishes to leave in the middle of a lease, he must either hand the property back to the landlord and give up his rights under the lease—known as 'surrendering' it—or he must find a tenant acceptable to the landlord to take over the lease. This is called 'assigning' the lease.

When a tenant leaves before the end of a lease, the landlord is entitled to the rent for the remainder of the period, though he has a duty to make reasonable efforts to find a new tenant. Provided that he does so, he can charge the old tenant for the period the house or flat is empty.

Frequently the tenant is liable under the terms of the lease to redecorate the flat or house to a certain standard and to carry out repairs to fixtures and fittings. If he does not meet his obligation, the landlord can have the work completed and sue him for the cost. Often, however, the person to whom a lease is assigned will be prepared to take over the responsibility for repairs.

The landlord may be anxious to regain possession of the flat rather than have the lease assigned to a new tenant. He may want to let it at a higher rent, live in it himself or redevelop it in some way.

It is worth while trying to strike a bargain. Sometimes the landlord will agree to forgo all claims for decorations and repairs for the sake of getting the tenant out.

If such an agreement is reached, make sure that the landlord gives his consent in writing. If there is any doubt, or if the amount of money involved is considerable, it may be worth consulting a solicitor to avoid the possibility of a future claim.

### Being made to leave

No one can lawfully be forced to leave his home until a court has given its consent. A landlord can try to obtain this consent by applying for an eviction order.

In most cases, however, the landlord must take preliminary steps before he can apply to the court for an eviction order.

### Notice to quit

The most common way of trying to get a tenant to leave is to ask or tell him to do so. In most cases the landlord supports his action with a formal letter, called a 'notice to quit'. This can be used when the tenant has no fixed-period agreement or lease, and pays his rent weekly or monthly.

The notice to quit need not be in writing, but it must give the tenant a minimum of four weeks' notice ending on a day when the rent is due to be paid.

If the wrong date is given, the notice will not be valid; nor should there be conditions attached to the notice. For example, if the notice says the tenant shall leave 'unless he fails to find alternative accommodation', it would not be valid.

The notice must cover the whole of the rented premises, not just a part.

There is no need for the tenant to challenge the notice (in fact there is no machinery for him to do so) because the landlord cannot force him to leave without going through the second stage—applying for an eviction order.

When the landlord makes his application there will be a court hearing, and the tenant has an opportunity to put his case.

### Forfeiting a lease

When the tenant has a fixed-term lease or agreement—say for three years—and the landlord wants to evict him before it expires, the landlord can go to court and start an 'action of forfeiture'. If the action succeeds, the tenant will forfeit his lease or agreement.

Actions of forfeiture can be brought only

on the ground that the tenant has broken one of the conditions of his contract in such a way that the tenancy must be ended. For example, a tenant may have failed to carry out repairs he has undertaken to do or he may have failed to pay the rent.

If the action succeeds, the tenant loses any rights he may have under a contract to stay on the premises. But he may qualify for the legal protection of a controlled or regulated tenancy—according to the circumstances. ☐ Rent and security: unfurnished property, p. 252; controlled tenancies, p. 256.

The right of a landlord to secure the forfeiture of a lease is carefully controlled.

First, the lease must state that the landlord has a right to resume possession of the property if the tenant breaks any covenant or clause in the contract.

Secondly, the landlord must usually serve the tenant with a special notice specifying the breach, asking him to remedy it, if it can be remedied, and requesting him to make cash compensation. No such notice is needed where the tenant has failed to pay rent or has assigned or sub-let his tenancy in breach of his contract with the landlord.

Thirdly, the landlord must not have waived the breach by, say, demanding rent when he was aware that the tenant had broken one of the conditions of his contract.

Fourthly, even where there has been a breach, the court can still refuse forfeiture. In the case of the tenant's failure to do repairs three or more years before the end of his lease, the landlord may not even be allowed to start proceedings for eviction unless he gets permission from the court.

As the law on forfeiture of leases is technical, the tenant should take legal advice at the first hint of action by the landlord.

People with controlled or regulated tenancies—but not furnished tenancies—are still protected from eviction even when a forfeiture action succeeds.

It is up to the court to decide whether there are sufficient grounds under the Rent Acts to order the tenant's eviction.

### When an agreement expires
If the tenant's lease or agreement has already run out, the landlord does not need to take any preliminary steps. He simply starts an action claiming possession of the premises. But the action does not succeed just because the agreement has expired.

### Applying for an eviction order
Once the necessary preliminary steps have been taken, a landlord can apply for an eviction order. A private landlord must apply to the county court; a local authority can apply to a county court or to a magistrates' court.

The landlord must then satisfy the judge

---

## A landlord's first move to gain an eviction

| Type of occupier | Preliminary steps a landlord must take |
| --- | --- |
| Tenant with fixed-period agreement or lease which still has some time to run | If the tenant has broken a term of his agreement, the landlord can ask a court to order the tenant to forfeit his lease—called an 'action of forfeiture' |
| Tenant with *expired* fixed-period agreement | None (tenancy has automatically expired) |
| Weekly, monthly or other periodic tenancy | Landlord must serve a legal document called a 'notice to quit' |
| Employee with accommodation provided by an employer to enable him to do his job more efficiently or conveniently | Proper notice of dismissal from his employment unless dismissed for misconduct.☐ Leaving the job, p. 639 |
| Tenants of the Crown, charitable trusts or registered housing associations | Landlord must serve a notice to quit |
| Council tenants on weekly, monthly or other periodic tenancies | Council must serve a notice to quit |

that he has followed the correct procedure and that there are grounds in law for requiring the tenant to leave.

### Going to the county court

The first warning of eviction which most tenants receive is a county court summons, giving the landlord's reason for wanting possession of the property.

The summons shows the costs the tenant must pay if he admits the claim and gives the date he is to appear in court.

With the summons will be another form for the tenant to state his side of the case. The tenant should immediately seek legal advice.

At the county court the landlord will try to establish grounds for eviction by giving evidence about the terms of the tenancy and why he wants the tenant to leave.

After each witness for the landlord has given evidence, the tenant or his legal representative can cross-examine him. The tenant can then give his evidence, call his witnesses and put all the legal arguments to the judge.

# Grounds for eviction

## Regulated or controlled tenancies

To make an order on grounds 1–12 the judge must consider that eviction would be reasonable

| | |
|---|---|
| **1. Alternative accommodation** | The landlord can provide an alternative home, which is about the same size and the same distance from the tenant's work, and rent and security are roughly the same as in the tenant's present home |
| **2. Rent arrears** | If rent arrears can be paid off in instalments the court will normally make a suspended order for possession—an eviction order which does not take effect as long as the tenant keeps up his payments. A possession order will normally be made only if the tenant has an extremely bad rent record. If the tenant pays all arrears before the case comes to court, no eviction order can normally be made |
| **3. Breach of agreement** | The tenant has broken a term of the tenancy by, for example, turning the property into a lodging house without authority. An eviction order may be refused if the breach is not serious and the tenant is prepared to remedy it |
| **4. Nuisance to neighbours** | The tenant or his lodger has been a nuisance to neighbours |
| **5. Illegal use** | The tenant or his lodger has been convicted of using the premises for an immoral or illegal purpose |
| **6. Damage** | The tenant or his lodger has damaged the property or made unauthorised alterations |
| **7. Change of mind** | The tenant refuses to leave after telling the landlord he would, forcing the landlord to cancel arrangements for re-letting the house or selling it |
| **8. Sub-letting** | The tenant has sub-let or assigned his tenancy without consent. The landlord is not entitled to an eviction order if the tenant keeps a part of the tenancy for himself |
| **9. Overcharging a sub-tenant** | The tenant has overcharged a lawful sub-tenant. This affects only controlled or regulated sub-tenancies where the maximum rent is fixed |

The judgment will then be given. Usually the judge will order the losing party to pay the winning side's costs.

If the landlord gets possession, the judge can postpone the day of eviction, usually by anything up to six weeks. With tenants employed in agriculture he can postpone the eviction for as long as he likes and must normally do so for six months. ☐ Rent: cases of limited protection, p. 264.

Where a landlord applies for an order because the tenant is in arrears with rent, the judge often makes an eviction order but postpones its operation as long as the tenant pays off arrears at so much a week, and continues paying his normal rent in full.

**Local council evictions**

A local council can get a tenant evicted more quickly from property it owns by applying to a magistrates' court under the Small Tenements Recovery Act 1838. These powers can be used only before October 1, 1972, when the Act is repealed.

| | |
|---|---|
| **10.** Employment | The tenant was let the property as an employee but no longer works for the landlord who needs the home for a full-time employee of himself or of a tenant of his |
| **11.** The landlord's needs | The landlord needs the property for himself or a member of his family and would suffer more hardship from being without it than the tenant would suffer from being evicted. Members of the landlord's family who qualify are a son or daughter over 18 years old or the landlord's parents. If the tenancy is regulated, the landlord's father-in-law or mother-in-law qualify. Tenants already living in the property when the landlord bought it cannot normally be evicted on this ground |
| **12.** Licensing offence | A tenant of controlled accommodation which includes off-licence premises has been convicted of a licensing offence, has been an unsatisfactory licence-holder or is refused renewal of his licence |
| **13.** Official orders | A closing, demolition, or clearance order has been made |
| **14.** The landlord's home | The landlord once used the property as his own home and warned the tenant that the tenancy was only temporary while he was away. This applies to regulated tenancies only |
| **15.** Church use | The tenancy is regulated and the property has been reserved for a minister of religion other than the Church of England |
| **16.** Agricultural premises | The house or flat consists of agricultural premises let to someone who is not a farm worker and it is needed by the landlord as a home for an agricultural employee. An employee or former employee or the widow of a former employee cannot normally be evicted on these grounds |

**Grounds for eviction in furnished tenancies**

| | |
|---|---|
| **17.** No right to security | The landlord has correctly served on the tenant a notice to quit, and any term of security granted by a Rent Tribunal has ended and the notice to quit has expired |
| **18.** Expired agreement | The tenant had an agreement for a fixed period and the agreement has expired |

The council must be able to satisfy the court on three important points:
1. That a proper notice to quit has been served.
2. That a 'notice of intention' to apply to the court has been served. This must be read or explained to the tenant or nailed to his door.
3. That the council needs the property to let to another tenant.

If the council proves these points the magistrate will issue a 'warrant of possession'. This can be put into force no sooner than 21 days after the warrant has been granted and no later than 30 days after. Entry on a possession warrant can be made only between 9 a.m. and 4 p.m., and not on a Sunday, Good Friday or Christmas Day.

### Eviction by bailiffs

If the tenant does not remove himself and his family after an eviction order has been granted to his landlord he can be forcibly moved by the court bailiffs. If he decides to resist, for example, by barricading himself and his family inside their home, the bailiffs can break down doors or windows to gain entry into the property.

But bailiffs are not permitted to force their way into a tenant's home except to carry out a court order. If they try to do so, they may lay themselves open to prosecution for harassment' or illegal eviction. ☐ Officials' rights of entry into the home, p. 293.

### Security of sub-tenant

Sub-tenants of a landlord whose agreement allows him to sub-let will not be evicted, even if their immediate landlord *is* ordered to leave.

If, however, the immediate landlord has sub-let without authority, the sub-tenant may be evicted. This applies also to any tenant of a landlord whose mortgage does not allow him to let any part of his property.

## When eviction is illegal

No tenant can be evicted without a court order, however badly he has behaved. If he receives a notice to quit, he need not leave until the notice has been confirmed by a county court order. If the landlord tries to evict him illegally, the tenant may call the police, but they can act only to stop a breach of the peace.

If a landlord or any person evicts or tries physically to evict the tenant without a court order, he is guilty of a criminal offence. He has a defence if he can convince the court that he had reasonable cause to believe that the tenant had already left the premises, but if he fails he may be fined up to £400 in a magistrates' court. If the case is heard by a Crown Court, he may be fined any amount or be imprisoned for up to two years.

Even if he does not resort to eviction by physical means, the landlord might still be found guilty of illegal harassment. For example, courts tend to regard it as harassment if a landlord cuts off the supply of gas, electricity or water, or if he interferes with a tenant's enjoyment of his home in some other way—perhaps by causing excessive noise or disturbance. ☐ The right to privacy, peace and quiet, p. 266.

The local authority prosecutes in cases of illegal eviction. Any landlord who acts without legal authority should be reported immediately to the legal department of the local council. If the council does not act, the tenant can prosecute privately.

Prosecuting the landlord does not regain the tenant's home for him.

One legal remedy is to try to regain entry. If the tenant can regain entry peacefully, he runs no risk. But if he has to use force, either to break a lock or to overcome the landlord's resistance, he may be breaking the law.

Another remedy is to ask for a court injunction ordering the landlord to allow the tenant to return and restraining him from trying to evict the tenant again. The tenant may be able to get legal aid for such action. Otherwise it could cost him £30 to £40, though most of this would be recoverable if he wins. ☐ Help with legal fees and costs, p. 710.

If the landlord disobeys the order, he can be sent to prison for contempt of court. The tenant can also sue the landlord for damages, and although this may take time, it has in some cases resulted in damages of up to £300.

If the tenant does not want to go back to his former home because of any unpleasantness, he can find a new home and may be able to sue the landlord for damages, covering the cost of any hotels or other emergency accommodation, plus incidental expenses such as the cost of removal vans and taxis.

Before taking this action, however, he should consult a solicitor.

# Homes: the third choice

*Finding and joining a co-ownership scheme*
*Moving in*
*Monthly payments*

*Living on a co-ownership estate*
*Moving out*
*The role of the 'parent' society*

THE house-hunter who does not want the initial expense of buying a property, and is also unwilling to meet the high running expense of rented accommodation, has a third choice: to live in a house or flat on an estate where the properties are owned collectively by all the residents. This arrangement is known as co-ownership.

A co-ownership home combines some of the advantages of renting property with some of the advantages of owning it. Deposit and legal fees are comparatively small; the co-owner can leave at short notice without expense; and, if he stays more than five years, he shares in any increase in the value of his home.

The principle is not new. Since the passing of the Industrial and Provident Societies Act in 1893 it has been possible for a group of people to register themselves as a non-profit-making housing society, seeking finance for their building project from local authorities, building societies and other lenders.

Co-ownership was given considerable impetus with the establishment of the Housing Corporation—a Government body—under the Housing Act 1964.

Many talented architects, frustrated by the conservative tastes of commercial developers, have been attracted to work on co-ownership schemes where they often have more freedom to try out new ideas. As a close watch is kept by the Corporation on design and standards of building, a co-ownership estate is likely to be of better design and quality than a similar private development.

Apart from the quality of the houses and flats themselves, considerable attention is usually given to communal amenities—such as landscaped gardens and play areas.

### How to find a co-ownership scheme
Although the Housing Corporation sponsored nearly 35,000 houses and flats in its first seven years of operation, the number of new homes available is limited. They are normally advertised in the local press, on notice boards at the site, and at the offices of the housing societies' managing agents.

For a complete list of current developments, write to the Housing Corporation's head office in Sloane Square House, Sloane Square, London SW1W 8NT, or its regional offices in Kings Road, London SW3 4TS, and in Edinburgh, Cardiff, Leicester and Manchester.

### How to join
It costs little or nothing to join the waiting list for a co-ownership house. Where a new development is being built, the prospective member may be able to have a house allocated immediately. But if all the planned houses are already allocated, he must wait for someone to withdraw or move out.

As soon as a house is available, the prospective member joins the housing society by buying a £5 share. This gives him a vote in the management of the estate.

Joint membership is also available—giving equal rights over the property to a husband and wife or two friends who wish to share a home. In these cases, only one of the joint members has the voting right.

### Moving in
A new member may be able to move in within a month of joining; but there could be a delay if the house or flat has been lived in for some time and needs redecorating.

Before he can take possession, the co-owner must pay a deposit—probably between £50 and £200. This will be held by the society in case he falls behind with his rent or causes damage to the property which he refuses to repair. When he leaves, the deposit will normally be returned.

The member enters into an agreement with the society which usually runs for a year at first, and is renewable. This is a relatively simple document, and the legal costs (only about £10) are paid by the member. The agreement provides, among other things, for all the outside repairs and maintenance, and the upkeep of common areas, to be carried out by the society. Any interior repairs or decoration are the responsibility of the co-owner.

### Monthly payments
The monthly payments for a co-ownership home depend on the total cost of the development, the interest the housing society has to

277

pay on its 100 per cent mortgage over 40 years with the Housing Corporation and a building society, the cost of external repairs and maintenance, insurance, central heating and the upkeep of communal gardens. The payments for each house will be based on its size and any extra amenities it may have.

The monthly payments are checked by the Housing Corporation when final costs are known and whenever a new member moves in. The amount of these payments is stated in each tenancy agreement, together with the actual cost of each house. However, if interest rates or running costs rise or fall, the society may adjust the payment.

This ensures that enough money is being paid into the society to enable it to repay its mortgage and also maintain, and even improve, the development. Over the years, the value of the homes is likely to increase. New members' monthly payments will then be based on the increased value.

Because the schemes are financed by a mortgage, the interest charges on the loan are allowable for income-tax relief. In most cases, housing societies choose to use the Government Option Mortgage scheme, which means that the interest they pay to the building society and the Housing Corporation is reduced, and so the payments are lower. In such cases, the co-owners are not able to claim tax relief on their payments. ☐ Applying for mortgage, p. 194.

### Living on a co-ownership estate

Every member of a housing society has an equal vote in the management of the estate— through an elected management committee, on which any voting member is eligible to serve. The society may employ full-time caretaking staff, or volunteer members may undertake such tasks. The costs are met out of the members' monthly payments.

The co-owner cannot sub-let, nor can he run a business from his house. He may have to seek the society's—that is, his neighbours'—permission to make any improvements. He is responsible for the rates, but the society is responsible for all other charges, except internal repairs and decorations.

Unlike the house-owner, the co-owner cannot sell his home to anyone he chooses when he leaves. The house usually goes to the next applicant on the society's waiting list. But if a co-owner dies, the agreement usually allows a husband or wife to take over.

If the co-owner stays for the full term of 40 years, his monthly payments will be reduced considerably for, after the end of the period, they need to cover only the cost of maintaining the estate.

He is in a similar position to the house-owner who has paid off his mortgage.

If a husband or wife has taken over the house or flat during the 40 years, the society counts the date as from the time the agreement was originally signed.

A co-owner can be evicted only if he breaks the terms of the agreement, perhaps by failing to make payments. But even where eviction is possible, the society must take action through the courts, in the same way as any landlord seeking to remove a tenant from unfurnished property. ☐ Grounds for eviction, p. 274.

### Moving out

Most agreements, after the initial year, operate on a month-to-month basis, though this may vary from one development to another. After the first 12 months, therefore, a member usually needs to give only one or two months' notice. If he wanted to leave within his notice period, he would have to pay the society the full payment due.

When a co-owner leaves, the society returns his initial deposit. But it deducts any charge for redecoration or repairs which may be necessary before a new tenant can move in.

In addition, the co-owner who has lived in his home for at least five years gets back a proportion of the money he has paid in and a proportion of any increase in the value of his home, when his dwelling has been re-let to a new member.

### Role of the 'parent' society

Anyone can join a co-ownership scheme, can live on a co-ownership estate and leave it without having the bother and hard work of starting such a scheme.

Normally at least eight people are needed to found a co-ownership scheme, and they must have the backing of the Housing Corporation. Some members of the group should have experience of house-building—architects, accountants, solicitors, surveyors and builders, for instance.

They will often find that, between them, they are able to do all that is required to get their project started. But they may employ outside consultants for anything they are unable to do themselves.

This group is the 'parent' housing society. It sees each scheme through, finds the tenants and manages the estates. From then on, the society is run by the co-owners through their committee. They have the expert guidance of the parent society to deal with external repairs, cleaning and gardening. This is done by a management agreement, renewable every five years.

It is therefore possible to be a founder-member of a co-ownership estate without helping to organise it.

All co-ownership schemes are non-profit-making. Members of a 'parent' society are entitled to their normal fees as architects, accountants and solicitors, but they do not make a profit on the development.

Their plans for the group of houses or flats, and a full account of the estimated cost, have to be submitted to the Housing Corporation.

If the project is approved, the Corporation lends the society one-third of the money it requires for the complete development at ¼ per cent above the current building society interest rate. The other two-thirds of the construction costs is obtained on a group mortgage from a building society, local authority or other lender.

Because both mortgages are repayable over 40 years, instead of the usual 25 or 30, the occupants' weekly or monthly payments are naturally lower than the mortgage repayments which have to be made by those who are not members of a co-ownership scheme.

## How the repayment is calculated

A CO-OWNER who leaves after five years or more will normally be entitled to a sum of money known as a premium payment. This is calculated in two parts.

First there is the 'basic payment' which is a proportion of the co-ownership value of the home when the member first moved in. That value is based, not on the market price of the house, but on the amount the society is able to charge as a monthly payment to its members. The proportion paid on moving out rises from 1 per cent after five years' occupation to a maximum of 80 per cent after 38 years.

Then there is the 'valuation amount'—a proportion of any increase in the co-ownership value of the house since the co-owner took it over. The proportion paid rises from a minimum of 50 per cent of the increase in the value after five years to 80 per cent after 20 years.

For example, the co-owner who lives for seven years in a house which was valued at £5000 when he took it over and is now valued at £7500 will be entitled to a premium payment of £1400. This is made up as follows:

| | |
|---|---|
| Basic repayment | |
| 3 per cent of original value (£5000) | £150 |
| Valuation amount | |
| 50 per cent of increase in value (£2500) | £1250 |
| Premium payment | £1400 |

The payment will be made to a departing co-owner as soon as the house is re-let. There is one limitation, however. The premium payment can never be higher than the 'security amount'—the difference between the value of the house when the co-owner leaves and the sum still to be paid on it.

| Number of years | Percentage of first value | Percentage of increase |
|---|---|---|
| 5 | 1 | 50 |
| 6 | 2 | 50 |
| 7 | 3 | 50 |
| 8 | 4 | 50 |
| 9 | 5 | 50 |
| 10 | 6 | 60 |
| 11 | 8 | 60 |
| 12 | 8 | 60 |
| 13 | 9 | 60 |
| 14 | 10 | 60 |
| 15 | 11 | 70 |
| 16 | 12 | 70 |
| 17 | 13 | 70 |
| 18 | 14 | 70 |
| 19 | 16 | 70 |
| 20 | 18 | 80 |
| 21 | 20 | 80 |
| 22 | 22 | 80 |
| 23 | 24 | 80 |
| 24 | 26 | 80 |
| 25 | 29 | 80 |
| 26 | 32 | 80 |
| 27 | 35 | 80 |
| 28 | 38 | 80 |
| 29 | 41 | 80 |
| 30 | 45 | 80 |
| 31 | 49 | 80 |
| 32 | 53 | 80 |
| 33 | 57 | 80 |
| 34 | 62 | 80 |
| 35 | 67 | 80 |
| 36 | 73 | 80 |
| 37 | 79 | 80 |
| 38 | 80 | 80 |
| 39 | 80 | 80 |
| 40 | 80 | 80 |

# Rights and responsibilities of running a home

*Protecting the home*  *Danger to passers-by and to visitors*
*Removing intruders*  *Duties to workmen*
*Squatters and trespass*  *Warnings and notices*

EVERY householder has the right to protect and defend his property and to keep out intruders and trespassers. But he also has a responsibility to protect legitimate callers or visitors from harm or injury while they are on his land or in his home.

## Protecting the home
The right to protect private property against trespassers includes the right to put up defences—for example, broken glass, nails embedded in the top of a wall, or barbed wire—provided they do not in any way infringe local by-laws.

But the householder cannot legally use dangerous instruments designed to kill or permanently maim intruders. Electric wires designed to electrocute an intruder, or dangerous booby-traps, are ruled out.

## Guard dogs
It is legitimate to keep a fierce-looking dog to warn off uninvited guests, but the law does not allow guard dogs so savage that they may attack and maim or cripple people.

It might be in order to keep a vicious dog to guard premises where there is no danger that the dog will injure anyone other than burglars—for instance, in a factory at night. But it would not be reasonable to use the same dog to patrol a field which children might walk across on their way to school.

Keeping a fierce dog is a serious responsibility and the owner would have to pay damages to any lawful visitors who were injured. ☐ Keeping animals, p. 287.

## Removing intruders
Householders are entitled to use 'a reasonable degree of force' to prevent a trespasser from entering, to control him while he is on the property or to get rid of him. This means that if force is used it must be in proportion to the degree of danger in which the householder reasonably believes himself to be.

The householder should not injure the trespasser unless the trespasser threatens violence. If there is time, the trespasser should first be asked to leave. If he refuses to go, the householder can lay hands on him and propel him from the premises using only as much force as is necessary. For instance, it would be considered unreasonable to attack an unarmed trespasser with a stick.

When the intrusion happens at night, the householder is legally entitled to use more force. The law recognises that at night an intruder is more frightening and allows householders to respond with greater vigour.

Similarly, if there has been violence, or any sign of intended violence, the householder has every right to reply in kind. If a burglar uses a gun, or looks as if he is about to use one, the householder may be justified in shooting him dead.

The householder does not have to wait until the intruder fires the first shot or strikes the first blow. Nor is he limited to using the same means or weapons as the intruder, provided always that the methods he employs are not excessive in the circumstances.

For instance, a householder who finds himself face to face with a violent intruder might reasonably hit him with a cricket bat, even if the intruder appeared to be attacking with only his bare fists.

The householder has a right to defend his family or guests if they are threatened with violence, and he can defend his property and possessions. He can use violence to prevent someone from taking away his goods illegally or to prevent someone from deliberately damaging his property.

But again he must act reasonably. He would not have any legal protection if he shot at a child raiding the apple tree or even at a thief trying to steal his car in the night.

## How to deal with squatters
Occupiers also have certain rights against squatters who take possession and try to stay in their property.

A landowner may find, for example, that gypsies or hikers have set up camp on his land without permission. If he wants to get rid of them, and they refuse to go, he can evict them by force. But he must not resort to any unreasonable methods.

If gypsies refuse to move after being asked to, the owner is entitled to tow their caravans off his land with a tractor. But he is not entitled to set fire to the caravans.

The householder who finds his home taken over does not have such a clear case for direct action, however.

Civil law allows him to use reasonable force to eject a squatter or to match force with force. But criminal law forbids forced entry—both by squatters *and* by the householder himself.

So, although the squatters will probably have broken the law and can be prosecuted for entering and holding the house, the householder who breaks down his own front door or hurls a brick through his own window to get inside to tackle them may find that he, too, is committing a criminal offence.

The law allows the householder to use force only if the trespasser has not yet legally assumed possession—that is, shown some intention to hold the property. Quick action after the house has been occupied might be legal if not too much force is required to re-occupy the premises and eject the trespasser. But if the squatters are numerous this should not be attempted as it might give rise to prosecution for riotous assembly.

The occupier could ask the police to eject the squatters, but it is unlikely that they would take action. This is because the police, generally, are reluctant to take sides in this kind of dispute or in civil disputes between landlords and tenants.

If there is a fight involving squatters, however, a householder should call the police on the ground that a breach of the peace is being committed or threatened.

It is better to apply to the county court for an order for possession of the premises, rather than risk a tussle which may get out of hand and end with both the squatters and the householder being prosecuted.

A squatter has no legal rights to the property unless he has stayed there for 12 consecutive years without the owner trying to get him out.

After 12 years, a squatter would automatically become the owner of the land by 'squatters' right'. This is a rare occurrence.

### Suing an intruder

Anyone who deliberately enters another person's land or property without permission or legal right is a trespasser and can be sued by the occupier. There is no need to prove that the trespasser caused any damage.

If he can prove that someone walked across his lawn or along his drive, or sat on a fence, or even just stood on the grass without permission, he would be able to take action.

But it would very rarely be worthwhile to sue for trespass unless damage had resulted. The compensation a court would award would normally be only nominal.

Postmen, milkmen and deliverymen do not commit trespass even though they have not been given explicit permission to enter the property. Because of their jobs, they have implicit permission. Door-to-door salesmen and canvassers do not commit trespass when they call at a house—unless there is a 'No hawkers or circulars' sign.

A policeman who wrongfully enters a home to search it without a warrant or other lawful excuse can be sued for trespass. It is also a trespass to put anything on someone else's land—for example, an abandoned car or garden refuse.

Airlines cannot be sued for trespassing in a landowner's airspace, but an occupier can sue for damages if anything falls on to the land from the plane, if the plane crash-lands on the property even though the pilot is not to blame, or if a plane flies unreasonably low—which is normally below 2000 ft for airliners and below 1000 ft for light aircraft.

### Damages

Where damage is caused, the compensation ordered by the court is usually the amount of the loss—not the cost of reinstating the property to its original condition. If a trespasser has caused a major fire he can be sued only for the value of the old house, not for the cost of building a new one.

### Danger to passers-by

Where the building overlooks a public road, the occupier must keep it in good repair. He is responsible if a defect causes damage to someone on the road.

If a chimney-pot falls on to the road and kills a passer-by, the occupier is liable even if he had no reason to suspect that the chimney-pot was in a dangerous condition.

### Protecting visitors

House-owners and tenants have a legal obligation to take reasonable steps to protect their visitors from injury. If they fail to do so, and someone is injured as a result, they can be sued for damages.

Regular repairs and maintenance should remove most sources of danger. Replace tiles or slates, for example, as soon as they begin to slip or crack. Repair faulty light switches or plugs and replace worn flex.

It is probably impossible to make sure that no one will ever be injured. But the householder can protect himself by insuring against the risk of being sued.

The premium for such a policy is low compared with the damages which might be awarded. ☐ Insuring the home, p. 216.

In law, the occupier has a responsibility to 'lawful visitors', who include tradesmen, salesmen, postmen and council or court officials.

Even certain kinds of trespassers become entitled to reasonable protection from injury. A householder's degree of responsibility depends òn the circumstances and on who the trespassers are. He has less responsibility to ensure the safety of burglars or poachers than he does to protect trespassing children, who have almost the same protection in law as people who are not trespassers.

➤ THE BOYS WHO WOULD NOT GO AWAY
*Mr W. Ferris decided to clear a stretch of land to prepare for some building work. The land had been derelict for a number of years and had been used by children as a playground.*

*There was one particularly big tree, a 60 ft elm. On the morning it was to be brought down the man in charge, Mr A. Poulter, an experienced nurseryman, twice chased children away—but each time they came back. Eventually the tree was held by only one root, and Mr Poulter gave the order to fell it. Three children were injured. One boy, ten-year-old Herbert Moulton, claimed damages for injury.*
DECISION *The court awarded £25 damages to Herbert Moulton because, although the children were trespassers, the nurseryman should have warned them at the critical moment when he cut the last root. (Moulton v. Poulter.)* ◄

**Duties to workmen**
Experts, unlike other visitors, are expected to avoid dangers with which they are supposed to be familiar and which they should have appreciated. The workman who comes to mend the hole in the roof could hardly sue if he fell through it.

But if he is injured because a rafter on which he stood was rotten and collapsed under him—or because of any other dangerous factor he could not alter—he is not necessarily barred from suing, even if he was told of the danger. In practice, unless he is self-employed, he is more likely to take action against his employer for failing to provide a safe place of work.

**Warning visitors**
If home-owner or landlord knows that there is anything dangerous about his property, he would be well advised to warn lawful visitors

as soon as they enter. A concealed ditch running alongside a drive, for example, should have some kind of guard rail, and should be lit at night: a loose floorboard that could cause a visitor to trip and break his ankle should be pointed out before the visitor goes into the room. Any visitor who ignores the warning has no claim for damages if he is injured as a result.

On the other hand, a visitor is protected only when he behaves as any reasonable visitor would. A guest who wanders upstairs to explore without the knowledge of his host cannot claim damages if he is injured.

A workman who borrows a defective tool without asking permission cannot sue if he is hurt—although he might be able to claim from his own employer for failing to provide adequate equipment.

Warn visitors if any work is being carried out which could be dangerous. If a visitor is injured as a result of a danger created by a workman—a defective light switch which gives a shock, for example—the occupier (as well as the workman and his employer) could be liable for damages unless adequate warning of the danger was given.

The occupier's only defence would be that he employed a competent workman, and could not be expected to do more than he did to supervise the work.

The duty to warn visitors about any danger also covers cases where the owner did not know about the danger but ought to have done. If the danger was one that he could not have discovered even with reasonable precautions, he would not be liable to anyone injured. But if the court decides he ought to have known about it, he can expect to have damages awarded against him.

A warning which would be considered adequate for adults may not be sufficient for children; and special care must be taken where young people are concerned to see that they are not injured.

Dangerous machinery or equipment must not be left within their reach. At the same time the property-owner is entitled to assume that very young children will not be allowed to enter his house or land without being accompanied by a parent or an adult.

**Public notices**
Many businesses avoid their liability for injury to visitors by putting up a notice saying that anyone entering does so at his own risk. Few private householders would use this means, but if they did it would have the same effect, provided it was clearly displayed.

# Disputes with neighbours

*Boundaries and driveways*      *Creating a nuisance*
*Overhanging trees*            *Disputes over personal property*
*Dangers to health*            *Objecting to plans*

GOOD relations between neighbours may break down because they do not know their rights and obligations. Who pays for repairs to a fence between two gardens? How much noise is a neighbour expected to tolerate? Who replaces something stolen while a neighbour was looking after it?

The law provides solutions to many such questions. In cases where a neighbour refuses to fulfil his obligations, or where there is still room for disagreement, the law also provides ways in which the dispute can be resolved.

### Determining the boundary
In any argument about the dividing line between two properties, the first step is to check the title deeds of the house, which may include land measurements or a plan.

If there is a mortgage on the house, the deeds will be held by the building society or other lender. They should allow the deeds to be inspected by the owner, provided they are given adequate notice. A tenant who wants to inspect the deeds will have to approach his landlord who will probably agree to let him see them, but is not obliged to do so.

In an increasing number of cases, however, the title deeds give no measurements and little boundary detail. The owner's only course of action in such a case, if no agreement can be reached in a dispute over boundaries, is to sue his neighbour for trespass—on the grounds that the dividing wall or fence is on his land.

This will be expensive, and evidence may be difficult to find. The court is likely to accept that any wall or fence which has stood undisputed for a reasonable period of time is the legal boundary.

OWNERSHIP OF FENCES A common difficulty with walls and fences is that the title deeds may not show who is the owner. Many people believe that the owner of the land upon which the supporting stakes of a fence or the buttresses of a wall stand is automatically the owner.

## Dealing with noisy neighbours

POLICE are often called by people who complain about noise from a neighbour's home. But apart from passing on the complaint to the neighbour, there is little they can do unless a serious breach of the peace, such as a fight, is likely to develop.

One way to deal with a noisy neighbour is to apply to a court for an order to make him stop the noise. This is likely to succeed only if it can be proved that the noise is both excessive and habitual.

If, for instance, a neighbour holds wild and noisy parties once or twice a year, little can be done. But if the parties are held once or twice a week, the court is likely to order them to be stopped.

Three or more neighbours acting together can complain at the local town hall, asking the authority to serve a notice requiring the offender to stop any noise which amounts to a nuisance. Failure to comply with this notice may be punishable in the magistrates' court. Musical instruments played in the home may annoy a neighbour. But in law it is considered reasonable to allow a child to learn to play the piano, no matter how unpleasant the neighbours may find the noise.

On the other hand, it would not be reasonable for a teacher to give late-night piano lessons five times a week.

The court would intervene only if the noise was more than a neighbour could reasonably be expected to put up with.

If, however, the neighbour can show that the noise is being made expressly to annoy him, he may succeed in getting the court to make an order stopping it.

In one case, the court stopped a neighbour from deliberately beating trays against a joint wall, although the level of noise was not so high that it would otherwise have justified any legal action.

There is, in fact, no rule of law to this effect and it is, at the most, a presumption which may not be upheld.

DITCHES Where there is a man-made ditch and a hedge, the owner on the hedge side of the ditch owns all the land up to the far edge of the ditch—unless deeds show otherwise.

## Shared driveways

In cases where two or more adjoining owners share a single driveway to their garages, the deeds of the houses should show who owns the driveway and who has a right to use it.

Possibly the most common arrangement is that each owns half of the driveway, and has a right of way over the other half. Less common is the situation where one owns the whole strip and the other has a right of way.

When a driveway is blocked by a parked car or other obstacle, first ask the owner to remove it. If he refuses, and if the obstruction is across the entrance to the driveway on a public road, the police can be asked to help.

If the obstruction is in the driveway itself, on private land, the person whose right of way is obstructed should not move the obstacle against his neighbour's wishes. Ask a solicitor to write to the neighbour. If this fails, apply to a court for an order compelling the neighbour to remove the obstruction in question.

The property deeds may state that the householder's right of way over land owned by his neighbour is for 'persons on foot only'. This means that he has no right to drive a vehicle over it, even if the owner does.

## Paying for repairs

In some cases the deeds of the property may make clear who is responsible for repairing shared driveways, walls and fences. Many deeds include conditions—called, in law, restrictive covenants—that have been accepted when the house was bought. □ Exchanging contracts, p. 205.

Where there is one owner, a restrictive covenant may oblige him to keep a wall or driveway in good repair. If he refuses to do essential repair work, those legally entitled to enforce the covenant may get an estimate for the cost of the repairs. They should show the estimate to the owner, have the work done and, if necessary, sue him for the cost.

The owner of a wall or driveway who is not bound by a restrictive covenant is normally under no legal obligation to carry out repairs. He will, however, have to pay for any damage to another person's property caused by defects of which he should have been aware.

A wall or fence jointly owned is called a 'party' wall or fence, and is treated in law as if severed vertically between the respective owners. Neither owner may actively do anything to his own half that is likely to endanger the other half.

Where the deeds do not specify that repairs to a wall, fence or driveway have to be done by one owner, it is best for neighbours to agree about sharing the costs. If they want to make sure that no one tries to get out of paying after the work has been done, they can exchange letters setting out precisely how the cost is to be shared, or they can get a solicitor to draw up an agreement.

If neighbours cannot agree and the deeds do not say who should pay, no one can be forced to contribute to the cost of any repairs that may become necessary.

## Overhanging trees

If overhanging trees cause disputes, neighbours may be entitled to remedy the problem themselves or, if necessary, take legal action.

If the owner of a tree refuses to trim overhanging branches, the neighbour is entitled to cut them off at the boundary line. The branches and any fruit belong to the tree-owner, and must be returned to him. Similarly, roots can be cut off at the border.

If cutting off roots or branches would be too difficult, an application may be made to a court for an order forcing the tree-owner to have them removed.

Damages can be awarded if financial loss is proved. Where roots have caused actual damage—perhaps to the foundations of the house—or where a lawn has had to be dug up to trim them, the owner of the tree can be sued for the amount of the loss the neighbour could prove he had sustained.

Fruit which falls into a garden from a neighbour's tree remains the neighbour's property, and cannot be used without his consent. But, strangely, the householder into whose garden it falls has no legal obligation to hand it back, or to give the neighbour access to retrieve it. There is, in fact, no legal action the neighbour can take to regain his property.

Where a tree is not encroaching on the neighbour's land but blocks some of the light from his house, a legal solution might be more difficult.

The neighbour would have to prove, under complicated law, that he had the right to the light—commonly known as 'Ancient Lights'—for perhaps 20 years.

TREE PRESERVATION A householder who hears that a neighbour is planning to cut down trees which he regards as having an amenity value to his area, can appeal to the local council planning department. If the council agrees that the destruction of the trees would be a real loss, a tree preservation order is granted. This procedure cannot be used to save trees that are the property of the council itself, however.

## Dangers to health
If a neighbour dumps rubbish in his garden, and the smell attracts flies or rodents causing a health hazard, the local authority public health department should be called in. The department's inspector can order the rubbish to be removed, and if the neighbour still does nothing, the local authority can seek a court order compelling him to obey.

## Creating a nuisance
A property-owner—and in some cases a tenant—may have grounds for legal action if his neighbour does anything that interferes unreasonably with his comfort and convenience—for instance, causing smell, fumes, noise, heat or vibrations.

The property-owner may be able to get a court order—known as an injunction—to make his neighbour stop whatever is causing the annoyance, or he might be able to claim damages. In either case the action is for what is known in law as 'nuisance'.

There will be grounds for action only if neighbours fail to act 'reasonably' towards one another. Neighbours generally have to tolerate the smoke and smell of occasional garden bonfires, for example; but the law gives them some protection against a steady flow of foul-smelling fumes.

The standard of what is reasonable varies from place to place. A judge in one case said: 'What would be a nuisance in Belgrave Square would not necessarily be so in Bermondsey.'

Nuisance to neighbours cannot be justified simply on the grounds that it produces an overall public benefit. A factory which causes a foul smell may be closed down by the courts, or the owners may have to pay compensation, even if the benefit to the public of the process greatly outweighs the inconvenience it creates for the neighbours.

Even if there is no other site for the activity, those carrying on an operation which the law would regard as a nuisance must either persuade the neighbours to accept compensation or stop the operation.

The fact that the occupier or firm has taken precautions to avoid creating a nuisance will not protect him from damages. If a claimant

## Duty to avoid danger to neighbours

An occupier who keeps something particularly dangerous on his land is responsible for the consequences. If a dangerous animal or substance escapes and damages a neighbour's property, the owner is normally liable for the damage, whether or not he was actually to blame for the escape.

His only defence will be to prove that the escape was caused by a trespasser or by something unexpected or extraordinary.

This strict standard applies whenever an occupier is not using his property 'naturally'. Natural use of property includes the keeping of farm animals, or the storing of gas or electricity for domestic purposes. A central-heating oil tank is probably a 'natural' use, but this has not been tested in the courts.

'Unnatural' use would be keeping dangerous animals or storing unusual amounts of dangerous substances—such as explosives or petrol. Even water, if stored in large quantities, could be regarded as dangerous because of the damage it can cause.

Where there is no proof of negligence, legal action can be taken only by a neighbour—an important limitation. Only in the case of fire can someone other than the owner or occupier sue for personal injury. On the other hand, where the occupier has been negligent, anyone affected can sue.

If the accident was the result of something that could not reasonably have been foreseen, an action based on negligence will fail. So if it is proved that a leaking central-heating oil tank had only just been inspected and that the leak was the result of an unusual form of metal fatigue, neither the house-occupier nor the heating firm would have to pay damages.

But if the leak was due to rust which should have been seen and dealt with by the occupier, he will be liable. If the inspector of the tank was incompetent and the fault should have been discovered, then the heating firm would probably be liable.

Special rules cover damage done by animals. ☐ Keeping animals, p. 287.

proves that he is affected despite those precautions it is then up to the occupier to show that he is not creating a nuisance.

## Taking action

Only the person who occupies the house or land can take legal action over a nuisance. This is strictly interpreted by the courts, and is held to prevent even the occupier's family from suing.

If the property is held by a tenant, normally only the tenant will have the right to sue. The owner would be able to sue only if he could show that his own interest in the property had been adversely affected. Action is normally taken against an occupier, but others, including the landlord, may also be sued. Even the person who started or created the trouble complained about—such as a workman who left premises in a condition that would cause a nuisance to neighbours—remains liable even after he has moved away.

A landlord may be liable for damages if his tenant causes a nuisance which the landlord knows about or should know about. He can escape paying only if he can show that the tenant promised not to continue whatever conduct is disturbing the neighbours.

If action is to be taken for injury or damage, the harm must be both substantial and actual. Fear of future damage is normally not enough. For instance, a wall in poor condition that seems certain to fall one day into a neighbour's property does not give grounds for a legal action—until the day it falls.

It is no defence to show that the nuisance was there before the occupier took the property. A person is legally entitled to buy a property and then try to stop the neighbour from continuing the nuisance which the previous owner had tolerated.

## Borrowing from neighbours

Anyone who borrows an article must, by law, return it as soon as the lender asks for it. The borrower must not use the article for any purpose that has not been agreed.

If the article is lost or damaged, the lender is entitled to compensation if he can prove that the borrower was negligent. But if the lender himself has contributed in some way to the damage—for instance, by entrusting his property to someone whom he should have known to be unreliable, such as a child—he cannot claim.

The lender also has an obligation to warn the borrower of any hidden defects in the article. He would be liable for any injury that resulted, for instance, if he lent a friend some chairs for a party and failed to give a warning that some of them were in a very dangerous condition.

## Looking after goods

When a neighbour or friend is asked to look after some article or property, it is generally quite difficult to secure compensation if it is lost or damaged while in his safe-keeping. If a neighbour took in something for safe-keeping while the owner was away, the neighbour would be liable for loss or damage only if he had been negligent in taking care of it.

## Lost property

A householder may find an article belonging to a neighbour on his property—say a child's football accidentally kicked over the garden fence, or an umbrella left in the home by mistake. Such situations are covered by two basic legal principles.

The first is that the owner of any article is always entitled to recover it. Secondly, the finder commits theft if he uses an article unless he believes (and can prove) that the owner cannot be traced by reasonable means.

There is no time limit within which the owner must reclaim his property. He can insist on its return even ten or more years later.

No one has a right to enter a neighbour's home to retrieve his property—technically a child is trespassing if he goes into a neighbour's garden without permission to collect a football. The neighbour is under no legal obligation to return the ball, or to allow anyone on to his property to retrieve it. He must not use it for his own benefit, however.

If the finder cannot give the article back—he may have sold it or given it away—the owner may claim its value from him.

## Objecting to plans

Householders have to be on the alert for anything which threatens to make their properties less pleasant to live in, or which may lower their market value.

For example, a neighbour who wishes to build a garage in front of the building line of his house does not have to tell people living near by. He will apply to the local council for planning permission, and the plans will be available for inspection. It is then up to the other householders to protect their interests.

A householder who objects to his neighbour's plans should write to the council, making his objection clear.

If he is not satisfied with the council's decision, there may be an opportunity to appeal further. ☐ Threats to the home, p. 300.

# Keeping animals

*Quarantine*  
*Preventing injury or damage*  
*Dangerous animals*

*Dogs attacking livestock*  
*Straying livestock*  
*How to get protection*

APART from dogs, nearly every form of domestic animal can be kept in Britain without any kind of a licence. The owner of a dog over six months old must normally get a licence from a post office and must renew it every year.

Exceptions for which no licence is needed are: guide dogs for the blind; two farm or sheepdogs on a farm; and hounds under a year old which have not been used with a pack, provided that all the other hounds in the pack have been licensed.

Farms over 400 acres can have more than two unlicensed sheep dogs depending on the size of the farm and the number of sheep, but a certificate must be obtained from a magistrates' court. Anyone who fails to take out a licence where one is required can be prosecuted and fined up to £10.

## Quarantine
All animals brought into this country from abroad must spend six calendar months in quarantine, in approved kennels, from the date of arrival. There are no exceptions, and the fact that the animal has been inoculated against rabies or vaccinated against other diseases makes no difference.

To get a licence to import a dog or cat into Britain the owner must:

**1.** Secure accommodation at a quarantine kennel approved by the Ministry of Agriculture. The Ministry will provide a list of such kennels on request.

**2.** Employ an authorised 'carrying agent' to whom the licence will be sent and who will meet the animal at the port of landing, clear it through Customs and deliver it to the kennels.

**3.** Send a licence application form to the Ministry of Agriculture, Fisheries and Food, Government Buildings, Hook Rise South, Kingston Bypass, Surbiton, Surrey. With this form should go written confirmation from the kennels that the booking has been accepted, together with similar confirmation from the carrying agent.

While it is being landed and taken to quarantine kennels the animal must be kept in a suitable box, crate or kennel, approved by the carrying agent. Anyone importing a dog over six months old must get a dog licence as soon as the animal is landed.

The costs of landing, transporting and keeping an animal in quarantine have to be paid by the owner, so an owner should find out the fee of the kennels and the agent before confirming bookings.

If the owner of a dog or cat decides to take it out of the country while it is in quarantine, it will be released without formality or delay.

## Preventing injury or damage
The law on responsibility for damage caused by animals rested mainly on the decisions of judges until the passing of the Animals Act 1971. The provisions of the Act made several significant changes.

Anyone who owns an animal, or is left in charge of it, has a legal duty to take reasonable care that the animal does not cause injury or damage. If he fails to fulfil this duty, he may be sued for damages.

Animals owned by young people under the age of 16 are the legal responsibility of the head of the household.

Similarly, an employer is expected to know of any dangerous characteristics in an animal he owns if they were known at any time to one of his employees who had been in charge of the animal.

An owner is normally responsible if the animal escapes—even if it has been let loose by someone else—and he remains responsible until someone else becomes the animal's keeper. However, a person who takes an animal in to prevent it from causing damage, or to keep it until it can be returned to its owner, does not become the keeper and is not responsible if the animal escapes again.

Generally an owner or keeper is responsible only when it can be proved that his negligence resulted in the injury, accident or damage caused by the animal.

An owner might be held to be negligent if, for example, he allowed a dog with a trailing lead to run free in a crowded street, and a shopper was tripped up and injured; or if he let his dog rush across a busy road and cause an accident.

There are three special cases, however,

where an owner will be held responsible even if he has not been proved negligent. These are when animals are dangerous; when dogs attack livestock; and when stray livestock cause damage.

**Dangerous animals**
Owners are normally liable for any injury or damage caused by dangerous animals—a description which covers two legal categories.

In the first are wild animals, either those not native to this country, such as lions, tigers, bears and elephants, or indigenous fierce animals such as foxes.

The second category covers domestic animals such as dogs and bulls which become dangerous for any reason.

The law says that a dangerous animal is one that, if not restrained, would be likely to cause damage, or one that was capable of causing severe damage.

For instance, tigers are dangerous because, if let loose, they are likely to cause injury or damage. A docile dog with an infectious disease such as rabies is dangerous because if it bites, the damage will be severe, even fatal. The well-known saying that every dog is allowed one bite has a legal significance in the sense that the owner of an apparently docile dog may not be liable if it bites unexpectedly. But once a dog has bitten without provocation, the owner can be sued for damages if it attacks someone a second time.

The dangerous characteristic need not be peculiar to one particular animal, for someone affected to claim damages. But the owner or keeper must know that his animal shares this characteristic. The dog owner who knows that his bitch with a litter is—like other bitches in a similar condition—prone to bite strangers, will be liable for damages if it does so.

The only defence which the keeper of a dangerous animal could use would be that the person hurt was in some way responsible.

If the keeper can show that the damage was entirely the fault of the injured person, he can avoid liability. If each was equally to blame, then damages would be halved.

Special rules apply when the person injured is a trespasser, and there is no liability if a trespasser is injured by a dangerous animal kept to protect persons or property—provided it was reasonable to keep that type of animal for that particular purpose.

## Cruelty to animals

CRUELTY to animals—by kicking, beating, hard riding, overloading or torture—is a criminal offence under the Protection of Animals Act 1911. It is also illegal to terrify an animal or have it carried in a way that would cause suffering.

The maximum penalty for cruelty is a fine of up to £50 and three months' imprisonment. The court may order that the animal which has been cruelly treated should be taken away from the person convicted.

Where someone has been cruel to a dog, the magistrates have power—under the Protection of Animals (Cruelty to Dogs) Act 1933—to ban him from ever again owning a dog or obtaining a dog licence.

Where cruelty to other animals is involved, the court can stop the convicted person keeping a particular animal or any animal of a specified kind, for a given time. But this power can be exercised only on a second conviction.

The most common cause of cruelty to animals is neglect. For example, an owner is guilty of cruelty if he fails to feed his dog, or keeps it tethered to a post for long periods.

But in these cases it is necessary to prove that the animal has been subjected to substantial and unnecessary suffering.

It is also an offence to abandon animals, leaving them to fend for themselves. For example, a person who goes on holiday and does not make arrangements for someone to look after his dog can be prosecuted under the Abandonment of Animals Act 1960. Here, it is unnecessary to prove that the animal has suffered; all that is required for a successful prosecution is that there should be proof that it was likely to suffer if left unattended.

Improper killing of animals is another example of cruelty. The law requires that all animals should be destroyed humanely. The humane killing of large animals such as horses requires the use of a gun or lethal injection.

Do not drown unwanted pets such as kittens or puppies. The Royal Society for the Prevention of Cruelty to Animals recommends that this be done humanely by a veterinary surgeon or an officer of the RSPCA or other animal welfare society. The RSPCA does not charge a fee for this service.

A person who keeps an alsatian to guard his home would not have to pay damages to an injured trespasser unless it was unreasonable to have so fierce a dog. For instance, it would not be reasonable to keep a vicious dog to guard an open field over which children frequently walk to school.

It is often thought that the owner of a cat is not liable for any damage or injury it may cause. But the law does not, in fact, make any distinction between cats and other animals. However, it is more difficult to prove that the owner of a cat has been guilty of negligence, as cats are more difficult to control than other domestic pets.

## Dogs attacking livestock
In 1971 more than 6000 sheep in England and Wales were either killed or injured by dogs. An owner can be made to pay damages if his dog attacks livestock, even though he has not been negligent.

In this case livestock means cattle, horses, asses, mules, sheep, pigs, goats, deer (other than wild deer) and poultry, which includes most varieties of fowl.

The only defence is that the livestock strayed on to the dog-owner's property. A dog, in other words, is allowed to injure livestock in its own territory.

In all other circumstances, a farmer is within his rights in shooting a dog if it is worrying livestock or about to do so, and there are no other reasonable means of stopping it.

The farmer can also shoot a dog which has been worrying livestock if it is still in the area, if it is not under the control of anyone, and if there is no way of finding out to whom the animal belongs.

The dog can be shot by the owner of the livestock, by the person owning the land on which the livestock was found, or by an employee of either of them. Anyone who kills or injures a dog must report the incident to the police within 48 hours.

## Straying livestock
When livestock stray on to someone else's land, the owner is normally liable for any damage even though he is not negligent. For example, damages might be claimed if a neighbour's donkey strayed into a garden and ate the prize geraniums there.

There are, however, two defences. One is that the animals strayed on to the land from the highway, where they had a right to be. This means that if a horse pulling a cart on the road bolts on to a householder's lawn, its owner would not have to pay damages unless he had been negligent. But this defence applies only if the animal was lawfully on the highway. It will not apply if the animal has strayed on to the highway.

The second defence is that the person claiming damages was to blame, or partly to blame—for instance, if he had failed to put up a fence which he was legally bound to build.

## The duty to fence land
The owner of any animal is responsible for any injury or damage caused if it strays on to the road, as long as he was negligent in allowing it to escape there.

Most property owners have a duty to put up fences to keep their animals from getting on to the road. The main exception is in remote country districts where there are few motorists and where it would be unreasonable to expect owners to fence great areas. On commons, where many people have the right to graze their livestock, no one has the right to put up fences.

A landowner is entitled to hold stray livestock until he gets compensation for any damage they have done. He must feed and water them, and inform the police and, if possible, the owner within 48 hours.

If the cost of the damage has not been paid within 21 days, and proceedings to secure the return of strays have not started, the person holding the animals can then sell them at a market or public auction. After amounts for damage and expenses are deducted, the balance from the sale goes to the animals' owner.

Selling the animals does not prevent the person whose property they invaded from suing for damages.

If the owner of the animals is not found, the person on to whose land they strayed is entitled in law to keep them.

## How to get protection
The best way to avoid costly bills for damage caused by animals is to take out insurance. Policies range from cover for the farmer whose employee is hurt by a dangerous bull, to insurance for the landowner who fears his livestock may stray on to a road and cause an accident. Most insurance companies offer such cover.

There are also policies which cover dogs, cats or other pets for death, veterinary fees, and loss. A personal liability policy will indemnify the pet owner against compensation he may have to pay if a pet causes death or injury, or damage to property.

The compensation limit on a personal liability policy is normally very high, and the cost of legal defence is included.

# Help in the home

Responsibilities of an employer
National Insurance and S.E.T.
Income tax

The right to sack an employee
A safe place to work
Foreign employees, including au pairs

PEOPLE who employ domestic help regularly—even a part-time gardener or cleaner—have many of the legal responsibilities of an ordinary employer. Others who would not normally need domestic help may find difficulty in running the home in an emergency—illness or a death in the family, for example—and can ask the local authority to provide a home help.

## Responsibilities of an employer
Anyone who pays people to work in the home may have to pay National Insurance contributions and (until April 6, 1973) Selective Employment Tax, and may have to deduct income tax from an employee's wages.

The employer is liable for damages if his negligence, or the negligence of any other person employed by him, results in injury to an employee on his property.

## National Insurance contributions
National Insurance stamps must be bought for every employee who works for more than eight hours a week and whose earnings are ordinarily more than £4 a week or include board and lodging.

The cost has to be paid partly by the employer and partly by the employee, whose contribution is deducted from his wages.

An employer must buy a National Insurance stamp each week from a post office, stick it on the employee's National Insurance card and cancel the stamp by writing the date over it in ink.

If the employee has no card, the employer must get one for him, unless the employee works for other people.

For example, if a cleaner works for three householders, the first one to employ her for eight hours or more a week must pay the National Insurance stamp if her wage is over £4 a week or includes board and lodging. The two others are exempt.

If the cleaner does not work more than eight hours for anyone, the householder who employs her first each week must buy the stamp. For this reason it can be cheaper to employ part-time domestic help later in the week, rather than earlier. Many householders

who share a domestic employee frequently arrange to share the cost of the stamp.

The cost of National Insurance stamps depends on the age and sex of the employee and the number of hours worked. The local Social Security office will give details of current rates and supply a leaflet explaining National Insurance for domestic workers.

Industrial injuries contributions must be paid for every employee, regardless of hours worked or earnings. If a National Insurance stamp is not necessary, a separate stamp covering industrial injuries must be bought.

## Selective Employment Tax
Until April 6, 1973, an employer must pay Selective Employment Tax for anyone working for him for more than eight hours a week at a wage of more than £4, or who receives board and lodging. The tax, which is abolished on that date, is included in the National Insurance stamp as part of the employer's contribution.

However, a domestic employer can obtain a full refund if:
1. The employee is helping or looking after someone over 70, someone who is ill, or a pregnant mother.
2. The employee is helping to look after a child under 16 who is living with only one parent or guardian who goes to work for more than eight hours a week.

A refund of two-thirds is payable if the employee is over 65. A refund of half the amount can be obtained if the employee is over 18 and does not normally work for that employer for more than 21 hours a week.

If the employee does not work for a period of a week or more—because of holidays or illness, for example—the employer still has to buy a National Insurance stamp. But he can obtain a refund of the S.E.T. portion of it.

## How to claim a refund
Only the employer who buys the National Insurance stamp is entitled to claim the S.E.T. refund. If two employers share the cost of National Insurance stamps, the claim can be made only by the one who is legally responsible for stamping the card. His household—not

that of anyone else for whom the employee works—must qualify for a refund.

The claim is made on a form supplied by the Department of Health and Social Security. An employer can apply for a refund after the tax has been paid for 13 weeks, or as soon as the employee has left.

## Income tax

Anyone who pays an employee more than £8 a week—or £34·50 a month—must deduct income tax from the wages.

For those who have never employed anybody before, a booklet can be obtained at the office of the local Inspector of Taxes, *The Employer's Guide to Pay-As-You-Earn*. The booklet sets out an employer's tax responsibilities. Forms, including tax tables and tax deduction cards, will also be sent.

If the employee has never worked before, the employer should tell the Inland Revenue inspector. The employee will be sent an income tax form and, after it has been completed and returned, the Inland Revenue will calculate his or her code number.

This code number, used against the tax tables, will show how much tax has to be deducted each pay day.

If the first week's wages are due to be paid before the employer has been told the employee's code number, the emergency deduction tables, supplied with the forms, can be used. Under this table, tax will be deducted as though the employee had only a single person's allowance.

The employee who has worked before should give his new employer a taxation form, called a P.45, from the previous employer. This will state the total wages paid in that financial year, the total income tax deducted, and the employee's code number.

The P.45 at that stage is in two parts. The employer keeps one and sends the other to his Inland Revenue office. Information on the P.45 will be used as the basis for deducting tax.

If the employee cannot supply the P.45, the emergency tax tables should be used.

An employer who pays an employee less than £8 a week is not normally responsible for deducting tax. But if he knows that an employee to whom he pays more than £1 a week has another source of income he still has to make a tax deduction, and should apply to the Inland Revenue for a code number.

A new employee who starts work after a period of unemployment may be entitled to a tax rebate—the figures will be given in the tables. The rebate should be paid by the new employer. If he cannot afford to pay the

amount due it can be credited against future deductions, or the office of the Inspector of Taxes will advance the money.

When an employee resigns or is dismissed the employer should complete the three parts of a P.45 form, sending one to his local Inland Revenue office and giving the other two parts to the employee.

The employer must send the income tax he has deducted to the office of the collector of taxes for his area each month. Each tax month ends on the 5th, and the money must be paid by the 19th.

The Inland Revenue is entitled to demand from employers any tax that should have been deducted from employees' wages, even if it was not deducted. It can also impose a penalty for non-payment of tax, which is fixed by the Inland Revenue Commissioners and is subject to appeal to the courts.

## The right to sack an employee

An employer of domestic servants has the same right to dismiss them as any other employer. Employees who have worked for more than six months must be given at least a week's notice, or a week's wages. □ Leaving the job, p. 639.

## A safe place to work

An employee injured because of the negligence of the employer or a fellow employee can claim damages. It is therefore in the employer's interests to insure himself against any possible claim. □ Insuring against business hazards, p. 695.

For instance, an employee who falls from a ladder which is rotten or broken may be entitled to damages if he can prove that his injury happened because the employer or a fellow employee was negligent.

The injured employee may be entitled to damages even if he is partly to blame.

## Foreign employees

All foreign domestic employees—except those working as au pairs—must have a work permit and a valid passport before arriving in the United Kingdom.

A work permit, granted only for resident and full-time workers, is issued by the Department of Employment only to employers. The employer then sends it to the employee he wants from abroad.

Employers can obtain an application form AR 1B from the Department's local offices.

Before completing it, employers should ensure that the foreign worker's health and character are satisfactory and that he knows the conditions of his future employment. If the worker is from Spain or Portugal, he also needs a permit from his own government to work abroad.

The application form states the date and place of birth, numbers and names of dependants, and details of previous visits to Britain.

Employers must agree to pay the cost of the employee's return to his own country if that is required by the authorities.

Permits will not be issued if the Department thinks that a suitable employee can be found in this country.

The Department must also be satisfied that the wages the foreign worker will receive are not less than those normally paid to a British worker in the same area. Conditions of employment, too, must be similar to those applying to British employees.

Foreigners under 18 or over 54 are not admitted to Britain to work. Nor are Italian girls under 21, or women with children, even if they have no intention of bringing them.

Single men will not be given a work permit if they have dependants. Married men are given a permit only when their wives are taking joint employment with them and there are no children.

Applications to employ a man and wife should be accompanied by a declaration from them that they have no children. This should be signed by their local mayor or clergyman.

If the couple are Spanish this declaration should be accompanied by a statement from a Spanish judge or from the secretary or registrar of the Civil Registry.

Italian couples should send a document— *Certificato dello stato di famiglia.*

If a foreign worker wants to leave the employer, he can do so. The employer is also entitled to dismiss a foreign worker.

However, a foreign worker must get permission from the Department of Employment before taking another job.

National Insurance stamps must be bought for foreign workers as usual. The worker should get a National Insurance card from the local Department of Social Security office.

**Au pair girls**

Foreign girls who come to Britain to learn English and live as a member of a British family are distinct in law from domestic employees. Au pairs take their meals with the family and receive pocket money— normally between £2·50 and £3·50 a week.

Neither the au pair girl nor the family has to pay National Insurance contributions during the first six months she is in Britain. But the au pair must register with the local officer of the Department of Social Security as a 'non-employed' person as soon as she has been in the country for 26 weeks.

If an au pair is being paid more than £6 a week, she—not the family—will have to pay National Insurance contributions, at the non-employed rate.

The booklet, *Au Pair in Britain*, lays down guidelines for the foreign girls and for the families with whom they stay. The booklet, published in seven languages, can be obtained from the Home Office, Immigration and Nationality Department, Princeton House, 271–7 High Holborn, London WC1V 7EW.

It advises families that an au pair should not be asked to work more than five hours a day, including time spent baby-sitting or caring for children.

The Home Office advises that the au pair and her hostess should do the household work on a partnership basis, and the hostess should not require the girl to do jobs that she would not do herself. The girl should do such jobs as make beds, wash up, tidy and dust rooms, and look after children. She should be given one day a week free, and have an opportunity to attend part-time classes.

An au pair can leave a family at any time. If she does not have another job and lacks the money to return home she should be put in touch with her Consulate or an organisation named in the Home Office booklet.

## National Health Service home helps

LOCAL authorities provide help in the home as part of the National Health Service, if the need is urgent. If a mother is ill, or having another baby, the council may supply a full-time help to look after the home and any young children.

If the children are at school the council will probably decide that part-time help will meet the need adequately.

Home help is also available for older or infirm people and for convalescents just out of hospital.

Any inquiries or applications should be made to the Home Help Organiser of the local council. The service is not always free. Charges vary from council to council and a person's ability to pay is taken into account.

# Officials' rights of entry into the home

*Landlords and local authorities*    *Post Office*
*Gas, electricity and water boards*    *Police and warrants*
*Customs and excise*    *Bailiffs and other court officials*

ALTHOUGH the law safeguards the privacy of an Englishman's home, very many public officials have the right to cross his threshold for one reason or another. It has been calculated that 10,000 officials of national or local government are entitled to enter private premises.

To these must be added the representatives of various boards who provide essential services (gas, water, electricity and telephones) and certain private individuals who have a right to look after their own interests inside other people's homes: landlords inspecting the property, and neighbours examining common walls or shared services.

Bailiffs and sheriff's officers are given wide powers to enforce court orders inside private homes. Officers known as 'certificated bailiffs' who operate under licences granted by the courts also have some of these rights.

Finally, there are the police, whose rights of entry vary according to the circumstances.

Most of these uninvited guests have to ask the householder's permission before entering, but if permission is refused they will usually be able to obtain a warrant from a magistrates' court giving them absolute authority to enter —and, in some cases, allowing them to use force to gain entry.

The Acts of Parliament which permit these incursions into privacy also assure a certain amount of protection to the householder. In some cases the officials have to give notice of their intention to enter; usually they can call only at reasonable times of the day; and except in cases of emergency—such as a gas leak— they may not enter by force unless they have a warrant from the local magistrates' court.

## Landlords

Leases and tenancy agreements usually give landlords the right to inspect their property at reasonable times—during the daytime and after notice has been given.

A landlord who calls without warning can be prevented from entering; if he enters without the tenant's permission and without giving notice, he can be regarded as a trespasser. In one case where a landlord had called unexpectedly, a court ruled that the tenant was right to refuse the landlord access to some of the rooms, and had not acted in breach of his agreement.

Tenants of unfurnished houses and flats with leases of less than seven years can make the landlord carry out structural and other repairs, but they must let him enter their home to do so at reasonable times of the day, provided they have received 24 hours' written notice.

Landlords of properties with very low rents have to make sure that the properties are fit for human habitation, and they are given similar rights of entry. Council officials can also request admittance to council houses and flats after giving 24 hours' notice.

Even after the expiry of a lease or the completion of an agreed period of notice, landlords have no right to enter a property to evict a tenant; they must apply for a court order. These orders can be enforced by a Writ of Possession in the High Court, carried out by a sheriff's officer, or a Warrant for Possession in a county court, executed by a bailiff. ☐ Leaving a rented home, p. 272.

## Local authorities

Council officials can enter private homes under the Public Health Acts (dealing with pest and vermin control, infectious diseases, and so on) and under the Housing and Planning Acts (overcrowding, demolition orders, slum clearance). Visiting officials must carry written authorisation from the council, stating the purpose of the visit. If the council official has no authority to enter the home, the householder has every right to keep him out.

In one reported case, a public health inspector attempted to enter a home without a valid right. This is how the judge described what happened: 'When the sanitary inspector from the council arrived, the appellant obstructed him with all the rights of a free-born Englishman whose premises are being invaded, and defied him with a clothes prop and a spade. He was entitled to do that unless the sanitary inspector had a right to enter.'

If a council official calls and demands entry, ask to see his authorisation and check that his reasons for wanting to inspect the property are valid.

293

HEALTH INSPECTORS A public health inspector may inspect any house in which he suspects that the occupiers are breaking some provision of the Public Health Acts, or where he has reason to believe that local bye-laws or building regulations are being ignored.

Where a building is shared by more than one family, called 'multiple occupation', the inspector has the right to enter without notice.

In all other cases, however, the inspector can be asked to give 24 hours' notice of a proposed inspection. If entry is still refused after the proper notice has been given, he can apply to the local magistrates' court for a warrant entitling him to use force to enter.

HOUSING INSPECTORS The law gives local council housing inspectors fewer powers to enter private property, but they are entitled to make an inspection in certain circumstances. He can assess a house for compulsory purchase; examine premises that may become subject to a demolition order; make sure that the provisions of a clearing or closing order have been met; or check that necessary repairs ordered by the council have been carried out.

Although the inspector may call without giving notice, a householder can insist that he delay the inspection for 24 hours. After that, the inspector is entitled to enter, but he has no powers to get a magistrate's warrant and he is not allowed to force entry.

PROSECUTION Any occupier who continues to refuse to admit a properly authorised public health or housing inspector can be prosecuted. The penalty is a fine of up to £20 for each occasion entry is refused.

## Gas and electricity boards

Officials from gas and electricity boards can enter premises to read meters, to inspect fittings, to repair faults or to cut off the supply. A householder is entitled to ask them to produce written evidence showing that they are employed by the board involved.

An official who is refused entry for proper purposes can apply for a magistrate's warrant authorising him to use reasonable force to get in. A householder refusing to admit an official with a warrant may be liable to a fine.

In an emergency, the consent of the occupier or the issue of a warrant is not needed. An authorised representative of a gas or electricity board can enter if he reasonably believes there is danger to life or property.

## Water boards

Water-supply authorities are entitled to enter any property to inspect meters and fittings, and to confirm suspected waste, pollution or misuse (use for undeclared purposes). If entry is refused, the board is entitled to cut off the supply from outside the property. If they suspect that a meter has been tampered with, they are entitled to apply for a magistrate's warrant which permits them to use reasonable force to enter.

Authorities also have a right to enter and survey land once they have been authorised to acquire it for water supply.

## Customs and excise

Customs officers are entitled to search premises for goods on which duty has been evaded. If refused entry they can seek a High Court search warrant (Writ of Assistance) or a magistrate's search warrant which permit the use of reasonable force. They can search at any hour, but must have a policeman with them at night.

Customs officers, coastguards, police or members of the armed forces can enter without a warrant to prevent signalling to smugglers.

## Post Office

Telephone subscribers are obliged to allow telephone engineers into their homes at all reasonable times. Television records inquiry officers can also ask to enter properties to check that householders have working TV sets if the officers trace a signal from a set which their records show is not licensed. These checks are carried out by officials in detector vans, operating on behalf of the Ministry of Posts and Telecommunications.

If refused entry, inquiry officers can apply for a magistrate's warrant.

## Police

Police officers cannot normally force their way into a private home without the owner's permission or without a magistrate's warrant unless they are trying to prevent a breach of the peace or make an arrest.

However, they have power to search for stolen goods on the written authority of a senior police officer alone when:

**1.** The present occupier, or any other occupier within the last year, has been convicted of handling stolen goods within the last five years.

**2.** The present occupier has ever been convicted of an offence involving dishonesty and punishable by imprisonment.

## Warrants

Householders are not notified when officials or police officers apply to the court for a warrant to enter their homes; there are no arrangements for householders to attend the court or opportunities for them to oppose the application. This is because the various officials already have an absolute right in law to enter premises. As long as certain conditions are fulfilled, magistrates may grant warrants confirming this right.

For instance, the Rights of Entry (Gas and Electricity Boards) Act 1954 provides that magistrates may grant warrants authorising officials to enter premises, by force if necessary, if sworn evidence is submitted to them in writing. This evidence must state that:
1. Admission to the building is reasonably required for a specific purpose.
2. The board is entitled to exercise its power of entry for this purpose.
3. The requirements of the relevant Act have been complied with.

## Bailiffs and other court officials
County courts have a staff of bailiffs, who are often retired police officers. They carry out court orders under the direction of the court registrar acting as High Bailiff.

High Court orders are carried out by a similar body of officers, known as sheriff's officers. They are employed under direction of the High Sheriff of each county, who has a traditional responsibility and legal authority to enforce the orders of the High Court; but in reality High Sheriffs, who are chosen by the Queen, now have only a ceremonial position, and the control of sheriff's officers rests with the county's Under Sheriff, who is usually a local solicitor.

Bailiffs and sheriff's officers have similar rights and powers of entry into private households; but they must be distinguished from private bailiffs, known as 'certificated bailiffs', who are not court officers and do not have similar rights—although they do hold a certificate which entitles them to seize people's goods to pay off debts.

Certificated bailiffs are private-enterprise officials who usually specialise in seizing goods, which are sold to pay taxes, rents and rates. The process is known as distraint or levying distress. They are licensed to operate under the various laws of distress, and their certificate is granted after an examination by the magistrate or registrar of a county court.

It is customary for firms of certificated bailiffs to work under contract for property companies, doing the job of seizing the goods of tenants who have failed to pay their rent. But it is no longer legal for landlords to employ their own certificated bailiff in their permanent rent collection department.

Although certificated bailiffs usually have no right to force entry into private dwellings, a householder's refusal to let them in can have damaging consequences. The fact that a tenant has knowingly barred access to a bailiff can provide a landlord with grounds for possession, or lead to a bankruptcy notice.

Sheriff's officers enforcing High Court orders act as officers of the court. Anyone who resists a sheriff in the proper execution of his writ—such as a squatter who ignores a sheriff's requests to leave the premises—is guilty of contempt of court which is a criminal offence.

Court officers trying to gain entry to seize goods or levy distress do not usually have a right to break open any outer door of a house or flat; they must not break a window or even put their hands through a hole in the door or through a broken window to undo a lock. But if a door is unlocked, the bailiff or sheriff's officer can turn the handle and enter; he can also climb in through a window, as long as it is already partly open, or climb over a fence. Inside, he is entitled to break open any locked doors.

Once distress has been levied, certificated bailiffs are entitled to use force to gain entry on a later occasion.

Bailiffs and sheriff's officers are not allowed to seize certain goods. They must not take any fixtures; any essential clothes (as opposed to mink coats) and bedding used by the tenant and his family; or any goods belonging to lodgers or any other person except the tenant, his wife and children. The tenant must also be left with tools of his trade up to a maximum value (depending on the type of debt).

Legally, all court officers are allowed to remove goods covered by credit-sale agreements, as these goods become the property of the purchaser after the first payment. Goods acquired under current hire-purchase agreements cannot be seized as they remain the property of the vendor or finance company until the last payment has been made.

This restriction does not apply to certificated bailiffs acting under a distress warrant for rent, who are entitled to take any effects to 'the order and disposition of the tenant'. But in practice they will rarely seize the item if a hire-purchase agreement is produced.

County court bailiffs and sheriff's officers are also empowered by possession orders and writs to enter properties to evict tenants or householders who have fallen behind with their mortgage repayments. In these circumstances, they are entitled to use whatever force is necessary to remove the householder and his family from the premises.

295

# When outsiders can enter a home without consent

| | GROUNDS | TIME | AUTHORISATION |
|---|---|---|---|
| **Landlords** | To inspect the property | Reasonable hours | Under the terms of the lease or tenancy agreement |
| | Eviction: Landlord has no right to evict except through the courts—see **Court Officers** | | |
| **Neighbours** | To repair or maintain shared services or common walls | Reasonable hours | Deeds sometimes give specific rights of access. Otherwise rights are assumed |
| **Electricity Board Officials** | To check fittings, read meters, or cut off supply | Reasonable hours | 1. Official carries a pass to prove his identity |
| | | | 2. Magistrate's warrant |
| | To check equipment or mend a fault when danger to life or property is suspected | Day or night | Official carries a pass to prove his identity |
| **Gas Board Officials** | To check fittings, read meters, or cut off supply | Reasonable hours | 1. Official carries a pass to prove his identity |
| | | | 2. Magistrate's warrant |
| | To check equipment or mend a fault when danger to life or property is suspected | Day or night | Official pass |
| **Water Board Officials** | To inspect fittings and to check if water is being wasted, misused or polluted | Reasonable hours | 1. Official pass |
| | | | 2. Magistrate's warrant |
| **Post Office Officials** | To inspect or remove telephones | Reasonable hours | Official pass |
| | To check that householders using TV sets have a valid television broadcast receiving licence | Reasonable hours | 1. Official pass |
| | | | 2. Magistrate's warrant |

| NOTICE | IF THE HOUSEHOLDER REFUSES |
|---|---|
| Varies according to the agreement | Landlord can seek permission in the courts |
| Reasonable | Force cannot be used; police will not assist. Neighbours must take court action |
| None | Official cannot gain entry at this stage; he must apply for a warrant |
| None | Warrant permits entry by force if necessary, but the Board must make good any damage caused, or pay compensation |
| None | Official cannot use force; he may ask a policeman to accompany him, to prevent a breach of the peace |
| Disconnection, 24 hours— otherwise none | Official cannot gain entry by force at this stage; he must apply for a warrant |
| None | Warrant permits entry by force if necessary, but the Board must make good any damage caused, or pay compensation |
| None | Official cannot use force; he may ask a policeman to accompany him, to prevent a breach of the peace |
| 24 hours | Official cannot gain entry by force. Where there is a metered supply he is entitled to apply for a warrant, which allows him to enter by force if necessary. He is also entitled to cut off the water supply from outside the property when householders refuse entry |
| None | Official who suspects that a meter has been tampered with in some way applies for a warrant that entitles him to enter by force if necessary. Again, he can cut off the water supply |
| None | Post Office engineer cannot force entry; Post Office can sue for return of property |
| None | Inspector cannot gain entry without permission of the householder; if refused, he must apply for a magistrate's warrant |
| None | Inspector can ask police to accompany him to prevent a breach of the peace after obtaining the warrant |

continued ▶

**When outsiders can enter a home without consent** continued

| | GROUNDS | TIME | AUTHORISATION |
|---|---|---|---|
| **Local Authority Officials** (Health or housing inspectors) | To investigate breaches of the Public Health Acts, bye-laws or building regulations | Reasonable hours | **1.** Official carries a letter of authority |
| | | | **2.** Magistrate's warrant |
| | To examine with a view to orders for compulsory purchase, demolition, closing, clearance or repairs | Reasonable hours | Official carries a letter of authority |
| **Police** | To prevent a breach of the peace or make an arrest | Day or night | Officer's warrant card |
| | To carry out investigations | Day or night | **1.** Officer's warrant card |
| | | | **2.** Magistrate's warrant |
| **Firemen** | To put out a fire, to protect from fire or to rescue people or property | Day or night | Any fireman on duty can exercise the power |
| **Customs Officers** | To search for contraband | Day or night | Writ of Assistance or magistrate's warrant |
| **Court Officers** (Sheriffs and Bailiffs) | To carry out court orders by seizing goods | Day or night, but not Sundays | Judgment summons, court order or distress warrant |
| | To carry out court orders by seizing particular goods (HP property, papers needed in a trial, etc.) | Day or night, but not Sundays | Warrant for delivery or writ of delivery |
| | To evict a tenant | Reasonable hours | Warrant for possession or writ of possession |
| | To seize anyone charged with contempt of court; to take possession of premises by court order | Day or night | Court order |
| **Certificated Bailiffs** | To carry out court orders by seizing goods and subsequently selling them to pay rent, rates or taxes | Between sunrise and sunset, but not Sundays | Distress warrant issued by landlord (rent), local authority (rates), or Inland Revenue (taxes) |
| **Valuation Officers** (Inland Revenue) | To assess improved or enlarged property (for rating purposes) | Reasonable hours | Official pass |

| NOTICE | IF THE HOUSEHOLDER REFUSES |
|---|---|
| None | First refusal leads to 24 hours' notice (except in investigation of multiple occupation, when no notice is required). After second refusal, inspector can obtain a magistrate's warrant |
| 24 hours | Inspector can force entry if necessary. In addition, refusal may lead to prosecution and a fine of up to £20 |
| None | After first refusal, 24 hours' notice given. If entry still refused, there is possibility of a £20 fine for obstruction. But official cannot obtain a warrant, or force entry |
| None | Police may use whatever force they consider necessary |
| None | Police cannot use force at this stage; they must apply for a magistrate's warrant, except when they want to search premises for property stolen or received by a former occupant |
| None | Warrant empowers police to use whatever force they consider necessary |
| None | Fireman can force entry, and the householder is liable to prosecution if he refuses. The penalty is a fine of up to £25 |
| None | Customs officers may use reasonable force to open doors, windows or containers. Between 11 p.m. and 5 a.m. they must be accompanied by a police officer |
| None | Officers cannot break in; they must enter through unlocked doors or windows which are already partly open |
| None | Officers can use any force they consider necessary to enter the premises and carry out the goods or documents |
| None | Officers can use any force necessary to secure an eviction |
| None | Officers may use reasonable force |
| None | Certificated bailiffs are not entitled to use force to gain entry to private dwellings, unless distress has already been levied |
| 24 hours | Officers cannot use force to gain entry but householders who wilfully bar valuation officers are liable to a fine of up to £5; officers who are unable to gain entry make their assessment on whatever information they can obtain |

# Threats to the home

*When an owner can be forced to sell*
*Bodies with compulsory purchase powers*
*How an order is made*

*Grounds for objecting*
*How compensation is calculated*
*The right to rehousing*

EVERY householder needs to be alert to anything that threatens to make his property less pleasant to live in or to lower its market value. The threat may come from a neighbour who is extending or altering his house; from a new road or development scheme which could change the character of the neighbourhood; or from a compulsory purchase order.

If a neighbour wants to alter his property, say by building a garage in front of the building line or adding another room, he has to apply for planning permission from the local authority. He is not obliged to inform people living near him, but the plans of what he proposes can be inspected in the local authority office. ☐ Repairs and improvements, p. 223.

A householder who hears that work is proposed on an adjoining property can inspect the plans to see if his interests will be affected. If he thinks they will be, he should write to the council immediately, making his objection. If the proposed development is large enough, he can also write to the Secretary of State for

## Recognising the danger signs

If a householder is to have any chance of success in opposing a development which threatens his home, he must act at the earliest possible moment.

He cannot rely on receiving personal notification of developments planned by either the local authority or by a private firm or individual. The only way to be sure is to consult the local council's planning department.

Some councils keep a 'development plan'. This shows the type of development allowed in different areas—industrial, residential, and so on—and the areas where no development is allowed. The development plan has to be approved by the Secretary of State for the Environment.

Other authorities prepare 'structure' and 'local' plans, which show planning proposals and areas where restrictions on development are in force. Specific development areas are clearly indicated by key symbols.

Whichever system is used, any objection which a householder wishes to make should be registered with the council's planning department as soon as the plan has been drawn up. Do not wait for a direct threat. It may then be too late.

A plan may, for example, indicate that the authorities intend to buy land compulsorily to develop a certain area. If a householder does not register an objection when the plan is first drawn up, his right of objection may be severely limited if a compulsory purchase order is subsequently served on him.

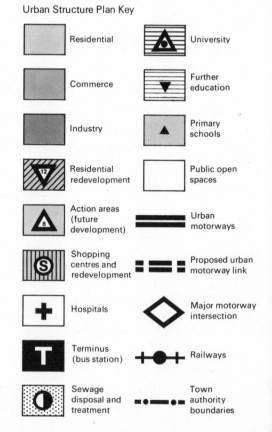

Urban Structure Plan Key

| | | | |
|---|---|---|---|
| Residential | | University | |
| Commerce | | Further education | |
| Industry | | Primary schools | |
| Residential redevelopment | | Public open spaces | |
| Action areas (future development) | | Urban motorways | |
| Shopping centres and redevelopment | | Proposed urban motorway link | |
| Hospitals | | Major motorway intersection | |
| Terminus (bus station) | | Railways | |
| Sewage disposal and treatment | | Town authority boundaries | |

the Environment asking him to 'call in' the planning application. The Secretary of State may then order a public inquiry at which objectors can state their case. ☐ How an inquiry is conducted, p. 304.

Sometimes, work may start on alterations without planning permission being granted. Anyone objecting can report the work to the local council. The developer will be ordered to stop work while the case is studied. If permission is not granted, he can be made to restore the site or building to its original state.

The same basic principles and procedures apply whether a neighbour wants to build another house in his grounds or a large company wants to put up a multi-million pound office block.

The usual grounds for objection are that the proposed development spoils an owner's enjoyment of his own property or lowers its market value. Much depends on what is

considered appropriate for a particular area.

For example, if a motor trader proposed to build a repair works in a residential area, the residents would have a good chance of successfully objecting. In a semi-industrial area, they would be less likely to succeed.

A surveyor can advise on grounds for an objection and on whether it is likely to succeed. He can also estimate the cost of being represented at an inquiry, and the threat to the value of a property if the work goes through.

Apart from planning objections, a householder may have grounds for action if a new development would block most of the light to the windows of his property. In law he must have used the property for at least 20 years before he can claim a right to what is known as Ancient Lights.

Anyone who believes his right to Ancient Lights is threatened should contact a solicitor. If an agreement cannot be reached with the

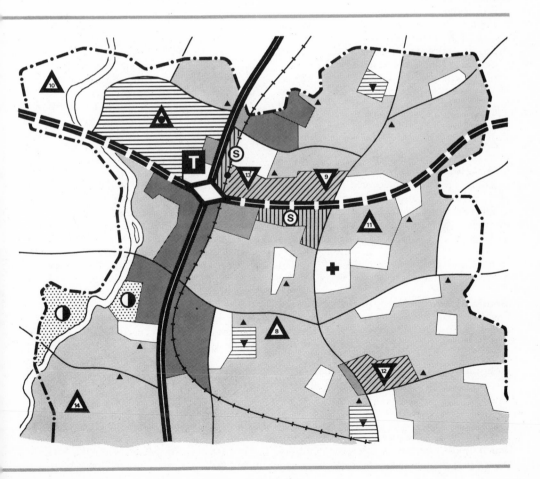

would-be developer, the solicitor may advise an application to the High Court for an injunction to enforce the right.

### When an owner can be forced to sell

If a private individual or company wants to buy a property, the owner may refuse to sell, however much money he is offered. But if the Government, a local authority or certain other public bodies wish to buy the property, in certain circumstances the owner can be made to sell and will be compensated. This transaction is called 'compulsory purchase'.

In some cases the authorities do not wish to buy the property but merely to use it in some way. For instance, they may wish to have the right—known as an easement or wayleave—to run a drain under it, or perhaps telephone or electricity cables over it.

If the owner does not consent to his property being used for such a purpose, the authorities can seek a compulsory purchase order.

Two methods of objection are open to anyone faced with a compulsory purchase order, or the likelihood of one.

First, there are legal rights of objection for owners and tenants. To make the best use of them, the advice of a solicitor will be necessary.

Secondly, the bodies which have the right to apply for compulsory purchase orders can be made to heed public opinion. Some—such as local authorities—are democratically elected and are therefore more likely to take note of public reaction.

Sometimes a private meeting can be arranged with the authority applying for the order. Householders who go armed with carefully prepared objections and practical alternatives may get proposals modified.

Where this fails, a public campaign is often more effective. Public opinion can be mobilised through protests to local councillors and Members of Parliament, and through letters to local newspapers. The national Press and television may also take an interest.

### Bodies with compulsory purchase powers

Several bodies have the power to buy your home under a compulsory purchase order.

LOCAL AUTHORITIES The vast majority of compulsory purchases are made by local authorities for slum clearance or some other form of redevelopment. Councils may also buy property for such projects as schools, sewage treatment works or local road schemes.

GOVERNMENT DEPARTMENTS The Department of the Environment is the department which most frequently uses compulsory powers—to acquire land for new roads and motorways. Other ministries have compulsory powers. The Home Office may want land for a new detention centre, or the Ministry of Defence may plan to build an Army camp.

STATUTORY UNDERTAKINGS Public bodies, such as British Rail, gas, electricity and water boards can buy land compulsorily for such things as laying lines, cables and pipelines.

NEW TOWN CORPORATIONS Land for the building of new towns may be bought from the owners by compulsory purchase.

### How an order is made

The usual steps involved in buying property by compulsory purchase are laid down in the Acquisition of Land (Authorisation Procedure) Act 1946. First, the authority wishing to acquire the land prepares a draft order, accompanied by a map showing the land which is involved.

An announcement that the order is being applied for is then published in at least one local newspaper for two consecutive weeks. It states where the draft order can be inspected, where objections can be made and what is the period allowed for raising objections. This must be at least three weeks.

A similar notice must be served on the owner, occupier or tenant of any land to be acquired, except tenants entitled to notice to quit of a month or less.

If no objections are made, a Government Minister will normally confirm the order. If there are objections, a public inquiry must be held or the objector must be given some other opportunity to state his case. The body applying for the order has the right to be represented. So have the objectors; if they are successful, the authority normally has to pay their costs; otherwise they must pay their own costs.

After considering the report of the Government inspector conducting the inquiry, the Minister will confirm or refuse the order.

The order comes into effect on the day it is announced. It can be challenged in the High Court, however, within six weeks. The grounds for such a challenge are that the interests of the person affected have been seriously prejudiced because the body which granted the order was acting beyond its legal powers, or because the procedure laid down by Parliament was not followed.

If the order was applied for by a local authority, the order will be confirmed by a Minister. In some cases, however, the same Minister both seeks the order and confirms it. For instance, the Secretary for the Environment would apply for land for a motorway and also confirm the order. In this case he must be scrupulous in keeping his two separate functions apart.

## Grounds for objecting
The best ground for an objection is that the proposed scheme is not the best solution to the problem. It might be possible to argue, for example, that a proposed route for a new road is not the logical one, and to counter by suggesting an alternative which would cause less disruption.

The original written objection need be only brief. The objector could confine himself in his letter to saying, 'I wish to object to the road scheme on the following grounds:
1. That the proposed route is wrongly sited and should be moved five miles to the east, where less property would be affected.
2. That South Street is a neighbourhood of attractive old houses and buildings which should not be destroyed.'

At the inquiry, it would be possible to produce a map, showing the alternative route proposed by the objector.

## Compensation
If all objections to the order are overruled and it is finally confirmed, the body compulsorily buying the property sends the owner and other people who have a legal interest in the property a document called a 'Notice to Treat'. This asks the person to whom it is sent to give particulars of his interest in the property, and offers to negotiate about any compensation which may be involved.

Once the Notice to Treat has been served, nothing the owner does to his property can increase his compensation. But compensation is based on the value of the property when the authority actually takes possession—or the date on which the price is agreed or fixed by arbitration, if this is later.

## How compensation is calculated
The price an owner receives is based on what it would fetch on the open market if the owner decided to sell. To this is added compensation for being disturbed, and for any other direct loss the purchase has caused.

Six basic rules are laid down by the Land Compensation Act 1961:
1. The owner is not entitled to an inflated price merely because the sale is compulsory.
2. The value is the price that the property 'might be expected to realise' on the open market. In practice, this means what qualified experts think it would have realised. The price is usually negotiated between the seller or his surveyor and an officer of the Board of Inland Revenue, called a district valuer. If the two cannot agree, the owner can appeal to a body called the Lands Tribunal, which will settle the matter (subject only to a right of appeal to the courts on a point of law).

If planning permission has been given to develop the property and make it more valuable, or is likely to be obtainable, this is taken into consideration in the negotiations. Any change in the value of adjoining land belonging to the owner will also be considered. Any drop in value because of the threat of acquisition will not, however, be allowed to affect the price.
3. Any special advantage of the property

## When neighbouring land is compulsorily purchased

A HOUSEHOLDER is not generally entitled to compensation for nuisance or loss of amenities caused by the compulsory purchase of a neighbouring property.

He has no right to compensation, for instance, if a motorway is built 50 yds from his home and noise from heavy traffic keeps him awake all night.

Even if a local authority wants to compensate such people, it is entitled to do so only in the rare cases where the properties concerned can be compulsorily purchased for some other reason—if they are in a slum-clearance area, for example.

Where property bought under a compulsory purchase order is subject to a restrictive covenant—an obligation placed on the owner or occupier for the benefit of neighbouring land—neighbouring owners cannot enforce the covenant on the purchasing authority.

This means that the authority could with impunity build a 10-storey block of flats on land which was previously limited to one detached house. But if the owner of neighbouring land or property consequently suffers damage he will be entitled to claim compensation from the authority.

Similarly, the loss of a right of support or the obstruction of a right to light could give rise to a claim for compensation.

which made it attractive to the body buying it cannot increase the price if there is no other demand for it. For instance, the fact that its situation makes it an ideal site for a reservoir would not have the effect of increasing its value on the open market.

**4.** If at the time of purchase the property was used illegally, that cannot be a basis for compensation—for example, if a large income had been made out of illegal overcrowding of residents in a house.

**5.** If the property is valuable to the owner because he can use it in a particular way, but it has no real value for that purpose on the open market, the price may be based on the cost of buying or erecting a suitable alternative. This applies to places like churches and schools.

The owner, however, must genuinely intend to set up a new establishment elsewhere.

**6.** The owner is entitled not only to the value of his interest in the property but also to compensation for any loss caused by being disturbed. For instance, a business owner can claim for loss of profits. All removal expenses are also a legitimate claim.

There is no compensation, apart from under rule 5, for the fact that the dispossessed owner may have to pay a higher price or rent for a new property. He can, however, claim that the compulsory purchaser buys fixtures at a fair price. If he decides to take fixtures, he can claim not only removal expenses, but also the cost of adapting fixtures such as curtains and carpets to the new premises.

## How an inquiry is conducted

INQUIRIES are held by Government departments for a variety of purposes—to hear planning appeals, for example, and to decide whether compulsory purchase orders should be confirmed. Procedures differ according to the subject, but the general principles are the same.

NOTICE Advance notice is given of the date, time and place of the inquiry. People directly concerned are informed by post; notices are also posted on or near the land which is the subject of the inquiry, and there are usually advertisements in local papers. In planning appeals, the local authority sends notices to all houses directly affected.

DOCUMENTS At least 28 days before the inquiry, the local authority or other official body involved issues a written statement of its case. It also lists plans and documents to which it may refer at the inquiry, including details of where they are available for inspection and copying.

The statement is sent to people directly involved; anyone else can usually get a copy on request.

When an inquiry is set up to hear a developer's appeal against refusal of planning permission, objectors to the development can obtain a statement of the council's reasons for refusing permission—but not of the developer's case.

If a Government department is supporting the local authority, a representative will attend the inquiry if any of the people involved give at least 14 days' notice.

The inquiry is conducted by an inspector appointed by the Ministry concerned; he is usually a qualified surveyor. Anyone who wishes to take part can appear in person or be represented by a barrister, solicitor, surveyor or anyone else.

The inspector calls in turn on the people involved to state their case, and to call witnesses if they wish. Witnesses do not normally take an oath, but they can be subjected to cross-examination.

At the close of the inquiry, the inspector goes with representatives of the people involved to view the site and locality.

THE DECISION The inspector makes a written report to the Minister, with recommendations. The Minister usually accepts the recommendations, but is not obliged to do so.

However, if the Minister disagrees with the inspector on a question of fact, or takes into account new evidence, he must inform the people and organisations represented at the inquiry. If they disagree, they can put their views in writing to the Minister, or ask for the inquiry to be re-opened.

A letter giving the Minister's decision is sent to the parties. They are also entitled to a copy of the inspector's report if they ask for it within a month of the decision.

In some smaller planning appeals, the inspector himself makes the decision.

COSTS In a compulsory purchase order inquiry, a successful objector has his costs paid for him. In planning appeals, the parties normally meet their own costs.

In addition to the six basic rules, the owner of a house has one other important right: if the compulsory purchaser wishes to buy only part of the property, and the owner considers it is not worth keeping the rest, the buyer can be required to take the whole property and pay full compensation—unless the authority can show that the part can be taken without 'material detriment' to the whole.

## Valuation of unfit property

A medical officer of health has powers to inspect property within his local authority area to see whether, because of such defects as structural instability or inadequate light and ventilation, it should be designated as unfit for human habitation.

This designation may affect the amount of compensation when such property is compulsorily purchased as part of slum clearance or comprehensive redevelopment.

Where an unfit house was occupied by the owner or a member of his family for two years before the date when proceedings began for declaring the property unfit, full compensation is paid. In some cases, full compensation can also be claimed by an owner-occupier who has lived in the house for less than two years. These rules apply to cases arising after April 23, 1968.

In all other instances, basic compensation is limited to the value of the site. This is increased, however, if the owner can prove that the house has been well-maintained at his own expense.

The addition, known as 'well-maintained house payment' is calculated at four times rateable value—or twice rateable value if the house is well-maintained inside but not outside, or vice versa.

Total compensation for an unfit house must not exceed the amount that would have been due if the house had not been unfit.

The difference in compensation for a 'fit' and 'unfit' property can be substantial, so anyone whose property is in danger of being bought as 'unfit' should consider taking professional advice. In some cases a surveyor may be able to successfully challenge an unfit classification.

## The right to rehousing

Not everyone who loses his home under compulsory purchase is automatically entitled to be rehoused. In the case of slum-clearance projects, however, the local authority has to show that a family can be rehoused before the Secretary of State for the Environment will confirm the compulsory purchase order.

When there are no stipulations about rehousing—for example, when homes are cleared for a motorway—rehousing will depend very much on the attitude of the local authority in whose area the development is taking place.

Some local authorities consider themselves obliged to offer to rehouse almost everyone affected by compulsory purchase. Others, with long council-house waiting lists, try to limit their rehousing to those residents whose chances of finding other accommodation are remote.

Single people, and lodgers who have lived with a family on a temporary basis for only a short period, are not normally rehoused. Nor is anybody who moves into a house after it has been scheduled for compulsory purchase.

Some local authorities start making preliminary arrangements for rehousing as soon as the development plans are drawn up. Others wait until the compulsory purchase orders are confirmed and a few leave it almost until the bulldozers move in.

In view of the varying attitudes, anyone seeking rehousing after compulsory purchase should seek information from the local authority housing department as soon as the order has been confirmed. They should ensure that the department knows their present address and that they are expecting the authority to provide alternative housing.

Frequently, an assurance that residents losing their homes will be rehoused is given at a public inquiry. If not, an individual approach to the local authority housing department may help to persuade them to consider providing other accommodation for those who are being displaced.

## Accepting a council home

Most owner-occupiers of 'fit' houses who receive the full, open-market value of their property together with reasonable removal expenses will prefer to buy another house rather than move into a council home.

Occasionally, however, owner-occupiers decide to accept council homes. In these cases councils sometimes attempt to reduce compensation, claiming that payment should be made for the cost of rehousing. This practice is disliked by the Department of the Environment, which advises councils to pay full compensation.

Any owner-occupier who finds that his property is down-valued because he accepts council accommodation should protest immediately. An appeal to the district valuer should result in full compensation being paid.

305

# Moving house

*Dealing with removers' forms*       *Preparing for the move*
*What the charge covers*             *Moving overseas*
*Insurance*                          *Putting furniture in store*

MOVING house is a difficult and time-consuming business, and one in which there are innumerable snags for the unwary. The first step in organising a removal properly is to approach a number of removal firms for an estimate. Do this well before the anticipated move, as it is difficult to get a reliable contractor at short notice.

Where possible, choose firms recommended by friends. Failing this, the yellow pages of the telephone directory give names and addresses under the heading 'Removal and Storage—Domestic'.

The firm's representative will call and quote a price for the removal. The customer should make sure to mention if he is moving to a flat—there may be an extra charge if it is higher than the second storey.

Normally, the estimate will be for a lump sum, but some firms quote so much an hour. A lump-sum quotation is usually best—an estimate on an hourly basis may look cheaper, but sometimes proves to be more costly. Make sure that the estimate is in writing.

One or two small firms, mostly in rural areas, may be prepared to do the job without asking the customer to sign a contract listing their terms and conditions. In such cases the law says that certain 'implied terms' will automatically cover the transaction.

If a removal contractor agrees to move household furniture for a price, without stipulating further conditions, the law says that he must carry out the work to a 'reasonable' standard. He must take 'reasonable' care of the customer's goods—and he is liable if the goods are lost or damaged through his negligence, or that of his employees.

In practice, a removal contractor who lost or damaged goods would find it difficult to prove that neither he nor his employees had been negligent. So the customer who can escape signing a form with the firm's terms and conditions is in a strong position.

## Removers' printed forms

The majority of removal contractors give an estimate on a printed form which incorporates, in tiny print, a variety of conditions. All of them are weighted against the customer.

The common law obligation to take reasonable care of the goods can be varied or

## Pitfalls of a removal firm's estimate

A customer who signs a remover's estimate usually agrees to be bound by the standard conditions printed in small type on the back.

The majority of these conditions cover the sort of difficulties that practice has shown are likely to crop up. For example, the estimate is subject to revision unless the customer accepts it within 21 days. It is given on the understanding that the contractors are allowed to decide the route and manner of removal. Most people will probably be content to accept conditions such as these.

Some of the other terms may attempt to take away from the customer his legal rights to adequate compensation if his property is lost or damaged. He can protect these rights by reading the small print closely and crossing out or amending any unacceptable clause before signing the form.

**12 (a)** The contractor shall not be liable for any loss or damage which is caused by or results from fire, however that fire is caused, and no claim can be entertained.

Fire risk In law, a remover normally has to pay for any damage caused by fire to other people's property if the fire was started as a result of his negligence or the negligence of one of his employees—if, for example, a fire broke out in the removal van because of an electrical fault which the remover knew about but failed to remedy. If the customer accepts this clause, the remover escapes all liability, and there is little point in going to law to fight an expensive action.

excluded altogether if the remover and his customer agree, and this is what some contractors try to do in the small print.

There are many conditions, and they are usually printed on the 'acceptance' part of the estimate, which the customer has to sign, date and return to the contractor.

### Altering the form

The contractor's estimate is an offer in the legal sense, which the customer is free to accept or reject. The customer is also free to strike out or alter any of the conditions which he does not like.

If he does this, and the contractor does not write back and refuse to do the job, then the conditions as altered will apply.

It may be, of course, that no contractor in the area will do the work other than on the 'standard terms'. In this case there is not much the customer can do but accept. Experience shows, however, that many of the larger firms will accept alterations.

Some contractors try to deal with alterations to forms by including a clause on the subject: 'All the above conditions shall apply to work done in relation to the furniture and effects, whether by way of removal out of the premises or re-delivery from the warehouse or otherwise whatsoever, and shall be deemed to be incorporated in any contract which may be entered into with regard to such work or in relation to such furniture and effects.'

The legal effect of this clause is not clear. The contractor is attempting to say that he will not do the job except on these terms. But if the customer strikes the clause out, and the alteration is accepted and the amended conditions are those acted upon, no court is likely to rule that the unaltered conditions apply.

### What the charge covers

Before deciding between the estimates, check what each one covers. Usually they include packing and unpacking of belongings, loading, unloading and the moving itself.

Charges may be lower if the householder opts to do some or all of the packing himself; but usually this is false economy. Packing is a specialist job, and if it is undertaken by the removal firm there can be no room for dispute about who is responsible for breakages.

Even where the customer does some of his own packing, he should always get an experienced tradesman to pack clocks, pianos, barometers and electrical equipment.

### Insurance

If the customer succeeds in altering the terms of the removal firm's estimate form, he may increase his protection against damage or loss during the move. He is still likely to have difficulty, however, in getting a remover to meet a claim, especially if the sum of money involved is large.

He can reduce the risk of financial loss by taking out insurance for the removal period. This cover, known as 'transit insurance', will compensate the owner if any belongings are damaged or lost in the move. The remover

---

**15** The liability (if any) of the contractors for any loss or damage shall be limited to either (a) the cost of repairing or replacing the damaged or missing articles or (b) £15 for any one article, suite or complete package and the contents thereof (including valuables), whichever is the smaller sum.

**16** All claims for damage to or loss of any goods shall be made in detail in writing (time being of the essence of the contract) within three days after delivery of the goods alleged to be damaged, or in the case of goods alleged to be lost, within three days of the time when the goods should have been delivered.

**Loss or damage** A removal firm has a duty in law to look after furniture and belongings, and to take reasonable steps to see that they are not damaged or lost. If the firm fails to do so, the customer has a right to claim the actual cost of repairs or replacement—often far more than the £15 to which he is limited if he accepts this clause.

**Time limit** Claims for goods lost or damaged must be made in law a reasonable time after the removal firm completes the job. No arbitrary limit is set, except that no action can be started more than six years after the event. Many people find it difficult to check every item within three days and genuine claims may be ruled out by this clause.

will often offer to arrange insurance, or the customer can make his own arrangements. If the contents are insured under a house-contents policy, the householder can ask for a temporary extension to cover loss or damage as belongings are packed, transported and unpacked in the new home.

Jewellery and other valuables are usually excluded from such a policy, and special cover must be obtained. Similarly, expensive items may have to be insured separately; some insurers pay no more than 5 per cent of the total insured sum for any one article.

Some transit-insurance policies exclude risks such as scratching, bruising and denting of articles, breakage of china, glass and brittle objects and of glass in picture frames, unless they are specially protected. Often, insurance companies make it a condition of the policy that the packing is done professionally.

### Preparing for the move

Fix the actual date for removal with the contractor—and try to avoid Saturdays and Sundays. Weekend removals are normally charged at overtime rates.

If the old or new house is difficult to find, let the remover have a simple plan of the streets, or a diagram with the precise address, description and directions.

Under the contract, removers claim the right to charge extra if they face delays caused by local parking, waiting or unloading restrictions. If these restrictions are likely to arise, tell the remover so that he can seek police co-operation in advance.

Refrigerators should be defrosted before removal, and any fixtures that are being taken should be made ready for loading. Unless the customer has specially requested it, the removal men do not take down curtain rails, light fittings or TV aerials.

Removal firms provide their own packing cases to transport crockery, books and all smaller objects. For an extra fee, some firms will supply wardrobe boxes in which clothes can be hung to save them from being folded.

When the removal men arrive, take the foreman round the house and show him what has to be removed. He will decide the best order to work in. The customer must be sure to point out anything to be taken from the garden or from any outbuildings.

The removal estimate usually covers the taking up of linoleum and carpets and taking down of curtains, but it does not normally include refitting at the new home.

It is the customer's responsibility to see that the place is cleared, so take a good look round before the men finally move away. Make sure that there is someone at the new house or flat to give the removers clear instructions about where each item of furniture should go.

When all the furniture has been moved in, the customer may be asked to sign a document which states that everything has been safely delivered. This often happens before he has had a chance to make a thorough check. In this case the customer should sign that he is satisfied 'subject to inspection'. This leaves him free to claim if any damage is found later. Be sure to make a full inspection as soon as possible, for removers are usually reluctant to meet a claim which has been delayed.

### Moving overseas

Removal firms accept even less liability when moving goods overseas. There is a range of insurance depending on the destination, and much depends on the risks in the country that goods are bound for.

It is important to insure the goods for their value at destination. An article worth £100 in Britain could be worth much more abroad. Removals to foreign countries usually require special documents, customs certificates and import licences. This work is best carried out by a firm specialising in overseas removals.

### Putting furniture in store

If the home contents are going into store, treat clothing and blankets, carpets and fabrics with moth and insect deterrent. Make sure no foodstuffs or inflammable liquids are included.

Under the contract, the remover usually accepts no liability for the goods while in store. It is therefore vital to insure against all risks, including fire.

It is possible to extend a transit policy to cover risks while in store. A house contents policy can also be extended—generally for fire only, occasionally for theft.

The insurance will not cover items packed by the customer in trunks, cases or drawers unless the contents have been listed and the details given to the insurer. Special insurance is necessary for valuables. Jewellery is best deposited with a bank.

The remover's agreement usually lays down what happens if the customer gets behind with paying charges for goods in store. Basically, if storage charges are two years in arrears, or if the contractor gives the customer notice to remove his goods and he fails to do so, the contractor is given power to sell the goods. The customer is entitled to the balance after the deduction of charges and costs.

# YOUR FAMILY

# Getting engaged

*The promise to marry*     *Returning gifts*
*Broken engagements*

GETTING engaged is a romantic and social event which involves no legal contract. People of any age can become engaged merely by agreeing verbally to marry. Permission from the couple's parents is not required for an engagement, although it is illegal for anyone under 18 to marry without the consent of their parents or a court.

### The promise to marry
Before 1970, when the law was changed, an engagement or a promise to marry was regarded in much the same way as other forms of legal contract.

If the promise was not kept, either the man or the woman could sue for damages; usually it was the jilted woman who sought redress.

Now such a promise is no longer binding in law, nor does 'breach of promise' give rise any longer to an action for damages.

Even a woman who, relying on the promise of marriage, has sexual relations with a man can no longer seek damages for breach of promise if the wedding does not take place.

The right to sue for breach of promise was abolished because it was generally recognised to be archaic. The Law Commission reported in 1967 that such actions were usually taken by people interested only in gold-digging.

The Commission suggested that it was wrong for the law to create pressures for people to go through with marriages which they would not otherwise undertake.

### Broken engagements
There are some instances, however, where the law protects the interests of the man or woman after the broken engagement.

If, for example, the couple had already bought a house or invested money in a business before breaking off the engagement, then either can apply to the courts to share out the money or property between them.

Any legal action must be brought within three years of the date when the engagement was broken off, and it is advisable to let a solicitor deal with it, since an application has to be made to a county court or High Court.

The court is asked to apportion whatever the engaged couple owned jointly, and it does

so in the same way as it decides who owns what after a marriage breaks down. □ After the divorce, p. 406.

The court is not concerned with compensating the man or woman for any losses arising from the broken engagement: the question is simply one of property law, not whether either was at fault.

In effect, somebody whose engagement ends is entitled to take out of the common pool a proportion of what he or she put into it, unless there was some specific agreement.

If the woman paid for a house and the man decorated and converted it, each would be entitled to a proportion of the total value.

Neither the couple nor any relative or friend has any legal right to reclaim money spent in anticipation of a wedding that does not take place.

The girl may have bought her trousseau and made the bridesmaids' dresses. The man may have paid for the honeymoon hotel booking. But they have no legal means of reclaiming their money. If a father has paid out money towards the wedding, he cannot claim compensation if the man jilts his daughter.

### Returning gifts
Gifts made to one another by the engaged couple on the assumption that they were going to marry can be recovered legally, no matter who broke off the engagement.

This does not apply to ordinary gifts, such as Christmas presents, since these would be made for the special occasion and not because of the intended marriage.

Engagement or wedding presents from friends or relations must be returned if the wedding is called off, since they were given specifically because of the intended marriage. If they are not returned, they can be claimed back in the courts.

The engagement ring, however, remains the girl's property unless the man gave it to her only on condition that they got married.

He might make the gift of an engagement ring conditional if, for example, the ring was a family heirloom used for engagements. The ring would then be regarded as his family property and would have to be returned.

# Deciding to marry: the legal consequences

THE law gives a woman who marries a number of legal and financial advantages over one who is content to live with a man without going through a wedding ceremony. Contrary to popular belief, there is no formal legal status of a common-law wife, and the position of a woman who lives with a man without a formal tie can be difficult in the event of a disagreement.

MAINTENANCE Unlike a legal husband, a man has no duty in law to maintain a woman with whom he lives, and the woman does not have the right to pledge his credit for certain goods as a wife is entitled to do. ☐ For richer, for poorer, p. 323.

The man does have a duty to maintain the children of the family, however, and the woman can take legal action for maintenance if he fails to do so. ☐ The unmarried mother and her child, p. 330.

SOCIAL SECURITY BENEFITS The woman is barred from claiming many of the Social Security benefits to which a wife is entitled, such as a widow's allowance, widowed mother's allowance, widow's pension; and maternity benefit on the man's insurance. But she can seek supplementary benefit for herself and the children of the family if they are deserted. ☐ State help in hardship, p. 550.

INSURANCE A man and woman living together unmarried cannot insure each other's lives because, as they are not formally related, neither has the 'insurable interest' in the other which is required by insurance law.

However, if he wishes, a man can insure his life and arrange for the policy to benefit the woman with whom he is living. A woman can do the same with a policy on her life. ☐ Life assurance, p. 518.

INCOME TAX A man and woman living together are automatically taxed separately, and the man can claim only a single man's personal allowance, even if he is wholly maintaining the woman.

If the couple look after children, the person who has legal charge of them can claim children's tax allowances as long as he or she maintains them. If, however, the woman has charge of the children—because she is an unmarried mother or they are the product of her marriage that has split up—the man cannot claim the allowance even though he maintains them.

INHERITANCE A legal wife has a right to a share of her husband's property and belongings if he should die without leaving a will. The common-law wife has no such rights. ☐ Distributing an estate, p. 430.

## Rights to the family home

Without a formal marriage, the right to remain in the family home in the event of a dispute may belong only to the partner whose name is on the rent book, lease or tenancy agreement of a rented home, or the title deeds of one that is owner-occupied.

RENTED HOME If the man is the official tenant of the family home, he can demand at any time that the woman with whom he is living should leave. He can even get a court order against her if she refuses.

When the man dies, the woman has no right to remain in the home, except where the house or flat is unfurnished, there are children in the household, and the tenancy is protected by the Rent Acts. ☐ Rent and security: unfurnished property, p. 252; Controlled tenancies, p. 256.

OWNER-OCCUPIED HOME A man who owns his own home, or is buying it on a mortgage, normally has the right to require a woman with whom he is living to leave whenever he wishes, and to obtain a court order against her if she refuses.

However, the woman is entitled to remain if she can show that the house is partly hers because she has helped in its purchase or because the man has given her a share in the property. The test is similar to that used to establish the property rights of a husband and wife. ☐ After the divorce, p. 406.

A court which is asked to decide the rights of the couple will inquire into their original intentions. A crucial factor is whether they decided that the home should be owned partly or wholly by the woman. A written document signed at the time would be powerful evidence.

But if her contribution to family finances amounted to looking after the home and the children in the normal way, this would not establish a right to any part of the property.

If it was bought in their joint names, this would indicate that each has a share. The court would then allocate the proportion of the sale price to which each is entitled.

# Getting married

People forbidden to marry
Formalities of marriage
Going to see the registrar

The ceremony
The register-office marriage
Marriage in different churches

MARRIAGE in England and Wales is controlled by the law in three ways. Certain people are not allowed to marry, and legal safeguards exist to ensure that they do not; the marriage ceremony itself must be properly conducted; and the marriage must be registered by an authorised person.

## People forbidden to marry
The law disqualifies people from marrying if they are already married, if they are too closely related, or if they are under 16 years of age.

ALREADY MARRIED Both parties must be either single, widowed or divorced. Polygamy (having more than one husband or wife) will be recognised in this country only in certain circumstances and provided neither party had his or her permanent home in this country at the time of the marriage. □ The law on polygamy, p. 318.

Anyone who is already married cannot marry a second or further partner in this country. If such a person does marry a second or further time he or she can be charged with the crime of bigamy. □ ABC of crime and punishment, p. 758.

UNDER AGE Marriage involving anyone under the age of 16 is not permitted in this country. However, such a marriage will normally be considered valid if the ceremony took place in a country where it is allowed—but not if either party had what is regarded in law as his or her permanent home in this country at the time the marriage took place. □ The law and where you live, p. 320.

Someone who is 16 or over but under 18 years old and wants to get married must normally have the consent of both parents (or guardians or adoptive parents). If the parents are separated or divorced only the parent who

---

## Relatives who may not marry

For centuries, only the Church had the authority to perform marriages and always prohibited those between close relations. These prohibitions are now established by statute, and the Marriage Act 1949 lists which relatives are forbidden to marry. A relative named in the list may be a whole-blood relation (people who are descended from the same parents or pair of ancestors), a half-blood relation (people related through one parent or ancestor) or certain people related by marriage or adoption—for instance, mother-in-law and son-in-law, stepson and stepmother, adoptive mother and adoptive son.

If a marriage ceremony is performed for relatives who are forbidden to marry, it has no legal effect, and the marriage is void in law. The partners have no rights or duties, and either can apply to a court for a decree of nullity. □ Ending a void marriage, p. 393.

Sexual intercourse between near relatives is a criminal offence. □ ABC of crime and punishment, p. 758.

| A man may not marry his | A woman may not marry her |
|---|---|
| grandmother | grandfather |
| stepgrandmother | stepgrandfather |
| grandmother-in-law | grandfather-in-law |
| mother | father |
| mother-in-law | father-in-law |
| mother's sister | father's brother |
| father's sister | mother's brother |
| stepmother | stepfather |
| adoptive mother | adoptive father |
| sister | brother |
| half-sister | half-brother |
| daughter | son |
| sister's daughter | sister's son |
| brother's daughter | brother's son |
| daughter-in-law | son-in-law |
| stepdaughter | stepson |
| granddaughter | grandson |
| stepgranddaughter | stepgrandson |
| granddaughter-in-law | grandson-in-law |

has been given custody need give consent. If the child is illegitimate, only the consent of the mother is required. When a local authority has assumed parental rights, perhaps because the child has been orphaned, or abandoned, or because the parents are considered unfit to look after the child, the authority must give its consent to the marriage. If a child is a ward of court, the consent of the court must be obtained.

If a person whose consent is required cannot be traced or is insane, the Registrar General at Somerset House, The Strand, London WC2 1LA (or in some circumstances the superintendent registrar of a district) can allow the marriage to go ahead. But permission can be given only after an investigation of the circumstances.

When at least one parent refuses consent, the couple can apply to a magistrates' court for permission to marry. The hearing is private and informal. The court's decision is final and there is no right of appeal.

Young people of 16 or over, but under 18, can still marry without parental consent in Scotland. But this is now more difficult than it used to be, since residence must be established for 15 clear days, following which public notice of the intended marriage must be displayed for seven clear days.

Where the parties are under age, the superintendent registrar will take all possible steps to ensure that written consent has been properly obtained. Forgery and perjury are offences which, if discovered, would be reported to the police who could prosecute.

If the marriage takes place without the necessary consent, it is not invalid. The law tries to ensure that young people do not get married without the approval of their parents, but it does not go as far as to say that those who do so are not properly married.

## Formalities of marriage

Before a couple can marry, the law requires certain checks to ensure that there is no 'impediment'—that is, that neither is legally disqualified from marrying. These checks are made either by a superintendent registrar or, if the couple are marrying in the Church of England or the Church in Wales, by the clergyman who is to perform the ceremony.

The Church of England is the established church, and its clergy are allowed both to perform the wedding ceremony and to register the marriage. The Church in Wales, though disestablished, is in the same position. No other church or religious body has the automatic right to register a marriage. Although

priests or ministers of other denominations may be authorised to register marriages, the couple must have a certificate permitting the marriage from the local superintendent registrar before the ceremony can take place.

## Going to see the registrar

Each district has its own superintendent registrar, whose office is listed in the local telephone directory under 'Registration of Births, Deaths and Marriages'.

The superintendent registrar can issue two types of certificate permitting marriage. The most common is the Certificate for Marriage, which takes about 21 days to obtain.

Alternatively, the superintendent registrar can issue a Certificate and Licence, provided certain conditions are met. This speeds up the process of getting married considerably. ☐ Cutting down delay, p. 314.

To qualify for a Certificate for Marriage the couple must have lived in the district for at least seven days before giving notice of their intention to marry to the superintendent registrar. If they live in different districts they must give notice to the superintendent registrars of both districts.

The superintendent registrar will note the couple's names, addresses, ages (he will usually ask to see birth certificates) and occupations. He needs to know whether they are single, widowed or divorced. A divorcee has to produce a decree absolute certificate, and a widow or widower a death certificate of the former spouse. The couple then sign 'solemn declarations' that they know of no legal reason why the marriage should not take place.

If one of the parties is under 18, he or she has to produce proof of parental consent to the marriage. Consent can be given either on a form supplied by the registrar or in a letter from the parents or guardians. A letter granting consent should name both parties, and if the consent of both parents is needed (as it normally is) both must sign it.

The superintendent registrar will ask where the wedding is to be held. It can take place in the register office or in any registered building in the district. This includes the churches and chapels of all recognised religious sects. Jews and Quakers (members of the Society of Friends) can marry in any building—even a private house—as long as the proper notice has been given to the superintendent registrar and he has issued his authority.

The ceremony can be held in a registered building outside the district of residence of either party if, for instance, one of the parties normally worships there, or belongs to a religious sect that does not have a place of worship in the registration district.

OBJECTIONS When the superintendent registrar has taken the particulars, a notice of the intended marriage is displayed in the register office for public inspection for 21 days. During this time anyone may lodge an objection to the marriage—for instance, on the grounds that one of the parties is already married, is under age, or is marrying without proper consent.

If after 21 days no valid objections have been received, the superintendent registrar issues the Certificate for Marriage, giving permission to marry. The certificate is valid for three months and if the wedding is not held during that time for any reason the process of giving notice must be repeated.

**The ceremony**

Whichever form of marriage ceremony is to be followed, and whichever religious denomination or sect may be involved, the basic legal requirements are the same. The marriage must be conducted by a person or in the presence of a person 'authorised to register marriages' for the district; the particulars are entered in the marriage register, which must be signed by both parties, two witnesses and the person authorised to register the marriage. The ceremony, unless it is a Jewish or Quaker one, must take place between 8 a.m. and 6 p.m.

Certain words set out in law, including a solemn declaration that they are free to marry, must be spoken during the marriage ceremony by both parties in the presence of a registrar or authorised person and two witnesses.

The man says: 'I do solemnly declare that I know not of any lawful impediment why I (full names) may not be joined in matrimony to (full names). I call upon these persons here present to witness that I (full names) do take thee (full names) to be my lawful wedded wife.' Then the woman repeats the same words, substituting 'husband' for 'wife'. No other words are required to be spoken by law.

**The register-office marriage**

The simplest form of marriage, with no religious involvement, is a short ceremony in a marriage room at the district register office. It must be held 'with open doors' so that anyone can attend.

The date and time of the ceremony are usually fixed with the superintendent registrar

---

## Cutting down delay

A COUPLE wishing to marry at short notice may do so by obtaining a Certificate and Licence or, if the marriage is taking place in the Church of England or Church in Wales, by applying for either a common licence or special licence. This is more expensive than the normal procedure.

To obtain a Certificate and Licence, notice need be given to only one superintendent registrar, even if the parties live in different districts. However, the party giving notice is required to have lived in the district for at least 15 days. On the day that notice is given, the other party in the marriage must be resident in England or Wales.

If there is no legal reason to prevent the marriage the registrar can issue a Certificate and Licence which allows the couple to marry after only one clear weekday (not including either Christmas Day or Good Friday).

**Common licence to marry in church**

In the Church of England or the Church in Wales, the equivalent of a Certificate and Licence is a common licence granted by the bishop of the diocese in which the wedding is to be held. Marriage can take place as soon as a common licence is issued.

The couple must apply to one of the bishop's deputies, known as surrogates. At least one of the parties must have lived in the parish for 15 days before applying for the licence.

**Special licence**

In rare cases the church allows a 'special licence' to marry, with no residence qualifications. But the licence, which comes formally from the Archbishop of Canterbury, is granted only for marriage according to Church of England rites and only in exceptional circumstances—for example, if the couple need to avoid publicity, or if one partner is dying.

The special licence permits the marriage ceremony to be performed in a place other than a church—for instance, in a hospital.

The application for a special licence to marry, together with sworn statements explaining why it is necessary, is made to the office of the Registrar of the Faculty, 1 The Sanctuary, London SW1P 3JS.

when the couple give notice of the marriage. Two witnesses have to be present, and before the ceremony begins the registrar checks with the couple the details on the certificate to permit the marriage. He will also ask for the names and occupations of the fathers, even if they are dead.

The superintendent registrar begins by warning the couple of the solemnity and binding nature of the vows they are about to take. Each of them must then make a solemn declaration that they are free to marry.

After that the man says to the woman: 'I call upon these persons here present to witness that I (full names) do take thee (full names) to be my lawful wedded wife.' Then the woman says the words, substituting 'husband' for 'wife'. It is customary—but not essential —for the man to say the words first. The couple legally become man and wife as soon as both have repeated these vows. The law says nothing about an exchange of wedding rings, but such an exchange may be incorporated into the ceremony at this point.

After the ceremony the registrar enters in the register the date, names, ages, pre-marital status and occupations of the couple, and the names and occupations of their fathers.

The couple then sign the register, the bride using her name before the marriage. The two witnesses and the registrar then sign. A copy of this entry, the marriage certificate, may be obtained from the registrar after the ceremony.

SECOND MARRIAGE There are no restrictions to prevent divorced people from marrying in a register office since it is a civil ceremony with no religious significance.

## Marriage in the Church of England

A clergyman of the Church of England (or Church in Wales) registers the marriage as well as conducting the religious ceremony.

All parishioners have a right to be married in their parish church, or at a different church if they usually worship there. But their names must normally be on the church electoral roll for the parish. To be on this roll it is necessary either to live in the parish or to attend the church regularly.

Instead of going to the registrar for a certificate, the couple usually have banns read in their respective parish churches.

Exceptionally, a clergyman may agree to marry a couple on production of a superintendent registrar's certificate, but in most cases he will conduct all the inquiries to establish their eligibility himself.

The couple fill in forms asking for the banns of marriage to be read, and much the same information must be given as would be required by the superintendent registrar: names, ages (again a birth certificate may be asked for), occupations, and in addition the places and dates of baptism.

The Church of England allows marriage between Anglicans and those of other denominations, but usually insists that a non-Anglican who is not a Christian is first baptised. Register-office marriages and marriages in other denominations are recognised by the Church of England.

THE BANNS If the clergyman does not know the couple, he will usually wish to check the facts given, and it may be seven days before the first banns are read in church. They must be read in both parishes if the couple live in different parishes and also in the church where the wedding is to take place if that is different.

The banns are the equivalent of the notice displayed by the superintendent registrar in his office. They must be read out on three Sundays during the morning service.

The fee for calling the banns is 75p for each church.

When one of the couple lives in a different parish from the one where the wedding is to be held, he or she must get a certificate from the local parish church to show that the banns have been called there. The cost of this certificate is 50p.

The banns can be read at sea if one party is in the Royal Navy.

The text of the banns is as follows: 'I publish the banns of marriage between (name of man and his status—bachelor or widower) of (name of parish) and (name of woman and her status—spinster or widow) of (name of parish). If any of you know cause or just impediment, why these two persons should not be joined together in holy matrimony, ye are to declare it. This is the first (or second or third) time of asking.'

The banns become void if anyone—say a parent—raises a valid objection to the marriage. If no one objects, the clergyman provides a certificate that the banns have been duly called. The marriage may then take place within three months. If it does not, the banns are void, a new application has to be made and new banns will be called.

SECOND MARRIAGE Officially, the Church of England allows divorced people to marry in church only when the other partner of the first marriage is dead.

However, much depends on the clergyman who is to perform the marriage. Many of the clergy now feel that the church should permit a religious ceremony if the person in question was the 'innocent' party in his or her divorce and has been a regular church-goer.

In the Church in Wales, it is never possible for a divorced person to remarry in church.

**Marriage in the Roman Catholic Church**
In addition to the law forbidding closely related people to marry, the Roman Catholic Church does not allow the marriage of first or second cousins without the consent of a bishop. Spiritual relationships are also a bar to Roman Catholic marriage: for example, a godmother may not marry her godson without a bishop's permission.

When a Roman Catholic couple first go to their priest asking to marry, he completes pre-nuptial inquiry forms for each to sign. These require details of parents' names, the place and date of baptism and confirmation, and the place and date of the proposed marriage. The couple have to state that they are free and willing to marry, and give details of any previous marriages.

In some dioceses, checks may then be made in every parish in which either has lived for more than six months since the age of 16, and a 'Letter of Freedom' is obtained stating that no marriage entry concerning the person has been made in a parish register.

The priest will also require a baptism certificate issued within the previous six months in the parish where baptism took place, complete with any amendments, such as confirmation, marriage or annulment.

If one partner is a non-Catholic, the pre-nuptial inquiry will not be completed until the non-Catholic has received instruction in the Catholic doctrine. In addition the non-Catholic will have to assure the priest that he will not prevent any children of the marriage from being brought up in the Catholic faith.

When the priest is satisfied that the couple are free to marry, the banns must be published in the parish or parishes where they live (or in the parish where the Catholic party lives).

The Roman Catholic Church states that the banns must be published on three consecutive days when a large congregation will be present, but many priests now publish the banns on a notice board outside the church instead.

## The cost of getting married

THERE is a set scale of charges for register-office marriages, but for a church wedding fees vary according to the religious denomination and the individual church.

If the minister is not authorised to register marriages, the registrar must attend and will usually charge the same fee as for a register-office wedding. The registrar's fee is £1·50 for attending the marriage and there is a 50p fee for the marriage certificate.

A minister authorised to register marriages will usually charge the same fees, but in addition there will be extra charges depending on the type and grandeur of the wedding. No attendance fee is charged for Jewish or Quaker marriages.

In the Roman Catholic Church there is no charge for the wedding itself if one or both of the couple belong to the congregation, but an offering is made instead.

Apart from these charges, the cost of any extras should also be taken into account. For instance, if an organist is engaged, it will cost about £2. For bell-ringers, a choir, or a soloist, the charges will be subject to an agreement with the church. It is usual also to pay for any floral decorations.

**FEES**

**Registrar's certificate**

| | |
|---|---|
| CERTIFICATE FOR MARRIAGE | |
| If couple live in the same area, the notice fee is | £1 |
| If couple live in different areas, the notice fee is | £2 |
| CERTIFICATE AND LICENCE | |
| Certificate | £1 |
| Licence | £5 |

**Marriage ceremony in register office**

| | |
|---|---|
| Attendance of registrar | £1·50 |
| Marriage certificate (copy of entry into marriage register) | 50p |
| (no other fees) | |

**Marrying in the Church of England or the Church in Wales**

| | |
|---|---|
| Calling the banns in each church | 75p |
| Certificate that banns have been called | 50p |
| or Common Licence | £4·50 |
| or Special Licence | £25 |
| (this is the set fee, but the actual cost of obtaining the licence may be very much higher—as much as £50) | |
| or Registrar's certificate | £1 |
| (rarely used for marrying in the Church of England or Church in Wales) | |

**The wedding in church**

| | |
|---|---|
| Marriage fee | £8 |
| Marriage certificate | 50p |

Occasionally, the bishop will agree to dispense with the publishing of banns if the couple have good reason to make such a request—for instance, to avoid unwanted publicity or to speed up the marriage.

Unlike in a Church of England marriage, banns published in a Roman Catholic church do not dispense with the necessity of giving notice to the superintendent registrar. A superintendent's Certificate for Marriage or Certificate and Licence must be obtained and given to the priest conducting the ceremony, together with the pre-nuptial inquiry form and any other documents giving evidence of the couple's personal history and status.

Some Roman Catholic priests are authorised to register a marriage. If the priest is not authorised, a registrar must attend. The church ceremony now incorporates the State formalities. Two marriage registers must be signed, as in all religious marriages outside the Church of England. One is for the district register office; the other for the church.

A Roman Catholic wishing to marry a non-Catholic in the Catholic faith can do so only with the permission of the bishop of the diocese. Normally church authorities require that Roman Catholics are married only by a Catholic priest in a Roman Catholic church.
SECOND MARRIAGE The Roman Catholic Church generally refuses to marry divorced people unless the former husband or wife is dead. However, it has its own procedure for declaring marriages void and for dissolving those that have not been consummated.

The priest to whom the couple apply will refer the request to a local Roman Catholic tribunal, which requires a marriage to be declared null or to be dissolved by a decree obtained locally or from Rome before either partner can marry again in church. If, however, the previous marriage was not recognised by the Roman Catholic Church, a second marriage will often be allowed by the tribunal.

### Marriage in the Jewish faith
A marriage in the Jewish faith is allowed only if the couple are both Jews.

Each synagogue has a secretary of marriages who is empowered to register marriages between members of the synagogue. He conducts pre-marriage inquiries to ensure that the couple meet certain requirements. If one of the couple, or his or her mother, was born outside the Jewish faith, Orthodox and Reform synagogues may require a conversion certificate issued by a rabbi. The Liberal (or Progressive) Jewish Synagogue accepts as Jewish those brought up in the faith with one

Jewish parent. Notice of the marriage must be given to the superintendent registrar, and his certificate to permit the marriage must be obtained.

In addition, Orthodox Jews must apply for the Chief Rabbi's permission to marry if their synagogue comes within his jurisdiction.

This is usually obtained by the secretary of marriages or the rabbi intending to marry them. He will need to produce the couple's Certificate for Marriage or Certificate and Licence, birth certificates and details of the places and dates of their parents' marriages. The Chief Rabbi will also want to know if their fathers were Cohens, Levites or Israelites.

A Jewish marriage ceremony does not necessarily have to take place in a synagogue—many Jews are married in private houses—and it can be held at any time of the day, although not on Saturdays, Jewish festivals, fasts and periods of 'sephirah' (semi-mourning).

The secretary of marriages, who must be present, records the marriage in the marriage register after the ceremony. The couple, two witnesses and the rabbi sign the Jewish marriage certificate, called a 'ketubah'.
SECOND MARRIAGE In the Jewish faith, Orthodox and Reform (but not Liberal) synagogues insist on a religious bill of divorcement, as well as a civil decree absolute, before remarriage. In addition, an Orthodox Jew descended from the tribe of Cohen may not marry a convert or a divorcee.

### Marriage in the Society of Friends
Although the Society of Friends has no clergy, each group of Friends appoints a registering officer who is permitted by law to make arrangements for marriages within the Society.

Both parties must complete a declaration of intention of marriage, and if either is not a Friend, he or she must complete a second form and produce a reference from two Friends.

The couple must obtain a certificate to permit the marriage from the superintendent registrar who, if either is not a Friend, will require a certificate from the registering officer authorising the marriage under Society rules.

The registering officer announces the forthcoming marriage at the end of a normal meeting of the Friends for worship, and also arranges a special meeting during which the marriage will take place. At this meeting the couple repeat the Society of Friends' marriage vows, and sign a Society marriage certificate which is read out by the registering officer and signed by all Friends present. After the meeting, the civil register is signed and witnessed, as in all marriage ceremonies.

SECOND MARRIAGE Quakers are not forbidden to divorce or to remarry. A second marriage of a divorced person or persons can take place within the Society, but the couple must convince the Friends' meeting that they have serious views on marriage, and they must be regular attenders at Society meetings.

## Marriage in the Free Churches

To marry in a Free Church—Methodist, Congregational, Evangelist, Baptist, Salvationist—either the bride or groom must live within the registration district where the church ceremony is to take place, or be a regular worshipper at that church.

Notice must first be given to the registrar and a Certificate for Marriage or Certificate and Licence obtained as usual.

Most Free Church ministers are authorised to register the marriage after the ceremony, but if the minister is not, a registrar must attend. Before the couple exchange their vows the minister asks if there is any known legal impediment to the marriage. When the service ends, two marriage registers are signed.

Inter-denominational marriages are usually allowed in the Free Churches.

In the Salvation Army, which is organised on a military basis with ministers (both men and women) referred to as officers and ordinary members of the church as soldiers, there is a special stipulation that no officer may marry a soldier. In practice, this means that a soldier and an officer who wish to marry must wait until the soldier has completed his or her training and becomes an officer (a full-time Salvation Army official). In cases where this is impossible, an officer may revert to being an ordinary soldier in order to marry. Otherwise, the Salvation Army procedure for marriage is as in other Free Churches.

SECOND MARRIAGE Most of the Free Churches allow a divorcee to marry in their churches, but the minister must agree. In the Salvation Army, cases of lay members and full-time officers who wish to marry after divorce are dealt with on their merits.

## Marriages in other religions or sects

Couples go through a civil marriage at the register office and then, on production of their marriage certificate to a minister or priest of their faith, have a marriage ceremony in their place of worship or house.

## The law on polygamy

A POLYGAMOUS marriage is one in which a man or woman takes more than one wife or husband. If such a marriage is allowed by the law of the country where both partners are normally domiciled it is generally treated as valid in Britain, and the children are regarded as legitimate. ☐ The law and where you live, p. 320.

A marriage that is only *potentially* polygamous—that is, when the law of the country where both partners normally live would allow the husband or wife to marry again, though neither has done so—is also regarded as valid in Britain.

No marriage contracted in this country can ever be polygamous, however. The second marriage in this country of someone whose own country recognises polygamy is void—even if the ceremony took place in a High Commission or embassy building.

Moreover, even if his or her first marriage was contracted in a country where polygamy is legal, the partner who is already married is guilty of bigamy.

From 1972 the Matrimonial Proceedings (Polygamous Marriages) Act allowed the partners in a polygamous or potentially polygamous marriage to take action in English law to seek a divorce, separation, annulment or maintenance order.

The procedure is exactly the same as for the partners of a monogamous marriage contracted in this country. ☐ Breakdown of marriage, pp. 386–407.

Until 1971, someone who was a party to a marriage that was or had been polygamous was restricted in his or her rights to social security benefits. Only in cases where a marriage had in fact been monogamous at all times were the partners entitled to full benefits, including family allowances and industrial injury benefits.

In 1971, the National Insurance Act gave the Secretary of State for Social Services powers to make special regulations to deal with polygamous marriages. The regulations had not been published in mid-1972, but it was generally expected that they would permit benefits to be paid in full to one wife of a marriage that was actually polygamous.

# For better, for worse

WHEN a couple marry, they have a legal duty to live together, and each must give the other the benefit of company and support—known in law as 'the duty of consortium'. Although this duty forms the legal basis of married life, the law does not set out precisely how each partner must behave. The law cannot force a husband to love or cherish his wife; nor can it force him to return if he leaves her.

In practice, neither party can take the other to court to enforce these duties while they are living together. But when a marriage breaks down, the question of rights and duties becomes very important, as any breach by one partner of the rules as to what is acceptable behaviour in a marriage will give the other certain legal rights—to a separation order or a divorce, for example.

Over many years, these rules of behaviour for husbands and wives have been laid down by divorce court judges, who have had to decide what type of misconduct is sufficient to justify the break up of a marriage.

These rules provide a guide to each partner's rights and duties in a normal marriage—rights and duties which vary according to the means, education, social position, health and other circumstances of the husband and wife.

In a wealthy household, it may be reasonable for the wife to refuse to do chores which could be done by a domestic help, whereas in the ordinary home a wife would not be entitled to insist on such help.

Again, a wife is normally expected to look after the house and the children while the husband provides the family income. But if the husband is chronically sick, the wife may reasonably be expected to earn money in order to support the family.

The law might regard it as reasonable for a wife to expect her husband to spend time with her instead of going drinking every night. But if the husband's absence was caused by his work, her demand for his company might not be regarded as reasonable.

There are no hard and fast rules. Each couple works out for itself its own pattern, and the law will normally not become involved in domestic disputes between husband and wife.

In any case, the law cannot compel one partner to return home or to behave as befits a husband or wife. Until 1970, a husband or wife could bring an action for the 'restitution of conjugal rights' to compel the other partner to resume living together. But this did not prove effective, and was abolished.

## The family home

Because the principal earner in a family has to live near his work, the husband generally has the right to say where the home is to be.

If, however, a wife provides a family's main income—because her husband is chronically sick, perhaps—her choice of a home may legally override her husband's wishes.

If the principal earner, normally the husband, has to move to another area because of his work, his wife cannot claim that she is being deserted if she decides not to go with him. As long as he intends to return or, if the move is more permanent, offers her a home with him and in the meantime continues to support her and the family, he is fulfilling his legal duty of consortium.

On the other hand, if the wife refuses to go with him, the husband may be able to prove that he has been deserted by his wife and that he need no longer support her.

➤ NO DUTY TO LIVE WITH A MOTHER-IN-LAW *After Mr and Mrs Munro's marriage in 1947, the couple went to live in the South of France in a villa owned by Mr Munro's mother. The mother was domineering, and Mr Munro was unemployed and addicted to drink. In March 1948, Mrs Munro left her husband and went to live in London. She felt that she was unable to reform her husband and she believed that his mother was a bad influence on him.*

*In May 1948, Mr Munro visited her in London, but he refused to resume cohabitation there with her. He suggested that she should return to the villa. Mrs Munro was not prepared to do this, although she was willing to make a home for her husband provided it did not involve living with his mother.*

*In 1950, Mrs Munro petitioned for the restitution of conjugal rights, and a restitution* order was served on her husband. Mr Munro appeals against this decision. His lawyer argued that, for the order to be well founded, the facts must show that the husband had withdrawn from cohabitation.

He claimed that, in this case, the wife had deserted her husband and therefore she was not entitled to a decree.

DECISION Mr Munro's appeal was dismissed, since his offer of a home in the villa was one which it was reasonable for his wife to refuse. She was entitled to ask her husband to provide a reasonable home away from her mother-in-law, which he could and should have done. Mrs Munro wanted to reform her husband, to get him to work and make a home for them both. She had every right to an order for the restitution of conjugal rights. (Munro v. Munro.) ◄

Where both husband and wife work, and the wife has a successful career which would suffer if she had to move, a court would be unlikely to decide that she had to follow her husband to another part of the country.

➤ A WIFE'S RIGHT TO KEEP HER HOME Mr King was 73 and retired, and his second wife 37 when they married in 1937. Both had homes in the same neighbourhood in Cornwall, but one of Mrs King's conditions of marriage was that they should live in her bungalow.

She insisted on this because she earned her living there by taking in guests, keeping cows and selling fruit and flowers. Mr King had not undertaken to provide for his wife either after the marriage or in his will.

After living with his wife for a few months, Mr King returned to his home and insisted that Mrs King go with him. She refused and he filed a petition for the dissolution of the marriage on the grounds of desertion.

Mrs King filed a cross-petition denying desertion and asking for dissolution of the marriage because of her husband's desertion.

## The law and where you live

EVERYONE is subject to the laws of the particular country in which they have their domicile—which is usually, but not always, where they live. At birth, a child automatically acquires the domicile of his parents.

On reaching the age of 18 everyone, except a married woman, can acquire a new domicile by settling in a new country with the intention of living there permanently.

By law, a wife takes the domicile of her husband. Even if a wife lives in a different country from her husband, she is still considered to be domiciled in whichever country he chooses to live in permanently. A wife cannot change her domicile unless the marriage has been ended by death or divorce.

If, for example, a husband deserts his wife and goes to live in Australia permanently, his wife is also considered to have Australian domicile, even though she decides to remain in the United Kingdom.

As soon as she is divorced, however, if she is living in England she automatically recovers her English domicile.

Domicile governs a variety of questions relating to family problems, such as the right to marry, legitimacy of children, and distribution of property on death. For example, although a person domiciled in England cannot marry under the age of 16, if the couple are domiciled in a country where the age limit is 15, their marriage would be valid in England.

Domicile is important in marriage if the marriage involves more than one system of law —for instance, if the partners are of different nationalities; or if one or both have lived, married or owned property in a country with a different legal system; or if they have lived in different countries and now want to get divorced. The main effect is not on the everyday problems of marriage, but on what happens when legal proceedings are taken.

The intention of permanent residence is important. If a man domiciled in England took a job in, say, Italy, there would be no change of domicile if he intended to retire to England, no matter how long he stayed in Italy. On the other hand, he would acquire a new domicile if he had intended to settle in Italy for good— even if he changed his mind after ten years.

No one can have a British domicile—he will be domiciled in Scotland, Northern Ireland or England and Wales. This is because England (with Wales), Scotland and Northern Ireland each has its own legal system. Similarly, there is no such thing as a domicile in the U.S.A., since each State has its own laws.

In most countries there is one system of law only; but where there are different systems each confers its own domicile.

DECISION *The court ruled in Mrs King's favour. It found she had good cause for refusing to leave her bungalow and that Mr King was guilty of desertion.*

*In view of Mrs King's economic dependence on living in her bungalow and the arrangement reached before the marriage, she had not acted unreasonably. (King v. King.)*◄

A wife would be entitled to refuse to go with her husband if she could show that her health would suffer or if the move would have a serious effect on her children's education.

►THE MOTHER WHO REFUSED TO MOVE *Mr Dunn returned to live in England in 1941 after four years in the Navy. He visited his wife twice at their home in Morpeth, Northumberland, but quarrels arose over money and the couple did not live together after 1941.*

*After that Mr Dunn was stationed at various places in England and several times asked his wife to go and stay with him for indefinite periods. She refused because her acute deafness made her unhappy with strangers and also because her son had just started work in Morpeth.*

*Mr Dunn petitioned for divorce on the grounds of his wife's desertion and asked the discretion of the court in respect of his adultery.*

DECISION *The judge accepted the wife's evidence and held that in the circumstances she did not desert her husband and was justified in the course she took.*

*The husband appealed unsuccessfully against the trial judge's decision. (Dunn v. Dunn.)*◄

Occasionally, a married couple may sign a legal agreement about where they are to live. If one partner breaks the agreement, the other can claim desertion—but only if the circumstances have not changed.

If, for example, the wife had agreed to live in Paris but later had a child allergic to that city's water, she would have the backing of the law in deciding to move away from Paris.

## Nationality
When a woman who is not a citizen of the United Kingdom and Colonies (abbreviated below to U.K. citizen) marries a man who is a citizen, she does not automatically become a U.K. citizen. But she is entitled to acquire that status by registration. She has to apply to the Nationality Division of the Home Office, Tolworth Tower, Surbiton, Surrey KT6 7DS.

A man who marries a United Kingdom citizen cannot become a U.K. citizen himself simply by registration on the strength of his wife's citizenship. He has to apply in the normal way for naturalisation if he is an alien, or registration if a Commonwealth citizen or citizen of the Republic of Ireland. ☐ Newcomers to the United Kingdom, p. 383.

A United Kingdom citizen who marries a foreigner does not automatically lose United Kingdom citizenship; but it can be given up by applying to the Home Office. There is no law in the United Kingdom forbidding dual nationality. But anyone holding two nationalities may be compelled by the laws of the other country to make a choice.

## Sex in marriage
Part of the law of consortium is that each partner has the right to reasonable sexual relations with the other. But the law gives no precise definition of what is 'reasonable'; it can rule only on what seem to be extreme cases.

Where sexual intercourse has never taken place, the marriage is null and void on the grounds of non-consummation, and either partner may sue for its legal dissolution. ☐ Ending a void marriage, p. 393.

In normal cases, where sexual relations take place but one partner refuses to have intercourse as often as the other would like, the situation is more complicated. Both the refusal to have intercourse and excessive demands for sexual relations have been successful grounds for divorce.

A husband cannot force his wife to have intercourse if she refuses. If he does so he could be accused of rape, though this is extremely rare. Such an incident would be more likely to be used as a ground for divorce.

Similarly, contraception is a matter for agreement between the marriage partners. A woman might be able to claim that her husband was being cruel—and so breaking up the marriage—if he invariably insisted on taking contraceptive precautions, despite her desire for children or the demands of her religion which forbade contraception.

On the other hand, it is unlikely that the husband would be at fault if he were taking precautions only because he reasonably thought they had enough children, that they could not afford more, or that the wife's health might be in danger if she had more.

In all these cases, the same would apply if it were the wife, instead of the husband, who chose to use contraceptives.

## Marriage secrets
In most marriages, both partners know a great deal more about each other than either might want anyone else to find out. In law,

husband and wife must each respect the other's confidence. If, for example, a wife has been told something by her husband in confidence, she must not divulge it to anyone.

Even if her husband were on trial, she could claim the right not to give evidence in court about what she had learnt from him in confidence.

This duty to keep marriage secrets continues even after the marriage has been ended by divorce.

▶ SECRETS BETWEEN HUSBAND AND WIFE *Margaret, Duchess of Argyll, was the third wife of the Duke. They married in March 1951 and were divorced, on the grounds of the Duchess's adultery, in March 1963. The Duchess had been married once before and both had children by previous marriages.*

*In 1964, the Duchess brought an action to restrain the Duke, the Editor of* The People, *and the proprietors of the newspaper from publishing articles which she claimed were in breach of marital confidence, involved earlier court actions and proceedings, and included evidence given at the hearing of the Duke's divorce petition at the Scottish Court of Session.*
DECISION *The judge granted an injunction restraining publication of secrets relating to the Duchess's private life, personal affairs or private conduct during her marriage. The court considered that confidential communication between husband and wife must be protected.*

*In this case, it ruled, publication of some of the passages complained of in the Duke's articles would be a breach of marital confidence.*

*The court also ruled that the Duchess's adultery did not nullify her right to the court's protection, nor did the fact that she had published articles of her own.*

*The protection did not apply only to the Duke, said the court, but also to persons into whose hands the confidences might come. Accordingly, an injunction was also granted against the Editor of* The People *and the proprietors of the newspaper. (*Argyll *v.* Argyll, The People *newspaper and its Editor.*) ◄

## Crime

A husband or wife can be prosecuted if either commits a crime against the other partner. The husband who steals from his wife, and the wife who attacks and injures her husband are just as guilty as if they had committed the crimes against any other person.

There is one situation in which the law regards husband and wife as one person: where the charge is one of conspiracy to commit a crime. No couple can be prosecuted for conspiring together, although either or both could be charged with conspiring with someone else.

In court, one marriage partner can be compelled to give evidence against the other only where a husband is accused of a crime against his wife, or *vice versa*.

In all other cases the partners can choose whether or not to give evidence against one another. A wife, for example, has the right to give evidence against her husband when he is charged with sexual offences against young children, though she cannot be forced to do so.

In all cases, one partner can give evidence in court in support of the other.

## Suing each other

Although, in some cases, the law treats husband and wife as one person, there are instances when they can sue each other.

This can be a valuable right—for example, if a wife is injured in a car crash caused by her husband's driving. It gives her a means of claiming against her husband's insurance by suing him for damages.

Other more trivial actions are likely to be dismissed by the courts. Judges and magistrates are unwilling to allow court time to be spent on actions based largely on vindictiveness, such as a husband claiming damages for golf clubs destroyed by his wife, or a wife claiming for a dress torn by her husband.

## Suing other people

Husbands—but not wives—have the right to sue outsiders for injuries to their partner if those injuries result in their losing their rights of consortium. It is possible, for example, for a husband to sue a car driver for the loss of his wife's services while she is in hospital after an accident caused by the driver.

The loss of a wife's services does not normally lead to heavy damages: loss of consortium would not usually result in an award of more than a few hundred pounds.

On the other hand, the husband can claim for any actual financial loss or expenditure resulting from injury to his wife. If, say, a wife were so badly injured that she had to spend the rest of her life in hospital, the husband would be able to claim a substantial sum from the person responsible.

It would be for the court to decide the amount that should be awarded to cover specific items such as medical expenses and the cost of employing a housekeeper, together with the amount due on more general grounds, such as the husband's grief and the loss of his wife's company.

# For richer, for poorer

A HUSBAND has a legal obligation to provide for his wife according to his social and financial position. Normally, for example, he is expected to provide her with at least a home and enough money to pay for groceries, clothes for herself and the children, and all necessary household goods.

The wife, on the other hand, has a duty to help conserve her husband's property. Her financial demands should not exceed what he can meet. Normally, for example, she is not entitled to spend his money on luxuries, such as expensive jewellery, without his consent.

Although a husband is under a common law duty to support his wife, a wife has no legal means of forcing her husband to give her more money as long as she continues to live with him. But a court might find that her husband's failure to provide adequate support had caused the breakdown of the marriage, thus providing grounds for divorce.

## The husband's credit

The law places a strict limit on the use a wife can make of her husband's credit. In her capacity as housekeeper, the law says that, if she is living with him, she has her husband's authority to commit him to pay only for 'necessaries' for the family.

'Necessaries' include adequate food, clothing, domestic articles, and the repair of domestic appliances or even of the house itself.

The only way the husband can avoid paying is by proving that he told the tradesman not to give his wife credit or that he gave his wife a large enough allowance to make it unnecessary.

If the husband has, in the past, paid certain bills, the tradesman is entitled to assume that the husband will continue to pay until specifically told by letter that he will not. If the husband merely puts an advertisement in the newspaper saying that his wife can no longer pledge his credit, he will still have to pay the housekeeping bills—unless he can prove that the tradesman has read the advertisement.

## How a wife can claim maintenance

A wife who is not being properly maintained and decides to enforce her legal rights has two choices: she can start proceedings for divorce, where grounds for this exist; or she can apply to the magistrates' court for a maintenance order against her husband. But the order cannot be enforced until she actually leaves. ☐ Four ways to separate, p. 388.

Moreover, a wife living with her husband has no legal right to know what her husband is earning, and she is therefore unable to know whether she is getting a fair share of the family resources for running the home.

## Ownership of property

When a couple marry, each retains his or her property, and the wife can go on acquiring new property after the marriage without her husband having any right to it.

Complications arise, however, when the husband and wife begin to use their own property to acquire new possessions for their common use. For example, the wife's building society deposit may be used to buy a house towards which the husband also makes a contribution and for which he takes on the mortgage repayments.

The question of 'who owns what' rarely crops up when the husband and wife are living together, but it becomes highly significant when the marriage breaks down.

In general, even if one of them has contributed much less than the other, both are often held to own an equal share of any property. This applies to the house, and to all jointly purchased property such as cars, television sets, washing machines and refrigerators. ☐ After the divorce, p. 406.

This situation contrasts with that of two people who are not married and who buy property by contributing unequal shares to the purchase price. In a dispute, each would normally be entitled to a share in the property proportionate to his or her contribution towards the purchase price.

Housekeeping money belongs to the husband; he provides it for the specific purpose of maintaining the home. If the wife manages to save from the money, both husband and wife have an equal right to the savings, and to the goods bought with them. If the wife buys herself a car out of the savings, she and her husband have an equal claim to it.

# Having a baby

*Making arrangements*
*The right of the father to attend the birth*
*Welfare and financial help*

*Childbirth benefits*
*Registering the birth*
*Claiming family allowance*

BECAUSE maternity hospital beds are scarce in some parts of the country, not every woman can choose to have her baby in a National Health Service hospital. A mother-to-be has no automatic right under the Health Service to go into hospital, but she will normally be admitted if the doctor thinks it necessary for medical reasons, or if her home is unsuitable. It is also common to go into hospital for the first baby or when more than one baby is expected.

The hospital accommodation and specialist services under the Health Service are free; but in some hospitals there are a few small wards, with additional privacy, which are available for a small charge.

A woman who cannot book a place in a Health Service maternity ward because she does not qualify on medical grounds, may be able to pay for private medical care and accommodation during childbirth.

Members of private health insurance schemes cannot usually reclaim the cost under the scheme. But they may be able to do so if the expense is due to 'an abnormality of maternity'—a Caesarean operation, for example.

**Making arrangements**
If the birth is to be at home, the family doctor usually recommends a local authority midwife or attends the mother at the birth himself. He may, alternatively, put her in the care of another general practitioner who specialises in maternity cases.

The doctor or the midwife arranges for all ante-natal and post-natal examinations to be carried out at a local authority clinic or performs them himself or herself.

It may be necessary for the mother to go into hospital at the last minute if extreme complications develop during a home confinement. If the birth is premature, the doctor arranges for an ambulance with an incubator to take the mother and baby to hospital. In an emergency the midwife can organise the move to hospital.

The local authority home help service is available to help the mother before and after the child's birth. This may be provided free, but most authorities make an hourly charge which may be based on the family's financial circumstances. ☐ National Health Service home helps, p. 293.

**The right of the father to attend the birth**
Many hospitals allow husbands to be present during a birth, but the father has no legal right to insist on being there.

The husband must accept that the hospital staff allow him to stay because it may help his wife. If the birth becomes difficult, he may be asked to leave.

If the husband refuses to leave a hospital, the authorities have power to remove him, using any necessary force. In a home confinement, the doctor or midwife has no similar right to get the father removed, but would have to rely on persuasion.

A pregnant woman who wants her husband to attend the birth should tell her doctor. He will be able to say whether the consultant, hospital or midwife approve. If not, he may be able to arrange for the delivery to be made by staff more sympathetic to the request.

**The best time for a family**
Family planning is rarely based on tax considerations, but there is an advantage in having a child born as late as possible in the tax year, which ends on April 5. The taxpayer is entitled to a full year's tax allowance for the child, irrespective of when in the year it was born. The later the birth, the fewer the expenses to set against the tax allowance.

**Twins insurance**
A family with a history of twins should consider twins insurance, which must be taken out before the end of the fourth month of the pregnancy. The premium depends on the insurance company's estimate of how likely it is that twins will be born. Many insurance companies do not issue a policy if a woman has been having treatment to increase fertility.

**Welfare and financial help**
A wide range of benefits is available to a pregnant woman, a mother, and her children. Neither the pregnant woman nor the father needs to have paid contributions to qualify for

many of the benefits, since they are provided under the National Health Service.

All medical services are free. Welfare foods are available at a subsidised price and, in certain circumstances, may be obtained free.

MEDICAL BENEFITS In addition to the free services of the doctor, consultant, midwife, health visitor and hospital, a pregnant woman also gets free prescriptions from the time her pregnancy is confirmed until one year after the baby is born.

Dental treatment is free during pregnancy and for a year afterwards. This includes the provision of dentures. Dental and prescription concessions end immediately if the woman has a miscarriage.

FREE MILK An expectant mother from a family which has a fairly low income, or is receiving family income supplement or supplementary benefit, is entitled to one free pint of milk a day. She is also entitled to one free pint a day for each child under five.

In families which do not qualify on income grounds, an expectant mother is entitled to one free pint of milk a day if she already has two children under five. She is also entitled to one free pint a day for each further child under five.

A physically or mentally handicapped child aged five or over up to and including 16 who is not attending an educational establishment is also entitled to free milk, regardless of the family income.

Leaflet W11, *Your right to free welfare milk and foods*, obtainable from post offices and clinics, explains how to claim free milk and gives details of the current income limits for those claiming on income grounds.

A family entitled to free milk receives a book of tokens which can be used to obtain either fresh milk or National Dried Milk.

If a child receiving free milk enters hospital or goes to live with someone else, the token book should be passed on with the child. An expectant mother should also take her token book with her if she goes into hospital.

Entitlement ceases if the child moves abroad or dies. In either of these cases, outstanding tokens should be returned to the Social Security office. This also applies when a woman has a miscarriage, though some tokens may be allowed for her to use during her convalescent period.

After the birth, if the mother is not breast feeding, she may use the token book to obtain one free 20 oz. pack of National Dried milk for her child each week. When dried milk is being given to a child under a year old, the mother can claim additional tokens at the local Social Security office for an extra 21 packs a year.

OTHER WELFARE CONCESSIONS In addition to milk, vitamin drops and tablets containing vitamins A, C and D are available free to any family with an expectant mother or a child under five if the family qualifies for free milk on income grounds, or is receiving supplementary benefit or family income supplement. Orange juice is no longer supplied, because of the dental hazard.

### Childbirth benefits

Two forms of benefit are paid for childbirth: a lump sum called a maternity grant, and a weekly benefit called a maternity allowance.

MATERNITY GRANT Most mothers qualify for the cash grant. The detailed qualifications relate to the contribution year and benefit year. ☐ The National Insurance scheme: what the terms mean, p. 605.

There are two ways in which a woman can qualify. In the first, she (or her husband) must have:

1. Paid 26 or more contributions between the time of entering insurance and the week in which the baby is expected, or is born.
2. And paid or had credited 26 or more contributions for the last contribution year before the benefit year in which the baby is born (or the contribution week in which the baby is due).

Alternatively, a woman may qualify for the grant if she (not her husband) has paid 26 full, flat-rate contributions in the 52 weeks immediately preceding the thirteenth week before the date on which the baby is due.

An unmarried mother, however, cannot claim on any insurance payments made by the man she claims to be the father, even if he admits paternity.

If a woman has opted out of paying full flat-rate insurance contributions, any contributions paid by her employer cannot be counted.

A maternity grant is payable if the child is still-born, provided that the pregnancy lasted for at least 28 weeks. When more than one child is born, an additional grant will be paid for each subsequent child which lives for 12 hours or more.

Maternity grants are paid in addition to other National Insurance benefits.

HOW TO CLAIM A maternity grant may be claimed at any time in the nine weeks before the expected date of birth or up to three months after the birth.

Any claim made more than three months after the birth may be disallowed unless there are valid reasons for the delay. If the delay is more than a year, the application is automatically refused. The claims should be made on Form BM4, which can be obtained from any Social Security office or child welfare clinic run by the local authority.

Return it to the local Social Security office with a certificate from the doctor or midwife (Mat B1 before the birth, Mat B2 afterwards), or the baby's birth certificate.

MATERNITY ALLOWANCE Mothers who do not go out to work do not qualify for the maternity allowance. The allowance is paid only to women who have been working and paying full flat-rate National Insurance contributions in the year ending 13 weeks before the baby is born. This year is known as the test period.

To qualify for any part of the allowance, a mother must have paid 26 full flat-rate insurance contributions as an employed or self-employed person in the test period.

To qualify for the full allowance, a woman must have 50 contributions paid by or credited to her in the test period. If a woman has less than 50 flat-rate contributions in the test period—but at least 26—she is entitled to a proportion of the full allowance.

Only a woman's contributions are taken into account. No allowance can be paid on the basis of any contributions made by the husband.

Contributions at less than the full flat-rate normally do not count. Contributions paid as a non-employed person do not count in the first 26 payments, but can count after that towards the total of 50, provided that the woman has paid or been credited with at least 39 contributions as an employed or self-employed person.

HOW TO CLAIM The allowance should be claimed on Form BM4, as for the maternity grant, between the fourteenth and eleventh week before the baby is expected. It is

## How childbirth benefits are paid

| | MATERNITY GRANT | MATERNITY ALLOWANCE |
|---|---|---|
| To whom payable | The mother; payable from nine weeks before confinement or for still-birth if pregnancy lasted at least 28 weeks | The mother—if she has been employed and has paid at least 26 insurance contributions in the year ending 13 weeks before the birth |
| Depends on the insurance of | Woman or husband. For an unmarried woman the insurance of the child's father does not count | Woman |
| When to claim | From nine weeks before, until three months after confinement | At least 11 weeks before expected date of birth* |
| Duration | Lump-sum payment | 18 weeks—from 11th week before expected week of birth |
| Disqualifications | None | 1. Receiving other benefit of a greater amount 2. Working in allowance period 3. Breaking rules of behaviour (e.g. refusing medical examination) |
| Increases for dependants Child | None | Yes |
| Adult | None | Yes, in exceptional cases |

*In the case of a premature birth more than 11 weeks before the expected time of confinement, the payments can be back-dated and the full 18 payments made up after the birth. The full number of payments are also safeguarded in a premature birth between 11 weeks and the expected date

important to claim at this time, as benefits are not usually paid in arrears.

If the claim is made after the birth, no benefits are paid for the time before the birth and the mother is paid only until the child is seven weeks old, unless the birth was earlier than expected. Delay in applying can result in loss of benefits unless it can be shown there was a special reason for the late claim. For example, a single woman expecting a child may have been ill and unable to apply at the right time.

EARLY OR LATE BIRTHS When the birth is premature, the allowance is paid in full, as if the birth took place on the expected day.

If the birth is late, the allowance is paid for six weeks after the birth, provided the mother informs the local Social Security office.

If an application is refused, there is provision for an appeal to the local National Insurance tribunal. ☐ Appearing before a tribunal, p. 735.

HOW THE ALLOWANCE IS PAID Maternity allowance is paid to the mother by weekly orders, issued in book form, which may be cashed at a post office. If the orders are not cashed within three months of the date on them, they will be replaced; but if they are left for a year or more, the benefit will be lost.

DISQUALIFICATIONS A woman is not entitled to maternity allowance for any week in which she does paid work. If she draws benefit for unemployment, sickness, injury, or as a widow, she will be paid whichever benefit is the larger, but not both.

She may be disqualified completely if she breaks the rules of behaviour—for example, by refusing to have a medical examination.

INCREASES FOR DEPENDANTS In some circumstances, the amount of benefit paid may be increased, to take account of the dependants of a pregnant woman. A husband incapable of supporting himself through mental or physical infirmity would qualify. So would a close relative who is living with and dependent on a pregnant woman.

Forms for making the claims, as well as advice on any particular question, can be obtained from all local Social Security offices.

## Notifying the health authorities

When a child is born, the local health authorities must be notified. This is usually done by the doctor or midwife. Written notice must be given to the medical officer of health for the area within 36 hours of a birth.

Although usually performed by the doctor or midwife, the duty to notify legally falls on the father, if he was living on the premises where the birth took place, or on anyone who attended the mother at the birth.

If the birth took place at home, the father should make sure that the midwife or doctor is making the notification.

PENALTY Failure to notify a birth is punishable by a fine of up to £1, unless the court is satisfied that the person being prosecuted reasonably thought that someone else had notified the health authorities.

## Registering the birth

The parents of a child born in England or Wales are legally obliged to give the local registrar of births and deaths details of the birth within 42 days.

Even a still-birth—where a child is born dead after at least 28 weeks of pregnancy—must be registered as a birth. The death of a child after birth is registered as a death. ☐ What to do when someone dies, p. 408.

If the child is legitimate, either the father or the mother may give the details of birth to the registrar. If the parents are dead or unable to register the birth personally, it must be done by the occupier of the house in which the child was born, by anyone present at the birth, or by anyone having charge of the child. Any of these people may be required by the registrar to visit his office.

REGISTERING AN ILLEGITIMATE CHILD Registration of an illegitimate child is basically the same as for a legitimate child, except that the duty to register does not fall on the father. In practice, in nearly a quarter of illegitimate births, the father does register the birth. If the mother is unable to register the birth, the duty passes to the same people as in the case of a legitimate birth. ☐ The unmarried mother and her child, p. 330.

FEES AND PENALTIES If the birth is registered within 42 days, no fee is charged. The registrar can order the informants to come to his office to make the registration and, if they do not come, he can prosecute them. The maximum fine is £2.

If the birth is not registered within three months, the qualified informants must pay a small fee and the register entry will be witnessed by the superintendent registrar as well as the registrar for the district. After a year, the fee is doubled and the written authority of the Registrar General is needed.

If the informants are unable to register the birth at the registrar's office, they may apply for the birth to be registered at their home. A small fee is charged.

Some registrars also regularly visit maternity hospitals in their district to register births.

INFORMATION THE REGISTRAR NEEDS
Parents or the person required to register a
birth must tell the registrar:
1. The date and place of birth.
2. The name, surname and occupation of the
father. If the child is illegitimate, this will
only be included at the request of both parents.
3. The name, surname and maiden name of
the mother.
4. The sex of the child.
5. The child's name or names. The child can
be registered without a name and the name
can be added later if a certificate of baptism is
produced. Both the informant and the
registrar have to sign the amendment.

If the child is still-born, the particulars to be
supplied are the same except that no name is
needed, and evidence explaining the child's
death must be given to the registrar.

### The birth certificate

A full birth certificate can be obtained from
the registrar at the time of registration for a
fee of 50p. An alternative, shortened form
of the certificate is available free. This short
form omits all details of parentage and gives
simply the Christian names or forenames and
surname of the child, his or her sex, and the
date and place of birth.

Both types of certificate can be obtained for
a fee after registration by applying to the local
registrar or to the General Register Office at
Somerset House, Strand, London WC2R 1LB.

Anyone is entitled to ask to look for any
birth, marriage or death certificate at the local
register office or Somerset House. A small
search fee is charged. Certified copies of any
register entries are also available on request.

### Naming the baby

A child usually takes the father's surname. It
can, however, be registered in its mother's
name—for example, if she is a celebrity or a
show-business personality, or if the child is
illegitimate. Often the parents choose the
child's forename or Christian name or names
long before it is born and give these when
registering the baby. But they can have
second thoughts and change the child's name
after registering, provided they do so within
12 months of the registration.

When the baby is not to be baptised, the
parents who want to change a forename in this
way apply to any registrar for a 'certificate of
name given not in baptism'. On this form they
insert the ·date of the child's birth and
registration, their names and the name or
names they want the baby to have. Then they
return the form to the registrar where the birth

was registered, within 12 months of the
registration of the birth.

When the baby is to be baptised, the parents
can get the Christian name changed by having
the child baptised with a different name or an
additional name to the one in the register.
They must fill in a 'certificate of name given
in baptism'. The clergyman who baptised the
child, or whoever normally issues the church's
certificate of baptism, completes the form and
the parents return it to the registrar who
registered the birth. He will amend the entry.
This can be done only if the baptism took
place within 12 months of the first registration.
Once the child has been baptised, a different
procedure has to be followed. □ Changing
your name, p. 366.

### Claiming family allowance

When a child is born, the mother may become
eligible for family allowance—a weekly benefit
paid through the post office.

Family allowances are paid for every child
who is eligible after the first. Those eligible
are children under school-leaving age and
youngsters under 19 receiving full-time education, or in a low-paid apprenticeship.

The allowance is paid for step-children,
adopted children, or a child being maintained
or fostered—unless the natural parents are
paying at least 90p a week for the child's
maintenance. In that case, the natural parents
may be able to claim the allowance.

The allowance can be claimed for a child in
hospital, at boarding school, or visiting friends
or relatives for less than 12 weeks.

Claims cannot normally be made for a child
committed to the care of a local authority by
court order, or over whom a local authority
has assumed parental rights—even though the
parents may be contributing more than 90p
a week to keep him.

No allowance can be claimed for a child
where a guardian's allowance is being paid.

Illegitimate children are treated as belonging to the mother rather than to the father. No
allowance would be paid where a man was
living with a woman who was not his wife and
they had two children under 16—one the
legitimate child of his broken marriage, the
other the woman's illegitimate child. This
would count as two families of one child each.

When the husband and wife are living
together, the family allowance belongs to the
wife, but the husband can draw it. If they are
separated, the allowance belongs to whichever
parent has custody of the child, or is contributing at least 90p a week towards its
maintenance. If both parents are eligible, and

cannot agree which is to draw the allowance, the Secretary of State for Social Services makes the decision.

RESIDENCE To qualify for family allowance, a husband or wife, born in the United Kingdom, must have lived in the U.K. for at least 26 weeks of the previous year.

Anyone from any other country must have lived in Britain for 26 weeks of the previous year and at least 156 weeks in the previous four years (52 weeks in the last two years in the case of a British subject or protected person).

There are less stringent residence conditions for people coming from certain European and Commonwealth countries. Similar concessions are granted to British residents on an extended visit to these countries. Details are given in leaflets FAM 32, *Families entering Great Britain*, and FAM 32A, *Families leaving Great Britain*, obtainable from the local Social Security office.

HOW TO CLAIM When a family has more than one child within the specified age limits, the allowance should be claimed for all of them except the eldest. The form for making a claim may be obtained at any post office. Send it to the local Social Security office. Disputes over eligibility are settled by the local National Insurance tribunal.

HOW IT IS PAID The family allowance is paid weekly at a named post office. It is liable to income tax and has to be included on the husband's tax return. The weekly orders, payable on Tuesdays, are valid for six months.

WHEN TOO MUCH IS PAID If, by mistake, too much family allowance is paid, no repayment need be made—provided the overpayment is not the result of carelessness on the part of the recipient and there has been no fraud or deliberate attempt to receive the extra money. If the Social Security authorities find that a family knew that it was receiving more than it should, they will demand repayment from the husband.

## Nationality of children

CHILDREN take the nationality of their parents or of the place where they were born or, sometimes, of both. A child born in the United Kingdom or one of its colonies is automatically a citizen of the United Kingdom and Colonies (abbreviated here to 'United Kingdom citizen'). But this does not apply to the children of foreign diplomats.

Children born on a ship, aircraft or hovercraft registered in the U.K. and Colonies are considered to have been born within the U.K. and Colonies.

For example, if a child were born on a BOAC flight over the Atlantic he would be a United Kingdom citizen. If he were born on a similar trip but on a Pan-American aircraft he would not be one, unless his father was a United Kingdom citizen.

Legitimate children born outside the U.K. and Colonies to fathers who are United Kingdom citizens are also classified as United Kingdom citizens.

But if the father was also born outside the U.K. and Colonies and is a United Kingdom citizen only because *his* father was one, the child does not qualify unless:

1. The child or his father was born in a Protectorate, Protected State, Mandated or Trust Territory. Or they were born in any place in a foreign country over which the Crown has or had jurisdiction at the time of the child's or the father's birth.

2. The child's birth is registered at a U.K. consulate abroad, normally within a year.

3. The father is, at the time of the birth, in the service of the Crown.

Illegitimate children born abroad to mothers who are United Kingdom citizens do not automatically take the nationality of their mother. But they can, in certain circumstances, be registered as citizens. If the father is a U.K. citizen and the parents later marry, the children normally take their father's nationality.

Any citizen of the U.K. and Colonies, or of one of the self-governing Commonwealth countries, is also a British subject or Commonwealth citizen.

There are two ways, apart from birth, of obtaining United Kingdom citizenship—naturalisation (for aliens) and registration (for Commonwealth citizens). If parents become naturalised citizens, this does not automatically make their children U.K. citizens, although the Home Secretary can, and normally does, register the children as citizens. ☐ Newcomers to the United Kingdom, p. 383.

A United Kingdom citizen can hold citizenship of another country if that country permits it. A person can renounce United Kingdom citizenship after the age of 18.

# The unmarried mother and her child

AN unmarried woman who becomes pregnant is entitled to the same ante-natal care as a pregnant married woman. But she can claim maternity benefit only on her own National Insurance payments, not on those of the man she claims to be the father, even though he may admit paternity. □ Having a baby, p. 324.

The unmarried mother may need extra help, especially if the father of her child is not prepared to support her. One source of advice is the National Council for the Unmarried Mother and Her Child, 255 Kentish Town Road, London NW5 2LX, which provides information about all aspects of the problem.

During pregnancy, the unmarried mother may decide what she intends doing with the baby after it is born—whether she wants to bring up the child herself, place it in a foster home, or have it adopted.

A mother cannot legally sign a form agreeing to have her baby adopted until it is six weeks old, and the adoption does not become final until the couple adopting the child have had it in their care for at least three months. □ How to adopt a child, p. 336.

## Registering the birth

All births in England and Wales, including those of illegitimate children, must be registered with the Registrar of Births and Deaths for the district in which the child is born. If a child is illegitimate, the information has to be given to the registrar by the mother or by the occupier of the house in which the child was born, or by anyone present at the birth or anyone having charge of the child.

The birth of an illegitimate child can be registered in the name of the mother only, or in the names of the mother and the father if they both sign the register. Even if the father does not sign, his name can be registered if he completes a statutory declaration that he is the father of the child. Forms for these declarations can be had from any local registrar's office. The registrar can also allow a birth to

## When a wife gives birth to an illegitimate child

IF a married woman has a child by someone other than her husband, that child will be technically illegitimate. When registering the birth, the mother has three choices:
**1.** She can register the child in her own name without mentioning the father.
**2.** She can register the child with the consent and participation of the true father, in which case it can be given either her surname or that of the father.
**3.** She can act as if her husband were the father of the child and register the birth as legitimate, if her husband consents.

The child will be regarded as legitimate if the mother is married unless there is strong evidence to the contrary, such as her husband's impotence or his absence from home at the time conception must have taken place.

Even a child who is registered as illegitimate can later be declared legitimate by, say, a divorce court. A married woman who has a child by another man and later goes to live with him may want to re-register the child.

If the child has been registered as the legitimate son of her husband, he cannot be re-registered in the name of his true father—even though she decides to divorce her husband and marry the father. On the other hand, if she has registered the child as illegitimate, he can be re-registered as legitimate after she marries the father.

The woman's former husband, though not the father of the child, has all the normal rights and duties of a father if the child was registered as legitimate.

He can have the child educated in a way that may be unacceptable to both the mother and her new husband. He may even be required in law to maintain the child, unless he can produce evidence that he was not the father.

be subsequently re-registered in the same way, to show the father's name, if the first registration showed only that of the mother.

A child born to unmarried parents becomes legitimate as soon as they marry, whether the birth was initially registered in the names of both parents or only in the name of the mother. Within three months of the marriage, the parents must inform the Registrar General of Births, and the child must be re-registered as legitimate. If they fail to do so, they may be fined £2; but such failure does not prevent the child from becoming legitimate.

## Claiming benefits
An unmarried mother can claim the same maternity grant and allowance as a married mother—provided she has the necessary National Insurance contribution qualifications. ☐ Having a baby, p. 324.

She can also claim support for herself and her child from the local Social Security office. ☐ State help in hardship, p. 550.

## Getting financial help
A mother choosing to bring up an illegitimate child herself is responsible for maintaining the child until the age of 16. If she wishes to get financial help from the father, she must instruct a solicitor to draw up a legal contract with him or get a court order, called an affiliation order, against him.

A private agreement between the father and the mother, in which he agrees to support the child, can be enforced by the courts like any other contract—provided both parties intended that it should be legally binding.

Even if the father is paying regularly under a private agreement, the mother can still apply for a court order against him. But the court will consider the agreement when deciding how much maintenance to award.

## Seeking an affiliation order
A woman who is about to give birth to an illegitimate child or has already done so can apply to a magistrates' court for an affiliation order requiring the alleged father to pay towards the maintenance of the child.

An application can be made by a single woman, a widow or a divorced woman. It can also be made by a married woman if she can prove in court:
1. That her husband is not the child's father.
2. That she and her husband are no longer cohabiting in the legal sense of the term.
3. That by her conduct she has lost the right to be maintained by her husband.

If the mother is cohabiting with her husband, she cannot apply for an order against the father of the child.

A couple may be cohabiting in law even though sexual relations between them have ceased; but they will not be cohabiting merely because they are living under the same roof. In areas of housing shortage, the courts sometimes rule that a couple living in the same house are not legally living together. The decision will depend on the facts of each particular case.

In one case the court said that a woman was legally single where she and her husband had no sexual relations, she had had a separate room for four years, and there was no evidence to rebut her claim that she and her husband had lived completely separate lives.

In another case, decided by the same court on the same day, the judges reached the opposite conclusion. There, also, husband and wife had separate bedrooms, they had not had sexual relations for some years and in most respects lived separate lives. But there were still some vestiges of family life. One of the children shared a room with the husband, and when the wife became pregnant, the other child shared the room with him, too. The wife bought the food and cooked the husband's evening meal and left it for him, and the husband in turn continued to support the wife and the children. Although husband and wife had no friendly contact, these few contacts were taken to be enough to deprive the wife of a right to sue the father of her illegitimate child for maintenance.

If the mother usually lives in the United Kingdom and the child is born in any part of the country, the court can make an affiliation order, even if the father is a foreign national and lives abroad. The court can also make an order if the mother is a British subject living permanently in the United Kingdom, even if the child is born abroad.

If the child is at any time committed to the care of the local authority, the father can be made to pay the money under the court order direct to the authority. Anyone else who has legal custody of the child can also apply to have the payments made to him or her—but only if the court order was originally made in favour of the mother. If the mother leaves the child to be looked after by someone else and never applies for an order, the person bringing up the child cannot claim any payments from the father.

HOW TO APPLY A woman wishing to apply for an affiliation order must go to a magistrates' court and ask for a summons to be served on the man she claims to be the father. When the summons has been served, there is a hearing at which the woman must give evidence, even if the man admits that he is the father.

The mother's statement must be supported in some way—for instance, by the father admitting the facts in court. But if the man contests the case, the woman must produce other evidence—a letter, perhaps, or a witness who can say that the man has admitted to being the father.

Evidence from witnesses that the couple were fond of each other beyond mere social friendship would count. So, too, would evidence that they had the opportunity to have sexual intercourse, provided it is supported by other evidence suggesting that intercourse had taken place. The mere fact that the man did not answer a letter or statement accusing him of being the father is not corroboration, unless it is evident that an innocent person would have replied.

BLOOD TEST If either party requests, the court can order a blood test on the child, the alleged father and occasionally the mother. But a test cannot be made on a person without his agreement. Consent for a blood test on an illegitimate child can be given by the mother.

A child will be given a blood test unless the court decides it would be against the child's interest—if, for example, a test might result in a decision which left the child without any certain father. But the child's interest is not the sole one to be considered.

A test which might prove that the mother's husband was not the father—so making the child illegitimate—was at one time thought to be against the child's interest. Today, however, with the stigma of illegitimacy less than it was, the courts will normally order a test.

A blood test can never positively prove that a particular person is the father, only that someone is *not*. Where a man is wrongly accused of paternity, blood tests give a 70 per cent chance that this can be discovered.

Where the tests show that the blood group of the alleged father and the child are the same, the probability that he is the father depends on how common that blood group is; the more common the group, the less weight can be attached to the fact that man and baby have the same classification.

If either the alleged father or the mother refuses a blood test, the court can take this into account when assessing the evidence of the case—but a refusal cannot be regarded as conclusive.

WHEN TO APPLY The mother must make an application to the court within 12 months of the birth of the child if an order is to be

granted. But if she has received payments from the alleged father during this period, she may be allowed to apply later.

If the supposed father leaves England during the first year, the 12-month period starts again when he returns. An order cannot be first made after the child is 13. If the mother dies before the hearing, no order can be made, since she must give evidence. But her death does not bring an order already made to an end.

## Duration of an order

An affiliation order usually lasts until the child is 16, but sometimes the court declares that it should stop earlier. When the child is 13, the mother has to apply to have the order confirmed, and this is usually done except in the rare case where the child is already working and supporting himself.

The father pays the money to the court and the mother collects her allowance from the court each week. If he fails to pay, the court might take further measures to enforce the order, such as ordering the man's employer to deduct the money from his wages each week.

When the child becomes 16, the mother can apply to have the order extended for further periods of two years each if the child is being educated or trained for a job. If the mother is dead or insane, the child himself can apply for an extension. An affiliation order may cease on the death of the father, or a judge can order payments to continue to be made out of the father's estate.

CHANGING AN ORDER An affiliation order can be varied if the circumstances of the father or the mother change. The father may lose his job, become ill, or acquire a second family and additional financial commitments and so may no longer be able to pay.

If his inability to pay is only temporary, he can apply to the court to relieve him of the need to pay during the period of crisis. He can also apply for a variation of the order if the mother marries someone who is willing to take on responsibility for the child.

Applications for a variation can be made at the court which made the order, or at another court, if that is not convenient, by producing a copy of the original order.

## Disputes over custody

The mother has a right to bring up her illegitimate child, but if the father wants custody he can apply to the court, which will decide who would make the better parent.

A father would be likely to get custody of his child if, for example, he could show that the mother was living a loose life and wanted to offer the child for adoption, while he could provide a comfortable home.

However, fathers are rarely successful in claiming custody. In a case in 1969, the father failed where the mother married another man and applied to adopt the child. Under an adoption order the natural father does not have access to the child. But the court decided it was better for the child to be made legitimate and live with the mother and her new husband than to remain illegitimate and have occasional visits from the natural father.

The choice of religion is normally the mother's, but the father can apply to the court if he objects. Again, the court will decide in the child's best interests. But almost certainly the decision will be in favour of the mother if the child is to remain with her.

## Inheritance

No illegitimate child may succeed to a title, or to property going with it. With this exception, an illegitimate child now has the same right to share in the property of his parents as legitimate children. This means that the recognised children of a marriage may occasionally find themselves in the position of having to share their father's property with someone that they may not previously have known existed.

However, a man with illegitimate children who does not want to provide for them out of his estate can exclude them from his will. An illegitimate child can claim that his father has failed to make adequate provision for him in the will. But the court is unlikely to give him much, unless he was receiving a regular allowance before the death of his father. ☐ Challenging a will, p. 422.

If the father or mother dies intestate—that is, without making a will—the illegitimate child's claim on the estate is equal to that of any legitimate child. Similarly, the parents can benefit when an illegitimate child dies without leaving a will. ☐ Distributing an estate, p. 430.

If, for example, such a child makes a fortune as a pop singer and then dies, his parents are entitled to inherit just as they would be if he were legitimate.

Another difference between the legitimate and the illegitimate child, from the point of view of inheritance, is that the illegitimate child does not have any automatic claim on the property of his grandparents. He cannot inherit unless they make a will in his favour, or one referring to grandchildren generally.

## When a child is legitimate

| The child | Status |
|---|---|
| A child conceived before and born after marriage | Legitimate |
| A child conceived in marriage, but born after the husband's death | Legitimate |
| A child born to unmarried parents, who at a later date decide to get married | Legitimate from the time the parents marry |
| A legitimate child of parents who are divorced at a later date | Remains legitimate |
| A child born to parents who were married to other people, but who later get divorces and then marry each other | Legitimate from the time the parents marry |
| A child of a marriage later found to have been null and void—for example, a bigamous marriage, or one in which one party was under 16, or was forced to marry | Legitimate, if at the time of the marriage, or of conception, one of the parents believed the marriage was valid |
| A child of a voidable marriage—that is a marriage which is not simply void, but becomes void only if either the husband or the wife gets a court decree | The child remains legitimate in the same way as a child of divorced parents |

# Becoming a foster parent

*Restrictions*  *Council supervision*
*How to apply*  *Financial help*

FOSTER parents are people who look after other people's children, taking on most of the responsibilities of normal parents. But usually they have no legal rights over, or claims to, the children, unless the children stay with them for so long that a court would be prepared to rule that it would be better for the foster parents to keep them.

Anyone considering becoming a foster parent, therefore, has to bear in mind that the natural parents can normally take a child back at any time—even if they are virtual strangers to the child.

As far as the law is concerned, a foster child is normally one under school-leaving age who is looked after by people other than his parents, close relatives or guardian for more than six days continuously.

If a couple do not take in children regularly, however, and the child is not going to stay with them for more than 27 days, it is not considered a case of fostering.

Not all children placed with foster parents remain with them for long periods. Sometimes they need a home for only a matter of weeks or months, because of a family crisis.

## Restrictions
People who have been convicted of offences involving bodily harm to children cannot become foster parents. Nor can anyone living in the same house as such a person.

The law governing fostering is the same whether the foster parents take in the child by a private arrangement or at the request of the local authority or a children's society. Nor does it make any difference if the couple are paid for looking after the child.

## How to apply
A couple may become foster parents in two ways: either by making private arrangements with the parents of the child or children concerned; or by applying to a local authority or a children's society.

If a couple decide to make private arrangements, they must give notice to the local authority social services department at least two weeks before the child is to arrive in their home. In an emergency they may take the child immediately, provided they notify the council within 48 hours.

If, however, the couple are already registered foster parents with a foster child, they do not need to advise the council of any new children they intend to take in.

A couple who wish to become foster parents for a local authority should write to the social services department for their area. They will then be asked to give full information about themselves, their home, anyone else living with them and the accommodation they can provide for the child.

They will also be asked to give as references the names of a number of people who know them well, usually including the family doctor. Sometimes they are also required to produce medical certificates.

The next step is an interview with a social worker, who will want to see the husband and wife in their own home. If the officer thinks the home would suit a particular child, the couple have to sign an undertaking to bring the child up as their own and to comply with a number of requirements. They must also agree to encourage him to practise his religion. Children are rarely placed with foster parents of a different religion.

Unless the case is an emergency one or concerns a young baby, the social worker normally arranges meetings for the child and the foster parents to get to know each other. Initially the child will probably stay for a few weekends, to adapt to new surroundings.

## Council supervision
Once the child moves into the new home the child-care officer will make regular visits—the first within a month of the child moving in. The frequency of further visits depends on how often they are considered necessary.

Children under five must be visited at least once every six weeks, and children over five at least once every two months. But after two years they need be visited only once every three months.

If the child is old enough, the social worker will arrange a private talk, perhaps over tea, so that the child can discuss any problems he may have. If the child is at school, the social worker will consult the teachers about the child's progress and welfare.

Within the first three months, a doctor must make a report on the child's physical and mental health. The child is then usually registered with the family doctor. He or she must be examined every six months and a report is sent to the children's department.

The social worker can visit the home at any time, and remove the child if he thinks it in the child's interest. The foster parents can appeal against this in the juvenile court.

### Financial help

Where the fostering is a private arrangement, the amount paid to the foster parents is a matter for them and the parents to decide.

Local authorities and children's societies pay for the child's keep, clothing and pocket-money. They also consider any other expenses that may arise—for example, holidays, guide or scout uniforms and music and dancing lessons. In some cases the council may, at its discretion, pay for tools for an apprentice or a bicycle for a child who has a long journey to make to school.

The amounts paid vary from one area to another, but the general aim is the same: to see that the foster parents are not out of pocket for looking after the child, but that they do not make an excessive profit. Some authorities pay enough, however, to make looking after several foster children a financially attractive alternative to a wife going out to work.

## Foster children: what the law demands

Foster parents are never given complete control of the child they are caring for.

When a couple are accepted as foster parents they are required, by Act of Parliament, to sign this form before taking over the foster child. They must promise (clause 6) to allow the local authority to take back the child at any time, without disclosing its reasons for doing so, irrespective of how long the child has been with the foster parents.

They must also agree (clause 5) to allow Ministry or council officials to visit the child at any time, or to inspect their home, and to notify the council (clause 4) of any serious occurrence affecting the child—for example, illness, a serious accident or an offence against the child.

In practice, all the conditions under which the child is placed with the couple are explained and discussed fully while the council is making inquiries into their application to become foster parents

### Borough of Barchester

SOCIAL SERVICES DEPARTMENT

**UNDERTAKING TO BE SIGNED BY FOSTER PARENTS**

We/I JOHN AND MARY BROWNING

of 59, MARKET STREET, LONDON W2B 3YH

having on the 3RD day of AUGUST, 19 71, received from the Barchester Borough

(hereinafter called "the Council") PETER PALMER who was

born on the 12th day of JUNE, 1966 and whose religious persuasion is

METHODIST, into our/my home as a member of our/my family undertake that:-

(1) We/I will care for PETER PALMER and bring him/her up as we/I would a child of our/my own.

(2) He/she will be brought up in and will be encouraged to practise his/her religion.

(3) We/I will look after his/her health and consult a doctor whenever he/she is ill, and will allow him/her to be medically examined at such times and places as the Council may require.

(4) We/I will inform the Council immediately of any serious occurrence affecting the child.

(5) We/I will at all times permit any person so authorised by the Secretary of State or by the Council to see him/her and visit our/my home.

(6) We/I will allow him/her to be removed from our/my home, when so requested by a person authorised by the Council.

(7) If we/I decide to move, we/I will notify the new address to the Council before we/I go.

(8) We/I undertake that in the event of our/my claiming or receiving a family or guardian's allowance as the result of the foster-child's presence in the foster-home, we/I will immediately notify the Council of the fact.

(Sgd.) J. Browning

(Sgd.) Mary Browning

Dated January 3RD 1971

# How to adopt a child

THERE are few legal obstacles, in principle, to prevent any adult—even a single person—from adopting a child, and more than 24,000 children are adopted in Britain every year. But since there are always more people wanting to adopt than there are children available for adoption, and since the interests of the child are of major importance, there are many practical limitations on who can adopt a child.

The law lays down that any child being adopted must be a British subject, under 18 and unmarried.

Married couples wanting to adopt must both be over 21, and one over 25, unless the child is a relative; in that case it is sufficient if both are over 21. No married person can adopt a child without the consent of the other partner; and a couple cannot adopt unless they are married.

Any single person seeking to adopt a child must be over 25, or 21 if the child is a relative. It is unlikely that a single man would be allowed to adopt a girl.

An adopter's nationality is not important, but anyone adopting a child in Britain must normally have a permanent home in Britain or intend to live permanently here.

Someone who does not live in Britain can, however, apply to the High Court or a county court for a provisional adoption order— virtually the same as a normal adoption order, except that the child does not qualify for certain property rights under settlements and inheritances. The order remains provisional until the applicant has legally adopted the child in his or her own country.

In addition, many agencies which help with adoption have rules. Couples are not normally considered until they have been married for at least five years, for example. In some cases there may be an upper age limit of 40 for a wife and 45 for a husband.

Local authorities arranging adoptions tend to prefer the couple to be about the same age as natural parents of the child would be.

Three out of ten applications for adoption come from a child's mother and step-father —when an unmarried woman later marries someone other than the father, or when a young widow re-marries. These applications are regarded as a formality to change the child's name and birth certificate and to give the step-father full legal rights.

## Finding the child

A couple seeking to adopt a child have several possible sources they may try. There are more than 70 voluntary charitable adoption agencies and societies, and the social services departments of most local authorities help to arrange adoptions. It is possible, too, that a local doctor, hospital matron or almoner, or a district nurse may have information about a mother seeking a home for her child.

The couple themselves may even know the parents of the child. But they should avoid following up any advertisement by people offering children for adoption. It is illegal for anyone, except an authorised agency or local council, to advertise for adoption. An offender can be fined up to £50.

Finally, the couple may be relatives or foster parents of the child they want to adopt.

ADOPTION FEES It is a criminal offence to pay or accept money or any other form of reward for arranging an adoption. An offender can be jailed for up to six months and fined up to £100. Registered agencies can make and receive payments for a child's maintenance.

## Preliminary checks

The adoption society or local authority first checks that the couple or person applying is eligible to adopt. Then it inquires into their background, to decide whether they would make good parents.

Many adoption societies are religious organisations, which may insist on parents who can provide a religious upbringing. One survey showed that 85 per cent of societies would not consider applicants who belonged to no religion, 75 per cent would consider only Christians, and 59 per cent would consider only regular church-goers.

There are societies, however, which are not concerned with religion, and local authorities tend not to place any emphasis on religion.

Couples must be prepared to answer personal questions about themselves and their marriage. If they are childless, they will probably be asked if they have taken medical advice on infertility.

It sometimes happens that a couple will try to adopt a child to save their marriage. Adoption authorities are on their guard to prevent children going to this type of family.

### How to apply

NOTIFICATION An adoption comes into force when a court makes an adoption order. Notice of an intention to adopt a child can be made as soon as the child is six weeks old. An adoption order cannot be made until three months have elapsed since this notice was given.

The first step is to notify the social services department of the local authority, by letter, that an adoption order is to be sought.

The letter should give the child's name and date of birth and the date on which the couple started looking after it, if they are already doing so. It should state that the couple wish to adopt the child, and should be signed by both husband and wife.

A mother adopting her own baby does not have to give this notice.

LOCAL AUTHORITY SUPERVISION Immediately the local authority acknowledges the couple's notification of intent, the child becomes 'protected'. During the minimum three-month period it takes from notification to the official court adoption order, the child stays with the adopting parents, and they must allow regular visits by social workers from the local council's social services department.

It is the job of these officials to supervise the child and to ensure that the couple and the child adapt to each other. If the child was found through an agency or society, its welfare worker will also wish to visit the home.

If the couple move, they must give the council at least two weeks' notice.

APPLYING TO THE COURT The formal application to adopt the child is made to a county court, a juvenile court, or sometimes the High Court (a more expensive procedure, because a solicitor and a barrister are normally required). The application may be made as soon as the council has been notified—in other words, after the child is six weeks old.

In most cases, the couple wanting to adopt must obtain from the registrar of the county court or the justices' clerk at the juvenile court an application form, a consent form, and two medical report forms.

The application form must be completed and signed by both applicants. They must give their names, addresses, occupations and ages, and state when they first started to look after the child. The form asks also for information

---

## Getting the agreement of the natural parents

THE law tries to serve the best interests of the child, the people adopting it, and the natural parents. One of the basic principles is that, unless the circumstances are exceptional, the parents or guardians of the child must be shown to agree to the adoption.

This does not apply, however, to the father of an illegitimate child. Only if he has been ordered to maintain the child need he be informed of any adoption proceedings. He can apply for custody of the child and, if he does, the matter must be settled before an adoption order can be made.

He can also ask the court to hear him at the adoption hearing.

The parents usually give their consent in writing before the court hearing. This should be witnessed by a magistrate, a justices' clerk or a county court officer. It can be withdrawn at any time before the adoption order is made.

The natural parents cannot take the child out of the care of the court, even if they change their minds. They must notify the court that they withdraw their consent and let it decide where the child should stay.

The court can decide that the consent has been withheld unreasonably, but it is usually reluctant to do so. The welfare of the child is one, but not the sole, factor which has to be taken into account.

The natural parents have rights, too, which the court will consider. Their mental health and the sense of responsibility they have shown towards the child are likely to carry weight.

A court can waive the parents' consent if it has not been possible to trace them. Normally it will require evidence to show that strenuous efforts have been made. It can also waive consent where parents have abandoned or ill-treated the child.

The only condition that the natural parents can impose on the adoption is that the child should be brought up in a certain religion.

HOW TO ADOPT A CHILD

about the child, and the couple must state if they are related to the child.

The names and addresses of the child's natural parents must be given on the form if they are known. The couple must also get the natural parents to complete a consent form.

Where the natural parents are known only to the local authority or the agency arranging the adoption, the authority or agency will arrange for the consent form to be completed and the adopters will not be told who the natural parents are. The natural parents have no legal right to secrecy, although their names are not usually revealed.

The adopting parents, however, can specify that they wish to be identified only by a serial number to protect their anonymity.

When the form is completed, it should be sent with the couple's marriage certificate, and two medical certificates which can be supplied by their own doctor for a fee.

The first medical certificate states that the couple are physically and mentally fit to adopt the child. This is not needed if one of the applicants is the natural parent of the child. The second concerns the child's health, and the doctor has a duty to warn the couple of any ailments or disabilities.

COURT GUARDIAN When the application is received, the court immediately appoints a guardian *ad litem*—meaning 'for the case'—to look after the child's interests until adoption.

Normally the guardian is the council director of social services, but if he has placed the child with the couple, the court can appoint a probation officer or a social services director from another district.

The guardian's job is to make sure that the would-be adopters understand the responsibility they are taking on. If the child is old enough—say over five—the guardian must also ensure that he wants to be adopted by the couple. The guardian visits the natural parents of the child, if they are known, and makes sure that their consent was given voluntarily, that they have not been paid, and that they have not changed their minds.

In general, it is his duty to gather any information which could help the court to reach a decision on the adoption. His report is confidential to the court and is not seen by the applicants or by the natural parents, unless the court, at its discretion, decides that they should see the report.

### The court hearing

The hearing at which the adoption order is made is private—with usually only the guardian and the adopting couple present.

The exception is in the High Court, where a solicitor and barrister are usually required. Normally it is a brief hearing.

Before it makes the adoption order, the court must be convinced that:

1. The child's natural parents agree to the adoption. They have the right to withdraw their consent at any time before the order is made. Alternatively, a court may allow the adoption to go ahead without the consent of the natural parents if, for example, it has been impossible to trace them or they have withheld their consent unreasonably.

2. The adoption is in the child's interests, and—if he is old enough to say—that he is happy about it.

3. No money has changed hands.

Normally, all the necessary inquiries have been made by the guardian, and the hearing is simple and informal. There is rarely any need for a lawyer, and costs are minimal.

However, if the court is not completely satisfied on any point, it can decide to make a provisional order for two years. The adopting parents would then have to re-apply. During the interim two years, they would be visited by council officers and welfare workers.

NOTIFICATION When the order is made, the clerk of the court informs anyone concerned who has not been at the hearing—for example, the natural parents. A copy of the order or interim order is given to the adopting parents. This order does not usually show the names of the natural parents, but the couple have the right to demand and receive the full order, which does give the details.

REGISTRATION The full order is also sent to the Registrar General. It can be inspected only with the authority of a court order. The main details—except particulars of the natural parents—are entered in the Adopted Children's Register at Somerset House.

Two kinds of birth certificate are then available. One is a short form, exactly similar to the shortened version of the normal birth certificate giving only the child's name, sex, and date and place of birth. It does not say that the child has been adopted.

A copy of this is given free to the adopting couple, and further copies are available from the Registrar General's office at Somerset House, London WC2 1LB, for 75p.

A full certificate, giving the same basic details, also contains the names, addresses and occupations of the adopting parents. It costs 75p. The date of the adoption order, the name of the court which granted it and the date of registration are included. The cost of a copy of this certificate is £1·25. It is often five to six months before the adoption is completed, owing to factors such as delays in arranging court hearings.

### The rights of an adopted child

An adopted child has most of the rights of a natural child, but loses all claims against its natural parents. If the child is illegitimate all affiliation claims on the father cease.

INHERITANCE An adopted child can inherit in the same way as any other—except that it cannot inherit a title or any land that goes with the title. Adoptive parents who own property overseas should take legal advice before drawing up a will, for the law of that country may be different on inheritance.

INCOME TAX Relief of income tax is given for adopted children.

FAMILY ALLOWANCES Once a couple take responsibility for a child, they can draw family allowance (if they qualify otherwise). ☐ Having a baby, p. 324.

## Time and procedure for adoption

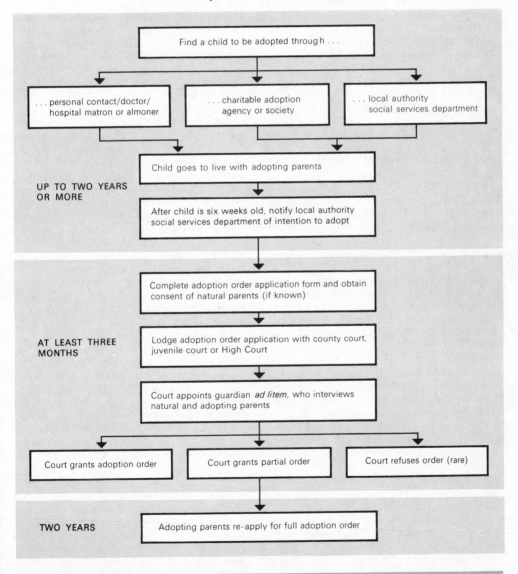

Find a child to be adopted through ...

... personal contact/doctor/ hospital matron or almoner

... charitable adoption agency or society

... local authority social services department

**UP TO TWO YEARS OR MORE**

Child goes to live with adopting parents

After child is six weeks old, notify local authority social services department of intention to adopt

**AT LEAST THREE MONTHS**

Complete adoption order application form and obtain consent of natural parents (if known)

Lodge adoption order application with county court, juvenile court or High Court

Court appoints guardian *ad litem*, who interviews natural and adopting parents

Court grants adoption order

Court grants partial order

Court refuses order (rare)

**TWO YEARS**

Adopting parents re-apply for full adoption order

# When children should have a guardian

THERE are several circumstances in which a child may need a guardian—a person appointed to supervise the child's upbringing, sometimes with the help of a parent. A guardian may be appointed when:

**1.** One or both parents are dead.

**2.** Both parents are going abroad for some time, leaving the child at home.

**3.** The father is going abroad and wants someone to assist the mother with the child's upbringing while he is away.

### How guardianship works

If a relative or friend takes charge of a child whose parents have been killed, he is not the child's legal guardian unless he has been properly appointed. In law, he is a foster parent and is subject to the control of the local authority and other rules of fostering children. ☐ Becoming a foster parent, p. 334.

It is better, in such a case, for the person left in charge of a child to ask the magistrates' court to appoint him the child's legal guardian. In this way he escapes the restrictions of the rules of fostering, and he does not have to apply to the court when decisions concerning the child's welfare have to be made.

A guardian will normally have custody of the child when acting alone. But when he is acting with one parent surviving, the parent will have first claim on the child, unless it can be shown that he or she is unsuitable.

When appointing a guardian, a parent may direct that the custody of the child be given to someone else—a solicitor might be made the child's guardian, while a relative has custody.

When this happens, the guardian must generally supervise the child's upbringing, while the person given custody would have ordinary, day-to-day control.

A guardian has the same right to discipline a child as a parent, and must see that the child gets a full-time education. ☐ Looking after children, p. 342.

A court can be asked to intervene at any time and can give custody to someone else if it is shown that the original person to have custody is morally unsuitable.

RELIGION A guardian must not change the child's religion. A child too young to have been taught any religion must be brought up in the religion of the last surviving parent.

If both parents died together, and they had different religions, the guardian would have to choose which religion to teach the child.

If there are two guardians and they disagree —or if one guardian disagrees with a parent— they must ask the court to settle the difference between them.

MAINTENANCE In general, a guardian need maintain the child only out of money or property belonging to the child. He can, however, be punished under the criminal law if he neglects the child by failing to provide a home and enough food and clothing.

A guardian who has custody of a child can ask the court to make a surviving parent pay towards the upkeep of the child.

LEGAL LIABILITY The responsibility of a guardian for a child's actions is the same as that of a parent. In particular, the guardian can be made to pay damages if he fails to control the child, and as a result the child causes injury or damage to someone else or their property. ☐ Looking after children, p. 342.

### Guardians and the child's money

Where the ward's property or money is concerned, the guardian is treated as a trustee. If he deals in the child's property, any profit he makes belongs to the child.

Dealings which benefit the guardian are suspect. When the child reaches the age of 18, he can challenge in the courts any transaction the guardian has entered into with his money or property, and ask for it to be cancelled.

In all these cases, the onus is on the guardian to show that he was acting in the best interests of the child. To protect himself in law, the guardian should ensure that the child is advised by an independent solicitor.

### How the State helps

A guardian is sometimes paid a weekly National Insurance allowance for each child in his care. This allowance is payable when both parents are dead, or perhaps when one is dead and the other is serving a long term in prison, or cannot be traced. If the child is illegitimate and the father is not known, however, the allowance is paid on the death of the mother.

Where parents have been divorced, the allowance can be paid to the guardian on the death of the parent who was granted custody of the child—provided that the other parent is not maintaining the child, and is not liable to do so under a court order.

The guardian can claim the allowance as long as the child is under 19 and receiving full-time education.

The allowance is normally payable only if at least one of the dead parents was insured under the National Insurance Acts—but if one of the parents lived or was insured in another country, this may count instead. If the guardian's allowance is paid, the guardian cannot also get the family allowance for the same child.

Details of the guardian's allowance are available in leaflet N.I.14, from the Department of Health and Social Security. Claims are made on Form B.G.1 from the same office.

**When guardianship ends**

The duties of a guardian generally come to an end when the minor reaches his 18th birthday.

The marriage of a minor under 18 will end the rights and obligations of a parent, but not those of a guardian of a young man under 18 unless the appointment included a clause to the contrary. It is not likely that a guardian would want to continue when a minor married, but he would be entitled to do so.

If the ward was a girl, and under 18, the guardianship would end automatically on her marriage. The husband then takes over the guardian's responsibilities.

Guardianship also ends if a sole guardian dies, but another guardian can be appointed by the court. If one of two guardians dies, the other guardian continues.

A guardian cannot resign without the court's permission. But if he does not want to go on as guardian the court will usually allow him to withdraw since it is obviously not in the child's interest to be looked after by someone who is unwilling or unable to carry out a guardian's obligations.

The courts have the power to take away a guardianship at any time. This could happen because of neglect, misconduct or a change in the guardian's circumstances.

The court might, for instance, appoint a new guardian if the original one was sent abroad by his employers and it was thought better for the child to be brought up and educated in this country.

## Appointing a guardian

THERE are three ways in which a guardian is appointed—by deed, by will or by applying to a court. No one can be made a guardian without their agreement.

BY DEED A deed is a formal statement drawn up and signed by the parents. It is witnessed under seal.

It is always advisable to employ a solicitor when drawing up a deed of guardianship. This will cost between £10 and £20.

BY WILL When one parent dies, the other automatically becomes the legal guardian of any children. But either husband or wife can also appoint a guardian, by deed or by will, to take over in the event of his or her death. This means that if one parent dies, the other will have the support of the additional guardian in bringing up the child.

If both parents die after naming two different guardians, both the people appointed are guardians and have to act together.

A guardian appointed in the will of a father (but probably not in that of a mother) has the power to appoint another guardian if necessary. For example, a father might leave in his will instructions that two friends be the guardians of his two children and that if one were to die, the survivor should be able to appoint another to succeed him.

BY COURT ORDER A court can appoint a guardian whenever it thinks one is needed. For example, a relative or friend who takes charge of a child whose parents have been killed can apply to a court to be appointed the child's legal guardian.

Another situation is where the dead parent did not appoint a guardian to act with the surviving parent and the survivor needs help with the children. A third is after a divorce, when the court thinks neither parent is fit to have charge of a child.

The person wanting to become a guardian has to apply to the court and the court will always try to appoint a relative or friend—someone already fairly well known to the child, and not a complete stranger.

# Looking after children

*Food and clothing*　　　*Punishing a child*
*Illness and injury*　　　*Property and contracts*
*When a child is in danger*　*Paying for a child's mistakes*

THE law cannot make parents love their children, but it does lay down minimum standards of conduct. In some cases, it is a criminal offence for parents to allow their standard of care to fall below the minimum—for example, failing to get proper treatment for a sick child or imposing excessive punishment. A child who is injured through his father's carelessness may sue him.

### Food and clothing
Parents have a legal obligation to feed, clothe and provide for their children properly, but this duty varies according to the family's standard of living.

A millionaire's son, for instance, would have a right to a higher standard of living and possibly a more expensive education than a farm labourer's son. Children must receive their full and fair share of their parents' worldly goods.

But although children have this right to be looked after adequately, there is nothing they themselves can do legally to force their parents to obey the law. There is no legal procedure for children to go to court to claim support for themselves.

Only the mother can take legal action—by suing the father for maintenance on behalf of the children if she believes that they are being neglected. Any order the court makes is enforceable only if the father and mother are living apart when the order is made, or if they begin to live apart within three months of the order being made.

If the mother convinces a magistrates' court that the child is in need, the court may order the husband to pay her so much every week towards the upkeep of the child. If necessary, the order may be enforced by deducting the amount from the husband's wages. But if she continues to live with her husband, she has no legal means of making him maintain the child.

Her only course is to inform the local council social services department. If social workers believe that there are good grounds for action, the department can ask the court to have the child taken into care—possibly in a local authority foster home or by a relative,

under the supervision of the council. ☐ Children in trouble, p. 356.

It may be possible for the mother to get legal aid to bring a maintenance action against her husband if they are living apart. But if the wife has a private income, legal aid may be given only in part or not at all, depending on her means. ☐ Help with legal fees and costs, p. 710.

### When a child is ill
Parents must take care of a child when he is ill, and they have a duty to ensure that he gets whatever medical treatment is necessary. To fail to do so is a criminal offence.

It would, for example, be an offence not to call a doctor if it seemed that one was needed. When the doctor advises some form of treatment, it may also be an offence for the parents to ignore his advice.

It makes no difference in law that the parents may refuse to allow an operation or blood transfusion because this is forbidden by sincerely held religious convictions. A court would be interested only in establishing whether their point of view seemed acceptable and reasonable to an ordinary man.

Where a child is in hospital requiring treatment, and both the parents refuse consent, the hospital sometimes informs the local council social services department, which then applies to a magistrate for an order taking the child into the care of the council. In such a case the council would be able to give the hospital the legal consent necessary for the child's treatment.

### When a child is injured
Parents have a duty to take reasonable care of their children and see that they are not injured. But it may happen that, through carelessness or accident, the parents are in some way to blame for a child's injury.

If they have been careless the child could sue his parents for damages through his 'next friend'—usually a close relative—since a child under 18 cannot bring civil proceedings on his own behalf.

When a child has been hurt in a car accident caused by his mother or father, he can sue his parents and—if they have suitable insurance—any damages awarded would then be paid by the parents' insurance company. The right to sue might also be useful in the rare cases where parents insure themselves against claims by their children—a young child might claim damages for negligence if he were injured while crossing a road unaccompanied, because his mother let him wander away in a busy street.

If a child is injured by someone else, the father or guardian can claim damages for what the law calls 'loss of services'.

The father can claim that he is entitled to the services of his child, so that if the child is injured he suffers a loss. In 1968, however, the Law Commission recommended that this kind of action should be stopped and that, instead, parents should be able to sue only for actual loss—say medical or legal expenses in connection with injuries to the child.

In addition to the parents' action, the child would also have the right to sue for damages in the normal way, through a 'next friend'.

## When a child is in danger

Parents have the same rights to defend their children as they have to defend themselves. If they believe that a child is in danger of attack, they may prevent the attack. In extreme cases, they might even be within the law if they seriously injured or killed an attacker. But they must be able to show that they really believed that the child was in danger of being killed or seriously injured.

Any force or violence must be proportionate to the danger. If would obviously not be reasonable to wound a neighbour seriously in order to restrain him from smacking a child. Nor would a court consider it lawful to assault a neighbour in revenge *after* he had admonished or smacked a child.

## Punishing a child

Parents and guardians have a right to control and discipline their children, but the punishment must not be excessive. There are no precise rules as to what is permitted, but the law requires people in charge of children to act with restraint. This applies to teachers, child-minders, baby-sitters and foster parents, as well as to parents and guardians.

Punishment which inflicts serious injury on a child is illegal, for the parent is subject to the normal law of assault, and he or she could be fined or even sent to prison for causing the child grievous bodily harm. Unnatural punishment, such as the locking up of a child for hours without food, is also an offence.

Cases such as these are usually discovered by a neighbour, who may reasonably suspect assault or cruelty. His best course is to report his suspicions to the nearest branch of the National Society for the Prevention of Cruelty to Children, which will send one of its officers to investigate the allegation confidentially. This confidential approach avoids embarrassment should the suspicions be unfounded.

A child who is being ill-treated in any of these ways, or a child who is completely beyond the control of normal parental discipline, can be brought before a juvenile court, taken away from the parents and put in the care and control of the local authority.
☐ Dealing with rebellious children, p. 354.

## Children's property and money

A child can own money and most forms of property in the same way as an adult. The most important exception is land. Under English law, no minor may be a landowner; land must be held in trust for him until he reaches the age of 18.

EARNINGS When a child is earning a small amount, perhaps by doing a newspaper round or when he gets pocket money from his parents, he is legally free to spend or save it as he pleases.

The position is more complicated when the child has left school and is working but still living at home. He may then be earning a substantial sum each week or month.

The parent has no legally enforceable right to any part of the child's earnings, but where the child is in a regular job the parent has the right to be paid for board and lodging at home.

The size of any contribution he could be asked to make would depend on how much he is earning but this is not an area where either side would normally have recourse to action in the courts.

GIFTS If a child is given money, at Christmas for example, the parents cannot insist that he share it to help pay household expenses, even if they are partly for the child's benefit.

If the child receives a gift that he is too young to manage, the parents hold it as trustees. For example, if a five-year-old child is given £10 as a gift, the parents would have the responsibility of looking after it for him—either saving the money or spending it on the child's behalf.

If the gift is only £1 the law might consider that even a five-year-old could normally be left to choose what he wanted to do with it. Most parents would allow the child to have the money in some form, or place it in a bank in his name.

TRUSTEES When a child inherits a large sum of money, or where he is earning a considerable amount—perhaps as a child actor or model—the parents, and possibly some outside party such as a solicitor or bank manager, are appointed trustees. Parents usually have the right to withdraw a given amount from a trust fund to maintain the child. But the money is not theirs and they must spend it only on the child. ☐ Setting up a trust, p. 526.

Parents should take legal advice before using any money held for a minor under trust, for if the child decides when he becomes 18 that they have used the money wrongly, he can take action in the courts to try to force them to repay it.

Parents who are also trustees must beware of transferring money from the trust either to themselves or to anyone else. Unless there is strong evidence to the contrary, the courts are likely to believe that the parents have had undue influence on the child. In that case the parents would have to reimburse the trust.

Whenever it is necessary to take decisions about trust property, engage a solicitor to advise the child independently. It is not advisable in such cases for the parents to use the same solicitor as the child.

Under normal circumstances, any action against parents for misuse of trust funds should be brought by a child within a short time—say six months—of attaining the age of 18. But it is quite possible for a young man or woman of 20 or 21 still to be considerably under the parents' influence, and in this case he or she could still bring the action.

## Children's contracts

Unless they have signed an indemnity or guarantee, parents are in no way liable for contracts entered into by children under 18 on their own behalf—and neither, normally, are the children.

Most contracts are unenforceable against a child, and the person with whom the contracts are made must bear any loss. The law states that a contract cannot normally be enforced against someone under 18—unless it is for necessities or to his advantage.

On the other hand, the minor or his parents can normally insist on the other party to the contract honouring it. ☐ The law on buying and selling, p. 442.

## Paying for a child's mistakes

Parents can sometimes be held responsible for injury or damage caused by their children.

Children can be sued just like anyone else;
but often the parents will find that they are being sued too—on the ground that they did not keep strict enough control over their child.

In deciding whether a minor has been 'negligent', the standard applied is that of a reasonably careful minor of that age. It would not be easy to prove, for example, that a seven-year-old who set fire to a haystack was negligent, because the law does not expect an adult's sense of responsibility in a child.

Usually there is little point in suing a minor because he probably has no money, and his parents do not have to pay damages simply because they are his parents. They can only be made to pay damages if they can be shown to have been negligent in bringing up and controlling the child.

If a three-year-old child runs out of his front garden into a road and causes a driver to swerve and be killed, the parents may be liable because they allowed the child to escape into the road. They would not, however, be expected to exercise the same control over an older child.

It might happen that a boy of 15, who is normally responsible and obedient, is given an airgun with proper instructions on how and where to use it.

Even if this boy unexpectedly injured another child with the gun, his parents would probably not have to pay damages because it could be held that they had acted with reasonable prudence and caution.

In reaching its decision, the court would be likely to pay particular attention to the boy's age. The younger the child, the less reasonable it will be for the parents to trust him and rely on his obedience and common sense.

If a boy is too young to be wholly trustworthy, it would not necessarily be a defence for the parents to show that they specifically warned him about the danger—or even forbade the action he took.

▶ THE BOY WHO MISHANDLED A GUN *A farmer gave his 12-year-old son a shotgun and taught him how to use it. He told the boy not to take it off the farm and forbade him to use it when other children were about. But he did not explain how he should handle the gun when other children were about. Despite this warning, the boy took the gun away from the farm. It went off and another boy was injured. The injured boy, through his father, sued the farmer for damages.*
DECISION *The farmer was held liable because he had been careless in not teaching his son how to handle the gun when other people were present. (Newton v. Edgerley.)* ◄

# Disputes over children

*How custody is decided*  
*The father's and mother's rights*  
*Religion*

*Medical treatment*  
*Education*

T HE most important of parents' rights over their children is the right of custody—the right to determine the manner and style of a child's life, how he is to be educated and what religion he is to follow. Normally the parents agree on all these points, and the question of custody has little significance. But where there are disputes between parents it becomes important.

## How custody is decided
The chief consideration in deciding who is to have custody of the child is always the welfare of the child. The interests, rights or wishes of the parents are of secondary importance.

When a marriage breaks up, the custody of very small children is normally given to the mother. If the child is old enough, he can give his preference and this will be considered. Wherever possible, brothers and sisters are not separated from one another.

A child's physical well-being, rather than his spiritual needs, will take precedence, even where the claim for custody arises out of a dispute between parents about the religion in which the child will be brought up.

So if a child is very young and is thought to be better off with his mother, the court will usually award custody to her, no matter what the father may say about religious upbringing.

## The father's and mother's rights
A mother can demand a say in how a child is brought up only if she applies to the court for custody under the Guardianship of Infants Acts. But normally she must have left or be about to leave her husband. If she is living with him, the father's wishes and decisions take precedence over hers.

It is theoretically possible, however, for a mother living with her husband to apply to the court to have the child brought under the court's guardianship as a ward. She could then try to persuade the court that her way of bringing up the child would be better for the child than the father's. This is a clumsy and expensive procedure and is rarely used in disputes over children's upbringing.

If one parent leaves home with a child, the remaining parent can apply immediately for custody of the youngster. If there is any danger that one partner may try to take the child out of the country, the other parent should consider applying to have the child made a ward of court.

## Religion
When the parents are living together, the father has the right to choose which religion the child is to follow. But the mother may feel strongly enough to ask the court to take charge of the child as a ward of court and then allow her to bring it up in her religion.

The court will consider first whether the child has already been taught one particular religion. For instance, if a father had at first agreed to have the child brought up as a Roman Catholic and then changed his mind, the court would probably rule that the child should be allowed to remain a Catholic.

If the parents are separating, the court will decide that the child should follow the religion of whichever parent is given custody.

If one parent is dead and there is a dispute between the surviving parent and any guardian, the court could be asked to decide. But unless it was thought to be against the child's best interests, the parent would probably be allowed to decide.

## Medical treatment
Where the parents belong to different religions it is possible that a dispute over beliefs could affect the child's medical treatment. Some sects, for example, do not believe in surgery or blood transfusions.

Where treatment is necessary, however, hospital authorities are likely to press the parents for their consent. When they do so the mother is just as entitled to sign a consent form for an operation as the father. □ Looking after children, p. 342.

## Education
As in religion, it is the father's will which prevails unless the mother goes to court. It is advisable, however, to consult a solicitor before taking action, since the issues are less clear-cut in most disputes over education than in those involving the choice of religion.

# When a child must go to school

EVERY child aged five and over but under 16 (before the 1972–3 school year, 15) must receive a full-time education, and this education must be geared to the child's age, ability and aptitude. If a child reaches the age of five during a school term, the school is not obliged to admit him until the beginning of the next term—but the decision on when the child will actually be admitted rests with the local education authority or even with the head teacher.

Schools are not bound to admit any child once a term has started unless the child has been ill, has been away from home with his parents or has been unable to attend school earlier for some other reason beyond the parent's control, such as moving house.

Local education authorities have a duty to provide sufficient schools in each area to give reasonable opportunities for primary and secondary education to all pupils.

### Responsibility for a child's attendance

Parents and guardians are responsible for a child's attendance at school—and the responsibility remains, even if the child is not living with his parents or guardians. In the case of an illegitimate child, it is up to the mother or guardian to see that the child goes to school.

If parents or guardians can give the child an education as good as, or better than, he or she would receive at school, they do not have to send the child to school. □ Learning at home, p. 347.

If the local education authority thinks that a child is not getting an adequate education, it can serve a school attendance order on the parents. The order tells the parents that they can name the school they choose for their child but if that school is already full, or if the local authority thinks it is too far away or unsuited to the child's needs, the authority can ask the Secretary of State for Education and Science to order the child to be sent to another school.

### Refusing to send a child to school

If a parent refuses to send the child to the school the authority chooses, despite the attendance order, he can be fined unless he proves that the child is receiving a suitable full-time education outside school.

A parent can be fined £10 the first time he is convicted of not complying with an attendance order. For the second and subsequent offences the fine is £20.

If the parent is absolutely determined to keep the child away from school, and is willing to be fined and even to go to prison, the local authority cannot itself use force to get the child to school. But it can ask a juvenile court to make an order that the child is in need of care and protection.

If the court agrees, it can send the child to a community home or put him in the care of a relative or friend who is willing to send him to the school chosen by the authority. Alternatively, the court could put the child in the charge of a probation officer. □ Children in trouble, p. 356.

### When a child can stay at home

Parents have to ensure that the child goes to school regularly. There must be a good reason, such as illness, for keeping a child at home.

If a child's illness is prolonged, it may be advisable to discuss with the school or the education authority whether a teacher should be provided at the local authority's expense to give home tuition.

Another reason for keeping the child away is if the child's religion demands that certain days be set aside for religious observance.

If the school is not within walking distance (2 miles for a child under eight, and 3 miles for a child of eight or over) and the local authority has failed to provide transport or boarding accommodation, a parent also has a right to keep his child away.

The qualifying distance is measured along the shortest usable route. It is no excuse, however, for a parent to say that the route the child has to take is unsafe.

If the child has no fixed address—for instance, if he or she lives on a canal barge—a parent can avoid prosecution if he can show that work requires him to travel from place to place, and that his child attends school as often as the father's work permits. However, a child aged seven or over must attend school for at least 400 half-days a year, and if he fails to do this the parent can be fined £10.

The local education authority would find it difficult to enforce the child's attendance in a case like this unless it sent him to boarding school at its own expense.

### Educating handicapped children

Local authorities must make arrangements to educate handicapped children. They have authority to examine any child of two or over living in their area so that they can estimate what special schools will be needed. Parents who refuse to have their child examined can be fined up to £5.

When a child is found to need special treatment, the parents are advised to arrange for this treatment. If they fail to do so, the local authority takes over the responsibility.

When a handicapped child has to be sent to a special boarding school, the local authority has to meet the cost and parents must be given 21 days' notice of the authority's intention to send the child away to school.

Parents who disagree with the local authority's decision can write to the Secretary of State for Education and Science, at Curzon Street House, Curzon Street, London W1Y 8AA, stating their objections.

If the child is sent away, the parents can insist that his case is reviewed each year.

Children needing special treatment are defined in ten categories: the blind, the partially sighted, the deaf, the partially hearing, the delicate, the educationally subnormal, epileptics, the maladjusted, the physically handicapped, and those with speech defects.

### Leaving school

A child whose birthday falls between September 1 and January 31 inclusive in 1972 or later has to stay at school until the end of the spring term following his or her 16th birthday.

A child with a birthday between February 1 and August 31 inclusive in 1972 or later must stay at school until the end of the summer term in the year of the 16th birthday.

Children whose 15th birthdays fall before September 1, 1972 are not covered by the raising of the minimum school-leaving age. Such a child may leave at the end of the spring or summer term following his or her birthday.

## Learning at home

PARENTS who wish to have a child educated at home can do so, provided that the education given is efficient, full-time, and suited to the child's age, ability and aptitude.

There is no legal requirement that parents must first ask a local authority for permission. It is only when the authority has reason to believe that the parents are failing in their duty that it has the right to call on the parents to show that the child is being educated.

An education authority cannot simply assume that a child is not being educated in accordance with the law merely because education is given at home.

The parents are allowed to bring evidence to the courts to show that they are providing efficient, full-time education at home.

Parents can educate the child at home even though neither is a qualified teacher, provided that the education is efficient and full-time.

➤WHEN HOME TUITION IS EFFICIENT *In 1911, Mr Shears's son was attending a local school near Pembroke when he was punished by the headmaster. Because of this, his father took him away and tried to send him to another school.*

*But Pembrokeshire education authority refused the transfer because they considered that Mr Shears's action was capricious.*

*The father then arranged for a tutor to educate his son. The education authorities sent the school attendance officer to the home and, on the day of his visit, he found that the child had received no tuition that day. The attendance officer filed a complaint, and Mr Shears was summonsed on the ground that he had unlawfully and without reasonable cause omitted to send his child to the local school.*

DECISION *The justices decided that the education the boy was receiving was efficient. They considered it irrelevant that his education might not have been as efficient as the schooling offered by the local school. The justices considered that the fact that he received no education on the day in question did not alter the basic proposition that the education was efficient. The summons was therefore dismissed. (Bevan v. Shears.)* ◄

The education provided by parents need not be as comprehensive or of the same form as given at a State school. There is no legal requirement that specific subjects must be taught.

# The parents' right to choose a school

IN theory, most parents have the right to choose the school where their children will be educated. In practice, other factors often override the parents' choice. The Education Act 1944 lays down that in most cases children going to State schools should be educated in accordance with their parents' wishes, but the Act also gives local education authorities the right to override parents' wishes if:

**1.** The parents' choice would mean that the child did not receive efficient instruction.

**2.** The parents' choice would involve the local authority in 'unreasonable expense'.

**3.** The school chosen by the parents can be shown to be unsuitable for the 'age, ability and aptitude' of the child.

### Choosing a primary school
In many areas, there is no choice of primary school, for only one is available. Even in towns where there are several schools, the local education authority limits parents' choice by dividing its district into zones or catchment areas, one for each of its schools.

Difficulties may arise when parents wish to have their children educated outside the zone in which they live. Where the choice is on religious grounds, most local authorities meet the wishes of parents, so long as schools do not become too overcrowded.

In other cases, where the choice is based on facilities or academic record, the authority may disregard the parents on the grounds that their choice would cause 'unreasonable expense' to taxpayers.

Where there is a newer school, and it proves to be more popular than the older ones, the authority may try to restrict entry to it by limiting its catchment area. In this case, the parents' only hope of getting their wishes followed is to persuade the Secretary of State for Education and Science that it is unreasonable of the local authority to refuse entry.

### Insisting on your choice
In many areas, the local education authority publishes a map of the region showing the sites of all primary schools. The parents may then make their choice and inform the local education officer. If the education officer finds that the school chosen is either outside the parents' zone, or that all places at the school have been filled, he tells the parents to choose another school.

Parents who wish to insist on their first choice must then send a written complaint to the education officer. The officer or his staff will consider the complaint and try to reach agreement with the parents.

If no compromise is possible, there are a number of steps parents can take. It is cheaper and often more effective to bring pressure on the local authority by seeking the support of local councillors and the Member of Parliament, and by trying to win sympathy by letters to local newspapers, than it is to take legal action. Advice on presenting a case may often be obtained from the local branch of the Campaign for the Advancement of State Education. Apply for the address to the local Citizens' Advice Bureau.

The parents may also appeal to the Secretary of State for Education and Science. If they can show that the school of their choice has places available, the Secretary of State may direct the education authority to admit the child to the school the parents prefer.

But if the local authority can prove that any vacancies are soon to be taken by children from within the school's zone, then the parents are likely to lose.

OMBUDSMAN It may be possible, in a rare case, for parents to appeal against a decision by the Department of Education and Science to the Parliamentary Commissioner or Ombudsman. But the Commissioner has powers to investigate only complaints alleging administrative injustice by a Government Department (not by a local authority). The Commissioner must be approached through a Member of Parliament and not directly.

The parents therefore have the difficult task of convincing an MP that the Department has not followed the rules. It is not enough simply to disagree with the Department's ruling.

SEEKING AN INJUNCTION If the parents disagree with the Department, they can seek a High Court injunction ordering the local authority to allow their child to go to the school of their choice. This is expensive and will rarely be successful. A solicitor will be able to advise on the chances of success. It is important to keep a record of all letters and meetings with the education authority.

### Choosing a secondary school

There is no uniform system of State secondary education and no standard way of selecting pupils. In general, parents have a limited choice of school.

Only where a local education authority has a fully comprehensive system can parents expect to be able to make a choice without regard to their child's examination results.

Even in such areas, they may have the same kind of difficulties as are encountered with primary schools, for most areas are zoned and the schools take only children from their particular neighbourhood.

If parents want to complain about a zoning restriction, the procedure is the same as for complaints over primary school selection. Where they can show that places are available at the school of their choice they are likely to be successful.

SELECTION In many areas some form of selection is still carried out when a child moves from primary school to secondary school.

More than one factor may have been considered: the child's examination result, if any

---

## The parents' right to choose a course

IN practice, the type of course the child will follow at school depends on the school, the head teacher, and the child's abilities.

In many cases, of course, the head teacher will take the parents' wishes into account. The head teacher may, for example, think a girl should take Greek and Latin, but agree in the face of her parents' insistence to allow her to take domestic subjects instead.

It is unlikely, however, that a head teacher could be persuaded to allow a girl to follow an academic course if he thought she was more suitable for a commercial or domestic course.

Parents who are dissatisfied may appeal to the local education authority against any decision by a head teacher. But to be successful they have to prove that the course they want for the child is suitable for his or her 'age, ability and aptitude'. Unless they have the support of educational experts—such as previous teachers or an educational psychologist—it is unlikely that parents will succeed.

### Religious instruction

All State schools include religious study in their courses, and unless the school is run by a particular denomination this must be non-denominational in character.

Parents can ask the school to allow their child to withdraw from a religious class or morning religious assembly. It may be possible for the child to be withdrawn from the main religious activities and to have separate instruction in his own faith. Some churches offer the services of their clergymen to schools.

In schools which have a religious backing—such as church schools—it is unlikely that any other religion than the one of the church authority would be taught. But the basic right to opt out of the religious classes still exists.

### Sex education at school

Many schools—including primary schools—run courses of sex instruction, with film and photographic illustration.

Generally, parents are invited by the local authority to express their views before the course begins and they may be allowed to withdraw their children from such courses.

If no notice is given, parents can complain to the head teacher and in most cases would probably be able to persuade the school to allow their child to withdraw.

But if sex classes are organised as part of the normal biology lessons it is unlikely that a parent could insist on his child not attending.

### The child's right of choice

Children have no legal right to choose their own school courses. In normal circumstances, though—especially after the minimum school-leaving age—the wishes of the pupil involved will at least be considered by the school.

Where there is a dispute between parents and child, the school is likely to follow the parents' wishes rather than the child's. But the school's chief duty is to do what is educationally right for the child.

A child of 15 or over (16 after 1972) cannot be compelled by a school to stay on at school. But if he is under 18, his parents have the right to insist that he stays on, and if he refuses the parents could have him taken into care.
□ Children in trouble, p. 356.

form of 11-plus examination is used in the area; the child's IQ, based on an intelligence test; and often, a grading from the child's teacher in the upper primary school class.

QUOTA SYSTEM Children are often chosen not only on the basis of examination results, but because they qualify for a place on a quota system. This happens when all the available places are divided among all the primary schools in the area.

Each school is awarded a number of places at the local grammar school on the basis of previous examination results. Later, after the examination, individual pupils are chosen.

If only seven places are available to a particular school, there may be many children with high marks in the examination who are left after the top seven are chosen.

## Complaining about selection

If you think your child has been selected for the wrong kind of secondary school, ask to see the head teacher at the primary school. Although he or she is not obliged to show parents their child's examination results, it is useful to enlist their help for an appeal to the local education officer.

The head teacher may advise that the authority's choice of school for the child is right. Or he may admit that there is a discrepancy between the examination marks and the assessment made by the child's teacher, and he might be willing to support the parents' complaint to the local education officer.

APPEALS TO THE LOCAL AUTHORITY When the result of the selection is known, dissatisfied parents should appeal in writing to the local education officer mentioning, if possible, that the primary school head teacher has offered support for the child's case.

APPEALS TO A GOVERNMENT DEPARTMENT If the education officer refuses to change his decision, the parents can appeal to the Secretary of State for Education and Science, at Curzon Street House, Curzon Street, London W1Y 8AA. They must be able to show that the local education authority has acted unreasonably.

The Secretary of State and the law take a narrow view of what amounts to unreasonable action and the verdict is likely to go against the authority only if it can be proved that the authority took into account irrelevant factors.

To support the case, parents may enlist the support of previous teachers, or they may have the child examined by an educational psychologist, who will give the child an IQ test. The names of such experts are available from the Secretary of the Association of Educational Psychologists. The local Citizens' Advice Bureau will provide the address.

THE OMBUDSMAN If the Secretary of State refuses to direct the local authority to admit the child to the school preferred, the parents can appeal through their MP to the Ombudsman or seek an order in the High Court.

For either course to be successful the parents must be able to show that there has been some administrative or legal mistake.

COURT ACTION If action is contemplated through the courts, consult a solicitor who is experienced in educational law.

If the parents have a good case, bringing pressure on the education authority is more likely to produce a change of mind in a dispute.

## If an appeal is lost

When parents keep a child away from school during a dispute over choice, they are breaking the law—unless they can prove that they are providing efficient full-time education suitable for the child's age, ability and aptitude at home. □ Learning at home, p. 347.

ATTENDANCE ORDERS When a child is kept away from school and the authority is not satisfied with the reason for the child's absence, an application can be made to a magistrates' court to have a school attendance order confirmed. This is served by the authority on the parents and puts them under an obligation to choose a school to which they will send their children.

Parents who are determined to continue the fight may name a school to which the authority has already refused to allocate the children. The authority can then apply to the Secretary of State for Education for a direction as to what school is to be named on the attendance order. The Secretary's decision is final.

DISOBEDIENCE A parent can be fined £10 for not complying with a school attendance order. For the second and subsequent offences the fine is £20. The local authority can also apply for a court order to take the child away from parents and place him or her in care. □ Children in trouble, p. 356.

## Discrimination on racial grounds

It is illegal for schools or local authorities to discriminate on the grounds of race, colour or national or ethnic origins. A parent who suspects such discrimination can complain to the local race relations conciliation committee, whose address can be obtained from the local authority offices.

Alternatively, a parent can complain to the Race Relations Board at 5 Lower Belgrave Street, London SW1W 0MR.

# School rules and discipline

*Rules about dress*　　*Punishment for breaking rules*
*Cleanliness of pupils*　　*Complaining about punishment*

SCHOOL authorities are entitled to lay down rules governing the discipline, behaviour, appearance and cleanliness of pupils. These rules can be applied not only in school but also on the way to and from school. If a pupil breaks the rules, the teachers are entitled to take appropriate disciplinary action. Schools have wide scope for making regulations, and no court would interfere unless the rules were entirely unreasonable.

### Rules about dress
A head teacher is entitled to lay down rules about dress and appearance. If the parents send a girl to school in a mini-skirt which the school thinks is too short, she can be sent home.

If the parents keep sending her in a short skirt, and she continues to be sent home, they can be prosecuted for not sending her to school. The same might apply if a head teacher thought a boy's hair too long.

The only defence would be that the headmaster's ruling was unreasonable and that he was depriving the child of his right to an education. It would then be for the magistrates to decide; or there could be an appeal to the Secretary of State for Education and Science.

### Cleanliness of pupils
The school can insist on standards of cleanliness in its pupils. To protect other pupils, a local authority also has the power to see that schoolchildren are free from vermin.

The school can warn parents that if children are not cleaned up within 24 hours, they will be cleansed at school. Examination of a girl can be carried out only by a doctor or by a woman.

### Punishment for breaking rules
The right of teachers to punish children at school is similar to that of parents. When a child is sent to school, the school authorities take over the parents' right of discipline.

Parents are legally considered to have delegated their authority—which means that they cannot intervene in the way the school exercises its disciplinary powers. A father cannot tell the teacher how or when to punish a child. The responsibility for deciding on punishment at school rests with the school. The

principle is that punishment must be moderate and in line with school rules. It should be the sort that a reasonable parent would think fitted the offence; and it must not be inflicted vindictively, or by a teacher who has lost his temper.

CORPORAL PUNISHMENT Corporal punishment is still allowed by law, in principle, though in practice many local authorities have prohibited it. Any instrument used should not be of a sort to cause serious injury. It would be reasonable to use a school cane, but a heavy walking stick might be considered dangerous by a court. A school must record corporal punishment in its 'punishment book'. A child who was beaten so severely that he was in considerable pain for several hours afterwards might be able to sue his teacher for assault, and claim damages.

The local education authority could also be sued as the teacher's employer.

The child, as a minor in law, would have to bring the action through his father or guardian. In a severe case, a teacher could be prosecuted for assault in a criminal court, just as a parent could be if he injured his child.

KEEPING A CHILD IN AFTER SCHOOL Detention in accordance with the school rules is normally lawful, even if it inconveniences the child's parents. It would not be legal, however, if the punishment were clearly out of all proportion to the misdemeanour of the child.

### Complaining about punishment
In most cases, parents do not wish to involve themselves in a court case; usually, they would be satisfied by an apology and an assurance that their child will not be the victim of unreasonable punishment again. If parents feel aggrieved at methods of discipline, they can complain to the headmaster, the governors or managers of the school, or the local authority education officer.

In one instance, parents complained to the local authority after their five-year-old son, who suffered from asthma, was gagged with sticky tape because he talked in class. The chief education officer ordered an inquiry, which resulted in apologies being offered to the parents by the teacher and the headmaster.

# Injuries at school

*Grounds for damages*     *Responsibility outside the school*
*Danger in the playground*

SCHOOL authorities have a legal duty to take reasonable care to see that children are not injured at school. The meaning of 'reasonable care' depends on the age of the child; a school must take greater care of a five-year-old than of a teenager.

If a child suffers a serious injury at school, it is worth while for parents to ask a solicitor if they have grounds for a damages claim.

A claim can be made even when the child is partly to blame for what happened, though damages would be reduced. If another child causes an injury, it may still be possible to take action against the school authorities.

Damages may have to be paid if a child suffers pain or is unable, even for a brief period, to enjoy life in the usual way. The school will be insured, and there is therefore little likelihood that any teacher found to be at fault will be required to pay damages.

## Grounds for damages
A wide variety of incidents have been ruled by the courts to constitute lack of reasonable care by a school or its teachers.

➤ A TEACHER'S NEGLIGENT ORDER *A teacher sent a 13-year-old girl to poke a fire and pull out the damper in a grate in the teachers' staff room. Her pinafore caught fire and she was severely burnt. She claimed damages.*
DECISION *The jury found that the teacher had been negligent and awarded the girl £300 damages. Later, the Court of Appeal said the local education authority was also liable because the teacher acted within the scope of her job.*◄

➤ THE UNGUARDED STOVE *Eleven-year-old Betty was burnt when her apron caught fire as she and classmates crowded around a stove during a cookery lesson.*
DECISION *The local authority was found to have been negligent. The judge said that the authority should have anticipated the danger and put a guard round the stove.* ◄

## Danger in the playground
Injuries in the playground may give parents grounds for legal action against the school for lack of supervision by the teaching staff.

➤ THE MILK-BOTTLE HAZARD *An 11-year-old girl was injured when she slipped and fell in the playground, cutting herself on glass from a broken milk bottle.*
DECISION *The Court of Appeal ruled that the school authority was liable for damages, as it should have insisted on a safer system of storing and carrying away empty milk bottles and should have provided supervision.* ◄

The school is not liable for every accident. Teachers cannot be expected to protect children against every possible danger, although they must take reasonable precautions.

➤ UNAVOIDABLE MISHAP *A boy lost an eye when he was struck by a golf ball hit by another boy through a doorway leading to the playground.*
DECISION *The court held that the school was not liable as there was no evidence of lack of supervision. In addition, there was no evidence that, if there had been more supervision, it would have prevented the accident.* ◄

The law recognises that it is not always possible for teachers to foresee dangers that could threaten schoolchildren. They have a reasonable right to assume that older children do not need constant supervision.

➤ UNFORESEEN DANGER *A 13-year-old boy was injured when a lorry that was delivering coal to the school dumped its load on him. The accident happened during the morning break.*
DECISION *The court ruled that there was no liability on the school. The headmaster did not know the coal was to be delivered that day, or that it would be delivered by a tip-up lorry, or that the lorry would come during the break period. It was held that he was not negligent in failing to supervise 13-year-old boys during every moment of their break.* ◄

➤ WHEN CHILD INJURES CHILD *A boy threw a ball of sand and lime from a barrow in the playground, injuring another boy.*
DECISION *The court held that the school should have anticipated the accident. The school did, in fact, recognise that the sand and lime which had been left in the playground was dangerous.*

*The contractor had been asked to take it away, but he had not done so. Both school and contractor were liable on the ground of negligence.* ◄

## Responsibility outside the school

The school can also be liable for an injury caused out of school but while the child is waiting to go home.

► WHEN PUPILS GO HOME EARLY *Five-year-old Sandra was injured by a car 250 yds from her school at 3.29 p.m.*

*The children were normally let out at 3.30 p.m., but on that particular day they were let out at 3.25 p.m. Sandra's mother arrived at 3.31 p.m. and would have intercepted her child before she reached the main road if the children had been let out at the normal time.*

DECISION *The court held that the school was liable for damages because it was negligent in allowing small children out even five minutes before the scheduled time, without telling parents that this would happen.* ◄

When small children are let out of school early, the school must see that they are supervised until their mothers arrive. Even if they are let out on time, a school owes a duty of care until it can reasonably assume that the parents will be there.

If the school is on a main road, it would be negligent of the teachers to allow small children to wait for their parents unattended on the edge of the road.

If, through the negligence of the school, a child runs into the road and causes an accident in which other people are injured or killed, the victims or their dependants would also be able to claim against the school.

► THE OPEN SCHOOL GATE *David, aged 3½, was a pupil at a nursery school. The class teacher was about to take him and another child for a walk, but she left them to go to the lavatory.*

*On the way back she bandaged another child who had fallen down, and was taking him to the headmistress when she met David, who had been brought in from the street.*

*During the ten minutes she had been away, he had run out on to the road through an open gate. A lorry driver who had had to swerve to avoid him hit a telegraph pole and was killed. The driver's widow sued the school.*

DECISION *The court decided that the teacher was not negligent but that the school was responsible for not preventing the accident. The unlocked gate was a crucial factor in the decision. The widow was awarded damages.* ◄

A school can be held liable not only for lack of supervision but also for injuries caused by faulty or dangerous school buildings. In these circumstances the standard of care required is usually higher, since the school is liable, without proof of blame, if it fails to comply with the statutory standards for school premises.

► THE DANGEROUS DOOR *A girl sued her school after she was injured by putting her hand through a glass door which was swinging towards her. She claimed that the school was liable because the glass was too thin.*

DECISION *The girl was awarded damages. The court said that the school authorities were negligent since they knew that the glass was not strong enough, but had not replaced it. They would have been liable, even if there had been no proof that they were at fault, since the door did not comply with statutory standards.* ◄

## Lost property

IF property belonging to a child is lost or stolen at school, the school or the local education authority may be required to pay compensation.

Normally the school is not liable unless either it or a teacher is seriously negligent. If a coat-stand is placed near an open door so that passers-by could easily steal a coat, this may be considered to be negligence.

If a teacher accepts something from a child for safe-keeping, the school is normally liable for its loss or damage if the parent can show that the teacher was negligent.

The question of negligence depends on the particular facts of the case. A parent who sends a child to school with an overcoat not marked with his name might find it more difficult to establish that the school was responsible for its loss than if it were properly marked.

Similarly, if children take to school valuable jewellery or transistor radios, in defiance of a school rule forbidding such items to be brought on to the premises, and they are not given to a teacher for safekeeping, it is unlikely that the authorities would be liable if they were lost, stolen or broken.

# Dealing with rebellious children

*The parents' authority*     *Help from the law*
*Help from an outsider*

WHEN the behaviour of children gives parents serious cause for concern, they may wish to turn to other people for help or advice. Only in extreme cases, however, can they expect the law to provide a solution to such family difficulties.

Although the law lays down general guidelines about the scope and duration of parents' authority over their children, it cannot turn a disobedient and rebellious son or daughter into a dutiful one.

## The parents' authority
The extent to which parents have a legal right to control the actions and behaviour of their children diminishes steadily as the children grow older.

The parents' legal rights to tell their child what to do end automatically when the child gets married, even if the child marries at the age of 16.

Where the child remains single, a parent's legal authority may continue until the child reaches the age of majority, 18. It may, however, end earlier.

Whether the parents' rights come to an end before a single child is 18 depends mainly on whether the child is in the 'custody' of his parents—that is, living at home and dependent on them for his or her food, clothes, care and attention.

This means that, if a child leaves home to take a job elsewhere and becomes self-supporting, he can for most purposes be considered a free agent and his parents will not be able to enforce their discipline legally.

➤ THE BOY WHO LEFT HOME TO WORK *On leaving school, a 15-year-old boy was placed by his father in a residential farm training centre. After several weeks of study, the boy moved on to practical training on a farm where he received his keep and wages. He worked there for some months, during which he received no allowance from his father. Furthermore, he paid his fares himself whenever he went to his parents' home at weekends.*

*In 1962, while travelling in a farm truck driven by another boy, he was injured when the vehicle ran into a tree. After spending a period*

*in hospital he returned to his parents' home for a period of care and convalescence.*

*His father considered bringing an action against the driver, but decided against it since he was unsure of the insurance position and also believed that his son would recover fully.*

*More than three years later, his son was still afflicted—he suffered from amnesia and a speech defect. The father was refused leave to bring an action because he had delayed too long. The boy therefore decided to bring an action himself when he was 21 (the age of majority at that time). Before he could do this, he had to obtain a court ruling that he was not in his parents' custody at the time of the accident.*

DECISION *Since the boy had left home and lived miles away, the court ruled that he had left his parents' custody. Furthermore, he was earning his own living and supporting himself completely, which meant that he was not in the effective care of his parents. Though his father had acted for him earlier, this was merely because, as a minor, he could not bring an action himself. As he had left his parents' custody, he was not disqualified by time from bringing an action when he became 21. (Hewer v. Bryant.)* ◄

While the child under 18 remains at home, however, the parents' wishes have to be respected—in theory, at least. In these circumstances, a parent has a right to decide whether his son can buy a motor cycle, whether his daughter can go on holiday with her boyfriend or whether a bright child can leave school at 16 for a dead-end job.

Although parents have this authority in theory, the law does not give them any effective means of enforcing it in practice.

If a 15-year-old daughter living at home is told by her father to be home by 11 o'clock at night but consistently comes in later, the father has a legal right to punish her himself. But there would be nothing a court could do to enforce his orders.

By the time a boy is 14 or a girl is 16, the courts will not enforce that part of the concept of custody which consists of control of the physical movements of the child.

If a 16-year old girl runs away, a court will not normally grant the parents a writ of *habeas corpus* to restore her to the family home unless they can be persuaded to make her a ward of court.

In the normal situation it is left to parents to control their own children, and if the children are disobedient a court is unlikely to intervene to help the parents.

### Help from an outsider

A more helpful way of dealing with unruly children may be to get help and advice from an outsider. Sometimes a child who refuses to respect the views of his parents can be persuaded to change his mind by someone outside the family circle.

HEADMASTER A confidential talk with the child's headmaster, or a teacher who knows him or her well, may help parents to understand their child's problems better and possibly suggest remedies.

The teacher may also be willing to talk to the child about his behaviour. If there is a good relationship between teacher and pupil, the talk may bring it home to the child that his behaviour is causing anxiety.

DOCTOR If the child appears emotionally disturbed, the family doctor may be able to help—possibly by referring the child to a psychiatrist or a psychiatric social worker who will try to solve the child's problems.

LOCAL AUTHORITY OFFICIALS The social services department of the local authority has experience of dealing with difficult youngsters. Officials will listen sympathetically to parents' problems and may be able to suggest suitable remedies.

A worried parent can also ask for the specialist advice of the local authority's probation or education departments.

### Help from the law

Parents who feel that their child's problems are too great to cope with have two legal remedies—to have the child taken into the care of the local authority, or to have the child made a ward of court.

Both solutions mean that the parents will have to surrender some of their rights over the child. Neither course is likely to be appropriate, except in extreme cases.

CHILDREN IN CARE Parents who feel they have lost control of a child can make arrangements for the local authority's social services department to take over their responsibilities.

The child will be sent to live with foster parents or in a children's home, and will be supervised by the department. He or she will be given similar treatment to that received by those children who are being looked after by the local authority because a court has found them to be 'in need of care and protection'. ☐ Children in trouble, p. 356.

Where a child is taken into care at the request of parents, however, the parents have the right to demand the return of the child at any time.

The social services department will also aim to return the child to its parents as soon as there are signs that the family can re-establish a happier relationship.

WARDS OF COURT To make a child a ward of court, one or both parents must apply to the Family Division of the High Court. The application is likely to be costly—at least £100—though legal aid may be available to those who cannot afford it.

The procedure is often used by parents trying to stop a daughter from eloping with a young man they think unsuitable. It is also used when parents are in disagreement as to how the child should be brought up.

Once an application has been made to the court, the child becomes a ward immediately, even before any hearing. This automatic wardship lapses after 21 days, unless the court has fixed a date for the hearing.

The court may instruct one of its officers, the Official Solicitor, to represent the child. In such a case, he sees both the child and the parents, and tries to find out as much as he can of the family situation. He then reports to the judge what he thinks is best for the child.

The court has extensive powers over the major decisions of a ward's life—for instance, whom he or she may marry, or where he or she should live or go to school.

When the court confirms the wardship, it appoints an official guardian to ensure that the child does not take any major step, such as marrying, without the specific consent of the court. But the court cannot, in the nature of things, effectively regulate the day-to-day behaviour of a child.

The wardship automatically ends when the child reaches the age of 18, but the court can end it at any time before, if a change in the circumstances make it no longer necessary.

Parents can discuss wardship with any solicitor or with the Official Solicitor to the Supreme Court, The Royal Courts of Justice, Strand, London WC2A 2LN.

Having a child taken into care or made a ward of court are both drastic steps which parents turn to only as a last resort.

But in some cases it is possible that, by explaining to a rebellious child what could happen, the parents may persuade him or her to be more co-operative in future.

# Children in trouble

*Keeping a child out of court*
*Help from the local authority*
*The child in court*

*When care and protection are needed*
*Action by the court*
*Dealing with criminal offences*

CHILDREN who get into trouble are regarded in law partly as a delinquency problem and partly as a social one. There is consequently no rigid distinction between the way in which the law deals with children who commit criminal offences and the treatment it provides for innocent children with unsatisfactory home backgrounds.

The thinking behind the Children and Young Persons Act 1969—which deals with the treatment of children who get into trouble —is that a boy or girl who persistently commits criminal offences such as shoplifting may be the victim of circumstances.

For instance, disruption of home life may be the root of the trouble—the parents may have died, the child may come from a broken home or may have been ill-treated by members of the family.

Conversely, a child who is not suspected of breaking the law can still be brought before a court if it appears that he or she is in need of care and protection—in other words, if the home life is not satisfactory.

A child might come to the notice of the authorities without committing an offence if he regularly played truant from school, for example, or if he were frequently found by the police to be staying out all night. A child is also considered to be in need of care if he or she leaves home, takes drugs or goes off with an older woman or man.

The law makes a distinction between a child, defined as someone under 14, and a young person, someone of 14 and over but under 17. In these pages, however, 'child' and 'children' refer to all youngsters under the age of 17, unless it is otherwise stated.

### Keeping a child out of court

If a child is believed to have committed an offence, or appears to be in need of care and protection, the police will almost always get in touch with the parents and the local authority social services department. If it is a first offence or a trivial matter, the police may exercise their discretion not to prosecute, and may drop the matter with a warning.

When a parent shows genuine concern for a child's welfare, the authorities can often be persuaded not to go to court. They may, however, ask the parents to agree voluntarily that the child should be taken into the care of the local authority for special supervision.

### Help from the local authority

When children are taken into care they go either to a children's home or to a foster home where they will be supervised by the local authority social services department.

If they have special needs because of a physical or mental handicap—for example, a speech defect or backwardness at school—they are sent to a special home.

For children of 15 and over, it is sometimes possible to find a place at a residential school, a nautical college or some other establishment where they can learn a skill.

LOCAL-AUTHORITY HOME The children's home, sometimes known as a community home, is not bolted and barred like a prison.

---

## Ages of criminal responsibility

THE law makes a distinction between a 'child'—someone under 14—and a 'young person'—someone turned 14, but not yet 17 years old.

UNDER 10 A child under 10 cannot be charged with any criminal offence. But a child of 8 and over suspected of a criminal offence can be dealt with in 'care' proceedings.

AGED 10–13 A child turned 10 but under 14 can be charged with a criminal offence, but the prosecution must prove that the child knew that he was doing wrong.

AGED 14–16 A young person turned 14 but under 17 can have his fingerprints or palm-prints taken. Furthermore, he can be ordered to pay damages or compensation instead of his parents having to pay. In criminal proceedings, a young person can be fined a sum of up to £50, or he can be sent to a detention centre.

It may be little different from an ordinary boarding school. The standard of discipline varies from place to place.

The warden is chosen for his experience and understanding of children and he should welcome letters, telephone calls and visits from parents.

Children in trouble are associated in many people's minds with 'Borstals' and 'approved schools'. In fact, no one under 15 can now be sent for Borstal training, and approved schools are being replaced by the community homes. Children from broken homes will not normally be sent to the same community home as delinquents who are in trouble and require training.
RETURNING THE CHILD Social services officials try to return the child to his home as soon as conditions become suitable.

If the arrangement was voluntary and the parents withdraw their consent, the local authority must return the child. However, if the department is not satisfied with the family home and circumstances, it can ask the local authority to pass a resolution depriving the parents of parental rights.

The parents can dispute this by appealing to a juvenile court within 28 days. The court will then confirm the resolution or quash it.

### The child in court

If the parents do not agree that the child should be taken into care, or if the authorities think the matter should be brought to the attention of the juvenile court, proceedings will be taken.

A juvenile court consists of three magistrates, at least one of whom is a woman. The magistrates are specially chosen for their skill and experience in dealing with youngsters.

There are two kinds of proceedings: deciding whether a child is in need of care and protection, and deciding whether the child has committed a criminal offence.

Any child or young person turned 8 but under 17 can be brought before the court under the 'care' proceedings.

These hearings do not lead to any form of criminal record and are not supposed to carry the stigma of criminal proceedings.

Both 'care' and criminal cases are heard in private—no members of the public are admitted to a juvenile hearing, only the parents, child, court officials and Press.

Though newspaper reporters may be present, they are not allowed to report the child's name and address or to give any information which might identify him or her unless the court directs otherwise.

In rare cases, the magistrates may decide that publicity is desirable—if, for example, a child is cleared of an offence and it is important to put an end to rumours and gossip.

### When care and protection are needed

A child can be brought before a court as being in need of care and protection even though no offence has been committed. The court has power in such a case to make an order if it considers that, because of the unsatisfactory nature of his home, he is in need of care and control which he will not otherwise get. In these circumstances, an order can be made on any one of five grounds:
1. That the child is being subjected to ill-treatment or neglect.
2. That the child is exposed to moral danger.
3. That another child in the family is being ill-treated or neglected.
4. That the child's behaviour is beyond the control of the parents.
5. That the child frequently fails to attend school without good reason—such as illness.

### Action by the court

If, after hearing the evidence, the magistrates find that a child is in need of care and protection, there are several courses open to them.
BINDING OVER The parents can be bound over so that, if they do not take proper care of the child and exercise adequate control, they will have to forfeit up to, say, £50 to the court.

A court might decide on this course if it thought the child had got into trouble because of the parents' neglect. The parents cannot be bound over unless they agree. If they refuse, some other sort of order is made.
SUPERVISION ORDER If the court makes a supervision order, the child remains at home with his parents but is placed under the supervision of the council's social services department. This order replaces the old probation order, which has been abolished.

A probation officer may, however, carry out the supervision order if the court wishes—for example, if the child or a member of the family has previously been in contact with the probation service.

A social services official or probation officer has wider powers under a supervision order than under the old probation order, and this is the main difference between the two.

The court may decide that the child should attend a college for special training. It then depends entirely on the officer supervising the order—whether a social services department official or a member of the probation service—to select the place and decide how often each week or month the child should attend. So the court makes its decision and the official carries out that decision as he or she sees fit.

The court order can also lay down that the child must live in a place chosen by the supervising officer for a certain time; for instance, the officer might insist on a boy staying at a hostel for a month. Alternatively, the court may say that the child must take part in certain activities, such as going to a youth club. The supervising officer can decide which hostel and which youth club.

As a general rule, the supervising officer cannot make a child live away from home for more than a total of three months during the order, or force him to do other things, such as attend evening classes or a youth club, for more than 30 days in any one year of the order.

The supervising officer's job is to advise the child and give help in any way he can. The child will usually have to visit the officer from time to time, and the officer will call on the child at home.

The officer will also try to help with family problems, especially those affecting the child.

Help may be needed in dealing with housing difficulties, getting a job or sorting out Social-Security claims.

Great importance is attached to helping the whole family to prevent future trouble. Money is sometimes available to pay for travel, special clothing or training.

A supervision order usually runs for three years but never extends beyond the young person's 18th birthday. As with taking into care, the child can come under supervision by agreement with the parents.

The supervising officer can apply to the court during the three years to have the order ended if he thinks the child has made so much progress that the order is no longer necessary. The parents can also apply to have the order ended. If the supervising officer does not agree with them, however, the parents would have to give a very good reason for wishing to terminate the order.

If the child does not obey the supervising officer's instructions, or if he gets into trouble again, he can be brought back to the court. The court may then give a warning and continue the supervision order, or it may decide that the child should be taken from home and placed in care.

TAKING INTO CARE When supervision has failed, the child may be taken into the care of the local authority. In this case, the child is in exactly the same position as if he had been

## What to do when a child is accused

THE parents, guardian or foster parents of a child who gets into trouble may receive a visit from the police. It is always best to invite the policeman in. If the child is accused of doing something wrong, he or she should be asked to go into another room while the matter is discussed.

The policeman will probably wish to ask the child some questions, and the parents should insist on being present. If the policeman decides to charge the child, he should do so only in the presence of the parents. Only rarely is it necessary to arrest a child.

If asked to accompany the policeman to the police station to make statements, the parents should go voluntarily. Sensible co-operation is likely to assist everybody.

In a serious case, however, it would be sensible and proper to refuse to answer questions—and to advise the child to refuse to answer questions—until a solicitor is present.

If the child is arrested, the police have the power to grant bail. If they refuse, the child will be brought before the magistrates, when

the parents can apply for bail and for legal aid if needed. If the magistrates refuse bail, an application can be made to a High Court judge.

The court may order fingerprints or palmprints of a young person turned 14 but under 17 to be taken, but the prints must be destroyed if the prosecution drops the case or the youngster is acquitted.

If a young person of 14 or over is accused of killing someone, the procedure is exactly the same as for an adult on a similar charge. The Press is often asked or directed not to report the name and address or other identifying particulars of the child.

Children can also appear in an adult court on less serious charges if they are accused with an adult. If the children are found guilty they are usually sent to be dealt with by the juvenile court.

Children awaiting trial or sentence can, on rare occasions, be kept in prison. The authorities are under instructions to avoid this as far as possible, but it can happen when there is no other suitable place to keep them.

taken into care by agreement with the parents, except that the parents cannot demand his return. The order normally runs until the child is 18.

The parents may appeal when the order is made and may renew the appeal every three months. They would have little chance of succeeding, however, unless they could show a marked improvement in the family home. On the other hand, the social services department has an obligation to restore the child to his own home as soon as possible.

If, during the first year, the parents do not visit the child often or keep in touch, the local authority will appoint a visitor to go to see the child and try to make friends.

If a child behaves exceptionally badly and keeps on running away, he may be sent to one of the few closed homes which are designed to prevent absconding.

The case of every child in a closed home must be reviewed every three months by a committee which includes at least one independent person who has no connection with the local authority.

HOSPITAL ORDER If two doctors certify that, because of his mental condition, a child needs hospital treatment, the court can make a hospital order. Under the order, the child can be released only when the hospital doctors decide that he is fit to be discharged.

The parents can apply to the Mental Health Review Tribunal to order the child's discharge. The hospital will give them the necessary forms and explain the procedure.
☐ Treatment for the mentally ill, p. 380.

GUARDIANSHIP ORDER As an alternative to the hospital order, the court can make a guardianship order, which places the child under the guardianship of the local health authority. The child can normally be released only when the doctors decide he is fit for discharge. But a parent can apply to the Mental Health Review Tribunal to order a discharge.

A 'care' order can be combined with a hospital order, but otherwise the juvenile court can make only one order at a time.

## Dealing with criminal offences

When a child is suspected of committing a criminal offence, the authorities can do one of two things. They can apply to the juvenile court for a 'care' order or other order, in exactly the same way as they would if the child were simply in need of care and protection. Or they can bring a criminal prosecution.

A child who has committed a criminal offence might be dealt with by a court under 'care' proceedings—rather than being charged

with the offence—if the social services officials believed that he or she was a victim of circumstance, such as an unhappy home life.

Sometimes, though, there is no possibility of criminal proceedings. A child *has* to be dealt with in 'care' proceedings if he is under the age of criminal responsibility—no child under 10 can be charged with a criminal offence.

A criminal prosecution against a child of 10 and over but under 17 can be brought only by the police, by an officer of the National Society for the Prevention of Cruelty to Children or by a social services department official. And even the police or N.S.P.C.C. officer must consult the department before prosecuting. It is not possible for a private person to prosecute a child.

Criminal proceedings are a last resort, when the police think that the case cannot be dealt with adequately by parents, teachers and social workers or that care proceedings will fail to deal with the case adequately.

If a child is in serious trouble, parents should ask a solicitor whether the child should admit or deny the offence and whether the child should be represented in court.

Parents who have difficulty in finding the money for legal fees may qualify for legal aid.
☐ Help with legal fees and costs, p. 710.

In criminal cases, the magistrates can make any of the orders applicable to 'care' proceedings. There are several additional remedies they can apply.

DISCHARGE The magistrates may decide not to impose a penalty although the case is proved. This is called 'giving a discharge'.

A discharge can be 'absolute', which means that it is the end of the matter and nothing more will be heard of it.

Alternatively, the discharge can be 'conditional', in which case the child can be brought back to court to be punished for the original offence if he gets into trouble again within a period decided by the magistrates. This period cannot be more than three years.

FINE OR COMPENSATION The juvenile court magistrates can impose a fine of up to £50 on the child (or his parents if he is under 14). They can order the parents or the young person to pay compensation of up to £100. This compensation might be due if the child has, say, smashed windows, uprooted shrubs or caused similar damage.

OTHER ORDERS The magistrates can send a boy of 15 or over to a Borstal institution, though this is unusual for boys of under 17. A boy remains at a Borstal for between six months and two years, depending on his conduct.

# All about coming of age

*Court proceedings*    *Marriage*
*Education*    *Medical treatment*
*Employment*    *Taxation*

YOUNG men and women become entitled to their full legal and property rights at the beginning of the day of their eighteenth birthday. The lowering of the age of majority from 21—under the Family Law Reform Act 1969—does not affect any will, agreement or arrangement made before January 1, 1970, the date when the change came into force.

If a will made before that date says that property is to be inherited when a person reaches his majority, it means 21—which was

## The ABC of minimum ages

| | |
|---|---|
| **Adoption** | A baby can be handed over to prospective new parents at any age, and formally adopted from $4\frac{1}{2}$ months up to the age of 18. The mother cannot sign a consent form until the child is six weeks old. ☐ How to adopt, p. 336. |
| **Alcohol** | A young person over 14 can be taken into a bar by an adult, but cannot buy or consume alcohol until he is 18. At 16, he can drink cider or beer with a meal in a room with no bar. ☐ Restaurants and public houses, p. 656. |
| **Bank accounts** | A baby can have a deposit bank account and own any interest. The child can draw on the account when the parents and the bank manager agree that he is responsible enough to handle money. A current account, with cheque book, can be used from the age of about 13, at the bank manager's discretion. A child can have a savings account in a post office from the age of seven. |
| **Blood donors** | A person can donate blood from the age of 18. |
| **Contracts** | A person under 18 can enter into contracts for 'necessary' purchases, employment or training, but a contract giving an interest in property is only partly valid as the boy or girl can withdraw at any time before reaching 18, and for about six months afterwards. Parents have no legal responsibility for contracts made by children under 18—unless they have given a guarantee on the youngster's behalf or authorised him to make the contract on their behalf. |
| **Court proceedings** | A child of any age can be brought before a court if thought to be in need of care and protection. At ten a child can be charged with a criminal offence and brought before a juvenile court. Offenders over 17 are dealt with in an adult court—and so, sometimes, are children under 17 who are jointly charged with an adult or charged with homicide. ☐ Ages of criminal responsibility, p. 356. |
| **Driving** | At 16, a boy or girl can get a licence to drive a tractor, at 17 a motor cycle or car, at 21 a lorry or bus. ☐ Learning to drive, p. 20; Motor cycles, p. 165. |
| **Earnings and income** | A child's income belongs to him at any age. ☐ Looking after children, p. 342. |
| **Education** | A child can go to a State nursery school from the age of two. He or she must usually start school by five and receive full-time education until the age of 16. ☐ When a child must go to school, p. 346. |

the age of majority when the will was made. Similarly, if a will says that property was to be inherited at a certain age—say, 20—it cannot be inherited earlier.

Some age qualifications remain unchanged. For example, no one under 21 can be a candidate at a local or Parliamentary election, or sit on a jury.

Among changes in the Act, young people can now marry at 18 without the consent of their parents, instead of waiting until 21. But the Act did not change the age at which they can marry with consent—this remains at 16.

Although students now become adults at 18, their parents are expected to contribute to their maintenance until they reach the age of 25 (or the age of 21 in the case of a married daughter), unless they have been self-supporting for three years.

Age limits a youngster's rights and responsibilities in two ways. First it disqualifies a youngster from engaging in certain activities—such as owning land, driving motor vehicles on public roads and claiming Social Security benefits.

Second, it makes it an offence to supply people who are under age with certain commodities—such as cigarettes and fireworks—though the youngster cannot be charged for possessing them.

| | |
|---|---|
| **Employment** | No child under 13 is allowed to work, except in the entertainment business, or in light agriculture or horticulture. At 13 a child can do light work permitted by local by-laws for two hours a day. Strict rules also apply for those between 13 and 18. ☐ When children can take a job, p. 593. |
| **Films** | A child can see a category U or A film at any age, though the British Board of Film Censors considers A films contain material which may be unsuitable for children under 14. At 14 a youngster can see an AA film, and at 18 an X film. |
| **Fingerprints** | Police need parents' consent to take fingerprints of anyone under 17; but if consent is refused, magistrates may order prints to be taken from anyone aged 14 or over charged with an offence punishable with imprisonment. Fingerprints must be destroyed if a minor is acquitted. |
| **Firearms** | A youngster can own an airgun at 14, and a shotgun at 15. Younger children can use arms under qualified supervision. ☐ Children and firearms, p. 141. |
| **Fireworks** | It is an offence to sell fireworks to a person under the age of 13. |
| **Flying** | A boy or girl can fly solo in a glider at 16. In other aircraft the minimum age is 17. |
| **Free travel** | Free travel on public transport generally stops at the age of three. A child is usually charged reduced fares until 14. ☐ Rights of the traveller, p. 162. |
| **Gambling** | A boy or girl aged 18 can gamble in a private home, take part in casino gambling, and enter a betting shop. ☐ Betting and gaming, p. 660. |
| **Jury service** | A man or woman may be required to serve on a jury at 21. |
| **Lotteries** | A lottery ticket may be bought in the name of anyone aged 16 or over. |
| **Marriage** | A young person can marry at 16, but until the age of 18 he or she must obtain the consent of parents or guardians—or, if they refuse, the consent of a court must be obtained instead. ☐ Getting married, p. 312. |
| **Medical treatment** | At 16, a person can consent to medical, surgical or dental treatment. Most hospitals require permission from a parent for operations on anyone under 18. |

continued ▶

## The ABC of minimum ages continued

| | |
|---|---|
| **National Insurance** | A minor pays National Insurance contributions at 16. Unpaid apprentices, people receiving full-time education, the unemployed, and sick are exempt. |
| **Owning land** | People can own land at 18, and have the freehold or leasehold of property in their name. Until then, the land or property must be held by an adult. |
| **Passports** | A child travelling abroad alone has to have a passport. Before a passport is issued, parental consent must be given. A child travelling with a parent can be registered on the parent's passport until the age of 16. |
| **Pets** | No one under 12 can buy a pet, but a child of any age can own one. |
| **Prison** | Youths and girls can be given a prison sentence at 14, though below this age they can be held in prison awaiting trial. |
| **Services** | A boy may join the Army or the Royal Navy at 15, and the Royal Air Force at $15\frac{1}{2}$, with his parents' permission. A girl may join the Women's Royal Army Corps, the Women's Royal Air Force or the Women's Royal Naval Service at 17, with parental permission. |
| **Sickness and supplementary benefit** | A person can draw sickness benefit at $16\frac{1}{2}$ and supplementary benefit in his or her own right at 16. ☐ State help in hardship, p. 550. |
| **Smoking** | At 16 young people are allowed to buy and smoke cigarettes. Anyone who sells to children under that age can be punished by a fine of up to £100. |
| **Suing and being sued** | People under 18 cannot normally bring a court action, except through a 'next friend', usually a parent or guardian. There is one exception—they can sue for loss of earnings up to £750. There is no definite age at which a minor becomes liable for civil damages. It is seldom worth suing anyway because the minor usually has no assets. It is not normally possible to sue parents for a wrong done by a minor, unless the parents themselves have been negligent. ☐ Looking after children, p. 342; Children in trouble, p. 356. |
| **Taxation** | Children's income is taxable. A parent is entitled to tax relief from the beginning of the tax year in which a child is born. The relief increases in the first full tax year after the child reaches 11. Relief stops at the end of the tax year in which the minor becomes 16, or when full-time education ends. ☐ How the income tax system works, p. 556. |
| **Transplants** | At 18, a person is allowed to give a body organ or tissue for transplant. |
| **Unemployment benefit** | A person must be $16\frac{1}{2}$ to draw unemployment benefit. |
| **Voting** | A person can vote in local or Parliamentary elections at 18, but cannot stand as a candidate until he or she reaches the age of 21. |
| **Wills** | A boy or girl under 18 who is left money or property in a will cannot receive it directly as he or she cannot give a valid receipt to the dead person's representative. A trustee must use any income or capital for the sole benefit of the beneficiary. No one under 18 can make a valid will, unless he is on military service, when the will is valid at any age. |
| **Witnesses** | A young child can give evidence in court if the judge thinks the child understands the duty to tell the truth. |

# Going to university or college

MANY young men and women who reach a certain academic level are able to obtain a university or college place and a local-authority grant. But a university place—unlike a place at school—is not an automatic right. Neither is a local-authority grant. Universities, colleges and local authorities have a wide discretion to choose among applicants. This means that a would-be student with an impressive academic record still faces the danger of being turned down because of a shortage of places.

## Obtaining a place
The first step for anyone interested in going to university or college is to find out which institutions run courses in the subjects he wishes to follow. His school careers master will be able to guide him.

Advice can also be obtained from the Advisory Centre for Education, 32 Trumpington Street, Cambridge CB2 1QY.

Applications for full-time first degree or first diploma courses at universities and university colleges in the United Kingdom are usually made through the Universities Central Council on Admissions. The address is P.O. Box 28, Cheltenham, Gloucestershire, GL50 1HY.

IF A PLACE IS REFUSED A university or college is acting within its rights in refusing to accept any applicant. In most cases, the would-be student will have no legal remedy.

Someone whose application was turned down, despite the fact that he had the necessary examination passes and had attended what seemed to be a satisfactory interview, might feel that the college was being unfair, or even negligent, in choosing students.

However, although colleges try to be scrupulously fair in selecting applicants, the law does not place on them any obligation to be fair or even careful.

If there are signs of serious irregularities— if the politics of the applicant seem to be involved in his rejection, for example, or if there was sustained antagonism between one of the interviewers and an applicant—the applicant should first complain to the registrar or the executive secretary of the college, or alternatively to the dean or head of the college department or faculty. If this is unsuccessful, the rejected applicant might consider enlisting the help of his Member of Parliament.

## Starting at college
When a university or college offers a student a place and this is accepted, there is a contract between the two. Indeed, in many colleges, the student is required to sign a document binding him to accept its rules.

Although the law is far from clear on this, the duties of the college under the contract would normally include giving the courses it had advertised in its current prospectus, or providing comparable courses; and providing qualified staff, adequate classes or tutorials, a library and facilities for private study.

The student, for his part, would be obliged to accept the university or college discipline and all reasonable directions of his teachers.
COMPLAINING TO THE COLLEGE If a student finds that the college is not carrying out its obligations he can, technically, take action for damages. However, this course is not normally necessary or worth while unless the harm caused is serious and all non-legal methods of solving the problem have failed.

For instance, if a student believes that the course or the standard of teaching is insufficient or incompetent, he can first complain to the dean of the faculty or the department head.

If this fails, and the student is still certain that his complaint is justified, he can go to the academic board, to the governing body— frequently called the 'Senate'—or to the registrar. The students' union may be willing to take up the complaint, or to help him prepare his case. Action in the courts would only have a chance of success in an extreme case, where the facts showed plainly that the student had not got what he contracted to receive from the college.

## Lodging problems
A student who takes lodgings—usually a bed-and-breakfast arrangement, though possibly it may include an evening meal—makes his own contract with his landlord. He will agree to pay weekly, monthly or possibly for a term,

and will arrange the period of notice required.

In law, the student who pays for board as well as lodging will probably be a lodger with no legal protection against eviction except the right to reasonable notice. ☐ Rent: cases of limited protection, p. 264.

If a student wants something more secure, he can take a furnished or unfurnished flat— if the university rules allow. ☐ Choosing the type of home to rent, p. 242.

Disagreements with landlords are best settled informally if possible. In cases of difficulty, the college or faculty dean, or the university lodgings bureau, may mediate.

If a large sum is involved and a friendly settlement is impossible, then legal advice should be sought by the student. ☐ Getting advice on a legal problem, p. 708.

## College regulations

When a student becomes a member of a university or college, he agrees in law to accept any reasonable regulations made by the authorities. This does not, however, prevent the student from trying to persuade the authorities to change the rules.

While the rules continue, the student has an obligation to attend any lectures or tutorials which the college makes compulsory, to wear a gown if instructed to do so, and to return at night to his lodgings, college or hostel at the time laid down by college regulations.

If a student fails to observe the regulations, this in itself will not give the university or college authorities the right to take any action in law. They will be entitled, however, to apply college disciplinary procedures.

The law gives colleges and universities wide scope for making regulations, and no court would interfere with these regulations unless the rules were entirely unreasonable.

## Students' privacy

Students living in college will probably be required to accept rules about the state of their rooms and the hours of visiting.

If there is excessive supervision, or if college officials violate students' privacy without cause, all a student can do is to complain to the warden or any other official responsible. He has no means of redress in law.

If this fails—possibly because the warden decides the policy—the students' union may be able to negotiate a change in the rules.

## Personal files

Universities and colleges usually keep records of all students, and their right to do this will be accepted by the courts. The student has no

legal right to see his records, which belong to the university or college authorities.

A college that chooses to do so will be entitled to show a student some—but not all— of the papers in his confidential file. Reports provided by headmasters and other people on condition they remain confidential can be used only by authorised college officers.

A student who suspects that a report contains information about his political activities has no legal remedy. People providing references have a right to be frank, and the law will generally protect them against actions for libel. If a student discovered that a report on him contained inaccurate or untrue statements, he would be able to claim damages for libel only if the report had been seen by un-authorised people, and the writer had made the untrue statements maliciously. ☐ The dangers of controversy, p. 666.

Damaging or taking records without permission may lead to prosecution for criminal damage or theft, as well as being an infringement of the college's own regulations.

## Disciplinary procedures

When a student joins a college or university, he agrees implicitly to be bound by its disciplinary procedures. These and the rights of appeal are contained in the institution's regulations, which the student is assumed to have read when he enrolls.

All university bodies making decisions which seriously affect the rights and status of a student must observe the rules of natural justice. This means that the student should be told the case against him and be able to make representations and that those hearing the case must act fairly.

Rights of representation vary at this type of hearing. A student may be entitled to appear himself, or only to send a letter. At some institutions, he may be entitled to be represented by a tutor, a member of his own or another department or a lawyer. When a student fears expulsion or other serious punishment, he should consult a solicitor.

It is normal for appeals against disciplinary decisions to be made to a special board of review, to the Vice-Chancellor or to an outsider, called the 'Visitor'. If the rules of natural justice have not been observed, the High Court can order a re-hearing.

## Double punishment

Where something forbidden by a university rule is also illegal—for example, stealing—a student who breaks the rule risks being punished twice: once by the university and a second time by the courts. But he fares no differently from those in other walks of life, such as a dishonest shop assistant who might lose his job as well as being prosecuted.

In many cases it may depend on the university whether a criminal prosecution is brought or not. The police may not know of the alleged offence unless they are informed of it by the university; or where the police already know, they may be persuaded to allow the university authorities to deal with it.

When a student appears on a serious charge before a university disciplinary body, therefore, he should ask if criminal proceedings are likely. He will be justified in reserving his defence and refusing to make a statement if the university refuses to undertake not to initiate a criminal prosecution. (Otherwise any admissions he made could be repeated in court by a witness who heard them.)

Even if the university gives such an undertaking, this does not rule out independent action by the police or anyone else affected.

However, any punishment which the university body had decided on could be cited in court as a reason why a student found guilty should be treated leniently.

All serious crimes suspected to have been committed within the university by students will normally be reported to the police by the authorities. In such cases, the university may make a solicitor available to the student.

## Demonstrations and sit-ins

A peaceful procession in a public place does not involve many legal risks in practice. Local bye-laws may require 36 hours' notice to the town hall or the local police, or both. The police will normally arrange for the procession to take place without causing unreasonable obstruction to other road users. ☐ Meetings, marches and demonstrations, p. 672.

If, however, a demonstration involves a disturbance of the peace and clashes with the police, anyone taking part risks prosecution.

Minor disturbances and angry exchanges of abuse may cause the police to stop a demonstration or meeting and ask people, possibly including bystanders, to disperse. If the disorder gets worse, people taking part may be charged with disorderly behaviour, obstructing the highway, obstructing the police in the execution of their duty or with threatening, insulting or abusive behaviour.

Conviction for such offences will, for a first offender, involve only a fine or being asked to give an undertaking, backed by the threat of forfeiting money, to keep the peace. If a student has been suspended but refuses to leave university or college premises after being ordered to do so by the authorities, he can be sued for trespass. Furthermore, the university may request the help of the police during a sit-in. But the police are unlikely to take action unless a breach of the peace has been caused or is likely to occur.

Such sit-ins can lead to prosecution if they involve breaking into rooms or buildings, assaults on university officials, damage to property, threats to those who oppose the action, or seizure of things found on the premises. Criminal charges that might be brought include conspiracy, causing an affray, forcible entry, criminal damage, riotous assembly, unlawful assembly and burglary.

A demonstration or sit-in which develops into a major disturbance—involving large numbers of people, fighting, assaults on the police, damage to property and causing bystanders to be in grave danger or fear of harm —may produce serious charges which may be tried in the higher courts.

When the police do not bring charges because the university asks to be allowed to cope, the students concerned, in effect, enjoy a privilege—they will have no criminal record as a result of the university's punishment.

## Examination failures

Students who fail examinations can be expelled, transferred from an honours course to a pass course or ordinary degree course or forced to take an extra year over the course. But the college must consider all relevant educational evidence.

The teachers taking the decision are not obliged to take into account the student's personal circumstances—for instance, illness or a domestic crisis. If they choose to do this, however, they have an obligation in law to allow the student, or someone authorised by him, to give evidence in person or in writing.

Any student who is asked to withdraw from a university partly or wholly because of his personal circumstances, without being allowed to present evidence, can apply to the High Court for an order quashing the decision.

If the order is granted, the court will probably instruct the university to re-hear the evidence and reconsider its decision. Proceedings in court must, however, be started as soon as possible, or the court will not intervene on the student's behalf.

Students who fail examinations sometimes feel they deserved to pass. Unless they have clear evidence of discrimination against them or of the examining authority's incompetence, no court action will succeed.

# Changing your name

*Christian names*  
*Forenames and surnames*  
*Three ways of changing a name*

*Marriage and divorce*  
*Living together*

ANYONE is legally entitled to call himself by any name he chooses—provided he does not do so for a fraudulent reason and that he gives his official name or names on all official and legal documents. In most cases no legal formality is needed to change a name, but there are several procedures for making known the change.

**Christian names**
It is more difficult to change a Christian name—one given in baptism—than it is to change any other first name or a surname. In 1946 Mr Justice Vaisey said that a Christian name, given in baptism, could be changed in only three ways—by Act of Parliament, by a bishop at confirmation and by the addition of a name on adoption. He added: 'Nobody can part with a Christian name by deed poll.'

**Forenames and surnames**
The first names, or forenames, of people who have not been baptised and anyone's surnames can be changed without legal formality. The person simply adopts a new name. But this method can lead to complications in personal matters such as National Insurance, income tax, getting a passport, having a bank account and even buying a house or shares, unless there is some sort of official notification. (It is assumed that the person wanting to be known under another name will make sure that his friends and business colleagues are informed that he has made this change.)

**Changing by advertisement**
The simplest and cheapest method of making an official notification that a person is adopting a new name is for him to advertise the fact in a newspaper circulating in the area where he lives. Anybody using this method should keep copies of the newspaper advertisement to show people, particularly tradesmen or firms with whom he may wish to open an account.

**Changing by statutory declaration**
There may be occasions when someone using a new name needs to prove legally who he is—for example when he is left money in a will under his original name. In such cases he can swear before a Commissioner for Oaths to the name he has been using and the name he was given at his birth. This is called making a statutory declaration.

If a solicitor is used to prepare the wording of the declaration, the total cost in fees to the solicitor and to the Commissioner for Oaths—who is also a practising solicitor, authorised by the Supreme Court to hear sworn statements—should be no more than £5·25.

A statutory declaration is like a statement made under oath in court. Anyone making a false declaration can be prosecuted for perjury, for which the penalties are severe—a maximum of seven years or a fine or both.

**Changing by deed poll**
The best and most official way to change a surname is by deed poll, which costs about £10.

The deed—which is simply a written statement of the person's original names and the names he now wishes to use—is drawn up by a solicitor. A legal seal is attached, the document is signed by the person changing his name, and witnessed.

The change does not need to be advertised unless the solicitor registers the deed at the filing department of the Central Office of the Supreme Court, Strand, London WC2A 2LN. Then it must be advertised in the official Government newspaper, the *London Gazette*. The filing department will supply a copy of the deed to people such as a bank manager or to a firm's pension fund if it is required.

If a copy is also registered at the Passport Office, Clive House, Petty France, London SW1H 9HD (any Employment Exchange will receive documents for forwarding to the Passport Office), a passport will be issued in the new name without the old name being mentioned. Otherwise the old name is given as well—unless the new name has been used for more than ten years, or since before the age of 18, or unless it results from legal adoption.

COLLEGE OF ARMS A deed poll can also be drawn up and recorded by the College of Arms, Queen Victoria Street, London EC4V 4BT. The person concerned does not need to have a Coat of Arms. This change is also published in the *London Gazette* and the total cost in a normal, straightforward case is £15·75.

WIFE AND CHILDREN The same deed poll can be used to change a wife's surname, but this must be written into the deed and signed.

The names of children under 16 normally change with those of the parents. But children of 16 and over have to sign the deed in the same way as their parents. A father can change a child's name without the consent of the mother, but the mother must have the father's consent to change her child's name.

## Marriage and divorce

When a woman marries, her new name is entered on the marriage certificate. That is all the proof required of her change of name.

But she can still use her maiden name, or any other name, if she wishes for professional or other reasons. If she is divorced she can continue to use her married name—or any of her married names if she has been divorced more than once—or revert to her maiden name. Similarly, a widow may revert to her maiden name or use the name of her late husband or anyone to whom she was previously married.

A woman must not use a former husband's name in a way which implies that he is still married to her. If she does, her former husband can seek a court injunction to stop her.

If by representing herself still to be her former husband's wife she implies that a woman he has later married is not his legal wife, she can be sued for libel or slander.

A woman who marries a peer of the realm—that is a duke, a marquis, an earl, a viscount or a baron—or who marries a knight or baronet, has a right to use the title she gains by marriage even if they are later divorced. But if she remarries, she loses the right.

## Living together

If a woman lives with a man to whom she is not married she can change her name to his by deed poll—or she may simply start using his name. She can write to the National Insurance and tax authorities and anyone else with whom she is likely to have business and tell them that in future she wants to be known by the man's surname. Documents such as insurance cards will then be made out in her new name.

➤ THE NAME MADE NO DIFFERENCE *Jessamine was the legitimate daughter of Mr and Mrs Knight. After her daughter was born, Mrs Knight went to live with a man named Roberts and continued to live with him for many years. Jessamine, although christened and registered as Jessamine Knight, was always known as Jessamine Roberts.*

*Arranging to get married, Jessamine told her intended husband her real name and on the advice of the vicar, it was agreed to publish the banns in the name of Roberts because the other name would mislead the public. Eventually Jessamine's husband applied to have the marriage annulled on the grounds that the true surname had not been given and the banns had failed to comply with the Marriage Act 1823.*
DECISION *The husband's plea was rejected. The court said that as the wife had agreed to her name being stated as Roberts, without any fraudulent intention, and that as Roberts had become her true surname by usage, she had complied with the Act. (Dancer v. Dancer.)* ◄

If anyone changes his name, or uses his proper name, only to get the benefit of some well-known trade name or to take advantage of the goodwill of a business or another person with the same name, that firm or person can apply to the court for an order prohibiting the action. Similarly, a court can order someone to stop using a sporting title which does not rightly belong to him. But the genuine champion has to prove that the person using his title has deprived him of his reputation or damaged his means of earning a living.

➤ THE DISPUTED BOXING TITLE *Hugh Serville became the official welterweight champion of Trinidad in 1952. In 1953, he came to England and although he held a licence to box he could not get any fights.*

*While in England, he discovered that another West Indian boxer, Hector Constance, was in Britain, billing himself as 'welterweight champion of Trinidad' and 'welterweight champion of the British West Indies'. Serville asked the High Court for an injunction to restrain Constance from using these titles or passing himself off as the holder because he had no right to the first title and the second did not exist.*
DECISION *The court ruled that Serville had not proved that Constance had acted with any intention of damaging Serville's means of earning a living, or that Constance even knew that Serville was champion. Serville had failed to establish that he held any reputation in England or that the public could confuse the two men. His case was dismissed. (Serville v. Constance.)* ◄

If a court orders someone to give up a 'borrowed' name or title, but he persists, he can be sent to prison for contempt of court and freed only if he agrees to drop the name and apologises to the court.

# Getting the best from a doctor

*How to choose a doctor*  
*Getting on to a doctor's list*  
*Changing doctors*

*Getting private treatment*  
*Obtaining prescriptions*  
*Complaints against a doctor*

EVERYONE in Britain, even a visitor to the country (provided he has not come *only* for medical treatment), has a right to medical treatment under the National Health Service, whether or not he pays National Insurance contributions. Alternatively, anyone can choose to pay for private medical treatment.

For those who want Health Service treatment, the first step is to register with a general practitioner. A National Health Service patient is entitled to choose any doctor in his area who treats patients under the Health Service and is willing to accept him.

### How to choose a doctor
Often, neighbours in a new area will be able to recommend a doctor. If not, a list of family doctors, with addresses, surgery times and the names of any partners, can be inspected

in the offices of the local National Health executive council. Lists should also be available in any main post office, public library or Citizens' Advice Bureau.

### Getting on to a doctor's list
A prospective Health Service patient takes his medical card to the doctor of his choice and asks to be taken on to his list. If the medical card has been lost, the doctor will provide an alternative form.

The prospective patient should not wait until he or a member of his family is ill. The doctor may have difficulty in treating a patient until he receives the medical records, which may take several weeks to arrive from the patient's previous doctor.

### If a doctor refuses a patient
Health Service doctors are not obliged to accept every patient who applies to them. A doctor can reject a patient because he already treats the maximum number of patients permitted by the Department of Health and Social Security. Alternatively, he may have set himself a lower limit. He does not have to give reasons for refusing to accept a patient.

Most patients who are refused a place on one doctor's list can find an alternative without difficulty. If, however, no doctor can be found, apply to the clerk of the local executive council, which has powers to insist that a local doctor take a patient. The address can be found in the telephone directory under 'National Health Service'.

While waiting for a place on a doctor's list, the patient is entitled to necessary treatment from any Health Service doctor—even one who refuses to accept him permanently.

### How to obtain treatment
The best way to ensure good treatment from a doctor is to treat him with consideration. Go to the surgery whenever possible instead of asking for a home visit, but do not make unnecessary calls or visits. If a home visit is necessary, make the request early in the day if possible. Always give the doctor as much information as possible about the illness.

A patient is entitled to treatment and to

---

## A doctor's qualifications

ANYONE who wants to check a doctor's qualifications can consult the Medical Directory—copies are kept by most public libraries. This lists the degrees and diplomas held by doctors, mentions some of the jobs they have held and may help the patient to find a doctor with special experience. Some of the additional qualifications are:

CHILD HEALTH Diploma in Child Health (D.C.H.).

PSYCHOLOGICAL MEDICINE Diploma in Psychological Medicine (D.P.M.).

CHILDBIRTH AND WOMEN'S DISEASES Diploma of the Royal College of Obstetricians and Gynaecologists (D.R.C.O.G.).

TROPICAL DISEASES Diploma in Tropical Medicine and Hygiene (D.T.M. & H.).

DISEASES OF THE EYES Diploma in Ophthalmology (D.O.).

EAR, NOSE AND THROAT DISEASES Diploma in Laryngology and Otology (D.L.O.).

home visits, but he cannot demand that the doctor treat him in a particular way, or ask the doctor to make unnecessary calls.

WHEN THE DOCTOR WILL NOT CALL If the doctor refuses a visit and you still feel it is necessary, call again, give the symptoms and stress the urgency.

If the doctor still refuses to call, tell him you plan to call another doctor or an ambulance, and do so if necessary. ☐ Claiming damages against hospitals and doctors, p. 381.

TREATMENT AWAY FROM HOME Patients away from home for less than three months can apply to any doctor on the Medical List for temporary treatment. It will be helpful if the patient can give the doctor his medical card or at least his Health Service number.

Anyone staying away from home for longer than three months should apply for a transfer to another doctor.

WHEN THE DOCTOR IS NOT AVAILABLE In the case of an accident or other emergency, when the patient's doctor or his deputy is not available, any available doctor on the Medical List must give necessary emergency treatment.

TREATMENT OVERSEAS Most countries do not offer free treatment to foreigners working or on holiday there, and medical expenses incurred abroad cannot be claimed back from the Health Service. But a few countries—New Zealand, Yugoslavia, Bulgaria, Poland, Norway, Denmark and Sweden—provide medical treatment at reduced rates for United Kingdom citizens. Full details can be obtained from the local office of the Department of Health and Social Security.

People visiting other countries can take out insurance to cover medical treatment. Health insurance for foreign travel is often covered in a package holiday, along with a personal effects and accident policy. ☐ Booking a foreign holiday, p. 142.

Anyone who may require one of a group of drugs controlled by the Misuse of Drugs Act 1970 while abroad, should ask his doctor for a letter to present to a doctor or hospital abroad, explaining his requirements. These drugs—morphine, for instance—may be exported only under Home Office licence. The traveller may also need an import licence in the country to be visited, and the Home Office will usually be able to give information about this.

Anyone returning from abroad with drugs, such as 'pep pills', which are included in the Act, needs to obtain authority in advance to bring them into this country.

People requiring a continuous supply of drugs, other than controlled drugs, for treatment while abroad for a short period may get them on the Health Service before leaving, but the doctor does not have to prescribe drugs in advance to cover illnesses which might occur on holiday—such as stomach upsets.

## Changing doctors

A patient can change doctors if he moves house—even if he does not move to a new area—simply by taking his medical card to the doctor of his choice.

If the patient has not moved house, there are two ways to change doctors. The first is to ask his present doctor to agree to an immediate transfer. The doctor signs a part of the card and the rest is filled in by the patient. The card is then taken or sent to the new doctor.

If the present doctor refuses to agree to the transfer, or if the patient is too embarrassed to approach him, the patient should send the card to the local executive council, whose address is on the card, with a letter stating that he wishes to change doctors. He should first secure the agreement of the new doctor to the change.

The card will be returned with a slip to be filled in and taken to the new doctor, who is authorised to accept the patient not earlier than 14 days from the date on which the application was received by the executive council. This authority to change doctors remains in force for one month.

If the patient needs treatment during the change-over, he can ask his old doctor.

## How a doctor can transfer a patient

The doctor can have a patient removed from his list by applying to the executive council. If the patient is undergoing treatment, he cannot be transferred until the doctor is satisfied that the patient will have another doctor, or that he does not need further attention for seven days.

## Getting private treatment

All doctors have the right to accept private patients. Some deal only with private patients, and the secretary of the local medical committee, whose address can be obtained from the clerk of the executive council, may be able to provide the names of doctors who are prepared to see patients privately.

Private patients have to pay the full price for any medicines or appliances that are prescribed for them by a doctor.

## Obtaining prescriptions

All necessary medicines—along with certain medical appliances—can be prescribed on the Health Service by a doctor.

When prescription charges are in force, they

have to be paid to whoever supplies the goods—a chemist, a hospital or the doctor himself.

Several categories of patient do not have to pay the prescription charge. They are:
**1.** Anyone under 15 or aged 65 and over.
**2.** Expectant mothers, or mothers with a child under 12 months old.
**3.** People suffering from a disease which needs continuous treatment, such as epilepsy.
**4.** People with a continuing physical disability which prevents them from leaving home without help.
**5.** War pensioners needing treatment for their war disablement.
**6.** Anyone receiving supplementary benefit or family income supplement—and dependants.
**7.** Anyone else who needs help to pay the charges—and his or her dependants.

## Complaints against a doctor

Patients dissatisfied with treatment by a doctor can complain to the local executive council. The council can punish the doctor, but cannot award compensation. The patient may, however, be able to recover any expenses resulting from the doctor's breach of his terms of service.

The patient can also complain to the General Medical Council, which has power to punish the doctor, but cannot award compensation. The patient may also sue the doctor for damages. ☐ Claiming damages against hospitals and doctors, p. 381.

Under their contracts with executive councils, family doctors agree to abide by certain 'terms of service'. The grounds of any complaint to the executive council, therefore, can only be that the doctor failed to comply with these. Most complaints make one or more of the following allegations:
**1.** That the doctor failed to give all the necessary treatment.
**2.** That the doctor failed to visit a patient who needed treatment at home.
**3.** That the doctor failed to arrange necessary hospital or specialist treatment.

Complaints may be made by the patient himself; by the husband or wife of the patient; by any person given authority by a patient unable to complain because of age or illness; or, if the patient is dead, by anyone.

➤ ASSUMPTIONS A DOCTOR CANNOT MAKE *The wife of a patient telephoned late one evening asking the doctor to call and examine her husband, who had abdominal pains. When she was told that the doctor's partner was on duty, she replied that she had tried to contact him, but could get no answer. She agreed to try again.*

*Later she rang the first doctor back to say that there was still no reply, and the doctor said he would try to get in touch with his partner himself. A few minutes later he telephoned, heard the engaged tone, assumed that the patient was talking to his partner, and went to bed.*

*Unhappily, he was wrong. The patient's wife was unable to get in touch with the partner until early next morning, when he examined the husband and had him transferred to a hospital where the man later died.*

*It was discovered afterwards that the partner's telephone had been temporarily out of order because of a storm. The wife made a complaint against the doctor.*
DECISION *The doctor was found to have failed to visit and treat his patient, whose condition required it, and was fined.*

*An appeal by the doctor was dismissed because the appeal committee considered that it was not reasonable for him to have assumed that contact with the partner had been made.* ◄

When a doctor fails to make a visit because he has not been given adequate information about the patient's illness, or because he has been misled, the committee is likely to find that the doctor has not failed in his duty.

➤ WHEN THE ILLNESS IS NOT STATED *A woman whose husband was suffering from abdominal pains asked her neighbour to call the doctor. The neighbour telephoned, but was unable to tell the doctor why a visit was necessary. The doctor declined to come.*

*Later a second doctor was called to examine the patient. He diagnosed a suspected perforated ulcer and sent the patient to hospital. The family made a complaint against the first doctor.*
DECISION *The service committee of the executive council dismissed the complaint. They accepted the doctor's defence that, on the information given, no visit was necessary.* ◄

A doctor can be expected to treat his patient only on the basis of the information he is given. When the patient fails to undergo tests or provide information, the doctor will not be held responsible if treatment is inadequate.

➤ THE DOCTOR WHO NEEDED MORE INFORMATION *A doctor was asked to see a girl who was said to be tired and generally unwell. When the girl arrived at the surgery, the receptionist told her mother that she had tried to telephone to ask that a specimen of urine be brought.*

*The doctor examined the girl, but found nothing definitely wrong. He said he would need the specimen before an adequate diagnosis could be made. No specimen was provided, however, and the following day, a Sunday, the doctor's partner was asked to call and see the girl. The partner declined, on the grounds that there seemed to be no new circumstances requiring the visit, and again stressed the need for a urine specimen to be provided.*

*The following morning the patient's condition got worse, and after two telephone calls the doctor visited her and transferred her to hospital, where she died in a diabetic coma. The patient's family complained to the executive council.*

DECISION *The complaint was dismissed. The doctor's receptionist gave evidence that repeated requests had been made for a specimen. Without this, the doctor could not have been expected to make an accurate diagnosis.* ◄

### How to complain

Complaints to the executive council must be made in writing to the clerk of the council (the address is on the patient's medical card) within six weeks of an incident.

If illness or some other reasonable factor causes delay, the service committee, which deals with complaints, may allow up to two months from the date of the incident. After this, the complaint can be heard only with the consent of the doctor or the Secretary of State for Social Services.

PROCEDURE If the chairman of the service committee considers that there is no case to answer, the matter may be disposed of without a hearing. The patient can appeal against this in writing, within a month, to the Secretary of State for Social Services.

Where there is a case to answer, the clerk of the council seeks the doctor's written observations on the complaint. These are then passed back to the complainant for his comments. The chairman considers the matter and decides whether a hearing is necessary.

In some cases, to prevent relations between doctor and patient from deteriorating, the complainant may be asked to agree to conciliation rather than an inquiry—although he will not lose his right to an inquiry if the attempt at conciliation fails.

Such a suggestion will not be made in a serious case, but in others it may be in the complainant's interest to agree.

If the case is heard by the service committee it will come before a lay chairman, three doctors and three laymen. Their decision will be by majority vote.

Both patient and doctor may conduct their own case or may have it presented by a friend. Solicitors, barristers or other paid advocates may advise but may not conduct the case.

The committee is entitled to determine its own procedure. Usually the complainant gives evidence and is then questioned by the doctor or his representative, and by members of the committee. Any witnesses the patient calls are also examined and cross-examined. The doctor's case is heard in the same way. Finally, both parties sum up.

The committee's recommendation is first reported to the executive council, after which copies of the report are sent to each party. Both patient and doctor can claim expenses.

### Penalties

If the doctor is found to have broken his terms of service, the executive council may:
1. Reduce the number of patients the doctor is allowed.
2. Order the doctor to pay any expenses incurred by the patient as a result of the doctor's error (not including the expenses of the hearing).
3. Fine the doctor.
4. Suggest that the doctor be removed from the Health Service Medical List. This would be considered by a special body called the Health Service Tribunal.

### Appeals

The doctor or patient can appeal against the executive council's decision to the Secretary of State for Social Services within one month.

The patient cannot complain on the grounds that any fine imposed was too small, although the doctor can complain that it was too big.

The appeal must be in writing, and should state the grounds for appealing. The patient should not merely repeat the original complaint, but he can stress facts which he believes received insufficient attention from the committee, or he may put forward new facts (provided this is done not less than a week before the appeal is heard).

He can also try to show that facts accepted by the committee were inaccurate, challenge the inferences drawn from those facts, or argue that the decision was against the weight of the evidence.

The Secretary of State for Social Services may dismiss the appeal without hearing the parties if he feels there are no reasonable grounds for the appeal. But normally he cannot do this if a doctor is appealing against an adverse decision.

Any such appeal will be held in private before not more than three people, appointed by the Secretary of State. Usually they include a legally qualified chairman and a doctor. Both sides can be represented by lawyers, trade-union representatives, family members or a friend; but legal aid is not available.

As in the original hearing, both sides may call witnesses and claim expenses. Costs are occasionally awarded to the successful party.

## Complaints to the Medical Council

The General Medical Council deals with doctors convicted in the courts or accused of serious professional misconduct. It is not concerned with minor misunderstandings and disputes, however unfortunate the results. The main circumstances which lead to doctors appearing before the GMC's disciplinary committee are alcoholism, drug addiction, advertising, or sexual relations with patients.

A patient who wishes to make a complaint must make a statutory declaration, sworn before a Commissioner for Oaths, and send it to the General Medical Council, 44 Hallam Street, London W1N 6AE.

If the complaint is thought to merit action, the doctor will be asked for an explanation. If further action is necessary, the case will pass to the disciplinary committee.

The complainant may present his own case, or he may engage a lawyer. If a patient cannot afford legal services, the council may allow its own solicitor to present the case.

The procedure is similar to that of a court of law. Witnesses can be required to attend, and evidence is given on oath. After their witnesses have been heard and cross-examined, each side sums up its case.

Generally the case will be heard in public, and the proceedings are likely to get coverage in the local and national Press.

## Punishment

If the disciplinary committee of the General Medical Council finds that a doctor has been guilty of infamous conduct, it can:

**1.** Admonish the doctor.
**2.** Put him on probation by postponing judgment for a specified period.
**3.** Strike him off the Medical Register.
**4.** Suspend his registration for a period.

If he is struck off the register or suspended, the doctor has 28 days in which to appeal.

Only a small number of cases are brought each year, and only 359 doctors were struck off the register between 1900 and 1969.

COSTS No costs can be awarded to the successful party by the disciplinary committee.

# Private health insurance

PRIVATE health insurance schemes normally ensure a private room and a choice of hospital or doctor. They may also provide after-care in a nursing home, private treatment from a general practitioner, or group medical care for company staff.

Premiums vary according to the age of the person to be insured and the type of cover required. In most cases there is an upper age limit of 65. Each scheme has different allowances for the cost of treatment covered.

There is usually a maximum for benefit payable in any one year.

The cover for in-patient treatment normally includes nursing-home or hospital-bed charges, operating-theatre fee, the expense of special nurses and the cost of drugs and medicines while in a nursing home.

In surgical cases, there are rates for operations, including surgeon's and anaesthetist's fees. In medical cases, expenses cover physician's fees, consultations, X-rays, physiotherapy and radiotherapy.

Out-patient treatment cover includes full expenses for operations, consultations with specialists, X-rays, tests, physiotherapy, nursing at home and convalescence.

In most schemes, no medical examination is required before insurance is taken out. Cover for dependants is normally at a reduced rate.

If a patient is already suffering from an illness when he joins the scheme, he will not normally be covered for treatment of that illness. Some schemes also set a time—say, three months—after joining before benefit is paid. The premium is normally a yearly one, and can be reviewed before renewal.

The insurance company, except in certain cases, will not refuse to renew a subscription because of heavy claims during the year. Normally, too, it will pay benefit for any type of treatment unless that treatment is specifically excluded on its application form.

There are a number of specialist health insurance companies, including: British United Provident Association, 25 Essex Street, London WC2R 3AX; Private Patients Plan, 157 St. John's Road, Tunbridge Wells, Kent; and Western Provident Association, 42 Baldwin Street, Bristol BS1 1NE.

# How to get specialist treatment

*At the dentist's*     *Care of the feet*
*Spectacles*          *Convalescing*
*Deafness*           *Drug addiction*

THE National Health Service provides a number of specialist services, including dental treatment, ophthalmic (eye) care, deafness aids and treatment, chiropody (care of the feet), treatment for drug addiction, and sometimes convalescent care and home help.

### At the dentist's
A patient wanting dental treatment under the Health Service does not need to register with a dentist as he does with a doctor, and can change dentists without having to fill in any official forms.

Not all dentists accept National Health patients. A list of those who do can be seen at any main post office.

Treatment under the Health Service is not free, except for patients in certain groups, such as expectant mothers. Apart from these, charges are related to approximately half the cost of the services provided. A list of the maximum fees a dentist can charge for Health Service treatment can be seen at the office of the local executive council, whose address is listed under 'National Health Service' in the telephone book or printed on the patient's medical card.

If the patient wants to be treated under the Health Service, he should make this clear to the dentist at the outset and, before starting treatment, should sign a Health Service treatment form. The dentist is entitled to ask for payment before he starts treatment.

Some dentists will not give certain types of treatment, such as capping teeth, under the Health Service. If this happens, the patient can either try to find Health Service treatment elsewhere or agree to have private treatment.

Again, a patient may want more expensive treatment or more expensive false teeth than those provided under the Health Service. The dentist may be willing to provide these, leaving the patient to pay the excess over the Health Service allowance; otherwise the patient will have to be treated privately.

EXEMPTIONS Expectant mothers and mothers who have had a child within the preceding 12 months do not have to pay for treatment.

All patients under 21 are exempt from the basic charge for treatment—though once over school-leaving age they have to pay for dentures and other forms of special treatment.

Patients already receiving supplementary benefit or family income supplement may claim reimbursement of the charges. ☐ State help in hardship, p. 550.

CANCELLED APPOINTMENTS If a patient breaks an appointment he can be charged at the dentist's discretion.

Patients accepted for a course of treatment whose condition requires a home visit from the dentist are entitled to this at any place within 5 miles of the dentist's surgery.

DENTAL TREATMENT IN HOSPITAL Patients are not charged for treatment if they are in hospital when it becomes necessary.

Out-patients who have treatment in dental teaching hospitals are also treated free. Would-be patients should check with their local teaching hospital for details.

COMPLAINTS Patients with complaints can go to the local executive council in the same way as patients of family doctors. ☐ Getting the best from a doctor, p. 368.

If the patient complains of inadequate dentures, his case may be dealt with by the denture conciliation committee of the executive council. This committee can recommend that the executive council permit the patient to attend another dentist, in order to have a new denture made without further charge.

Complaints should be made to the clerk of the executive council.

Complaints about conduct can also be taken to the General Dental Council, 37 Wimpole Street, London W1M 8DQ.

### Spectacles
If a patient wants a first pair of spectacles under the Health Service, he must get a form from his family doctor authorising a sight test. He can then take this form to any ophthalmic medical practitioner (who tests sight and prescribes glasses) or to any ophthalmic optician (who tests sight, prescribes glasses and may also supply them). Both can be found through the Medical List available at any main post office.

After the first sight test, the patient can have tests at any time without applying to his doctor. However, if he needs a second test within a year, he must obtain permission from his local executive council.

There is no charge for eye-testing at the optician's premises. But the patient may be charged if he asks for a test at his home.

CHARGES There is a fixed charge for each single-vision lens, and a higher one for each bifocal lens. A patient has to pay extra for plastic or safety lenses.

The adult patient must also pay for the frames for his spectacles. He should insist on being shown the range of National Health Service frames, which are available at various prices. As an alternative, he will be offered privately supplied frames which are considerably more expensive. He will also be charged privately for lenses if Health Service lenses will not fit the privately supplied frames he has chosen.

Children under the age of ten can obtain Health Service lenses and frames free. People already receiving supplementary benefit or family income supplement may claim back money spent on Health Service glasses.

No charge is made for Health Service lenses supplied to youngsters under 16 or to older people receiving full-time education.

If the patient wants rimless glasses or specially shaped lenses, the whole transaction, for lenses as well as frames, becomes a private arrangement. Charges should be agreed in advance with the optician.

Ophthalmic treatment may also be obtained through a hospital if the patient's doctor agrees. This is usual if the opinion of a consultant ophthalmic surgeon is needed.

The cost of repairs or replacements must be paid by the patient, unless he can prove that the loss or damage was due to something other than lack of care on his part.

Complaints are made to the executive council—as they are for doctors and dentists. ☐ Getting the best from a doctor, p. 368.

## Deafness

A patient suffering from deafness should first consult his family doctor who will, if necessary, refer him to a consultant to see whether surgery or a hearing aid is required.

If an aid is necessary, the Health Service body-worn aid, known as the Medresco, can be obtained free of charge from the ear, nose and throat departments of hospitals and audiology clinics.

Commercial aids range in price from £25 to £100. Never buy one without a free trial first.

Additional information about hearing aids and treatment for deafness can be obtained from the Royal National Institute for the Deaf, 105 Gower Street, London WC1E 6AH.

The institute also tests hearing aids free, and issues a list of hearing aids with information about their performance and price.

## Care of the feet

There is no comprehensive Health Service chiropody service—though some hospitals, local authorities and voluntary services treat old people, the infirm and expectant mothers. A family doctor or the health department at the local council offices will advise.

## Convalescing

Though there is no standard service, convalescence after an illness is available, where medically necessary, as part of the hospital service. The patient's family doctor, a hospital doctor, medical social worker or the council health department will give advice.

## Home nursing and home helps

Invalids or elderly people who need home nursing or home help should consult their doctor or the local health department. Schemes vary throughout the country. ☐ National Health Service home helps, p. 292.

## Invalid chairs and cars

Invalid chairs and cars are provided in appropriate cases. As a first step, patients should consult their general practitioner—or a consultant, if they are attending hospital.

## Hardship

Patients who cannot pay Health Service charges can get aid. They should ask their doctor, dentist, chemist or whoever else may be concerned—or go to the local office of the Department of Health and Social Security.

## Drug addiction

Drug addicts can obtain treatment at a number of centres around Britain which are run by doctors licensed under the Misuse of Drugs Act 1970. These centres are normally in the psychiatric sections of hospitals; a list is available from the Department of Health and Social Security.

The Department advises that addicts, or those concerned with them, should first go to their family doctor or to a general practitioner who will then recommend treatment.

There is no power to compel a person's admission to hospital solely because of his addiction, though he may be compulsorily admitted if his mental health is affected as a result. ☐ Treatment for the mentally ill, p. 380.

# Ending a pregnancy

*Grounds for termination*    *The cost*
*How to apply*    *Criminal abortion*
*Advisory services*

A WOMAN whose health or welfare is threatened when she becomes pregnant may be permitted by law to have an operation to end the pregnancy. She may be able to have the operation privately or free under the National Health Service.

### Grounds for termination
The Abortion Act 1967 says that a pregnancy can be brought to an end if two doctors agree that any of the necessary circumstances are present. These are:

**1.** That continuation of the pregnancy would present a risk to the mother's life.

**2.** That continuation of the pregnancy would endanger her physical or mental health more than if the pregnancy were terminated.

**3.** That continuation of the pregnancy would endanger the physical or mental health of any other children of the family more than if the pregnancy were terminated.

**4.** That there is a substantial risk that the child would be born with a severe physical or mental abnormality.

Unless one of these four conditions is present, induced abortion is unlawful. Except in an emergency, the operation must be performed in a Health Service hospital or in premises licensed for such operations by the Department of Health and Social Security.

A doctor who has conscientious or religious objections can decline to take part in abortion operations, except where it is necessary to save the life of the mother or prevent serious mental or physical injury to her.

### How to apply
A woman should first consult her family doctor. If this is inconvenient she can consult another general practitioner privately.

Normally a patient will not be seen by a specialist unless she has been referred by her doctor. But with abortion operations, where some doctors have moral objections, some consultants may see patients without a doctor's reference. If a doctor refuses the woman's request to be considered for a Health Service abortion she may ask to see a specialist. If the specialist agrees that the pregnancy should be terminated, he can send her to another

doctor. If this doctor also agrees, the operation can legally go ahead.

CONSENT A woman does not always need the consent of her husband to have her pregnancy terminated. If the father is not the patient's husband he has no rights in the matter. Unmarried girls do not need parental consent unless they are under 16. ☐ Treatment in hospital, p. 376.

### Advisory services
To help women whose doctors are unwilling to advise on termination, voluntary advisory services have been set up in several parts of the country. If they cannot secure a Health Service operation for the woman, they can usually provide an introduction for a private operation at a fee considerably cheaper than those charged by private clinics.

Among the main advisory centres are: Pregnancy Advisory Service, 40 Margaret Street, London W1N 7FB; Marie Stopes Memorial Centre, 108 Whitfield Street, London W1P 6BE; Pregnancy Advisory Service, 1st Floor, Guildhall Building, Navigation Street, Birmingham B2 4BT; and Southern Pregnancy Advisory Service, 138 Dyke Road, Brighton, Sussex BN1 5PA.

### The cost
Health Service abortions are free, but the cost of private operations varies. One reason is that the operation becomes more difficult the longer it is delayed. It will be cheapest before the thirteenth week of pregnancy.

Abortions through an advisory service would rarely cost more than £100 and could be as low as £55. A private abortion operation, which may be obtained through a doctor or specialist, or by applying direct to a private nursing home which deals with such cases, could cost £130–£150, perhaps more.

### Criminal abortion
Anyone having any part in terminating a pregnancy when none of the necessary circumstances laid down by the Abortion Act 1967 is present, is guilty of a criminal offence. If the pregnant woman dies, all concerned can be charged with manslaughter.

# Treatment in hospital

*All about going into hospital*  
*Consent for treatment*  
*The patient's right to information*

*Visiting and staying with children*  
*Discharge or transfer from hospital*  
*Complaints about hospital treatment*

I N an accident or an emergency, a patient will normally be admitted to hospital automatically and without delay. Otherwise the patient can be admitted only if his family doctor thinks he needs hospital treatment. He cannot *demand* hospital treatment.

If the doctor refuses to send him to hospital, and the patient disagrees, he may ask his doctor to obtain a second opinion, which the doctor should do if he considers it medically necessary. Otherwise, there are two courses of action open to the patient.

The first is to go to the casualty department of the local' hospital and hope to be referred to one of the out-patients departments. But this is inadvisable. It is an abuse of the casualty service, and a casualty officer may merely send the patient back to his doctor, who will not be pleased at the patient's going behind his back.

The second, and probably more satisfactory course, after the patient has tried to discuss his problem frankly and amicably with his doctor, is to change doctors. ☐ Getting the best from a doctor, p. 368.

The patient is not limited to the hospitals in his own area. He can go further afield if his doctor agrees. The patient, however, has no right to be admitted to a particular hospital, though the waiting period for admission to one hospital may be shorter than another.

Private patients—even those of a doctor who is not on the Health Service list—are entitled to free hospital treatment, and so is a patient seen privately by a consultant.

If any patient wants a particular specialist, he should ask his family doctor. Strictly speaking, the patient is not entitled to demand a particular specialist, but a doctor will probably try to accommodate the patient's wishes as far as possible.

Patients can also be referred to hospital by a company doctor or from the school health service. Patients can attend venereal-disease clinics (often known as special clinics) without being referred there by a family doctor.

## Choosing the type of hospital

Occasionally the family doctor may want to refer his patient to a hospital specialising in a particular class of disease. Otherwise the choice of hospitals is between teaching and non-teaching. There may be little to choose between them as far as quality of treatment is concerned, but some people may dislike the practice in teaching hospitals of allowing medical students—as well as hospital staff— to examine patients.

If the patient does object, he can ask the family doctor to send him to a non-teaching hospital. The doctor will probably agree. Sometimes, however, the right type of treatment may be available only at a teaching hospital. The patient is entitled to ask that no student should be allowed to examine him. The Department of Health and Social Security advises hospitals not to make admission conditional upon the patient's agreeing to students' examinations.

If the patient asks not to be seen by students it may mean that he will have a limited choice of consultants. This, however, should not affect his treatment.

Teaching hospitals prefer patients to consent to being examined by students. One of the strengths of British medical teaching over that of many other countries is that students are taught at the patients' bedsides and not just in a classroom.

## Waiting lists

Hospital waiting lists vary considerably. The patient should ask the hospital how long he will have to wait before he can be admitted. If this seems too long, he should ask his family doctor to try another hospital.

A patient may sometimes be able to jump the queue if he is prepared to go into hospital at a few hours' notice when beds may become available through cancellations.

## Getting the best from the hospital service

Before attending hospital—especially in cases where the diagnosis is still in doubt—the patient should check that he has told the family doctor all his symptoms and all relevant family and personal history.

This is also the time for the patient to consider how much he wants the hospital specialist to tell him about his illness. The patient who takes an intelligent interest in his illness will usually get adequate information. Every Health Service hospital should provide the prospective patient with a handbook containing useful information. Details of visiting hours will be included; if relatives are unable to fit in with them, the ward sister may be able to make special arrangements.

## Amenity beds

There is no charge for hospital treatment under the Health Service, unless a patient chooses special accommodation.

Some hospitals have a number of single rooms, or rooms with two or three beds, known as amenity beds. A patient wanting a degree of privacy can ask if such a bed is available. If the patient needs such accommodation for medical reasons, he will get priority—and will not have to pay. Otherwise he will be charged a small daily fee laid down by the Department of Health and Social Security. The treatment is exactly the same as that in a general ward.

## Consent for treatment

The patient can refuse any operation or type of examination or treatment. It may be an assault on the patient for a doctor to examine or treat him against his will. It may also be an assault for a surgeon to operate without the patient's consent. In both cases the patient may be entitled to compensation.

But the patient should bear in mind that if he refuses a certain treatment, the hospital may say it is impossible to treat him. For example, the patient may decline to accept a blood transfusion, and his surgeon may then decide that he is not prepared to operate. In cases where patients object to blood transfusions, most surgeons will refuse to promise in advance that no transfusion will take place —they may simply say that they will bear the patient's objections in mind. In serious cases they may take upon themselves the risk of legal action, rather than allow a patient to die.

Similarly with children, the surgeon may agree to respect the parents' objections if reasonably possible—but he will not allow a child in his care to die.

THE CONSENT FORM Consent is normally required before an operation, though in an emergency the surgeon may take such action as he reasonable believes the patient would wish were he aware of his condition. Consent is usually written, but it does not have to be. Patients aged 16 or over can sign their own consent form. If a patient is under 16 years of age, the consent form is generally signed by a parent or guardian. Patients or relatives should not sign until they have an adequate explanation of what is intended.

Avoid signing a consent form permitting the surgeon to carry out 'whatever may be necessary'. Such consent is too widely drawn to provide the patient with adequate warning of what treatment he is to receive. Instead, insist that an adequate description of the treatment to be carried out is entered on the form. If the description is too narrow, a further operation · might be required for something unforeseen.

If the patient is worried that the operation will include something he does not want done, he can write on the form that he refuses consent for that particular part of the operation.

He should also ask the surgeon to explain any factors which might influence him in deciding whether or not to have the operation. ORGAN TRANSPLANTS Consent for part or parts of the body of a dead person to be used for organ transplants or medical research purposes is covered by the Human Tissue Act 1961. This states that when a person has, in writing, or verbally in the presence of two witnesses, requested that his body or any specified part of it be used after death in this way, the person lawfully in possession of the body may authorise the removal of the parts or organs specified. The person lawfully in possession is normally the nearest relative or, if no relative is available, the hospital authority.

If the circumstances of the death require that an inquest be held—for example, if the death resulted from a road accident—the doctor must notify the coroner and obtain his consent before any organ is removed. ☐ Investigating a sudden death, p. 410.

When the dead person has not given permission, organs may be removed only after all reasonable inquiries have been made to establish that he did not object to such operations and that his relatives do not object.

Anyone wishing to donate his body or specific organs after death to a medical school can get forms from the Inspector of Anatomy at the Department of Health and Social Security, Alexander Fleming House, Elephant and Castle, London SE1 6BY. Those who want to help others by donating organs can carry a written document with them stating their wishes.

CONSENT BY HUSBAND OR WIFE If a wife needs to have an operation which may affect her capacity to bear children or have sexual intercourse, the surgeon may ask the husband to sign a consent form.

This is largely a matter of courtesy, and even if the husband refuses, the surgeon is still able to proceed if he feels it to be in the wife's best interests and if she herself consents.

However, the consent of the other partner would probably be considered essential in the case of a sterilisation operation carried out on a husband or wife purely as a means of birth control. But legal action taken against a surgeon for operating without the other partner's consent would have little chance of success.

### The patient's right to information

The patient has, in general, the right to be told what is wrong with him, though a doctor does not have to tell a patient everything—especially if he thinks it would be prejudicial to the patient's interests.

The rights of a relative to know what is wrong with a patient are not as clear. Doctors have an ethical obligation not to disclose any secrets they learn from their patients.

In most cases, of course, it is in the patient's interests that his close relatives know the nature, probable duration and outcome of his illness. But there are exceptions. For instance, a doctor in charge of a maternity case where the husband and wife were separated would probably not—without the wife's consent—inform the husband that she was in hospital to have a baby. Similarly, the outlook for the patient in a mental hospital will probably not be divulged to a husband seeking divorce until the doctor is satisfied that his patient's interests are being properly represented.

### Ownership of case notes and X-rays

The Health Service patient has no right to insist on seeing his case notes, X-rays or laboratory notes. These documents are owned by the hospital authority. However, if the patient thinks that the diagnosis was wrong, and decides to take legal proceedings, he can apply for a court order instructing the hospital to make these documents available for inspection and copying. Hospital authorities will generally make documents available if there is a hospital inquiry.

A patient who has an X-ray taken privately does not necessarily have the right to keep it, unless this was specifically agreed beforehand. What he is paying for is the radiologist's opinion, and it is arguable that the films themselves are merely the basis on which that opinion is founded. However, a private patient is entitled to the specialist's opinion in writing.

### Visiting and staying with children

The importance of children having regular visits from their parents, especially if they are expected to have a long stay in hospital, is generally recognised. The Department of Health and Social Security has recommended that hospitals should be generous when setting visiting hours.

If the parents think that the hospital visiting hours are inadequate, they can ask for special consideration or take up the matter with the hospital secretary.

Some hospitals provide accommodation so that mothers can stay with young children. Often, the facilities are not publicised because they are limited. The mother can write to the matron asking about such facilities before the child is admitted. In the case of an emergency admission, the parents should have a word with the matron or the ward sister about accommodation. Mothers, however, have no absolute right to demand such facilities.

Accommodation, but not necessarily board, is free for mothers staying in hospital unless the child is in a pay bed, when a charge is made for both mother and child.

### Expenses for patient or visitor

Anyone who is receiving supplementary benefit and has to go to hospital for outpatient treatment can get a refund of necessary travelling expenses. The money can be collected from the medical social worker's office at the hospital, on production of a supplementary-benefit order book.

Travelling expenses are not normally paid to people visiting hospital patients. But the Supplementary Benefits Commission will help if the cost of such travel will cause any hardship. However, the payments will cover only the cost of the visit.

People who do not qualify for supplementary benefit and people in full-time employment cannot normally get financial aid towards travel expenses, unless their income is only slightly above the qualifying level for benefit or if an expensive journey has to be made.

A person may also get aid if he is summoned to the bedside of a close relative who is seriously ill in hospital, and cannot meet the expense of the journey.

For more details contact the local office of the Department of Health and Social Security.

ACCOMMODATION Visitors who want to stay close to the patient during a long illness can see the medical social worker at the hospital, who should be able to recommend reasonable accommodation near by.

SPECIAL HOSPITALS Visitors to patients detained in the three special hospitals—Broadmoor, Berkshire; Rampton, Nottinghamshire; and Moss Side, near Liverpool—and to the State Hospital at Carstairs in

Lanarkshire are entitled to receive contributions towards the cost of travel by public transport, including air travel if necessary.

This assistance can be given only to visitors who are not already receiving supplementary benefit. Application forms can be obtained at the hospital and travel tickets must be produced.

## Discharge or transfer from hospital

A patient can discharge himself from hospital at any time, but he will not be discharged by the hospital until his treatment is completed.

A patient who wants to leave against the doctor's advice will be asked to sign a statement that he is discharging himself.

Sometimes the hospital may try to discharge the patient against his will—or perhaps transfer him to a long-stay hospital. Pressure to reduce waiting lists means pressure on patients to return home as soon as possible. If the patient feels he should remain longer, he should ask to see the consultant to check whether the decision can be changed.

AGED PATIENTS Before an aged patient is discharged, the medical social worker at the hospital should see that satisfactory arrangements are made for looking after him or her.

The patient's family cannot be forced to look after him. But the local authority will generally help the family with such facilities as a home help and a laundry service.

The family should not allow themselves to be rushed into taking the patient home. They should be given reasonable notice to enable necessary arrangements to be made.

CHECKS BEFORE DISCHARGE Before leaving, a patient should:

1. Check if and when he must attend the outpatients' department.
2. See that he has a supply of any necessary tablets to last until he visits his family doctor.
3. Collect any necessary sickness certificate.
4. Find out what effect the treatment may have on his work, diet, fertility, sexual activity and so on.

AFTER-HOSPITAL CARE Patients recovering from a serious illness may be able to get convalescent treatment. But this varies throughout the country. The patient should consult the medical social worker at the hospital for details of facilities available.

## Complaints about hospital treatment

Complaints about trivial matters often arise from misunderstandings. They should be mentioned to the ward sister or doctor, and can usually be dealt with on the spot.

More serious complaints are best taken up with the consultant. If he fails to give a satisfactory explanation, complain in writing—tactfully and fairly—to the hospital secretary.

The hospital secretary will either deal with the case himself or pass it to the hospital management committee, or board of governors in the case of a teaching hospital. If it is a very serious complaint, it will probably pass to an even higher authority—such as the regional hospital board.

Less serious complaints are dealt with by a committee of inquiry set up by the hospital authority, usually with a legally qualified chairman. The members of the committee should not be connected with the hospital involved in the complaint.

If the complaint is against a doctor, a doctor of similar experience would probably be appointed to the committee.

The complainant and the people against whom the complaint is made will probably be allowed legal representation, and the complainant should receive a copy of the committee's report.

There is no formal right of appeal. But if the complainant is dissatisfied, he can try to pursue the case with a higher authority such as the regional hospital board or the Department of Health and Social Security, which may order a further inquiry. Support from an independent source such as an M.P. may help.

COSTS Committees of inquiry have no power to award costs or damages, but may recommend to the hospital authorities that out-of-pocket expenses and legal expenses should be covered. The hospital authority can also discipline a doctor for professional misconduct or incompetence.

Where the hospital staff or an individual specialist seem to have been negligent in providing treatment, the patient or a relative may have grounds for an action for damages against the hospital. ☐ Claiming damages against hospitals and doctors, p. 381.

HEALTH SERVICE OMBUDSMAN When the relevant legislation comes into force, patients can also complain to an independent official called the Health Service Commissioner (or 'Ombudsman'). The Commissioner deals with complaints of injustice or hardship through bad administration or failure to give necessary treatment; but he cannot investigate actions based on a medical man's clinical judgment, or actions of anyone not employed by the Health Service.

When the Commissioner is ready to begin investigations—probably in 1974—details of how to apply are available from local Citizens' Advice Bureaux.

# Treatment for the mentally ill

As far as possible anyone who needs treatment for serious mental illness is admitted to hospital informally, and is treated with other patients, instead of being isolated.

INFORMAL PATIENTS Anyone who feels he needs treatment for mental illness can go to his family doctor, who can arrange for admission to hospital just as for someone who is physically ill.

COMPULSORY ADMISSION A relative or a local council official called the 'mental welfare officer' can apply to a hospital to admit a patient for observation or treatment there. The applicants must have seen the patient within 14 days of the application being made (if the admission is a matter of emergency, within three days).

The application has normally to be accompanied by two medical recommendations—one, if possible, from a doctor who knows the patient. It can be made on the grounds that admission is required for the patient's health or for the safety or protection of others; or on the grounds of severe subnormality and—in the case of a person under 21—psychopathic disorder or severe subnormality.

When a mental welfare officer applies for a patient to be admitted for treatment, he must consult the closest relative, unless this would involve unreasonable delay or is impossible for some reason. If the relative objects, the officer has to apply to the county court.

If the relative's objection is considered unreasonable, the county court may order that someone else—possibly the local authority—should make the decision.

A patient admitted for observation cannot be detained for more than 28 days unless a further application is made for treatment. A person detained for treatment can be held first for a year, then for a further year, and for periods of two years after that. At each stage his case is reviewed by the hospital.

EMERGENCIES In an emergency—for example, if the patient is violent—a relative or a mental welfare officer can apply for a patient to be admitted to a mental hospital, supporting the application with only one medical recommendation, if possible by a doctor who knows the patient.

Detention in this case is limited to 72 hours. It can be extended by a second medical recommendation for a maximum of 28 days, including the first 72 hours. But if no second recommendation is received by the hospital managers, the patient will be discharged.

APPEALS A patient who is compulsorily admitted to hospital for treatment can apply to the local Mental Health Review Tribunal for discharge within six months of admission. He can also apply to the tribunal if he or his relatives object to a renewal of the treatment period. Relatives can also appeal to the tribunal if the medical officer objects to an order for discharge applied for by the relatives.

A hospital authority has a duty to ensure that the patient and his relatives know of their rights of appeal to the tribunal. The patient can be examined in the hospital by a doctor, chosen by himself or his relatives, who will advise on the merits of applying to a tribunal at any particular time.

There is a review tribunal for every hospital region in the country. The hospital authority will provide the necessary forms.

GUARDIANSHIP ORDERS A guardian can be appointed for a person suffering from mental disorder, either in the patient's interest or for the protection of other people.

The guardian—either the local health authority or someone acceptable to it—has the same powers as a father has over a child under 14. □ Appointing a guardian, p. 341.

COURT ORDERS Courts can make hospital or guardianship orders for persons concerned in criminal proceedings, who need treatment.

## Management of a patient's affairs

The Court of Protection, an office of the Supreme Court of Judicature, manages the affairs and property of people unable to look after their own interests because of mental disorder. This includes the management, sale, purchase, exchange or settlement of property, the making of a will and the conduct of legal proceedings concerned with property.

Patients are visited by people known as the 'Lord Chancellor's Visitors', who consider a person's capacity to manage his affairs. Any relative affected—or, in some cases, even the patient himself (where he is mentally capable)—can appeal to the Court of Appeal against activities of the Court of Protection.

The address of the Court of Protection is Staffordshire House, 25 Store Street, London WC1E 7BP.

# Claiming damages against hospitals and doctors

*A doctor's duty*  *Collecting evidence*
*Deciding who to sue*  *When to bring an action*
*Seeking legal advice*  *Operations without permission*

APATIENT who is dissatisfied with the treatment he receives in hospital or from a family doctor may have grounds to sue for damages. If the patient feels he has received poor treatment, he may be able to sue on the ground of negligence. If he has been subject to an operation or a course of treatment for which he did not give his consent, he may be able to claim damages for assault.

**A doctor's duty**
No doctor guarantees that his patient will come to no harm from the treatment he prescribes. But the patient is entitled to expect that the doctor should use reasonable skill and care. If he fails to do so, and the patient suffers loss or injury, the patient can claim that the doctor has been negligent.

➤ THE PATIENT SENT HOME WITH 18 BROKEN RIBS *Mr Wood was taken to hospital after being hurt in a road accident. The doctor who saw him failed to diagnose any serious injury. The following day, Mr Wood died. He had 18 broken ribs and congestion of a lung.*
*The doctor, who was sued, pleaded that the faulty diagnosis was caused by the patient's inability to give an account of the accident and his dulled reaction to pain, due to alcohol.*
DECISION *The doctor was found to have been negligent. The judge said that, because of the patient's condition, the doctor should have been particularly careful. (Wood v. Thurston.)* ◄

Generally speaking, it is up to the person suing to prove that the hospital or doctor has been negligent.
The exception is where the most obvious explanation for what has happened is the negligence of the medical staff. In such a case, the facts appear to speak for themselves. This is known as the principle of *res ipsa loquitur*—and it is up to the doctor or hospital to prove that negligence was *not* the cause of any harm that came to the patient.

➤ 'CURE' MADE THINGS TWICE AS BAD *A patient went into hospital to have an operation on two fingers which were stiff due to contraction of the tendons. When he came out of hospital,*

*not two, but four fingers had become stiff. He sued the Ministry of Health for negligence.*
DECISION *The Court of Appeal ruled that this was a case of* res ipsa loquitur. *It was not for the patient to prove that the hospital had been negligent, but for the hospital to explain how the other fingers became stiff without negligence. (Cassidy v. Ministry of Health.)* ◄

A patient who claims that the facts of a case speak for themselves may nevertheless have to go to court ready to make out a case against the doctor he is suing. For if the court refuses to uphold the principle of *res ipsa loquitur*, the onus of proof will be on the patient. If he is unable to prove his case, he will lose.

➤ A HAZARD OF DENTAL TREATMENT *When her jaw broke while the dentist was extracting a tooth, Mrs Fish took the view that the facts spoke for themselves, and sued the dentist.*
DECISION *The court held that this was not a case of* res ipsa loquitur—*there is always the chance of a fracture of the jaw when a tooth is extracted. Since Mrs Fish had offered no evidence to support her claim that in this case the dentist had been negligent, her action failed. (Fish v. Kapur.)* ◄

A doctor or hospital need not have given the wrong treatment to be considered negligent. They can also be made to pay damages for failing to give treatment when it was their responsibility to do so.

➤ PATIENT COULD NOT CONTACT SURGEON *Mrs Corder was operated on for the removal of excess fat below the eyes. She was told that if there was bleeding within 24 hours of the operation she had to telephone the surgeon.*
*Bleeding did occur, but Mrs Corder was unable to contact the surgeon because there was no answer to his telephone. Because she had no treatment, her face was disfigured. She sued the surgeon for negligence.*
DECISION *Damages were awarded to Mrs Corder. The court held that the surgeon had a duty to give post-operative care. Having asked to be called, he should have had the telephone efficiently manned. (Corder v. Banks.)* ◄

To succeed in a negligence claim, a patient needs to show that the doctor or hospital did not give the treatment that a competent practitioner would have given. Where injury results from an unforeseeable danger, the patient has no valid case.

➤ MISADVENTURE IS NOT NEGLIGENCE *Mr Roe was given an injection which caused paralysis of his legs. He sued the Ministry of Health in 1954. The evidence showed that paralysis was caused, not by the anaesthetic, but by a substance called phenol, which had seeped through invisible cracks in a glass container, contaminating the anaesthetic.*
DECISION *The case was dismissed. The possibility of such an occurrence was unknown before this case, and Mr Roe's paralysis had resulted from misadventure and not from negligence. (Roe v. Ministry of Health.)* ◄

### Deciding who to sue
When a patient feels that his family doctor has been negligent, he can sue the doctor himself. In a claim against a hospital, however, he may not be sure who to take action against. In practice, the difficulty is easily overcome. Hospital authorities, as employers for the Department of Health and Social Security, are liable for the acts and omissions of their staff, both doctors and nurses. All the patient need do is sue the employing authority —the hospital management committee, or the board in the case of a teaching hospital.

Alternatively, he can sue the hospital authority together with any other person whose negligence seems to have been involved.

### Seeking legal advice
In almost all cases, a patient who sues will have to consult a solicitor in the early stages.

Often the patient will be in some doubt as to whether he has a case for a claim at all. The first thing to do is to write a letter of complaint to the hospital secretary, keeping a copy. If the reply is not satisfactory, he should take the letters to a solicitor.

The patient may ask for a hospital inquiry at the same time as deciding to sue for negligence. If so, the legal proceedings will probably be delayed until the inquiry is over. A patient who is in any doubt about how to proceed should consult his solicitor. ☐ Treatment in hospital, p. 376.

### Collecting evidence
A court can make its decision only on the evidence presented to it. Therefore the patient will normally have to obtain expert medical

evidence to support his view. This is frequently the main difficulty experienced by patients in this type of case, because legal aid may not be granted until a sound case is shown to exist. The cost of obtaining medical evidence is often high.

In cases of difficulty the British Academy of Forensic Sciences, Department of Forensic Medicine, London Hospital Medical College, Turner Street, London E1 2AD, will supply a solicitor with the name of a medical expert.

The case is not as good as won, however, just because the patient finds an expert who supports him. The hospital's or doctor's side will probably be able to produce *their* expert witnesses as well. Doctors are not expected all to think alike, and the courts are most unlikely to find negligence if a course of treatment has the support of a responsible body of medical opinion.

The patient's experts will have to persuade the judge—personal injury cases seldom come before a jury—that, on the balance of probabilities, the course adopted by the doctor was one which no doctor of reasonable skill would have adopted if acting with reasonable care.

### When to bring an action
In personal injury cases, the patient has three years from the date of the negligence or assault in which to issue a writ. If the injury does not make itself felt until after three years, the patient can still start proceedings—but only within one year of discovering it.

The solicitor, after trying to get an admission of liability and an out-of-court settlement, will issue the writ. If the case is not settled out of court, it could take two or three years to come into court.

### Operations without permission
A doctor who carries out treatment without the patient's consent may sometimes be sued for assault. These cases are not common and often arise from a misunderstanding over the operation or treatment intended.

For example, many doctors recommend that women who have had three babies by Caesarian operation should be sterilised, and it is common practice to carry out sterilisation at the time of the birth of the third baby; but it would be quite wrong to sterilise a woman without her valid consent.

A patient who feels that a wrong or unnecessary operation has been performed should speak to the consultant. If the consultant cannot explain satisfactorily why the operation took place, the patient should consult a solicitor.

# Newcomers to the United Kingdom

*Conditions for admission*  
*Entry for relatives and dependants*  
*Tourists, businessmen and students*

*Port of entry procedure*  
*Deportation and newcomers' rights*  
*How to become a U.K. citizen*

PEOPLE from abroad who wish to visit or make their homes in the United Kingdom are divided in law into two main groups: those with an unrestricted right to enter and live in the U.K., who are known as patrials; and those who need consent to enter, or can be refused entry, called non-patrials.

Non-patrials seeking to enter the U.K. must meet two requirements:

**1.** They must be able to prove they have the necessary qualifications.

**2.** They must also seek permission to enter, at a recognised port of entry, from a Home Office official called an immigration officer.

The categories of patrial and non-patrial, and the regulations which cover people in them, apply from the date on which the Immigration Act 1971 comes into force.

## People born or naturalised in the U.K.

Anyone born or adopted in the United Kingdom is a patrial with an unrestricted right to enter and live in the U.K. So are people who acquire citizenship of the U.K. and Colonies by naturalisation or in certain cases registration in the U.K.

Children of people in the above categories, and women Commonwealth citizens married to people in the above categories, are patrials.

## Citizens of the Irish Republic

Citizens of the Irish Republic travel freely to and from the United Kingdom. But they are non-patrial, and individuals can be prevented from entering if the Government considers it in the public interest.

## Immigrants from the Commonwealth

Commonwealth citizens, sometimes known as British subjects, consist of citizens of the United Kingdom and Colonies; and citizens of independent Commonwealth countries.

CITIZENS OF THE U.K. AND COLONIES The following citizens of the U.K. and Colonies qualify as patrials:

**1.** Those born or adopted in the U.K.

**2.** Those with one parent, or in some cases one grandparent, born in the U.K.

**3.** Those who have been resident in the U.K. for the last five years.

**4.** Those who acquire citizenship of the U.K. and Colonies through naturalisation or in some cases registration in the U.K.

**5.** Women married to patrials.

A citizen of the U.K. and Colonies who is not a patrial is admitted to the U.K. only if he or she qualifies as a worker, relative or dependant, tourist, businessman or student. In addition, he may qualify by obtaining a special voucher from the nearest U.K. representative before setting out. These are issued mainly to Asians living in Kenya and Uganda.

CITIZENS OF COMMONWEALTH COUNTRIES The following citizens of Commonwealth countries qualify as patrials:

**1.** Those born or adopted in the U.K.

**2.** Those with a parent born in the U.K.

**3.** Those who acquire citizenship of the U.K. and Colonies by naturalisation in U.K.

**4.** Those who have been resident in the U.K. for the last five years and register as citizens of the U.K. and Colonies.

**5.** Women married to patrials.

A citizen of a Commonwealth country who is not a patrial is admitted to the U.K. only if he qualifies as a worker, relative or dependant, tourist, businessman or student.

PATRIALS COMING FROM ABROAD A patrial wanting to enter the U.K. needs a passport and—if his passport is not issued in the U.K. or the Irish Republic—a certificate of patriality, obtainable from the nearest U.K. representative. The birth certificate of any parent born in the U.K. may have to be produced.

## People coming to work

Non-patrials who want to come to the U.K. to work may be admitted if they obtain a work permit before entry. Permits are issued only to employers, who must show that there are unlikely to be suitable applicants locally. An employer who obtains a permit then sends it to the worker he wishes to engage. The issue of permits is controlled by the Department of Employment.

Permits must normally be renewed annually. A holder may not change his job without Government permission. A permit holder who has been working here for five years, has sufficient knowledge of English (or Welsh), and is not considered undesirable by the Government, can apply for registration as a citizen of the U.K. and Colonies. He then no longer needs a permit.

The following people do not require permits: people taking jobs in Government Departments or international organisations; representatives of foreign firms not already represented in the U.K.; foreign journalists; ministers of religion; doctors and dentists taking up professional appointments; tem- porary workers, such as seamen; and seasonal workers in agriculture.

Qualified nurses and midwives may be admitted without permits to find work. But they must take jobs approved by the Depart- ment of Employment within six months of their arrival.

Young Commonwealth citizens can take jobs incidental to a holiday. They may normally stay for up to three years.

### When aliens come to the U.K.
Aliens are citizens of countries outside the Commonwealth. All are non-patrial, and con- ditions of entry to the United Kingdom depend on nationality.

ALIENS FROM COMMON MARKET COUNTRIES From the date on which the U.K. enters the Common Market (European Economic Com- munity), nationals of the other Market coun- tries are free to come to the United Kingdom, though individuals may be refused entry for reasons of public order, safety or health. The countries concerned are: France, Germany, Italy, Belgium, Holland, Luxemburg (the original 'Six'); and Norway, Denmark and the Irish Republic.

ALIENS FROM OTHER COUNTRIES Aliens from countries outside the Common Market are subject to immigration control.

A visa is required by all stateless persons (except refugees), and by nationals of Albania, Bulgaria, Czechoslovakia, Hungary, Poland, Rumania and the U.S.S.R.; and people from all non-Commonwealth countries in Asia and Africa, except Israel, Japan, Kuwait, Maldive Islands, Republic of Korea, Turkey, Algeria, Ivory Coast, Morocco, Tunisia and South Africa.

Any other alien who wishes to live in the U.K. is advised to apply for a letter of con- sent to the Home Office Immigration and Nationality Department, 276 High Holborn, London WC1V 7EW, or to the nearest U.K. representative.

Aliens from outside the Common Market need a work permit if they wish to seek employment. After Britain joins the Common Market, permits are not needed by nationals of Market countries.

### Entry for relatives and dependants
Relatives and dependants who do not qualify to enter the U.K. in their own right are subject to special rules.

DEPENDANTS OF COMMONWEALTH CITIZENS Dependants can join a Commonwealth citizen in the U.K. only if they obtain an entry certificate from a U.K. representative.

DEPENDANTS OF ALIENS Relatives of aliens from countries to which visa requirements apply require a visa themselves.

MEN COMING TO MARRY A non-patrial man with an entry certificate, visa, or Home Office letter of consent can enter the U.K. to marry provided the ceremony will take place within three months and the couple will leave the U.K. shortly after.

WOMEN COMING TO MARRY A woman may be admitted for up to three months to marry in the U.K. An entry certificate or letter of consent is advisable.

HOW APPLICATIONS ARE DECIDED Normally, permission for children to enter the U.K. is granted only if both parents will be with them—only one parent if the other is dead, or physically or mentally incapable of looking after the child, or if the child is joining a parent resident in the U.K. who has sole responsibility for the child.

A child over 18 normally has to qualify in his own right. A husband is admitted to join his wife only in cases of hardship. Other relatives are normally admitted only if 65 or over, living alone and in poverty, and the U.K. relatives can support and house them.

### Tourists, businessmen and students
Visitors can normally come to the U.K. for a short trip with little formality—provided they can support themselves without working and can meet the cost of return.

If the immigration officer suspects that a visitor wants to find work and settle, he may refuse entry. Visitors may find it easier to prove that they intend to leave at the end of their trip if they carry return tickets.

The normal limit for visits is six months. If a visitor later wants to stay longer he must apply to the Home Office.

BUSINESSMEN A businessman is admitted as a visitor, though if the stay is for more than six months an entry certificate, Home Office letter of consent or visa is needed. He may transact business without a work permit.

STUDENTS Anyone accepted at a U.K.

educational institution for a minimum of 15 hours a week of organised day-time tuition may be admitted provided he has an entry certificate, visa or letter of consent.

A student is normally admitted initially for 12 months, and may be permitted to do part-time work to help to support himself. Trainee nurses and midwives, and doctors and dentists on full-time post-graduate study are treated as students.

### Port of entry procedure
Anyone subject to immigration control may enter the U.K. only at a recognised port of entry and with permission from an immigration officer, who decides how long he may stay and whether he may take a job. Anyone with a criminal record, or regarded as a danger to national security or public health can be refused entry, even if he has all the other qualifications.

RETURNING RESIDENTS An immigrant resident in the U.K. who has been absent for two years or less is admitted without condition. Someone who has lived in the U.K. most of his life can return at will after a longer absence. But a person whose stay in the U.K. was subject to a time limit has no automatic claim to re-admission.

Entering the U.K. without the consent of an immigration officer is a criminal offence. Offenders can be deported.

### Rights of newcomers
ALIENS Once in the U.K., an alien may own property and obtain Social Security benefits. But he cannot vote, sit on a jury or hold public office.

An alien of 16 or over may be required to register with the police if he is a student, if his visit is for more than six months, or if he is working in a job for which a work permit is needed. He must inform the police of any change of address, occupation, or marital status, and be able to produce his registration certificate to a policeman or immigration officer at any time.

These requirements continue until an alien is accepted for permanent settlement in the U.K., usually after four years.

COMMONWEALTH CITIZENS A Commonwealth citizen admitted temporarily or permanently has the same rights as any U.K. citizen.

### When newcomers can be deported
Any non-patrial can be deported on the orders of the Home Secretary if he breaks a condition imposed on his stay in this country, or if the Home Secretary considers it in the public interest. He can also be deported if he is convicted of an offence for which he could go to prison and the court decides to recommend him for deportation.

If a man is ordered to be deported, his wife and children under 18 can be deported with him. If a woman is ordered to be deported, her children under 18 can be deported with her, but not her husband.

EXEMPTIONS A non-patrial Commonwealth citizen or citizen of the Irish Republic cannot be deported on the grounds of the public interest if he has lived continuously in the U.K. since the Immigration Act 1971 came into force. He cannot be deported for breaking a condition of admission or be recommended for deportation by a court if he has been resident in the U.K. for the last five years. These exceptions do not, however, extend to cover aliens.

RIGHTS OF APPEAL Appeals in immigration cases are heard by a judicial officer called an adjudicator, by a body called the Immigration Appeal Tribunal and, occasionally, in the courts. There is no appeal against the refusal of a work permit, nor against decisions which are taken on the grounds of an applicant's political views.

### How to become a U.K. citizen
Commonwealth citizens or people from the Irish Republic can become citizens of the U.K. and Colonies by applying for registration after five years living in the U.K. or in the service of the Crown abroad. Registration is also available to any alien woman who is, or has been, married to a citizen of the U.K. and Colonies.

An alien can become a citizen of the U.K. and Colonies by applying for naturalisation after five years' residence. If the five-year period is not continuous, the applicant must have been resident in the U.K. or in Crown service abroad for at least the previous 12 months and for four of the last seven years. Residence in a colony or protectorate counts towards the four years.

The applicant must intend to live in the U.K. or in a protectorate or colony.

Statements from four citizens of the U.K. and Colonies willing to be sponsors must accompany the application. There is a fee of £30, or £33 for a husband and wife. Alternatively, the wife can await her husband's naturalisation and then apply for registration at a fee of £2.

MINORS A child under 18 can be granted registration, but not naturalisation.

# Trying to save a marriage

*Reconciliation attempts*  
*When reconciliation attempts fail*  
*Leaving the home*

*Paying for the home*  
*The children's position*  
*Money for the wife*

TODAY it is recognised that the law should not try to perpetuate a marriage if the love and respect on which it was based have ceased to exist. Since the Divorce Reform Act 1969 became law in 1971, it has been possible to end marriages amicably and honestly, proving only that a partnership has broken down irretrievably.

The law's main concern is to ensure that neither party is suddenly deprived of a home or financial support and to ensure that children are properly provided for.

### Reconciliation attempts
When serious trouble threatens, the couple should discuss the future thoroughly—and if necessary seek advice—for even where the law allows divorce by consent, judges must be satisfied that every possible effort has been made to save the marriage. □ Grounds for divorce, p. 395.

Many people turn to friends, a priest or their doctor for help. There are also many specialist agencies which exist to give advice when a marriage breaks down.

MARRIAGE GUIDANCE COUNCIL Volunteer counsellors who have been trained to listen to, diagnose and advise on matrimonial troubles, staff more than 100 Marriage Guidance Council branches throughout the country. Husband and wife are seen either individually or together. They can get expert advice from doctors, psychiatrists and solicitors.

FAMILY PLANNING ASSOCIATION Advice on birth control and sexual matters which may threaten a marriage can be obtained from the Family Planning Association. By solving a contraception problem, for example, they may be able to remove a fear of pregnancy which has been hampering sexual relations.

FERTILITY CLINICS If the marriage is breaking down because the couple cannot have a child, it may be helpful to seek advice from a fertility clinic (sometimes known as a sub-fertility clinic). These are run by hospitals as part of the National Health Service, and the husband and wife have to be referred to one by a doctor or a family planning clinic.

PROBATION OFFICERS Although more frequently used by people referred to them by a court, probation officers are often able to help in exploring the possibilities of reconciliation. The address of the local Probation and Aftercare Service is in the telephone directory.

CHILD CARE OFFICERS If the cause of the trouble is an unruly child, a child care officer at the social services department of the local authority may be able to help.

HELP AT WORK If either partner in a failing marriage works for a large company, the firm's personnel and welfare department may be able to help.

The discretion of all these agencies and individuals can be relied upon and it is in the interests of both parties to confide in them fully. They cannot give evidence about anything they hear or discover, if there should be court proceedings later, unless both parties give their permission.

The law encourages reconciliation. If a solicitor is consulted about divorce, he is expected to discuss the possibility of reconciliation and to tell his client of people qualified to help. Even when the case reaches court, the judge may adjourn the hearing if he thinks there is a chance of a reconciliation.

### When reconciliation attempts fail
When separation is inevitable, the husband and wife must decide which of them is to move out of the family home and who is to have care of the children.

Sometimes, it is possible for the couple to stay in the same house yet live separately, but this is at best a temporary solution. At worst, it will cause added bitterness and suffering, particularly to the children.

### Leaving the home
When husband and wife cannot agree on who is to leave the home, cases that have been decided offer some guidance.

ONE OWNER A husband does not have an automatic right to turn his wife out of the home simply because he owns it. Nor can the wife evict her husband if she owns the house. The partner who is not the owner can, under the Matrimonial Homes Act 1967, remain in or return to the home with the permission of the High Court or a county court.

This right of occupation can be ended only by a court order or by divorce or death of the partner who is not the owner. The court has complete discretion and might order the partner who is not the owner to leave if, for instance, he or she is committing adultery and wishes to live in the house with his or her lover; or if the owner has provided adequate accommodation elsewhere.

There is always a danger that the partner who owns the house may try to sell it. To guard against this, the partner who is not the owner can register his or her interest in the home at the Land Registry (if ownership of the house is registered) or else in the Land Charges Register. It is best to register as soon as matrimonial differences arise, and a solicitor will do this quickly and cheaply. Once this is done, it will be almost impossible for the owner to sell or mortgage the house. But even if it is sold, the other partner has the right to stay until a divorce is granted or a court orders them to leave.

JOINT OWNERS If the house is owned in the names of both husband and wife, both have the right to occupy it, and neither is allowed to sell without the consent of the other. Neither partner jeopardises the right to ownership by leaving the other in sole possession during a separation.

This protection extends to a partner whose name does not appear in the deeds, but who has a part share in the house through contributing to the purchase or to improvements.

If one partner refuses consent to sell the family home, the other must obtain a court order before the sale can proceed. The court allows the sale only if it would not be unjust to the objecting partner.

RENTED HOUSES Similar protection is given under the Matrimonial Homes Act in the case of a rented home. The partner who is not the named tenant has the same right of occupation as the partner who is named. A husband who rents a home in his own name has no legal right to turn his wife out. If he does, a court can order him to allow her back. ☐ Renting a home, pp. 252–65.

### Paying for the home

Rent or mortgage instalments must be paid as usual when a marriage breaks up. If a husband leaves home and stops paying his rent or mortgage repayments, the wife must either pay herself or face eviction. This can be particularly hard for a deserted wife who lives in rented property.

In practice, the wife in mortgaged property has a better chance of keeping her home. It takes some time for a lender to get possession of a house, and if the wife acts promptly, she should be able to get a court to give a maintenance order against the husband before there is any risk of eviction. The wife, or her solicitor, should write to the building society or other lender at an early stage, explaining the circumstances.

When the house is owned by a local council, the housing officials may help a deserted wife to find other accommodation—but usually only after she has a divorce or a separation order. If she has custody of the children, they will usually either transfer the tenancy to her or provide another tenancy.

### The children's position

In most cases the custody of the children is settled between the husband and wife; but sometimes both genuinely believe that they can give the children the better home.

If there is a dispute, one or both parents should apply to the local magistrates' court—or, if divorce proceedings have started, to the divorce court—as quickly as possible to resolve it. If a solicitor is not being retained, this can be done by calling at the office of the clerk to the magistrates. In any court dispute, the magistrates will give priority to the interests of the children. ☐ Custody and care of children, p. 403.

### Money for the wife

In many cases a wife will be left, after a separation, with insufficient money for her own day-to-day expenses. Her need for maintenance will be even more urgent if she is taking care of any children of the marriage.

A solicitor will advise her on the amount she can reasonably ask from her husband, and on the best way to ensure payment.

A firm letter from a solicitor may be sufficient to ensure payment. If not, she can apply to the local magistrates' court or to a divorce court for a maintenance order. It is not necessary for a wife to be living apart from her husband before obtaining an order—but (in the case of a magistrates' order) if she wants to enforce it, they must separate within three months of the order.

If a magistrates' court grants an order, the husband has to make regular payments to the clerk of the court, who holds them until the wife collects them from him. The divorce court will order payments to be made direct. If the husband falls behind with the payments, either court can order deductions from his wages. If he continues to ignore the order, he can be sent to prison for wilful failure to pay.

# Four ways to separate

*The informal agreement*
*The separation or maintenance deed*
*Magistrates' court order*

*Grounds for the application*
*Temporary orders*
*Judicial separation*

WHEN a marriage has broken down for good and the partners are living separately, it is usually wise to make the legal position clear. The choice is between a separation and a divorce. Today if a couple really want a divorce, they can get one, either very quickly if there has been what used to be known as a 'matrimonial offence', or by consent after two years' separation.

The alternative, for those who do not want a divorce, is some kind of legal separation, which has most of the legal effects of divorce —although, of course, it does not give the partners the freedom to re-marry.

There are four ways to separate:
1. By informal agreement.
2. By separation or maintenance deed.
3. By magistrates' court order.
4. By judicial separation.

**The informal agreement**
The partners can come to an agreement, either verbally or by an exchange of letters, that they will in future live apart on certain terms. The husband may agree, for example, to pay the wife a certain amount each year, and he may let her stay on in the house with the children.

This is the cheapest and simplest sort of separation, but it is difficult to enforce in the courts because such agreements are regarded as mere domestic arrangements. So, if an agreement is reached, it pays to have it drawn up legally by a solicitor in the form of a deed.

**The separation or maintenance deed**
If there is no dispute about the arrangements, a solicitor acting for both parties can draw up a deed of agreement.

But if husband and wife do not agree on all the major matters—such as custody of children and maintenance and provision of a home—they should have separate solicitors to work out a compromise.

It is important to make some provision for maintenance, however small, at the outset. The terms can be varied later by applying to the court if circumstances alter materially, or if the deed fails to provide properly for any child of the family. If no early provision is made for maintenance, a wife may find that

it is more difficult to get help when she eventually applies to the court.

No contract between man and wife can prevent the court from hearing an application for maintenance, or from altering an agreement. But where two people have signed a deed, after being advised by lawyers, the court will assume that the sums agreed were right in the circumstances existing then. It is thus vitally important to fix a proper figure and not simply to agree to a sum without careful consideration.

To save the expense and trouble of a later application to vary the order, the deed may provide that the payments shall vary in line with changes in the husband's income.

In some cases, especially where the income is substantial, advice should be taken from an accountant as well as a solicitor. The tax position may be important.

When husband and wife are living separately under a deed or an order of the court—sometimes even when informally separated—they are taxed as two people. Whether this is an advantage depends on their joint incomes and whether the money is earned or unearned. Where the joint earned incomes are over £4005 a year, they will pay less tax between them after the separation—and still less if the income is unearned. ☐ How the income-tax system works, p. 556.

The effect, if any, of the earned income allowance, child allowance and the total children's income on the tax position of the parent who has custody must be considered if there is a substantial sum involved.

**The effect of a deed on divorce prospects**
The terms of the separation deed need to be carefully considered, for they can in some circumstances affect the chances of obtaining a divorce later.

A husband or wife who plans to seek a divorce, and believes that the other partner will not give consent, may wish to petition on the grounds that he or she has been deserted. In this case the deed, while dealing with maintenance and other matters, will have to omit any reference to separation. If the deed states that the couple have agreed to part, it will not be possible to establish desertion. Where both husband and wife want a divorce, a deed mentioning separation will eventually be no obstacle, for divorce by consent is permitted after two years of living apart.

## Magistrates' court order

A wife may need protection from a cruel husband who refuses to leave the home or who keeps pestering her; or a husband may want to be free to live apart from a nagging wife. These are among the obvious instances where the magistrates' court provides a quick way of settling matrimonial problems by making a separation order, either permanently or as a prelude to divorce.

The advantages of the magistrates' court are that it is accessible, private, cheap and quick. The justices can make all of the orders that the divorce court judge can make, except the divorce decree itself, which allows the parties to re-marry.

When hearing domestic disputes magistrates sit in closed court: no one except the parties and their lawyers is allowed to be present, so there can be no publicity in newspapers.

When magistrates make a maintenance order, payments are usually made through the court. If payments are not made regularly and arrears mount up, the court can make an order for the money to be deducted from the husband's earnings by his employer, who then sends it to the court. This is known as an 'attachment of earnings' order.

To seize a man's earnings through his employer may seem a good idea, but in practice it often does not work satisfactorily. A husband determined not to pay has only to change his job and move away from the district, and it may be months or years before the court or his wife can catch up with him.

However, the threat of an attachment of earnings order is often useful, because a man in regular employment may not want to risk his employer finding out about the order. He is therefore encouraged to pay regularly.

## Later proceedings

Even if divorce proceedings are ultimately to be taken, it may be a good plan to apply to a magistrates' court for a separation order right away. Questions of money and children are then quickly disposed of, and any finding by the magistrates, on an allegation of adultery or persistent cruelty, for example, can be relied on in divorce proceedings as proof of breakdown without calling all the witnesses again.

In this way any costs incurred in the magistrates' court are not wasted, and legal aid may meet them in whole or in part. Another

---

## Effects of separation

WHEN a husband and wife separate, whether by agreement, magistrates' court order or divorce court order, their rights and obligations change. The couple are then under no duty to live together, so neither can be accused of desertion.

Maintenance payments, whether fixed by agreement or by court order, can be varied by a court.

The custody, care and control of children can be dealt with by magistrates or a divorce court. Where separation is by agreement, court proceedings will have to be taken if either partner wishes to change the provisions for the children.

Husband and wife are taxed separately. The husband loses the marriage allowance and the two incomes can no longer be added together for tax purposes.

The child allowance can be claimed by the parent who has actual custody of the child, unless otherwise agreed.

---

advantage is that since the order is not final, it gives the injured party a breathing space before seeking a divorce. Where there is some chance of reconciliation this is desirable.

## Grounds for the application

An application to a magistrates' court for a separation order can succeed only if the complainant can prove desertion, cruelty, adultery, neglect, one of a number of sexual offences, habitual drunkenness or an addiction to drugs by the other partner.

DESERTION To prove desertion it must be shown that one partner left the marital home or forced the other partner out of it. Two elements are essential for desertion: the deserter must want to bring married life to an end and there must be a definite separation to different homes.

The leaving or driving out must be without good reason. If, for example, a husband reasonably feels forced to leave his wife because she is committing adultery, or because she nags him unmercifully, or neglects him so that his health is suffering, he is not deserting her.

A temporary parting is not desertion: many husbands have to go overseas in the Services or in the course of their jobs. If, on the other hand, while he is away, a husband makes it clear that he has no intention of returning to married life, then he is deserting his wife—from the time he comes to the decision not to return to the family home.

The desertion does not need to have been going on for any particular length of time. But the magistrates must be satisfied that the defendant has been away long enough to make it reasonably certain that he or she intends to abandon the family.

CRUELTY Persistent cruelty is conduct by the defendant that has caused, or is likely to cause, danger or injury to the health of the complainant or to a child of the family. A complaint may be made if one partner has been convicted of an assault on the other partner.

Physical violence, except of a minor nature, is cruelty; but physical violence is not the only type of cruelty. Mental cruelty is recognised by the courts as being just as serious a threat to health. Such things as drunkenness, nagging, neglect, gambling, associations with a member or members of the other sex, and even sulking and prolonged silences may be cruelty if they cause or threaten injury to health.

Physical violence may be corroborated by witnesses who have seen it happen or have seen the resulting bruises. In mental cruelty cases, evidence of injury to health is important. It should, if possible, be given by a doctor. If the cruelty has been condoned or forgiven, no order can be made unless there has been further cruelty.

ADULTERY Although it can hardly ever be proved by direct evidence, the courts will find adultery proved if they are convinced that, on the evidence, the defendant had both the inclination and the opportunity to commit adultery and very probably did so.

For example, if the husband gives evidence that his wife was frequently in the company of another man; that she refused to give the man up when asked to do so, saying that she loved him dearly; and that they went away for a weekend together—then the magistrates will have little difficulty in assuming that adultery took place.

If the wife and her lover both give evidence that although they were very fond of each other and went away together, they did not commit adultery, it will be for the magistrates to decide whether to believe them or not.

The magistrates will not make an order if the adultery has been condoned—if, that is, the complainant takes the guilty spouse back into the home, or continues living with him or her (whether having sexual intercourse or not) after finding out about the adultery.

Sexual intercourse is very strong evidence of condonation, but in certain circumstances (if, for instance, a wife has difficulty in repelling her husband's advances) it will not be considered to amount to forgiveness.

NEGLECT If a husband fails to give his wife a reasonable amount of housekeeping money, he can be shown to have wilfully neglected her and any children of the marriage.

What is 'reasonable' is a matter for the magistrates to decide. The more a man earns, the more he is expected to provide for his family. But if he is out of work through no fault of his own, he would only be able to give them what he gets from National Insurance or supplementary benefits. Husbands who do not give their wives most of their Social Security benefits may be found guilty of neglecting their families.

A husband whose earning capacity is impaired by age or illness, so that it would be reasonable for the wife to contribute to the

## How to apply to the magistrates

THE procedure for applying to the magistrates for a separation is simple and quick, especially if the case is not being defended.

First consult a solicitor, which can be done quickly and cheaply. If the case appears straightforward he may advise the applicant to deal with it by himself. If there are any likely difficulties he will handle it and apply for legal aid if the applicant is eligible.

The applicant should go—with a solicitor if one is being used—to the local magistrates' court and make a formal complaint on oath

before a magistrate. If the magistrate accepts the complaint he signs it and issues a summons against the marriage partner, giving the date for the hearing of the case.

This summons must then be handed to the police either by the applicant's solicitor or by the clerk to the justices. It is served by the police on the defendant.

Even without legal aid, the case is not likely to be expensive unless it is being strongly defended with witnesses and a barrister for either side. ☐ The cost of parting, p. 402.

## When adultery is not condoned

MAGISTRATES cannot make a separation or maintenance order in favour of an applicant who is proved to have committed adultery which has not been condoned.

For instance, a court would not grant a wife a maintenance order for herself on the grounds of her husband's cruelty if he could prove that she had committed adultery which he had not condoned. But the magistrates would not penalise children and would probably grant a maintenance order for them.

However, even a wife who has committed adultery may be given maintenance during divorce proceedings, although the adultery may affect the eventual result.
☐ Grounds for divorce, p. 395.

support of the family, may complain that his wife has wilfully neglected to provide, or contribute to, reasonable maintenance for himself or any child of the family.

A magistrates' order for maintenance cannot be enforced unless the parties have separated within three months of its being made. This remedy is therefore of no use to a wife who wishes to go on living with her husband.

SEXUAL OFFENCES If either partner is found guilty and convicted of a sexual offence on a child of the family there will be grounds for a complaint. There will be grounds, too, if either partner allows or insists on having sexual intercourse while knowingly suffering from a venereal disease.

A wife may also complain if her husband has forced her into prostitution or to indulge in certain sexual perversions.

DRUNKENNESS OR DRUG ADDICTION A complaint may be made if the other partner is a habitual drunkard or a drug addict.

### Time limits for a complaint

The complaint must be made within six months of the matters complained of, or of their discovery. For instance, if a husband has been committing adultery the complaint must be made to the court within six months of the discovery of his adultery. In the case of persistent cruelty the complaint must be made within six months of the last act of cruelty. The case will come up for hearing quickly—within a week or two—unless it is going to be defended, when it may take the complainant's solicitor time to trace witnesses, take statements and perhaps instruct a barrister.

### The hearing

If, when the complainant gets to court, the defendant is not there, or attends court and admits that he or she is guilty of the conduct complained of, the applicant usually need give only a short statement on oath stating the complaint. A court, however, may ask for supporting evidence even in an undefended case.

If a solicitor is not being employed, the clerk to the justices helps the applicant by asking questions. It is usually a short hearing.

### The defended case

When the case is defended—that is, when the other partner opposes the granting of a separation order—evidence has to be given at much greater length and it is wise to be represented by a solicitor or barrister who knows what questions to ask to make the case clear.

The complainant's legal representative, if one is used, will open the case by giving the magistrates an outline of the marriage, putting forward any relevant arguments of law.

After giving his or her main evidence, the complainant is cross-examined by the other partner or by his or her legal representative. Then witnesses can be called and cross-examined. At the end of all the evidence the defendant or the defending lawyer addresses the court to urge that the complaint should be dismissed. If the defence raises any points of law in this address the complainant's legal representative has a chance to reply.

The magistrates will then decide whether they find the complaint or complaints proved.

### What magistrates may order

When they have reached a decision, the magistrates may make a number of orders.

SEPARATION ORDER They may order that 'the complainant be no longer bound to cohabit with the defendant'. This means that the marriage partners have the right to live apart, but it does not bring all the duties of marriage to an end. It is only a legal separation and is not final.

MAINTENANCE ORDER The magistrates may order that maintenance be paid to the wife (or in rare cases to the husband) and for any child of the family. The order will be for an amount that the magistrates think is reasonable, taking into account the partners' earnings or earning capacity and their liabilities.

The magistrates try to ensure, as far as possible, that the wife and children do not suffer financially as a result of the breakdown of the marriage. This can be done easily where there is enough money, but normally where the husband is not earning a large amount the result of having to run two homes instead of one will be that both husband and wife suffer. ☐ After the divorce, p. 406.

CARE AND CUSTODY OF THE CHILDREN Whether or not the magistrates make a separation order, and whether or not they find the complaint proved, they have the power to make any order they think appropriate in relation to the children.

These include custody orders, orders for access (to allow the parent who is not granted custody of the children to see them regularly), maintenance orders and orders that the children be put under supervision of the local authority or committed to its care.

While the magistrates will take into consideration the wishes of the parents in making these orders, they are guided by the rule that the welfare of the child comes first.

'Welfare' does not necessarily mean the child's immediate happiness. In some cases the magistrates will decide that it is more beneficial for the child to live with one parent although at the moment the child seems happier with the other. Or they may decide that a child should be educated in a way that is contrary to the child's own wishes. It is the ultimate good of the child that has to be considered. ☐ Custody and care of children, p. 403.

### Temporary orders
Sometimes, if the magistrates cannot come to a final decision on the day when the case is brought, or when one party asks for an adjournment to obtain legal aid or representation, the court will make an interim order.

This cannot last for more than three months, and if within that time the case is not brought back before the magistrates, the order lapses and the complainant has to start again.

Magistrates can adjourn the hearing of a case at any stage. They may do this at the request of one of the parties, or because they want to allow time for a probation officer to see the husband and wife to help them towards a reconciliation, or because they want a children's officer to investigate.

The magistrates will not usually hear a case if a divorce petition has been filed, or if one is about to be filed. But a husband cannot stop his wife from getting a maintenance order simply by telling the magistrate that he is about to file a petition for divorce, since the magistrates can make an interim order for maintenance. If the husband does file a petition, the wife can apply to the divorce court for a maintenance order.

### Right of appeal
There is a right of appeal within 21 days from the decision of the magistrates to the Family Division of the High Court. But it would be unwise to try to decide whether an appeal is worth while, or to conduct such an appeal, without legal advice and representation.

In the Divisional Court, three (or sometimes two) High Court judges review the notes of evidence made by the clerk at the magistrates' hearing and consider the magistrates' reasons for arriving at their findings.

The judges hear legal argument by barristers. Evidence is given only in exceptional circumstances—and then not in person but by a sworn statement, known as an affidavit.

If the judges think that the magistrates did not pay due regard to the evidence as set out in the notes, or otherwise dealt with the case wrongly, they may send the complaint back for re-hearing before other magistrates in the same area. They would do this, for instance, if the evidence showed there was conduct amounting to legal cruelty but the magistrates had dismissed the complaint. But if they find that the magistrates were wrong on a point of law the court can reverse the decision of the magistrates, or make a new order.

### Judicial separation
It is also possible to obtain a separation order from a divorce court and in that case it is known as a 'judicial separation'. The grounds for a decree of judicial separation are virtually the same as those for a divorce—except that the petitioner does not have to prove that the marriage has broken down irretrievably. ☐ Grounds for divorce, p. 395.

If the case is not defended, an application may be made to a county court. If it is defended, on the other hand, the case has to go before the High Court.

However, since magistrates can now award unlimited maintenance—under the Family Law Reform Act 1969—judicial separation seems likely to become less common, since it not only takes longer but is also a more expensive procedure.

It is likely to continue to be used mainly when the husband or wife wants the marital property to be divided—wants, that is, all the consequences of divorce except the right to re-marry. Decisions concerning property can be made only by a divorce court, not by a magistrates' court.

# Ending a void marriage

*When a 'marriage' is void*  
*When a marriage is voidable*  
*Failure to consummate*

*Defences to a nullity petition*  
*Other grounds for a nullity decree*  
*How to get a nullity decree*

SOME 'marriages' are never legally recognised. In legal terms, they are 'void marriages'. The courts recognise as marriage only a voluntary and lawful union between one man and one woman, entered into for life. Other marriages, while perfectly legal unions at the beginning, can be set aside by the courts because of some serious physical or mental defect in one of the partners.

### When a 'marriage' is void
In this country, certain marriages are never legally marriages at all—a bigamous marriage, for example, where there is already a husband or wife; or a sham marriage such as might take place between actors on the stage or in a charade; or a union between two people of the same sex. In each instance, the marriage is void from the beginning.

Normally, polygamous marriages fall into the same category, though the law recognises as valid an immigrant's polygamous marriage which takes place in a country where polygamy is legal. ☐ The law on polygamy, p. 318.

There are no legal rights or duties in a void marriage and, if asked to do so, a court will grant a decree of nullity declaring such a marriage null and void.

There are other unions which are void because they are illegal—those which contravene some Act of Parliament, such as marriages between close relatives, or where one of the parties is under 16. ☐ Getting married, p. 312.

A marriage is also void if there was something fundamentally wrong with the marriage ceremony—if, for instance, the wrong words were used, or the wrong names were given for either partner. ☐ Getting married, p. 312.

### When a marriage is voidable
Some marriages, although not void from the beginning, may be annulled by a court for some other reason. They are called voidable.

A marriage which is not truly voluntary is voidable. But the claim that it was contracted under duress is difficult to prove. There must have been a powerful influence such as fear that prevented one of the parties from exercising independent judgment and freedom of action during the ceremony.

► THE GIRL WHO MARRIED IN FEAR *An 18-year-old Hungarian girl wanted to leave her country in 1949. She feared that if she stayed she would be imprisoned because of her family's social and economic position.*

*In March 1949 she married a French citizen, obtained a French passport and came to England to live. The couple never lived together, and the marriage was not consummated.*

*After arriving in England, the girl petitioned for a nullity decree on the ground that she was induced to be a party to the marriage by fear.*

*Two other Hungarian women gave evidence for the girl. They said that they had married in fear to get foreign passports, and that their marriages had been dissolved.*

DECISION *The girl was granted a decree of nullity. Although English law insists on the consent of both parties to a marriage, consent can be cancelled if one of the parties was in fear at the time. The court held that the girl believed she would be in peril if she remained in Hungary, and that she married in fear. (H. v. H.)* ◄

Again, if a man is so drunk at his wedding that he is quite incapable of knowing the nature of the ceremony, there are grounds for saying later that it was not a true marriage.

Similarly, the marriage will be held to be voidable if a woman is forced to marry under a threat, or if either party is deceived about the true nature of the ceremony.

► THE COUNT WHO DID NOT CONSENT *Count Jerome Valier, an Italian living in France, went through a marriage ceremony at a London register office in September 1916 with May Winifred Davis, an English girl. The couple never lived together and the marriage was not consummated. Later, Count Valier married the Marchesa Balbi in Italy.*

*Two actions eventually went to court. Count Valier asked for a declaration of nullity on the grounds that he did no know the nature of the contract at the time, and that he did not consent or intend to marry. He said he had believed that the ceremony he went through with Miss Davis was one of betrothal, not of marriage.*

*May Winifred Valier sued the Count for divorce, on the grounds of desertion and of*

393

*adultery with the Marchesa Balbi. She also claimed that the Count's marriage to the Marchesa was invalid, because he was married at the time of the ceremony.*

DECISION *The court decided that there was no valid marriage between the Count and Miss Davis. It held that at the time he did not know what he was doing and that there was nothing in his subsequent conduct that amounted to ratification of the marriage.*

*The court found that the Count did not easily understand English. It also took notice of the two stages of contracting a marriage in Italy—a 'solemn espousal', which is an exchange of promises, and the actual marriage ceremony.*

*The court also found that the Count did not intend to marry, because 'marriage is the acceptance by the mutual consent of the parties of the married state with knowledge of the nature of the undertaking and consequences'. (Valier v. Valier.)* ◄

In order to prove a marriage to be voidable, it is not sufficient to show merely that one of the parties to the marriage went into it unwillingly or with reservations. Nor can a marriage be said to be voidable simply because one party deceived the other about his or her circumstances, financial or otherwise.

### Failure to consummate

Complete refusal to allow sexual intercourse in marriage is usually a ground for a decree of nullity, because marriage is a contract and is rendered voidable if not consummated.

But a decree of nullity will be granted on the ground of non-consummation only where there has been no sexual intercourse at any time since the marriage. Pre-marital intercourse between the partners is disregarded. One act of intercourse is enough to consummate a marriage.

In the case of wilful refusal, only the partner who has been refused intercourse can petition for nullity—not the one who has refused.

There may be no intercourse because one of the parties is incapable of a normal sexual relationship. The man may be impotent, or the woman may have some physical defect or suffer from a nervous condition which makes intercourse impossible.

Any of these reasons would be a ground for a nullity decree. If intercourse had occurred after the marriage, subsequent refusal, or incapacity, might be grounds for divorce as unreasonable behaviour. □ Grounds for divorce, p. 395.

In the case of impotence, either partner in the marriage may bring a petition—an impotent man may petition for nullity on the ground of his own incapacity, provided that the wife was unaware of this condition in her husband at the time of the marriage.

### Other grounds for a nullity decree

Even where there has been full consummation of the marriage, there are other grounds for a nullity decree, which were introduced by the Matrimonial Causes Act 1937.

These are that, at the time of the marriage, one of the parties was suffering from a mental disorder, epilepsy or veneral disease, or the wife was pregnant by another man.

### Defences to a nullity petition

A court cannot grant a decree of nullity on the ground that the marriage is voidable if the other partner defends the case and the judge finds that the petitioner behaved in such a way that his or her partner believed he or she would not seek to have the marriage dissolved.

But before refusing a decree, the judge must be satisfied that the petitioner was aware of his right to an annulment at that time. He also has to be satisfied that it would be unjust to the other partner to award a decree.

It is possible the partners might have agreed before marriage that there should be no sexual relations since they wanted only companionship and that, after marrying, they intended to live as brother and sister.

This could happen where a man advertised for a housekeeper and suggested marriage simply as a convenience. In a case like this, a court might infer such an agreement from the facts presented to it and, in the circumstances, would not grant a decree of nullity.

Nor would a decree be granted if the partners had accepted the situation and treated the marriage as a proper one.

In some cases, proceedings must start within three years of the marriage. In others, a decree cannot be granted if it is shown that the petitioner was aware of the circumstances which make the marriage voidable at the time of the ceremony.

### How to get a nullity decree

To petition for a nullity decree, first consult a solicitor. In many cases medical advice is essential and legal aid may be possible.

A petition, as in divorce, is made to a county court. If it is defended it is heard in the High Court.

Maintenance may be obtained before and after the decree. If the case is proved, the judge will grant a decree nisi which can be made absolute (final) after three months.

# Grounds for divorce

*Proof of breakdown*  *Desertion*
*Adultery*  *Living apart*
*Unreasonable behaviour*  *Incurable insanity*

UNTIL 1937, the only ground for divorce was adultery. Then the late A. P. Herbert, the author and M.P., steered through Parliament, against much opposition, an Act which made divorce possible on the grounds of desertion, cruelty and incurable insanity, as well as adultery.

In 1969 there was another major change— the Divorce Reform Act, championed by Mr Leo Abse, M.P., which came into operation on January 1, 1971. This is intended to make divorce easier, less painful and, in most cases, free from guilt or shame.

It is no longer necessary to prove that one party has committed a 'matrimonial offence'— cruelty, desertion or adultery—before getting a divorce. Now the only test is whether the marriage has broken down irretrievably, although the old matrimonial offences may provide evidence of a breakdown.

Divorce by mutual consent is permitted after two years' living apart, and divorce without the consent of the other partner after five years' living apart. These periods of living apart are accepted in law as proof of the breakdown of a marriage.

TIMING OF THE ACTION Only in exceptional circumstances can divorce proceedings be started within three years of the date when the marriage took place.

To get leave to apply for a divorce within this time, the person seeking the divorce, called the petitioner, must convince the judge that he or she will suffer 'exceptional hardship' if not allowed to start proceedings without delay. Alternatively the petitioner may show that the other partner (the respondent) has behaved with 'exceptional depravity'.

Alleged unreasonable behaviour, for example, must be so bad that it is causing grave injury to health or danger to life. Adultery would cause exceptional hardship where, because of his wife's adultery, the husband had to maintain another man's child. Sexual perversions or prostitution could also give grounds for an application.

Even if one of these facts is proved, the judge cannot grant leave to apply for a divorce until he is satisfied that there is no hope of reconciliation. The judge must also take into account the best interests of any children of the marriage.

If leave to apply for a divorce is refused, a wife can seek a maintenance order in the High Court or ask for a separation order (with maintenance) in a magistrates' court. ☐ Four ways to separate, p. 388.

## Proof of breakdown

In the more common divorce proceedings— that is, where the partners have been married for at least three years—the person seeking the divorce must convince the court that the marriage has broken down irretrievably.

Under the Act there are only five ways in which breakdown may be proved. They are:
1. Adultery.
2. Unreasonable behaviour.
3. Desertion for two or more years.
4. Living apart for two years (if both parties seek the divorce).
5. Living apart for five years (even if the other partner refuses consent).

## Adultery

Anyone who petitions on the grounds of adultery must prove that the other partner has committed adultery and that the petitioner finds it intolerable to live with him or her. (Adultery need not be the reason the petitioner finds it intolerable to live with his or her partner. He or she may simply want to separate or re-marry.)

Under the Act, adultery in itself is no longer a ground for divorce if the marriage has not broken down. Thus a single act of adultery, committed during a period of separation or under the influence of drink, and regretted afterwards, may not be a ground for divorce.

Adultery is defined as *voluntary* sexual intercourse between a married person and someone of the opposite sex other than the marriage partner. In law, both the married person and the lover are adulterers.

The voluntary aspect is important. If a woman is raped, that does not amount to adultery by her, although a married man who commits rape is guilty of adultery.

Any intercourse taking place while either person is so drunk, or so affected by mental illness, as to be incapable of understanding what is happening, is not usually regarded as adultery on the part of the drunk or ill person, although it is adultery by the other if either of them is married to someone else.

Proof of adultery is seldom by direct, visual evidence, but usually by confession or by circumstantial evidence. In the normal undefended divorce case alleging adultery, written confessions are taken from the adulterers in conditions which do something to ensure that they are telling the truth.

They are seen by an inquiry agent, who explains that he wants evidence for divorce, that they need not make statements unless they wish to do so, and that any statements they do make may be used in evidence in divorce proceedings. The agent makes sure that he has got the right people and can convince the court of their identity.

The courts always look at confessions carefully and are suspicious when the marriage partner refuses to name the co-respondent. It is only too easy for a person who wants a divorce to make a false confession.

CIRCUMSTANTIAL EVIDENCE Confessions are obtained only if the adulterers are willing to make them. Otherwise proof is generally by inference—called 'circumstantial evidence'.

All the evidence the court needs to establish adultery—in the absence of a denial or explanation—is a sufficient combination of inclination ('guilty passion' is the old-fashioned term) and opportunity.

Inclination may be shown by evidence of familiar behaviour, and opportunity by evidence that a couple were alone together in circumstances suggesting that their relationship was not innocent.

For example, if a wife has been staying out late without offering any explanation; if love letters have been found in her possession; if neighbours have seen her often in the company of another man, and have seen that man arrive at her house when the husband was away; and if the divorce case is undefended—then the judge may infer adultery from the circumstantial evidence.

But if the case is defended and the wife and the man deny on oath that they committed adultery, it will be for the judge to decide whether or not he believes whatever explanation they give of their indiscreet behaviour.

If both parties deny adultery, the aggrieved husband or wife may think it worth waiting for the five-year period of living apart before bringing divorce proceedings. The other partner's denial of adultery or objection to a divorce would then make no difference.

ILLEGITIMATE CHILD Another method of proving adultery is to show that the wife gave birth to a child on a date which makes it certain that the husband could not be the father—perhaps because of his long absence overseas.

To prove this, the husband must give evidence that he has inspected the register of births and seen the dated entry of the child's birth and his wife's signature.

It may be possible to prove, by blood tests of the husband, mother and child, that someone other than the husband may have been the father. In about 70 per cent of cases where the husband is not the father, blood tests will prove positively that he is not.

The blood tests cannot prove who *is* the father, but sometimes they can eliminate a man who is not. A wife contesting a divorce petition might be advised not to consent to the tests, since they can go against her. But in certain circumstances where it is in the interests of the child, the court may order blood tests. If tests are ordered, no one can be forced to submit to them, but refusal suggests guilt and is held against the person refusing.

WHAT IS INTOLERABLE? Once adultery has been proved, the judge has to be satisfied that the person seeking the divorce finds it intolerable to live with the other.

The adultery itself need not be intolerable; it may be that the adultery, or some other factor, makes life together intolerable. For example, it may be that the adultery proves the last straw: a wife who has put up with her husband's unkindness for years, may find even a single act of casual adultery enough to make her decide that she cannot go on with the marriage. If the case is undefended and the petitioner gives evidence that adultery has been committed and she cannot bear to go on living with him for any reason, that will probably be enough.

A husband or wife is unlikely to get a divorce merely by pretending that he or she regards further life together as intolerable. For one thing, solicitors and barristers are prevented by their professional code of ethics from putting forward any witness to say on oath what they know to be untrue.

It does not matter if a lawyer *suspects* his client's story, for he is not the judge. But if he has been told by the client that he did not mind his wife's adultery in the least, or actively encouraged it, and is quite happy to go on living with her, then the lawyer cannot continue with the case if the client proposes to swear on oath that the marriage was intolerable to him.

In addition, perjury is a criminal offence.

Even if the husband or wife is not prosecuted, the giving of false evidence may result in the failure of the divorce action.

COSTS If the judge finds that adultery is proved with a named man (the co-respondent) he may, and usually will, order that the co-respondent pay the costs incurred by the husband in bringing the case to court. Whether an order for costs is made is a matter for the discretion of the judge. A co-respondent can no longer be ordered to pay damages to the husband for the loss of his wife (unless the petition was filed before January 1, 1971).

## Unreasonable behaviour

It is not necessary to prove either physical violence or injury to health to get a divorce; it is enough to show that the partner's conduct was such that the petitioner would not reasonably be expected to live with him or her, and so caused the marriage to break down.

Until the new law has been in operation for some time it is not possible to say precisely what the courts will consider constitutes unreasonable behaviour.

Certainly all conduct which could have been cruelty under the old law—violence, habitual nagging, serious neglect, sexual perversions, refusal to have children, long-continued insulting behaviour, habitual drunkenness and obsessive gambling—will be capable of being unreasonable behaviour. But it will no longer be necessary to prove actual or threatened injury to health, and it should be easier to prove such conduct than it was to prove 'cruelty' under the old law.

The test to be applied under the new law is really a commonsense one: would a reasonable person expect any husband or wife to put up with such conduct in marriage?

Evidence by the petitioner that the conduct complained of did in fact cause him or her such distress that he or she really could not go on with the marriage any longer, will usually be sufficient. But it is important to have supporting evidence from witnesses if this is possible.

The judge will have to decide whether the petitioner reacted reasonably to the other party's conduct. Differences in health, social class and other circumstances will have to be taken into account.

Forgiveness is important in deciding whether the conduct complained of should be tolerated by the petitioner. And one of the clearest signs of forgiveness is considered to be willing sexual intercourse.

If the intercourse was unwilling, or undertaken without full knowledge of the facts (for instance, in the false belief that the other person had given up an adulterous relationship) it will not be taken to imply forgiveness.

Going back to living together after 'unreasonable' conduct does not now affect the court's decision—as long as the period or periods of living together do not exceed six months in total. This concession has been introduced into law to encourage attempts at reconciliation of the partners.

However, if a marriage has broken down completely—if one partner left the other because of marital unhappiness and not just for convenience—the conduct of one or the other is very likely to fall under the heading of unreasonable behaviour.

## Desertion

Desertion means that one partner has abandoned the other. But it is not always easy to decide who has deserted whom.

One common issue in the divorce courts is who has the right to say where the family will live—that is, to choose the location of the matrimonial home. In English law there is no rule that the husband has an absolute right to decide where the matrimonial home is to be. It is a matter of what is reasonable.

If, for example, a husband decides to move to Lancashire because he has been offered a good job there, and the wife refuses to leave Surrey, where all her family and friends are and where she has a job as a part-time typist, she will be considered to have deserted him. But if she were a doctor in general practice in Surrey and her husband chose to move to Lancashire from a perfectly satisfactory job simply because he preferred to move, the courts might well decide that she was deserted.

A similar yardstick would apply if, say, the husband wanted to go overseas. If he simply wanted to move to a new job in some other country, his wife's wanting to stay in Britain and refusing to go with him could be considered reasonable. On the other hand, if he worked for a firm in Britain which asked him to spend three years with its overseas subsidiary, after which he would return home, it might be unreasonable of the wife to refuse to go with him—especially if the temporary move abroad would further his career. □ For better, for worse, p. 319.

If a husband leaves his wife and later wants to come back, his offer to return, if it is genuine, brings his desertion to an end. But if his wife refuses to have him back, *she* may become the deserter and will have no claim for financial support.

But if she has good reason to refuse to have

him back, the courts would decide differently. For instance, if she can show that he is returning only to avoid a maintenance order, or if she has good reason to believe that he has been committing adultery while away, she is entitled to refuse to have him back. He will then continue to be the deserter.

If a wife who has been deserted commits adultery while her husband is away, she may no longer be able to claim that he has deserted her. But if she can prove that the husband does not know or care about the adultery, it has no effect and the deserted wife can still get a divorce after two years.

To prove breakdown of the marriage, the desertion must have started at least two years before the date on which the divorce petition is sent to the court. But the living apart need not be continuous—that is, the husband and wife may have lived together for up to six months in all in two and a half years. This is to encourage reconciliation.

Suppose, for example, a husband leaves his wife on June 1, 1971, and says that he is not coming back. He has no good reason for leaving, and his wife wants him back. A month later she telephones him and asks him to try again. He comes back for six weeks, but then leaves her again. After three months, the husband suggests they go on holiday together for a fortnight, which they do, but on their return he leaves his wife for good.

She can petition for divorce only when they have been apart for a total of two years, not counting the total of two months of attempted reconciliation—that is, on or after August 1, 1973 (not June 1, 1973)—two years and two months after the first separation.

Desertion may be proved even if a couple continue to live in the same house, as long as they do so as two separate households. This may not be the case if they have meals together, or spend their evenings together watching television, when the courts will probably regard them as still living together.

### Living apart for two years

If a husband and wife have lived apart for two years or more, for whatever reason, either can petition for a divorce and will be able to prove breakdown of the marriage on this ground alone—but only if the other consents.

The separation must be reasonably complete. It is not sufficient, for example, for the husband to be away all week, if he returns home at the weekends. A husband and wife who run two separate homes and visit each other from time to time, perhaps staying overnight, will probably not break into the

two-year period. The court will have to decide whether they have been living in separate households for two years or more.

If both parties want a divorce, an enforced separation resulting, say, from service overseas or a prison sentence, will not necessarily be sufficient grounds, unlike the position in cases of desertion. The parties must have regarded the marriage at an end at the beginning of the two-year period.

The law encourages attempts at reconciliation. One or more breaks, not exceeding six months in total, do not end a period of separation. But the couple must live apart for at least two years in addition to any period of trial reconciliation.

SETTLEMENTS A divorce by consent can usually be obtained only after the couple have agreed about arrangements for property, money and the children.

For example, a wife may formally consent to a divorce on condition that the husband transfers the house to her free of any mortgage, that she has the custody of the children, and that he agrees to a maintenance order.

If the husband agrees, the wife gives her consent to the divorce, and he will be granted a decree nisi. This is the provisional decree which says that the marriage is to be dissolved unless sufficient cause is shown why the decree should not be made absolute, and the divorce granted.

But then if the husband finds that he cannot pay off the mortgage and is unable to keep up such a high maintenance order, the wife may decide that agreeing to a divorce was a mistake. She can then apply to have the decree nisi set aside.

If the judge feels that she gave her consent to the divorce under a misapprehension about her husband's ability or willingness to pay, he will cancel the decree and there will be no divorce. But she must make her application before the decree is made absolute—generally within six weeks of the divorce hearing. Once the final decree is made, it cannot be set aside simply because the wife consented to a divorce under a misapprehension.

The law gives further financial protection to the divorced partner who applies to a court for such protection after a decree nisi based upon living apart for two or five years. The judge will consider all the circumstances of the couple, such as age, health, earning capacity, conduct and financial position. He will not make the decree absolute until he is convinced on one of three grounds:

1. That the petitioner has made reasonable provision for the divorced partner.

**2.** That the petitioner has promised to make such provision for the other partner.

**3.** That the person being divorced does not require maintenance from the other partner.

### Living apart for five years
When a husband and wife have lived separately for five years or more, the law presumes that the marriage has broken down without hope of repair, and either partner can be granted a divorce even if the other refuses to consent.

The only ground on which the person being divorced can oppose the case is that the divorce will cause grave financial, or other, hardship and that in all the circumstances it would be wrong for the court to grant a decree. This usually applies only to a wife.

Then, unless the judge considers that the wife has been fairly treated and will not lose too much financially by the divorce, he may refuse a decree.

He may also take into account the interests of any children or other persons concerned, including any woman with whom the husband is now living and any children he has had by her. For instance, the husband may want the divorce to marry the other woman and make these children legitimate.

The judge has to balance the interests of the aggrieved wife, who may suffer by the divorce, against the interests of the new family, and the public interest in having the situation made legal.

A woman who in the past has not been a dutiful wife may find it difficult to persuade the judge not to grant a divorce, even if she stands to lose financially. And a long-lasting relationship between the man and another woman which has produced children will strongly influence the judge in favour of granting a decree, however hard this may be on the wife.

In such a case both parties should be represented by solicitors and, in many cases, the solicitors will advise that a barrister should be briefed. There could be as much evidence and argument as in a defended divorce based on alleged adultery, and the lawyer's art of persuasion is just as necessary.

### Incurable insanity
A divorce can no longer be obtained on the sole ground that a wife or husband is incurably insane and has been receiving treatment for mental illness. The petitioner must now prove to the court that the marriage has broken down by establishing one or more of the situations already outlined.

Somebody who is mentally ill cannot legally consent to a divorce, so divorce by mutual consent after a two-year separation period is not possible. A divorce can, however, be granted if it is shown that the couple have lived apart for five years, and that the respondent is insane. This has to be proved by medical evidence.

In many cases of insanity it is not necessary to wait five years before the divorce. The sick partner may behave in such a way that the other cannot reasonably be expected to live with him or her.

A divorce can then be sought on the grounds of unreasonable behaviour at any time after three years of marriage. It is not necessary in this case to prove that the partner is incurably insane.

However, there is no possibility of getting an easy, quick divorce from somebody whose mind is disordered. In the first place someone must be appointed to act for the sick partner in the divorce proceedings. This person is called a guardian *ad litem*—that is, a guardian for the case. Although any responsible person could act as guardian, he will usually be the Official Solicitor—a legal officer employed by the Crown to care for the interests of infants and insane or disabled people involved in court actions.

All the papers, including the divorce petition, will be served on the guardian, who does not even show them to the respondent if the doctors think it unwise.

In order to protect a helpless respondent's interests, the Official Solicitor may decide to defend the case. He investigates the circumstances and if he thinks that there is anything which may cause injustice to his client he will defend the case and instruct a barrister to appear for the respondent.

The barrister cross-examines the petitioner and other witnesses if necessary, and makes submissions to the judge. In certain cases, he may oppose the divorce. But usually his main object is to see that his client is financially looked after.

Even a patient in a National Health Service hospital needs money for extra comforts, and whether the husband or wife is the petitioner, the judge may order a contribution to be made to the patient's maintenance.

If the person bringing the divorce proceedings is well off, a substantial order may be made, or even an order for a lump-sum payment. This will be held by someone in charge of the respondent and used to ensure the best possible treatment or, perhaps, to re-establish the patient in normal life after he or she is released from hospital.

# How to get a divorce

*Filing a petition*     *Giving evidence in court*
*The legal procedure*    *When a court delays divorce*

ANYONE is allowed to conduct the proceedings in his or her own divorce case, but it is not wise to do so because there are many pitfalls requiring expert legal knowledge. People who cannot afford the cost of being represented by a lawyer can usually obtain legal aid for divorce proceedings.

A solicitor can save a great deal of anxiety and time through knowing precisely the grounds on which the courts are likely to grant a divorce. If, for example, he thinks that his client's account of the breakdown of the marriage would not satisfy a court, he will make further investigations. He may advise that an inquiry agent should be employed to find out if adultery is taking place. Alternatively, he may write a suitable letter to the other partner which will enable the case to be established on the grounds of desertion.

PRELIMINARY ARRANGEMENTS When filing a petition, the solicitor is required by law to certify whether or not he has discussed with the petitioner the possibility of a reconciliation, and whether or not he has given the petitioner the names and addresses of persons qualified to help in bringing about a reconciliation. However, most marriages are beyond repair by the time a solicitor is consulted.

Even in undefended cases, where the other partner does not oppose divorce, there are usually other matters to be settled—who will be given custody of the children of the family, and how joint property, such as a house, is to be shared. It is important to obtain legal advice on these matters because they often raise difficult questions of law.

If the petitioner is seeking legal aid, there may be a short delay while the solicitor makes the necessary application.

**Filing a petition**
The first step is to file a divorce petition at the nearest county court which has divorce jurisdiction, or alternatively at Somerset House, Strand, London WC2R 1LB. The petition must follow the form laid down in the divorce court rules and must contain certain statements of fact. These include date and place of marriage, names and dates of birth of children of the family, and a summary of allegations supporting the contention that marriage has irrevocably broken down.

Petition forms are available from any legal stationer. It is possible for the person seeking divorce to complete the form without assistance, but it is advisable to leave it to a solicitor. Although some petitions may be simple, others need to be carefully framed, and must include any application for maintenance or any other financial claim.

Where there are children, a separate statement of the present and proposed arrangements for them must be filed with the petition.
MAINTENANCE The dependent partner—either a wife with little or no means, or a sick husband who has to rely on his wife for support—can obtain maintenance while waiting for the divorce to be heard. The right to maintenance is not affected by the fact that the dependent partner is being cited.

The amount needed can be agreed through the solicitors. But if no agreement is reached, application can be made to the court for maintenance pending the hearing.

**The legal procedure**
The court sends the completed petition to the other partner, together with a document called a 'Notice of Proceedings' and a form called an 'Acknowledgement of Service'. On the second document, the respondent, as the other partner is called, is asked whether he or she wishes to oppose the petition, consents to divorce on the ground of two years' living apart, or would like to be present to give evidence to the judge on financial matters or on custody of the children of the marriage.

If the respondent has no intention of defending, the form is returned to the court, signed by him or his solicitor. The case is then put on the court list to take its turn, after which it may take between six weeks and three months to get a hearing, depending on how busy the court is.
DEFENDED DIVORCES Most petitions are undefended, but it is nevertheless wise to consult a solicitor before deciding whether to defend. If the respondent denies the charges made in the petition, an answer is filed. The answer contains the denials and any counter-charges

and may also seek a divorce decree, in which case it is then called a 'cross-petition'.

Sometimes, a husband or wife files a defence in order to gain a better bargaining position over money, property or the children, or because allowing the charges to go unchallenged would put him or her in a bad light. If the charges are untrue, silence would imply that they were admitted.

REACHING A COMPROMISE In many cases the parties reach a compromise, and the case is not fought over in court.

In a typical example, a wife petitions on the ground of her husband's unreasonable behaviour, but he denies the charge, and cross-petitions, alleging her adultery. She then admits the adultery, but says it was not the reason why the marriage broke down, claiming that this happened after she was driven out by her husband's conduct. She now wants to re-marry, and she claims a share in the matrimonial home.

Her solicitors offer to drop her case and let the husband have a divorce for adultery if he will settle her claim to a £1000 share in the house. Rather than fight and risk a finding of unreasonable behaviour and payment of costs, the husband offers £750. The wife accepts.

Such a bargain used to be known as 'collusion' and, before the Divorce Reform Act 1969, it could prevent a divorce, unless found by the court to be acceptable in the circumstances. The Act now gives people more freedom to make such bargains, although they must not conspire to mislead the court.

## Giving evidence in court

Unless the case is defended, only the petitioner and his or her witnesses need attend the hearing. If it is defended, both partners with their witnesses have to attend. A divorce hearing is held in public, but there are restrictions on what may be published in a newspaper. Such a report must be confined to:

1. Names, addresses and occupations of the people involved.
2. The charges, defences and counter-charges in support of which evidence has been given.
3. Submissions on points of law arising from the proceedings and the decision of the court.
4. The judgment of the court, and the judge's observations in giving judgment.

Before the case is called, the solicitor or barrister takes his client through the evidence at a 'conference'.

When the case is called, the petitioner or partner seeking the divorce goes into the witness box and takes the oath. In an undefended case, his or her lawyer asks questions

designed to draw out the story of the breakdown of the marriage in the shortest and least painful manner.

The judge himself may ask some questions. He is usually particularly anxious to satisfy himself that the children of the family are being properly provided for. A 'final decree' cannot be granted until he is satisfied.

After the petitioner's evidence, witnesses may be called or documentary evidence produced. For instance, an inquiry agent may produce confession statements to prove adultery, or a doctor may give evidence that the health of the wife or husband suffered as a result of the other partner's conduct.

This simple procedure for undefended cases may all be over in a few minutes. Where a case is defended, however, there could be many more witnesses, cross-examination of both sides, and lengthy arguments by lawyers. The hearing may then last for several days.

THE DIVORCE DECREES If the judge finds the case proved, he will make out an order giving a 'decree nisi' of divorce. This means that the final decree, called a 'decree absolute', can be obtained in six weeks' time. This delay allows any irregularities to be discovered before the marriage is finally dissolved.

In rare cases—for example, where a woman is expecting a baby or if a man has to go abroad on public service and wants to re-marry first—the judge may direct that the decree should be made absolute earlier.

## When a court delays divorce

If the court has been grossly misled by anyone in order to obtain a decree, either the respondent or the Queen's Proctor may bring the case before the court again, and so delay the final decree until the matter is resolved.

The Queen's Proctor is an official who intervenes in divorce cases if there are grounds for believing that for some reason a decree should not be granted.

The court can ask his help if suspicions are aroused, during or after the hearing, which suggest, for example, that there has been fraud or a conspiracy between the parties to deceive the court in order to get a decree. However, the most likely reason for any delay is that the arrangements for the children may be incomplete or unsatisfactory.

In a case of divorce by consent, a partner who feels that he or she gave consent on the basis of misleading information can apply to the court to have the decree nisi set aside.

For example, a husband's misleading statement about his ability to provide maintenance would be sufficient cause to make such an application, though there is no certainty that the application would succeed.

If the divorce was on the ground of living apart—whether by consent after two years, or after five years without consent—the court can refuse to make the decree final until it is satisfied with the arrangements made to provide for the dependent partner.

It is widely believed that adultery during the six weeks before a decree becomes absolute can jeopardise the divorce, but this is not correct. This misunderstanding survives from the time when the Church dealt with matrimonial law.

When making the decree nisi, the judge may also make orders about the custody of the children and about maintenance, if these questions have been agreed. If there is no agreement, the arguments are heard later by the judge or by a registrar, in private.

After six weeks, the solicitor should get the decree absolute from the court. Once this document has been obtained the marriage is ended, and both parties are free to marry again.

Additional copies of the decree can be obtained from the court where the case was heard, or from the Registrar General, Somerset House, Strand, London WC2R 1LB.

## The cost of parting

DIVORCE need not be expensive. The cost can vary considerably—depending on how complex a case is, how much work is involved for a lawyer, both before and during the court hearing and, particularly, on whether or not the case is defended.

A childless couple who agree to end their marriage after two years' separation may get a divorce for £85–£100. Any other undefended divorce normally costs about £120. But if there is a dispute, if custody of the children has to be decided, or if financial arrangements have to be negotiated, costs can run into hundreds of pounds. Evidence from an inquiry agent to prove adultery, or from a doctor to prove cruelty, adds to the expense. Inquiry agents and doctors, including Health Service doctors, charge fees and expenses if they give evidence.

The costs for one side in a three-day defended hearing would probably be about £300, but could be more if a leading barrister, or more than one, were used. These costs would not cover the subsequent settling in the judge's chambers of the details for custody, maintenance and other financial arrangements. This could add a further £60–£100; much more if there is a prolonged dispute over children or money.

### Recovering costs

Costs may be awarded against either party or against a co-respondent. For example, if a husband proves that his marriage broke down because of his wife's adultery, the court may order the other man to pay the husband's costs. Similarly, a wife who shows that her husband deserted her or behaved badly towards her might be given costs against him.

The person against whom costs have been awarded does not, however, have to pay any amount the opposing lawyers choose to charge. His own lawyers can send the bill to a court official, who decides what is a 'fair charge', and the court official would not allow any expense that he considered unreasonable. For example, he would not allow a witness's air fare from New York, if the evidence could have been sworn on oath in New York.

This procedure for checking a bill is called 'taxation'. The unsuccessful respondent has to pay the amounts allowed by the court, and the balance of the petitioner's costs are paid by himself or herself. The 'taxation' official rarely allows all the petitioner's costs to be charged against the losing party.

### Legal aid

In many cases, legal aid is available to the petitioner. If it is, he may have to pay nothing at all or only a contribution to the costs.

### Costs in a magistrates' court

It is impossible to give more than a rough guide to the cost of a matrimonial case—such as an application for a separation order—in the magistrates' court. It depends on the lawyer employed, the length of the case and the number of witnesses. But an uncomplicated case conducted by a solicitor should cost £15–£20. If there is a dispute between the parties which goes on for two or more days, the costs will be much higher.

Ask the solicitor to quote a fee at the outset, but remember that it may rise if the case lasts longer than expected. ☐ Four ways to separate, p. 388.

# Custody and care of children

*Deciding who has the children*  
*How a court decides on custody*  
*When neither parent gets control*

*Parents' rights to see their children*  
*When an order is broken*  
*Maintaining the children*

A CHILD inevitably suffers as a result of a broken marriage, and in dealing with the question of custody a county court, High Court or magistrates' court strives to act in the child's best interests. A court normally acts on the principle that a stable, affectionate relationship counts for more than a blood-tie.

The aim is to provide for the true needs of young children, even if it means that they are brought up in another household or perhaps within a second marriage. But young children, particularly girls, are seldom taken away from their mothers.

The welfare aspect is regarded as so important that no court will grant a divorce or nullity decree, or make a separation order, without being satisfied about the arrangements for the children of the family.

The only exception would be if the children were living abroad, so that the court could not be satisfied about the conditions.

## Children of the family
In law, 'children of the family' are:
1. Any child born to the wife during or before the marriage—provided that her husband is the father.
2. Any child adopted by both husband and wife. This does not include children boarded out to them under fostering arrangements.
3. Any child who has been treated by both husband and wife as a child of the family. This includes an illegitimate child of the wife, provided that the husband treated the child as one of the family—that is, if he allowed the child to live under his roof and maintained it as if it were his own, even though he was aware that he was not the father. This same legal state also applies to an illegitimate child of the husband living in the home.

## Deciding who has the children
The law requires that children of a broken marriage must live in some permanent home, and the court can, on the application of either party, decide which parent shall have them.

Where there is agreement between the parties, the judge makes a custody order at the same time as he grants a divorce decree, provided he is satisfied that the agreement is in the best interests of the child.

Where there is a dispute over custody, he will delay making an order at the divorce hearing until he has received evidence 'in chambers'—at a private hearing attended only by the husband and wife and their lawyers. This avoids any publicity, which might be harmful to the children.

At this hearing, evidence is given in sworn statements called 'affidavits'. These are read to the judge by the solicitor or barrister, and either side may question the other on this written evidence. Evidence from schoolmasters, doctors, relatives or friends of the family may also be given by affidavit, with the same rights of cross-examination.

## How a court decides on custody
There is no *rule* that a mother gets the custody of young children, but this is generally the case because it is usually in their best interests.

However, if the father can provide a good home for them, with a proper 'mother substitute' such as a housekeeper, relative or even a second wife, he may be awarded their custody; but, in practice, this seldom arises.

After hearing all the evidence, and the arguments on both sides, the court takes into account the child's age and sex; the amount of contact the child has had with each parent; the record of each party as a parent (any neglect or cruelty will obviously be important); the accommodation each can offer; and educational facilities offered.

Another important consideration is where the children have lived up to the time of the court hearing. Courts do not like to disturb children by moving them around, and if the couple have separated, a custody case is heavily influenced in favour of the parent who has had the children all the time.

When the child is old enough to have formed definite views about which parent he wants to live with—usually taken to be the age of 12—his views also may be considered, and the court may ask to see the child privately.

Where the court feels it does not have enough information from which to make a decision, it may call in a court welfare officer for a report on both parties and the sort of home that each is able to offer.

GUILTY PARTY The 'guilt' of either party leading to the break-up of a marriage is of relatively little importance in deciding who should have the children, since a bad husband or wife is not necessarily a bad parent.

The courts try to protect children from the bad example of a parent—one having an adulterous relationship, for example. But if, on balance, it is better for the child to live with a parent who has committed adultery, then even the presence in the home of a mistress or lover will not automatically prevent the court from making a custody order in favour of the 'guilty' parent. However, if a mother were leading a thoroughly immoral life—as a prostitute, for example—she would have little chance of keeping her children.

### When neither parent gets control

In some cases, neither parent can provide a satisfactory home for the children and the court may then order that the children be committed to the care of the local authority.

Again, if the court is unsure of the capability of the parent to whom it proposes awarding custody, the court may make a supervision order, giving the local authority social services department the right and duty to visit and watch over the child's upbringing.

The court may also grant custody, in suitable cases, to someone other than a parent— a grandparent, for example.

SPLIT ORDERS A court order concerning children can cover a wide field.

Usually, the parent who is given custody has the children to live with him or her, has day-to-day control of them, and decides on their education, religion and upbringing.

But—except in a magistrates' court— custody may sometimes be awarded to one parent and 'care and control' to the other.

A split order like this could be made where, for example, the mother is the natural person to look after two very young children although she is not in other ways a responsible person, while the father is a devoted and wise parent but would find it difficult to give enough time to the children.

In such circumstances, the father might be awarded custody of the children and the mother care and control.

This would grant the mother day-to-day charge of the children, but would give the father the right to be consulted on, and in most cases decide, major matters such as education.

JOINT CUSTODY On rare occasions a court will grant joint custody. Normally this does not prove to be a satisfactory arrangement, unless both parents are in complete agreement over the welfare of their children.

### Parents' rights to see their children

The rights of access to the children of a broken marriage often give rise to disputes, usually as an extension of the matrimonial quarrel.

Often the court will stipulate that the parent who is not awarded custody should have 'reasonable access' to the children, and leave the arrangements to the parties.

But where there is likely to be any dispute, the affected party should seek specific rights.

The amount of access will depend on the circumstances of each case. For instance, where parents live within a few miles of each other and the children are at day school, access might be for a whole day each weekend.

If distances are greater, the children might go to stay with the other parent for one weekend a month. Where the child is at boarding school, or the homes are far apart, access might be for a week during the Christmas and Easter holidays and for three weeks in the summer. The court would probably order that the parents take it in turns to have the children at Christmas and Easter.

REFUSING ACCESS A parent is refused access to a child only if he is likely to seriously harm the child's development.

A habitual drunkard, for example, may be kept away from the children, or may be allowed to see them only in the presence of someone else; certainly a man convicted of sexual offences against children, or of gross violence, will not be allowed to see them without safeguards, and may be refused all access.

### When an order can be changed

No order need be regarded as permanent. There is always the right to appeal where a parent thinks the court is wrong. A child custody order normally continues until the child reaches the age of 16. Either parent may go back to the court to ask for a variation of the order if the circumstances change.

### When an order is broken

Failure to obey a court's order about custody of, or access to, children is contempt of court, and may be punished by imprisonment.

On the first offence, the offending parent will generally be cautioned; but a second act of contempt usually results in imprisonment.

REMOVING THE CHILD When a child is the subject of a custody order made by a court, neither parent may take the child to a country out of the jurisdiction of the court—not even to Scotland or Northern Ireland—without the written consent of the other parent.

If this consent is refused, permission to take the child may be sought from the county court—but normally the court will give consent only when there is no danger of the child remaining outside England or Wales. INJUNCTION Where there is a chance that one parent may try to take the child out of the country, the court can be asked for an injunction—an order restraining the parent from carrying out his or her suspected intention.

To apply for an injunction, a parent should see a solicitor. The cost will not be high, and emergency legal aid is available if necessary.

If an injunction is granted, the Home Office should be informed—a solicitor will do this—so that all ports and airports can be alerted.

### Maintaining the children

Where a court has awarded custody to the mother, it normally makes an order at the same time for the children's maintenance. The father is usually ordered to pay.

Even if a wife is better off than her husband, she is still entitled to ask for an order, although she may be expected to contribute something towards the children's upkeep from her own income.

In deciding the size of a maintenance order, the court first considers the child's financial needs—for instance, a 15-year-old obviously needs more food and more expensive clothes than a three-year-old.

The court also considers the family's previous standard of living, and tries to put each child into a financial position similar to the one it would have had if the marriage had not broken down.

The conduct of either husband or wife which led to the ending of the marriage has nothing to do with who pays or receives a child's maintenance. If a 'guilty' mother is given custody of children, she is entitled to exactly the same maintenance for the children as if she were 'innocent'.
SECURITY If the person ordered to pay maintenance is wealthy, the court can make an order tying up part of his capital, so that the income from it can be used to pay either all or part of the maintenance. The court would not tie up all a man's capital in this way, nor would it tie up capital needed for his business.
LUMP SUM The court can order the payment of a lump sum for the benefit of any child of the family. This might be a final settlement of all claims against the parent; but the court is more likely to order maintenance payments

as well. The court will, in some cases, order regular payments, provision of security *and* the payment of a lump sum.

### Deciding on the amount of maintenance

Although the court actually makes the order, the lawyers for the husband and wife normally work out an agreement between them. An order for maintenance is made in general terms at the hearing in which a decree nisi is made. Details are settled in chambers—a private hearing, when press and public are not admitted.

### Variation of orders

Maintenance orders can always be varied by the court that made the original order. This may result in the amount fixed being reduced or increased, depending on whether the father's income has gone up or down.

Courts are most often asked to vary an order because the father's circumstances have changed—because he has lost his job, or been given promotion and a higher salary, or acquired a second family. But the needs of the first family take precedence over those of the second.

The fact that a mother re-marries will bring to an end a maintenance order in her favour; but the order for the children will continue. The mother's second husband is not required to maintain her children of the earlier marriage unless their father is incapable of doing so and the second husband has accepted them as part of his family.

If a father loses his job or becomes ill, he should immediately tell the court to which payments are made. The court will not then take action for non-payment. Indeed, it may advise the father to apply for a variation of the order for a period.

Normally a maintenance order runs out when the child reaches 17, but it can be extended until the child is 18, or even 21, if the child is still receiving full-time education.

### Collection of payments

Most orders for maintenance payments are made by, or registered with, a magistrates' court, and payment is usually made to the court. The mother is generally required to collect the money, though a few courts may send money by post.

If the father does not pay, despite the court order, the court can tell an employer to deduct the maintenance from his wages or salary.

A parent who refuses to pay can have his or her goods seized and sold. If all else fails, a defaulting parent can be sent to prison.

# After the divorce

*Dividing the family possessions*  
*How the judge decides ownership*

*Maintenance for the wife*  
*How the amount is fixed*

O NCE a divorce is made absolute, the husband and wife revert to single status. Both are free to re-marry, though the fact that one may have to pay maintenance to the other can make it difficult financially.

If one dies without making a will, the other is no longer entitled to inherit. But either party may apply to the court for some financial provision from the other's estate. For example, a wife who has been getting maintenance from her former husband may be given either a lump sum or continued maintenance if he dies leaving a substantial estate.

If the only will in existence was made before the marriage broke up, references to 'wife' or 'husband' are still valid.

The income tax authorities regard the former husband and wife as single people.

**Dividing the family possessions**  
Married couples normally share a home and everything in it. But if the marriage breaks up they usually divide their possessions.

Even while they are married, a husband or a wife can apply to the High Court or a county court to settle disputes about ownership. In the event of a divorce or an annulment, they have three years in which to apply to a court.

If a court decides that husband and wife have equal claims to property—furniture, say —it could make an order for that furniture to be sold and the proceeds shared equally.

Since the sale might not bring in what the property is worth, a more sensible course is for both parties to agree to try to divide it fairly.

**How the judge decides ownership**  
In deciding who owns what, the court first tries to establish the intention of the husband and wife at the time each article was bought.

Where only one party made any contribution to the purchase—for example, where the husband buys furniture out of his earnings and the wife pays nothing, or where the wife buys a washing-machine out of a legacy—the property clearly belongs to the buyer. But very often there is no such clear-cut certainty.

For example, a husband might pay the deposit on a washing-machine and make some hire-purchase payments, but when he is short of money his wife might keep up payments from her earnings or by thrifty housekeeping. In such cases the courts have normally ruled that ownership is shared equally.

SHARED PROPERTY Where one party owns property and the other contributes substantially to its improvement, the latter is entitled to share in the sale proceeds.

An example of shared entitlement would be where the wife owned the house and the husband paid for an extension. The husband would be entitled to a proportionate share of the proceeds of any sale and would have similar rights if he built the extension himself.

THE HOME The house the couple lived in is usually the most important piece of property owned by either or both of them.

The decision to purchase in one name or the other, or in both names, is important since ownership of a house is generally determined by the courts according to what is in the original transfer documents.

In law, a wife who leaves her husband for another man would normally still be entitled to her share of the matrimonial home if it was bought jointly in both names.

But no matter who, on paper, is the legal owner of the house, the court takes into account any contributions towards the purchase.

For instance, if the house is in the husband's name only, but the wife contributed half the deposit or made a substantial part of the mortgage repayments out of her earnings, she would be given a share in the proceeds of sale.

This share will not necessarily be in proportion to the contributions. Courts have tended to look on these as showing an intention by both parties to buy the house as a joint matrimonial home and, where it is impossible to discover the precise contributions and intentions of the partners, to award equal shares in its value.

But a court can share the proceeds of a sale in any way which it thinks right in the particular circumstances.

Although the wife's contribution must be money or money's worth, it need not consist of direct payments. She might, for example, use her wages for housekeeping, leaving her husband to make the mortgage repayments, or she might contribute to the value of the property by making improvements.

Similarly, the couple's earnings might be 'pooled' and payments on the house made out of the 'common purse'. In this case the wife would be entitled to her share in the house, even if her husband earned much more.

BANK ACCOUNTS The money in joint bank accounts belongs equally to both husband and wife. Judges usually hold that both are entitled to half the money in the account, regardless of how much each has contributed. WEDDING PRESENTS In general, wedding presents are considered to be the property of the party whose friend or relative made the gift. Any presents given by one marriage partner to the other belong to the receiver.

**Transfer of property**
The court has power to order one partner to transfer property to the other, and can alter any deed or arrangement made by or in the interests of the parties or their children.

In deciding ownership, the judge applies the law and takes no account of the parties' conduct or their needs. But he can make transfer orders irrespective of ownership in any way he considers right. So a woman who has no claim to the matrimonial home because she has made no contribution may have the house transferred to her because the judge considers it best, taking into account both the parties' conduct and their respective needs.

**Maintenance for the wife**
When a couple are divorced, the court can order one to pay maintenance to the other. Usually husband must provide for wife.

This can be done through periodic payments, an amount deposited as security, or payment of a lump sum and reduced periodic payments. The periodic payments and the security arrangements can be changed later by the court at the request of either party, but a lump sum cannot be changed.
INCOME TAX If a man is ordered to make regular maintenance payments, he can deduct tax at the standard rate from them. But, as the former wife is now taxed as a single woman, the amount deducted is usually more than she is due to pay. She can claim the excess amount from the local tax inspector.
LUMP SUMS The court may make an order for a lump-sum payment, but normally only if the husband has substantial capital. The court may order a lump sum to be paid to the wife for a specific purpose, such as a house deposit.

For the husband, it is often more satisfactory to make a lump-sum payment on condition that no further claim is made on him. If the woman is likely to re-marry she is better off with a lump sum, as periodic payments cease once she marries again. Similarly, if she wants to emigrate or to set up a business, she will be well advised to take a lump sum, with or without reduced maintenance payments.

**How the amount is fixed**
In cases where there is a dispute, the question of how much maintenance a divorced wife should receive is argued out by lawyers for the two sides. If they cannot agree, a judge decides in his chambers. Usually, each side gets a statement of the other's financial affairs which has been sworn on oath to be true. This means that if false figures have been given knowingly, the person concerned can be prosecuted for perjury. In fixing the amount or deciding whether property should be transferred, the court is bound by law to consider:
1. The income, earning capacity, property and other financial resources of the couple.
2. The financial needs and obligations such as mortgage and hire-purchase repayments and maintenance of a second family.
3. The standard of living enjoyed by the family before the marriage broke up.
4. The age of each party.
5. The length of time they were married.
6. The contribution made by each party to the welfare of the family, including looking after the home and bringing up the children.
7. The value of any pension or benefit that either party may lose because of the divorce.
8. The conduct of the two parties.

The court also considers these matters in deciding whether to transfer property.

Take the case of the middle-aged woman who has run the home and brought up a family. Her husband then leaves her through no misconduct on her part. She will get more than an equally innocent, childless young woman who has been married only a few years and who can return to her previous career.

A woman with three children to bring up, who broke up her marriage by her own adultery and was not being maintained by another man, would get only the minimum necessary for essentials, plus an unchanged amount for any children.

The aim is, as far as possible, to put everyone concerned into the financial position they would have been in if the marriage had not broken up. There are no rules, but a good working guide is to add together the incomes of husband and wife, give each member of the family enough for a bare living, and divide the rest as fairly as possible between them.

# What to do when someone dies

*Registering the death*    *Disposal certificates*
*Death certificates*    *Death at sea*

As well as sorrow, a death in the family brings many practical problems. Relatives have to comply with formalities of registering the death, and if death was accidental or unexpected, a post mortem may be held. Then there is the funeral to be arranged. ☐ Investigating a sudden death, p. 410; Arranging a funeral, p. 412.

Bereavement also has its financial side. Dependants may need immediate financial support; they may be able to claim damages if the dead person was killed in an accident. Finally, the dead person's property has to be divided up. ☐ Ready cash for the bereaved, p. 414; Claiming damages for fatal accidents, p. 417; What happens to property and belongings, p. 420.

Normally, the last doctor to attend a person who dies issues a medical certificate stating the cause of death. This must be sent, either by the doctor or by a relative, to the local registrar of births, deaths and marriages.

If the doctor has not been in attendance during the 14 days before death, or if the death is sudden or caused by an accident or neglect, the doctor must report it to the coroner. ☐ Investigating a sudden death, p. 410.

### Registering the death
A death has to be registered in person—normally within five days, or within 14 days if the registrar has previously been informed of the death in writing. The death must be registered with the registrar of the district in which it took place.

For deaths at home or in hospital, the following people—in order of preference—can register the death:
**1.** Any relative present at death, attending the dead person during their last illness, or living in the district.
**2.** Anyone else present at death.
**3.** The head of the house, if he knew of the death, or anyone else staying in the house.
**4.** Anyone arranging burial or cremation.

Where death happens elsewhere, or a body is found, death can be registered by any relative; anyone present at death; anyone finding or in charge of the body; or anyone arranging burial or cremation.

The registrar needs to know the date of death and where it took place. He also requires the full name, address, sex, date of birth, marital status and occupation of the dead person. Whoever gives the registrar this information must also give his own name, address and relationship to the dead person and why he qualifies to register the death.

The register is then signed by the registrar and the person registering the death.

### Death certificates
When the death is registered, the registrar issues a death certificate, which confirms the registration, for a small fee. This is used to claim widow's benefit and State death grant.

Separate certificates can also be obtained for dealing with wills, and insurance and pension policies. Certificates are available at a reduced fee for claiming money from friendly societies, the National Savings Bank, trustee savings banks, savings certificates and premium bonds. ☐ Ready cash for the bereaved, p. 414.

Special death certificates are needed to claim where a child has insured the life of a parent or grandparent. Only one certificate is issued, so if more than one insurance company is involved, the claimant should ask for the certificate to be sent back by each company in turn. ☐ What happens to property and belongings, p. 420.

If any certificates are lost or destroyed, or if extra ones are needed, copies can be obtained from the registrar who registered the death or —if it is more than a year after the death took place—from the General Register Office, Somerset House, London WC2R 1LB.

### Disposal certificates
No burial or cremation can take place until a disposal certificate has been issued. This is usually done by the registrar when the death is registered.

The registrar may issue a certificate before the death is registered—but only if he has received all the necessary information, and is merely waiting for the register to be signed. This situation could arise when the person who supplied the information is in hospital.

Until a disposal certificate is available, it is advisable to make only provisional arrangements for the funeral.

When a certificate is received it should be taken to the undertaker, the church or the cremation office. However, a disposal certificate issued before the death is registered is not accepted by cremation authorities.

## Death at sea

What happens when someone dies at sea on a British-registered ship is largely left to the ship's master. The death is recorded in the ship's log and the entry witnessed by a crew member and, if possible, by a doctor.

This entry in the log is valid as a registration of death as soon as it is witnessed. Forms have to be completed later which eventually enable relatives to obtain a copy of the registration from the General Register Office in London.

If the next-of-kin is on board and gives permission, the captain can allow the burial to take place at sea. If there are no relatives on board he will try to contact them and find out their wishes; but he is entitled in law to bury a body entirely on his own authority.

FOREIGN SHIPS If the death occurs on a foreign-registered ship, the laws of that country will apply and the regulations for bringing a body back from abroad will have to be followed if relatives want to hold the burial in this country.

---

# Bringing a body into England and Wales

THE death of a British subject abroad has to be registered according to local regulations. It helps to register the death with the British consul in that country as copies of the death certificate may then be obtained later from the Registrar General at Somerset House.

If the body is brought back to Britain, the Customs will want to see a certificate of death or an authorisation for the removal of the body from the country of death.

The registrar where the funeral is to take place requires evidence—such as the British consul's certificate—that the death occurred outside Britain.

If the body is to be cremated, a doctor's certificate stating the cause of death has to be sent to the Home Office, Romney House, Marsham Street, London SW1P 3DY, so that a cremation authorisation certificate can be issued by them.

If death occurred in Scotland or Northern Ireland, but the funeral is to take place in England, the death certificate issued there will be accepted as evidence of death.

## Service deaths

If a serviceman dies while serving abroad, the Ministry of Defence arranges and pays for his funeral there. The Ministry will fly the body home if the family prefers, but the family is then responsible for the funeral. In this case the Ministry provides the coffin and makes a contribution of £5 towards the expenses. If the family provides the coffin the Ministry makes a grant of £10.

Such deaths are registered by Service Registering officers, and certificates can later be obtained from the General Register Office, Somerset House, London WC2R 1LB.

## Sending a body abroad

If a body is to be sent out of England or Wales, even to Scotland, the coroner of the district in which the death took place must be informed. The necessary Form 104 can be obtained from the registrar.

The body must not be moved until four days after the coroner has acknowledged receipt of the notice. The four-day limit can be waived by the coroner in special cases, such as that of an Orthodox Jew, whose body is required by religious rules to be buried as soon as possible after death.

The consular office of the country to which the body is to be sent will be able to advise the family of any special regulations which have to be met in that country.

The British Customs need one copy of the death certificate, and one or more copies will be needed in the country to which the body is being sent.

These documents may have to be translated and authenticated at the consulate or embassy of the country. There may be a charge for this. The consulate will also advise on what arrangements can be made in advance and what formalities are required when the body arrives in its country.

The coroner in the district where death occurred must be told of a proposed burial at sea. Anyone can be buried at sea at least 3 miles beyond the low-water mark.

# Investigating a sudden death

*Post mortem examinations*     *When a child is stillborn*
*Attending an inquest*

I F there is anything unusual about a death, the district coroner must be informed. The coroner—who is either a lawyer or a doctor or, sometimes, both—has to be told of all cases of sudden death; all cases where death is caused, even indirectly, by an accident; where there is anything suspicious about a death; and where the cause is not known.

He has to be told if death happens during a hospital operation, in prison, or where the cause may have been suicide or drugs, abortion, alcoholism or poisoning.

When there are reasonable grounds for supposing that a death was due to violent or unnatural causes, the law requires an inquest to be held.

When a death is reported to the coroner, the registrar cannot register it until the coroner authorises him to do so. This means that the funeral also has to wait until the coroner gives his permission.

The coroner is usually informed by the hospital, if death occurred there, or by a doctor, the police or the registrar. But anyone who is concerned or uneasy about the cause of death can also give information to the coroner, who may investigate any death reported to him. His address is listed in the local telephone directory under 'Courts'.

The involvement of the coroner can be distressing for the dead person's family, and he is therefore careful not to intervene unless he feels there is no alternative.

The coroner's officer, usually a policeman, will make a preliminary inquiry to see if there are grounds for the coroner's intervention.

If the coroner is satisfied that the cause of death is adequately explained, he sends the registrar formal notice and the death can then be registered.

A disposal certificate is issued in the normal way, and the funeral can take place.

If, however, the coroner is in doubt, he can order either a post mortem examination or an inquest, or both.

Scotland has no coroners, but unexpected or violent death is investigated in the same way by a law officer, the 'procurator fiscal'.

## When death is presumed

N O death certificate can be issued unless there is a body. The lack of a certificate can cause difficulties when a person is presumed to have died, though there is no definite proof. Someone could die in an air crash or drown at sea, for example, and the body might not be found.

In these cases, relatives who want to deal with the missing person's estate and other belongings, or a widow who wants to re-marry, can apply to the High Court for an order that the missing person is presumed dead. The order dissolves any marriage in the same way as a divorce decree.

An application cannot usually be made until seven years after a missing person disappears. In an accident such as an air crash, however, where it is virtually certain that death has occurred, an application can be made immediately.

**Post mortem examinations**
Coroners commonly order a post mortem— a medical examination to establish the cause of death. There is no appeal against this decision. The post mortem is usually carried out at the mortuary by a doctor or a pathologist. It is supervised by the coroner's officer.

A relative has the right to be told the time and place of a post mortem and may ask to be represented by a doctor at the examination.

If the post mortem shows that death was from natural causes and the circumstances need no further inquiry, the coroner informs the registrar, who can then register the death.

The coroner is not obliged to tell the dead person's next-of-kin the result of the examination, but in some districts the coroner's officer or a policeman will call on the family.

Unless there is an inquest the body is returned to the family after the post mortem.

Post mortem examinations are common where death occurs in hospital. They may be ordered by the coroner. Hospital authorities who wish to make their own investigation into the cause of death must have the signed consent of the next-of-kin, who may refuse.

A relative who goes to the hospital after a death, if not the next-of-kin, should be in a position to say whether the next-of-kin will be prepared to give his consent. Relatives may ask for the result of the post mortem.

### Attending an inquest

Inquests, called public inquiries in Scotland, are held in about 20 per cent of cases reported to coroners. Their purpose is to investigate publicly the circumstances of death more fully than is possible by a medical examination—to establish who the dead person was; how, when and where he or she died; and to inquire into any unusual or suspicious circumstances.

The coroner can often make the decision himself about whether or not to order an inquest. But in some cases he is obliged to hold one—for example when death results from a road accident, when it takes place in prison, or when there is a suspicion that it was violent or unnatural. This could include death by lightning or even from a poisoned finger.

Notice of the inquest is normally given by a policeman, who informs the next-of-kin and other people concerned—such as an employer, if someone has died at work.

The coroner usually holds the inquest on his own, but in certain cases he has to call a jury—if, for instance, he has reason to believe that the cause of death was murder, a car accident, or industrial disease.

An inquest is primarily an investigation, not a trial. Witnesses at the inquest are under oath, but the proceedings are less formal than in an ordinary court. The coroner questions witnesses and can allow questioning by anyone with a proper legal interest—that is, the personal interest of a close relative, not an interest on behalf of an organisation.

A witness is not obliged to answer any question which would tend to incriminate either himself or his wife by exposing them to criminal proceedings. He is not, however, protected from answering questions which might be relevant in any subsequent civil proceedings, such as an action for damages.

Witnesses cannot refuse to begin giving evidence. The privilege of declining to answer can be claimed only after the question has been asked. The coroner then decides whether a witness may refuse to answer. Anyone who defies a coroner's instruction to answer can be sent to prison for contempt of court.

If there might be a claim for compensation, as can happen if death is caused by a road accident or an industrial accident, it is sensible for the next-of-kin to be represented at the inquest by the solicitor acting for them.

If, before the verdict has been reached, the coroner is told that someone has been charged with causing the death, he adjourns the inquest until criminal proceedings are over.

An inquest may be opened and adjourned after evidence of identification only. This can happen where the police have further inquiries to make, or where the coroner has not completed his investigations although the medical cause of death is not in dispute. Further adjournments are at the coroner's discretion.

The coroner can then authorise burial or cremation and will give the next-of-kin an order for burial or a certificate for cremation. This has the same effect as a disposal certificate from the registrar.

VERDICTS A coroner or his jury can bring in one of a number of verdicts. They are: murder or justifiable homicide; manslaughter; infanticide; suicide, often 'when the balance of the mind was disturbed'; criminal abortion; accident or misadventure; and death from industrial disease, or death from natural causes. A verdict may be left 'open' if there is not enough evidence to record any other verdict, as happens when it is impossible to determine between a death by suicide or by accident.

Where a coroner's jury finds that death was caused by murder, manslaughter, infanticide or criminal abortion, and the person apparently responsible is known, the court has power to commit that person for trial. If the police think that the jury's verdict cannot be sustained, the prosecution offer no evidence at the trial, and the accused is discharged.

### When a child is stillborn

The stillbirth of a child—one born dead after the twenty-eighth week of pregnancy—has to be registered in the same way as a normal birth. ☐ Having a baby, p. 324.

The death of a foetus before the twenty-eighth week of pregnancy is a miscarriage—which is not registered.

If a doctor or midwife is present at the stillbirth, he or she will issue a certificate of stillbirth, stating the cause of death and the duration of the pregnancy. If no doctor or midwife is there, anyone present can make a declaration on Form 35 (obtainable from the registrar), saying that to the best of his or her knowledge, the child was stillborn.

If there is any doubt that the child was born dead, the coroner should be informed. He will issue a certificate stating the cause of death when he has completed his investigations.

# Arranging a funeral

ARRANGEMENTS for a funeral can be made entirely by relatives or friends, but normally an undertaker is engaged. No one person is responsible in law for authorising funeral arrangements, so the family should agree about who takes charge. Another matter for family discussion is whether to put an announcement of the death and of the time and place of the funeral in the newspapers. An undertaker will arrange this if required.

Usually the wishes of the person who has died determine whether the body is to be buried or cremated. In law, relatives are not bound to observe these wishes.

### Choosing the undertaker

At a time of grief, many people do not like to start thinking about finance. But the financial aspects of a funeral have to be considered. After deciding on the type of funeral required and how much can be spent, contact a number of undertakers and compare the charges and services. The undertaker should be asked for an itemised estimate of costs, which are based on the type of coffin and services. They vary throughout the country.

The National Association of Funeral Directors, 57 Doughty Street, London WC1N 2NE, lists a minimum-price funeral, consisting of a simple coffin, hearse, one car for mourners, bearers and the services of the undertaker. This costs up to £60.

But in high-cost areas, such as London, the minimum-price funeral is likely to cover only the basic service. Extra expenses may increase the price to somewhere between £80 and £100.

The most common extra is about £5 to remove the body from home or hospital—this usually includes preparing the body. The undertaker will also charge for each day the body is on his premises.

Other extra costs include fees for graves, grave-digging and additional cars; and there is an additional charge if the cemetery is more than about 5 miles away from the funeral director's premises. Any extra journey which has to be made to move the body and coffin will also add to the cost.

Cremation fees range from £6 to £13, which may include the medical referee's fee,

use of the crematorium chapel and the chaplain's fee. The cost of a church service will be additional to the undertaker's bill.

### Deciding whether to embalm

Embalming, which costs about £5, involves replacing blood with a preservative called formalin. If there is any objection to embalming, tell the undertaker.

Embalming can be carried out only when a doctor has signed a medical certificate of cause of death. It is unwise to embalm until a disposal certificate—which allows the undertaker to proceed—has been issued by the registrar.

If a death has been reported to the coroner, the body must not be embalmed until the cause of death has been established. □ Investigating a sudden death, p. 410.

### Authority for the funeral

The disposal certificate from the registrar or coroner should be given to the undertaker before funeral arrangements are confirmed.

If he has to collect the body from hospital, he needs written authority—such as the disposal certificate, or a form signed by the executor of the estate or a relative.

### Burial

Everyone is entitled to be buried in the churchyard of the parish in which he had his home —whether or not he died there or was a Christian. A burial fee of about £3·50 is normally charged.

A vicar may also allow burial in the churchyard for someone who did not live in the parish. Burial fees in such cases may be higher. The church decides the position of the grave, and payment of the burial fee does not ensure exclusive use of the grave. This can be acquired by applying in advance to the diocesan registrar for what is called a 'faculty'.

Separate permission has to be obtained, and a separate fee paid, for a headstone. The church or cemetery must approve the inscription before the stone is set up.

BURIAL IN A CEMETERY Most cemeteries are run by local authorities and are non-denominational. A few, however, may be reserved in part or completely for members of a particular faith. Exclusive grave space can be bought. Fees for all graves, whether reserved or not, depend on size and position.

PRIVATE BURIALS Burials outside churchyards or cemeteries—in the dead person's own garden, for instance—require permission from the local planning authority, the local health department and the Department of the Environment. If there are objections, the burial must take place at a recognised site.

## Cremation

Cremation involves more formalities than burial. Usually, four official forms have to be completed. The aim of this procedure is to prevent cremation before the cause of death has been definitely established.

Form A, the application for cremation, has to be completed by the next-of-kin or the executor of the will and countersigned by a householder who knows the executor.

Form B is signed by the doctor who last attended the dead person. Form C is signed by another doctor, to confirm the first doctor's Form B. Each doctor will usually charge between £3·15 and £6·30. Forms B and C

are not needed if the body has been in the coroner's charge.

Form F is signed by the crematorium doctor or medical referee. His fee is usually included in the crematorium charges.

## Local authority funerals

Where there are no relatives, or none willing and able to pay for a funeral, it is arranged and paid for by either a hospital or by a local authority. Costs are recovered by claiming from any State grant which may be due.

The Department of Health and Social Security will arrange and pay for a simple funeral for anyone receiving a war disablement pension who dies as a direct result of that disablement. If the widow wishes to arrange a slightly more expensive funeral, she can pay extra to supplement the service offered.

Next-of-kin should contact the local War Pensions' office immediately if they want the Department to arrange the funeral. Alternatively, the Department will make a grant equivalent to the full State death grant for any war-disabled pensioner, even if he had not qualified for the full State death grant.

## The right to a Government death grant

THE Government makes a lump-sum payment, called a death grant, to the next-of-kin of a person who has died, or to the person paying for the funeral.

Particulars of the deceased must be given on a form, and the applicant has to state in what capacity he is making the claim. Evidence of death may be required.

The dead person's birth certificate and, if applicable, marriage certificate, his National Insurance contribution card and any other State payment books not previously returned must also be sent.

Qualification for a grant is based on National Insurance contributions—usually those made by the dead person. If 45 or more contributions have been paid or credited in the last complete contribution year before death, or before the dead person reached pensionable age, the grant will be paid in full.

If that condition is not met, it will still be paid if the dead person paid or had credited a yearly average of at least 45 contributions between July 5, 1948 (or his sixteenth birthday, if later), and the end of the last contribution year before death. If the average is under

45 a year but more than 13, a reduced grant may be paid. If less than 13, no grant at all is payable.

Men born before July 5, 1883, and women before July 5, 1888, do not qualify for a grant. If they were born in the ten years after those dates, the grant is reduced.

Grants for children under 18 are all reduced. No death grant is payable for a stillbirth.

The claim can be based on the dead person's own insurance contributions or those of a husband or wife, whether or not he or she is still alive. A grant may also be paid on the record of a close relative if the dead person has never been able to work or to pay National Insurance contributions.

The grant should be claimed, within six months of the death, from the local office of the Department of Health and Social Security on Form BD1. Application can also be made on the back of the free certificate of registration of death (Form BD8).

Even if a body has been bequeathed for medical research and will not be buried for some time, the grant should be claimed immediately after death.

# Ready cash for the bereaved

*Getting help from the State*  
*Claiming widow's benefit*  
*Types of widow's benefit*

*Industrial and war benefits*  
*Child's special allowance*

WHEN a man dies, a widow or close relative may need to raise ready cash. Holdings of up to £500 in the National Savings Bank can be withdrawn easily. The widow or relative sends the claim form with a copy of the death certificate and evidence that the applicant is entitled to draw the money. Such evidence can be provided by a marriage certificate or a copy of the will.

If the next-of-kin is not the widow, his or her birth certificate has to be sent, as well as a copy of the will. A relative or friend can claim only if named in the will. Where there is no will, a relative other than the widow must wait until the estate is distributed.

Deposits in savings accounts with friendly societies, or insurance money, may often be withdrawn easily by the widow or by the next-of-kin named in a will. These people may also

be able to claim from an employer's pension fund. To find out the exact position, write to the organisation concerned, explain the circumstances, and ask for a claim form.

If the dead person has arranged his finances wisely—say by nominating who should receive his savings—the procedure is more simple. The nominee need produce only the death certificate and evidence of identity.

**Getting help from the State**
A widow may be entitled to financial help from the State provided that her husband had paid at least 156 flat-rate National Insurance contributions since he last started to pay them or had them credited every week. If the couple were already married on July 4, 1948, and the husband was insured on that date, contributions paid before then are taken into account,

## How to apply for benefits

| Benefit | When payable | Who qualifies | How to claim |
|---|---|---|---|
| Widow's allowance | For first 26 weeks of widowhood | Lawful widow who was under 60 at time of husband's death or whose husband was not a retirement pensioner | Complete Form BW1, obtainable from the local office of the Department of Health and Social Security. Send it with widow's birth and marriage certificates and the death certificate |
| Widow's supplementary allowance | For first 26 weeks of widowhood | Lawful widow whose husband was not entitled to a retirement pension at the time of his death but whose earnings give entitlement to an earnings-related supplement | As for widow's allowance |
| Retirement pension | After 26 weeks of widow's allowance | Lawful widow aged 60 or over at death of husband; he must not have been a retirement pensioner but his or her contributions must qualify for a pension. □Qualifying for a State pension, p. 525 | As for widow's allowance |
|  | Immediately | Lawful widow aged 60 or over at death of husband; he must have been a retirement pensioner | Complete Form BD8 (on back of death certificate) and send to the local office of the Department of Health and Social Security |
| Widowed mother's allowance | After 26 weeks of widow's allowance | Lawful widow under 60, with a child or children under 19 | As for widow's allowance |

and the qualifying number of contributions is usually 104 instead of the normal 156.

If a widow is to get the full allowances, her husband must have paid or had credited an average of 50 flat-rate contributions for each complete year of insurance. An average of 13 to 49 contributions a year qualifies her for reduced benefit. An average of less than 13 means that she receives no benefit.

Only someone regarded in law as a widow can benefit. A woman who has been living with a man to whom she was not married does not qualify when he dies. Nor does a woman whose marriage has ended in divorce or has been annulled—though she may receive a child's special allowance. If a lawful widow re-marries, or lives with a man as his wife, she ceases to be entitled to any widow's benefit from her previous marriage.

## Claiming widow's benefit

A widow completes Form BD8 (the back of the death certificate) and sends it to the local office of the Department of Health and Social Security. If she is 60 or over when widowed and her husband was receiving a retirement pension, the office will adjust her retirement pension or arrange one for her. If she is under 60 or her husband was not a retirement pensioner, the office will send her Form BW1, on which to claim widow's benefit.

The widow should complete Form BW1 and return it to the office, together with her birth and marriage certificates (if available) and the death certificate (unless one has already been sent). If a claim for widow's benefit is made more than three months after the husband's death, benefit may be lost.

Usually a widow is told about two weeks after sending back the form whether her husband's National Insurance contributions entitle her to receive benefit. If her claim fails, she can apply to the local National Insurance appeal tribunal within 21 days.

## Types of widow's benefit

Normally, a widow whose husband's contributions entitle her to financial help gets a widow's allowance for 26 weeks, provided that she was under 60 at the time of her husband's death or he was not a retirement pensioner.

QUALIFYING CHILDREN For each qualifying child in her family the widow gets extra benefit. A child qualifies if he is under school leaving age; or if he is under 19 and receiving full-time education or is an apprentice with

| Benefit | When payable | Who qualifies | How to claim |
|---|---|---|---|
| Widow's pension | After 26 weeks of widow's allowance or when widowed mother's allowance ceases | Lawful widow between 40 and 60 at husband's death, or when widowed mother's allowance ceased | As for widow's allowance |
| Widow's industrial death benefit | Immediately | Lawful widow whose husband died as a result of an industrial accident or disease | As for widow's allowance. If possible, also send evidence of cause of death, such as written evidence of the inquest verdict |
| Industrial death benefit for others | Immediately | A dependant of a person who died as a result of an industrial accident or disease | Complete Form BI 200, obtainable from the local office of the Department of Health and Social Security. Return it with death certificate (and marriage certificate if a widower) |
| Widow's war pension | From date of husband's death, but application must be made promptly | Lawful widow whose husband's death was caused by service in the armed forces | Contact either the local Social Security office or the Department of Health and Social Security, Norcross, Blackpool FY5 3TA |

For a widow to qualify at all for widow's benefit (widow's allowance, widow's supplementary allowance, widowed mother's allowance or widow's pension) her husband must have paid at least 156 flat-rate National Insurance contributions since he last became insured (104 contributions if the couple were already married on July 4, 1948, and the husband was insured on that date). There are no contribution conditions for either industrial death benefit or widow's war pension.

low earnings; or if he is under 16 and cannot work because of prolonged illness or disability.

After 26 weeks, a widow may be entitled to a widowed mother's allowance or a widow's pension, or (if 60 or over) a retirement pension. WIDOW'S ALLOWANCE For the first 26 weeks, a widow is entitled to a widow's allowance, with extra benefit for each qualifying child.

While receiving widow's allowance, a woman may be eligible for extra benefit related to her husband's earnings, provided that he was not entitled to a retirement pension. This is called a widow's supplementary allowance.

A woman receiving a widow's allowance is credited with flat-rate National Insurance contributions, so that she can later claim a retirement pension based on her contributions. WIDOWED MOTHER'S ALLOWANCE After receiving widow's allowance for 26 weeks, a widowed mother with a child of her own under 19 living with her gets a widowed mother's allowance. This is made up of benefit for herself and each qualifying child.

A woman pregnant by her late husband may get the widowed mother's allowance after receiving widow's allowance for 26 weeks. WIDOW'S PENSION If a widow has reached the age of 50 when her husband dies and does not qualify for a widowed mother's allowance, she can receive a full widow's pension after drawing the widow's allowance for 26 weeks. Similarly a widowed mother who has reached 50 when her widowed mother's allowance ceases can qualify for a full widow's pension.

A widow aged between 40 and 50 in these circumstances can qualify for a reduced-rate pension.

If a widow is 60 or over when her husband dies and he was not a retirement pensioner, she will receive a widow's allowance for 26 weeks. After that, whether she is retired or not, she is entitled to a retirement pension based on her own contributions or her husband's— whichever is the greater.

A widow can receive, with her own retirement pension, half of any pension increase her husband earned by deferring retirement and paying contributions after December 25, 1961. She is entitled to half the graduated pension earned by his contributions, in addition to her own graduated pension.

### Industrial and war benefits

Whether or not a widow qualifies for benefit under the National Insurance scheme, she may qualify for death benefits under the industrial injuries scheme, or she may be eligible for a dependant's war pension. She cannot claim these benefits as well as National Insurance widow's benefit. But if she receives either and it is less than she would receive in National Insurance widow's benefit, the difference is made up by the local Social Security office. INDUSTRIAL DEATH BENEFIT The widow of a man who dies as the result of an accident at work, or from one of the classified industrial diseases, may be entitled to special benefits. If she claims on Form BW1 that his death was caused by such an accident or disease, she must send the full death certificate and, if possible, further evidence, such as written evidence of the inquest verdict (obtainable from the coroner's court).

For the first 26 weeks, a widow who qualifies is paid a pension at the same rate as the widow's allowance. After 26 weeks, a widow who was under 50 at the time of her husband's death gets a small pension and the widow of 50 or over gets a larger one.

A younger widow who was pregnant when her husband died, or who is permanently unable to support herself, will receive the same pension as a widow of 50 or over. A widow with qualifying children gets the larger pension. If she is 40 or over when this entitlement ceases, her pension continues at the higher level, instead of reverting to the lower rate. INDUSTRIAL DEATH BENEFITS FOR OTHERS A man who is permanently unable to support himself, and whose wife contributed over half the cost of his support, is entitled to a pension if his wife dies from an industrial accident or from a classified industrial disease. The widower claims on Form BI 200, obtainable from the local Social Security office, sending the full death certificate and his marriage certificate with the form.

Other close relatives who were dependent on the dead person may also claim benefit. WAR PENSION A woman whose husband dies as a result of service in the armed forces is usually entitled to a widow's war pension. If she thinks her husband's death was due to service in the armed forces, she should contact the local Social Security office, or write to the Department of Health and Social Security, Norcross, Blackpool FY5 3TA.

### Child's special allowance

A woman whose marriage has ended in divorce or has been annulled may receive a child's special allowance. It is payable after her former husband dies provided that she has a qualifying child in her family; that her former husband was contributing or was liable to contribute to the support of the child; and that she has not re-married. Claim on Form CS1, from the local Social Security office.

# Claiming damages for fatal accidents

*Those who can benefit*  
*How to claim*  
*What losses will be compensated*

*Assessment of damages*  
*Deductions from potential damages*

WHEN somebody is killed in an accident, it may be possible to claim damages from the person responsible. Relatives or heirs may have grounds for two different kinds of legal action:

1. Dependants can claim damages for loss of financial support. These claims are made under the Fatal Accidents Acts.

2. The executor or administrator, acting on behalf of the dead person's estate, can claim damages for the cutting short of the dead person's life and for any pain and suffering which was caused to him or her.

To be successful, the claimant must prove that the person being sued was wholly or partly responsible for the death.

If death was caused by a road accident, or by an accident at work, the person responsible will probably be covered by third-party motor insurance or some form of employer's liability insurance.

The claimant can then be reasonably certain that compensation will be available. It is also likely that the claim will be settled by negotiation, as insurance companies do not normally go to court in straightforward cases.

Furthermore when a death occurs at work, a State benefit called industrial death benefit may be available to the dependants. □ Ready cash for the bereaved, p. 414.

## Those who can benefit
Relatives who can benefit from claims if they were financially dependent on the dead person include a wife (but not a common-law wife), or husband, parents, children and stepchildren; grandparents and grandchildren; brother, sister, uncle or aunt.

An adopted child is regarded as the child of its adopters, and not of the real parents, for the purposes of claiming damages. An illegitimate child is entitled to benefit in the same way as a legitimate child.

## How to claim
All dependants who wish to sue under the Fatal Accidents Acts must do so in one action, which is usually brought in their name by the dead person's executor or administrator. An action against the party responsible must be

started within three years of the death, or it will be legally barred. However, the dependants can themselves sue if a personal representative has not been appointed, or if he fails to start the action within six months of the death.

In many cases, the widow herself is the representative. If so, she should get legal advice on the possibility of a successful action.

Each dependant is entitled to individual damages. In most cases, the court apportions damages between the different dependants. If a successful action is brought by a widow in her own name and in the names of her children, there will be separate judgments for her and for each of the children.

Although a representative can settle a claim with the insurance company, or with any other party being sued, by agreeing to take a lump sum for himself, this cannot be done when the claim involves others.

In such cases all claimants must agree to the settlement and, if any of them are under 18, a court must approve it.

## What losses will be compensated
Damages for loss of support are based on actual or potential financial loss—not on grief, sorrow or any kind of mental distress.

Relatives can succeed only if they can prove either that they were dependent on the dead person, or that they would probably have received support from him or her, had he or she lived.

For this reason it is difficult to assess damages for the loss of a child. The mere possibility that a child would, when grown up, contribute to the support of his parents is not enough. There must be reasonable expectation of support.

However, where a child is serving an apprenticeship, and would soon be earning full wages, courts find that there is a reasonable expectation, and award damages.

The case is much the same for the loss of a wife. The amount her husband or children are entitled to claim is limited by the extent to which she contributed to the support or upkeep of the home when she was alive. The courts have held that services given in the home without payment are to be regarded as the equivalent of financial support, and they now award damages based on this.

PARTIAL LOSS When a widow claims on behalf of herself and her children, she does so because she has lost the total support of the bread-winner. However, a claim can be made for loss of partial support.

For example, a crippled father was awarded damages for the loss of occasional financial help given by his son who was killed in an accident; so, too, was a father who received voluntary help in his work from his son.

The claimant does not have to prove that he had a right to support. It is enough to prove that there was a reasonable expectation of financial benefit if the dead person had lived.

PAIN AND SUFFERING Where the action is taken on behalf of the dead person's estate for pain and suffering and loss of expectation of life, the award is usually small. Typical damages are, for a child £200 to £300, an adult £500, an elderly person about £100.

## Assessment of damages

The purpose of damages is to make good the financial loss which is suffered by dependants as a result of death—that is, to compensate a family for the loss of support provided by a bread-winner. The courts award a lump sum to take care of the family in the future.

The courts usually work out the amount of damages in relation to the dead person's age and earnings and to the time the claimants would have been dependent on him, on the following lines:
1. They find the dead person's net annual income by taking his total income at the time of death and subtracting income tax and National Insurance contributions. They add any other contribution he made—for example, if he did repairs around the house this would raise the value of the contribution.
2. They find how much he spent on himself.
3. They calculate his net contribution to the household by subtracting point 2 from point 1 and then taking into account any special features that would increase the contribution. The figure reached is called the 'dependency'.
4. They deduct money which the dependants received as a result of the death which they would not have received otherwise.
5. They multiply this 'net dependency' by a figure—called the multiplier—which estimates the expected working life and earning prospects of the dead person.

The courts seldom use a multiplier greater than 15, even when the dead person's probable working life would have exceeded 15

years, because a certain reduction is made to allow for the possibility that the dead person would die of natural causes in less than 15 years. Apart from this, they presume that damages will be invested, and so remain intact whilst earning interest for dependants.

The multiplier varies from about 15 for a man under 40, to about nine for after 50, to about three or four after 60.
6. The courts also take into account the age, health and general circumstances of dependants. Until 1971, an important factor in deciding damages used to be the remarriage prospects of the widow—she received lower damages if she was thought likely to remarry.

Under the Law Reform (Miscellaneous Provisions) Act 1971, the courts will not now take remarriage prospects into account—even if the widow is already engaged, or has re-married, by the time the case is decided.

If, as a result of the injury that caused his death, damages were owing to the dead person before he died, these can be passed on to his legal representative. Such damages become part of the estate and belong to the heirs.

FUNERAL EXPENSES Reasonable funeral expenses may be recovered as part of the damages even if there is no other claim.

## Deductions from potential damages

Money may sometimes be deducted from potential damages if the dependants receive some financial benefit as a result of the death —if money or property is inherited under the dead person's will, for example.

If an elderly parent receives money from his dead child's estate, for example, this will be a clear gain. Normally, the parent would have died before the child. In this case, the court will deduct the amount inherited.

On the other hand, if a professional man is killed before reaching the peak of his earning capacity, the small amount of money accumulated at his death would not compensate for the much larger sum that would have come to the widow and children in the future, and therefore it will not be deducted.

Similarly, if the dead person was elderly, and the dependants would have inherited the money anyway, their only gain is to get it sooner. The court will make a small adjustment, usually downwards, in such a case.

The following sums are not deducted from potential damages:
1. Money payable under any insurance policy.
2. Any pension (including the return of contributions) and any lump-sum payment in respect of the dead person's employment.
3. Any benefit under the National Insurance

Acts, such as widow's benefit, guardian's allowance and death grant.

**4.** Any financial benefit other than those mentioned above, such as a payment made to a widow by her husband's employers.

**5.** No deduction is made for the value of the home, furniture, car or other personal belongings of the dead person if the dependants had the use of them before the death, and inherited them from him.

Money awarded to a widow for her children is usually paid to the court, which invests and controls it. The court will occasionally release capital for approved purposes—to pay for children's education, for example. When children reach 18, their money is released to them.

Other claimants are paid their damages direct. Before 1971, money awarded to a widow for herself was also subject to the court's control. Since that date, however, the money has been paid direct, and any widow who had money under court control in 1971 may now apply to have it paid to her.

## How damages might be assessed

Mr Andrews was killed in a car accident for which the other driver was wholly to blame. Mr Andrews's dependants are therefore entitled to damages. If Mr Andrews had been wholly to blame, no claim could be made. If he had been partly to blame, damages would be reduced proportionately.

| | | | |
|---|---|---:|---:|
| Take the dead person's annual income at his death, less tax and National Insurance contributions | **MR ANDREWS'S NET ANNUAL INCOME** | | |
| | Earned income after tax and insurance | £1550 | |
| | War disability pension | £200 | |
| | Income from investments of £12,500 (after tax) | £400 | |
| If the dead person was a handyman, contributions—such as house repairs—are added | **OTHER CONTRIBUTIONS** | | |
| | Value of repairs and decorations carried out around the home by Mr Andrews | £50 | |
| | Total financial contribution | | £2200 |
| A proportion of certain shared household outgoings is included in the list of the dead person's spending, as well as his direct expenses. His expenditure less his total financial contribution gives the 'dependency' | **MR ANDREWS'S ANNUAL EXPENDITURE ON HIMSELF** | | |
| | Lunches, travelling, haircuts (£7 a week) | £364 | |
| | Drinks: about £2 a week at home, shared with his wife (half share £1) | £52 | |
| | Car: quarter of £4 a week charged to him because his car was used by all the family | £52 | |
| | Life insurance | £52 | |
| | Housekeeping: a total of about £25 a week, of which £4 could be attributed to Mr Andrews | £208 | |
| | Holidays: a total of about £120 a year, £40 for Mr Andrews himself | £40 | |
| | Annual gift of £52 to a former employee counts as expenditure on himself | £52 | |
| | Total spending on himself | | £820 |
| | **Financial dependency of family** (net income less total spending) | | £1380 |
| Any money which the dependants received as a result of the death is deducted from the dependency | **IMMEDIATE FINANCIAL BENEFIT TO FAMILY** | | |
| | Widow's share of war disability pension | £65 | |
| | Investments: widow inherited investments worth £10,000 (remaining £2500 left to other people), on which she paid £1500 estate duty. Annual interest on balance | £300 | |
| | Total benefits | | £365 |
| | **Net financial dependency** | | £1015 |
| The 'multiplier' is a figure based on the dead person's expected working life and salary prospects | **FINDING THE MULTIPLIER** | | |
| | The judge decides that Mr Andrews might have worked for a further 10 years, so he uses a multiplier of 10. The financial dependency is multiplied by this figure | | £10,150 |
| Any additional expenses after death are finally added, to give the figure for total damages | **ADDITIONAL EXPENSES AFTER DEATH:** | | |
| | Funeral | £150 | |
| | Driving lessons for Mrs Andrews, because her husband had driven the car | £100 | |
| | | | £250 |
| | **Total damages** | | **£10,400** |

# What happens to property and belongings

*When little is left*
*Larger estates*
*Who handles the estate*

*Applying for authority*
*When a solicitor should be employed*
*The cost of handling an estate*

UNDER English law the property and belongings of someone who has died—his estate—do not pass directly to the heirs; they go first to the personal representatives of the dead person, who pass them to the heirs only after they have administered the estate. The personal representatives are known as executors if there is a will, and as administrators if there is no will.

The first step for relatives winding up an estate is to find out if there is a will. It may be at the bank or with the solicitor who drew it up, or among personal papers.

If no will can be found—even though the relatives are certain one has been made—the estate must usually be administered as if none had been made. In exceptional circumstances it may be possible to prove the contents of a missing will without producing the will itself—if, for example, the solicitor who drew up the document has kept a draft.

### When little money or goods are left
If the dead person left only a small amount of cash—in the form of bank notes and coins—and personal effects of a limited value such as clothes and furniture, no official steps may have to be taken before the estate is distributed.

The relatives simply divide his effects informally according to the will if there was one or, if there was not, according to official rules governing what happens when there is no will. □ Distributing an estate, p. 430.

### Larger estates
Where the estate is considerable or involves more valuable assets such as a house or stocks and shares, it is usually necessary for the personal representatives to put the matter on a proper legal basis.

The details of what happens depend on whether there is a will, but fundamentally the task of the dead person's personal representatives is to decide who is going to be responsible for the estate.

When this is decided, the personal representatives of the dead person must:
1. Find the value of the estate and the extent of the debts.
2. Prepare documents required by the Princi-

pal Registry of the Family Division, or one of the district probate registries. This department issues authority for dealing with an estate and, unless a solicitor is employed, prepares forms for the Estate Duty Office.
3. Obtain legal authority to handle the estate. Probate fees and estate duty must be paid and the documents sworn at the Registry before this is granted.
4. Gather in the assets of the estate.
5. Pay any debts.
6. Pay legacies and bequests, and distribute or invest the rest of the estate.

### Who handles the estate
The choice of a person to be responsible for winding up the affairs of a dead person depends on whether or not there is a will.

WHEN THERE IS A WILL The estate of someone who has left a will is usually handled by the executors named in the will. It is common for the solicitor who drew up the will, or the dead person's bank, to be joint executors with a relative.

The executors apply to a probate registry for official permission to handle the estate. This is known as 'grant of probate'.

In cases where the dead person has made a will, but not appointed executors, an application must be made for a 'grant of letters of administration'. Like probate, this grant gives the applicant authority to deal with the estate. The application must be sent with the will, and the distribution of the estate is as laid down in the will.

The person who is named in the will as trustee for the residuary estate—what is left after all claims have been met—has the first right to apply for this grant. For instance, if a man leaves £100 to his sister, and the rest to his wife in trust for the children, then the wife is the first person entitled to the grant.

If there is no named trustee, others can apply, including anyone entitled to the balance of the estate or anyone who receives a bequest.

Even a creditor, whose interest is in collecting the assets of the estate so that he can be paid money due to him, is allowed to apply.
IF THERE IS NO WILL When no will is left, the nearest relatives apply for the grant of

letters of administration. It is best that someone closely involved with the final distribution of the estate should also be involved with the administration.

The surviving husband or wife would normally want to take the grant and is the first person entitled to apply.

The children (or grandchildren, if their parents have died), are next entitled. If there are no children or grandchildren, the parents of the dead person can apply, followed by brothers and sisters or their children.

When a person dies leaving neither will nor relatives, the business of winding up the estate can be referred to the Treasury Solicitor (Treasury Solicitor's Department, 35 Old Queen Street, London SW1H 9JA).

Application to the Treasury Solicitor is usually made by somebody with a possible claim on the estate, by the bankers of the dead person, by the coroner, or the hospital where the person died.

What is left of the estate after all claims have been met is described by the Latin words *bona vacantia*—meaning 'unclaimed goods'—and reverts to the Crown.

Usually there is only one administrator, but if anyone under 18 is entitled to an interest in the estate there must be two. Again, if someone is entitled to the estate only while he is alive instead of being able to dispose of it as he wishes (in law, if he has a life interest in it) there must also be two administrators.

### Applying for authority

Representatives can either handle the estate themselves or employ solicitors or a bank to help them. If the dead person has appointed his bank to be one of the executors, the burden of administration will be handled by the bank.

If the decision is taken to handle the estate personally, write to or telephone the Personal Application Department, Principal Registry of the Family Division, Room 111, South West Wing, Bush House, Strand, London WC2B 4QR, Tel. 01-836 7366. Alternatively, contact one of the district probate registries, whose address is in the telephone directory.

The Personal Application Department deals with both grants of probate and letters of administration. Its officials will explain what has to be done and assist with the forms, but they cannot give legal advice.

The grant of probate or letters of administration, both obtained from the local probate registry, are short documents naming the representatives and giving them legal authority to deal with the estate. Extra copies of the grant will be needed by the various institutions —banks, insurance companies and building societies—who hold the dead person's assets. The grant provides those giving up the assets with a guarantee that these are going to the properly authorised representative.

### When a solicitor should be employed

There are several situations in which it is advisable to employ a solicitor to handle the estate: where there is no will and some of the estate is to go to children under 18; where the estate is insolvent or so heavily in debt that there are not sufficient assets to pay both debts and legacies; when there are trusts to be administered; and when the dead person's estate includes a business or is worth more than a few thousand pounds.

### The cost of handling an estate

The costs of employing a solicitor or bank (or its subsidiary company) are payable out of the estate, so they are really paid by the person entitled to what is left from the estate when all debts and specific bequests have been paid.

Solicitors' fees depend on the amount of work done, the complexity of the estate and its value. It is worth asking a solicitor roughly how much he might charge.

Bank charges for handling an estate vary in much the same way. In 1972, for example, a subsidiary company of one of the Big Four banks made the following charges:

ACCEPTANCE FEE When the grant of probate or letters of administration were obtained, the company made a charge on the gross value of the estate:

| | |
|---|---:|
| On the first £5,000 | £1.25 per £100 |
| On the next £15,000 | £1 per £100 |
| On the next £20,000 | 75p per £100 |
| On the next £20,000 | 50p per £100 |
| On the next £15,000 | 25p per £100 |
| On the balance | 15p per £100 |

WITHDRAWAL FEE When assets were withdrawn, to be distributed to beneficiaries for example, the company charged £1 per £100 of their value (minimum £25).

ANNUAL MAINTENANCE FEE On assets remaining in their control, the company charged a twice-yearly fee of 10p per £100, plus 50p per £100 for investments (minimum £5).

OTHER FEES There were further fees for buying or selling investments; for dealing with income-tax matters; and for any 'unusual or exacting' administrative duties.

On top of bank and solicitors' fees are probate registry fees, commissioners' fees for oaths—sworn statements are needed in proving a will—and certain other expenses.

# Challenging a will

IF a will has been made properly and there is no evidence of 'undue influence', fraud or mental instability, it is almost impossible to have it set aside—even when a relative seems to have been deprived. ☐ Advantages of making a will, p. 530.

It may, however, be varied. An immediate dependant, such as a widow, can ask the court to vary the terms of a will to provide support, as a lump sum or as income from the estate.

A court will also intervene in cases where there is no will if it thinks that the normal rules of intestacy—the rules which govern distribution when there is no will—will not make reasonable provision for a dependant. ☐ Distributing an estate, p. 430.

Take the case of a widower who leaves two children—a daughter, married to a rich man, and a 14-year-old son, still at school. Under the intestacy rules, they would both get the same. Yet the son's need is clearly greater and he could ask a court to vary the rules.

## Who can apply
The only dependants who can apply to the court to alter a will are a wife or husband, an unmarried daughter, a son under 21, or a child who, because of physical or mental incapacity, is unable to support itself. An illegitimate child has the same rights as a legitimate child.

## How to apply
A solicitor is needed to dispute a will. With estates of £750 or under, the case can be heard in a county court; cases involving estates of any size can be heard in the High Court. County court procedure is not complicated. Applications to the court must normally be made within six months of the date probate was granted or letters of administration taken out. However, the court can extend the time if it thinks the limitation unfair.

## How the court decides
In assessing reasonable provision, a court will consider the amount of the estate, the standard of living of the dead person and of the applicant, the applicant's finances, and the dead person's moral obligation to the applicant.

The main question is whether the will is unreasonable—bearing in mind the circumstances in which the person died and any events that should have been foreseen.

➤WHEN A MISTRESS GETS PRIORITY *In 1941 Mr A left his wife and agreed to pay her £1 a week as long as he lived. He left his estate, worth £370, in trust for life to the woman with whom he was living, and on her death to their two illegitimate children. The wife, who had an income of £190 a year, complained that her husband had not made adequate provision for her.* DECISION *The wife's application failed. The court said the husband had been reasonable in providing for the mother of his children, rather than for his wife. (Re. Joslyn.)* ◄

## Former husbands or wives
The court can order that special provision be made for a former husband or wife, if it is satisfied that it would have been reasonable for the dead person to have done so.

This, however, covers only a former husband or wife who has not remarried and whose home is in England or Wales.

➤A BRUTAL HUSBAND'S MORAL OBLIGATION *A Norfolk publican, whose wife left him, made a will leaving most of his money to another woman. His wife had left him because of his physical violence. She had been loyal for 14 years and had helped to build up his business.*

*He was violent also to the second woman, who had also worked hard for him for three years.*

*In 1966 he shot himself, leaving his wife £416 a year and the rest of his estate to his mistress and her son by a former marriage. His wife challenged the will.* DECISION *The court awarded his wife another £234 a year because his moral obligation was greater to her than to his mistress. But the mistress still had more of the estate than the wife. The court said that a man could make whatever provisions he liked, as long as he did not leave his dependants destitute. (Thornley v. Palmer.)* ◄

## Variation of court orders
The courts can order money to be paid from the estate in regular payments or a lump sum.

A court can be asked to vary an order if some material fact was not given to the court when it originally made the order, or if one of the dependants' circumstances have changed substantially since that time.

A dependant could ask for more if another dependant had a football pool win and no longer needed all the money awarded.

# Working out the value of an estate

*Listing and valuation of assets*     *Valuation of a business*
*Personal belongings*                 *Debts*
*Stocks and shares*                    *Capital gains tax*

THE property of a dead person cannot be divided up according to his will, and estate duty cannot be paid, until his representatives or close relatives have worked out what the estate is worth. The first step is to list all the dead person's assets. These have to be supplied to the Government department which deals with estate duty—the Estate Duty Office—which enters them on a form called the Inland Revenue Affidavit. The affidavit is completed even where no duty is payable.

## Listing the dead person's assets
Find out what assets the dead person had—including his National Savings Bank account, savings certificates, or Premium Bonds. There may be a bank account, insurance policies, stocks and shares, and a house or flat.

Where an item has a fixed value, such as a bank balance or savings certificates, ask for a statement. Give the authority for making the request—either as an executor or as administrator of the will.

INTEREST AND PROFIT For any asset which collects interest, the representative must know the interest credited to the account up to the date of the death.

Any interest which accrues after death is exempt from estate duty, but it may be liable for income tax. It may be used for paying debts and expenses of administration. Anything left after the estate is distributed goes to whoever gets the residue of the estate.

Payments on shares, and sometimes on stocks, are called dividends and are normally paid by a dividend warrant. There are two parts to this: a cheque which is paid into a bank, and a voucher, showing the tax deducted, which has to be shown to the Inland Revenue.

If any dividend warrants were due to the dead person before the date of his death, they must be included in the list of assets.

In the case of a with-profits insurance policy, the profits up to the date of death will have to be stated.

RENT If the dead person let any of the property he owned, his assets will include rents owing to him up to the date of his death. As with interest, rents due after the death go first to the administrators, who have to pay

income tax on the amount they receive. What is left then goes to the heirs.

PENSIONS If the dead person was receiving a pension, State or private, write to the Government department or firm paying it and ask whether there are any arrears due. Payments under the National Insurance scheme are made for the whole of the week in which death occurred.

If the pension scheme also provided for a pension for the widow, her pension will not form part of the husband's estate.

Sometimes a pension scheme provides for a capital sum to be paid out to whoever the fund managers nominate as the beneficiary. When it is paid directly to the widow, or another dependant, the money is not considered part of the estate.

If, however, it is paid to the executors it is included in the dead person's assets.

TAX REBATE The estate may qualify for a tax rebate on the dead person's earnings, particularly if he paid tax by Pay As You Earn.

To discover the precise position, write to the Inspector of Taxes who dealt with the dead person's income tax. The dead person's former employer will have the address.

INCOME AFTER DEATH Income tax and sometimes surtax are payable on any income from the dead person's estate after his death —such as rents, interest on bank accounts and stocks and dividends from stocks and shares. This tax must be paid by the executors or administrators until the assets are finally distributed. The income is then treated retrospectively as having been the income of the person receiving the asset, and he must ask the Inland Revenue to make any necessary tax adjustment.

## Valuation of jointly held assets
The valuation of a jointly held asset—such as a house or a bank account—presents a special problem. The Inland Revenue Affidavit requires only the value of the share owned by the dead person to be supplied. What that share amounts to must be established. Usually a purchase has been made for the general good of the family, with no thought of accounting for who owns what. The Inland

Revenue will normally assume that joint owners held the property in equal shares.

BANK ACCOUNT There are special rules for deciding how much of a joint bank account should be included in the estate when one of the joint holders dies.

If contributions to a joint account are made by only one partner, and the other draws on the account only as a convenient way of paying household bills, the whole account forms part of the estate of the contributing partner, and duty has to be paid only when that partner dies.

If, however, the non-contributing partner is free to draw on the account for personal expenditure, then half the account belongs to the estate of one partner, and half to the other. Half of the account is therefore included in the estate of the first of the joint holders to die.

If both partners contribute to the account, half of the balance is regarded as belonging to the estate of one partner and half to the other. This rule applies irrespective of the actual amounts of money which each of the joint holders has contributed.

THE HOME Normally, if the husband has paid for the home and then put it into joint names, only half of it is treated as his property and is liable for duty on his death.

If, however the husband lives for less than five years after the property is put in the couple's joint names, the whole house is treated as his property. If he lives for more than five, but less than seven years, any duty payable is reduced.

The same principle does not apply to property bought by the wife and put in the joint names of husband and wife.

In that case, the whole value of the house is treated as the wife's and if she dies first it all becomes part of her estate.

An exception is made where it can be proved that the wife intended to make a gift of part of the house to her husband. That part of the house escapes estate duty on the wife's death if she survives for seven years after the gift; and it qualifies for a reduced rate of duty if she survives more than five years, but fewer than seven.

The value of a house is its market value, with vacant possession. The value is reduced if there is a sitting tenant protected by the Rents Acts. □ Choosing the type of home to rent, p. 242.

The value is also reduced in the case of joint ownership because the surviving widow or widower is entitled to stay on in the house.

The district valuer will value the house for the Inland Revenue. If his figure seems too high, an independent professional valuation may help in persuading him that he has over-valued the property.

The amount of any outstanding mortgage which has to be repaid further reduces the value of the house. The building society or other lender will give details.

## Personal belongings

The value of furniture, clothing and personal effects is what they would fetch if sold second-hand. Try to fix figures based on the original cost, modified by a realistic allowance for depreciation or appreciation.

Most items lose rather than increase in value. The chief exceptions are coins, stamps, paintings, valuable furniture and jewellery.

If the dead person left valuables among his assets, it is often worth getting a professional valuation. Do not be tempted to undervalue such items. If a value is set unrealistically low and the item is later sold, the seller may have to pay capital gains tax on the increase in value between the value stated on the Inland Revenue Affidavit and the sale price.

Goods on hire purchase should be included in the list of assets, at their second-hand value; the remaining instalments due are debts.

## Stocks and shares

A rule of thumb is used to value stocks and shares for estate duty. If the shares are quoted on the London Stock Exchange, the value is based on the stock exchange quotation on the day of death. If death occurred at the weekend, the price which applied on either Friday or Monday can be used.

The price can be found in the official Stock Exchange list, available at most public libraries or at a bank. The list gives two prices—a minimum and a maximum—for the day. These are not necessarily the same as the prices given in newspapers, which are usually the closing prices. Take care to give the share's market price, and not the nominal price. □ Stocks and shares, p. 514.

FIXING THE VALUE The value of a share for estate duty is its minimum price plus one-quarter of the difference between that and the maximum. For instance, if the shares had a maximum selling price on the day of death of 60p and a minimum of 50p, the value is one-quarter of the difference between 60 and 50, or $2\frac{1}{2}$p up from 50p. The share value would therefore be $52\frac{1}{2}$p.

If the shares are not quoted on the London Stock Exchange, or not quoted at all, valuation is best done by the company's auditors, a stockbroker or an accountant.

UNIT TRUSTS If the dead person held units in a unit trust, the financial newspapers or the Stock Exchange list will give their value. Two prices are quoted—the price at which the units are sold to the public and the bid price at which the trust managers will buy back their own units. The bid price is the one that has to be given for valuation purposes. If in doubt, write to the secretary of the trust and ask for the bid price on the date of death.

### Valuation of a business
If the dead person owned or controlled a business or was a partner in one, professional assistance, probably from an accountant, will be needed to value the concern.

If a wife contributed to the value of her husband's business by her work, the value of the business represented by her contribution will pass to her on his death and will therefore not be counted as part of his estate for estate duty purposes.

### Debts
The account of the dead person's estate has to include a statement of his debts. Personal representatives should try to trace debts. This is in the interest not only of the estate, but also of the executors or administrators.

If, after the administration of the estate is completed, someone turns up who can show that he was owed money by the dead person, the personal representatives will have to pay the debt out of their own pockets.

The representatives can claim the money from beneficiaries; but, in practice, this can be embarrassing and difficult. Beneficiaries could hold the representatives responsible because they had failed to tidy up the estate.

ADVERTISEMENTS The way to avoid disputes over debts is to place an advertisement, paid for out of the estate, in the *London Gazette* and in a local newspaper. If the dead person lived in one area and owned property in another, advertise in both districts and in a national newspaper. The advertisement should invite creditors to claim by a specific date—not less than two months from the time of the advertisement. Any claim after the stated date must be made against the beneficiaries, and not against the personal representatives.

Debts include what the dead person owes the grocer, or the gas or electricity boards and outstanding hire-purchase instalments.

A bank overdraft counts as a debt; so do reasonable funeral expenses.

Items that are hired do not count as either assets or debts. The estate is affected only if there is any payment due from before the date of death, or if the estate is owed money by the hire company for the period between an advance payment and the date of death.

### Capital gains tax
If the dead person owned shares or a house he let to tenants, capital gains tax may have to be paid on the increase in value between what he paid and the open market price on the day of his death. The tax, a debt on the estate, applies only if the person died before March 30, 1971. When it is charged, the first £5000 of any increase in the value of an asset is exempt. However, this £5000 may be reduced if the dead person took advantage of the £10,000 exemption from capital gains tax which he was allowed to do on his retirement. Total death and retirement exemption must not exceed £10,000.

Capital gains tax is deducted from the property when assessing assets for estate duty.

Capital losses can be set against gains made by the dead person in the year of death, or the previous three years.

Capital gains—or losses—may also be made between the time of death and the time the assets are sold. Such gains or losses are considered to have arisen on death, and are dated accordingly. ☐ Capital gains tax, p. 574.

## Clearing up debts

### MRS WINIFRED JONES DECEASED

Pursuant to the Trustee Act, 1925 Any person having a CLAIM or an INTEREST in the ESTATE of Winifred Jones, formerly of The Close, Eggars Lane, London W4, who died on March 13, 1972, is required to send particulars thereof in writing to the undersigned Executor, James Alfred Jones, on or before July 31, 1972, after which date the Executor will proceed to distribute the assets having regard only to claims and interests of which he has had notice.

### JAMES ALFRED JONES
The Close, Eggars Lane, London W4

A newspaper advertisement inviting creditors to make their claims prevents disputes over debts. Successful claims after the estate is settled are then paid by beneficiaries, not by personal representatives

# Obtaining authority to handle an estate

*Applying for the grant*     *Swearing the documents*
*Assessing estate duty*      *Paying duty and fees*
*Compiling the affidavit*    *Receiving the grant*

B EFORE the personal representatives of the dead person can gather in the assets of the estate and pay legacies and bequests, they must obtain the necessary legal authority. They do this by providing information for a number of official documents, swearing them to be true, and paying court fees and estate duty (commonly known as death duty).

The legal department which grants this authority—the Principal Registry of the Family Division of the High Court—then issues either a grant of probate (where executors are named in a will), or of letters of administration.

Either document enables the personal representatives to proceed with winding-up the affairs of the dead person.

The documents are compiled by the Registry from forms filled in by the executors or administrators, or by their solicitor.

## Applying for the grant

Anyone who decides to handle the estate personally should apply at the Probate Personal Application Department of the local probate registry or sub-registry by telephone, letter or by calling in person. Officials are always ready to explain the procedure.

Form 38 is the personal application for the grant of probate or letters of administration. Not all the executors named in the will need apply. The applicants first have to indicate at which registry or office they wish to swear the documents.

The form asks for basic information about the dead person and the applicant(s), and the place and date of the death.

It also asks whether there is a will. If there is, and the applicants are not executors, they must say whether the will names anyone under the age of majority—now 18. Names of executor(s) not applying must be given. The form also asks about the dead person's surviving relatives.

## Assessing estate duty

Estate duty is assessed by the Estate Duty Office, working closely with the probate registry. The task of the Office is to prevent the evasion of estate duty in the administration of an estate.

Duty is based on a statement called the Inland Revenue Affidavit, which is compiled from information given on forms filled in by the executors or administrators, or prepared by a solicitor, and signed by the applicants for the grant of probate or letters of administration.

Estate duty is charged on estates exceeding a certain value. If no solicitor is employed, the amount is assessed by the Estate Duty Office. It is subject to adjustment after the grant has been issued to the applicants. ☐ How estate duty works, p. 540.

## Compiling the affidavit

FORM 44 This form is headed 'Return for Estate Duty'. The first part of this form deals with property which, though not strictly part of the estate, may be liable for estate duty—such as gifts worth more than £500 given by the dead man in the seven years before death.

In the second part of this form, known as Account 1, details should be given about everything owned by the dead man in the United Kingdom. It should also include any sums payable on his death, even if these amounts have already been received.

The third part of this form—Account 2—includes a statement of the dead man's debts. There are also spaces for details of funeral expenses and any outstanding mortgage.

FORM 37A If the dead person owned any freehold or leasehold property—such as houses, building land, woodland and pasture —Form 37A must be filled in. There is space for details of any sales of such property which may have taken place.

FORM 40 A statement of holdings of stocks or shares need be completed on Form 40 only if the dead person had more stocks and shares than can be entered on Form 44. ☐ How to fill in the forms, p. 428.

## Where to send the forms

The completed forms, together with the death certificate and will, should be taken or sent to the Probate Personal Application Department of the local probate registry or sub-registry. If the dead person held National Savings

Certificates, either a letter from the Savings Department certifying the value or a list of the certificates showing their purchase date and value at the time of death, must be sent.

Make and keep a copy of the will, and if the papers are sent by post, register the letter.

**Swearing the documents**
The Probate Registry asks the applicants to go to the registry or office to pay estate duty and fees, and to swear the documents. The applicants formally swear the Inland Revenue Affidavit, and an oath relating to the performance of their duties as executors or administrators, on the Bible or by affirmation. The applicants may also have to obtain a guarantee (usually from an insurance company) to be responsible if the representatives mis-appropriate the estate or pay out to the wrong beneficiaries.

An officer of the High Court first goes over the affidavit with the applicants and tells them what estate duty and probate (court) fees will have to be paid. Both depend on the value of the estate.

If the forms have been sent in by post and there is no major difficulty, swearing of the affidavit and oath take place on the first visit. Otherwise a second visit to the registry or office is necessary.

GUARANTEE In some cases, the oath has to be supported by a guarantee given by sureties. The main ones are if the application is made by one of the following:
**1.** A creditor.
**2.** Someone who does not stand to benefit from the estate.
**3.** Someone who is resident outside the United Kingdom.
**4.** Someone who is acting for a minor, or for a person incapable of managing his own affairs (because of mental illness, for example).

Two sureties are required unless the estate is worth less than £500, in which case one is sufficient. The registry has lists of insurance companies willing to act as sureties.

Anyone who asks personal friends to be sureties, instead of an insurance company, should explain that, if the administrators default on their duty or make a mistake, the sureties may be liable for the loss caused up to the gross value of the estate.

**Paying duty and fees**
When the personal representatives swear the documents, they have to pay probate fees and estate duty at the same time (though duty on certain parts of the estate can be paid by instalments). Often money is needed urgently.

The dead person's own bank may allow his account to be used. Usually, however, the bank will not release money until probate or letters of administration have been granted, so there is often a gap to be filled.

Normally, banks lend money to pay estate duty and probate fees against the security of the property in the estate.

If the dead person had no bank account, the personal representatives may be able to make arrangements with their own bank.

Special arrangements can be made to enable money to be used for this purpose from the dead person's National Savings Bank account, or from his savings certificates or Premium Bonds. An application form is obtainable from the registry. It is sent to the Savings Department with the relevant certificates or bank books. The money is paid direct by the Savings Department to the registry.

If none of these sources of funds is available, the personal representatives have to find some other lender.

**Receiving the grant**
Between one and three weeks after the documents are sworn and the duty and fees paid, the Probate Registry issues the grant. This states that administration of the estate is vested by law in the personal representatives whom it names. It is their authority for dealing with the estate. Ask the registry for extra photocopies of the grant, to use when gathering the assets. They cost 10p each.

## Arranging an interview

REPRESENTATIVES must attend at least one interview when they apply for authority to handle an estate. They may arrange for this to be held at a probate registry, a sub-registry or a local probate office. Most representatives will find one of these in their nearest town.

The representatives can return the forms by post to the probate registry or sub-registry and indicate where they wish the interview to be held. They are then sent a notice of an appointment.

Alternatively, representatives may take the completed forms in person to the probate registry, sub-registry or probate office during office hours and ask to be interviewed then. This will be arranged if it is convenient.

# How to fill in the forms

## Form 44 Return for estate duty

**1. Settled property**

A settlement is an arrangement under which a person transfers property, usually money or stocks and shares, to somebody else and directs that the income be paid to a third person or group of people. The capital is usually shared by others when the first beneficiary dies. A common example is a marriage settlement when a wealthy father gives property to trustees on the understanding that the income is paid to his daughter during her life, and that on her death the capital is divided among her children.

**3. Gifts**

Put in details of outright gifts and also of gifts with 'strings' attached. The dead person might have given his house to his married daughter on condition that she let him live there rent-free Personal representatives who are close family members are likely to know of such gifts; if they do not, they should ask people likely to have received them or to know who has. Gifts count as part of the estate and must be described here. ☐ Ready cash for the bereaved, p. 414.

**4. Policies of assurance, other than those included in Account 1**

The dead person may have a policy providing for a payment directly to his widow or crippled son rather than into the estate generally. The money might still, however, be liable for estate duty; details must be included here.

**5. Nominations**

The dead person may have asked that a savings-bank account or savings certificate be handed over to someone, such as a business associate, at the time of his death. Such requests should be described here.

**6. Superannuation benefits**

Under an employer's pension scheme a widow could become eligible for a pension. In this case, answer 'Yes' and give details of the payments.

**7. Property held jointly**

This is to establish how much of the joint holding belonged to the dead person and is liable for estate duty—for example, a joint bank account or joint ownership of a house. ☐ Working out the value of an estate, p. 423.

## ACCOUNT 1

**1. British Savings Bonds, Development Bonds, War Loan and other government securities**

The value of War Loan is given in the official Stock Exchange list. Defence Bonds are worth the amount stated on them plus any capital additions due and interest since the last date of payment.

**4. Other stocks, shares or investments including unit trusts**

If there is not enough room, use Form 40 to enter details, put the final figure in the right-hand column and add 'see Form 40 for details'.

**6. Cash at bank**
**7. Money in savings banks or in building, co-operative or friendly societies**

Give the balance (or amount overdrawn) in the dead person's account. Enter joint bank account details under Item 7, page 2.

**8. Policies of insurance on life of deceased**

Give the names of insurance companies, and the amounts of the policies.

**9. Policies of insurance on the life of any other person**

This applies, for example, to business partners insuring each other's lives. Such a policy is valued as part of the estate of the person who took it out, and the surrender value which the insurance company will give should be entered.

| | |
|---|---|
| **12.** Other assets not included above or at Items 13–16 | This includes arrears of retirement pension, tax refund due from the Inland Revenue and superannuation payment unless it is made to a civil servant (see under Item 14). |
| **13.** Post-war credits | Post-war credits, payable to those who were paying income tax during the Second World War, have already been cashed by most people. If the credits have been paid, leave the item blank. If not, the Inspector of Taxes will give their value. The amount the credits are worth also appears on the certificates. |
| **14.** Civil servant's gratuity | This gratuity is payable to civil servants on retirement, or to their estate if they should die before they retire. |
| **15.** Business assets | A professional valuation is advisable. |
| **16.** Freehold and leasehold property | This means any interest in property which continues after death and for which the dead person paid rent, such as a 70-year lease with four years to run. If the rent was the full market rate for that kind of property, its value to the estate is nil. If the dead person was paying a low rent, the amount to include is the figure for which the lease could be sold at the time of death. A professional valuation from an estate agent or surveyor is advisable. See also Form 37A. |

## ACCOUNT 2
**Estate out of the United Kingdom**

Enter details of all types of asset—a house in the South of France, for example, or a partnership with a real-estate broker in New York.

## Form 40

| | |
|---|---|
| **Name and class of share or stock** | Enter a full description—for example, Marks and Spencer £1 Ordinary share or 5 per cent Preference share. |
| Unit of quotation | Put in the value of the unit quoted on the Stock Exchange. The unit for shares is usually one share and the unit of quotation of stock is usually £1. |
| Holding of shares or stock | For example, 37 shares or £37 worth of stock. |
| Market price at date of death | ☐ Working out the value of an estate, p. 423. |
| Source of market price if other than London Stock Exchange List | Enter shares quoted on provincial or foreign exchanges. If the share is not quoted, valuation is best done by a stockbroker or accountant. A bank manager may also be able to help. |

## Form 37a

| | |
|---|---|
| **2.** Description of dead person's property | The District Valuer values the property for the Inland Revenue, normally after receipt of the completed forms. |
| **3.** Tenure | This includes limitations on the use of property, such as forbidding its use for business purposes. Covenants are normally in the title deed to the property, but if in doubt consult a solicitor, preferably the one who handled the transfer. |
| **4.** Name of tenant **6.** The rent payable | If the house is owner-occupied, write 'owner-occupied—not applicable'. If the property is normally let but vacant at the time of death, put in the gross estimated rental if it were let. |

# Distributing an estate

*Paying the debts*
*Estate duty clearance*
*Distribution under a will*

*Transferring the home*
*Distribution when there is no will*
*When there is no widow or widower*

BEFORE the beneficiaries and creditors can be paid, the assets of an estate have to be gathered together. This is done through the opening of an executorship (or administratorship) account at a bank, so as to keep all the money from the estate completely separate.

If the dead person's bank account is in credit, send the bank a copy of the grant of probate or letters of administration, and ask the bank manager to transfer the money to the executorship (or administratorship) account.

Insurance companies usually want their own withdrawal form signed by the executors.

With stocks and shares, the grant must be registered with the company. The company's registered office can be found in *The Stock Exchange Official Year Book*, available in most public libraries. This also states whether the company charges a registration fee, usually small. The company needs the share certificates and the grant, or a copy of the grant, which has been sealed and issued by the Probate Registry.

If a dividend warrant has been issued in the name of the dead person it will have to be returned before being transferred to the executor, unless the bank allows it to be paid directly into the executorship account.

## Paying the debts
The first priority in discharging debts is to pay estate duty. Any other debts owed by the estate can then be settled.

All outstanding debts may be paid from the executorship account. Keep copies of all letters sent with cheques, and ask for receipts.

If there is not enough ready cash to pay debts and death duty, it may be necessary to raise money by selling some of the assets.

## Estate duty clearance
Before distributing the estate, write to the estate duty officials at the local tax office, asking for a clearance certificate, which shows that the right amount of duty has been paid.

A clearance certificate protects the administrators against being made to pay the balance of estate duty if the estate has been undervalued. There is no need for a certificate if the estate is worth substantially less than the figure at which estate duty becomes payable (£15,000 from March 21, 1972). If the estate is on the borderline, it is advisable for the personal representatives to get a certificate in case it is later found to exceed the limit.

The value of the property for the clearance certificate is not necessarily the same as that for the return known as an affidavit, which is required by the Inland Revenue. For the affidavit, the value of a house included in the estate is given by the dead person's personal representatives. Before the certificate is issued, the value has to be confirmed by the district valuer, who may put a higher price on it.

A new or corrected affidavit may have to be sworn if the estate's value rises. It could happen that a new debt owed by the dead person is discovered, which will result in the estate getting a rebate on the estate duty paid.

## Distribution under a will
When all expenses and debts have been paid, it is possible to go ahead with distribution.

The first step is to pay legacies. If there is any uncertainty about where a beneficiary lives, write to his last known address, to find out if he still lives there, before sending the cheque or goods.

If a beneficiary lives outside the sterling area, the money can be sent without the need for Bank of England consent, provided the clearing bank making the transfer is satisfied that it is a genuine legacy. ☐ Sending money abroad, p. 440.

If the legacy is a personal item, such as a gold watch, ask the beneficiary to take delivery and to give a receipt. The cost of sending items such as this cannot be charged to the estate unless the will says so.

If the will assigns stocks or shares to a beneficiary, they must be transferred by the executors on a stock-transfer form obtainable from the Solicitors' Law Stationery Society, Oyez House, Breams Buildings, London EC4P 4BU, or from a bank or stockbroker.

Stamp duty in transferring stocks and shares to a beneficiary is charged at a flat rate of 50p. Transfers to a beneficiary where there is no will may be exempt from stamp duty, but in this case consult a bank, stockbroker or solicitor. After completing the stock-transfer form, send it to the company for registration. The company will issue a new share certificate in the name of the new owner.

If the dead person included in his will an item which he no longer owns, the person who was to receive it has no claim.

When the item left in a will has been transformed in some way—for example, in the case of shares involved in a takeover transaction—the problem calls for legal advice.

BENEFICIARIES UNDER 18 If the person who benefits under the will is younger than 18, anything to which he or she is entitled will usually be transferred to trustees, except where the bequest is small.

Sometimes executors will pay money into a joint account where cheques have to be signed by both the trustee and the young person.

TRANSFERRING THE HOME In selling a house to distribute the proceeds to a number of beneficiaries, the executors or administrators have full authority. When property is to be transferred to a single beneficiary, the process is known as 'assent'.

For registered land, this involves filling in the Land Registry Form 56, obtainable from H.M. Stationery Office or the Solicitors' Law Stationery Society.

The completed form, together with the grant of probate and the Land Registry fee, is then sent to the appropriate Land Registry district office.

The Land Registry fee is calculated at a rate of 50p per £1000 (or part) of value, up to a maximum of £250.

Assent for transferring unregistered land does not have to be registered anywhere, and no stamp duty has to be paid. It can even be written by the executor himself on an ordinary sheet of paper. The assent is kept by the new owner, together with the other documents concerning the house.

If there is a mortgage outstanding, write to the building society or other lender before completing the assent and find out if they will allow the beneficiary to continue the mortgage.

If the mortgage is to be paid off, write to the building society and ask how much is still owing. As soon as the balance of the mortgage is paid off, the society will send the deeds of an unregistered property to the personal representatives.

Where the land is registered, the society sends a charge certificate and a formal acknowledgment—Form 53 (Co). Both these documents are then sent to the Land Registry, which in turn supplies a land certificate,

showing that ownership of the property is free of claims.

If the house was in the joint names of husband and wife, what happens to it depends on the form of ownership.

If the couple were what is known in law as joint tenants, the share of the dead person passes automatically to the survivor on death. No assent is needed.

If, however, the couple were tenants in common, the share of the dead person passes either to whoever is named in his will, or—when there is no will—to whoever is entitled in law to inherit (in most cases, probably the husband or wife). Personal representatives must then follow the normal rules about assent and registration of the transfer.

DISTRIBUTING PERSONAL EFFECTS When personal effects such as furniture or clothes are to be shared among relatives, they decide on how to divide them. It may save arguments if all or part of the effects are auctioned, and the proceeds divided.

**Distribution when there is no will**
When there is no will, distribution is carried out according to what are known as intestacy rules. When an estate is worth less than £15,000 after expenses, the surviving husband or wife takes everything.

WHERE THERE ARE CHILDREN If an estate is worth more than £15,000, the surviving husband or wife takes all personal effects, the sum of £15,000 plus interest at 4 per cent as from the date of death, and a 'life interest' in half the remainder. The children take the other half of the remainder. A life interest means that the survivor can invest that half and take the income, but cannot spend the capital.

The survivor can, however, take the life interest as a lump sum. This eliminates small sums of interest spreading over a lifetime. The choice must be made within 12 months.

The children divide their half at once and, when the surviving father or mother dies, they share his or her half in the same way. The survivor can ask for the matrimonial home as part of the claim to the first £15,000 and this choice, too, must be made within 12 months.

For example, if the estate of a man with two children is valued at £20,000 after expenses, his widow would get his personal belongings, £15,000 outright and a life interest in £2500—half of the £5000 left. The children would share £2500 at once. On their mother's death, they would share her part equally.

If either of the children died before their father, and left children of their own, those children would take their parent's share divided equally between them. Children of a previous marriage, and adopted or illegitimate children, are also eligible.

Income from money left in trust for children under 18, and up to half the capital, is usually used for their education or maintenance.

WHERE THERE ARE NO CHILDREN If the dead person left a widow or widower but no children, the widow or widower takes the personal effects, the first £40,000 and half of the remainder entirely for herself or himself.

The remaining half is shared between the parents, if they are living; if the parents are dead, the brothers and sisters share it. The share of a brother or sister who died first, but left children, is divided among these children.

If there are no children, parents, brothers, sisters, or children of brothers or sisters, the widow or widower takes all.

WHEN THERE IS NO WIDOW OR WIDOWER If there are children, but no widow or widower, the children share the whole estate equally. The share of a child who has died before the person whose estate is being distributed is divided equally between his children.

For example, if the dead person leaves £10,000 and is survived by three children and two grandchildren—daughters of his eldest son who had been killed in a road accident— the three living children each take £2500 and the two grandchildren each take £1250.

Where only parents survive, they take the whole estate in equal shares. If only one is living, he or she takes the whole estate.

If neither direct descendants nor parents survive, the estate goes to the first group of relatives in the following list surviving at the time of the dead person's death. (Members of each group take equal shares; and if any member is dead, his share is divided equally between his children.)

1. Brothers and sisters.
2. Half-brothers and sisters.
3. Grandparents.
4. Aunts and uncles of the whole blood.
5. Aunts and uncles of the half-blood.

Where there are none of these relatives, the estate belongs to the Crown. Sometimes the Crown will distribute the estate, or part of it, to deserving relatives not listed above.

### When the beneficiary dies first

When there is a will, a bequest of a specific amount of money or a particular article is normally ignored if the person for whom it was intended dies first. The beneficiary's heirs are not entitled to inherit.

An exception is made where money or property is left to a son or daughter who dies first. The children of that son or daughter are then entitled to receive the bequest.

Anything left to any other beneficiary who dies first goes to whoever gets the residue, or remainder, of the estate. If the residue beneficiary dies first, the residue is distributed as if there were no will. This situation is known as a partial intestacy.

In a partial intestacy, a beneficiary may qualify under both will and intestacy rules. In this case, distribution is as follows:

1. Bequests and legacies under the will are paid to all beneficiaries *except* those also entitled under the intestacy rules.
2. The remainder is provisionally divided according to the intestacy rules.
3. *Either* the bequest under the will, *or* the amount due under the intestacy rules, whichever is the greater, is paid to those who qualify under both.
4. What is left is distributed to the remaining beneficiaries in proportion to their claims under the intestacy rules.

Consider the case of a father who dies leaving only a son and daughter. In the will he leaves the sum of £500 to the son and no other provisions are made.

If the estate is worth £750 there will be a partial intestacy of £250. Under the intestacy rules the son and daughter would share the original £750 equally; but, as the will takes precedence, the son will take his £500 bequest, and the remaining £250 goes to the daughter.

If the estate is worth £1000, the son keeps the £500 bequest and the daughter receives the remaining £500. Where the estate is worth over £1000, son and daughter share the amount over £1000 equally.

### Closing the administration of a will

When everyone has been paid, the final accounts can be prepared. They should show all payments into and out of the estate, and all the assets that made up the estate and how they were dealt with.

The usual form is a simple cash account, showing money paid out of the estate on the right-hand side, and money paid in on the left.

When a debt or legacy is paid, write, for instance, 'Income tax arrears paid, June 5, 1972, £49' on the right-hand side. When money is received, write, for example, 'Insurance moneys from Standard Life, July 11, 1972, £4500', on the left.

Personal representatives can charge the costs of administration—postage, forms and fees—to the estate, but they cannot charge any other fee unless the will says so. Solicitors' and bank fees are paid out of the estate.

# YOUR MONEY

# Using a bank

THE banks most generally used by the public are known as 'clearing banks'—they operate a system of collecting payment for cheques paid into their branches through the Bankers' Clearing House, which is based in London.

The four major clearing banks are the National Westminster, Lloyds, Barclays and the Midland. The smaller ones include Coutts, and Williams and Glyn's.

The services they provide are similar: they hold their customers' money, provide facilities for money to be paid to third parties, handle customers' regular payments and lend money to customers. Banks also give advice on investment, act as agents in the buying and selling of shares, and provide foreign exchange and traveller's cheques.

## Choosing the account

CURRENT ACCOUNT The most commonly used banking service is the current account. The customer deposits his money and the bank issues him with a cheque book. He may withdraw money from a current account at any time, either by making out a cheque for cash, or by paying a cheque to someone else.

A current account holder can arrange for the bank to take care automatically of his regular payments—mortgage repayments, for example. There are two systems. The customer may make out what is known as a 'standing order', under which the bank pays the building society each time a payment is due. Or, under the 'direct debit' system, he authorises the bank to make payments regularly on application by the building society. In both cases, there is no need for further action by the customer until he wishes to cancel the arrangement.

The customer may be able to arrange for loans or overdrafts on a current account.
☐ Choosing the type of credit, p. 490.

BUDGET ACCOUNT A variant of the current account is the budget account, designed to help the customer to spread his regular expenses evenly over the year. The bank and the customer agree on the total amount likely to be needed for regular expenses in a year—such as gas, electricity, rates, and mortgage or rent. Each month the bank then transfers one-twelfth of this amount from the customer's current account to his budget account.

The customer is given a cheque book for the budget account, but he may issue cheques on it only to meet expenses agreed with the bank as part of his budget. Because payments are spread over the whole year, the customer is allowed to overdraw on the account if a number of bills arrive at the same time.

DEPOSIT ACCOUNT The simplest account is the deposit account. The customer's money is used by the bank in exchange for interest.

Seven days' notice is usually required to withdraw money. No cheques are supposed to be drawn on a deposit account, though this is sometimes allowed in certain areas.

The rate of interest on a deposit account is normally 2 per cent below the bank's 'base rate'—the rate used for calculating interest on various types of loan. This varies from time to time and from bank to bank.

SAVINGS ACCOUNTS Money left in a savings account earns a fixed rate of interest—sometimes below, sometimes above that on a deposit account. These accounts are intended to be used for small regular savings.

## Opening a current account

Unless the customer is introduced by someone known to the bank, he is asked to provide at least one reference when he opens a current account. To safeguard its customers' money, the bank tries to establish that any prospective customer is honest and responsible.

The customer has to give the bank a specimen of his signature. If he is operating a joint account with his wife or with a business partner, the bank will also require a copy of the signature of the other person who is to sign the cheques, alone or jointly.

## The clearing system

A cheque is 'cleared' when the branch on which it is drawn has paid the branch at which it is paid in or cashed.

When a customer pays in a cheque, the branch receiving it sends it to the Bankers' Clearing House in London, where banks exchange with one another cheques which have been presented to them. The clearing departments of the individual banks then send the cheques to the branches on which they are drawn. The branch makes sure that the cheque is properly drawn and signed and confirms that the amount is covered by a credit balance in the account or by an agreed overdraft limit. The bank honours (pays) the cheque by cancelling it and deducting the amount from the customer's account.

Any cheques which cannot be paid—because there is not enough money in an account to meet them, for example—are returned to the branch where they were paid in. The branch informs the customer that the cheque has not been paid. The clearing process usually takes four working days, though foreign cheques can take a month or more.

Although a cheque is usually credited to the customer's account immediately it is paid in, the bank is not bound to honour cheques made out by the customer on the strength of the credited cheque until that cheque has been cleared.

If a customer wants speedy clearance of a cheque he has received, he can—for a small fee—have his bank send it direct to the branch on which it is drawn. This bypasses the clearing system, and usually means that he can find out within a day whether or not the cheque is being honoured.

Similarly, a customer paying in a cheque at a branch other than his own can arrange to have it sent direct to his own branch, instead of through the Clearing House. This ensures that there are funds available earlier to meet any cheque he wishes to issue.

Not all cheques pass through the Bankers' Clearing House in London. If cheques are paid in or cashed at branches of the same bank, they are dealt with by the bank itself.

## Cheque books and writing cheques

A cheque is simply an order to the customer's own bank to pay money out of his current account to the person or company named on the cheque. In theory, a cheque can be made out on any piece of paper or other material, but the special forms issued by the bank are generally used.

DRAWER The person who signs and issues a cheque is the drawer. When he writes out a cheque he is 'drawing' on his bank.

DATE No bank pays a cheque until the date given on it. If a cheque is issued without a date, the person receiving it is entitled to write in the date; but he must not alter the date.

A cheque with a non-existent date, say November 31, is normally paid on or after the nearest actual date preceding it—in this case November 30. A cheque which has a long-expired date—usually more than six months before—is not paid by the bank, but is returned as being out of date.

NAME Take care to give the correct name of the person or company to whom the money is to be paid—the 'payee'. If a wrong name is given, the payee may nevertheless get the money by signing the cheque on the back—called endorsing it—in the style used by the person who issued it, adding—if he wishes—his proper signature.

AMOUNT When issuing a cheque, give the amount in writing (showing pounds in words and pence in figures) and again in figures. Do not leave spaces which could be filled in.

If the amount in words differs from the amount in figures, the bank will not normally pay out, but will return the cheque. It may, however, pay the smaller of the two amounts.

## Crossed and open cheques

There are two kinds of cheques—open and crossed. The payee can cash an open cheque, which has no crossing lines on it, at the branch of the bank on which it is drawn.

A crossed cheque is one with two parallel lines ruled across it, or the name of a bank written across it. The payee cannot cash such a cheque at a bank. Payment can be obtained only by paying it into a bank account, which is a safeguard if the cheque falls into the wrong hands. If the cheque has to go through an account, the person presenting it can be traced, which increases the possibility of recovering the money. When an open cheque is cashed by someone not entitled to it, the money may never be recovered.

To cross an open cheque, simply draw two parallel lines across it. Many banks issue books of cheques which are already crossed.

The words '& Co.' are often written in the crossing, but they have no legal significance. The practice stems from the time when the payee's bank was generally named.

BEARER CHEQUES A cheque payable to 'John Smith *or bearer*' may be passed from one person to another, and the bank pays the person who finally submits it. No one needs to endorse the cheque. Bearer cheques are rarely used, since there is a risk of fraud.

ORDER CHEQUES If a cheque is made payable to 'John Smith *or order*', John Smith can, if he wishes, endorse it and make it payable to someone else.

Many cheques already have the words 'or order' printed on them. The holder who wants to make sure that a cheque is paid personally to the individual named, can cross out the words 'or order' and make the cheque payable to 'John Smith only', adding the words 'not transferable'. The drawer must initial or sign these alterations.

The same result can be obtained by writing 'A/c payee only' within the crossing, with or without the name of the payee's bank.

## Making a cheque 'not negotiable'
Once the payee has endorsed a cheque it becomes negotiable—that means it can be transferred to someone else without the drawer's permission.

The drawer can get some protection by writing the words 'not negotiable' through the crossing. This does not mean that the cheque cannot be transferred or endorsed—that is, passed on to others—but the people who receive the cheque legally have no better title to it than had the person who gave it to them.

If someone steals a cheque payable to 'order' and passes it in payment of a genuine debt, the person receiving it has no legal right to payment; nor has anyone else to whom he might give it.

If a cheque is endorsed and later dishonoured by the bank on which it is drawn, the person finally presenting it will have to seek payment from whoever passed it to him or from any endorser.

First write to the drawer and tell him of the refusal and then tell the endorser or endorsers. It is then possible to sue any of the people who passed it on for payment. Notice of dishonour must be given within 24 hours to all those liable except the drawer, who is not entitled to any formal notice.

## Cashing and paying in cheques
The only person who can obtain cash on a crossed cheque is the holder of the account himself, or his known agent. The account holder writes between the crossing the words 'Pay cash' and signs it (initials only are not accepted). The cheque can then be cashed at the account-holder's branch of the bank.

Anyone else must pay a crossed cheque into his own account and cannot obtain cash.

However, an open or uncrossed cheque can be cashed by the payee at the branch named on the cheque.

BANK CARDS A customer can usually get cash only from the branch at which he holds his account. If he wants to cash cheques elsewhere, he can make special arrangements with his bank and with the branch of his choice.

Alternatively, some banks give the customer a cheque guarantee card or a credit card, which guarantees payment of an amount usually up to £30, though some banks allow more. This enables him to cash cheques at most banks and also with most shopkeepers.

CASH DISPENSERS For customers wanting to draw cash outside bank hours, main banks have installed machines called cash dispensers, fixed to an outside wall of the bank. The customer obtains from his bank a cash dispenser card; when he needs money, he places it in the dispenser, which checks it electronically and issues a packet of banknotes.

PAYING IN CHEQUES Cheques drawn on British banks may be paid into the payee's own account without being endorsed. This does not apply to foreign cheques, those from the Republic of Ireland, and those with a box marked 'R' on the face of the cheque.

The letter R indicates that the receipt form on the back of the cheque must be signed before it can be paid. Similarly, traveller's cheques and bills of exchange must be endorsed before they are honoured.

Where an endorsement is required, the payee must sign his name in exactly the style used by the person issuing the cheque. If his name has been mis-spelt or an initial omitted, he must sign it in the way it is written.

## When a cheque 'bounces'
The bank must honour a correctly drawn cheque if there is money in the customer's account to cover it, or if the customer has made an arrangement to overdraw, and the limit has not been exceeded.

If there is not enough money in the drawer's account to cover a cheque, and he has not arranged an overdraft or has exceeded the agreed limit of an overdraft, a cheque may 'bounce'. A 'bounced' cheque is one that is returned to the person who paid it in, with the words 'refer to drawer' or R/D on it. It means that the bank will not pay the money and the payee must contact the drawer to obtain payment.

There are several other reasons why a cheque may not be honoured. The customer may have died or have been declared mentally ill, or a court may have ordered the bank to stop payments or the drawer may have stopped the cheque. The bank may also refuse payment if the words and figures on the cheque differ, or if the cheque is out of date or badly mutilated.

A bank is not able to pay a post-dated cheque—a cheque with a future date—if it is presented before it is due.

When a cheque is not honoured, it is returned to the bank of the person to whom it is made out. The bank then informs him that the money has not been paid. His own account, which will already have been credited with the amount of the unpaid cheque, is immediately reduced by that amount.

RE-PRESENTING He may then decide either to approach the person who issued the cheque direct and ask for payment—usually by postal or money order; or instruct his bank to return the cheque to the bank which issued it.

This is called re-presenting the cheque, and if the reason for its original non-payment was a temporary shortage of funds, it may be met on re-presentation.

If the cheque has not been paid because the drawer has died or has been declared mentally ill, the payee must apply to the drawer's executors or to a guardian appointed by a court, to collect payment.

STOPPING PAYMENT A drawer may stop a cheque by asking the bank to refuse payment. The cheque is then returned to the presenter with the words 'orders not to pay' on it.

There is nothing in law to prevent a drawer stopping payment on any cheque, provided he does not do so fraudulently. It would be fraudulent, for example, to stop a cheque for perfectly satisfactory goods or services, with the intention of avoiding payment.

But if a customer is dissatisfied with goods or services, he will be within the law in stopping payment until the shopkeeper or dealer has dealt satisfactorily with his complaint. If the dispute cannot be resolved, it will be open for the dealer to sue for payment in full, just as for any other debt.

### Bank giro

An alternative to paying by cheque is the banks' credit-transfer system—bank giro.

The customer fills out a form for each firm or individual he wants to pay, and hands them to the bank with the total amount involved in cash or a cheque. The bank then transfers a payment to the account of each payee at the indicated branch of any bank in the country. When there are several payments to be made at the same time, this is cheaper and easier than sending individual cheques. Even people who do not have accounts can pay in money at any bank for such transfers.

### Lost and forged cheques

When a cheque book is lost, it is the customer's duty to inform the bank immediately and to stop payment on the cheques in it. If he does not know how many cheques were left in the book, he should stop payment on all his cheques. He can later re-issue a cheque to anyone who is not paid because of this.

FORGED CHEQUES If a signature is forged or a cheque is forged by being altered in some way, the bank is normally responsible if it pays out. But if the drawer has enabled the

---

## When the bank makes a mistake

THE bank has a duty to honour cheques correctly drawn and presented when there is enough money in the account or when definite arrangements have been made for an overdraft. This is part of the contract between the customer and the bank. In theory, therefore, if the bank wrongly returns the cheque when there is money in the account, the customer could sue for breach of contract.

In practice, however, this is not often done, because in legal actions for breach of contract the person suing has to prove that he has suffered financial loss. This is difficult to show in a case where the bank has simply not paid out a customer's money.

It is more common, in such cases, to come to some agreement with the bank, whereby it accepts responsibility for the error and makes known its mistake to the person who had the cheque unpaid. If, however, the customer feels that his reputation has been seriously damaged by the bank's mistake, his main recourse in law is an action in libel.

▶THE BOOKMAKER WHO WON *Mr John Davidson operated a bookmaking business from his home in South London. He issued a cheque for £2 15s. 8d. to Mr S. Marks. The cheque was returned to Mr Marks by Mr Davidson's bank marked 'not sufficient'. Because of a clerical error, it was believed that there was not enough money in Mr Davidson's account.*

*Mr Davidson sued the bank for libel, claiming that the words 'not sufficient' meant that he was unable to pay the £2 15s. 8d. and that it was not safe to transact business with him.*

DECISION *The court decided that the aspersions on Mr Davidson's credit-worthiness were unjustified. He was awarded £250 damages, and costs. (Davidson v. Barclays Bank Ltd.)* ◀

forgery to be made, by writing the cheque so badly that extra amounts could be written in, the bank might be able to claim that the customer did not take proper precautions, and it may refuse to stand the loss from his account.

In one case, a customer who made out cheques to 'Brown', leaving space in front of the name for the wrong initials to be filled in, was held by a court to be partly responsible for the loss he suffered, and was not able to recover from his bank all the money lost.

### The customer's right to secrecy

The bank has no right to divulge details of any customer's account, except in special circumstances. Police, for example, are entitled to information on production of a court warrant—or a court may itself order details to be disclosed.

The bank can, however, make disclosures when it can show that it is in its own interest to do so—for example, if it is suing a customer to recover an overdraft.

Similarly, the bank must in law provide the Inland Revenue Department with the names of any customers who are earning more than £21 interest on deposit accounts in a year.

Otherwise, the bank must keep silent about the accounts and dealings of its present and former customers.

REFERENCES Banks are often quoted as references—in applications for credit or other business arrangements. Normally a bank gives such references only through other banks, not to members of the public or to companies. If information is required about a potential customer, it saves time to ask your own bank to make inquiries at the customer's bank.

References are usually given in guarded terms. A bank is unlikely to use a form of words that could be considered damaging, or might give rise to legal action.

A reference hedged with qualifications probably indicates that the bank is unwilling to commit itself wholeheartedly.

Customers have no right to be told what has been said by a bank or by anyone else from whom they have sought a reference. However, a person who is able to prove that he has suffered loss as a result of a negligently prepared reference might be able to sue the bank concerned for damages.

### Checking the bank statement

A bank statement may be obtained as often as the customer wants it. Many banks issue statements automatically every quarter.

The information given in the statement—whether or not it names the payee of cheques,

for example—depends on the bank's policy. If a customer wants more information, he has to arrange it with his local manager.

A customer who thinks his statement is wrong should challenge it immediately. Similarly, the bank is entitled to correct any error it discovers itself. If, for example, the bank overstates the amount in a customer's account, and the customer then overspends, the bank may not be held legally responsible for any cheques it returns unpaid—although a sympathetic branch might be willing to pay the cheques and accept repayment from the customer over some months.

If the customer could show that he spent the money only because he thought that he had it, and so relied on the bank, he could demand that the bank stand the loss by meeting the cheques. The onus of proving that the bank misled him is the customer's.

### Bank charges

Every bank charges for the services it provides. Charges are based on the amount in the account and the use the customer makes of the services.

The customer is not usually told of the charges until he sees the item debited on his statement. If he thinks they are too high he should complain to the manager and try to have them reduced.

If the bank deducts a charge for services without warning, leaving insufficient funds to meet a cheque that a customer has issued, it leaves itself open to legal action—either for breach of contract or possibly for defamation if the bank dishonours the cheque.

To win his case, the customer would have to prove that he could not have known that the bank was about to charge him.

### Other banks

Other organisations which use the term 'bank' in their title provide differing services.

TRUSTEE SAVINGS BANKS The network of trustee savings banks offers a particular type of banking service—a store for money. They also operate accounts with cheques, but do not lend money to private customers. ☐ Keeping money on deposit, p. 512.

MERCHANT BANKS Much of the financing of business and commerce is carried out through merchant banks. Their work is specialised, and they have few private customers.

BANK OF ENGLAND The central bank in Britain is the Bank of England, responsible, under the Treasury, for issuing cash. All clearing banks have accounts with the Bank, but it has virtually no private customers.

# Using National Giro

*Paying in money to Giro*
*Drawing cash and making payments*

*When funds are insufficient*

NATIONAL Giro is a special bank run by the Post Office. It specialises in the speedy transaction of deposits and payments, is relatively cheap and gives frequent statements of account—daily if required.

Giro's main advantage is convenient cash withdrawal from a post office outside normal banking hours. But unlike commercial banks, it does not lend money or allow overdrafts—though account holders can apply through Giro for loans from a finance house. □ Personal loans and second mortgages, p. 506.

It does not offer facilities such as safe deposits, advice on tax and investment, or references for customers. But it does handle international payments, and can provide foreign currency and travellers' cheques.

Anyone aged 15 or over can open an account by completing the application form available at any post office. The minimum deposit is £1.

Instead of periodic bank charges, Giro sets a fixed price on all its transactions.

## Paying in money to Giro

Cash can be paid in at any post office, but cheques and crossed postal or money orders must be posted to the National Giro Centre, Bootle, Lancashire GIR OAA. The account holder may not draw against a cheque paid into the account until it is cleared through the banks—usually four working days later.

PAYMENTS FROM OUTSIDE GIRO A person without a Giro account who wishes to send money to a Giro account holder may pay in cash or postal orders, but not cheques, at a post office, by completing an 'in-payment form'.

## Drawing cash and making payments

A Giro account holder can name two post offices at which he wishes to draw cash. He can draw up to £20 at either, provided withdrawals are not on successive working days.

To withdraw larger sums, a Girocheque must be sent to the National Giro Centre, from which it will be returned 'authenticated' in two or three days. Authenticated cheques can be cashed at any post office. Those for over £50 may be cashed only at the post office named on them, though this need not be one of those named in the holder's account.

PAYMENTS THROUGH GIRO Payments between Giro users are made by a transfer/deposit form, which can be sent direct to the payee or to the National Giro Centre.

The holder of a Giro account can pay Girocheques to people who do not hold Giro accounts. He should write the payee's name on the top line of the Girocheque, fill in the rest of the cheque, and write the payee's name and address on the back. The cheque is then posted to the National Giro Centre, which authenticates it and passes it to the payee.

If the payee is to deposit the Girocheque in his bank, it should be crossed and sent to him, not to the National Giro Centre.

STANDING ORDERS Regular payments from one Giro account into another—for rent, for example—can be made by standing order.

AUTOMATIC PAYMENTS Regular bills—for gas, for instance—can be paid through the Giro automatic debit transfer service.

DRAFT PAYMENTS For large payments a Giro draft, obtainable from the National Giro Centre, can be used. The customer's account is debited by the amount on the draft. It must be paid in within three months, otherwise the draft will be invalid and the account will be credited again with the amount.

## When funds are insufficient

If the money in an account is not sufficient to cover a Girocheque, it is returned unpaid. If funds are insufficient to meet a transfer or standing order, payment is made if there is enough in the account on any of the three following days. If not, the transfer is returned to the account holder or, in the case of a standing order, account holder and payee are notified that payment has not been made.

PROSECUTION A Giro customer needs to be on his guard against overdrawing. If he does so, and it can be shown that he had no reason to believe that the money drawn was available, he can be prosecuted for obtaining money by false representation.

LIABILITY Giro accepts responsibility for its mistakes and will correct them; normally it is liable for any loss arising from a forged cheque. But it does not accept legal liability for the *consequences* of mistakes.

# Sending money abroad

*Making gifts*      *Imports*
*Buying property abroad*     *Studying abroad*
*Investing abroad*

**M**ONEY transactions between United Kingdom residents and people overseas are controlled by the Treasury under the Exchange Control Act 1947. A resident of the United Kingdom—generally speaking, someone who has lived here for three years or intends to stay for three years—requires permission to send money to countries other than the U.K. (which includes the Isle of Man and the Channel Islands) and the Republic of Ireland.

For exchange-control purposes, overseas countries are divided into three categories:

*Category A:* British Commonwealth (except Canada and Rhodesia), Bahrain, Iceland, Kingdom of Jordan, Kuwait, Pakistan, Qatar, South Africa and South West Africa, United Arab Emirates and Republic of Yemen.

*Category B:* All countries not included in Category A, except Rhodesia.

*Category C:* Rhodesia. Transactions with residents of Rhodesia are not covered by the rules given here, and the advice of a bank should be sought in every case.

Banks or National Giro, under permission given by the Bank of England, are able to arrange many transactions for customers with residents of countries in Categories A and B,
including most types of current payment.

Where the payment is not covered by the permission, the bank concerned or the National Giro will apply to the Bank of England for specific consent. ☐ Using a bank, p. 434; Using National Giro, p. 439.

Sometimes payments may also be made through the Post Office overseas money-order service. Do not send cheques or bank notes, as this may contravene the regulations.

In case of difficulty, guidance can be obtained from the Bank of England (Exchange Control), New Change, London EC4M 9AA.

BORROWING OVERSEAS A United Kingdom resident must obtain Bank of England approval to borrow foreign currency from, or pay interest to, someone who is not resident in the U.K. or the Republic of Ireland.

PENALTIES Anyone who breaks the exchange-control regulations is liable to imprisonment or a fine. He may also have to forfeit the money or assets involved in the offence.

## Making gifts

In any calendar year, a U.K. resident can send gifts through his bank of up to £1000 to residents of Category A countries, and up to £300 to residents of Category B countries.

---

## Going to live abroad

**A** UNITED KINGDOM resident going to live for more than three years in a country outside the U.K. and the Irish Republic should apply through his bank to be treated as resident in the new country for exchange-control purposes.

An individual, or husband, wife and children under 18, may take normal household and personal effects to the new country.

Those going to Category A countries can transfer up to £20,000 in sterling assets on departure; for Category B countries, the limit is £5000. These limits may be increased for people taking jobs in Category A countries or in the enlarged Common Market (Belgium,
France, Western Germany, Italy, Luxembourg, Netherlands, Denmark and Norway.

Assets not eligible for transfer on departure are held in the U.K. as 'blocked assets', though they may be used immediately to buy currency in the investment currency market.

Any income from U.K. assets, whether blocked or not, can be taken out at the official exchange rate. Foreign currency assets may be transferred immediately and in full.

After four years, anyone with blocked assets can apply to take them out of the country.

The four-year restriction period is not usually applied to foreign nationals returning to the country of their nationality.

Gifts can be in cash, Premium Bonds or Savings Certificates.

He may seek Bank of England permission to exceed this limit in special cases—for example, a wedding or if someone is in need and there is hardship.

Gifts of securities which come within the relevant annual limits can also be made if the Bank of England approves.

In addition, gifts in kind worth up to £100 (excluding insurance and freight) may be sent. Special Customs permission is required to send diamonds out of the country.

LEGACIES No special permission is needed to transfer assets left in the will of a U.K. resident or distributed under the intestacy rules. ☐ Distributing an estate, p. 430.

### Buying property abroad

A United Kingdom resident who wants to buy a home or land outside the U.K. and the Republic of Ireland, even if he is buying from another U.K. resident, must get exchange-control permission from the Bank of England. Usually a bank handles the transaction and only one property is allowed to each family.

Where the property is to be purchased from a foreign resident, the buyer has to obtain the money to pay for it from the investment currency market.

This market, which was established to avoid a drain on reserves, increases the costs, because the price of investment currency is higher than the official exchange rate.

This additional cost—the difference between the official exchange rate and the price of the investment currency—is called the premium and is expressed as a percentage.

For example, if the investment currency premium is 30 per cent, every £100 worth of currency costs £130. This means that currency for a £5000 holiday home in Spain will cost a U.K. resident £6500.

The premium varies according to the demand and the amount of investment currency available. The pool of investment currency is replenished when U.K. residents sell certain foreign currency securities and property outside the U.K. and the Republic of Ireland.

### Investing abroad

When a U.K. resident wants to buy assets outside the U.K. and the Republic of Ireland, such as a share in a foreign business he intends to manage, or take part in managing, he has to get Bank of England permission.

If, however, he wishes to buy foreign currency securities—for instance, shares in a

Japanese car firm quoted on the Tokyo Stock Exchange—generally no special permission is needed. Normally a bank, a solicitor or a stockbroker makes the purchase. The money to pay for the securities has to be bought from the investment currency market in the same way as for buying property abroad.

Alternatively, where stocks or shares are quoted on a United Kingdom stock exchange, they may be purchased for sterling. The sterling quotations for foreign currency securities include the investment currency premium in the price quoted. There is no difference in cost whether the securities are purchased in the United Kingdom for sterling or abroad for foreign currency.

To ensure that all transactions in foreign currency securities are carried out in accordance with the exchange-control rules, all securities have to be held under the control of a bank, solicitor or stockbroker.

SELLING Anyone who sells foreign securities for payment in the currency of a Category A country may sell the whole of the proceeds on the foreign currency market. He may also sell the securities for sterling.

The holder of foreign securities which pay interest in or are sold for the currency of a Category B country is permitted to sell 75 per cent of the foreign currency sales proceeds on the investment currency market. The remaining 25 per cent has to be sold at the official rate of exchange.

If such securities are sold for sterling, the seller has to buy investment currency equivalent to 25 per cent of the sales proceeds and sell it at the official exchange rate.

### Imports

Most foreign goods can be obtained in the U.K. from the producer's U.K. branch or their agent—a firm of importers, for example. Anyone who needs to import goods directly should check whether a licence is needed at the Import Licensing Branch, Department of Trade and Industry, Sanctuary Buildings, 20 Great Smith Street, London SW1P 3BT, naming the goods and their source. Payment must be made through a bank and import duty is usually payable.

### Studying abroad

A United Kingdom resident who takes an educational course abroad is allowed up to £2000 each academic year in foreign exchange for enrolment, tuition, accommodation and cost of books. When leaving the U.K. he will be entitled to a traveller's allowance. ☐ Booking a foreign holiday, p. 142.

# The law on buying and selling

*The rules governing a contract*
*Goods on display*
*When the shopper can change his mind*

*Protection for the customer*
*When young people buy goods*

BUYING and selling involves making a contract—an agreement or a set of promises which can be enforced by law. There are a few cases where the law says that the agreement must be written down in full—such as a hire-purchase contract. In other cases, some supporting written evidence is normally required—a contract to buy a house, for instance. Otherwise, verbal agreements between two parties are enforceable by law.

### The rules governing a contract
Simple contracts have three elements: an offer, an acceptance and a consideration.
OFFER An offer may be the basis for bargaining—an offer for a second-hand car—or it may be the standard terms on which a firm does business (known in law as a 'firm offer').
ACCEPTANCE An offer is binding only when accepted. Until then it can be withdrawn.
CONSIDERATION The law does not enforce bare promises. Each party must confer a benefit on the other—goods for money, for instance.

When a customer buys a pound of butter, she makes an offer by telling the assistant what she wants. The assistant accepts the offer by handing her the butter. The customer provides the consideration by paying.

### Goods on display
If a shop puts the wrong price tag on an article in the window by mistake, it is not obliged to sell at the marked price. The price tag on goods in the shop window or on the shelves is not an offer in the legal sense. It is an 'invitation to treat', or an invitation to the customer to make offers. The customer has no redress if the shopkeeper refuses to sell at the marked price, or even if the shopkeeper refuses to sell at all.

### When the shopper can change his mind
These rules of contract can work in a shopper's favour. For example, the customer has a legal right to back out of a transaction right up until the time he has made his offer and the shop has accepted.

In a self-service store, for example, the housewife does not make an offer in law until she takes the groceries to the check-out

counter and offers to pay. But if she damages the goods before making the offer, she has a legal obligation to pay for them.

►CONTRACT AT THE CASHIER'S DESK *By law, certain drugs can be sold only under the supervision of a registered pharmacist. Boots Cash Chemists Ltd opened a self-service store and some of these drugs were displayed on the shelves, where customers selected them.*

*A pharmacist was stationed at the cashier's desk, but not near the drugs. In 1951, Boots were convicted of selling drugs without the necessary supervision. They appealed.*
DECISION *The Court of Appeal quashed the conviction, holding that the self-service system did not amount to an offer to sell, but was an invitation to customers to make offers to buy. The customer's offer was accepted at the cashier's desk under the supervision of the pharmacist. (Pharmaceutical Society of Great Britain* v. *Boots Cash Chemists Ltd.)* ◄

### Protection for the customer
When expensive goods are bought and sold, the shopkeeper and the customer often expressly agree on the contract terms—the shopkeeper gives his word that the goods work efficiently, or promises to repair any defects.

In smaller transactions, however, customer and seller do not normally discuss such matters. Nevertheless, the law states that certain terms can be assumed to apply in every case, except where the parties agree otherwise. These are the 'implied terms' of the contract, and they are set out in the Sale of Goods Act 1893.

If the shopkeeper breaks the implied terms, the customer's legal rights are normally limited to a claim for the cost of putting the defect right. If it cannot be put right, the compensation amounts to the difference between the price paid and the value of the goods with the defect. In practice, traders normally take back defective goods.

The three most important implied conditions are that the goods must fit the description, must be without serious defect and, if the customer asks for them for a particular purpose, must fulfil that purpose.

DESCRIPTION If a customer orders goods by description, they must correspond to the description. If, for example, a man asks for a rubber hot-water bottle and is given one made of plastic, the seller has not fulfilled his side of the bargain.

QUALITY If a customer buys anything by description from anyone who deals in the product, it must be of 'merchantable quality'. The goods must fulfil their function, and must be up to the standard a reasonable man would expect for the price.

SUITABILITY The general principle of the law is expressed in the Latin phrase *caveat emptor*—let the buyer beware. This means that the customer is supposed to examine goods carefully before agreeing to buy. But the Sale of Goods Act 1893 makes an important inroad into that principle. It says that in certain circumstances goods must be reasonably fit for the purpose for which they are bought. Three conditions must be satisfied:

**1.** The goods must be of a kind which the dealer normally sells. A customer is not protected if he buys a watch from a grocer's shop, unless the grocer usually sells watches.

**2.** The customer must make known to the seller the purpose for which he wants the goods, so as to make it clear that he is relying on the shopkeeper's skill and judgment.

**3.** If a customer asks for something by its brand name, he is not protected, because he is not relying on the seller's skill and judgment. But if the customer consults the shopkeeper who then recommends particular branded goods, the customer will be protected.

The protection given to the customer by the Sale of Goods Act is extensive, but any conflicting terms that he agrees with the seller will cancel his rights to this protection.

### When young people buy goods

People under 18 often find difficulty in buying goods unless they pay cash at the time of ordering. The reason is that if a customer under 18 fails to pay for something he orders, the shopkeeper may not be able to take legal action to claim the money owing.

A contract for 'goods supplied or to be supplied' can be enforced against someone under 18 only when it is for 'necessaries'. Expensive photographic equipment may be 'necessary', for instance, for a young fashion photographer but may not be for a teenager who uses a camera for holiday snapshots only.

The practical outcome of this is that shopkeepers will not supply goods on credit to people under 18 unless they can persuade an adult to promise to undertake responsibility for the bill if the youngster defaults.

---

## The rules of legal tender

ONLY certain bank notes and coins are legally valid in Great Britain. They are called legal tender. A 10p piece, for example, is legal tender but the old half-crown is not.

NOTES The £1, £5, £10 and £20 bank notes issued by the Bank of England are legal tender. Notes issued by banks in Scotland and Northern Ireland are not legal tender anywhere, though some shopkeepers and businesses accept them.

Local notes and coins issued on Jersey, Guernsey and the Isle of Man are legal tender only on those islands.

COINS The 50p, 10p and 2s., 5p and 1s., 2p, 1p and ½p coins are all legal tender. So is the old 6d. coin until it is withdrawn.

There is a limit on the number of coins in separate or mixed denominations that can be used as payment. For example, a shopkeeper is entitled to refuse eleven 2p coins, or any combination of ½p, 1p and 2p coins, for an article which costs 22p and to require the buyer to pay in coins of larger denomination.

On the other hand, when high denominations of notes or coins are offered for a small payment, shopkeepers and others are usually prepared to give change. But strictly speaking they are not required by law to do so. So if a bus passenger has only a note to pay his fare, and the conductor or driver is unable or unwilling to change it, the passenger (if he wishes to continue his journey) must pay the note and hope that, by giving his name and address, he will be sent the change.

| NEW CURRENCY | |
|---|---|
| 50p pieces are legal tender | up to £10 |
| 10p and 5p pieces (in separate or mixed denominations) | up to £5 |
| 2p, 1p and ½p pieces (in separate or mixed denominations) | up to 20p |

| OLD CURRENCY | |
|---|---|
| 6d. pieces | up to £5 |
| There is no legal limit on bank notes. | |

# Buying groceries

*Meats, fish and poultry*  *Dairy produce*
*Fruit and vegetables*  *Preserves and beverages*
*Bread and flour*  *Labelling*

THE preparation and sale of food and groceries are strictly controlled by law. Detailed regulations seek to ensure that the food is of good quality, free from harmful chemical additives and prepared in hygienic conditions; that minimum standards of composition are met—the fruit content of tins of fruit, for example, or the amount of meat in sausages—and that labelling is clear, informative and not misleading.

Many of the controls are applied long before the food gets to the customer. Others provide a set of standards which help the customer to judge value for money. □ What to do about faulty goods, p. 460.

## Meats

All meat must be sold by weight, and the buyer must be told the weight before paying or taking it away. 'Meat' includes offal and any food consisting substantially of meat. It does not include meat pies, meat puddings or Bath chap, which do not have to be sold by weight. The treatment of meat with acids to keep it fresh-looking is illegal.

MINIMUM CONTENT There is a regulation minimum meat content for various products:

| | |
|---|---|
| Beef sausages | 50 per cent |
| Pork and other sausages | 65 per cent |
| Fresh frankfurter, salami and Vienna sausages | 75 per cent |
| Tinned frankfurter, salami and Vienna sausages | 70 per cent |
| Meat pastes | 55 per cent |
| Jellied meat, luncheon meat and meat with cereal | 80 per cent |
| Meat loaves and meat rolls | 65 per cent |
| Stuffed meat loaf | 50 per cent |

## Fish

Fresh and frozen fish and products consisting mainly of fish—whether raw, cooked or processed—must be sold by weight. The weight regulations do not apply to fried fish, shellfish in the shell, jellied or pickled fish.

Fish cakes or paste bearing the name of a particular fish must contain at least 70 per cent of the named fish. In cases where the name comes first, as in 'salmon fish cakes', the fish content of the product must be higher than where the name on the label follows, as in 'fish cakes: salmon'.

## Poultry

Like meat, poultry must be sold by weight, and the customer must be informed of the weight before paying or taking the bird away. This does not apply to unpacked cooked poultry or to poultry pies.

## Fresh fruit and vegetables

Fruit and vegetables do not have to be labelled with type and variety, but a trader can be prosecuted for false or misleading labels—for example, for calling potatoes King Edward's when they are not.

POTATOES A shopkeeper can sell potatoes only by net weight. Pre-packed potatoes can be sold only in packs of ½ lb., ¾ lb., 1 lb., 1½ lb. and multiples of 1 lb. The packs must be marked with the net weight.

GREEN VEGETABLES Many green vegetables must be sold by weight. They include beans, brussels sprouts, brussels tops, curly kale, peas, spinach, spring greens and sprouting broccoli.

The weight of these vegetables must be made known to the customer before he pays or takes them away.

SOFT FRUIT AND MUSHROOMS Some soft fruit can be sold only by weight, and some by weight or number. Fruit which can be sold only by weight includes bilberries, cherries, blackberries, blackcurrants, cranberries, raspberries, red and white currants and strawberries. This regulation covers mushrooms.

OTHER PRODUCE Fruit or vegetables which can be sold either by weight or by number include apples, apricots, bananas, beetroot, carrots, corn-on-the-cob, greengages, leeks, mandarins, nectarines, onions (not spring onions), oranges, parsnips, peaches, pears, plums, shallots, swedes, tangerines, tomatoes and turnips.

Bunches of carrots, spring onions, turnips and beetroot need not be sold by weight.

Easily countable fruits and vegetables may be sold by number. Up to eight items may be sold pre-packed without the number being marked, provided the wrapping is transparent.

Similarly, collections of mixed fruit or vegetables—for example, Christmas fruits, or vegetables for a stew—need not be sold by weight.

## Canned fruit and vegetables

Standards have been set to ensure that cans of fruit and vegetables contain a certain percentage of the named fruit or vegetable. The same minimum limits, expressed as a percentage of the total content by weight, apply to processed fruit and vegetables.

FRUIT Minimum limits for tinned or processed fruit include:

| | |
|---|---|
| Apple puree | 91 per cent |
| Apples (solid pack) | 81 per cent |
| Apples and blackberries mixed, and rhubarb | 55 per cent |
| Apricots, bilberries, blackberries, blackcurrants, loganberries, peaches, pears, pineapple, raspberries, red currants, strawberries, mixed raspberries and red currants | 58 per cent |
| Fruit salad and fruit cocktail | 54 per cent |
| Cherries, damsons, greengages and plums | 60 per cent |

VEGETABLES The minimum limits for named vegetables, in cans or processed, include:

| | |
|---|---|
| Butter beans (dry) | 26 per cent |
| Runner and stringless beans | 47 per cent |
| Broad beans, beetroot, carrots, celery, macedoine, parsnips, fresh garden peas, swedes and turnips | 63 per cent |
| Peas (processed, soaked and scalded), marrowfats | 47 per cent |
| Peas and carrots mixed | 54 per cent |
| Potatoes (other than mashed) | 63 per cent |
| Leaf spinach | 67 per cent |
| Puree spinach | 94 per cent |

BEAN AND PEA SIZES Tinned peas and beans are graded according to their regulation sizes.

Small peas, or *petits pois*, are up to $\frac{11}{32}$ in. in diameter; medium peas are from $\frac{11}{32}$ in. to $\frac{13}{32}$ in.; large or standard are more than $\frac{13}{32}$ in.

Small stringless beans are up to $\frac{7}{32}$ in. in width; medium beans are up to $\frac{9}{32}$ in. in width; large are over $\frac{9}{32}$ in. in width.

FRUIT SYRUPS There are four grades of fruit syrups, according to density and sugar content. They are, in ascending order: light syrup, syrup, heavy syrup and extra-heavy syrup.

## Bread and flour

Bread must be sold by net weight if the amount exceeds 10 oz. Loaves weighing more than 10 oz. must be sold in multiples of 14 oz.

MILK BREAD Anything called milk bread must contain not less than 6 per cent milk solids and, if skimmed milk is used, this must be stated.

STARCH-REDUCED BREAD There must be less than 50 per cent carbohydrate, based on dry weight.

PROTEIN BREAD The minimum permitted content of protein is 22 per cent.

WHEATGERM BREAD There must be not less than 10 per cent added processed wheatgerm.

BROWN OR WHEATMEAL BREAD The special flour used must contain at least 0·6 per cent of fibre, and up to 5 per cent soya or rice flour may be added.

WHITE BREAD The flour must contain a proportion of chalk to increase the calcium content, as well as added vitamins and iron.

FLOUR may be sold only by net weight. Prepacked flour must be sold only in fixed quantities: 1, 2, 4, 8 or 12 oz., 1 lb., $1\frac{1}{2}$ lb. or multiples of 1 lb.

## Dairy produce

Strict hygiene regulations cover the processing and distribution of dairy produce—milk, cream, butter and some fats.

MILK All fresh milk sold to the public must be from tuberculin-tested cows (cows tested to detect tuberculosis). Nearly all of it must be heat-treated, the exception being a small quantity bottled on farms. Milk comes in the following grades:

PASTEURISED MILK has been heated quickly and kept at a temperature of at least 72°C (161°F) for 15 seconds, to retard fermentation.

HOMOGENISED MILK has been heat-treated and processed so as to disperse the fat globules evenly throughout the milk. It costs slightly more than pasteurised.

STERILISED MILK has been homogenised, then heated in the bottle at 100°C (212°F). It has a different taste and lasts longer.

UHT MILK has been subjected to 'ultra heat-treatment' at 132°C (270°F) for one second. It keeps in an unopened carton for up to five months without refrigeration.

CHANNEL ISLAND/SOUTH DEVON MILK has at least 4 per cent butter fat and costs more than pasteurised. It must come from cows of Channel Island or South Devon breed.

COLOUR CODE Some dairies have adopted a voluntary colour code for their bottle tops: silver for pasteurised; red for homogenised; gold for Channel Island and South Devon.

Pre-packed milk must generally be sold in quantities of one-third of a pint, half a pint or multiples of half a pint. If the container is not a transparent pint or half-pint bottle, the quantity must be marked. The exception to this rule is milk sold from a vending machine, which can come in any quantity and at any price—but the quantity must be marked on the carton and the machine.

DRIED MILK Varieties of dried milk on sale range from full-cream with at least 26 per cent milk-fat content to skimmed milk with less than 0·5 per cent milk fat. The label must state the equivalent number of pints of liquid milk.

CONDENSED AND EVAPORATED MILK Milk sold in condensed or evaporated form must contain not less than 9 per cent milk fat and 31 per cent milk solids.

CREAM Containers must be marked with net weight of contents or capacity measurement. 'Double cream' must contain not less than 48 per cent milk fat, and 'single cream' must have at least 18 per cent milk fat.

BUTTER By law, only natural colouring can be used, and not more than 16 per cent water may be added. Butter must have a minimum milk-fat content of 80 per cent and a maximum 2 per cent of milk solids. If the salt content exceeds 3 per cent, the butter must be described as 'salted'.

MARGARINE Vegetable oil, or a mixture of vegetable with animal or fish oils, is used to make margarine. The law states that it must contain added vitamins.

Margarine may be blended with up to 10 per cent butter and, like butter, its water content must not exceed 16 per cent.

## Preserves

JAM If mixed fruits are used to make jam—for example, apple and blackberry—the first-named fruit must usually be not less than 50 per cent and not more than 75 per cent of the fruit content, though this does not apply when the second fruit is strongly flavoured.

The jam must contain a certain minimum of fruit (which varies between 25 and 40 per cent). Only citric, tartaric and malic acids may be used, and the amount of sulphur dioxide in the jam is controlled.

MARMALADE Generally, the regulations are as for jam, but it must contain not less than 20 per cent citrus fruit.

OTHER PRESERVES The contents and composition of other preserves are also controlled. The basic rule is that none of them may contain less than 65 per cent soluble solids.

## Soft drinks, tea, coffee and cocoa

It is an offence to use the wrong name to describe a drink.

A CRUSH is a soft drink containing fruit juice for consumption without dilution.

CORDIAL is a clear citrus crush for consumption without dilution. The fruit content is squeezed juice from the flesh of the fruit only. Cordials and crushes must have at least 5 per cent of fruit juice by volume, and at least 4½ lb. of sugar added per gallon. A limited quantity of artificial sweetener is permitted.

SQUASH is a soft drink containing fruit juice and intended to be diluted. Citrus squashes must have at least 25 per cent of fruit juice by volume and at least 22½ lb. of added sugar per 10 gallons. A limited quantity of artificial sweetener is permitted. Non-citrus squashes need have only 10 per cent of fruit juice. (A clear citrus squash may also be called a 'cordial'—the customer must read the label and see if it is intended for dilution or not.)

'DRINK'—for example, 'orange drink'—may be prepared for drinking diluted or undiluted. The fruit content is obtained by squeezing the whole fruit. If intended to be drunk undiluted, it must have at least 2 lb. of citrus fruit per 10 gallons. If it is to be diluted, it must have at least 10 lb. of fruit per 10 gallons.

LOW-CALORIE SOFT DRINKS 'Slimming drinks' must not contain more than 7½ calories per fluid ounce if not intended to be diluted. The label must state that it is low calorie.

There are no regulations about the composition of tea, cocoa and drinking chocolate.

LIQUID COFFEE ESSENCE must be made from coffee—at least 4 lb. of coffee for each gallon of essence. In 'coffee and chicory essence', there must be 2 lb. of coffee for each gallon.

VIENNESE COFFEE is a mixture of 85 per cent coffee and 15 per cent figs.

FRENCH COFFEE is a mixture of coffee and chicory, with a minimum of 51 per cent coffee. The label must state that it is French coffee.

Coffee, coffee mixtures, tea, cocoa and drinking chocolate may be sold by net weight or pre-packed in 1, 2, 4, 8 or 12 oz., 1 lb., 1½ lb. or multiples of 1 lb.

## Labelling

From January 1, 1973, controls over labelling and food advertising, including slimming and other 'medicinal' products, become stricter.

Pre-packed foods have to be labelled with the common name of the contents—as distinct from brand-names. An exception is made for brand-names that have become household words over a period of 30 years before January 1971, such as Bovril and Marmite.

The majority of pre-packed foods must have a complete list of ingredients, including additives, on the label, arranged in weight order.

Other regulations cover the composition of special or medicinal foods. If a manufacturer claims that a product provides energy, calories, proteins, vitamins or minerals, these claims must be clear and substantiated. Nothing can be called a 'slimming aid' unless it has been proved to help slimming.

**The value of trading stamps**

The issue and use of trading stamps is governed by the Trading Stamps Act 1964. Trading stamps must be printed with a value expressed in current coin of the realm. Their cash value is less than many people imagine—

it takes nearly 32 stamps of one leading brand to make one new penny.

Once the shopper has collected stamps worth 25p face value, they can be cashed—or 'gifts' chosen.

The customer exchanging stamps for goods should take even more care to examine what he is getting than if he were buying for cash.

The customer who pays cash normally has rights in law if the goods are defective. The trading-stamp customer almost always loses these rights under the terms of the scheme.

---

## What to do if you are accused of shoplifting

IN supermarkets and other big stores, it is sometimes easy for an absent-minded housewife to walk off with goods without paying for them. This can lead to prosecution for theft.

A woman who is suspected of shoplifting is usually approached by a store detective, or some other member of the store's staff, and asked to go to the manager's office. At this stage the suspect is under no legal obligation to comply.

If she refuses, the detective may either let her go or arrest her. The detective has no special legal status, and his right to arrest is that of the ordinary private individual.

Contrary to popular belief, the detective does not have to wait until a suspect leaves the store before making an arrest, though if he does it may be easier to prove that the shopper had no intention of paying. In fact, the detective can make an arrest both inside and outside a shop. He can even follow a suspect into another shop and arrest her there.

Even if she is completely innocent, the shopper is best advised not to resist arrest.

Once she is in the store manager's office, the shopper does not have to answer any questions, and can ask to be allowed to telephone a solicitor to ask his advice. If possible, speak to the solicitor out of earshot of the store's staff, for any damaging statement they overhear could be repeated as evidence in court.

If the shopper realises that she has taken something from the store by mistake without paying for it, she can try to avoid prosecution by explaining how she came to make the mistake. A possible disadvantage of doing this is that what she says may again be taken down and repeated in court.

If a solicitor agrees to come at once to the manager's office—and he will probably

be reluctant to do so—it is best to leave any explanation until he arrives.

If the shop manager accepts the shopper's story, or if he begins to doubt the detective's evidence, the store may simply drop the matter. To secure a conviction for shoplifting —a form of theft—the prosecution has to prove beyond reasonable doubt that the shopper intended to avoid paying.

If the store decides to prosecute, the shopper must be handed over to the police as soon as possible—within an hour at the most.

A shopper who is arrested by a store detective, and later acquitted, may have grounds to sue for damages for false imprisonment and—if the detective used force—for assault. To defend the action, the detective would have to prove not only that he made an honest and reasonable mistake, but that someone else committed the offence.

A shopper who won the action might receive increased damages if she had been detained in the shop manager's office for an unreasonable period, or had suffered exceptional embarrassment or humiliation.

On the other hand, a shopper who agrees to go to the manager's office without being arrested cannot sue.

If the detective, or another member of the store's staff, accuses a customer of shoplifting in front of witnesses, and the shopper is found not guilty, she may also be able to claim damages for slander. ☐ What to do if you are libelled or slandered, p. 671.

Anyone convicted of shoplifting is normally tried in a magistrates' court and can be fined up to £400 or sent to prison for up to ten years. A light sentence, or none at all, may however be imposed where there are mitigating circumstances, such as emotional stress.

# Buying household goods

MAKING full use of the protection provided by the law is an essential part of buying household goods. The housewife shopping for fruit can usually tell whether she is getting value for money by examining the goods beforehand; but the customer buying a complex piece of machinery, such as a refrigerator or a washing machine, cannot be sure it is mechanically sound before he buys. He has to rely on the assurances of the shopkeeper and the manufacturer, while protecting his rights in law to claim compensation if they prove to be wrong.

Many of the choices to be made in shopping depend on the customer alone; only he can decide the best colour, pattern or finish.

Where there is doubt about which piece of equipment will do a particular job best—a lawn-mower for cutting grass in a paddock, or a washing machine for boiling nappies—it is wise to get advice from a specialist shopkeeper.

No shopkeeper should take lightly the duty of advising his customers. In law he can be made to account for any false information he gives, even if it is given innocently.

Where the customer makes clear to the seller the purpose for which goods are required, he has a right under the Sale of Goods

## What's in a label

Descriptive labels or tags on goods are a useful guide for the prospective buyer. They make it possible for the shopper to compare the claims of different manufacturers, and to decide which article is best suited to his purposes.

Some of the labels are sponsored by trade associations, who set minimum standards for their members, and others by independent bodies such as consumer protection organisations.

Some are a guarantee of quality and safety, while others are intended only as a guide to the use or treatment of goods—washing instructions for garments, for example. Use of these labels is strictly controlled by their sponsors. Anyone using them without authority risks prosecution.

Labels claiming that products are 'approved' by prestige organisations such as youth associations or yacht clubs should be regarded as a guide to quality only if such organisations have facilities for rigorous and scientific product testing.

A **Gas Council** seal means that the appliance has been tested for safety, performance and durability in accordance with British Standards specifications, and with the gas industry's own requirements

The **Woolmark**, used by licensees of the International Wool Secretariat, assures performance and quality of pure new wool products, backed up by extensive testing

BRITISH CARPET CENTRE

The British Carpet Centre is the authoritative body representing leading British manufacturers of Axminster and Wilton carpets

**British Carpet Centre** labels apply to genuine Wilton and Axminster carpets and indicate suitability in five categories:
**1.** Light domestic use (in bedrooms, for example). **2.** Medium domestic use. **3.** General domestic and/or light contract (commercial) use. **4.** Heavy domestic and/or medium contract use. **5.** Luxury domestic and/or heavy contract use

Act 1893 to rely on the skill and judgment of the seller. If the shopkeeper normally sells that type of goods, and he recommends a product which turns out to be unsuitable, the customer can demand compensation or, if the goods are seriously defective, he can get his money back.

This does not apply when the customer buys goods under a patent or trade name—if he asks, for example, for an 'Icecold' refrigerator. But if he asks for a refrigerator, and the dealer says: 'I suggest that you have an Icecold', this is not a sale under a patent or trade name and the dealer remains responsible for any advice he gives.

### When a deposit must be returned
A customer should not hand over any money —even a deposit—until he has decided exactly what he is going to buy and is given an assurance that the shopkeeper can supply the goods by the time he requires them.

A deposit is almost invariably paid as part of the purchase price and is an indication that the customer intends to accept the goods and pay the balance on collection or delivery.

Therefore, if a customer pays a deposit and then decides that he does not want, or cannot afford, the goods he has ordered he is not normally entitled to a refund.

It may be possible, however, to get the shopkeeper to agree that the deposit is to be returned if the goods cannot be supplied on time, or if they are not, after all, needed. Most pram dealers, for example, offer to refund a deposit if the customer finds that, because of a miscarriage, the pram is not required.

Get written confirmation of any special agreement about the deposit, possibly a note written on the receipt—'Refundable in full if the goods are not delivered by . . .'

### Order forms and sales agreements
A customer buying a major item of household equipment may sometimes be asked to sign an order form or sales agreement. While it might

The British Electrical Approvals Board's mark indicates an appliance approved as safe in accordance with British Standards. It is no guarantee of quality or performance

Home Laundering Consultative Council tags give advice on washing, including recommended water temperatures

The Teltag scheme, devised by the now defunct Consumer Council, is still used to give details of composition, size, performance and use of appliances. Tags do not recommend 'good buys', but give the customer a way of comparing different brands

The Design Centre label indicates products selected by the Centre on the grounds of their fitness for purpose, appearance, quality, ease of maintenance and value for money

The Kitemark of the British Standards Institution shows that goods comply with basic standards of quality as published by the Institution

The Retail Trading-Standards Association's labels show which washing or dry-cleaning methods should be used for garments and textiles. The Association is particularly concerned with the quality of school uniforms

appear to do no more than confirm the customer's order, the form often takes away many of his most valuable legal rights.

Where there is no order form or other written agreement, the customer has a right to redress under the Sale of Goods Act 1893 in three main circumstances:

**1.** If the goods do not match the description he was given of them or tally with the sample he was shown.

**2.** If a reasonable man, knowing the condition of the goods, would not have bought them for the price.

**3.** If the goods are not fit for the purpose the buyer told a specialist shopkeeper he wanted them for.

In any of these cases, the customer can normally claim compensation for defective or unsuitable goods; if they are virtually worthless he may be entitled to have his money back.

☐ What to do about faulty goods, p. 460.

In addition, the customer has a right to claim damages from the manufacturer if a product causes injury or damage because of negligence in its manufacture. ☐ Faulty goods: suing the manufacturer, p. 464.

Many sales agreements and order forms contain 'exclusion clauses' which aim to exclude the protection given by these rules. They may offer other guarantees, and it depends on the customer whether he prefers these to the protection given by law. If an order form takes away a customer's legal rights and offers less protection in return, he can try to avoid signing it. Alternatively, the clauses to which he objects can be deleted, but this is effective only if the seller accepts the alteration.

If he refuses, the customer may be best advised to shop elsewhere, unless it seems that other suppliers of the goods do the same.

The conditions on a sales agreement or order form which rob the customer of his rights are often printed in small type on the back. They are binding on the customer, even if he has not read them, provided the seller has drawn the customer's attention to them. It is sufficient to print on the front of the form, for example, the statement: 'subject to the conditions printed overleaf'.

➤ NO REDRESS OVER A FAULTY MACHINE *In 1934, a salesman working for F. Graucob & Co. Ltd persuaded Miss L'Estrange, who owned a cafe at Llandudno, Caernarvonshire, to buy an automatic vending machine for selling cigarettes.*

*Miss L'Estrange signed a 'Sales Agreement' which contained a great many clauses in small print, one of which stated that 'any express or implied condition, statement or warranty, statutory or otherwise, is hereby excluded'.*

*Miss L'Estrange did not read the agreement before signing it, and later said that she did not realise what she was signing. When delivered, the machine proved defective. She refused to pay for it and sued to recover her deposit.*

DECISION *Her claim failed. The High Court held that the clause formed part of the contract. Miss L'Estrange, said Lord Justice Scrutton, 'having put her signature to the document and not having been induced to do so by fraud or misrepresentation, cannot claim to say that she is not bound by the terms of the document because she has not read them'. (L'Estrange v. F. Graucob & Co. Ltd.)* ◄

Miss L'Estrange might have failed even if she had not signed the agreement; if, for example, the terms of the agreement had been brought to her attention in some other way—say by a printed notice or verbal advice.

**The pitfalls of guarantees**

On the face of it, a manufacturer's guarantee appears to provide a benefit for the customer by promising to repair some or all defects which appear in the product within a specified period. In practice, the customer may be worse off with a guarantee than he would otherwise be.

Most guarantees are a kind of exchange—they replace the customer's rights in law with a set of promises, generally from the manufacturer. Only if the customer gains more than he loses is it worth accepting the guarantee.

BENEFITS IN LAW The customer who relies on his rights in law can claim against the *shopkeeper* if the goods are defective or unsuitable, and against the *shopkeeper* and *manufacturer* if they are dangerous or if they are improperly made and cause injury or damage.

BENEFITS UNDER GUARANTEE The customer who relies on a guarantee makes whatever claims the guarantee allows against the manufacturer—not against the seller.

It is not as curious as it might seem for the manufacturer to appear to take on some of the responsibilities of the retailer; for the retailer who faces a claim from a customer over defective goods would have a right to claim in turn against the manufacturer. All the manufacturer is doing, therefore, is short-circuiting the process.

In doing so he often provides less protection for the customer than the law does.

Some guarantees, for example, provide that the manufacturer will pay for new parts, but not for the cost of labour to fit them. By law, the seller of defective goods is responsible for paying for both labour and parts.

Many guarantees exclude claims against the manufacturer for injuries or damage. Claims could otherwise be made in law.

Guarantees often exclude claims for losses caused by the defect—damage done to clothes by a faulty washing machine, for example. An arbitrary time limit which would not apply in law may also be put on claims.

On the practical side, there may be benefits under even a limited guarantee. A claim in law is costly and frequently unrewarding to pursue if the seller refuses to meet it. A claim under guarantee, on the other hand, will usually be cheap and straightforward by comparison.

No one need accept a guarantee unless he chooses to do so, although some retailers may not sell to a customer who refuses one. When a customer is sold goods without accepting a guarantee, he retains his protection under the law. Many guarantees require the buyer to sign and return a card to the manufacturer. All the buyer has to do to reject the manufacturer's guarantee is to keep the card.

### How to judge a guarantee

Ideally, all manufacturers' guarantees should provide positive assurance for the customer that the manufacturer will:

**1.** Accept responsibility for the quality and suitability of the goods.

**2.** Repair or replace defective items or parts free of charge.

**3.** Pay compensation for loss or damage caused by these defects.

**4.** Accept his responsibilities under common law and Acts of Parliament.

**5.** Allow disputes to be referred to any independent arbitrator and not try to prevent them from being taken to court.

Few guarantees meet this standard.

Guarantees are seldom given with second-hand goods, other than vehicles. If they are, they are given by the retailer and usually limit his legal obligations.

If the customer accepts a guarantee, the manufacturer or retailer who gives it is under a legal obligation to carry out its terms. This is so even where the customer has no card to sign, and no written undertaking addressed to him by name. The fact that the customer has never dealt directly with the manufacturer, but only with a retailer, does not weaken his legal right to benefit under the guarantee.

➤ THE MEDICINE THAT FAILED *Mrs Carlill was delighted to read the Carbolic Smoke Ball Company's advertisement. It gave a guarantee that the company's remedy, used in the prescribed manner, would 'positively cure' influenza and 17 other ailments.*

*So confident were the advertisers that they offered £100 to anyone who caught influenza after using the smoke balls as directed.*

*Mrs Carlill bought a smoke ball and used it as directed, but she still caught influenza. She claimed the £100 from the manufacturers, but they refused to pay. So she sued.*

DECISION *The company had to pay Mrs Carlill £100. The Court of Appeal said the advertisement was an offer, addressed to the public at large. Anyone could accept the offer by doing what the advertisement required, namely purchasing and using the remedy as directed. (Carlill v. Carbolic Smoke Ball Co.)* ◄

## Good and bad guarantee clauses

This warranty is in addition to the buyer's statutory and other legal rights which are not diminished in any way by its acceptance

Any warranty or guarantee form which includes a clause similar to this is worth accepting, for it offers the customer valuable rights in addition to those which are provided under the common law and Acts of Parliament

In substitution of any statutory or other warranty or condition express or implied, the company guarantees this unit for twelve calendar months from the date of delivery to the original user. In the event of dispute the company's decision will be final

The customer's rights under the Sale of Goods Act 1893 are excluded by this clause. In place of them, he receives a more limited and less valuable form of guarantee, and he also forfeits his right to carry any dispute to independent arbitration or to the courts. A customer who is offered this type of guarantee may sometimes be better off refusing it and relying on his legal rights

# How the law controls sales cards

Many shoppers regard the normal price of goods as an indication of their quality, particularly if quality cannot be gauged by a quick examination. In a sale, for example, they tend to regard a watch marked '£25 reduced to £10' as of a higher quality than one marked '£15 reduced to £10'. If, therefore, the shopkeeper inflates the 'normal' price to make the sales reduction seem greater, the customer is likely to be misled.

To prevent this happening, the Trade Descriptions Act 1968 makes false claims about prices illegal. A seller commits an offence if he indicates falsely that he sold the goods at a specified higher price, or if he claims falsely that he is selling goods at less than a recommended price.

The practice of marking special lines, bought for use at sale time, as though a higher price had previously been charged, is thus discouraged.

It is also an offence for the seller to give a false idea of the total price the customer eventually has to pay—to say, for example, 'Yours for only £3', when £3 is a deposit on the goods, not the total price.

Goods must have been offered at deleted price in same shop (or one in same chain) for 28 consecutive days in last six months. If prosecution can prove otherwise, shopkeeper has broken the law

The shop must have offered the goods at the higher price on only one day in the previous week—unlike the 28-day period needed for tickets showing straight price reductions

A 'recommended' price is usually the one set by the manufacturer. But the manufacturer may legally inflate the 'recommended' price to make 'reductions' look more impressive

This card gives no guarantee of a bargain, for the shopkeeper who invents the 'price elsewhere' is breaking the law only if it might be taken to be the one recommended by the manufacturer

No control is exercised by the Act over the price described as 'Today's value'. Such a price can be a wholly fictitious figure applied to goods bought specially for a sale

'Seconds' are goods offered at a cut price because of small defects or faults. The buyer cannot expect perfect goods or a replacement for them if they prove defective

'Special-purchase' goods are bought specifically for a sale. The ticket must not indicate that the price is a genuine reduction on the price at which the goods are normally sold in the shop

The seller of 'imperfect' or 'substandard' goods may indicate a price for such goods in perfect condition so long as the perfect samples have been sold in that shop or shops elsewhere

A shop may offer 'sub-standard' or 'imperfect' goods at a sale price without indicating a price for 'perfect' samples, but the buyer cannot expect to get a refund if he is not satisfied

# Buying at auctions

*Conditions of sale*          *Bidding at auctions*
*Backing out of a sale*       *Bidding by the seller*
*The reserve price*           *Where auctions can be held*

AN auction is a sale at which goods are sold to the highest bidder, and it is governed by the same basic principles of the law on contracts as apply to any other sale. There are also special rules which apply only to sales by auction.

At the sale, the auctioneer's request for bids is merely an attempt to set the ball rolling. It is not an offer to sell in the legal sense. The bidder makes the offer by bidding, and the auctioneer is free to accept or reject the bid. The final tap of the hammer—usually the third—indicates that the sale is complete. Until then, any bid may be withdrawn.

Auctions are primarily cash sales and only a well-known and regular customer can expect to get credit for anything he buys.

## Conditions of sale

Auctions are governed by conditions of sale, drawn up by the auctioneer. They are drafted in the interests of the seller and the auctioneer, not primarily in those of the buyer. If there is a catalogue, the conditions are usually printed inside the cover; but they may be posted up in the sale room or simply read out by the auctioneer, who has a legal obligation to draw them to the customers' attention.

Sometimes the sale catalogue states that the sale is 'subject to the auctioneer's usual conditions', displayed on a notice in the saleroom.

The conditions form the basis of the contract and, unless they are wholly unreasonable, the courts will regard them as binding.

Bargains at auctions are rarer than many people think. Anyone who plans to make a bid has to examine the goods carefully beforehand. The guiding principle is *caveat emptor*—'let the buyer beware'. Goods sold at auctions are normally second-hand, and the buyer is expected to be aware of any defects when he bids. The goods are sold 'subject to all faults'. If a table turns out to be riddled with woodworm, for example, the buyer has no redress.

Even when new goods are sold, the printed conditions of sale invariably exclude liability for any defects.

A buyer who wants to be sure can try asking the auctioneer: 'Is that sideboard free from woodworm?' or 'Is that car mechanically sound?' Usually the auctioneer will not be drawn. But if he does vouch for something, this will cancel any disclaimer of responsibility in the printed conditions of sale.

➤ THE HEIFER THAT DIED *Mr Couchman, a farmer, bought a heifer for £29 at an auction.*

*The sale catalogue, which described the animal as 'unserved', also stated that the auctioneers would not be responsible for any error or mis-statement. However, both the owner, Mr Hill, and the auctioneer verbally confirmed*

---

## The law against dealers' 'rings'

THE law protects the person who is selling goods at an auction from attempts by dealers to keep prices artificially low. The aim is to prevent dealers from getting together and agreeing not to bid against each other, in the hope that one of them will be able to buy the goods at a low price.

The dealers then hold a private auction, called a 'knock-out', among themselves.

It is illegal for dealers to form a 'ring' for this purpose, though the law has proved difficult to enforce. It applies only to dealers,

and not to members of the general public—although it is an offence for any person to pay someone else not to bid for a lot. If such an arrangement is made, the auctioneer is entitled to refuse to part with the goods.

The penalties for taking part in a ring are a fine of up to £400, or imprisonment for up to six months, or both.

A copy of the Auctions (Bidding Agreement) Act 1927, setting out the law on dealers' rings, must be conspicuously displayed in the auction room throughout the sale.

*the animal's description when Mr Couchman questioned them before making his bid. They gave their answers in good faith.*

*A few months later, the heifer died as a result of carrying a calf at too young an age. Mr Couchman sued Mr Hill for damages.*

DECISION *Mr Couchman was awarded damages. The Court of Appeal decided that the answers to Mr Couchman's inquiries overrode the conditions of sale in the catalogue. (Hill v. Couchman.)◄*

Because of the dangers involved in misstatement, auctioneers are careful about how they describe antiques and works of art. If there is some doubt about who painted a picture the auctioneer protects himself by stating that a painting is 'attributed to Constable'.

### Backing out of a sale

If a buyer bids a high price for goods in the belief that they are worth more, and the goods are knocked down to him, he cannot back out. But there are a few cases in which a mistake can enable the buyer to avoid the contract.

►THE BUYER WHO DID NOT KNOW WHAT HE WAS BUYING *Hemp is a fibre used for making cordage and rope, and for weaving into strong fabrics. Tow is the unworked fibre of flax and is unsuitable for these purposes.*

*Scriven Bros. & Co. instructed Mr Northcott, an auctioneer, to sell a large quantity of Russian hemp and tow for them. Samples were on show in the auction rooms. The sale catalogue indicated only the number of bales, in two lots—one of hemp, the other of tow. It did not say which was which.*

*A buyer for Hindley & Co. inspected only the lot containing hemp. This was knocked down to him at the auction. Thinking the other lot was hemp, too, he bought that, but it was tow.*

*Hindley & Co. refused to accept the lot when they discovered it was not hemp. Scriven Bros. sued Hindleys for £470, the price of the tow.*

*Mr Northcott claimed that he announced the second lot as tow. This was denied. Hindleys said that their buyer had not been told that the tow was marked in a similar way to the hemp.*

DECISION *The court dismissed the action because the sale was void. The parties were never in agreement as to the nature of the materials. One was selling tow, the other thought he was buying hemp—so there was no contract of sale. (Scriven Bros. & Co. v. Hindley & Co.)◄*

If a buyer at an auction is persuaded to bid by false statements made about the goods by the auctioneer or the seller, the buyer will be entitled to give the goods back, refuse to pay, or claim his money back. Alternatively, he is entitled to claim compensation from the person who made the false statements for any loss he suffers because the goods are not what they were made out to be.

### The reserve price

The conditions of sale for an auction often contain a clause stating that 'all lots are subject to a reserve price'. This is a price below which the goods will not be sold, and the auctioneer is not bound to disclose what the reserve price is. If the reserve price is not reached by the bidders, the goods will be withdrawn from the sale.

English law has never decided whether the auctioneer is obliged to sell the goods to the highest bidder, even when the reserve price has not been reached. It is therefore uncertain whether a disappointed would-be buyer could force the auctioneer's hand in these circumstances. Most well-drawn conditions of sale state that the auctioneer may refuse any bid.

Even where the auction sale is advertised as being 'without reserve', it is doubtful whether this amounts to a definite offer to sell to the highest bidder. The general rule is that any sale is incomplete until the final rap of the hammer, and a Scottish court has held that a sale 'without reserve' is not a legally enforceable offer to sell. An English court would probably decide this point in the same way.

### Bidding at auctions

The bids at an auction can be made verbally or by signs. For example, a buyer who wants to remain anonymous may have arranged with the auctioneer to bid by nodding his head, rubbing his nose or perhaps by tapping his ear with a rolled newspaper.

It is most unlikely that a spectator could, by making a move at the wrong moment, suddenly find himself the owner of a painting or piece of furniture worth thousands of pounds. The story of a man who bought a Rembrandt by waving to a friend across the auction-room floor is a myth.

Because it is part of an auctioneer's skill to know who is bidding at any moment, disputes are unlikely to arise over who actually made the final bid for a lot—though if a dispute occurs the auctioneer has the right to put the lot up for sale again.

The auctioneer also has the right to start the bidding at a certain level and to insist that bids are made in certain amounts. This is common in bigger salerooms, where many of the lots may fetch high sums. To save time, and to help the bidding reach any reserve price, the auctioneer may accept bids only in, say, thousands of pounds. As the bids rise, the auctioneer may cut the size of the bid units.

## Bidding by the seller

In some cases the seller himself is allowed to bid, to inflate the price. He can do so, however, only if he reserves the right to bid. The auctioneer must announce this when the lot is put up for sale; or, if all the lots belong to one person, the seller's right to bid can be stated in the printed conditions of sale.

## Where auctions can be held

Auctions can be held anywhere—in a sale-room, in the open air provided they do not cause an obstruction, or in a private house. The auctioneer is an agent for the seller,

working for commission, and he does not make a contract with the buyer.

The actual contract is made between the buyer and the seller, with the auctioneer as intermediary. The auctioneer is liable for negligence in conducting the sale. His liability is, however, to the seller of the goods.

The auctioneer must also display a clear notice containing his name and address. If he fails to do so, he can be fined up to £20.

The fact that an advertisement states that an auction will be held at a certain time and place does not legally oblige the auctioneer to hold the sale. One would-be buyer sued to recover travelling expenses when an auction was cancelled. His action failed.

The same principle applies if advertised goods are withdrawn from the sale.

## How the law protects the buyer

AUCTIONS at which people are tricked into buying shoddy goods at inflated prices are prohibited by law.

At one time, these 'mock auctions' were a regular feature at fairgrounds, seaside resorts and town markets. People were tricked into buying third-rate goods.

Mock auctions worked in this way: one man, known as a 'pitcher', lured a crowd with promises of an auction at 'give-away' prices. Some genuine goods, which were never sold, were displayed to support his claims.

Then the auctioneer, known in the trade as the 'top man', opened the sale by offering goods at ridiculously low prices—for example, a watch for 25p. A buyer paid his money, got the watch—and some money back.

He was encouraged to hand the watch round in the crowd to show what a bargain it was. Small, cheap articles were given away free, to keep the crowd interested.

The auctioneer used a skilful flow of patter, interlaced with gifts and 'sales' at low prices, to build up buying fever in the crowd. Bidders came to believe that they would get valuable articles for a fraction of their real price.

As the buying urge grew stronger, the auctioneer offered more expensive items, such as canteens of cutlery.

Buyers paid, say, £5 for a canteen, thinking that they would get both the cutlery and a refund of part of the price. The auctioneer's assistants would make a show of trying to stop such a 'generous' sale, but the auctioneer

would insist and hand over sets of tightly wrapped cutlery to the eager buyers. This time there would be no money refunded to the buyers by the auctioneer.

Later, buyers would find that the 'bargain' cutlery was of low quality, often worth about half what they paid.

Usually by the time the buyers found out, the auctioneer had disappeared. Even if he had not, the buyer had no redress.

To combat such practices, Parliament passed, in 1961, the Mock Auctions Act, making it an offence to promote or conduct or assist in the conduct of a mock auction.

A sale is a mock auction in any of the following cases:

**1.** If a lot is sold to a person at a lower price than his highest bid, or if part of the price is repaid or credited to him, unless to cover a defect discovered after he made his bid.

**2.** If the right to bid is restricted to people who have already bought, or agreed to buy, one or more articles.

**3.** If any of the articles are given away or offered as gifts.

The Act applies only to lots including or consisting of: plate or plated articles, linen, china, glass, books, pictures, prints, furniture, jewellery, household, personal or ornamental articles, musical instruments and any pieces of scientific apparatus.

Penalties for a breach of the Mock Auctions Act are prison sentences of up to two years or a fine of up to £1000.

# Buying on the doorstep

*Salesmen's tricks*   *Returning the goods*
*The 'cooling-off period'*   *Charity collections*
*Signing an agreement*

THE purpose of much doorstep selling is an immediate sale with no after-sales service. However, reputable firms employ doorstep salesmen, too, and it is only by close questioning that a buyer can distinguish the genuine from the suspect.

Where the purchase is from a reputable firm, the buyer has the same prospect of redress if he has any complaint as he would have against the ordinary shopkeeper. ☐ What to do about faulty goods, p. 460.

If any salesman misleads or makes false claims about his goods, a purchaser may be able to sue the firm under the Misrepresentation Act 1967. The firm may also risk prosecution under the Trade Descriptions Act 1968.

## Salesmen's tricks

Beware of the salesman who claims to be something else. Encyclopaedia salesmen may, for example, give the impression that they represent the local school or education authority. Another trick is to ask parents to take part in an 'educational survey'.

Some salesmen canvassing for subscriptions to magazines claim to be students working their way through college. There have been cases of the wrong magazines arriving, or no magazines arriving at all, after people have paid out money for subscriptions.

Some representatives of central-heating firms describe themselves as 'consultant engineers conducting a survey'. They may suggest that having central heating installed qualifies for an improvement grant from the local council. This is not usually so, but in some cases the local council may pay part of the cost of central heating if it is part of full-scale modernisation of the house. ☐ Repairs and improvements, p. 223.

Fire-extinguisher salesmen sometimes claim to be local-authority inspectors, and insist that it is an offence not to have an extinguisher. The local fire service will give advice.

SWITCH-SELLING Some firms may advertise, say, an 'almost new washing machine, fully automatic, £50'. The salesman who calls in response to an inquiry then 'regrets' that the advertised machine has been sold and he offers something else which usually costs more.

'WORK' AT HOME Housewives and the housebound should be wary of advertisements which offer 'a steady income from work at home'. Often they are from firms selling knitting machines, or something similar, who offer to buy the goods made with them. An offer like this may be genuine, but the small print in the contract often enables the firm to avoid buying the goods or to get them cheaply. Meanwhile, the customer has to pay for the machine.

## The 'cooling-off period'

When goods are acquired on the doorstep under either a hire-purchase or a credit-sale agreement, the salesman is usually obliged to give the customer a copy of the contract, and to send a second copy by post within seven days. The contract must contain a red box warning the customer of the type of agreement, and a notice advising him of his right to withdraw.

The customer has four days from the time he receives the second copy of the agreement to change his mind and cancel the contract. This is called the 'cooling-off' period.

The customer's right of cancellation during the 'cooling-off period' applies to hire-purchase agreements of up to £2000 if the customer signs the agreement anywhere other than at the dealer's or finance company's premises. Beware, therefore, of being asked to sign the agreement 'down at the office'.

If it is a credit sale, the deal can be cancelled only if the total cost is more than £30 and less than £2000. Some central-heating companies dodge this by splitting up their installations into lots costing less than the £30 minimum. The buyer then cannot cancel the deal.

Unscrupulous firms may try to deny the customer his legal rights by failing to leave a copy of the contract and by not sending a second copy, as the law demands. In such cases it would be difficult for the customer to cancel because he might not have an address at which to find the company.

But his right to cancel continues. He can therefore refuse to go ahead with the agreement, and even if the goods are delivered, he can refuse to pay for them.

When a customer decides to cancel, it is enough to send a letter to the finance company or the dealer saying that he is exercising his right of cancellation; but it is better to refer precisely to the transaction, and to quote any reference number for it. Send the cancellation by recorded delivery and keep a copy.

The letter must be signed by the person who signed the original agreement. ☐ Hire purchase, p. 498; Credit sale, p. 503.

### Signing an agreement
To protect yourself when signing a hire-purchase or credit-sale agreement:
**1.** Make sure that all the blank spaces on the agreement have been completed in ink.
**2.** Check that the cash figures are those agreed.
**3.** Never sign a blank form, even if the salesman says that he will complete it later.
**4.** Get a copy of the agreement when signing.
**5.** Never sign a form without the red-box warning. It will not be a hire-purchase or credit-sale agreement. It may be a simple hire agreement, under which the goods never become the customer's property. ☐ Hiring goods, p. 466.
**6.** Never sign a second form. It may concern a 'split agreement', a method used by some firms to avoid the hire-purchase laws.

### Returning the goods
If the customer exercises his right to cancel the agreement within the four-day time limit, and the goods have been delivered, he does not have to return them. The seller must make his own arrangements to collect the goods, and the buyer is not liable for any charge.

The customer need not even hand over the goods unless the seller sends a written request for them; he may hold on to them until any deposit he has paid is returned and he receives back any goods he has given in part-exchange.

But while the customer has the goods, he must take reasonable care of them and he must not use them; otherwise he may be liable for any damage caused to them.

Some doorstep salesmen try to force the buyer to pay 'rental' while the goods have been in his possession, or to pay for 'wear and tear'. The buyer need make no payment at all.

### Charity collections
House-to-house collections for charity are subject to special rules which provide a limited safeguard against dishonest collectors. The collector must have a police licence and should wear an identifying badge.

A common trick is to offer goods 'made by blind people' or 'made by the severely disabled'. Always ask for identification, and see that the caller has authority to collect. If in doubt, contact the police.

There is no need to tolerate persistent callers. It is an offence to 'importune any person to his annoyance or to remain in or at the door of any house if requested to leave by the occupant'.

## Buying stolen goods

IT is an offence knowingly to buy stolen goods. Anyone convicted of handling stolen goods can be sent to prison for up to 14 years. It must be proved, however, that the person who is handling the goods knew or believed them to be stolen. Anyone who handles them innocently does not risk punishment. But an innocent buyer may find that the goods he has bought no longer belong to him if they were stolen.

The person who sells stolen goods has no right to sell them and the buyer can be made to restore them to the true owner.

The main exception to this comes from what is known as 'sale in market overt'—open market. The shopper who buys stolen goods from any shop in the City of London, if it is the shop's usual type of merchandise, or from any market held by charter, authority of Parliament or by local custom, has a good title to them. Although the law says that if the thief is convicted the goods should be returned to their true owner, criminal courts are reluctant to order this and prefer to leave the question of 'true ownership' to the civil courts.

### Goods on hire purchase
Where goods are bought and prove later to have been on hire purchase or subject to a conditional sale agreement, the buyer cannot become the true owner because the seller was not entitled to make a sale.

However, there is one important exception. A private person who buys a motor car unaware that it is on hire purchase or conditional sale is protected by the Hire Purchase Act 1964. If, in good faith, he buys a car which was on hire purchase, he is allowed to keep it.

# Buying by post

THE customer who buys goods by post has the same legal protection as the customer who buys from a shop. Goods must be of a reasonable quality in relation to the price paid, and fit for the purpose for which they are bought. Furthermore, advertisements must not be misleading. If these conditions are not met, the customer has the right to claim compensation or, if the goods are totally unusable, to return them and claim his money back. ☐ The law on buying and selling, p. 442.

There may sometimes be risks in buying by post. The customer may have no opportunity to examine the goods before he places an order; in some cases he parts with his money before receiving the goods, so running the risk of fraud. Though such incidents form only a small proportion of all postal buying, two rules apply to all mail-order transactions. Deal only with established companies; and never send money to any organisation which does not give its address in full.

## Goods advertised in the Press

Much of the mail-order business in Britain is conducted through advertisements in magazines, national and local newspapers. When the advertisement states that the money will be refunded if the customer is not satisfied, this promise is enforceable in law. In most cases, advertisements give the customer some protection for, under the Code of Advertising Practice, publishers generally insist that advertisers refund money if a customer has reason to be dissatisfied with goods.

Although this code is not enforceable by law, publishers can exert pressure by refusing further advertisements from doubtful firms.
COMPLAINTS First take up any complaint with the firm concerned. If this fails, inform the advertisement manager of the publication concerned, or the Advertising Standards Authority, 1 Bell Yard, London WC2A 2JX.

## Mail-order catalogues

The other main system of postal buying is by catalogue. The law says that the goods offered in a catalogue must be accurately described. If the goods supplied do not correspond to the description, the customer has the right to return them and claim his money back, provided he gets in touch with the firm promptly.

## Cancelling an order

In law, a sale is not binding until one party has made an offer and the other has accepted. An advertisement or catalogue, however, is not an offer in the legal sense, but an 'invitation to treat'—that is, an invitation to potential buyers to make offers.

▶AN ADVERTISEMENT IS NOT AN OFFER *In 1968 Mr Arthur Partridge put an advertisement in a bird fancier's magazine offering for sale 'Bramblefinch cocks and hens, 25s. each'. These birds are, in fact, protected and in most cases it is illegal to sell them.*

*Mr Anthony Crittenden, an RSPCA inspector, brought a prosecution against Mr Partridge, on the grounds that the advertisement was an 'offer for sale' of a protected bird.*
DECISION *The High Court found him not guilty. It held that the advertisement was an 'invitation to treat' and not an offer for sale in the legal sense. (Partridge* v. *Crittenden.)*◀

When goods are ordered from an advertisement or catalogue, the sale is not binding until the seller accepts the customer's offer to buy. This usually happens at the moment when the goods are actually dispatched by the seller—not when the buyer sends his money.

Until then the buyer can change his mind, and cancel the order. The letter of cancellation should be sent by recorded delivery.

The seller can refuse to go ahead with the sale—under these same rules—perhaps because he has sold all the goods on offer. But if he does so he must refund any money sent with unfulfilled orders.

Where the customer does not write direct to the mail-order firm, but buys through an agent, then the contract becomes binding at the moment the agent accepts the order.

Where the seller offers a specific item and the offer is addressed to the customer by name, this constitutes an offer in law and the contract is binding as soon as the customer sends a letter of acceptance. He does not have the right to cancel the sale just because he changed his mind—unless of course the goods have been offered on approval.

The point at which the contract is made can have an important effect if a dispute between buyer and seller goes to court. The case is heard in the county court for the area where the contract was made.

### Paying for goods by post
The customer should keep the counterfoil of any postal order or cheque sent in payment for mail-order goods. It is advisable, too, to keep a copy of the newspaper advertisement or catalogue from which the goods were ordered.
GOODS ON CREDIT Many of the goods bought by post can be paid for in instalments—either direct to the company or to a local agent.

### Goods on approval
It may be advisable to take advantage of an offer in a newspaper advertisement or catalogue to have goods sent on approval—even if a deposit is required. If the goods are not satisfactory, or if the customer simply changes his mind, he is entitled to return them to the company without obligation and reclaim his deposit. Take care to unpack and rewrap the goods carefully, for the customer is responsible for any damage caused by carelessness.

If the goods have to be signed for when they are delivered, add the words 'accepted unexamined'. This protects the customer if the goods have been damaged in transit.
RETURNING THE GOODS Be sure to obtain a certificate of posting or a receipt from the railway or parcels office. If the goods are then lost before they arrive at the company's address, the customer cannot be held responsible. Always include your name and address with any goods returned.

### Unsolicited goods
People sometimes receive goods they have not ordered. This may be due either to a mistake or to a hoax order. Reputable firms, on being notified what has happened, will either refund return postage or arrange for collection.

Legally, the receiver of unsolicited goods is not obliged to pay for them, nor is he obliged to return them to the sender.

Anyone who receives goods which he has not agreed to accept or to return has two courses open to him.
1. His safest course is to write to the sender saying that the goods are unsolicited, and giving his own name and address and the address from which the goods can be collected. This helps to establish that the goods were not ordered. In the meantime he should keep the goods in a safe place.

From the time he receives the goods until 30 days after he posts his letter, the recipient must not unreasonably refuse to allow the sender to collect the goods. If the sender does not recover them in that time, they become the recipient's property.

To avail himself of this procedure, the recipient must post his letter to the sender not more than five months after receiving the goods (strictly, at least 30 days before the end of six months from receipt).
2. Alternatively, the recipient is entitled to keep the goods for six months from the date he receives them without having to notify the sender. Again, he must keep them safe and not unreasonably refuse to allow the sender to take them back during that time. If, at the end of six months, the goods have not been collected, they belong to the recipient.

Once the goods become his property, the recipient may do whatever he wants with them. Until then, he must not use them in any way, give them away or damage them deliberately—though a court would be unlikely to hold him responsible for accidental damage.

Demanding payment for unsolicited goods without reasonable cause to believe that there is a right to payment is an offence under the Unsolicited Goods and Services Act 1971. An offender can be fined up to £200—or up to £400 if he puts the recipient on a list of defaulters, or threatens to do so; threatens legal action; or invokes or threatens to invoke any other collection procedure.

Naturally, none of these provisions applies to unsolicited advertising material and samples, which become the property of the recipient as soon as he receives them.

### Cash-on-delivery
The Post Office system of cash-on-delivery—where a customer orders goods by post and pays the postman on delivery—is sometimes misused to obtain money by deception. Think carefully before paying for a parcel delivered C.O.D. If no goods have been ordered, refuse to accept it.

If the customer accepts the parcel and pays the postman, he cannot ask the Post Office to take it back later, nor can he get money refunded—even if there was nothing in the parcel.

Report any such incident to the Post Office and the police immediately. The sender is not only breaking Post Office regulations, but he is also guilty of an offence under the Theft Act 1968. The Post Office investigation branch prosecutes where the sender can be found.

# What to do about faulty goods

*A customer's right to change his mind*
*The customer's right to choose*
*Defective or unsuitable goods*

*If the customer is misled*
*Tactics of making a claim*
*Bringing pressure on the shopkeeper*

A CUSTOMER may be dissatisfied with a purchase for several reasons: food may be bad or short weight; goods may be damaged or faulty; a piece of furniture may not fit; a new carpet may be different from the shop's sample; electrical apparatus may be dangerous or may fail to do the job the salesman said it would do.

In some of these cases the customer has the right to legal redress; but he first has to establish legitimate grounds for complaint.

When the grounds are established, there are four ways to pursue the complaint.

COMPLAINING TO THE SHOP In almost all cases, the first step is to take the complaint to the person who sold the goods. The vast majority of genuine complaints, reasonably pursued, will be remedied by the shopkeeper.

BRINGING PRESSURE If the shopkeeper deals unsatisfactorily with a complaint, the customer may get results by complaining to a trade organisation to which the shopkeeper belongs.

PROSECUTION A shopkeeper who gives a customer reason for dissatisfaction may also have broken the law—by selling food unfit for human consumption, for example. In this case, the customer can report the matter to the authority responsible for prosecuting.

CLAIMING DAMAGES When all else fails, the customer may be entitled to take legal action —usually against the shopkeeper, but sometimes against the manufacturer.

If the complaint concerns the quality or suitability of the goods, only the buyer has a right to claim—not, for example, a person to whom the goods were given as a gift. The claim is made against whoever sold the goods —not the manufacturer.

If the complaint is about dangerous goods which have caused injury or damage, the claim is normally made against the manufacturer. Anyone affected is entitled to make a claim— not just the buyer. ☐ Faulty goods: suing the manufacturer, p. 464.

Whichever way the customer decides to pursue his claim, he must act quickly—delay weakens his case. If the bill is unpaid, he will be justified in withholding the money until his complaint is looked into.

Shops are obliged to exchange goods, or to give a customer his money back, only where the law gives the customer specific rights.

Many of these rights can be surrendered if the customer signs an order form, sales agreement, credit-sale agreement, hire-purchase agreement—or even, in some cases, a guarantee. ☐ Buying household goods, p. 448.

### A customer's right to change his mind

Some shops allow customers to change goods no matter what the reason for their dissatisfaction. Where this policy is publicly stated— on a notice or in advertisements—the shop has a legal obligation to keep its promise.

So if the shop promises 'Money back if you are not delighted', it must make the refund when asked to do so, even if the customer's dissatisfaction arises solely because he made a bad choice in the first place.

If a shop has no such policy but an assistant promises that goods will be exchanged, the shop must keep its word. When given no such undertaking, a customer has no legal right to change goods which are not defective.

### The customer's right to choose

Where the customer describes what he wants, the goods supplied must fit the description. This requirement is laid down by the Sale of Goods Act 1893. If the customer asks for a rubber hot-water bottle and receives one made of something else, the shopkeeper must, in law, take it back and refund the money.

The customer cannot complain if he asks for a hot-water bottle by a trade name. If he demands a 'Cosynite', thinking it to be made of rubber, and 'Cosynite' turns out to be metal, he has no right to change it.

When a customer chooses goods from a book of samples in the shop—a carpet, for example, or cloth for a made-to-measure suit— he must be supplied with goods which match the sample.

However, both these rights can be overruled by a written agreement with the shop.

### Defective or unsuitable goods

A customer has grounds for a complaint if the goods fail to meet a certain standard. The Sale of Goods Act says they must be of 'merchantable quality'. This does not mean that the goods must be without blemish. The test is whether a reasonable person, knowing their condition, would still buy them for the price.

The customer has no right to redress, however, if he examines the goods before he buys and afterwards finds a fault which his original examination should have revealed.

In law, expensive goods are expected to be of a higher quality than cheaper ones. Conversely, someone who pays a 'bargain' price, or buys an item in a sale, cannot usually complain if the goods are not of the same quality as goods sold at the normal, higher price.

The customer has a right to claim compensation from a shopkeeper who sells unmerchantable goods; and if the goods cause injury or damage, he may have a right to claim against the manufacturer. ☐ Faulty goods: suing the manufacturer, p. 464.

The terms of an order form, guarantee, sales agreement or credit-sale agreement may deprive the customer of his right to compensation for injury. A similar clause may also rule out compensation for unmerchantable

quality, though such a clause will not protect the shopkeeper if the goods are found to be fundamentally defective.

A customer who obtains goods on hire purchase, no matter what he signs, has a right to claim compensation for unmerchantable goods in all but three circumstances.

The three exceptions are: if the goods are sold as second-hand; if the shopkeeper brings to his notice, before he takes the goods, the fact that they are defective; or if the customer examines the goods before taking them, and should have noticed the defect.

Goods which prove unsuitable for their everyday purpose will give grounds for a complaint under the Sale of Goods Act if they are of a type normally sold by the seller.

But if they prove unsuitable for a special purpose, the customer has grounds for complaint only if he clearly told the seller what he wanted the goods for (and if goods of that type. are normally sold by the seller). Buying a car for towing a heavy caravan might be considered a special purpose.

A customer with special needs—because of

## Repairs under guarantee

FAULTS in manufacture usually occur early in the life of a product, and most manufacturers accept responsibility for the first months or sometimes years of a product's life. After this limited guarantee period, repairs and maintenance generally become the responsibility of the customer.

Read the terms of the guarantee carefully. A typical guarantee states that the manufacturer 'will supply a replacement for or repair any component . . . which is faulty or below standard by reasons of inferior construction or material'.

Some guarantees cover only new parts, and charge the customer for labour. Where a small item has to be sent to the manufacturer's service depot for repair, the customer sometimes has to pay return postage. Under some guarantees, repairs and replacements are not free but a reduced charge is made.

Some guarantees can be used only by the person who buys the goods, not by someone to whom the goods are given as a present or by someone who buys them from the original purchaser during the period of the guarantee.

Where the product has a guarantee, make sure that it is valid. Many manufacturers

refuse to carry out repairs unless, at the time of purchase, the customer posts back the 'registration card' which the customer was given with the original purchase.

Next, find from the terms of the guarantee what the customer has to do to get a repair done. In some cases he must send the product back to the manufacturer, and in others he has to contact an approved local dealer. With large items, such as washing-machines and refrigerators, the customer normally contacts the local service organisation, the address of which will be in the local telephone book.

REJECTED CLAIMS If the manufacturer claims that the guarantee is invalid—perhaps because a card was not filled in and sent off at the time of purchase—the customer may be able to make a claim against the shopkeeper for selling defective goods.

If the guarantee has just expired and a costly repair is necessary, it may be possible to get the manufacturer to share the cost.

Alternatively, there may be grounds for making a claim against the shopkeeper, if this is not prevented by anything the customer has signed (including a guarantee registration card).

illness or allergy, for example—must make this clear to the seller, otherwise there is no claim if those needs are not met.

►THE WOMAN WITH SENSITIVE SKIN *Mrs Griffiths bought a tweed coat in 1939 from a shop belonging to Peter Conway Ltd. Unknown to the salesman, Mrs Griffiths had unusually sensitive skin, and as a result of wearing the coat she suffered a skin complaint—dermatitis. She sued for damages, claiming that the coat was not fit for its usual purpose—that is, for wearing.*
DECISION *Mrs Griffiths lost. Nothing used in making the coat would have harmed the skin of a normal person. Since Mrs Griffiths did not tell the shop that she had abnormally sensitive skin, she could only expect the coat to be reasonably fit for the purpose of being worn by a normal person. (Griffiths v. Peter Conway Ltd.)* ◄

The right to claim compensation because goods are not fit for their purpose can, however, be taken away by something the customer signs, or by a notice displayed in a conspicuous place in the shop.

## Short-weight or poor-quality food
Any shop selling food has an obligation, under the Weights and Measures Act 1963, not to give short weight or measure. ☐ Buying groceries, p. 444.

If the customer gets short weight, he can demand that the shop puts it right. The shop is also committing an offence and can be reported to the local council's weights and measures inspector, who may prosecute.

If convicted, the shopkeeper may be fined up to £100, or imprisoned for up to three months, or both. For a later offence, the maximum fine is increased to £250.

A shopkeeper has an obligation to see that the food he sells is of good quality, fit for human consumption, free from harmful additives and kept in hygienic conditions.

If a shopkeeper sells food which does not meet these standards, the customer has a right to claim. He can also report the shop to the council's public health inspector (in towns) or the weights and measures inspector (in rural areas). A shopkeeper found guilty can be imprisoned for up to three months or fined up to £100 or both. He can also be fined £5 for each day an offence continues.

## If the customer is misled
A customer may be unhappy with what he has bought because it fails to live up to the standards claimed for it by the shopkeeper. In these circumstances, two types of legal action

may be possible. He may have a claim in law against the shopkeeper under the Misrepresentation Act 1967; and he may be able to report the shopkeeper to the weights and measures inspector with a view to prosecution under the Trade Descriptions Act 1968.
GETTING MONEY BACK An untrue statement of fact—a 'misrepresentation'—made by a shopkeeper to induce a customer to buy can give the customer grounds for complaint.

If a second-hand car salesman states that 'this car has been fully and comprehensively overhauled', or 'the tyres have done only 1000 miles', these are statements of fact. If they prove to be untrue, they are misrepresentations, and the customer who can show that he was induced to enter into the contract by a misrepresentation has the right to revoke the contract and ask for his money back. Alternatively, he can claim compensation.

It makes no difference to the claim whether the false statement was made fraudulently or innocently, unless the salesman can prove that he had reasonable grounds to believe, and did believe, up to the time the contract was made, that the statement was true.

However, statements of opinion, or sales 'puffs', give no such right. If the salesman says that a car is 'a real bargain at the price', this is a matter of opinion, not fact, and the customer has no right to rely on the statement.

Where a customer thinks he is entitled to get his money back, he must act quickly. If what a court would regard in the circumstances as an unreasonably long time has elapsed, he will not be able to cancel the contract, although he may still be able to claim compensation.

Anyone who wants to claim under the Misrepresentation Act has to prove that the statements were made and that they were false.
PROSECUTING THE SELLER A shopkeeper or other trader who applies to goods a false trade description or a false indication of price is committing a criminal offence under the Trade Descriptions Act—whether or not he intends to mislead.

A customer who suffers as a result can report the matter to a weights and measures inspector, who has powers to prosecute.

The Act defines a 'trade description' as any description, statement or other indication, direct or indirect, about any one of a number of matters listed in the Act. These include:
The quantity, size or gauge of goods (for example, 'this bedspread is 70 in. × 90 in.').
What they are made of ('pure cotton sheets').
Their fitness for purpose, strength, performance or accuracy ('unbreakable cups').

Any other physical characteristics they possess ('this car is fitted with disc brakes').

Any statement that the goods have been tested or approved ('approved by the Good Housekeeping Institute').

Where the goods were made, when they were made, and who made them.

Any other information about their history ('this car has had only one owner').

False indications of price that are illegal under the Act include:

Descriptions or comparisons between a trader's current price and his own previous price. For example, 'sheets specially reduced from £3·50 a pair'.

False comparisons with a recommended retail price ('recommended retail price for a standard double bed is £59·50, our price is only £50').

Any other indication that a price is less than it really is.

The false description of any of these points can be in writing, or by means of an illustration or other marking on the goods themselves, or in advertising matter. It would, for example, be an offence to show the British Standards Institution Kite Mark when in fact its use was unauthorised. The false description can also be a verbal statement by the trader—but verbal statements are difficult to prove.

Statements made in the Press, on radio, and in films and television broadcasts are not regarded in law as 'trade descriptions' unless they form part of an advertisement.

### Tactics of making a claim

Once a customer is satisfied that he has grounds in law for asking a shop to make amends for something it has sold, he can set about pressing his claim.

Always make the complaint, in the first place, to the shop concerned, and give it a chance to put the matter right. Be sure to speak to the manager, or to the owner if it is a small business.

If a personal approach fails, write a polite but firm letter. Keep a copy of the letter and of any ensuing correspondence.

At this stage it is better not to try to state the legal basis for the claim. Simply set out the complaint fairly and ask what the firm proposes to do about setting the matter right.

### How the shop must make amends

A shop which sells defective or unsuitable goods—or breaks a term of its contract with the buyer—has no right to deny responsibility and simply pass on a customer's complaint to the manufacturer. The buyer can insist that the shop itself makes amends. The only claim a customer can make against a manufacturer is for injury or damage caused by the manufacturer's negligence.

The fact that the shopkeeper did not know, or could not have known, about a defect does not absolve him from responsibility. The law gives him the right to claim against the manufacturer for selling *him* defective goods.

Where there is a fundamental defect or unsuitability in what he has bought, the retail customer has a right to demand his money back. He can refuse to accept a replacement, or credit, at the shop.

Where there is a defect that is not fundamental, the customer is entitled to demand his money back only if he discovers the defect before he is considered in law to have accepted the goods—which usually happens after he has taken the item home and has had a reasonable opportunity to examine it.

After this, he is entitled only to a refund of part of the price to compensate him for the defect. If a reduction in price is agreed, he has a right to cash, not credit.

The customer may be entitled to make further claims. He can claim for damage resulting from the defect—such as the cost of clothes ruined by a washing machine.

In special circumstances, he may be entitled to claim the cost of hiring a replacement while the defective purchase was repaired. He would have to show that the hiring was absolutely necessary—and he might find the court taking a strict view of what is necessary.

### Bringing pressure on the shopkeeper

A shopkeeper who refuses to meet a reasonable claim may be persuaded to change his mind if the complaint is pursued through a trade organisation. □ Complaints: how to bring pressure, p. 478.

Pressure may also be brought to bear through local consumer groups, Citizens' Advice Bureaux and similar organisations.

### Taking legal action

If all else fails, the customer can take his case to court. There are, however, several disadvantages. Going to court involves delay, and a customer with a just cause can still lose his case through lack of the right evidence.

Going to court also costs money, and even the successful customer who wins and is awarded costs cannot expect to recoup all the money spent in bringing the action. If his claim is for less than about £30, he may find that his legal costs swallow up any damages he is awarded. Legal aid is seldom available.

# Faulty goods: suing the manufacturer

*Grounds for claiming*     *Claiming against the retailer as well*
*Who can claim*

T HE customer who is sold faulty or defective goods normally has to seek redress against the seller. But if the goods cause injury or damage because of negligence in the way they were made, the customer or anyone else affected may be able to claim damages from the manufacturer.

The law makes the manufacturer liable for loss or damage caused by his own negligence or that of one of his employees.

### Grounds for claiming

In law, for a claim against a manufacturer to succeed on the grounds of negligence, it must be shown that:

**1.** The manufacturer had a duty of reasonable care to the person claiming damages from him.
**2.** The manufacturer failed in his duty by not taking reasonable care.
**3.** The damage done, which the manufacturer should have reasonably foreseen, was caused by his failure to take reasonable care.

If, for example, a housewife receives a severe shock when she uses an electric iron, and an investigation by a qualified electrician shows that the wiring inside the iron (*not* the plug fitted by the housewife), was wrongly connected, making the earthing system ineffective, the housewife would have a valid case against the manufacturer.

She would be able to claim that he had a duty of care towards her because she was the type of person he would reasonably expect to use the iron. He would also have failed in his duty of care by allowing the iron to be wrongly connected, while the shock she received, which could and should have been foreseen by the manufacturer, was caused by the wiring being wrongly connected.

### Who can claim

Exactly who is entitled to claim damages from a manufacturer depends on the circumstances of the case. But the scope is much wider than with claims for damages against a retailer over defective goods. Claims against a retailer can be made only by the person who purchased the goods and, by doing so, established a contract between himself and the retailer. Claims against a manufacturer can be made by anyone who could reasonably be expected to suffer through his negligence.

If a husband buys a defective iron and his wife or *au pair* girl is injured while using it, they—not the husband—have the right to sue the manufacturer.

▶ THE SNAIL IN A BOTTLE *Mrs Donoghue was bought a bottle of ginger beer by a friend in a café in Paisley, Scotland. The bottle was of dark glass, and neither suspected that it contained anything other than ginger beer.*

*The café proprietor poured some of the ginger beer into a tumbler which contained ice-cream and Mrs Donoghue drank some. As her friend poured the rest of the ginger beer from the bottle into the tumbler, a decomposing snail floated out.*

*Mrs Donoghue subsequently claimed that, as a result of the ginger beer she had already drunk, and the sight of the decomposing snail, she suffered shock and gastro-enteritis. As she had not bought the drink from the retailer, she had no contract with him, and therefore could not sue him. So she sued the manufacturers of the ginger beer. In 1932, the case was taken to the House of Lords.*

DECISION *Mrs Donoghue's right to claim damages was upheld and she received a settlement of £100. The law lords ruled that, although there was no contract between Mrs Donoghue and the ginger beer manufacturers, they owed her a general duty of care in that she was the ultimate consumer. This same principle would also apply to other products. (Donoghue v. Stevenson.)* ◀

A manufacturer may escape paying damages if he shows that, although he or his employees were negligent, it could not have been foreseen that the person injured would use the product.

It is also doubtful whether a manufacturer could be held responsible if someone was injured using his product for some purpose for which it was not intended.

Generally, the manufacturer will not be liable unless damage or injury has been done. If, for example, in addition to giving an electric shock, an iron caught fire, ignited the ironing-board cover and burnt a pair of curtains, damages could be claimed to compensate for the loss of all these items, since the damage was foreseeable and not too remote from the cause.

If the manufacturer can show that the defect was not his fault—that the iron had been tampered with since it had left his factory, for instance—he would not be liable.

It would not be a satisfactory defence, however, for a manufacturer to show that he produced a million irons in the previous 12 months without a hint that any were defective. The fact that one defective iron *did* slip through would usually cancel this defence.

Often, the manufacturer has no defence. If an iron is incorrectly wired there is usually no doubt that he was negligent.

➤ SEEN, TRIED AND APPROVED—BUT STILL DEFECTIVE *A company director, Mr Herschtal, obtained for his firm a car on hire purchase from Stewart & Ardern Ltd. He was driven about 3 miles in the car by one of the garage employees and then signed a receipt for it, stating that it was in good condition and 'seen, tried and approved'.*

*Next morning a wheel fell off the car. Mr Herschtal suffered shock and consequently had to incur medical and other expenses.*

*It was found that the wheel nuts had not been properly tightened for some time and that the threads were stripped. In 1940, Mr Herschtal sued the garage for damages for negligence.*

*Stewart & Ardern claimed that he had been given an opportunity to inspect and adjust the wheel before using the car and that they had no duty to do this for him.*

DECISION *Mr Herschtal won his case. The court ruled that the garage, knowing that the car was to be used immediately, was negligent in not ensuring that it was in a safe condition. The test was not whether the person buying the car had ample opportunity for an inspection of the vehicle, but whether such an examination could reasonably be anticipated by the garage. (Herschtal v. Stewart & Ardern Ltd.)*◄

### Claiming against the retailer as well

The customer who suffers injury or damage may be able to claim damages against the retailer. Two types of action are possible—claiming damages for negligence in selling goods which the retailer should have known to be defective; and claiming damages under the Sale of Goods Act 1893 for failure to supply goods of 'merchantable quality'.

☐ What to do about faulty goods, p. 460.

RETAILER'S NEGLIGENCE A housewife injured by a faulty iron is not likely to have a legitimate claim for damages against the retailer for negligence unless it can be proved that he had good reason to suspect that the goods were defective, but took no action. She might also be able to claim if he did not take sufficient care to see that the iron was safe.

If, for example, people who had bought irons had already returned them and complained that they were given electric shocks, the retailer who, knowing this, sold another would be liable along with the manufacturer.

Anyone who sues both a manufacturer and a retailer for negligence does not receive twice the damages. The amount awarded is paid by the manufacturer and retailer according to the negligence apportioned to each party.

MERCHANTABLE QUALITY Even where the retailer has no reason to know of the dangerous condition of the goods he sells, he should usually repair or replace them when the defect is discovered. In law they will not be of 'merchantable quality'. If he refuses, the buyer can sue for damages, which would be added to those obtained from the manufacturer.

➤ THE CHEMICAL LEFT IN THE WOOL *Dr Richard Grant, of Adelaide, South Australia, bought a pair of underpants manufactured by Australian Knitting Mills Ltd from retailers John Martin & Co. Ltd in 1931. The day after he first wore the pants he contracted dermatitis.*

*Dr Grant claimed that the dermatitis was caused by a chemical in the pants, which had not been removed during the manufacture. He sued Australian Knitting Mills Ltd for negligence in not ensuring that the pants were free from harmful chemicals, and John Martin & Co. Ltd, on the grounds that the pants they had sold him were not fit for the purpose for which they were required and were of unmerchantable quality.*

DECISION *Dr Grant received damages from both the manufacturer and the retailer. The presence of the chemical was a hidden and latent defect which could not be detected by any examination that a customer could reasonably make. Therefore the manufacturers were negligent, and the retailer was held to be liable for a breach of an implied condition of sale. (Grant v. Australian Knitting Mills Ltd.)*◄

Where there are grounds for suing both retailer and manufacturer, it is normally better to start by suing the manufacturer because he is more likely to be able to pay any damages awarded. But a claim can be made against the retailer as well, if the manufacturer shows signs of defending the case. This avoids the danger that, if a claim against the manufacturer fails, one against the retailer will be lost through failure to start it in time.

# Hiring goods

*Down-payments*      *'Snatch-back' and rental increases*
*Copies of agreements*     *Sending the goods back*
*Ending the hire*

T HE hire of a wide variety of goods is be-coming increasingly common. Ordinary hire transactions include everything from a floor-sander or a mechanical roller to radio and television sets. In almost all cases the customer is likely to be met with 'terms and conditions'. If a firm is going to lend an expensive piece of equipment, it needs to protect its investment. A hire company will do this in two ways.

Firstly, it may ask for a deposit, which may range from a small sum to several pounds.

Secondly, the firm will try to protect itself by producing a set of standard terms and conditions of contract; and invariably these bind the customer because they are incor-porated in the hire documents he is asked to sign before taking the equipment.

The best way to judge the advantages and disadvantages of a hire firm's conditions is to compare them with what would be the customer's rights in law if no special conditions were imposed by the hire firm.

LEGAL RIGHTS Normally, the person who hires out the goods has some responsibility to maintain them so that they are fit to do the job they are hired for.

In most cases, the hire firm (known in law as the owner) would be liable to repair any defect in the goods.

HIRER'S OBLIGATION If no special condi-tions are agreed, the hirer has an obligation in law to take delivery of the goods and pay the agreed rental.

The hirer must take reasonable care of the goods while they are in his possession, and he is liable for ordinary negligence; but he is not responsible for fair wear and tear.

HIRE FIRM'S CONDITIONS Except in rare cases, the customer cannot obtain conditions quite like this. He has to accept the goods on terms dictated by the hire firm. But in some fields—television rental, for example—he has a wide choice, and it pays to compare the various agreements.

Few firms allow potential customers to take a copy of their agreement away to study before it is signed, but it can usually be seen in the firm's showrooms.

A customer who comes across a particularly unfair clause can strike it out and ask the shop to accept the amendment. If it will not, he can try to obtain better terms elsewhere.

### Down-payments

There are times when Government regulations require that a down-payment equivalent to the rental charges for a certain period of hire must be made when the agreement is entered into. Unfortunately, the regulations do not say to what purpose that payment shall be devoted.

In most cases the deposit covers the rent for the minimum hire period. In some instances, however, payment of rent starts immediately and continues throughout the hiring, so that the down-payment is an extra charge.

A variation is for the down-payment to cover the rent for a specified interval follow-ing a long period of hiring—sometimes called, misleadingly, a 'rent-free period'.

There is no ready way of learning which of these three situations applies, and only a study of the agreement will reveal the terms the hire firm is imposing.

### Copies of agreements

A firm which hires out goods has no obligation in law to give the customer a copy of the agreement he has signed. Nevertheless, the customer should insist on being given a copy of the agreement, so that he is not left without a check list of his rights and obligations.

### Ending the hire

Whether the customer can terminate the con-tract by giving notice depends on the terms of the agreement. In the case of a short-term hire —for example, of a floor-polisher—the agree-ment is likely to run from day to day. In a longer-term hire—say, of a television set— there may be a minimum hire period, possibly the one laid down by Government regulations, with a break-clause after that period.

It is usual for the owner to reserve the right to terminate the agreement in specified cir-cumstances—if the hirer falls behind with the payments, for example, or goes bankrupt. Some clauses go on to stipulate that, in these circumstances, 'the owner shall be at liberty to remove the goods forthwith without notice, for which purpose it shall be lawful for him to enter into or upon any premises where the goods may be, without prejudice to any other rights that the owner may possess'.

This clause does not give the firm the right to use force to break in, but it places the hirer under an obligation to allow the firm's representatives in to take away the goods.

In practice, the firm is not likely to exercise its right to terminate the hiring and repossess the goods, except as a last resort. Anyone who has something on long-term hire and gets into financial difficulties should approach the firm and discuss this problem.

Some of the television rental firms offer an insurance scheme covering payments during illness or unemployment. It is worth paying a small charge to obtain this extra benefit.

### 'Snatch-back' and rental increases

In hire-purchase transactions, once the customer has paid one-third of the price of goods worth under £2000, no steps can be taken to repossess the goods without the leave of a county court. This is valuable protection where, for example, the hirer dies and his widow wishes to continue with the transaction.

But under a simple hire contract, there is nothing in law to prevent the hire firm from inserting a clause in the agreement giving it the right to take back the goods if the customer falls behind with even a single payment. This may operate harshly in some cases, and it is advisable to try for an agreement where the rental firm cannot 'snatch back' the goods until a number of payments have become overdue.

Hire customers should also be on their guard against agreements which allow the owner to increase the rent payable after a period; it is sometimes possible to obtain an undertaking that the rent will not be increased for a specified period.

Normally, the rent decreases as the years go by until a period of minimum payment is reached. At this stage, some companies demand an increase—usually with a view to getting the customer to take new goods at a higher rent. Usually there is nothing in the agreement to forbid higher charges, and if the customer objects, the firm may terminate the hiring and remove the goods.

### Sending the goods back

Finally, the agreement will usually contain a clause dealing with what happens if the hirer wants to give up the goods before the end of an extended hire period (perhaps to return a black and white television set and obtain a colour set from another firm). The agreement will probably state that, in this situation, the 'hirer shall then pay to the owner a sum equivalent to the rental hire still payable, or which would have been payable for the remainder of the contract, in full and final settlement of all claims, less an allowance for accelerated payment'.

This is a typical 'liquidated damages' clause, representing the owner's assessment of the loss he is likely to suffer as a result of the agreement being terminated. If it is fair and reasonable, it will be upheld in court.

It is only if the sum is unreasonable and out of all proportion to the greatest possible loss that the owner would suffer, that it will be irrecoverable. □ Hiring a car, p. 61.

---

## Damage and repair clauses in hire agreements

The hirer is responsible for the safekeeping of the goods and for their use in a proper and workmanlike manner, and is strictly liable for any loss of or damage to the goods, from whatsoever cause arising, fair wear and tear excepted

The hirer shall not repair or attempt to repair the goods, but shall forthwith notify the owner at his usual business address of any breakdown which occurs while the goods are in his safekeeping

In law, the hirer is responsible if he carelessly damages the property. This clause also seeks to make him responsible for loss or damage through accidental fire or theft. It puts an unfair burden on the customer, unless the hire firm also offers insurance for the goods at a reasonable premium.

If the hirer breaks the terms of this repair clause and does his own repairs he can be made to pay for any damage that results. Better firms may add the undertaking: 'The owner will, on receipt of written notification from the hirer, forthwith repair and maintain the goods as necessary'.

# Repairs and services

*Repairers' legal obligations*
*Problems over sub-contractors*
*Faulty repairs and uncollected goods*

*Laundries and dry-cleaners*
*Complex electrical and clockwork goods*
*Developing and printing films*

THE law gives valuable rights, in theory, to the person who pays to have his property repaired, processed or serviced. They cover, among other things, what happens if repairs are badly done, or if the customer's property is lost or stolen at the repairer's. In practice, it often proves difficult to find a firm which will repair goods without imposing on the customer less favourable conditions than the law allows.

The first step in trying to ensure value for money is to find a firm whose standard conditions of work are fair, or one which will agree to waive some of its more oppressive terms.

**Repairers' legal obligations**
When a customer engages a firm to carry out a repair or service, there is in law a contract between them—a contract for work done and materials supplied.

In such a contract, the firm will be obliged, unless other terms are agreed with the customer, to see that after repair the goods are fit for their intended purpose. A repaired television set must be capable of receiving sound and vision, and a repaired washing machine must be capable of washing clothes.

This applies as long as the purpose is made known to the repairer before he starts work, the repair work is the type the repairer usually performs, and the customer is relying on his skill and judgment.

These terms ensure that, if a repair is done badly, the customer will be entitled to have it done again free of charge and, in certain limited circumstances, to claim compensation —if clothes are damaged, for example, as the result of a faulty washing-machine repair.

Unless other terms are agreed with the customer, a repairer has a duty to take care of goods entrusted to him and to protect them from damage, fire and theft. If the goods are lost or damaged, he will normally be obliged to compensate the customer.

These conditions apply only where the customer and the firm carrying out the repair or service have no special terms agreed between them. In practice, this is rare.

What usually happens is that the firm accepts work under a standard set of conditions, many of them less favourable to the customer than those implied in law.

The firm's own conditions apply as long as the firm observes two rules.

First, the customer must be made aware of the conditions *at the time* he arranges for the repair or servicing. This can be done by handing him a ticket with the conditions printed on it, or by displaying a notice setting out the conditions in a prominent place on the firm's premises.

The customer does not have to read the conditions to be bound by them, but he must be given the opportunity to read them. In cases where the customer receives a ticket from an automatic machine, he must be able to see the notice before he puts in his money.

Secondly, no member of the firm's staff must give the customer a misleading impression of the effects of the standard conditions. If such an impression is given, a court might hold that the standard conditions do not apply.

➤THE WEDDING DRESS DAMAGED AT THE CLEANERS *In 1951 Mrs Curtis took her wedding dress for cleaning to a shop belonging to the Chemical Cleaning and Dyeing Co. The assistant told her that she would have to sign a 'receipt' form, and Mrs Curtis asked why. She was told that it was because the company would accept no liability for damage to beads or sequins. Thus reassured, Mrs Curtis signed.*

*When Mrs Curtis collected her dress it was badly stained. She claimed the cost of a new dress but the company refused to pay, pointing out that the receipt she signed contained a condition exempting the cleaners from liability for damage. Mrs Curtis sued.*
DECISION *Her claim was successful. The court held that the company was not able to rely on the clause because, through the assistant, they had misrepresented the effect of the conditions— albeit innocently. (Curtis v. Chemical Cleaning and Dyeing Co.)*◄

After this case firms began to print conditions saying that no employee had authority to alter or vary the conditions. But a clause to this effect is unlikely to be upheld in law except in very unusual circumstances.

➤THE MOTORIST WHOSE LUGGAGE WAS STOLEN *On January 25, 1967, Mr Alfred Mendelssohn drove a Rolls-Royce into a London garage owned by Normand Ltd. He was going on holiday with his wife, and a suitcase on the back seat contained jewellery.*

*As Mr Mendelssohn was about to lock up his car, an attendant told him that he could not do so. Mr Mendelssohn pointed out that the luggage was valuable, and the attendant agreed to lock the car when he had moved it to its parking place.*

*He failed to do so, and the suitcase was stolen. Mr Mendelssohn claimed £200 from the garage as compensation for the loss of his suitcase, and the garage refused to pay. The owners pointed out that Mr Mendelssohn had been given a ticket containing 'conditions on which vehicles are accepted'. They included:*

*'. . . (The garage owners) will not accept responsibility for any loss or damage sustained by the vehicle, its accessories or contents however caused . . . No variation of these conditions will bind (the garage owners) unless made in writing signed by their duly authorised manager.' Mr Mendelssohn sued.*

DECISION *Mr Mendelssohn won his case. Although the printed conditions formed part of the contract, the attendant's statement that he would look after the car took priority. He had the necessary authority to make the representation, and the court found that his statement was an inducing clause of the contract. (Mendelssohn v. Normand Ltd.)*◄

## Problems over sub-contractors

Sometimes a repairer will accept a job and later pass it on to another firm—perhaps because of pressure of work, or because it is a job which, like cleaning suede or repairing an antique clock, calls for special skill.

This can lead to disputes over responsibility for bad work, and the only sure way to avoid these disputes is to make it clear at the outset that a sub-contractor must not be used.

Where the customer makes no such stipulation, a sub-contractor may be employed in either of two ways: the repairer may ask the customer to choose the sub-contractor; or the repairer can choose the sub-contractor himself.

If the customer chooses the sub-contractor and the work is not done satisfactorily, he will probably have a claim only against the sub-contractor. This may often be unsatisfactory, since the customer will have had no opportunity to inspect or discuss the terms on which the sub-contractor accepts work.

If, however, the repairer makes his own choice of sub-contractor—and he is entitled to do so without asking specific consent,

unless the customer has forbidden it—then the original repairer will be responsible in law for any loss or bad workmanship.

The practical difficulty here is that many repairers are unwilling to compensate a customer for loss or damage caused by a sub-contractor unless legal action is taken.

➤THE STOLEN MINK *In 1962 Mrs Morris sent her mink stole to Mr Beder, of Brook Street, London, to be cleaned. She agreed that it should be sent to C. W. Martin & Sons Ltd, one of the country's largest cleaners. Mr Beder, contracting on his own behalf, entrusted Martins with the fur on conditions which provided that 'goods belonging to customers' were held at customers' risk and that the cleaners would 'not be responsible for loss or damage, however caused'.*

*Martins also agreed to 'compensate the customer for the loss or damage of the goods during processing by reason of the company's negligence or that of its servants or agents but not by reason of any other cause whatsoever'.*

*Mrs Morris's fur was stolen by one of Martin's employees and she claimed damages.*
DECISION *Mrs Morris was entitled to damages because Martins were liable for their employee's act. They could not use the exemption clause because the 'customer' was the furrier, Mr Beder, and the fur was not 'goods belonging to' the furrier. (Morris v. Martin & Sons Ltd.)*◄

## What to do about faulty repairs

The best way to ensure satisfactory repairs is to make sure that the terms are right at the outset. If the repairs are then not done properly, the customer will be legally justified in refusing to pay until they are.

If the customer has already paid the bill, one of the best ways of bringing pressure on the repairer is to complain to a trade organisation to which the repairer belongs. ☐ Complaints: how to bring pressure, p. 478.

If the complaint concerns the repair of something valuable, it may be worth while taking legal advice. Sometimes a solicitor's letter is effective. In other cases it may be necessary to consider suing the repairer. Unless a large amount of money is involved —at least £30—it is unlikely to be worth while.

## Uncollected goods

Anyone who accepts goods in the course of business for repair must keep them safe. In most cases, a repairer can refuse to hand them over until his charges have been paid. He has what is called in law a 'lien' on the goods.

If a customer fails to collect his property, the repairer may have the right, under the

Disposal of Uncollected Goods Act 1952, to dispose of them by public auction.

To avail himself of this right, the repairer must display a notice stating that acceptance of goods is subject to the Act. After a period of 12 months from the time the goods were ready, the repairer can sell them. But first he must send a letter to the customer's last known address giving notice of his intention.

The repairer cannot make a profit on the sale. The balance between the money raised and the amount due is payable to the customer and must be held until he collects it.

## Laundries and dry-cleaners

Small dry-cleaners and laundries sometimes impose highly restrictive conditions which include such terms as:

'Goods accepted at the customer's risk.'

'Compensation is limited in any case to half the cost of the garment or ten times the cleaning charge, whichever is the greater.'

Many laundries use a guarantee drawn up by the Guild of Professional Launderers and Cleaners. This is very much in the customer's favour. One condition states:

'We accept full responsibility for every article entrusted to our care. We undertake to re-process, free of charge, any article considered unsatisfactory, and to compensate fairly in case of loss or damage.'

A list of firms which operate the Guild's guarantee can be obtained from the Guild of Professional Launderers and Cleaners, 16 Lancaster Gate, London W2 3LL. Make sure when choosing a member of the Guild that there are no conflicting terms and conditions which might limit the value of the guarantee.

The same guarantee is operated by some members of the Association of British Launderers and Cleaners, which also investigates complaints about members of the Association. ☐ Complaints: how to bring pressure, p. 478.

## Electrical goods

When a complex piece of electrical equipment breaks down—an electric toaster or a television set, for instance—expert attention is nearly always essential. Once more the customer is likely to be met with widely phrased conditions limiting the repairer's liability.

There are several bodies in the electrical goods field which deal with complaints. ☐ Complaints: how to bring pressure, p. 478.

## Watch and clock repairs

Watches and clocks are delicate and costly pieces of equipment, and they need to be repaired by specialists. This is a field in which it pays to shop around. Many shops have 'minimum charges', and the best way to get value for money is often to take a broken watch to a craftsman with his own business.

Look out for terms and conditions displayed in the shop, and take care if you are asked to sign anything. Terms which can limit the rights of the customer include:

'All work is undertaken by the firm at customer's risk only.'

'All goods belonging to customers, whether upon or in the company's premises, are held or transported at the customer's risk and the company shall not be liable for loss or damage howsoever caused.'

Several trade organisations in the field will investigate complaints against their members. ☐ Complaints: how to bring pressure, p. 478.

## Developing and printing films

Most films taken by customers to the local chemist's shop are processed in a central laboratory. Alternatively, a customer can send a film to the central processing department of the makers. A customer often has to do this with colour film from which slides are made, because he has already paid for the processing in the purchase price. Work is likely to be accepted only subject to the following condition, which is broadly fair:

'We will replace with an equivalent amount of unexposed material any film, negative or print lost or damaged when in our possession for processing or copying. Apart from such replacement and refund of any processing charges paid to us for the said service, we undertake no further liability for loss, damage or delays of whatever nature.'

The customer who takes his film or camera to a photographic dealer may find that the dealer is a member of the Photographic Dealers' Association, which will investigate a genuine complaint about a member. The Association will urge a dealer to settle a justified complaint. ☐ Complaints: how to bring pressure, p. 478.

## Other repairers

The principles involved in dealing with other repairers are the same. Always watch out for onerous clauses trying to shift responsibility for loss of goods or damage to them. If possible, find a repairer who does not impose such conditions.

In some cases, there are no general complaints bodies—in the case of footwear, for example—but the local Citizens' Advice Bureau or a consumer group can often help to bring pressure at local level.

# Calling in a contractor

*How to commission work*  *Calling in an expert*
*Accepting an estimate*  *Work in an emergency*

THERE are many jobs about the house which any competent handyman can do, but sometimes professional help is needed—not only for such jobs as building and decorating, but also for the installation of central heating and plumbing.

## How to commission work

Before calling in a contractor, decide exactly how much work has to be done, then obtain quotations from at least three contractors, telling each one that other estimates are being obtained, so each knows there is competition.

Where the estimates are subject to 'conditions of contract', read the conditions carefully. Once the estimate is accepted, those conditions form part of the contract.

The conditions vary with the type of work, but most of them are drafted to give the contractor more rights and fewer responsibilities than he would have if he accepted work without imposing his own terms on customers.

The contractor may accept no responsibility for bad workmanship, or he may limit his responsibility to defects discovered during a short period after the work is completed.

He may accept no responsibility for defective materials, or limit his responsibility to any compensation he can recover from the manufacturer or his supplier.

The contractor may refuse to accept responsibility for injury or damage resulting from the work or the negligence of his employees.

He may reserve the right to increase the price, and to take away any of the customer's materials (bricks, piping, etc.) which are replaced during the work.

A condition which is common on many contractors' forms is that any dispute arising out of the contract must be referred to an arbitrator. In some circumstances this is a valuable provision for the customer. It binds the contractor to a form of settling disputes which is swift, decisive and relatively inexpensive. ☐ Going to arbitration, p. 719.

There are, however, drawbacks to the clause. It prevents the customer from going to court over the contractor's work. In some disputes the threat of court action—where a contractor's bad workmanship may attract damaging newspaper publicity—may persuade a contractor to meet a claim.

The customer can strike out the clauses he objects to, but the contractor may then be unwilling to accept the job.

WHERE NO CONDITIONS ARE IMPOSED Some smaller contractors do not impose conditions, in which case the work is carried out under rules laid down by common law.

These can be summed up in the words of Lord Justice Edmund Davies who said in a case about a builder in 1968: 'In every building contract, there is to be implied (in the absence of express words to the contrary) a three-fold undertaking by the builder: (a) that he will do his work in a good and workmanlike manner; (b) that he will supply good and proper materials; and (c) that the house will be reasonably fit for human habitation.'

The contractor is also liable for his workmen's wrongful or careless acts, and for damage to customer's property.

THE CUSTOMER'S CONDITIONS The customer can also lay down conditions, although the contractor may not agree to them. The Consumer Council, an independent public body which operated between 1963 and 1971, produced a set of conditions for house decorating and repairs which are very much in the customer's favour.

The set consists of a wallet containing three coloured forms. There is a blue one for the customer to forward his request to the contractor for a quotation and to state exactly what he wants done.

The form has eight conditions printed on the back (with space for extra conditions). The customer fills this in, sends it to the contractor and keeps a copy.

There is also a green form to be sent to the contractor for him to set out his estimate. If the customer is satisfied with the estimate, he sends the yellow acceptance slip.

The conditions on these forms state, in essence, that the contractor will be responsible for doing a good job, and that he will provide suitable materials. He will also be responsible if his employees damage property. The price is not to be altered except for agreed extras, and the value of any materials belonging to the customer which have to be removed will be deducted from the bill.

Distribution of the forms has now been taken over by the Consumer's Association. Sets can be obtained at 5p each from the association's Membership Services Department at 14 Buckingham Street, London WC2N 6DS.

## Accepting an estimate

When deciding which estimate to accept, avoid the temptation to accept the lowest price irrespective of the competence of the contractor. A householder who employs an incompetent contractor runs the risk not only of extra expense to have defective work

put right, but also of claims for damages from anyone injured by the faulty work.

Once the customer has chosen an estimate he should write to the contractor accepting the quotation and instructing him to start work. Keep a copy of this letter (and any subsequent correspondence with the firm).

In the letter it is advisable to say that 'extra work shall be carried out only on my written instructions'. Otherwise extra work will have to be paid for.

## Calling in an expert

On big jobs such as conversions or building an extension to the house, it often pays to call in an architect to help with problems of design,

# Reading the small print on a builder's estimate

Conditions on builders' estimate forms are typical of those used by many other contractors. The chances are that a customer will have to accept them if he wants the work done.

The provisions often attempt, in the interests of the builder, to alter the conditions under which work is carried out by limiting or removing the legal protection the customer would otherwise have If the customer signs the form or agrees that

the work be done on these terms, the small print will be binding in most cases.

The alternative is for a customer to find a contractor who does not impose such terms, or to strike out the clauses which he objects to. A customer is quite free to do this provided he tells the contractor. But where a customer decides to exercise this right, he runs the risk that the contractor will refuse to take on the job

WORKMANLIKE JOB Defects which appear within three months from the completion of the works if proved to be caused by workmanship or materials which are not in accordance with the estimate will be made good by the builder at his own cost. Notice in writing must be given to the builder before the period expires

The contractor is not accepting *full* responsibility for bad workmanship—only for that which is proved to be 'not in accordance with the estimate'. This liability lasts for only three months from the date the work is completed, and the customer must write to the builder before the end of that period, notifying him of any defects that have appeared. In the absence of a clause of this sort, the

contractor's liability in law continues as long as any defects can be positively attributed to his work and not merely to subsequent changes or to wear and tear. This is subject to the rule that a court action must be started within six years of an alleged breach of contract.

If legal action is taken, the court will decide the extent of the contractor's liability

MATERIALS REMOVED Unless otherwise specified, credit has been allowed for any materials necessarily removed to allow the execution of the work

If, during the course of the job, the contractor has to remove the customer's materials (a damaged copper back boiler, for example), this clause gives him the right to keep them without reducing the charge given in the estimate. In cases where, as is

common, no allowance is shown on the estimate for materials removed, such a clause may give the customer cause for suspicion that materials removed, with scrap or re-use value, merely represent an added profit for the builder

planning permission, and so on. ☐ Repairs and improvements, p. 223.

The architect may recommend the use of a form of contract called the R.I.B.A. Agreement for Minor Building Works. Under this, the contractor's obligation is 'with due diligence and in a good and workmanlike manner to carry out and complete the works to the reasonable satisfaction of the architect'.

**Work in an emergency**
When a pipe bursts or a roof starts to leak, there may be no time for estimates. The customer needs repairs done at once.

This does not mean, however, that the customer has to pay whatever the contractor chooses to charge. In these circumstances, the law says that unless the customer has agreed a higher figure with the contractor he is bound to pay only a 'reasonable charge'.

If the contractor's bill seems high, the customer can challenge it. He can also ask other contractors in the same business what would be a 'reasonable charge' for the job, and use this in his negotiations with the original contractor. If he refuses to lower his charge, the customer can pay what he considers reasonable, and invite the contractor to sue for the balance.

The question on which such a case will be judged is: would a contractor in the same line of business consider it reasonable?

---

DEFECTIVE MATERIALS Materials are supplied subject to conditions of sale attached by the manufacturer or supplier. If any materials prove faulty, the builder's liability is limited to such amount as may be recovered from the manufacturer or supplier

Although the contractor agrees to provide all necessary labour, materials and equipment, and to take every care, he does not accept responsibility if materials or goods are faulty. His liability is limited to the amount of money he can recover from his supplier

---

DAMAGE TO PROPERTY The customer should satisfy himself that he is adequately covered by insurance against loss or damage by fire or other risks during building operations. The builder is not liable for loss or damage by fire to the works, materials on site or any property of the customer

The contractor is not responsible for damage to materials or goods he is installing for the customer, even if it is caused by his men's negligence. Nor is he liable if the customer's property is damaged in any way by his employees. Without such a clause the builder would normally insure against the risk. Instead, the clause saves the builder money by throwing the responsibility for insurance on to the customer, who then faces a possible increase in premiums if a claim is made

---

PRICE The words 'prime cost' or 'p.c.' indicate the net amount proposed to be paid by the builder for the supply and/or fixing of the item concerned, together with any cash discount not exceeding 5 per cent the builder can obtain. Should the net amounts paid for prime cost or p.c. items together with such cash discounts prove to be higher or lower, then the difference shall be added to or deducted from the quoted price.
The words 'provisional sum' indicate the amount included to cover a specific item and the estimate is subject to adjustment by substituting for the provisional sum, where the item of work is carried out by a sub-contractor, the amount payable to such sub-contractor, plus a supervisory charge not exceeding 5 per cent, or where the item of work is carried out by the builder a price agreed therefor

By marking items on the estimate as provisional sums, the contractor is covering himself against rises in the price of materials. In fact, it means that he can later increase the price for almost any reason. In practice, the contractor may state: 'Washhand basin to customer's choice, £30 provisional sum'. If the customer chooses a more, or less, expensive basin the price is varied accordingly

# What to do about bad workmanship

*Deducting from the bill*  *Going to a solicitor*
*Appointing an arbitrator*  *Appealing to a trade organisation*

ANYONE who engages a contractor to do a job for him, and finds it done badly, is entitled in law to have the work brought up to standard. This principle applies to a wide range of installation, repair and maintenance work, from servicing a car to installing central heating in a home.

In law, as soon as a craftsman accepts a job and the customer agrees to pay him for doing it, a contract is made, even if nothing is written. The customer's precise rights under the contract depend on the agreed terms, but two conditions apply in almost every case.

First, the customer is entitled to have the work done as requested, using exactly the measurements, materials and finishes specified. If the contractor wishes to make any change in the work, he must get the customer's agreement before going ahead.

Secondly, the customer is entitled to have the work done to what an expert in the relevant trade would consider to be a proper and workmanlike standard (unless otherwise agreed).

Whether the contractor fails to do what is asked of him, or does it badly, the first step in getting the defective work put right is always the same: show him what has gone wrong, ask him to put it right and confirm this request in writing, keeping a copy of the letter.

The defect may be the result of shoddy work by an employee that had gone unnoticed; if so, it will probably be put right without delay. The contractor has no right to charge extra for this, or for repairing any damage which resulted from his firm's bad workmanship.

If, however, the contractor denies that his work was at fault and refuses to put the defect right or demands extra payment for doing so, the surest remedy is to put the matter in the hands of a solicitor, and be prepared, if necessary, to go to court. For those not prepared to spend the time or money, there may be three other courses open: deducting from the bill, appointing an arbitrator or appealing to a trade organisation.

## Deducting from the bill

If the work has not been paid for, the quickest method is to have the defect remedied by another contractor, and deduct all the costs

involved in doing this from the first tradesman's bill; but it is important to follow the correct procedure.

STAGE ONE As soon as bad workmanship is suspected, ask the contractor to put it right. Confirm the request in writing and keep a copy of the letter.

STAGE TWO If he refuses to remedy the fault, it is wise to take the precaution of not paying for the work until it is completed as agreed. Technically the householder may be at fault in doing this, for he is probably breaking his side of the contract. But the contractor whose work is defective will also be at fault, and for this reason a court would be likely to regard the householder's action as justified.

The householder must ensure that he could prove bad workmanship in court, if necessary. How this is done depends on whether the contractor has failed to do what he agreed, or has simply done it badly.

The householder who thinks the contractor has not followed instructions should check against the contract (if there is one), or the estimate or his copy of the letter commissioning the contractor to carry out the work. Any of these may give proof that the contractor has failed to follow his instructions. Where there is no written proof, or where the written evidence is unclear on the point in dispute, there can be no short cut in getting redress; the advice of a solicitor will be essential.

If, on the other hand, the complaint is of work done badly, the customer will need an expert's assessment.

Suppose a lean-to sun-lounge with a sloping glass roof has been built on to a house. A few days after the builder leaves, panes of glass in the roof work loose in a rainstorm, and water pours in, damaging the paintwork. The builder denies that his work is at fault, puts in a bill for £480 and demands full payment.

Unless it was a freak storm or the owner has damaged the roof, bad workmanship must be a prime suspect. To confirm this, call in an expert who can report on the cause of the damage and the likely cost of repair.

This expert may be an independent specialist of high standing (in this case, an architect or surveyor), or a well-regarded craftsman in the relevant trade. The craftsman should be more experienced than the original builder, and preferably an official of the local trade organisation. A professional man may impress a court more if the action ever comes to be tried; but another craftsman may be more convenient, for he can also carry out repairs.

The professional man—but probably not the builder—will charge a fee for his report, say £15·60 together with expenses in this case, but this can also be deducted from the original builder's account if bad workmanship is confirmed by the expert.

The householder should make sure at the outset that the expert who assesses the damage will be willing to repeat his findings in court if necessary.

Suppose, in this case, that a surveyor is called in and finds that a patent glazing system has been used in the construction of the sun-lounge roof, but that the manufacturer's instructions have not been followed. As a result, the roof is not completely waterproof; and the panes of glass have become loose in a strong wind.

He estimates that to remove all the broken panes and replace them correctly will cost about £60. Redecorating the sun-lounge will come to about £20.

The builder's failure to follow the manufacturer's instructions gives the householder good grounds to claim that this is a case of bad workmanship.

Not all cases will be as clear as this, of course. Where there is doubt, the usual test which a court would apply is: would a competent and experienced craftsman in the same trade have done differently?

As soon as there is proof of bad workmanship, again ask the first builder to rectify the defect. If he refuses, the customer can then get another builder to put it right.

STAGE THREE Consider paying part of the original builder's account, while leaving a generous margin to cover the cost of the extra work. In this case the bill is £480, and the architect's fee plus estimated cost of repairs and redecoration come to nearly £94, so it is safe to pay £350. With the cheque should go a letter saying that this is a payment on account, and that any balance will be paid when the cost of the repair work is known.

Paying part of the bill may be useful if the builder decides to take legal action, for it could help to convince the court that the customer has acted reasonably in the dispute —an important consideration when it comes to the award of costs.

On the other hand, the householder may prefer to withhold all payment in the hope that this will persuade the original builder to do the necessary repairs. If the builder does do this, the householder should pay the bill, deducting only the cost of the survey.

STAGE FOUR When repair work has been completed, the householder can settle the bill with the first builder. From his original account, £480, take the cost of bringing the work up to standard, £93·20, and the earlier payment on account, £350, and send him the balance, which is £36·80.

If the contractor feels strongly enough about it, he can take the householder to court; but the householder has no reason to fear this. If the contractor threatens legal action, either personally or through a solicitor, reply by stating that the action will be defended.

If the contractor sues the householder for breaking the contract by not paying in full, the householder's reply should be that he was justified in doing so because the contractor had already broken his side of the contract by not doing the job properly. Technically, this reply might be in the form of either a defence to his claim, or a counter-claim. Either way, the case would then centre on how well the contractor had done the job.

This method is not open, however, if—as in the case of cars and small electrical goods —the bill has to be paid before the goods are returned. The owner of a garage or electrical repair shop is usually within his rights in keeping the goods until he is paid.

At each stage it is important to be able to produce evidence of faulty workmanship— photographs, diagrams and even, where relevant, defective materials.

## Appointing an arbitrator

A useful method of resolving disputes, whether or not the bill has been paid, is to agree to appoint an arbitrator—a qualified, impartial outsider who will examine the facts and decide between conflicting claims.

If there is a contract, it may contain a clause under which customer and contractor agree to refer disputes to an arbitrator and accept his decision; alternatively, the customer may suggest arbitration to the contractor at the time the dispute arises.

The arbitrator will naturally require a fee for his work, but it will often be less, in a straightforward dispute, than the cost of going to court. It is best to decide beforehand who is going to pay this fee—each side may pay half, or the losing side may pay all. Once an arbitrator is appointed, both parties are usually barred from taking the dispute to court, except in unusual circumstances—where the arbitrator has been guilty of misconduct (by taking a bribe, for example) or has made a mistake on a point of law.

### Going to a solicitor

In all cases of faulty workmanship, the ultimate remedy is legal action. If the amount of money involved is large, or the consequences of bad workmanship likely to involve the householder in losses, it may be best to go to a solicitor at the outset.

The law exists to remedy breaches of contract, and a solicitor's training and advice can often be invaluable in sorting out the strengths and weaknesses of his client's own case, and bringing pressure on the recalcitrant contractor to make amends. The great majority of cases are settled without going to court.

If a solicitor is asked to take up the case, he will have to be paid and other legal expenses may arise. A decision on whether to go ahead with the claim will normally depend on the amount of money involved, and the likely cost of legal proceedings. (Even if the householder wins a court action and has costs awarded in his favour, he will usually be left to pay about a third of the legal fees.)

A solicitor will advise whether court action is likely to be financially worth while. It may

## The case of the sun-lounge that let in the rain

A householder is entitled in law to have bad workmanship put right. If a builder's work on a new sun-lounge proves to be shoddy, for example, the householder can take action to have it put right—even if this involves employing another contractor. But the householder must take care to follow the correct procedure and keep the original builder fully informed of his intentions and actions.

---

16 Fernden Way,
Westover

8 March 1971

Dear Mr Wilkinson,

I thought it might be helpful if I sent you written details of the trouble with the sun-lounge which I mentioned on the telephone this morning.

As you probably know, your workmen finished here on Friday. During the heavy rain on Sunday evening we noticed water seeping through the joins between panes of glass in the roof of the sun-lounge. Later whole panes started sliding down the roof, and three came off altogether and fell into the garden. Unfortunately, the rainwater made quite a mess of the inside paintwork.

I am sure that, in view of your reputation for high standards of workmanship, you will want to give the matter your immediate attention.

Yours sincerely,

A. N. Cameron

M.A. Wilkinson Esq.,
Lane, Thorpe and
Clifford (Builders) Ltd,
Seabridge Lane,
WESTOVER

---

REPORT ON DAMAGE TO SUN-LOUNGE
AT No 16, FERNDEN WAY, WESTOVER.

Prepared by:

SPROCKET & RIDGE F/ARICS.,
CHARTERED SURVEYORS,
23, HIGH STREET,
WESTOVER.                    25 March 1971

A report was requested on water penetration through the roof of a new sun-lounge built at the above address.

It is understood that in a recent heavy storm with strong winds there appeared to be some movement in the glass panels of the roof accompanied by severe water penetration which has caused damage to internal

---

16 Fernden Way,
Westover

29 March 1971

Dear Mr Wilkinson,

Thank you for your letter of 16 March, in which you say, 'Examination reveals that the original work on the roof was correctly carried out, and any damage must have been caused by misuse or exceptionally high winds.'

I have had the roof examined by a surveyor, and enclose a copy of his report. He says that the roof leaks because the asbestos cords and storm clips recommended by the manufacturer have not been fitted.

In the light of this, I must ask you again to repair the roof, make good the faulty installation and redecorate the stained paintwork. I cannot agree to your suggestion that I should pay extra for this, since it appears to be necessary solely because the original installation was faulty.

Yours sincerely,

A. N. Cameron

M.A. Wilkinson Esq.,
Lane, Thorpe and
Clifford (Builders) Ltd,
Seabridge Lane,
WESTOVER

---

**Stage one** The sun-lounge is completed, and the builder sends in his bill for £480. Then comes the storm, and the roof begins to leak. Telephone the builder, and send him a firm, polite letter, taking care to keep a copy.

**Stage two** The builder is adamant: no repairs without extra payment. He feels confident that the work is not at fault. But the surveyor you call in finds otherwise. Delay payment, and again ask the builder to make amends.

be possible to obtain legal aid to meet part or all of these legal expenses. ☐ Help with legal fees and costs, p. 710.

### Appealing to a trade organisation
Many of the organisations set up within individual trades undertake to look into complaints against their members. Some give a form of guarantee against major defects. Where the system is as good as this, an appeal to the trade organisation will usually be the first recourse of anyone who fails to get satisfaction from one of its members.

However, no trade organisation operates an effective complaints system for disputes arising from alterations and additions to houses.

The powers of trade organisations to investigate complaints and bring pressure to bear on their own members vary enormously. Check the complaints procedure of the organisation involved before deciding whether to rely on this remedy alone. ☐ Complaints: how to bring pressure, p. 478.

Often it may be safe to complain to a trade organisation while also taking action against the bad workman in one of the ways detailed here. This can be to the public good; a rebuke from his trade organisation is more likely to make a contractor improve his standards than a complaint from an individual.

---

**LANE, THORPE & CLIFFORD (Builders) Ltd.**
Seabridge Lane, Westover  Tel. Westover 334

A.N. Cameron,
16 Fernden Way,
Westover.                                    10 April 1971

    re: Sun-lounge at 16 Fernden Way, Westover.

Dear Sir,

    Thank you for your letter of 29 March and the report you obtained from Sprocket and Ridge. I have

---

16 Fernden Way,
Westover
11 April 1971

Dear Sir,

    Thank you for your letter of 10 April.

    I note that you have read the surveyor's report of the cause of damage to the sunlounge roof. I also note that, despite this, you are not prepared to make good the defective work and redecorate the damaged paintwork without further payment.

    I have therefore decided to have the work done by another contractor. I shall deduct the cost of this from your final account.

    Please find enclosed my cheque for £350, being payment on account of part of your bill of 7 March 1971. The balance, if any, after deducting the cost of this extra work, will be forwarded as soon as final figures are known.

                        Yours faithfully,

                        A.N. Cameron

M.A. Wilkinson Esq.,
Lane, Thorpe and
Clifford (Builders) Ltd,
Seabridge Lane,
WESTOVER

**Stage three** A second refusal from the builder means that you are free to get the repairs done elsewhere. Whatever it costs, you can then deduct from the first builder's bill. In the meantime, send the builder a payment on account.

---

**LANE, THORPE & CLIFFORD (Builders) Ltd.**
Seabridge Lane, Westover  Tel. Westover 334

A.N. Cameron,
16 Fernden Way,
Westover.                                    14 April 1971

    re: Sun-lounge at 16 Fernden Way, Westover.

Dear Sir,

    I am in receipt of your letter of 11 April and the cheque for £350 as part payment of our bill for

---

16 Fernden Way,
Westover
9 May 1971

Dear Sir,

    I have now received notification of the cost of repairing and redecorating the sunlounge built by you at this address, and am able to make a final settlement as follows:

Your account dated 7/3/71                       £480

LESS:
    Surveyor's fees           £15.60
    Repairs to roof            55.10
    Redecorating inside
    walls                      22.50
                                              93.20
                                             386.80
LESS:
    Payment on account dated 11/4/71           350

Cheque enclosed in final settlement         £36.80
                        Yours faithfully,

                        A.N. Cameron

M.A. Wilkinson Esq,
Lane, Thorpe and
Clifford (Builders) Ltd,
Seabridge Lane,
WESTOVER

**Stage four** When the work has been done by a second builder you can make your final settlement with the first. Faced with a serious case of bad workmanship, you have had the defects put right without ending up out of pocket.

# Complaints: how to bring pressure

*Gas and electricity*  *Toys and games*
*Furniture and carpets*  *Cleaners and launderers*
*Clocks, watches and jewellery*  *Cars, motor cycles and car hire*

CUSTOMERS with complaints about defective goods, poor repairs or bad service may be able to enlist the help of a trade organisation to get the matter rectified. Many run complaints investigation services to protect the name of their trade.

►THE MISLEADING DRESS LABEL *Mrs P. complained to the Association of British Launderers and Cleaners Ltd that her dress labelled 'Dry-clean only' had faded during dry-cleaning by one of its members. The association discovered that the makers had attached the wrong label. It should have recommended that the dress be washed, not dry-cleaned.* DECISION *The dressmakers admitted that they were at fault and compensated Mrs P.*◄

All complaints should first be taken up with the retailer, dealer, repairer or—in limited circumstances—the manufacturer.
☐ What to do about faulty goods, p. 460; Repairs and services, p. 468.

If they are unwilling to remedy the fault or refuse to replace the article, the customer can then contact the trade organisation. But it is wise to find out first what provision the organisation makes for dealing with complaints and assess the chances of obtaining a fair settlement. Some organisations, for example, refuse to consider complaints arising out of work done by a member's sub-contractor.

Write in the first instance to the secretary of the organisation. Set out the complaint fully and fairly and give the name of the retailer and manufacturer and any relevant registration numbers. Send copies of receipts or guarantees, not the originals. It is not advisable to send the defective article until asked to do so.

In most cases, any obligation on a trade

## Organisations which can help the customer

### CARAVANS AND CARAVAN PARKS
National Caravan Council
40 Piccadilly
London W1V 0ND

**Membership**
750 members, including manufacturers, distributors, caravan-park operators and component manufacturers
**Complaints procedure**
The council will investigate complaints provided the matter has not already been referred to a solicitor for action. If the council cannot settle a dispute it may appoint an arbitrator acceptable to both parties. But if the complaint is not proved, his fee may have to be paid by the customer
**How to find a member**
List available from council

### CAR AND VEHICLE HIRE
British Vehicle Rental &
Leasing Association
47 Windsor Road
Slough, Bucks

**Membership**
400 members, representing well over 60 per cent of the industry
**Complaints procedure**
The association sets standards of operation and vehicle safety for its members and investigates all complaints against members. It first acts as mediator. If this fails to resolve the dispute, there is a right of appeal to its committee of management. A dispute may also be referred either to the association's legal adviser or to an independent arbitrator
**How to find a member**
Look for the association's sign

organisation either to investigate a complaint or deal with it satisfactorily is moral, not legal. But where an organisation gives a guarantee it will be obliged to comply with the terms of the guarantee.

➤THE CRUMBLING BUNGALOWS *Sixteen people who bought new bungalows at Rushyford, Co. Durham, found within a year of moving in that floors were subsiding and internal walls cracking. They complained to the builder, who did some repairs, then went into liquidation.*

*The buyers approached the National House-Builders Registration Council, which had guaranteed the houses. The council discovered that the wrong material—red colliery shale—had been used beneath floor slabs.*
DECISION *The N.H.B.R.C. paid for two of the bungalows to be demolished and rebuilt and for major repairs to five others. The cost varied from £1000 to £5000 per bungalow. The council also met the cost of accommodation for seven families who were evacuated while work was carried out.* ◄

Action taken on complaints varies widely from one organisation to another. Some do no more than urge their members to make amends. Others have powers to discipline or expel members who repeatedly give poor service. A minority follow a strict complaints procedure and call in an arbitrator if they are unable to settle the dispute themselves.

➤A WRANGLE OVER CAR REPAIRS *After a garage belonging to the Motor Agents' Association had repaired his car, Mr J. complained that their charge was excessive and that some of the work was unsatisfactory.*

*An independent engineer called in by the M.A.A. confirmed that, while the charges were reasonable some of the work was defective. Neither Mr J. nor the garage accepted this report, but agreed to the M.A.A.'s offer of independent arbitration.*
DECISION *The arbitrator confirmed that the charges were fair, but directed the garage to pay Mr J. compensation to cover the cost of rectifying the work which was defective.* ◄

Some organisations even have funds to recompense any customer who suffers through one of their members going out of business.

Anyone considering consulting a solicitor to press his complaint should not wait until the trade organisation has completed its investigation, as delay may prejudice his legal claim and lead to evidence being lost.

---

## CLEANERS AND LAUNDERERS

Carpet Cleaners Association
P.O. Box 3
Harpenden, Herts.

**Membership**
118 full members and 12 associate members
**Complaints procedure**
If the association cannot settle a dispute, it gets an independent assessment from either the Dyers' and Cleaners' Research Association or the Retail Trading-Standards Association
**How to find a member**
Write to the association

---

Association of British
Launderers and Cleaners
22 Lancaster Gate
London W2 3LL

**Membership**
Nearly 2000 members, representing 85 per cent of the laundry trade and 70 per cent of the dry-cleaning trade
**Complaints procedure**
If the association's services advisory bureau cannot resolve a dispute between a customer and a member, the association's fabrics investigation committee will examine the garment and make an independent assessment
**How to find a member**
List available from the association

---

NOTE: This directory of trade organisations includes several independent, non-trade bodies which either give consumer advice or investigate consumer complaints

continued▶

## Organisations which can help the customer continued

### CLOCKS AND WATCHES

British Horological Institute
35 Northampton Square
London EC1V 0ET

**Membership**
3500 members, representing about 45 per cent of the clock and watch servicing industry
**Complaints procedure**
The institute tests any clock or watch which is the subject of a complaint. If the institute finds that the complaint is justified, the member is asked to put the repair in good order without charge. The repaired clock or watch is then tested again by the institute before being returned to the complainant
**How to find a member**
Look for the certificate of membership or emblem which members display, or write to the institute for the name and address of the nearest member

British Watch and Clock
Makers' Guild
65 Clyde Road
London N15 4LS

**Membership**
About 1500 members, representing the retailing, distribution and repair sections of the watch, clock and jewellery trade
**Complaints procedure**
The guild offers help and advice in disputes with members and non-members alike. If the dispute cannot be resolved it may be referred to the guild council, which consists of experts from all branches of the trade
**How to find a member**
Look for the guild emblem, which most members display

### COAL AND SOLID FUEL APPLIANCES

Coal Utilisation Council
19 Rochester Row
London SW1P 1LD

**Membership**
1100 coal merchants, 500 solid-fuel appliance distributors and 3000 appliance installers are members of the council's service schemes. The 1100 coal merchants registered under its diploma scheme account for about half of all domestic solid-fuel sales
**Complaints procedure**
The council deals with complaints about solid-fuel appliances or heating systems. The quality or delivery of solid fuels are outside its scope, although any substantiated complaint against a coal merchant holding the council diploma will be investigated
**How to find a member**
Look for council symbols, or contact the regional office

Approved Coal Merchants'
Scheme
Derbyshire House
St Chad's Street
London WC1H 8AE

**Membership**
Represents nearly all retail coal merchants
**Complaints procedure**
All complaints, except those about prices, are dealt with under the scheme. Regional panels act as arbitrators. Complaints about panel decisions go to the independent chairman of the National Panel
**How to find a member**
Look for the emblem of the scheme at coal merchants' offices and on delivery lorries

Domestic Coal Consumers'
Council
Thames House South,
Milbank
London SW1P 4QE

**Membership**
Independent body representing the interests of coal consumers
**Complaints procedure**
The council handles any complaints not resolved by the Approved Coal Merchants' Scheme. Write to the secretary of the council

## CREDIT AND HIRE PURCHASE

Hire Purchase Trade
Association
3 Berners Street
London W1E 4JZ

**Membership**
2750 members, but excluding those hire-purchase companies who are members of the Finance Houses Association (next entry)
**Complaints procedure**
Ask the local citizens' advice bureau to contact the association. The association then acts as an independent assessor
**How to find a member**
Look for the membership plaque or write to the head office

---

Finance Houses Association
14 Queen Anne's Gate
London SW1H 9AA

**Membership**
33 members, who transact 85 per cent of all instalment credit business undertaken by finance houses in the U.K.
**Complaints procedure**
The association will take up legitimate complaints by the public against its members, but if this does not result in a settlement it is unlikely that an independent arbitrator will be called in
**How to find a member**
List available from the association

---

## CYCLES AND MOTOR CYCLES

National Association of Cycle
and Motor Cycle Traders
31a High Street
Tunbridge Wells
Kent

**Membership**
1500 members, representing 60 per cent of the retail cycle trade and 40 per cent of the lightweight motor cycle trade
**Complaints procedure**
Most complaints dealt with by the association are made by customers against manufacturers, although it will also handle complaints against member retailers. Complaints about work carried out by a sub-contractor are excluded. The association does not refer unresolved disputes to an independent party. Nor can it provide redress if a customer suffers because one of its members goes out of business.
**How to find a member**
Look for the association's symbol in the dealer's window

---

Cycle and Motor Cycle
Association
Starley House
Eaton Road
Coventry CV1 2FH

**Membership**
150 members, representing manufacturers and wholesalers of bicycles, mopeds, scooters, motor cycles, three-wheelers, accessories, components and specialised clothing
**Complaints procedure**
The association investigates complaints against members, but it cannot impose a solution. There is no independent assessment
**How to find a member**
Ask the dealer if he belongs to the association

---

## ELECTRICITY AND ELECTRICAL INSTALLATIONS

Electricity Consultative
Councils

**Membership**
There is an electricity consultative council for each of the areas served by the electricity boards. Members are appointed by the Government to represent the interests of consumers
**Complaints procedure**
Complaints should first be made to the local electricity board office. If the dispute is not resolved, it should be passed to the secretary of the area consultative council for investigation.
Addresses of the area boards and consultative councils are in the telephone directory

continued ▶

## Organisations which can help the customer continued

Electrical Contractors'
Association
55 Catherine Place
London SW1E 6ET

**Membership**
2300 members, representing more than 85 per cent of all electrical-installation work carried out by private contractors
**Complaints procedure**
The association guarantees the work of its members against bad materials or workmanship. The complaint must be made within 12 months of the completion of the contract and the association will appoint a competent engineer to inspect and report. If the report is adverse, the association will see that the defect is rectified either by the original contractor or, if necessary, by another firm. The association will also investigate complaints which are made against members' activities as electrical-equipment retailers, but no separate guarantee of this equipment is offered
**How to find a member**
Look for the symbol of the association, write to the association's head office or consult the area electricity board

National Inspection Council
for Electrical Installation
Contracting
Trafalgar Buildings
1 Charing Cross
London SW1A 2DT

**Membership**
6700 electrical contractors are on the council's roll of approved electrical-installation contracts
**Complaints procedure**
The council deals with all complaints about the work of approved contractors on its roll, including complaints about his sub-contractors. If a complaint is made, the council's local inspecting engineer meets the contractor on site, together with the complainant if possible. If the inspecting engineer finds the work is not up to the standard of the Regulations for the Electrical Equipment of Buildings, published by the Institute of Electrical Engineers, then the contractor must put it right without charge
**How to find a member**
The council's roll of approved electrical-installation contractors is available in all citizens' advice bureaux, electricity board showrooms and most public libraries

### FOOD, DRINK AND DAIRY PRODUCE

National Dairymen's
Association
Freeth House
37 Queen's Gate
London SW7 5HS

**Membership**
About 5000 members, handling 85 per cent of milk which is sold by private dairymen
**Complaints procedure**
Complaints are investigated either by a regional secretary or by the head office
**How to find a member**
Write to the association

Rice Council
2 Hampstead High Street
London NW3 1PT

**Membership**
The council has no members as such, but exists to promote United States rice, which is handled in Britain by about 30 producers and packers and accounts for about 60 per cent of the total market
**Complaints procedure**
The council handles complaints about the condition of rice products at the time of purchase and their performance in cooking. Complaints are taken up with producers or packers and the purchase is usually replaced by them
**How to find a member**
Products promoted by the Rice Council bear its symbol

## FOOTWEAR REPAIRS

St Crispin's Boot Trades
Association
St Crispin's House
Desborough
Nr Kettering
Northants

**Membership**
Approximately 4500 members, representing almost three-quarters of
the shoe-repair trade
**Complaints procedure**
The association deals only with complaints against shoe repairers
(*not* manufacturers). Its technical adviser will make a free check on
the article, but if this does not resolve the dispute, he may refer it for
independent assessment to the Shoe and Allied Trades Research
Association, to which St Crispin's is affiliated
**How to find a member**
Look for the association's sign

## GAS SUPPLY AND INSTALLATIONS

Gas Consultative Councils

**Membership**
Gas Consultative Councils have operated by Act of Parliament since
the gas industry was nationalised in 1948. Their members consist of
all types of gas users, advised by gas industry experts
**Complaints procedure**
Complaints should first be made to the local gas board office or
showroom. If the dispute is not resolved it should be referred to
the secretary to the area consultative council
Addresses of the area boards and councils are in the telephone
directory. Lists of members and council secretaries are displayed in
gas board offices and showrooms

## HAIRDRESSING AND WIGS

Incorporated Guild of
Hairdressers, Wigmakers
and Perfumers
4 The Broadway
Woodbridge Road
Guildford, Surrey

**Membership**
The guild has 3000 members
**Complaints procedure**
The guild will try to settle complaints about wigs and hairpieces, al-
though in practice few are found to involve its members. If the guild is
unable to resolve a complaint against one of its members, it is usually
able to give advice about putting the case to the local authority's
weights and measures department or help with obtaining legal advice
**How to find a member**
Look for the membership plate

## HEATING AND VENTILATING

National Heating Centre
34 Mortimer Street
London W1N 8AR

**Membership**
Nearly 200 heating engineers, all of whom are legally committed to
give a two-year guarantee backed by insurance
**Complaints procedure**
The centre investigates all complaints concerning domestic heating
systems installed by its members which are still covered by its two-
year guarantee. This insures each installation against fault. If the
guarantee has expired, the centre refers the complaint to the registered
engineer and asks him to put it right. The last resort is arbitration, and
the complainant pays the costs if the decision goes against him.
Charges for inspecting a system are £3·15 (3 gns) an hour. Where,
due to bankruptcy or liquidation, repairs cannot be done under the
guarantee by the installing engineer, the centre commissions another
registered engineer to do the work free of charge
**How to find a member**
Write to the centre

continued ▶

## Organisations which can help the customer continued

National Heating Consultancy
Gardner House
188 Albany Street
London NW1 4AP

**Membership**
41 members, all professionally qualified, self-employed consultant engineers. It is a condition of membership that they have no vested interest in manufacturing, marketing, installation or fuel supply

**Complaints procedure**
The consultancy, a non-profit-making body, will (among other services) investigate complaints about defective domestic-heating installations. The fee for its services, including inspection and report, is £3·90 an hour, plus expenses. If requested to do so by both parties, the consultancy acts as mediator and, if necessary, as arbitrator. It also provides expert witnesses in legal actions

**How to find a member**
Members work through the head office. Write to the consultancy, giving full details of the complaint and asking for an estimate of the inspection fee

---

Heating and Ventilating
Contractors' Association
Coastal Chambers
172 Buckingham Palace Road
London SW1W 9TD

**Membership**
Nearly 800 members, 500 of whom are in the domestic heating and ventilating business

**Complaints procedure**
The association operates a scheme which guarantees the installation against faulty performance, bad workmanship or defective materials for two years. Any faults are rectified by the association, if necessary at its own expense.

The scheme also provides that if a member goes bankrupt or into liquidation the association honours the guarantee at its own expense, to a limit of £250 per installation and £1000 per member. If a dispute under the guarantee goes to an arbitrator the complainant pays a deposit of £25, which is refunded if he wins

**How to find a member**
Write to the association

---

Insulation Glazing Association
6 Mount Row
London W1Y 6DY

**Membership**
200 members representing about 85 per cent of the double-glazing work carried out in Britain

**Complaints procedure**
All complaints against the workmanship of members are investigated. If the complaint appears to be genuine, the association urges the member to put the matter right.

It makes no provision for independent assessment of a dispute, but it will provide the names of independent consultants to whom a complainant may refer

**How to find a member**
Write to the association

---

### HOLIDAYS AND DOMESTIC AND FOREIGN TRAVEL

Association of British
Travel Agents
50-57 Newman Street
London W1P 4AH

**Membership**
Over 4000 travel agents and tour operators

**Complaints procedure**
The association refers complaints to a special department for evaluation. The association will provide an alternative agency to arrange a replacement holiday free of charge if a member goes out of business through insolvency

**How to find a member**
Look for the ABTA symbol, or write to ABTA for a list of members

National Villa Association
57 North Hill
Colchester,
Essex

**Membership**
Four members, who are engaged in renting holiday villas abroad
**Complaints procedure**
The association has an independent tribunal, composed of a barrister, an accountant and a journalist—none of whom is connected with the travel trade. Complaints are referred to the tribunal, the findings of which are binding on NVA members
**How to find a member**
Write to the association

## HOUSEHOLD GOODS AND APPLIANCES

Federation of British
Carpet Manufacturers
Brook House
2-16 Torrington Place
WC1E 7JP

**BRITISH CARPET CENTRE**

**Membership**
43 members, all carpet manufacturers (*not* retailers) representing about 80 per cent of the trade. Fourteen of these sponsor the British Carpet Centre which advises the public on Axminster and Wilton woven carpets
**Complaints procedure**
On receiving a complaint, the federation contacts the manufacturer. If no settlement can be reached the dispute may be referred, by agreement, to the federation's panel of arbitrators.
   A member of the panel will visit the complainant and inspect the carpet; the merits of the case are decided by his report. The panel's services to the consumer are free.
   Alternatively, the complainant and manufacturer may submit the matter to an independent textile-testing house. The cost is likely to be around £5 and must be paid by the 'loser'
**How to find a member**
Look for the British Carpet Centre symbol and/or a brand label stating that the manufacturer is a member of the federation

Tufted Carpet Manufacturers'
Association
Royal Liver Chambers
8 Silver Street
Bury
Lancashire BL9 0EX

**Membership**
30 members, representing 80 per cent of the trade. Membership restricted to *tufted* carpet manufacturers operating within the U.K.
**Complaints procedure**
If a dispute is not settled after being referred to the manufacturer, the association advises the complainant to take the matter to the Retail Trading-Standards Association, which acts as an independent arbitrator. The cost of a technical analysis of carpet by the Retail Trading-Standards Association is not less than £6·30 (6 gns), which is charged to the complainant if the RTSA finds in favour of the manufacturer
**How to find a member**
Contact the association

National Association of
Retail Furnishers
3 Berners Street
London W1P 3AG

NATIONAL ASSOCIATION

OF RETAIL FURNISHERS

**Membership**
1650 members with 4000 shops, representing about 70 per cent of the trade by value
**Complaints procedure**
The association investigates most complaints about furniture (but *not* usually carpets). The complaint is taken up with the retailer if he is a member of the association, and if the dispute is not then satisfactorily resolved the association may appoint an arbitrator agreed by the customer, retailer and supplier. This is usually another retailer. There is no charge for this service
**How to find a member**
Look for the association's symbol or write for a local list

continued ▶

## Organisations which can help the customer continued

National Federation of
Ironmongers
20 Harborne Road
Edgbaston
Birmingham B15 3AB

**Membership**
6500 members, representing about 50 per cent of the hardware, ironmongery and D.I.Y. trade
**Complaints procedure**
Complaints are passed first to the director, then referred either to the appropriate department or to one of the 43 local associations which comprise the federation.

The federation tries to ensure that the retailer puts the matter right at his own expense. No provision is made for independent assessment of a dispute
**How to find a member**
Look for the symbol of the federation, which is displayed in most members' shops

---

Sewing Machine Dealers'
Association
5 Great James Street
London WC1N 3DA

**Membership**
300 members, representing about 55 per cent of the domestic trade and 90 per cent of the industrial trade
**Complaints procedure**
Unresolved disputes are referred for arbitration to the association council, which appoints a member to inspect the machine. The council's decision is final.

Most association members sell new machines under the SMDA guarantee. If the dealer goes out of business while the machine is still covered by guarantee, the association assumes liability and appoints another dealer to carry out repair work without charge for the remainder of the guarantee period.

Under the Reciprocal Service Scheme a machine which is still under guarantee may be serviced or repaired by a dealer other than the one who sold it. No charge is made, except for the cost of collection and delivery
**How to find a member**
Look for the association's badge, which is displayed by most members, or contact the association

---

### HOUSES, FLATS AND MAISONETTES (NEW)

National House-Builders'
Registration Council
Hill House
Hill Avenue
Amersham, Bucks.

**REGISTERED
HOUSE-BUILDER**

**Membership**
About 17,000 builders and developers, representing 99 per cent of all firms building homes for sale
**Complaints procedure**
The council investigates complaints against member-builders under the terms of its House Purchaser's Agreement. In general, the builder agrees to put right at his own expense any defects which may arise as a result of his failure to comply with the council's standards of workmanship and materials. This covers both major and minor defects for up to two years. The council will step in if the builder is unable or unwilling to do the work.

Any major structural defects will be investigated for up to ten years after the issue of the certificate, but the purchaser must pay an investigation fee and the first £15 of any valid claim after the sixth year. The council can also recompense a house-purchaser by up to £1000 if the builder goes bankrupt
**How to find a member**
Look for the symbol on new housing estates or consult the council's official register which is available in public libraries, citizens' advice bureaux and building-society offices

## INSURANCE COMPANIES AND BROKERS

Corporation of
Insurance Brokers
15 St Helen's Place
London EC3A 6DS

**Membership**
Nearly 4000 elected members, representing 1156 firms

**Complaints procedure**
The member firm is asked for an explanation, which is usually sufficient to settle disputes. There is no provision for helping members of the public who suffer from a member firm going bankrupt. But every firm has to prove its solvency each year and must take out an indemnity policy for not less than £100,000

**How to find a member**
Write to the corporation

---

British Insurance Association
P.O. Box No. 538
Aldermary House, Queen
Street, London EC4P 4JD

**Membership**
286 members

**Complaints procedure**
The association takes each complaint to the chief executive of the company concerned. If disputes are not settled there is no provision for independent arbitration

**How to find a member**
Write to the association or ask at the local citizens' advice bureau

---

Association of
Insurance Brokers
Craven House, 121 Kingsway
London WC2B 6PD

**Membership**
About 2000 individual members in about 1000 firms

**Complaints procedure**
The association deals only with complaints against members and will act as an arbitrator

**How to find a member**
Look for the association's badge and certificates and the words 'Associated Insurance Brokers' after the firm's name. Individual members can use the letters F.A.I.B, A.A.I.B or M.A.I.B after their names

---

## JEWELLERS AND GOLDSMITHS

National Association of
Goldsmiths
St Dunstan's House
Carey Lane, London EC2V 8AB

**Membership**
2800 retailers

**Complaints procedure**
The association deals only with complaints against members, and takes them up with the retailers concerned. There is no provision for independent assessment of complaints

**How to find a member**
Look for the association's emblem in retail jewellers' windows or ask the retailer whether he is a member

---

## LEATHER AND LEATHER GOODS

Leather Institute
Leather Trade House
9 St Thomas Street
London SE1

**Membership**
The institute exists to promote the British leather trade and looks after its interests

**Complaints procedure**
The institute deals with complaints and inquiries about leather goods and arranges for allegedly defective goods to be tested by the British Leather Manufacturers' Research Association. The complainant may be charged a small fee. If a complaint is justified, the institute asks the firm involved to put the matter right

**How to find a member**
Look for the leather symbol to ensure that an article is genuine leather, not imitation

continued ▶

## Organisations which can help the customer continued

---

### MAIL ORDER PUBLICATIONS

Association of Mail Order
Publishers
1 New Burlington Street
London W1X 1FD

**Membership**
15 firms, all those foremost in the mail order publishing business
**Complaints procedure**
The association has set up the Mail Order Publishers' Authority for the purpose of investigating complaints and enforcing a Code of Practice. Write, initially, to the director of the association outlining the facts and quoting, if possible, the reference number allotted by the mail order firm
**How to find a member**
Membership lists and copies of the Code of Practice are available free from the association. Members show the association sign on their promotional literature

---

### MOTORING—GARAGE SERVICES

Scottish Motor Trade
Association
3 Palmerston Place
Edinburgh EH12 5AQ

MEMBER OF
THE S.M.T.A.

**Membership**
1900 members, representing about 75 per cent of the retail motor trade in Scotland
**Complaints procedure**
The association's investigations committee takes up customers' complaints with members. A dispute which cannot be resolved by negotiation may be referred to arbitration if both sides agree to accept the findings
**How to find a member**
Look for the membership badge. Most members also display the association's emblem on their stationery

---

Motor Agents' Association
201 Great Portland Street
London W1N 6AB

**Membership**
18,500 members (including members of the Scottish Motor Trade Association), covering about 90 per cent of the trade
**Complaints procedure**
The association deals with all complaints except those about guarantees on new vehicles, which should be taken up with the manufacturer and dealer. Other complaints should be made to the association within three months of the transaction. In cases where the association cannot resolve the dispute, it has facilities to appoint an independent arbitrator if the customer and the association member agree to accept his findings. Both parties have to pay a £5 deposit. If the arbitrator finds in the complainant's favour, the deposit he has paid will be refunded
**How to find a member**
Look for the association's sign or ask the garage if they are members

---

### PHOTOGRAPHIC SALES AND SERVICES

Photographic Dealers'
Association
1 Bedford Square
London WC1B 3QS

**Membership**
4000 members, representing more than 75 per cent of annual turnover in the retail trade
**Complaints procedure**
In the case of members, the association urges the dealer to resolve a justified complaint. Disputes which cannot be resolved in this way are referred to the association's governing body, the National Council of Photographic Dealers.
The association does not take up complaints against non-members
**How to find a member**
Look for the sign of the association which many members display

---

## RADIO AND TELEVISION SALES AND RENTALS

Radio and Television
Retailers' Association
100 St. Martin's Lane
London WC2N 4BD

**Membership**
2500 members, representing two-thirds of the total sales turnover of television sets and about half the turnover in rentals

**Complaints procedure**
The association deals with all complaints against members, including cases where the public suffers as the result of a member going out of business. If a dispute cannot be resolved, the association asks the complainant's permission to submit it to an independent expert

**How to find a member**
Look for the association's symbol in the dealer's window

## TOYS, GAMES AND PLAY EQUIPMENT

British Toy Manufacturers'
Association
Regent House, 89 Kingsway
London WC2B 6RS

**Membership**
350 members, representing more than 90 per cent of toy production

**Complaints procedure**
When complaints cannot be satisfactorily resolved through the retailer, the association will refer complaints against members to the manufacturer. When a complaint is considered valid the manufacturer is urged to make good the defect or provide a replacement

**How to find a member**
Contact the association

## TRANSPORT—BRITISH RAILWAYS

Transport Users'
Consultative Committees

**Membership**
Committee members are appointed by the Secretary for the Environment from nominations by public bodies, industry, commerce and voluntary and social organisations to represent as wide a cross-section of rail transport users as possible

**Complaints procedure**
The committees consider any matter affecting the facilities and services provided by British Railways. Complaints should first be made to the railways. If they are not resolved, the secretary of the area committee should be contacted

**How to find a member**
Railway stations will provide the address of the secretary of the area T.U.C.C. Their addresses are also shown in telephone directories

## GENERAL ADVICE ON CONSUMER COMPLAINTS

Citizens' Advice Bureau
(National Council)
26 Bedford Square
London WC1B 3HH

**Membership**
Independent, national body with local offices

**Complaints procedure**
A citizens' advice bureau can help inquirers to seek solutions to their problems by offering practical information and advice, by explaining legislation, and by putting them in touch with the appropriate person, organisation or local authority or Government department. For example, a citizens' advice bureau knows which local solicitors are on the Legal Advice Panel list (although they do not make recommendations), which local builders are members of the National House-Builders' Registration Council, and which local authority department deals with various types of consumer complaint

**How to find a member**
Citizens' advice bureaux are usually found in large towns and some smaller market towns. Addresses and telephone numbers can be obtained from public libraries, post offices and local councils

489

# Choosing the type of credit

*Where to go for credit*  *Checking a customer's credit-rating*
*Split agreements*  *Credit-rating classification*
*Promissory notes*

SEVERAL types of credit are available for people who cannot afford, or do not wish, to pay cash for goods or services. The two factors to consider when making a choice are what interest is charged and what conditions are imposed.

Find out, for example, whether the credit agreement is likely to limit your right to compensation if the goods prove faulty or unsuitable. Is it possible to get a reduction in interest charges by repaying the money early? If illness or accident reduce income unexpectedly, can the goods be sent back and payment stopped? At what stage can the goods be sold? What undertakings have to be given to the lender by the prospective client to obtain credit?

## Where to go for credit

BANK LOANS Apart from interest-free terms offered by some shopkeepers as an added inducement to buy, a bank overdraft or personal loan is frequently the cheapest form of credit. The sum borrowed is usually repaid over an agreed period, not necessarily in fixed instalments falling due on stated days. Interest is charged periodically on the outstanding debt, not on the full sum originally borrowed. Depending on current income-tax legislation, some or all of the interest paid by the borrower may qualify for tax relief.

Bank loans and overdrafts are subject to Government restrictions, and from time to time customers may be able to borrow only for favoured purposes—extending a house, for example, or financing a business. ☐ Personal loans and second mortgages, p. 506.

HIRE PURCHASE In law, hire purchase is an agreement under which the customer rents the goods with the right to buy them after a certain number of payments have been made.

The goods do not become the property of the customer until the final payment has been made, and he cannot sell them earlier without the permission of the owner—the shop or a finance company. The owner of the goods can normally take them back if the customer does not pay, or breaks some other condition of the agreement. ☐ Hire purchase, p. 498.

CONDITIONAL SALE Similar in most respects to hire purchase is the conditional-sale agreement. But there is a technical difference in law between the two. In the case of hire purchase, the customer has the right to buy the goods at the end of the agreement—but he is not obliged to do so. With conditional sale, the customer agrees at the outset to purchase the goods. This form of agreement is not common as a method of obtaining credit.

CREDIT SALE When a customer buys the goods and pays for them by instalments, this is known as credit sale. The customer owns the goods as soon as he signs the agreement and they cannot be taken back by the finance company. If the customer cannot meet the repayments he is entitled to sell the goods and repay the debt. ☐ Credit sale, p. 503.

CREDIT CARDS A customer with a credit card buys goods on credit and pays monthly to the company issuing the card. Interest is charged only if the monthly bill becomes overdue.

BUDGET ACCOUNTS Many stores operate budget accounts, sometimes known as revolving credit, which give the customer the right to buy goods up to an agreed figure with a set monthly repayment. As each payment is made, further credit is available up to the maximum allowed to the customer.

CHECK TRADING The customer buys checks or vouchers from a check-trading organisation. He pays for the checks by instalments and uses them to buy goods from stores which grant this facility. ☐ Credit for small purchases, p. 509.

PERSONAL LOAN Personal loans are granted either by finance houses or by 'fringe' banks. Repayment is made at regular intervals and interest charges vary. National Giro recommends a company operating a similar loan scheme. There is no restriction on the purpose for which a loan can be used. It can even be used for a completely different purpose to the one for which it is granted. Depending on current income-tax legislation, part or all of the interest may qualify for tax relief.

Since there may be no connection between the organisation granting the loan and the person selling the goods, the customer has no right to send the goods back if he has repayment difficulties. If he fails to pay, the lender can sue to recover the money.

SECOND MORTGAGE If the customer is a householder, and can offer part of the value of his house as security, he can apply for a second mortgage. The terms are similar to those for personal loans, but second mortgages are easier to obtain.

PAWNBROKERS A loan for a small amount over a period of about six months can be obtained by 'pledging' goods with a pawnbroker—leaving them as security against the loan. If the loan is not repaid in time, the pawnbroker has the right to sell goods on which he lent up to £2, to recover his money. Goods on which more than £2 has been lent have to be sold at a public auction. The owner can claim, within three years of the sale, any profit made by the pawnbroker.

MONEYLENDERS A loan from a moneylender is the most expensive way of borrowing money and interest rates of up to 150 per cent are charged, though the moneylender may not be able to take legal action to claim unpaid interest over 48 per cent. ☐ Personal loans and second mortgages, p. 506.

PRIVATE BORROWING An individual who borrows money privately may be asked to sign an I.O.U. as an acknowledgement of the debt. If the debt is not repaid, the I.O.U. itself does not give grounds for legal proceedings. However, the lender can take action to recover the debt, and the I.O.U. document is useful evidence if there is a dispute. ☐ Suing to recover a debt, p. 725.

### Split agreements
Sometimes a customer is offered two contracts to sign—one a cash-sale agreement with the dealer, and the other a loan agreement with the finance company. In law, these two transactions are in no way tied. They are commonly known as 'split agreements'.

Many home improvements—such as central heating—are sold in this way. Often the contractor arranges for the purchaser to borrow the money and pay him in cash.

Split agreements have a major disadvantage for the customer. If the goods turn out to be faulty he cannot withhold instalments as a way of bringing pressure on the contractor, since the money is owed not to the contractor but to a finance company.

Many garages which offer cars for sale on 'easy terms' operate split agreements of this kind. Most of the sources of finance are reputable companies, and they normally require the vehicle to be assigned to them as security for the loan. This gives them the right to 'snatch back' the vehicle if the buyer falls behind with payments. Moreover, true

interest rates charged by finance companies on such loans are often as much as 30 per cent.

Equally unfavourable split agreements are sometimes found in the retail television trade, when a TV set is bought with a loan and repayments are made through a coin-collecting device attached to the set.

### Promissory notes
Other similar agreements require the borrower to sign a promissory note for repayment. When he does so, the customer acknowledges his debt for the full amount of the loan and promises to pay it back by instalments. If he defaults, the finance company may sue for the whole amount outstanding even if the goods are returned.

Sometimes the technicalities of a credit arrangement can work in a customer's favour.

►THE CAR THAT WAS RETURNED *Arthur Stimson paid a first instalment of £70 to a dealer in Stanmore, Middlesex, for a £350 Austin. He took the car away two days after signing a hire-purchase agreement form. However, in law, it was not an agreement but merely an offer by Mr Stimson to enter into a hire-purchase agreement with a company called Financings Ltd.*

*One clause on the form read, 'this agreement shall become binding on the owner (Financings Ltd) only upon acceptance by signature on behalf of the owner, and hiring shall begin then'.*

*After two days, Mr Stimson returned the car*

## Drawbacks of a personal loan

**4** I/We further understand that the loan will be secured by an instalment promissory note and the whole amount payable under the note will become payable immediately in the event of default in making any payment for one month from its due date.

Personal loans from finance houses usually require the borrower to sign a promissory note. If he falls behind by a single month's payment, the whole debt becomes due at once. The hire-purchase customer in a similar position may be allowed by a court to make reduced payments. The personal-loan borrower with defective goods cannot return them and end the agreement, as can the hire-purchase customer

to the dealer, saying he no longer wanted it. He was unsatisfied with its condition and performance. The night before the acceptance was signed by Financings Ltd—four days after the car was returned—it was stolen from the dealer.

Eventually the car was recovered, though badly damaged. Financings Ltd then claimed damages from Mr Stimson for breach of contract. DECISION The claim failed on two grounds. First, said the Court of Appeal, by returning the car to the dealer, Mr Stimson had revoked his offer before it had been accepted. Secondly, Mr Stimson's offer was conditional on the car being in substantially the same condition at the time of acceptance as it was when the offer was made. As this was not so, Financings Ltd's 'acceptance' was of no effect. Mr Stimson even got his deposit back. (Financings Ltd v. Stimson.)◄

**Checking a customer's credit-rating**
Anyone over the age of 18 can obtain credit, provided he or she is considered to be a good risk. The credit-worthiness of applicants for some types of credit is determined by making inquiries about their ability to meet the instalment payments and their past records in similar transactions.

The customer fills in an application form giving his name, address, occupation, place of work, age, the type of accommodation he lives in and whether he rents, leases or owns it.

If a person gives false information on a proposal form when applying for any type of credit, he can be prosecuted for committing a criminal offence. Some people are tempted, when applying for an advance, to overstate their income or underestimate their expenses, so as to give a more favourable picture of their circumstances.

► THE MISLEADING MORTGAGE APPLICATION Mr Webb, a partner in a Staffordshire motor-repair firm, applied to a building society for a mortgage. On the application form he stated that he was earning £1250 a year, though in fact he was earning much less than that. He also claimed that he was manager of the firm.

The building society wrote to the firm for confirmation of these facts. Mr Webb intercepted the letter and forged his partner's signature on the reply. As a result, the building society granted the mortgage advance and issued two cheques to him.

When the true facts became known, the Director of Public Prosecutions was informed. He decided to prosecute and Mr Webb was tried at the Staffordshire Assizes in 1961. DECISION The court sent Mr Webb to prison for six months, after he had pleaded guilty on three charges, one of which was causing the building society to execute cheques by false pretences. This had resulted from the false information he had given. (R. v. Webb.)◄

If the customer is under 18 or lives in furnished accommodation, he will almost certainly be asked to provide a guarantor—someone who will assume the liability to pay if the person responsible fails to do so. The guarantor fills in a similar form and he then becomes the main subject of inquiry.

Application forms are sent by the shop or dealer to the finance company, which passes details to a credit-checking agency. NATIONAL CREDIT REGISTER The register contains details of outstanding debts to companies which subscribe to it. It also has information about court judgments, bankruptcy judgments, and distress warrants against persons who have defaulted with their rent. It is sometimes known as the credit 'blacklist', though it gives information which is favourable to the customer as well as that which is unfavourable.

If the customer has bought anything on credit before, there is likely to be a file on him, which can be compared with the personal details supplied on the credit application form. Provided they agree—or can be explained if they differ—and the file is 'clean', no further inquiries are normally necessary.

Even an unfavourable entry on the file does not necessarily bar the customer from getting credit. It may show, for instance, that a county court order was made against him ten years earlier. If he can prove that his financial circumstances have since changed for the better, he may still get credit.

But an order made, say, only two years previously would almost certainly bar him. OTHER AGENCIES If the applicant is not listed on the National Credit Register, many finance companies use credit-investigation agencies which keep files—usually local—similar to those of the Register.

The address the customer has given is checked. Most agencies have copies of the electoral registers for the areas they cover. These show whether a customer is over 18 and, by marking people's names with a letter J, indicate that they are eligible for jury duty. Such people are considered good credit risks unless there is evidence to the contrary.

If the customer is not listed on the files or on the electoral register under the address given, an agent may make personal inquiries.

Local government officers may be persuaded

to confirm addresses and establish whether the applicant is a house-owner or tenant. An individual policeman may be willing to check whether the applicant has a criminal record, and trades groups can vouch for his standing with local shopkeepers.

### Credit-rating classification

When the agent completes his inquiries, the applicant is classified confidentially as: a fair risk; a fair risk, provided that he offers a suitable guarantor; or a bad risk.

A customer classified as a bad risk is not likely to be granted credit, unless he can convince the shopkeeper or finance company that the classification is a mistake.

The company is not obliged to give a reason for refusing credit, and a customer who suspects that he has been wrongly classified as a bad risk may have no way of confirming his suspicions or challenging the classification. Where a customer believes a mistake has been made, he should nevertheless draw it to the attention of the person responsible in the finance company concerned, and ask for it to be rectified.

## Working out the true interest rate

A CUSTOMER obtaining goods on credit often has difficulty in discovering the true rate of interest he is paying. The dealer or finance company is obliged by law to state the cash price, number of instalments, amount of each instalment and the total sum to be paid. But there is no obligation to cite the rate of interest.

The dealer or shopkeeper may mention a rate, but this will probably be the flat rate—a misleading figure, since it is calculated as if none of the money borrowed were repaid until the end of the period, whereas, of course, the amount outstanding will be gradually diminishing.

A true rate of interest is one that is calculated periodically on the amount of loan outstanding. As a rough guide, the customer can find the true rate by multiplying the flat rate by 1·8.

A more precise way to work it out is given by the table. First divide the total amount borrowed by the monthly repayment. Take that figure, find the figure nearest to it in the appropriate repayment column and read off the true interest rate on the left.

Take the case of a £200 loan, repayable on monthly instalments of £10 over two years and quoted at a flat rate of 10 per cent interest. To convert to a true rate, divide the total amount borrowed (£200) by the monthly repayment (£10), giving an answer of 20. The figure in the table under 24 months closest to 20 is 20·030. Read the true rate of interest on the left—18 per cent.

REPAYMENT PERIOD in months

| TRUE INTEREST RATE | 6 | 9 | 12 | 18 | 21 | 24 | 27 | 30 | 48 |
|---|---|---|---|---|---|---|---|---|---|
| 5 | 5·913 | 8·815 | 11·681 | 17·307 | 20·067 | 22·794 | 25·487 | 28·146 | 43·423 |
| 6 | 5·896 | 8·779 | 11·619 | 17·173 | 19·888 | 22·563 | 25·198 | 27·794 | 42·580 |
| 7 | 5·879 | 8·743 | 11·557 | 17·040 | 19·710 | 22·235 | 24·914 | 27·448 | 41·760 |
| 8 | 5·862 | 8·707 | 11·496 | 16·909 | 19·536 | 22·111 | 24·635 | 27·109 | 40·962 |
| 8½ | 5·854 | 8·689 | 11·465 | 16·844 | 19·449 | 21·999 | 24·497 | 26·941 | 40·571 |
| 9 | 5·846 | 8·672 | 11·435 | 16·779 | 19·363 | 21·889 | 24·359 | 26·775 | 40·185 |
| 9½ | 5·837 | 8·654 | 11·405 | 16·715 | 19·277 | 21·780 | 24·224 | 26·610 | 39·804 |
| 10 | 5·829 | 8·636 | 11·375 | 16·651 | 19·192 | 21·671 | 24·089 | 26·447 | 39·428 |
| 10½ | 5·820 | 8·619 | 11·344 | 16·587 | 19·108 | 21·663 | 23·955 | 26·285 | 39·057 |
| 11 | 5·812 | 8·601 | 11·315 | 16·524 | 19·023 | 21·445 | 23·822 | 26·125 | 38·691 |
| 12 | 5·795 | 8·566 | 11·255 | 16·398 | 18·857 | 21·243 | 23·560 | 25·808 | 37·974 |
| 13½ | 5·771 | 8·514 | 11·167 | 16·212 | 18·611 | 20·931 | 23·174 | 25·342 | 36·933 |
| 15 | 5·746 | 8·462 | 11·079 | 16·030 | 18·370 | 20·624 | 22·796 | 24·889 | 35·931 |
| 16½ | 5·722 | 8·411 | 10·993 | 15·850 | 18·133 | 20·324 | 22·428 | 24·447 | 34·969 |
| 18 | 5·697 | 8·361 | 10·908 | 15·673 | 17·900 | 20·030 | 22·068 | 24·016 | 34·043 |
| 21 | 5·649 | 8·260 | 10·740 | 15·327 | 17·448 | 19·461 | 21·372 | 23·186 | 32·294 |
| 24 | 5·601 | 8·162 | 10·575 | 14·992 | 17·011 | 18·914 | 20·707 | 22·306 | 30·673 |
| 27 | 5·554 | 8·066 | 10·415 | 14·668 | 16·590 | 18·389 | 20·072 | 21·645 | 29·170 |

# Comparing the type of credit

| | HIRE PURCHASE | CREDIT SALE |
|---|---|---|
| Deposit/ premium or security | Minimum deposit may be fixed by Government regulation on many goods | Minimum deposit may be fixed by Government regulation on many goods |
| Period and method of repayment | Up to three years in weekly, monthly, or quarterly instalments. Maximum period sometimes fixed by Government regulation | Up to three years in weekly, monthly, or quarterly instalments. Maximum period sometimes fixed by Government regulation |
| Interest | Between 5 and 15 per cent flat is normal but *TRUE* rate of interest is often almost double | Between 5 and 15 per cent flat is normal, but *TRUE* rate of interest is often almost double |
| Right to cancel | Customer can cancel within three days of receiving second copy of agreement —but only if first copy was signed away from trade premises. However, on goods worth over £2000 there is no right to cancel | Customer can cancel within three days of receiving second copy of agreement if total credit price is over £30 and not more than £2000 and agreement is signed away from trade premises |
| Rights if goods are faulty. ☐ What to do about faulty goods, p.460 | Company must repair or replace faulty goods free of charge unless defects are specified in agreement. In many agreements over £2000, customer's rights to free repair or replacement are excluded | Customer's rights to free replacement or repair are excluded by many agreements |
| Right to send goods back if customer cannot afford payments | Customer can send goods back (though not if they cost over £2000) if he cannot afford payments. But he must normally make up half of total purchase price and pay all outstanding payments at the time he sends goods back | No right |
| When customer can sell goods | Goods must not be sold until the final payment without the written consent of the dealer or finance company | Goods can be sold at any time, but agreement may require balance of debt to be paid off immediately |
| What happens if customer fails to pay | Dealer or finance company can repossess the goods only by obtaining a court order if one-third total purchase price has been paid. However, in most cases involving £2000 or more, owner can repossess immediately without court order | Owner can sue to recover the debt, and the court may order customer's goods to be seized |
| What happens if customer repays early | Customer may receive a small rebate | Customer may receive a small rebate |

| BANK LOAN/OVERDRAFT | FINANCE-HOUSE LOAN | SECOND MORTGAGE |
|---|---|---|
| Security such as shares required for a large loan or overdraft | No security needed | Security provided by mortgage on customer's house |
| Period by arrangement; customer pays into account at regular intervals | Up to ten years by monthly repayments | Up to ten years by monthly repayments |
| Overdrafts a certain percentage above bank's base rate. Loan is about 12 per cent *TRUE* | 10 to 15 per cent flat but *TRUE* rate is about double | Varies between 15 and 25 per cent *TRUE* rate |
| No right | No right | No right |
| Same as if the customer pays cash | Same as if the customer pays cash | Same as if the customer pays cash |
| No right | No right | No right |
| At any time | At any time, but agreement may require balance of debt to be paid off immediately | At any time |
| Owner can sue to recover the debt, and the court may order customer's goods to be seized | Owner can sue to recover the debt, and the court may order customer's goods to be seized | Finance company can apply for court order to force sale of property to repay the loan |
| Interest ends when customer stops using overdraft. He may receive small rebate on the loan but he could have to pay full interest charge | Customer will usually receive a rebate, but could have to pay full interest charge | Customer will usually receive a rebate, but could have to pay full interest charge |

continued ▶

## Comparing the type of credit continued

| | INSURANCE LOAN | CREDIT CARD |
|---|---|---|
| Deposit/ premium or security | Surrender value of policy—that is, the current paid-up value | No security needed |
| Period and method of repayment | Usually repaid with policy premiums, though terms vary and loan may be carried separately | By monthly repayments, usually up to about one year |
| Interest | General *TRUE* rate is about 8 to 10 per cent, though it can be lower and may be written into policy | No interest if account is cleared within one month. About 20 per cent *TRUE* rate payable on overdue accounts |
| Right to cancel | No right | No right |
| Rights if goods are faulty. ☐ What to do about faulty goods, p. 460 | Same as if customer pays cash | Same as if customer pays cash |
| Right to send goods back if customer cannot afford to pay | No right | No right |
| When customer can sell goods | At any time | At any time |
| What happens if customer fails to pay | As long as interest is paid the loan may often be allowed to carry on, since the policy's value increases all the time with premiums | Customer can be sued for debt and the court may order his goods to be seized to pay the debt |
| What happens if customer repays early | Interest stops when loan is repaid | Interest stops when loan is repaid |

| BUDGET ACCOUNT | CHECK TRADING | MONEYLENDER | PAWNBROKER |
|---|---|---|---|
| First instalment paid in advance usually serves as deposit, unless goods are subject to Government regulation minimum deposit | First instalment is accepted as deposit | No security needed | The item pawned is security for the loan |
| By weekly or monthly instalments up to agreed number (usually 8 to 12), unless fixed by regulation | By weekly instalments over about 21 weeks for checks; up to 100 weeks for vouchers | By weekly or monthly instalments. No fixed limit | Goods returned if loan is repaid within six months |
| Around 5p in the £. *TRUE* rate is about 10 per cent | Checks at 5p in the £ (but *TRUE* rate is up to 25 per cent). Vouchers at $12\frac{1}{2}$ per cent (*TRUE* rate is much higher depending on repayment period) | Between 15 and 150 per cent *TRUE* rate. Over 48 per cent, courts may refuse to enforce excess | Between 20 and 25 per cent, depending on loan. If loan is over £5, more interest can be charged |
| No right | No right | No right | No right |
| Same as if customer pays cash but, as the seller is being paid, customer may be in better position to withhold instalments | Same as if customer pays cash, though check firm may intervene to help the customer | Same as if customer pays cash | Same as if customer pays cash |
| No right | No right | No right | No right |
| At any time | At any time | At any time | At any time |
| Customer can be sued for debt and the court may order his goods to be seized to pay the debt | Customer can be sued for debt and the court may order his goods to be seized to pay the debt | Customer can be sued for full amount owing, plus interest charge. But the court may re-examine interest rate if excessive | After six months, goods worth £2 or less become the pawnbroker's. If worth more, they are sold by public auction and the owner can claim any profit within three years of sale |
| Customer may receive a small rebate | No rebate | Rebate unlikely | No rebate |

# Hire purchase

*How the law helps*  *Sending the goods back*
*Early repayment*  *Arrears in payments*
*Cancelling the agreement*  *Signing an agreement*

THE most common form of credit is hire purchase. The customer pays a deposit on the goods, a finance or hire-purchase company pays the dealer the balance, and the customer then repays the balance in instalments to the finance company.

Hire purchase is most commonly used for articles which retain a substantial value if they have to be repossessed during the period of the agreement—like furniture and cars. It offers the customer one of the safest forms of credit available, if the total sum involved is less than £2000.

Special safeguards under the Hire Purchase Act 1965 apply to agreements of £2000 or under and ensure that the customer receives a fair deal if he wants to return the goods or if he cannot pay for them.

However, he is not allowed to sell or dispose of the goods during the period of the agreement. If he 'fails to keep up the payments, the company may be entitled to take back the goods. TERMS From time to time, Government regulations lay down minimum deposit and maximum repayment periods permitted on hire-purchase transactions.

## How the law helps
A hire-purchase agreement is defined in the Hire Purchase Act 1965 as one under which the customer takes the goods on hire initially, with a clear option to become the owner at a later stage, if he so wishes.

Where the cost of the goods plus the cost of credit is £2000 or less, all forms of hire purchase are covered by the Act, though the provisions of the Act in some cases differentiate between new and second-hand goods. Where the total of price and charges is over £2000, the customer has no special rights other than those in the agreement.

In transactions of less than £2000, the customer is protected in three important ways.
1. The owner or seller guarantees that he has the right to sell the goods. This is a technical matter and simply means that if someone else is able to prove that the goods belong to him, then the customer can reclaim the money he has paid to the owner or seller. So if a car has been repossessed by a finance company and a second customer has taken it on hire purchase, the second customer is protected if the first customer tries to get it back.
2. The goods must be free from serious defects—in the condition the law calls 'merchantable quality'. Goods are considered in law to be not of merchantable quality if a reasonable man, knowing of any defects in them, would refuse to take them for the price.

This protection for customers who are sold defective goods applies to hire-purchase agreements for new goods of £2000 and less. It will even apply where the customer has to sign an agreement which appears to rule out claims of this sort—*unless* the firm can show that the exclusion clause was brought to the customer's attention, and its effect made clear to him, before he signed.

This protection does not extend to goods which are second-hand or sold as defective.

If the goods are unsatisfactory, the customer should write immediately to the finance company, or the supplier, asking for a replacement or a free repair. If the goods supplied are seriously defective, he is entitled to repudiate the agreement and claim his money back; or he can ask for—and if necessary sue for—a reduction in his payments.
3. The goods must be reasonably fit for the purpose for which they are required, provided that the customer makes known what he wants them for—or that this is obvious.

Dealers or finance companies can include a clause in the agreement which absolves them of this liability, but they must show it to the customer and explain it before he signs.

## Early repayment
If the customer decides to repay the amount outstanding in a lump sum at any time during the period of repayment, the law gives no special right to have the interest charges reduced. The finance company may grant a small rebate for early settlement.
NEGOTIATED REBATES If the dealer gives an undertaking—if, say, he promises there will be a rebate for prompt or early payment—this may be binding on the finance company.

The Hire Purchase Act 1965 makes the dealer the agent of the finance company for any representation made about the goods. So any promise he makes to induce the customer to take the goods is binding on the company.

► A CAR SALESMAN'S PROMISE *On September 19, 1952, Mr George Andrews was driving along in a small 1934 saloon which he had bought second-hand from a Leeds motor dealer. The car swerved suddenly and collided with a lorry. An inspection showed that the steering column was badly worn and that various other things were wrong or missing. Mr Andrews, who was badly injured, sued on the grounds that the salesman who had supplied the car on hire-purchase terms had described it as a 'little beauty' and promised he would have 'no trouble with it'.*
DECISION *The motor dealer was ordered at Leeds Assizes in 1956 to pay Mr Andrews damages of £645 on the grounds that his sales manager's statement amounted to a warranty that the car was in good condition and reasonably safe for the road. (Andrews v. Hopkinson.)* ◄

## Cancelling the agreement

In most cases, once the agreement has been signed it is too late to cancel it—that is, to end the agreement without incurring any liability. An exception is when the sale was made 'outside of regular trade premises'—on the doorstep or in the home. The customer is given a copy of the agreement and is sent a second copy by post. He has three days from receiving the second copy in which to cancel. ☐ Buying on the doorstep, p. 456.

An agreement cannot be cancelled outright because the customer discovers that he cannot keep up the payments. If payments stop, the customer is liable for the agreed balance.
INSURING AGAINST FAILURE TO PAY Some finance companies offer free insurance against inability to keep up repayments on a loan because of sickness, unemployment or death. The insurance provides for continuation of regular payments.

Where the company does not provide insurance, the customer can arrange his own.

## Sending the goods back

If the customer cannot afford to continue the hire-purchase payments or wants to return the goods, he can return them only if he pays or has paid the equivalent of half the total amount of the agreement, and all instalments due up to the date when the goods are returned. But if this would be unfair and would give the owner an unreasonably large profit, a county court could reduce the amount.

The customer must also pay for any damage caused by his failure to take reasonable care of the goods while in his possession.

The right to return the goods is valuable when the customer feels he has made a bad bargain. It may be better from his point of view to send the goods back and pay half the money due rather than to keep them.

If he wishes to pay less, he can wait for the finance company to sue him and then try to persuade the court to reduce the amount.

## Arrears in payments

If the customer falls behind with payments, the finance company may be entitled to take the goods back. Once one-third of the total price has been paid, however, the company cannot do so without a court order.

When a finance company applies for a repossession order, the court generally makes an order allowing the customer to keep the goods as long as he pays reduced instalments.

When a customer dies before the agreement is completed, his widow has no legal right to keep goods on hire purchase, but many finance companies write off the outstanding balance.

## Signing an agreement

Every hire-purchase agreement must contain a 'red box', warning the customer that it is a hire-purchase agreement and that he will be legally bound by its terms.

The agreement must contain a statement of the cash price and the total purchase price, including the hire-purchase charges. The customer must also receive a copy of the agreement at the time of signing.

The customer who takes a few simple precautions when he signs the agreement avoids difficulties later on. Make sure all blank spaces on the agreement have been filled in with ink and check that cash figures are those agreed. Do not sign a form without the 'red-box' warning—it may well be a simple hire agreement under which the customer never owns the goods.

Never sign a second form. It could be a 'split agreement'—a method sometimes used to avoid hire-purchase legislation. ☐ Choosing the type of credit, p. 490.

## When hirer becomes owner

An essential feature of a hire-purchase agreement is that the ownership of the goods does not pass to the hirer until he exercises his option to purchase. The option is a written provision stating that if certain conditions are complied with—notably making all the payments required by the agreement—the hirer may buy the goods for a nominal sum.

# Reading the terms of a hire-purchase agreement

Hire-purchase agreements provide shoppers with a safe form of credit for sums of less than £2000; but in return for the safeguards conferred by the Hire Purchase Act 1965, the customer has a number of obligations towards the seller of the goods, known as the owner. These obligations are set out in detail on the agreement form he signs. There is no standard form, though Form HP1, prepared by the Hire Purchase Trade Association, is widely used where the total cost of goods and interest charges is less than £2000. Even the design of parts of the form, such as the red box containing the warning to the customer, is controlled by law.

**2** Provided the Hirer shall have meanwhile duly performed and observed all the terms and conditions of this Agreement the goods shall become the Hirer's property if and when the total amount paid under Clause 1 hereof shall equal the total hire purchase price thereof, but until such time the goods shall remain the sole property of the Owners and the Hirer a mere bailee thereof. The Hirer shall be fully responsible for maintaining the goods in good order and condition and for all loss thereof or damage thereto however occasioned (fair wear and tear only excepted) but nothing in this clause contained shall authorise the Hirer to create or allow to be created a lien upon the goods or any of them in respect of repairs or otherwise.

## THE AGREEMENT

The customer must keep the goods safe and not allow anyone to take them because of a debt—called taking a lien on the goods. This might happen if a garage kept a car because the customer could not pay for repairs

**3** The Owners do not let the goods subject to any warranty or condition express or implied save those set out in the Hire Purchase Act. Furthermore it is hereby expressly **Agreed** and **Declared** that the condition as to fitness for a particular purpose which would otherwise be implied by the Hire Purchase Act shall be wholly excluded, and that the condition as to merchantable quality shall be:

(a) wholly excluded where the goods are let as second-hand and stated to be so in the Schedule:

(b) where the goods are new and let as being subject to defects, excluded only in respect of such defects as are specified in the Schedule.

If the goods are second-hand or defective, this must be brought to the customer's attention before he signs the agreement. Otherwise the goods must be free from serious defects—what the law calls of 'merchantable quality'. Unless he can persuade the owners to delete this clause, the customer has no right to replacement or compensation if the goods are later found to be unsuitable for the particular purpose for which he wanted them

**4** The Hirer shall keep the goods in the Hirer's actual possession and control and shall not remove them or any of them from the Hirer's address as set out in the Schedule or any other permitted address without the previous written consent of the Owners, who may by themselves, their servants or agents inspect them at any time on demand.

If the customer wants to move from the place where he has the goods, he must get the owner's consent in writing before taking the goods with him. This clause gives the owners the right to inspect the goods whenever they may wish to do so

**5** The Hirer shall punctually pay or cause to be paid, and at any time on demand shall produce or send to the Owners their servant or agent, the last receipts for all rents, rates, taxes and other outgoings (including payments due under any mortgage or charge) in respect of the premises whereon the goods may be, and shall keep the goods free and exempt from any distress for rent, execution or other legal process (including any action taken by a receiver appointed pursuant to any mortgage or charge).

The finance company reserves the right to check on the customer's private affairs, and to see receipts for rent, rates, taxes and mortgage repayments. It does so because, if the customer fails to pay his bills, the goods might be seized in error, along with his other property, under a court order

**6** The Hirer shall not sell, let, assign or otherwise dispose of the goods or any of them or of the benefit of this Agreement or the option of purchase herein contained, or attempt so to do nor commit any act of bankruptcy nor compound or negotiate for any composition with the Hirer's creditors.

The customer has to agree not to sell, let, give away or otherwise let the goods out of his care while they are still covered by the agreement. Nor must he at any time default on any other debt so that he risks going bankrupt

**7** The Hirer shall repay to the Owners on demand all expenses, legal and other charges incurred by the Owners in ascertaining the whereabouts of the Hirer or the goods or in taking steps to resume possession of the goods or in applying for or enforcing payment of any sums payable by the Hirer to the Owners under this Agreement, including, in the case of an inspection of the goods by the Owners at a time when the Hirer is in default under this Agreement, the travelling expenses of the Owners, their servant or agent from their Office to and from the place of inspection.

The customer must pay the finance company's costs if it has to repossess the goods, if it has to take legal action, if it has to trace the customer, or if it has to employ a collector to obtain payment from the customer

**9** In case of any and every breach by the Hirer of any of the terms and conditions hereof (except those in respect of payment of hire rentals) or should it transpire that any part of the information contained in the 'Particulars of Hirer' section of the Schedule or in any relevant proposal form is in any material respect inaccurate the Owners shall thereupon become entitled to recover possession of the goods and, if they see fit, the Owners may:

(a) (Subject to the provisions of the Hire Purchase Act) without prejudice to their claim for arrears of hire or damages for breach of this Agreement or any other rights hereunder forthwith and without notice or demand repossess themselves of and remove the goods

or

(b) By written notice sent (by post or otherwise) to or left at the Hirer's last known address forthwith and for all purposes absolutely determine and end this Agreement and the hiring thereby constituted, whereupon the Hirer shall no longer be in possession of the goods with the Owners' consent nor shall either party thereafter have any rights hereunder, but such termination shall not discharge any pre-existing liability of the Hirer to the Owners.

If the hirer breaks the agreement in some way other than by not paying promptly, or if he gives false information about himself on the agreement form—for example, by exaggerating his salary to make sure he gets the credit—the owner can repossess the goods immediately or end the agreement by giving notice in writing.

In repossessing the goods or ending the agreement, the finance company does not lose any of its rights to take the hirer to court to recover the full amount due under the agreement

**11** This Agreement, and the consent of the Owners to the Hirer continuing in possession of the goods, shall automatically and without notice determine if the landlord of any premises on which the goods may be by himself or his agent shall take or threaten to take any step to distrain upon the goods or any of them, and no payment subsequently accepted by the Owners without knowledge of such automatic determination shall in any way prejudice or affect the operation of this Clause.

If, as sometimes happens, a landlord seizes or 'distrains' the goods for non-payment of rent, the agreement is automatically ended. The goods then revert to the finance company which can take steps to recover them. This automatic termination applies even if the company has continued to accept payments without knowing that the goods have been seized

**TERMINATING THE AGREEMENT**

**1** The Hirer may put an end to this Agreement by giving notice of termination in writing to any person who is entitled to collect or receive the hire rent.

The customer can end the agreement—but must do so in writing

continued ▶

## Reading the terms of a hire-purchase agreement continued

**2** He must then pay any instalments which are in arrear at the time when he gives notice. If, when he has paid those instalments, the total amount which he has paid under the Agreement is less than [5] £ . . he must also pay enough to make up that sum, unless the Court determines that a smaller sum would be equal to the Owner's loss.

The figure entered in this clause must be not more than half the total purchase price. A court may fix a lower figure

**4** The Hirer should see whether this Agreement contains provisions allowing him to put an end to the Agreement on terms more favourable to him than those just mentioned. If it does he may put an end to the Agreement on those terms.

The agreement may be better than the minimum permitted by law, so there is a reminder to read all of the terms before ending the agreement

**5** [After [6] £ . . has been paid then] unless the Hirer has himself put an end to the Agreement the Owner of the goods cannot take them back from the Hirer without the Hirer's consent unless the Owner obtains an order of the Court.

If one-third or more of the total purchase price has been paid, the owner can recover the goods only by getting a court order

**6** If the Owner applies to the Court for such an order the Court may, if the Court thinks it just to do so, allow the Hirer to keep either:

(a) the whole of the goods, on condition that the Hirer pays the balance of the price in the manner ordered by the Court; or

(b) a fair proportion of the goods having regard to what the Hirer has already paid.

The court may allow the hirer to keep the goods in certain cases, provided he agrees to pay for them on a basis fixed by the court. Alternatively, it may allow him to keep part of the goods already paid for by him

> This document contains the terms of a hire-purchase agreement. Sign it only if you want to be legally bound by them.
>
> Signature
> of hirer_____
>
> The goods will not become your property until you have made all the payments. You must not sell them before then.

This warning to the hirer, printed in a red box, must be included on all hire-purchase agreements where the cost of goods plus the cost of credit is less than £2000. It must say whether the agreement is for credit sale or hire purchase

**1** The cash price of the goods was declared to me either by a Ticket or Label or in a Catalogue or Advertisement or in some other manner of writing otherwise than in the Agreement itself.

**DECLARATION BY THE HIRER**
By accepting this clause, the customer agrees he was told the true price—therefore check the amount before signing, as later complaints may be rejected

**2** [[7](A) I carefully examined the goods and am satisfied that they are in every respect satisfactory and suitable for my purpose.]
[[7] (B) I acknowledge that the defects specified in the Agreement were brought to my notice.]

Before signing, the customer should ensure he knows of any defects. This clause takes away his rights to argue later

Form ©The Hire Purchase Trade Association, 3 Berners Street, London W1E 4JZ.

# Credit sale

*Cancelling an agreement*     *Protection for the customer*
*When goods can be sold*    *Reading the agreement*
*Repossession of goods*    *Red-box warning*

IN a credit-sale agreement, the customer becomes the owner of the goods at the outset—unlike the hire-purchase customer, who does not become the legal owner until all the instalments have been paid. Credit-sale payments are made by instalments in the same way as hire-purchase payments, and interest rates are similar. ☐ Comparing the type of credit, p. 494.

RIGHT TO CANCEL Since the goods are owned by the customer from the outset, he does not normally have the right to cancel the agreement or to return the goods. But if the agreement is not signed on trade premises, and the total of interest and repayments is more than £30, the customer has three days to cancel. ☐ Buying on the doorstep, p. 456.

In addition, the customer may be able to cancel because of fundamental defects or unsuitability, in the rare cases where this right is not excluded under the terms of the agreement.

SELLING The customer may sell the goods at any time, but if he does so, the terms of the agreement may require that he repays the balance of the loan immediately.

REPOSSESSION The company financing the loan has no right to repossess the goods. If the customer falls behind with payments, the company can only sue him for debt. A credit-sale agreement usually provides, however, that the full amount outstanding becomes due if the customer defaults on payments.

PROTECTION Where the goods turn out to be unsatisfactory, the credit-sale customer's position is exactly the same as in a cash sale. The Sale of Goods Act 1893 gives him specific rights if the goods he has purchased prove to be seriously defective or unsuitable; but the terms of credit-sale agreements will usually deprive the customer of these rights. The shopper who buys by credit sale, unlike the hire-purchase customer, can lose his legal protection as a result of a written agreement. ☐ What to do about faulty goods, p. 460.

## How credit sale binds the customer

**3** The Sellers do not sell the goods subject to any warranty, condition or stipulation either express or implied.

The customer's legal rights are excluded by this clause. He normally has no remedy in law if the goods are defective or unsuitable

**4** If the buyer:
(i) makes default in payment of any one instalment and remains so in default for a period of seven days after due date, or
(ii) sells, pledges, lends, lets on hire or otherwise parts with the property in or possession of the goods
then and in either such case the whole of the balance of the total purchase price then outstanding shall become due and payable forthwith.

If the customer sells the goods before he has finished paying for them, or if he lends them, hires them out, uses them as security for a loan, or parts with the goods in any other way, he is liable to repay immediately the whole of the balance that is outstanding

**5** This Agreement is not subject to cancellation by the Buyer, and no indulgence or forbearance shown or extended to the Buyer by the Sellers shall in any way prejudice the Sellers' strict rights hereunder.

The customer's right to change his mind is limited—he can cancel within three days an agreement not signed on trade premises if the cash price and interest exceed £30. Otherwise the company is entitled to full payment

continued ▶

## How credit sale binds the customer continued

6 This Agreement shall only become binding on the Sellers upon acceptance by signature on their behalf and shall be deemed to be made on the date on which it is so signed. If the Sellers shall decline to accept the same then any monies actually paid to the Sellers hereunder shall be returned to the Buyer who shall have no further claim against the Sellers.

The agreement becomes binding not when the customer signs it, but when the company accepts. If the company rejects the agreement for any reason, the buyer gets his money back, but he has no right to compensation—for inconvenience, for example

## SCHEDULE

| Description | Retail Cash price | Purchase price under this agreement |
|---|---|---|
| Automatic washing machine Type XB 901 | £69.80 | £81.66 |
| TOTALS | £69.80 | £81.66 |

The Schedule, which must be completed on the agreement form before it is signed, leaves three spaces. One is for a full description of the goods which are the subject of the agreement.

This is followed by a column for the retail cash price and, next to it, the full purchase price under the agreement—that is, the total price after interest

and credit charges have been added to the original price of the goods.

The buyer should check these two columns carefully before signing the agreement, to ensure that the interest he is being charged is not too high.

If it is, then he can always try for a better bargain elsewhere

The Buyer has read the above Agreement and acknowledges that before he entered into it the cash price of the goods as shown above was separately stated to him otherwise than in the Agreement either by a ticket or label or in a catalogue or advertisement, or in some other manner of writing, and that the particulars given in the Schedule are correct.

If the customer checks all points in the Schedule and is satisfied with the agreement, he declares this in the form shown. He says that he was told the full cash price, but he does not have to be told the true interest rate (though he can find it from the table on p. 493)

This document contains the terms of a credit sale agreement. Sign it only if you want to be legally bound by them.

Signature of Buyer _____

RED-BOX WARNING For all credit sales over £30 the agreement must, under the Hire Purchase Act 1965, carry this description, printed in a red box, which warns the customer of the type of agreement he is signing. Failure to observe the strict rules which govern the design of the box may mean the agreement cannot be enforced.

Form © Hire Purchase Trade Association, 3 Berners Street, London W1E 4JZ

# Guaranteeing a credit agreement

*Why a guarantor is needed*        *The guarantor's legal position*
*What the 'guarantee' form means*

Acustomer who obtains goods on credit may be asked to name a guarantor—someone who agrees to make good any failure to meet the obligations incurred under the terms of purchase. A guarantee of this sort is usually required when the customer is not considered a good risk by the finance company.

A customer under the age of 18, for example, must always produce a guarantor, because it is uncertain whether the finance company could take legal action if he defaulted on the debt. ☐ The law on buying and selling, p. 442.

A customer who is not a householder may similarly be required to find a guarantor, because he is more likely to change his address and so become difficult to trace.

Anyone who is asked to sign as a guarantor to a credit agreement should make sure he knows what is involved. The terms of the 'guarantee' may commit him to more than the minimum liabilities of the customer himself.

In the strict sense, a guarantee is an undertaking by one man to meet the obligations of another in the case of default. But many of the finance-company forms headed 'guarantee' are forms of legal indemnity under which the so-called guarantor accepts a liability that is often larger than the customer's.

In hire-purchase agreements, for instance, a customer who finds himself in difficulties with payments can hand back the goods and the most he can be called on to pay is half the original purchase price.

But the guarantor may have to pay *all* the outstanding payments and compensate the finance company for any loss or expense caused by the customer's defaulting on payments or making off with the goods. Expenses in this context might include tracing the defaulter and sending someone to recover the property.

In addition, the terms of most indemnity forms deprive the guarantor of the right to sue the defaulter for the money.

These guarantee or indemnity documents have no 'red-box' warning as hire-purchase agreements have, and the unwary can be trapped into guaranteeing large sums on behalf of people they know only slightly.

The finance companies are interested only in ensuring that they get their money back, with a profit. They do not allow the wording on indemnity clauses to be altered in any way.

It is therefore important to read and understand the wording of the vital indemnity clauses before signing a guarantee form. Anyone who decides to sign should be fully prepared to meet the commitments it contains.

## Pitfalls of signing a hire-purchase guarantee form

The guarantor agrees to meet the finance company's losses and expenses whenever the company asks for payment. There is no obligation on the company to wait until the hire-purchase customer is a particular number of instalments in arrears, and no obligation to take the usual steps to recover the debt before claiming money from the guarantor.

A guarantor who signs this form can be made to pay more than the hire-purchase customer himself. If the customer defaults, the guarantor may be required to meet the remainder of the payments due under the hire-purchase agreement, together with any money the hire-purchase company spends trying to recover the debt.

These could include the cost of tracking down a customer who has defaulted.

**1** I/We will indemnify and keep indemnified you your successors and assigns from all loss or damage suffered and all claims costs and expenses made against or incurred by you in any way arising out of or consequent upon your having entered into such Agreement whether arising out of a breach by the customer of any of the terms and conditions thereof or otherwise including any such loss or damage etcetera as aforesaid as may arise from the said Agreement being (for whatever reason) unenforceable against the customer.

Form © Hire Purchase Trade Association, 3 Berners Street, London W1E 4JZ

# Personal loans and second mortgages

*Bank loans*　　　　　　　　*Giro loan scheme*
*Finance-house advances*　　*Raising money on insurance policies*
*Second mortgages*　　　　　*Moneylenders and pawnbrokers*

A CUSTOMER who wants to obtain goods on credit will frequently be offered the opportunity to pay a deposit, take the goods immediately and make up the balance over the following months or years. The alternative is to seek a personal loan, often from a source completely unconnected with the supplier of the goods, and pay cash to the shopkeeper or dealer. Depending on the purpose for which the money is required, and the security the customer can offer, such loans may be available from banks, finance houses, insurance companies, moneylenders or pawnbrokers or through National Giro.

One advantage of a personal loan over hire purchase or credit sale is that some or all of the interest on the money borrowed may qualify for tax relief. This depends on the tax laws in operation at the time the money is borrowed, and may apply only to loans for certain approved purposes.

## Bank loans

One of the cheapest ways of raising money is by borrowing from a bank, because rates of interest are generally lower than those charged by finance companies and moneylenders, and the interest charge becomes lower as the balance outstanding is reduced.

But banks are sometimes selective about the people to whom they lend money, and the purposes for which it is lent. There are two ways of obtaining a bank advance: through an overdraft or by a personal loan.

OVERDRAFTS Banks sometimes agree to pay a customer's cheques when the customer has no money in his account. This facility, known as an 'overdraft', is the most common form of bank advance.

However, overdrafts have a major disadvantage—they can be withdrawn whenever the bank wishes, without notice. The bank will then refuse to meet payment on any further cheques and press the customer to repay the amount already owed. Banks may take this course when the customer tries to exceed the overdraft limit or fails to reduce his debt in accordance with his agreement.

The interest on an overdraft is usually fixed at $\frac{1}{2}$-4 per cent above base rate—the rate used by the bank concerned as a basis for calculating interest rates on various types of loan. Interest is added either quarterly or, more usually, at the half year.

For a bigger overdraft, some form of security, such as share certificates or a life-assurance policy, may have to be provided.

PERSONAL LOANS Most clearing banks operate a personal-loan scheme under which the amount of the loan is credited to the customer's account and the customer has to make regular repayments, usually monthly.

This costs more than an overdraft because interest is charged on the whole loan, whether it is all taken up at the same time or in stages. So the true interest rate is about half as much again as the rate quoted. It is important to get the loan terms clear from the start. ☐ Working out the true interest rate, p. 493.

## Finance-house advances

A personal loan can sometimes be obtained from a finance house, particularly if the loan is tied to the purchase of goods or services. Finance houses often operate personal-loan schemes as an alternative to a credit-sale or hire-purchase agreement.

Some of these schemes are operated in conjunction with gas and electricity boards, oil companies and the National Coal Board, to enable the customer to install central heating or other home improvements.

Under such agreements the customer has fewer rights in law than he might have, for example, under a hire-purchase agreement. He cannot claim against the finance house if the goods are defective, nor can he return the goods and pay only half the price.

Whether or not he can make a claim against the supplier of defective or unsuitable goods depends on the terms of any agreement he signs. But in any case, he cannot hope to bring pressure on a supplier by withholding payment, since the money is owed not to the supplier but to a finance house. ☐ Buying household goods, p. 448.

The true interest rate on finance-house loans is usually between 18 and 25 per cent, and the repayment period is normally about three years, though it may be up to ten for central-heating installations. No security is normally needed, but in some cases it may be necessary to provide a reference or a guarantor —for example, where the customer is a minor or not a householder. ☐ Guaranteeing a credit agreement, p. 505.

If the repayments are not kept up, then the whole of the amount outstanding on the loan becomes due, and the finance house can claim the balance immediately. They can also ask for the whole loan to be repaid if they find that the customer gave misleading information when he applied for the advance.

## Second mortgages
Finance houses also arrange second mortgages, that is loans on the security of property.

A few years after a house is bought, it is normally worth more than the original purchase price. Furthermore, repayments made on a building-society (capital repayment) mortgage give added security.

This security is known as the 'equity' in the house. Say a householder borrowed £3000 from a building society for a £4000 house four years ago and the house is now worth £5500. His equity in it is the additional value (£1500), plus his original stake (£1000), plus whatever repayments have been made on the first mortgage, say another £1000. Thus the total security he has available for a second mortgage is £3500.

Borrowing money on a second mortgage is expensive—the true interest rate can be as high as 25 per cent. The customer may also have to pay initial charges for survey and legal expenses, which could add substantially to the cost of the loan.

The customer must usually give at least six months' notice or pay six months' interest if he wants to sell the house during the second-mortgage repayment period. Some agreements even allow the lender to charge the full amount of interest due on the loan if the house is sold and the loan is repaid early.

If the customer falls behind with payments on a second mortgage, the whole of the balance will usually become due immediately, and the finance house will have the right to sell the house if the customer cannot pay. Finance houses have been known to use this power to recover relatively small sums, although they must first obtain a court order.

Second mortgages can also be arranged by guarantee companies and mortgage brokers, who in turn go to finance companies for the loan. This is even more expensive, as they, too, must take a share of the profits.

Before signing a contract with a guarantee company or a second-mortgage broker, have it approved by a solicitor, as there are some companies who take advantage of an applicant's lack of knowledge of the law.

Home-owners seeking money for house conversion or improvement can sometimes obtain an advance to cover part or all of the cost from the building society with which they already have a mortgage. The terms and interest rate on a building-society loan will invariably be better than on a second mortgage. ☐ Repairs and improvements, p. 223.

## Giro loan scheme
National Giro does not itself offer loans, but account-holders may be advanced money through Giro's link with a finance house. There is no automatic limit to the loan, and interest is charged at a true rate of 18 per cent a year—a rate similar to that charged on hire-purchase agreements.

## Raising money on insurance policies
Money can be raised on life-insurance and endowment-insurance policies, provided they have been in force for at least two years.

Policy-holders can borrow up to 80 or 90 per cent of the policy's surrender value—the amount the insurance company pays if the policy is given up. ☐ Life assurance, p. 518.

The customer should ask the company to quote the values for surrender and loan, since these vary among companies. As a rough guide, the surrender value is usually about the sum of the premiums paid *minus* those paid during the first two to three years.

The terms of insurance loans vary from company to company, but true interest rates are about 8–10 per cent. The loan can be repaid at any time the borrower wishes.

## Moneylenders
Moneylenders advertise loans without security. They usually charge extremely high interest rates—up to 150 per cent true rate.

Only in extreme circumstances, where all other ways of obtaining credit have been exhausted, can it be worth while going to a moneylender. The customer is given some limited protection by the Moneylenders Acts 1900 and 1927, but this does not prevent him paying heavily for what he borrows.

Moneylenders have to be licensed annually by the local authority. Most refer to themselves as 'loan companies'.

The interest they can charge on loans is not fixed by law, but if the true rate exceeds 48 per cent, it is likely to be regarded in law as excessive. It is not illegal to charge an 'excessive' rate—in fact many moneylenders do so—but if the moneylender sues a customer for non-payment, the court may refuse to allow him to recover the whole of the interest.

On the other hand, the moneylender may be able to convince the court that the rate was justified in the circumstances.

The moneylender is not allowed by law to make any other charges for the loan except interest. If he does so, the borrower can take legal action to have the agreement set aside.

### Pawnbrokers
Pawnbrokers lend money, usually in small amounts over a short term, on the security of goods deposited with them.

They have to be licensed by the local council and their application has to be supported by a character certificate from the local magistrates. The interest they charge on loans below £5 is restricted by law to a true rate of 20–25 per cent, depending on the amount of the loan. Where the loan is more than £5, the pawnbroker can charge more interest by agreement with the borrower.

The borrower can 'redeem his pledge'—that is, repay the loan and get his goods back—within six calendar months plus seven days of grace. After that time, if the article is pledged for £2 or less it becomes the pawnbroker's absolute property.

A pledge over £2 in value can be sold by the pawnbroker if the loan is not repaid, but the borrower is entitled to receive any surplus produced, provided that he claims it within three years of the sale.

## The true price of a second mortgage or finance-company loan

Anyone borrowing on the security of a second mortgage or from a finance company should be aware that it is expensive and that there may be many hidden extras. For instance, make sure that the survey fee is the total one, and that you will not be called upon to pay any more. Legal charges, registration fees, holding fees and insurance to cover the loan can mount up considerably. In this case, Mr Davis will receive less than £200 of the £250 advance, but he will repay more than £370 over the three-year period.

The customer must usually give at least six months' notice or pay six months' interest if he wants to sell the house during the period of the second mortgage

38 Hollyhead Road, Leytonstone, London East 11, Telephone 539 1314, Telegrams Banex London, Telex 391243

Mr W. R. Davis,
30 Hill Drive,
London E11.
8th February 1971.                                    Your ref. wrd/5

Dear Mr Davis,

   We are in receipt of your application and are pleased to confirm having procured on your behalf an offer of an advance subject to references, confirmation of income, valuation and survey, contract and the undermentioned conditions.

   OFFER OF ADVANCE

   1. Second mortgage secured on 30 Hill Drive, London E11.
   2. Advance £250.
   3. Period of repayment 3 years.
   4. Interest payable on advance at a flat rate of 15 per cent per annum.
   5. Monthly repayments of principal and interest of £10.35.

   CONDITIONS OF OFFER

   1. Surety - Mrs W. R. Davis, 30 Hill Drive, London E11.
   2. Group life-assurance policy to be effected.
   3. Accident, sickness and unemployment policy to be effected.
   4. Survey fee of £4.20 payable upon acceptance of offer.
   5. Returnable holding fee of £15 payable upon acceptance. This is returned upon completion of advance.
   6. Our registration fee, payable when the advance is made or, if after acceptance, when the offer is declined, is £15.
   7. The borrower to pay legal fees - approximately £30-35.

Yours sincerely

*H. Webb.*

H. P. Webb

# Credit for small purchases

*Credit cards*      *Credit trading*
*Budget accounts*   *Check trading*
*Credit clubs*

**H**IRE-PURCHASE and credit-sale arrangements tend to be used to buy expensive items such as cars, washing machines and refrigerators. But there are credit schemes which enable the customer to defer payment on lower-priced items. The terms under which these schemes operate differ from company to company.

## Credit cards

Credit cards are issued by banks or private companies to enable holders to obtain a wide range of goods and services without using either cash or a cheque book.

When the holder makes a purchase from firms in the scheme, he shows his credit card and signs the bill. The account is then sent to the credit-card company for payment.

The customer receives a monthly account from the company, which generally has to be paid within a month. Interest of $1\frac{1}{2}$ per cent per month (about 20 per cent per annum) is normal on outstanding accounts.

If a card is lost the holder is responsible for any debts which are incurred on it unless he informs the company immediately.

HOW TO JOIN A SCHEME Membership of a credit-card scheme is open to anyone who can satisfy the company of his credit-worthiness. Prospective members are asked to complete a searching application form.

## Budget accounts

Many retailers operate 'budget accounts' which allow a customer making monthly payments to claim continuous credit up to a maximum sum—usually nine or twelve times the monthly payments. As soon as he makes a payment, the customer can buy further goods to bring the amount outstanding up to the agreed maximum. The retailer usually makes a service charge, which may be 5 per cent. The true interest rate, however, is usually about 10 per cent. □ Working out the true rate of interest, p. 493.

Alternatively, the charge may be added to each item the customer buys.

RESTRICTIONS When Government credit controls are in force, it may not be possible to use a budget account for expensive goods.

Budget accounts are normally too short-term for larger amounts, and there may not be provision for the minimum deposit required by law.

## Credit clubs

A scheme similar to a budget account is run by co-operative retail societies, usually through 'credit-club' vouchers, which can be used in any department of the store. The charge is 5p in the £ and the loan is normally repayable by weekly instalments.

## Credit trading

The credit-trading system is similar to budget-account credit, but it is handled by door-to-door traders selling items such as clothing, soft furnishings and bedding. Customers generally pay a fixed sum each week or month.

## Check trading

Two forms of credit are used by check-trading companies—the check system and the voucher system. The trading company provides a brochure listing the shops which accept its checks and vouchers.

Check-trading companies employ local agents who call each week to collect instalments. New customers fill in an application form to show their credit-worthiness.

THE CHECK SYSTEM Checks are issued for £5, £10 or £20, and can be used at retailers in the issuing company's scheme.

Interest, at a flat rate of 5 per cent, is added to the check when it is issued. A customer who wants a £20 check pays the £1 interest. The agent gives him the check and collects the balance in instalments over 20 or 21 weeks.

The true rate of interest on this loan comes to almost 25 per cent per annum. □ Working out the true rate of interest, p. 493.

THE VOUCHER SYSTEM Vouchers are given for larger amounts. They are usually issued for up to £250 and the issuing company has to approve the purchase in advance.

There is usually a rebate for prompt settlement on the agreed date, and there may be a bigger rebate for earlier settlement. The true interest is nearly double the flat rate of 12 or $12\frac{1}{2}$ per cent. Vouchers are repaid through the company's collector by weekly instalments.

# Finding and keeping

*The owner's rights*
*Tracing the owner*
*Found—on the finder's own property*

*Found—in a public place*
*Found—on someone else's property*

WHETHER a person who finds an article can keep it depends on where it was found—whether on property which the finder owns, in a public place, or on property which belongs to someone else. Two basic principles govern all three situations. The owner can always claim; and the finder must try to trace the owner.

### The owner's rights
The owner is always entitled to recover an article from the person who found it. If the finder is not able to return it—for instance if he has sold the article or given it away—then the owner may sue the finder for its value.

There is no time limit set for reclaiming an article. A person who finds a watch, for example, can be forced to return it, no matter how long it is since it was found. If it has been sold the owner can recover its full value, but generally he must sue for the proceeds within six years of the sale of the item.

### Tracing the owner
The person who finds an article is guilty of theft unless he takes reasonable steps to trace the owner. It is never enough for the finder to do nothing merely because he believes that the owner is unlikely to be found.

The question of theft arises as soon as the finder has taken possession of the article. For example, if a person picks up a wallet which is lying on the pavement, he will have taken possession of it and he must immediately attempt to trace its owner.

The safest way is to hand the article to the police and let them make inquiries. This shows that the finder is acting honestly. The police hold the article on the finder's behalf —for a month if it is worth up to £30, and for up to six months if it is worth more. If the owner cannot be traced in that time, the article is handed back to the finder.

If he does not want it, the article is auctioned and the proceeds are given to police funds.
REWARDS Most people are glad to show their appreciation for the return of their property. But no one has the right to insist upon a reward or compensation—not even for expenses incurred in tracing the owner of the lost goods. If a reward has been offered, though, it must be paid to anyone who fulfils the conditions stated in the offer.

### Found—on the finder's own property
When land or a house is transferred, everything that is fixed to the land or forms part of the structure of the house is generally transferred with it. The owner is therefore entitled to keep anything dug up in the garden— except treasure trove—or found hidden in the house. Even if it was lost by the previous owner, it becomes the property of the new owner. Anything other than treasure trove which is discovered in rented accommodation belongs to the owner of the property.
TREASURE TROVE Hoards of coins and any objects made of gold, silver or plate buried in the ground by an unknown owner who intended to remove them later are known as treasure trove. Ownership of treasure trove never passes with the land.

Anyone who finds what might be treasure trove must report it to the police. The local coroner holds an inquest to decide if it was deliberately buried. If it was, the article is treasure trove and belongs to the Crown. It is usually sent to a national or local museum and compensation is paid to the finder.

If treasure trove is not reported but kept by the finder, and is later discovered by the authorities, it is confiscated and the finder may be prosecuted. The penalties are a fine or imprisonment, with no fixed maximum.
SECOND-HAND FURNITURE OR CLOTHES Articles found in second-hand furniture or clothes generally belong to the original owner and must be returned. They can be kept only if the finder can prove that the article was intended to be part of the sale.

This principle applies to gifts. For example, if a wardrobe containing a sum of money has been given as a gift or is being held temporarily, the finder would have to prove that the money was also intended as a gift.

### Found—in a public place
A public place is any place which the public is entitled to use, including roads, squares, public-transport vehicles and parks. Anyone

510

finding an article of value there must try to trace the owner—preferably by advertising or by informing the police.

The owner can always recover the article, unless he has deliberately abandoned it; but as long as the article is not claimed by the owner, the finder can keep it.

If an article is abandoned and the former owner later claims it, the finder will have to hand it over unless he can prove that it was abandoned. It is usually impossible to do so if the article has any value.

Public places also generally include any place which members of the public are encouraged to visit—the public parts of shops, cinemas, theatres, public houses, restaurants and hotels. But there, it is advisable for the finder of an article of value to take it to the owner of the public place or his authorised representative—for example, the manager of the shop or cinema.

BYE-LAWS Some public places—buses, trains and certain parks, for example—are controlled by bye-laws which may lay down rules for property found in them. Usually, for example, articles found on a train or bus must be handed to the guard or conductor.

ARTICLES WHICH ARE NOT OWNED An article which has never been owned is treated in the same way as one which has been abandoned. The principle applies to fish found in the sea or, say, wild birds, moths or butterflies. However, many of these are protected by conservation laws.

It is not always easy to decide whether an article has an owner or not. Wild flowers by the wayside belong to the person who owns the apparently 'waste' land. And in most cases fish in a river may be caught only with the permission of the owner of either bank.

## Found—on someone else's property

In general, anything found on someone else's property must be handed over to him.

➤ THE CLEANER WHO STRUCK GOLD *Mr Sharman was employed by the South Staffordshire Water Company to clean out a pool on land which it owned. During his work Mr Sharman found two gold rings. The water company claimed them but Mr Sharman refused to hand them over. He had tried to trace their real owner but had failed.*
DECISION *The company was given the rings because possession of the land included possession of everything attached to it in the absence of a stronger claim. (South Staffordshire Water Company v. Sharman.)* ◄

In two circumstances articles may be kept. The first is where the public is encouraged to use parts of the property. In one case, for instance, a person was allowed to keep unclaimed bank notes found on the floor of the public part of a shop.

The second exception is where the owner of the property has never occupied it.

FINDS BY EMPLOYEES Anything found at work must be handed to the employer, who is obliged to attempt to trace the owner. Roadsweepers are not entitled in law, for example, to keep what they find in the street, nor is the dustman legally entitled to keep what he finds in refuse from homes or offices.

## Found—in the sea or on the seashore

ANYTHING found in the sea or on the seashore which came from a ship or which is part of a ship is technically 'wreck' and should be handed to the local receiver of wrecks. He can be contacted through the nearest customs post.

Failure to give up wreck to the receiver is a criminal offence punishable by a fine of up to £100. Anyone who fails to hand over wreck can also be made to pay twice the value of the property to the owner.

The owner has one year in which to claim his property. After that, it is sold and the proceeds belong technically to the Crown.

However, the finder is sometimes given part of the proceeds as a reward. If he took an active part in recovering the wreck—perhaps by towing it to land or bringing it up from the sea bed—he can claim a reward for salvage.

The basis of a reward claim for salvage is that the finder has put himself to cost, trouble or risk to save maritime property—a ship, its cargo, wreck or the lives of passengers or crew who were on the vessel.

The property or survivors must have been saved from danger, and the amount of the reward depends on the degree of danger, the value of the property, and the amount of labour and skill spent on the salvage operation by the finder.

# Keeping money on deposit

*Bank deposits*  *Building societies*
*Trustee savings banks*  *Fringe banks*
*National Savings*  *Local government loans*

THE simplest form of investment is the loan of money to the Government or an institution which uses it to make a profit and pays interest on the loan. Money lent in this way is said to be 'on deposit'. The interest rate depends on how long the money is committed for and the risk it runs, as well as on the general economic climate.

## Bank deposits
Money in a bank deposit account can be withdrawn after giving seven days' notice, although most banks allow money to be withdrawn on demand if it is urgently needed.

Because the money is readily accessible, the interest rate on a deposit account is comparatively low. Clearing banks pay 2 per cent below their base rate—the rate used for calculating interest on a variety of loans.

A bank deposit account is useful as a temporary 'home' for money until a more rewarding investment is found.

## Trustee savings banks
Trustee savings banks operate ordinary savings accounts with an interest rate of $3\frac{1}{2}$ per cent. They also have investment accounts, with an interest rate of up to $7\frac{1}{2}$ per cent, where a month's notice may be required to withdraw money. As the funds are lent to the Government, the investment is secure.

## National Savings
The safest schemes in which to put money are savings schemes run or guaranteed by the Government. One of the most popular, in spite of the low rate of interest it offers, is the National Savings Bank. The main attraction is the ease and speed of withdrawal facilities. At any of 20,000 post offices, up to £20 can be withdrawn on demand by any saver who has at least that much in his account. Larger amounts can be obtained within seven days.

Interest is paid at the rate of $3\frac{1}{2}$ per cent a year, and the first £21 of interest is free of income tax. Before April 6, 1973, it is liable to surtax; after that, the interest is free of income tax at the basic and higher rates.

Interest is calculated on whole pounds on deposit for complete calendar months, so that a deposit made, say, on July 2 and withdrawn on August 30 would earn no interest.

INVESTMENT ACCOUNT When £50 has been invested in an ordinary savings account at $3\frac{1}{2}$ per cent interest, an investment account can be opened at an interest rate of $7\frac{1}{2}$ per cent. One month's notice must be given to withdraw money. The interest is paid gross—that is, without deduction of tax—and is taxable.

SAVINGS CERTIFICATES A longer-term investment is in National Savings Certificates. Interest rates vary, but savings certificates usually pay more interest than the National Savings Bank, provided they are retained.

The £1 certificates earn 25p tax-free interest after they have been held for four years. If they are cashed within 12 months, no interest is paid. Between 12 months and four years, interest is paid on a sliding scale.

No one is allowed to hold more than 1000 units of a new issue, but earlier issues may be held in addition. After maturity, savings certificates continue to earn interest if held for a minimum of three or four months (depending on the issue). But the holder can usually get a better return on his savings by cashing matured certificates promptly and purchasing new ones, or putting the money into some other form of investment.

SAVINGS BONDS British Savings Bonds are issued in multiples of £5, and pay interest at 7 per cent gross, which is taxable. The bonds can be cashed at one month's notice. If they are held for the full five years, a 3 per cent tax-free bonus is paid.

PREMIUM BONDS The interest rate on Premium Bonds is $4\frac{3}{4}$ per cent, but instead of the money being paid to holders of the bonds, it goes into a prize fund. From this fund, prizes are distributed to bond-holders whose bond numbers are selected by a computer in a weekly and monthly 'draw'. The prizes range from £25 to £50,000, and are tax-free. Winners of £25 and £50 prizes are paid automatically by a crossed warrant. The £100 up to £50,000 winners are notified and must indicate on a claim form whether they would like to receive their winnings in cash or by cheque, or have the money paid into a National Savings Bank account.

TAX RESERVE CERTIFICATES A type of saving useful for self-employed people who have to pay income tax direct is the Tax Reserve Certificate, issued in units of £5.

Provided they are used to pay income tax, these certificates earn interest—usually about 4 per cent. They can be held indefinitely, but no further interest is earned after two years. They can be obtained at banks and Inland Revenue offices. The certificates enable the taxpayer to spread his tax burden over a period. Tax reserve certificates are abolished from January 1, 1974.

## Building societies

Building societies provide a compromise between the safety of Government-guaranteed deposits and the higher risk and higher possible returns offered by stocks and shares.

The societies exist to provide mortgage loans to people who want to buy their own homes, and they raise these funds from savers and investors by offering complete security and competitive rates of interest.

Most societies are members of the Building Societies Association, which lays down standards of operation and recommends the interest rate the societies should charge borrowers and pay investors. The investor may be able to find a small society which offers a slightly higher rate.

Because building societies' funds are invested in traditionally sound ways, mainly in first mortgages for owner-occupied homes, those which are members of the Building Societies Association are almost as safe as Government-backed bodies.

SHARE ACCOUNT The usual method of investment in a building society is the share account. This is different from a share in a company, because a building society share can be withdrawn on notice, according to the particular society's rules.

Repayment terms of share accounts vary slightly from one society to another. For instance, some societies insist on a full period of notice, sometimes up to six months.

DEPOSITS Although a building-society investment carries almost no risk, the investor can protect himself even further by asking for a 'deposit' investment. This gives the investor the legal status of a creditor. If the society becomes insolvent, he has priority of payment over the shareholders. The interest rate is usually about ¼ per cent lower.

SUBSCRIPTIONS For people who are prepared to save regular amounts, most societies offer a better rate of interest for 'subscription' shares. Schemes vary from one society to another, but the best of them offer favourable terms, with immediate withdrawal facilities. However, some societies may charge a high price for early withdrawal, and the saver may lose up to three months' interest.

INTEREST RATES Some building societies offer a fixed interest rate on money placed with them for longer periods; but this rate is not usually much higher than the rates offered for other types of building-society investment.

Other building-society interest rates fluctuate according to general lending conditions. To attract money, the building societies must offer keenly competitive rates of interest.

Most building societies pay tax on interest, at a reduced rate, direct to the Inland Revenue. The investor himself does not have to pay basic rate income tax on the amount he receives.

This makes an investment in a building society a good one for the taxpayer. People who do not pay much tax, however, get the same rate of interest with no tax benefit. For this reason, a building society is not a good investment for them.

A building-society investment is not the most profitable form of investment, either, for the man who pays surtax or, after April 6, 1973, the higher rates of income tax. When he collects his interest he has to pay surtax (or the difference between income tax at the basic rate and his highest personal rate) not on the money he actually gets, but on the amount he would have received if the society had not already paid tax on it. ☐ How the income-tax system works, p. 556.

## Fringe banks

Other institutions accepting deposits include finance houses and property investment companies. They are called 'fringe banks'.

Interest paid by these organisations is liable to tax, and it is generally similar to the true rate (taking the tax into account) paid by the building societies on a share account. But people who do not pay income tax receive a better return from a fringe bank than they would from a building society.

However, the financial reliability of fringe banks varies widely. Without knowledge of the way they are managed, it is not always safe to invest large sums with them.

## Local government loans

Many local authorities accept deposits for periods of up to five years at fixed rates of interest. These deposits are as secure as Government loans, and they offer a higher return. Loans are for a fixed period, but sometimes early repayment is offered if required.

# Stocks and shares

*Shares and their value*      *How business is transacted*
*Rights of shareholders*     *Bulls, bears and stags*
*Types of stock*              *Rules for takeover bids*

THERE are two basic ways of investing money on stock exchanges. The investor can buy shares in a public company or he can invest in stocks, lending money to a public body such as the Government, and receiving interest on the loan. Whichever he does, it is called investing in 'securities'.

## Shares and their value
The most usual form of security is a share. The people who have bought shares—the shareholders—own the company between them.

Each share is given a nominal value when it is first issued, say £1 or 25p, but this is not necessarily the price the buyer pays.

The actual price paid on the stock exchange for a share goes up or down according to how well the company is doing or is expected to do.

The amount of profits to be divided among shareholders is decided by the directors. When these profits are divided, each shareholder's portion, or dividend, is usually announced as a percentage of the nominal value. So if a company announces a dividend of 10 per cent for the year, each shareholder gets 10 per cent of the nominal value.

Suppose, for example, that a 10 per cent dividend is declared on a share with a nominal value of £1, when the current price of the share on the stock exchange is £2. The return for anyone buying at the current price would be only 5 per cent. This is called the yield.

Yield was used as a yardstick to assess shares when, in general, profits were distributed. Now that the tendency is to plough back a high proportion of the profits, another method is often used.

This is called the 'price/earnings' or P/E ratio. It is calculated by dividing the market price of all the company's shares by the total annual profit. The figure represents the number of years it would take the profits, if they continued at the same rate, to add up to the present value of the company shares.

## Rights of shareholders
Companies issue different types of share and each has different rights. There are two main kinds, 'ordinary' and 'preference'. The latter usually entitle the holder to a percentage of the profit before ordinary shareholders are paid. They may also give the holder priority if the company is dismantled or 'wound up'.

ORDINARY SHARES Holders of ordinary shares are entitled to any profit left after preference shareholders have been paid. Ordinary shares are known as the company's 'equity'.

PREFERENCE SHARES A fixed rate of interest is normally quoted on preference shares—for instance '5 per cent preference shares'. This means that the holder of the share must receive 5 per cent of its nominal value before the company's profits can be shared between other shareholders. There are several kinds of preference shares:

**1.** Cumulative preference shares give the holder a right to dividends which the company has failed to pay in past years, before anyone else can be paid.

**2.** Participating preference shares give a right to a share in the rest of the profits as well as the fixed dividend.

**3.** Redeemable preference shares give the company the right to buy back shares at, or near, their nominal value, although the holder cannot demand that the company buys them back at that value.

## Voting rights
Shareholders own the company—they are entitled to share the profits of a company, and they can share out the proceeds between them if the company is sold or wound up. But it is the directors who control the business. They have a duty to run the company in the best interests of the shareholders, but do not simply carry out the shareholders' instructions.

The way the shareholder exercises his ownership is through his vote. The vote goes with the share, so that a man with 50 shares has 50 votes.

Directors have to be voted on to the board of the company, and they elect a chairman. The chairman and the directors can also be voted off the board. In the last resort, the whole board of directors can be voted out of control and replaced by a new board.

Not all shares have votes. Preference shares, for example, do not normally give the holder a vote unless the company has fallen into arrears with the fixed dividend which the shareholder is entitled to receive.

The ordinary shareholders normally hold the voting power in a company. Sometimes, however, ordinary shares are issued that are specifically called 'non-voting'. These are issued when a board fears that, if new shareholders were given a vote, it might lose control.

As these shares carry no right to a voice in the company, their price is lower, although their nominal value is the same as that of ordinary shares. Sometimes non-voting shares are labelled simply 'A' or 'B' shares.

ANNUAL GENERAL MEETING The directors of a company must, under the Companies Act 1948, hold a general meeting of shareholders every year and give all shareholders 21 days' written notice of where and when it is to take place. The shareholders have to approve the dividend, appoint directors to replace those retiring, and pay the company's auditors. They can also discuss all the company's affairs and policies.

If there is no disagreement on policy, resolutions put before the shareholders are passed by a 'show of hands' by the people who attend the meeting. In this case each shareholder has one vote, no matter how big or small his shareholding is.

But if there is a dispute on an important matter, those dissenting or those present have a right to demand a poll. The people at the meeting then vote according to the number of shares they hold. Those not attending the meeting can authorise someone else to attend and vote for them by proxy if a poll is held.

### Shareholders' rights to new issues

From time to time shareholders receive notices from the company about the issue of new shares. It can be a 'scrip' issue or a 'rights' issue, and there are important differences between the two.

SCRIP A scrip issue (sometimes wrongly called a 'bonus' issue) is really a book-keeping adjustment. The shares are issued when a company has built up profits which have not been shared out and other assets have acquired a greater cash value over the years because of inflation. If a company wishes to transfer this added value to its capital account, it issues shares free to its shareholders.

They receive new shares in proportion to their shareholding—say one new one for every three shares held.

It may seem that the shareholder has got something for nothing. But, unless the total amount of dividends increases, he will receive the same return on his money, spread over

four shares instead of three. Similarly, nothing has altered the total value of the company, so the value of his total holding is unchanged.

RIGHTS A rights issue is made when a company wishes to raise more capital. It gives the shareholder the right to buy more shares in proportion to his holding—say one new share for every three held.

The new shares are normally offered below the market price, so there is what is called a 'bonus element'. The shareholder is forced to pay for more shares or see his investment whittled away by the lower share value.

If he does not want to or cannot afford to take it up, he can sell his 'rights' in the open market. It is usually a good idea to consult a stockbroker or bank manager about a rights issue. A bank will sometimes advance a customer the money to buy the new shares.

### Types of stock

Stock exchanges also deal in loans. There are two main types: loans raised by public bodies, called 'gilt-edged' securities, and those raised by companies, which are called debentures.

GILT-EDGED SECURITIES Loans raised by the Government are called 'gilt-edged' securities because they are guaranteed by the issuer.

An investor lends his money by buying loan stock on the open market. He withdraws it by selling the stock to someone else or waiting until the loan is redeemed—that is, repaid—by the original borrower.

The stock has approximately the face value of the original loan and carries a fixed rate of interest, but its price fluctuates considerably. These fluctuations depend on how long the loan is to last, the rate of interest, the reputation of the borrower and the general state of the investment market. Dated stock carries a date, or range of dates, within which it is to be repaid. It has the advantage that, even though its market value may become depressed, it must gradually recover as the redemption date approaches.

The Government also issues 'undated' gilt-edged stocks, such as 'consols' and 'war loan'. The loan is never redeemed but the Government guarantees the interest indefinitely. The price varies according to interest rates and the state of the money market.

The complexities of dealing in stock make this a field in which only experts can have much hope of success.

DEBENTURES Loan stocks raised by companies, as opposed to official bodies, are called debentures. The holder is entitled to a fixed annual interest. If this is not paid, he has a high priority claim to the company's assets if it is wound up. The interests of debenture holders are watched over by a trustee, usually an insurance company or bank.

The original amount of the loan may be redeemable at a fixed time, or at so much a year, or never. Sometimes a company makes more than one issue of debentures and they are ranked in order of preference, much like first and second mortgages on a house.

Sometimes debentures carry the right, after a certain time, to convert them into equity shares. If the company has prospered since the debentures were issued and the shares have gone up accordingly this can represent a considerable capital gain for the holder.

### How business is transacted

Buying or selling shares is known on the stock exchange as a 'bargain'. Only a stockbroker can buy or sell and he generally charges 1¼ per cent commission for his services.

Although the stockbroker is dealing on behalf of a client, under stock-exchange rules he is responsible personally for the transaction. If, for instance, he sells shares for a client and the client fails to deliver them, the stockbroker must buy the equivalent number to deliver, even if it involves him in a heavy loss.

If a stockbroker fails to fulfil his commitments and a client loses money as a result, a stock-exchange fund will compensate the client for the loss even if he has no legal claim against the stockbroker.

JOBBING On the London Stock Exchange the buyer's stockbroker and the seller's stockbroker do not deal with each other directly. They sell to or buy from a stock-exchange dealer called a 'jobber'. Like any other dealer, the jobber hopes to sell for more than he buys—he earns his living out of this profit which is called the 'jobber's turn'. There are, therefore, two prices for a share—the price at which the jobber is prepared to buy and the price below which he is not prepared to sell.

CONTRACT NOTES When the bargain is completed, the stockbroker sends his client a 'contract note' giving details of the bargain. This should be kept, because the tax authorities require evidence of the transaction.

REGISTERING THE TRANSFER OF SHARES The document which gives evidence of an investor's ownership of shares is called the share certificate. When shares are bought and sold, the seller's stockbroker sends his client a transfer form to sign and return with his share certificate.

The seller's stockbroker then forwards this old share certificate and the transfer form to the company's registered offices and the transfer is registered in the company's books. The old certificate is destroyed and a new one, showing the name of the buyer (the new owner) is issued to him. The company can charge a registration fee of a few pence but often does not do so.

SETTLEMENT DATE The stock exchanges work in two-week periods—sometimes three-week periods at holiday times—called 'accounts'. All money owing on the sale and purchase of shares is paid at the end of this period. The buyer's stockbroker expects a cheque from his client and the seller's stockbroker sends his client a cheque.

The only exceptions are gilt-edged securities and new issues, which must be paid for on the day after the bargain. If a client buys and sells shares in the same account, the stockbroker charges one commission for both bargains.

### Bulls, bears and stags

Because payment is not made until the end of the account, speculators buy shares for which they have not got the money in the hope of selling them at a profit before the end of the account. Or they sell shares they do not possess in the hope of buying them for delivery at a cheaper price before the end of the account. Certain stock-exchange expressions have grown out of such practices.

A 'bull' is a man who buys in the expectation that shares will rise in value. A 'bear' is a man who sells in the expectation that shares will fall in value. A 'stag' is a man who subscribes to a new issue hoping that he will be able to sell at a profit as soon as dealing in the shares commences on the stock exchange.

### Rules for takeover bids

One company can obtain control of another by buying a majority of its shares direct from the shareholders instead of through the stock exchange. Usually, the company making the bid makes an offer and gives shareholders a time limit for acceptance.

A panel, with a full-time director-general and staff, was established in May 1969 to govern the conduct of takeovers and defend the interests of shareholders involved in takeover situations. The panel consists of representatives of City institutions such as the Stock Exchange and the clearing banks.

It has no legal powers, but tries to ensure that companies involved in takeovers adhere to a voluntary set of rules known as the takeover code. The code requires, for example, that shareholders who accepted earlier offers for their shares shall be entitled to be paid the value of the final offer.

# Putting money into unit trusts

*Buying and selling units*        *Tax on capital gains*
*What the managers may charge*    *Investment trust companies*

IN a unit trust, people with small amounts to invest pool their money, making up a large sum which is invested for them by professionals over a wide field, reducing the chance of serious loss. An insurance company, bank or other financial institution acts as trustee to see that all the money received is used in the interests of the subscribers, and the Department of Trade and Industry has power to supervise unit trust operations.

The legal basis on which a unit trust operates is a trust deed. This lays down the sort of investments that can be made and the basis on which people can take a share.

Within this framework, professional investment managers—for example, a merchant bank or a firm of stockbrokers—use subscribers' money to earn income and increase the capital value of units. Because it is a trust and not a company, there is no fixed capital.

## Buying and selling units
The managers of a trust deal directly with the public, attracting new investors mainly through newspaper advertisements. The price at which the units are offered to the public is supervised by the trustees and the Department of Trade and Industry. It is calculated by computing the current market value of all the securities the fund holds. To this figure is then added the brokerage charges, stamp duty and the managers' commission, and the total is divided by the number of units.

BLOCK OFFERS To make dealings easier, the trust deed may authorise a fixed-price offer of blocks of units to be made, usually valid for a week—provided that this price is not more than 2½ per cent more or less than the properly calculated price.

An investor who buys units just after a distribution of interest has been announced, but before it is paid, will not qualify to share in the distribution. Such a purchase is termed 'ex-dividend' or 'ex-distribution' and the letters 'xd' are added to the price of the unit —for example '64p xd'.

The trust is bound to buy back units if the investor wants his money back. The repurchase price is again based on the price the trust's investments would fetch on the open market, but this time expenses are *deducted* before dividing by the number of units.

Because expenses are added on to the basic value to arrive at the purchase price, and deducted to produce the selling price, this would result in a gap between buying and selling prices of about 10 per cent of the total investment. Many trusts increase the repurchase price, to reduce the gap to 5 per cent. This is usually what it would cost to buy and sell the same investments through a broker.

## What the managers may charge
The charges made by investment managers tend to be similar from one trust to another. They can consist of two parts:
1. An initial service charge of between 3p and not more than 5p per £ invested, payable when the units are bought.
2. A half-yearly fee, paid out of the trust fund's income, of between 20p and 50p for every £100 in the fund.

The Department of Trade and Industry lays down that initial and half-yearly charges, taken over 20 years, must not come to more than 13¼ per cent of the investor's total stake.

## Tax on capital gains
The notice which an investor receives with each distribution of interest tells him what will be his share of the capital gains on which the trust is taxed. The investor may add that amount to the cost price of the unit when calculating his own gain or loss when he sells his holding. This ensures that tax is not paid twice on the same underlying profit.

## Investment trust companies
For people with, say, £300 or more to invest there are also investment trust companies, which follow the same principle of widely investing subscribers' money. Their shares, quoted on the stock exchanges, must be bought and sold through a stockbroker.

An investment trust company can raise part of its capital in preference shares and debentures, giving the management greater capital to work with at a fixed interest. If the management is successful, there will be greater profits to divide among ordinary shareholders.

# Life assurance

Choosing the type of policy
Choosing the company
Taking out a policy

Getting a loan
Converting and assigning a policy
Home service assurance

---

TAKING out a life-assurance policy is one of the best-known ways of long-term saving and at the same time protecting the family with a substantial sum of money from the time the first premium is paid. A wide variety of policies is available. It is, however, difficult to get truly independent advice. Many brokers do not represent sufficient companies to be able to offer their clients a wide choice; and all agents are under pressure to sell policies which provide them with the highest commission.

TAX RELIEF The Government encourages saving through life assurance by allowing tax relief on premiums paid to assure the life of the taxpayer and the taxpayer's husband or wife, but not the lives of children, parents or anyone else. Annual premiums of up to 7 per cent of the sum assured qualify for tax relief —any excess is ignored. A taxpayer can claim relief on total premiums of up to one-sixth of his income.

Two-fifths of allowable premiums paid before April 6, 1973 qualify for relief. With income tax at 38·75 per cent, this amounts to a tax saving of up to 15½p on every £1 paid.

With the introduction of unified tax, premiums paid on or after April 6, 1973 qualify for relief at half the basic tax rate. Where this rate is 30 per cent, tax saving is up to 15p on every £1 paid.

WHO CAN BE INSURED An individual can take out an assurance policy on anyone in whom he has an insurable interest—that is, anyone whose death will cause him financial loss.

A businessman, for example, may take out an assurance policy on the life of a partner and husband and wife may take out policies on each other's lives.

But a parent has no insurable interest in the life of a child, nor a child in the life of a parent. So a parent cannot take out a policy on the life of a child; the policy must be in the child's name, or—for the child's benefit—on the life of one of the parents.

## Choosing the type of policy

TERM ASSURANCE The basic life-assurance policy is temporary or term assurance which protects the family during a specific period of years. It covers only the risk that the policy-holder may die before the end of that period; if he outlives the term, he gets nothing back.

Provided a person is in reasonable health, the cost of a term assurance policy is relatively low—far less than any other form of life assurance. For this reason it is often the best choice for a young man with a limited amount to spend on assurance who wants to provide a substantial sum for his family in the event of his death.

A common form of term assurance is the mortgage-protection policy, where the amount of insurance cover decreases at the same rate as the sum of money outstanding on a building-society or local-authority mortgage. If the policy-holder dies, the policy pays off the outstanding mortgage.

Another form of term assurance is the family income assurance under which no lump sum is paid if the policy-holder dies during the term, but annual payments, usually tax free, are made to the dependants until the end of the term.

Term assurance is often combined with other benefits—to give a larger sum assured if the policy-holder dies in the early years of the policy, for example, or to provide regular payments to support children until a specific date, in addition to the regular sum assured.

WHOLE-LIFE ASSURANCE Under a whole-life assurance policy the assurance company agrees to pay a fixed sum when the policy-holder dies. It is similar to term assurance except that the sum assured is payable on the death of the policy-holder at any age, not just during a specific period.

Premiums, which depend on the sum assured and the age of the insured person, are paid throughout his life, and the sum assured is paid to dependants after his death.

As people do not usually continue to earn throughout their lives, assurance companies have an alternative type of policy under which premiums end at a certain age, such as 65, although the policy continues.

Where payments are arranged to come to an end in this way, premiums must, of course, be higher. The younger the insured person, the lower his premiums. Whole-life policies can also be taken out 'with profits'—that is, the company pays bonuses based on its profits in addition to the fixed sum. This is a valuable 'hedge' against inflation.

ENDOWMENT ASSURANCE Most people want to be able to use their savings in retirement, so they take out another type of policy—endowment assurance. This protects the family and provides a sum of money at the maturity date—that is, at the end of the agreed term of years—or on death, if it occurs first.

The term of the policy can be as long or as short as the person wishes, although for tax reasons policies for terms of less than ten years are not common. Premiums depend on whether the policy is with or without profits, the age of the insured person, the sum assured and the term of the policy.

An endowment policy can also be combined with a mortgage as protection against the premature death of the borrower. This is not to be confused with a mortgage-protection policy.

The borrower takes out an endowment policy on his own life, and pays the premiums and the interest on the loan. If he dies before the end of the loan period, the endowment policy automatically pays off the loan.

If he survives, the policy matures at the end of the loan period and the loan is paid off in one lump sum. The advantage is that there is tax relief on both the premiums and the interest. □ Applying for a mortgage, p. 194.

## Policies with and without profits

A person who takes out a whole-life or an endowment policy can qualify for a share of the profits earned by the assurance company on its investments. The share, or bonus, is added to the original sum assured so that at maturity there is a much larger lump sum.

This is known as a 'with-profits' policy and counters the effects of inflation as, during periods of inflation and high interest rates, bonuses are likely to be high, too.

It is difficult to quote a precise figure on maturity 25 or 30 years ahead because the profits earned by an assurance company will vary according to changes in its management, or in the economic climate, and fluctuations in the stock market. Estimates of bonuses should be treated with caution.

'Without-profits' policies do not carry any right to share in surpluses, but they incorporate a degree of profit as the total premiums paid are usually less than the sum assured.

Premiums for with-profits policies are always higher than for without-profits policies, because the holder is not only paying to have his life assured, but he is also to be entitled to a share in the company's financial success. Many companies also pay terminal bonuses when the policy matures. They are paid out of the increased value of the stocks and shares the companies hold. The size of the terminal bonus varies with the attitude of the company and the capital appreciation at the time the policy matures and is paid.

## Unit-linked policies

The growth of the unit trust movement has led assurance companies to offer unit-linked assurance under which most of the premium is invested in a named unit trust.

When the policy matures or is surrendered, the insured person receives either the value of the units bought by the premiums or the actual units themselves.

Units are bought out of each premium payment, with a small amount retained to cover the company's expenses and the death risk. The company may use part of that amount to guarantee that the eventual value of the units at maturity will not be less than the actual premiums paid. Normally, the value should be much more, since the income from the units is re-invested in buying more units.

If the insured person dies during the term of the policy, his dependants receive the value of the units bought up to that date, or a guaranteed sum of money, whichever is greater.

There are many combinations of all these types of policy. For example, some policies are 50 per cent without profits and 50 per cent unit-linked; others allow the holder to increase the sum assured by paying larger premiums on the policy without having to take a further medical examination.

BUILDING-SOCIETY-LINKED POLICIES A policy can provide for the bulk of each premium to be invested in a deposit in a named building society, bearing interest at that society's normal rate, or at a similar rate.

Although the earnings on such a policy are similar to a conventional one, there is the advantage that, if the holder wants to cancel the policy, he is usually guaranteed the return of the amount in the deposit account. With an ordinary policy, there is no such guarantee.

The whole of the premiums on such policies may qualify for tax relief, giving the saver a means of depositing money with a building society and qualifying for a tax reduction.

## Choosing the company

Compare the premium rates and the rate of bonuses paid out on life policies in previous years by companies offering the type of policies required. Look also at their estimated figures for the future. Remember, however, that these figures are no more than estimates. COMPARING THE TERMS It is possible to surrender or cash in a policy before it matures, though it is rarely financially advisable, except in unit-linked or building-society-linked insurance policies.

The payment the policy-holder receives is known as the surrender value. For the first two or three years, there is no surrender value at all. For several years after that, the surrender value is small and usually does not even cover the amount of the premiums paid.

Few British insurance companies specify surrender values in their policies, so it is difficult to estimate future performance. Where surrender values are given, they are included in a schedule which shows what the policy-holder can expect to receive at various stages in the life of the policy.

A company will always work out a surrender value if it is asked to. There is no charge to the policy-holder, or any commitment on his part. SPECIAL CONDITIONS AND RESTRICTIONS Try to ensure that there are as few conditions as possible attached to the policy. Some policies, for example, exclude people who are pilots or who live abroad permanently.

One restriction common to most policies, however, is suicide. Companies do not usually pay out in full where a policy-holder has killed himself, unless he was mentally ill at the time. For what is called 'insane suicide', companies will pay out. The insurance company's intentions in a case of a suicide where the victim is not mentally ill are usually clearly defined by the terms of the policy.

## Taking out a policy

Any mis-statement or omission of material facts may give the company the right to refuse payment. This is because a life-assurance policy is known as a contract 'of the utmost good faith'. This means the company must have details which will enable it to assess the risk involved so it can decide whether to issue a policy and at what premium.

The law provides that if any false statement can be proved, the company will be free to avoid the contract—that is, not pay out.

Great care should therefore be taken in answering questions, particularly about past health or about proposals which other companies may have accepted on special terms. If there is any doubt, answer 'not to my knowledge' rather than 'no'.

The assurance company usually wants to know about the habits of the applicant and the health history of his family. The company may also ask him to undergo a medical examination, for which it will pay the doctor's fee and make the necessary arrangements. If a person is in reasonably good health for his age, however, most companies accept him without an examination at the normal premium rate.

Once a person is rejected, or accepted with loaded premium—that is, a higher charge than the published rate for his age—his name is placed on a list shared by the insurance companies. This does not necessarily mean he will also be rejected or charged more by other companies, as standards differ among them. They may instead investigate the matter thoroughly or impose special conditions.

Most companies do not pay out on a claim or on maturity without proof of age. It saves trouble if proof is given when the policy is taken out, by supplying a birth certificate.

## Getting a loan

Life-assurance policies are also useful as security for a loan or other credit. Many assurance companies are prepared to give loans on the security of a policy of up to 90 per cent of the surrender value. Banks also regard a life-assurance policy as one of the best forms of security for a loan. □ Choosing the type of credit, p. 490.

If a policy-holder finds it difficult to pay his premium in any one year, the company may lend him the amount of premium for that year, and even for the following year, rather than lose the policy altogether.

## Converting and assigning a policy

A policy can usually be changed if it ceases to meet the holder's requirements. This is better in most cases than cashing in the policy and taking out a new one, but is still wasteful and expensive to the policy-holder.

PAID-UP POLICIES A policy-holder who decides to stop paying a premium can ask to have the policy converted to a 'paid-up' policy, instead of surrendering it and losing all benefits. This means that a sum of money, based on the amount paid up, is paid when the person dies, or on maturity in the case of an endowment policy. The amount is obviously less than would be payable under the original policy and, since it ignores compound interest, it is also poor value for the policy-holder.

An assurance policy can be made over to someone else by means of an assignment, a legal document transferring ownership to a third party. A simple way to vest benefits in a wife or children is provided by the Married Women's Property Acts. This usually requires the help of a solicitor. Such a policy then belongs to the person to whom it is assigned.

A policy also can be assigned to or deposited with a third party as security for a loan. The insured person keeps up the payments and gets the policy back when the loan is repaid.

The assurance company should be notified in writing of any assignment. To avoid possible disputes, send the notification in duplicate and ask the company to stamp the copy and return it as an acknowledgment.

A policy may contain a provision making it non-assignable. Any assignment would then be invalid, and any person accepting the policy would not be paid.

## Home service assurance

A well-known form of life assurance is home service assurance or industrial life assurance where premiums are collected regularly from the home. Usually only small sums of money are involved. Benefits, too, are generally small and tend to be poor value. These policies normally contain a prohibition against assignment.

# Accident and illness insurance

INSURANCE can provide protection against an unexpected fall in income as a result of an accident or illness. The three main forms of insurance for such circumstances cover:

**1.** Death by accident. The premium for this policy is relatively small and is a useful supplement to any other life assurance.

**2.** Death or loss of limbs or eyesight by accident. This policy may include an agreed sum to be paid weekly for any other temporary incapacity caused by an accident.

**3.** All accidents and sickness. There is also an alternative—at a lower premium—whereby the policy-holder can choose to insure only against certain diseases.

TICKET INSURANCE The simplest form of accident insurance—'ticket insurance'—is obtained from booking office clerks or vending machines at airports and railway stations. It gives cover only for a particular journey within a specified period of time.

## A permanent policy

One of the best forms of accident insurance is the one with a built-in non-cancellation clause. Under this policy the company cannot cancel the insurance, no matter how many claims for sickness the holder has made, provided that the terms of the policy have been kept. Nor can it force the holder to give up the policy by raising premiums to a prohibitive level. The holder, however, can choose to discontinue the policy if he wishes.

This policy is usually called permanent sickness and accident insurance. The holder may have to have a medical examination. People are usually accepted between the ages of 20 and 55, with the insurance cover ending between 55 and 65.

Costs can be reduced by choosing to receive no benefits for the first one, three, six or 12 months of a claim. An employer may, in any case, continue to pay wages during this period.

RESTRICTIONS Under most policies, the company is entitled to refuse a claim if the insured person is injured or killed taking part in some unusually hazardous activity, such as pot-holing, or if the accident occurs as a result of some act of war.

If the policy-holder was under the influence of drink or drugs at the time of an accident, the company might refuse payment, even if he was not responsible for the accident.

Companies usually specify which illnesses are not covered; cerebral abscess may be included, but not cerebral thrombosis.

A customer taking out almost any type of accident or sickness policy has to fill in a detailed proposal form giving particulars of his job, medical history and physical condition. Non-permanent policies are renewed every year; increasing age usually results in higher premiums, as does a tendency to accidents, leading to a large number of claims.

The insurer wants to know about the pastimes of the person to be insured; for example, a keen skier or mountaineer would attract a higher premium than a bowls enthusiast.

## How to choose

Examine and compare closely the benefits offered by the various policies of the different companies. How many weeks will they pay in the event of incapacity? How much will they pay per £1 of premium? What kinds of accidents and illnesses are covered? When are payments made? What are the lump sums on death or loss of limbs?

Look for these real differences between policies, not only for low premiums.

# Planning for retirement

*Employers' pension schemes*     *Buying an annuity*
*Living off savings*             *Private pension policies*

THE greatest financial change in most people's lives comes when they retire. Standards of living reach their peak in the middle and later years of a working life. But on retirement, income falls sharply to the bare subsistence level provided by the State retirement pension, unless some provision has been made to supplement this.

People looking ahead to retirement can provide themselves with an additional income by joining an employer's pension scheme, investing sufficient savings to provide a regular income from interest and dividends, or by taking out an individual annuity or pension policy with an insurance company.

### Employers' pension schemes
Many firms operate superannuation or pension schemes, and a person working for such a firm has many of his retirement problems solved for him.

If the scheme is voluntary, the employee will want to consider whether it will be worth while joining. If it is compulsory, the value and cost of the pension scheme may be among the factors the employee takes into account in deciding whether to take a job.

Most schemes replace part of the National Insurance graduated pension, and this has to be considered in assessing whether a particular scheme offers value for money. ☐ Qualifying for a State pension, p. 525.

More important is what happens to pension rights and the cash paid in if you decide to change your job and move to another employer. The employee who changes jobs rarely receives as much benefit as if he stayed —and the time to find out what might be lost is before starting the job.

Whether or not the employee can withdraw money from the scheme if he leaves before retirement depends on whether the pension scheme is contributory or non-contributory. In a contributory scheme, the employee contributes to the pension fund as well as the employer; in a non-contributory scheme, only the employer pays.

A person in a contributory scheme is entitled to withdraw all or most of his contributions when he leaves. If he leaves his money in the scheme, he will usually obtain a reduced pension based on his own and his employer's contributions to the fund.

In a non-contributory scheme there is no cash refund on leaving, but some employers grant a reduced pension based on the contributions they have paid.

Be wary of schemes where benefits are payable only at the employer's discretion or which depend on the profitability of the business. If possible, avoid taking a job on these conditions. Find out whether the pension is transferable from one employer to another, as it is for example in the printing industry.

Not all schemes provide for payments to dependants, such as widows and orphans, if the employee dies before retirement. Find out whether the pension ceases when the employee dies after retirement, or if it continues (usually at a reduced rate) for the widow.

TAX RELIEF Most, but not all schemes, are approved by the Inland Revenue, with the result that the premium paid is treated as an allowable expense and is deductible from the employee's earnings before tax is charged. For every £1 he spends in pension payments, the taxpayer saves at least 30p in tax (given an effective tax rate of 30 per cent).

Pension contributions go into a pension fund, and the money is then invested. The pension fund does not pay tax on its income, so its growth is usually quicker than any personal investments a private individual might build up.

When it is paid, the pension is taxable as earned income. But the pensioner may qualify for age exemption, reducing considerably the tax he has to pay.

There may be provision for the payment of a lump sum to the employee when he retires, combined with a smaller pension than he would otherwise have received. In such cases, the lump sum is normally tax free.

### Living off savings
People whose employers do not provide a pension scheme, or who are self-employed, have to make their own arrangements to supplement the State pension.

One way is for the saver to invest his money

in stocks, shares and deposits. If he is able to build up substantial investments by the time he retires, the interest on them might provide an adequate income.

In practice, few people have enough money to be able to live off the interest and dividends alone, and if they are relying on their investments for an income, they are forced to cash a proportion of the investment at regular intervals during retirement.

The difficulty of this course lies in knowing how much of his investment the saver can afford to cash each year.

A person in normal health retiring at the age of 65 could, in theory, work on the basis of average expectation of life—14 years for a man, 17 years for a woman—and invest his savings with a view to living on capital and interest together. Everything would then be used up at death, on the same principle that a building-society mortgage is repaid in equal instalments.

The major drawback of such a scheme, however, is that if the saver is among the thousands of people who live for much longer than the average, he will be in some financial difficulty once he has used up all his capital and is wholly dependent on the State pension.

One way to avoid this is by negotiating a private pension policy—often called a retirement annuity contract—with an insurance company. Provision for retirement can also be made by means of an ordinary endowment assurance policy with annuity options.

## Buying an annuity

Insurance companies sell annuities—which provide a guaranteed annual income until death—based on the average expectation of life. This means that the people who live longer are supported by the contributions of those whose life span is shorter than average.

If a person is in bad health, investing his savings in an annuity will not be beneficial unless the insurance company is willing to give special terms for impaired lives.

Alternatively, for a slightly smaller annuity at the same cost, it is possible to make an agreement that the company will pay for a minimum number of years, say five or ten. If the holder dies in this period, the balance from the insurance company will be paid as a lump sum to his estate.

It is possible to provide a wife with an income if her husband dies first by making it a condition that the annuity is to continue for her lifetime should she outlive her husband.

Other types of annuity are also available. Some people, for instance, arrange that if they die before they have had their 'money's worth' in payments under an annuity, the difference between the price they paid for it and the money they have had back from the insurance company will be paid into their estate.

Another possibility is an increasing annuity, under which payments are increased—for example by 3 per cent a year—to keep pace with the rising cost of living.

The annuity market is highly competitive and when interest rates are high, better terms can be obtained. If interest rates fall, annuities already bought are not affected, and this often adds to the attraction of annuities over other forms of investment.

IMMEDIATE ANNUITIES Annuities which begin to pay a regular income as soon as they are bought are called immediate annuities. They are purchased for a lump sum and can provide quarterly, half-yearly or annual payments for the purchaser.

Immediate annuities are suitable for someone who has retired or is just about to do so.

DEFERRED ANNUITIES A saver can prepare for retirement by paying regular premiums for a deferred annuity which pays out when he or she reaches a specified age.

Deferred annuities are often linked with life-assurance policies so that the saver may be able to claim tax relief. Effectively the annuity then becomes a life-assurance policy, with an option for the sum assured to be used to buy an immediate annuity on maturity. For every £1 he pays in premiums, the taxpayer saves about 15p in tax (given an effective tax rate of 30 per cent).

With a deferred annuity it is possible, by paying extra, to arrange that premiums paid will be refunded to the saver's estate if he dies before he receives any payments or has received only a few payments.

Such policies also have the advantage that they can be surrendered for cash if the holder needs money in an emergency. They can also be used as security for a loan.

TAX ON ANNUITY PAYMENTS For income-tax purposes, payments under an annuity are considered to be in two parts, one representing a repayment of the purchase price and the other the payment of interest.

The repayment part is calculated by dividing the cost of the annuity by the number of years it is expected to run, based on average mortality rates. The figure which results is deducted from the annual payment and is free of tax. The balance is regarded as income and is subject to tax.

The amount of tax payable depends on what allowances and other income the buyer of the annuity has. The income is regarded as unearned (or investment) income, but age relief often applies. ☐ How the income-tax system works, p. 556.

## Private pension policies

Someone who is not in a company pension scheme, or is self-employed, can get tax exemption on the whole of the premiums (up to a set limit) paid for a private pension, or retirement annuity contract.

It is a condition of such a policy that the pension cannot be surrendered, and money cannot be borrowed against it. In addition, the pension cannot be prematurely assigned —made over to someone else.

The maximum annual premium allowed is £1500 or 15 per cent of what the policy-holder earns in non-pensionable employment or self-employment, whichever is the lower. A husband and wife may each pay premiums up to the permitted maximum.

Until April 5, 1971 a lower limit of £750 or 10 per cent of income was set on premiums. But anyone born before 1916 who was not entitled to a pension from full-time employment was allowed to pay premiums up to the following figures:

| TAX RELIEF LIMIT | | |
|---|---|---|
| Year of birth | Limit | Percentage |
| 1914 or 1915 | £825 | 11 |
| 1912 or 1913 | £900 | 12 |
| 1910 or 1911 | £975 | 13 |
| 1908 or 1909 | £1050 | 14 |
| 1907 or earlier | £1125 | 15 |

If the premium exceeds the percentage limit in any one year the excess can be carried forward and added to later premiums so that relief can be claimed in the later year.

Normally a year's tax allowance is calculated by reference to premiums paid that year. But an allowance can be claimed for premiums paid up to six months after the assessment for the year has been made, provided that a claim is made to the Inspector of Taxes within the same six months.

An employee who already contributes to a company pension scheme, and gets tax relief on his payments, may want to take out an additional private pension policy to boost his retirement pension. He will qualify for full tax relief on the pension policy payments only if they are made out of some source of income which provides no pension—such as freelance earnings or a part-time job.

Many variations can be arranged to meet individual circumstances, within the limitations imposed by the Inland Revenue for tax relief on pension premiums. The pension which is eventually received is taxable as earned income and qualifies for earned-income relief.

UNIT-LINKED PENSION POLICIES The feeling that fixed cash benefits do not hold their value, because of inflation, has led to a type of pension policy where the premium, less the insurance company's expenses, is invested in a unit trust selected by the policy-holder. ☐ Putting money in unit trusts, p. 517.

Income from the units in the pension fund is tax free and is re-invested in further units.

Premiums can be varied from time to time so that instead of being committed to fixed payments for years to come, a person can alter the amount he pays if his income rises or falls. If at some stage the price of the units appears to be low, he can pay in a lump sum and have the units added at that price, just as if he were making a direct investment.

Similarly, if a person stops paying he is not penalised, for the units already allotted to the policy continue to be held for him, and the income from them will be re-invested, until he reaches retirement age.

For some people, this is more attractive than the usual practice with life-assurance policies, where the ending of a policy can be unprofitable and where flexibility of payments is not so easily arranged.

A unit-linked policy may provide for the units in the person's holding to be sold for his estate if he dies early before having received the full amount due. The pension may be fixed at retirement according to the value of the investment at that time, or it may fluctuate with changes in unit prices. The choice is often available to the insured person.

Because the policy is represented at all times by a known quantity of units, with a regularly published price, it is usually possible to vary the age at which payments of the pension are started. In this way a man who takes out a unit-linked pension policy does not necessarily have to wait until the age he originally specified for receiving the pension. He could decide to start drawing the pension earlier if, say, the value of the units had reached a level which would provide him with the income he required.

The unit trust in which the premiums are invested can also be changed. For example, a person can have a long-term growth trust while he is contributing, in order to achieve maximum growth of his savings, and he can then change to one offering a higher income but smaller growth prospects when he retires, so that he has the greatest possible income at his disposal in these later years.

# Qualifying for a State pension

THE State pension scheme depends on contributions from worker and employer. It provides an income for anyone who has retired from full-time work after paying regular National Insurance contributions and has reached pensionable age—65 for men, 60 for women.

The State scheme has two parts—the flat-rate retirement pension, which can be paid regardless of any private pension arrangement; and the graduated pension, which provides extra retirement income where there is no suitable employer's scheme available.

**Flat-rate retirement pension**
To qualify for the flat-rate retirement pension, an employee must have paid at least 156 flat-rate contributions between the date he enters the scheme and the date he reaches 65 (60 for a woman). To qualify for a standard-rate retirement pension, an employee must have averaged at least 50 contributions a year throughout the time he has been insured.

These can include 'credits'—contributions credited on his insurance card during, for example, sickness or unemployment, when he need not pay.

A reduced rate of pension will be paid if the average is less than 50 contributions a year. The pension is cut roughly in proportion to the amount by which contributions have fallen short. No pension at all will be paid if the average is less than 13.
PENSIONERS WHO WORK People who take the pension at 65 (60 for a woman) but continue to do paid work are allowed to earn a limited amount in any week without a cut in pension.

Anyone who carries on with regular work after retirement age can earn a bigger eventual pension by continuing to pay contributions. In any case, a man of 70 (or a woman of 65) is assumed, for pension purposes, to have retired, and can receive a full pension regardless of any earnings.
WIVES A wife aged 60 or over may qualify for a flat-rate pension in her own right, because she has worked and paid contributions, or through her husband's contributions.

To get a pension on her own insurance, a wife must have paid, or been credited with, contributions for at least half the weeks between her marriage and her 60th birthday.

A wife qualified on her own insurance can draw her pension if she retires before her husband. But a wife whose pension depends on her husband's contributions must wait until he retires.

A husband who draws a State pension, but whose wife is not yet 60, can claim an allowance for her as a dependant. If his contributions record is below the 50-a-year average, the allowance is reduced. To qualify for the allowance he must either be living with his wife or paying at least the amount of the allowance towards her maintenance, and she must not be drawing any other National Insurance benefit or earning more than the amount of the allowance.

A divorced woman can use her former husband's contribution record before and during the marriage, if it is better than her own record, to help her to qualify for a pension.
CHILDREN Allowances are paid for children supported by pensioners. The allowance ends when a child reaches 16, although for children staying on at school, students and some apprentices the age limit is 19.

An additional allowance may be payable for a woman taking care of the pensioner's child, so long as his wife is not receiving a State pension and he is not receiving a dependant's allowance for her.

**Graduated pension**
Most employees pay into the graduated pension scheme. Contributions are calculated as a percentage of weekly earnings within certain limits. The age rules are as for the flat-rate scheme. The amount of the pension, too, depends on the total contributions paid.

An employee need not subscribe fully to this scheme if the Registrar of Non-Participating Employments is satisfied that he is adequately covered for retirement and allows the *employer* to 'contract out' of the graduated scheme. The *employee* has no individual option.

Contracted-out employees pay a higher flat-rate contribution and a reduced graduated contribution which counts for graduated pension in the normal way.
WIVES A wife can get a graduated pension on her own contributions, but not on her husband's. A wife who is not entitled to a separate flat-rate pension, but who has paid graduated contributions, can draw her graduated pension by itself, once she is 60, even if her husband has not yet retired.

# Setting up a trust

*Reasons for a trust*  
*Choosing the type of trust*  
*What the trust does*

*Choosing the trustees*  
*Duties of trustees*

A TRUST is a legal arrangement by which people called trustees are put in charge of assets such as money or property which they use for the benefit of other people known as the beneficiaries. The trustees are the legal owners of the assets, but cannot benefit from them; the beneficiaries are not the legal owners, but do benefit.

Trusts usually involve a transfer to trustees of money or other assets which they are to hold as capital. This is called the trust fund.

The person who sets up the trust decides how he wants the trustees to deal with the trust fund itself and with the income it will produce when it is invested.

### Reasons for a trust

The creator of a trust can use it to make a gift to a person who cannot receive such a gift directly—for example, a boy or girl under 18 who cannot legally own a house or land. Anyone wishing to make a gift of property to a child can transfer it to trustees with instructions to hold it until the child is 18 and then transfer it to him.

The trust can also be used to benefit someone who is suffering from mental illness or who is incapable for some other reason of managing his own affairs.

Protecting family assets from extravagance or the risk of bankruptcy is another reason for setting up a trust. A man might wish to leave money to his widow or children but fear that they would squander the money if they were given a free hand with it. He can lessen the chances by appointing responsible trustees with the power to decide how much of the money can safely be paid to the beneficiaries at any one time.

A trust can be designed so that if a beneficiary goes bankrupt, the money passes to other members of the family rather than to the bankrupt's creditors.

The trust can be used to set aside assets to be used in a flexible way in the future. Thus, a man with three young daughters may set up a trust in his will, leaving the trustees money to distribute as they think best amongst the daughters when they grow up. If two of them marry when they are of age and the other does

not, the trustees may, for example, give one-quarter to the two married daughters and half to the unmarried one if she is poorer.

Trusts can also be used to channel money to charity, or to pay for the upkeep of a pet.

Trusts play a part in certain tax-saving schemes. Most schemes are drawn up individually in consultation with lawyers and tax experts, and anyone wishing to use a trust in this way should take professional advice.

A trust can also be a method of saving estate duty. ☐ How estate duty works, p. 540.

### Choosing the type of trust

Before setting up a trust the creator should consider what he wants to achieve for the beneficiaries and which type of trust best provides this. There are basically three types of trust—simple, discretionary and protective.

SIMPLE TRUSTS Anyone who wishes to lay down precisely how the capital and the income of the trust fund should be used will set up a simple trust.

Take the case of a man who puts £2000 into trust and directs that the income shall be paid to his wife for as long as she lives, and that after her death, the money (or the investments which then represent it) shall be divided equally between their children.

The wife is called an income beneficiary and she is entitled to all the income which the £2000 produces, but not to the capital.

The children are known as the capital beneficiaries. When their mother dies they share the £2000 bequest equally. Unless the trust instrument—the document which sets out the terms of the trust—provides for it, the children do not receive any income from the fund during their mother's lifetime.

There can be more than one income beneficiary at the same time.

DISCRETIONARY TRUSTS A trust which allows the trustees to decide, as circumstances change, how the capital and/or income of the trust fund shall be divided among the named beneficiaries is known as a discretionary trust.

It is a useful form of trust for a man who wants to provide for several dependants, but cannot foresee who will need the most.

The trustees of a discretionary trust may

also be given power to transfer capital to the beneficiaries at whatever time, and in whatever proportions, they think fit.

PROTECTIVE TRUSTS Someone who wants to provide for another person may hesitate to make an outright gift which might be squandered or seized if the recipient goes bankrupt. The solution is to set up a protective trust.

The beneficiary is given the income from the trust fund for life, unless certain specified events occur—such as going bankrupt. If he does anything to deprive himself of the right to receive this income, the trust changes to a discretionary trust. Then the trustees have to divide the income as they see fit among the beneficiary and members of his family.

A person cannot legally protect himself in this way from the effects of his own bankruptcy. ☐ Debts and bankruptcy, p. 580.

HOW A TRUST IS CREATED The deed or will by which the trust is created is known as the trust instrument. Because the law of trusts is complex, it is best drawn up by a solicitor.

## What the trust does

Generally a trust allows the trustees to invest the capital, make advances to beneficiaries, and use income from the trust fund to take care of any children who will be entitled to the capital when they are grown up. If the creator wishes, the trust instrument can specifically exclude some of these powers.

INVESTMENTS The trust instrument should say how trust funds are to be invested, and the trustees must follow any instructions which it gives about investments.

If the trust instrument does not specify how the fund is to be invested, the trustees have investment powers under law.

These allow them to divide the trust fund into two parts (which must initially be of equal value) and to invest one part in substantial public companies which show a potential for growth. The other part must be invested in gilt-edged and other fixed-interest securities, including Government stock, National Savings Certificates and building-society deposits.

The duties of trustees in making investments are laid down by law. In some cases the law makes it necessary for them to seek professional advice before investing, and it is always desirable to do so.

If the creator of the trust wants to give special powers to the trustees—for example, to allow them to keep a particular block of shares which would not be an authorised investment under the general law of trusts—he should say so in the trust instrument.

When considering investment possibilities the creator of the trust and the trustees must bear in mind the often conflicting needs of the different beneficiaries.

If, for example, the income from a trust fund is to go to a woman during her lifetime and the capital to her brother when she dies, it is in her interests that a large proportion is invested to yield high income, even if there is little prospect of capital growth.

On the other hand, it is in the brother's interests that a high proportion of the fund should be put into investments likely to grow in capital value, even if this means that the income will be smaller in the meantime.

The creator of the trust may indicate whose interests are to be paramount; if he does not, the trustees must try to strike a balance between the two.

ADVANCES The trustees can usually advance capital to a beneficiary before he is entitled to receive it, if he is in need. If the creator wants to prevent such a situation, he must exclude this power in the trust instrument.

If nothing is said on this point, the trustees can make an early advance of up to a half of the capital which the beneficiary would expect to receive from the trust.

Even if the beneficiary is entitled to the full amount only when he fulfils some condition—such as getting married—and he does not fulfil that condition, he does not need to refund the money advanced.

But if he does become entitled to the capital of the trust fund and is one of several people who are to share it, then the amount of his share is reduced by the amount of the advance he has already had (unless the creator of the trust provides otherwise).

If there is an income beneficiary and a capital beneficiary, then the income beneficiary must give his consent before any arrangement can be made to advance a share of the capital to the other beneficiary. This is because any reduction in the amount of capital in the trust fund has the effect of reducing the income from it in most cases.

CHILDREN A trust can be used to provide for children's maintenance, education or benefit up to the age of 18. The trustees can usually make payments either to the parents directly or to the school or any other body involved.

Parents have to pay income tax on any money obtained from a trust which is used before April 5, 1972 for the benefit of their children. After that date, such money may be taxed as the child's unearned income.

If the trustees do not use all the income for these purposes, they must re-invest the surplus income and keep it until the child reaches 18. If the child is then entitled to the capital under the terms of the trust, he will also receive the accumulated income.

## Choosing the trustees

After the terms of the trust have been decided upon, the next step is to choose the trustees. This is done by the creator of the trust.

When a trust is created by will, the executors are usually made trustees. Solicitors are also often appointed as trustees. They charge for acting in this capacity.

Most banks have executor and trustee companies or departments which accept trusteeships on behalf of customers. There is a Government department, the Public Trustee (24 Kingsway, London WC2B 6JR), which used to accept the role of trustee, but is currently being wound up.

Banks also charge for acting as trustees. They are often more expensive than solicitors.

A person who creates a trust which will be effective in his own lifetime may himself be one of the trustees. He can give himself the right to appoint new trustees when the need arises; or he can give the right to someone else, to be exercised after his death.

If he does not confer upon himself or another person the right to appoint new trustees, or if the trust is to come into effect after his death, then the remaining trustees normally have the power to nominate successors if one of them dies or retires.

COST When a trust is created by will it does not greatly increase the cost of making a will. Wills which contain simple trusts are often drawn up for £5 or less, and even a will containing a complicated trust is not likely to cost more than about £20.

It may be more expensive for the person who creates a trust by separate deed in his lifetime, and anyone thinking of doing this should consult a solicitor to find out how much it is likely to cost.

Where a house, land or stocks and shares are put into a trust, separate conveyance or transfer documents are required to pass the property into the trustees' ownership, and this also adds to the cost.

Stamp duty is payable at the rate of £1 for every £100 of the value of many types of asset put into a trust of this sort.

## Duties of trustees

Anyone over 18 can be appointed as a trustee, but before agreeing to become one, it is worth examining carefully a trustee's tasks.

In general, a trustee is not entitled to any payment for his services, and even if all goes well he may have to contend with complaints from unhappy beneficiaries.

Anyone who acts as a trustee has a legal obligation to observe the terms of the trust. If he fails to do so—innocently or intentionally—he may have to make good from his own pocket any money wrongly distributed.

However, the creator of the trust can ensure that his trustees do not suffer financially because of an honest mistake by having a clause inserted in the trust instrument which protects them in such a situation.

PROFESSIONAL ADVICE The wisest course for a trustee not professionally qualified in administering trusts is to appoint an expert to do this for him.

Under the general law a trustee may instruct solicitors to undertake all the routine administration of the trust, and appoint solicitors or accountants to prepare trust accounts and to work out tax liability. The solicitor or accountant appointed in this way can be paid out of the trust fund.

But the trustee must make the final decisions in any matters affecting the trust—and he is responsible for them.

PAYMENT Trustees are entitled to recover all expenses incurred in connection with the administration of the trust. But they can charge for their services, or for the time they spend administering the trust, only when one of the following applies: firstly, the trust instrument specifically authorises such payment; secondly, all the beneficiaries agree to a charge being made (if they are adults with no mental disability); thirdly, a court authorises the trustees to make a charge—which it will do only in exceptional circumstances, such as where a trustee contributes a special skill.

If the creator of the trust wants to have a professional trustee such as a solicitor, he must give him power in the trust instrument to charge for his services.

CONFLICTING INTERESTS Unless the trust instrument or all the beneficiaries authorise it, the trustee must not place himself in a position where his own interest conflicts with that of the beneficiaries. For this reason, a trustee cannot usually buy property from the trust, even at a fair market value.

He is not allowed to keep any profit which he makes from his position as a trustee, even if the trust does not suffer. If, for instance, he is agent for an insurance company, and arranges for the trust assets to be insured, he must pay any commission received to the trust.

BREACH OF TRUST If the trustees do not observe the terms of the trust, a beneficiary may be entitled to sue for damages. If the beneficiary's 'breach of trust' action succeeds he may be entitled to compensation for any loss he has suffered as a result of the breach.

The usual grounds for such cases are that the trustees have invested trust money in unauthorised assets; that they have been dishonest in administering the trust; that they have paid out to the wrong beneficiary; or that they have not paid out the correct amount to one of the beneficiaries.

In law, each trustee is responsible for the administration of the trust. This means that every trustee must keep himself informed on all matters of administration—even if most of the work is being done by other trustees or by solicitors appointed by the trust.

RETIREMENT There are only four circumstances in which a trustee can normally retire:
1. If the trust instrument allows him to.
2. If another person is appointed in his place.
3. If he leaves a minimum of two trustees, and the others consent to his retiring.
4. If all possible beneficiaries are over 18, suffer from no mental disability, and consent to the retirement.

Otherwise, he can apply to the court to be discharged from his duties; but this is rare, and should not be necessary.

## Benefiting from a trust

WHETHER a trust is set up during the lifetime of its creator or by his will, the beneficiaries are entitled to be informed about the trust by the trustees.

There is no public register of trust deeds, so someone who believes he may have been named as a beneficiary but has not been informed should contact the solicitors of the person making the trust. The contact can be made personally or through another solicitor.

If he believes the trust is contained in a will of someone who has died, he can check this by paying a search fee of 5p to inspect a copy of the will at the Registrar General's Office, Somerset House, Strand, London WC2R 1LA. Alternatively, he can write to the solicitors acting for the executors of the will.

Those named to benefit from a trust are entitled to accounts and information from the trustees enabling them to check that they are getting their due, and that the trust is being properly administered.

The trustees are bound by law to inform beneficiaries if, for example, any changes are made in the investment of the trust fund. But these details are not supplied automatically—the beneficiary has to ask for them.

An income beneficiary is entitled to accounts from the trustees showing the income of the trusts. A capital beneficiary is entitled to accounts showing dealings with all capital assets. The trustees' responsibility is only to *show* these accounts to a beneficiary. They need not send a copy of accounts for the beneficiary to keep, although in practice they usually do so.

A discretionary beneficiary—one who does not benefit from the trust automatically but can do so at the discretion of the trustees—is entitled to see accounts even if the trustees have not exercised their discretion in his favour.

ENDING THE TRUST A sole beneficiary can, if he is over 18 and has no mental disability, bring the trust to an end—even if the person who set up the trust intended it to go on for a longer period. Similarly, if there are several named beneficiaries all over 18 and they all agree, they can bring the trust to an end. Suppose, for example, that a widow is entitled to the income from a trust for her life and that on her death the capital is to be divided between her two sons. As soon as both are 18, they can, with their mother, end the trust if they wish, and share the capital.

This saves estate duty if the mother dies, because it would otherwise be assessed on all the assets and income of the trust. If the trust is broken and only part is left with the mother, estate duty is saved on the remainder.

Because of the complications involved, it is necessary to break a trust through a solicitor, who can advise on the fair distribution of the capital. It is not possible to end a trust by agreement if unborn heirs are included among the beneficiaries.

If any person who might benefit from a trust is under 18, or if there are unborn beneficiaries, any variation in the trust must be made through a court. The court protects the interests of those who are not adults by ensuring that the arrangement is fair before sanctioning it.

Unless the total value of the trust fund is more than £20,000, it is not usually worth making an application to a court, because of the cost involved.

# Wills I : advantages of making a will

*Putting the will in writing*    *Changed circumstances at death*
*Who can make a will*    *Keeping the will safe*
*Making the will clear*    *Altering a will*

**M**ANY people think that because they own little property or few possessions there is no point in making a will. Others believe that when they die their family can sort out their belongings and valuables and distribute them fairly.

They may even leave a letter or other informal paper setting out their wishes which, although not a valid will, indicates what they want done with their belongings. The law, however, makes definite provision, under what are called the intestacy rules, for the division of property after death when there is no valid will. □ Distributing an estate, p. 430.

These rules are based on what are assumed to be the average person's obligations. But unless a proper will is made, there is no guarantee that property will be divided as the dead person would have wished.

For example, in law the surviving husband or wife is always entitled to the first £15,000 of any estate, in addition to the dead person's household goods, if there is no will. Since many people die leaving much less, this rule may mean that children receive nothing.

ESCAPING DEATH DUTY Making a will is also an important method of escaping death or estate duty—the tax that may have to be paid when someone dies on the value of his property and belongings (which are known in law as his estate).

Take the case of a man who wants to leave everything to his wife. If he fails to make a will and his widow dies shortly after him, estate duty may be charged twice on the same property (the second time at a reduced rate). A will overcomes this risk.

Again, a husband may prefer to leave property to his wife in such a way that the remainder passes to their children when she dies. A will can make this possible without estate duty being charged on the death of the widow.

## Putting the will in writing
The person making a will, known in law as the testator, must put it in writing. A spoken request by a dying man has no legal validity. The only exception—known as a privileged will—is for a will made by a member of the armed forces on active military service.

USING A SOLICITOR There is no need to have a solicitor draw up a will. But using one is a form of insurance which may avoid disputes about the meaning of the will after death, and the testator gets the benefit of legal knowledge and practical advice.

A solicitor's charge for a simple will is about £8 to £12. Many ask less and some have a tradition of charging an uneconomic fee, especially to established clients.

## Who can make a will
Anyone over the age of 18 can make a will provided he is of sound mind, memory and understanding. There is no age limit for members of the armed forces on active service.

MENTAL ILLNESS A court can declare a will invalid if the relatives are able to prove that the deceased was not of sound mind at the time of making it. But unless there is evidence to the contrary, it is presumed that the maker of a will was sane.

To be considered sane for the purpose of making a will the testator must be fully capable of comprehending three points:
**1.** He must know that he is making a will giving his property to the various beneficiaries.
**2.** He must know the extent of the property which he has for disposal.
**3.** He must understand the nature and extent of the claims which people who might expect to benefit may have on him.

Incapacity to understand any of these three points need not be the result of actual mental illness. It could arise from senility, physical illness or drunkenness at the time the testator makes the will.

The fact that the testator was suffering from insane delusions would not necessarily invalidate his will, if it could be shown that they did not affect his capacity to understand the three points at the time of making the will.

FORCE OR INFLUENCE The law states that a will must be a product of the man or woman's own mind. It will not be valid if it is obtained by force, threats, fraud or what the law calls 'undue influence'.

Attempts to influence someone who is making a will by appealing to his sense of family affection or ties of kindred or gratitude for services rendered are not undue influence. But bullying the testator or lying about the character of someone who is to benefit might invalidate the will.

DISABLEMENT A person who is blind, deaf and dumb, paralysed or illiterate can make a will, but the will should include a clause which refers to his disability and shows that he understood and approved the will despite the disability. ☐ Making a simple will, p. 532.

SERIOUS INTENTION A will must be made on purpose and in earnest. It is invalid if it is made as a joke, without any intention of its having legal effect, or if it is signed by mistake without the testator realising that he is putting his signature to a will.

**Making the will clear**
A will is unique among legal documents for, when it becomes effective, the person who made it is not there to explain what it means.

This has led the courts to be very strict in interpreting wills. The testator must therefore ensure that there can be no doubt about names, addresses or property described.

Words are interpreted by the courts in their strictest sense unless the will itself shows that the testator used them in some other way. 'Grandchild' does not normally include a great-grandchild. 'Dependants' may be too vague an expression to have any effect.

The courts make great efforts—by examining the past circumstances of the deceased—to decide what is meant in the will.

➤ WHICH NIECE DID THE AUNT MEAN? *A woman left a will in 1912 which divided all her residuary estate between 'my brother Walter Jeffrey, his wife and their daughter'. But Walter Jeffrey had five daughters. The High Court was asked to decide which one was meant. It took into account evidence that the aunt was particularly fond of one girl, Phoebe, and had made an earlier will (later revised) naming her specifically. Several letters between the aunt and the niece were also produced in court showing the tie of affection.*
DECISION *The court found that evidence of intention was strong enough to show that Phoebe should receive a one-third share with her parents. (In re Jeffrey.)* ◄

Even where a testator gives apparently precise instructions, the courts may decide that the general rules of law must apply.

➤ PROBLEM OF WHO DIED FIRST *Dr Trevor Rowland made a will in 1956 before taking on a job in the South Pacific. He left everything to his wife, but said that if her death 'preceded or coincided' with his, his property was to go to his brother and nephew.*

*Dr Rowland and his wife were both lost in a shipwreck in the South Seas. There was no evidence of what happened, so it was impossible to say, as the will required, that Mrs Rowland died first or at the same time as her husband.*
DECISION *The general rule of law was applied which presumes that the older person dies first. That was Dr Rowland. His property went to his wife and then, as she also was dead, it descended under her will to her relatives instead of to his relatives. (In re Rowland.)* ◄

That was probably not what Dr Rowland wanted, but the Court of Appeal said that the will had to be strictly interpreted.

**Changed circumstances at death**
A will is said to 'speak from death', which means that it is read as if it were the testator's last words. When it speaks of 'all my property', it means all the property when he dies, not at the time of writing.

Similarly when it speaks of 'all my grandchildren' it is not restricted only to those who were alive when the will was made.

But if the testator writes 'my grandchildren' and then names those alive at the time, any others born later will be excluded.

**Keeping the will safe**
A will should be kept carefully. It can be lodged with the bank or the family solicitor, or it may be kept at home. The testator, however, should ensure that his executors know where to find it when he dies.

When a will is destroyed by accident or not found on the death of the testator, the estate must be divided as if no will had been made, unless it is clear that the testator did not intend to revoke the will and it is possible to prove what its contents were. ☐ Distributing an estate, p. 430.

**Altering a will**
A will, once made, need not be final—the testator can change it at any time by adding a codicil or making a new will. A testator also has to make a new will when he or she marries, as marriage usually revokes an existing will. ☐ Changing a will, p. 539.

When the testator dies, relatives who feel they have not been provided for adequately in a will can sometimes get its contents varied by a court. If they can prove it was not properly made, they may be able to get it set aside. ☐ Challenging a will, p. 422.

# Wills II : making a simple will

*Introduction to the will*  *Signatures on the will*
*Appointing executors*  *Witnesses to a will*
*Disposal of property*  *Will forms*

THERE are four essential points which must be included in a will to make it valid. First, it must contain an introductory statement. Then it needs a clause appointing at least one executor. Thirdly, it must give instructions for the disposal of property. Finally it must be signed by the person making the will in the presence of at least two witnesses, and by the witnesses themselves in his presence.

## Introduction to the will

Every will should begin by stating that it is a will, and naming the person making it—called the testator or, if it is a woman, the testatrix. Men usually add occupation and women marital status, though this is not essential.

The will must be dated and it must make clear that it supersedes any previous will, or amendment to a previous will, called a codicil.

## Appointing executors

The person who sees that the terms of the will are carried out and arranges payment of estate duty is called an executor, or executrix in the case of a woman. At least one executor or executrix should be named in the will.

Sometimes, even in the simplest will, part of the money has to be held in trust for children. In such cases the executors are normally also named as trustees—although there is no reason why other or additional people should not be trustees. ☐ Setting up a trust, p. 526.

Be sure to get the prior agreement of anyone who is to be named as an executor or trustee; no one is obliged to accept either position. If, when someone dies, the executors named refuse to act, anyone with an interest in the estate can apply to administer it. ☐ What happens to property and belongings, p. 420.

## Disposal of property

The testator should make sure that all his property is covered by the will. The simplest solution is to make his only gift a 'residuary' one—a gift, that is, of 'all my property'.

It is inadvisable simply to dispose of everything he owns, item by item, for he is likely to own other things by the time he dies. In

these circumstances only the items detailed would be covered by the will. Any new items would be dealt with as if there were no will and would be covered by the intestacy rules.

If the testator wants to make specific gifts, he should make sure that he leaves the 'residue' of all the rest of his property to a named person. Otherwise anything he has not specifically mentioned will have to be distributed according to the intestacy rules. ☐ Distributing an estate, p. 430.

## Signatures on the will

The will must be signed by the testator in the presence of at least two independent witnesses, who are not beneficiaries, and they must sign below his signature and in his presence.

Although it may be sufficient in law for the testator and the witnesses merely to sign their names, in practice it is essential for the will to include a clause saying that the testator signed in their presence and that they then signed in his. This is known as the attestation clause.

If there is no such clause, it may be difficult for the executors to obtain legal authority to handle the estate (the grant of probate). The witnesses must be traced and asked to swear an 'affidavit of due execution' setting out when and where the will was signed and witnessed. If either of them has died or cannot be found, the will is declared invalid.

If the testator is unable to sign, it can be signed for him by someone else, but it must be done in his presence. The will must have been read to him and he must have acknowledged in the presence of the two witnesses that it represents his wishes. In such cases an attestation clause must also indicate that the will was signed by someone other than the testator, and that the other formalities have been complied with.

WHERE TO SIGN Normally the signatures on a will should be at the end. It is advisable for the testator to sign immediately after the wording, leaving no room for additions.

If the will covers more than one page, the testator's signature is required only at the end. If the testator signs only the first page, the rest of the will is invalid.

After the will has been written but before

it is signed, the testator may make alterations. These will be valid if the testator and witnesses all sign each alteration.

## Witnesses to a will

Anyone, except a blind person, can witness the signature on a will, although it is best to choose someone over 18. But any gift made to a witness is invalid. It will go into the residue or be dealt with under the intestacy rules. Similarly, the wife or husband of a witness cannot benefit from a will—unless they were married after the will was signed.

There is one exception to this rule. If there are two witnesses who do not stand to benefit from the will either personally or through their husbands or wives, further witnesses will be strictly speaking 'surplus to requirements', and any bequests to them will be valid.

A professional man, such as a solicitor or an accountant, who has agreed to become an executor, will not be able to claim a fee for his work if he has signed the will as a witness. He will, however, be entitled to expenses.

Witnesses do not need to see the contents of the will. They are only required to witness the testator's signature and should not sign unless they actually see him signing.

## Will forms

Most stationers sell will forms costing about 10p each. Although there is no need to use these forms—any piece of paper is satisfactory—a standard form helps the testator to remember the points to be included.

One disadvantage of a standard will form is that the restricted space may make the testator turn to the back of the form or try to fit legacies in by some other way. If he and the witnesses then sign at the front of the form—instead of at the end as the law requires—the later part of the will becomes invalid.

---

## The clauses of a simple will

The completed standard simple will form must give the name and address of the person making the will, called the testator. The will must be fully dated and all former wills and codicils should be revoked. Give the name and address of the executors. If the testator wishes them to receive a fee or a gift for their services he should make a clause to this effect in the will, as they will otherwise be barred from claiming anything. If the testator makes gifts of money or items of property before the residuary gift, these will normally be free of estate duty unless they are gifts of freehold land or houses —in which case the person to whom they are given will have to pay any estate duty attributable to them. If the testator wants the duty to be paid out of the residue of his estate instead, he should say that it is 'free' of duty. It is a good idea to say this even when the gift is not a house or land

> This will is made by Thomas James Johnson, Salesman, of 12 Highwood Close, Birmingham 17, on the 9th day of March 1971.
>
> 1. I hereby revoke all former wills and codicils made by me.
>
> 2. I appoint James Edward Robinson of 12 High Street, Newton, Kent, and William Jeremy Johnson of 2 Acacia Avenue, Newton, Kent, to be executors and trustees of my will.
>
> 3. I leave £100 and my grandfather clock to my nephew, Thomas John Johnson, of 49 Birdwalk Avenue, Birmingham 19, and the residue of my estate to my wife, Sylvia Margaret Johnson.
>
> Signed by the testator in our presence and then by us as witnesses in his presence.
>
> *T. Johnson*
>
> Thomas J. Johnson
> Testator
>
> *Jas R. King*
>
> Jas R. King,
> 10 Highwood Close,
> Birmingham 17
>
> Cabinetmaker
>
> *P. Baker*
>
> Penelope Baker,
> 14 Highwood Close,
> Birmingham 17
>
> Spinster

# Wills III : making a complex will

*Gifts of property and money*　　*Disposing of the body*
*The residue of the estate*　　*Simultaneous deaths*
*Giving to charity*　　*Imposing conditions on gifts*

SOMETIMES a simple will is not enough to express the intention of a testator. He may want to make a number of special gifts to his friends, for example, and then divide what is left among two or more beneficiaries.

The drafting of a complex will is usually entrusted to a solicitor. An unqualified person who does it himself runs the risk that his intentions will not be carried out because of an ambiguity in the drafting of the clauses.

The solicitor will first deal with the special gifts, separating the gifts of property or belongings from the money gifts.

## Gifts of property
Leaving an article in a will to someone does not prevent the testator giving it away to someone else or selling it before he dies. If the article is not part of his property at the time of his death, the gift is invalid.

➤ THE GIFT THAT WAS SOLD *In 1921 Hannah Sikes made a will in which she gave what she described as 'my piano' to her friend Mrs Crossley. In May 1923 she sold the piano.*

*Later that month she bought an electric motor player piano for which she paid £228 18s. She still owned that piano when she died, and Mrs Crossley claimed that it was hers under the will.* DECISION *Mrs Crossley did not get the piano. The one mentioned in the will had been sold and it made no difference that Hannah Sikes had later acquired another. (Re Sikes.)* ◄

To prevent this type of dispute, the solicitor will usually make sure that the gift is precisely defined; alternatively, if the testator intends to leave property which he has yet to acquire, the will can be made to read, for instance: 'I give to X any piano which I own at the date of my death.'

CHOOSING SOUVENIRS Sometimes a testator wants to give a member of his family or some other group a souvenir from his possessions without specifying a particular article. This object can be achieved by allowing the executors to give the people named something they ask for.

Anyone making these arrangements should make sure that the will defines clearly who is entitled to souvenirs, and places a limit on the value of any one souvenir. A limited time should be allowed for choosing, so that the winding-up of the dead person's affairs is not delayed longer than necessary.

MORTGAGES AND ESTATE DUTY If a testator makes a specific gift of property which is mortgaged—and this applies only to freehold land and buildings—the person receiving the gift has to take over the burden of the mortgage on the property.

The testator can relieve the recipient of this burden by saying in the will that the gift is to be free of the mortgage. The mortgage will then be paid off out of the residuary estate.

In the case of *leasehold* land and buildings and other property, the mortgage is paid off out of the residuary estate automatically, unless the testator directs to the contrary.

If the intended recipient feels that a property left with a mortgage outstanding would be a burden, he need not accept it. No one is obliged to accept anything left in a will.

AN OPTION TO BUY A testator may want a particular person to have something that he owns, but may not feel able to make a free gift of it to him. He might want his eldest son to have the family home, but if the house forms the bulk of the estate there might not be enough left, if he made an outright gift of the house, to allow fair shares for the other children. The solution is to give the son an option to buy the property from the estate.

Any option clause should specify a time limit so that there is no undue delay in distributing the estate. The price to be paid under the option must also be stated. One solution is to state that the price will be that fixed for estate-duty purposes. This is usually on the conservative side, so the beneficiary gets a good bargain.

Take, for instance, the case of the eldest of four sons—who are to share the estate equally —being given the chance to buy a house valued at £10,000 for estate duty. After payment of debts, estate duty and expenses, the estate as a whole, including the house, is valued at, say, £16,000—making £4000 for each son. The eldest son has to pay £10,000 for the house, but that money goes into the estate in place of the house, and he is entitled to a quarter share. So he receives £4000 back and each of his brothers gets the same.

OPTION TO CHOOSE Where the testator wants to give someone the chance to claim something of value, but is not sure whether they will want it, he may make them a money gift and at the same time give them the option to buy the item for that sum.

### Gifts of money

When money is bequeathed there is no need to state the sum in both words and figures. But if this is done and the two disagree, whichever is written second counts. A special kind of money gift can be made by writing off a debt which would otherwise have to be repaid to the estate.

If the total sum of money bequeathed exceeds the value of the property left, each gift is reduced in proportion.

PROPERTY INSTEAD OF MONEY Executors may usually give beneficiaries the testator's possessions or investments to the value of the money gift, provided the beneficiaries agree.

It is also possible for the testator to insert a clause in his will removing the need for the executors to obtain the beneficiaries' consent.

The main advantage of this option—without the beneficiaries' consent—is seen when the person making the will owns a large amount of stocks and shares. If on his death they are to be sold to raise the money needed to pay all the beneficiaries, the estate would have to pay a considerable sum in stamp duty.

The executors may not under any circumstances give one beneficiary, in exchange for money, any article already bequeathed by the will to another beneficiary.

### The residue of the estate

Leaving the residue of the estate—after all the special gifts are made—to one person is the simplest way to dispose of it.

In practice, more complicated arrangements are sometimes made. For example, the testator

## Dividing up the residue

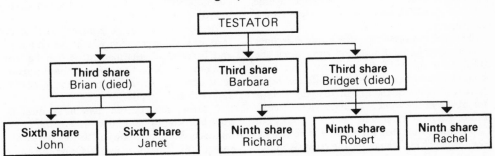

Arrangements for dividing the residue of an estate can go any way down the family tree. The will can direct that if a beneficiary dies before the testator his share is to be divided among his descendants.

This means that the beneficiary's children will inherit; if *they* are all dead the bequest will pass to the testator's grandchildren, and so on. But beneficiaries lower down the family tree than grandchildren should only be included if they are alive at the date the testator dies. Otherwise the gift may become void, because property cannot be bequeathed in perpetuity. A solicitor will advise about such gifts.

When a bequest of this kind is made, it is usual to stipulate that the beneficiary's children (or grandchildren) should have an equal share of the original beneficiary's share, not a share equal to that of the other beneficiaries. To ensure this, the testator adds that the descendants of the original beneficiary shall, in the Latin phrase used in wills, take equally *per stirpes*.

Consider the case of a man who has three children—Brian, Barbara and Bridget—and leaves the residue of his estate to be divided equally between them. Suppose that Brian and Bridget die before their father and that Brian left two children of his own—John and Janet—and that Bridget left three—Richard, Robert and Rachel. There will be six people to share the residuary estate: John and Janet (sharing Brian's one-third); Barbara; and Richard, Robert and Rachel (sharing Bridget's one-third). The money goes equally between each branch of the family—it is not shared equally between the six people entitled to benefit.

might want the residue of his estate to be divided between two or more people. Or he might want one person (his wife, perhaps) to receive the income from it during her lifetime, leaving the property itself to be divided up (among the children, for example) after she dies. He may also wish to make provision for the possibility of one or more of the beneficiaries dying before he does.

In any of these more complicated cases, a solicitor drawing up a will usually puts in a clause known as a 'trust for sale'.

This makes a gift of the residue to the executors with a direction to sell everything but allows them to delay the sale indefinitely. They are told what to do with the proceeds and the testator's directions are the 'trusts' on which they hold the property.

The law regards the sale as having taken place even if it has not, simply because the executors have a duty to sell the remainder of the property. It therefore looks on the residuary estate as money, the one thing that can always be divided equally.

INCOME FOR LIFE A testator may direct that one person should receive an income from the residue until he dies, at which date it is finally divided up. Often a widow is given income only for her lifetime without the right to use the capital.

This has the advantage that estate duty does not have to be paid a second time when she dies, as it might if the property had been bequeathed to her outright. A wife can similarly restrict her husband's share to the income for life from the residue of her estate. ☐ How estate duty works, p. 540.

To make sure that the income is sufficient, the testator can arrange for the trustees to pay a lump sum from the residue to someone entitled only to income (a widow, for example) when *they* think necessary. If she were able to insist on payment, any provisions about the residuary estate would be invalid since, in effect, she would be receiving it as a gift. The testator should also ensure that should his widow become the only trustee—perhaps if the others die—she will not be able to pay herself lump sums from the residue. If she could, the estate duty advantage of the arrangement might be lost.

HOUSEHOLD GOODS A husband wanting his wife to receive interest on his property, but not the property itself, should nevertheless make an outright gift to her of all household goods, as there can be unwanted complications if these are tied up in trust.

The gift of household goods should be made in the special gift section of the will. The best

way to do it is to rely on a lengthy legal definition, by giving her 'my personal chattels as defined by the Administration of Estates Act 1925'. The income from the property that remains can then be dealt with.

DEATH OF BENEFICIARIES It is also advisable to cover the possibility that people named to benefit in the will may die before the person who made the will. One solution is to direct that if anyone named in the will dies before the testator, *his* children can benefit as soon as they reach the age of 18. ☐ Dividing up the residue, p. 535.

The testator can state that if one beneficiary dies, the others should divide his share. For example, a testator with four brothers can direct that however many of them happen to outlive him should take equal shares. So if only three are living at the date of his death, each takes a third of the inheritance.

## Providing for children

A testator can ensure in his will that, if he dies before his children reach the age of 18, there will be someone to take charge of their upbringing. He does so by finding someone who will agree to take on the responsibility and appointing him or her the children's guardian in his will.

Because it cannot be known which of the testator's children, if any, will be under age and in need of guardianship when he dies, and others may be born after the will is made, it is normal to refer to them generally, rather than by name.

A father may decide that, if he dies, the guardian should help his wife to bring up the children. More often he will want the guardian to act only if both he and his wife die before the children are 18. He can achieve this by appointing a guardian to act only from the date of his wife's death, and then jointly with anyone she appoints. ☐ When children should have a guardian, p. 340.

MONEY FOR CHILDREN Where property has been left to children but they are not yet entitled to take it, the trustees may be entitled in law to use its income, and even its capital, for the children's benefit—to pay school fees and expenses, for example.

If the only reason why a child cannot take the property is because he is a minor, the Trustee Act 1925 allows the trustees to use the income for his benefit (any income not used is accumulated and added to the capital). But in exercising this power the trustees must take into account the age, requirements and circumstances of the minor and the availability of income from any other fund. An over-cautious trustee may therefore pay out less than he would do if he had a completely free hand, and the testator may prefer to relieve him of restrictions.

The same Act allows the trustees, if they think it necessary, to use up to a half of the child's share of the capital for his benefit before he becomes entitled to take it. If the testator wishes, he can extend this power so that the whole share can be used in this way.

The power to use income and to 'advance' capital is usually desirable, but both powers can be taken away from the trustees if the testator so desires.

ILLEGITIMATE AND ADOPTED CHILDREN The word 'children' in a will includes illegitimate children, who have the same legal right to inherit from their parents as legitimate children, except in the case of a title or property attached to one. If the testator does not want an illegitimate child to benefit, this must be stated explicitly in the will.

Adopted children are covered by the expression 'children' if an adoption order is in force before the will is made. Any children who might be adopted in the future can be included only by adding a specific clause covering them in the will.

## Investing the estate

If the will benefits children, or gives an income to a widow for her lifetime, some or all of the estate will have to be invested. The executors are normally entitled to invest only in trustee investments—those laid down by law as being very reliable, with little chance of losses, such as gilt-edged securities.

The testator may own certain shares that he particularly wants the trustees to keep, even though they are not trustee investments. These could be shares in a family business or some bought for sentimental, charitable or personal reasons. The executors can be given special authority to retain them.

## Giving to charity

Anyone who wants to leave a gift to charity should take care to get the name of the charity right.

The name of the charity can be checked in the *Annual Charities Register and Digest,* available in most public libraries. A register of most charities is also kept by the Charity Commission at St Albans House, 57–60 Haymarket, London SW1Y 4QX. Lists of educational and similar charities are held by the Department of Education and Science, Curzon Street House, 5 Curzon Street, London W1Y 8AA.

PROVIDING FOR PET ANIMALS A testator who wants to leave money for the care of a pet animal may direct his executors to pay money for the pet's benefit. Such a clause is, however, unsatisfactory from a number of points of view. First, a gift in this form has to be for a specified amount, and it is obviously difficult not to leave too much money or too little. Secondly, no legal action can be taken if the executors fail to carry out this part of the will, since a pet is not able to take legal action.

A more satisfactory solution is to give income to someone, possibly to a charity, on condition that they look after the pet, and to stipulate that if they fail to do so the money will go to someone else. This type of gift needs careful wording by a solicitor.

## Disposing of the body

The testator has the right to state in the will his wishes about the disposal of his body, though what he says is not legally binding (except if he prohibits cremation). It is essential to tell relatives of such wishes, in case there is a delay in finding or reading the will.

Any clause covering the disposal of the testator's body should usually be included at the beginning of the will, immediately after the introduction giving the testator's name and revoking all former wills.

A testator who wants any of his organs to be used after death for transplants or research —heart, kidneys, eyes, and so on—should make separate arrangements. There is no point in mentioning this in the will because by the time it is read, it is usually too late to use them in this way. □ Treatment in hospital, p. 378.

ANATOMICAL EXAMINATION The testator can, however, state in his will that he wishes to give his body to a medical school to be used for anatomical examination. If no near relatives object, and the body is suitable, it is collected by the medical school, which also arranges for the body to be buried when the examination is concluded.

If the relatives do object, the bequest is not legally enforceable.

An explanatory leaflet is available from HM Inspector of Anatomy, Department of Health and Social Security, Alexander Fleming House, Elephant and Castle, London SE1 6BY, or from the professor of anatomy at any university medical faculty or medical school.

## Simultaneous deaths

If a beneficiary under a will dies at the same time as the person who made the will, or shortly after—perhaps as a result of an accident in which both were involved—there are two immediate consequences.

First, the gift will be in danger of being subject to estate duty twice, once as part of the estate of the testator and again as part of the estate of the beneficiary who has died. An estate-duty relief known as 'quick-succession relief' will reduce the second charge.

The second consequence is that the gift may then be distributed according to the will of the beneficiary and possibly to a person or organisation which the original testator would not have wanted to benefit.

If it is impossible to know which of the two died first, then there is a legal presumption that the older died first. Therefore, the property left to the younger would pass to him normally and be distributed according to his will or, if there was no will, according to the intestacy rules.

The solution is to direct that the gift is to take effect only if the beneficiary survives the testator by, say, three weeks.

It is usually worth taking these precautions only in the case of a gift of the residue of an estate left to a close family relative.

### Imposing conditions on gifts

Conditions imposed on gifts left in a will have to be carefully phrased. They can be held to be invalid if, for example, they are not sufficiently clear or require something to be done of which a court disapproves.

If clauses in a will are held to be invalid, the result is that either the condition is ignored and the gift takes effect without it, or the whole gift fails.

To ensure that a condition attached to a gift takes effect, it is important to make certain that three rules are followed.

**1.** Make the condition something that must be done, or avoided, *before* the gift is taken not something which is liable to take the gift away again afterwards.

It is better, for instance, to say 'I give £100 to my daughter Jane if she is living in Britain at the date of my death' rather than 'I give £100 to my daughter Jane which she is to forfeit if at any time after my death she goes to live abroad'.

A small gift made to an executor 'if he shall prove my will' is common and valid as a reward for attending to the details of administering the estate.

**2.** Make quite sure it will be easy to tell whether the condition has been fulfilled.

One testator made a will which said that no one was to take a benefit under it who had married 'out of the Jewish faith'. A judge said

that this was sufficiently clear to be enforced. But when another testator left money to his grandchildren if they married people 'of the Jewish race', the judge in that case held that this was too vague. The difference presumably lies in the difficulty of checking on a person's ethnic background, compared with the greater ease of discovering the religious faith to which he subscribes.

**3.** Avoid conditions which require illegal acts, or ones on which the law is likely to frown. Examples of conditions which have been held invalid are those dissuading people from marrying by taking money away if they do, and conditions aimed at stopping children from living with their parents.

If a testator is determined that his will should impose a condition and he wants to make absolutely certain that it will be acted on, he should consult a solicitor to ensure that the clause is properly framed.

### Appointing professional executors

Solicitors, accountants or corporate bodies such as banks can be appointed professional executors and trustees. A testator may want to do this, particularly if he cannot think of a relative or friend who would accept the task.

A solicitor will usually have to be employed in the winding-up of the estate and the administration of the trusts (if there are any), so it is often convenient to appoint him executor and trustee.

If the testator is wealthy or has complicated financial affairs, he may want to appoint his solicitor and his accountant. A solicitor may be needed even when a corporate executor and trustee is appointed, though the corporation will do some of the administration work involved.

A clause should be included in the will allowing a professional executor and trustee to charge for his services. This is essential, for executors and trustees are not normally allowed to charge for services unless the will gives express permission.

BANKS AS EXECUTORS Banks, and some insurance companies who also act as executors, publish scales of fees which they charge for their professional services. The clause appointing them should refer to this scale. Every major bank branch can supply a specimen wording and give details of fees. □ Advantages of making a will, p. 530.

PUBLIC TRUSTEE The Public Trustee is a Government department which acts as an executor and trustee for private individuals. However, the work of the department is currently being wound up.

# Wills IV : changing a will

*Making a codicil*  *Reviving a will*
*Cancelling a will*

ALTERATIONS to a will—even those made before it is signed—must be signed by the person making the will, the testator. The only exceptions are changes in a serviceman's will, which are valid if only initialled.

Otherwise, an unsigned alteration is valid only if it can be proved to have been made before the testator signed the will. Where unsigned alterations cannot be validated, the executors must follow the original text.

### Making a codicil
When the will has been signed and witnessed, it can be amended at any time by the testator to include new bequests or take account of new developments. This is done by adding new clauses in separate documents called codicils.

A codicil should refer to the will it is amending and explain what parts of that will are affected. It should make clear that the rest of the will is still valid. Codicils must be signed by the testator and his signature witnessed by two people who do not stand to benefit from the codicil. The witnesses need not be those who witnessed the will.

### Cancelling a will
Once a will is made it governs what happens to the testator's estate—until he cancels it. In law, cancellation is called revoking the will.
MARRIAGE A will is automatically revoked when a testator marries, even though he marries the main beneficiary. The only exception to this rule is when the will is expressly stated to have been made in contemplation of marriage to a named person.

If the marriage does not take place, the will remains effective unless the testator marries someone else or states that the will is valid only if the marriage takes place. If a testator is married when he makes a will, the will is not revoked by a subsequent divorce.
DESTRUCTION A will is not revoked until it is superseded, or burnt or torn up by the testator or in his presence and on his instruction.
LATER WILL OR CODICIL A will is revoked by a later will or codicil only if the later document states this explicitly, or if there is proof that this was the testator's wish.

If, for example, a testator who made a will in 1970, makes in 1972 a new will or codicil which is not designed to deal with his whole estate, and which does not state that 'this will revokes my previous will' both documents are valid. Only the parts of the first will which conflict with the second are revoked.

### Reviving a will
A will that has been revoked can be revived. The testator can sign it again with a new date and have his signature witnessed by two people—not necessarily the original witnesses.

Alternatively the testator may make a codicil stating that his original will is being revived.

## Drawing up a codicil

I, James Jenkins, of Flat 8, Bevere House, Panton Street, London S.W.1, declare this to be a first codicil made on the 5th day of February 1971, to my will dated 1st day of October 1969.

1. By my will, I appointed Henry Adams and William Jenkins to be my executors and trustees, but Henry Adams has since died. Now, therefore, I appoint Philip Wilson of 10 Church Road, Oxford, to be an executor and trustee in place of Henry Adams and jointly with William Jenkins.

2. By my will, I gave the sum of £100 to Patricia Mary Watson. Now I give her the sum of £150 instead of the sum of £100.

3. In all other respects, I confirm my will.

The codicil must refer to the will it is amending and clearly explain the amendments. It should also indicate that, apart from the amendments, the rest of the will is still valid. The codicil must be signed by the testator and his signature witnessed by two people, though they need not be the same people who witnessed the original will.

# How estate duty works

*Property left to a marriage partner*
*Duty on jointly owned property*
*Duty on trusts and gifts*

*Life-assurance policies*
*Duty-free property and exemptions*
*How duty is calculated*

WHEN someone dies, his executors or the administrators of his estate may have to pay tax on the value of the belongings he leaves. This tax, called estate or death duty, is payable where the value of the dead person's estate—money, land, buildings, goods, shares, patents and copyrights, any interest in a trust, and debts due to him—exceeds the estate duty threshold.

This threshold, which is changed from time to time, was fixed at £15,000 from March 22, 1972. In addition, property worth up to £15,000 passing from one marriage partner to the other was duty-free.

Duty is charged on a rising scale: the smaller the estate, the lower the rate.

The duty is payable on all assets which the dead person owned and could dispose of for his own benefit during his lifetime. A life-assurance policy which becomes part of the holder's estate when he dies may therefore be subject to duty, for he can cash it or give it away while he is alive. A life policy payable to someone else, which does not benefit the assured, may escape duty.

Even where the dead person was not able to dispose of his property—for the purposes of law 'property' means assets of all kinds, not just buildings and land—duty may still have to be paid. This situation may arise where the person who died was an infant or was mentally ill and not able to manage his affairs. The fact that in law the property was not his to do with as he pleased does not preclude it from ranking as part of his estate.

## Property left to a marriage partner
Part of the property passing to a widow or widower on the death of the first partner is excluded from the estate for calculating duty. The value of exempt property, which may change from time to time, was fixed from March 22, 1972 at £15,000.

This relief applies whether the surviving marriage partner receives the property as a gift, under a will, under the rules for distributing an estate where there is no will, under a trust or as an annuity. (Marriage partner here means surviving widow or widower, not partner in any other sense.)

The exemption for property passing between marriage partners applies in addition to the exemption for property below the estate duty threshold. So if a man died in April 1972 leaving £15,000 to his widow in a will, the first £30,000 of his estate was duty-free, whoever was left the other £15,000.

## Duty on jointly owned property
When a house is owned jointly by a husband and wife, only half of the house is counted for the purpose of assessing liability to estate duty when the first of them dies. (When the survivor dies, the whole house *may* be included, depending on the circumstances.)

In the case of joint bank accounts, rules for deciding how much of the account should be included in the estate of one of the joint holders are more complicated.

If contributions to the account are made by only one partner, and the other draws on the account only as a convenient way of paying household bills, the whole account forms part of the estate of the contributing partner, and duty has to be paid only when that partner dies. If, however, the non-contributing partner is free to draw on the account for personal expenditure, half the account belongs to each partner's estate.

If both partners contribute to the account, half is regarded as belonging to the estate of one partner and half to the other, irrespective of the actual proportions each contribute.

## Duty on trust property
Duty is paid only where the deceased held property for his personal benefit. If he was a trustee holding property for beneficiaries other than himself, that property is exempt when he dies.

Where the dead person was a beneficiary, the trust's capital is liable to duty in proportion to the dead person's share of the annual income received from the trust.

Take the case of a trust which has an annual income of £1000, from which it pays £100 a year to a beneficiary. When that beneficiary dies, one-tenth of the trust's capital is added to the dead person's estate for the purpose of calculating duty. The duty on that one-tenth is then paid by the trust, not by the dead person's estate.

Similarly, duty is payable on a proportion of the capital in the trust on the death of a trustee who received a fee for his services, except if he provided those services in a professional capacity—for example, as an accountant or solicitor.

If the dead person was not entitled to fixed payments from a trust, but received money at the trustees' discretion, duty is payable only on the part of the trust's capital corresponding to the proportion of income paid to him in the seven years before death. However, if he ceased to benefit within seven years of death, the dutiable part of the capital is calculated from the proportion of trust income which he received during the last seven years in which he *did* benefit, or might have benefited.

If the trust has come to an end and a lump sum has been paid in settlement to the beneficiary, estate duty is paid out of his estate when he dies on whatever part of that sum remains in his possession.

When one beneficiary dies, other beneficiaries who have received lump sums within the previous seven years may also have to pay estate duty on the amounts they have received. Anyone who receives a large capital sum when a trust is wound up is well advised to insure against having to pay duty. ☐ Insuring against estate duty, p. 543.

Where property is put into a trust from which both husband and wife can benefit, the property is liable for duty when the first partner dies, but it is not liable when the second dies. The estate duty rule which makes this possible is known as the 'surviving spouse exemption'.

This concession applies even if, at the time of the first partner's death, the value of the estate is below the estate duty threshold, and so not liable to duty, but increases above the threshold by the time of the second partner's death. ☐ Setting up a trust, p. 526.

## Duty on gifts
In law, gifts made by a person in the seven years before his death are liable to estate duty when he dies. Part of a gift may, however, escape duty. When the donor dies more than four years after the date of the gift, 15 per cent of the gift escapes duty; after five years, 30 per cent is duty-free; and after six years, 60 per cent escapes duty. No duty at all is payable after seven years.

To escape duty, even a gift made seven years before death must be a complete one, with no benefit for the donor.

If, for example, a mother transfers the house in which she lives to her son, but continues to live in it while the son stays elsewhere, she must pay him a commercial rent and meet all the outgoings herself if the gift is to escape duty.

If, on the other hand, the mother pays a commercial rent, but the son meets the cost of rates, repairs and similar bills, estate duty still has to be paid.

Another way in which the mother can avoid this danger is by transferring to her son all the house, except for one or two rooms kept for her own use. If the son then lives in the rest of the house, duty will eventually have to be paid only on the value of those rooms which the mother kept for herself.

The seven-year rule applies even to gifts between husband and wife, but there is a slight relaxation in the case of the matrimonial home where the giver retains an interest. If a husband lives for seven years or more after giving the home to his wife, the house is not liable to duty on his death even if he continued to benefit from the property by living there.

Gifts worth less than £100 in total to any one person are free from duty. This limit is increased to £500 if the gift is an outright one, with no conditions attached which give the donor a benefit from it.

DISGUISED GIFTS Where the dead person sold something to a relative in the seven years before his death for only part of the real price, the Inland Revenue assumes that he intended to make a gift of the balance, which is therefore included in his estate for duty purposes. This rule is intended to discourage disguising gifts as sales.

Take the case of a relative who pays one-third of the real price. If the seller dies within seven years, duty may have to be paid on two-thirds of the value of the property at the date of death.

The rule does not apply where the owner sells something to a non-relative for less than its worth, not because he wants to make a gift, but because he makes a bad bargain. In this case, no duty is payable.

MARRIAGE SETTLEMENTS Up to certain limits, gifts to people about to be married or given in trust for the benefit of themselves and their children are exempt from estate duty on the death of the donor. Where the donor is the parent or ancestor of either party to the marriage the limit is £5000. If there is no close relationship the limit is £1000.

Where the gift is above the maximum allowed only the excess is dutiable.

To be exempt, the gift must be made before

or at the time of the marriage, or as a result of an earlier agreement to make the gift.

GIFTS FOR A LIFETIME If a gift of property is made on the basis that it is returned to the donor on the death of the recipient, no duty is payable when the recipient dies. But if the donor dies first, two lots of estate duty become payable—one when the donor dies and a second when the recipient dies.

Where the gift has been made by a husband to a wife or *vice versa*, payment of duty is often postponed until the death of the second partner. This is not possible, though, if the donor has in some way benefited from the property, or if the property was originally owned by the recipient.

GIFTS TO CHARITY No duty is payable on gifts to charity if they are made at least one year before death. If the gift is made in the year before death, or is left in a will, duty has to be paid only on the excess over £50,000.

The donor must, however, surrender his full interest in the property. If the gift is to end at a future date or when a particular event happens—if, for example, a charity is to receive the income from letting a building only until, say, 1980 or until it completes a particular research programme—then duty has to be paid on the property on that date unless it is transferred to another charity.

PUBLIC GIFTS Land (and money for land maintenance) given to the National Trust is exempt from estate duty. The exemption can also apply to gifts to some Government departments, local authorities and non-profit-making bodies which are responsible for preserving public buildings.

GIVING AWAY AN INTEREST IN A TRUST Where someone is entitled during his lifetime to receive money under a trust and gives his life interest away, the gift becomes valueless on his death, since his interest ceases.

Nevertheless, if he dies within seven years of making the gift, duty will have to be paid on the proportion of the fund from which that income was derived.

Moreover, if the person giving away an interest in a trust is not entirely excluded from benefiting under that interest, it is liable for duty even after seven years. The position is the same if the interest is sold.

### Life-assurance policies

Gifts of reasonable amounts made out of income which can be shown to be part of the dead person's normal expenditure are usually exempt from estate duty. To qualify for relief, the gifts must have been habitual or usual and, after making the gifts, the donor must

have been left with enough money to maintain his normal standard of living.

Assurance premiums can count as gifts for the purpose of this exemption. For instance, a husband can take out an assurance policy on his own life, payable to his widow. He can pay the premiums or give his wife enough money to pay the premiums and, provided these premiums are not excessive, they are regarded as part of normal expenditure and are not subject to duty. When he dies, payments to the widow under the policy also escape duty.

Policies taken out on or after March 20, 1968 qualify for total exemption only if the level of premiums is what would be regarded as the 'normal and reasonable expenditure' of the dead person. If the premiums went beyond this reasonable expenditure, the assurance will be included in the main estate. But, under the seven-year rule for gifts, not all the assurance bought in the fifth, sixth and seventh years before death is liable to duty.

Suppose, for example, that a husband took out a policy on his own life 15 years before his death and assigned it to his wife. If she receives £15,000 under the policy when he dies, this represents a gift of £1000 for each year the policy existed and for each annual premium paid. If the annual premium is considered excessive by the Inland Revenue, duty is payable on the equivalent of this gift for the last seven years of his life—that is, on £7000—less the deductions under the seven-year rule.

Assurance policies taken out before March 20, 1968 qualify for exemption under slightly different rules.

Policies on the dead person's life taken out and paid for by someone else, such as a widow, are not normally dutiable.

To qualify for exemption, assurance policies must be payable to someone other than the dead person.

### Duty-free property

Some types of property—works of art, for example—do not incur estate duty on death, only when the recipient sells them.

WOODLANDS Where the estate of a dead person includes land on which timber is growing, the value of the timber is not added to the value of the estate in fixing the rate of duty. When the timber is sold, duty is payable on its value at the date of death and at the rate fixed for the whole estate.

WORKS OF ART Inherited works of art and items of scientific or historical interest are exempt from death duty as long as two conditions are met. They must not be sold or otherwise disposed of; and any undertakings required by the Treasury (a ban on the export of a painting, for example) must be observed.

If they are sold within three years of death, or if there is a breach of undertaking in that time, duty is payable on the value at the time of death. This value is added to that of the rest of the estate to determine the rate payable. If they are sold after three years, duty is payable on the amount received, and this amount is added to the rest of the estate to calculate the rate of duty.

BUSINESS PLANT There is a reduced rate of duty (55 per cent of the applicable rate) on agricultural property or industrial buildings or on business machinery and plant.

## Special exemptions

Estate duty is not applied, or applies at a reduced rate, in certain special circumstances.

MILITARY SERVICE All property of someone who dies on active service or who dies as the result of a wound received while on active service is exempt from duty.

DEATHS IN QUICK SUCCESSION Reduced rates of duty are charged when property becomes liable for duty twice within five years because of deaths in quick succession.

The duty payable is reduced by 75 per cent if the second death occurs within three months of the first. The reduction for longer periods is: second death within one year, 50 per cent reduction; within two years, 40 per cent; within three years, 30 per cent; within four years, 20 per cent; and within five years, duty is reduced by ten per cent.

SIMULTANEOUS DEATHS When two people die in circumstances which make it impossible to tell who died first, and property passes from one to the other, duty is charged only once.

## How duty is calculated

To calculate duty, an estate is in effect divided into slices. The first dutiable slice is taxed at the lowest rate, the next at a higher rate, and so on. Rates are liable to change; but from March 22, 1972, the first slice—from £15,000 to £20,000—was charged at 25 per cent, and the top slice—everything over £500,000—at 75 per cent.

## Who must pay the duty

When an estate is liable to duty, the money usually has to be collected and paid by the executors or administrators of the estate.

Where the property on which duty is charged is part of a trust under which the dead person benefited, the tax is paid by the trustees. Duty on jointly owned property must be paid by the surviving owner.

Where the property was given away within seven years of death, the duty must be paid by the individual who has received the gift.

Trust property liable to duty, and gifts in the seven years before death, are added to the main estate so that the average rate of duty can be fixed. However, if the value of the estate is below the estate duty threshold, the estate and the trust property are treated separately, so that no duty is paid on the estate. Special rules cover duty when the estate is slightly over the threshold.

## Insuring against estate duty

ANYONE receiving a gift is liable to have to pay duty on it if the donor dies within seven years. He can, however, insure against any possible claim. The policy is taken out on the life of the donor, and payment is made if he dies within seven years. It should be for a sum equal to the amount of the duty that might have to be paid.

The advice of a solicitor or accountant is usually necessary in establishing what sum to insure for. Remember that the tax is on the value of the gift at the time of death, not its value at the time it was given.

When insuring against possible death-duty claims on gifts, pay the policy premiums out of your own money, not out of the gift, particularly if the gift is in the form of a trust. If money received from the dead person has been used to pay the premiums, the whole policy may be counted as part of the gift and further duty may have to be paid on it.

There is no problem in assessing duty on a gift when it is cash, or when it is still owned by the recipient. It may happen, though, that the person receiving a gift other than cash disposes of it before the donor dies. In that case duty is payable on the amount he received by selling the gift. If he exchanged it for some other piece of property, duty is paid on the value at the time of death of whatever he received in exchange—not on the value at the time he received it.

# Re-arranging family finances

*Mortgages and rents*     *Gas, electricity and telephone bills*
*Insurance policies*     *Rate demands*
*Hire purchase and loans*     *Maintenance payments, debts and tax*

WHEN a family's income drops—perhaps because the husband has suffered illness or injury, or because he has been forced to take a lower-paid job or has lost his job altogether—the couple will need to re-arrange their finances as soon as possible. Social Security or supplementary benefits may be available, but these rarely restore the family income to its original level. ☐ State help in hardship, p. 550.

Creditors should be approached immediately it is known that commitments cannot be met. They are likely to show more sympathy to a debtor who explains his circumstances and offers a reduced payment than to one who confesses only after a series of unpaid bills.

## Mortgages and rents

Most families give top priority to retaining their home. If unemployment is the cause of financial difficulties, supplementary benefit may be available to meet the cost of housing.

Otherwise, if the home is being bought on a mortgage, a building society or local authority may allow the home-owner to make 'interest only' repayments for a stipulated period. He would then have to make increased monthly repayments as soon as possible, to clear the arrears on repayment of the loan itself.

This will not assist anyone whose mortgage has been running for only a short time, since in the early stages of a capital-repayment mortgage a large proportion of the monthly repayment consists of interest.

A building society is unlikely to agree to suspend repayments, though it may extend the loan period. As a last resort, it will sell the house to clear the mortgage.

A home-owner with an endowment mortgage may find that the insurance company is prepared to waive premiums for a time, leaving him to pay only interest on the loan.

Anyone buying on a mortgage who suffers a substantial drop in income and sees no prospect of his situation improving may be able to reduce his repayments by converting his mortgage to an option mortgage. ☐ Applying for a mortgage, p. 194.

COUNCIL-HOUSE RENTS Tenants of council houses who, in similar circumstances, find they are unable to pay their rent, should contact their local authority housing department. In cases of genuine hardship, some councils allow the rent to run into arrears for a specified time. Others accept a reduced rent until the hardship is over. Either way, the tenant is expected to clear arrears once his finances improve.

If a tenant falls into serious arrears over a long period, he may find that he is rehoused in lower-grade accommodation at a reduced rent. Usually he will not be evicted without alternative accommodation being offered, since the local council is legally obliged to try to accommodate homeless people.

If the local authority operates a rent-rebate scheme, a tenant whose income drops may qualify for a rent rebate, especially if he can show that his income has remained reduced for nine months to a year. ☐ How rent rebates and allowances are calculated, p. 263.

PRIVATE RENTS Private landlords may occasionally be willing to accept reduced rents from tenants in financial difficulties if it appears that these difficulties will be short-lived. However, this is rare.

The best course of action for a tenant facing a long-term drop in income is to seek cheaper accommodation as soon as possible.

## Insurance policies

A policy-holder who finds he is unable to meet his life-assurance policy premiums can surrender the policy for cash, provided it has run for the minimum period laid down by the insurance company. If the holder wants to continue the policy, the insurance company will usually agree that the holder need pay no premiums—they are advanced as a debt against the policy's surrender value. If this goes on for so long that there is no surrender value left, the policy will lapse.

When his financial circumstances improve, the policy-holder can either pay increased premiums until the full surrender value is restored, or continue paying the agreed premium and take a lower payment when the policy matures.

In some cases, the insurance company may be prepared to allow the policy to remain

IF THE FAMILY INCOME DROPS

static, as a paid-up policy, until the policy-holder can continue his premiums. If premiums on other types of policy cannot be paid —motor insurance, for example—the policies usually lapse. □ Life assurance, p. 518

### Hire purchase and loans

Hire-purchase or loan agreements with finance companies occasionally include insurance against the customer's inability to pay due to illness, injury or unemployment. With this type of agreement the customer should write immediately to the company, which usually asks for details of the circumstances.

When the agreement contains no such provisions, the customer should contact either the store which supplied the goods or the finance company and explain the difficulties.

If a hire-purchase agreement has been running for only a short time, the store or company may agree to take back the goods. The customer will invariably have to forfeit payments already made.

In addition, the agreement may require the customer to pay a substantial minimum payment. However, when the hire-purchase price is less than £2000, the customer can terminate the agreement at any time by paying the difference between what he has already paid and *half* the hire-purchase price. If this seems more than the finance company's actual loss, the customer can offer a lower payment.

Should this be refused, he can simply return the goods and discontinue payments, leaving the company to take legal action to recover the debt. When this happens, the court has powers to decide that the customer should pay less than half the price.

If more than one-third of the hire-purchase price has been paid, the customer is within his rights in refusing to surrender the goods unless the company applies for a court order.

Generally, the court tries to give the customer a second chance, and allows him to keep the goods while he pays reduced instalments. □ Hire purchase, p. 498.

PERSONAL LOANS A borrower who explains his difficulties *before* he gets into arrears is usually allowed to make interest-only payments for a period. Technically, the finance company may sue for all the money owing as soon as a payment is overdue. □ Personal loans and second mortgages, p. 506.

### Gas, electricity and telephone bills

Anyone unable to pay a gas, electricity or telephone bill should contact the board accountant or local telephone manager, who

may agree to a period of extended credit. All three bodies are reluctant to disconnect supplies if there seems a reasonable chance of the account being settled eventually.

Extended credit is often allowed for a widow who does not have much cash at her disposal; but board accountants and telephone managers are given discretion to apply this procedure in other cases of genuine hardship.

Sometimes a small, regular payment may be accepted if it will clear the account before the next bill. If not, the gas or electricity board may install a coin-in-the-slot pre-payment meter. Alternatively, gas, electricity or telephone authorities may try to set a limit on the next quarter's bill.

Before helping a customer in difficulties, most board accountants and telephone managers look at his payment record. The person who has paid bills promptly invariably gets a more sympathetic hearing.

TELEVISION RENTAL Television rental companies usually expect customers to honour their agreements, irrespective of personal circumstances. Many refuse to take back the set before the hire period has expired, or to make a refund of rentals already paid. If they do, many will insist on the customer making a payment to compensate for the breaking of the hire agreement.

### Rate demands

The householder whose income drops may also qualify for a rate rebate. The local council offices can advise the ratepayer on this. □ How to apply for a rates reduction, p. 221.

### Maintenance payments and debts

If his income drops, a man who is making maintenance payments to an ex-wife, or to children, or to both, should apply to the court to reduce the order.

If there is a judgment debt against a person whose income drops, he should apply to the court and ask to pay by instalments. If he is already doing this, he should ask for the instalments to be reduced.

### Tax refunds

Income tax deducted from wages and salaries under the Pay-As-You-Earn scheme is calculated on the amount the taxpayer is expected to earn in a full tax year. If the taxpayer's income drops, he may qualify for a refund of part of the tax already paid. The refund will be automatic if wages or a salary continue to be paid; but people who lose their jobs must make a claim for any refund due from their local tax office.

# Recouping money lost through injury

*Accidents on private property*    *Accidents on public property*

ANYONE whose income drops through an accident caused by someone else's negligence may be entitled to claim damages. Two things must be proved for the claim to succeed. Firstly, it must be shown that the person responsible for the accident had a duty of care towards the person who was injured. Secondly, it must be proved that he acted with such negligence and disregard for the safety of the injured person that he broke that duty of care and injury resulted.

If the injury is caused by a road accident, it may be possible to claim from the person who caused the accident—even a pedestrian. ☐ Grounds for claiming damages, p. 121.

If the accident happened at work, the injured person may be able to claim from his employer, or occasionally from a workmate or colleague who has been negligent. ☐ What to do if you are injured, p. 629.

If the injury was caused by an animal not being kept under proper control, it may be possible to claim against its owner. ☐ Keeping animals, p. 287.

Anyone injured by something bought by them or someone else may be able to claim against the manufacturer or against the dealer who sold it. ☐ Faulty goods: suing the manufacturer, p. 464.

Occasionally, too, sporting accidents give grounds for damages claims. ☐ Accidents at sporting events, p. 131.

It may also be possible to claim damages for accidents in a number of other circumstances, including those that occur on private or public property.

## Accidents on private property

Visitors and people who enter private property lawfully have a right to expect the occupier of the premises or land to extend a reasonable level of care towards them.

They have a right to be warned about any potential dangers which may exist and about which the occupier knows or ought to know. So the visitor to a friend's house who is not warned about a loose stair-carpet and trips, breaking his ankle, may be entitled to claim damages from his friend. Though he may be reluctant to do so because of friendship, he may find that his friend will suffer no loss, since he is insured against such claims under a household insurance policy.

If the danger is obvious—a clearly visible barbed-wire fence, for example—or if the visitor has been warned about it, he cannot normally claim damages if he is injured.

Any caller who is on his lawful business is entitled to claim—the milkman, postman, door-to-door salesman or even political canvasser. Trespassers cannot expect the same consideration, though they must not be subjected to intentional harm.

Where the premises are rented, anyone who is injured may be entitled to sue the landlord if the accident happens:

**1.** In a part of the building for which the landlord is responsible, such as a stairway.

**2.** Or in a part which he has a duty to repair, and he has been notified of the defect which causes the injury. ☐ Repairs: whose responsibility?, p. 268.

WARNING NOTICES Anyone injured on property where there is a conspicuous notice stating that the public enter at their own risk is unlikely to succeed in a claim for damages provided the nature of the danger is clear.

Generally, the law regards a sign of this type as sufficient to absolve the occupier of responsibility. But such a notice would have no effect if the injured person had entered the premises *before* he had an opportunity of seeing the notice.

When an accident is caused through the negligence of an employee acting in the course of his employment the employer, as well as the employee, is normally liable.

When children are involved in accidents, the law does not expect them to be as alert to danger as adults. A child who is injured despite a warning may still be able to recover damages unless it is shown that he deliberately disregarded a persistent caution which he was old enough to understand, or that the person responsible for causing the injury took all reasonable precautions.

Warning notices, therefore, cannot normally be considered a valid defence in cases where a child under the age of, say, 12 is claiming damages. The courts tend to rule that an owner or occupier has a duty of care to child trespassers if he knows, or ought to know, of their presence.

## Accidents on public property

People injured on public property may also be able to claim damages against the responsible authority. If a pedestrian falls on a badly maintained pavement or road, for example, he may be able to sue the local council.

A child injured in a public park or swimming-pool may be entitled to claim against the local council if the accident happened during the normal opening hours.

Vandalism is a foreseeable risk in parks, so a child injured, for example, on a slide damaged by vandals might have a valid claim.

ROADSIDE PROPERTY It is possible for someone using public property to be injured by private property. This could happen if, for example, a pedestrian on a public street is struck by a slate or tile which falls from a private house.

In such cases (or where an excavation is made or a cellar is not properly maintained), anyone injured while using the public road and not actually on private property does not have to prove that negligence was involved. The occupier or owner whose premises skirt public property has an absolute liability to ensure that the structure and any excavations are safe. If the occupier rents the property, a passer-by who is injured can sue the landlord if the accident is caused by a defect which existed when the tenancy began, or by one which the landlord has a right or duty to repair. There is no need to prove that the occupier or landlord either knew or ought to have known of the defect.

But this principle does not extend to natural features such as trees. If the passer-by is injured by a branch falling from a tree, the occupier of the land on which the tree stands is liable only if it can be shown that he has been negligent.

Where premises are used for a purpose which endangers members of the public passing by, the occupier and owner are liable for injury if, through negligence, they fail to take reasonable precautions. If there is a realistic danger of accidents—perhaps when a golf club sites a tee too near the road and a passer-by is injured by a golf ball—it may not be necessary to prove negligence.

## Compensation for criminal injuries

PEOPLE who are victims of crimes of violence are in some cases entitled to compensation from public funds. The Criminal Injuries Compensation Board has power to award compensation for:

1. Injuries directly attributable to a crime of violence, including arson or poison.
2. Injuries caused when trying to prevent, or helping the police to prevent, a crime.
3. Injuries caused when trying to arrest, or helping the police to arrest, a suspect, including injuries caused to an innocent bystander.

Compensation is paid in a lump sum, assessed on the basis of court damages. The injury must usually have been reported to the police without delay.

No claim will be considered if the injured person and his attacker were living together in the same family, or if the injury was caused by a traffic offence (other than deliberate running down).

When criminal injuries result in death, or when someone suffers criminal injuries but dies from another cause, claims can be made by close relatives and dependants.

AMOUNT OF AWARD There are three main limitations to awards. First, Social Security benefits are deducted in full. Second, part of a widow's pension paid by either public or private employers may be taken into account when calculating the award. And third, any amount awarded for loss of earnings or earning capacity is based on an earnings rate which cannot exceed twice the average industrial earnings figure in the victim's trade at the time of the injury.

HOW TO APPLY Claims should be submitted as soon as possible after the event on an application form obtainable from the Criminal Injuries Compensation Board, 10–12 Russell Square, London WC1B 5EN.

The applicant may be asked to undergo a medical examination and also to allow the board to make enquiries with his own doctor, his employers and the police.

A decision on the application is normally taken by a single member of the board. If the applicant wishes to challenge the decision, he can apply for a personal hearing before three board members.

# Recouping money lost through fraud

*What to do if you are deliberately misled*
*What to do if you are innocently misled*

ANYONE who believes he has been the victim of fraud—perhaps he has been tempted by false promises to invest his savings, or has paid money for a house to someone he now finds is not entitled to sell—has two types of legal remedy open to him.

If he thinks a criminal offence has been committed, he can take steps to see that those responsible are prosecuted. If he has lost money, he can make attempts to recover it by suing for damages.

PROSECUTION Many types of fraud constitute either theft or criminal deception. A victim should hand all the evidence to the police, who will prosecute those responsible if there is a strong enough case. ☐ ABC of crime and punishment, p. 757.

If the victim has bought something on the basis of false statements made by the seller, it may be possible to prosecute under the Trade Descriptions Act 1968. Suspected offences should be reported to the local weights and measures inspector, not to the police. ☐ What to do about faulty goods, p. 460.

SUING FOR DAMAGES A successful prosecution will not recover lost money. To do this, the victim must sue for damages.

If he has lost money through being deliberately misled, he can bring an action under common law for deceit. If he was given false information, but it is not possible to prove it was given deliberately, he can take action under the Misrepresentation Act 1967.

**What to do if you are deliberately misled**
Anyone who loses money through being deliberately misled may be able to claim damages for deceit. For his claim to be successful, he must be able to show:
**1.** That the defendant made a 'representation of fact' which was false—an untrue statement or a promise he never intended to keep.
**2.** That the defendant knew the statement was false, or made it recklessly, not caring whether it was true.
**3.** That the defendant intended the statement to be acted upon.
**4.** That the claimant did, in fact, act upon it.

If the action arises out of a contract between claimant and defendant—if, for example, one was buying from the other—proving these four points will be sufficient to establish a claim. Otherwise, the claimant must also show that he has lost money as a result of the false information or promise.

FALSE STATEMENT A wide variety of statements, or even gestures, can amount to the false representation of fact that must be proved in a deceit action.

For instance, it is a false representation of fact for a businessman to make a promise he never intends to carry out—when, for example, the promoters of a business attract funds by saying that they intend to prospect for nickel in Australia, though they have no intention of using the money that way.

Silence could also amount to a false representation of fact if there was an implicit obligation to clarify the situation by speaking up. A company might be held to be guilty if, for example, it sold plots of land in Portugal for holiday homes and withheld from investors the fact that fresh building had been banned in the area.

RECKLESSLY OR KNOWINGLY An action for deceit cannot succeed unless the defendant recklessly or knowingly makes a false statement, without caring whether it is true. If he says in a reference that an applicant for a job can safely be entrusted with large sums of money, he lays himself open to an action if he knows that the applicant has been in prison for dishonesty. He may also be liable if in fact he does not know whether the applicant can be trusted.

DEFENDANT'S INTENTION A false statement does not give grounds for action unless it is made with the intention that the person concerned should act on it. A car dealer, for example, can be sued if he tells a prospective buyer that a car is mechanically sound even though he knows it to have defective steering. In this case, he intends his hearer to act on the statement—by buying the car. If, however, he makes the same statement about a vehicle in an exhibition which is not for sale, no action is possible because the statement cannot be acted on.

PLAINTIFF'S ACTION The claimant must also show that he relied on the statement and acted on it. If he knows that a statement is false—for example, if he sees that the car's steering is defective but still accepts the vehicle—he has no grounds for action.

Similarly, a coin collector offered what is claimed to be a rare coin for £50 has no grounds for action if he recognises it as counterfeit and agrees to pay only £1.

As a rule any misrepresentation gives grounds for action, whether it is written, spoken or merely implied. Action for deceit over a statement about a person's creditworthiness, however, can be taken only if it has been given in writing and the person making it has signed it. Where a statement has been made by a person acting for someone else, expert advice is essential before deciding to take legal action, as this branch of the law—known as the law of agency—is complicated.

**What to do if you are innocently misled**
Anyone who is persuaded to enter into a contract on the basis of false information may also be able to claim damages even if no fraud is involved or where none can be proved. The action is taken under the Misrepresentation Act 1967.

A garage, for example, may tell the buyer of a second-hand car that the vehicle has done only 10,000 miles when the true figure is 50,000. In this case it may be difficult to prove that the false information was given knowingly or recklessly, since the mileometer may have been turned back by the previous owner without the knowledge of the seller.

The buyer would be entitled to sue for damages under the Misrepresentation Act, however, if he could prove:

**1.** That a false representation was made.
**2.** That it was made with the intention of being acted on.
**3.** That it induced the buyer to enter into the contract—that is, it was acted on.

In effect, anyone taking action under the Misrepresentation Act has to prove three of the elements necessary for an action for deceit; he is relieved, however, of the need to prove the remaining one—that the false statement was made knowingly or recklessly without caring whether or not it was true.

## Claiming damages for bad advice

ANYONE who asks for advice from someone in a profession or business—a banker, for example, or a stockbroker or surveyor—is entitled to expect him to exercise the proper standard of skill and care in the circumstances in giving his opinion, even if the advice is given free and there is no contract involved. If the professional man fails to do so, and the person who asked for the advice suffers physical or financial loss or nervous shock as a result, he may be sued for damages.

A professional man who gives advice negligently can face claims not only from his own client—the person who may be paying for advice—but also from others adversely affected. In law, he has a duty towards anyone he knows is going to rely on his opinion.

This does not mean that the action can be taken on all negligent or careless mis-statements. If, for example, an accountant is asked for an opinion on a tax question at a party, such an off-the-cuff view would not make him liable if his statement is negligently wrong.

People whose profession or business it is to give advice or opinions—such as valuers, bankers, doctors, accountants or estate agents —are particularly liable to be sued.

The risk is not confined to these classes of people only, however. The limit of those liable is still being worked out by the courts. It appears to cover anyone who claims to be in a business or profession which involves the giving of advice, or anyone who gives advice for a fee, or probably anyone who gives advice in which he has some financial interest. It has also been held to apply to a local authority—for example, after a building inspector had negligently approved the laying of foundations on a rubbish tip.

The basis of any claim is that the person giving the advice has set himself up as someone competent to give such advice, and by doing so has made himself liable if his advice is given negligently.

To be actionable, a careless statement need not be in writing, although if it is, it may be easier to persuade a court that it was a situation where the maker of the statement ought to have been more careful.

If, however, the person making the statement also makes it clear that it is made without legal liability, he cannot be sued even though he may have been negligent and someone else has suffered as a result.

# State help in hardship

*Qualifying for supplementary benefit*
*Special help for women*
*How benefit is calculated*

*Obtaining additional benefit*
*When benefit can be reduced*

ANYONE who suffers hardship because of low income may be eligible for one of a number of State benefits. If he or she is working full-time and supporting at least one child under 16 (or still at school), it may be possible to claim a weekly addition to wages. There are also State benefits for people out of work through sickness, unemployment or industrial injury. □ Help for low-paid families, p. 555; Claiming sickness benefit, p. 602; Qualifying for unemployment benefit, p. 650; How the State helps the injured, p. 632.

Anyone who is not eligible to claim these benefits, or who faces hardship even after receiving one of them, may qualify to claim supplementary benefit. This may be either a weekly allowance or a single payment to meet an exceptional need.

Payment is controlled by the Supplementary Benefits Commission, an independent body set up by the Government.

## Qualifying for supplementary benefit

Basically, supplementary benefit may be claimed by people who are over retirement age (65 for a man, 60 for a woman) and by people of 16 and over who are registered as unemployed at an employment exchange or who are unable to work for other reasons.

Payments are made to people in full-time work only in situations of urgent need. For example, help might be given to a family man who had lost his wage packet or to a man or woman who needed the fare for a long-distance journey to visit a critically ill relative. Occasionally these cash benefits are paid to help people after floods and fires. Grants of this kind may have to be repaid eventually.

When an employee starts a new job, he may be able to claim benefit to cover living expenses for up to 15 days before the first full wage packet.

No one who is taking part in a strike, whether official or unofficial, is entitled to benefit for himself. However, he may be able to claim for his dependants.

STUDENTS Supplementary benefits are not paid to people who are still at school or studying full-time at a university or technical college, although children and students may be counted as dependants in parents' claims.

However, a local authority grant made to a student may not take into account his dependants—perhaps because he married after the course started or because his wife had a child more than six months after the start of the course. In such cases, supplementary benefit may be payable for the dependants.

A student can claim for dependants only if he is taking a course for which local authorities can make grants. He is not able to claim if he is a post-graduate student or if his only dependant is a wife who is capable of working.

YOUNG PEOPLE A school-leaver who is looking for a job can claim after his 16th birthday, even if he is still living with his parents. Before 16 he is considered to be dependent on them.

DISABLED PEOPLE A disabled person cannot claim benefit if he is in a full-time job. But a self-employed disabled person may be given benefit if his earnings are abnormally low for the kind of work he is doing.

HOSPITAL PATIENTS In cases where a husband and wife are drawing benefit and one of them is admitted to hospital, the couple's entitlement to benefit is generally unaffected for the first eight weeks. After that time the benefit is reduced by £1·35, and no further adjustment is made unless the patient remains in hospital for more than two years.

Visiting expenses can normally be met from the saving in living costs resulting from the provision of free board and lodging for the patient. But additional benefit can be awarded if visiting expenses exceed this saving.

If a dependent child of a family drawing supplementary benefit has to go into hospital, no adjustment is made in the parents' allowance until the child has been in hospital for 12 weeks. After this time the benefit is usually reduced.

A supplementary benefit of £1·35 a week can be paid to single people in hospital to cover their personal expenses, and additional payments are made to meet outside commitments, such as rent and rates.

People not receiving regular supplementary benefit can still get help with the cost of hospital visiting if their income is only slightly above supplementary-benefit level. If they are working full-time, help can be given only in an urgent case—for instance, if a close relative is seriously ill.

## Special help for women

A married woman living with her husband cannot claim supplementary benefit. But if her husband claims, her needs and resources will be taken into account in deciding the benefit.

Benefit can be paid to women who are separated, divorced or unmarried with children. If they have children to look after, they do not have to be registered as unemployed to qualify for benefit.

SEPARATION If a husband who is separated from his wife and children fails to maintain them, or if the maintenance payments are not sufficient to meet their needs, the wife can claim supplementary benefit.

In this case, it is the policy of the Supplementary Benefits Commission to encourage the wife to apply to the magistrates for a maintenance order against her husband. She cannot be compelled to apply but if she refuses, the Commission may take the husband to court. If the husband refuses to maintain the wife and children, the Commission can take criminal proceedings against him.

If the wife qualifies for supplementary benefit in addition to any maintenance her husband is ordered to pay, she can have the maintenance money paid to the Social Security office. To do this, she simply authorises the magistrates' clerk to pass on the payments. The advantage is that even if her husband falls behind with his maintenance payments she still receives her full weekly benefit, including the amount due under the court order.

A similar arrangement can be made if the wife has to apply for benefit because the maintenance payments, though sufficient to raise her income above supplementary-benefit level, are not made regularly. If over a period the husband's payments exceed the benefit paid, the balance is handed over to the wife and the arrangement is cancelled.

UNMARRIED MOTHERS A single mother who obtains an affiliation order against the father of the child may be able to claim benefit if the amount she receives is less than the supplementary benefit she would be entitled to.

Again, if the mother qualifies for supplementary benefit, the advantage of arranging to have money due under the court order paid to the Social Security office is that she is guaranteed regular payments.

The mother of an illegitimate child may not want to apply for an affiliation order or to disclose the father's name or whereabouts to the Supplementary Benefits Commission. She is nevertheless entitled to benefit.

The Commission can attempt to find the father and take him to court to obtain a maintenance order for the child.

COUPLES LIVING TOGETHER A woman who lives with a man as his wife even though she is not married to him cannot claim benefit for herself. However, she may obtain benefit for children for whose support the man is not responsible, at least for a few weeks while she adjusts to the new situation.

The result of this rule is that a single woman or a deserted woman who would otherwise qualify may be refused benefit if it is thought she is living with a man as his wife.

## How a claim is made

Applications for supplementary benefit must be made in writing. Ask for an application form at any post office or at the local employment exchange. For people under State pension age who cannot work, the form required is S1. Form B1 is used for those who are available for work. People over pensionable age should ask for Form SP1.

If financial help is required urgently, claims can be made in person at most local Social Security offices.

Anyone who applies has to give detailed information about his and his wife's income and savings, and about all his dependants.

## How benefit is calculated

The amount of supplementary benefit to which an applicant is entitled is calculated by an officer of the local Social Security office. It consists of two parts:

1. A basic allowance laid down by Parliament. This changes from time to time, and current rates are given on the benefit application form. This basic rate may be reduced if the applicant has income from other sources or savings over a certain level.

2. An allowance for rent, based on the rent that the applicant actually pays.

## Working out the basic rate

The applicant and his wife are allowed to earn a small amount from part-time work before a reduction is made in the benefit payable. This allowance changes from time to time, but account is taken of any expenses made necessary by the part-time job.

National Insurance retirement pensions count as part of the applicant's income, and can affect the amount of supplementary benefit. Only widowed mothers are allowed part of the pension before it is counted as income.

Other State benefits—family allowances, National Insurance and industrial-injury benefits—and maintenance payments are all taken in full as income. Items disregarded are a part of war and industrial disablement pensions (up to £2 a week in 1972) and a part of most other income (up to £1 a week in 1972).

In working out how much benefit is payable, the Social Security officer ignores the value of the applicant's home, and the family is allowed to have a certain amount of savings. In 1972 it was up to £325.

Where the family savings were £325 or more, the applicant was considered in 1972 to have a weekly income of 5p for every £25 between £300 and £800. The weekly income was assessed at 12½p for every £25 savings over £800.

But since the first £1 of weekly income was ignored, a claimant with no other income could have up to £824 in savings without affecting his rate of benefit.

## Working out the allowance for rent

Once the basic allowance has been decided, the total benefit is calculated by adding an amount for housing.

With rented property this amount is the sum paid in rent and rates. With owner-occupied property, the rent allowance is the sum of mortgage interest, rates and an amount for repairs and insurance.

The rent allowance depends largely on the cost of housing in the applicant's area. Either the actual rent—or as much of it as is considered 'reasonable in the circumstances'—must be taken into account. A deduction is made if the rent covers lighting and heating.

When rent seems higher than what is 'reasonable in the circumstances', the Social Security officer has power to reduce the amount allowed.

In such a case the Social Security officer must consider whether there is cheaper adequate accommodation available to the applicant and whether it is reasonable to expect the family to move to it. This last consideration would depend very much on whether the applicant is likely to require supplementary benefit for any length of time.

It is not usual for an applicant to be expected to move if his financial crisis is likely to be over soon—if, for example, his earnings drop temporarily because of illness. If it is felt that an applicant ought to move, the full rent should always be allowed while he looks for alternative accommodation.

Where a high rent is being paid for some special reason—shortage of adequate housing, or where a single woman has a child and is unable to find any other home—the full amount may be paid on the grounds that it is reasonable in the circumstances.

Whether or not the claimant is already getting a rent rebate or allowance from the local authority, the Social Security office will tell the authority he is receiving supplementary benefit, and after eight weeks (if he is still on benefit) the authority will award a rebate or allowance according to special rules. His supplementary benefit will normally be adjusted to leave him the same spending money as before.

ALLOWANCES FOR NON-HOUSEHOLDERS
In the case of a lodger, board and lodging are normally paid in full (together with an allowance for personal expenses) only if the amount is considered reasonable. For example, a man living in a hotel and paying £12 a week would not receive the full £12.

The same rule applies to the cost of board and lodging in nursing homes, but the amount considered reasonable would be higher.

An applicant who lives in someone else's home is normally entitled to a small rent allowance, together with a fixed sum for personal expenses, regardless of how much he pays towards the rent.

SUB-LETTING If an applicant for supplementary benefit sub-lets part of his home, the rent allowance may be reduced by the net amount the sub-tenant contributes to the rent. Wear and tear to furniture are allowed for, and so is the cost of the sub-tenant's electricity if this is included in the rent.

For example, a family may pay £6 a week rent and sub-let a room for £3, including electricity worth 55p, with wear and tear estimated at 35p. The net income from sub-letting is £2·10; so the rent allowance, therefore, would be £3·90.

PAYING OFF A MORTGAGE Although anyone buying a house on mortgage may be entitled to an allowance for interest, no allowance is made for capital repayments. But since the interest forms the biggest part of the mortgage repayment during the first years of house purchase, the allowance could be substantial. While the family's income is reduced it may be possible to arrange with the building society or insurance company to pay only interest. □ Re-arranging family finances, p. 544.

## Obtaining additional benefit

In some circumstances more benefit than the basic rate may be obtained. This is paid either weekly or as a lump-sum grant.

Extra weekly payments ('discretionary

additions') cover such items as special medical diets, extra fuel, domestic help and heavy laundry expenses.

Other special needs which can be met in this way include storage charges, hire-purchase payments for essential furniture and kitchen goods, and even pocket money for a child at boarding school.

In deciding whether to give extra benefit, the Social Security officer can take into account income and savings which are disregarded in calculating the basic rate.

LUMP SUMS Most lump-sum payments are for such items as clothing, bedding, furniture and removal expenses. But a payment may be made for any necessary expense that cannot reasonably be met out of normal weekly income or from savings.

A lump-sum payment is not normally made if the person would still be left with more than £100 of his own savings after meeting the emergency.

Extra payments may also be refused if the money could be obtained elsewhere. The cost of school uniforms, for example, will not be met, because a grant can be made by the local education department. But applicants should never be expected to seek charitable help if a cash grant can be made.

It is unlikely that an 'exceptional needs' payment would be made to clear an unreasonable debt. But sometimes a payment may be made to cover an outstanding hire-purchase commitment.

The cost of clothing usually has to be met out of the normal weekly benefit. But where a person—especially one who has been receiving benefit for some time—has difficulty in meeting an immediate clothing need, a lump sum may be paid.

HELP FOR IMMIGRANTS An immigrant and his family may be eligible for a special grant to help them return home, but this is done only if they are most unlikely to settle successfully in Britain, and if their return home is likely to save public money. Help is not given if the immigrant can afford to pay the fare back to his own country without assistance.

Immigrants who are not receiving supplementary benefit can obtain help of a similar sort under a scheme run for the government

## How to draw the money

SUPPLEMENTARY benefit is paid by vouchers which can be cashed each week at a post office. Pensioners have their supplementary benefit added to their pensions and a new book of vouchers is issued for the combined payment.

Vouchers should be cashed within three months of the date stamped on them. If the money is not claimed within this time, it can be obtained by making a new application to the local office of the Department of Health and Social Security. But if this is not done within one year, the money will be lost.

Only people who are entitled to a regular weekly benefit are paid by voucher. If benefit is needed only for a short time it is sent through the post in the form of a Giro order or, very exceptionally, handed across the counter of the local Social Security office.
☐ Using National Giro, p. 439.

Unemployed people looking for work draw their benefit when they sign on at the local employment exchange.

If the applicant is not able to draw the benefit himself, because of illness, he can sign the authorisation section on the back of the benefit voucher and name a relative or friend who should be allowed to collect the money on his behalf.

Similarly, if the applicant is unable to manage his own affairs for some other reason the Social Security office can be asked to allow a friend or relative (called in law an appointee) to collect the benefit.

PAYMENT IN KIND The Supplementary Benefits Commission can pay benefit in the form of goods or vouchers, instead of cash, if this seems the best way of meeting a need. For example, a person with no fixed address may be given a voucher to pay for a bed at a hostel, instead of a cash allowance.

When several people need help in an emergency, perhaps if their homes have been flooded, meals and other help in kind may be provided either by a cash grant or vouchers with which to buy food and other necessities.

ASSIGNING BENEFIT It is illegal to try to give a supplementary-benefit voucher to someone else—say as security for a loan. But the local Social Security office can be asked to pay all or part of the benefit to someone—as rent to a landlord, for example.

by International Social Service, 39 Brixton Road, London SW9 6DD. Applicants should send full details in writing.

**When benefit can be reduced**
When the supplementary benefit an applicant would normally receive is more than he could earn full-time in his normal work, the amount he actually receives is reduced accordingly. This rule, called the wage stop, applies to all cases where the applicant is unemployed, unless there are exceptional circumstances.

In calculating what would be an applicant's normal wage, the Social Security office includes the amount of any family-income supplement which he is entitled to draw. □ Help for low-paid families, p. 555.

Occasionally, to avoid hardship to children, part of the wage-stop reduction is added back, so that even if the benefit paid is still less than the normal rate it is more than the man could earn in normal circumstances.

SICKNESS A sick person can be wage-stopped only if his sickness is temporary—which the Supplementary Benefits Commission interprets as meaning that he is expected to be fit for work within three months.

DISABLEMENT If a disabled person is regarded as fit for work and is required to register at the employment exchange to claim benefit, he can be wage-stopped. But if a man is unemployable through age, disability and other factors, the wage stop is not applied.

VOLUNTARY UNEMPLOYMENT If an unemployed person is disqualified from receiving unemployment benefit because he left his job voluntarily, was sacked for misconduct, or has refused a reasonable offer of work, then his supplementary benefit is reduced by 40 per cent of the basic allowance for a single person. If this would cause hardship a smaller deduction is made. □ Qualifying for unemployment benefit, p. 650.

In areas where jobs are readily available, unskilled single men under 45 who are physically and mentally fit are given four weeks to find work. After that, benefit is cut off unless the man reapplies and the Supplementary Benefits Commission accepts that he is not to blame for still being unemployed.

Other people under 45—married men or women, skilled or unskilled—who are neither handicapped nor have dependants who would suffer hardship, are allowed to draw benefit for three months before a four-week warning to find work is given.

If an unemployed man persistently fails to make efforts to maintain himself or his family, he can be taken to court. He can be jailed for up to three months or be fined up to £100.

---

## Appeals over supplementary benefits and FIS

ANYONE dissatisfied with a Social Security officer's decision over a claim for either family income supplement (FIS) or supplementary benefit has the right to appeal to the Supplementary Benefit Appeal Tribunal.

If he is appealing over FIS, the applicant should first ask the Social Security office to explain the decision he objects to. If the explanation seems unsatisfactory, the applicant should appeal as soon as possible.

In a dispute over the amount of supplementary benefit, first ask the Social Security office for a breakdown of how the figure was arrived at (called a notice of assessment).

If the applicant feels that the officer's decision is wrong or unfair, and the officer refuses to change it, he should appeal to the Tribunal within 21 days.

Apart from dissatisfaction with the amount allowed, the applicant can also appeal against a decision to pay all or part of his benefit in kind, or to pay his benefit to some other person.

He can appeal against the requirement that he register at an employment exchange as a condition of drawing a supplementary allowance. Finally, he can appeal against a decision to recover benefit paid while he was in full-time work or was waiting for National Insurance benefit or family allowance to be paid.

HOW TO APPEAL An appeal can be made to the tribunal through the local office of the Department of Health and Social Security, either by letter or on a special form.

Appeals usually take between two weeks and a month to arrange. If the need is urgent, ask for an early hearing, and explain why it is important to get a quick decision. □ Appearing before a tribunal, p. 735.

HELP WITH AN APPEAL Legal aid is not available for a tribunal hearing. If help is needed with the appeal a trade-union official or a social worker can often assist. Help can also be sought from the Citizens' Rights Office, 1 Macklin Street, London WC2B 5NH.

# Help for low-paid families

*Who qualifies for the supplement*   *Rights of appeal*
*How the amount is decided*

PEOPLE in full-time work who are earning low wages and supporting at least one child under 16 or still at school may be entitled to claim from the State a weekly addition to their wages.

The addition, known as the family-income supplement (FIS), is paid under the Family Income Supplements Act 1970.

How low a family's income must be to qualify for the supplement depends on the number of children in the family. At the end of 1972 a family with one child qualified if their income was below £19·80 a week. A family with four children qualified if their income was below £25·80 a week.

## Who qualifies for the supplement

FIS can be claimed by anyone who fulfils the following three conditions (including unmarried mothers and unmarried couples living together as man and wife):

**1.** The claimant, or the man if a couple is claiming, must be in full-time work—that is, he or she must normally work 30 hours a week or more.

**2.** He or she must support at least one child who is under 16 years of age, or still at school. This includes an adopted or illegitimate child. A foster child can be included only if no boarding-out allowance is paid by the local authority or an approved voluntary body.

**3.** The family must have an income below a certain level—known in law as the 'prescribed amount'. At the end of 1972 the prescribed amount for families with one child under 16 or at school was £19·80; for each additional qualifying child, the prescribed amount was increased by £2.

HOW TO MAKE A CLAIM To claim FIS complete the form obtainable at the post office and send it in with the necessary evidence of income. If full evidence is not available at once, the form should still be sent without delay, as the supplement will be awarded only from the date of the claim.

## How the amount is decided

Anyone who qualifies for FIS receives half the difference between their gross income and the prescribed amount, up to a maximum which at the end of 1972 was £5 a week. The income of husband and wife (or of two people not married but living as man and wife) is added together for this purpose. Children's income is disregarded. Gross income means wages before tax and National Insurance contributions are deducted. Family allowances are regarded as part of income.

In calculating gross income, the only money *not* taken into account is:

**1.** The first £2 of a war-disablement pension.

**2.** A constant-attendance allowance paid under the industrial-injuries and war-pension schemes, and the attendance allowance for the very severely disabled.

**3.** The boarding-out allowance paid to foster parents by a local authority or approved voluntary body (but a child for whom such an allowance is paid is not counted as part of the family when a claim for FIS is decided).

Wages are generally averaged over the five weeks preceding the week in which the claim is made or, if the claimant is paid monthly, over the preceding two months.

FIS is normally fixed for 26-week periods. If the family's circumstances change, no adjustment is made until the end of the 26 weeks, when the supplement is reassessed in the light of the changed circumstances.

Rates of FIS, and the level of the prescribed amount, change from time to time; up-to-date figures can be obtained from the local Social Security office.

HOW THE MONEY IS PAID People receiving FIS are normally given a book of weekly orders which can be cashed at a post office.

## Rights of appeal

Whether or not an applicant qualifies for FIS, and if so how much he or she should receive, is decided by the Supplementary Benefits Commission. Anyone who is dissatisfied with a decision on his case can appeal to the Supplementary Benefits Appeal Tribunal. ☐ Appeals over supplementary benefits and FIS, p. 554.

FALSE INFORMATION It is an offence to give false information to obtain FIS. Anyone who does so can be fined up to £100, or sent to prison for up to three months, or both.

# How the income-tax system works

*Three ways of taxing income*
*How wage-earners are taxed*
*How self-employed people are taxed*

*Tax on the income of wives and children*
*Reform of the tax system*
*Tax avoidance and evasion*

MOST forms of income are subject to tax—wages, commission, bonuses, tips, most types of interest, dividends, rents, profits and pensions. Income tax is also charged on some business expense allowances, on fringe benefits such as a rent-free flat, and even on some State benefits.

Nobody pays tax on the whole of his income, however. Two types of deduction—for outgoings and allowances—are made before the tax due is calculated. Tax-free outgoings include mortgage interest, fees to professional bodies and maintenance payments to a wife or children which are made under a court order. Allowances are made for a wife, children, other dependent relatives, life-assurance premiums, and so on.

When these deductions have been made,

tax is charged at the prevailing rate, which may be altered from year to year according to the Budget and the Finance Act which makes the Budget law.

TYPES OF INCOME For tax purposes, income is divided into earned income (mainly wages, salaries and profits of sole traders and partnerships) and unearned or investment income (from rents, dividends and so on). Generally, unearned income over a certain amount is taxed more heavily than earned income.

**Three ways of taxing income**
Tax is paid in three different ways according to the source of income and the financial and personal circumstances of the taxpayer.
**1.** Tax on the wages and salaries paid to employees has to be deducted by the employer

## Which types of income are liable to tax

|  | TAXABLE | NOT TAXED |
|---|---|---|
| Earnings | All salaries, wages, commission, bonuses and tips and other income from employment. Profits from business or professions | Luncheon vouchers up to 15p a day |
| Expenses | Expenses allowances paid by employer but not spent entirely on the firm's business | Money paid to re-imburse a PAYE taxpayer for expenses incurred wholly, exclusively and necessarily in the course of his job. The taxpayer must show he personally obtained no benefit from the expenses he was paid |
| Benefits in kind | Fringe benefits, such as use of house or car. Most free accommodation. Certain share options granted to directors or employees and disposed of by them (but approved schemes liable only to capital gains tax) | Payments in kind not convertible into cash or money's worth—unless paid to a director or to an employee whose earnings (including the benefits being considered) are £2000 a year or more. Rent-free accommodation occupied by someone other than a director for the purpose of carrying out the duties of the job (a caretaker's flat, for example) |

and sent to the Inland Revenue. This system is known as Pay As You Earn (PAYE).

**2.** Tax on the earnings and profits of most people who are self-employed is paid direct by the taxpayers themselves.

**3.** Tax on dividends—such as unit-trust distributions—is deducted at source. This means that the unit trust (or other payer of dividends) deducts tax at the current rate before it pays the dividend to the investor. If more tax is deducted than the investor is liable to pay, he claims money back from the Inland Revenue.

For tax purposes, income is divided into six categories or Schedules. The two which most affect the average taxpayer are Schedule E and Schedule D.

SCHEDULE 'E' Anyone who is an employee receiving a wage or salary is taxed under Schedule E. The tax calculation is made on the amount of money earned during the current tax year, even if the earnings, such as commission, are not paid until a later year. Tax under Schedule E is usually collected through PAYE.

SCHEDULE 'D' A self-employed person is taxed under Schedule D. This schedule covers income from trades, professions or vocations, interest, income from abroad, and profits from letting furnished property.

The amount of tax that has to be paid is usually based on the income which was received in the previous year.

### How wage-earners are taxed

Most wage and salary-earners are taxed under Schedule E, and the money is deducted from their wages by PAYE. The taxpayer supplies the Inland Revenue with information about his income and outgoings, and the allowances he wishes to claim, on a form called the Tax Return. From this the Inland Revenue calculates his tax liability, and sends him and his employer a code number. The employer uses this code number to work out from the tax tables how much tax to deduct each week or month.

If the taxpayer fails to supply the Inland Revenue with details of his income, or fails to claim the allowances for which he is eligible, he is likely to be given a low code number—or an emergency code. This may mean that more tax than necessary is deducted temporarily from his income. If the taxpayer's code is wrong, the employer is nevertheless

|  | TAXABLE | NOT TAXED |
|---|---|---|
| Pensions | Retirement pensions. Widow's war pension and widow's benefit not paid for the maintenance of children | War disability pensions and the part of widow's benefit paid for the maintenance of children. The general increase in rates for the second half of 1972/3 |
| Other State benefits and grants | Family allowances | Unemployment and sickness benefits. Supplementary benefit. Maternity benefits and grant. Educational grants and awards |
| Rents | Rents from property (less expenses such as repairs) | |
| Interest and dividends | Dividends, bank, loan and annuity interest. Trustee and National Savings Bank interest over £21 | Interest on National Savings Certificates, Save-As-You-Earn deposits. First £21 from Trustee and National Savings Bank interest. 'Capital element' of annuity payments. ☐ Planning for retirement, p. 522 |
| Prizes and winnings | | Premium Bond prizes, winnings from gambling, betting or football pools |
| Redundancy payments | Compensation for loss of office over £5000 | Redundancy pay. Compensation up to £5000 for loss of office |

obliged by law to continue using it to work out how much tax to deduct until he receives a new code from the Inland Revenue. The taxpayer will then be paid back the tax he has overpaid.

To calculate or check a taxpayer's code number, the Inland Revenue sends him a Tax Return form, usually in the spring, which he is obliged to complete and return. The form requires information about his income, outgoings and claims for allowances.

The taxpayer himself can also ask for a form if, say, he believes he is not being granted all the allowances to which he is entitled. The PAYE taxpayer gets a Form P1.

At other times the PAYE taxpayer receives two other Inland Revenue forms giving details of his total income and amount of tax he has paid—Forms P60 and P45.

At the end of each tax year—which runs from April 6 to April 5—every employee should receive Form P60 from his employer. This gives his total earnings for the year and the amount of tax paid.

Keep the P60 for at least a year from the date of issue because delays may arise if it cannot be produced when claiming Social Security benefits. It is a useful record for checking assessments for income tax.

When he leaves a job, the PAYE taxpayer should receive from his employer Form P45. This gives the date on which he leaves, the total income he has received during the tax year so far, the amount of tax he has paid on it, and his code number.

Do not lose this form, for a new employer is unable to deduct the correct amount of tax without it. The P45 can also be used when claims are made for unemployment or other Social Security benefits.

Some time after the end of the tax year, the PAYE taxpayer may receive a form—the Notice of Assessment—giving details of his income, allowances and tax paid in that year. The form also indicates whether too much or too little tax has been paid. Tax overpaid in a previous tax year can be claimed from the tax office, and is paid direct to the taxpayer. Underpaid tax is often added to the taxpayer's weekly or monthly PAYE payments for the rest of the current year.

Any taxpayer who wants to check that the correct amount of tax has been deducted in a previous year is entitled to ask the tax inspector to supply him with a Notice of Assessment if he has not been sent one.

### How self-employed people are taxed

Anyone who is self-employed—whether a freelance writer, a small shopkeeper or a doctor in private practice—is assessed on his annual profits. The amount of tax payable

---

## What happens about incorrect Returns

IF incorrect Returns have been made, by error or design, it is best to take professional advice from an accountant or solicitor before informing the tax inspector.

In deciding what action to take, the Inland Revenue takes into account whether the incorrect Return was reported by the taxpayer or discovered by the Inland Revenue. If the taxpayer (or an accountant on his behalf) reports a mistake, penalties and sometimes even interest on unpaid tax may be waived.

The Inland Revenue has many ways of finding out about sources of income which the taxpayer might be tempted—illegally—to conceal. Firms are obliged by law to give details of payments they make, even to freelance and casual workers. Investigations are often started by the authorities after insurance claims on stolen jewellery, local newspaper reports of 'good living' or large parties, the purchase of investments, or the entry of investment income on a later year's Return.

The income-tax authorities work closely with the Estate Duty Office and if the size of an estate gives grounds for believing that the dead person may have concealed his income, dependants may have the trouble and expense of an inquiry. The administration of the estate will be delayed until the inquiry ends.

Where it appears that the full income has not been entered on a Tax Return, a common method of calculating the extent of the error is what is known as a 'back duty investigation'. This may be carried out by the Inland Revenue or by the taxpayer's own accountant, usually at the option of the taxpayer.

The method of calculation is to work out, often for each year, increases in wealth, the total known income and known outgoings, including reasonable living expenses, and to regard any 'deficiency of income' as having been omitted from Tax Returns.

under Schedule D is usually based on the previous year's income. He receives the yellow Return Form 11P, which is similar to the P1 but allows more space for the greater amount of information required.

When the Return has been completed, the Schedule D taxpayer sends it to the tax inspector with a copy of his accounts and eventually receives a statement of the amount of tax due—an assessment. If there is any error or disagreement about the assessment, he has 30 days in which to appeal.

If no appeal is made within that time, and the taxpayer has no good reason for failing to appeal, he has to pay the amount demanded.

If, because a self-employed taxpayer delays presenting his accounts, the inspector makes an estimated assessment which is too high, it is important to lodge an appeal within 30 days, saying that the accounts will be sent shortly.

Tax is payable by self-employed people in two equal instalments, on January 1 and July 1 every year. If the tax bill has not been agreed by January 1, the inspector is entitled to demand a reasonable sum of money on account of the first instalment due.

BUILDING WORKERS Some people in the building industry who supply their own labour, or that of other people, to a main contractor, are classified as self-employed. They are sometimes known as workers 'on the lump', or labour-only subcontractors.

On income received before April 6, 1972 they pay tax direct, like other self-employed people. To be allowed to do so after that date, a subcontractor must apply for a certificate of exemption. This will be granted if he has a permanent place of business in the United Kingdom and is submitting Tax Returns or accounts, or convinces the tax authorities that he will do so. Anyone refused a certificate can appeal. ☐ Appealing against the tax bill, p. 578.

If a subcontractor does not apply for a certificate, or one is refused, a main contractor is required to deduct 30 per cent from payments made to the subcontractor—except those which cover the cost of materials he has supplied. These deductions are sent to the tax collector as payment on account of the subcontractor's income tax. Any difference between this amount and the tax the subcontractor is actually liable to pay is rectified when he receives a tax assessment.

## Tax on a wife's income

A working wife need not normally make a separate Return from her husband. His Return covers her income and allowances, and any demands for payment of tax debts will be made to him. A working wife taxed with her husband is entitled to have the equivalent of a single person's allowance deducted from her earnings before tax is charged. This is called wife's earned income allowance.

If, however, the husband and wife wish to pay their tax separately, they can ask the inspector for a separate assessment. This does not alter the total amount of tax they pay on income received before April 6, 1972—it merely allocates their separate debts.

From April 6, 1972 a husband and wife who apply for separate assessment are taxed on their earned income as single people. Each receives a single person's allowance, instead of the husband receiving the married man's allowance, but the wife no longer receives wife's earned income relief. If the couple are in the higher-income bracket because of the wife's earnings, they pay less tax than if they had been assessed jointly.

The unearned income of the wife continues to be taxed with her husband's income, however. And the husband is entitled to claim any allowances for children of the marriage.

SEPARATED COUPLES Husbands and wives are automatically taxed individually if they are separated by court order or deed of separation, are permanently living apart, or if one lives in the United Kingdom and the other is abroad.

## Tax on a child's income

A child is assessed for tax in the same way as any other taxpayer if his income is large enough to warrant it. The child must complete a separate Tax Return, and is entitled to claim the usual allowances.

The point at which a child becomes liable to tax may change from Budget to Budget, but in 1972–3 a child's income was taxable if he earned more than £591 or had investment income of more than £460.

If the child's income exceeds a certain amount—in 1972–3, £115—the parents' tax allowance for that child is reduced. For every £1 over the limit, the allowance is reduced by £1.

A student's educational grants are not counted as income for tax purposes.

If a young person under 18 receives income from investments given to him by his parents, the income is added to that of the parents for tax purposes. Investment income from any other source is regarded as the child's.

Different rules apply to investment income received by a child before April 6, 1972. The child's income from investments bought by parents is taxed as part of the parents' income until the child reaches 21; investment income from any other source is taxed with the parents' income until the child reaches 18 (or 21 if the child is not working).

### Rates of tax

Tax rates, which used to be expressed as so much in the £, are given as percentages, so that tax at 7s. 9d. in the £ becomes tax at 38·75 per cent.

Before April 6, 1973 income tax is charged at a single rate. The reduced rates of 4s. and 6s. in the £ were abolished by the Finance Acts of 1969 and 1970. People with high incomes may have to pay an additional tax called surtax. ☐ Paying surtax, p. 561.

### Claiming refunds for overpayment

Anyone who has paid too much income tax can apply for a refund. Overpayment may occur when a PAYE taxpayer marries, or when tax is deducted at source from payments made to people liable to pay little or no tax (for example, dividends which are paid after deduction of tax).

To claim a refund, write to the tax inspector. The taxpayer may then be asked to complete a Repayment Claim Form and produce evidence of the payment received net of tax.

### Reform of the tax system

Major changes in the system of personal direct taxation come into force on April 6, 1973. Their main aim is to simplify the operation of the tax system.

OLD SYSTEM Before that date, the income of private individuals and partnerships is subject to two forms of direct tax—income tax and (if the taxpayer's income is high enough) surtax. The two taxes are calculated at different times, according to different rules and by different departments.

The standard rate of income tax is set for unearned or investment income (from dividends, rents and so on)—despite the fact that this accounts for only 5 per cent of all the income which is taxed.

Since the aim of successive Governments has generally been to tax earned income (from wages and salaries) less heavily than unearned income, a complicated system of allowances has to be applied to earned income to reduce the tax paid on it. In effect, tax is paid at the standard rate on only a proportion of earned income—in 1972–3, on seven-ninths of earned income up to £4005 and on 85 per cent of earned income above that.

One disadvantage of this system is that tax appears to be higher than it really is. When the standard rate of tax is 38·75 per cent, many people imagine that each £ they earn is taxed at 38·75 per cent (after allowances are used up). People who earn £10 in overtime, for example, believe that they have to pay tax at the full rate on the extra £10, leaving net earnings of just over £6. In fact, they pay tax at the standard rate on only seven-ninths of the £10, leaving nearly £7 after tax (assuming total earned income to be less than £4005).

The old system also gives a misleading impression of the value of personal allowances. In 1972–3, for example, a married man's personal allowance is £600. For anyone with earned income, however, the amount of his income which escapes tax is larger than this, because of the effect of earned-income relief. It is in fact £772.

NEW SYSTEM Under the new system, income tax and surtax are replaced by a single tax, sometimes known as unified tax. The basic tax rate is set for *earned* income (instead of unearned income), and this becomes the rate at which earnings are taxed after allowances have been used up—for many people, it is the rate charged on overtime payments, for example. There is a surcharge on unearned income above a certain level, and unified tax at higher rates replaces surtax.

As a consequence of these changes, figures for personal allowances are altered, though their effect on the amount of tax charged remains the same. The new figures represent the true value of these allowances to people with earned income.

Most people who pay tax by PAYE also receive new code numbers, though again this does not affect the amount of tax they pay (unless their circumstances have changed since the last coding).

### Tax avoidance and evasion

There are legal and illegal ways of paying less tax. Legal methods are termed 'tax avoidance', and consist of arranging one's affairs to take advantage of the rules in the system. 'Tax evasion', which is illegal, entails making incorrect statements and Returns which mislead the tax inspector into undercharging.

It is an offence to try to evade tax by failing to make a Return. The maximum penalty is £50, plus a maximum of £10 a day for each day that no Return is made after the failure has been declared by the Commissioners of Income Tax.

If failure to make a Return results in tax

being undercharged, the taxpayer has to pay the balance due, as well as any penalty which may be imposed on him.

In practice, however, prosecutions for failing to make a Return are rare. The inspector has more effective ways of encouraging the taxpayer to make a Return.

A self-employed person who fails to make a Return may find that the inspector assesses him on estimated profits which are far higher than his actual profits.

A PAYE taxpayer who makes no Return may find that he has not been given all the allowances to which he is entitled—and is therefore paying more tax than is necessary.

Any false statement or representation in a Return carries a penalty of up to six months' imprisonment. If an error is made negligently, without the intention to mislead, the maximum penalty is £50, plus the amount of any tax due. The tax also has to be paid to the Inland Revenue.

If a Return or statement is deliberately fraudulent, there is again a maximum penalty of £50, plus twice the amount of tax lost, and the tax itself must still be paid.

## Paying surtax

SURTAX is an extra tax, on top of income tax, which may have to be paid on income received before April 6, 1973. The point at which an individual becomes a surtax payer depends on what allowances he can claim. A married man with £1500 in outgoings and allowances would not start paying surtax until he earned more than £6501.

Surtax is assessed from the ordinary income tax Return Form and is paid to the Surtax Office in a lump sum on January 1 of the year following that for which it is assessed.

HOW INCOME IS CALCULATED All the money included in an individual's income when income tax is calculated forms part of his income for surtax purposes. Increasing rates of surtax are charged on successive slices of income. In 1970–1 surtax started at 10 per cent and rose to a maximum of 50 per cent.

If a surtax payer receives 'tax-free' interest from a building society—that is, interest from which tax has already been deducted—he is regarded as receiving the hypothetical gross amount before tax was deducted. Calculating the gross amount is known as 'grossing up'.

For surtax, the first £21 interest on National Savings and Trustee Savings Bank accounts counts as part of income and is grossed up.

Certain outgoings are deducted before surtax is charged—mortgage interest, approved pension contributions, retirement annuity payments and business losses.

SURTAX ALLOWANCES Many, but not all, of the allowances deducted from income before surtax is charged are the same as for income tax. These are: allowances for children; housekeeper; dependent relative; daughter's services; blind people; additional personal allowance for children; the difference between a single man's and a married man's allowance.

But single person's allowance, relief for wife's earned income and for premiums paid on life-assurance policies are not deducted.

After allowances, surtax is charged on the net amount exceeding the starting-point, which in 1970–1 was £2000. But a taxpayer with a net amount of not more than £2500 in 1970–1 or £3000 in 1971–2 is exempt from surtax. If his figure is over these limits, surtax must not exceed 40 per cent of the excess.

SPECIAL RELIEF ON EARNED INCOME A surtax payer is allowed basic earned-income relief at the income-tax rate—in 1970–1, two-ninths of income up to £4005 and 15 per cent of anything else.

If the earned income less earned-income relief exceeds a basic sum (£2000 in 1970–1), a further relief is granted to reduce it to that basic sum. But the relief must not exceed a prescribed maximum (£2000 in 1970–1). Within that maximum, enough relief is granted to reduce net earned income to a low figure (£2000 in 1970–1).

ABOLITION OF SURTAX Surtax is abolished from April 6, 1973 and replaced by higher rates of unified tax. The basis of calculation is similar to surtax, but personal and wife's earned income allowances are deducted from income, and the first £21 interest from National Savings and Trustee Savings Banks is not grossed up.

Unlike surtax, higher rate tax is paid during the year to which it applies, and is deducted under PAYE where appropriate.

During 1973–4, people liable to the higher rate for the current year, and surtax for the previous year, may defer part of the tax to January 1, 1975 and part to January 1, 1976.

# How to make a Tax Return

*Earnings, pensions and State benefits*  
*Interest, dividends and rents*  
*Other forms of income*

*Allowable outgoings*  
*Allowances for wife and children*  
*Claiming other allowances*

EVERY year the Inland Revenue sends out to most taxpayers a form called a Tax Return. The most common ones are the P1 for PAYE taxpayers and Form 11P for Schedule D taxpayers. Not all taxpayers receive one every year. If an individual's circumstances do not change much he may receive a form only at irregular intervals.

If you are sent a Return form, complete it and return it to the inspector as soon as possible. The Inland Revenue needs the information given on the form to work out

## A step-by-step guide to completing the form

**Earnings**  
Form 11P deals with these earnings under the heading Employment or offices

Details of earnings from the PAYE taxpayer's own full-time employment need not be entered as his employer has to give this information to the Inland Revenue. Taxpayers completing Form 11P can find information about PAYE earnings on Form P60 which the employer has to give to every employee paying tax under PAYE.

If husband and wife are taxed together, include details of a wife's earnings from her P60. If the couple have asked to be taxed separately, the wife should complete a separate Tax Return, covering her earnings and claims for allowances.

If a wife works for her husband he should declare any wages he may have paid her.

Declare here any income received from part-time employment—working as a barman in the evenings, for example. Do not include part-time earnings which are not from working for someone else but from, say, freelance articles for the local newspaper or magazines or from giving music lessons. Such earnings should be included as 'Profits from trade or business' in Form P1.

Include all tips and incidental receipts, such as gifts from an employer if these are relatively expensive.

Include all bonuses from your employer which are given annually or which you are entitled to receive as part of your contract. Bonuses given as 'personal tributes' (e.g., a cricketer's benefit) are not taxable. Receipts of this kind are declared under 'Any other profits or income'.

If the taxpayer is provided with living accommodation by his firm, its value must be included—unless he is an employee (not a director) and the terms of his employment require him to live where he does to do his job properly. For example, a manager living above his shop, or a night watchman with a flat in an office block, is not taxed on the value of his accommodation and so need not enter it here.

**Pensions and Social Security benefits**  
These are the same on both forms

Pensions are regarded as earned income and are liable for tax. A pension from an employer may already have had tax deducted under PAYE. The pre-tax value of the pension should be given, together with the employer's name and address.

Enter the full amount of any State pension received (though the Autumn 1972 increases are not taxed in 1972–3 only).

A wife entitled to her own pension, through having paid full

how much tax has to be paid on your income. Any taxpayer who does not receive a form, but believes he is paying too much or too little tax, should write to the tax inspector detailing the changes in his circumstances or asking for a Return form. If necessary, a PAYE taxpayer will then receive a new code number.

The taxpayer is likely to need a new code number when he marries or when his wife has a child; when a child of his starts full-time work; when he takes out a life-assurance policy on his own or his wife's life; and when he takes out or ends a mortgage.

The Return deals with two years; it looks back at income, outgoings and capital gains in the past tax year and covers claims for allowances for the coming year. A tax year runs from April 6 to April 5.

Ensure that all entries you make on the Return are complete and accurate and be sure to claim all the allowances to which you are entitled, otherwise too much tax may be deducted. Take care to declare all taxable income; failure to do so can lead to steep bills for unpaid tax and possibly prosecution, fines and even imprisonment.

Form P1 and Form 11P are similar; in the following guide to the Returns the headings from P1 are given, followed by the equivalent sections on Form 11P.

---

**Pensions and Social Security benefits**
continued

National Insurance contributions herself, qualifies for a wife's earned-income relief which is equivalent to the personal allowance she would receive if single. Put a cross in the box so that the tax inspector knows she is entitled to the relief.

State where any other pension comes from—for example, a widow may receive a pension from a firm which used to employ her late husband—and how much it is.

The weekly and yearly amounts of family allowances have to be given so that the tax inspector can check on the number of children for whom the taxpayer is claiming. Family allowances are taxed as earned income and a deduction may be made to 'claw back' increases in family allowances from taxpayers with higher incomes.

Enter the total yearly amount received in State widow's benefits.

Other benefits which have to be included are guardian's allowance and the special child's allowance paid to a divorced mother.

Do not include sickness, unemployment or maternity benefits, or redundancy pay. None of these is taxable.

On Form P1, give details of any pension which you and your wife, if she is not separately assessed, expect to receive in the coming year. This avoids under or overpayment of tax.

---

**Interest not taxed before receipt**
This entry is the same on both forms

All interest received or credited without deduction of tax must be entered. Income-tax relief is allowed automatically on the first £21 of interest received by a husband or wife (or both) on Ordinary accounts in the National Savings Bank and Trustee Savings Banks and the Savings Department No. 2 of the Birmingham Municipal Bank. Before April 6, 1973, the interest does not escape surtax, however.

Enter the name of any other bank and the amount of interest received or credited. Tax is payable on all such interest received.

Include all other interest which has not been taxed before it is received, such as Co-operative Society deposits (but not dividends on purchases), National Development Bonds, Savings Bonds, Government stocks bought through the Post Office or a Trustee Savings Bank, War Loan or Defence Bonds, or annuities on which tax has not been deducted.

If you are not sure whether tax has been deducted from interest received, consult the organisation making the payment.

continued ▶

## A step-by-step guide to completing the form continued

**Interest from building societies**
This is the same on both forms

Give the name of the building society and the amount of interest received or credited. Building societies agree a special rate of tax with the Inland Revenue, below the standard rate, to be paid on building-society interest. Income tax is not payable on it again but before April 6, 1973 it may be liable to surtax. If, after that date, you are liable for income tax at a higher rate, you have to pay the difference between that and the basic rate.

No repayment can be claimed if the taxpayer would not normally have been liable to pay tax.

**Dividends, interest, trust income, and annuities taxed before receipt**
This is the same on both forms

To simplify tax collection most investment income has tax deducted before it is paid. If a taxpayer would not normally have been liable to tax he can claim a repayment. Where, before April 6, 1973, surtax is payable, it is calculated on the hypothetical gross amount before the deduction is made. This is the figure to be entered. If, after that date, you are liable for income tax at a higher rate, you have to pay the difference between the tax already deducted and this higher rate.

**Rents from furnished or unfurnished lettings or hirings**
This appears on Form 11P under the heading Property

If a person lets property—and this includes part of his own house, a holiday cottage or a garage—he must complete this section.

-If the income from these sources is large, consult an accountant. Otherwise give the names and addresses of the properties and the full rents received and any profit made from gas or electricity meters.

Enclose a statement of expenses incurred—rates, legal fees, ground rent, repairs and decorations, costs of collecting rents, and insurance premiums. They may be allowable against tax.

**Profits from trade or business**
This appears at the beginning of Form 11P as Trade, profession or vocation

Enter any income not taxed under PAYE—from giving private lessons, writing or doing accounts for a small business, for example. Give details of profits and losses and the type of business concerned, and the address from which it is carried on. If possible, supply the tax inspector with proper accounts.

Expenses are allowable if they are wholly and exclusively incurred for the purpose of business. It may therefore be possible to claim some part of the cost of running a car or a house. But this has to be agreed with the tax inspector.

The help of an accountant is usually necessary to get the full benefit; his fees may be allowed against tax. If the accounts have not been completed, enter 'accounts to follow' and return the form.

**Maintenance or alimony received**
Enter this under Other profits or income on Form 11P

Only payments under a court order or a legally enforceable agreement need be included. Any other payments are tax free. State whether the amount received is gross, or net of income tax and expenses.

**Income from abroad**
There is a separate section for untaxed income from abroad on Form 11P

Tax is payable on any income which is received from abroad.

If it is earned—a pension, for example, or profits from a business carried on abroad—tax is usually payable only on that part of the income brought into this country during the tax year.

If overseas income is unearned—dividends or interest from investments, for example—it is taxable even if it is kept abroad and not brought back to this country.

A taxpayer may be entitled to relief from double taxation if any income he receives has been taxed already in the country of origin. Where this occurs it is advisable to consult an accountant.

**Any other income not entered elsewhere**
The Form 11P heading for this section is Any other profits or income

Include any income received which is not entered anywhere else in the form, such as payments for irregular freelance activities.

Remember to offset against it any expenses for postage, telephone, stationery, etc. Include a separate account to show what expenses have been deducted.

**Outgoings:**
**Expenses against earnings**
On Form 11P this section is called Expenses in employment

A number of trade unions have agreed a fixed-expenses deduction with the Inland Revenue. To claim, enter a cross in the box on Form P1. A union member who can prove that he necessarily incurred greater expenses than the agreed deduction may be able to get a larger allowance. In this case, give full details of all claims, including items normally covered by the fixed allowance.

Where there is no agreed deduction, give details of expenditure, and a description of the job as well as the amount claimed. These expenses must be necessary for the performance of that particular job.

**Fees or subscription to professional bodies**
Enter under Expenses in employment on Form 11P

Tax relief is given on subscriptions to professional bodies but not for trade union dues unless membership is recognised by the Inland Revenue as being necessary for the taxpayer's job.

**Superannuation contributions (other than to a trade union)**
Include in Expenses in employment on Form 11P

Tax relief is allowed on the whole of a taxpayer's contributions to any superannuation fund approved by the Inland Revenue—usually a pension scheme operated by his employer. The taxpayer should find out from his employer whether the fund is approved.

If the employer pays all the contributions and the employee pays nothing—that is if it is a non-contributory pension scheme—the employee is not entitled to claim relief.

If his firm requires him to make a contribution for a deferred annuity for his wife or children, this is allowable against income tax.

A PAYE taxpayer with freelance income can also get relief if he contributes to a pension scheme approved by the Inland Revenue or if he makes regular payments over a number of years to buy a retirement annuity. Relief is allowed on a maximum premium of £1500 a year or as 15 per cent of the taxpayer's non-pensionable earnings, whichever is the lower figure. Up to £500 of this £1500 (or 5 per cent of the taxpayer's earnings) can be used as premiums on an annuity payable to his wife after his death.

Husband and wife are always considered separately. The husband cannot get relief on his wife's pension policy and her income is not added to his before calculating the 15 per cent.

**Claim for interest paid on loans for purchase or improvement of land, buildings, etc.**
This comes under the same heading on Form 11P

The taxpayer need not enter the amount of interest paid to a building society as the Inland Revenue obtains this from the society. Give the society's name and address and the roll or account number.

Mortgage repayments to a building society are deductible in part, but not payments under the Government's option mortgage scheme.

Whether or not interest on loans for other purposes qualifies for relief depends on current tax laws. In 1972–3 most interest is eligible, except hire-purchase interest and the first £35 interest paid on loans for purposes other than buying and improving property. In 1971–2, no relief is allowed on most loans other than those for property purchase and improvement.

Enter the amount of interest paid, the purpose of the loan and the date on which the money was spent.

continued ▶

## A step-by-step guide to completing the form continued

**Other interest and payments**
Form 11P calls this section
Other interest and outgoings

Give the total amount of alimony or maintenance payments made and the name of the person who receives them.

Enter the amount of any gift made under a deed of covenant—that is, a legally binding agreement to pay a fixed amount each year. Enter the gross figure, but before making the payment, be sure to deduct tax at the standard or basic rate, so as to obtain any relief due. In practice most deeds of covenant are in favour of charities, which can later reclaim the tax from the Inland Revenue.

Give the total amount of rent paid on property in the U.K. to anyone who normally lives abroad. Enter the gross figure, but remember to deduct tax at the standard or basic rate before making the payment.

**Alterations in income or outgoings**
This section is the same on both forms

Enter any changes during the previous year which might alter tax liability—interest on a new deposit account, completion of payments on a mortgage and so on. Describe the changes with dates—the amounts should already have been entered.

**Capital gains**
This section is the same on both forms

Anyone who has capital gains to declare is likely to have to list them on a separate sheet. Give a brief description of the assets, state when they were bought and when they were sold and the figures for both deals. State what profit was made, but remember to deduct any expenses involved in the purchase or sale. □ Capital gains tax, p. 574.

**Allowances:**
**Wife living with or wholly maintained by husband**
**Children**
These two sections are the same on both forms

Anyone who has married or remarried during the tax year should state the date of the marriage and his wife's maiden name.

Parents are entitled to an annual allowance for each child under 11, and an increased allowance for a child between 11 and 16.

If the child receives full-time instruction at a school, college or university, or is training for more than two years for a trade or profession, the allowance can continue to be claimed until the child's education is completed.

**Housekeeper or person looking after children**
The Form 11P heading is the same

A widow or widower can claim an additional personal allowance if he or she employs a resident woman housekeeper. The same allowance can be claimed by an unmarried man or woman who maintains a mother or other woman relative living with him or her to look after a brother or sister for whom a child allowance is given.

**Additional personal allowance for children**
The sections are again the same

A widow with a child for whom she is entitled to claim the ordinary child allowance is entitled to claim an additional children's allowance. This additional allowance can also be claimed by a married man whose wife is prevented by ill-health from looking after the children; by a man entitled to a single person's allowance; and by a single, separated or divorced woman who is either in full-time employment or totally incapacitated.

The taxpayer is not entitled to claim both this allowance and the allowance for a housekeeper. Check with the tax inspector's office which is currently the larger (usually it is the additional children's allowance) and claim that one.

**Dependent relatives**
The heading is the same on Form 11P

The taxpayer may claim an allowance if he supports or contributes to, or has living with him his widowed, divorced or separated mother or mother-in-law, or any other relative of his or his wife who is unable to work because of old age or infirmity.

If the total value of the maintenance the taxpayer pays to the

| | |
|---|---|
| **Dependent relatives** continued | dependent relative is less than the maximum allowance, then the allowance is reduced. If more than one person contributes towards maintaining the relative the allowance is shared.<br><br>If the relative's income exceeds a maximum (the tax office will supply the current figure—normally about the retirement pension figure) the allowance is reduced by the amount of the excess.<br><br>A single woman—spinster, widow, divorced or separated—is entitled to a higher allowance if she looks after an infirm or elderly relative who lives with her. |
| **Relief for persons born before April 6,19—** The sections are the same on both forms | Before April 6, 1973 a taxpayer can claim this relief if he or his wife are over 65 or reach the age of 65 during the current tax year. This relief is given if income is below a certain amount and there are different rates for single and married people. |
| **Daughter on whose services you are compelled to depend** The sections are the same on both forms | A taxpayer who maintains his daughter to take care of him or his wife because he or his wife is in bad health can claim this allowance. He cannot claim both this allowance and the housekeeper's allowance. Anyone who fulfils the conditions for both should claim the larger.<br><br>The taxpayer who qualifies for both the daughter's services allowance and the blind person's allowance is again entitled to choose the larger—but he may not claim both. |
| **Blind person's allowance** The Form 11P section is the same | A blind person, or the husband of a blind person, is entitled to an allowance which is reduced by any tax-free disability benefit received. If both husband and wife are blind, the allowance is doubled. |
| **Death and superannuation benefits** There is no equivalent section on Form 11P | A deduction is allowed if any part of the taxpayer's contribution to a trade union is for death and superannuation benefits. Give the name of the union, the full contribution for the year and the proportion applicable to death and superannuation benefits. |
| **Retirement annuity payments** This section appears only on Form 11P | A person whose job is not pensionable or who is self-employed can in some circumstances claim a deduction for payments made to provide a pension. To qualify, the payments must be made under a contract approved by the Inland Revenue or to an approved trust scheme which provides a life annuity in old age.<br><br>The deduction may not exceed 15 per cent of earnings or £1500, whichever is less. Up to £500 of this £1500 (or 5 per cent of the taxpayer's earnings) can be used as premiums on an annuity payable to his wife after his death. |
| **Life insurance** The sections are the same on both forms | Part of the premiums on policies taken out by the taxpayer on his own or his wife's life are deductible, up to 7 per cent of the sum assured—but not those on children or other relatives. Until April 6, 1973 relief is normally given on two-fifths of premiums which total £25 a year or more, subject to a maximum of one-sixth of the taxpayer's income. If total premiums amount to more than £10 but less than £25, relief is allowed on £10. After April 6, 1973 relief is normally given on one-half of premiums. If total premiums are less than £10 the full amount is allowed.<br><br>If the policy is in its first year and premiums are more than £26 a year, the taxpayer has to send a Life Assurance Premium Certificate, issued by the insurance company, giving details of the policy.<br><br>This relief does not extend to surtax or higher rate tax. |

# Checking the tax bill

*Checking the Notice of Coding*
*Checking the Notice of Assessment*

**M**OST taxpayers are given an opportunity at least once a year to check that the amount of tax they are being asked to pay is correct. People who receive a regular wage or salary may be sent two forms by the tax inspector's office:
**1.** A Notice of Coding, which lists what allowances have been agreed by the tax inspector and gives each taxpayer a code number. The employer uses tables issued by the Inland Revenue to calculate from the code number how much tax to deduct from each employee under the Pay-As-You-Earn system.
**2.** The Notice of Assessment, which shows the amount of tax due, and the amount deducted, in a previous tax year. The Notice of Assessment is sent to a PAYE taxpayer only if the wrong amount of tax was paid in a previous tax year, or if he has requested one.

People who are self-employed, or whose income is unearned, receive a similar Notice of Assessment which sets out how much tax

## Checking the Notice of Coding in detail

| | |
|---|---|
| **Expenses, etc.** | Before April 6, 1973 multiply by 9/7 to get the actual figure allowed by the tax office. If the result is less than the figure claimed, ask the tax inspector for the reason for the reduction.<br><br>From April 6, 1973 expenses shown on the Notice of Coding are identical to those on the Tax Return unless the tax inspector has reduced a particular item, or disallowed it entirely. |
| **Superannuation** | This section is for payments to an employer's pension scheme or a trade-union pension or death-benefit scheme (not the State scheme). Before April 6, 1973, multiply by 9/7 to get the actual figure allowed. If the claim has not been allowed in full, it may be because only part of the payments qualify to be set against tax. Check with the employer whether this could be the case.<br><br>If there is no entry at all, it may be because your employer operates a Net Pay arrangement under which superannuation is deducted from salary before it is entered on the tax records. Alternatively, it may be because the scheme is not 'approved' by the Inland Revenue—not all are. Check with the employer. |
| **Building-society interest payable** | Mortgage interest paid to an assurance company or local authority—as well as to a building society—should be shown in this section. Before April 6, 1973, multiply by 9/7 to get the actual figure allowed. Then check this figure against the figure for interest paid during the year given on the statement supplied by the building society (or other lender). The figures may be slightly different if the lender's accounting year is different from the tax year.<br><br>Where there is a marked discrepancy (more than a few pounds), or where no statement has been received from the lender, ask the lender how much interest was paid during the tax year. This figure is normally supplied by a building society direct to the tax authorities, and may occasionally be wrong because of a clerical error on the part of the tax office or the building society. |

they will have to pay in the current year.

The calculations on the Notice of Coding and Assessment are normally based on details supplied by the taxpayer himself on the Tax Return. The tax inspector's office decides whether, in its view, the taxpayer is entitled to the outgoings and allowances claimed on the Return. The inspector can allow a claim in full, reduce it if he thinks the taxpayer has claimed more than he is entitled to, or refuse a claim altogether.

Often the first indication a taxpayer receives that his claims have been allowed, reduced or rejected comes when he is sent either the Notice of Coding or Assessment. The forms list outgoings and allowances, and it is left to the taxpayer to check whether his claims have been allowed in full, and if not to consider whether to appeal. ☐ Appealing against the tax bill, p. 578.

For this reason it is important to keep a note of entries on the Tax Return form, and to check them against the figures shown on the Notice of Coding and Assessment.

It is also possible that either form may contain an error of calculation which, if not reported, will affect the amount of tax deducted. So check that additions and subtractions have been correctly made.

**Checking the Notice of Coding**
The Notice of Coding—Form P2—contains much of the information given on the Tax Return form, but the way in which certain items are described is different. The form is headed 'coding allowances' but the word 'allowance' is used in two different senses.

In the first section of the notice, 'allowances' covers *expenditure* such as expenses, superannuation payments, and interest on a mortgage,

| | |
|---|---|
| Personal<br>Wife's earned income<br>Housekeeper<br>Additional personal<br>Children<br>Dependent relatives | Figures for these allowances should be given as claimed. Check with the Tax Return Guide, the information leaflet provided by the tax inspector's office, that the correct allowances have been given, and notify the inspector of any errors<br><br>If an allowance has been claimed under these headings but is not entered here, ask the tax inspector if the allowance has been deliberately disallowed, and if so, why. |
| Life insurance | The figure given here is seldom the amount the taxpayer pays in premiums, except where small amounts are concerned. Usually it is a proportion of premiums—two-fifths before April 6, 1973, and after that date one-half.<br><br>Other restrictions may limit the relief allowed. No taxpayer is allowed to claim life insurance relief on more than one-sixth of his total income. In addition, annual premiums exceeding 7 per cent of the amount payable on death do not qualify for relief.<br><br>Where less than the full relief is allowed, check the regulations currently in force as given in the Tax Return Guide before contacting the tax inspector. |
| Allowances given against other income | This is a convenient way for the Inland Revenue to tax, under the PAYE system, small amounts of income from sources other than the taxpayer's main income. The tax inspector simply deducts such income from the total allowances which are given in the first section of the Notice of Coding.<br><br>Where the 'other income' is substantial—say more than £300 in all—an alternative method is used to collect the tax due. The tax is assessed independently of PAYE and the taxpayer receives a separate bill which he must pay direct.<br><br>What the Notice of Coding calls 'Other income' includes for tax purposes small amounts of income from property, interest on investments, pensions and family allowances. |

continued ▶

and *income-tax allowances* such as the personal allowance and the child's allowance.

The second section, 'Allowances against other income', deals with small amounts of income from sources other than the taxpayer's main income—freelance short-story writing, for example. It shows an amount which will be deducted from allowances in order to tax the income from other sources. In tax jargon, the allowances are 'exhausted' or 'consumed' by the other income.

In all other cases, three items on the Notice of Coding relate to money paid out by the taxpayer and deducted from his gross income before tax is charged. These allowances are for expenses, superannuation and building-society interest payable.

Before April 6, 1973 the figures on the notice are less than those on the Tax Return because of an accounting technicality which does not affect the amount of tax eventually paid. The figures show what has been allowed,

*reduced* by an amount for earned-income relief. The tax tables used by employers to calculate how much tax to deduct from pay compensate for this reduction.

From April 6, 1973 earned-income relief is abolished with the introduction of a unified system of income tax. After that date, the figures on the Notice of Coding and the Tax Return are identical, unless a claim is reduced or disallowed.

When, as in 1971–2, earned-income relief on the first part of earned income is two-ninths, the figure shown on the Notice of Coding is seven-ninths of the amount allowed (85 per cent if your income is high enough to take you over the £4005 limit of earned-income relief). To check, therefore, whether you have been allowed the full amount of your claims multiply the figures by 9/7.

Take the case of the man who claims £45 superannuation and £36 expenses, and receives a Notice of Coding showing £35 and

---

**Checking the Notice of Coding in detail** continued

| | |
|---|---|
| **Income from property** | This figure—which includes such items as rent from letting a room or letting half a house as a flat—is an estimate of the income likely in the coming year, based on the amount of income the taxpayer actually received in the previous year. As the coding has to be assessed before the end of one financial year and the start of another, even the figure for the previous year will be an estimate.<br><br>If the property has been disposed of, or is unlikely for some other reason to produce income in the year under review (because it is to be occupied rent-free by a relative, for example), inform the tax inspector and an adjustment will be made.<br><br>If the income actually produced is likely to be only slightly different from the anticipated income, there is no need to inform the inspector at this stage, for any tax overpaid will be refunded automatically when an assessment is made some time after the end of the financial year. |
| **Interest** | This figure, which is for interest received, is a prediction, based on previous years, and it is necessary to inform the inspector and ask for a re-coding only if the true figure is likely to be substantially different —because investments have been sold, for example, or a deposit account has been closed.<br><br>The entry here should not include any tax-free interest, such as the first £21 on National Savings or Trustee Savings Bank deposits, or on an account with the Birmingham Municipal Bank Savings Department No. 2. |
| **Pension** | Money received from retirement pensions is classed as earned income and before April 6, 1973, is eligible for earned-income relief at a rate of two-ninths. To allow for this, the tax inspector enters here only the remaining taxable seven-ninths. After 1973 the full amount claimed is shown.<br><br>The part of widow's benefit which the widow receives for herself |

£21 respectively. He works out how much the inspector's office has allowed like this:

---

**SUPERANNUATION**

| Take the figure on the Notice of Coding | £35 |
| Multiply by $\frac{9}{7}$ | £35×$\frac{9}{7}$=£45 |

**EXPENSES**

| Take the figure on the Notice of Coding | £21 |
| Multiply by $\frac{9}{7}$ | £21×$\frac{9}{7}$=£27 |

---

The calculation shows that the tax inspector's office has allowed the claim for £45 superannuation payments, but only part of the expenses claim—just £27, instead of the £36 claimed. It is then up to the taxpayer to decide whether to challenge the ruling.

A taxpayer who has unearned income, in addition to his main earned income, is entitled to have mortgage interest or similar outgoings deducted from the unearned part of his income. But superannuation and expenses, which relate to income from employment, must be deducted from that earned income.

Before April 6, 1973 a taxpayer gains from having allowances deducted from unearned rather than earned income, since he qualifies for earned-income relief on a greater slice of his earned income while also receiving the full tax-free allowances on unearned income. This may be shown by an entry against 'Other adjustments' at the bottom of the form.

It is not always possible for the taxpayer to work out how the inspector reaches this figure, but if an adjustment is shown on the Notice of Coding he can ask the tax office for a copy of the detailed calculation.

Where a taxpayer's income is almost entirely unearned, his Notice of Coding may show little or no income tax allowances to be set against his small amount of earned income. Instead, allowances and deductions are set against the unearned income and

---

| **Pension** continued | is regarded as earned income and will be entered in this section, less the amount of earned-income relief. But the amount she receives for her children is non-taxable.<br><br>Other non-taxable pensions and benefits are disability pension, family income supplement, sickness and unemployment benefit, supplementary benefit, maternity allowance and death grant. |
| **Family allowance** | Family-allowance payments are classed as earned income. If, for example, £46 is received in family allowance during a tax year before April 6, 1973, the amount entered is £46 less the two-ninths free of tax as earned-income relief—that is, £36.<br><br>From April 6, 1973 earned-income relief is abolished and the full amount received is entered here. |
| **Family allowance deduction** | This deduction for family allowances is to ensure that increases in allowances brought in during 1968 and later years are paid back by those whose income does not qualify them to receive the extra allowance. This is what is known as the 'claw back'.<br><br>This claw-back entry for family allowances may also vary from year to year. It consists of a deduction for each child who qualifies for an allowance. |
| **Net allowances** | The total in the section headed 'Allowances against other income' should be deducted from the total of allowances in the first section. Check that the deduction has been correctly made.<br><br>The taxpayer should have received separate notification—often on the Assessment form—if he has paid less tax than was due in previous years. If there is an entry here, and no notification has been sent, ask the inspector for details.<br><br>An adjustment to recover tax unpaid in previous years is deducted from the net allowances to arrive at the final figure of allowances which are given against pay. |

included on the separate Assessment he receives for his main tax bill.

A table of PAYE codes, Form P3, is often sent with the first Notice of Coding for the taxpayer to check his coding. Keep this form to check against any revised Notice of Coding.

**Checking the Notice of Assessment**
At the end of each tax year, the inspector works out precisely how much tax an individual should have paid. He takes into account earnings from full-time and part-time jobs and fees paid for freelance work, all of which will usually have been notified by the person or firm making the payment. He also considers the information given by the taxpayer on the Tax Return form.

If an individual pays tax under PAYE, this precise calculation of tax due is then compared with the actual amount of tax he has paid. An adjustment is made to the code number for the following year to take account of any

## How the Notice of Assessment is set out

The amounts of income earned, allowances given and tax deducted are detailed on a Notice of Assessment for PAYE —Form P70 C. Before the unified system of income tax is introduced on April 6, 1973 it is set out as follows:

**Part I** This should show gross income—from which expenses, superannuation or retirement annuity payments and mortgage interest payable are deducted

Earned-income relief is then deducted, and further allowances listed as on the Notice of Coding. Check these figures, add them up and subtract the family allowance figure to find the total allowance

An assessment is made for allowances given against other income and deducted from allowances—in the same way as on the Notice of Coding

The net allowances are then deducted from the gross income to find the amount of income on which tax has to be charged

Any relief from Part IV was (before it was abolished) carried over and the amount deducted to give the total tax assessed; from this deduct any overpayment of tax in previous years or add underpayments

Deduct from the resulting figure the amount of tax paid already to find whether there has been any under or overpayment

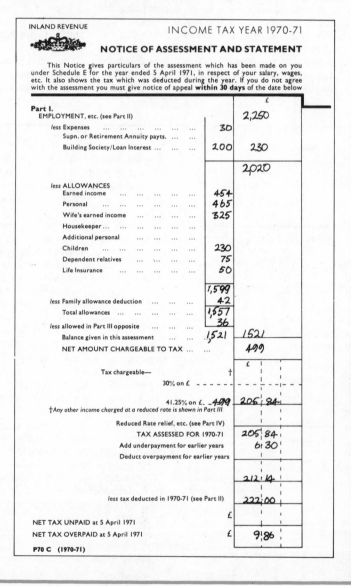

underpayment. An overpayment is, of course, refunded to the taxpayer.

Where the taxpayer has paid more or less than was due, he receives from the inspector a Notice of Assessment, setting out the detailed calculation of his tax liability. If the inspector believes that the correct amount of tax has been deducted, no Assessment is sent unless the taxpayer asks for one.

Anyone who receives a Notice of Assessment should check immediately that it is correct, as there is a strict time limit of 30 days in which to appeal. A taxpayer who fails to appeal within that period cannot challenge the amount for which he has been assessed, unless he can produce a valid reason for not appealing within the time limit—that he was out of the country, for instance.

The Notice of Assessment received by a person who pays tax under Schedule D is similar to that sent to a PAYE taxpayer but it is arranged in a different order.

---

SALARIES AND WAGES

**OF TAX UNPAID OR OVERPAID**

In any communication please quote

NVM/ 00-52624 AG

in accordance with the directions in Note 9 overleaf. If notice of appeal is given it will be appreciated if you will enclose this form for any necessary amendment.

This Notice is addressed to you personally as is required by law, but **if you have a professional adviser or agent it is desirable that you should bring it to his immediate attention.** Other information is given overleaf.

Issued by
H.M. INSPECTOR OF TAXES

James Gant, Esq.,
14 Green Lane,
Bromwich
Oxon

**Part II. Particulars of employment, etc., and of net tax deducted**

| Employment, etc. | Earnings | Expenses | Tax deducted |
|---|---|---|---|
| | £ | £ | £ |
| Jellow Industries Bromwich | 1,750 | 30 | 196 |
| Elgon Supermarkets | 500 | | 26 |
| less Tax refunded other than by employer | | | |
| | 2,250 | 30 | 222 |

**Part III. Allowances set against other income**

| | Earned Income Age Relief | Allowances | Income charged at 30% |
|---|---|---|---|
| Interest | | | |
| National Insurance pension | | | |
| Family allowances | 46 | 10 | 36 |
| Total allowances set against other Income | | — | 36 |

**Part IV. Reduced rate relief, etc.**

| | | £ |
|---|---|---|
| (i) Relief (where due) on dividends, etc., at 11.25% on £ | | |
| (ii) | | |
| (iii) | | |

**Part V.**

Earned income relief calculation

Net income     2020

Dividends     20

2040

2/9ths of 2040 = 454

Reproduced by permission of the Controller of H.M. Stationery Office

---

**Part II** Gross earned income is made up from wages or salary from full-time and part-time employment, together with earnings from occasional freelance jobs. Check the figures against Form P60 supplied by the employer, and against any other notifications of earnings. If you have only one employment, the figures will be entered on Part I without being shown here

**Part III** Allowances set against other income covers small amounts of income, such as rents of up to £300 a year, which are deducted from allowances instead of being separately assessed for tax. These are shown in the same way as on the taxpayer's Notice of Coding. Check amounts carefully

**Part IV** A person's income may be too low for him to pay tax. Yet if he receives income from dividends on shares, it may have been taxed before being distributed. This may mean that he is entitled to a rebate. No rebate will be shown unless the taxpayer has made a claim

**Part V** In Part V of the Notice of Assessment the inspector may show any other calculations —for example how he has assessed earned-income relief, or the amount of relief due on insurance premiums

# Capital gains tax

*How a gift is taxed*
*How a dead person's property is taxed*
*Tax on houses and land*

*Tax on furniture and jewellery*
*Tax on stocks and shares*
*How the tax is paid*

WHEN an individual or a company makes a profit by selling something which has risen in value since it was acquired, the State usually demands its share of that profit. Sometimes, as in the case of a shopkeeper selling goods, income tax will be paid on the profit; or in the case of a company selling its products, corporation tax will be charged. But when stocks and shares, businesses, land or buildings are sold or disposed of, the profit is liable to capital gains tax.

There are some exceptions—an owner-occupier, for example, does not pay capital gains tax on the sale of his home.

Until April 6, 1971 there were basically two forms of capital gains tax—short-term capital gains tax charged on the profit made on assets held for less than a year, and long-term capital gains tax on the profit from assets held for more than a year.

From April 6, 1971, however, short-term capital gains tax was abolished, and all gains made after that date are taxed at the same rate. LOSSES A taxpayer who makes a capital loss, by selling an asset for less than he paid for it, may generally deduct this loss from profits made on other transactions in the same or any future tax year to arrive at the gain to be taxed.

If the total sale proceeds are under £500, certain deductions must be made before a loss can be carried forward to a subsequent year.

For losses before April 6, 1971, deduct any gain made in the tax year in which the loss was made. For losses after that date, deduct the difference between £500 and the total gain.

### How a gift is taxed
A gift worth more than £100 is treated as though it were a sale at open-market value and the donor has to pay capital gains tax on any increase in the value of the gift since it came into his possession, or its estimated increase in value since April 6, 1965 if he acquired it before that date. Even gifts worth less than £100 become subject to the tax if, in a single tax year, the value of the gifts made to one person is more than £100.

Gifts of family heirlooms, jewellery, furniture and other personal belongings—what the law calls 'personal chattels'—are not liable to capital gains tax unless their value is more than £1000. Gifts of any value made to charities after March 21, 1972 are exempt.

The man who gives away all or part of a family business is normally subject to capital gains tax. But if he has controlled the business for ten years, at 65 he is allowed the first £10,000 of any gain he makes tax free. For the man giving up his business between the ages of 60 and 65, there is a partial exemption.

### How a dead person's property is taxed
When a taxpayer dies he is regarded as having sold all his property to his executor or administrator, but no capital gains tax is charged on the estates of people who died after March 30, 1971.

People who receive the assets of the dead person are not liable to the tax unless they dispose of them. Then tax is paid on any increase in value since the date of death.

### Tax on houses and land
Land and buildings—with the exception of owner-occupied homes—are generally subject to capital gains tax.

If owner-occupied homes and gardens are used partly for business purposes they are not fully exempt. Tax has to be paid in proportion to the part used for business.

Property bought and sold with the sole intention of making a profit is always liable to tax. ☐ Tax on the sale of property, p. 241. DEVELOPMENT Since the abolition of the betterment levy in 1970, development value is taxed as a capital gain when the property is disposed of.

LEASES Land or property held on a lease with 50 years or less to run is treated as a wasting asset—that is, as though its cost price were gradually exhausted over its life. The cost is held to decline until it reaches zero or a nominal price. Capital gains tax is charged on the amount by which the sale price exceeds the 'cost' of the unexpired life of the asset. The precise 'cost' of the unexpired life of a lease is calculated from a table published in the Finance Act 1965.

For example, a lease on a house which cost

£1000 when it had 50 years to run would be regarded as having cost £811 if it were sold after 25 years. After 40 years, the price would be considered to have fallen to £467. If, when the property is disposed of, there is a sub-lease, the main lease is not treated as a wasting asset until the sub-lease has expired.

ACQUISITIONS BEFORE 1965 Where land or buildings liable to the tax were acquired on or after April 6, 1965, tax is charged on any increase in value when they are sold.

If they were acquired before that date, it is assumed that the value has risen—or fallen—at a constant rate between the date of acquisition and the date of sale. On this basis, capital gains tax is charged on the part of the increase assumed to have accrued since April 6, 1965.

The date of purchase and sale, for this purpose, is taken as the day on which the contract was made, not the date when the bills were paid.

The taxpayer has an alternative (which must always be applied where there is development value); he can choose to pay

## Exemptions from capital gains tax

SEVERAL types of property are exempt from capital gains tax, even though a profit may be made on them when they are sold.

PRIVATE HOMES One owner-occupied dwelling at a time with up to an acre of adjoining garden or land is exempt. Extra land is allowed where it is judged necessary for 'reasonable enjoyment'.

A house does not become liable to tax just because the owner leaves home for a period. As long as he is not away for more than three years (four if the reason is work, or any length of time if the work is abroad) he is not liable to pay tax when he disposes of the house—provided he does not own and occupy another dwelling meanwhile, and returns to the house before he sells it. Moreover the last 12 months of ownership are allowed as if occupation continued, even if the owner moved elsewhere, while arranging the sale, for instance.

Where only part of the house is owner-occupied, or the house is let for part of the period of ownership, the appropriate proportion of the gain remains exempt.

Property occupied rent-free by a dependent relative, or by beneficiaries under a trust or settlement, is also exempt.

PRIVATE CARS Any vehicles bought for personal use are exempt.

GOVERNMENT BONDS British Savings Bonds, National Development Bonds, Defence Bonds, Savings Certificates and most Government Stocks escape tax. Gilt-edged securities are exempt from capital gains tax if held for more than a year.

LIFE-ASSURANCE POLICIES No tax need be paid on payments from life-assurance policies, unless these were acquired from a third party.

GOODS SOLD FOR LESS THAN £1000 No tax is payable on goods sold for less than £1000.

MOVABLE GOODS WITH A LIMITED LIFE Where the life of goods is estimated at less than 50 years, they escape capital gains tax.

GAMBLING Winnings from gambling are not subject to capital gains tax.

SMALL GAINS Gains which totalled less than £50—after deduction of losses—in any tax year before April 6, 1971 are exempt from capital gains tax. On gains marginally over £50, tax is no more than the excess over £50.

The exemption limit for total sales in any tax year from April 6, 1971 is £500, and tax on gains over this figure is not usually more than half the excess. Gains made by a husband and wife are added together for assessment.

TIMBER Profit on the sale of standing timber and underwood is exempt.

GIFTS UNDER £100 Gifts are exempt if they total less than £100 in a tax year.

GIFTS TO CHARITIES Any gift to charity made after March 21, 1972 is exempt.

HANDING OVER A BUSINESS A man retiring at 65 who disposes of the whole or part of a business which he has controlled for 10 years or more pays no tax on the first £10,000 of profits. If he sells or gives away the business between the ages of 60 and 65, he is entitled to a smaller exemption.

WORKS OF ART OR OF SCIENTIFIC VALUE Where these are exempt from estate duty, they may also escape capital gains tax in certain circumstances. ☐ How estate duty works, p. 540.

FIRST £5000 ON DEATH Though the property of anyone who died before March 30, 1971 is treated as property sold, for the purpose of capital gains tax, the first £5000 of gains 'realised' in this way is exempt—provided that total exemptions since retirement do not exceed £10,000.

tax on the actual increase in value since April 6, 1965 by having the asset valued as at that date. The claim must be made within two years of the end of the tax year in which the property was sold, although the tax inspector may extend the time allowed.

Once the choice has been made it is irrevocable. The Inland Revenue does not give its view on what the April 6, 1965 value was until after the taxpayer has formally chosen to be taxed on that basis. Professional advice is usually necessary before making such a choice.

PART DISPOSALS Where only part of an asset is disposed of, that part is valued and taxed as a separate asset.

### Tax on furniture and jewellery

Movable property, such as furniture or jewellery, is subject to capital gains tax only if the proceeds of the sale of each article or set of articles come to more than £1000. Even then, tax cannot amount to more than half the excess over that sum. Losses on such sales, however, are not allowed against tax.

Furniture and jewellery acquired before April 6, 1965 are valued by the same methods as apply to buildings and land.

### Tax on stocks and shares

Stocks and shares sold or disposed of at a profit are liable to capital gains tax. Equally, losses can reduce the tax bill.

Retain all contract notes when shares are bought or sold, in order to have proof for the Inland Revenue of the prices paid and received.

The date of a transaction for tax purposes is the date on which stocks or shares are actually bought and sold (contract day) and not the date on which the bill is paid (settlement day).

The general rule for assessing tax on dealings in stocks and shares is that all purchases of one specific security—say, one company's ordinary voting shares—form a pool, and the average cost price is calculated. Any shares bought and sold on the same day, or held for someone else, are not included.

All shares held on April 6, 1965 normally form a separate pool from those bought after that date, and they are considered to have been disposed of first when any sale is made.

If the shareholder makes a loss on a sale of gilt-edged securities and then buys identical shares within a month (or within six months if they are bought privately and not through a stock exchange) he cannot claim tax relief on the loss, except against a future sale of those same shares.

Where there is more than one purchase on the same day, the day's deals are combined and no notice is taken of the precise time of each deal. Similarly, two sales on the same day are combined.

When shares are exchanged—in a takeover, for example—the deal is not considered as a disposal, but the new holding is treated as if it dated back to the original share purchase. If cash is given for shares in a takeover, the transaction ranks as a disposal, and tax is payable on this basis.

Bear deals are always subject to capital gains tax. These are deals in which a person sells shares he does not yet own and then makes a profit by buying them later in the account period at a price lower than the amount he sold them for.

UNIT AND INVESTMENT TRUSTS When a unit trust pays capital gains tax on the shares it buys and sells, the trust notifies each unit-holder how much tax has been paid on his holding. In calculating tax liability when he sold them, the unit-holder used to add the amount of the gain to the cost of his units so that he did not pay tax twice.

But this complicated calculation was abolished in April, 1972. Now, the total capital gain is worked out on the normal method for shares, then a tax allowance of 15 per cent of the gain is set against tax due.

Unit-trust holders learn the amount of their gain from the distribution warrant, which is sent out twice a year by the trust. It is wise to keep these warrants as evidence for the Inland Revenue; if they are lost, copies can be obtained from the managers of the trust. Similar rules apply to investment-trust company shareholders.

WORTHLESS ASSETS When a company goes into liquidation and the shares become worthless, shareholders can deduct their losses from any gain they make in the same or any future tax year and so reduce the profit on which tax has to be paid.

BONUS OR RIGHTS ISSUES If a holding of securities is increased by special issues—such as bonus or rights issues—these are treated for capital gains tax assessment as part of the taxpayer's original holding.

### The 'Doomsday' system for securities

The date when capital gains tax was introduced—April 6, 1965—is sometimes referred to in financial circles as 'Doomsday'. Stocks and shares bought before that date and sold since are liable to tax.

There are two ways of working out how much capital gains tax should be paid.

**1.** Normally, a taxpayer who profits on a sale

can compare the price he gets for his holding either with the price he paid for it or with its value on 'Doomsday'. Choosing whichever is higher reduces taxable profit.

But if he makes a loss and wants to offset it against future gains he must take the lower figure—either the 'Doomsday' price or the price he actually paid for the shares—when calculating how much he has lost.

Sales at prices which fall between the cost price and the 'Doomsday' price are regarded as producing neither a profit nor a loss.

**2.** For sales after March 19, 1968, the seller has the option of choosing to take the value on April 6, 1965, in any circumstances. There could be an advantage in choosing this alternative if the cost price is lower than the 'Doomsday' price. If the selling price is lower than both the other prices it would increase the amount of losses to set against future gains, and if the selling price is between the other two prices it could turn an actual gain into a loss for tax purposes.

The claim must be made in writing to the inspector of taxes within two years of the end of the tax year in which the seller first disposed of any of the assets concerned. Once made, the choice cannot be changed. Moreover, the choice will apply to all other ordinary shares held by the taxpayer if he made it in connection with a sale of ordinary shares, or to all other fixed-interest securities if his choice was in respect of fixed-interest securities.

HOW TO VALUE SHARES To find out how much a share was worth on April 6, 1965, consult a stockbroker, accountant or bank manager, or ask the company itself.

When declaring the value of shares, take into account any rights or bonus issues. This may mean that the number of shares sold is more than the number held on 'Doomsday', which may reduce the average price. Unit-trust prices on 'Doomsday' can be obtained from the trust managers. The figure needed is one midway between the buying and selling price of the units.

ASSETS IN PRIVATE COMPANIES Shares in private companies are not quoted on stock exchanges and do not always change hands for money—they may be inherited, for instance. When they are later sold, capital gains tax will be due if a profit is made; and if a loss is made it will be possible to offset that loss against tax due.

To establish the value of shares in a private company acquired by any means other than buying them, the tax authorities estimate an 'open-market value' for the shares. This is the price at which they would have changed hands

on the open market in a sale between a willing, but not necessarily anxious, buyer and a seller in a similar frame of mind.

Where there are restrictions on the transfer of shares, the taxpayer must assume that the buyer would be allowed to buy the shares, but would later expect to have the restrictions apply to him when he sold them. This kind of valuation can be difficult, and an accountant's help is necessary in almost all cases.

There is difficulty, too, in assessing the value of a minority holding in a family company. The willing buyer might make an allowance for what is known as 'family understanding' or might cut his offer, thinking that the combined family vote would be against paying a dividend even though the company was making a profit.

Again, professional advice from an accountant or solicitor is necessary. The valuations finally have to be negotiated with the Inland Revenue authorities.

**How the tax is paid**
One section of the income tax Return Form demands details of any acquisition on which capital gains tax might one day be due.

The taxpayer should enter the value of his house and any costs incurred in improving it, even though he expects to remain an owner-occupier and therefore exempt from capital gains tax on his home.

DEDUCTING EXPENSES At its simplest, the rise in value of an asset is measured by subtracting what it cost to buy from what it brings in when it is sold.

When calculating capital gains tax, the owner is allowed some expenses as part of his costs. These include expenses involved in purchase and sales proceedings—fees and commissions for surveyors, valuers, agents, accountants and lawyers.

Advertising costs and stamp duty are allowed, as are any expenses in establishing, preserving and defending rights of ownership. Generally, an accountant's fee for calculating tax liability is not allowable.

RATES OF TAX There are two ways of assessing capital gains tax, and the inspector of taxes will automatically choose whichever produces the smaller amount of tax.

The first method is to charge tax at a flat 30 per cent of the gain. This will usually be more advantageous for the taxpayer whose income is high enough to warrant surtax.

The alternative method allows half of any gain up to £5000 tax free. The other half, and any amount over £5000, is added to ordinary income and is subject to income tax and surtax.

# Appealing against the tax bill

Appealing to the tax inspector
Appealing to the commissioners
General commissioners

Special commissioners
Appealing against the commissioners

A TAXPAYER who disagrees with his tax assessment has a right of appeal—first, to his tax inspector; second, to an independent panel of people called Tax Commissioners appointed to hear income-tax appeals; and third, in some cases, to the courts.

The fact that the taxpayer does not have the money with which to pay the tax he owes is not a legitimate ground of appeal.

### Appealing to the tax inspector
There are two kinds of Inland Revenue officials—H.M. Inspectors of Taxes and Collectors of Taxes. The inspectors assess how much tax has to be paid and the collectors receive the money.

An appeal against the amount of tax assessed must be made firstly to the inspector of taxes. It is a waste of time to complain to the tax collector—simply tell him that you are appealing against the assessment and ask him to delay collection until after the appeal has been decided.

If there is any dispute over taxes, remember that the tax inspector is not an impartial judge. His job is to obtain for the Inland Revenue the maximum amount of tax the law permits.
TIME LIMIT ON APPEALS An appeal against a tax assessment must be made within 30 days of the date of the assessment. An appeal will be considered after 30 days only if the taxpayer was away from home, ill, or unable to appeal in time for 'other reasonable cause'. What is a 'reasonable cause' will be decided by the tax commissioners, if the tax inspector refuses to accept the explanation.
LODGING THE APPEAL The first stage of an appeal is to write to the inspector giving the grounds for objecting to the assessment.

If this information cannot be collected within the time limit, the letter need not go into detail. It might say, for example:

'I wish to appeal against your tax assessment for the year 1970–1, dated May 1, 1971, on the grounds that it is excessive and does not accord with accounts to be submitted.'

This is a formal appeal to keep the matter open. It cannot damage the taxpayer's position and it gives him more time to prepare his case.

A delay in appealing, however mistaken the assessment may seem, can result in the appeal being rejected by the tax inspector.

If the person appealing is paying tax under the PAYE system, it may speed the case to give evidence of any item not allowed, so that his code number can be changed promptly.

The grounds for the appeal should be put to the inspector fully as soon as possible—perhaps after seeking an accountant's advice. All the inspector's questions should be answered in full.

Where the tax inspector's interpretation of the law is in question, an accountant may ask him to quote the sections of the Income and Corporation Taxes Act or the Finance Act on which his decision is based.

In general, it is wise to keep the debate with the tax inspector to letters.
THE TAX INSPECTOR'S DECISION There are two ways in which an appeal to the inspector can be settled. Firstly, the taxpayer can drop the appeal. If he does, the position is as if he had not appealed in the first place. He must pay the tax demanded, or accept that he is not entitled to a rebate.

Secondly, the taxpayer and the inspector may reach an agreement on how the amount of tax to be paid should be revised. The inspector has the power to amend an assessment and this is the way most cases are solved. Once an agreement is reached, it is binding and there can be no further appeal.

### Appealing to the commissioners
Sometimes the taxpayer and the inspector may fail to come to an agreement.

If the appeal is rejected and the taxpayer is not satisfied, he is entitled to ask the inspector to refer the case to one of the bodies specially set up to hear appeals against tax assessments.

There are two such bodies—the general commissioners, who deal with the bulk of appeals, and the special commissioners, who normally consider more complex and technical disputes. The general commissioners are comparable to lay magistrates, whereas the special commissioners are equivalent to professional judges.

If a taxpayer's appeal is based on a technical point or on intricate legal grounds, he would be advised in most cases to ask for a hearing before the special commissioners.

However, he loses one advantage if he chooses to go before the special commissioners. In cases heard by the general commissioners, the tax inspector must put his side of the dispute in terms which laymen can understand. But if the hearing is before the special commissioners, the inspector is entitled to present his argument in technical terms that might make it difficult for the taxpayer to follow.

Both general and special commissioners have the power to increase the assessment, as well as to reduce or cancel it.

## General commissioners

If there is to be a personal hearing, the taxpayer receives a notice of the time and place. It is wise to be early because the first to arrive are sometimes the first heard.

The hearing is informal and in private: Press and public are not admitted. The taxpayer is not asked to take an oath and he may be invited to remain seated when addressing the commissioners.

One major difference between the commissioners' hearing and a court is that the onus is on the taxpayer to prove that the assessment is excessive. The taxpayer is, as it were, guilty until proved innocent. On the other hand, the taxpayer does not have to pay costs, even if the case goes against him.

The general commissioners are impartial, but they are not necessarily experts in tax law. They are usually retired businessmen, retired Service officers and civic leaders.

However, they have a clerk—usually a solicitor, accountant or a retired tax inspector —to help them on points of tax law. There must be at least two lay commissioners and a clerk present.

If the amount of money in dispute is large, it is worth being professionally represented by a barrister, a solicitor or an accountant.

The hearing begins with the taxpayer or his representative explaining the reason for his appeal to the commissioners. He may produce documents as evidence, and he can call witnesses. For example, a witness might vouch that the taxpayer had a certain amount of money at a certain time and therefore his new motor car was not bought out of profits from his business.

The tax inspector then explains to the commissioners why he has rejected the claim. When he has finished, the taxpayer or his representative can question him.

The taxpayer has the last word. He can answer points the inspector has made and give any explanations he thinks necessary.

The commissioners then confer. If the appeal is complicated, the taxpayer may be asked to leave the room while, with the clerk's help, they reach a decision. If the taxpayer is asked to leave, the tax inspector should leave, too. He has no more right to add further points to his argument than the taxpayer has.

Decisions are usually given immediately. If the commissioners need time to consider, the taxpayer is informed of the decision by post.

## Special commissioners

More complicated cases are dealt with by the special commissioners—tax lawyers, based in London, who visit the larger towns in the provinces about twice a year to hold hearings. The tax inspector informs the taxpayer when hearings are due.

It is advisable to be represented by a barrister or solicitor at a special commissioners' hearing. The procedure is basically the same as at a general commissioners' hearing.

## Appealing against the commissioners

Once the commissioners—either general or special—have given their decision, an appeal to the courts can be made only if the commissioners' decision is thought to be wrong in law. In this case the taxpayer must immediately express dissatisfaction with the decision and then, within 30 days, write and ask the clerk for a 'case to be stated'. This costs £1.

The clerk has a summary of the case prepared, giving the commissioners' reasons for reaching their decision.

When the taxpayer gets the summary, his legal advisers can decide whether it is worth the cost of further appeals. If the case merits it, these can be made to the High Court, the Court of Appeal and, in certain circumstances, to the House of Lords.

The ordinary taxpayer should take expert legal advice before proceeding with an appeal to the courts. While he pays nothing towards the cost of the commissioners' hearing, the loser pays both sides' costs in the courts.

APPEALS BY THE TAX INSPECTOR If the inspector of taxes is dissatisfied with the outcome of a commissioners' hearing, he is entitled to appeal to the courts in the same way as the taxpayer. If the inspector wins his case, the taxpayer is liable for the Inland Revenue's costs and his own costs.

When the taxpayer appears in court in person, however, it is not the Inland Revenue's practice to ask for costs, although they are legally entitled to do so.

# Debts and bankruptcy

*Methods of collection, legal and illegal*
*Taking a debtor to court*
*Petitions for bankruptcy*

*Receiving order and public examination*
*Voluntary bankruptcy*
*Getting discharged*

CUSTOMERS can face legal action for debt for a variety of reasons. They may run up a bill and fail to pay; they may withhold payment for defective goods or refuse to meet part of the bill of a tradesman who is overcharging; or a firm may claim payment for goods that have already been paid for, or were never ordered or received.

In all these cases, the procedure which must be followed by the person or organisation claiming the money is the same. At each stage, the law gives the customer the opportunity to challenge an incorrect demand for payment, or to pay off a genuine debt by regular payments geared to his income and commitments. It tries to ensure that no one who is being pursued for money which he does not owe need have cause for anxiety as long as he takes steps at each stage to deny the debt.

A different procedure applies to the collection of arrears of rents and rates. ☐ Rates: how the system works, p. 219; Unfurnished property, p. 252; Controlled tenancies, p. 256; Furnished property, p. 259; Council houses and flats, p. 262.

For all other cases, the creditor usually sends reminders of the debt by letter, and may call personally. If the debt is disputed, make it clear at this stage.

Sometimes firms that are owed money employ debt-collecting agencies to call on the debtor. Such collectors have no special powers, and there is no legal obligation to answer their questions. They can, however, give a valid receipt if the debtor pays them.

**Illegal methods of collection**
A creditor is entitled to seek payment by legal means only. If he harasses a debtor, he is guilty of a criminal offence under the Administration of Justice Act 1970.

Under the Act, the creditor or anyone acting on his behalf has to observe certain rules:
**1.** He must not harass or bully the debtor in such a way as to subject him and his family to alarm, distress or humiliation—by threatening him with publicity, for example.
**2.** He must not tell the debtor that criminal proceedings are to be taken when, in fact, the debt is purely a matter for a civil court.

**3.** He must not ask for payment in such a way as to suggest that he is acting in an official capacity; nor must he send a demand in a form which suggests that it is an official document. Debt-collecting agencies have sometimes used documents that look like county court official forms. All documents coming from the court bear the court's seal, and this should always be checked if a document looks suspicious. The seal is in the form of a crown, with the name of the court running round it.

If a debtor thinks he is being 'harassed' in any of these ways, he should report it to the police. The offence is punished by a penalty of up to £100 for a first offence.

**Arranging to pay**
Eventually the creditor, or more often his solicitor, writes to demand the money. The solicitor's letter will say that failure to pay, or to put forward a satisfactory proposal for repayment, will result in legal proceedings within a certain period.

Creditors often accept an offer to pay off a debt at so much a week or month rather than go to court, particularly if the person owing the money includes a payment with his offer as a token of good faith. An offer to pay is therefore often a way to avoid the extra costs of court proceedings.

**Taking a debtor to court**
If his solicitor's letters fail to recover the money, the creditor may decide to take action through the county court or the High Court. (Actions for debts over £750 can be heard only in the High Court.) If the court finds that there is a debt outstanding, it makes an order for it to be paid—a judgment summons —usually by regular instalments. The debt is then known as a judgment debt.

If the defendant continues to withhold the money, the creditor can apply to the court for the debt to be enforced in a number of other ways.

He can ask for an order allowing the county-court bailiff to seize the debtor's goods and sell them, for example. Or he can apply for an attachment of earnings order—a court order instructing the defendant's employer to deduct a regular sum from his pay. □ Legal action II: suing to recover a debt, p. 725.

### Petitions for bankruptcy

It sometimes happens that whatever measures a creditor takes—personal pressure or action in the courts—a debtor may prove unable to pay because he is insolvent: his total debts exceed the value of his property. The debtor usually goes bankrupt, either by choice or on the insistence of his creditors.

When an individual goes bankrupt, his assets are shared out fairly among his creditors, according to the sums he owes them. There are severe limitations on the activities

of the bankrupt himself until he has given a full and public account of his finances, and has repaid his creditors at least 50p of every £ he owed them.

If an individual is genuinely insolvent, bankruptcy is often the best solution. But to anyone who is still solvent, bankruptcy is an unnecessary disaster and everything possible should be done to avoid it.

No one can be made bankrupt unless his actions have made it clear, in one of the ways recognised by the law, that he cannot pay his debts. There are ten such ways, known as 'acts of bankruptcy':

**1.** Failing to comply with the terms of a bankruptcy notice—a court document which is served on the debtor and tells him that

---

## What it means to be bankrupt

THE law places severe limitations on the activities of a bankrupt. His financial affairs remain in the hands of the Official Receiver or trustee; he may be required to notify them periodically of his earnings or other income; and any surplus over and above what he needs to support himself and his family he may have to pay for the benefit of his creditors. His employer may be ordered to pay over part of his income at source.

A bankrupt may not, without the permission of the court, act as a director of a company, nor may he manage a company, directly or indirectly. Many professions and public offices are closed to him—he may not be an M.P., for example, a local councillor or a magistrate.

A bankrupt may not obtain credit for more than £10 without telling the person granting him credit that he is a bankrupt.

There is nothing in law to prevent a bankrupt opening a bank account. If he does so, however, the bank has a legal obligation to report the fact to the Official Receiver, who usually orders the account to be closed and the money in it handed over.

A bankrupt who runs a bank account without the permission of the Official Receiver or trustee, runs the risk of committing an offence if, for example, he has an overdraft.

If he is a trustee of anyone else's money, the bankrupt must resign, or he will be removed.

ACQUIRED PROPERTY If a bankrupt comes into any money before he is granted his discharge—for example, if he inherits money —this goes to the Official Receiver for

the benefit of the bankrupt person's creditors.

PENALTIES A bankrupt can be sent to prison if he does not observe the conditions laid down by law. If he obtains credit for more than £10 without admitting he is a bankrupt, for instance, he can be prosecuted under the Bankruptcy Act 1914, and jailed for up to two years. If he becomes a company director, he can be sent to prison for up to two years.

### The bankrupt's wife

In bankruptcy a husband and wife are treated as separate individuals. On the bankruptcy of her husband, the wife can keep anything she can show belongs to her—what she owned before marriage, or bought out of her own earnings or was given to her by persons other than her husband.

If the couple jointly own a house, the husband's half share passes to the trustee. Usually, the house is sold and, after repayment of the mortgage, the proceeds are divided between the wife and the trustee. Sometimes the wife can manage to buy the trustee's share and so become the sole owner.

Anything given to the wife by her husband within two years of the bankruptcy can be taken back by the trustee. Gifts made between two and ten years before bankruptcy can also be recovered unless the bankrupt can show he was solvent at the time.

The wife of a bankrupt is not barred from running a business or employing her husband to help her, but the trustee may need proof that it really is her business, and not his.

unless he pays a judgment debt, or provides security for it, he will have committed an act of bankruptcy.

**2.** Having his goods seized by the sheriff or bailiff for the purpose of paying judgment debts, and allowing the goods to be sold or held for 21 days.

**3.** Taking steps to avoid his creditors, such as moving from his usual address without leaving a forwarding address, or going out of the country and remaining abroad.

**4.** Notifying his creditors that he has suspended or is about to suspend payment of the debts he owes them.

**5.** Notifying a court that he can no longer pay his debts.

**6.** Giving everything he owns to a trustee for the benefit of all his creditors.

**7.** Giving all or part of his property to someone else in a way which would give unfair preference to one creditor compared with the others if he were declared bankrupt.

**8.** Fraudulently conveying any part of his property (for example, giving his house, or his share of it, to his wife).

**9.** Making an application for his financial affairs to be administered by the county court. A debtor can apply for such an order, known as an administration order, when he is unable to pay a judgment debt and the total amount he owes is not more than £300.

**10.** Having an order made against him to supply a list of creditors. This may happen when one of his debtors applies for an attachment of earnings order—a court instruction to his employer to deduct a regular sum from his wages or salary to pay debts. ☐ Legal action III: suing to recover a debt, p. 725.

In practice, most bankruptcies are based on a failure to comply with a bankruptcy notice, which demands payment within seven days of a judgment debt.

The notice is applied for by a creditor and issued by the county court for the area in which the debtor lives or has his business.

If the debtor lives in London, or has his business there, or if the creditor is unable to find out where he lives, the notice may be issued in the High Court.

When the Inland Revenue brings bankruptcy proceedings—because the debtor fails to pay income tax or surtax, for example—the petition is normally heard in the High Court. If, however, a High Court petition would cause the debtor undue hardship, perhaps because of the distance of the court from his home, he may apply for the proceedings to be transferred to a local county court.

The bankruptcy notice must be handed personally to the debtor—in law, 'served' on him—within a month of its date of issue, unless the court extends this time limit.

The creditor, his solicitor, or someone employed by them may serve the notice, or it may be served by the court bailiff. The notice must give the name and address of the solicitor who applied for it.

If the debtor cannot be served with the notice personally, because for example he is deliberately avoiding service, the creditor can apply for an order of 'substituted service'. In this case the notice may be sent by post or advertised in a newspaper.

The result of this procedure of substituted service may be that the debtor does not receive personal notice of the proceedings, and may miss his opportunity of opposing the bankruptcy proceedings. He will have to pay the costs of substituted service, which are greater than the cost of serving the notice on him personally.

The debtor who wishes to avoid bankruptcy should do everything in his power to pay the judgment debt within the seven days allowed. If he does so, the creditor has no grounds to proceed with his petition.

If, however, the debtor thinks he has a counter-claim against the creditor which equals or exceeds the amount of the debt, he has three days to apply to the court to cancel or 'set aside' the notice.

An application form to set aside a bankruptcy notice is obtainable from the county court office. When it is returned, the debtor must also send a statement sworn before a commissioner for oaths setting out the details of his counter-claim.

If the registrar of the court thinks the application is valid, he fixes a time for a hearing and extends the bankruptcy notice until then.

A debtor can also apply to have the notice set aside if the correct procedure has not been followed by the creditor's solicitor—if, for example, the details of the judgment debt have been stated incorrectly on the notice.

**Creditor's petition**

A creditor or group of creditors can apply to have a debtor brought before a bankruptcy court if the debtor owes them a total of £50 or more. This is known as petitioning for bankruptcy and presenting the petition to the court is called filing it. The petition must be on the ground of an act of bankruptcy not more than three calendar months earlier than the date on which it is filed.

If the debtor has not already been served with a bankruptcy notice, the first official indication he receives that there will be a bankruptcy petition is when the petition is given to him. It is served in the same way as a bankruptcy notice and he must receive it at least eight days before the date fixed for the court hearing of the petition.

The petition asks the court to make an order placing the debtor's financial affairs in the hands of the Official Receiver—an official appointed by the Department of Trade and Industry. The order is called a receiving order.

If either the creditor or the debtor requests it, the registrar can appoint the Official Receiver to take charge immediately of the debtor's financial affairs. The registrar will not do this unless he is satisfied that the appointment is necessary to safeguard the debtor's property. The application must therefore be accompanied by an affidavit giving the reasons for it.

When the petition is delivered to the court, the registrar appoints a day for the hearing, usually four to six weeks ahead. He informs the Chief Land Registrar immediately so that the debtor cannot sell any buildings or land he is known to own.

If the debtor wishes to oppose the making of a receiving order, he must file a notice with the registrar setting out the statements in the petition which he wishes to dispute.

He must also post copies of the notice to the petitioning creditor or creditors and their solicitors not later than three days before his case is to be heard.

HEARING THE PETITION The petition is heard by the registrar in private, with only the creditors, the debtor and their legal advisers and witnesses present.

The petitioning creditor must swear and produce at the hearing an affidavit that the money is still owing. A creditor who does not wish to attend the hearing personally may be able to get the permission of the court to be absent. Without such permission he must appear in court or the bankruptcy petition may be dismissed.

The creditor and the debtor are each entitled to file affidavits sworn by themselves or other witnesses. They may also apply for subpoenas, ordering witnesses to attend and give evidence at the hearing.

For his petition to be successful, the petitioner has to prove four things:
1. That the debtor lives or works within the area covered by the court.
2. That the money mentioned in the petition is owed, and that after taking into account any security held by the creditor the sum outstanding comes to not less than £50.
3. That the petition was served on the debtor.

4. That the act of bankruptcy mentioned in the petition was committed.

If the debtor contests the petition the registrar will hear both sides and then decide whether to make a receiving order. An order can be made in the debtor's absence if the registrar is satisfied that the bankruptcy notice has been served on him, or if he has notified the court of his consent.

### Receiving order
Once the order is made the Official Receiver takes complete charge of the debtor's financial affairs. All claims against the debtor and payments that are due to him are dealt with by the Official Receiver. The debtor is protected from any further claims by his creditors; but those who have loaned money on the security of a particular asset, such as a building society that has advanced money for house-purchase, can take steps to have the asset sold so that they can be repaid.

The Registrar informs the Department of Trade and Industry that the receiving order has been made, and the Department places an announcement in the *London Gazette*. An advertisement is also placed in the debtor's local newspaper.

### Cancelling the receiving order
If the debtor can prove that he is able to pay all his debts, or if he is able to come to an arrangement with his creditors about repaying them, he is entitled to apply for the receiving order to be cancelled and the bankruptcy petition dismissed.

A similar order may be made if he proves that the receiving order ought not to have been made in the first place.

### Preparing the statement of affairs
Provided the receiving order is not cancelled, the debtor must prepare a statement of all his assets and liabilities—called a statement of affairs—under the supervision of the Official Receiver. The Receiver must find out about the debtor's assets so that they can be turned into cash and shared among creditors.

Any transfers of money or property made by the debtor to other people before he went bankrupt are investigated closely. Money can be recovered from people who received gifts up to ten years before the bankruptcy. If the creditor can prove that the debtor was unable to pay his debts at the time, the Official Receiver can obtain a court order against the person who received the money or property.

The debtor may offer to make an arrangement with his creditors—say, by paying each a certain amount immediately after selling assets and more later. This is called a 'composition' with the creditors.

The offer is made at the meeting of creditors called by the Official Receiver when the statement of affairs is completed. The meeting must be called within 14 days of the receiving order being made, unless an extension is ordered by the court, so that the Official Receiver can explain the debtor's financial position. A minimum six days' notice of the meeting of creditors is given in the *London Gazette* and a local newspaper. The debtor is given three days' notice.

If the creditors agree to the composition, the debtor or the Official Receiver can ask the court to approve it and cancel the receiving order. Before the composition can be submitted to the court, however, it must be approved by a majority of the creditors who are owed between them at least three-quarters of the total value of proved debts.

If the creditors do not agree to a composition (and they rarely do) a 'trustee in bankruptcy' is appointed to take over the debtor's affairs from the Official Receiver. The trustee is usually a chartered accountant whose fee is paid out of the assets. If there are very few assets, the Official Receiver becomes the trustee. Generally, the trustee is supervised by a committee of inspection composed of creditors.

The Official Receiver continues to supervise the case. He has power to institute criminal proceedings against the debtor if he has committed fraud or bankruptcy offences. ☐ What it means to be bankrupt, p. 581.

### How the debtor becomes bankrupt
If the creditors decide to press for the debtor to be adjudged bankrupt, the Official Receiver applies for a court order. The debtor is entitled to oppose this application if he can show that he is intending to pay his creditors in full, or if he is proposing a composition with them.

If the debtor is adjudged bankrupt, this is advertised in the same way as the receiving order by an announcement in the Press.

### Public examination
The debtor then has to appear before the registrar in open court. At this public examination he must answer, on oath, questions put to him by the Official Receiver, the trustee in bankruptcy, his creditors or their legal representatives, and the registrar himself. If he refuses to answer or fails to appear he can be sent to prison for contempt of court.

The debtor is questioned about his assets and his prospects of earning money in the future. He is also asked to explain why he allowed himself to get into the position where he could not pay his debts.

Anyone can attend the public examination and the Press can report the proceedings.

If the registrar is satisfied with the debtor's answers, he concludes the examination. After a suitable period of time has elapsed, the debtor is then entitled to apply to the court for a discharge from bankruptcy.

If the registrar is not satisfied with the debtor's answers, he can adjourn the hearing until a later date for inquiries to be made.

If he finds that the debtor is failing to make a proper disclosure of his financial affairs, he can adjourn the examination *sine die*, that is, indefinitely. The debtor is not then entitled to apply to be discharged from bankruptcy until the public examination has been resumed and concluded.

### How the money is divided
The trustee takes almost everything belonging to the debtor, and turns it into money to divide among the creditors. The only assets and income which the debtor is allowed to keep are:

Personal income, including family allowances and certain pensions.

The debtor's beds, bedding and personal items of clothing.

Tools of the debtor's trade, up to a total value of £20.

In certain circumstances the debtor may even be required by the trustee to make a contribution from these assets to the money that is distributed to creditors.

There is, however, an order of preference among the creditors.

SECURED CREDITORS The first people to be paid are those who lent the debtor money against the security of a particular asset. They are called 'secured creditors'. For instance, if the debtor is buying a house on mortgage, the building society has to be repaid out of the proceeds of selling the house before any money can be shared among other creditors.

PREFERENTIAL CREDITORS Certain other debts have priority once the secured creditors and the costs of the bankruptcy proceedings have been paid. These include employees' wages (limited to services rendered during four months before the bankruptcy and not exceeding £200), National Insurance contributions, income tax and rates.

UNSECURED CREDITORS What is left is divided among the rest of the creditors. The trustee works out how much can be paid for every £1 owed. This repayment is called a 'dividend'—for instance, 25p in the £. Any surplus after all the creditors are paid comes back to the debtor.

## Voluntary bankruptcy

Debtors are normally made bankrupt by their creditors, but they can petition for their own bankruptcy if they see no possible way of paying their debts in full and wish to make a new start.

A debtor who wishes to be declared bankrupt can get the necessary forms to petition the court from his local county court offices.

He must first deposit £5 with the Official Receiver and obtain a receipt for it.

He must also pay a fee of £5, which can be waived if the Official Receiver gives the debtor a certificate saying there are reasonable grounds to think his assets are sufficient to cover any administrative costs.

The debtor must then present the court with copies of four documents.
1. The petition. On the form provided by the court, the debtor gives details about himself, his debts and the people to whom he owes money. If he does not intend to suggest an arrangement with his creditors, he should ask the court to declare—or 'adjudicate'—him bankrupt.
2. Three copies of the receiving order. This places everything the debtor owns in the hands of the Official Receiver. These forms are also filled in by the debtor for the registrar to sign if the order is made.
3. Two copies of the draft adjudication order which will declare him bankrupt, if he is asking to be adjudicated bankrupt.
4. The receipt for the deposit.

If the debtor has been trading as a firm, or in partnership, documents giving the names and addresses of other partners or members of the firm, and their consent to the petition, are required. The forms can be obtained at the county court offices.

If the documents are in order, a receiving order is made and an adjudication order is made too, if one has been asked for. The registrar informs the Inspector General of Bankruptcy of the orders and they are published in the *London Gazette*.

## Getting discharged

Because of the handicaps of being bankrupt, it is in the bankrupt's interest to end his bankruptcy, to be 'discharged', as it is called, as soon as possible. The discharge releases the bankrupt from all the debts involved in the bankruptcy. He can apply at any time after he has been adjudged bankrupt, provided that his public examination has been concluded.

If it has not, he must apply to the court for the examination to be resumed and satisfy the registrar that he has given a full and honest account of his financial affairs so that he will conclude the examination.

To apply to the court for his discharge, the bankrupt completes a form and returns it to the court accompanied by a certificate from the Official Receiver listing all the creditors of whom he has had notice, whether or not they have proved the debts.

The county court registrar fixes a date for the hearing and gives the Official Receiver at least 28 days' notice of it. He gives all the creditors at least 14 days' notice and the hearing is announced in the *London Gazette*.

At least seven days before the hearing the Official Receiver sends the court a report of the bankrupt's affairs. He sends a copy of this report to the bankrupt by registered post or recorded delivery.

Once the report has been filed at the court, any creditor is entitled to inspect it on payment of a small fee.

The Receiver's report deals with the bankrupt's conduct before the bankruptcy, and the reasons for going bankrupt. The Receiver also gives details of how the bankrupt's assets have been turned into cash, the assistance he has given to the Official Receiver and the trustee, and how much he has contributed towards the payment of his debts.

The Receiver's report also contains any facts that might prevent the court from giving a discharge. The court attaches great importance to the Receiver's report, and the chances of obtaining a discharge are greatly increased when the report is favourable.

In practice, there is little point in applying for a discharge from bankruptcy without the agreement of the Official Receiver. The county court is unlikely to grant a discharge until the Official Receiver reports that all the bankrupt's assets have been realised and that no more money can be obtained from him to pay what he owes his creditors.

If the bankrupt applies to be discharged at too early a date, or before the assets have been realised and dividends paid, his application may be dismissed as premature.

If the debtor intends to dispute the Official Receiver's report he must file a notice with the court at least two days before the hearing, indicating the parts of it which he intends to challenge. He must also serve a copy of the notice on the Official Receiver at least two days before the hearing.

A creditor who intends to object to the

discharge for any reason that is not given in the Official Receiver's report must also give two days' notice to the court and serve copies on the Official Receiver and the bankrupt.

If they wish to oppose the discharge, creditors are entitled to appear at the hearing without giving notice, and to state their objections. Normally, a creditor would oppose the discharge only if he had reason to believe that the bankrupt still had concealed assets.

ANNULMENT If a bankrupt is able to pay his debts in full, with interest and the costs involved, then he may apply to the court to have his bankruptcy annulled. This is an alternative to a discharge.

The result of an annulment is as though he had never been made bankrupt. Annulment is, however, a privilege, and may be denied to a bankrupt who has conducted himself badly.

TYPES OF DISCHARGE The court can grant the discharge, refuse it, grant a conditional discharge or grant a suspended discharge. A conditional discharge might stipulate that the bankrupt should continue to pay so much a month to his creditors. A suspended one might say that the discharge does not become effective until after a certain period of time or until so much in the £ had been paid.

Suspended or conditional discharges do not automatically free the debtor from the restrictions of bankruptcy. For example, a conditionally discharged bankrupt would have to get the court's permission to open a bank account or become a director of a company.

In certain circumstances the court cannot give an unconditional discharge:

**1.** If less than 50p in the £ has been paid to creditors (unless the bankrupt could not be held responsible for a lower dividend).

**2.** If the bankrupt had not kept proper books for the three years preceding his bankruptcy.

**3.** If he continued trading after realising that he was insolvent.

**4.** If he incurred debts without any reasonable expectation of being able to pay them.

**5.** If he has failed to account to the Official Receiver for any missing money.

**6.** If the bankruptcy was due to the bankrupt's extravagance or gambling, or culpable neglect of his business.

**7.** If the bankrupt has put any of the creditors to needless expense by engaging in pointless legal actions.

**8.** If he gave preferential treatment to one of his creditors in the three months before he was made bankrupt.

**9.** If he borrowed money in an attempt to make his total assets up to 50p in the £ of his debts.

**10.** If, on a previous occasion, he has been adjudged bankrupt or has entered into a composition—the arrangement to pay mentioned earlier—with his creditors.

**11.** If he has been found guilty of any fraud or breach of trust.

**12.** If he has been found guilty of any indictable offence in connection with his bankruptcy, such as destroying accounts.

If the court refuses an absolute discharge, it may indicate that a further application may be made either after a specified time, or when the bankrupt can provide proof that he has reformed himself.

**After the discharge**

Once the discharge has been granted, the bankrupt is no longer subject to legal restrictions. But public offices, such as being an M.P., a magistrate or a councillor are still normally closed to him for a period of five years after his discharge.

This ban can be lifted if, when the bankrupt's petition for discharge is heard, the court grants a 'certificate of misfortune' saying that the bankruptcy was not caused by his misconduct.

The discharged bankrupt must also continue to co-operate with the Official Receiver who can re-open any matters which come to light in connection with the bankruptcy—for instance, evidence that the bankrupt lied about his assets. The Receiver can re-open the case and the court has power to rescind the discharge at any time in the light of new evidence about the debtor's financial conduct before or since he became bankrupt.

If an application for a discharge is not made the bankrupt remains a bankrupt forever. On his death, no one is entitled to inherit anything from him, unless there is a surplus of assets after all outstanding debts have been paid out of his estate.

**The right to appeal**

The debtor has a right to appeal against any court orders made during the course of bankruptcy proceedings. Legal aid is available for such appeals, which are heard by the Chancery Division of the High Court.

The debtor can also apply for the order against which he is appealing to be held up until the result of the appeal is known.

Such an order, which is known as a 'stay of proceedings' or a 'stay of advertisement', avoids a person being publicly declared a debtor or a bankrupt, for example, until the matter which is in dispute in the appeal is resolved by the higher court.

# YOUR JOB

# Applying for a job

*Checking on pay*
*Hours and conditions of work*
*The duties of an employee*

*Starting and ending a job*
*Jobs with special conditions*
*The letter of appointment*

EVERY employee starting a new job makes a legal contract with his employer—whether the word 'contract' is mentioned or not. The terms of the contract may be agreed between them in the course of an interview, set out in a letter of appointment, or covered by a collective agreement. The contract usually comes into effect as soon as the employee starts work.

Anyone applying for a position, therefore, needs to get agreement on all the aspects of the job which are important to him before he decides to take it. He should use his interview to establish what would be required of him if he took the job; the terms and conditions of work; his duties and status in the firm; and his prospects.

It is too late for an individual employee to try to change the conditions after he has started work. By that time he is regarded in law as having accepted the terms negotiated with the employer.

Where no mention was made of one of the conditions of the job, it is assumed—as soon as he has been with the firm for a reasonable time without questioning the condition—that the employee has agreed to be bound by the firm's usual practice.

Find out, for example, not only how many weeks' holiday the firm gives, but also if there are any limitations on when employees are allowed to take holidays.

➤ EXPENSIVE OVERSIGHT *A man who joined a computer company as its operations manager signed a written agreement which stipulated that he was entitled to four weeks' annual leave. He had already booked a two-week holiday in Morocco in May for himself and his family.*

*But after starting work he found that the firm did not allow holidays before June or after August, so he had to cancel the booking and forfeit £110 cancellation fees. He could take no action against his employer, for there had been no breach of contract. The mistake was his own.*◄

An applicant should take particular care to find out whether he will be classed as an employee or self-employed in the new position. If he is to be self-employed, he should be aware of the legal consequences and study the advantages and disadvantages, including the income tax position. ☐ Employed or self-employed: the differences, p. 594.

## Checking on pay
Ask not only what the wage or salary is, but also how it is calculated—monthly, weekly or hourly. Find out how wages are paid—by cash, cheque, or credit transfer to the employee's bank—and when.

For most manual workers (technically those covered by the Truck Acts 1831–1940) wages must be paid in cash. Under the Payment of Wages Act 1960, payment by cheque, credit transfer, postal or money order to workers covered by the Truck Acts must not be a condition of employment; but wages may be paid in any of those ways at the employee's request if the employer agrees.

PIECE-WORK AND COMMISSION If there is a piece-work system—under which the employee is paid according to the work he completes—ask how pay is calculated and get written confirmation before the job starts.

Some firms use a combination of a basic wage and piece rates—so much for so many hours worked, plus a bonus for items made. Similarly, sales staff often get commission.

An employee who is paid on the basis of the work he does, needs to be sure that work will always be available. Find out from the company itself, or from local union officials or fellow employees, whether the company has a record of laying men off or putting them on short time. If so, ask what work prospects are. ☐ How wages are protected, p. 598.

Find out if the piece-work or commission rates vary, and ask the employer to explain the system. A girl starting work at a factory, for example, may at first be paid £5 for the first dozen pairs of pyjamas she makes, with extra payments for additional pairs.

When she has gained experience, however, the company may require her to make five dozen for £5, before she qualifies for bonus payments. This is known as a 'leading-in allowance', and may be phased over a period of four weeks.

Seek written details of how piece-work

or commission rates can be changed if this information is not already included in the original agreement. Most piece-work and bonus schemes are governed by trade-union agreements. If there are doubts about the system, seek advice from union officials.

PAY INCREASES Beware of accepting a job at an unsatisfactory salary on a vague promise of pay rises and promotion after a set period. If promises are made, ask for them to be confirmed unambiguously.

'FRINGE' BENEFITS Managerial staff will want to know about 'fringe' benefits, such as pension schemes, free or cheap life assurance and medical insurance, the use of a company car, cheap loans for house purchase, etc.

EXPENSES Rules about expenses paid by the firm should be made clear. If the firm offers to make exceptions to its rules, they should be written into the agreement.

When an employee uses his own car on the firm's business, increased insurance premiums often have to be paid. Find out if the firm pays these, and contributes to running costs.

SICK PAY Whether an employer has to pay an employee when he is away from work due to illness depends on the usual practice of the industry. But if the employer and employee agree to arrangements for sick pay, these arrangements will apply even if they conflict with the practice of the industry.

If sick pay is part of the contract, ask for how long it is paid in full or in part. Find out whether it is based on average earnings or basic rate, and whether National Insurance sickness benefit is deducted. Women should inquire about maternity leave, since it may be paid, part-paid or unpaid.

EQUAL PAY FOR WOMEN Women should also ask if they are entitled to equal pay when they do the same work as men. In 1975 equal pay for the same work is compulsory.

CHECKING THE OFFER An applicant who wants to check the employer's offer can ask at the local office of the Department of Employment whether the pay offered is in line with local rates or not.

In many industries, wages are determined by Wages Councils. These councils can tell prospective employees about agreed pay and overtime payments, holidays and holiday pay, and other conditions. ☐ Industries with minimum wages, p. 601.

**Hours and conditions of work**
Check that the hours and conditions of work are acceptable, and find out if there is compulsory overtime, or shift-work.

Senior managers may be required to serve on outside committees, government bodies or public inquiries. It is a good idea to have any such requirements stated in writing.

HOLIDAYS Before starting work, agree on holidays. Find out how many weeks' annual holiday may be taken at any one time, and if and how holiday pay accrues.

Make sure that the company is willing to allow holidays already arranged. Once an employee starts a job, the firm's holiday practice becomes legally binding, unless special arrangements have been made.

PENSIONS Pension schemes are often explained in a pamphlet: ask for a copy. Check whether pension rights are transferable to a new firm if you change jobs. Be sure of the retirement age, and find out the amounts

---

## Racial discrimination in jobs

ANYONE applying for a job who feels he has suffered discrimination on the grounds of race, colour, or national or ethnic origins can complain to his local conciliation committee, whose address is obtainable from any Department of Employment office; to the Race Relations Board in London; or the Secretary of State for Employment.

The rejected applicant need not make the complaint himself. It can be made on his behalf by someone else, as long as the worker involved is named.

The complaint, which must be made within two months, may be dealt with by a body set up by employers and unions within the industry to deal with race issues. An appeal can be made against any decision of such a body to the Race Relations Board.

If conciliation proves impossible, or the employer refuses to give an assurance that he will put the matter right, the Race Relations Board can refer it to the County Court.

The court, which sits with a judge and two laymen experienced in such issues, can either issue an injunction ordering the employer not to commit further discrimination, or else can make an award of compensation to the worker who suffered discrimination.

contributed by both employer and employee. Ask whether the employee's contributions receive full or only limited tax relief.

DANGEROUS JOBS If the job involves danger, ask what extra pay is given. Make sure that proper safety precautions are taken. If you are an independent contractor, take out your own insurance against injury and sickness. A good insurance broker will give free advice about different forms of insurance. ☐ Safety, health and welfare, p. 608.

TRAVEL Those whose work involves travel should find out if fares are paid in advance.

INVENTIONS AND COPYRIGHT If the work is creative, negotiate the best possible terms for anything you may invent, design or write in direct connection with the job. Unless this is done, the basic rule is that inventions and copyright belong to the employer. ☐ Who benefits from inventions, p. 612.

**The duties of an employee**
Firms such as goldsmiths and jewellers, which make very valuable products, or companies that deal with scientific inventions or money, take special precautions to protect their

## Weighing up the letter of appointment

Check the written particulars carefully before signing and returning the letter of appointment—once signed, it becomes legally binding

**1.** Note the title of the job. Be careful of any distinctions which may denote a substantial difference in status and responsibility

**2.** Make sure the salary figure is the one quoted at the interview. Do not be afraid to point out any discrepancy—it may be a clerical error

**3.** The letter should state when the salary or wages are paid. The employer must not pay later than this stated time

**4.** The starting date must be given so that there is no problem of proving the date when calculating notice or redundancy payments

**5.** Ensure that the periods of notice are at least the minimum laid down by the Industrial Relations Act. An employee may resign after the legal minimum one week's notice

**6.** Check that the letter states what holidays you are entitled to, gives the qualifying period

**FUNGICIDE LIMITED**
Head office
270 Archway Road, Manchester M40 4TZ
Tel. 061-795 1188
Works office
Coronation Works, Zinc Street, Sale, Cheshire
Tel. 061-973 0001

Our Ref. RFPN/J1/287          20 November 1970

Mr M.T.Fiske
73 Parkdale,
Manchester M37 2PX.

Dear Mr Fiske,

    This is to confirm your appointment as assistant data-processing manager **1** of Fungicide Ltd, at a salary of £1,950 per year **2** to be paid monthly on the 25th of every month. **3** You are asked to start work on January 17 1971 **4** and to continue until such time as the company gives you notice. Fungicide Ltd agrees to give one week's notice after 13 weeks employment, two weeks' notice after one year and four weeks' notice after two years. **5**

    You will be entitled to one week's paid holiday in the first calendar year worked, and three weeks a year thereafter, **6** plus all Bank Holidays or six days in lieu of Bank Holidays. **7**

and the amount of holiday which can be taken at any given time

**7.** If you might have to work on Bank Holidays and receive days off in lieu, check when such days can be taken—a holiday in January may be less useful than one in August when schools have their holidays. Ensure that there is no objection to taking days off work for any religious festivals associated with your faith—for instance, the Jewish Passover

business interests and safeguard their goods. Find out at the start whether you are likely to be searched when leaving work. The employer cannot do so without your consent.

SECRETS In certain types of work, employees must sign an agreement to keep the employer's secrets. All civil servants, for example, have to sign a declaration binding them to the provisions of the Official Secrets Acts 1911 and 1920. Some firms require employees not to write to the Press about the firm.

PRIVATE WORK Ask the employer whether he allows his staff to do other work in their own time—some firms forbid taking an evening job as a barman, for example.

Many insist, too, that employees agree not to work for a competitor if they leave. Such conditions may not be legally enforceable, but trouble can be avoided by seeing that the terms are reasonable in the first place.
☐ Restrictions after leaving the job, p. 653.

MARRIAGE Single women should inquire about the firm's rules on marriage. Some firms refuse to employ married women.

PREVIOUS EMPLOYMENT Avoid the temptation to give misleading answers about your

---

-2-

Mr M.T.Fiske                    20 November 1970

The company agrees that you may have a further week's unpaid holiday in the first year — and that the two weeks may be taken together from July 5 to July 19. **8**

You will be required to join our staff pension plan after six months' service **9** and details of this plan are enclosed. You will be expected to take a medical examination and X-ray subject to which your appointment is final. **10**

Your hours will be from 9 a.m. to 5.30 p.m. every weekday, Monday to Friday, with some evenings when a new programme goes on the computer. **11** Salary reviews normally come at 18-month intervals or less. **12** You, on your part, agree that you will not reveal any information concerning Fungicide's activities to rival firms or any other parties outside the company. **13** Any computer programmes that you may write will remain the property of the company. **14**

We look forward to a long and happy association.

Yours sincerely,

*R.F.P.Noakes.*

R.F.P.Noakes
Managing Director

**8.** If you have arranged a holiday at a certain time, get written confirmation that you can have time off at that date

**9.** Find out whether the company has a pension scheme and if membership is compulsory for employees. If so, check the terms of the scheme before accepting the job. Be sure of the retirement age and how much you must contribute. Discover also whether you can transfer pension rights if you change your job later

**10.** Sometimes there is a compulsory medical examination. An employee who refuses to take this may not get the job

**11.** Notice that no payment is specified for overtime here. Some firms give extra days off instead, and allow a day off as soon as possible after eight hours' overtime

**12.** Read the clauses about future salary rises—a regular review, as opposed to regular increments, does not always guarantee an increase

**13.** Even without a contract or a letter of appointment, an employee has a duty not to disclose his employer's secrets to rival organisations. See if the firm will permit staff to contribute articles with no commercial value to technical journals, or lecture on business topics

**14.** Look closely at the wording of any statement in which the company claims the rights to what an employee invents or writes. While it is reasonable for a company to reserve rights in anything an employee produces in connection with his job, few people would be happy to surrender anything they write or invent outside work

previous salary or employment. An applicant who gets a job as a result of dishonesty can be dismissed without notice if the true facts are discovered.

UNION MEMBERSHIP Check if employees are required to join a union and whether you will be allowed to do so by the union concerned. Generally, the employer cannot insist on a person joining a union unless he has an agency shop agreement with the union concerned. ☐ The law on union membership, p. 618.

If the job is covered by a union agreement, ask the local branch secretary or a shop steward to show you or to give you a copy. Such agreements are often legally binding.

DISCIPLINE Works rules or office practice may include detailed disciplinary procedure.

Ask at the interview if employees can be fined, suspended or dismissed for breaking certain rules. ☐ When an employee can be disciplined, p. 616.

### Starting and ending a job
Make sure that the date of starting work is given in writing, for that date determines any eventual redundancy pay, period of notice due, seniority within the firm and length of holidays to which an employee is entitled.

If the contract is for a set period, the date for ending the job should also be in writing. If not, find out how much notice an employee must give if he leaves.

The law insists on certain lengths of notice based on length of service. Under the Contracts of Employment Act 1963, as amended by the Industrial Relations Act 1971, an employee must be given one week's notice after 13 weeks' continuous employment; two weeks after two years, four weeks after five years, six weeks after ten years, and eight weeks after 15 years. Employees must give at least one week's notice. An employer or employee may agree to more notice, but not to less. ☐ Leaving a job, p. 639.

### Jobs with special conditions
Certain types of employment have special terms and conditions, and special methods of calculating pay.

SEAMEN AND DOCKERS Merchant seamen and dock workers have special contracts under the Merchant Shipping Acts 1894–1970 and the Dock Workers (Regulation of Employment) Act 1946.

Every docker is entitled to a permanent contract of employment with a single employer. If his wages fall below a guaranteed weekly minimum wage, his employer must make up the difference.

All British merchant seamen, officers and masters must carry a card issued by the Department of Trade and Industry. Generally a person under school-leaving age cannot be employed in the merchant navy.

GOVERNMENT WORK Civil servants have no legally enforceable contract. But they do have the right to employment until a minimum pensionable age, through what is called 'security of tenure'. Many of their terms of employment are governed by the 'established code' laid down by the Civil Service.

TEMPORARIES Temporary employees usually have a contract with their employment agency, not with any employer to whom they may be sent. The agency is responsible for their terms of employment.

APPRENTICESHIPS Apprentices in some trades sign a special type of contract called indentures. The 'master' or employer undertakes to teach the apprentice his trade, and the apprentice agrees to learn and to obey.

Apprenticeship agreements must be signed by both parties. If the apprentice is under 18, his parent or guardian must also sign.

### The letter of appointment
Most employers are obliged by the Contracts of Employment Act to give all new employees written details, known as the written particulars of employment, within 13 weeks of starting the job.

These written particulars are not themselves the contract of employment. The object is to give employees a clear understanding of their rights and obligations.

It is the agreement reached before work is started that is in fact the contract of employment. So it is desirable to ask for a letter of appointment setting out all the points raised. Clear up any misunderstanding and get any mistake put right before starting work.

### When an applicant is rejected
An applicant refused a job seldom has grounds for legal action—except if he has been turned down because of his race, colour or national or ethnic origins. ☐ Racial discrimination in jobs, p. 589.

BAD REFERENCES Anyone who suspects he has been rejected because of a bad reference from a previous employer has no right to see the reference. If he happened to read it, he might be successful in an action for libel only if he could show that the reference writer included errors of fact with a reckless disregard for the truth, or acted from an improper or ulterior motive. ☐ The dangers of controversy, p. 666.

# When children can take a job

No child under school-leaving age may be employed full time, and there are severe restrictions on the kinds of work children can be employed to do on a part-time basis. Generally, no child under 13 can be employed except for light agricultural work. Between 13 and 15 a child cannot be employed for more than two hours on any schoolday or Sunday. The law, however, varies because children are protected not only by Acts of Parliament, but also by local bye-laws.

Check with the local council before allowing a child of school age to take a job.

### Jobs that are barred
Many jobs are barred to children completely. Under the Children and Young Persons Acts 1933 and 1963, for example, it is illegal to employ anyone under 15 to do dangerous work or to lift heavy objects. They cannot work in manufacturing, demolition, mining, building or transport industries. An employer breaking the rules can be fined up to £100.

In addition, most areas have bye-laws which forbid the employment of children in kitchens, cake shops, restaurants, slaughterhouses, billiard saloons, any gaming or betting establishment, or any business requiring door-to-door selling or touting.

The Factories Act also forbids young persons (those under 18) from working at certain jobs that may be hazardous to health, such as the processing of lead.

### Jobs that are allowed
Even where children can be employed, the parents may have to obtain permission from the local education authority. The employer also has to observe the bye-law restrictions on how long and at what time of day children can be employed.
NEWSPAPER ROUNDS Although children are not allowed to sell from door to door, bye-laws in most areas permit them to deliver newspapers before and after school hours, though not before 6 a.m. or after 8 p.m. In some districts they may also be allowed to sell newspapers on the streets, though no other type of street trading is permitted.
HARVESTING In many country areas, children are allowed special school holidays to help with potato harvesting and similar jobs.

If the local council has no such scheme, parents should seek permission from the education officer before keeping a child away from school to do harvesting work.

The children of farmers and market gardeners may do light work on their parents' holdings during school holidays without the need to obtain such permission.

### Children on the stage
The most profitable form of employment for children is in public entertainment. However, a child under school-leaving age must have a licence from the local education authority before taking part in:
1. Any performance which members of the public pay to watch.
2. Any performance on licensed premises.
3. Any performance which is to be broadcast (including films and television commercials).

The licence lays down the times during which the child is allowed to be absent from school and the local authority must ensure that the work does not interfere with the child's education or health.

If the entertainment is to be outside the United Kingdom, a magistrate's permission is needed in addition to the licence granted by the education authority.

If the child is under 14, there is a further restriction. Unless the proposed performance is in an opera or ballet, it must be proved that the part the child is to play could not be played by an older child.

Children under school-leaving age may not take part in any potentially dangerous types of entertainment (such as trapeze acrobatics). It is illegal to train children under the age of 12 for this type of entertainment.
EXCEPTIONS No licence is normally needed for a performance organised by a school or similar body, unless the child is being paid more than just expenses.

### Children under contract
An employer cannot normally enforce the terms of a contract with a child under 18 who decides to stop work. Nor can a child be held to an agreement if a court orders him to quit a job because it considers the work is bad for him, or that a contract is not to his advantage.

The rule is that the child can be held to an agreement by an employer only if the contract is clearly to the child's benefit.

# Employed or self-employed: the differences

*How to find out which you are*
*How the court decides*

AN EMPLOYER may offer to take on an applicant as a self-employed, independent contractor, rather than as an employee. Before agreeing, consider the advantages and disadvantages.

The self-employed person has greater freedom of action, but fewer legal rights. He can claim a wider range of expenses against income tax, but he is not eligible for a number of State benefits if he is injured at work, unemployed or made redundant.

### How to find out which you are
There are a number of tests which the individual can apply to find out whether he is an employee or self-employed.

First, he should find out whether his tax is to be deducted under the PAYE system, or whether he is responsible for paying it direct to the tax office. Find out, too, who is responsible for stamping the National Insurance card —the company or the individual worker. In practice, the difference between a self-employed person and an employee is that the employee pays tax under PAYE and has his card stamped by the employer.

These tests, however, are not infallible, for a worker is not regarded in law as self-employed simply because he and his employer choose to consider him self-employed.

The law tries to protect workers from being classed as self-employed by an employer simply to save himself money and avoid his legal responsibilities. Similarly, it tries to prevent someone who is really an employee from gaining the tax advantages of the independent contractor. ☐ How the income tax system works, p. 556.

Where there is any doubt, the Department of Health and Social Security decides the issue—subject to appeal to the courts. The Department is responsible for determining whether a man must pay National Insurance contributions at the employed rate or as an independent contractor.

### How the court decides
If an employer or self-employed person wishes to challenge the ruling of the local office of the Department, he can appeal directly to the Secretary of State's office in London. If the local office's ruling is upheld, the employer or the individual worker can ask the High Court to decide whether the contract between the employer and the person working for him establishes what the law calls a master-servant relationship or whether it shows that the worker is genuinely self-employed, and contracted to the employer for a particular job, or for a set time.

The courts have worked out a number of complicated tests to find what the contract really establishes. No one test is conclusive; all must be considered together. For example, the courts define an employee as a person who is controlled by the employer not only in *what* he does but also in *how* he does it.

In 1952 Lord Denning said that what mattered was the relationship between the person doing the work and the enterprise for which he was working. If he was an 'integral' part of that enterprise, he was an employee, but if he was not then he was an independent contractor. A chauffeur, a reporter and a ship's captain would therefore be employees; the owner-driver of a taxi, a freelance journalist and a ship's pilot would all be independent contractors.

Another test is that of 'economic realities'. A genuinely self-employed person usually owns or hires all the tools of his trade. He keeps the profits and is responsible for his own financial losses.

Most employees, on the other hand, use tools, machines, equipment and premises belonging to their employers. The judge has to take into consideration all of these tests.

➤THE EMPLOYEE WHO SET HER OWN HOURS *Mrs Ann Florence Irving was engaged by Market Investigations as a part-time interviewer. She could choose when she worked, provided that she met the deadlines set by Market Investigations. Once she had been given addresses to visit, she was not under the direct control of the firm. But she was given very detailed instructions as to how to conduct the interviews and which people to interview.*

*Market Investigations asked the Minister of Social Security whether Mrs Irving and other* similar interviewers were employees or self-employed. The case went to the High Court.

DECISION *The court upheld the Minister's decision that Mrs Irving was an employee. She was under a substantial degree of control by her employers, but that in itself was not conclusive. The fact that she was an interviewer only part time and could work for other people, did not prove that she was self-employed.*

*Mrs Irving's contract did not make any provision for time off, sick pay, holiday periods or* dismissals, but the judge held that this did not mean that it was not a contract of employment.

*Finally, the judge applied the test of 'economic realities'. If Mrs Irving had been in business on her own account, or provided her own tools for her work, or risked her own capital, or made her own profits out of the way she conducted her business, then she would have been an independent contractor. Since none of these circumstances existed, she was an employee. (Market Investigations v. Ministry of Social Security.)*◄

## Advantages and disadvantages of two ways of working

|  | EMPLOYEE | SELF-EMPLOYED WORKER |
|---|---|---|
| Holidays | Normally entitled to take holidays with pay | No paid holidays (although it is customary in some industries to give 'holiday pay') |
| Sickness | Entitled to State sickness benefit, and earnings-related supplement. Often entitled to wages during sickness | Entitled to basic State sickness benefit only. Usually no wages during sickness |
| Injury at work | Entitled to State industrial-injury benefits. May have grounds for claim for damages | No industrial-injury benefits. May have grounds on which to claim for damages |
| National Insurance contributions | Paid partly by employer and partly by employee | Paid wholly by self-employed person, but at a lower rate |
| Income tax | Limited expenses can be deducted from income before tax is charged. Tax deducted from wages or salary under Pay-As-You-Earn scheme | Wider range of expenses can be deducted. Tax is paid under Schedule D in two instalments during the year after the money is earned |
| Legal liability for injury to other people | Both employer and employee are liable for the employee's negligence. In practice, injured people are more likely to claim against employers | Self-employed person is liable for his own negligence unless the company accepts responsibility. He is more likely to be sued than an employee |
| Pension | May be eligible to join firm's pension scheme under which employer pays part or whole of contribution | No company pension scheme, but eligible for tax relief on private pension or annuity premiums |
| Notice | Entitled to minimum notice laid down by law | Entitled only to notice stipulated in contract |
| Unemployment | Eligible for unemployment benefit | No unemployment benefit |
| Redundancy | Normally eligible for State redundancy pay | No redundancy pay |
| Dismissal | Protected from dismissal for unfair reasons | Protected only by terms of the contract (if any) |

# Checking the contract

*Signing a detailed contract*          *Altering the conditions of employment*
*If there is no detailed contract*

WHEN an employee starts a new job, the terms of his contract are often unwritten. Nevertheless there is still a contract in law, based on what was agreed verbally at the interview. Such verbal agreements can be difficult to prove, however.

To avoid misunderstandings or disputes, an applicant for a new job should ask for a letter from a new employer offering the job and outlining the main terms, such as the rate of pay, before giving notice to his present employer. □ Applying for a job, p. 588.

### Signing a detailed contract
In many jobs—particularly apprenticeships and senior posts—the employer asks each employee to sign a full agreement before he starts work. This should be checked, clause by clause, before signing, because once it is completed it becomes the legal contract, no matter what was agreed verbally before.

### If there is no detailed contract
The employer is usually bound, by the Contracts of Employment Act 1963, to give every employee a written statement of the terms under which he is employed within 13 weeks of the date on which the employee starts work. The employer does not have to do this, however, if he has given the employee a full contract which covers all the points required in the statement.

Others not entitled to such a statement—called the 'written particulars'—are:
**1.** People who are normally employed for fewer than 21 hours a week.

## What the written particulars must show

The written particulars given by an employer to a new employee must, by law, contain certain information, including the names of the two parties to the contract. The statement must also contain:

| | |
|---|---|
| The date of appointment | Holiday entitlement and, possibly, benefits such as pensions, pay increments and redundancy pay, are based on length of service, so it is important to have a record of when the employee's service began. If the employee begins as a temporary worker, the date he or she is to join the permanent staff should also be stated |
| Wages or salary | Wages or salary can be stated as a weekly, monthly or annual amount. Alternatively, the method of calculating remuneration, perhaps on a piece-work or commission basis, should be stated. Overtime rates, where applicable, and agreements covering increments, must be given |
| Time and method of payment | The employee must be told when he will be paid—for instance, weekly or monthly, in arrears or in advance. Payment by cheque or through a bank cannot be made a condition of employment for workers covered by the Truck Acts 1831–1940, that is, most manual workers |
| Sick pay | In addition to stating how much sick pay, if any, is given and when, the employee should be told when a doctor's certificate is required |
| Hours of work | As well as regular hours, the statement should make it clear if the employee is expected to work late on occasions or, perhaps, be on call at weekends. It should also state if and when overtime is paid |

**2.** Registered dock workers, merchant seamen and fishermen.

**3.** Civil servants.

**4.** Employees who work abroad.

**5.** An employee who is the father, mother, husband, wife or child of the employer.

If the written particulars differ from what was agreed and the actual conditions under which the employee is working, he should take the matter up with his employer immediately, unless the difference in the stated terms is in his favour. Although the written particulars are not in themselves the contract of employment, the courts would consider them as evidence of what had been agreed if there was a dispute later.

Check, too, that the written particulars cover all the points required by law. If they do not, take the matter up with the employer as soon as possible.

If an employee fails to get satisfaction from the employer over the written particulars—because the employer fails to supply them at all or because they are unsatisfactory—he can appeal to his local industrial tribunal. These bodies, set up by Parliament, consist of a trade-union representative, an employers'

representative, and a lawyer as chairman. A trade union or the local office of the Department of Employment will explain where and how to lodge the appeal.

The tribunal hears evidence from both employer and employee, and can then confirm the particulars of employment as they were given, add to them, or alter them. It can give damages for breach of contract. Appeals can be made to the Industrial Relations Court.

The employer is not always obliged to give full details of the conditions of work in the particulars. Instead, he may refer to other documents which set out pay and conditions, such as orders issued by wages councils or collective agreements with trade unions, and say where they are available for inspection.

**Altering the conditions of employment**

If the employer wishes to alter the conditions of employment, he must inform the employee in writing or display a conspicuous notice in the place of work. This must be done within one month of any change. But he cannot alter the contract without the agreement of the employee. A change in the contract must be notified by a change in the written particulars.

| | |
|---|---|
| Paid holidays | The length of annual holidays and how holiday pay is calculated if an employee leaves, must be stated. The document must also give particulars about other public holidays |
| Pension provisions | The employer must state whether the firm is contracted in or out of the Government Graduated Pension Scheme. If there is a private scheme the employee must be told when he can join, whether it is compulsory to join, and the rules and conditions |
| Period of notice | The employee must be told what notice must be given by himself and the employer. Once the employee has been in the job for 13 consecutive weeks, he is entitled by law to at least a week's notice. This goes up to two weeks after two years, four weeks after five years, six weeks after ten years and eight weeks after 15 years. After the 13 weeks, the employee must also give one week's notice, the legal minimum, however long his service with the firm. Longer periods of notice may be arranged by mutual consent |
| Trade-union membership | The employee must be told about his rights to join or not to join a trade union and about any agency or closed-shop agreement. ☐ The law on union membership, p. 618 |
| Grievances | The employee must be told who will hear any grievance he has about his employment and how the grievance will be handled |

# How wages are protected

*Time-rate or piece-rate*    *Defining a manual worker*
*How wages are paid*      *Deductions from pay*

IN most industries and professions there is no statutory minimum wage. How much a man is paid is entirely a matter for negotiation with the employer, either by the individual employee or by his union. As important as the actual weekly or monthly sum to be paid is the basis on which the amount due to the employee is calculated.

### Time-rate or piece-rate

Many people are paid on a time basis—a fixed rate for a given number of hours. Their basic wage is the same, no matter how much or how little work they do.

OVERTIME Where a time-rate system is operated, there is a fixed working week to distinguish normal hours from overtime. In most cases, overtime work earns a higher rate of pay. The employer is not legally bound to pay more unless he has agreed to do so.

PIECE-RATES In many industries wages are calculated on a productivity or piece-rate basis. In agreements of this sort a worker is paid a basic wage plus a bonus according to the amount of work he does rather than the time he puts in. Sometimes a group of people working together share a total payment for the job or for their joint output.

Piece-workers' wages can suddenly be reduced if the firm has no work, so collective agreements between managements and unions and wage-regulation orders usually include clauses allowing for fall-back pay. This means that the company agrees to pay its workers not less than a certain amount. This may be a fixed minimum or it may be calculated as an average of pay received in previous weeks.

Where there is no collective or individual agreement, the employer has a legal duty to make sure that work is available for employees who are paid on a piece-work basis.

➤THE WORKMAN WITH NO WORK TO DO *Rosser and Sons owned the Cilfrew Tin-plate Works in Glamorgan. In February 1903 some of their machinery broke down, forcing them to close the factory for five weeks. Orders fell off so badly that on July 20 they had to close altogether, giving Mr Devonald, one of their tin-plate rollermen, six weeks' notice. Mr Devonald was*

# How to check your payslip

Payslips vary from firm to firm. Every employee should check the details to make sure that the correct deductions have been made

**Tax period** indicates the tax month (or week, for weekly paid workers) numbered from April (or the first week in April), the start of the tax year

**Tax code**, allocated by the tax office, enables the employer to calculate tax deductions. Check against Form P60

| | | TAX PERIOD | TAX CODE | BASIC PAY | | OVE |
|---|---|---|---|---|---|---|
| JELLOW INDUSTRIES | | 6 | 600 | 183 | 35 | |
| NAME JAY ROBERT MR | NATIONAL INSURANCE | GRADUATED PENSION | TAX | TAXABLE PAY TO DATE | | GRADUAT TO |
| | 3 \| 52 | 6 \| 37 | 33 \| 90 | 1100 \| 00 | | 35 |
| WORKS NUMBER | DEPARTMENT | PAY METHOD | PAYMENT DATE | MISCELLANEOUS DEDUCTIONS | | |
| 429 | 9 | CR–TFR | 30. 9. 71 | 6 \| 95 | 2 \| 82 | |

**Pay method** indicates how the particular employee is paid— either by credit transfer, cheque or by cash

**National Insurance** shows the amount of the contribution paid by the employee to the Government scheme

**Graduated pension** shows the amount of the employee's contribution, based on his salary before other deductions

*on piece-work and, with the factory closed, he had no opportunity to work or earn money. He sued Rosser and Sons for six weeks' wages.*
DECISION *He was awarded £14, calculated on an average weekly wage of £2 6s. 8d. The employers had a legal obligation either to find work for Mr Devonald, or to pay him as if he had been working. (Devonald v. Rosser.)* ◄

LAYING-OFF When workers are laid off due to circumstances beyond their employer's control—for example, because of a strike in another factory supplying components—they are not normally entitled to be paid. But when the employer *is* responsible, perhaps because of a decline in orders, the workers must be paid.

The only time this rule does not apply is where a contract of employment sets out the circumstances in which workers are not entitled to pay when they are laid off.

They may be able to claim unemployment or supplementary benefits during the period when they are out of work. In certain circumstances workers may, by giving notice to the employer under a fixed procedure, claim redundancy payment after a long period of lay-off or short-time working. □ Claiming compensation for redundancy, p. 645; Qualifying for unemployment benefit, p. 650.

### How wages are paid

Wages are generally paid in cash, by cheque or directly into a bank account, usually at weekly or monthly intervals. The agreed method of payment is normally written into the contract of employment. A merchant seaman, for instance, is generally paid in full when he leaves his ship. If an employee subsequently finds that he is not being paid regularly—for instance if instead of getting his money each week as agreed, he sometimes waits for three weeks before he is paid—he can sue for breach of contract.

At the end of each day's work an employee has earned a payment, under the Apportionment Act 1870, for the portion of the wage period—which is usually a week or a month—that he has worked.

This means that if he agrees to leave without notice he is, in most cases, entitled to payment for the proportion of the wage period he has worked. Even if the employee is dismissed for gross misconduct he is still entitled to the wages owing to him.

This does not apply if the employer and employee have agreed that payment should be made only when the work is completed.

A manual worker must by law be paid in cash unless the worker and employer agree otherwise. All other workers must agree a method of payment with their employer.

If a manual worker consents in writing he can be paid by cheque, postal or money order, or credit transfer direct to his bank—this is permitted under the Payment of Wages Act 1960. Although other employees may take part of their income in kind—for example, a company employee may agree to take shares

Overtime pay is not always given. Some employers give the employee a day off after he has worked a set number of hours

Other payments could include special fees or holiday pay due to an employee leaving before he takes his holiday

Non-taxable allowances cover expenses—for entertainment or for hotel accommodation while travelling for the firm, for instance

| on | TAX CODE | BASIC PAY | | OVERTIME | | OTHER PAYMENTS | | | NON-TAXABLE ALLOWANCES | | O |
|---|---|---|---|---|---|---|---|---|---|---|---|
| | 600 | 183 | 35 | | | | | | | | |
| TAX | | TAXABLE PAY TO DATE | | GRADUATED PENSION TO DATE | | TAX DEDUCTED TO DATE | | TOTAL PAY | TOTAL DEDUCTIONS | NET PAY | O |
| 90 | | 1100 | 00 | 38 | 22 | 202 | 65 | 183 | 35 | 53 56 | 129 79 |
| MISCELLANEOUS DEDUCTIONS | | | | | | OTHER DEDUCTIONS | | DETAILS OF MISCELLANEOUS DEDUCTIONS 1. SPORTS AND SOCIAL CLUB 2. UNION DUES 3. MISCELLANEOUS | | | O |
| 82 | | | | | | | | | | | |

Miscellaneous deductions could include superannuation payments or repayments of advances in salary

Taxable pay, Graduated pension and Tax deducted list the accumulation of these items since the start of the tax year

Total deductions adds up insurance, tax, pensions and other deductions given in the second line of the payslip

or payments under profit-sharing schemes—it is illegal for a manual worker to be paid in kind, irrespective of whether or not he consents. This rule was laid down by the Truck Acts to end the abuse of workers being paid in inferior goods, or in tokens which could be exchanged only at company shops and in return for goods at inflated prices.

## Defining a manual worker

The fact that employees use their hands does not make them manual workers. A typist, for example, works with her hands, as does a surgeon, but neither would be thought of as a manual worker. Neither is therefore protected by the Truck Acts.

Men employed to dig ditches are obviously manual workers, but there are many arguable borderline cases. The Truck Acts deals with only one borderline case, that of domestic servants, who, it says, are not manual workers. Apart from this ruling it has been left to the courts to decide.

They have ruled that a manual worker is someone whose physical labour is the substantial part of his employment, as opposed to the workman whose physical labour is only incidental to the job. For example, a foreman working with his own hands and a seamstress operating a sewing-machine and an iron have been held to be manual workers.

➤WHEN A DRIVER IS A MANUAL WORKER *In the early days of motor buses the driver was expected to carry out repairs en route, in addition to driving. Mr Smith, a driver with the Associated Omnibus Company, was cranking the engine of his bus when the starting handle flew back, breaking his wrist.*

*In 1907 he sued his employers, claiming that because he was a manual labourer he was entitled to compensation. The bus company had provided him with spanners and wrenches to enable him to carry out repairs.*
DECISION *The court considered these tools to be necessary, and as strength was needed to use them this amounted to manual labour. The driver was judged to be a 'workman' entitled to compensation. (Smith* v. *Associated Omnibus Co.)◄*

Nowadays, however, a bus driver is not considered to be a manual worker since he is not generally expected to repair his bus.

## Deductions from pay

There are only a few deductions which an employer can make from a manual worker's pay without the employee's agreement in writing. Among them are income tax, National

Insurance contributions and payments under attachment of earnings orders. But even with agreement in writing, deductions can be made only for certain items specified in the Truck Acts—medical expenses, food provided on the premises, housing or education, for instance. Other deductions are absolutely prohibited.

Written agreement is not needed where the money is paid by the employer at the employee's request to a third person with whom the employee has a contract. This covers trade-union dues, holiday funds and or savings schemes.

Employees other than manual workers have no such legal safeguards, although in practice the situation may be covered by a collective agreement or an individual contract.

➤A PACKER'S BACK PAY *Mr Pratt joined a firm of wholesale drapers in 1900 as a packer of straw hats. After Army service during the First World War, he applied for his old job back. He was told by the general manager that his wages would be 53s. a week, plus free dinner and tea.*

*'You will agree', the manager said, 'that your dinner and tea are worth another 10s. a week.' Mr Pratt agreed.*

*In December 1935, the firm handed over part of their premises to the men so that they could set up their own canteen. To compensate for the loss of free dinner and tea, they were paid an extra 10s. a week in cash. Mr Pratt sued the firm for £397 10s., claiming that they had unlawfully been deducting 10s. a week from his wages since his re-engagement.*
DECISION *He won his case on the grounds that there had never been an agreement or contract in writing 'to stop wages in respect of victuals'. (Pratt* v. *Cook.)◄*

FINES BY THE EMPLOYER An employee can be fined by his firm—for being late, for instance—and have the money deducted from his pay. But this can be done only if the employee has previously agreed, in writing, to the fines system. Manual workers do not have this protection, although the employer would have to show that they knew about the fines system and had accepted it. ☐ When an employee can be disciplined, p. 616.

SICK PAY Everyone who has worked for more than 13 weeks full-time should know what pay to expect if he is absent from work through illness. The rate of sick pay, and for how long it is paid, must be included in the written particulars of employment which has to be provided by the employer.

Employers are entitled to opt out of the duty to pay employees who are absent because of illness—but this must be part of the contract of employment. If it is not, an employee who falls ill is covered by the common-law rule that every employee must be paid in full for as long as he is ill. Most employers limit their liability to pay full wages indefinitely, and provided the employee is informed, they are allowed to do so.

➤ NO SICK PAY FOR FISHWORKER *Samuel Petrie was hired by Macfisheries in 1930 to work in their smoke-hole.*

*Illness kept him away from work for short periods in the next few years and he received half pay. This was according to the firm's rule, prominently displayed on a notice board in the smoke-hole. It said that an employee who fell sick would be paid half wages for up to three weeks in any one year. These payments, the notice added, were* ex gratia—*a gesture of generous employers who did not consider themselves legally bound to pay.*

*In July 1938 Mr Petrie went sick again and* was away from work for about six months. He received three weeks' half pay, but claimed full pay for the whole period. When his employer's refused to pay he sued them for £82 17s. 6d. DECISION Mr Petrie lost his action. The court said that by laying down these provisions for sick pay, even if they were ex gratia, and by publishing them on the notice board, the company was considered to have suspended the common-law rule. By accepting pay on at least three previous occasions, Mr Petrie had agreed to the firm's policy. (Petrie v. Macfisheries.) ◄

In addition to whatever the employer may pay during illness, every employee is entitled to sickness benefit under the National Health insurance scheme—provided that he has paid enough weekly contributions. The amount of the State benefit received is usually deducted from the employee's sick pay, although there is no legal reason why the employee should not receive both these payments. ☐ Claiming sickness benefit, p. 602.

## Industries with minimum wages

M OST people are paid as much as they or their union can persuade the employer to pay. For the majority of workers, there is no national minimum wage laid down by law.

There are exceptions for certain groups of workers however. Employees of any firm working for the Government, of local authorities or of any of the nationalised industries must not be paid less than the current minimum paid in the private sector of the same industry.

Since 1891, the House of Commons has periodically passed Fair Wages Resolutions—the latest in 1946—to ensure that firms employed by the Government do not pay their workers less or observe less favourable hours and conditions of employment than those established by negotiation, arbitration or by standard practice.

These resolutions do not have legal force, but firms which fail to comply with the terms of the resolution may lose their Government contracts. The contractor must also make sure that the resolution is observed by any sub-contractors he may employ.

An employee whose firm is engaged on Government work and who thinks he is being under-paid compared with people in the same branch of private industry should raise the matter with his employer. If this fails to produce a satisfactory result, the individual or his union can complain to the local employment exchange, or to the Ministry for whom the work is being done.

WAGES COUNCILS In industries or parts of industries where unions are weak and where employees do not have strong individual negotiating positions, there is another form of protection. Employees in these industries are covered by Wages Councils, some of which were first set up in 1909 as Trade Boards.

Each council lays down minimum wages for workers in the industry which it covers, and controls overtime payments, holidays and holiday pay. Anyone who is not paid at least the minimum rate can sue his employer, although in practice such cases are dealt with by the Wages Inspectorate of the Department of Employment, on behalf of the worker. The Department can prosecute an employer who does not comply with wages regulation orders.

The councils consist of an independent chairman, two other independent members, and equal numbers of members from both employers and employees in the industry.

A list of industries which have wages councils is kept by local employment exchanges who will provide copies on request.

# Claiming sickness benefit

*How to claim*

*How benefit is paid*

*How much benefit is paid*

*The duration of benefit*

*When benefit may be refused*

*When benefit may be reduced*

LOSS of earnings through illness can be partly made up by the State sickness benefit scheme. Anyone paying National Insurance contributions can claim sickness benefit for himself and his dependants when he has been off work for at least four days excluding Sundays. After six months' illness, sickness benefit ceases and is replaced by invalidity benefit.

A claimant must satisfy two conditions:

**1.** Since he started work, he must have paid at least 26 National Insurance contributions. Any contributions credited during unemployment or a previous illness do not count.

**2.** He must have at least 26 contributions to his credit in the 'contribution year' preceding the spell of sickness. To get benefit at the full rate, 50 contributions must have been made. Benefit is at a reduced rate if fewer than 50 but at least 26 contributions have been paid or credited in the contribution year. ☐ The National Insurance scheme: what the terms mean, p. 605.

PENSIONERS Men and women who continue working after the age at which they become eligible for a State retirement pension (65 for a man, 60 for a woman) are entitled to benefit until 70 (65 for a woman).

Because the amount of sickness benefit in this case is the same as the pension a man would get if he retired at 65, the contribution test for retirement pensions applies. ☐ Qualifying for a State pension, p. 525.

## How to claim

To claim benefit, obtain from a doctor a National Insurance medical certificate stating that you are unfit for work, and send the completed certificate to the local Social Security office.

There are two types of certificate. The more common, closed certificate, covers up to seven days and gives the day on which the doctor thinks the patient can return to work.

If the patient is still too ill to work he must obtain a new certificate from the doctor. An employee who returns to work before the date shown on the certificate should inform his local Social Security office immediately. The second type of certificate, the open certificate, can cover up to 28 days and the doctor gives it if the illness is likely to last more than seven days. It does not name a date for return to work.

This type of certificate must be renewed on the date given by the doctor. Keep a note of this date so that the doctor can be asked for a new one as soon as it is needed. Gaps between certificates may result in loss of benefit.

If the patient is still unfit at the end of 28 days, the doctor may issue a certificate for any length of time up to 13 weeks.

The first certificate should be sent to the local Social Security office within six days, excluding Sundays, of the onset of illness (21 days if you have never claimed before). If there is any break between the start of the illness and the date on the certificate, explain the reason. If further certificates are needed, they must reach the office within ten days of the beginning of the period to which they relate, excluding Sundays.

If it is not possible to send a medical certificate within the time allowed, write to the Social Security office saying that a claim for benefit is being made and giving the following details: the full name of the patient, his or her date of birth, address, and if possible National Insurance number.

PENALTIES Any claimant who makes a false statement to obtain benefit—either for himself or someone else—may be fined up to £100, or be sent to prison for up to three months, or both. The Department of Health and Social Security can deduct from future payments any amounts of benefit which have been overpaid, or take legal proceedings to get the money back unless the claimant can show that he used due care and diligence to avoid the over-payment.

## How benefit is paid

Sickness benefit is paid by National Giro order, posted to the applicant. An invalidity pension, unless expected to be of short duration, is paid by means of a book of orders, to be cashed weekly at the post office. Sickness benefit can be paid the same way.

If the first medical certificate is 'closed'— giving the date on which the doctor thinks the claimant will be fit for work—payment is made on the last day of sickness or soon after. Otherwise, payment is made about a week after the first completed certificate has been sent. After that, a weekly payment is made on the same day of each week.

The person to whom the money is to be paid is always named on the Giro order he receives. Unless the order is crossed—when it must be paid into a bank—it can be cashed at any post office.

If the claimant cannot get to a post office to cash the order, there is a space on the order for him to authorise someone else to collect the money on his behalf. Whoever cashes the order should take evidence of the identity of the person named on the order—a driving licence, a club membership card or official correspondence addressed to the claimant.

If the Giro order is not cashed within three months of the date stamped on it, a new one must be obtained. If the order is not cashed within 12 months without good reason, benefit may be lost altogether.

### How much benefit is paid

SICKNESS BENEFIT Rates of sickness benefit can change, and information on current rates can be obtained from the local Social Security office. Rates are calculated weekly, and one-sixth of the weekly flat rate is paid for each day off work.

There are additional allowances for a wife, children and other dependants. But no extra is paid for a wife earning more than the dependant's allowance. Her earnings are assessed after allowance has been made for necessary expenses.

Claims can be made for all children under 15, for those up to 19 if they are at school or university, and for apprentices who earn less than a fixed amount each week. A man who is

## Earnings-related supplement

EXTRA money can be claimed on top of most flat-rate State benefits. This is called the earnings-related supplement and depends on earnings during the previous tax year. It can be claimed by people between 18 and 65 (60 for a woman) who pay tax under PAYE or the Marine Tax Deduction Scheme.

Self-employed people and those over pensionable age—even if they have continued working—cannot receive earnings-related supplements. Nor can married women who have not paid flat-rate insurance contributions. Working widows can get the supplement while sick or unemployed if they have paid National Insurance contributions.

CALCULATING THE SUPPLEMENT The amount of supplement to be paid is calculated on the claimant's weekly 'reckonable' earnings in the previous tax year—the total earnings on which he paid tax by PAYE, divided by 50. Other earnings are not taken into account. If the claimant was off work for part of the preceeding year, this will reduce his weekly reckonable earnings and, therefore, the supplements payable.

The supplement is based on earnings between an upper and a lower limit. Until January 1974 the limits are £9 and £30 a week. The payment made is usually one-third of the amount by which the claimant's income exceeds the lower limit. For example, no one earning less than £9 a week in the previous tax year can claim the supplement. If he earned £25 a week, a claimant is entitled to one-third of £16.

If his reckonable earnings were £35, however, he is not entitled to one-third of the difference between £9 and £35—only to one-third of the difference between £9 and £30, for income over £30 a week does not qualify for the supplement. The maximum earnings-related benefit is therefore £7.

From January 1974 the limits are £10 and £42, and the supplement is one-third of reckonable earnings between £10 and £30, and 15 per cent of the rest. From January 1975 the upper limit is raised to £48.

HOW TO CLAIM The forms on which claims for flat-rate benefit are made include a space for a claim for the supplement.

Earnings-related supplement is not paid for the first 12 days off work, but separate periods of illness can be added together to make up these qualifying days—provided there is no spell of more than 13 weeks between each period. The supplement is paid for a maximum of 156 days, not including Sundays.

The total benefit paid—including flat-rate benefit, allowances for dependants, and earnings-related supplement—must not be more than 85 per cent of the claimant's reckonable earnings in the previous tax year.

divorced or separated can claim for a child living with his wife or former wife if he contributes to the child's support. He can also claim for any child of a woman living with him whom he supports, even if the child is not his own. He can claim for a woman other than his wife who lives with him, or who is maintained or employed by him, or who looks after his children.

MARRIED WOMEN A working wife can get sickness benefit for herself even if her husband is working.

If her husband is incapable of self-support or is not living with her, she can also receive benefit for any dependent children, provided her husband does not himself receive State benefit for them. She can also get extra benefit for her husband if he is an invalid and cannot support himself—but only if she pays at least half the cost of supporting him.

INVALIDITY BENEFIT An invalidity pension is paid at the same rate as sickness benefit, but the allowances for dependent children are higher and the amount a wife can earn before her allowance is reduced or cut off is also higher.

An invalidity allowance is payable in addition to the invalidity pension if the incapacity began before 60, for a man, and 55, for a woman. At the end of 1972 the allowance was £1·15 per week if incapacity began before the age of 35, 70p if it began between the ages of 35 and 44, and 35p if it began at the age of 45 or more.

### The duration of benefit

A claimant is not paid sickness benefit for the first three days of illness unless these occur not more than 13 weeks after a previous period of illness for which benefit was paid. Anyone not entitled to benefit for these three days may be able to claim supplementary benefit. ☐ State help in hardship, p. 550.

Provided the claimant has paid at least 156 National Insurance contributions during his working life, and has paid or been credited with 26 in the previous year, he can draw sickness benefit for up to six months, after which he receives invalidity benefit. Contributions credited during unemployment or a previous sickness do not count towards the total of 156.

If fewer than 156 contributions have been paid, sickness benefit is paid for a maximum of 312 days—in effect for a year, because Sundays are not counted.

To qualify for benefit after that, 13 more contributions must be made for 13 weeks worked. If it is not possible to work

those 13 weeks, an application can be made for payments under the supplementary benefits scheme. ☐ State help in hardship, p. 550.

### When benefit may be refused

Two payments cannot normally be made from public funds for the same purpose. He is generally paid whichever of the benefits is the greater.

ABSENCE ABROAD Sickness or invalidity benefit is not normally paid to anyone outside Great Britain, Northern Ireland and the Isle of Man. It may be paid if the claimant was unable to work for at least six months before going abroad, or if he left the country for treatment.

IMPRISONMENT Sickness or invalidity benefit is stopped for any period a claimant is in prison or in custody on remand. If he is acquitted or only fined, back payments may be claimed.

### When benefit may be reduced

If an allowance for a child or other dependant is already being paid as part of some other benefit, such as a war pension, the additional sickness or invalidity benefit for the child is reduced by the amount of that allowance.

Benefit is not reduced, however, simply because a claimant continues to receive his wages or if additional sickness benefit is paid by a friendly society or trade union.

HOSPITAL IN-PATIENTS If a man or his wife spend more than eight weeks in hospital receiving National Health Service treatment, benefit is reduced.

### How to appeal

Claims are decided by the local insurance officer. If any dispute arises, the first appeal is to the local National Insurance appeal tribunal. All the claimant needs to do is to write to the local Social Security office about it.

The claimant can attend the hearing and state his case, or he can be represented by his trade union, a lawyer or a friend. ☐ Appearing before a tribunal, p. 735.

If he is dissatisfied with the tribunal's decision, he or his trade union can appeal to the National Insurance Commissioner.

There is no appeal against the Commissioner's decision except on points of law.

The case may be reviewed if facts come to light which were not known at the time the decision was made by the tribunal or the insurance officer. A decision by the Commissioner can be reviewed only if there is fresh evidence which could not reasonably have been brought forward at the time.

# The National Insurance scheme—what the terms mean

WHEN a person applies for National Insurance benefits, he may not receive the full amount. This is usually because he has not satisfied the contributions requirements laid down by the various Acts and Regulations. These requirements and the terms used to explain them are the same for most types of benefit.

FLAT-RATE CONTRIBUTIONS Each weekly National Insurance contribution is normally stamped on the insurance card. The rate of contribution an individual must pay depends on which class of insurance he is in. These are: Class 1 (employed): people working for an employer, including paid apprentices. Class 2 (self-employed): those people working for themselves. Class 3 (non-employed): people who do not work, for example, a person living off investments or a student.

CREDITS Contributions are credited on a person's card without payment when the insured person is sick or unemployed.

CONTRIBUTION YEAR The period of 52 or 53 weeks for which any National Insurance card is in use is called the contribution year. There are four contribution years, which begin on different dates—the first Monday in March, June, September and December of each year. The contribution cards for each year have different colours and each is indicated by the letters A, B, C or D, printed on the front of the card after the National Insurance number. Each insured person is given one letter when he starts work for one of these four contribution years, and retains it throughout his working life.

The number of National Insurance contributions paid or credited in a contribution year decides whether a claimant qualifies for benefit (provided other conditions are satisfied) and how much he can receive.

BENEFIT YEAR The contributions paid in one year are used to determine the amount of benefit paid in what is termed the benefit year. This begins five months after the end of the contribution year for flat-rate benefits.

The five-month gap is because of the accounting and technical system at the Department of Health and Social Security. Five months is needed to deal with the paper work involved. So, since contribution year 'A' ends in March, the claimant is entitled to benefit on that year's contributions from the first Monday in August. The letter at the end of the National Insurance number signifies the year covered by the employee's contribution card:

| Letter | Contribution year | Benefit year |
|--------|-------------------|--------------|
| A | March 1, 1971 to March 5, 1972 | Aug. 7, 1972 to Aug. 5, 1973 |
| B | June 7, 1971 to June 4, 1972 | Nov. 6, 1972 to Nov. 4, 1973 |
| C | Sept. 6, 1971 to Sept. 3, 1972 | Feb. 5, 1973 to Feb. 3, 1974 |
| D | Dec. 6, 1971 to Dec. 3, 1972 | May 7, 1973 to May 5, 1974 |

If a man has paid or had credited 50 contributions during the contribution year March 1, 1971, to March 5, 1972 and he becomes ill six months after the end of the contribution year—say in August 1972—he is normally entitled to sickness benefit at the full rate.

If he becomes ill three months after the end of the contribution year, he is still entitled to benefit. However, in this instance it is calculated on the basis of the contributions he paid in the previous contribution year—March 2, 1970, to February 28, 1971.

School leavers are automatically credited with 'pre-entry' contributions and are entitled to benefit once they have paid a minimum of 26 qualifying contributions.

Similar rules usually apply to a student who has just finished his course.

If, however, he has worked for more than six months before his course began, he will be required to satisfy the usual contribution conditions.

There are, however, some special rules which might enable the student wishing to claim National Insurance benefits to count any class 3 contributions which he has paid during his course as though they had been paid as class 1 contributions.

EARNINGS-RELATED BENEFIT YEAR The period of one year which begins on the first Monday of May each year is known as the earnings-related benefit year and it is used in calculating the payment of earnings-related supplements.

From 1973, the earnings-related benefit year will start from the first Monday of January.

APPEALS Any appeal over a contributions record must be made to the Secretary of State for Social Services in the first instance.

# Hours of work

*Restrictions in certain jobs    Rules for women and young people*

THE hours a man works usually depend on a trade-union agreement, or an individual arrangement with his employer. There are, however, legal restrictions on how many hours a week women and young people may work in certain industries—indeed, there are times of the day when they cannot be employed.

There is no legal requirement for an employer to pay higher rates for overtime—except in some trades covered by wages councils. Generally, overtime rates are paid under individual or collective wage agreements. ☐ How wages are protected, p. 598.

Some jobs involving public safety have restrictions on hours. The Secretary of State for Employment can limit the number of hours worked by employees in industries controlled by the Factories Acts, and in some cases Parliament imposes limits.

BAKING People employed to bake bread and cakes and to wrap them cannot start work on a day shift before 5 a.m. or finish after 10 p.m. If they are dough-makers or tend ovens, they may start at 3 a.m.

Bakery workers are permitted to work a night shift, between 6 p.m. and 6 a.m., if the employer gives notice to the Department of Employment. But no one is allowed to work these shifts for more than four consecutive weeks, or for more than 26 weeks in a year.

PUBLIC TRANSPORT Drivers of public-service vehicles—buses and coaches—carrying fare-paying passengers must not spend more than five-and-a-half hours continuously at the wheel, or be on duty of any sort for more than 11 hours at a time.

Between duties there must be at least 11 hours free, except for once a week, when there can be a minimum of nine-and-a-half hours. A driver may not be on duty for more than 72 hours a week.

PRIVATE HIRE COACHES Drivers of vehicles not in the public service carrying more than 12 passengers, such as hired motor coaches, must comply with the same regulations covering shifts and working hours as public-transport drivers—except that they are limited to 60 hours on duty in a week.

FLYING An airline pilot must not be on duty continuously for more than 16 hours, including ground duty as well as flying time. He must then go off duty for a minimum of 18 hours. In any 28 days, he must not be at the controls of an aircraft for more than a total of 100 hours.

MINING There is no restriction on the number of hours a man over 18 may work in a mine or quarry. But anyone under 18 is not allowed to do mine or quarry work for more than 48 hours in any week or for more than nine hours in a day.

ROAD FREIGHT A lorry driver must not drive for more than five-and-a-half hours without taking half-an-hour's rest. Nor must he work a shift of more than 11 hours, or ten hours at the wheel.

In a maximum working week of 60 hours, all lorry drivers must have 24 consecutive hours off duty.

SHOPS Shop assistants are not allowed to work more than six hours (five if they are under 18) without a 20-minute break. They must have at least one full day and one half day off duty every week.

### Rules for women and young people

The working hours of women and young people under 18 employed in industry are regulated by law. Young persons in shops are also covered, but office workers may be required to work any hours.

The total working time allowed in one week for women and young people in industry is 48 hours (44 hours for those under 16). Generally, the earliest possible starting time allowed is 7 a.m., and the latest finishing time 8 p.m.—or 1 p.m. on a Saturday.

Women and young people may not work more than an 11-hour shift in a factory where a six-day week is worked. And they must be given adequate rest and meal breaks.

In factories working a five-day week, the limit for a shift is raised to 12 hours, with a maximum of ten hours actual working time. But the maximum hours worked in any week must still be 48 (44 for those under 16).

Women and young people must be given a break of at least half an hour after four-and-a-half hours of continuous work, or after five hours continuous work if they have been given a ten-minute interval.

Every employer must display a notice in his factory stating the permitted hours of work for women and young people. If this is not done, any employee can report the omission to the district factories inspector.

OVERTIME Women, and young people aged 16 but under 18, can work overtime in factories but not more than six hours a week or 100 hours a year, and they must not work overtime in more than 25 weeks of one year. The number of hours worked, including overtime and meal breaks, must not exceed 12 hours on a weekday and six hours on a Saturday. If a woman works overtime she must finish by 9 p.m.

There is no limit on women's hours of overtime in shops, but young persons may work a total of only 40 or 44 hours a week, depending on age.

SUNDAYS Women and young people are not allowed to work in factories on Sundays—except where the Jewish Sabbath is observed, where milk, fish, fruit and vegetables are treated or preserved, or with the permission of the local factories inspector. Male young persons may work Sunday maintenance shifts which are essential for production. Women, but not young persons, may also work on Sundays in bakeries. Both women and young people may work in shops on Sundays.

NIGHT WORK The Employment of Women and Young Persons Act 1920 and the Hours of Employment (Conventions) Act 1936 prohibit the employment of women and young people at night for most categories of manual work. Night is defined as a period of 11 consecutive hours including the hours between 10 p.m. and 5 a.m.

Exceptions may be made for a woman holding a non-manual management job. In these cases the local factories inspector must give his permission.

## Arranging a holiday

THERE is no law that everyone must have a paid holiday each year. This is a matter for agreement between employers and unions or with employees individually.

In industries which are regulated under the Wages Councils Act 1959, holidays and holiday pay are fixed by wages councils and the Agricultural Wages Board. ☐ Industries with minimum wages, p. 601.

The regulations may determine the length of holiday, when it may be taken, and what pay, if any, shall be given.

Apart from these provisions, entitlement to holidays and holiday pay (including any extra payment such as a Christmas bonus) depends on the terms of each employee's contract.

HOLIDAY AGREEMENTS Holidays vary from one industry to another and from one type of employee to another. Usually an employee is required to work a certain time with a company before he becomes entitled to part or all of the agreed holiday.

If there is no agreement on the subject, the date on which a new employee can take his first holiday will depend on the way in which the employer calculates the holiday year—say from April to March, instead of January to December. An employee who starts work in February, and is entitled to one week after four months, might not be able to take any time off before August—six months after starting work, but only four months after the beginning of the firm's holiday year.

In some industries—building and civil engineering, for example—a holiday entitlement may be carried from one employer to another.

In some jobs a certain number of days' absence (unless because of sickness or other legitimate cause) reduces the employee's holiday entitlement. In others, contracts of employment lay down that the employee must work a specified time before and after the holiday to become entitled to holiday pay.

TIME OF YEAR Trade unions and employers usually agree that holidays should be taken mainly between May and September. Although some firms close for an annual holiday, most companies stagger holidays. Decisions on the particular weeks which an employee may take are a matter for individual agreement —usually between the employee and the head of his department or, possibly, the company's personnel officer.

BANK HOLIDAYS Bank holidays, such as Christmas Day and Easter Monday, are regarded as holidays for everyone, but not all employees can claim them as a right. Only women and young people whose conditions are controlled by the Factories Acts are guaranteed a day off or a day in lieu.

# Safety, health and welfare

*Who is responsible for safety*     *Property stolen at work*
*When the rules are ignored*

THE safety of an employee at work is the responsibility of the employer, the employee -himself and his colleagues. Because he controls the premises and equipment, the employer has the major responsibility. But employees must observe safety regulations so that they do not endanger themselves or other workers.

Detailed regulations covering the safety, health and welfare of employees are laid down in the Factories Act 1961, the Offices, Shops and Railway Premises Act 1963, and a number of Acts and regulations governing particular industries and processes.

The regulations are enforced in factories by factory inspectors, working under the Department of Employment, who have the right to examine any factory and to report on its safety precautions. In shops and offices this responsibility rests with local authorities, who have similar powers.

Every accident that causes the death of an employee, or causes an employee to be absent for more than three days, must be reported to the appropriate authority. ☐ What to do if you are injured, p. 629.

Employers must pay the costs of meeting the safety regulations, unless they are specifically allowed under the Acts to charge employees. An employee who is asked to pay for safety clothing or equipment can consult his trade-union representative or the factory inspector before doing so.

**When the rules are ignored**
All premises covered by the Acts must have a summary of them prominently displayed. An employee who thinks that a safety regulation

## Safeguarding the employee

The regulations controlling safety and health at work are detailed. An employee is entitled to check that his own place of work complies with the regulations. To do so, he should first find out from the shop steward or personnel department which Act applies to his workplace. The employer must display placard copies of the relevant regulations, some of which are summarised here.

| | |
|---|---|
| Access | Employees must have safe access to all parts of their work 'so far as is reasonably practicable'. An employee working in a place from which he could fall more than 6 ft 6 in. must be provided with a safety device, such as fencing, where this is 'reasonably practicable'. |
| Cleanliness | Dirt and refuse must not be allowed to accumulate. Floors in all places of employment must be cleaned thoroughly at least once a week. In factories, dirt and refuse should be cleared daily from floors, benches, staircases and passages. Factory walls with smooth surfaces should be washed down at least every 14 months, and repainted at least once every seven years. |
| Clothing | Space must be provided for employees' special clothing or outdoor wear, and drying arrangements provided where required. |
| Drainage | Floors which are liable to become wet and dangerous during working hours must be drained adequately. |
| Drinking water | Fresh drinking water must be provided for all employees. |

is being broken should first draw the management's attention to the breach. If no satisfactory action is taken, factory employees should inform the local factories' inspector; employees in shops, offices or railway buildings should inform the local authority.

An occupier of premises—usually the employer—who fails to comply with any of the safety regulations can be prosecuted. A subordinate can be prosecuted instead, if the breach is his fault.

PENALTIES An occupier convicted of breaking the regulations can be fined up to £60— or up to £300 if the offence could have caused death or serious injury. If the occupier fails to put right the breach of regulations, he can also be fined up to £15 for every day that the offence continues after his conviction.

A negligent employer can also be sued for damages by an employee who has been injured or who suffers ill health as a result of the negligence. ☐ Suing an employer after an accident, p. 636.

ACTION AGAINST EMPLOYEES Employees who break the regulations can also be fined a maximum of £15, or £75 if the offence could have caused death or serious injury.

In theory, an employee who breaks the regulations can be sued as well if, as a result, a fellow employee is injured. But in practice, most injured workers choose to sue the employer because he is more likely to be insured and therefore more likely to be able to pay any damages awarded. The employer can be sued because he is legally responsible for the actions of the employee who was at fault. ☐ What to do if you are injured, p. 629.

**Property stolen at work**
An employee whose personal property is stolen at work is entitled to compensation from his employer only if he works in a factory. Under the Factories Act, employees must be provided with adequate and suitable accommodation for clothing not worn during working hours. This includes clothing removed when the employee puts on overalls or other working garments.

An employer must take reasonable care to prevent the theft of workers' personal property in a factory, and a claim against him for damages could fail if he showed that the facilities were reasonably safe in the circumstances.

However, employees in offices and shops cannot sue their employers. They can only report any thefts to the police.

| | |
|---|---|
| Dust and fumes | All practicable measures must be taken to extract harmful dust and fumes. Employees must be provided with masks or other suitable means of protection against breathing them in. |
| Fire safety | Adequate means of escape in case of fire must be provided, along with fire-fighting equipment. Doors must not be fastened in any way which makes them difficult to open from inside. Where fire risk is high—for instance, in premises where inflammable materials are used, or where more than 20 people work in the same building above the first floor—fire instruction must be given.<br><br>Local fire authorities have powers to bring fire-safety precautions up to standard by requiring factory and office occupiers to apply for a certificate of fire safety.<br><br>Fire-fighting equipment must be provided and be accessible in every factory, office and shop covered by the Acts. |
| First aid | A first-aid box must be provided in every workplace, with one box for every 150 employees. The proper contents of these first-aid boxes are specified in the Acts. Most chemists sell boxes already made up to the legal specifications. |
| Floors, passages and stairs | All floors, steps, stairs, passages and gangways must be kept safe and free from obstruction. Staircases must have handrails, and any openings in floors must be fenced, unless the job makes this impracticable. |

continued ▶

## Safeguarding the employee continued

**Goggles**

In industries where there is the slightest risk of injury to the eyes, goggles must be supplied or effective safety screens provided.

**Heavy loads**

Workers should not be required to lift or carry heavy loads which might cause them injury. Maximum weights for loads are set out in regulations for various industries.

Cranes and other lifting machines are also dealt with separately. They must be examined at least once every 14 months and, when in use, precautions must be taken to ensure they do not endanger people working in the vicinity.

**Humidity**

Where processes are used which involve a humid atmosphere—such as in the textile industry—the local factory inspector must approve the health, safety and welfare standards of the plant.

**Lighting**

Adequate lighting is required by law in workplaces. It can be either artificial or natural. There must also be adequate lighting in any part of a factory to which the employees are likely to go. If windows provide the light, they must be kept clean.

**Machinery**

Dangerous machinery, including transmission machinery and prime movers, must be securely fenced or be situated where employees cannot come into contact with it. Manufacturers and suppliers must ensure that the machinery is safe to use, with all dangerous features guarded. But the occupier of the premises is responsible for the safety of staff who use the machinery. The Factories Act covers power plants, transmission machinery, self-acting machinery and other types. Special regulations apply to hoists and lifts, which must be regularly examined and not used to carry dangerous loads.

Industrial equipment, such as steam boilers, air receivers and gas-holders, is covered by regulations in the Factories Act. Detailed requirements specify conditions of use and maintenance.

**Meals**

Employees must not eat meals in areas where lead, arsenic or other poisonous substances are used. The employer must provide them with somewhere to eat their meals.

**Overcrowding**

Workplaces should not be so overcrowded that there is a risk of injury to employees' health. The law says that a minimum of 400 cubic ft (or 40 sq ft of floor space) should be allowed to each employee. But the 400 cubic ft does not take into account any space which is 14 ft above floor level.

**Seating**

Seating must be provided if employees have the opportunity to sit during their work, or if they do the whole job sitting down.

**Temperature**

A reasonable temperature must be maintained in places of work. Where no strenuous physical effort is called for, a temperature below 16°C (61°F) is not considered reasonable by the law. Each workroom must have a thermometer in a place where the employees can see it, so that the temperature can be checked. Any heaters or cooling systems must not give off harmful fumes.

**Underground work**

Factory inspectors must approve all premises where work takes place below ground level.

| | |
|---|---|
| Ventilation | All workplaces must be properly ventilated. Fumes, dust and other harmful substances given off in the course of work must be extracted from the working atmosphere. |
| Washing facilities and lavatories | There must be an adequate number of lavatories, with separate lavatories for men and women where both are employed. Employers must also provide proper washing facilities, including hot and cold running water, soap and clean towels, or other suitable means of cleaning and drying. Lavatories and washing facilities must be kept clean, sufficiently lit and adequately ventilated. |
| Women and young people | Women and young people are not allowed to work in some industries where there is a health hazard, such as lead manufacture.<br><br>No one under the age of 18 may remain employed in a factory longer than 14 days unless medically examined by an appointed factory doctor and given a certificate of fitness for that employment. The certificate must be renewed annually.<br><br>Women and young people are not allowed to clean certain machinery while it is in motion, or if it is dangerous. No young person can work on any dangerous machinery unless supervised or fully instructed in its use. |

## Safety laws in special industries

Certain industries are not covered by the two main safety Acts, but have their own safety laws.

| | |
|---|---|
| Agriculture | Separate safety laws for agricultural workers cover the safeguarding and safe operation of farm machinery, the safe use of dangerous chemicals, and the avoidance of accidents to children. These rules are contained in the Agriculture (Poisonous Substances) Act 1952, and the Agriculture (Safety, Health and Welfare Provisions) Act 1956.<br><br>The Ministry of Agriculture, with a staff of inspectors, enforces the provisions of these Acts. Other safety provisions for agricultural workers are similar to those in the Factories Act. |
| Mines | The National Coal Board has a legal duty to provide for the safety, health and welfare of its employees. Office staff are covered by the Offices, Shops and Railway Premises Act, but people engaged in mining itself are covered by the Mines and Quarries Act 1954. This lays down regulations about the provision of airshafts, and such things as the lifting gear which takes miners up from and down to the coal face. The Act also makes it an offence for a miner to take cigarettes, tobacco or matches to a place in the mine where they could be dangerous. The maximum fine, on conviction, is £20. |
| Quarries | Detailed regulations for the working of quarries are also laid down by the Mines and Quarries Act. They cover such items as the measures the management must take if an operation is sending up dust that could injure the health of employees. |
| Shipping | The Merchant Shipping Act 1970 sets out safety regulations aboard vessels, and such things as facilities for medical treatment. It also sets minimum standards for the crew's accommodation on board ship. |
| Transport | The Department of the Environment can require the use of safe equipment on railways and make rules for safe railway operation. |

# Who benefits from inventions

*The rights of the inventor*  
*Restrictions on State employees*

*Company 'suggestion' schemes*  
*Creative work and copyright*

SPECIALIST staff usually have a clause in their contracts setting out who is legally entitled to benefit from anything they invent during their work. In most cases, the employee has to agree that any inventions he makes in connection with his job are the property of his employers.

In return, he is usually promised some financial reward—possibly even a share in the profits. But this is a matter for negotiation, and the employee must try to get the best terms for himself when he agrees to take the job. ☐ Applying for a job, p. 588.

Where there is no such provision in the contract, any invention the employee makes in the course of his work belongs to his employer, whether the employee agrees or not. He is entitled to no part of it, nor to any reward—even if it is highly successful.

➤ PATENT IN DISPUTE *Mr Scorah invented a method for making acrylic acid (used in certain types of glass) while working for Triplex, a glass firm. Later he left them and set up in business on his own as a glass manufacturer. He was granted a patent for his invention. When Triplex applied for a patent on the same invention, they found that Mr Scorah had already obtained one. They asked the court to say that they were entitled to the patent, and that Mr Scorah was not.*  
DECISION *Triplex won the case. There was nothing in Mr Scorah's contract to cover the situation that had arisen, and the method had been invented during working hours and using the firm's materials. In these circumstances, an invention or discovery made as a result of what the employee was engaged and instructed to do was the property of the firm for which he worked, not the employee. (Triplex v. Scorah.)*◄

Even where the employee's invention is not part of the work he was specifically instructed to do, it must be given to the employer if it is connected with the employee's job.

➤ THE INVENTION THAT WENT WITH THE JOB *While Mr Homewood was working for the British Syphon Co. Ltd as chief technician, he invented a device for dispensing soda water and did not inform the firm. Instead, he patented the invention and left to work for a rival company. British Syphon asked for a court injunction restraining the rival firm from using the device, and applied for the patent.*  
DECISION *The court decided that Mr Homewood was not entitled to patent the invention. The patent belonged to his employers because he had worked on it in the course of his employment. (British Syphon Co. Ltd v. Homewood.)*◄

The law, however, takes note of whether the invention is something the employee could not reasonably be expected to develop as a result of his work.

If a man making bicycle wheels designs a new type of gear wheel, the invention belongs to his employer. But if the invention has nothing to do with the man's own job—if, say, the employee designs a new type of bicycle bell—his employer has no claim, and the employee can patent it. ☐ Protecting commercial ideas, p. 697.

Similarly, if an engineering student takes a holiday job as a factory sweeper and notices how a machine could be improved, his invention is entirely his property. The employer cannot claim any part of it, because the invention did not spring from the student's job as a sweeper.

Again, if a man invents something completely unconnected with his work—if, say, a machine-setter invents a new golf club—his employer has no claim on it, even if it was developed during working hours and using materials belonging to the firm.

### Restrictions on State employees

The Crown owns any invention made by State employees, even if the invention is unconnected with their work. If it has no value to the State, the employee will usually be allowed to patent it himself.

Where the invention is retained by the Government, the inventor can apply for an award through his departmental head.

A State employee who is dissatisfied with the payment he receives can appeal to the Central Awards Committee at the Treasury.

Employees in nationalised industries have the same general rights to the proceeds of their inventions as employees in private industry. The restrictions which apply to Crown employees—people employed directly by the Government—do not apply to them. But some State industries—for example, the National Coal Board—run invention award schemes of their own. The amount paid for an invention depends on whether it belongs to the employee or whether the employer is entitled, under the contract of employment, to claim full or partial rights to it.

### Company 'suggestion' schemes

Many factories and offices ask employees to submit ideas to improve efficiency, sales or productivity. Where the company pays for any idea, benefits from it belong to the firm. The employee is entitled to no further reward, no matter how much money his idea makes or saves for the firm.

The price paid for suggestions—whether it is in cash, or in the form of a holiday for the employee—usually depends on how the company's experts value the suggestion.

### Creative work and copyright

Writing, designs, films, photographs, records, broadcasts, paintings, sculpture, architectural plans and other creative work, where skill is involved, is protected by the law of copyright. Artistic merit is irrelevant.

But ideas cannot be protected in this way. Only when an idea has been put down in some written form can the law help the creator, by prohibiting the reproduction of the idea in any way without a suitable payment.

The copyright in any creative work which is produced in the course of a man's employment—that is, when he is working on something he is specifically employed to do such as writing or designing—belongs to his employer.

A newspaper, for example, owns the copyright of any article a staff journalist writes as part of his normal duties. But if the same man writes an article in his spare time, the copyright belongs to him.

> THE ACCOUNTANT WHO TURNED AUTHOR
*A book based on experience and knowledge gained during his employment was written by Mr D. F. Evans-Hemming, an accountant. The book included the text of lectures given by the author while he was working as an accountant for Stevenson, Jordan and Harrison. Another part of the book was material written as part of an assignment for his firm. The firm sued the publishers, Macdonald and Evans, claiming that the copyright was theirs.*
DECISION *The court found that copyright in the part of the book relating to the special assignment belonged to the employer. But copyright in the part containing the lectures belonged to the author, because the lectures made use of his own special knowledge and expertise, and not his employer's. (Stevenson, Jordan and Harrison v. Macdonald and Evans.)* ◄

If a writer is self-employed, copyright in his work always belongs to him, unless he assigns it to someone else.

Disputes between writers and employers over copyright can be settled only in the High Court, with possible appeal to the Court of Appeal. But first a solicitor should be consulted.

## Settling disputes over inventions

IF there is a dispute over the ownership of an invention, it is usual for either the employer or the employee to apply for a patent. If the other side challenges the application, the Comptroller-General of Patents arranges a hearing. Both the employer and the employee can be legally represented.

An application should be made to The Patents Office, Southampton Buildings, Chancery Lane, London WC2A 1AY. □ Protecting commercial ideas, p. 697.

This procedure is available only if neither the employer nor the employee is given exclusive rights to any invention in the contract of employment. If one side has the legal rights to an invention, there can be no arbitration.

After the hearing, the Comptroller may decide in favour of the employer or the employee, or he may apportion the rights in the invention between them.

The Comptroller's decision is legally binding. But either side can appeal—firstly, to the Patents Appeal Tribunal, which consists of two High Court judges who are specialists in patent law. Then—on points of law only—further appeals can be made to the Court of Appeal and to the House of Lords.

# Duties to the employer

*Obeying the employer's orders    Keeping the employer's secrets*
*Giving faithful service*

IT is the legal duty of every employee to obey his employer's orders, to give faithful service, to protect his employer's interests and to keep his employer's trade secrets. If he does not fulfil these duties, the employer is normally entitled to dismiss him without notice for breach of contract.

**Obeying the employer's orders**
There are two main exceptions to the general rule that an employee must obey his employer's orders.
**1.** An employee must not be required to break the law. For instance, if an employer asks him to steal another company's secrets or to ignore the safety provisions in the Factories Acts, the employee is entitled to refuse.
**2.** An employee may refuse to do work for which he has not been employed. An accountant may refuse to operate a machine; a chauffeur may refuse to act as a gardener.

In such circumstances an employee does not break his contract if he refuses to carry out his employer's instructions—but the employer should be told why his orders are being disobeyed.

In almost every other case, however, the employee cannot ignore his employer's instructions without risking dismissal. The employer need not necessarily be right: his orders may be unreasonable or absurd, but they must be obeyed. Even when a highly skilled employee knows more about the job than his employer, he must do as he is told.

➤ THE GARDENER WHO REFUSED TO PLANT *Major Webb employed a gardener named Sydney Pepper, whom he considered inefficient and unco-operative. Finally, one day in 1967, Mr Pepper refused to do some planting and swore at his employer. He got the sack. Mr Pepper sued Major Webb for wrongful dismissal.* DECISION *Mr Pepper lost his case. The court said he had broken his contract both by his outright refusal to obey orders and by his earlier intransigence. (Pepper v. Webb.)* ◄

UNION ORDERS A union may instruct its members not to do something. But in law an employee's first obligation is to his employer.

Provided he is not being asked to do a job that is not his, and the order is lawful, he must obey his employer, not the union.

➤ THE MINERS WHO REBELLED *A group of 34 miners reported for work at the Bowes and Partners coalfield on December 20, 1892. One was a non-union man and the others refused to go down to the coal-face in the same lift with him. The under-manager would not let them use the next lift and they had to wait all morning at the pithead, missing their shift.*
*The same thing happened on the two following days. Bowes and Partners sued Robert Press, one of the union men. They maintained that by refusing to go down with the non-union man he had disobeyed a lawful order and broken his contract with the company.* DECISION *The court held that the owners were entitled to compensation. Press and the other union men were in the wrong. (Bowes v. Press.)* ◄

WHEN OBLIGATIONS CONFLICT When an employee disobeys an order because of loyalty within the company, the law may take a lenient view, although still holding that orders *should* be obeyed.

➤ THE SECRETARY WHO REMAINED LOYAL *Miss Laws worked as a secretary for the London Chronicle Ltd, and was present at a meeting in 1959 between her immediate superior and the managing director. During an argument, the man for whom Miss Laws worked got up to leave the room and she rose to follow him. The managing director told Miss Laws to stay, but she left with her superior and was dismissed without notice. She sued for wrongful dismissal.* DECISION *The court said that her action was, strictly speaking, wrong. However, the law in civil cases has the right to take special circumstances into consideration. The court decided that her action was not serious enough to justify dismissal, and awarded her damages. (Laws v. London Chronicle Ltd.)* ◄

**Giving faithful service**
It is an implied condition of every contract of employment that the employee has a duty to be honest and to give his employer faithful

service. In law, this is called the 'duty of fidelity'. An employee who makes himself unfit for work, or is negligent, or acts in a way that harms his employer's business is in breach of his duty.

ABILITY TO DO THE JOB An employee who says he is able to perform certain tasks also gives his employer a contractual guarantee that he is competent to do them. Degrees of skill vary, but if an employee deceives his employer by claiming to be able to do work he is not able to do, he will have failed in his duty of fidelity to his employer.

AVOIDING A CONFLICT OF INTERESTS An employee must not take bribes, use his employer's property without permission to make money for himself, or take advantage of his employment to make any secret profit.

►BONUS FOR THE BOSS *Mr Ansell, managing director of the Boston Deep Sea Fishing Company, received a sum of money as commission from a firm supplying boats to the company, and held shares in another firm which supplied it with ice. When they found out, his employers took legal action against him for breach of contract.*
DECISION *The court held that it was wrong for the managing director to be in a position where his own interests could conflict with those of his employers, and made Mr Ansell account for commission he had earned and interest and bonuses paid on his shares. (Boston Deep Sea Fishing Co. v. Ansell.)* ◄

**Keeping the employer's secrets**
Employees often learn trade secrets while at work—a special manufacturing method, or details of a new product about to be launched, or even a list of customers. In law, such information is the employer's property and must not be given away or sold.

The principle was put clearly by Lord Shaw in the House of Lords in 1916. 'Trade secrets, the names of customers, all such things which are denominated objective knowledge—these may not be given away by a servant; they are his master's property,' he said.

Only where an employer has in some way broken the law by possessing them does the employee have a right to divulge such secrets.

►THE SALESMAN WHO SOLD A STORY *When Mr Putterill resigned as sales manager for Initial Services, he took with him confidential company files about price increases and price fixing. He passed these on to the* Daily Mail, *which published a story about them, revealing that there had been breaches of the Restrictive Trade Practices Act 1956. In 1967, the company sued Mr Putterill for breach of his duty of fidelity, and argued that its own admitted breach of the Act gave him no valid defence.*
DECISION *The court found that, although the employee was under a duty not to disclose confidential information, in exceptional cases the public interest required him to do so.*

*This, said the court, was probably one of those cases, and Initial Services lost their case. (Initial Services v. Putterill.)* ◄

In almost every other case, the employee's duty to his employer must take priority over all other loyalties.

PART-TIME JOBS An employee must not in his spare time earn money from another company by using the knowledge gained from his full-time job unless his full-time employer has given his consent.

►THE SPARE-TIME EXPERTS *Employees of Hivac Ltd, skilled in making midget valves for hearing aids, went to work in their spare time for a rival firm, Park Royal Scientific Instruments. Although there was no evidence that the employees had passed on secrets, Hivac complained that their activities did the company a great deal of harm and, in 1946, asked the court to stop Park Royal from using Hivac employees.*
DECISION *The Court of Appeal said that the employees were wrong to work for Park Royal in their spare time. In general, an employee could use his skills in any way he wanted, particularly in his spare time; but he was not entitled in law to use them to harm his employer. (Hivac v. Park Royal Scientific Instruments.)* ◄

The Hivac case was an unusual one, however. Because there were only a few workers in the country trained to do this type of job, any work the Hivac employees did for any other firm was helping to destroy Hivac's sales monopoly.

WHEN THE JOB ENDS The employee's responsibility to keep his employer's secrets does not end when he leaves the job. He is entitled to earn a living elsewhere, but he may use only his own skills, not his former employer's secret techniques.

An employer's list of customers is also considered a trade secret. If an employee in a new job remembers the names of some of his former employer's customers and solicits business from them, he may be entitled in law to do so. But he must not deliberately memorise or write down a list of names with the intention of using them to his own benefit in new employment. ☐ Restrictions after leaving the job, p. 653.

# When an employee can be disciplined

*When warnings are given*  *When an employee can be dismissed*
*When fines can be levied*  *Right of appeal*
*Suspension from work*  *Where to get help*

INDIVIDUAL contracts and collective agreements in many industries contain details of how workers can be disciplined for various offences. They cover warnings, fines, suspensions and, finally, dismissal itself. Any such disciplinary procedures will be upheld by law only when individual employees have consented to them. This consent can be signified by signing a contract, accepting a union agreement, accepting an established custom in a firm, or by agreeing to the disciplinary action at the time.

An employee fined without his consent can sue for the return of any money deducted from his wages; similarly, someone who is suspended can sue for lost earnings.

The employer's only right, if there is no code of discipline for the company staff, is the right of dismissal when this is justified. □ Leaving a job, p. 639.

## When warnings are given
It is common for accepted disciplinary procedures to lay down that an employee must be given a certain number of warnings at specified intervals before any more serious disciplinary step is taken. Some agreements require such warnings to be given in writing.

Where an agreement provides for warnings, the employee can take legal action if he is disciplined without warning. He can sue for wrongful dismissal, for example, if he is sacked without being warned first. But if there is no warning procedure, he need not be warned. If he is, it has no significance.

## When fines can be levied
No worker can be fined or have money deducted from his wages without his agreement—unless he is a manual worker in a firm which has an accepted fines system. □ How wages are protected, p. 598.

Even when he does agree, the fine or deduction made from his wages has to be reasonable. In practice, his agreement with the employer usually limits the fine, whatever the cost to the employer of the action which led to the fine.
MANUAL WORKERS Certain conditions stipulated by the Truck Act 1896 must be satisfied before fines or deductions can be made from the wages of manual workers. In addition to the normal provision that the employee must agree, manual workers have to be told in advance what offences are punishable and how much the fines may be. In some factories, for example, workers who are more than five minutes late are fined half-an-hour's pay. Where details of offences and fines are included in, say, a notice on the factory wall, and not in the employee's own contract, the employee must have agreed to the terms before he took the job—and the employer must have proof that he did so.

The employer must give details of the fine and the offence to the employee in writing. If the employee wants to recover any wrongful fines, he has to sue his employer within six months. But the employer is also liable to be prosecuted if he ignores the Truck Act provisions. The penalties are a fine of £5–10 for a first offence, £10–20 for a second offence, and up to £100 for a third offence.
BONUSES In general, a firm has complete freedom to withhold a bonus as a punishment, unless the employer and employee have clearly agreed that the bonus is part of the employee's remuneration. Otherwise, no employee can take legal action if his employer does not pay a bonus: such payments are not regarded as wages, but are discretionary—called *ex-gratia* payments in law.

## Suspension from work
An employee can be suspended from work only if he agrees either before he takes the job or at the time his employer wants to suspend him.

If an employee is suspended to keep him away from work before his case is heard, he may be kept on full pay because the suspension is not disciplinary.

But where the suspension is used as a means of discipline, the employee is not usually paid. This does not mean that his contract has ended, and he may not be able to claim unemployment benefit because he is not available for other work. If he is in need, he may be able to claim supplementary benefit. □ State help in hardship, p. 550.

An employee who thinks he was wrongly

suspended can sue his employer for damages within six years of the suspension.

APPRENTICES An employer cannot usually suspend an apprentice because he has agreed to train him for a specified time. But he can suspend him and extend the apprenticeship by an equivalent period.

## When an employee can be dismissed

An employee may lose his job without being given notice if he is guilty of grave misconduct or if he is negligent or incompetent.

But not every type of misconduct will give the employer the right of instant dismissal. An unprovoked assault on a foreman would generally give the right. But nobody can be fired without notice for occasional unpunctuality unless his contract authorises it. If it does not, he can take action. ☐ Claiming compensation for dismissal, p. 641.

Persistent lateness, on the other hand, would probably be regarded as grounds for instant dismissal. ☐ Leaving a job, p. 639.

If his contract lays down specific circumstances in which the employee can be dismissed on the spot, and he is instantly dismissed for any other reason, it will be wrongful. This is so even when, without the contract, the employee's conduct would have justified instant dismissal.

If there are no dismissal provisions in the contract, an employer does not have to give reasons; but where summary dismissal is concerned, he must dismiss the employee at the time of the incident and not, say, a month after it happened. If he delays, he forfeits his right to dismiss the employee.

A worker dismissed for proven misconduct is not entitled to compensation. ☐ Claiming compensation for dismissal, p. 641.

## Right of appeal

Some agreements may entitle an employee to a hearing before he is dismissed. The employee is usually asked to appear before a committee of both labour representatives and management. He can explain his case personally or someone may be allowed to plead for him—a friend, shop steward or solicitor, for instance. If the employee does not accept the decision, he may have a further right of appeal, usually to higher management.

## Where to get help

An employee who feels he has been wrongly fined, suspended or dismissed will usually be able to consult his union officials. The union may provide free legal advice and help with costs of an action. In most cases, however, employers and union officials will settle disputes without going to court.

If the employee cannot get union help, the Citizens' Advice Bureau may assist him. But consultation with a solicitor is vital before legal action. Fighting a case is often costly; any damages awarded are unlikely to cover more than lost earnings or the amount of any fine.

---

## When an employer can sue

AN employer, instead of dismissing or disciplining a worker, can sue him for damages if the employee's negligence has resulted in financial loss.

The employee is bound by law to act in a reasonable way and not to be negligent. He must, for example, exercise care in operating his employer's machinery and equipment.

If he accidentally slips on a factory floor and knocks over expensive equipment which must be replaced, an employer will probably not be able to sue him for damages. But if he misuses equipment and damage results, he may have to pay for the cost of repairs.

➤THE CARELESS LORRY DRIVER *A lorry driver named Lister, employed by the Romford Ice and Cold Storage Co. Ltd, negligently backed his truck into his father, who was also employed by the firm.*

*The father, who was injured in the accident, sued his employers for damages, which the employers' insurance company paid. The insurance company then took up the master's right to sue an employee, and brought an action against Lister for repayment of damages they had paid his father.*

DECISION *The son was ordered to repay the damages to the insurance company because of his negligent driving. The House of Lords' judges all agreed that there was an implied term in a worker's contract that he must 'perform his duties with proper care'. Lister had broken the implied term of his contract by not exercising enough care. (Lister* v. *Romford Ice and Cold Storage Co. Ltd.)* ◄

# The law on union membership

EVERY worker has the right in law to decide whether or not he wants to belong to a trade union. Once he has made his decision, he is protected by the Industrial Relations Act 1971 against victimisation by his employer, the union or his fellow workers.

The law gives special protection to members of registered unions—that is, unions that are registered with the Chief Registrar of Trade Unions and Employers' Associations. There is no such protection for members of unregistered unions, which are called in law only 'organisations of workers'.

## Joining a union
If an employee's work puts him in a category covered by a union, he must not be refused membership without good reason.

An application may be refused, however, on reasonable grounds—if the applicant has previously been a member of the union and has consistently fallen into arrears with his subscriptions, for example. The union is then entitled to refuse the application until the arrears have been paid.

REMEDIES FOR UNFAIR REJECTION If a worker feels that his application for membership of a trade union has been unfairly rejected, he can appeal to one of two authorities. If the union is registered, he can bring his case before the Chief Registrar of Trade Unions and Employers' Associations. Alternatively, complaints against registered or unregistered unions can be made to an industrial tribunal. ☐ How workers can complain against a trade union, p. 622.

## Protection for union members
An employer must allow a worker to belong to the registered trade union of his choice, and to play a full part in its activities. And he must not interfere with the right of the worker not to belong to a trade union—whether or not it is registered.

If an employee believes his rights have been infringed, he can complain to an industrial tribunal. ☐ Union membership: what to do if you are victimised, p. 619.

When an employee belongs to a registered union, his employer must not prevent him from attending union meetings, speaking publicly at events organised by the union, or standing for union office. This does not mean that the worker can carry on these activities during working hours. This is permitted only if there is a specific agreement on these points between the union and the employer.

It is considered an unfair industrial practice for an employer to attempt to penalise the worker in any way for his trade-union activities—for example, by suggesting that he is jeopardising his chances of promotion.

The worker is also protected against dismissal on the grounds of union activities, sometimes even where these take place during a strike. Until 1971, an employee who was dismissed because of his union activities had no redress provided he was given appropriate notice or paid wages in lieu.

An employee unfairly dismissed for union activities has the right to appeal to an industrial tribunal. ☐ Claiming compensation for dismissal, p. 641.

## The law against the closed shop
For many years it was the practice in some industries—such as entertainment, the docks and printing—for employers to take on only workers who belonged to a particular trade union. Sometimes employers agreed with unions that if a vacancy occurred it was to be filled by a person recommended by the union; this is known as a 'pre-entry closed shop' (closed, that is, to anyone who is not already a member of the appropriate union).

Any such agreement is now unenforceable, and any attempt to continue the practice by industrial pressure constitutes an unfair industrial practice. If a worker is told by an employer that he must be a member of a particular trade union before being employed, he can complain to an industrial tribunal.

In the past, trade unions have threatened to strike, work to rule or ban overtime to enforce a closed shop. If this happens now, the prospective employee who is not a union member can complain about the union to an industrial tribunal.

If he can show that he was rejected because of union pressure, he can claim compensation from the union, the employer or both. So, too, can an employee who loses his job because he is not a union member.

## Refusing to join a union

Some employees have an unrestricted right to refuse to join a union. Others must pay the equivalent of the union subscription to charity if they do not wish to join. This situation can arise through what are known as approved closed shops and agency shops.

APPROVED CLOSED SHOP In some industries a type of closed shop is still permitted if an employer and a registered union jointly obtain the permission of the Industrial Relations Court. This is the approved closed shop. Non-union members are given jobs on condition that they join the union (unlike the pre-entry closed shop—which is no longer permitted—where only people who are *already* union members are given jobs).

In an approved closed shop an employee with a conscientious objection to union membership can apply to the union for exemption. If this is refused, he can appeal to an industrial tribunal. If he is declared exempt, he need not join a union, but must pay the equivalent of the union subscription to charity.

AGENCY SHOP An employer may have an agreement with a registered trade union that, unless he objects, any new employee taken on should join the union—assuming he is not already a member.

If he wants to object, all he has to do is to inform the union of his intention not to join. He must then pay the union subscription without becoming a member, or pay a similar sum to charity.

## Starting and ending an agency shop

If an employer refuses workers' requests for an agency shop, a registered union can apply to the Industrial Relations Court for a secret ballot among the employees affected. If a majority of those eligible to vote, or two-thirds of those voting, are in favour, the employer must operate the agency shop. When the ballot goes against an agency shop, no further application can be made for two years.

In an agency shop, an employer can penalise or dismiss a worker who refuses to join the union or pay subscriptions in lieu. A union may also put pressure on an employer by industrial action to dismiss the worker without risking a claim for compensation.

ENDING AN AGENCY SHOP Anyone working in an agency shop may apply to the court for a ballot to find out whether the majority of the workers affected want the arrangement to end. The application must have written support from one-fifth of those covered by the agreement.

If the agency shop was created by ballot, no application can be heard for two years. In any new ballot a two-thirds majority of those voting or a simple majority of those eligible is needed to end the agency shop.

---

## Union membership: what to do if you are victimised

ANY worker who feels that he has been the victim of an unfair industrial practice—perhaps through an employer's refusal to give him a job because he does not belong to a union—can complain to an industrial tribunal.

The tribunals, which sit in various parts of the country, consist of a legally qualified chairman, a member nominated by trade unions, and another member nominated by employers' organisations.

HOW TO COMPLAIN Application forms for a hearing before an industrial tribunal are obtainable from the local office of the Department of Employment. After completing it, the worker is told when the hearing will take place. He may present his own case or he can ask a lawyer or union official to do it for him.

A worker refused a job because he is not a union member may first be granted an order saying that he is entitled to be employed. If the worker has been out of work for, say, six weeks before obtaining another job, the tribunal may award him the equivalent of six weeks' wages, plus expenses, to be paid by the employer who refused him a job.

If the job for which he was turned down had better prospects than the one which he later obtained, he might also be awarded an additional sum as compensation. Any award is limited to a maximum of £4160.

The employer has to pay the worker the sum awarded. If he fails to pay, the award is treated like any other debt and the worker can sue in the county court.

An appeal against a decision of a tribunal can be made to the Industrial Relations Court —but only on a point of law, not on the facts.

# Workers' rights within the union

*The right to attend meetings*
*The right to take part in elections*
*When a member can stand for office*

*Contributing to political funds*
*The law against 'kangaroo courts'*
*Resigning from the union*

ONCE a worker becomes a member of any trade union, the law gives him the right to take part in its activities, and protects him against the misuse of powers by union officials. The Industrial Relations Act 1971 lays down guiding principles which registered and unregistered unions (and employers' organisations and associations) must observe in dealing with their members.

A union which fails to comply with these principles commits no criminal offence. But any member whose rights are infringed is entitled to claim compensation. ☐ How workers can complain against a trade union, p. 622.

Sometimes the guiding principles laid down by law may conflict with the union's own set of rules. In this case the union must observe the guiding principles; it will not escape liability to pay compensation by pleading that it was only following its rule book.

### The right to attend meetings
Every member has a right to attend meetings of the trade union section or branch of which he is a member, unless it is reasonable to limit attendance at a particular meeting.

What is regarded in law as an acceptable reason for excluding members from a meeting depends partly on the size and organisation of the union in question. It is not unreasonable, for example, for a large union to insist that only elected delegates can attend a conference to decide policy, since it would be impracticable to hold a general meeting of hundreds of thousands of members.

But if a union section regularly takes major decisions at hastily convened meetings, so that members who are not present in the works at the time cannot attend, the absentees are likely to be regarded as unreasonably excluded.

### The right to take part in elections
When elections are held within a union for local representatives or national officers, no member must be unfairly excluded from nominating candidates or from voting. Similarly, when a ballot is held members must be given a reasonable opportunity to vote.

It might be regarded as fair for certain classes of members—such as probationary members, or honorary life members who have retired—to be excluded from nominating candidates or from voting.

All ballots and elections must be secret, and conducted so that no one is able to discover how any particular member cast his vote.

### When a member can stand for office
The guiding principles lay down that no union member should be unreasonably excluded from standing for any union office or, if he is elected, from holding office.

It might therefore be considered unfair for a union to prevent even a new member from standing for the committee of a small local union branch.

But it might not be unreasonable for the rules to stipulate, particularly in a complex industry, that no one can stand for president until he has been in the union for some years.

It is also lawful for the rules to bar members who do not pay a political levy from any office where they would administer the political fund.

### Contributing to political funds
A union cannot spend money on party politics from its ordinary funds: the cash must come from a special political levy. Any member who does not wish to contribute can contract out of doing so by completing a form obtainable from union offices or officials.

### The law against 'kangaroo courts'
Most unions give their officials powers to discipline members who break union rules. Usually, penalties can be imposed, including fines, suspension and expulsion.

Loss of union membership can have serious consequences, especially in cases where a union has exclusive rights to bargain with the management. By expelling a member, a union can effectively deprive him of any say in its proposals about pay and conditions.

The law therefore lays down a number of conditions which a union must observe in taking disciplinary action against members.

A union is not entitled to try a member in what is sometimes known as a 'kangaroo court'. In such a 'court', a member would be brought before a hastily summoned meeting and faced with charges of which he had been given no previous warning. He might then be tried on the spot—sometimes by his accusers—and fined, suspended or expelled.

To prevent this sort of injustice, the Act says that any charges against a member must be set out in writing and given to him in time for him to prepare a defence.

If the matter is complex it is not satisfactory for a union to give the member, say, ten minutes or a quarter of an hour in which to put his defence. The time given must be reasonable in all the circumstances.

Furthermore, the body which is set up to hear the case should not include people who may be personally involved in the dispute.

These are among the principles of natural justice which apply to the procedures by which decisions are arrived at. These principles covered union disciplinary procedures even before the passing of the Act.

Once the case against the member has been heard, together with his defence, the findings of the body set up to hear the case must be given to the member in writing.

If the union rules state that appeals must be made within a certain time, no penalty—such as a fine or suspension—may be enforced until the time limit for appealing has expired or the appeal has been heard.

SUBSCRIPTION ARREARS These rules do not apply if the reason for ending a worker's membership is his failure to pay his subscriptions. In this case, the union is obliged only to give the member reasonable notice that his membership is being ended and to set out its reasons for taking this action.

Any organisation or individual who takes any action or threatens any action contrary to these guiding principles is guilty of an unfair industrial practice. The worker who feels he has been unfairly treated can then claim compensation from the union. □ How workers can complain against a trade union, p. 622.

**Special protection in registered unions**
Under the Industrial Relations Act, a trade union can register with the Chief Registrar of Trade Unions and Employers' Associations. To find out if a union is registered contact a union official or ask at the local office of the Department of Employment.

Registration gives the union certain legal rights—for example, the right to secure proper recognition in collective bargaining—in return for certain legal controls over its rules. These controls are designed to ensure that all its members have adequate information about the union's activities and finances and that they have the right to elect officials and, if necessary, vote the governing body out of office.

The rules of a registered union must cover 12 major points. They must:
1. Make it possible for the governing body of the union to be removed—by laying down a specific length to a term of office or providing for elections to be held at fixed intervals.
2. Lay down rules for the election, appointment and removal of officers and officials.
3. Set out the powers given to the union's governing body.
4. State the procedure under which the rules themselves can be changed.
5. Set out the way in which union elections are to be held, and state who is eligible to vote.
6. Lay down a procedure which must be followed if a ballot is taken.
7. State the amount of union contributions and the penalties which can be imposed on a member who falls into arrears or fails to pay.
8. Describe the conduct which can lead to disciplinary action, together with the nature of and procedure for the disciplinary action.
9. Set out regulations for keeping properly audited financial records, and allow members to inspect the books and financial records.
10. Lay down what happens if the union is dissolved.
11. List the officials who can instigate industrial action and specify the circumstances when they can do so.
12. Specify a procedure whereby members can complain about officials' breaches of the rules.

In addition to complying with these regulations, every union must make an annual report to its members about its activities.

Organisations and associations other than trade unions which represent people working in a particular field can apply to be entered on a special register if they negotiate terms and conditions of employment for their members.

Such organisations and associations could, for example, include the British Medical Association or the British Veterinary Association.

Once these organisations are registered, their members have most of the same rights and obligations as trade-union members.

**When the rule book is ignored**
As well as the protection given by the 1971 Act, every member or ex-member of a registered or unregistered union has the right to complain to the ordinary courts if his union does not comply with its rule book. This procedure, which existed before 1971, may be the only course open to members of an

unregistered union, for the industrial tribunals can consider breaches of a rule book only if they are also contrary to the guiding principles of the Act.

► MUSICIAN WHO WAS EXPELLED *Mr Bonsor, a musician, was 52 weeks in arrears with his union subscriptions. This entitled the union to expel him, but the expulsion was carried out by the local branch secretary and not, as the rule book laid down, by the branch committee. Mr Bonsor's widow later brought an action against the union for damages.*
DECISION *The court held that the union was in breach of contract and awarded his widow* *damages to cover the earnings he had lost by not being able to work as a musician. (Bonsor v. Musicians' Union.)*◄

### Resigning from the union

In the past the rules of a few unions made a member who wanted to resign follow such a complicated procedure that he seemed virtually unable to leave the union voluntarily.

The law now lets a man end his membership at any time, on giving notice and meeting any reasonable conditions. But in an agency or closed shop, he must go on paying the equivalent of his subscription. ☐ The law on union membership, p. 618.

---

## How workers can complain against a trade union

COMPLAINTS can be made against a registered or unregistered union by members or former members who object to the way in which it is run, and by non-members who consider they have been wrongly refused membership. The law gives them the right, as a last resort, to have their complaints heard by an independent body.

First, however, a person with a grievance against a registered union may take the matter up in the way set out in the union rules. If, when this has been done, he still feels that he has been unfairly treated, he can ask the Chief Registrar of Trade Unions and Employers' Associations to make an investigation. Alternatively, he can apply to the Chief Registrar direct, without first going through the union's own appeals procedure.

A worker must make his request for an investigation within four weeks of the action about which he is complaining, within four weeks of its coming to his notice, or within four weeks of exhausting the union procedure for hearing complaints. The Registrar can extend the time limits if he is satisfied that there are special reasons for doing so—if, for instance, the worker has been unable to take action through illness or injury.

The Registrar investigates the complaint and makes a report of his findings to the worker and to the union. If he finds that the complaint is justified, he tries to promote a settlement. For example, he may find that a union member has been suspended from membership in breach of the rules, and may try to settle the dispute by discussions with both sides, perhaps suggesting that the union should lift the suspension and pay compensation to the member. If a settlement is not reached the Registrar can pass the matter to an industrial tribunal. In serious cases he may refer it to the Industrial Relations Court.

A worker who is a member of an unregistered trade union can complain to an industrial tribunal. This direct procedure can also be used by members of registered unions, without first complaining to the Registrar.

A worker must complete the correct form, obtainable from the local office of the Department of Employment, and return it to them. He will then be told of the date of the hearing. ☐ Appearing before a tribunal, p. 735.

Whether the case is referred to the tribunal by the Registrar or directly by the individual concerned, the remedies are the same.

Where a case is decided in favour of the worker the tribunal can order the union to pay him compensation and also any expenses he may have incurred. The amount of compensation is limited to 104 weeks' pay and the maximum pay considered is £40 a week so that the maximum a worker could be awarded is £4160.

If a dispute has been taken to the Industrial Relations Court, the court has the power to order the union concerned to refrain from acting wrongly and to insist that it does not repeat its action.

If a member of a registered or unregistered trade union feels that the rule book has not been observed, he can also take the matter to the ordinary courts. This may, however, be an expensive and lengthy procedure and he should first consult a solicitor.

# How the law controls collective bargaining

*Dealing with inter-union disputes*
*Finding better ways to settle grievances*

*The employee's right to information*
*Making agreements legally binding*

MOST disputes between employers and their workers are settled by discussion, without reaching the open conflict of strikes or lock-outs. This process of negotiation between unions and management is known as collective bargaining.

In order to encourage the peaceful settlement of disputes, the Industrial Relations Act 1971 lays down guidelines for the conduct of collective bargaining. The Act:
**1.** Establishes procedures for avoiding disputes between registered unions themselves—for example, disputes over which union is to represent the workers in a company.
**2.** Lays down procedures for settling disputes between registered unions and employers.
**3.** Encourages registered unions and employers to make agreements legally binding.
**4.** Establishes the right of employees to basic information about the company or firm for which they work.

### Dealing with inter-union disputes
When more than one union claims to represent the same group of workers in a firm, there is danger of industrial unrest.

When this situation arises, the employers or a registered trade union can inform the Secretary for Employment that they intend to ask the Industrial Relations Court to settle the dispute. He can try to settle it himself, but if he fails, it will be referred to the court. The Secretary also has the power to refer a dispute to the court after consulting the employer and the unions.

An employer, a registered union or the Secretary for Employment all have the right to ask the court to decide which group of workers has terms of employment that can be determined at the same negotiations. This group is known as a bargaining unit.

In addition, the union may ask for the right to take part in negotiations on behalf of the employees in a bargaining unit. The union may go further and suggest that it should be recognised as having exclusive bargaining rights. It would then be known as the sole bargaining agent.

If, after hearing the arguments from both sides, the Industrial Relations Court feels that no further progress can be made by discussion, it may refer the question to the Commission for Industrial Relations.

The Commission is a body established under the Industrial Relations Act to assist both employers and registered unions in working out ways of settling industrial disputes.

Disputes in which the help of the Commission is needed may occur where an employer is unwilling to recognise more than one union, or where bargaining is fragmented because there are many large unions in the company.

The Commission investigates the dispute and may hold a hearing in public or in private at which witnesses give evidence and the unions and employers present their cases.

The Commission may recommend that a sole bargaining agency be established, but its recommendation takes effect only after the employer or the union has applied to the court to make it binding. This must be done within six months.

The court asks the Commission to arrange a ballot of all the employees in the bargaining unit. If a majority votes in favour, the court must make an order directing that only the union in question can be recognised by the employer as a bargaining agent for those employees.

If at any time a group of workers is not satisfied with the union which represents them in the bargaining unit, it can ask the court to reconsider the matter. The court cannot make an order covering the same workers within two years. If it has already made an order, more than two years previously, the workers' application must be supported by two-fifths of all employees in the bargaining unit. In all other applications, a request from one-fifth of the workers is enough.

While a dispute over the right to take part in collective bargaining is being considered by either the Commission or the Industrial Relations Court, neither employer nor union must bring pressure to settle the dispute. To do so is an unfair industrial practice, and may give grounds for a claim for compensation or for a court order. □ Claiming compensation over an industrial dispute, p. 627.

Once the court has decided that a registered

union is sole bargaining agent, it is also an unfair practice for the employer to negotiate with any other union over the pay and conditions of workers in the sole agent's bargaining unit, or to refuse to engage in serious collective bargaining with the proper union.

It is unfair, too, for a union without bargaining rights to bring pressure on an employer to negotiate with it, or not to negotiate with a union which has bargaining rights. Again, compensation may be claimed by anyone who suffers loss as a result of unfair actions of this kind. ☐ Claiming compensation over an industrial dispute, p. 627.

### Finding better ways to settle grievances

In some companies and industries, the machinery for dealing with workers' grievances or for settling industrial disputes is poor. There may be frequent strikes, lock-outs and other forms of industrial action. In some cases there may not even be an agreed procedure for settling disputes.

In these circumstances, the Industrial Relations Court can be asked to inquire into the matter by the Secretary for Employment, a registered trade union, or an employer. If the court believes that the system is defective, it refers the question to the Commissioner for Industrial Relations.

The Commission makes an investigation and submits a report to the court, setting out its recommendations for improving the disputes machinery. Copies of the report are sent to the organisations involved in the dispute.

The Commission may also try to arrange peace talks between those involved. If these talks fail, the Industrial Relations Court can make an order enforcing a remedy.

Once a negotiating procedure has been laid down by the court, both sides must make genuine attempts to use it. If either fails to do so, it is guilty of an unfair industrial practice and can be made to pay compensation.

### The employee's right to information

If collective bargaining is to be successful, trade-union representatives often need information about the company with which they are negotiating. For example, if they are discussing a bargain under which their members will be given a pay increase in return for higher productivity, the unions will need to know production figures and costs.

The employer is therefore obliged by law to give such information to registered unions, and a union which is refused relevant information without good reason can complain to the Industrial Relations Court. If the court upholds the complaint, it can grant the union the right to refer a claim for improved terms and conditions to the Arbitration Board. Any award it makes is binding on the employer.

ANNUAL STATEMENTS In any firm where more than 500 people are employed, the employer also has a duty to issue an annual written statement to his workers not more than six months after the end of the period to which it refers. The information that must be included is laid down in regulations made by the Secretary for Employment.

The employer does not have to reveal information which is against the interests of national security or which has been given to him in confidence. He need not give information about an individual if it is prejudicial to someone who has not agreed to its being revealed; and apart from matters concerned with collective bargaining, the employer does not have to give any facts which might prejudice his business.

### Making agreements legally binding

When unions and management bargain over wages, conditions of work and rules for solving industrial disputes, the terms they agree may be set out in two types of agreement.

**1.** Those parts of the deal which relate to the individual worker's conditions of employment may be incorporated into each worker's contract of employment.

**2.** The full terms they have agreed may be included in a collective agreement signed by management and trade-union representatives.

If a worker subsequently breaks the terms of his contract, the employer has grounds for legal action. ☐ Leaving a job, p. 639.

If the union breaks a term of its agreement with the management (by calling a strike without using the agreed procedure for settling disputes, for example) the employer may take legal action.

A written collective agreement is assumed to be legally binding unless it contains a statement saying that it is not. Similarly, any decision of a negotiating body established under voluntary negotiating procedures is legally binding unless both sides agree that it is not.

Any party which breaks an agreement which is legally enforceable, or fails to take all reasonable steps to prevent officials and members from breaking such an agreement, is guilty of an unfair industrial practice and may be made to pay compensation to those affected. Such claims can be heard only by the Industrial Relations Court. ☐ Claiming compensation over an industrial dispute, p. 627.

# Taking industrial action

*Industrial and non-industrial disputes*
*When a strike must be postponed*
*Holding ballots on strike action*

*Sympathy strikes and 'blacking' goods*
*The right to picket*
*Intimidation and conspiracy*

ANYONE who feels he has a grievance against his employer is entitled to go on strike or take other industrial action, as long as he has not agreed in his contract to refrain from doing so. The law does not force a worker to remain at work against his will, and he does not lay himself open to legal action if he follows the correct procedure.

PROCEDURE FOR STRIKING Anyone who wishes to strike has a legal obligation to follow any dispute procedure laid down in his contract or included in a trade union agreement by which he is bound. If no such procedure is laid down, or if the procedure is exhausted, the worker must give notice of his intention to strike, either personally or through his trade union. The period required is the same as if he were resigning. ☐ Leaving a job, p. 639.

Failure to follow this procedure is technically a breach of contract, and gives the employer the right to claim damages.

**Industrial and non-industrial disputes**
Different rules apply to industrial action when it is in support of an industrial dispute and when it concerns non-industrial issues.

INDUSTRIAL DISPUTES In law, an industrial dispute is one that involves workers *and* employers and is concerned with terms and conditions of work, engagement and dismissal, demarcation and procedure agreements.

Registered trade unions (or employers'

---

## The legal consequences of going on strike

IMPRISONMENT Legal action cannot be taken against anyone simply for going on strike. But if a court order has been made in respect of a particular strike—for example, ordering a cooling-off period—any strike *organiser* who disobeys it can be fined or imprisoned for contempt of court.

DISMISSAL Employees who go on strike and are then dismissed for that reason cannot normally claim compensation for unfair dismissal, though there are exceptions. ☐ The law on union membership, p. 618.

STRIKE PAY An employee on strike will not usually be given strike pay by his union unless the strike is official. Strike pay is given at the union's discretion.

UNEMPLOYMENT BENEFIT An employee on strike is not entitled to unemployment benefit. Anyone out of work because of a strike can qualify for benefit only if he can prove that he is not taking any part in the strike; that he is not helping to finance it; that he does not belong to the class of workers engaged in it— those employed at his place of work immediately before the stoppage; and that he does not stand to benefit from it. ☐ Qualifying for unemployment benefit, p. 650.

SUPPLEMENTARY BENEFIT An employee who is out of work because of a strike cannot get supplementary benefit for himself, but allowances may be paid for his wife, children and other dependants. Any strike pay he receives will be taken into account when these allowances are calculated. A striker may also obtain a loan from the supplementary benefit authorities in the first 15 days back at work. ☐ State help in hardship, p. 550.

REDUNDANCY PAYMENTS An employee who is dismissed because of redundancy and then goes on strike during his period of notice may be required to work the remaining days of his notice after the strike.

If he refuses to do so he may find that he has forfeited his right to redundancy pay.

If the strike occurs during a period of notice given by the employer, the contract ends with the strike and no wages are due afterwards. If the employee gives notice and then goes on strike, he is not entitled to pay for any part of the notice period.

Strike periods are deducted when assessing length of employment for redundancy pay, but do not break continuity. ☐ Claiming compensation for redundancy, p. 645.

associations) and their authorised officials are entitled to induce others to break their contracts in furtherance of such a dispute.

But if any person or group of people not authorised by a registered trade union tries to persuade workers to break their contracts—if, for example, a shop steward defies a registered union or if an unregistered organisation starts a strike—those responsible commit what is termed an unfair industrial practice and can be sued for compensation by anyone affected.

The same applies to any unauthorised person or group which persuades someone to break a commercial contract—say, by persuading suppliers or customers to stop dealing with the employer in the dispute.

Any registered trade union (or employers' association) which decides to make its members' unofficial and unlawful actions official at a later stage is allowed to do so without becoming liable to pay compensation. But it may have to pay compensation for the period the strike was unofficial, if it did not try to stop the unlawful industrial action.

The law covers strikes staged to compel an employer to dismiss an employee unfairly, to agree to a pre-entry closed shop or to stop negotiating with a sole bargaining agent approved by the Industrial Relations Court.

Organising a strike in defiance of an enforceable trade union agreement is also unfair.

It is even an unfair practice to threaten to organise a strike for any of these reasons—or to organise some lesser form of action, such as a go-slow. Organising a work-to-rule, however, provided that it does not involve any breach of the workers' contracts, is allowed.

NON-INDUSTRIAL DISPUTES A dispute between groups of workers or employers, or one about political issues or personal disagreements, is classed in law as non-industrial.

Anyone who organises a strike or other industrial action, even if notice is given, to pursue a non-industrial dispute loses any protection given by the Industrial Relations Act and may be guilty of unfair industrial practice. Those who suffer as a result may be able to claim compensation from the organisers, or seek a court order forbidding the unfair practice.

### When a strike must be postponed
There are also times when even a registered trade union can be required by law to postpone a strike. In an emergency, the Government is entitled to apply for a court order instructing the organisers of a strike to defer taking industrial action. This order may be sought for one of two purposes.

1. To provide a 'cooling-off' period during which further attempts can be made to find a solution to the dispute.
2. To give time for a secret ballot to be taken among the workers concerned to discover the extent of support for strike action.

In either case the court has powers only to order strike *leaders* to delay organising industrial action. It has no power over the activities of individual strikers.

The grounds for asking for a cooling-off period or a ballot are the same: that the strike is likely to damage the national economy, endanger the lives or health of a substantial number of people, threaten national security or produce public disorder.

### The 'cooling-off' period
When the Government feels that the necessary grounds are present, the Secretary for Employment can make an application to the Industrial Relations Court for an order to prevent anyone organising a strike or other industrial action for a 'cooling-off' period or periods up to a maximum of 60 days.

If the court is satisfied that there is a threat to the nation's economy, order or security, or to the health of the community, it issues the order which names those responsible for calling or inducing the strike.

If anyone named disobeys the order, he is in contempt of court and—like anyone who fails to comply with any court order—he can be fined or imprisoned until he apologises.

Anyone else who tries to *organise* industrial action—for example, unofficial committees of militants—is also in contempt.

If, however, ordinary workers decide of their own accord to go on strike despite the order and the notices issued by their union executives, no action can be taken against them or the union leaders.

If at the end of the cooling-off period the unions still decide to go ahead with the strike, they are entitled to do so unless a secret ballot is ordered.

### Holding ballots on strike action
Sometimes when a strike is called—even after a cooling-off period—it is doubtful whether the action has the support of most of the workers involved. If the Secretary for Employment thinks that such industrial action might threaten the nation's economy or security or public health or order, he can ask the court to order suspension of the strike until a secret ballot of members is held to find out whether there is a majority in favour.

The court may ask the Commission on

Industrial Relations, or a union, to supervise the ballot. The result of the vote is reported first to the Commission on Industrial Relations, which makes a report to the Industrial Relations Court. All the court can do is to publish the result of the ballot. It cannot compel the trade union to abide by the result unless the rules of that union lay down that

the results of ballots are binding. But if a ballot shows the majority of workers are against industrial action a union is unlikely to go ahead.

**Sympathy strikes and 'blacking' goods**

Sympathy strikes—where employees in one place take action in support of colleagues elsewhere—are lawful, provided that those

---

## Claiming compensation over an industrial dispute

ANYONE guilty of an unfair practice during an industrial dispute may face claims for compensation from those who suffer, or are likely to suffer, as a result. Claims, which are usually decided by the Industrial Relations Court, can be made by employers, trade unions and occasionally by individuals.

CLAIMS BY EMPLOYERS An employer might claim compensation:

Against a union which breaks a collective agreement or fails to take all reasonable steps to prevent a breach of the agreement—unless the agreement contains a clause specifically stating that it is not legally binding.

Against a union which brings pressure on him to negotiate when another union has sole bargaining rights.

Against anyone not authorised by a registered trade union who incites any sort of industrial action.

Against any individual or organisation which incites industrial action in support of unauthorised or unfair industrial action.

Against any individual or organisation which declares 'black' his goods and services if they are not involved in the dispute.

CLAIMS BY UNIONS A trade union might claim compensation:

Against an employer who breaks a collective agreement—unless the agreement specifically states that it is not legally binding.

Against an employer who refuses to supply information about his company which is essential to productivity bargaining.

If the union is recognised as sole bargaining agent, it might also claim compensation against an employer who negotiates with another union; or against another union which brings pressure on the employer to negotiate.

CLAIMS BY INDIVIDUALS Occasionally an individual will also be entitled to claim compensation—for example, against union members who picket his home, or a union which organises such action.

Also, anyone who suffers from unfair industrial action can sue for compensation or apply for an order against those responsible.

LIMITS OF COMPENSATION Most claims for compensation are decided by the Industrial Relations Court, although some cases are decided by an industrial tribunal.

Compensation is based on the losses incurred by the person or organisation making the claim. These include expenses and any benefits which might have been expected if the unfair industrial practice had not taken place.

But the amount awarded must take into account any action by the person claiming which contributed to the situation.

The amount of compensation that can be awarded against an employer is unlimited. A limit is imposed, however, on the amount which can be awarded to an individual—no more than £4160, based on a maximum wage of £40 a week for 104 weeks.

A limit is also imposed on the amount which can be awarded against a registered trade union, depending on the size of the union. A union with fewer than 5000 members cannot be made to pay more than £5000; for those with between 5000 and 25,000 members the limit is £25,000; those with membership of between 25,000 and 100,000 pay a maximum of £50,000; unions with more than 100,000 members have a top limit of £100,000.

There is no limit on the amount that can be claimed from an unregistered union.

**Action in other courts**

Court actions over matters not covered by the Industrial Relations Act—for example, over allegations of conspiracy or intimidation—are usually heard in other divisions of the High Court, or in the county court.

Anyone affected can apply for an injunction to forbid the action complained of, or can seek damages. There is no automatic limit to the amount that can be awarded.

involved give proper strike notice and provided that the original strikers have a genuine industrial dispute and are not pursuing unlawful objectives.

But if the object of the sympathy strike is to force an employer who is not directly involved in the original dispute to break his commercial contracts with an employer who is, then the sympathy action is unfair.

In the same way, if goods are blacked to stop a firm that is not involved from delivering or obtaining goods from an employer who is involved, any union which orders the blacking is acting unlawfully. All those directly responsible—officials, shop stewards and the union itself—may be made to pay compensation individually.

But if the supplier or purchaser of the goods is giving direct support to the strike-hit employer, blacking is not unlawful. Companies within the same group are not necessarily taken to be acting in direct support of each other.

Where blacking is directed only against the employer in the dispute, it is allowed provided that it is started by a registered union or its officials.

### The right to picket

No one must be forced to go on strike against his will. But there is nothing in law to stop strikers trying to persuade workmates to join them. For this reason, the law allows peaceful picketing under certain conditions. A group of strikers can picket a factory where a strike is taking place to persuade employees still working to join the strike. But they are not entitled to picket to further an unfair industrial practice—to persuade workers to join a sympathy strike, for example.

Workers on a lawful picket may give information to non-strikers—such as the facts of the dispute—and seek information from them, perhaps about their reasons for remaining at work. But they must use only peaceful persuasion, and must never picket a worker's home. Pickets run the risk of prosecution for other offences. ☐ Meetings, marches and demonstrations, p. 672.

Often the police are present when picketing takes place, and they are entitled to use their discretion in directing pickets if they fear a breach of the peace. Pickets who disobey reasonable police requests may be charged with obstructing the police.

➤ THE PICKETS WHO WENT TOO FAR *During an official strike by draughtsmen at the English Electric Company Ltd factory at East Lanca-* *shire Road, Liverpool, in 1964, about 40 pickets walked round and round in a circle in a service road which was part of the highway near the main entrance to the factory.*

*The police asked the strikers' leader, Harold Kenneth Tynan, to call off the pickets. He refused to do so and was arrested and charged with obstructing the police in the execution of their duty.*

*Mr Tynan pleaded that since picketing was specifically allowed under the Trade Disputes Act 1907 he could not be convicted.*

DECISION *Mr Tynan was found guilty. The court held that the circling manoeuvre obstructed the highway and was a nuisance in law.*

*It therefore went beyond the provisions of the Trade Disputes Act. (Tynan v. Balmer.)* ◄

### Intimidation and conspiracy

Anyone who tries to bring pressure during any type of dispute by threatening to commit a civil wrong, such as trespass, lays himself open to claims for damages for intimidation. He may also be liable for damages if he threatens to commit a crime.

Claims for damages or for an injunction forbidding the unlawful action can be made by anyone who suffers.

Again, if two or more people agree to do something illegal—such as destroying property—they may face claims for damages for conspiracy. They may also be liable if they conspire to commit an unfair industrial practice, such as picketing a worker's home.

NON-INDUSTRIAL DISPUTES In disputes which are not classified in law as industrial, workers can face further claims for damages.

Anyone who induces a breach of employment or commercial contract by bringing pressure on a party to that contract lays himself open to claims for damages.

Anyone who threatens to break his contract, or to induce others to break their contracts, may have to pay damages for intimidation. In a non-industrial dispute, he does not have to threaten to commit a crime or a civil wrong other than breach of contract to be liable.

Two or more people who agree to do something which will harm another person are liable for damages—even if such an act would not be unlawful if done by one of them alone. They will not be liable, however, if they are acting to protect what the courts call a legitimate trade interest—such as conditions of work or wage levels.

Claims are usually heard in the High Court. But if they involve allegations of unfair industrial practice, the claim is transferred to the Industrial Relations Court.

# What to do if you are injured

*Reporting the accident*
*Getting a medical certificate*
*Gathering evidence*

WHEN an employee is injured at work his interests are protected by law in two ways. He can claim State benefit under the Industrial Injuries Scheme for any accident which happens 'in the course of and arising out of his employment', whether the accident was the employer's fault or his own. And he can sue his employer for damages—provided he can prove that the accident was wholly or partly the fault of either the employer or another employee for whose carelessness the employer was responsible.

Whichever course he eventually decides to take—and he may follow both—there are certain steps that any injured employee should take as soon as possible after an accident to protect his future interests.

**Reporting the accident**
An accident should be reported as soon as possible to the employer, or to someone in authority—for example, a supervisor or safety officer. If the worker is too badly injured to report the accident himself, he should ask someone else to do it for him.

All factories, mines and quarries where ten or more people are employed must have an accident book or some form of record of

## Recording an accident

The Factories Act requires that where ten or more people work in a factory an injury must be recorded in an accident book. But where there is no accident book, an injured employee must record accident details in a letter to his employer

**1.** State the basis of any future claim—that the accident happened in the course of the job

**2.** Give your name, home address and position or job

**3.** Say when and where the accident happened

**4.** State how the accident happened—but do not suggest you were in any way responsible

**5.** Give a full account of the injuries—and leave open the question of any future developments or complications

---

The Manager
Supership Stores Ltd
54 High Street, Exworth

Exworth Hospital
Exworth, Essex
August 1, 1971

Dear Sir,

I wish to notify you that I have been injured in an accident in the course of my employment with you.

My name: James Edward Clark.
My address: 18, Acacia Terrace, Exworth.
My occupation: Shop assistant.
Date of accident: July 25, 1971
Time: Approximately 11.45 a.m.
Place of accident: Store-room.
Cause of accident: Slipping off an insecurely fastened ladder while stock-taking.
Nature of injuries: Bruises and lacerations on the right arm, bruises and sprains on legs.
A final diagnosis of injuries cannot be made at this stage.

Yours faithfully
J. E. Clark.

accidents. Details of accidents must be entered in the book; this is a requirement of the Factories Act 1961.

A worker who is too badly injured to write the details in the book himself should ask someone else—a friend, a workmate, or a trade-union official—to make sure that the details are recorded.

Where there is no accident book—in many shops and offices, for example—or where the employee cannot arrange to have details entered in the book, he should write a letter, or get someone else to write, informing his employer of the accident.

Any fatal accident, or any accident which causes an employee to be off work for more than three days, must be reported by the employer to the district factory inspector or, for shops and offices, the inspector appointed by the local authority.

### Getting a medical certificate

A worker injured in an industrial accident should see his doctor even if the injury does not seem serious enough to keep him off work. The visit is necessary in case there are later complications which result in a claim.

If the employee is unable to work because of the injury, his doctor will give him a medical certificate with which he can claim from the Social Security office both sickness benefit and injury benefit. Sickness benefit is paid after three days off work; it is replaced by the higher-rate industrial-injury benefit if his claim is successful. ☐ How the State helps the injured, p. 632; Claiming sickness benefit, p. 602.

If the injury is not serious and the doctor thinks that the employee can return to his job within a week, he normally issues a 'closed' certificate, stating the date on which the employee should be fit to return. Otherwise he issues an 'open' certificate, which covers up to 28 days and can be renewed.

GOING BACK TO WORK An employee who goes back to work before the date given on a closed certificate must inform the Social Security office immediately. If he has an open certificate and is still off work after 28 days, he needs to get another certificate and send it to the Social Security office.

When he does return to work, he should always have a closed certificate, which the doctor issues when he has recovered.

### Gathering evidence

If an employee is likely to take legal action after an accident, the employer or the firm's insurance company usually carries out an investigation into what happened, and compiles a detailed report.

The injured worker is unlikely to be shown this report even if he asks. But he should gather his own evidence to establish any case he might eventually want to make.

A badly injured worker should not wait until he is fit enough to collect evidence. He should try to get a workmate or perhaps a trade-union representative or solicitor to make enquiries for him.

Either the injured worker, or his solicitor, can then make a realistic assessment of his chances of success if he decides to sue the employer for damages.

TAKING PHOTOGRAPHS It may be worth hiring a professional photographer to take photographs of the scene of the accident. Remember, however, that the employer is under no obligation to allow outsiders to inspect his premises or property, or to take photographs. But if his permission is asked—perhaps through a trade-union representative—soon after the accident, he is less likely to refuse the request.

Should permission be withheld, the employee can still go ahead. Provided he does not force an entry or enter the premises at night, the worst that can happen is that he can be asked to leave. Alternatively, he can apply to the High Court for an order permitting inspection and photography.

If the accident involves, say, unguarded machinery or faulty stairs, or arises from the layout of the factory, make sure the photographs give an all round view of the scene of the accident. Choose a photographer who agrees in advance to appear in court if necessary. He may be required to verify the photographic evidence of the accident area. Keep a note of his name and address.

Notes on the accident or plans of the scene made soon after it has happened can also be useful. A court is more likely to pay attention to a statement made at the time or soon after, when the incident is still fresh in the memory. Most cases are not heard by the courts until several years after the accident occurred.

LISTING WITNESSES Names and addresses of witnesses should be obtained as soon as possible—if there is a delay it may not be possible to trace them. If the injured worker takes legal advice he should give a list of witnesses to his solicitor so that statements can be taken.

The injured worker, or his solicitor, can make a reluctant witness attend court by applying to the court for a witness summons, known as a subpoena.

## Financial help for an injured worker

Anyone in an accident at work may qualify for State benefits. While off work, he seeks industrial injury or sickness benefit. For long-term effects, he claims disablement benefit. ☐ How the State helps the injured, p. 632; Claiming sickness benefit, p. 602; Claiming disablement benefit, p. 635.

He may also seek compensation from his employer. ☐ Suing the employer, p. 636.

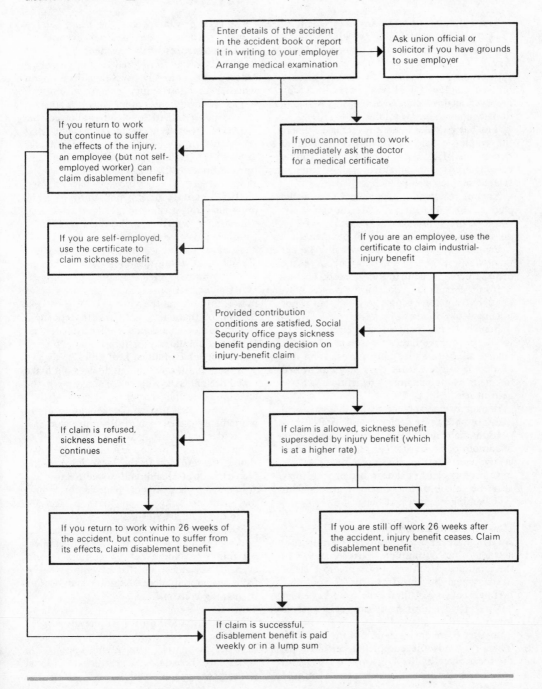

# How the State helps the injured

*How to claim injury benefit*
*What to do if a claim is rejected*
*How claims are decided*

*Accidents 'in the course of employment'*
*Accidents 'arising out of employment'*
*When the employee is to blame*

A N employee injured in an accident at work can claim a weekly National Insurance industrial-injury benefit. Almost all employees, including unpaid apprentices, are covered for injury benefit, but self-employed workers are not. They can, however, claim sickness benefit. □ What to do if you are injured, p. 629.

The basic rate of benefit is increased where the employee has a wife, children or other dependants. He may also be able to claim an earnings-related supplement. □ Earnings-related supplement, p. 603.

Anyone receiving injury benefit will not be paid sickness benefit as well—though if his employer pays his wages while he is away, he does not lose the injury-benefit payment.

Payment of injury benefit—which is higher than sickness benefit—is not linked to the insured person's contribution record.

Injury benefit is paid during public holidays, but not for a single day's absence, nor is it paid for Sundays.

Benefit is not paid in any circumstances for the first three days of absence. However, anyone likely to suffer hardship through loss of income in these three days may be entitled to claim supplementary benefit. □ State help in hardship, p. 550.

Benefit is not subject to income tax, and does not have to be declared on Tax Returns.

Industrial-injury benefit can be paid for a maximum of 26 weeks. Anyone still off work at the end of that time as a result of his injuries can claim sickness benefit. He may also be eligible for disablement benefit. □ Claiming disablement benefit, p. 635.

### How to claim injury benefit
An employee off work because of an industrial accident should complete Parts A and B of the National Health Service medical certificate, which he gets from his doctor. The first part covers a claim for the sickness benefit he may receive if there is any delay before injury benefit is allowed.

In Part B, he enters details of the accident. Then he sends the completed certificate to the local office of the Department of Health and Social Security. If the person injured consults a private doctor, he must send a private certificate and a brief account of the circumstances of the accident.

All claims are considered by the insurance officer, who normally gives his decision on whether to allow injury benefit within two weeks. During this time, sickness benefit can be paid; and if the claim is allowed, the difference between sickness benefit and the higher injury benefit is paid later. However, if the claim is refused, the applicant can continue to draw sickness benefit.

TIME LIMIT If the worker has claimed neither sickness benefit nor injury benefit previously, he is allowed 21 days, excluding Sundays, in which to make the claim. If he has previously received either benefit, he must make his claim within six days. If claims are not made within the time allowed, benefit may be reduced or lost.

MINOR ACCIDENTS Many people receive minor injuries in the course of their work. Not all of them may seem worth reporting, but to protect his rights to benefit later, an employee should report any injury which is painful or which fails to heal quickly.

If he does so, even though he does not make a claim right away, he can claim later if the condition becomes worse.

In these cases the employee should apply immediately, or as soon as the injury worsens, for a declaration that the accident was an industrial one. The application form (BI 95) should be returned to the local office of the Department of Health and Social Security.

Even if a claim is not made at this point, the insurance officer can make a decision while the facts are fresh.

Such decisions are filed and can be used if injury or disablement benefit is claimed later. An employee should claim for injury benefit even if he is uncertain that his injuries arose from his employment. Nothing can be lost by making a claim.

### What to do if a claim is rejected
When the insurance officer disallows a claim, he writes to the claimant, giving reasons. He also sends the address of the local National Insurance appeals tribunal, to which the

employee can appeal. It costs nothing to do so. Even if the claimant is unsuccessful, he does not have to pay the costs of the hearing as he would if he lost a case in a civil court. He can even claim expenses (according to a scale) for attending the hearing.

The insurance officer may also refer a claim to the tribunal if he is in doubt about it. If the dispute is about the claimant's past earnings, it must first be referred to the Secretary of State for Social Services for his decision. If an appeal is then made to the tribunal, it will be heard only if the chairman of the tribunal agrees.

Appeals must first be made in writing, giving reasons for contesting the decision. An employee's case will be strengthened if he can refer to similar claims that have been allowed. Such information can be obtained from the local Social Security office. Claimants can often seek the help of their trade union in making a claim, and at the hearing.

If the employee is not satisfied with the tribunal decision, he or his union can appeal, within three months, to the National Insurance Commissioner—an independent official.

An appeal to the commissioner is made in writing through the appeals tribunal. The insurance officer may also appeal. Before making such an appeal, an employee should take legal advice.

### How claims are decided

The question of blame does not affect industrial-injury claims. To succeed, the claimant need merely show that he is off work because of an accident 'arising out of and in the course of' his employment—generally, while the employee was at work and while he was carrying out his employer's business.

An accident, if it is to be the basis of a claim for benefit, must be a particular, unexpected happening which took place at a definite point in time. Normally, an injury must have been the result of a single event.

There are exceptions to the general rule, however, and some claims have succeeded where the employee has been able to prove that, although the injury developed as a result of repetitive work, it was in fact caused by a series of specific minor accidents.

Nervous shock—caused by seeing a fellow

---

## Claiming benefit for industrial disease

An employee is entitled to claim industrial-injury or disablement benefit if he becomes ill with one of a number of diseases which the State classes as 'industrial'—that is, caused by the work he does.

A list of these diseases is available from the Department of Health and Social Security. Each disease is linked only to certain industries, operations or processes. Claims are likely to be allowed only if the claimant contracted a particular disease while working in one of the specified industries.

HOW TO CLAIM The procedure for a claim begins with a medical certificate, which must be completed and returned to the Social Security office. To claim disablement benefit, complete Form BI 100B. A medical examination is then carried out by a doctor appointed by the Social Security office. If a claim is refused on medical grounds, a written appeal should be made within ten days to the local Social Security office. The claim will then be considered by a medical board consisting of two doctors.

If the claimant does not agree with the finding of the medical board, he has a right of appeal, within three months, to a medical tribunal. The decision of the medical-appeal tribunal is final on medical grounds; but if there has been an error on some point of law, an appeal can be made to an independent insurance commissioner appointed by the Crown.

If a claim for benefit is rejected on grounds other than medical—for example, that the employee has not worked in a job linked to that disease in the official list—an appeal can be made to the National Insurance appeals tribunal, again in writing, through the local Social Security office. If the claimant is still not satisfied, he can appeal to the commissioner.

WHEN BENEFIT STARTS Injury benefit for an industrial disease starts on the 'date of development'—the first day a claimant is away from work as a result of the disease. If disablement benefit is claimed, the 'date of development' is normally the day the disablement started. There can be a difference between the two, because an employee does not necessarily have to be off work or prevented from working to qualify for disablement benefit. Some of the benefit is likely to be lost if the employee delays in making the claim.

worker crushed in a machine, for example—is considered a personal injury.

Catching a cold at work does not qualify as an accident, even if it leads to a more serious illness. But injuries through freak weather conditions, if they are among normal risks of the job, can give rise to benefit.

▶ THE FARM WORKER WHO WAS KILLED BY LIGHTNING *A farm worker sheltered under an ash tree in the field where he was working when a thunderstorm began. He was struck by lightning and killed. His dependants claimed industrial death benefit.*
DECISION *The claim was allowed on the grounds that his job caused him to look for the nearest convenient shelter.* ◄

To qualify for industrial-injury benefit an employee must show that the accident was the main cause of his injury. In certain cases, expert medical evidence may be called for.

**Accidents 'in the course of employment'**
One of the tests of whether an accident happened 'in the course of employment' is if it occurred during normal working hours. This covers lunch and tea breaks or time spent going to the lavatory or washroom.

When the period of employment is broken by some activity outside working hours an employee may not be covered.

Similarly, if a person is working but breaks off for some purpose of his own, he can be disqualified from benefit.

An employee who goes to a part of the premises where he is not allowed can also find that he is not entitled to benefit.

In certain cases, accidents which happen outside specified working hours have been held to be 'in the course of employment'.

▶ THE CIVIL SERVANT WHO ARRIVED EARLY *A civil servant whose job required her to stand all day always caught an early train to work to avoid travelling in the rush-hour. She spent the time before she was due to start work reading at her desk. One morning, at about 7 a.m., she injured herself when trying to open her office window.*
DECISION *It was held that she was entitled to compensation, because her habit of arriving early was in the interests of her employers, since it enabled her to work more efficiently.* ◄

**Accidents 'arising out of employment'**
If an employee is injured while engaged in any activity connected with his work—even though it might not fall directly within the

scope of his employment—he might nevertheless be entitled to make a claim for industrial-injury benefit.

▶ TRADE-UNION MEETING WAS WORK *An employee claimed benefit after he was injured during a lunch-hour trade-union meeting which was held in his workshop.*
DECISION *Benefit was allowed. The union meeting, held with the employer's permission, related to his terms of employment.* ◄

EMERGENCIES If an employee is injured while helping to put out a fire at his employer's premises, or helping someone who is in danger, he can qualify for benefit if his action is in some way connected with his job.

▶ THE HELPER WHO WAS INJURED *A lorry driver stopped to assist a motorist whose car and caravan were across the road and apparently causing an obstruction. He was injured while returning to his lorry and claimed injury benefit.*
DECISION *His claim was allowed.* ◄

TRAVEL TO AND FROM WORK Going to and from work is not normally considered as being within the course of employment.

But if the employee travels in a vehicle provided by the employer, the situation is different. If, say, a minibus or a coach owned or provided by the employers carrying workers to and from their factory crashed, any of the firm's employees injured might be able to claim benefit.

If an employee drives a company car, van or lorry, and is allowed to use it to and from work, he is covered by the industrial-injuries scheme. An employee travelling on duty is entitled to benefit if he is in an accident.

A milkman injured in a crash on his rounds is covered. But if it happened as he was making an unofficial detour, he would not be.

When accommodation is provided for an employee, an accident which occurs on the employer's premises outside working hours may also give rise to a claim.

**When the employee is to blame**
Injuries caused by the misconduct, skylarking or negligence of another person during working hours give grounds for a claim for benefit. If the accident arose from the misconduct of the employee himself, he would be refused benefit.

An employee who takes an unnecessary risk—like jumping from a moving bus, or crossing a railway line in an unauthorised place—is acting outside the scope of his employment and will not receive benefit if he is injured while endangering himself in this way. Similarly, an employee who is hurt while doing something entirely for his own pleasure or convenience may not get benefit.

Extra duties taken on by an employee—for example where an operator mans a different machine from the one he was employed to work—may also be taken as not arising out of the employment.

Injuries arising from recreation during duty hours have also been judged as outside the scope of employment. A policeman was refused benefit after he was injured while playing in a football match for the police team during duty hours.

But some recreations have been held to be part of employment. For instance, firemen are expected to keep fit as part of their employment duty. In their case, even sports during permitted breaks have been held to be part of their employment.

---

## Claiming disablement benefit

ANYONE suffering from the effects of an injury at work or industrial disease may claim tax-free disablement benefit. In law, disablement includes the loss of a limb, an injury limiting physical activity, disfigurement, and the psychological consequence of injuries.

### When a worker can claim
A worker can claim disablement benefit:
1. If he has been off work, has drawn industrial injury benefit until it finishes after 26 weeks, and is still unfit for work.
2. If he has gone back to work, yet is still suffering from his injury or its effects.
3. If he is partially disabled, but not so seriously that he has to stop work altogether. In this case, he is not entitled to injury benefit, but can claim disablement benefit from the fourth day of his incapacity. If his disablement then gets worse and keeps him away from work, he is not entitled to injury benefit—only to sickness benefit, which is paid at a lower rate.

To claim disablement benefit the employee fills in a form available at Social Security offices—BI 100A, which covers accidents, or BI 100B, for industrial disease.

### How claims are decided
A medical board assesses the degree of disablement and how long it may last, but only after a ruling by an insurance officer—who also decides the amount of benefit payable—that the cause was industrial.

An appeal against the board's decision can be made within three months. An appeal against the insurance officer's decision must be lodged within 21 days. Further appeal is to the National Insurance Commissioner.

The medical board can decide that the claimant has suffered only partial disablement as a result of his accident. Or it may rule that he has suffered no disablement at all—in which case he is not entitled to benefit.

### How benefit is calculated
Disablement is worked out in percentages. Injuries such as loss of sight or both hands count as 100 per cent.

If disablement is assessed at less than 20 per cent, benefit is awarded as a lump sum payable, if desired, by instalments. Otherwise, benefit is paid as a pension.

### Additional allowances
Benefit can be increased by certain supplementary allowances in special circumstances.
SPECIAL HARDSHIP ALLOWANCE A person fit enough to work but unable to earn as much as he used to may get a special hardship allowance during rehabilitation or training.
UNEMPLOYABILITY SUPPLEMENT If a disabled person can earn only a tiny sum each year (from October, 1972, up to £234) he may claim an unemployability supplement.

Unemployability supplement and special hardship allowance are never paid together.
CONSTANT ATTENDANCE ALLOWANCE A person who is 100 per cent disabled and in need of constant attendance at home can claim this allowance in addition to his pension.
HOSPITAL TREATMENT ALLOWANCE A claimant in hospital for treatment can have his pension raised to the 100 per cent rate. But if he has been paid a lump sum, this is deducted.
SEVERE DISABLEMENT ALLOWANCE The severely disabled worker can claim an extra weekly fixed allowance.
ALLOWANCES FOR DEPENDANTS People receiving unemployability supplement or hospital treatment allowance may claim allowances for dependants.

# Suing the employer after an accident

*Dangers at the workplace*       *When safety precautions are ignored*
*Risks from workmates*            *The employee's right to special care*
*Dangerous tools and machinery*   *When the employee is also to blame*

An employee who has an accident at work is in a different position to a motorist involved in a road accident or a shopper who falls down the stairs of a department store. Their accidents owe nothing to any previous relationship between them and the person whom they may hold responsible.

The employee, on the other hand, relies on his employer for the safety of his job. He has little choice but to take the conditions of work as he finds them; and in many kinds of employment he literally depends for his life on precautions taken by the employer.

Everybody has a general duty in common law to manage his affairs with reasonable care so as not to cause injury by negligence. But because of the special nature of the 'master–servant' relationship, the statutory duties of an employer towards his employees are more specific and positive. They are:

1. To provide a safe place of work.
2. To provide safe plant, tools and appliances.
3. To employ competent staff.
4. To maintain a safe system of work.

In addition, the employer has the duty to take safety precautions laid down by Acts of Parliament and regulations. Failure to observe these statutory duties makes him liable for damages if it causes injury.

It is no excuse that providing statutory protection would be costly, unreasonable, or even contrary to common sense.

➤ THE TOP MAN WHO FELL *Alfred Boyton was top man, or mattock, in a firm demolishing a warehouse, when he fell from the fourth floor and was severely injured. Evidence showed that putting up guardrails would have been dangerous, and any resulting benefit not worth the risk.*
DECISION *The Court of Appeal held in 1971 that since it was physically possible to erect guardrails, the firm had failed to comply with a mandatory requirement and were liable for a breach of a statutory duty. (Boyton v. Willment Brothers Ltd.)* ◄

The most important of these statutory duties are those laid down by the Factories Act 1961 and by the Offices, Shops and Railway Premises Act 1963. ☐ Safety, health and welfare, p. 608.

An employer cannot be expected to check personally to see that every danger or risk is guarded against. In practice, some acts that lead to injury of an employee are the acts of other employees. In law, however, the employer must bear responsibility. In legal language, he has a *vicarious liability* for their acts.

Anyone who becomes ill or injured at work may have a claim against his employer. The advice of a solicitor or an experienced trade-union official is essential.

If union help is not available, an employee may be eligible for legal aid. Details are available from the Citizens' Advice Bureau. ☐ Help with fees and costs, p. 710.

The adviser will need full details of the accident or illness, and statements from reliable witnesses. Evidence of the extent of the injury and of the employee's personal and financial losses is also likely to be required.

If the solicitor considers that the injured person is entitled to compensation he will first attempt to settle the matter with the employer or his insurance company. If an employer disputes the claim or makes an unsatisfactory offer, the solicitor may advise suing. ☐ How a damages claim is decided, p. 124.

### Dangers at the workplace

The employee's working environment must be made safe by his employer. Where there are dangers, he must take all reasonable steps to remove them.

The employer must also ensure that his staff have safe access to work. There must be, for example, adequate lighting, and floors and passageways should be free of obstructions.

➤ THE UNLIT ROAD *In the half-light of an October morning, Mrs Thornton, a factory cleaner, was walking to work along a factory road. She tripped over a coil of wire and injured herself. The lights along the road were not turned on at the time. She sued her employers, Fisher and Ludlow Ltd, for damages.*
DECISION *Mrs Thornton was awarded damages in 1968 because her employers had failed to provide sufficient lighting in all parts of the*

*premises and to ensure that the roadway was clear of obstruction. (Thornton v. Fisher and Ludlow Ltd.)◄*

The employer who sends men to work on a building site is just as responsible to make reasonable provision for their safety.

►THE WINDOW CLEANER'S FINGERS *In 1952, Mr Christmas, a window cleaner, fell and was injured when a window sash came down on his fingers. His employers, General Cleaning Contractors Ltd, had provided safety belts; but he could not use them because, on the building where he was working, there were no hooks to which they could be fixed. He sued.*
DECISION *Mr Christmas was awarded damages. The employer should not have left the safety precautions to his men, said the House of Lords. It was not the employee's job to fix the safety hooks. (General Cleaning Contractors Ltd v. Christmas.)◄*

An employee injured on someone else's property may be able to sue the occupier of the premises, even if his employer was not negligent. ☐ Rights and responsibilities of running a home, p. 280; Recouping money lost through injury, p. 546.

### Risks from workmates
If an employee causes injury to a fellow worker, it is the employer who is liable under the Law Reform (Personal Injuries) Act 1948 —even in cases where the employer does not personally hire his staff. When an employer learns that an employee has behaved in a way that could endanger other workers, he must dismiss the man or move him to another job.

The employer's obligation in common law to operate with competent staff means that, for some jobs, the number of workers must not fall below the minimum for safety. Undermanning could make a safe job dangerous. Similarly, in some kinds of work the employer may have to ensure that his employees are supervised by responsible overseers.

### Dangerous tools and machinery
Every employer is bound by law to see that all equipment his employees have to use is safe. Transmission machinery which is moving or dangerous must be guarded.

Machinery, in the legal sense, is not only a tool or appliance. A crane has been defined as machinery, for example.

Even when an employer is not directly to blame for defective tools or equipment—for example, they may have been supplied in a

dangerous condition by the manufacturer—he can be made to pay compensation to any worker who is injured. In turn, the employer may take action against the manufacturer of the defective equipment.

### When safety precautions are ignored
An employer runs a double risk if he disregards the safety provisions of the Factories Act 1961, the Offices, Shops and Railway Premises Act 1963, and any Acts relating to particular industries. He can be prosecuted for breaking the law, and he is also open to a damages claim if an employee is injured as a result of his negligence.

For example, failure to provide goggles, safety aprons, boots, safety belts and other protective devices can give an injured employee grounds to claim damages. Moreover, the employer can also be prosecuted for ignoring the safety regulations.

It is the employer's responsibility to make sure that his workers are aware of the safety laws affecting them. If he does not do so, he can be made to pay damages if an employee is injured—even though the employee broke the regulations.

►THE PAINTER'S LADDER *Patrick Boyle, a painter working for Kodak Ltd, fell off a ladder in 1969 while painting a 30 ft high storage tank, and was injured. The Factories Act states that 'every ladder shall so far as is practicable be securely fixed so that it can move neither from its top nor from its bottom points of rest'. In this case, the ladder was not fixed; in fact, Mr Boyle was going up to fix it.*
DECISION *Damages were awarded to Mr Boyle. The House of Lords held that if the employer knew that his workmen were carrying out a dangerous job covered by the safety regulations, he should have seen to it that they were properly informed of these regulations. (Boyle v. Kodak Ltd.)◄*

If, however, the employer can prove that he took all possible care, he may not have to pay damages.

Employees are entitled to safe conditions in all parts of the premises where they work; an employer must also make sure his workers are safe even when they are taking part in non-working activities, such as making tea.

►THE SLIPPERY DUCKBOARD *Mrs Davidson worked in Handley Page's workshops, where liquid used for oiling lathes often spilt on to the floor. Labourers cleaned the floor and put sawdust on it. She stood on a duckboard to wash her*

*teacup; but the duckboard was slippery because no sawdust had been put on it, and she fell off. Later she claimed damages for personal injuries.*
DECISION *A county court judge held that Mrs Davidson was not entitled to damages because, at the time of the accident, she was not engaged in an activity directly connected with her work. However, the Court of Appeal said that the employer's duty extends to all activities reasonably connected with work, and she was awarded damages. (Davidson v. Handley Page Ltd.)*

## An employee's right to special care

The employer's duty to his workers is not just a general observance of the safety laws. Different steps have to be taken according to the different needs and physical condition of each employee. There is an individual responsibility to an employee with, say, an infirmity which makes his working situation different from other employees.

▶THE CASE OF A MAN WITH ONE EYE *Mr Paris, a garage fitter, had only one eye. He was hammering to remove a bolt on a vehicle when a chip of metal came away and flew into his good eye, leaving him totally blind. His employers had not provided him with goggles. They told the court that they did not think it necessary to do so, since men working in garages on maintenance or repair work did not normally require a pair of goggles.*
DECISION *The House of Lords said that the employers should have realised that Mr Paris was in danger of going blind from an accident of that kind, and guarded against it. 'The employer owes a particular duty to each of his employees,' said Lord Simonds. 'All circumstances relevant to that employee must be taken into consideration.' (Paris v. Stepney Borough Council.)◀*

The employer owes a less strict duty to employees who are experienced and appreciate the risks involved than to those who are not.

## If non-employees are involved

The employer must make sure that no member of the public is harmed by his negligence, and can be made to pay damages if he fails to do so. ☐ Recouping money lost through injury, p. 546.

But the employer owes the specific duties of safety and care only to someone who is one of his own employees and is acting in the course of his work.

▶ THE DRIVER AND THE DRUM *Under a long-standing agreement between British Road Services and Imperial Chemical Industries Ltd,*
*a driver from BRS was unloading a drum from his lorry at an ICI depot when it slipped and injured him. Driver O'Reilly sued ICI for failing to provide a safe system of work.*
DECISION *The Court of Appeal held that ICI was not responsible, since the driver was not one of its employees. (O'Reilly v. Imperial Chemical Industries Ltd.)◀*

## The employee who is partly to blame

If the injured employee is partly to blame, the damages awarded are split or apportioned by the court, which makes an estimate of the degree of blame of each party.

The employee also has a duty to observe safety regulations and, although his employer may have to pay damages if he is injured, the court takes into consideration any breach of the rules by the injured worker.

## The employee who is entirely to blame

If there is a breach of the law that is entirely the employee's fault, he may have his responsibility for the accident assessed at 100 per cent—which means he is not entitled to receive any damages at all.

Where two employees are jointly to blame for the same accident, the employer is liable to each of them for the negligence which was shown by the other.

However, if both of them do something rash and are injured as a result, the employer does not have to compensate either of them.

There is in law a principle known as *volenti non fit injuria,* which means that anyone who voluntarily accepts a risk cannot expect someone else to compensate him if he is injured as a result.

▶BROTHERS HURT IN EXPLOSION *Two brothers were on a shot-firing job in 1964 in which, according to the regulations, they had to take shelter before testing the circuit connected to the explosives. They made the test without taking shelter, and both were seriously injured. One of the brothers sued the employer.*
DECISION *It was held by the House of Lords that each brother had fully aided and assisted the other to break the regulations, and therefore they had voluntarily undertaken to accept the risks in doing so. The claim failed. (Imperial Chemical Industries Ltd v. Shadwell.)◀*

However, a man cannot be said to have voluntarily accepted a risk unless he had the freedom to avoid it. An employer could not, therefore, successfully defend an action by claiming that an employee was free to avoid danger by finding himself a job elsewhere.

# Leaving the job

AN employee can leave or lose his job in a number of ways: by giving notice, by receiving notice, by mutual agreement with his employer or because his contract has come to an end. He is entitled to leave without giving notice only if the employer has broken a term of his contract. This would happen, for instance, if the employer did not pay the agreed wages, or insisted that the employee should carry out some job for which he was not employed in the first place.

Similarly, an employee cannot be dismissed without notice (or pay in lieu of notice) unless he has been guilty of grave misconduct.

### How to resign
An employee is entitled to leave his job at any time (unless he has a contract which ends on a specified date) simply by telling his employer, preferably in writing, that he intends to leave. He must, however, give his employer proper warning, in accordance with the terms of his contract of employment.

In some cases, an employee may want to be released earlier, to take up a new job. Whether he is allowed to do so depends entirely on his present employer. The worker cannot force the employer to agree; and if he leaves before his notice period ends, he is in breach of contract.

Where the employee's own contract does not lay down a fixed period of notice, and there is no generally accepted period in his job, he must give one week's notice, provided he has been with the firm for more than 13 weeks. If he has been with the firm for less than 13 weeks, no period is laid down by law.

WITHDRAWAL OF NOTICE Once an employee has given notice, he has no legal right to withdraw it, unless his employer agrees.

WHEN NOT TO RESIGN An employee asked to resign is often well advised to refuse, because by agreeing he may lose his right to unemployment benefit and redundancy pay.

### When you are told to leave
An employer who decides to dismiss an employee must comply with the terms of the contract or any collective agreement. This means he must give the employee the required period of notice, or pay him wages in lieu

of notice, or pay him until the end of his fixed period, if there is one.

In some industries—printing, for example—employees made idle because of a strike in which they are not directly involved are sometimes given 'protective notice'. This has the same status in law as the usual notice, but is rescinded if the dispute is settled before the end of the notice period.

LENGTH OF NOTICE Where there is no fixed-term contract, the employee must be given the minimum notice required by law, unless his contract provides for a longer period. ☐ How notice is calculated, p. 640.

The law protects most employees who have worked for the same employer for more than 21 hours a week for 13 weeks.

Registered dock workers, seamen, civil servants, members of the forces, people normally employed abroad and most employees on a fixed-term contract are not covered, but rely on agreements with employers.

Generally, an employee may not be dismissed without the notice required by law, or pay in lieu of notice, unless he has committed an act of gross misconduct. ☐ When an employee can be disciplined, p. 616.

WHEN NOTICE STARTS Many people give notice on pay day. But legally, notice can be given on any day, and starts from the beginning of the employee's next working day.

### Pay during notice
Employees are entitled to pay during periods of notice provided they are ready and able to work. If they fall sick or go on holiday during their notice period, they are entitled to their basic weekly pay. This will be the pay, without overtime or additional payments such as a bonus, which they would normally have received if they had not been dismissed or resigned.

Even when there is no work for them to do during that time, they must be paid their normal wage. A piece-rate worker with normal working hours, and covered by the Contracts of Employment and Industrial Relations Acts, as most employees are, has an extra guarantee. He must be paid a weekly rate of not less than his average earnings during the last four weeks he worked before he gave or was given notice.

An employee with no normal working hours must be paid at the average weekly rate he received in the 12 weeks before notice.

If the employee wants to leave before his notice expires, his employer need not pay him for any days off work.

WAGES IN LIEU OF NOTICE If an employee is offered wages equal to those he would have earned by working out the period of notice, and is told to leave immediately, he is obliged in law to leave at once. But an employee has no right to choose between pay in lieu of notice or working out his notice.

His rights to redundancy pay and unemployment benefit are not affected, except that the contract ends at the beginning rather than the end of the period of notice, and this could affect qualifying periods. ☐ Qualifying for unemployment benefit, p. 650.

### When civil servants are dismissed

Civil servants who work for Government departments or in the Services (but not those in nationalised industries or Government corporations) are not covered by any of the provisions of the Contracts of Employment Act and can be dismissed without notice. But in most Government departments special procedures have been agreed.

### Fixed-term contracts

An employee who has a fixed-term contract can leave when it ends, whether or not his employer agrees. No notice is required by either party, because the contract itself states when the job is to end.

If the employee wants to leave before the end of a fixed-term contract, he can do so only when he has his employer's agreement.

THE GOLDEN HANDSHAKE When an employer decides to end a fixed-term contract, the employee is entitled to any amount which may have been agreed in the contract as compensation should the employment end prematurely. This is known as a 'golden handshake'—the amount a firm pays an employee to leave.

If no sum is stipulated in the agreement to cover a 'golden handshake', the employee may be able to bring an action against his employer for breach of contract.

### Taking action against the employer

An employee who has been dismissed may be able to claim compensation from his employer on one or more of three grounds:

**1.** If he has been unfairly dismissed.
**2.** If he has been dismissed on the grounds of race, colour, or ethnic or national origins. ☐ Claiming compensation for dismissal, p. 641.
**3.** If he has been made redundant. ☐ Claiming compensation for redundancy, p. 645.

These claims can be made irrespective of how much notice the employee is given. An employee dismissed without proper notice and who receives no pay in lieu of notice may also be able to sue his employer for breach of contract, unless he has committed an act of gross misconduct. ☐ Claiming compensation for dismissal, p. 641.

## How notice is calculated

THE minimum notice to which an employee is entitled depends on how long he has worked *continuously* for his employer:

| Service | Notice |
| --- | --- |
| 13 weeks–2 years | 1 week |
| 2 years–5 years | 2 weeks |
| 5 years–10 years | 4 weeks |
| 10 years–15 years | 6 weeks |
| 15 years and over | 8 weeks |

Any week in which less than 21 hours are worked—disregarding absence because of illness, injury or holidays, or because a worker has been laid off—breaks continuity. So does an absence of more than 13 weeks because of sickness, injury or holidays. Once continuity is broken, only the period following the break is taken into account.

A piece-rate worker will not be affected by the 21-hour qualification if there is a custom in his trade, or an agreement, that short weeks do not break continuity.

If an employee is kept away from work because of a strike or a lockout, the weeks during which he is out do not count towards qualifying him for longer service, though they do not break continuity.

Normally, only employment with the present employer counts; but if a firm is bought or merged with another firm, the employee's service is usually counted from the time he started with the original firm.

# Claiming compensation for dismissal

*What to do about unfair dismissal*
*Dismissal on racial grounds*
*What to do about inadequate notice*

*When the contract is frustrated*
*Contracts ended by death or winding-up*
*Where cases are heard*

ANY employee dismissed from his job may have grounds to claim compensation. If he is told to leave without good reason he can claim for unfair dismissal. If he is given less than the minimum notice required by law, and does not receive pay in lieu, he can sue for damages.

If he is dismissed because the work for which he was employed has ceased or diminished, he may be entitled to redundancy pay. ☐ Claiming compensation for redundancy, p. 645.

### What to do about unfair dismissal
In law, an employer is justified in sacking a member of his staff on the grounds of:
1. His ability and qualifications for the job.
2. His conduct at work.
3. Redundancy.
4. Any other substantial reason.

Dismissal for reasons other than these is presumed by the Industrial Relations Act 1971 to be unfair, and gives the employee the right to claim compensation or ask for reinstatement.

An employer cannot normally be compelled by law to take back someone he has dismissed, but if he refuses he may have to pay increased compensation.

In every case, it is up to the employer to prove that he gave notice for one of the reasons which the law regards as fair. In addition, he must show that dismissal was fair and reasonable in all the circumstances.

The Act gives an employer the right to dismiss a worker who proves incompetent at the job for which he was originally employed. But it is considered unfair dismissal to sack him for inability to do a more skilled job.

A maintenance engineer, for example, cannot be fairly dismissed for incompetence if he is employed for several years without his work being questioned, but proves unable to cope when transferred to production work.

An employee who disobeys an instruction and is dismissed for misconduct is not normally entitled to compensation, unless he can show that the order was illegal or unreasonable. For example, a lorry driver would be justified in refusing to take out a vehicle with inefficient brakes; but he would have no claim in law if he were dismissed for consistently refusing to call at a weighbridge.

An employee who is dismissed for joining, or refusing to join, a trade union, or for taking part in union activities can claim compensation, though if he is sacked because he is on strike he may not be regarded as dismissed unfairly. ☐ The legal consequences of going on strike, p. 625.

An employee who is locked out by his employer, and not offered reinstatement, has grounds for a claim unless the employer can show that his actions were fair. The locked-out employee who is offered reinstatement, however, has no claim.

WHO CAN CLAIM An employee who has been unjustly dismissed can usually claim compensation if he has been with the same firm for two years or more. But where union membership or activity is the ground for dismissal, an employee can claim irrespective of his length of service.

Some workers fall outside the scope of the unfair-dismissal provisions, and cannot claim compensation: anyone working for an employer with no more than three permanent employees, for example, and husbands and wives of employers. Certain categories of employees are also excluded: registered dock workers, fishermen who share the profits of their catch, people working less than 21 hours a week and employees who normally work outside Britain. No one over pensionable age (65 for men, 60 for women) can claim.

HOW TO MAKE A CLAIM An employee who considers he has been unfairly dismissed and wishes to press for reinstatement or compensation should, if he belongs to a trade union, first contact his union representative. Otherwise he should make his claim through the local employment exchange.

### How the claim is decided
Claims for compensation for unfair dismissal are decided by an industrial tribunal, set up by the Department of Employment, which hears evidence from employer and employee. ☐ Appearing before a tribunal, p. 735.

Both employer and employee may call witnesses. For example, an employee dismissed for incompetence may be able to get satisfied clients or technical experts to give evidence of the quality and standard of his work.

An employer may call other employees to give evidence that they regularly complied with an order which the dismissed man had refused, and that they considered the order reasonable or essential to the job.

If the tribunal rules that the dismissal was unfair, compensation is calculated on the financial loss which the dismissal has caused, and is likely to cause, the employee—loss of wages, for example, and of employment prospects.

The tribunal also has power to order anyone else responsible for an unfair dismissal to pay part of the compensation—a shop steward who gets a non-union man dismissed, for example, or an executive who maliciously engineers the dismissal of a colleague.

The maximum compensation for an unfair dismissal is £4160, or the equivalent of 104 weeks pay for the claimant, whichever is less.

If the employee has not found another job and refuses to be reinstated when his former employer is willing to accept him, compensation will be reduced or may not be paid at all unless the employee has good reasons for not returning. When an employee rejoins an employer by mutual agreement after an order by the tribunal, no compensation is payable.
REDUNDANT OR UNFAIRLY DISMISSED? Some employers, faced with a claim for compensation for unfair dismissal, may try to claim that the employee was redundant. From the employer's point of view, this has the advantage that any compensation he has to pay for redundancy—but not for unfair dismissal—is subsidised by the State.

In such a case, the job of the industrial tribunal will be to decide what was the true reason for the dismissal.

### Dismissal on racial grounds
An employer who dismisses a member of his staff on the grounds of race, colour, or national or ethnic origins may commit an offence under the Race Relations Act 1968, though there are exceptional cases where discrimination is not illegal. The employer's action also amounts to unfair dismissal under the Industrial Relations Act.

Anyone affected is entitled to claim compensation for unfair dismissal in the normal way. Alternatively, he can take up his complaint with the appropriate race relations bodies. ☐ Racial discrimination in jobs, p. 589.

The race relations bodies will try to conciliate between employer and employee; if

discrimination is proved, they may also seek an assurance from the employer that it will not be repeated.

If the race relations bodies fail to achieve a conciliation, the case is dealt with by an industrial tribunal as a claim for compensation for unfair dismissal.

### What to do about inadequate notice
An employee sacked without the notice to which he is legally entitled, or payment in lieu of notice, can sue for damages—whether or not the dismissal itself was justified. ☐ How notice is calculated, p. 640.

An employee can also sue where he can show that he left of his own accord because the employer broke the terms of the contract. For example, the employer may have tried to make him take on a more dangerous job.
WHAT DAMAGES ARE PAID Before deciding to sue, the employee should first consider what damages he is likely to get. A man wrongly dismissed without notice whose contract provided for three months' notice or money in lieu, would be awarded only that amount. That is the only loss which is a direct consequence of the breach of contract.

In the case of a piece-rate worker who has no fixed weekly wage, the court awards damages based on average earnings over the 12 weeks before dismissal.

If an employee suing for damages has been able to find another job immediately, at the same pay, the court will award only nominal damages. If he has taken a job at a lower salary, the court will award him only the difference between his old and his new pay for the period of notice to which he was entitled.

If an employee has not tried to find work during his notice period, the court will estimate how much he might have earned if he had made an effort to get a job, and then deduct the amount from his damages.

This does not mean he would have to take a totally unsuitable job. A civil engineer, for example, would not be expected to take a job as a labourer. But the fact that another job as a civil engineer carried a lower salary than he received previously is not necessarily a valid reason for refusing it. The longer he is out of work, the more reasonable it would be to expect him to take a lower salary.

If an employee has made a substantial part of his income from commission, tips or bonuses, the court takes these into account.

▶ THE HAIRDRESSER'S TIPS *A hairdresser, Mr Manubens, received wages and commission from his employer and an approximately equal*

*amount in tips from customers. He was dismissed without notice, and sued for compensation.*
DECISION *The court held that Mr Manubens was entitled to be compensated for the loss of wages, commission and tips since there was an implied term in his contract that his employer would not prevent him from receiving the income from these sources. (Manubens v. Leon.)* ◄

DEDUCTIONS FROM DAMAGES No tax is levied by the Inland Revenue on the first £5000 of damages awarded for loss of income due to wrongful dismissal. But the courts deduct an amount equivalent to the tax the employee would have paid if he had received the money as income in the normal way.

For example, if a man is said to have lost £5000 in earnings, he is not paid that amount; if the rate of tax he would normally have paid is 30 per cent, the court would deduct that from the £5000. His employer would therefore pay £3500.

Any allowances to which the man was entitled would be taken into account before the amount of tax which would have been payable is calculated.

If the damages awarded amount to more than £5000, the employee is paid the full amount of the excess and is responsible for paying whatever tax is assessed on this excess.
NATIONAL INSURANCE Any money normally deducted by the employer for National Insurance contributions is also deducted by the court.
STATE BENEFITS Unemployment benefit paid after dismissal is usually deducted from potential damages. So is part of any sickness or industrial injury benefit he receives.
OTHER DEDUCTIONS Any other deductions normally made from a man's earnings—such as union dues or pension-fund payments—are not usually deducted from damages.

The courts do not deduct the amount of any supplementary benefit received by the employee. Nor do they deduct any sum he receives as a result of a personal-insurance policy covering loss of income, or from an employment pension. Gifts from charitable organisations or from personal friends are not taken into account.

## Protection for public employees
Holders of public offices—such as police officers, town clerks and court officials— cannot be dismissed without a hearing. In the case of a policeman, this may be held by the local watch committee.

The hearing must be conducted according to the rules of 'natural justice'. The person

whose job is at stake must be allowed to put his case or be represented. Any person directly involved in his dismissal must not be a member of the tribunal.

When a public employee is dismissed, the dismissal will be unlawful if it breaks a regulation or statute on which the contract of employment is based.

Holders of public offices dismissed contrary to the rules of natural justice, and public employees given notice in breach of their contract of employment can ask for a court declaration that the dismissal was unlawful.

This declaration has no binding force in law, but in practice, the employer usually takes into account the court's ruling and reinstates the employee.

Civil servants, however, can legally be dismissed at the will and pleasure of the Crown.

The contracts of some public employees state that notice can be given only for certain reasons. If the employee is dismissed for reasons other than those in the agreement, there may be a breach of contract.

► SACKED FOR GETTING MARRIED *Mrs Elizabeth McClelland was employed as a senior clerk with the Northern Ireland General Health Services Board. Her appointment was said to be permanent and pensionable. After the appointment was confirmed, a further condition was inserted in the staff conditions of service, stating that the Board would ask for the resignation of any women members of staff who got married.*

*Mrs McClelland later married, and was dismissed. She sought a declaration that she had been wrongfully dismissed.*
DECISION *The House of Lords said in 1957 that the Board had broken the contract, because marriage was not a reason for dismissal allowed by her contract. She was reinstated. (McClelland v. N.I. General Health Services Board.)* ◄

PROTECTION FOR UNION OFFICIALS An elected trade union official who is threatened with dismissal for serious misconduct is also entitled to a hearing of his case. Such a hearing must be conducted according to the principles of natural justice.

## When the contract is frustrated
If a contract becomes meaningless because of something which could not be foreseen by the employer or the employee, and which is not the fault of either, the law considers that the contract has been frustrated and is ended.

For example, a contract would be frustrated if someone entered into an agreement to act as a firm's manager in a specified country, and then that country banned foreign nationals.

Where an employee is entitled to sick pay, prolonged absence through illness may not be considered to frustrate his contract. There are times, however, when illness can make it impossible to fulfil an agreement.

►THE OPERA SINGER WHO LOST HER JOB
*An opera singer, Mme Poussard, was engaged to sing in London but became ill during rehearsals and did not recover until after the first four performances. The employers had meanwhile engaged another singer, and when Mme Poussard asked to return, they refused to take her back. In 1876 she sued for wrongful dismissal.*
DECISION *The court held that she could not get damages. Her illness frustrated the contract; there was no contract left for her to sue on and the employers were under no obligation to take her back. (Poussard v. Spiers.)*◄

## Contracts ended by death or winding-up
If a firm goes out of business or an employer dies, the contracts of employment of the workers are automatically ended. A shop owner, for example, may employ a number of assistants to help him to run his business. Contracts are made directly between him and his employees. If the owner dies, the contracts of employment automatically end.

The contracts cannot be transferred to another firm or employer—although someone else may offer to take over the dead man's business. The original contract is ended and, if the business is taken over, any employees who are retained must agree new contracts with the new owner.

An employee's contract is not affected by the death of someone who does not directly own the business employing him. For instance, the managing director or general manager of any business concern may hire staff, but his death does not bring the employees' contracts to an end.

If a firm is wound-up—that is, if it goes out of business—the contracts between it and its employees come to an end in the same way as when the owner dies. The employees are entitled, in either case, to any wages due to them up to the time of the employer's death or the winding-up of the company. They are also entitled to receive any holiday pay they have accrued to date.

The employees have first claim on any money available, before unpaid creditors; but wages in lieu of notice are not treated as a preferential claim. ☐ Claiming compensation for redundancy, p. 645.

## Where cases are heard
Most claims for compensation for dismissal, whether on the grounds of inadequate notice, redundancy or unfair dismissal, are heard by industrial tribunals, where the procedure is quicker, cheaper and less formal than in court.

Claims involving allegations of inadequate notice can also be heard in a county court or the High Court, though the court has power to transfer the action to an industrial tribunal if it thinks fit. Actions for declarations or injunctions are heard only in the courts.

Appeals against tribunal decisions go to the National Industrial Relations Court. Appeals against decisions in county courts and the High Court are heard in the Court of Appeal.

---

# When a worker breaks his contract

An employee who breaks his contract, perhaps by walking out without giving notice, or by leaving after giving insufficient notice, can be sued by his employer. In practice, this is rare.

An employer can claim only losses he has suffered as a direct result of the employee's decision to leave. The employee cannot be held responsible for an entire plant's lost production, only for his own share of the losses.

The employer cannot be awarded more in damages than his actual loss. Some account is therefore taken of any replacement he has found. The employer may be able to prove that the employee who left was of value to him, in which case he could be judged to have incurred some loss, even if the work in the plant is continuing.

Even though the courts do not compel an employee to return to an employer, they do sometimes grant an injunction to enforce a clause in a contract which restricts the right of an employee to work for a firm in competition with his former employer.

If an injunction is granted, the employee's right to work in a particular area, or to do a certain job, may be limited. ☐ Restrictions after leaving the job, p. 653.

# Claiming compensation for redundancy

*Workers who qualify for payments*
*Working out the notice*
*When redundancy is disputed*

*When an alternative job is offered*
*Change of ownership*
*How the payment is calculated*

AN employee who is sacked because the work for which he was employed has ceased or diminished is regarded in law as redundant. Most workers who become redundant, whether they are on time-rate, piece-work or regular wages, are entitled by law to redundancy payment.

So is an employee who has not been sacked but chooses to leave his job because he has been laid off or put on short time for an extended period.

Redundancy money is paid in a lump sum, free of tax, and can be claimed even if the worker immediately finds a new job.

## Workers who qualify for payments
Only people aged 18 or over, but under 65 (60 for a woman), can qualify for redundancy payment under the Redundancy Payments Act 1965. The dismissed employee must have worked for an employer for not less than two years, putting in at least 21 hours a week.

Even among people who meet these requirements, there are exceptions. Civil servants, members of the Armed Forces, dock workers, or fishermen whose earnings depend on their share of a fishing boat's catch are not entitled to redundancy payments under the Act. Husbands and wives of employers are also excluded where the business is not a limited company.

An employee on a fixed-term contract for two years or more is not entitled to redundancy pay after the term expires if he made the contract before December 1965. If the contract was made after 1965, he should get payment, unless there is written agreement to the contrary.

The Secretary of State for Employment can exempt from the redundancy-payment law people who are guaranteed redundancy pay under the terms of a collective agreement between their trade union or staff association and the employer.

If you belong to a union or association, ask your local representative if you are covered in this way.

The terms of the agreement must not be inferior to those in the 1965 Act; and both parties must agree in advance to take any dispute which arises about redundancy payment to an industrial tribunal. ☐ How to claim redundancy pay, p. 646.

## When redundancy pay is withheld
Redundancy money is usually paid automatically when the employee is dismissed. If he does not get it, he should write to his employer claiming payment as soon as possible, or at the latest within six months. A written claim does not have to be made if the employee has complained of unfair dismissal to an industrial tribunal. ☐ Claiming compensation for dismissal, p. 641.

An employee whose firm is going into liquidation should apply immediately to the local office of the Department of Employment. All employers must contribute to a national redundancy fund, and if the firm is unable to meet its obligations, the State pays the employee. The employer is asked to repay the fund later, unless he is bankrupt.

An employer who refuses a claim must prove that he dismissed the man for a reason other than redundancy. Disputes are settled by an industrial tribunal.

## Working out the notice
An employee who is declared redundant should work out the full term of his legal notice, even if he is offered a job with another firm during that time. If he leaves earlier, without the agreement of his employer, he breaks his contract and may lose his right to redundancy pay.

Similarly, an employee offered a different job in the same firm should accept only on a trial basis. Otherwise he forfeits his right to redundancy pay if he finds the new work unsuitable. He should get the employer to agree in writing, or before a witness, that the new job is for a specified trial period only.

► THE MAN WHO ACTED RASHLY *Mr Carney, a grinder employed by Pilkington Brothers Ltd, became redundant on August 24, and was given written notice expiring on September 21. On August 30—well before his notice had expired— he accepted an alternative job in his employers' sheet works and started work on September 4.*

*He worked for 11 days and then asked his employers' permission to leave because of a bad ankle. They agreed, and Mr Carney left on September 16 and claimed redundancy pay. The local industrial tribunal rejected his claim and Mr Carney appealed to the High Court, claiming that he had been dismissed from work.*

DECISION *Mr Carney's appeal was unsuccessful. His notice had said: 'If alternative employment can be found and you accept, the notice will, of course, be withdrawn.' As he had accepted the job, his termination notice was withdrawn. But the court pointed out that if he had not rashly accepted the job but had said, 'I will try this alternative employment as an experiment', he would have won his case. (Carney v. Pilkington Brothers Ltd.)* ◄

## When redundancy is disputed

An employer may be able to escape liability for paying a dismissed worker redundancy money if the dismissal was not because of redundancy. A worker dismissed for misconduct, for instance, would not be entitled to redundancy pay.

Sometimes, too, it is difficult for a worker to claim that his employer has made him redundant, because the scope of his job has not been clearly defined.

► THE FITTER WHO WAS NOT REDUNDANT *George Arnold, a skilled motor fitter, ran an emergency breakdown service on alternate nights and at weekends for his employers, Thomas Harrington Ltd.*

*He lived in a flat on company premises and when the company decided to sell their bodybuilding division, they wanted vacant possession of Mr Arnold's flat.*

*They offered to re-employ him as a fitter but without the rent-free flat. Mr Arnold refused the offer and another fitter was taken on in his place. But the emergency breakdown service stopped because none of the fitters*

---

# How to claim redundancy pay

WHEN a worker is dismissed simply because there is no more work, his employer should make whatever redundancy payment is due automatically. If the payment is not made and no reason is given, the worker or his union must apply in writing to the employer. Then, if the employer disputes the claim, the employee can ask the local office of the Department of Employment for help and, if necessary, appeal to an industrial tribunal.

## Lay-offs and short-time

An employee who receives less than half a week's pay for four consecutive weeks, or for six weeks out of a total of 13, can choose to leave the job and claim redundancy pay for being put on short-time work, or laid off.

He must give written notice that he intends to claim within 28 days of the lay-off or short-time finishing or within 28 days of the end of the 13-week period. He should also give whatever notice is necessary to leave the job.

The employer may challenge the claim within seven days, if there is a reasonable prospect of 13 weeks of normal work for the employee. These 13 weeks must start within 28 days of the employee giving notice to claim redundancy pay.

If the employer can provide the work, he must write to the employee within seven days saying he will contest the claim. It is then up to the employee, if he wants to go ahead with his claim, to refer it to a tribunal for decision. There are time limits which the employee must observe in giving notice to leave:

1. Where the employer does not challenge the claim, the employee must give notice to leave within four weeks of his notice claiming redundancy pay.

2. Where the employer challenges the employee's claim, then withdraws the challenge, the employee must give his notice within three weeks of the date on which the employer's challenge is withdrawn.

3. Where the tribunal makes an award, the employee must give his notice within three weeks of the date of the award.

## Appeals to industrial tribunals

When an industrial tribunal considers disputed claims for redundancy pay, the employee can be represented by a lawyer, a trade-union official or a friend. He is not entitled to legal aid to help pay his costs.

If the tribunal decides in favour of a redundancy payment, it is paid either by the employer or by the Department of Employment. ☐ Appearing before a tribunal, p. 735.

An appeal can be made to the Industrial Relations Court—but only on a point of law.

lived near enough to the garage. Mr Arnold claimed redundancy pay.

DECISION *The High Court said that Mr Arnold was not entitled to redundancy pay because the emergency service was not work of 'a particular kind', but simply fitters' work. As another fitter had been employed in his place, the amount of work for fitters had not decreased. (Arnold v. Thomas Harrington Ltd.)* ◄

RESHAPING THE FIRM If, in a firm's re-organisation, an employee is unable to adapt to the new techniques he may be fired for incompetence. His employers could then reject a claim for redundancy payment.

► THE MANAGER WHO COULDN'T ADAPT *Mr Alexander Butterwick worked for the same garage for 30 years and became manager of the repairs workshop. In 1965, North Riding Garages took over the garage and introduced new methods in the workshop. The firm said that Mr Butterwick could not adapt himself to the new methods, and sacked him. A new manager was appointed. Mr Butterwick claimed redundancy pay, but the firm said he was not entitled to it because he had been dismissed for inefficiency and incompetence.*

DECISION *The High Court held that the need for work of a particular kind had increased. No actual redundancy existed, and therefore Mr Butterwick was not entitled to redundancy payment. (North Riding Garages v. Butterwick.)* ◄

### When an alternative job is offered

An employee who is demoted or shifted to an unsuitable new job is normally entitled to claim redundancy pay if he refuses the new job and is sacked. But he must have refused the alternative employment, and not have resigned of his own accord.

► THE MAN WHO QUIT *Mr Saunders was employed by Paladin Coachworks as a cabinet maker in 1953, and promoted to stores manager in 1962. He was put in charge of seven stores and had four men on his staff.*

*Soon, two of his men were given other jobs and the other two left because there was too much work. Mr Saunders became ill and while he was off work received a letter from his employers telling him that he was no longer needed as stores manager, and that he would be transferred.*

*When he returned to work, he refused the new job but gave two weeks' notice and left. He claimed redundancy pay.*

DECISION *The industrial tribunal held that Mr Saunders had not been dismissed and was therefore not entitled to redundancy pay. It*

added that *he could have refused to work because the employers had changed his contract without agreement. If Mr Saunders had done this, he would probably have been dismissed. But by giving notice himself, he terminated his contract and this did not amount to dismissal. (Saunders v. Paladin Coachworks Ltd.)* ◄

### Suitable alternative employment

An employer may avoid paying redundancy money if he offers suitable alternative employment. The offer should normally be made in writing. If, however, he offers a job in another town, the employee may have a good reason for refusing it—for example, if his children's schooling might be disrupted. He will then be entitled to redundancy pay.

But if the employee originally agreed to travel as part of his job and subsequently refuses, his employer can sack him without redundancy pay for breaking his contract.

An employee may be offered suitable alternative work which does not even have to be in the same place. He may, for example, be offered day work instead of night work. If the employee rejects the new conditions, the industrial tribunal decides if the difference is enough to justify redundancy pay.

In one case, an employee was offered a similar job to his old one, but without overtime. His original contract, however, included overtime work as part of the job, and he appealed to the tribunal and was given redundancy pay. The general principle is that the employee's refusal to accept the new terms must be reasonable in the light of his own personal circumstances.

### Change of ownership

When a business changes hands, an employee's continuity of employment is not interrupted provided that the new owner carries on the same kind of business. As long as the employee has worked for a total of 104 weeks in his job, he qualifies for redundancy payment if he is dismissed.

But continuity of employment can be interrupted if, because of a change of ownership, he is given new work to do.

► THE MISSING THREE WEEKS *Mr Percy Else was employed by Jacksons, a manufacturing company, from 1933 until 1962, when the business was transferred and the premises put up for sale.*

*In 1964, Dallow Industrial Properties bought the premises to lease out in small units to other manufacturers, and Mr Else was kept on as a maintenance worker. After Dallow had owned the premises for 101 weeks—three weeks less than the vital 104 weeks needed to qualify for redundancy pay—Mr Else was given notice.*

*An industrial tribunal decided he was entitled to payment because Dallow had taken over Jacksons' responsibilities. Dallow disagreed, and appealed to the High Court.*

DECISION *The High Court said there was no transfer of the trade or business carried on by Jacksons, but a sale only of the building. The premises were being used for quite different purposes by the new owner.*

*The two periods of employment, for Jacksons and then for Dallow, could not be added together to make the required 104 weeks. Mr Else was not, therefore, entitled to redundancy pay. (Dallow Industrial Properties v. Else.)* ◄

## How the payment is calculated

A redundant employee has to be paid one-and-a-half weeks' pay for each complete year he has worked for the firm from the age of 41 to 65 (60 for a woman); a week's pay for each continuous year's service from 22 to under 41; and half a week's pay for each year from 18 to under 22. □ Working out the amount of redundancy pay, p. 649.

However, no more than 20 years' continuous employment can be counted; the highest weekly wage taken into account in 1972 was £40; and the maximum redundancy payment an employee was entitled to—whatever his length of service and normal weekly wage—was £1200.

The normal wages are those paid at the time of the redundancy, and will usually have been agreed in the contract. If an employee has worked shorter or longer hours than those stated in the contract, and he is paid by the hours he works, the redundancy pay will be calculated as though he had worked the hours stated in the contract.

► THE CONTRACT—NOT THE PRACTICE *Mr Truelove was dismissed by Hall Services and given redundancy pay based on a 40-hour week—the hours he actually worked each week with his employer's permission. But his actual contract of employment was for a 54-hour week, and Mr Truelove asked an industrial tribunal to base his redundancy pay on this.*

DECISION *The tribunal in 1968 found for Mr Truelove and said that the contract, not the practice, should be the basis for redundancy pay. (Truelove v. Hall Services Ltd.)* ◄

If there is a discrepancy between the hours in the contract and the hours quoted in a trade union's local agreement, the contract hours are the hours that count for redundancy-pay calculations, unless the local agreement is held to be part of the contract.

► THE GENTLEMAN'S AGREEMENT *Mr Loman and Mr Henderson were employed in road haulage by Merseyside Transport Services. They were dismissed because they became redundant. The local industrial tribunal awarded them redundancy pay, but Mr Loman and Mr Henderson disagreed with the amount of the award, and appealed to the High Court.*

*They claimed that a local agreement between their employers and trade-union officials stated that 'payment shall be on the basis of a 68-hour week', and that their redundancy pay should be based on that agreement. The national agreement provided for only a 41-hour week, and the tribunal had ruled that this should be the basis for redundancy pay calculations.*

DECISION *The appeal was dismissed. A former manager of the firm told the court that the local agreement was 'in the nature of a gentleman's agreement' and was not a binding contract. The court agreed with the tribunal that redundancy pay should be based on the national 41-hour week agreement which was incorporated into the contract of employment. (Loman and Henderson v. Merseyside Transport.)* ◄

If a worker has to do overtime as part of his job, and not from choice, his overtime payments will be taken into account in calculating redundancy payment.

An employee who takes part in a strike after he has been given notice of redundancy does not lose his right to payment, provided that at the end of the strike he stays on at his employer's request to make up for days lost during the strike.

## When retirement is near

In the last year before pension age—when a man is 64 and a woman 59—redundancy payments are scaled down because those receiving them will soon be entitled to claim State pensions.

The payment is reduced by $\frac{1}{12}$ for each month worked during that year. If a man is made redundant when he is 64 years one month old, for example, he gets $\frac{11}{12}$ of the total redundancy pay to which he would be entitled. If he is made redundant on the day he is 65, he gets nothing.

If the firm operates a private-pension scheme the employer may be allowed to reduce or eliminate the redundancy payment according to a prescribed formula, usually based on an early but reduced pension.

# Working out the amount of redundancy pay

A quick way of working out how much redundancy pay a dismissed worker is entitled to is to use this ready reckoner. First, find the employee's length of service (in complete years) at the top of the table. Run your finger down the figures in this column until you come to the one opposite his age (given in the vertical column on the left). This is the number of weeks' pay to which he is entitled, subject to a maximum (in 1972, £1200). Only men can claim for service at the age of 60 or over. Any service before the week in which an employee reached the age of 18 is disregarded.

| AGE | NUMBER OF YEARS' SERVICE | | | | | | | | | | | | | | | | | | |
|---|---|---|---|---|---|---|---|---|---|---|---|---|---|---|---|---|---|---|---|
| | 2 | 3 | 4 | 5 | 6 | 7 | 8 | 9 | 10 | 11 | 12 | 13 | 14 | 15 | 16 | 17 | 18 | 19 | 20 |
| 20† | 1 | 1 | 1 | 1 | — | | | | | | | | | | | | | | |
| 21 | 1 | $1\frac{1}{2}$ | $1\frac{1}{2}$ | $1\frac{1}{2}$ | $1\frac{1}{2}$ | — | | | | | | | | | | | | | |
| 22 | 1 | $1\frac{1}{2}$ | 2 | 2 | 2 | 2 | — | | | | | | | | | | | | |
| 23 | $1\frac{1}{2}$ | 2 | $2\frac{1}{2}$ | 3 | 3 | 3 | 3 | — | | | | | | | | | | | |
| 24 | 2 | $2\frac{1}{2}$ | 3 | $3\frac{1}{2}$ | 4 | 4 | 4 | 4 | — | | | | | | | | | | |
| 25 | 2 | 3 | $3\frac{1}{2}$ | 4 | $4\frac{1}{2}$ | 5 | 5 | 5 | 5 | — | | | | | | | | | |
| 26 | 2 | 3 | 4 | $4\frac{1}{2}$ | 5 | $5\frac{1}{2}$ | 6 | 6 | 6 | 6 | — | | | | | | | | |
| 27 | 2 | 3 | 4 | 5 | $5\frac{1}{2}$ | 6 | $6\frac{1}{2}$ | 7 | 7 | 7 | 7 | — | | | | | | | |
| 28 | 2 | 3 | 4 | 5 | 6 | $6\frac{1}{2}$ | 7 | $7\frac{1}{2}$ | 8 | 8 | 8 | 8 | — | | | | | | |
| 29 | 2 | 3 | 4 | 5 | 6 | 7 | $7\frac{1}{2}$ | 8 | $8\frac{1}{2}$ | 9 | 9 | 9 | 9 | — | | | | | |
| 30 | 2 | 3 | 4 | 5 | 6 | 7 | 8 | $8\frac{1}{2}$ | 9 | $9\frac{1}{2}$ | 10 | 10 | 10 | 10 | — | | | | |
| 31 | 2 | 3 | 4 | 5 | 6 | 7 | 8 | 9 | $9\frac{1}{2}$ | 10 | $10\frac{1}{2}$ | 11 | 11 | 11 | 11 | — | | | |
| 32 | 2 | 3 | 4 | 5 | 6 | 7 | 8 | 9 | 10 | $10\frac{1}{2}$ | 11 | $11\frac{1}{2}$ | 12 | 12 | 12 | 12 | — | | |
| 33 | 2 | 3 | 4 | 5 | 6 | 7 | 8 | 9 | 10 | 11 | $11\frac{1}{2}$ | 12 | $12\frac{1}{2}$ | 13 | 13 | 13 | 13 | — | |
| 34 | 2 | 3 | 4 | 5 | 6 | 7 | 8 | 9 | 10 | 11 | 12 | $12\frac{1}{2}$ | 13 | $13\frac{1}{2}$ | 14 | 14 | 14 | 14 | — |
| 35 | 2 | 3 | 4 | 5 | 6 | 7 | 8 | 9 | 10 | 11 | 12 | 13 | $13\frac{1}{2}$ | 14 | $14\frac{1}{2}$ | 15 | 15 | 15 | 15 |
| 36 | 2 | 3 | 4 | 5 | 6 | 7 | 8 | 9 | 10 | 11 | 12 | 13 | 14 | $14\frac{1}{2}$ | 15 | $15\frac{1}{2}$ | 16 | 16 | 16 |
| 37 | 2 | 3 | 4 | 5 | 6 | 7 | 8 | 9 | 10 | 11 | 12 | 13 | 14 | 15 | $15\frac{1}{2}$ | 16 | $16\frac{1}{2}$ | 17 | 17 |
| 38 | 2 | 3 | 4 | 5 | 6 | 7 | 8 | 9 | 10 | 11 | 12 | 13 | 14 | 15 | 16 | $16\frac{1}{2}$ | 17 | $17\frac{1}{2}$ | 18 |
| 39 | 2 | 3 | 4 | 5 | 6 | 7 | 8 | 9 | 10 | 11 | 12 | 13 | 14 | 15 | 16 | 17 | $17\frac{1}{2}$ | 18 | $18\frac{1}{2}$ |
| 40 | 2 | 3 | 4 | 5 | 6 | 7 | 8 | 9 | 10 | 11 | 12 | 13 | 14 | 15 | 16 | 17 | 18 | $18\frac{1}{2}$ | 19 |
| 41 | 2 | 3 | 4 | 5 | 6 | 7 | 8 | 9 | 10 | 11 | 12 | 13 | 14 | 15 | 16 | 17 | 18 | 19 | $19\frac{1}{2}$ |
| 42 | $2\frac{1}{2}$ | $3\frac{1}{2}$ | $4\frac{1}{2}$ | $5\frac{1}{2}$ | $6\frac{1}{2}$ | $7\frac{1}{2}$ | $8\frac{1}{2}$ | $9\frac{1}{2}$ | $10\frac{1}{2}$ | $11\frac{1}{2}$ | $12\frac{1}{2}$ | $13\frac{1}{2}$ | $14\frac{1}{2}$ | $15\frac{1}{2}$ | $16\frac{1}{2}$ | $17\frac{1}{2}$ | $18\frac{1}{2}$ | $19\frac{1}{2}$ | $20\frac{1}{2}$ |
| 43 | 3 | 4 | 5 | 6 | 7 | 8 | 9 | 10 | 11 | 12 | 13 | 14 | 15 | 16 | 17 | 18 | 19 | 20 | 21 |
| 44 | 3 | $4\frac{1}{2}$ | $5\frac{1}{2}$ | $6\frac{1}{2}$ | $7\frac{1}{2}$ | $8\frac{1}{2}$ | $9\frac{1}{2}$ | $10\frac{1}{2}$ | $11\frac{1}{2}$ | $12\frac{1}{2}$ | $13\frac{1}{2}$ | $14\frac{1}{2}$ | $15\frac{1}{2}$ | $16\frac{1}{2}$ | $17\frac{1}{2}$ | $18\frac{1}{2}$ | $19\frac{1}{2}$ | $20\frac{1}{2}$ | $21\frac{1}{2}$ |
| 45 | 3 | $4\frac{1}{2}$ | 6 | 7 | 8 | 9 | 10 | 11 | 12 | 13 | 14 | 15 | 16 | 17 | 18 | 19 | 20 | 21 | 22 |
| 46 | 3 | $4\frac{1}{2}$ | 6 | $7\frac{1}{2}$ | $8\frac{1}{2}$ | $9\frac{1}{2}$ | $10\frac{1}{2}$ | $11\frac{1}{2}$ | $12\frac{1}{2}$ | $13\frac{1}{2}$ | $14\frac{1}{2}$ | $15\frac{1}{2}$ | $16\frac{1}{2}$ | $17\frac{1}{2}$ | $18\frac{1}{2}$ | $19\frac{1}{2}$ | $20\frac{1}{2}$ | $21\frac{1}{2}$ | $22\frac{1}{2}$ |
| 47 | 3 | $4\frac{1}{2}$ | 6 | $7\frac{1}{2}$ | 9 | 10 | 11 | 12 | 13 | 14 | 15 | 16 | 17 | 18 | 19 | 20 | 21 | 22 | 23 |
| 48 | 3 | $4\frac{1}{2}$ | 6 | $7\frac{1}{2}$ | 9 | $10\frac{1}{2}$ | $11\frac{1}{2}$ | $12\frac{1}{2}$ | $13\frac{1}{2}$ | $14\frac{1}{2}$ | $15\frac{1}{2}$ | $16\frac{1}{2}$ | $17\frac{1}{2}$ | $18\frac{1}{2}$ | $19\frac{1}{2}$ | $20\frac{1}{2}$ | $21\frac{1}{2}$ | $22\frac{1}{2}$ | $23\frac{1}{2}$ |
| 49 | 3 | $4\frac{1}{2}$ | 6 | $7\frac{1}{2}$ | 9 | $10\frac{1}{2}$ | 12 | 13 | 14 | 15 | 16 | 17 | 18 | 19 | 20 | 21 | 22 | 23 | 24 |
| 50 | 3 | $4\frac{1}{2}$ | 6 | $7\frac{1}{2}$ | 9 | $10\frac{1}{2}$ | 12 | $13\frac{1}{2}$ | $14\frac{1}{2}$ | $15\frac{1}{2}$ | $16\frac{1}{2}$ | $17\frac{1}{2}$ | $18\frac{1}{2}$ | $19\frac{1}{2}$ | $20\frac{1}{2}$ | $21\frac{1}{2}$ | $22\frac{1}{2}$ | $23\frac{1}{2}$ | $24\frac{1}{2}$ |
| 51 | 3 | $4\frac{1}{2}$ | 6 | $7\frac{1}{2}$ | 9 | $10\frac{1}{2}$ | 12 | $13\frac{1}{2}$ | 15 | 16 | 17 | 18 | 19 | 20 | 21 | 22 | 23 | 24 | 25 |
| 52 | 3 | $4\frac{1}{2}$ | 6 | $7\frac{1}{2}$ | 9 | $10\frac{1}{2}$ | 12 | $13\frac{1}{2}$ | 15 | $16\frac{1}{2}$ | $17\frac{1}{2}$ | $18\frac{1}{2}$ | $19\frac{1}{2}$ | $20\frac{1}{2}$ | $21\frac{1}{2}$ | $22\frac{1}{2}$ | $23\frac{1}{2}$ | $24\frac{1}{2}$ | $25\frac{1}{2}$ |
| 53 | 3 | $4\frac{1}{2}$ | 6 | $7\frac{1}{2}$ | 9 | $10\frac{1}{2}$ | 12 | $13\frac{1}{2}$ | 15 | $16\frac{1}{2}$ | 18 | 19 | 20 | 21 | 22 | 23 | 24 | 25 | 26 |
| 54 | 3 | $4\frac{1}{2}$ | 6 | $7\frac{1}{2}$ | 9 | $10\frac{1}{2}$ | 12 | $13\frac{1}{2}$ | 15 | $16\frac{1}{2}$ | 18 | $19\frac{1}{2}$ | $20\frac{1}{2}$ | $21\frac{1}{2}$ | $22\frac{1}{2}$ | $23\frac{1}{2}$ | $24\frac{1}{2}$ | $25\frac{1}{2}$ | $26\frac{1}{2}$ |
| 55 | 3 | $4\frac{1}{2}$ | 6 | $7\frac{1}{2}$ | 9 | $10\frac{1}{2}$ | 12 | $13\frac{1}{2}$ | 15 | $16\frac{1}{2}$ | 18 | $19\frac{1}{2}$ | 21 | 22 | 23 | 24 | 25 | 26 | 27 |
| 56 | 3 | $4\frac{1}{2}$ | 6 | $7\frac{1}{2}$ | 9 | $10\frac{1}{2}$ | 12 | $13\frac{1}{2}$ | 15 | $16\frac{1}{2}$ | 18 | $19\frac{1}{2}$ | 21 | $22\frac{1}{2}$ | $23\frac{1}{2}$ | $24\frac{1}{2}$ | $25\frac{1}{2}$ | $26\frac{1}{2}$ | $27\frac{1}{2}$ |
| 57 | 3 | $4\frac{1}{2}$ | 6 | $7\frac{1}{2}$ | 9 | $10\frac{1}{2}$ | 12 | $13\frac{1}{2}$ | 15 | $16\frac{1}{2}$ | 18 | $19\frac{1}{2}$ | 21 | $22\frac{1}{2}$ | 24 | 25 | 26 | 27 | 28 |
| 58 | 3 | $4\frac{1}{2}$ | 6 | $7\frac{1}{2}$ | 9 | $10\frac{1}{2}$ | 12 | $13\frac{1}{2}$ | 15 | $16\frac{1}{2}$ | 18 | $19\frac{1}{2}$ | 21 | $22\frac{1}{2}$ | 24 | $25\frac{1}{2}$ | $26\frac{1}{2}$ | $27\frac{1}{2}$ | $28\frac{1}{2}$ |
| 59* | 3 | $4\frac{1}{2}$ | 6 | $7\frac{1}{2}$ | 9 | $10\frac{1}{2}$ | 12 | $13\frac{1}{2}$ | 15 | $16\frac{1}{2}$ | 18 | $19\frac{1}{2}$ | 21 | $22\frac{1}{2}$ | 24 | $25\frac{1}{2}$ | 27 | 28 | 29 |
| 60 | 3 | $4\frac{1}{2}$ | 6 | $7\frac{1}{2}$ | 9 | $10\frac{1}{2}$ | 12 | $13\frac{1}{2}$ | 15 | $16\frac{1}{2}$ | 18 | $19\frac{1}{2}$ | 21 | $22\frac{1}{2}$ | 24 | $25\frac{1}{2}$ | 27 | $28\frac{1}{2}$ | $29\frac{1}{2}$ |
| 61 | 3 | $4\frac{1}{2}$ | 6 | $7\frac{1}{2}$ | 9 | $10\frac{1}{2}$ | 12 | $13\frac{1}{2}$ | 15 | $16\frac{1}{2}$ | 18 | $19\frac{1}{2}$ | 21 | $22\frac{1}{2}$ | 24 | $25\frac{1}{2}$ | 27 | $28\frac{1}{2}$ | 30 |
| 62 | 3 | $4\frac{1}{2}$ | 6 | $7\frac{1}{2}$ | 9 | $10\frac{1}{2}$ | 12 | $13\frac{1}{2}$ | 15 | $16\frac{1}{2}$ | 18 | $19\frac{1}{2}$ | 21 | $22\frac{1}{2}$ | 24 | $25\frac{1}{2}$ | 27 | $28\frac{1}{2}$ | 30 |
| 63 | 3 | $4\frac{1}{2}$ | 6 | $7\frac{1}{2}$ | 9 | $10\frac{1}{2}$ | 12 | $13\frac{1}{2}$ | 15 | $16\frac{1}{2}$ | 18 | $19\frac{1}{2}$ | 21 | $22\frac{1}{2}$ | 24 | $25\frac{1}{2}$ | 27 | $28\frac{1}{2}$ | 30 |
| 64* | 3 | $4\frac{1}{2}$ | 6 | $7\frac{1}{2}$ | 9 | $10\frac{1}{2}$ | 12 | $13\frac{1}{2}$ | 15 | $16\frac{1}{2}$ | 18 | $19\frac{1}{2}$ | 21 | $22\frac{1}{2}$ | 24 | $25\frac{1}{2}$ | 27 | $28\frac{1}{2}$ | 30 |

* For women aged between 59 and 60, and men aged between 64 and 65, the cash amount due is to be reduced by $\frac{1}{12}$ for every complete month by which the age exceeds 59 or 64 respectively.

† In some cases, employees whose 20th birthday falls a few days after they become redundant may have the necessary 104 weeks' qualifying service.

# Qualifying for unemployment benefit

*Who is entitled to benefit*　　*Employees dismissed for misconduct*
*When benefit is refused*　　*Offers of other work*
*Employees who resign*

UNEMPLOYMENT benefit is available under the National Insurance scheme for anyone who loses his job or is temporarily laid off by his employer, provided he can satisfy the following conditions:

**1.** He must have been an employee, not a self-employed person.

**2.** At some time in the past he must have paid at least 26 National Insurance contributions as an employed person.

**3.** He must register at his local employment exchange for another job.

To qualify for the full rate of benefit, a claimant must have paid, or been credited with, 50 contributions as an employed person in the previous contribution year. But he can receive part benefit for 26 or more contributions. ☐ The National Insurance scheme—what the terms mean, p. 605.

To qualify for immediate benefit, he must have been dismissed (not for misconduct) or have some justifiable reason for leaving.

### When benefit is refused
There are times when an employee cannot receive unemployment benefit, even though he has paid the necessary contributions and fulfilled most of the other conditions.

WAGES IN LIEU OF NOTICE An employee who is dismissed but who is paid wages in lieu of notice cannot draw benefit until the end of the period of notice for which he has been paid. If he is dismissed and given pay in lieu of a holiday he would have taken later, however, he is usually allowed immediate benefit. Similarly, a man who is dismissed while on holiday can generally draw benefit from the time his contract is terminated.

STRIKES No one who stands to benefit from a strike at his place of employment is allowed unemployment benefit while the strike is on. Nor is he eligible for supplementary benefit to meet his own needs—although he can claim it for his wife and children.

This means that if workers on one part of a production line strike, others who are involved, though they have nothing to do with the dispute, may not be able to claim unemployment benefit if they lose their jobs. This applies only if they—or other employees in

the same grade or class of employment—are taking part in the strike, likely to benefit from the outcome or are helping to finance it (for instance, if the union to which they belong is giving strike pay to strikers). The disqualification applies only to people employed in the same place, which means that only one department could be involved.

PENSIONS If a man is receiving a private pension from a previous employer he may not be entitled to the full benefit.

PART-TIME JOBS An unemployed man may have his benefit reduced or stopped if he takes a part-time job which breaks certain conditions. These are:

**1.** Earnings must not exceed a certain amount. In 1972 it was 75p a day.

**2.** The part-time job must not prevent the man from being available for full-time work.

**3.** The part-time job must not be the claimant's usual main occupation.

Part-time firemen and lifeboat men are, however, allowed to continue their part-time work without affecting the right to benefit.

ABSENCE ABROAD Normally, unemployment benefit is not payable to anyone living or going abroad. But agreements exist with some countries to provide benefit for unemployed British subjects. Full details can be obtained from the Department of Health and Social Security, Overseas Group, Newcastle upon Tyne NE98 1YX.

### Employees who resign
Anyone who leaves of his own accord must show he had good cause if he wants to claim benefit. Otherwise he can be disqualified for up to the first six weeks he is unemployed.

Personal dislike of his boss or a fellow employee is not regarded as a good cause for leaving. But if an employee can show that he was victimised or bullied by a supervisor, say, or that his employer had broken his contract, he is normally allowed benefit.

➤ A DISPUTE OVER PIECE-RATES *An employee who refused to accept his firm's reduced piece-rate payments was dismissed.*
DECISION *The Insurance Commissioner decided that the man did not have to accept the new*

*rates, and that his employer had broken the contract. The employee was therefore allowed unemployment benefit.* ◄

A man who resigns after receiving a firm offer of a new job, and then finds the offer withdrawn, is entitled to benefit.

► THE JOB THAT FELL THROUGH *An employee, offered a job by another firm, gave his notice. But the job never materialised.*
DECISION *It was ruled the man had 'just cause' to leave and qualified for benefit.* ◄

In very limited circumstances personal considerations may be thought to give a man sufficient reason to leave a job or an area.

► A HOME OF THEIR OWN *A man who lived with his wife and child in two rooms found a house in another town, left his job to live there, but was out of work for a time.*
DECISION *The Commissioner said that the move to a new house constituted a 'just cause' for leaving and the man was therefore entitled to receive benefit.* ◄

**Employees dismissed for misconduct**
Where an employee has been dismissed because of his misconduct, he can be refused benefit for up to six weeks.

► MISSING CASH MYSTERY *The manager of a chemist's shop was acquitted of embezzlement after some of his takings were missed, but the*

---

## How to claim benefit

ON the first day of unemployment anyone eligible to claim benefit should go to the local Employment Exchange. Those under 18 must report at the Careers Office (Youth Employment). A claimant should take his National Insurance Card or, if it is not available, state his National Insurance number if he knows it.

The employment officer will take details of the kind of work the applicant does. If there is no suitable job to offer, a claims officer will help the applicant to fill in an application form for benefit.

As long as an employee is out of work and receiving benefit, his National Insurance card is credited with contributions as though he were working. Unemployment benefit is paid once a week in cash.

FALSE CLAIMS A person who knowingly makes a false statement to obtain benefit may be jailed for up to three months.

LATE CLAIMS Any claim made more than a year after the period of unemployment finished will not be considered.

### How much benefit can be paid
The local insurance officer decides whether benefit can be paid and how much. There are lower rates for married women, and for people under 18. Payments are also made for dependants—a wife who does not work, for instance, and children under 16 (or under 19 in the case of young people still at school, students and some apprentices.) A woman who loses her job can claim for her husband if he is dependent

on her, and incapable of supporting himself because of physical or mental illness.

To close the gap between normal earnings and unemployment benefit, there is an additional allowance called an earnings-related supplement which depends on the amount earned in the last tax year. ☐ Earnings-related supplement, p. 603.

NO-BENEFIT DAYS Unemployment benefit is not paid for public holidays unless a claimant normally works on those days. If a claimant ordinarily works a four-day week, he receives unemployment benefit for only four days.

### How to appeal
An applicant who disagrees with the insurance officer's decision can have the case considered by the local appeal tribunal, by writing to the local Social Security office.

Anyone not satisfied with the tribunal's decision can appeal to the National Insurance Commissioner. It is best to let a union, staff association or solicitor handle the case.

Disputes about the number of insurance contributions paid or credited or about reckonable earnings are referred first to the Secretary of State for Social Services.

His decision can be challenged—only on a point of law—in the High Court, or it can be referred direct to the High Court by the Secretary of State. Legal aid may be available. ☐ Help with fees and costs, p. 710.

An appeal on a question arising from the Secretary of State's decision can be heard by the local tribunal only if its chairman agrees.

*company none the less dismissed him from its employment.*
DECISION *The Commissioner held that the man should be disqualified from benefit because he had been 'negligent in the discharge of his duties'.* ◄

An employee can lodge an appeal—which is considered by a National Insurance tribunal or the Commissioner—on the ground that the reason for which he was dismissed was not misconduct.

A man dismissed because he has been convicted of a criminal offence relevant to his suitability for the job is unlikely to get unemployment benefit—even if the offence is unconnected with his work. But an employee would not be refused benefit if he was dismissed only because his employer discovered he had a previous criminal conviction.

➤ THE ACCOUNTANT'S SECRET *A middle-aged chartered accountant kept secret a previous conviction when he was given a job with a large firm. The firm eventually heard about it and he was dismissed.*
DECISION *The accountant was allowed unemployment benefit.* ◄

The maximum period for which anyone can be disqualified from benefit is six weeks, but the tribunal or the Commissioner can allow a shorter period if it is justified.

➤ THE JOB LOST FOR 6½p *A British Rail labourer was found guilty of stealing sacking worth 6½p. He thought nobody would object if he took it, but he was fined £5 and lost his job.*
DECISION *The Commissioner reduced the disqualification period from six to two weeks.* ◄

Similarly, the insurance officer, tribunal or Commissioner can disagree with the employer and find the dismissal unjustified.

➤ BROKEN RECORD *A bus driver had a clean driving record for 21 years. One night his bus collided with another as he was turning it around in a dark street. The driver was dismissed as a result.*
DECISION *The Commissioner held that the driver should not be disqualified from benefit because the accident was not caused by an act of misconduct but was due only to an 'isolated error of judgment'.* ◄

### Offers of other work
Every employee who claims unemployment benefit must be available for other work. He may be disqualified from benefit for up to six weeks if he turns down any reasonable job that is found through the Department of Employment or refuses to attend a training course.

There are occasions when he can reject the offer of a job without disqualifying himself from benefit. For example, a man would be justified in refusing to accept a job that is vacant because of a strike—he is not expected to blackleg. He is also entitled, for a reasonable period, to refuse a job which offers substantially lower wages or poorer conditions than he normally has.

➤ A CUT IN SALARY *After being out of work for ten days a man was offered a job at a salary £300 a year less than he had in his previous job. He refused the job and made a claim for unemployment benefit.*
DECISION *It was held that his refusal of the job was reasonable, and benefit was allowed.* ◄

If the same man had been out of work for a long time, he might not have been given benefit. It is not always enough to say that the job offered is not as good as the previous one. The authorities take into account how long a man has been out of work and whether he was previously paid above the local rate, or given better than usual conditions.

➤ UNPAID TEA BREAKS *A middle-aged fitter refused a job because tea breaks were not allowed without loss of pay. He said that he had been paid for tea breaks in his previous job.*
DECISION *He was not allowed benefit because paid tea breaks were not customary in the area.* ◄

A worker's conscience and personal dislikes do not justify refusing a new job offered through the Department of Employment.

➤ THE WOMAN WHO WAS AFRAID *A young woman who had been out of work for some time refused a job in a Royal Ordnance factory because she thought the work was dangerous.*
DECISION *The Commissioner ruled that the work was no more dangerous than any other job, and upheld the insurance officer's decision not to pay unemployment benefit.* ◄

PENALTIES A man who refuses jobs which are considered suitable for him, or who refuses to carry out reasonable recommendations made by the local office of the Department of Employment aimed at helping him find suitable employment, can have his benefit stopped for up to six weeks. He can still claim supplementary benefit, though at a reduced rate. ☐ State help in hardship, p. 550.

# Restrictions after leaving the job

*How restrictions are limited*
*Taking action against an employer*
*Setting up a rival business*

SOMETIMES an employer may try to restrict the kind of job an employee can do if he leaves, or limit the area in which he can work. These restrictions, called restraints of trade, may be written into the employee's contract or letter of appointment.

Even if the employee has signed to acknowledge his agreement to a restriction of this kind, the employer must apply to the courts before he is entitled to enforce it.

The employer asks for an injunction to prevent the employee from breaking his contract. The injunction will not be granted unless the employer can show that the restriction imposed on the employee is reasonable and necessary to protect not only his interests but the interests of the public.

Some of the skills and knowledge acquired by an employee in his work belong to the employee himself. He can sell this acquired skill and knowledge to the highest bidder when looking for a new job.

But the interests of the employer are protected, too. A former employee is not entitled to pass on confidential information which he learnt in the course of his work.

An employer can also ask the court to grant an injunction preventing a former employee from persuading clients to switch their business to his new employer.

## How restrictions are limited

The courts may accept as reasonable an agreement that an employee cannot work at the same job for a different firm for a certain time after he leaves the job. But they do not allow sweeping restrictions on an employee's freedom of action covering long periods.

If a restraint clause tries to prevent an employee from working somewhere else, it must be specific, not worded in general terms.

➤ THE TAILOR WHO JOINED A COMPETITOR *In 1920, a department store tried to prevent Mr Lamont, one of its tailors, from going to work for a rival store. His contract said that he could not work for any department of any store in competition with his employers.*
DECISION *The court held that the restriction on Mr Lamont should have applied only to his* *working in the tailoring department of another store. Therefore the restraint clause was too wide and unenforceable. (Attwood v. Lamont.)* ◄

KEEPING INFORMATION SECRET The courts usually consider it reasonable for an employer to try to stop confidential or exclusive information going to a rival through an employee, but only if it is information the employee could not have got elsewhere.
AGREEMENTS BETWEEN EMPLOYERS People seeking a new job may find their former employer and companies in the same line of business have agreed not to employ one another's ex-employees.

➤ A 'NO POACHING' PACT *Kores and Kolok, who were competing firms, agreed that neither would take on an employee within five years of his leaving the other company. When Kolok later employed a research chemist who had just left Kores, Kores sued them.*
DECISION *In 1959, the agreement between the two firms was held to be not valid. A five-year ban on employees, including manual workers, was far too long, the court held. (Kores Manufacturing Co. v. Kolok Manufacturing Co.)* ◄

## Taking action against an employer

Courts usually refuse to uphold a restrictive clause in an agreement if it is contrary to the public interest—for example, keeping a skilled man out of work for which he is trained.

If an employee suffers because of a restrictive agreement or because a restraint clause in his own contract seems unreasonable, he can apply to the court to declare it void.

## Setting up a rival business

An employee who leaves to set up in business on his own can use the general knowledge and expertise he has gained with his former employer—unless the employer is likely to suffer unfairly from this.

For example, it might be reasonable for an employer to try to prevent an employee taking customers with him when he leaves. Much would depend on the terms of the contract. But the court would support such a restriction for a limited period only.

# Retirement: claiming a State pension

*Collecting a pension*     *Pensions for older people*
*Pensioners who work*     *How to appeal*

A PERSON nearing retirement age (65 for a man, 60 for a woman) normally receives a pension application form from the Department of Health and Social Security about four months before his State retirement pension is due. The form should be completed even by people who do not intend to retire. If no form is received, apply to the local Social Security office.

A wife claiming a pension on her husband's insurance should notify the department separately. Any claims for dependants must be made on separate forms.

A pension is not backdated for more than one month before the department is notified of retirement, unless there is good reason for delay. It is never backdated for more than 12 months, whatever the circumstances.

The size of pension which a claimant is entitled to receive may depend on the record of National Insurance contributions made during his or her working life. □ Qualifying for a State pension, p. 525.

## Collecting a pension
Pensions are usually paid from the first pension pay-day after retirement (normally a Thursday). They are paid weekly in advance in the form of orders which can be cashed at a named post office.

The pension must be cashed within three months of the date on which it is due to be paid, otherwise a new order has to be obtained. Graduated pensions and other additions are paid with the main pension.

Pensions can also be paid every four weeks or every quarter in arrears by a crossed order which must be paid into a bank account. Retirement pensions can be paid in any overseas country but if a person lives abroad, he may not receive the periodic increases paid to pensioners in Britain.

## Pensioners who work
Pensions are reduced if the pensioner earns more than a certain amount weekly during the first five years following retirement age.

In 1972 the limit was £9·50. For the first part of any additional earnings (up to £11·50 in 1972) half the excess is deducted from the pension. Any earnings above that further limit are deducted in full.

A working widow under 65 can have deductions made only until her retirement pension is reduced to the level of the widow's pension to which she would otherwise be entitled.

Any expenses incurred by working—such as the cost of employing someone to look after a pensioner's dependant—are set against earnings in calculating any pension reduction.

A man's pension is not affected by his wife's earnings unless he is drawing an increased pension because she is under 60. A woman's pension is not affected by her husband's earnings, even though it may be paid on account of the husband's insurance qualifications.

## Pensions for older people
Anyone aged 80 or over who is not entitled to a National Insurance Pension can claim an old person's pension, which is paid at a lower rate (in October 1972, it was £4·05, or £2·50 for a married woman).

INCREASES FOR THE OVER-80's All pensioners aged 80 or over, whether they are receiving the normal National Insurance retirement pension or the old person's pension, are entitled to an age addition (in 1972, 25p per week).

## How to appeal
A claim for a pension goes first to an insurance officer at the local Social Security office. If the person claiming the pension or allowance is not satisfied with his decision, he can appeal to the local tribunal.

But if the claim was refused on the ground of the contributions record, the Secretary of State must settle this issue before the appeal can go ahead. Even then the chairman of the tribunal can refuse to hear the appeal.

The local tribunal consists of an independent chairman and two members, one drawn from a panel of representatives of employed persons and one drawn from a panel of persons representing employers. □ Appearing before a tribunal, p. 735.

A final appeal can be made within three months to the National Insurance Commissioner, who is appointed by the Crown.

# YOUR SOCIAL LIFE AND POLITICS

# Public houses and restaurants

*When young people are admitted*
*Permitted hours of opening*
*Opposing a publican's licence*

*Betting, gaming and lotteries*
*Obtaining credit*
*Rights in public restaurants*

No one has an automatic right to be allowed into a public house or restaurant. These establishments are private property, and are regarded in law as shops—premises where retail trade is carried out. The licensee of a public house, sometimes called a landlord or publican, or the proprietor of a restaurant has no obligation to give a reason for not admitting or for refusing to serve a customer.

The only formal legal restriction on a restaurant proprietor's or licensee's right to exclude a customer is the Race Relations Act 1968. A licensee or proprietor cannot legally refuse to serve a customer on the grounds of race, colour or ethnic or national origin.

Anybody who thinks he has been barred on these grounds can report the incident to the Race Relations Board which, if there is evidence of discrimination, can try to negotiate a settlement. If this fails, the board may decide to prosecute the licensee or restaurant proprietor. The board's address is 5 Lower Belgrave Street, London SW1W 0MR.

If the grounds for exclusion are not race or nationality but still seem unreasonable—if, for instance, a man is refused service in a public house because he is wearing overalls—a complaint can be made to the brewer if it is a tied house (that is, owned by a brewer and leased or run by a tenant or a manager).

A publican, to be able to sell intoxicating drinks, has to obtain a licence from the local licensing magistrates.

The licence has to be renewed annually by the magistrates, and anyone with a complaint can oppose the renewal. For instance, a person who felt that he had been excluded unreasonably from a public house would have a ground on which to oppose renewal of the publican's licence.

If he succeeded, and a new licence was refused, the licensee would in effect be put out of business.

## When young people are admitted

Children under 14 are not allowed into licensed bars during licensing hours. A bar is defined as any place which is exclusively or mainly used for the sale and consumption of intoxicating liquor. But children living on the premises are allowed in bars, and children are permitted to go through a bar on their way to, say, an inner restaurant, lavatory or playroom which some public houses provide.

Young people aged 14 and over but under 18 are allowed into bars but are not allowed to drink intoxicating liquor there. If they do, an offence is committed both by the person who bought the drink and by the publican who sold it. The drinker under 18 can also be fined up to £20.

The licensee is liable to a fine of up to £25 for a first offence, £50 for a second offence, and he may also forfeit his licence for a second or subsequent offence.

Young people between 16 and 18 may order beer, porter, cider or perry—but not wine—with a meal eaten at a table in a bar (or elsewhere on licensed premises) if part of the bar is customarily set aside for serving meals to the public.

Children over five can drink beer, wine or spirits on licensed premises other than in a bar, provided they do not make the purchase themselves. No one under 18 may collect intoxicating drink from the off-licence part of a public house or an off-licence shop.

## Permitted hours of opening

Generally, a public house is allowed to serve drinks for only nine hours on a weekday and five and a half hours on a Sunday.

The Licensing Act 1964 lays down licensing hours as, generally, from 11 a.m. to 11 p.m., with a break from 3 p.m. until 5.30 p.m. on weekdays; and 12 noon to 10.30 p.m., with a break from 2 p.m. to 7 p.m. on Sundays, Christmas Day and Good Friday.

Licensing hours can be extended with the permission of the local licensing magistrates. The magistrates also have powers to alter the hours to suit particular local conditions. Some areas—parts of Wales and Monmouthshire—have Sunday closing by law.

Scottish licensing laws are also different. Each weekday, public houses are open from 11 a.m. to 2.30 p.m. and 5 p.m. to 11 p.m. On Sundays, public houses are closed, and only hotels sell intoxicating liquor—from noon to 2.30 p.m. and from 6 p.m. to 10 p.m.

Licensees may apply to the licensing magistrates for an extension of licensing hours to cater for a particular event, such as a wedding reception, which is being held on their premises. If the function is taking place on unlicensed premises—for example at a public hall or cricket club pavilion—a licensee must apply for an occasional licence which, in effect, extends his existing licence to these premises for a specified time.

In addition, there are various special licences and certificates—for example a supper hours certificate which allows intoxicating drinks to be sold only with meals and may be restricted to certain months of the year.

A special order of exemption can be granted to extend licensing hours for General Elections and on certain Bank Holidays.

Permanent modifications of licensing hours, known as general exemption orders, can be obtained by licensees catering for people in certain trades—for instance some public houses in London's Smithfield Market open at 6.30 a.m. to serve market workers.

The licensing hours apply only to the buying and selling of drink: the customer is allowed ten minutes at the end of each period of permitted hours for 'drinking up'. He is also allowed to take out of a public house during the 'drinking-up' period any bottles of intoxicating drink he has bought during licensing hours.

Although a customer is expected to leave licensed premises after trading hours, there is nothing in the Licensing Acts which says he must leave. But he is trespassing if he stays without the licensee's consent. A licensee may eject a customer, but is not allowed to use unnecessary force.

Outside licensing hours a licensee may provide drink at his own expense to friends or employees on any part of his premises. But customers cannot be regarded as friends for the purpose of evading the law. If charges were made against a licensee, he would have to prove that he was entertaining genuine friends, who were not paying for their drinks.

A licensee selling drinks on licensed premises outside the permitted hours is liable to a fine of £100, and may lose his licence. The after-hours customer is also liable to be charged and fined up to £100.

A licensee is not required by law to stay open during all the licensing hours. But if he frequently and unreasonably closes, the renewal of his licence may be opposed.

OTHER COMPLAINTS Customers can oppose the renewal of a licence on other grounds; consistently bad service, for instance, or unfavourable structural alterations. But opposition should be a last recourse after complaining first to the landlord and then, if the public house is owned by a brewery company, to the company itself.

## Opposing a publican's licence

Any person can oppose the granting or renewal of a licence to a publican by appearing and making a complaint at the annual meeting of the local magistrates' licensing committee—known as the 'Brewster Sessions'. The local Press normally publishes the date when it is to be held. The date can also be obtained from the magistrates' clerk at the local court.

Anyone opposing a licence should be represented by a solicitor and should have other people to support his complaints against a licensee. Magistrates must be convinced that a licensee has failed to provide a reasonable service to the public.

A licensee must be given seven days' notice before the sessions open that the renewal of his licence is being opposed, and also the reasons for opposing it. The clerk to the licensing magistrates must also be informed.

## Betting, gaming and lotteries

Betting and the passing of betting slips on licensed premises is an offence, except where there is a room licensed for betting.

Customers may play all games of skill, such as billiards, skittles and darts, for money, with no restriction on the amount of stakes. But for such games as dominoes or cribbage stakes must not be high—only a few pence. Other card games can be played on licensed premises for small stakes of a similar kind, provided that the licensee obtains a permit from the licensing justices.

Lotteries and sweepstakes can be held and licensed premises are also allowed under certain conditions to have gaming machines.
☐ Betting and gaming, p. 660.

## Obtaining credit

It is against the law for a licensee to allow credit for liquor drunk in a public house. But drinks sold with a meal can be included in the bill for the meal and credit allowed on the total sale of food and drink. Credit can also be given for all off-licence sales.

## Lost property

A customer who leaves property in a place provided by a licensee or restaurant proprietor—such as a hat and coat on a wall peg—can make a claim if his property is lost. A claim cannot be made, however, if a conspicuous notice warns customers that property is left at the owner's risk.

### Rights in public restaurants

A restaurant customer is not entitled to expect to be served a particular dish even though it is on the menu. If the dish is 'off' he has no legal grounds for complaint. But if he has ordered from the menu and the order has been accepted, he has the right to expect the food to be as advertised on the menu. It must also be of reasonable quality, in relation to the price and the type of establishment.

If the food is not what was ordered or if it is dirty or badly prepared, the customer may refuse to accept it, or to pay. He is not obliged to accept a substitute.

The customer can make the same protest against other irritations, such as slowness of service or dirty cutlery. But in all such cases it is essential that the customer personally explains his complaint to the manager and offers his name and address before leaving.

The proprietor may want to take civil action to recover the bill. If the customer refuses to give his address, the proprietor is entitled to detain him and call the police.

A public house or restaurant which has unclean food, equipment or premises may be breaking the hygiene regulations of the Department of Health and the Ministry of Agriculture, Fisheries and Food. The establishment may also be contravening local bye-laws. If a licensee or the proprietor of a restaurant has broken the hygiene regulations, he is liable to a fine of £100 or three months in prison, or both, and a continuing fine of £5 a day if he allows the offence to continue.

If a complaint is justified, the proprietor is unlikely to risk prosecution. He may offer a substitute meal or drink. This does not make him immune from prosecution, but the customer may be persuaded not to sue.

Anyone who wishes to proceed with a complaint about cleanliness in a catering establishment should contact the local council public health officer.

A customer who considers he has been overcharged for a meal has no rights of redress. But if he is charged more than is shown on a menu, he can refuse to pay the excess. A cover charge or service charge should not be included in the bill unless it is shown on the menu or in some other place where it can be clearly seen by customers before the meal is ordered.

Anyone who becomes ill from eating contaminated food can claim damages from the restaurant. To succeed, he has to show that the proprietors or their staff were negligent in the preparation of the food.

Even where there is no negligence, the person buying the meal (but not his family or guests) can claim for breach of contract if he suffers personally, since there is an implied term of the contract that the food is safe to eat.

☐ Suing for damages, p. 731.

---

## Measures for drinks

GIN, whisky, rum and vodka must be offered in certain fractions of a gill (one-sixth, one-fifth or one-quarter) and a notice must be displayed saying what the measure is. This regulation does not apply to other spirits, such as liqueurs.

Draught beer or cider must be sold only in quantities of one-third, one-half, or multiples of one-half, of a pint. In practice, most establishments offer only pints and half pints.

Glasses or mugs used for draught beer or cider must be of the same capacity as the liquor ordered, except when the glass has an engraved line to show the correct measure, or if automatic-measure pumps are installed.

A customer who thinks he has been given short measure or diluted beer can complain to the local authority's weights and measures inspector, whose address can be found in the local telephone directory.

The customer should preferably have witnesses to support his complaint. A weights and measures inspector can demand to be allowed to test the specific gravity of beer or spirits on licensed premises to check whether they have been diluted.

The penalty for diluting beer is a maximum fine of £500 or imprisonment not exceeding three months, or both.

The penalty for giving short measure is a maximum fine of £100 for the first offence or three months' imprisonment, or both. For second and subsequent offences, the maximum fine is £250. If the barman gives *more* than the exact measure (the 'long pull') he is breaking the law and is liable to a fine of £30.

# The rights of club members

*A club's constitution*      *When a club may be sued*
*Drinking in clubs*          *When a member may be expelled*

CLUBS have the right to confer or refuse membership at their discretion. They are restricted only by the law forbidding racial discrimination. If a club is genuinely private with a restricted membership it is not affected by the Race Relations Act 1968. But a club, such as a local political club, which admits new members so freely that it is virtually open to the public will be breaking the law if it rejects an application on the grounds of colour or race.

## A club's constitution

There are two main types of club—members' clubs, owned and run by a committee of members, and proprietary clubs, run by a private individual for profit.

In a proprietary club, the proprietor provides club facilities for the members, but the members have no control over him. If they object to his way of running the club, there is little they can do other than resign.

In a members' club, the members themselves choose the form of organisation—the club's constitution. This forms the contract between each member and the others. Once adopted, it must, in law, be observed.

CLASSES OF MEMBERSHIP The rules of a club often set out different types of membership—full, probationary and so on. The rights and responsibilities of each class are whatever the rules say they are. There is nothing in law to prevent a club giving the power to make decisions to only a few members.

TRUSTEES The assets of a members' club belong to its members, and not to the club itself. Since this is obviously inconvenient, clubs usually appoint trustees to hold property 'for the use and benefit of the club and its members in accordance with the rules'.

SUBSCRIPTIONS The amount of subscriptions and when and how they should be paid will usually be laid down by the rules. Once a member has paid his first subscription he has a legal obligation to pay until he resigns.

## Drinking in clubs

Generally the hours during which clubs can sell alcoholic drinks are the same as the hours which apply to most licensed premises in the area. ☐ Public houses and restaurants, p. 656. There are circumstances, however, when clubs can sell drinks to members outside these hours:

**1.** A club with a restaurant can serve drinks with meals for an hour after the end of normal licensing hours.

**2.** A club providing entertainment can sell drinks with meals until 1 a.m. from Monday to Saturday.

**3.** A club registered with the licensing justices may also apply for a special-hours certificate to sell alcoholic drinks between 12.30 p.m. and 3 p.m., and between 6.30 p.m. and 2 a.m., if the premises are covered by a music and dancing licence and meals are served. The 'special hours' may be extended until 3 a.m. in the London Metropolitan Area, but not in the City of London.

DRINKS FOR NON-MEMBERS A club can legally sell drinks to non-members if its rules for doing so are approved by the magistrates.

## When a club may be sued

A members' club which is not a company cannot be sued in its own name, for it is not a legal entity.

If an action against a club concerns its property, then the trustees are the defendants. If someone is injured on club premises, for example, he can take action against the trustees as legal holders of the club's property.

Alternatively, court action could be brought against the committee members as representatives of the members of the club.

## When a member may be expelled

Most club rules provide for expulsion. These must be followed carefully when a member is expelled. The methods of enforcing them ought not to be contrary to 'natural justice'.

Suppose, for instance, that a club tried to expel a member because he had not paid his subscription. If he could show that it was his bank's fault and that he had not been given a chance to put the matter right, he might get a court to declare that the expulsion was unlawful and that he was still a member, especially if membership of the club affected his professional reputation.

# Betting and gaming

*The law on gambling debts*

*Placing bets with bookmakers*

*Disputes with bookmakers*

*'Investing' in football pools*

*Taking part in bingo*

*Gaming in clubs and casinos*

MOST forms of gambling are subject to a wide variety of controls and restrictions. The main object of the various Acts of Parliament is to ensure that gambling is properly conducted, and that the odds are not unfairly stacked against the player.

The only exception is gaming in private houses which can be carried on without restriction so long as players are not charged an entrance fee.

## The law on gambling debts

The most far-reaching legal provision affecting gambling is laid down by the Gaming Act 1845, which says that all wagering contracts are, in law, 'null and void'.

This means that no dispute about a wager or bet can be settled in the courts. If cash has been paid, it cannot be recovered. A punter who has been given credit cannot be made to pay if he loses; nor can a bookmaker or gaming club be forced to pay winnings.

In practice, anyone who runs up a bill with a bookmaker and fails to pay is likely to be blacklisted, and to find that his bets will not be accepted in future. He may also be pressed for the money, possibly by a debt-collecting agency. As long as the bookmaker or agency does not harass him, there is nothing illegal about this. □ Debts and bankruptcy, p. 580.

Any agreement which is essentially a device to compel a punter to honour his debts under a wagering agreement is also unenforceable. If, to avoid being named as a defaulter, a person agrees to pay unpaid debts, the subsequent agreement is just as unenforceable in the courts as the original wager or wagers.

It is only wagers that cannot be enforced in the courts—not all bets. Legally, a wager is a bet in which both the gambler and the person or organisation accepting the bet stand only to win or lose money or money's worth on the outcome of some event whose result is not yet known. If only one side stands to win or lose, then the bet is not a wager, and the gambler can sue or be sued for debt.

When a gambler stakes money at roulette, for example, a gaming contract is made, because both the gambler and the casino proprietor are playing a game of chance with each other for money. Similarly, when a punter places a bet with a bookmaker, that bet is a wager, because either of them can win or lose, depending on the result of the race.

But a punter who bets with the 'Tote' is not making a wager, for the Tote cannot lose money on the outcome of a race. The Horserace Totalisator Board gets its income by deducting expenses from the bets placed, then shares out what is left among the winning punters. Since bets with the Tote are not wagering contracts, the board can sue in the courts to recover debts.

▶THE BET THAT WAS NOT A WAGER *Miss Barbara Smoker laid her bets on horses with Tote Investors Ltd, a company which accepted bets on behalf of the Horserace Totalisator Board. Miss Smoker was allowed credit, and when her horses lost she was unable to pay the bill, which amounted to £23 13s. 8d. Tote Investors sued Miss Smoker to recover the debt. She pleaded that the debt could not be recovered because it arose from a wagering contract.*
DECISION *Miss Smoker had to pay. The court held in 1967 that since the Totalisator Board can neither win nor lose, a bet with them is not a wager. The Board is legally obliged, under the Betting, Gaming and Lotteries Act 1963, to pay winners, and is therefore entitled to recover debts. (Tote Investors Ltd v. Smoker.)*◀

GAMBLING SYNDICATES If a group of people form a syndicate to gamble, the agreement they make among themselves is not a wagering contract, so they are free to take legal action against one another to recover debts or winnings. If one member usually submits entries for the group, who each pay a share of the entrance money, and the bet is successful, the other members may recover their share of the winnings from him.

But if the bet is not placed they cannot sue him for what they would have won, since any winnings would arise from an unenforceable wagering contract.

STAKEHOLDERS If two people making a bet ask a third person to hold the money until the bet is decided, the stakeholder has a legal obligation to do with each person's money whatever he is asked to do by that person.

This situation can have curious consequences. If the stakeholder pays over the stakes to the winner, the loser cannot recover his money from the stakeholder, who has simply done what he was authorised to do. But the winner cannot sue the stakeholder for the loser's money because his right to it depends on an invalid wagering contract.

On the other hand, if the stakes have not yet been paid to the winner, either party can recover his own stake from the stakeholder. If the loser makes such a request and the stakeholder then pays the stake to the winner, he will be liable to the loser because he will have acted outside his authority.

## Placing bets with bookmakers

Bets can be placed with a bookmaker or his accredited agent at a horse or greyhound racing track; by post; by telephone; at a licensed betting office; or in a factory or hostel, provided both the person making the bet and the person receiving the stake money work or live there.

Betting is prohibited in streets and in public places (apart from racecourses). The definition of a street is wide, and includes such places as bridges, footways and subways, and any doorway opening on to a street or on to ground adjoining and open to the street.

It is an offence to bet with anyone under 18, or to employ people under 18 to place bets. It is also an offence to use premises other than a licensed betting office as a place to which people resort to bet. The offence is aimed at 'resorting to bet', not just betting.

THE BOOKMAKER'S RULES Always ask a bookmaker for a copy of his rules, if they are not displayed in his office. They show any limit he sets on winnings—which may range from about £2000 to no limit at all depending on the size of the business—and how odds are decided. The rules usually provide for disputes to be settled by arbitration since betting disputes, being wagering contracts, cannot be resolved in court.

PUNTER'S AGENTS A man employed on commission by a punter to bet or carry out other wagering transactions for him, is known as a punter's agent. The punter cannot sue the agent if he fails to carry out instructions.

The agent is, however, liable to pay to his employer any winnings he has received. He cannot escape this liability. Yet the agent who puts on a bet as instructed and loses cannot claim the stakes back if the person who has employed him to bet fails to pay.

POSTAL BETTING The main pitfall of postal betting is that the punter can never be sure that his bet will arrive on time; and the rules always provide that 'proof of posting will not be accepted as proof of delivery'.

More important, the rules of postal bookmakers contain clauses which entitle them to declare certain bets void. A bookmaker can refuse to pay out on bets received after a stated time before the race; on those where

## Pitfalls of paying money to tipsters and forecasters

BACKING winners or winning on the pools is, for most people, a matter of luck. The serious gambler, of course, studies 'form', and there are reputable organisations which provide technical information to help him. But there are also some tipsters whose activities are misleading and sometimes dishonest.

The approaches of tipsters vary. One may say, for example, that he has information 'hot from the stable'. Another may offer to send 'winning telegrams' on the day of the race.

Newspaper investigations show that, if all their tips to different clients are compared, some tipsters tip all the horses in a race.

They send different 'tips' to different clients throughout the country, and then later claim that they have tipped the winner. Some may even offer a 'money-back guarantee'. Even if this were enforceable in theory, it may be difficult to rely on the guarantee in practice, since many tipsters operate from accommodation addresses.

A variation on this theme is to ask for recruits to a 'syndicate' which will back the tipster's own selections. The window-dressing is very good—attractive figures of previous winnings are quoted, and there are usually very detailed rules; but the effect is usually that the client cannot sue the promoter for any winnings due to him.

Anyone who pays money to a tipster and later suspects fraud should report the case to the police. If the tipster's address was obtained from a newspaper advertisement, a complaint to the paper's advertising manager may save people from being caught in the future.

the post-mark is indistinct; and on those where, in the bookmaker's opinion, 'there are any suspicious circumstances whatsoever'. These rules are inflexibly enforced.

## Disputes with bookmakers

Because, in law, all wagering contracts are null and void, a bookmaker cannot recover his money by means of legal action if a losing punter fails to pay. Nor can a punter successfully sue the bookmaker for his winnings, even if the bookmaker has given a cheque and later stops it.

Disputes may arise over a bookmaker's interpretation of his rules, or over the amount of winnings. Though the punter cannot take legal action, he can appeal to one of the national bodies governing racing or bookmaking. The punter can also oppose the renewal of the bookmaker's licence, without which he cannot legally operate.

BOOKMAKERS' ASSOCIATION The National Association of Bookmakers Ltd, 26–27 Cow-cross Street, London EC1M 6DQ, helps to decide betting disputes through its affiliated associations. This service is free.

The association's jurisdiction extends only to members, though on most racecourses the local association has power over non-members as well. Before taking a dispute to the association, find out if the particular bookmaker is a member. He will usually indicate that he is a member in his rules booklet, or the punter can ask the association.

The dispute or claim is heard by a committee of the local affiliated association. If the committee is satisfied that a claim has been established, it makes an order for payment. A bookmaker ignoring the order can be expelled from the association.

It is possible to appeal to the National Association against the local committee's decision. But the appeal must be based on technical grounds or on the belief that there were irregularities at the hearing.

TATTERSALLS' COMMITTEE If a backer has a dispute with a bookmaker (whether or not a member of the National Association of Bookmakers Ltd) and it relates to horse racing, he can apply to Tattersalls' Committee to adjudicate on it. The address is 7–9 Hatherley Road, Reading RG1 5QA.

The committee charges a hearing fee, which is non-returnable and varies according to the amount of the claim. If the committee decides in the punter's favour, it makes an order for the bookmaker to pay. If he refuses, he is listed as a defaulter, and is not able to 'lay off' bets with the larger national bookmakers.

TRACK COMMITTEES Tattersalls' Committee has jurisdiction only in the case of horse racing. A dispute with a bookmaker over a bet on greyhound racing can be referred to the advisory committee of the track concerned which can, if necessary, prevent a defaulter from setting up his stand again.

ARBITRATION It is always open to punter and bookmaker to agree that the matter be decided by an independent arbitrator. □ Going to arbitration, p. 719.

OPPOSING THE PERMIT A punter who feels he has been treated unfairly by a bookmaker can appeal to the licensing committee of the local magistrates not to renew his permit.

The permit comes up for renewal annually, and usually expires in May, which is the end of the licensing year. The bookmaker's application for a permit to be granted or renewed must be advertised in a local, national or sporting newspaper circulating in the area concerned. Anyone who wishes to object may do so by writing to the Clerk of the committee.

Two copies of the grounds for objection are required, and the objector is then given notice of the time and place of the hearing. If an objection is made and is not withdrawn, the objector has a right to be heard. He can be legally represented if he wishes.

## 'Investing' in football pools

Pools promoters cover their running costs and make their profits by deducting in advance a percentage of the total stakes. They do not stand to win or lose according to the outcome of the bet, and a football-pool entry is therefore not a wagering contract. In theory, it is enforceable in law.

The pools promoter is, however, free to lay down conditions, and in practice pools firms insert a clause saying that the transaction is 'binding in honour only'. This effectively bars legal action.

➤ THE ENTRY LOST IN THE POST *Mr Jones completed a football-pool entry and posted it to Vernon's Pools Ltd. It was a winning coupon, but Vernon's said that they had never received it. Mr Jones sued for the winnings allegedly due.*
DECISION *Mr Jones lost his action. The court said he could not enforce payment because the 'honour clause' made it clear that there was no intention to create legal relations; it was simply an 'agreement', and not an enforceable contract. (Jones v. Vernon's Pools Ltd.)* ◄

POOLS COLLECTORS Coupons can usually either be posted or handed to a collector. However, the use of a collector involves severe disadvantages. The rules usually say that a collector, though employed and paid by the pools firm, is an agent of the customer. So if the collector loses or fails to send in a winning entry, the customer has no claim in law against the pools firm.

LOST ENTRIES If an allegedly winning coupon is lost, the punter cannot sue either the pools firm or the Post Office. The Post Office is protected against claims of this sort. It is liable (within certain limits) only for the loss of registered and recorded-delivery packets. Pools coupons cannot be sent in this way, as there is then no time stamp.

INCORRECT ENTRIES The onus is on the punter to see that his permutations and entries are correct. There are frequent cases of punters who have submitted incorrect permutations, and discovered this only when they thought they had won. In these circumstances, the pools company may agree to return the stakes of the entry declared void—usually by giving the customer a credit note.

If the punter has sent in the same invalid entry all season, he cannot get his money back for the whole of the season. The pools companies keep the back coupons only for a week or two, and will return stakes only for the period for which they retain the coupons.

DISQUALIFIED ENTRIES There is a formidable list of disqualifications in the rules. An entry can be disqualified 'if in fact or in the opinion of the (pools firm's) accountants':

**1.** It is not accompanied by a remittance, or the form of remittance is invalid (cheques are usually not accepted unless arrangements are made in advance).

**2.** It is sent in by a defaulter (that is, someone who has been blacklisted by a pools firm) or anyone acting in concert with him.

**3.** Its envelope is not properly postmarked or

## Why pools firms can't be sued

*'I agree to abide by the company's Rules, which govern all entries and agree that this transaction is binding in honour only'*

The pools promoter is free in law to make his own rules, within certain limits, and usually includes the so-called 'honour clause'. This makes the entry a 'gentleman's agreement'. The result is that the client cannot sue the pools company for any winnings which he claims are due.

fails to reach the pools firm in the time allowed by the rules, 'or if the genuineness of any forecast therein is doubtful'.

**4.** It is not signed or is illegible, incorrectly completed, ambiguous or damaged.

**5.** There is any other breach of the rules.

### Taking part in bingo

Bingo is strictly controlled by the Gaming Act 1968. Commercial bingo clubs must be licensed by the local magistrates. Before anyone may apply for a licence, he must obtain a certificate of consent from a Government body called the Gaming Board. No one can play until he has been a member of the club, or of one of its branches, for at least 24 hours.

DISPUTES WITH A CLUB In practice, members' rights in bingo clubs are governed by the Gaming Act and the club's 'house rules' which are drawn up by the promoter, usually in consultation with the Gaming Board. A general rule is that a member is expected to make his call heard, and if he does not, he loses his chance to win.

If a player makes a mistaken call (known as a 'bogey' call), most rules provide for the card to be disqualified. Usually, the rules say that the management's decision is final.

Anyone who has a complaint about a bingo club which is part of a chain, and who cannot get satisfaction at local level, should write to the managing director. If a member believes that the game is not being conducted properly, he can address a complaint to The Secretary, The Gaming Board of Great Britain, Berkshire House, 168–173 High Holborn, London WC1V 7AA. The board has powers to object to the renewal of a club's licence.

### Gaming in clubs and casinos

Gaming is also controlled by the Gaming Act. Different rules apply to gaming in commercial clubs, to members' clubs (those from which no individual stands to make a profit) and to games played in public houses.

COMMERCIAL CLUBS Proprietary gambling clubs require a certificate of consent from the Gaming Board, as well as a licence from the local magistrates' court. The certificate is granted only after strict investigation.

There are important restrictions on membership. A member may not participate in gaming until he has belonged to the club for 48 hours or, in the case of clubs having several premises, has given notice 48 hours in advance that he intends to play at a particular branch. Members can introduce guests, but the guests can only be charged for gaming within the limits of the Act. Other members of the public cannot be admitted. People under 18 are not allowed in the room in a casino when gaming is taking place.

Casinos may provide facilities for equal-chance gaming and for certain games in which there is a banker—roulette, the various forms of baccarat (*baccarat banque, punto banco* and *chemin de fer*), blackjack and dice. Roulette may not be played with more than one zero, and some wagers and odds in blackjack and dice excessively favourable to the bank are not allowed.

It is an offence for the proprietor of a casino, or for anyone acting on his behalf, to make a loan or give other credit to enable someone to take part in gaming or to cover his losses. It is not illegal, however, for a friend unconnected with the club to lend money for gaming.

Casinos are allowed to accept cheques given by patrons in return for gambling chips, but must pay them into the club's own bank account within two banking days. A winning gambler who has cashed a cheque must not be given his own cheque back. The club has to pay the winner his money in cash (or give him a cheque of its own). If a gambler's cheque is dishonoured, the club can sue.

MEMBERS' CLUBS Genuine members' clubs and miners' welfare institutes with more than 25 members which do not have gaming as a main activity can be registered for gaming with the local magistrates. They can then charge their members up to £1 a day for gaming facilities, and in addition to equal-chance games, pontoon and *chemin de fer* may be played. Bridge and whist clubs are also permitted to register, and to make charges, even though their primary object is gaming.

PUBLIC HOUSES Certain types of gambling for modest stakes are allowed in public houses. ☐ Public houses and restaurants, p. 656.

NON-PROFIT-MAKING FUNCTIONS Limited gaming is allowed at certain social functions which are held for purposes other than private gain. ☐ Raising money by raffles, whist drives and bingo, p. 665.

## Other forms of gambling

Money—or money's worth—can be staked in other ways on the outcome of a future or un-ascertained event, and so rank as gambling.

PRIZE COMPETITIONS To be legal, a prize competition, whether conducted in a newspaper or by a trader, must depend 'to a substantial degree on the exercise of skill'. The rules of the competition will usually decide any dispute.

If two or more people enter a newspaper competition jointly, sharing entry fee and postage but putting the entry in only one of their names, the members can sue one another for their share if an entry wins.

➤ THE WINNER DENIED HER SHARE *Miss Simpkins had been living as a lodger for four years with Mrs Pays and her granddaughter, Esmé. All three liked a little flutter, and from about the beginning of May 1954, for some seven or eight weeks, they clubbed together to send in a coupon for the 'Empire News' fashion competition. Each of them contributed a forecast and Miss Simpkins filled in the coupon—but it was made out in the name of Mrs Pays.*

*There was an informal arrangement about sharing the costs of postage and entry, the costs sometimes being paid by one of them and sometimes by another. They had agreed to 'go shares' if an entry was successful. In the contest for the week of June 27, 1954, one of their lines was successful, and Mrs Pays was paid the prize of £750. She refused to pay Miss Simpkins a share of the prize. Miss Simpkins brought an action at Chester Assizes claiming a third of the £750 winnings.*

DECISION *Miss Simpkins won her case. Mr Justice Sellers awarded her £250 plus the costs of the action. Although the agreement was an informal one, from a legal point of view it was an enforceable contract. (Simpkins v. Pays.)* ◀

LOTTERIES English law allows lotteries only in limited circumstances. Many people in England and Wales receive through the post books of tickets for the Malta National Lottery or for the Irish Sweep—which are perfectly legal in Malta and the Republic of Ireland, but are not lawful in this country.

It is an offence in England and Wales for anyone to sell, distribute, offer or advertise for sale, or even to have in their possession, a ticket for an unlawful lottery. It is also forbidden for anyone to send or attempt to send any money or document relating to the sale or distribution of these lottery tickets out of the country.

The Post Office has power to confiscate any money or counterfoil relating to an illegal lottery which it may find in the post.

Despite the legal restrictions, many people in the United Kingdom do take part in the Maltese lottery and the Irish Sweep, and the published lists of prize-winners contain the names of many United Kingdom winners.

In practice, the police are unlikely to take action against somebody who merely bought a ticket for himself, if this came to light. But someone in Britain selling these tickets on a large scale might well be prosecuted.

# Raising money by raffles, whist drives and bingo

PEOPLE raising money for a good cause, not for private gain, are permitted to organise various forms of gaming and lotteries, provided they observe the rules laid down by law. These cover among other things, the value of prizes and the amount allowed for expenses.

## Organising a raffle

Raffles are a form of lottery—a distribution of prizes by lot or chance; the people taking part pay for a chance to win, but do not exercise any skill. Lotteries are permitted by law only in limited circumstances.

RAFFLES FOR CHARITY The most common form of lawful lottery is the raffle promoted to raise funds for charity, or for a club or political association. The organisers must first register their society with the local authority. Once it has been registered, the society may run a raffle or other type of lottery provided it keeps to certain rules.

The promoter must be a member of the society and if he, or anyone employed by him, is engaged in the betting business, he cannot be paid for his work. No prize must be worth more than £100, and not more than half the proceeds may be used for prizes.

No ticket may cost more than 5p and the price must be given on the tickets, all of which must cost the same. Not more than £750-worth of tickets may be sold, including tickets for any other lotteries the society may be holding on the same day.

The raffle may be advertised only on the premises of the society or in notices sent exclusively to members. Tickets can be sold to the public, but they can be sent through the post only to members of the society. Tickets must not be sold to anyone under 16.

The name of the society and the name and address of the promoter must appear on the tickets, which must not be sold at less than their full value. Expenses must not exceed 10 per cent of the proceeds. All profits, after deducting the cost of prizes and expenses, must go to the society or charity.

Within three months of the draw, a return must be sent to the local authority, giving the total proceeds, the amount spent on prizes and expenses, how the profits were used, and the dates between which tickets were sold.

PRIVATE RAFFLES A private lottery—one organised among people who all live or work on the same premises—must be promoted by a member of the group. All proceeds, after expenses have been deducted, must go to pay for prizes or, if a society is involved, towards the purposes of the society.

It is against the law to send tickets through the post, and they may be bought only by members of the group or society.

Tickets must all cost the same and must not be sold at less than their face value. Every ticket must include on it: the price; the name and address of the promoters; who is allowed to participate; and a statement that no prizes shall be given to anyone other than the buyers of the winning tickets.

The raffle may be advertised only on the premises, and the cost of printing and stationery are the only expenses that may be deducted from the proceeds.

RAFFLES AT SOCIAL EVENTS Raffles are allowed only at those social events which are not organised for private gain. Tickets may be sold only at the event, and the result of the draw must be declared there.

Not more than £10 may be deducted from the proceeds to pay for prizes, and no prizes may be given in cash. There is no objection to larger prizes as long as they are given to the organisers and not bought from the proceeds of the raffle.

The balance of the proceeds, after deducting prize money and expenses, must go to the cause for which the social event was organised.

## Fund-raising at social events

Apart from raffles, the betting and gaming laws allow three other types of fund-raising at social events such as dances, bazaars, fêtes and sporting events. These are games such as bingo and whist, side-shows, and slot machines.

Two conditions are common to all these activities: the events at which they take place must not be for private gain; and all proceeds, after deducting permitted expenses and prize money, must go to the cause for which the event is organised.

Games such as bingo and whist are allowed at social events, subject to certain rules. Players may make only a single payment to cover entrance fee, stake and any other charges made in respect of the gaming, and this must not be more than 50p. The total value of prizes must not exceed £50.

# The dangers of controversy

*Ways to avoid legal action*
*What makes a statement defamatory*
*Choosing the right time to speak*

*The safeguard of checking the facts*
*The safe way to comment*
*When the motive is crucial*

ANYONE who takes part in public controversy—or speaks his mind too freely in private—runs the risk of becoming involved in legal action if he criticises or accuses others unwisely. The law protects the good name of individuals and companies, and gives the right to claim compensation if that good name is damaged unjustly.

In law, unjust damage to reputation is known as defamation. There are two main types: defamation in a permanent form, such as writing, is libel, and defamation in a transient form, such as private conversation or public address, is slander.

Suing for libel or slander is open only to those who can afford the expense. But people in all walks of life can find themselves having to defend an action—councillors, trade-union officials, members of voluntary organisations and private individuals.

➤ THE PROTEST THAT LED TO COURT *In January 1965, the local Press in Ramsgate reported that negotiations were taking place for exporting cattle from Ramsgate harbour. There were protests from local organisations who feared that this would harm the town's holiday trade. The chairman of the Better Ramsgate Group, Mr J. Langelier, organised a petition demanding the dismissal of the harbour-master, Mr J. G. Hardy, who had entered into correspondence with a Belgian firm about exporting cattle.*

*The petition claimed that Mr Hardy's services were prejudicial to the interests of the town. More than 9000 people signed.*

*Next month the Mayor of Ramsgate reported that negotiations had been abandoned. He added that Mr Hardy had carried out his duties as an official instructed by the council and had not sought to influence council policy. The following day Mr Langelier handed in his petition to the mayor. Mr Hardy sued for libel.*

DECISION *Mr Hardy received a full apology from Mr Langelier, who also agreed to pay damages and costs. (Hardy v. Langelier.)* ◀

Being sued for libel or slander usually involves uncertainty and anxiety, particularly for anyone of modest means. It may also mean that a defendant has the embarrassment of a public apology and the expense of paying his own and his opponent's legal costs, in addition to compensation. Legal aid is not available.

## Ways to avoid legal action
The best way to avoid being sued successfully is to seek legal advice before making a controversial statement. Where this is not possible, the individual needs to bear in mind the principles of defamation law.

For a statement—or any other material, spoken, written or pictorial—to give grounds for legal action, the law says that four conditions must be satisfied:

**1.** The statement must be defamatory.
**2.** It must be understood to refer to the person (or company) taking legal action.
**3.** It must be communicated to a third person.
**4.** None of the valid defences must apply.

A plaintiff can take action against anyone who helped to communicate the defamatory matter—in law, anyone who published it.

## What makes a statement defamatory
If an action comes to court, it is normally for the jury to decide whether material is defamatory. In such a case, it depends on the opinion of ordinary men and women.

For this reason, defamation has not been comprehensively defined, though several definitions have been suggested:

'A false statement about a man (or woman) which is to his (her) discredit.'

'Anything which tends to lower a man in the eyes of right-thinking members of society.'

'Anything which tends to bring a man into hatred, ridicule, contempt, dislike or disesteem with society.'

Not all statements which might appear to fall within these definitions are equally liable to provoke legal action. Words of vulgar abuse, for example, or words spoken in jest are not defamatory.

On the other hand, there are certain types of statement that are particularly perilous.

It is defamatory, for example, to attack an individual's morals—to say that a landlady sleeps with her lodgers.

Similarly, there will usually be grounds for legal action in any statement which alleges dishonesty—for example, that a salesman doubles his income by falsifying expenses.

Any suggestion that a man or woman is incompetent at a job, or is unfit to hold a particular office, is particularly dangerous.

►THE CRITICISM THAT COST £1000 *In 1959, Dr Phyllis Wade was in charge of a department at the Royal Free Hospital, London, where Miss Grace Cochran was the superintendent radiographer. Dr Wade complained to the hospital officials that Miss Cochran was 'a source of chaos' in the department. She claimed that Miss Cochran often took her holidays a few days at a time and on several occasions did not mention that she would be absent. As a result of Dr Wade's complaint, Miss Cochran was dismissed. Miss Cochran sued for slander.*
DECISION *The jury decided in 1966 that Dr Wade had slandered Miss Cochran. It ordered Dr Wade to pay £1000 damages and costs. (Cochran v. Wade.)* ◄

DANGERS OF INNUENDO A statement which, on the face of it, is innocent enough can still give rise to a libel or slander action if, because of facts not given in the statement but known to the reader or hearer, its secondary meaning is defamatory. For example, the statement, 'Mr Bowen has lunch every day at the best hotel in town' appears to be safe. Its surface meaning—what lawyers call the 'natural and ordinary meaning' of the words—gives no grounds for complaint.

But if Mr Bowen is a pensioner with no other income, and is raising money for a campaign to increase pensions, the statement might be held to suggest that he is spending the money he collects on himself. As such, it would clearly be defamatory.

This sort of implication in the meanings of words is known in law as an 'innuendo'.
IDENTIFYING THE SUBJECT Anyone who makes a statement about a large class of people has no need to fear civil actions for libel or slander. No action will succeed unless it can be shown that ordinary people understood the statement to refer to a particular person or company.

If a writer on food and wine says, for example, that London chefs run unhygienic kitchens, no individual chef has grounds for

---

## The difference between libel and slander

ACTIONS for defamation fall into two categories—actions for slander and actions for libel. The main difference between them is the method of communication.
SLANDER When the defamatory matter is in a transient form—spoken words, a song or a gesture circulated only among the people present at the time—the action is for slander.
LIBEL When the defamatory matter takes a permanent form, the action is for libel. This covers all forms of written material, films, photographs, paintings, records, tape recordings and radio and television broadcasts.

If, in a libel action, the defendant can raise no valid defence, the plaintiff is entitled to damages without proving actual damage. In actions for slander, the general rule is that the plaintiff must prove actual financial loss.

Damages can, however, be claimed without proof of loss for four types of slander:
1. A statement which tends to disparage an individual in his profession, calling, trade or business, or in any office he holds.
2. A statement which suggests that the plaintiff has committed a crime for which, if convicted, he could be imprisoned.

3. A statement which suggests that a woman has acted immorally.
4. A statement which suggests that the plaintiff has an infectious or contagious disease, particularly a venereal disease.
OTHER TYPES OF ACTION Statements which are damaging, but not defamatory, may give rise to actions of a different sort. To say that a flourishing firm has closed down is not defamatory, since firms close for honourable reasons. Yet the statement obviously injures the firm's business.

Such statements, if they are made maliciously, may give grounds for actions for injurious falsehood.

Legal action can also be taken for 'slander of goods', a damaging but non-defamatory statement (spoken or written) about a firm's goods; and 'slander of title', a similar statement about a person's right to his property.

Statements in permanent form, which tend to cause financial loss, give a right to damages without proof of loss. So does any statement, spoken or written, which tends to cause financial loss in an occupation or business. In other cases, actual financial loss must be proved.

action, because it is a generalisation. To say the same of a particular chef by name would certainly be defamatory.

It would also be defamatory to make a general statement which could be taken by the people who read or hear it to refer to a particular individual—to mention the Greek chefs of a particular area of London where there were only two Greek restaurants.

Anyone who makes statements about groups of people may also run other legal risks. If he vilifies racial groups, he may be charged with inciting racial hatred. If he makes such extreme comments that they are likely to cause public disorder or a breach of the peace, he may be charged with criminal libel. Prosecutions for these offences are rare. ☐ Meetings, marches and demonstrations, p. 672; When libel is a crime, p. 669.

A speaker or writer cannot avoid legal action simply by not naming the person he intends to criticise. If his listeners or readers understand him to be referring to a particular person, then the necessary element of identification is present, and his statement is potentially defamatory.

DEFAMING THE DEAD Only the person (or company) libelled or slandered is entitled to sue. This means that there can be no civil action over defamation of the dead, though surviving relatives may be able to sue if the statement affects their reputations as well.

## Keeping criticism private

No defamatory statement gives grounds for a civil action unless it is communicated to someone other than the person about whom it is made. In law, it must be 'published'—by word of mouth, by radio, television, in writing, pictures or gestures.

This requirement can sometimes be used to advantage. Take the case of a supermarket manager who suspects a cashier of failing to record all the sales for which she receives money, and of pocketing the proceeds.

If he interviews her in the privacy of his own office, with no one else present or able to overhear the conversation, nothing he says will give grounds for civil action—even if he accuses her outright. The essential ingredient of any successful action—that the defamatory matter has been communicated to a third party—will be absent.

If, on the other hand, he writes her a letter which contains defamatory material, he risks legal action. For although the letter may be addressed to the girl personally, there is always the possibility that a third party—someone who opens it in error, for example—may see

its contents. The fact that it was not intended that the third person would read the letter is not necessarily a defence.

## Choosing the right time to speak

The law recognises that there are occasions when, in the public interest, individuals should be able to speak with impunity—witnesses giving evidence in court, for example. The law therefore accepts that statements made at such times should be protected against actions for defamation. The people who make them are speaking, in the legal phrase, 'on a privileged occasion'.

Privilege protects many statements which might otherwise give grounds for successful legal actions. There are two types of privilege, qualified and absolute.

QUALIFIED PRIVILEGE Anyone who makes a defamatory statement is protected from legal action if all the following conditions apply:
1. The person making the statement has a legally recognised interest or duty to do so.
2. The person to whom he communicates the information also has a legally recognised interest in it or duty to receive it.
3. The person making the statement is not activated by any dishonest, ulterior or improper motive (what is known in law as 'malice').

If all three conditions apply, the person making the statement is protected by qualified privilege—qualified because there is no privilege where there is an improper motive.

The householder who sees a neighbour's property being broken into, for example, and believes he recognises the intruder, has a legally recognised interest in reporting the matter to the police, and the police have a legitimate interest in receiving the report. Even if the householder is completely mistaken, and his report to the police causes embarrassment and anxiety to an innocent man, he is normally protected against an action for defamation, provided he can show that he acted in good faith.

If, however, the householder makes a dishonest report to the police, falsely naming an enemy as the intruder with the intention of settling an old score, he is not protected by privilege. His ulterior motive—to get even with a rival—removes the protection.

Again, the shop manager who suspects a cashier of dishonesty may prefer to interview her in the presence of the firm's security officer who investigated the case. Any accusations the manager makes during the interview are then communicated to a third person— the security officer. But the manager, if he acts in good faith, may expect to be protected against a successful action for defamation because both he and the security officer have what the law recognises as a legitimate common interest in the accusations.

If, however, the manager makes his accusation in the hearing of a representative of another firm, the cashier may be able to sue successfully because the defamatory matter has been communicated to someone who does not have a legally recognised interest.

For privilege to apply, the interest must be one recognised by the law. It is not enough that the hearer has an 'interest' in the accusations merely out of idle curiosity.

Other situations covered by qualified privilege, provided there is no improper motive, may in certain circumstances include the writing of character references and meetings of local councils.

If, for example, a councillor makes a defamatory remark during a council meeting in the council chamber, and it properly arises out of the subject under discussion and there is no suggestion of an ulterior motive, no action for defamation is likely to succeed against him. But if he makes the same statement in an election address, or at a public meeting, or repeats or enlarges on his accusations in an interview with a newspaper, he is not normally protected by privilege.

ABSOLUTE PRIVILEGE In some circumstances, an individual is protected against actions for defamation whether or not his motives were proper. Anyone taking part in court proceedings in the United Kingdom, for example, has this protection.

A member of the House of Commons or Lords also has absolute privilege for anything he says from his seat in the House during a debate, and for anything published in *Hansard*, the official Parliamentary report.

Absolute privilege also protects statements made by a client to his solicitor, and reports made by officers of the three Services to their superiors, and by officers of State to their heads of department.

## The safeguard of checking the facts

In theory, the safest way to ensure that a defamatory allegation does not lead to a successful action for damages is to make sure that it is true. Truth is a complete answer to any defamation action.

In practice, however, truth—or 'justification', as it is called—is often a difficult defence to establish. The law assumes the allegation is false, and the defendant must prove its truth, under the normal rules of evidence.

Anyone who intends to publish a damaging statement of fact, therefore, needs to be certain

## When libel is a crime

LIBEL is normally a civil wrong—what the law calls a 'tort'—but it can also be a criminal offence if the prosecution shows that the libel caused, or was likely to cause, a breach of the peace. Such prosecutions are rare because the person libelled normally prefers to seek damages in a civil action; for even if someone is found guilty of criminal libel, the person defamed does not get damages.

A criminal libel need not be 'published'— that is, seen by a third person. It is sufficient for the statement to have been made to the person defamed. The statement must be written or in some other permanent form.

Nor is it any defence to prove that the statement is true. The saying 'the greater the truth, the greater the libel' applies to criminal libel. The only valid defence is that the statement was made in the public interest.

Another difference between civil libel and criminal libel relates to dead people. If a speaker or writer defames a dead person, the

relatives cannot bring an action unless they themselves are defamed, perhaps by innuendo.

For example, if it was alleged, wrongly, that a dead woman had not been legally married, her children might claim that this implied that they were illegitimate. But if a dead person is libelled in such a way that his relatives are understandably angered into a breach of the peace, the writer might be prosecuted for criminal libel.

The maximum penalty for criminal libel is imprisonment for up to two years. In addition, the defendant is usually ordered by the court not to repeat the libel on pain of imprisonment. SEDITION There is also a criminal offence of seditious libel, relating to statements written or recorded in a permanent form. This offence covers vilifying the Sovereign or the Sovereign's family or urging people to overthrow the constitution by violent action.

Prosecutions for sedition are a rarity, however. No maximum penalties are laid down.

that he can prove the allegation is true if it is challenged. In some cases it may even be possible to obtain signed statements or affidavits from potential witnesses before the statement is made.

## The safe way to comment
Anyone making a defamatory statement which consists of comment, as opposed to statements of fact, can protect himself by taking pains to see that his comment is honestly made, and is on a matter of public interest, and that he has no improper motive. If he takes these precautions, he may be able to rely on the defence called 'fair comment'.

For example, a councillor speaking at a public meeting (which is never covered by privilege) needs to ensure that any comment or observations he makes come into the category of 'fair comment'.

This means, among other things, limiting himself to comments on matters of public interest. In law, what is a matter of public interest is not necessarily what interests the public. Rather it is those matters in which the public is entitled to take an interest because they are of genuine public concern.

So if the councillor comments on the state of the town's street lighting, an increase in the rates, or the services provided by the local hospital, these are all matters in which the public has a legitimate interest. But comments on the sexual morality of private or even public figures are not likely to be considered matters of public interest.

If the comment includes, or is based on, facts, the councillor must also take care to see that he can prove the facts are correct.

Anyone who writes a review of a film, book or stage play will usually rely for his protection from successful defamation actions partly on fair comment and partly, where statements of fact are concerned, on justification.

If the critic writes that a particular character forgot his lines eight times, it is obviously defamatory. The only defence, since this is a statement of fact, is justification—that the actor did, in fact, forget his lines eight times. If the critic names the wrong actor as forgetting his lines, he can be sued successfully for defamation.

If, on the other hand, he writes that the leading lady played her part incompetently, this too is an expression of opinion which he is entitled to make, provided he does so honestly and without an improper motive, such as pursuing a personal vendetta.

For the defence of fair comment to succeed, it is not necessary to prove that all reasonable men would agree with the comment, but merely that a fair-minded man could have made it honestly, and that the comment was in fact honestly made.

## When the motive is crucial
Two defences against actions for defamation —qualified privilege and fair comment—both fail unless the offending statement is made honestly and without an ulterior or improper motive. In law, there must be no element of 'malice' involved.

'Malice' in this context has a specialised meaning. It means almost any improper motive, not just spite. A shop manager who falsely states in a reference that a colleague is dishonest is considered in law to be activated by malice if he makes his comment to get even with a rival. The defence of qualified privilege which normally covers references will not apply.

Similarly, the critic who writes a hostile review might be considered to be acting maliciously if the author of the play he is reviewing had recently been appointed to a job for which the critic was also a candidate.

The best advice for the shop manager and the critic in these circumstances is to avoid giving the reference or writing the review.

There are many situations, such as these, in which even though an individual acts honestly, he may find it difficult to convince a jury that no malice was involved.

## Other defences against defamation
The other defences against actions for defamation apply only in limited circumstances.

WHEN THE VICTIM CONSENTS No one can sue successfully for defamation if he has agreed to publication of the defamatory matter.

INNOCENT DEFAMATION If an individual makes a statement which is 'innocently' defamatory—if he accidentally chooses the name of a real person for the villain in his novel, for example—he is able, in some circumstances, to defend a defamation action by offering to publish a correction and an apology. This defence is technical and requires the advice of a solicitor at the earliest possible moment.

For such a defence to succeed, he has to be able to prove that he took all reasonable steps to guard against the defamation.

This defence may also be open to someone who makes a statement which he later discovers is defamatory by innuendo if he can show that he did not know of the circumstances which made the statement defamatory, and took all reasonable care.

# What to do if you are libelled or slandered

A derogatory statement about a man or woman does not, on its own, amount to libel or slander. To have any chance of success in a defamation action, a plaintiff must be able to show that the statement damaged his reputation among right-thinking people, and that none of the recognised defences applies.

Not only is the law itself complicated, but the choice of the best legal tactics is difficult and the advice of a solicitor essential. Awards of damages for defamation are not always high, and costs can be heavy, especially if you lose. Legal aid is not available.

Anyone taking legal action for defamation has to prove three things:
**1.** That the material was published in the legal sense—that is, communicated to a third party. In the case of slander, this involves ensuring that there is at least one witness who heard the words spoken. If no one else was present but yourself and the proposed defendant, there is no civil case. In the case of libel, if the statement was made in, say, a newspaper, a copy of the newspaper is normally evidence enough.

In the case of a letter, however, it may be necessary to show that a third person saw it. If one man writes something defamatory about a second and sends it to that person marking the letter 'personal' or 'private', that does not constitute publication. But if he dictates the letter to a secretary or sends it to the recipient's office where someone else opens his mail, that is publication (though the letter may be privileged).
**2.** That it is defamatory. If the case comes to trial, the question of whether a statement is defamatory is dealt with in two stages. Firstly, the judge rules whether the words used are *capable* of being defamatory; secondly, the jury (or the judge if there is no jury) decides whether, in the circumstances in which the words were used, they *were* defamatory.
**3.** That the statement would be understood to refer to the person bringing the action.

## Deciding the best form of action

A solicitor may advise his client that he has no case. Alternatively, if there are grounds for action, the solicitor may advise one (or more) of three main courses: seeking an apology, with or without a statement in open court; applying for an injunction to prevent the libel or slander from being repeated; and suing for damages.

SEEKING AN APOLOGY If all that is wanted is that a mis-statement should be put right, the person concerned can ask for an apology, preferably with the help of a solicitor.

If the libel is published in a newspaper, the best results are obtained by going to a solicitor within hours of the newspaper appearing, and getting him to contact the paper on the same day—usually through a specialist barrister. If the newspaper agrees to publish a correction, it usually agrees to pay the legal costs of the person libelled.

ASKING FOR AN INJUNCTION When it is essential to stop an allegation immediately, one course is to ask for a court injunction. If granted, this forbids any repetition of the statement complained of until the injunction expires. Anyone who disobeys the order may then be sent to prison for contempt of court.

Anyone who has reason to expect that he is likely to be defamed in the future—a councillor, for example, who sees a proof copy of a leaflet attacking him—can ask for an injunction to prevent the further publication of the defamatory material.

The courts are reluctant to grant injunctions, especially if the publisher resists the application. An injunction will always be refused if the defendant intends to plead justification or qualified privilege in any libel action that may be brought.

SUING FOR DAMAGES For anyone determined to sue, the first thing to decide is whether the case is strong enough and whether the damages are likely to be sufficiently high to justify the costs involved.

Most libel and slander cases never reach the courts but are settled by lawyers acting for the two sides. They agree on a sum of damages and on the wording of an apology, usually to be made by a lawyer in open court.

If there is no apology, the case may go to a hearing. Then damages can range from thousands of pounds to a nominal halfpenny. If the case is heard with a jury, it is the jury that decides on the amount of damages, and it is not given any guidance by the judge on awards in similar previous cases. It is therefore difficult to estimate damages.

If they are considered unreasonable, the Court of Appeal sometimes orders a re-trial.

# Meetings, marches and demonstrations

*Planning a meeting*　　　　　*Keeping order at meetings*
*When meetings can be banned*　*Demonstrations in London*
*Pitfalls for organisers*

EVERYONE has a right to campaign publicly on whatever issue he chooses—to preserve a historic building, for example, to oppose the closure of a commuter railway line, or to protest against Government policy. This freedom of speech is one of the basic rights of British democracy.

But the campaigner has no special privileges. He is not immune to the laws forbidding the incitement of violence and racial hatred, and he must observe the rules about obstruction of the highway which apply to any other road-user. In some areas there are also bye-laws covering meetings in public places.

## Planning a meeting

In general, anyone can hold a peaceful meeting in a public place without police permission. But the organisers normally require the consent of whoever owns the site.

MEETINGS IN THE STREET Anyone planning to hold a demonstration in the street should check with the local authority whether there are bye-laws which have to be observed.

In general, the public has a right to pass and repass on the highway or across it, but not to use the highway for any other purpose. Therefore, anyone wanting to hold a stationary public meeting in a street theoretically has no right to do so without first getting the consent of the local authority.

Whether or not a procession needs consent depends on its size. If only a small number of people take part, in single file, they might be considered to be simply exercising their right to pass along the highway.

Where larger numbers are involved, however, the people taking part are doing more than exercising their normal rights because they are to some extent obstructing traffic, and in doing so are interfering with other people's rights to use the street.

The courts have held that a procession is lawful unless it constitutes an unreasonable use of the street. What is unreasonable depends on the circumstances.

Anyone making unreasonable use of the highway is likely to be prosecuted for obstruction. This may constitute the common law offence of public nuisance (penalty: any fine or term of imprisonment which the court thinks fit). Obstruction is also a specific offence under the Highways Act 1959 (penalty: a fine of up to £50). Or it may be an offence against local bye-laws.

The offence of obstruction is committed by anybody who prevents the public from exercising the right to pass and repass on or across the street. It is not necessary for the police to prove that any individual was actually obstructed, though they must show that the act of obstruction was intentional or reckless. Much depends on the discretion exercised by the police in deciding who to prosecute for obstruction.

The fact that public meetings have often been held in a place before will help to establish that the use of the street was reasonable. But it is not necessarily a complete defence to a charge of obstruction.

MEETINGS IN PUBLIC PLACES Many places open to the public are owned and controlled by the local authority—parks, public walks and even open ground. Where the ownership of the prospective site for a meeting is not certain, check with the local authority.

Many public places are covered by local bye-laws which ban meetings altogether, or permit them only at certain times.

Sometimes, written permission is needed from the local authority in advance of holding a meeting. Notice generally has to be given at least 36 hours before, and the proposed route and times of a procession have to be supplied by the organiser.

MEETINGS ON PRIVATE PROPERTY Get the consent of the owner of any hall or ground at which a meeting is to be held well in advance. Be sure to make clear the purpose of the meeting, to avoid the danger of a last-minute cancellation by an owner opposed to its aims.

Again, if the ownership of any property is in doubt, check with the local authority.

INFORMING THE POLICE If a meeting or demonstration is likely to be a big one and there is any possibility of trouble from opponents, it is advisable—though not essential—to warn the police in advance.

The chief constable for the area can sometimes impose conditions on a meeting or procession. For instance, he can stipulate the route that a procession must follow, the time of a meeting, or the place where it is to be held.

## When meetings can be banned

The fact that a meeting may constitute trespass, or that criminal offences such as obstruction may be committed by those taking part, does not give the authorities the right to ban it. The power to ban meetings in advance is extremely limited.

One way for the authorities to prevent a meeting from taking place is to refuse permission for it to be held. But this can be done only in cases where their permission is required—either under bye-laws, or where the authority owns the prospective site.

There are wider powers covering processions. Where serious public disorder is anticipated, the chief constable can ask the local authority to make an order banning either all processions, or a particular class of procession, for up to three months. The authority must first obtain the consent of the Home Secretary.

## Pitfalls for organisers

There are several other ways in which the organisers of public demonstrations can come into conflict with the law.

ADVERTISING THE MEETING Always get the permission of site owners before erecting posters on their property—failure to do so can lead to prosecution. Another type of consent—local authority planning consent—is needed for some posters. But if the purpose of the meeting is religious, political, cultural, educational, social or recreational, planning consent is not needed for posters which are no more than 6 ft square and do not obstruct the highway.

LOUDSPEAKERS The police should be given 48 hours' notice if a loudspeaker is to be used at a public meeting or to announce it.

Making unreasonable noise can bring a prosecution for creating a public nuisance; and the use of loudspeakers, megaphones, or any other kind of amplifier in the streets between 9 p.m. and 8 a.m. is usually against bye-laws. Loudspeakers may also constitute an offence under the Noise Abatement Act 1960. In either case, those responsible for the noise can be fined a maximum of £5.

LITERATURE Most local authorities have regulations controlling the distribution of literature in the streets. The police cannot seize leaflets unless material in them is obscene, or is likely to cause a breach of the peace, or to stir up racial hatred. Written material which is published or distributed must bear the name and address of the printer and publisher, otherwise there can be a fine of £5 for every leaflet distributed. The fine can be imposed on the publisher, the printer and the distributor.

COLLECTING SIGNATURES Provided no obstruction is caused, people may be stopped in the street and asked to sign petitions. Signatures may also be collected on the doorstep.

COLLECTING MONEY Police permission is not needed for house-to-house collections of money for political organisations. Nor is consent needed in order to collect money at a public open-air meeting, unless local bye-laws forbid such collections.

UNIFORMS No uniform of a political organisation can be worn publicly unless it is approved by the police with the consent of the Home Secretary. Permission is not normally needed, however, to wear emblems, badges, ties or medals.

INCITING RACIAL HATRED Normally, the law is not concerned with the content of a public speech—only with its effect. An important exception is the offence of inciting racial hatred. Any speech or written material which is likely to stir up hatred against one section of the community because of colour, race, or ethnic or national origins is against the Race Relations Act 1965, even if it does not result in, or even incite, disorder.

A prosecution can be started only with the Attorney General's consent. Magistrates can fine an offender up to £200, or send him to prison for six months, or both. The penalty can be as high as £1000 with a two-year sentence if the case is sent for trial by jury.

## Keeping order at meetings

Heckling at a public meeting is not an offence, provided it does not seriously interfere with the meeting. But anyone who breaks up a meeting by preventing the speakers from being heard can be prosecuted and fined up to £100, or sent to prison for three months. There are special penalties for disturbing meetings during an election campaign.

EJECTING TROUBLE-MAKERS If a meeting is being held on private property, the occupier or his employees can eject trespassers—that is, anyone who is not wanted at the meeting. They can use their own stewards to keep order, or they can call the police. No more force than is reasonably necessary under the circumstances should be used.

Anyone who uses threatening, abusive or insulting words or behaviour in a public place or at a public meeting with the intention of provoking a breach of the peace is guilty of an offence, and can be arrested without a warrant. The offence is committed if a breach of the peace is likely from that particular audience—even though the audience's reaction is unreasonable. The penalty is a fine of up to £100, or three months in prison on conviction by magistrates, or a £500 fine or 12 months in prison for anyone who is convicted by a jury.

The police can enter private property uninvited if a breach of the peace is taking place, or if they have good reason to believe that a breach of the peace is likely to occur.

► THE UNINVITED POLICEMAN *Police went to a protest meeting against the Incitement to Disaffection Bill in a Welsh town in 1934. The promoters asked the police to leave. There was a struggle between a constable and one of the promoters. The promoter sued for battery.*
DECISION *The magistrates decided that the constable acted lawfully, and he was found not guilty. The police thought that, if they were not at the meeting, there would be a breach of the peace and that seditious speeches would be made. The High Court rejected the promoter's appeal. (Thomas v. Sawkins.)* ◄

### Demonstrations in London

There is stricter control of public meetings and demonstrations in London than elsewhere.
MEETINGS NEAR PARLIAMENT Open-air political meetings of more than 50 people are generally forbidden within one mile of the Houses of Parliament on the north side of the Thames on days during which Parliament is sitting. Any person at the meeting can be fined up to £20. The object of this is to keep access to the Houses of Parliament open to Members.
TRAFALGAR SQUARE It is illegal to make a speech in Trafalgar Square without permission from the Department of the Environment (previously the Ministry of Public Building and Works). The Department's permission is required for any organised meeting or procession. If permission is refused, there are no facilities for an appeal.
LOUDSPEAKERS The police must be given 48 hours' notice if a loudspeaker is to be used. Even with consent, the loudspeaker must not be used to call people to a meeting, only to announce in advance that a meeting is going to take place.
PLACARDS Police permission is needed before placards or notices may be carried within a six-mile radius of Charing Cross. This applies also to distributing leaflets.
OBSTRUCTION The Metropolitan Police Commissioner can make regulations to prevent obstruction of streets or thoroughfares. He can also give police directions to keep order and avoid obstructions. The Commissioner can ban a meeting or procession with the consent of the Home Secretary. This power has been used sparingly in the past.

## When a demonstration causes injury or damage

ANYONE who is injured or whose property is damaged in a demonstration is entitled to claim compensation from those directly responsible. But usually it is difficult to identify who was responsible.

Only in strictly limited circumstances is it possible to sue the organisers of the demonstration. Even then, no legal action can be taken against a political party or any other organisation, but only against its officers. To succeed, it would have to be shown that the officer had a personal responsibility for violence—not simply that he organised a demonstration which later became violent.

Anyone injured in a violent demonstration may be entitled to compensation from the Criminal Injuries Compensation Board. For his claim to succeed, he would have to show that his injury resulted from a criminal act, though the culprit need not have been prosecuted. But the claimant might have to show that he had no connection with the demonstration. □ Compensation for criminal injuries, p. 547.

A householder, shopkeeper or property owner whose property is damaged in a riot can sue the police for compensation under the Riot (Damages) Act 1886. But he has to prove first that there was a riot—where a crowd acted violently—and that it was 'tumultuous'. This means the police should have been aware of the danger and should have prevented it.

Legally a 'crowd' can be as few as three people who get together with the intention of using force against anyone who tries to interfere with them. A claimant who brings an action for compensation needs a witness who was 'alarmed' by the situation.

# The right to vote

*Getting on the register*   *Voting by post*
*Casting a vote*   *Voting by proxy*

THE right to vote at both parliamentary and local-government elections depends on a number of qualifications. A person must have reached the voting age of 18 by the date of the election, and his name must appear on the register of electors, which is brought up to date each year.

To qualify for inclusion on the register a person must, on October 10:

1. Be a resident in the constituency—the electoral area—where he wants to vote (not an occupant of business premises).

2. Be a citizen of the United Kingdom, of an independent country within the Commonwealth or of the Republic of Ireland.

3. Not be subject to a legal incapacity to vote. People with legal incapacities which bar registration include peers—who may vote in a local government election, but not in a parliamentary election—people of unsound mind, those in legal custody, aliens (foreigners living in Britain who have not taken United Kingdom nationality) and people convicted of a corrupt or illegal electoral practice.

A person's name should be included when the register of electors is revised if he is already over 18 or if his 18th birthday comes before the following February 16, the date when the register comes into force.

In addition, the register contains the names of people who will reach voting age during the lifetime of the register—that is, before February 15 of the year following the one in which it comes into operation. These new voters have their date of birth printed after their names. For example, a name followed by the numbers 6/7 means that the elector reaches voting age on July 6 and can vote at elections held on or after that date.

## Getting on the register

Each autumn the local electoral registration officer—usually the clerk of the council—compiles a list of voters. He normally sends a form known as Form A to every house in the area, asking for the names of all people over 16 years 8 months who are resident there on the qualifying date, October 10.

Householders who fail to complete and return the form can be fined up to £50.

PEOPLE AWAY FROM HOME People working away from home on October 10 may still be registered in their home constituency, provided they can establish that they have a permanent address there. This applies even if their homes are sub-let for a short period.

Merchant seamen are regarded as living at their home addresses or at the club or hostel where they normally stay.

MOVING HOUSE People who move house must wait for the next qualifying date before they become eligible for inclusion in the register of electors for their new area, but they may still vote, in person or by post, in their former constituency.

ELECTORS ON TWO LISTS Some electors are permitted by law to be registered in two or more constituencies. For example, in 1970 court ruling established that young people studying away from home may be registered at their college addresses and at their homes. They may vote in both constituencies in council elections and parliamentary by-elections, but they must not vote twice in a parliamentary general election. The penalty is a fine of up to £100.

VOTERS WHO ARE OMITTED A provisional list of electors is published on or before November 28 and displayed in public libraries and main post offices.

Anyone left off the provisional list who thinks that he is entitled to be included can ask the returning officer before December 16 for his name to be added.

APPEALS Anyone who thinks that the returning officer has acted unfairly by refusing to register him can appeal by giving notice to the officer not more than 14 days after he is told of the refusal.

He should give his grounds for appealing and these are then forwarded to the county court for a decision. The voter or his representative must appear at the appeal hearing. If he is still dissatisfied, he has the right to appeal to the High Court.

## Casting a vote

Before polling day at a parliamentary election, each registered elector should receive a notice from the returning officer giving his number on the electoral roll and the name of the polling station at which he can vote. In local elections the returning officer is not required by law to send voters this notification. Voters can, however, find out where to vote from election literature supplied by the candidates, or by inquiring at the local council offices.

Inside the polling station, the voter gives his name and address to a clerk who hands him a ballot paper with the official mark.

A vote is cast by marking an 'X' beside one selected candidate's name. If there is any other mark on the ballot paper, or any crossing out, the paper is spoilt and may not be counted. If a voter marks his 'X' and then wishes to change his mind, he should take the ballot paper to the returning officer who will give him a new one.

In some local elections the voter has to choose several candidates and must therefore mark more than one 'X' on his ballot paper. In such cases, a notice in the polling station will say how many votes can be cast.

After marking his 'X', the voter folds the ballot paper to conceal his vote, and before placing it in the ballot box shows the official mark to the presiding officer. When he has finished voting, he must leave the polling station immediately.

It is illegal to vote more than once or to take someone else's place except where permission, which is known in law as a proxy, has been granted. These offences carry a maximum fine of £100 and anyone found guilty of an electoral offence can be barred from voting for five years.

## Voting by post
The local electoral registration officer can agree in certain specified cases to allow people who are unable to go to the poll in person to vote by post. There are three main categories:
1. Voters who have physical difficulty in getting to the polling station—the very old, the disabled or the blind.
2. Voters who have moved to another constituency since the register was made.
3. Voters who know in advance that their work will take them to another part of the country on polling day.

People on holiday at the time of an election are not allowed a postal vote.

OBTAINING A POSTAL VOTE To apply for a postal vote, in either local or parliamentary elections, write as soon as the election is announced to the local registration officer, who is usually the clerk of the local council. Explain the reason for needing a postal vote. An application form will be sent and when this is returned the registration officer decides if the request is justified. If illness is involved, the form may have to be signed by a doctor.

Any appeal against the officer's decision must be made within 14 days and will be heard by the county court.

Servicemen can apply to vote by post if they are stationed in some part of Britain other than the constituency in which they are registered.

## Voting by proxy
People likely to be out of the country at the time of an election because of their jobs can have their vote cast by someone else. This is known as voting by proxy.

Applications for a proxy vote in a General Election must be made in writing to the local electoral registration officer at least 12 days before polling day (not including Sundays and Bank Holidays).

In local-government elections applications for proxy votes must be made at least 14 days before polling day. Proxy votes are not permitted in parish council elections.

The registration officer will send a form requiring the reasons for absence and the elector's first and second choice as proxy voters. Any elector who agrees can be chosen to vote as a proxy.

The person picked as first choice proxy is notified of the decision to appoint him as proxy by the registration officer. If he does not accept the position, the elector's second choice is then approached.

The registration officer, once satisfied that a proxy is prepared to act in this capacity, sends him a notice of appointment. A proxy can be cancelled or changed by the elector giving notice to the registration officer.

A proxy voter who does not live in the elector's own constituency or already has a postal vote of his own, can obtain a postal vote by applying to the electoral registration officer for Form RPF 11.

Anyone who appoints a proxy may still vote in person if he arrives at the polling booth before the proxy. But once a vote has been cast—either by a proxy or by the voter personally—it cannot be cancelled.

Servicemen, Crown employees and members of the staff of the British Council who are overseas—together with their wives or husbands if they are with them—are allowed proxy votes under what is known as a 'service qualification'. A registration officer will register a service voter who has signed a service declaration. It must contain the address where he is to be registered, which should be his home.

# YOUR BUSINESS

# Setting up in business

*Trading under your own name*    *Choosing between public and private*
*Setting up a partnership*      *Choosing between limited and unlimited*
*Forming a company*          *Registering the company*

FOR the man who wants to set up in business there are three choices. He can become a sole trader; he can join other people in a partnership; or he can set up a company. Professional legal and financial advice should be sought to make sure that the best type of organisation is chosen.

### Trading under your own name
The simplest way to start a business is for a man to trade under his own name—called, in law, being a sole trader.

The sole trader receives all profits from the business, but he also has to bear any losses. He is *personally* responsible for all debts incurred by his business—and if he is not able to pay, he can be made bankrupt. His belongings may have to be sold to pay his creditors. ☐ Debts and bankruptcy, p. 580.

He can trade under his own name—John Smith, J. Smith, or simply Smith. But if he uses another title—for example, Smith Motor Spares—he is required to register the title within 14 days with the Registrar of Business Names, Companies House, 55–71 City Road, London EC1Y 1BB. If a married woman carries on business in her maiden name, it must be registered. ☐ Registering a business name, p. 679.

A sole trader is regarded by the Inland Revenue as self-employed and pays tax under Schedule D. He pays National Insurance at the self-employed rate. ☐ How the income tax system works, p. 556; Employed or self-employed: the differences, p. 594.

### Setting up a partnership
If two or more people want to go into business together they can form a partnership. There are no compulsory formalities, and the partnership agreement need not even be in writing—although it is advisable to have a written agreement setting out the terms of the partnership. When there is no agreement at all, relations between the partners are regulated by the Partnership Act 1890.

Where there is a written agreement, it usually lays down that certain steps cannot be taken without the consent of all the partners. Such joint decisions may range from negotiating the terms of a contract to deciding whether the partnership should expand into a different line of business. However, if there is no agreement on how such matters are to be settled, and no specific provision for dissolving the partnership, a partner who is consistently outvoted by the others may choose to quit, taking his share of the assets with him. (He remains liable for his share of the partnership debts, however.)

The partnership does not have to be registered—but if it uses any title other than the names of all its existing partners, that title has to be approved within 14 days by the Registrar of Business Names.

The accounts of a partnership are not open to inspection by the general public, nor do they have to be sent to the Registrar of Companies. There may be tax advantages to be gained by forming a partnership, depending on how the profits are divided. ☐ How businesses are taxed, p. 700.

LIMIT ON NUMBERS Partnerships are restricted to a maximum of 20 members, except for firms of solicitors, accountants and stock-brokers, who can have any number.

SHARING PROFITS No partner is entitled to be paid a salary for the services he gives to a partnership; he gets only his share of the firm's profits. That share, however, can be a fixed annual sum. Unless the partnership agreement fixes proportions in which they are to be divided, the profits or losses must be shared equally among the partners.

When a partnership is dissolved, the assets are divided among the partners according to the provisions of the agreement. Where there is no agreement, each partner first receives whatever amount he has contributed towards the capital of the firm. The remaining assets, including profits, are divided equally.

RESPONSIBILITY FOR DEBTS Each member of a partnership can be made personally liable for the whole of its debts—not just for a share. He is entitled, in turn, to recover contributions from other partners. Creditors can sue an individual partner, or a group of partners, or the firm itself. A partner who is sued can be made bankrupt if he fails to pay the debts or to obtain contributions from the other partners in time, even though the debts were incurred by another partner.

If members of a partnership are sued jointly for a firm's debts, the proportion each has to pay is normally the same as the share of the profits to which he is entitled. Contracts made by one partner are binding on all the others, provided the contracts are within the ordinary course of the firm's business.

LIMITING THE RISK The only way in which a person can have a share in a partnership without being wholly liable for its debts is through a limited partnership.

Such a person, usually known as a 'sleeping' partner, cannot legally take part in the management of the business. He cannot make contracts or draw cheques on the firm's account. All he can do is inspect the firm's books and give advice to the other partners— at least one of whom must be fully responsible in the normal way for the partnership debts. The 'sleeping' partner is liable for debts only to the amount that he has invested.

Such partnerships must register with the Registrar of Limited Partnerships, Companies House, 55–71 City Road, London EC1Y 1BB.

ENDING THE PARTNERSHIP If one partner agrees with the others that he should leave, the partnership ends. If there is no agreement on how the partnership is to be dissolved, any partner can at any time give notice to the others that he wants to end the partnership. The partner who leaves can sell his share to someone else only with the agreement of the other partners.

Technically, the partnership also comes to an end when one partner dies or becomes bankrupt—unless the formal agreement makes other provisions for such events.

If a partner is replaced, a new agreement is automatically needed, although—apart from the addition of the new name—it can be precisely the same as before.

**Forming a company**
The alternative to becoming a sole trader or forming a partnership is to set up a company, in which the founders become shareholders.

A company is regarded in law as having an existence of its own, separate from that of the members who hold its shares. This means that when the company is sued or fined, the

---

## Registering a business name

AN application to register a business name must be made on a form which is obtainable from the Registrar.

The Registrar can refuse to register a name which in his opinion is undesirable. A small business is unlikely to be allowed to use the words 'Imperial', 'Commonwealth' or 'International'. A name which suggests royal patronage is not normally permitted.

A businessman who wants to use the words 'investment trust', 'bank', 'bankers' or 'banking' in the title of his firm has to prove that this truly describes the firm's business.

An organisation cannot describe itself as a building society unless it is in fact a building society and has been registered with the Registrar of Friendly Societies.

☐ Registration does not give sole rights to a name, nor does it give protection against duplication. There is no guarantee that a registered business name will be accepted as a company name, if one is formed later.

It is in the interest of a businessman who wants to register a name to check whether it has been registered as a trade mark. He can do this at the Trade Marks Registry, Patent Office, 25 Southampton Buildings, Chancery Lane, London WC2A 1AY. The person or company with rights to the trade mark can seek an injunction to prevent it being used, and can also sue for damages.

HOW TO APPEAL If an application is rejected, the applicant can appeal to the Department of Trade and Industry within 21 days.

**Displaying the certificate**
When he approves a name, the Registrar issues a certificate of registration, which must be prominently displayed at the main place from which the business operates. All business letters, catalogues, circulars and show cards bearing a registered business name must also show the first name or initials and surname of all the proprietors of the business. Where the nationality of a partner is not British, his nationality must be shown.

**What to do when circumstances change**
If there is any change in the registered particulars—such as change of address, new proprietors or the closure of the business— the Registrar must be told within 14 days.

individual shareholders are not responsible for paying the damages or the fine. No shareholder can make any contract in the company's name unless he is authorised by the directors, or he is an officer of the company acting within his apparent authority.

All companies must be registered with the Registrar of Companies before they can begin trading or enter into contracts. Registered companies can be limited or unlimited, public or private.

### Choosing between public and private

Private companies are the most common. They are cheaper and simpler to form than a public company. They need have only one director and two shareholders—for example, a man and his wife.

A private company cannot have more than 50 shareholders, excluding past or present employees. When it grows beyond that limit, it automatically becomes public.

A private company can start business immediately it has been registered, unlike a public company, which must obtain a trading certificate from the Registrar.

A public company, on the other hand, is usually one whose shares are quoted and can be bought and sold on a stock exchange. It must have at least seven shareholders, two directors and a company secretary. There is no upper limit on the number of shareholders.

A company may, however, be classed in law as public even if its shares are not quoted on a stock exchange. The number of shareholders could, for example, exceed the 50 limit for a private company, making it public, even though shares are held by one family.

### Choosing between limited and unlimited

An advantage of forming a limited company is that its debts are its own responsibility, not that of the shareholders. A creditor cannot sue a shareholder for payment, and there is therefore usually no risk to the personal wealth of the shareholder. All the assets of the company, however, are available for paying the debts; it is only the shareholder whose liability is limited.

When a limited company is wound up, the shareholder may lose his money, though usually only the amount he has invested in the company's shares.

A limited company must make public its accounts by depositing them annually with the Registrar of Companies, who then allows anyone to inspect them for a small fee.

An unlimited company is one in which there is no limit on the liability of each of the shareholders if the company runs into debt. Their liability is similar to that of members of a partnership. An unlimited company does not normally have to reveal to the public the size of its profits, neither does it have to deposit accounts with the Registrar.

Other advantages of the unlimited company are that it can reduce its capital without applying to the courts for permission, and it is allowed to buy its own shares. In addition, the shares of an unlimited company are likely to have a lower valuation for estate duty.

COMPANY LIMITED BY GUARANTEE The liability of members of a slightly different type of company may be restricted to an amount which they have previously agreed to contribute towards debts if it goes out of business. This arrangement is known as a company limited by guarantee.

It is a form of organisation commonly used for clubs and charitable or other non-profit-making associations, and is of little value to the businessman, mainly because he would always have the prospect of selling personal belongings to meet his contribution for debts.

### Registering the company

The documents required for registering a company have to be drawn up and delivered to the Registrar of Companies, Companies House, 55–71 City Road, London EC1Y 1BB. Though anyone is allowed to do the job, it is usually carried out by a solicitor or by a firm known as law agents.

THE DOCUMENTS The founders of a company, known officially as the promoters, must send the Registrar of Companies a number of documents. They are:

**1.** A declaration, sworn before a commissioner for oaths, saying that all the requirements of the Companies Acts 1948 and 1967 have been complied with.

**2.** The memorandum of association, which regulates the company's relations with the general public.

**3.** The articles of association, which define how the company is to be run internally.

**4.** A statement of the authorised, or nominal, capital which the company has.

Any member of a group which intends operating as a company should be certain that he knows the precise meaning of clauses in the memorandum and articles of association, so that if disagreement, death or any other unforeseen event occurs, the provisions contained in the constitution assist the group, rather than add to their difficulties.

Every limited company (unless it is limited by guarantee) must have a nominal capital—

that is, the maximum number and value of shares which may be issued to shareholders. In small companies, the nominal capital is usually £100. The full amount does not necessarily have to be issued immediately; in fact, the minimum number is two members, each having one share.

Two other documents are usually provided for the Registrar before registration, although they do not need to be sent with the others. Within 14 days of the company's formation, the Registrar must be told the address of the registered office. He must also be given details of the directors and secretary within 14 days of their appointment.

WHAT THE MEMORANDUM MUST CONTAIN
The memorandum of a company is drawn up by the promoters covering five main points.
1. A name must be chosen. If the liability of the shareholders is to be limited, the last word must be 'limited', but it is not necessary to use the word 'company'. In certain circumstances, however, a licence can be obtained from the Department of Trade and Industry, absolving the company from the need to use the word limited. It is usually granted if the department is satisfied that the company is to be formed for the purpose of promoting art, science, religion, charity, or any other useful object— provided any profits are used to promote those objects, and not to pay any dividend to members of the company.

A company can change its name only with the approval of the Registrar of Companies. If it intends to trade under a name different from the one registered by the Registrar of Companies it must be approved by the Registrar of Business names. The registered name must be shown outside the office or place where business is carried on. The name must also be carried on all business communications. The names of directors, and their nationality, if they are not British, must also be given on company literature.
2. It must be specified whether the registered office is to be in England, Wales, Northern Ireland or Scotland.
3. The purpose for which the company was formed and the means by which it may do business must be stated. If the company takes any action beyond the powers defined in the memorandum—known in law as *ultra vires*—that action is not valid. The company cannot use that action as a basis for suing someone else, nor usually can any other person sue the company on the basis of an action taken *ultra vires*.
4. The memorandum must say whether the company is limited by shares or guarantee,

and give details of the amount of the share capital and how it is divided—that is, the face value of each share.
5. Each promoter named in the memorandum must also agree to take one or more shares in the capital of the company.
ARTICLES OF ASSOCIATION A company's articles of association are the internal regulations by which it is run, defining such matters as the appointment of directors and their individual powers.

A company limited by shares does not need to register articles; but if it does not do so, it is considered in law to have adopted the relevant set of model articles contained in the Companies Act 1948—that is, one or other of Tables A–D.
OFF-THE-PEG COMPANIES A cheaper and quicker way of going into business is to buy a company 'off the peg'. There are a number of firms with offices in the City Road area of London selling such 'off-the-peg' companies for £35–£40.

These off-the-peg companies are often suitable for small ventures, and it is usually possible to choose a company which has objects which cover adequately the proposed activities of the new business. Such companies have already been registered, with a 'ready-made' name, by the firms of law agents which sell them.

When a customer buys one, he is given share-transfer forms signed by the existing shareholders—the law agents—to make out in his own favour. Having completed the transfers and had them passed by the director, or directors—usually himself—he then becomes the new owner of the company. The change of ownership has to be notified to the Registrar of Companies only when the company makes its next annual return. The name of the company can be changed if the Registrar approves.

Short-term economy, however, can produce long-term complications, since the clauses of the constitution of off-the-peg companies are widely drawn and could be interpreted in many ways.

For example, the clause defining the purposes for which the company is established could have several different meanings. Alternatively, the clause may later be found too narrow to permit the company to branch out into an allied trade.

### The company file
When the Registrar receives the documents required he makes sure that they are in order, that there are no objections to the proposed

name—on the grounds, for example, that it is in use already—and that the purposes for which the company is being formed are legal.

He issues a certificate of incorporation—the company's birth certificate—and once this is received the private company can officially begin trading. There is usually a delay of between three days and a fortnight between lodging the registration papers and completion of registration.

Contracts made on behalf of the company before it is registered cannot be enforced either by the company or by the person with whom the contract has been made. The promoter would, in fact, be personally liable for any contracts made. However, the company can simply make new contracts in its own name after it has been registered.

When the Registrar has examined the documents and issued the certificate of incorporation, the documents are placed in a file at the Companies Registry at Companies House. Each year, an annual return—and, in the case of a limited company, the annual report and accounts—is also placed in the file.

Any member of the public may inspect a company's annual report and accounts.

A public company must also obtain a trading certificate from the Registrar before it can . start business. This can be avoided, however, by forming a private company and later converting it to a public company.

## Carrying goods by road

ROAD hauliers and businesses using their own transport must comply with laws governing the carriage of goods by road. Under the Road Traffic Act 1960, a goods vehicle is any vehicle or trailer which is adapted to carry goods. The regulations relate mainly to heavy vehicles, weighing more than 30 cwt when unladen or more than $3\frac{1}{2}$ tons laden.

### Operators' licences
Special operating licences are needed for heavy vehicles. The licences are granted by Department of the Environment Traffic Commissioners for each traffic area. Their address is available from the local council or the police.

Applicants must give details of how vehicles are to be used and the name of the person who is to be the licensed transport manager. Other information which may be required concerns the likely working hours of drivers, the maintenance facilities, the operator's financial status and his previous record as an operator.

### Excise licences
All goods vehicles must have an excise licence (which used to be called the Road Fund licence) before they are allowed to operate. The licence can be obtained from the Motor Taxation Centre at Swansea.

### Road restrictions
Goods vehicles are restricted to travelling at a speed of 40 mph, except on motorways where the limit is 60 mph. There are lower limits for those with trailers. Vehicles with trailers and goods vehicles over 3 tons unladen must not use the offside lane of a three-lane motorway except when it is necessary to pass an exceptionally wide load. The noise from vehicles of this weight must not exceed 92 decibels.

### Testing of goods vehicles
The construction and size of a heavy goods vehicle, and its equipment, are controlled by law. When a heavy vehicle is one year old it must be tested at a Department of the Environment testing centre. This must be followed by annual tests.

If a vehicle fails the initial test, the owner can have it repaired or modified and can then apply immediately to the testing centre for another examination. If he thinks the vehicle was wrongly failed, he can also apply to have it re-tested immediately.

If the vehicle is failed again, he can appeal to the Department of the Environment's area mechanical engineer—at the same address as the Area Traffic Commissioners—within ten days. If he is still not satisfied, he can appeal to the Secretary of State for the Environment.

### Weight plates
New goods vehicles must display for a year, 'in a conspicuous and readily accessible position', a manufacturer's plate showing, among other things, the maximum gross weight and axle weight authorised by the maker.

Heavy goods vehicles more than one year old must display a Department of the Environment plate at the back, showing the gross weight of the vehicle. This is supplied when the vehicle is first tested.

# Taking on staff

*Finding the right person*
*Drawing up the contract*
*What an employer can expect*

*Paying for industrial training*
*Dismissing an employee*
*Making redundancy payments*

WHEN a business proprietor takes on staff for the first time, the rate of pay may be a matter for negotiation; but in many jobs there is a set rate which has been agreed between employers and trade unions. An employer who wants to know the established rate can ask the Department of Employment or an official of the trade union concerned with the particular job.

He can also join an employers' organisation which may negotiate rates of pay with the trade unions. If these negotiations result in enforceable agreements, he will be bound to pay the rates.

Employers' organisations can be registered under the Industrial Relations Act 1971. Members are then protected against arbitrary disciplinary action or expulsion in the same way that members of registered trade unions have legal protection. ☐ Workers' rights within the union, p. 620.

### Finding the right person

The employer should decide what duties he wants his staff to perform, describe them accurately in advertisements and explain them fully at interviews. An employee who is later asked to do a job for which he was not engaged is entitled to refuse, or to leave without giving notice.

The employer should question applicants carefully about their qualifications, past career and health. Unless he is asked, the applicant is under no legal obligation to disclose matters which might damage his chances of getting the job—such as having been dismissed from his previous post. However, he must answer questions honestly. If an employer later finds that an applicant for a job has given him misleading information, he is entitled to dismiss the employee without notice.

An employer can usually employ anyone he chooses. But if he rejects someone on racial grounds, he may be committing an offence against the Race Relations Act 1968. ☐ Racial discrimination in jobs, p. 589.

If he employs more than 20 people, he must take on a quota of disabled workers.

He has certain obligations under the Industrial Relations Act. He has no right to refuse to engage someone because he is a member of a registered trade union. Nor can he make union membership a condition of employment, unless the Industrial Relations Court has agreed that a closed shop or agency shop should operate in his firm. ☐ The law on union membership, p. 618.

The employer must choose employees carefully because he has a legal obligation to other staff to provide them with competent fellow-workers. If he fails to do so, and a worker is injured as a result, the employer could be sued for negligence.

But if an employer makes an error of judgment—as opposed to negligence—in employing a particular person, this is not in itself grounds for an action for damages.

➤THE EXPENSIVE JOKER *Mr Hudson was injured by a fellow employee who played a foolish trick on him while he was working. The employee had a reputation for horseplay at work and had been warned repeatedly by the employers, the Ridge Manufacturing Co. Ltd. Mr Hudson sued the company for damages.*
DECISION *The employers had to pay because they had not stopped their employee's misconduct. (Hudson v. Ridge Manufacturing Co. Ltd.)*◄

REFERENCES One way an employer can assess the abilities of an applicant is to ask for references from former employers. It may also be useful to telephone the referee, who may be prepared to give more information in an informal conversation than he is willing to provide in writing.

Though many references tend to be couched in glowing terms, an employer has a right to regard a reference as a faithful guide to the character of his applicant. This is because anyone who writes a reference has an obligation in law to take care in doing so. If the writer is negligent, a prospective employer who suffers as a result may be entitled to take action for damages.

For instance, a referee who says that a wages clerk is honest and trustworthy when he knows that the man has convictions for dishonesty, might be sued successfully for damages if the clerk stole from his new employer. However, such an action is unlikely to succeed against an employer who states in a reference that it is given 'without liability'.

## Drawing up the contract

When the employer decides which applicant he wants to employ, he makes an offer either orally or by letter. The job must be offered and accepted to establish a contract in law. Once the offer has been accepted, the employer is not entitled to withdraw it. If he does go back on the offer, the applicant can claim damages. Usually the damages are equivalent to the amount he would have been entitled to if he had been hired and then dismissed with pay in lieu of notice. Technically, an employer can also claim damages from an applicant who accepts a job and then fails to take it. But an action on these grounds is unlikely to be financially worthwhile.

Many of the terms of a contract may be covered by collective agreements negotiated with trade unions. Alternatively, an employer can use standardised contract of employment forms, obtainable from law stationers, which cover a wide range of eventualities.

In some jobs the employer may be required by law to observe minimum wages and conditions laid down by wages councils or by fair wages resolutions. The prospective employer can find out from the Department of Employment, his employers' organisation or a trade union. ☐ Applying for a job, p. 588.

If any part of a contract is illegal, the whole of the agreement is void.

➤ THE ILLEGAL CONTRACT *Mr Miller made an oral contract of employment in 1945 under which he was to be paid £10 a week, plus travelling expenses, to cover the exact amount of his income tax. Only a small proportion of these 'expenses' were actually attributable to travelling. When he was dismissed, Mr Miller claimed arrears of salary from his employer, Mr Karlinski. He based his claim on both the agreed £10 a week and travelling expenses.*
DECISION *The Court of Appeal held that the agreement about expenses was illegal in so far as it was not a genuine agreement about travelling expenses, because it was an attempt to defraud the Inland Revenue. The whole contract was therefore illegal, and the employee was not entitled to enforce it. He could recover neither his 'expenses' nor his £10-a-week agreed wages. (Miller v. Karlinski.)* ◄

Whatever is agreed, the employer is bound by law, under the Contracts of Employment Act 1963, to give most employees a written statement setting out the main conditions of work. These particulars must be provided within 13 weeks of the day on which the employee joins the firm. If these details are included in a written contract which the employee receives on joining, no further action by the employer is necessary.

It is not necessary to give written particulars to people who are employed for less than 21 hours a week, or to a father, mother, husband, wife, son or daughter of an employer. ☐ Checking the contract, p. 596.

## What an employer can expect

The employee must give personal service—he cannot send a substitute to do his job unless this has been agreed beforehand. He must obey reasonable orders within the terms of his contract. But he will be within his rights in refusing to do a job for which he was not hired. If a man is taken on as a ledger clerk, his employer has no right to expect him to sweep the floor.

An employee must look after his employer's property and give an accurate account of any of his employer's money for which he is responsible. He is not allowed to make a profit for himself out of his employer's money; if he does, the employer can insist that the employee surrenders it to him.

The employee must exercise skill and care in carrying out his job. It is also his duty to be faithful and loyal to his employer. ☐ Duties to the employer, p. 614.

## Paying for industrial training

In some industries and businesses the employer may be required to pay a levy towards training to ensure a supply of trained staff for the industry. The amount which each employer has to pay is related to the number of staff he employs. He should check with the Department of Employment to see if any levy applies.

An employer can challenge the assessment of the amount which is levied on him by appealing to an industrial tribunal, which may rescind or reduce the levy.

An employer who decides to appeal should first write to The Secretary, Central Office of the Industrial Tribunals, 93 Ebury Bridge Road, London SW1W 8RE, and ask for a copy of Form IT1.

He must complete the form in duplicate and return it to the Central Office. Normally a hearing before a tribunal follows.

A tribunal consists of one person with legal qualifications and two lay members. The employer may be represented at the hearing by a barrister or solicitor. An appeal against the tribunal's decision can be made to the High Court, but only on a point of law.

## Dismissing an employee

In law, an employer is justified in sacking an employee only if he is unable to do the job, if his conduct is unsatisfactory, if he is redundant, or if there is some other *substantial* reason—for example, that he is dishonest. To dismiss a worker for any other reason may be considered under the Industrial Relations Act to be 'unfair', and the employee may be able to claim compensation. ☐ Claiming compensation for dismissal, p. 641.

In most cases the employer must also give the dismissed member of staff the minimum period of notice set out in the written particulars of his contract—or pay his wages for the period in lieu of notice. This applies even where a worker is sacked before he has received the written particulars. ☐ Leaving the job, p. 639.

The only occasions on which an employer is entitled to dismiss a worker without notice or without wages in lieu are when the worker has misbehaved or been dishonest. But the action to dismiss him must be taken immediately the misconduct or dishonesty is discovered.

If there is any doubt that notice is required, it is advisable to pay in lieu.

## Making redundancy payments

If an employer is dismissing workers because they are redundant, he must obtain a copy of Form RP1 from the Department of Employment for each employee dismissed.

The completed forms must be returned to the Department at least 14 days before the employee is due to leave. If more than ten employees are involved, 21 days' notice must be given. Redundancy occurs when an employer decides to dismiss an employee who is no longer required because the work for which he was engaged, or which he has been doing for a substantial period, has diminished or no longer exists.

This can occur if there is a recession in trade or perhaps if there is a change in the character of the employer's business.

For example, a shopkeeper may find after turning his shop into a self-service store that he needs less staff. The assistants he dismisses become redundant.

Even if the shopkeeper has to take on more people to work in his storeroom, with the result that his total number of staff is unchanged, the dismissed shop assistants are still regarded in law as redundant. The shopkeeper's need for employees of a particular kind—shop assistants—is reduced.

Redundant employees are entitled to a sum of money from their employer known as a redundancy payment. The amount to be paid depends on the length of an employee's service. ☐ Claiming compensation for redundancy, p. 645.

The employer must give the employee a written statement saying how the amount of the payment has been calculated. He can do this on an official form, RP3, supplied by the Department of Employment.

If the employer fails to provide the written statement, the employee is entitled to ask for one to be supplied within a week. An employer who then fails to provide one can be fined up to £20 for a first offence and up to £100 for any further offence.

Once the employer has made a redundancy payment, he can reclaim half the amount from the Department of Employment. He makes his claim on Form RP2, which is similar to RP1, from which details can be copied. When he sends RP2 to the Department he must also attach Form RP3, signed by the employee. If he wishes to give Form RP3 to the employee as his written statement, the employer has to make two copies. The rebate must be claimed within six months of making the payment to the employee.

Employers make a weekly contribution to the Government Redundancy Fund. This fund is used to make payments to employees whose employers cannot pay—for instance, because of bankruptcy. It also provides the cash to pay rebates to employers.

Contributions are collected as part of the flat-rate National Insurance contributions, which have to be paid for all men between 18 and 65 and women between 18 and 60.

The employer is allowed to claim as expenses against tax both the contribution to the fund and any amount paid to employees.

If the employer dismisses a worker wholly or mainly for some other reason than redundancy—say, gross disobedience—he does not have to give redundancy pay.

When an employee disputes the cause of his dismissal and claims that it was due to redundancy and not to inefficiency or any other reason given by the employer, the matter has to be settled by a hearing before an industrial tribunal.

It is then the employer who must prove that the worker was not redundant. Either party can later appeal to the Industrial Relations Court, but only on points of law.

# How business premises are controlled

Responsibility to employees
The shop and the law
Keeping a food shop

The control of offices
Opening a factory
Safety rules for outside work

ANYONE wishing to build a shop, an office or a factory, or to use another type of building—even a garage or a garden shed—for commercial purposes, must first obtain permission from the local planning authority. This is usually a county, borough, urban or rural district council.

First, approach the authority's planning officials informally to find out if the site chosen is acceptable. Most land is zoned as residential, industrial or green belt (rural land which should generally remain in its natural state). A council may indicate, for instance, that a shop may not be built among a block of houses, but only next to other shops.

If a local authority indicates that a site for new premises would be acceptable, formal application forms must be obtained from it for permission to build. There are two forms:
1. A certificate which must be completed by the applicant showing the ownership of the site. If the applicant is not the owner he must show that he has the agreement of the owner to build on the land.
2. A development application which must give information about the applicant, the proposed premises and their use.

The forms must be returned to the authority accompanied either by an outline plan of the premises or by detailed plans.

Under the Town and Country Planning Acts, Government approval is needed for the building of a factory, the conversion of premises to industrial use and the building of office blocks over certain sizes—for example, in central London where the size of the building exceeds 3000 sq. ft.

Consult the local authority to find out how best to proceed with an application.

When a planning authority considers an application to build premises it takes into account, after approving the site, the design of the premises, the materials used and the building's appearance. If preliminary planning permission is obtained after the submission of an outline plan, a further detailed plan of the premises must be drawn up and submitted for approval.

If planning permission is refused, there is a right of appeal within 42 days to the Department of the Environment, Whitehall, London SW1P 3EB.

Local-authority permission is also required if premises are to be extended or altered.

**Responsibility to employees**
Anyone running a business is responsible, under the Offices, Shops and Railway Premises Act 1963 or the Factories Act 1961, for the working conditions of the people employed on his premises. If a firm does not own the building it occupies, the owner is responsible for complying with some regulations.
☐ Safety, health and welfare, p. 608.

Premises in which an employer has only relatives working for him, or employees who work less than 21 hours a week, are exempt.

The regulations covering the treatment of employees vary according to whether the premises in which they work are legally defined as factories, shops or offices.
FACTORIES Broadly, a factory is a place where something is made, repaired, finished, cleaned, or altered from its original form, usually by machinery, and where more than two people are employed. Building sites, shipyards and dry docks, small workshops behind shops, and property stores at theatres where repairs are done, are all factories in law.
SHOPS Legally a 'shop' is a building or any part of a building devoted to retail or wholesale trade. This definition includes all the usual kinds of retailers and also covers hairdressers, private lending libraries and auction rooms. Semi-permanent stalls inside market halls are regarded as shops, but stalls in open-air markets are not. Mobile shops—those run by travelling grocers and greengrocers and ice-cream sellers—are covered where practicable by the regulations that apply to shops.

A canteen attached to a shop may be governed by the same regulations as the shop, if the local authority so decides.
OFFICES Under the Offices, Shops and Railway Premises Act, an office is defined as a place where administration, handling of money, telephoning, telegraphy and clerical work take place. The regulations which govern conditions in offices cover most office workers and staff in office canteens. Staff in canteens

serving both office and factory workers are controlled by the regulations decided upon by the local authority. It can decide that such canteens should be covered by the provisions of the Factories Act.

## The shop and the law

Anyone planning to take over an existing shop or open a new one must inform the shops inspector at the local council offices. The inspector is responsible for enforcing the Food and Drugs Act 1955, which deals particularly with hygiene, and the Offices, Shops and Railway Premises Act, which sets standards for working conditions.

He also enforces the Shops (Early Closing Days) Act 1965 and the Shops Act 1950, which regulate hours of opening, early-closing days, Sunday trading, employees' meal times, and the employment of young persons.

The inspector also has authority over public houses and restaurants, for these fit the definition of a 'shop'.

Apart from the Acts of Parliament governing shops, local authorities also have their own bye-laws, and the inspector should always be asked about them before any shop is opened for business.

He is entitled to inspect any shop at any time during working hours and he is allowed to exercise discretion when it is impractical for a shop to comply with regulations.

The owner of a shop must take precautions against fire. There must be adequate means of escape for staff and customers, and fire-fighting equipment must be provided. Shops employing more than 20 people, or more than 10 people on any floor except the ground floor, must be inspected by the local fire authority for a certificate of approval.

## Keeping a food shop

The siting of new shops which sell mainly food is carefully controlled by the local authority under the guidance of the shops inspector. For instance, food shops are not normally allowed near premises which give off fumes or smoke likely to cause contamination, or which attract rats or other vermin. The structural design of food shops, including restaurants, must also meet the standards set by the local authority.

A goods entrance separate from the customers' entrance is usually required. The yard or area where food is unloaded from transport has to be cleaned regularly.

Walls and floors must be easy to clean. Cracks must not be allowed to remain in walls or floors because they harbour germs. Any dampness is not usually tolerated by shops inspectors, because it encourages pests.

The size of premises, particularly restaurants, must be adequate so that they do not become overcrowded with equipment or people. A kitchen, for instance, must have a ceiling not less than 8 ft high and a minimum floor area clear of equipment of 100 sq. ft—the minimum size is increased if more than three people are employed in the kitchen.

Rooms for keeping food which is not packed or sealed against contamination must be well-lit and ventilated and must not be situated close to lavatories. Food rooms must not house washing equipment.

In shops selling food there must be sufficient sinks for washing equipment—in addition to hand basins used by staff. There must be hot water, except where a germ-killing agent is used with cold water. This applies also to public houses where glasses are washed.

DISPLAYING AND HANDLING FOOD Shops that display food openly must ensure that it cannot be easily contaminated. Unwrapped food—other than vegetables—must be displayed at least 18 in. from the floor.

Some food—meat, eggs and milk, for instance, and items made up from them—must be stored at certain temperatures. These foods can, however, be displayed openly for sale for a limited number of hours. The shops inspector will advise on the regulations.

People who handle food must keep themselves and their overalls clean. They must not smoke near open food. If anyone working in a shop catches, or knows that he is a carrier of, certain infectious diseases—for example, German measles, salmonella or typhoid—the shopkeeper must contact the local medical officer of health immediately.

MOBILE SHOPS Vehicles trading as mobile shops are controlled by local bye-laws which differ from one local authority to another, so anyone intending to operate a mobile shop should consult the local shops inspector.

MARKET STALLS Anyone intending to run a street market stall must first obtain a licence from the clerk of the local authority. Regulations for stalls are more lenient than those for fixed shops. But there are special requirements. A fish stall, for example, must be screened on three sides. There must be facilities for waste and a water supply near by.

## The control of offices

Office premises must usually comply with the provisions of the Offices, Shops and Railway Premises Act. The exceptions are local-authority premises (including council offices), schools and police stations, which come under the Factories Act.

Local authorities are responsible for enforcing regulations for those office premises which come under the Offices, Shops and Railway Premises Act.

Overcrowding is prohibited by the Act, which lays down that every employee must have at least 40 sq. ft of floor space and at least 400 cu. ft of breathing space where the ceiling is lower than 10 ft. No room should be so overcrowded as to cause the risk of injury to persons working in it.

The floor-space measurement formula does not apply to public offices, but the general prohibition against overcrowding does. This is because offices to which the public have access for interview or inquiry may have considerable floor and air space for the benefit of the public although employees could be overcrowded in one part of the room.

The temperature of every office must be reasonable. Where a person is required to work in a room for more than short periods on a job which does not require severe physical effort, the temperature after the first hour must be maintained at 16°C (61°F) or more. But this rule does not apply to an office or room where it is not practicable to maintain the temperature, or where a temperature of 16°C would damage goods. In such instances there must be a room where employees can warm themselves.

A thermometer must be prominently displayed on every floor of the building.

## Opening a factory

Before work can start in a factory, whether newly built or converted to industrial use, a month's notice must be given to the factories inspectorate, a section of the Department of Employment. This is not necessary where there is only a change in ownership.

The factories inspectorate should be consulted before sending in the notice, but the main details required are: the name of the firm or people owning the business; its address; the type of work to be done; and the machines, if any, that are to be used.

A new industrial plant may, for example, include furnaces which, under the Clean Air Act 1968, are not allowed to emit smoke. There are restrictions also on the amount of grit, dust and fumes that can be emitted. Factory chimneys must be high enough to prevent fumes harming the health of people in the neighbourhood.

A certificate approving fire-safety precautions for new or changed premises is also needed from the local fire authority. The authority inspects the premises and may insist that alterations be made.

HEALTH AND SAFETY Large factories should have an expert or a department devoted to the health, safety and welfare of employees. The Department of Employment has published a series of booklets on the legal requirements.
☐ Safety, health and welfare, p. 608.

APPOINTMENT OF DOCTORS Industrial firms are required by law to safeguard the health of their employees while at work. Large firms have doctors appointed to them by the superintending inspector of factories responsible for an area. The doctors are paid by the factory owner and can be employed full-time.

Factory doctors work according to Department of Employment rules and have the right to examine employees or ask to see documents relating to their work.

If a factory is considered by the inspectorate to be too small to have a doctor of its own, it may be put under the supervision of the local medical officer of health.

Certain notices must be posted at the main entrance to a factory or in a conspicuous position. These include a summary of the Factories Act; the address of the district inspector and the superintending inspector of factories (see the local telephone directory or contact the Department of Employment); the name and address of the appointed factory doctor; and a notice saying which clock, if any, is used for clocking in and out.

A factory inspector has the right to enter a factory at any time during working hours. If, after he has proved his identity, he is prevented from entering to carry out an inspection, he can call the police to force entry.

If the inspector believes that health and safety regulations are being broken in a factory, he can act as prosecutor in a magistrates' court against the firm or against any of its employees alleged to be at fault.

## Safety rules for outside work

Businesses which employ people on outside work must ensure that employees are in no danger when using machinery or equipment. Building operations and work on docks or quays are covered by the Factories Act.

Farmworkers are protected under the Agriculture (Safety, Health and Welfare Provisions) Act 1956.

Many of the rules for the farm are similar to those for factories. A list of regulations for the use of machinery, particularly covering the safety of young people, can be obtained from any office of the Ministry of Agriculture.

# Selling goods and providing services

*Dangers of misleading advertising*
*Conditions of sale*
*Complaints about goods sold*

*Credit for customers*
*Restrictions on prices*
*Contracts for repairs and services*

ANYONE whose business involves selling goods or providing services needs to be aware of the legal provisions protecting both himself and his customers. Even where there is no written contract, any deal he makes is subject to safeguards and restrictions.

## Dangers of misleading advertising
Anyone offering goods for sale must avoid giving them false or misleading descriptions. These can lead the seller into two different kinds of legal problem.

**1.** A customer who can prove in court that he bought goods on the strength of a false or misleading statement can sue the seller to get his money back, plus his legal expenses. This claim is made under the Misrepresentation Act 1967. It makes no difference whether the false or misleading statement was made deliberately or innocently.

The misleading statement must, however, relate to facts and not opinions. The buyer cannot sue on the basis of a statement such as: 'This is today's best bargain.' But he could sue over the statement 'This article is made of pure silk' if, in fact, the article was not made of pure silk.

**2.** The trader can be prosecuted under the Trade Descriptions Act 1968, which makes it an offence for anyone offering goods for sale to give misleading information which may persuade someone to buy the goods.

For instance, a bottle of Spanish-made whisky with a Scottish Highland scene on the label would be misleading because it implies that the whisky was made in Scotland.

Trade descriptions cover details such as the quality or size of an article, its composition, its place and date of manufacture or a statement that it meets a certain standard or has been approved by a particular person, organisation or authority. ☐ What to do about faulty goods, p. 460.

It is also an offence to indicate wrongly—on price tickets, for instance—that goods are being sold at less than the normal price. Detailed regulations lay down how price reductions must be expressed to keep within the law. A sales card saying 'Reduced from £3 to £2', for example, is lawful only if the article

was displayed for sale at £3 in the same store or group of stores for a continuous period of 28 days in the previous six months. ☐ How the law controls sales cards, p. 452.

POSSIBLE DEFENCES A trader who is accused of an offence under the Trade Descriptions Act has four possible defences:

**1.** That he made no false or misleading statements to the buyer.

**2.** That the alleged offence was due to a *genuine* mistake—for instance, the label advertising the price or quality may have been placed on the wrong article.

**3.** That he had relied on information from someone whose word he should be able to accept, such as the manufacturer of the goods.

**4.** That it happened through someone else's fault—for instance, that a child playing in the shop had changed the labels round or an employee had made a genuine slip.

➤ **THE SHILLING THAT DIDN'T COME OFF**
*Tesco Supermarkets Ltd were accused of an offence under the Trade Descriptions Act after charging a pensioner the full price for a packet of washing powder they advertised at '1s. off'. In their defence they claimed that the mistake had been made by an employee—the supermarket manager—and that they had taken all reasonable precautions to avoid such errors by themselves or by anyone under their control. Tesco were fined £25 but appealed.*

DECISION *The conviction was quashed. The House of Lords ruled in 1971 that a mistake by a shop manager could be regarded as a mistake by the company only if the company had delegated to him its entire responsibility. Tesco employed supervisors, but remained in control of selling. (Tesco Supermarkets Ltd v. Nattrass.)* ◄

The trader must show that he took all reasonable precautions to avoid the offence. If he claims that the alleged offence was someone else's fault, he must notify the prosecution at least seven days before the hearing.

## Conditions of sale
The Sale of Goods Act 1893 places a number of obligations on a seller which he cannot escape without obtaining the explicit agree-

ment of the buyer. These obligations, which are known in law as the implied terms of the contract, are:

**1.** The seller guarantees that he owns any goods he sells, or that he has authority to sell them, as in the case of an auctioneer.

**2.** Goods sold by description—which could be simply a name or a detailed specification—must correspond to the description. Similarly, if the buyer has been shown a sample, the goods must correspond to the sample.

**3.** If the buyer tells the seller what he wants to use the goods for and has relied on the skill and judgment of the seller, who normally sells that particular type of goods, the goods supplied must be reasonably fit for the purpose the buyer stated.

**4.** The goods must be of a reasonable quality or what the law calls 'merchantable' quality in relation to the price which the customer has to pay for them.

If the seller fails to observe any of these conditions without the agreement of his customer, the customer will be entitled to claim compensation from him.

The trader can exempt himself from any of these conditions, provided he makes it clear that he is doing so. He may, for instance, sell old or defective stock cheaply by indicating with a label 'all conditions or warranties implied by the Sale of Goods Act 1893, are hereby excluded'.

OWNERSHIP PASSED TO THE BUYER The ownership of goods passes from seller to buyer when the two parties themselves agree that it should.

Normally this is not a question which the two people concerned discuss in specific terms. When the goods are identified at the time of the sale and are ready for delivery, ownership passes immediately the bargain is struck between them.

This applies even when, say, the seller agrees to wait a few days for payment or the buyer agrees that it would be more convenient to him for the seller to delay delivery of the goods for a short period.

Sometimes, however, a buyer may order goods which the seller has not yet manufactured or bought from his own supplier. This is not accepted in law as a 'sale' but is an 'agreement to sell'.

There are several important differences from the seller's point of view. In the case of a 'sale', if the buyer fails to pay, the seller can sue for the actual price of the goods. But if the buyer defaults on an 'agreement to sell', the seller can sue only for damages to cover any *loss* he has incurred, say for inconvenience,

not necessarily for the full price of the goods covered by the agreement.

Similarly, if the seller is not able later to provide the goods he has agreed to sell—perhaps because he has let a more favoured customer have them—the buyer can sue for any loss he has incurred.

There is also a difference if the goods are damaged or destroyed. If there has been a 'sale', they are the property of the buyer and he must stand any loss even if they are still in the possession of the seller. The seller, however, must take reasonable care of them and can be sued for negligence by the buyer if he has not done so and they are damaged.

If, on the other hand, there has been only an 'agreement to sell', and the goods are damaged or destroyed before the agreement is fulfilled, the seller must stand the loss.

SALE OR RETURN Great care should be taken before parting with goods on a 'sale or return' basis. If the customer sells the goods before he has paid for them, he passes on legal ownership to his buyer.

This means that the original seller cannot recover the goods. He can reclaim the price only from his original customer, not from the present owner of the goods.

STOLEN GOODS An owner cannot recover his shirts, say, if they are stolen and subsequently sold in a clothing shop or an open market—that is, a market held by statutory authority, by local custom or by Royal charter.

However, if the shirts are sold in, say, a public house, on a doorstep, or in a shop that does not normally deal in shirts, the person from whom they were stolen remains the owner and has a right to recover them.

## Complaints about goods sold

The seller has an obligation in law to compensate a customer who returns goods as unsatisfactory. The obligation applies if the customer's complaint satisfies one of three main conditions:

**1.** If the goods are not what the customer asked for or if they do not match any sample that he was shown.

**2.** If the goods are defective or of poor quality in relation to the price paid (unless they were sold as defective or 'seconds').

**3.** If the goods are not suitable for the purpose for which the customer told the seller he wanted them.

However, the customer is not entitled to compensation if he examined the goods before he bought them and found—or could reasonably have been expected to find—the defects of which he is subsequently complaining.

Where a customer has legitimate grounds for complaint, the seller is normally under an obligation to make amends, even where the goods were sold with a manufacturer's guarantee. Though many customers are happy to have a defect repaired under guarantee, the seller has no right to pass a complaint to a manufacturer if the buyer demands that he deal with it himself. ☐ Faulty goods: suing the manufacturer, p. 464.

The way in which the seller must provide compensation varies with the type of complaint. Only when there is a fundamental defect, or when goods are totally unsuitable for the buyer's stated purpose, is the seller obliged to refund the purchase price or provide a replacement. In all other cases he can meet his obligations by giving the buyer a refund of part of the purchase price and allowing him to keep the goods. An example of a fundamental defect which would compel the trader to provide a replacement or refund the whole purchase price, would be an electrical fault in a toaster which made it useless for toasting.

In cases where the trader can meet his obligations by making a partial refund, the size of the refund depends on the seriousness of the complaint. Theoretically, it should be the amount of damages a court would award. The customer has a right to a cash refund if he asks for it.

If the customer agrees, a free repair is often the most satisfactory form of compensation, though again the customer has a right to demand financial compensation and have the repairs done elsewhere.

In a dispute with a stubborn or unreasonable customer, a seller who has been paid for the goods is in a strong bargaining position. If the customer rejects all reasonable offers, the seller can retain the full purchase price and invite the customer to take legal action. Because of the cost of doing so, the customer is not likely to sue unless a substantial sum of money—say, over £30—is at stake.

A seller who refunds money to a buyer for defective goods may have the right to claim in turn against the manufacturer, as he is himself a buyer from the manufacturer.

### Credit for customers
Traders can give customers credit by a variety of methods. A small shopkeeper, for example, may agree that a regular customer can pay for groceries the following weekend, at the end of the month, or by instalments.

Once the goods have passed to the buyer, the trader has no further legal claim on them,

even if his customer fails to pay. All he can do, if debt-collection methods fail, is to sue the buyer for the money. For small shopkeepers, this may not be worthwhile. ☐ Recovering business debts, p. 699.

Traders dealing in substantial items such as washing machines, furniture, clothing and cars cannot usually afford to have a large part of their stock producing only deferred payments under hire-purchase or credit-sale agreements. They may therefore come to an agreement with finance companies.

When a customer wants to obtain goods on a hire-purchase or credit-sale agreement, the trader gets the customer to fill in a finance-company form. The completed form is then sent by the trader to the finance company. If it accepts the customer, the company purchases the goods from the trader and enters into a hire-purchase or credit-sale agreement with the customer.

The finance company is then legally the owner of the goods and it is liable for all claims if the goods are found to be defective or unsuitable for their purpose.

However, it is usual for finance companies to protect themselves by a permanent agreement with the trader. Under the terms of such agreements, the trader undertakes to pay the finance company for any loss the company may suffer through a hire-purchase agreement introduced by him.

So, in practice, if a customer finds the goods unsatisfactory and demands that the finance company replaces or repairs them, the company can usually claim against the trader.

### Restrictions on prices
Shopkeepers cannot generally be prevented from selling goods below the price offered by competitors or below that recommended by manufacturers. Nor, generally, are there any upper limits set on what a retailer may charge.

Most resale-price agreements, by which traders were not allowed to cut prices for various goods below minimum levels, were made illegal by the Resale Prices Act 1964.

In certain circumstances, however, a manufacturer can still prevent a shopkeeper from selling his goods below his 'recommended' price. To do so, the manufacturer must satisfy the Restrictive Practices Court that the maintenance of his price at a fixed minimum is in the public interest.

Traders wishing to challenge illegal price-fixing must be able to show that a group of manufacturers producing similar goods has a minimum price agreement not sanctioned by the Registrar of Restrictive Practices. The traders can then take action through the Restrictive Practices Court to prohibit such an agreement.

However, a trader may suspect a manufacturer of putting pressure on him not to sell below the recommended prices. If he thinks his business is suffering because a manufacturer withholds supplies or reduces his discount on goods, he can apply to the High Court for an injunction to prevent the manufacturer acting in this way.

If the trader suffers financial or other business loss, he can also sue the manufacturer for compensation. A trader considering an action of this type should consult a solicitor immediately.

### Contracts for repairs and services

The business which provides services—a launderer, dry-cleaner, hairdresser and so on —can protect itself against legal action by imposing conditions on the service.

For example, a dry-cleaner or laundry can have a condition that goods are accepted only at the risk of the owner.

A firm is entitled in law to impose any conditions its customers are prepared to accept, and these will usually be effective as long as the firm displays the conditions in a prominent place on its premises where they can be seen before the contract is made. Or the firm can print them on the back of its ticket or receipt, with a reference on the face of the ticket—for example, the wording: 'subject to conditions overleaf'.

The conditions hold good in law only if none of the firm's employees misrepresents

them to the customer in any way. ☐ Repairs and services, p. 468.

If a firm undertakes repairs and other services, the work it does must be of a reasonable standard and the materials it uses must be fit for the purpose for which they are intended. For example, if a hairdresser uses a dye of a reasonable quality on a customer who happens to be allergic to the dye, the customer cannot normally claim damages.

If, however, she had told the hairdresser beforehand that she was allergic to the dye, she could sue him for negligence.

In the repair business, once goods have been repaired they must function properly—a vacuum cleaner must be able to clean a carpet. If it does not, the customer is entitled to have the repair done again free of charge. He may even be able to claim compensation for damage caused by a faulty repair.

SUB-CONTRACTORS A firm can sub-contract a repair job as long as the customer has not expressly forbidden this. However, unless the sub-contractor is chosen by the customer, the original contractor is responsible for any bad workmanship on the part of his sub-contractor. ☐ Repairs and services, p. 468.

The sub-contractor may charge more for his services than the original contractor does, but the original contractor can pass on the price increase to his customer only if he did *not* agree on a price with the customer before sub-contracting.

Most firms protect themselves by giving the customer an estimate, or by a clause concerning price fluctuations inserted in their conditions for undertaking work.

## Opening hours of shops

SHOPS are required by law to close for a half day during the week, unless the local authority approves otherwise. On such half days they must close not later than 1 p.m. The day for half-day closing can be chosen by the individual shopkeeper. A notice stating the early-closing day must be displayed.

Generally, every shop must be closed to customers not later than 9 p.m. on one 'late day' and 8 p.m. on every other weekday. Off-licences are an exception and are granted a special licence by the licensing justices.

Most shops must stay closed on Sundays. But those that sell newspapers, tobacco, confectionery and medicines can open. Food

shops can open if permitted by the local authority, but they must not sell fresh meat, fried fish or pet foods. Some authorities allow bread to be sold during restricted hours. All shopkeepers should consult the local authority before trading on a Sunday.

The regulations for trading hours are laid down by the Shops Act 1950, and the Shops (Early Closing Days) Act 1965. But late opening hours can be varied within the limits set down by the Acts or bye-laws.

Local authorities, through their shops inspectors, normally inform shop-owners of decisions on trading hours. Shopkeepers who ignore regulations can be fined up to £200.

# Dealing with value added tax

*How VAT works*
*Traders who must operate VAT*
*Transactions liable to VAT*

*Calculating how much tax to charge*
*Registering as a VAT trader*
*Settling accounts with Customs*

VALUE added tax (VAT) is a charge paid mainly by customers on the price of most goods and services bought on or after April 1, 1973. On that date purchase and selective employment tax are abolished.

Most businesses meet the ultimate cost of the tax on only a small proportion of their purchases. They are, however, heavily involved in the administration of the tax:
1. Initially, they pay VAT on most of the goods and services which they purchase.
2. They collect VAT on most of the goods and services they sell.
3. In most cases, they deduct tax paid to suppliers from tax collected from customers, and pay the balance to the department administering VAT, Customs and Excise.

There are exceptions to most of these rules.

### How VAT works
Value added tax is collected at various stages along the line of production and distribution. Each trader generally charges tax on the price at which he sells goods and services. But because of the refund system, the person who meets the cost is the final consumer.

Consider a product bought by a retailer for £35 plus VAT, and passed on to the public for £45 plus VAT. If the retailer were to account to Customs and Excise for this transaction alone, the calculation would be:

| | | |
|---|---|---|
| Sale price to customer | £45 | |
| VAT collected | | £4·50 |
| Purchase price from wholesaler | £35 | |
| VAT paid | | £3·50 |
| Balance due to Customs and Excise | | £1·00 |

In practice, traders calculate VAT on total tax collected and paid in an accounting period.

### Traders who must operate VAT
Everyone in business who is classed as a 'taxable person' (the term includes companies and partnerships) pays VAT on supplies of goods and services, and normally adds it to the prices charged to customers.

A trader with annual sales of £5000 or more is automatically a taxable person. Anyone with sales of less than this figure is usually exempt unless he applies to Customs and Excise to be classed as taxable. A trader who is not automatically taxable needs professional advice on the advantages and disadvantages of applying to be classed as taxable.

Exempt traders are often at a disadvantage compared with taxable competitors—particularly when dealing with business customers. Though the exempt trader does not charge his customers VAT, he pays the tax on his materials and—because he cannot reclaim it—may have to raise his prices.

On the other hand, a competitor who is a taxable person charges VAT, but his business customer is entitled to claim a refund from Customs and Excise. So in the long run the goods or services of an exempt trader may be more expensive to a business customer than those of a taxable person.

### Transactions liable to VAT
VAT is charged on the supply in the U.K. of goods or services in the course of business.

Supply of goods covers all forms of transfer and includes sale, part exchange, hire, hire purchase and loans (of goods).

Businesses importing goods pay tax on imports, and get a VAT credit against the tax they charge on sales.

Supply of services includes any activity that does not involve the transfer of goods; for example, the services of solicitors, electrical repairers, landladies, and hairdressers. Services are taxable only if paid for.

ZERO RATING Some goods and services are given what is called a zero rating. A trader selling them does not charge VAT. But he is entitled to reclaim from Customs and Excise any VAT he pays business suppliers.

A grocer, for example, who buys a refrigerator to sell frozen foods has to pay VAT on the refrigerator. But since food is zero-rated, he is able to reclaim the tax.

Zero-rated goods and services include most food (except restaurant meals); agricultural produce; books and newspapers; fuel and power (but duty remains on petrol); building; passenger transport other than taxis; residential caravans; drugs; and exports.

EXEMPT GOODS AND SERVICES A trader selling goods or services which are classified as exempt does not charge VAT but, unlike in the case of zero-rating, he cannot reclaim the VAT he pays suppliers.

Exempt supplies include: financial services, such as banking and insurance; dealings in land except holiday accommodation etc; education; youth club facilities; certain medical services; burial and cremation.

Some traders sell both taxable and exempt goods. They must apportion the tax they pay on purchases of goods and services between those relating to taxable sales (which they can recover from Customs and Excise) and those relating to exempt sales (which they must bear themselves).

GIFTS People in business who make donations (to clients for example) must account to Customs and Excise for VAT on gifts which cost them £10 or more.

OWN USE OF STOCK If a trader takes items from stock for his own or his family's use, this is treated as a sale to himself at cost price, and he must pay VAT on them.

CAPITAL EXPENDITURE A trader pays VAT when he buys capital goods such as plant and machinery, and deducts this from the VAT he collects in the normal way. A trader selling capital goods charges VAT and accounts for it to Customs and Excise.

BUSINESS EXPENSES AND CARS A trader is not allowed to claim a refund of the VAT he pays on buying motor cars or on entertaining clients, except clients from overseas.

## Calculating how much tax to charge

In general, tax is calculated on the price paid and at the rate in force when the goods are supplied, unless the contract says otherwise.

Goods or services paid for partly by part exchange are taxed on open market value. Goods supplied with a discount for prompt payment are taxed on the reduced price, whether or not the buyer pays promptly.

TAX AVOIDANCE To prevent traders avoiding tax by agreeing to sell goods to one another at a reduced price, Customs and Excise may assess tax on open market value.

## Registering as a VAT trader

Everyone in business who is not exempt through low turnover must register with Customs and Excise after September 1972. Details of procedure are available from Customs and Excise.

A trader who is exempt but whose turnover subsequently exceeds £5000 must register at once. A registered trader whose turnover falls below £4000 for a period of two years may apply to be de-registered.

Failure to register with the intention of avoiding tax is punishable by a fine of up to £1000 or three times the amount of tax involved, whichever is the greater; or by imprisonment for up to two years; or by both fine and imprisonment.

KEEPING VAT RECORDS A taxable trader must show VAT as a separate item on invoices to other taxable traders. He must keep a copy, and provide one for the purchaser. Records should be kept for at least three years.

Customs and Excise can inspect these records and other documents, demand information, and enter premises at any reasonable time. They may obtain a search warrant if they suspect a tax offence. They may also take samples to determine how goods are made.

Failure to keep records can lead to a fine of up to £1000, and a penalty of £10 for each day that the records are not kept.

## Settling accounts with Customs

The taxable trader must settle accounts with Customs and Excise every three months. He must add up all the tax which he has collected or is due to him for goods sold and services supplied during the three months, and add up all the tax which he has paid or is liable to pay for goods and services purchased by him during that time.

For this purpose, the date on which tax is due to the supplier is taken to be whichever of the following happens first: when goods are delivered or collected; three months after they are made available to the buyer if they remain uncollected; the date on which services are performed; or when payment is actually made.

The trader must send tax owing to Customs and Excise within a month of the end of the accounting period. If more tax has been paid than has been collected, he may claim a refund.

If a return is not made, or if Customs and Excise suspect that a return is inaccurate, they may charge the amount of tax that they think is due, and the trader will be faced with the problem of convincing them otherwise.

BUSINESS CHANGES When a business changes hands, the new proprietors take over existing VAT credits and liabilities, but no additional tax has to be paid. When a business closes down, the proprietors are treated as having disposed of all the goods in stock, and must account for VAT on this notional sale.

APPEALS Disputes over VAT are heard by the Value Added Tax Tribunal, with a further appeal on questions of law to the ordinary courts. ☐ Appearing before a tribunal, p. 735.

# Insuring against business hazards

*Arranging the policy*
*Special insurance*
*Keeping the insurance up to date*

*Making a claim*
*When claims are settled*

No business, whatever its size, can operate without a degree of risk. A tobacconist may lose his stock in a burglary, or a factory may be destroyed by fire. However, adequate insurance can protect almost any business against these and many other hazards.

Exactly what to insure against depends largely on the nature of the business and the premises from which it operates. Generally, the advice of a good insurance broker, or an insurance company specialising in business insurance, is indispensable. A broker seldom charges for such advice, since he is paid a commission by insurance companies.

## Arranging the policy

Most insurance companies offer a special shopkeeper's or small businessman's combined policy which usually gives wide protection under a single policy.

A combined policy insures business premises and stock against damage in a variety of circumstances—usually fire, lightning, earthquake, explosion, burglary, riots, strikes, civil commotion, labour disturbances, malicious acts, storm, tempest, flood or impact by a vehicle or aircraft or anything dropped from an aircraft. Damage during a war is excepted. It can also include cover against some or all of the following:

PUBLIC LIABILITY Everyone in business risks being faced with claims for damages from the public. For example, a grocer may unwittingly sell contaminated food and can be sued for damages; a builder may leave equipment where a passer-by trips over it and injures himself. Public-liability insurance would meet these claims.

EMPLOYER'S LIABILITY All private businesses need cover against the possibility that employees may be injured at work and claim compensation from their employer. ☐ Suing the employer after an accident, p. 636.

MONEY The theft of money, postal orders, cheques, or National Insurance or postage stamps can be included in a combined policy. If money is regularly taken to and from a bank or post office or held by collectors, special insurance should be arranged.

CONSEQUENTIAL LOSS When business premises and stock are damaged or destroyed, the loss which a business suffers is not always made good by repairs or replacement—trade may be disrupted or orders lost. Consequential-loss insurance gives cover against these effects, and some insurance companies also meet the extra expenses incurred in trying to get business operations back to normal.

FIDELITY GUARANTEE Pilfering of money or stock by staff can be compensated for by what is known as fidelity-guarantee insurance. This can be restricted to particular groups of employees such as cashiers or it can cover an entire work force.

PLATE GLASS Shop windows and glass doors are usually expensive to renew. Plate-glass policies usually give cover against accidental damage only. Cover against damage through burglary and vandalism can be arranged under fire and burglary policies.

## Special insurance

There is a risk of under-insuring through using a general policy. The amounts payable on any claim may be limited, unless specific sums or circumstances are agreed and written into the policy.

Claims for loss of money, for instance, may be limited to £300, or £25 when the premises are closed. Theft, dishonesty or fraud by an employee may be covered only if it is discovered within seven days. Damage to neon signs, vending machines, refrigerators and their contents is often excluded.

It is, therefore, essential to negotiate with the insurance company if a combined policy appears too limited. Usually extra insurance can be added to a combined policy. Occasionally, a separate policy is needed.

Generally, the size, situation and construction of the shop or business premises, plus the value and vulnerability of stock, are the main factors considered in basic premises and contents insurance.

Insurance companies are usually prepared to discuss ways to reduce premiums before a final figure is reached, and it is often possible to get a premium reduced by taking precautions. For instance, a businessman may be able to cut the cost of insurance by installing a sprinkler system or some other form of fire extinguisher.

Premiums for employer's liability insurance vary according to the type of work done. Shop assistants and light delivery staff can be insured at comparatively low rates. But the premiums for machinists, demolition workers or other employees whose jobs carry an element of danger are high.

Some businesses, because of the specialist nature of their operations, may need insurance to cover exceptional items or circumstances. For example, the proprietor of a seaside pleasure-boat business may wish to protect himself against loss of profits due to an exceptionally wet summer season. Many insurance companies offer such cover, but the premium is often high.

Insurance companies decline proposals for anything that could be against the public interest. For instance, although a publican could insure against losing his licence through circumstances beyond his control, such as the actions of an employee, he would not be allowed to take out insurance against losing his licence through the results of his own behaviour—for example, because of dishonesty or drunkenness.

Though not strictly insurance, businesses can arrange for an indemnity firm to provide compensation for the face value of dishonoured cheques—up to an amount agreed with the firm in advance.

## Keeping the insurance up to date

It is essential to bring an insurance policy up to date immediately circumstances change—to cover increased stock, for example. Do not wait until the policy has to be renewed.

Insurance companies always stipulate that property must be insured to its full value, except in a few special cases such as agricultural insurance. If it is not, the insurance company is technically entitled under many policies to refuse to pay any part of a claim. In practice, however, the company is likely to regard the policy-holder as his own insurer for the balance.

This is called the rule of average. Any loss is carried by *both* parties, the insurance company and the policy-holder.

For example, a businessman may value his stock at £5000 and insure it for this amount. During a slack period, deliveries of additional stock may arrive before earlier consignments have been sold. As a result, the total value of stock on the premises could rise to, say, £8000. Unless the insured amount (and thus the premium payable) has been increased, the businessman is insured for only five-eighths of stock value. In these circumstances, if stock worth £800 is stolen, the insurance company is entitled to refuse to pay more than five-eighths of the claim—£500.

The company should also be told of changes which may affect the policy—converting a store into a shop extension, for example, or storing inflammable goods in a warehouse previously used for 'safe' stock.

There is no advantage to be gained by over-insuring. Policy-holders are not allowed to recover more than the actual loss.

## Making a claim

Immediately there is any likelihood of a claim, telephone the insurance company so that it can arrange without delay to inspect damage or interview the policy-holder or his staff. Then complete a claim form.

Anyone who makes a false or exaggerated claim on an insurance company risks prosecution under the Theft Act.

Only urgent necessary repairs should be made before the insurance company has been notified. Always get the insurance company's consent before engaging contractors to carry out extensive repairs to the premises.

If the extent of the damage or of the loss through theft is not immediately apparent and the insurance company presses for details, sign the claim form but add that the total is the amount being claimed 'at this date'. If the insurance company accepts this, the policy-holder can present an additional claim when the true amount is known. If it does not, the insurance company is bound to give the policy-holder a reasonable time to prepare his claim.

Sometimes, when a fire or burglary has occurred, a person describing himself as an insurance assessor offers, for a fee, to negotiate a claim with the insurance company on the policy-holder's behalf. Try to check the reliability of the assessor before considering his services, and beware of signing an agreement which would give him a disproportionate percentage of any damages claimed.

## When claims are settled

When an insurance company pays a claim, the policy-holder is asked to sign and return a form stating that its cheque is in 'full and final settlement' of the claim.

Before doing this, ensure that all the amounts claimed have been paid. If not, do not present the cheque for payment at a bank, but take up the discrepancy with the company's claims department.

# Protecting commercial ideas

*How to apply for a patent*    *Trade marks*
*How to register a design*

WHEN the success or failure of a business rests on a new commercial or artistic development or invention, it is important to ensure that it cannot be used by a competitor. The extent to which an invention can be protected depends largely on its nature and whether it has been developed.

There is no protection in law for the inventor or creator until he has described his thoughts—in writing or by producing a first model or specimen. Only then can he prove that he developed the idea first.

INVENTIONS A means of producing an article or of improving some existing manufacturing process—both classified as inventions—can be protected by patent.

To do this the inventor registers it with the Patent Office, 25 Southampton Buildings, Chancery Lane, London WC2A 1AY. When an invention has been patented, only the inventor and people authorised by him are legally entitled to manufacture it, use it or benefit from it during the following 16 years.

This protection applies only to the United Kingdom and the Isle of Man. If the inventor wants to stop his invention being used in countries overseas, he must apply separately for a patent in each country. The International Convention for the Protection of Industrial Property, which has been signed by most countries, gives an inventor priority to register his process in any convention country within 12 months of his first getting a patent in his own country. A list of the convention countries can be obtained from the Patent Office.

DESIGNS When only the appearance of an article is to be protected, the design can be registered with the Designs Registry branch of the Patent Office. This gives protection in Britain for five years and gives the designer priority to register it in other convention countries within six months. A designer must apply before selling or offering for sale in the United Kingdom any quantity of articles made to the design he wants to patent.

ARTISTIC WORKS Literary, musical and other artistic works—such as sculptures and designs for medals or stamps—do not have to be registered. The sole right to benefit from them—called copyright—belongs to the crea-

tor throughout his life and passes to his heirs for 50 years after his death. The creator—or after his death, his heirs—can sell some or all of these rights at any time.

## How to apply for a patent

To establish a claim for a patent, the inventor must show that his invention differs in some important way from anything that has been patented before. This involves having a search made of the Patent Office records and submitting a detailed specification. Both can be done by a specialist in this field, known as a patent agent. A list of registered agents and their fees can be obtained from the Chartered Institute of Patent Agents, Staple Inn Buildings, London WC1V 7PZ.

For the inventor who wants to do the work himself, the Patent Office provides advice in a number of free publications.

THE COST Having an invention patented can be expensive. Probably £50 is the minimum cost for completing the procedure on a simple invention, and with the growing need to patent inventions internationally, £500 would not be exceptional. For this reason it is possible for an inventor to submit his idea in two stages—a provisional specification and a complete specification.

PROVISIONAL SPECIFICATION Once an inventor decides that he has a good process, he should register a provisional application. He can make a search beforehand to establish that his idea really is new, but this may lose him valuable time, as it is important to have the invention registered provisionally and establish the claim before anyone else.

Unless the inventor already has considerable experience of patent law, he is advised to obtain the help of a patent agent.

A form for a provisional specification can be obtained from the Clerk of Stationery at the Patent Office. The inventor has to give a clear description of the invention, but drawings are not usually required at this stage.

The description must define the precise scope of the monopoly rights claimed. If the inventor does not give sufficient detail someone else could make or patent something similar without infringing his rights. When the provisional specification has been submitted, the inventor has a year to consider whether his process is worth pursuing before he incurs the heavier costs of a complete specification and having a search made of the Patent Office records. This period can be extended to 15 months for an extra fee.

COMPLETE SPECIFICATION If he decides to go ahead, the inventor must submit a complete specification on forms obtainable from the Clerk of Stationery at the Patent Office. Full details and precise drawings must be given. It is at this stage that the advice of a patent agent is most needed.

A Patent Office examiner's search to see if the submitted design conflicts with any existing patent can take up to a year.

MAKING AN APPEAL If an applicant disagrees with the examiner's report, he can ask for an interview to put his case or he can apply for a formal hearing before an official appointed by the Patent Office comptroller. If he is still not satisfied, he has 14 days to appeal to the Patents Appeal Tribunal, and the case is heard by a High Court judge.

ACCEPTED SPECIFICATIONS If the specification is accepted, either by the examiner or on appeal, the comptroller of patents informs the applicant and advertises in the *Office Journal (Patents)* that the specification has been accepted and is open for public inspection. Three months are allowed for objections to the patent to be filed.

If there is no objection, or if any objections have been overruled, the inventor should apply to have the patent granted or 'sealed'. This application must be made no later than four months from the date the Patent Office published the complete specification. If the applicant can show that his failure to observe the time limit was unintentional, it may be accepted up to six months late.

Once the patent is granted, anybody using the invention without the patent-holder's permission can be sued for damages. This protection lasts 16 years.

TIME LIMITS The law allows a maximum of two years nine months for the whole process of applying for and receiving a patent. If the application is not in order or has not been accepted within that time, it becomes void. If the inventor wants to persist with it he has to start again from the beginning.

### How to register a design

Most designs have to be registered at the Designs Registry, Patent Office, 25 Southampton Buildings, Chancery Lane, London WC2A 1AY. Textile designs are registered at the Designs Registry, Baskerville House, Browncross Street, Salford M3 5FU.

An applicant, who may engage a patent agent to act for him, must present:

1. An official application form.
2. Four identical specimens of the invention.
3. A statement identifying the design feature or features for which novelty is claimed. After registration, the statement is open for public inspection.

GRANTING THE APPLICATION A search is made at the registry and, if the design appears to be novel, a certificate of registration is issued. If the certificate is refused, the appeal procedure is similar to that for a patent.

A design can usually be registered within two months. The formalities must be completed within a year of the date of application, but an extension of three months can be sought. If an application is not completed within 15 months, it is assumed that it has been abandoned.

COPYRIGHT Although it is not necessary to register copyright within the United Kingdom, an author or creator may wish to protect his copyright in other countries. Under international conventions the holder of the copyright can improve his protection by marking his work with the symbol © followed by his name and the year of publication.

If copyright is infringed, the holder of the copyright may sue for damages.

### Trade marks

Anyone in business can register with the Patent Office a trade mark which indicates that certain goods were produced or selected by him. The mark must contain or consist of at least one of the following:

1. The name of a company, individual or firm represented in a special way. The name alone is not enough, as it might be confused with that of a trader of the same name.
2. The trader's signature.
3. An invented word or words. But the word or words must not make any claim for the goods which would prejudice the claims of anyone trading in the same field.
4. An existing word or words which, again, make no claims prejudicial to other traders.
5. Some distinctive, pictorial mark.

Under common law, a businessman is protected against 'passing off'—an attempt by a rival to pretend that goods were made or supplied by the businessman or his firm. Having a registered trade mark gives further protection, making it easier for the businessman to secure an injunction to stop a rival firm encroaching on his business.

# Recovering business debts

*Personal debt-collecting*      *Employing a debt-collection agency*
*Recovery through the courts*

THERE are three main courses of action open to the businessman who is owed money by customers or clients. He can try to recover it himself, he can sue the debtor through a county court or the High Court, or he can call in a debt-collection agency.

### Personal debt-collecting
The businessman is entitled to act as his own debt-collector. Usually all he can do is send reminder letters to the debtor or arrange to call regularly to collect instalments. But he must not harass the customer or client. If he does, he is guilty of an offence under the Administration of Justice Act 1970. The penalty for a first offence is a fine of up to £100, and up to £400 for a subsequent offence.

To avoid harassing a debtor, the creditor must observe certain rules. He must not bully the debtor with threats of publicity, and he must not take any action that would distress, humiliate or alarm the debtor's family.

A shopkeeper, for example, who displays a list of debtors in his window may be guilty of 'harassing' them.

Requests for payment must not suggest that the creditor is acting in an official capacity—as a police officer, for instance. Nor should the creditor send a demand which resembles a document from the court. □ Debts and bankruptcy, p. 580.

### Recovery through the courts
If attempts to persuade a debtor to pay have been unsuccessful, a businessman can start legal proceedings—in the county court if the claim is for less than £750, or in the High Court. □ Legal action II: suing to recover a debt, p. 725.

### Employing a debt-collection agency
In many cases it is not worth while trying to recover a debt through a court. The amount owed may be small compared with the expense of legal action, even if costs are awarded, and the publicity which can follow a court hearing may be harmful to business.

In these circumstances, instead of writing off bad debts altogether, a businessman can try calling in a debt-collection agency.

Debt-collectors rely on persuasion to recover debts. They are not solicitors, and do not usually bring legal action against debtors.

Anyone can set himself up as a debt-collector and no special registration or qualification is required. So the businessman should make sure that the agency is entirely reputable, since any illegal practices it may adopt—harassment, for example—could make him liable to prosecution.

He could be guilty of an offence if he employed a disreputable firm to act on his behalf, because he would be 'concerting with others' in taking illegal action.

The best way to find a reliable agency is through personal recommendation. Alternatively, the Association of British Investigators Ltd (by guarantee), 2 Clements Inn, London WC2A 2DX, will recommend members who undertake debt recovery. The association checks the character and operating methods of all prospective members.

AGENCY METHODS Some agencies 'buy' the trader's debts, and the right to collect them, for a percentage of their value. Others keep a percentage of all money they recover—in effect a 'no-recovery no-fee' system.

For the small shopkeeper with perhaps a total of £50 owing from about a dozen customers the straight sale of the debts may seem the best available solution, especially if he has already tried to recover the money himself. By selling them even at only 20 per cent of their value, he can at least reduce his losses from £50 to £40.

But putting debts entirely in the hands of a debt collector on this basis may injure a businessman's reputation. Since he has forfeited all interest in the debts, he has no control over the debt-collector's activities.

When debts are released to a debt-collector on a 'no-recovery no-fee' basis, the businessman and collector are in fairly regular contact. It is easier then for the businessman to stipulate exactly how far he wants the debt-collector to go to recover his money.

Many firms that are anxious to protect their reputations keep a tight rein on the agency's activities and stipulate that no calls are made to a debtor's home.

# How businesses are taxed

*Working out taxable profit*  *How partnerships are taxed*
*Tax and the sole trader*  *Tax on companies*

ALL businesses have to pay tax on the profits they earn. A person trading on his own, and members of partnerships, are regarded in law as self-employed, and are taxed under Schedule D of the income tax system. Companies, however, have their own separate legal status and they are not liable to income tax, but to corporation tax.

Most people running businesses employ accountants to ensure that they present properly prepared accounts to the inspector of taxes, and do not pay more tax than they are legally obliged to pay.

### Working out taxable profit
Income or corporation tax is charged on the profits a business makes—that is, the excess of income over expenditure allowable for tax purposes. The profit figure in a business's own accounts is not necessarily the one on which it is taxed.

First, in calculating its taxable profit, a business is allowed to deduct from income only those expenses incurred wholly and exclusively for the purpose of the business.

A shopkeeper, for example, who uses an estate car for deliveries may find it convenient to include the entire cost of buying and running the vehicle in his business accounts— even if he also uses the car for weekend pleasure trips. But in arriving at his taxable profit, he is entitled to deduct motoring expenses only in proportion to business use of the vehicle.

Again, when a business prepares its own accounts, it may deduct from gross profit a charge for depreciation of assets such as plant and machinery. In some cases, the entire cost of buying an asset such as a vehicle may be deducted in the year in which it is acquired.

Neither of these items—depreciation and capital expenditure—can be included in accounts submitted for assessing tax liability. Instead, the business may be entitled to claim capital allowances and writing down allowances which spread the cost of capital equipment over a period.

The rate at which capital expenditure can be set against tax varies from Budget to Budget, and is not the same for all classes of expenditure. In the 1972–3 tax year, for example, the entire cost of many types of equipment and furniture can be set against profits in the period of the accounts in which they are purchased. But the rate for motor cars is only 25 per cent a year.

### Tax and the sole trader
A sole trader (a man in business on his own, without partners) pays income tax—and surtax or higher rate tax if he is earning enough—on his net profits, after his allowable expenses have been deducted.

The final figure is often a matter of negotiation between him or his accountant and the tax inspector. If accounts are not submitted, the inspector can assess tax at any figure he thinks reasonable.

### How partnerships are taxed
The taxation of partnership profits is more complicated than the taxation of a sole trader because more than one taxpayer is involved. A partnership pays income tax, not corporation tax.

At the end of the tax year the partnership must submit returns of its income, expenditure and profits to the inspector of taxes. Legally, this should be done by the partner whose name appears first in the partnership agreement. But the tax inspector can require any partner to give him the information.

In addition to the return of the business's finances, the inspector may call for a copy of any partnership agreement.

DISTRIBUTION OF PROFITS A partnership is assumed in tax law to distribute all its profits to the partners. It is not possible for a partnership to save paying tax by holding back any of its profits—even if the profit is invested in the business.

The tax inspector considers the partners' total net profits after deducting business expenses. Unless provisions for special commencing or closing years apply, those profits form the basis of assessment of the partners for the tax year following the end of the accounting year.

The assessment is divided among the partners according to how they divided the profits of the tax year—not the year in which the profits were made. The senior or first-named active partner must tell the inspector how profits are divided. Under the Partnership Act 1890, the profits are split equally, unless the partnership agreement says otherwise.

When the profits have been apportioned in this way, the inspector considers the personal claims of each partner—for his wife and children and so on. Unless a partner is completely inactive, the profits he receives are treated as earned income. The inspector then finds how much tax each partner should pay.

The partnership receives a demand for the total amount due and this is allocated among themselves according to their respective individual liabilities. But it is the partnership as a body which is legally bound to pay the tax; if any one of the partners does not contribute towards the tax bill, the other partners may have to take civil action to recover the money.

## Tax on companies

A company is involved in two kinds of tax on profits: corporation tax which it pays itself on the profits it makes; and income tax which it has to deduct from every dividend paid to shareholders. Corporation tax has to be met out of company funds; tax on dividends is borne by the shareholder by deduction from the dividend itself.

CORPORATION TAX The company makes a return of all its income, expenditure and profits, together with its claims for allowable business expenditure. The tax inspector assesses net profits for corporation tax.

DISTRIBUTION OF PROFITS After corporation tax has been paid the company can distribute profits among its shareholders in the form of dividends. From all dividends the company must further deduct and account for income tax at the standard rate.

If a shareholder is not liable to tax at the standard rate, he is responsible himself for applying for a refund. ☐ How to make a tax return, p. 562.

DOUBLE TAXATION Before April 6, 1973, company profits distributed as dividends are effectively taxed twice—once when corporation tax is paid, and again when they are subject to income tax.

From April 5, 1973, the income tax which a company pays on the dividends it distributes is treated as payment on account of corporation tax owing—so that nominally there is no double taxation.

There is often an advantage for a director who holds shares to take as much as possible out of the company in fees, rather than dividend. Fees are deducted from profits before they are assessed for corporation tax, provided that they qualify as expenses wholly, exclusively and necessarily incurred by the business. So only income tax (and surtax or higher rate income tax, where appropriate) is charged on directors' fees. Even after double taxation is abolished, this may be less than corporation tax on the same amount.

The amount of money that can be paid free of corporation tax in directors' fees, however, is controlled by the tax inspector. He allows only what he considers reasonable for the size of the company and the nature of its business. If the fees are challenged then it is almost always a matter of personal negotiation with the tax inspector.

The tax inspector has no power to limit the amount that is actually paid in fees. His discretion matters only where the company applies to have such payments treated as free of corporation tax.

HOLDING BACK PROFITS It is to the advantage of shareholders who already pay higher rates of personal tax to have as much as possible of the company's profit ploughed back into the business. Instead of receiving a highly taxed dividend, part of the profits go to increase the value of the company, and of their shares. There are, however, regulations limiting the more obvious forms of tax avoidance.

---

## When tax is due

SOLE TRADERS and partnerships are normally required to pay tax on the profits they made in the accounting year ending in the preceding tax year.

That means that in 1972/3 they pay tax on the profits made in the accounting year ending on March 31, 1971, as if these were the profits for the tax year 1972/3. The tax is payable in two instalments on January 1 in the tax year and the following July 1.

There are special complex rules covering how businesses are taxed in their opening and closing years, and the advice of an accountant is essential.

COMPANIES Corporation tax is normally paid by companies nine months after the end of the accounting year in which the profits were earned. Income tax is payable almost immediately dividends are paid.

# Taking business decisions

*General meetings*     *Protection of minority shareholders*
*Notice of meetings*    *When the company is being run badly*
*Resolutions*

A SOLE trader decides for himself how to run his business. Similarly, in partnerships there are few restrictions involved in running the business. Provided that the partners observe the conditions of their partnership agreement, they are free to take important decisions with little formality.

Companies, however, have to be run according to the rules laid down in the Companies Acts 1948 and 1967. While directors are given day-to-day control, shareholders must be consulted before any fundamental decision affecting the company can be taken.

Anyone, therefore, who wants to propose a fundamental change in the direction of the company's business must do so at a general meeting of the shareholders.

## General meetings
There are three different types of company meeting—the statutory meeting, which is held just after the company is set up; the annual general meeting (AGM); and the extraordinary general meeting (EGM).

THE STATUTORY MEETING A public company must hold a statutory meeting not less than a month or more than three months from the date on which it is entitled to start business. A report, called the statutory report, certified by two directors, must be sent to all shareholders 14 days in advance, stating the number of shares allotted, the money received from their sale, and listing the company's directors, auditors, managers and secretary. A copy of the report must be sent to the Registrar of Companies.

Private companies are not required to hold a statutory meeting; they differ in certain other respects from public companies, but generally they are affected by the same laws. ☐ Setting up in business, p. 678.

ANNUAL GENERAL MEETINGS Only one AGM need be held in the first two years after a new company is formed, as long as that meeting is held within 18 months of the incorporation date. Afterwards, however, an AGM must be held every year, and there should not be an interval of more than 15 months between one meeting and the next. At an AGM, the shareholders approve the accounts and balance sheet for the last financial year; appoint auditors for the forthcoming year; vote on the auditors' remuneration; receive the report of the directors and auditors; declare the final (or only) dividend (if any); and elect their directors. Other business, called special business, can also be dealt with.

EXTRAORDINARY GENERAL MEETINGS Any meeting which is not the statutory meeting or an AGM is an extraordinary general meeting. An EGM may be called by the company's directors; it may also be summoned by any group of shareholders holding at least 10 per cent in face value of the voting shares—even if this action is against the wishes of all the directors. This provision enables shareholders to assert their rights of control and dismissal over directors.

## Notice of meetings
Shareholders must be given 21 days' notice of the place, date and time of an AGM. They must normally be given 14 days' notice of any other meeting. If, however, a resolution is to be put making major changes in the articles or objects of the company (what is known as a special resolution), 21 days' notice is needed. They must also be given the text of any special resolutions.

Shorter notice of an AGM can be given only with the agreement of all shareholders entitled to attend. For any other meeting, shorter notice can be given only if 95 per cent of those entitled to attend consent.

SPECIAL NOTICE Twenty-eight days' special notice must be given to the company of any resolution calling for the removal of a director or an auditor, or for the appointment of a director over the age of 70.

WHO CAN ATTEND If a shareholder is unable to attend, he can send a proxy on his behalf; but unless the articles of the company provide otherwise, a proxy can vote only in a ballot—not when a decision is taken by a show of hands. A proxy may speak at a meeting of a private company but not at a meeting of a public company unless the articles specifically permit this.

Certain groups of shareholders—preference shareholders, for example—may be barred from voting under the company articles. If the articles do not lay down what the quorum for company meetings is to be, the rules of the Companies Acts must be followed: three members must be present in person at a meeting of a public company; two members must be present in person or by proxy at the meeting of a private company.

## Resolutions

Resolutions which can be considered by a general meeting fall into three categories—ordinary resolutions, special resolutions and extraordinary resolutions.

ORDINARY RESOLUTIONS Only a simple majority is needed to pass an ordinary resolution. If the vote is on a show of hands, each person voting has one vote. However, any shareholder can ask for a vote by poll or ballot, and in this case each member's voting power depends on the number of shares with voting rights that he holds.

SPECIAL RESOLUTIONS Any resolutions calling for major moves such as a change in the company articles or a change in the objects set out in the memorandum are known as special resolutions. Twenty-one days' notice must be given, and a resolution is not carried unless it has at least three-quarters of the votes cast in person or by proxy.

EXTRAORDINARY RESOLUTIONS Sudden emergencies in the life of a company can be met by extraordinary resolutions; for instance, the procedure might be used to call for the winding up of a company. Usually notice of the extraordinary resolution is given at the time of summoning the meeting at which the resolution will be considered. But in extreme emergency only a few days' notice is required.

The resolution is not carried unless it has at least three-quarters of the votes cast in person or by proxy.

The wording of all extraordinary and special resolutions has to be filed at the Companies Registry within 15 days of being passed by the shareholders.

## Protection of minority shareholders

Minority shareholders are vulnerable to attempts by larger shareholders to alter the company and its affairs.

The Companies Acts and the courts, however, provide them with limited protection. For example, they are generally protected against any move to vary their share rights. A variation occurs when the company has two or more classes of shares, and it is proposed to vary directly the voting rights of one but not of the other. If the company's articles

follow those listed in Table A of the Companies Act 1948, no variation of rights is possible except at a special meeting of the shareholders of the class affected. At least one-third of them must be present, and at least three-quarters must be in favour. Alternatively, three-quarters of those affected can give written consent to the change.

Certain indirect variations, however, may be permitted by the courts.

►THE SHAREHOLDERS WHOSE POWER GREW *Shares in Arderne Cinemas Ltd were divided into two classes—10s. shares and 2s. shares. Each share had one vote. Then the company decided, by an ordinary resolution, to subdivide the 10s. shares into 2s. shares. This gave the holders of the old 10s. shares five times as many votes for the same holdings, thus taking voting control from the 2s. shareholders. A minority shareholder appealed to the court.*
DECISION *The court held that this was not a variation of the rights of the original 2s. shareholders, and allowed the subdivision to stand. (Greenhalgh* v. *Arderne Cinemas Ltd.)* ◄

In a quoted public company, the Stock Exchange rules give minority shareholders added security.

However, the apparently watertight protection provided in the company's articles or in the Stock Exchange rules is not enough unless the memorandum backs up these rights; for the Companies Act 1948 allows this protection to be abolished or changed by a special resolution passed by all the shareholders. Once this has been done, another special resolution could sweep away the rights of any one class.

## When the company is being run badly

Minority shareholders who think the company is being run badly can apply to the courts for action. For example, if there has been a change in the memorandum, any individual or group holding 15 per cent of the face value of the company's shares can ask the court to have the change set aside.

If the company is being run oppressively but the shareholder does not want to petition for it to be wound up, the court can order those in control of the company to buy his shares at a price fixed by the court.

If an individual or a group, holding not less than 10 per cent of the shares, thinks the company is being run fraudulently or improperly, they can ask the Department of Trade and Industry to investigate. But good reasons must be given for this request.

# Formalities of winding up

*Choosing to stop trading*　　*Realisation of the company's assets*
*Being forced to wind up*　　*Paying creditors and shareholders*
*The winding-up hearing*　　*The dissolution of the company*

A SOLE trader is free to close his business whenever he wishes. Similarly, a partnership can stop trading at any time, provided that its members comply with the partnership agreement. A company can cease trading—or wind up, as it is known in law—either on its own initiative or because it is forced to do so by a creditor, a shareholder or certain public officials.

If a sole trader or members of a partnership cannot pay their business debts, they can be made bankrupt by their creditors since they are personally liable for business debts. ☐ Debts and bankruptcy, p. 580.

Winding up has a similar effect on a company as bankruptcy does on an individual, since the main purposes of winding up are:

**1.** To convert everything the company owns, including property and capital, into cash.

**2.** To pay as many of its debts or liabilities as possible.

**3.** To pay the shareholders any surplus after the creditors have been paid.

**4.** To dissolve the company.

## Choosing to stop trading

A company may decide to stop trading because it is no longer able to pay its way, or it may simply want to change the type or direction of its business.

A company can change its business by amending the objects clause in its memorandum of association. But it may prefer to have its original name struck off the list of companies held by the Registrar of Companies, and to start trading again under a new name.

To wind up a company voluntarily, the shareholders pass a resolution at a special general meeting. If, within the five weeks before the meeting, the company sends to the Registrar of Companies a sworn statement made by its directors that it can pay its debts —a declaration of solvency—the closure is known as a members' voluntary winding-up.

The advantage of a members' voluntary winding-up is that the company can appoint its own liquidator—the person responsible for the legal work in winding up a business.

If the directors do not file a declaration of solvency with the Registrar of Companies, the winding-up is known as a creditors' voluntary winding-up. In this case, the creditors—the people and firms to whom the company owes money—must be asked to attend a meeting on the day, or the day after, the members decide to wind up. At the creditors' meeting, the company's directors must give a full statement of the company's affairs. The creditors can then appoint a liquidator themselves. If their choice of liquidator differs from that of the company, it is their nominee who becomes liquidator, subject to any order made by the court.

## Being forced to wind up

Anyone who wants a company to be wound up has to petition the county court—or the High Court if the company's paid-up capital is more than £10,000—to make an order that the company be compulsorily wound up. But only certain people have the right to do so:

**1.** A creditor owed more than £50 whose demand for payment has been ignored by the company for at least three weeks.

**2.** Any shareholder who has held shares for at least six months in the last 18, and who holds shares for which he paid less than the nominal price—he is called a 'contributory'.

**3.** The company itself, if a meeting of its members resolves that a compulsory winding-up would be preferable to a voluntary one.

**4.** The Department of Trade and Industry, if it believes that the company is being run contrary to public policy.

**5.** The Official Receiver, if the company is already being voluntarily wound up and he thinks that the winding-up should be done under the supervision of the court.

## Presenting the petition

To petition for a compulsory winding-up, the applicant must obtain the appropriate form from the county court registrar or High Court public office. He must state on the form the date on which the company was first formed, its principal objects, its registered address, the amount of its nominal capital and the amount of its paid-up capital.

The completed petition is returned to the court, which sets a time and place for a hearing.

This is known as endorsing the petition. The petitioner has to confirm that he is petitioning within four days of presenting the petition. He does this by verifying by affidavit —sending in a written statement which he has sworn under oath is true.

The petitioner must advertise his petition, in *The London Gazette* and in a local newspaper circulating where the company has its registered office, seven days before the hearing. The company must receive a copy of the petition in a sealed envelope.

A petition can be presented on the grounds that the company is insolvent; that the reasons or objects for which it was formed no longer exist; that its articles provide for winding up in the circumstances prevailing at the time of the petition; that the company is really a partnership which could be wound up in the present circumstances; or that the shareholders have passed a resolution calling for a compulsory winding-up.

Less common grounds for a petition are that there is total deadlock between the owners of the company, or that it is being conducted in an arbitrary or oppressive way.

Anyone wishing to oppose the petition must file an affidavit within seven days of the date on which the affidavit verifying the petition was filed. The petitioner can then file affidavits in reply within three days.

## The winding-up hearing
The hearing is attended by the petitioner and the company or their legal representatives, and by any shareholder who bought shares at less than their nominal value (a contributory) or creditor who wishes to do so. If a creditor or contributory wants to give evidence, he must tell the petitioner before 4 p.m. on the day before the hearing.

## When the order is made
If the court makes a winding-up order, it takes effect from the day on which the petition was presented. The Official Receiver becomes the provisional liquidator until he, or someone else, is appointed official liquidator. The company must then stop trading. But the liquidator, with the court's permission, can trade on the company's behalf if he considers it beneficial to the winding-up. He may, for example, think he can raise more money by continuing the business for a time than he can by closing it immediately.

Once the order has been made, the company cannot dispose of any of its property, transfer any of its shares or alter the status of any of its members without the court's permission.

The directors have no more say in the company affairs, and its employees are immediately dismissed.

Within 14 days of the company's being placed under a winding-up order, it must send a statement of its assets, debts and liabilities, and particulars of its creditors, to the Official Receiver who makes a report to the court. He then arranges, within a month of the order, separate meetings of the company's creditors and contributories.

He advertises these meetings, seven days in advance, in *The London Gazette* and a local newspaper. The purpose of the separate meetings is to decide whether the Official Receiver should continue to be liquidator, and if not, who should take over.

The meetings also decide whether there should be a committee of inspection, consisting of creditors and contributories, to act with the liquidator. If the meetings disagree, the court decides on the liquidator.

## Realisation of the company's assets
It is the liquidator's job to realise the company's assets—to turn them into cash. He has the power to sell and transfer the company's property, and to process and sign all deeds and documents. He can ask contributories to pay the difference on their unpaid shares—so if a contributory paid 75p for a £1 share, he has to pay the 25p difference.

## Paying creditors and shareholders
Once the liquidator has realised the company's assets, he has to get the court's clearance before he can pay any class of creditor in full or before he comes to any arrangement with a creditor, contributor or debtor.

The liquidator advertises, in *The London Gazette* and a local newspaper, the time limit within which creditors must notify him of claims against the company. Creditors must prove the truth of their claims with affidavits. These must also state whether the creditors hold mortgages, deeds or insurance policies against the company as security for debts.

The liquidator then has 28 days to admit, reject or require further evidence on any creditor's claim. If he rejects a claim, the creditor can appeal within 21 days to the court which is dealing with the winding-up.

## Who is paid from the assets
Creditors of a company which is being wound up are divided into different classes and are paid in a strict order laid down by the law. But within each class of creditor, everyone must be treated equally. No one can be

paid in preference to a creditor of the same class. Secured creditors—those who have proved that they hold security for a debt—have priority over all other creditors. Once they have been paid, the liquidator's expenses and remuneration are settled.

The next class of creditors to be paid are those known in law as preferential unsecured creditors. Debts which must be paid to this class of creditor include: rates; purchase tax; National Insurance contributions and payments in lieu of graduated-pension contributions; corporation and other assessed tax.

Employees also rank as preferential unsecured creditors. They are each entitled to up to £200 in wages or salaries for services during the four months before the date of the winding-up order. They are also entitled to any holiday pay due. If they cannot be paid in full, they are given an amount proportionate to the size of their claims.

The last creditors to be paid are those known as ordinary unsecured creditors. These are people who neither hold security for the money they are owed nor have any special rights to be included in the list of preferential creditors.
SHAREHOLDERS Only after all the other debts have been settled can any of the company's surplus assets be distributed among the company's members—in proportion to the nominal value of the shares they hold. If the company is insolvent, shareholders do not usually get £1 for every £1 invested.

How much a shareholder is paid depends on the amount of his investment and on his rights as laid down in the company's memorandum of association.

People holding preference shares have priority over members holding ordinary shares. However, unless otherwise stated in the company's articles, a preference shareholder does not get preferential treatment with regard to any assets the company may have after the repayment of share capital. He then ranks equally with the other shareholders.

## The dissolution of the company

When the liquidator has converted the company's assets and paid its debts, he can ask the court, after sending notice of his intentions to the contributories and creditors, to order that the company is dissolved.

Within 14 days of the court making an order that the company be dissolved, the liquidator must send a copy of the dissolution order to the Registrar of Companies. At the same time, he applies to the Department of Trade and Industry for his release as liquidator. Once the company is dissolved, no one is liable for its debts.

## Making an arrangement with creditors

A SOLE trader, or members of a partnership, in financial difficulties can sometimes come to an agreement with their creditors out of court. By entering into such an agreement, known as a deed of arrangement, the debtor makes over his assets to an accountant, who acts as his trustee.

The debtor submits the deed of arrangement to his creditors. They are asked to reject or approve the deed and the appointment of the trustee. If the creditors reject the deed, a resolution for bankruptcy is usually passed. If a substantial majority approve the deed, assent forms are circulated for signature. The trustee deals with the dissenting creditors.

The deed of arrangement is executed by debtor and trustee in the presence of a witness. Within seven days, the deed must be registered in London.

A majority of the creditors must assent within 21 days of registration. If not enough assents are returned, the deed is void. The trustee may have to ask for the time in which the assents are to be returned to be extended, or he may serve notice on creditors who have not assented. Any creditor who has not assented to the deed can present a bankruptcy petition within three months of execution of the deed.

Once the necessary number of assents have been returned, the trustee can sell the debtor's property and divide the money among the creditors in fair proportions.

The trustee can make no payments until three months after the execution of the deed. Expenses must be paid first, but the trustee himself is not entitled to payment. Dividends are payable only to creditors.

Before final payment is made, the trustee may give notice in a local newspaper. Unclaimed dividends may be paid into the court two years after registration of the deed. Any surplus is returned to the debtor.

After the trustee has filed the final accounts, he is released from his duties.

# THE MACHINERY OF THE LAW

# Getting advice on a legal problem

*Using reference books*
*When officials can help*
*Other sources of free advice*

*When a solicitor or barrister is required*
*What a solicitor charges*

THERE is no one source of information and advice about the law, and even a book such as this can never be so comprehensive as to cover every problem that can arise. The layman with a legal problem can try to find out more about how the law affects him from books and official publications; he can ask civil servants or local-government officials for information; he can seek advice from unofficial or voluntary advice services; or he can consult a solicitor.

### Using reference books
Because the law in England and Wales has developed partly from Acts of Parliament, partly from regulations laid down by local or central government, and partly from decisions of courts in previous cases, the layman cannot hope to find the answer to every legal problem in any one publication. But he can consult a book such as this, where the problems have been approached from the layman's standpoint.

If further information is required, there are many sources open to him. Acts of Parliament and government regulations and orders are published by Her Majesty's Stationery Office —which has branches throughout the country, and whose main distribution office is at 49 High Holborn, London WC1V 6HB.

If the problem is based mainly on local regulations or bye-laws, the local council offices or the reference library will have copies.

For information on how previous cases have been decided by the courts, lawyers rely on the law reports. But there is no easy way for someone without detailed knowledge of the law to find out which cases are relevant. The layman can consult a legal textbook dealing with the subject required. But he will be ill-advised to base any action on his own reading of specialist publications.

### When officials can help
One of the most common sources of legal advice is the staff of local and central government offices. They can offer information and advice, but they cannot take any action on behalf of the citizen with a legal problem.
CITIZENS' ADVICE BUREAUX The same is true, to some extent, of the national network of Citizens' Advice Bureaux, financed mainly by local councils. Their staff, who are not lawyers, usually have wide experience of the more common difficulties such as divorce, consumer problems, disputes between landlords and tenants or between employers and employees. They give advice and will sometimes write letters or make telephone calls, but they will not normally take further action for a client.
THE POLICE Free advice on many problems may be obtained at any police station. In some cases the police may intervene. If they cannot take action they can say whether professional advice is needed.

### Other sources of free advice
Many national and local newspapers operate free confidential advice services for readers. They are usually staffed or advised by lawyers.
FREE LEGAL-ADVICE CENTRES Some large towns and cities have free legal-advice centres run by lawyers and voluntary helpers. The centres can give preliminary advice and write letters on behalf of anyone who consults them. A few provide lawyers to represent clients in court; but most refer people needing help beyond mere advice to a local solicitor.
TRADE UNIONS Members of trade unions are often able to get legal advice from their head office if they have a legal problem arising out of their work. The union can often arrange for a member to get free advice from a local solicitor, who is paid an annual fee by the union for such work.
MEMBERS OF PARLIAMENT Most Members of Parliament hold regular meetings in their constituencies. The times and places where they are available to talk to constituents may be published in the local Press, or they can be obtained from the party agent or the constituency association.

The advice service offered by MPs cuts across party political barriers: it is open to all constituents, not just to those who support the individual MP's political party.

Where a local council or Government department is involved, the main advantage of consulting an MP is that he can take direct action, and thus is often able to get a more satisfactory settlement than would be possible by a person taking legal action.

OMBUDSMAN In cases where a citizen has a complaint against civil servants, an appeal to the Parliamentary Commissioner (Ombudsman) may be the only way to solve the problem. But individuals must first see their MP or write to him—or to another MP if their own will not take the case—and it is the MP who decides whether the matter should be referred to the Ombudsman.

## When a solicitor or barrister is required

Many legal problems can be solved only by taking professional legal advice. The legal profession is divided into two branches— solicitors and barristers. A solicitor has direct contact with his client and undertakes day-to-day legal business, such as the purchase and sale of property, and drawing up wills. He can also represent clients in the magistrates' courts, county courts and before tribunals.

A barrister can represent clients in the lower courts and has the sole right to appear in the High Court, Court of Appeal and the House of Lords. He can be approached only through a solicitor, who submits particular legal problems to him and 'instructs' him if a case involves litigation in the higher courts.

A barrister who has been practising for a number of years can apply to the Lord Chancellor to be made a Queen's Counsel or 'take silk' (because a Q.C. wears a silk gown in court). Q.C.s are sometimes known as leaders because they cannot appear in court without a junior—a barrister who has not taken silk.

CHOOSING A SOLICITOR The best way to choose a solicitor is on the personal recommendation of a friend or professional acquaintance—a bank manager, for example.

Where a personal recommendation is not possible, lists of solicitors can be found in the local classified telephone directory, and from the *Law List*—generally available in public reference libraries.

None of these sources, however, can give the layman advice on which solicitor to choose. The best choice may be the one nearest to the client's place of business or home. But where the problem is specialised, or where a criminal charge is concerned, the client may have to approach several firms before he finds a solicitor willing to act for him.

He can usually get some idea of the kind of work various local solicitors handle from an office of the Citizens' Advice Bureau. Alternatively, the client can telephone or write to any solicitor's office giving an outline of the work involved, and ask whether he deals with that type of work—and, if not, whether he can recommend a local solicitor who does.

SEEING THE SOLICITOR Although it is not necessary to see the solicitor when he is first engaged, it is better to do so. Give him details of the case, including any papers or letters concerned. After the first meeting, make a point of sending the solicitor a confirmatory letter setting out all the details.

### What a solicitor charges

In some cases it is possible to get a solicitor's advice at a reduced charge, or State help to pay some or all of the solicitor's fees. The client who wants these subsidised services should make it clear to the solicitor at the outset. If the solicitor does not handle cases on that basis, he can refer the client to another solicitor. If he does, he can arrange for the necessary forms to be completed. ☐ Help with legal fees and costs, p. 710.

Most solicitors will give a client a broad indication of how much their services will cost. For some services there are fixed scales of fees. If, however, the client agrees at the outset, the solicitor is entitled to charge more.

Apart from this, a solicitor may charge what he likes, as long as the charge is reasonable. The method of calculating may be by the hour, by the number of consultations and letters written, by a percentage of the sums of money involved—or a mixture of all three.

Fees vary widely from one case to another, but the following list gives a broad indication (at 1972 prices) of the possible costs:

Acting as executor of a will involving a £10,000 estate—£200.

Negotiating compensation for a leg broken in an accident—£25 upwards, depending on the amount of work involved. If the other party admits liability, he pays the fees.

Dealing with an undefended petition for divorce—between £90 and £140.

Buying a £6000 house—£100. (With a £5000 mortgage, an additional £35–£45 would be added to the total cost.)

Drawing up a tenancy agreement for rented accommodation—between £12 and £15.

Where the client is paying his own fees, and no scale is involved, it is advisable to set a limit on how much expense can be incurred by the solicitor without fresh instructions from the client.

Solicitors seldom charge more for their work than the amount involved in the case. For even where a client wins his case, and the other side pays his costs, he is still liable to pay for some of his solicitor's work. ☐ The cost of legal action, p. 751.

# Legal aid I : help with fees and costs

*Two ways to get advice and assistance*
*Help in court cases*

NOBODY in Britain needs to fight a legal battle entirely on his own, simply because he cannot afford to pay a barrister or a solicitor. He can get legal advice, and in many cases the full services of a lawyer, through two schemes which exist to help people in need.

One, the State Legal Aid and Advice Scheme, provides three kinds of aid—for written and oral advice; for assistance with a legal problem which goes beyond advice but falls short of representation in court; and for representing a client in court.

The other scheme, the Voluntary Legal Advice Scheme, provides advice only.

The State scheme operates on the principle that the poor get free legal aid and those with limited means get legal aid if they agree to make a contribution towards their legal costs. Application forms are available from the

## Step-by-step guide to getting advice or legal aid

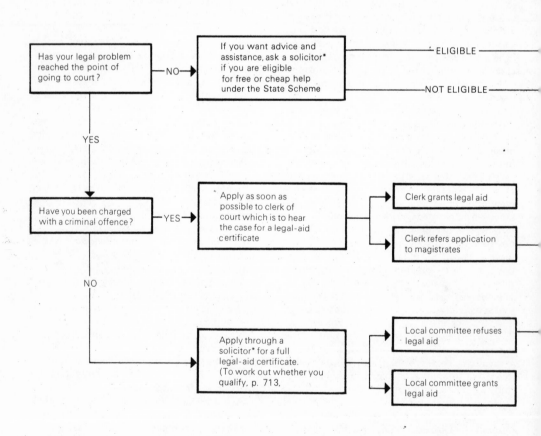

Citizens' Advice Bureau offices, court offices, the Law Society's Legal Aid offices and some police stations and solicitor's offices. Citizens' Advice Bureau staff, or a solicitor, will help complete an application form if necessary.

There are no restrictions on age, nationality or residence. Children and the mentally sick can apply through their parents or guardians.

**Two ways to get advice and assistance**
A person who needs legal advice or assistance may qualify under the rules of either the State scheme or a voluntary scheme run for people who would not otherwise qualify for cheap or free help.
THE STATE SCHEME The State's legal advice and assistance scheme is run by the Law Society, the solicitors' professional body. Help is free for those whose disposable income is

less than £11 a week and whose disposable capital is less than a certain sum (in late 1972 it was £125, but likely to be raised).

For people whose disposable income is between £11 and £20 a week, help is available under the scheme provided that they make a sliding-scale contribution of between £1 and £12. A single man would qualify if his take-home pay were £20 a week or less, a married man with three children if his take-home pay were up to nearly £30.

The income and savings of a husband and wife are considered jointly, unless they are living apart or unless advice is being sought on a matter in which they have conflicting interests—for example, divorce. ☐ Advice and assistance under the State scheme, p. 713. THE VOLUNTARY SCHEME Until 1972 the Law Society provided a scheme for people not

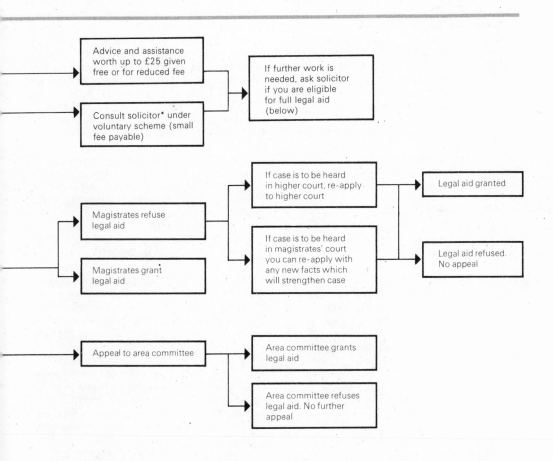

*Not all solicitors accept work under the State and voluntary schemes. ☐ Finding a solicitor, p. 712.

eligible to benefit from the State scheme of legal advice and assistance. Anyone, irrespective of means, could on payment of £1 obtain up to half-an-hour's advice from any solicitor who had agreed to participate in the Voluntary Legal Advice Scheme. In 1972, however, the Law Society decided that this scheme could be continued only if the amount payable by the client was increased—possibly to £3·50.

### Help in court cases

With a few exceptions, legal aid can be granted for bringing or defending any kind of action in any court, including a juvenile court. The exceptions are: appearances in a bankruptcy court; bringing or defending actions for libel and slander; and most applications for bail.

Legal aid can be granted to people appearing before the Lands Tribunal and the new National Industrial Relations Court. But it is not available before other tribunals such as those concerned with National Insurance, tax, rent, planning appeals, or claims for compensation for unfair dismissal. Anyone who qualifies for legal advice and assistance can, however, get a solicitor to draft the arguments that he should present when he appears at the hearing himself. The client may have to pay a contribution for such work, but it could be well worth while to pay a small amount for qualified help.

Again, before a grant can be made the local legal aid authorities must be satisfied that the applicant's financial status brings him within the legal aid scheme and that his case warrants the spending of public money.

---

## Finding a solicitor

NOT all solicitors work under the legal aid and advice schemes. To find one who does, ask at the local Citizens' Advice Bureau, at court offices or at any solicitor's office.

The names of solicitors accepting work under these schemes are also given in the Law List, available in the reference departments of most public libraries.

The letter 'S' in brackets after a solicitor's name means that he will accept work under the State scheme. The letter 'A' after his name means that he will accept work under both State and voluntary schemes.

Any solicitor whose name is on the panel for the State or voluntary scheme may be chosen by an applicant.

---

These tests are applied slightly differently in civil and criminal cases.

CIVIL CASES Legal aid for civil proceedings may be granted free or on condition that the applicant pays part of his costs himself.

It is estimated that more than half the adult population of England and Wales would be entitled to some form of State legal aid if they were involved in civil proceedings.

Usually a man will get free legal aid if his take-home pay, after deductions for dependants, income tax, accommodation and other essentials, is not more than £6 a week. Because of the number of allowable deductions a man with three children could earn nearly £23 a week and still qualify for free legal aid. His savings and assets, after deductions, must be below £125.

Anyone earning over these limits may be offered legal aid on condition that he makes a contribution himself. The contribution depends on how much money he has. But anyone whose disposable income (that is, income after deduction of necessary outgoings) is more than £950 or who has more than £500 capital is not entitled to legal aid at all. Again, because of the allowable deductions a person with three children still qualifies if he earns up to £42 a week. □ Legal aid II: help in civil cases, p. 714.

CRIMINAL CASES Legal aid is available for defending any case in a criminal court. It may be free or subject to a contribution.

There is a wide disparity in the granting of legal aid for trials in magistrates' courts. Lawyers claim that identical cases can be presented to two different courts and while one applicant will be granted legal aid the other will be refused.

For trials in the higher criminal courts there is no evidence of local variation, however. The great majority of people who find themselves facing trial in these courts are now granted legal aid, sometimes subject to making a contribution, which is dependent on their means.

In criminal cases, contributions are always assessed after the case has ended—in the light of the penalty if the defendant is convicted. □ Legal aid III: help in criminal cases, p. 716.

THE DOCK BRIEF Undefended people who face trial in the higher courts without legal aid are entitled to the services of a barrister for a nominal fee under the oldest form of legal aid, the Dock Defence, more commonly known as the Dock Brief. Under this traditional scheme, an accused person is permitted to point to any robed and wigged barrister in the court and require his services.

This fee is now fixed at £2·25. In recent

years the increased provision for legal aid has made dock briefs rare.

Under the Legal Advice and Assistance Act 1972, both magistrates and county courts have power to invite a solicitor who happens to be in the court building during a case to represent someone who does not have a representative and who is thought to need the help of a lawyer.

If this procedure is followed, the person who gets representation would have to make the same contribution to his defence costs as someone who had sought help under the legal advice and assistance scheme.

The Court of Appeal has also ruled that an unrepresented person can be accompanied by a friend whether he is a qualified lawyer or not. The friend is entitled to take notes in court, to make suggestions quietly and to give advice.

---

## Advice and assistance under the State scheme

THE State Legal Advice and Assistance Scheme provides help for people with small or moderate incomes and little savings.

The help can be given by a solicitor in his office or elsewhere—for example in the client's home if he is bedridden, or in a police station or prison if he has been taken into custody or sentenced.

### What work can be done

The scheme covers oral and written advice and preliminary legal work such as negotiating, letter-writing or drafting of documents. But it must not involve work costing more than £25. If the problem requires further action by the solicitor, he must apply for what is called an 'extended certificate' to allow him to undertake it. If the problem involves court representation, the client must apply formally either for legal aid for civil proceedings or for criminal legal aid. ☐ Legal aid II: help in civil cases, p. 714; Legal aid III: help in criminal cases, p. 716.

But the solicitor is entitled under the State advice and assistance scheme to give his client written guidance on how he should present his own case in court or at a tribunal hearing.

### Working out whether you qualify

When an applicant seeks advice or assistance, the solicitor acting under the State scheme is obliged to question his means. Whether he gets cheap or entirely free help depends on his disposable income and disposable capital.

Disposable income is take-home pay after tax and National Insurance contributions have been deducted, and after deduction of the same allowances for wife and children as apply in legal aid for civil cases. ☐ Legal aid II: help in civil cases, p. 714.

Disposable capital is savings after certain deductions have been made. Any Citizens' Advice Bureau or solicitor will advise in a particular case on what deductions can legitimately be made.

Free or cheap help is available under the scheme provided that after deductions, the applicant's disposable income is less than £20 and his disposable capital less than £125. The government has power to vary the qualifying rates at any time, and it is thought likely that the £125 limit for savings may be raised.

When an applicant qualifies but has a disposable income of more than £11 a week, he has to make a contribution towards the advice and assistance obtainable under the scheme. The contribution is assessed out of his disposable income only:

| Disposable income per week | Contribution by client |
| --- | --- |
| Under £11 | nil |
| £11–£12 | £1 |
| £12–£13 | £3 |
| £13–£14 | £5 |
| £14–£15 | £7 |
| £15–£18 | £10 |
| £18–£20 | £12 |

The maximum contribution is therefore £12, but it is officially estimated that more than half of the people using the scheme will be entitled to help without having to make any contribution.

When a contribution has been assessed by the solicitor he is entitled to payment immediately or within any period he considers fair. In some cases he may be willing to accept payment by instalments or he may even waive his right to the contribution.

When a solicitor informs an applicant that he is not eligible for help under the State scheme, he should ask for assistance under the Voluntary Legal Advice Scheme.

# Legal aid II : help in civil cases

*Working out whether you qualify*
*Working out how much you have to pay*

*What happens if you lose*
*What happens if you win*

APPLICATIONS for legal aid in civil cases are considered by the local legal aid certifying committee. The Supplementary Benefits Commission assesses the applicant's means to decide whether he qualifies for legal aid; at the same time the certifying committee considers whether the legal action he wishes to take or defend merits the spending of public money. The certifying committee will also decide, if it grants a certificate, what contribution the applicant shall be called on to pay towards the cost of the proceedings. This may not exceed the maximum contribution assessed by the Supplementary Benefits Commission.

If the local committee refuses legal aid, the applicant can appeal to the area committee. The applicant, or his representative, is entitled to appear and argue the case. But even if this second application is successful, the aid granted will not pay the costs of the solicitor appearing at the area committee hearing.

EMERGENCY CASES If the matter is urgent, an applicant can apply for an emergency certificate. If this is granted, the application for a full certificate will go forward normally.

**Working out whether you qualify**
In deciding whether an applicant's means entitle him to legal aid, the Supplementary Benefits Commission takes into account his disposable income and disposable capital. (Figures given here for disposable capital were recommended in 1972 by the Lord Chancellor's Legal Aid Advisory Committee, but had not been confirmed by the Government at the time of going to press.)

FREE LEGAL AID Anyone whose disposable income is less than £300 a year *and* whose disposable capital is less than £325 is entitled to free legal aid for bringing or defending civil proceedings. The capital test may be waived if the Supplementary Benefits Commission considers the applicant cannot make a contribution towards the costs.

LEGAL AID SUBJECT TO CONTRIBUTION Anyone whose disposable income is between £300 and £950 a year *or* whose disposable capital is between £325 and £1500 is entitled to legal aid provided he agrees to make a contribution to the costs of the case himself.

A contribution is also required from an applicant whose disposable income is below the £300 limit if he has disposable capital of more than £325. Similarly, an applicant with a disposable income of up to £950 a year and no disposable capital will be expected to make a contribution.

NO LEGAL AID If an applicant's disposable income is more than £950 a year *or* if his disposable capital is more than £1500, he is not entitled to any legal aid. In the case of capital exceeding that limit, the committee has a discretion to grant a certificate.

CALCULATING INCOME To calculate disposable income, first take the gross yearly income of the applicant, plus the income of the applicant's husband or wife (unless they are living apart or are on opposite sides in the case). For a self-employed person, his yearly net profit is regarded as his income. From this total income, deduct:

1. Income tax and National Insurance contributions for the year.
2. For a householder, mortgage repayments, upkeep and insurance. For a tenant, rent less profits from sub-letting. In other cases, a reasonable amount for accommodation.
3. Up to a total of £2 a week (£104 a year) for sick pay the applicant receives from a trade union or friendly society; private pensions, but not retirement, widow's or orphan's pensions or payments; disablement benefit and any workman's compensation payments.
4. Reasonable expenses incurred in connection with the applicant's employment.
5. The following annual allowances for dependants living with the applicant (weekly figures in brackets):

| | |
|---|---|
| Husband or wife | £213 (£4·10) |
| Child under 5 | £99 (£1·90) |
| Child 5 and over, but not yet 11 | £117 (£2·25) |
| Child 11 or 12 | £143 (£2·75) |
| Child 13 and over, but not yet 16 | £177 (£3·40) |
| Child 16 and over, but not yet 18 | £211 (£4·05) |
| Other dependants 18 and over | £270 (£5·20) |

An extra deduction is allowed for expense due to a dependant's age or illness.

**6.** The amount paid by the applicant for maintaining a dependant not living with him.
**7.** Necessary expenses in the case of a student living on a grant.
**8.** A set allowance of £104 for normal household expenses.

CALCULATING CAPITAL To calculate disposable capital, add together the applicant's savings, other financial interests, and personal possessions, plus those of a husband or wife unless they are living apart or are opposing parties in the case. Personal possessions other than clothing, essential furniture and effects and the tools of the applicant's trade—which are all exempt—are assessed at their value if they were sold, not the original cost.

Part of the value of a house or flat is included if the applicant owns it or is buying it on mortgage, provided that, after deducting any money owing on the mortgage, it is worth more than £7500. To arrive at the figure to be included, take the market value of the house, deduct what is owing on the mortgage, and then deduct a further £7500; the figure to be included is then *half* of what remains.

The value of a life assurance policy is considered to be the extent of a loan which could reasonably be raised on it, although the first £325 of any such loan is discounted.

From total assets, deduct:
**1.** £150 for the first dependant (husband/wife/child/other relative).
**2.** £100 for a second dependant.
**3.** £50 for any subsequent dependant.

Finally, if disposable *income* is not more than £700, the applicant can deduct from his disposable capital the balance between his disposable income and £700.

## Working out how much you have to pay

When legal aid is granted for a civil case, a fixed formula is used to calculate how much the applicant must pay towards his own legal costs. The formula is in two parts. The first part of the contribution is one-third of any disposable income over the 'free legal aid' limit of £300. So disposable income of, say, £650 automatically warrants a contribution of £116·66½, which is £650 minus the 'free limit' of £300, divided by three.

Secondly, the whole amount of any disposable capital over the 'free limit' of £325 is calculated as contribution. So disposable capital of £375 warrants a contribution of £50.

The two contributions are added together to give the *total maximum* contribution the applicant may have to make.

If the local committee considers that the costs of a case will be considerably less than the applicant's possible maximum contribution, it may offer legal aid subject to a lower contribution. Alternatively, if the costs of the case are less than the figure anticipated, the applicant will get a refund.

The local committee will write to the applicant offering legal aid subject to a stated contribution. If the applicant wants to accept, he signs his acceptance and returns the form.

Contributions out of income are normally paid by 12 monthly instalments. Contributions out of capital are normally paid in a lump sum on acceptance of the offer of legal aid.

## What happens if you lose

Anyone who accepts legal aid can be sure that he will not pay more than his maximum assessed contributions towards *his own costs*.

But if he loses he may be ordered to pay something towards the costs of *the other party*. These costs will be decided by the court. In practice, they are limited to a sum equivalent to a maximum of 12 times the monthly contribution he makes to his own costs.

Therefore when deciding whether or not to accept legal aid an applicant can reckon that if he loses the case his maximum liability will be his contribution, plus a further 12 monthly instalments. With free legal aid he normally pays nothing to the other party's costs.

## What happens if you win

If a legally aided person wins, he may be awarded damages and costs. The money goes to the Legal Aid Fund which deducts his own costs and pays him the balance.

On the other hand, the winning party may occasionally be awarded damages but not costs. The fund then deducts his costs from the damages and pays him the balance.

In some cases, costs will be greater than damages. If this happens, the Legal Aid Fund receives the whole of the damages, and takes the balance of the bill from any contribution which the legally aided person has agreed to make. The result may be that the legally aided person receives none of the damages awarded to him and has to pay some of the costs.

A similar situation may occur when his opponent is granted free legal aid and therefore makes no payment for the winner's costs, or when his opponent is granted legal aid subject to a contribution which is less than the costs of the case.

In addition, costs awarded against a losing party are often less than the actual costs of the case, and this can have the same effect of reducing any damages awarded. ☐ The cost of legal action, p. 751.

# Legal aid III : help in criminal cases

*Making a down-payment*
*Assessing the contribution*

NYONE seeking legal aid to defend criminal proceedings applies to the clerk of the court in which the case is to be heard. The defendant completes an application form and a second form giving particulars of his means.

For legal aid to be granted, the applicant must establish that the defendant needs legal aid 'in the interests of justice', and that he cannot afford to pay his entire legal costs. He is entitled to the benefit of any doubt.

The application form asks if there are any special circumstances which make legal aid necessary. The case may involve conflicts of evidence or points of law which the defendant might have difficulty in arguing himself, or he may have a poor knowledge of English.

If the applicant intends to plead not guilty, he will usually be granted legal aid. Even when he intends to plead guilty, if the offence is serious or if he has a bad record, legal aid ought to be granted so that any mitigating circumstances can be presented.

The form asks the defendant to name the solicitor he wishes to act for him. If a solicitor is not named the court will assign one.

Details of income and capital are required, and the same allowances are made as for civil cases. In criminal cases, however, there is no upper limit of income or capital above which legal aid cannot be granted. □ Legal aid II: help in civil cases, p. 714.

### Making a down-payment

Any defendant who appears to have sufficient money can be asked for a down-payment towards the cost of his case. This will not normally be more than £5 for a magistrates' court hearing or £25 in higher courts. If a down-payment is made, it is set against any contribution which a defendant is ordered to make when the case has ended; if he is not ordered to make any payment, his down-payment will be refunded.

If legal aid is refused, the defendant has no right of appeal, though he is entitled to re-apply to the same court with new facts.

Alternatively, if the magistrates refuse legal aid for proceedings in a higher court such as the Crown Court, the defendant can make a fresh application to the higher court at which he is due to appear.

Legal aid in a magistrates' court covers representation only by a solicitor unless the case is particularly complicated or serious, in which event a barrister may also be engaged. In the higher courts legal aid is normally for the cost of both a barrister and a solicitor.

Legal aid for trials in Crown Courts and in magistrates' courts pays for advice on the prospect of an appeal as well as preparation of the case and representation.

### Assessing the contribution

In criminal cases the defendant's contribution towards legal aid, if any, is assessed by the court when the case has ended. But when a case ends the court rarely knows the exact costs incurred by the defence, so if a figure is given it will normally be based on a guess. The court will probably bear in mind the official figures for average costs of legal aid cases.

The defendant will not have to pay anything at all if he is receiving supplementary benefit or if his income during the past year, after deducting income tax and National Insurance contributions, was not more than £250 and his savings are not more than £25. For a married defendant living with his wife these are increased to £450 joint income and £40 joint savings.

A person can be required to make a contribution even if he is acquitted. The court's final assessment of what he must pay depends, however, on all the relevant circumstances. Anyone heavily fined or sent to prison obviously has fewer resources. In practice, contributions out of income are unlikely to be greater than in a civil case. □ Legal aid II: help in civil cases, p. 714.

The assessment for capital and savings is also the same as in civil cases.

A defendant who thinks he has been ordered to pay too much can ask the court or the clerk to refer his contribution to the Supplementary Benefits Commission for investigation.

When the court has finally decided the amount of the contribution, if any, the defendant is told whether it must be paid in a lump sum or in instalments.

# Three ways of settling disputes

*Negotiating to solve problems*   *Nine types of civil action*
*Arbitration, tribunals and courts*

MOST civil disputes—between private individuals and organisations, public companies and sometimes the State— are settled by negotiation between the parties themselves, or between their solicitors. Such negotiations cover a wide field.

For example, a householder might claim that a decorator has done inferior work, and persuade him to accept a reduced payment. Or a woman whose husband has left her might demand financial support and secure, through her solicitor, a binding agreement on maintenance. Or an injured man might claim that he has received less sickness benefit than he is entitled to, and obtain a higher figure from the Social Security office.

Legal principles underlie all these settlements. The decorator is entitled to payment only at the appropriate rate for the standard he has achieved; a husband usually continues to have an obligation to maintain the wife he leaves; and sickness benefit has to be paid according to rules laid down by Parliament.

## Arbitration, tribunals and courts

It is only when the parties to a dispute are unable to reach an agreement among themselves that the law becomes actively involved. There are then three types of legal machinery for producing a settlement: arbitration, a tribunal hearing, or taking action in court.

ARBITRATION A dispute can be referred for a decision to an independent outsider known as an arbitrator, if both sides agree to abide by his decision. There is no set procedure, and anyone acceptable to both sides can act as arbitrator. Arbitration, which can be cheap, simple and private, is commonly used in disputes between commercial organisations— such as garages, builders and so on—and their customers. An arbitration clause does not totally oust the jurisdiction of the courts, but in most cases the arbitrator's decision is final. The courts can be asked to intervene only if the decision is contrary to law or the arbitrator has misused his powers. □ Going to arbitration, p. 719.

TRIBUNALS Where the machinery exists, a dispute can be put before a tribunal—a special administrative 'court' set up to deal with a particular issue, usually involving central or local government.

The Income Tax Commissioners, for example, are a tribunal to hear appeals from people disputing their tax assessment, and the Rent Tribunal fixes a fair rent for tenants in furnished accommodation.

There are also professional tribunals whose function is to exercise disciplinary control within a certain profession. For example, the Disciplinary Committee, a tribunal set up by Act of Parliament, has the power to suspend a solicitor from practice if it finds that he has been guilty of unprofessional conduct. □ Appearing before a tribunal, p. 735.

TAKING LEGAL ACTION In all other cases, people who cannot solve a dispute themselves can take legal action.

## Nine types of civil action

There are several kinds of civil action open to people who have suffered loss, or whose rights have been infringed. To choose one type of action does not rule out the use of any other. For example, a claimant can ask for the return of his land or goods, seek damages for their temporary loss, and persuade a court to make sure that the person sued cannot dispose of them before the claim is heard.

DEBT A person to whom money is owed can ask a court to recover the sum for him.

REPOSSESSION OF LAND A person who has been deprived of property—such as a house— can go to court to have it restored to him.

RECOVERY OF GOODS A person whose possessions have been taken by another can get an order from a court for their return.

DAMAGES Anyone who suffers a loss or injury can seek compensation in the courts.

*Special damages* cover losses that can be precisely calculated—loss of wages or profits.

*General damages* cover items that cannot be exactly calculated—pain, inconvenience, or any lessening in the capacity to enjoy life.

*Exemplary or punitive damages* punish the defendant for bad conduct, such as oppressive or unconstitutional action by a civil servant, or where the defendant planned to make a profit by defaming someone.

*Nominal damages* are awarded if a man claims

717

that his legal rights have been infringed, but cannot show that he has suffered any loss. For example, he can claim from a trespasser on his land, even if no damage was caused to his property by the trespasser.

*Contemptuous damages* are awarded when the court wants to show that the claimant deserved the injury or loss he suffered.

➤ HALFPENNY FOR DEATH CAMP DOCTOR
*Dr Wladyslaw Alexander Dering of North London sued Mr Leon Uris for libel in 1964. He complained that Mr Uris's novel, Exodus, suggested that he had taken part in 17,000 experimental operations at the Nazi concentration camp of Auschwitz, in Poland. It was shown that Dr Dering had taken part in a substantial number of operations, but not 17,000.*
DECISION *The jury awarded a halfpenny damages and Dr Dering was ordered to pay most of Mr Uris's costs, estimated at tens of thousands of pounds. (Dering v. Uris.)* ◄

SPECIFIC PERFORMANCE OF A CONTRACT
If a person fails to fulfil the terms of a contract, a court can be asked to order him to do so. Such an order is usually refused, however, if damages are considered to be sufficient compensation for the other party to the contract. Employment contracts and other contracts of personal service cannot be enforced by an order for specific performance.
ACTION FOR AN ACCOUNT If a person—say a rent collector or business partner—holds money for someone else, a court can ask him to explain the existing financial situation.
ACTION FOR A DECLARATION A person who simply wants to clarify his personal status—say to establish if he is validly divorced—can ask a court to set out his legal position.
INJUNCTION Before the hearing of a civil action the court may agree to freeze the situation temporarily. This is called granting an interim injunction, an order prohibiting someone from doing a wrongful act or requiring him to carry out a legal obligation.

An injunction can also be obtained as a remedy in the case itself. For example, an injunction can be issued by a court to stop a husband molesting his wife during and after a divorce case.
PREROGATIVE ORDERS Anyone who is the victim of wrongful acts by public authorities or officials can apply to the High Court for a prerogative order:
*Prohibition* is an order to prevent something from being done. It can, for instance, order a court not to try a case it has no right to try.
*Certiorari* is an order quashing a decision of anybody who is required to act in a judicial way. This may be an immigration officer, a local council, a government minister acting in a semi-judicial way, or any other public body. The basis for the court's decision is normally that there has been an error of law or a breach of the rules of natural justice.
*Mandamus* is an order compelling a person to carry out a legal duty. For example, *mandamus* might be used to make a local authority produce its accounts for a ratepayer.

## The changing court system

UNDER the new court system effective from 1972, the Crown Court hears criminal cases in continuous sessions in the main towns and cities throughout England and Wales. Civil cases are heard by the High Court, sitting in various parts of the country.

The introduction of the new system meant the abolishing of two of the oldest courts in the country—the assize court and the quarter sessions.

Assize courts were established in the early 13th century, to weld local customs into a consistent body of law.

Two or more judges from the High Court in London travelled in a circuit from one major town to another, visiting each three times a year. This system, which consisted of seven circuits, made it possible for people to have their cases heard locally. In modern times the assizes covered criminal cases passed on from magistrates' courts and civil cases not handled by county courts.

Quarter sessions started in the 14th century. There were two types—county quarter sessions presided over by a group of magistrates, and borough quarter sessions presided over by a barrister known as a recorder.

In criminal matters assizes overlapped with quarter sessions, and assizes dealt with the gravest offences.

A Royal Commission, set up in the late 1960's, found that the system of assizes and quarter sessions was not working effectively, and proposed the new system.

# Going to arbitration

*Choosing an arbitrator*    *Appealing against the decision*
*How arbitration is carried out*    *Paying the costs*

D ISPUTES over agreements and contracts can be settled by a third person acceptable to both sides instead of by a court or tribunal established by the State. Such a person is called an arbitrator. Arbitration is common in consumer situations—in disputes between motorists and garages or between customers and builders. It is also used widely in commercial affairs.

Often a clause is included in a contract stipulating that any dispute will be settled by arbitration, and laying down the procedure. Even where there is no arbitration clause, the parties in dispute can agree to allow the matter to be resolved by an arbitrator.

If there is an arbitration clause, either of the parties can insist on arbitration and the courts will refuse to hear an action arising out of the contract until the arbitration has been completed. But if both parties prefer to go direct to court, they may do so.

Arbitration keeps the dispute private. It is less formal than court proceedings. Lawyers can be employed but need not be. The hearing can be at a time and place convenient to the parties and can usually be arranged more quickly than a court hearing.

The cost is also likely to be less than the cost of going to court. Legal aid is not available for arbitration.

## Choosing an arbitrator
The choice of arbitrator is usually a matter for the parties in dispute. Often a contract lays down that, if they cannot agree, the arbitrator will be chosen by the current president of a professional body such as the Law Society (the solicitors' professional organisation) or the Institute of Arbitrators, 16 Park Crescent, London W1N 4BB.

The Institute also provides general information about arbitration procedure and some guidance on what arbitration will cost.

Disputes about union membership, unfair dismissal and similar industrial matters are sometimes dealt with by a body called the Industrial Arbitration Board. The board acts as arbitrator at the request of the Industrial Relations Court or of both parties to a dispute.

Local chambers of commerce and professional organisations are sometimes able to supply someone who is prepared to act as an arbitrator—he needs no legal qualification if both the parties agree to accept his decision. Many trade associations arrange arbitration in disputes between members and the public.
☐ What to do about faulty goods, p. 460.

Another common source of expert arbitrators in matters involving substantial sums is the London Court of Arbitration. The Court —so-called, although it is not a court of law— has offices at the London Chamber of Commerce, 69 Cannon Street, London EC4N 5AB.

If the parties cannot agree on an arbitrator, the High Court can appoint someone suitable.

## How arbitration is carried out
There is no fixed procedure for arbitration, though many professional and commercial arbitration bodies have sets of rules. A hearing is usual, but is not required if the parties agree to submit written evidence only.

## Appealing against the decision
An arbitration clause cannot totally oust the jurisdiction of the courts, but in most cases an arbitrator's decision is final. The courts can be asked to intervene only if the decision is contrary to law or the arbitrator has misused his powers in the case.

If the parties, or one of them, wish to take the arbitrator's decision to the High Court, the arbitrator is usually asked to 'state a case' by setting down his factual findings and the conclusions in law.

The courts cannot take a different view of the facts, but they can draw different inferences and correct the decision if the arbitrator's conclusion is wrong in law.

ENFORCEMENT If the losing side ignores the arbitrator's award, the successful party can take court proceedings to recover any money.

## Paying the costs
The question of costs depends on what was agreed either in the original contract or when the two sides decided to go to arbitration. It may be left to the arbitrator to award costs, or the parties may agree to pay their own.

# Legal action I : how the system works

*ABC of civil actions*
*Where appeals are heard*

ANYONE who is involved in a civil action may have to attend one of three types of court—a county court, the High Court (which has several Divisions, each dealing with different classes of case) or a magistrates' court.

Minor cases, such as claims for small debts, tenancy disputes and disputes over hire purchase, are all handled by a county court, which is the lower court in civil matters.

The High Court, which can also handle these minor cases, deals especially with claims for damages for personal injury, breach of contract, recovery of debts, and libel and slander. There is no upper or lower limit to the damages that can be claimed. Other minor actions over debts, guardianship, and maintenance for unmarried mothers and deserted

## Time limits on claims

All actions in which criminal law is not involved have to be started within a certain time of the action complained of. These time limits vary according to the type of case. For example, anyone injured in an accident normally has only three years to start his case. A person who wishes to recover land has 12 years. Once the limit has expired no writ can be issued, because out-of-time law suits are considered unfair to those against whom they are brought.

There are special rules for children under 18 and people of unsound mind. If the person entitled to take action is under 18 and in the custody of a parent, the limit runs from when he becomes 18. If he has been of unsound mind, but recovers, the limit runs from his recovery.

| CAUSE OF ACTION | TIME LIMIT |
|---|---|
| **Personal injury** | |
| Personal injury or death in an accident in the U.K. | Normally three years from the accident or from the date when it is or ought to be known that there is a cause of action |
| Personal injury or death in accidents in international waters or air space | Two years from the accident |
| Personal injury due to the slow development of a disease or injury | With the permission of the court, three years from the discovery of the disease; or if the injured person died without knowing of the disease, his relatives can claim within one year |
| 'Second injury' | Time starts afresh if the injury results from similar circumstances |
| **Contract actions** | |
| Breach of contract | Six years from the time the contract was broken |
| Debt | Six years from the date the debt was incurred or from the date when the debtor admitted liability, if later |
| Faulty work | Six years from when the work was completed |
| Action against guarantor | Six years from when the money guaranteed was demanded |

wives are handled by magistrates' courts, which hear mainly minor criminal cases, not civil ones.

## ABC of civil actions

ACCIDENT CLAIMS A person suing for damages as a result of an accident sues either in the county court or in the Queen's Bench Division of the High Court. He should not attempt to do so without first seeking the help of a solicitor. ☐ How a damages claim is decided, p. 124.

BANKRUPTCY AND WINDING-UP When a company is being wound up, or liquidated, the petition is heard in the county court if the company's nominal capital is less than £10,000. If the capital is above that figure, or if the company has its registered office in London, the action has to be taken in the High Court. ☐ Formalities of winding-up, p. 704.

Bankruptcy proceedings against an individual start in a county court (if he lives in London, outside England or his address is not known, they start in the High Court) after the Official Receiver has applied for a court order. ☐ Debts and bankruptcy, p. 580.

CHILDREN AND FAMILIES Magistrates' courts have a wide jurisdiction in domestic matters. They can make decisions on the custody of children, adoption and guardianship. They also make separation, maintenance and affiliation orders. Any disputes arising from such decisions made in the magistrates' court are dealt with on appeal in the Family Division of the High Court. ☐ Four ways to separate, p. 388.

| CAUSE OF ACTION | TIME LIMIT |
| --- | --- |
| **Civil wrongs** Trespass | Six years from the date of trespass |
| Libel and slander | Six years from the time when the libel or slander was last published. In the case of a book, a libel continues to be actionable throughout the period that the book is on sale |
| **Property disputes** Repossession of property | Six years from when property was wrongfully taken. If property is lent or comes into someone's possession innocently, six years from the date when the holder refuses to give it back |
| Land claims | Action to get possession of land must be brought within 12 years from when the cause of action first arises |
| Eviction of squatters | Twelve years from when continuous squatting began. Limit starts afresh when squatting has been interrupted |
| Rent claims | Six years from the last unpaid rent |
| **Other disputes** Actions based on fraud or the consequences of a mistake | Six years from when the fraud or mistake is discovered |
| Action against a trustee | No time limit for a claim by a beneficiary under a trust for fraud or for the return of assets |
| Action to get account of money being held by someone else | Six years from when the person holding money should account for it |
| Action against public authorities for breach of public duty | One year from when the wrong occurred |

COMMERCIAL INTERESTS The Commercial Court, a sub-division of the Queen's Bench Division of the High Court, hears disputes involving commercial law—usually major claims for damages between industrial firms. CONTRACTS Disputes over contracts are heard either in the county courts or in the Queen's Bench Division of the High Court.

Many contracts state that any dispute should go first to arbitration. If either party insists on arbitration, no court will intervene until it is completed—and then only if the arbitrator is thought to have made a mistake in law or misused his powers.
DEBTS Most attempts to recover debts are dealt with by county courts (for sums of up to

# How civil courts are organised

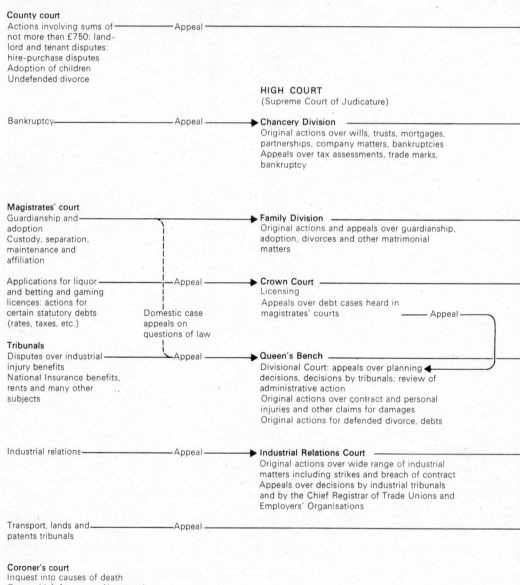

**County court**
Actions involving sums of ————— Appeal ————
not more than £750: land-
lord and tenant disputes:
hire-purchase disputes
Adoption of children
Undefended divorce

**HIGH COURT**
(Supreme Court of Judicature)

Bankruptcy ————————— Appeal ————➤ **Chancery Division** ——————
Original actions over wills, trusts, mortgages,
partnerships, company matters, bankruptcies
Appeals over tax assessments, trade marks,
bankruptcy

**Magistrates' court**
Guardianship and —————————➤ **Family Division** ——————
adoption
Custody, separation,
maintenance and
affiliation
Original actions and appeals over guardianship,
adoption, divorces and other matrimonial
matters

Applications for liquor ——————— Appeal ————➤ **Crown Court** ——————
and betting and gaming
licences: actions for
certain statutory debts
(rates, taxes, etc.)
Licensing
Appeals over debt cases heard in
magistrates' courts ——— Appeal ———
Domestic case
appeals on
questions of law

**Tribunals**
Disputes over industrial ——————— Appeal ————➤ **Queen's Bench** ——————
injury benefits
National Insurance benefits,
rents and many other
subjects
Divisional Court: appeals over planning ◄—
decisions, decisions by tribunals: review of
administrative action
Original actions over contract and personal
injuries and other claims for damages
Original actions for defended divorce, debts

Industrial relations ——————— Appeal ————➤ **Industrial Relations Court** ——————
Original actions over wide range of industrial
matters including strikes and breach of contract
Appeals over decisions by industrial tribunals
and by the Chief Registrar of Trade Unions and
Employers' Organisations

Transport, lands and ——————— Appeal ————
patents tribunals

**Coroner's court**
Inquest into causes of death
Ownership of treasure. No appeal

£750) or the Queen's Bench Division of the High Court, which deals with sums of any size. ☐ Debts and bankruptcy, p. 580.

Statutory bodies, such as the electricity and gas boards, are allowed to recover debts in the magistrates' courts.

DEFAMATION Actions for defamation—that is, libel or slander—can be heard in the county court or in the Queen's Bench Division of the High Court. ☐ What to do if you are libelled or slandered, p. 671.

DIVORCE Undefended divorce cases are heard in the county courts. Defended cases are heard in the Family Division of the High Court which also deals with matters arising from divorces, such as the custody of the

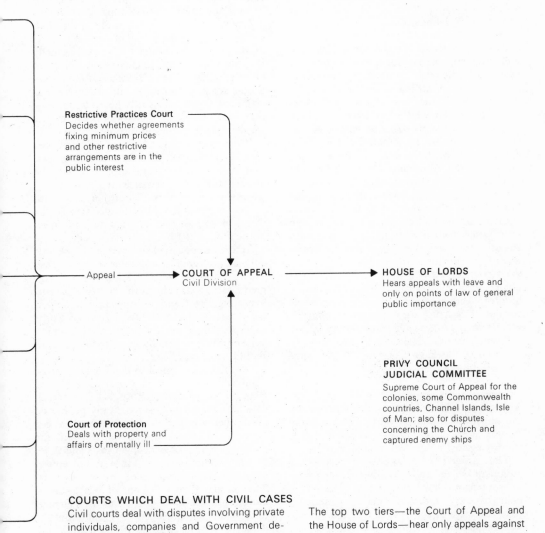

**Restrictive Practices Court**
Decides whether agreements fixing minimum prices and other restrictive arrangements are in the public interest

Appeal

**COURT OF APPEAL**
Civil Division

**HOUSE OF LORDS**
Hears appeals with leave and only on points of law of general public importance

**PRIVY COUNCIL JUDICIAL COMMITTEE**
Supreme Court of Appeal for the colonies, some Commonwealth countries, Channel Islands, Isle of Man; also for disputes concerning the Church and captured enemy ships

**Court of Protection**
Deals with property and affairs of mentally ill

**COURTS WHICH DEAL WITH CIVIL CASES**
Civil courts deal with disputes involving private individuals, companies and Government departments. The courts are in four tiers. The lowest level is made up of county and magistrates' courts and tribunals, which give a first hearing to the more straightforward cases.

The top two tiers—the Court of Appeal and the House of Lords—hear only appeals against decisions of lower courts. In between come the divisions of the High Court, which deal both with appeals and with original actions in more specialised or difficult cases

children and maintenance for the wife and children. ☐ How to get a divorce, p. 400.

EVICTION ORDERS County courts deal with actions for the eviction of tenants. ☐ Leaving a rented home, p. 272.

HIRE PURCHASE Hire-purchase disputes and the recovery of hire-purchase debts are dealt with either by the county courts or by the Queen's Bench Division of the High Court. ☐ Hire-purchase, p. 498.

INDUSTRIAL DISPUTES Though most industrial disputes can be dealt with by tribunals or arbitration, action over breach of contract and strikes can be taken in the Industrial Relations Court. ☐ Taking industrial action, p. 625.

LIQUOR LICENCES Whether or not there is a dispute, applications for liquor licences are heard in magistrates' courts. The renewal of licences and the settling of drinking hours for a district are decided annually by magistrates at what are known as Brewster Sessions. ☐ Public houses and restaurants, p. 656.

MARITIME MATTERS A sub-division of the Queen's Bench Division of the High Court, known as the Admiralty Court, deals with maritime matters such as collisions at sea.

MENTAL ILLNESS A special division of the High Court—the Court of Protection—deals with the affairs and property of people who have been certified as mentally ill, and with any disputes over their property. ☐ Treatment for the mentally ill, p. 380.

RESTRICTIVE PRACTICES A division of the High Court—the Restrictive Practices Court—decides whether certain commercial practices such as price-fixing are in the public interest. WILLS AND TRUSTS Disputes arising out of wills and trusts are dealt with in the Chancery Division of the High Court. ☐ Challenging the will, p. 422.

## Where appeals are heard

Anyone not satisfied with a court judgment can appeal to a higher court. The Court of Appeal (Civil Division), in London, hears appeals against judgments in civil matters.

The grounds for appealing against a judgment are generally that the original judge interpreted the law wrongly (an appeal on a point of law), or that the damages awarded were excessive or too low, or that the verdict was against the weight of the evidence (an appeal on a question of fact).

However, not all appeals are heard in the Court of Appeal. For example, if a magistrate's decision on licensing or on a claim for a debt is disputed, the appeal must go to the Crown Court. The Family Division of the High

Court hears appeals against decisions of magistrates' courts on issues affecting the family, such as separation, maintenance and affiliation orders.

All appeals against county court judgments except those concerning bankruptcy cases go to the Court of Appeal (Civil Division). Bankruptcy appeals are heard in the Chancery Division of the High Court.

But if the debt or damages claimed is less than £200 no appeal can be made on a question of fact. On a point of law, appeals can be made without the judge's permission if the amount in dispute is more than £20.

Appeals from the civil divisions of the High Court also go to the Court of Appeal.

POWERS OF THE APPEAL COURT Normally the Court of Appeal can change any judgment given in a lower court. However, if the appeal is against a jury decision—a rare occurrence as civil matters are not usually heard by juries—the Court can vary damages only with the consent of the parties in dispute.

If the parties do not consent and the Court of Appeal disagrees entirely with a jury decision, it must order that the case go back to the original court for a retrial with a new jury.

HOUSE OF LORDS A plaintiff or defendant who is not satisfied with the decision of the Court of Appeal can, as a last resort, appeal to the House of Lords.

Appeals can be made to the House of Lords only on points of law of general importance.

Some appeals against High Court judgments can go straight to the House of Lords, bypassing the Court of Appeal, but only if the Court of Appeal or the House of Lords have previously made a decision on a similar issue or if it involves how an Act of Parliament should be interpreted.

Permission to appeal to the Lords must be obtained either from the Court of Appeal or from the House of Lords Appeal Committee.

THE COST OF APPEALING Many people do not bother to appeal as the costs involved can be heavy. If the appeal is unsuccessful the losing party must pay his own costs and those of the winning side not only at the appeal stage but also the costs of the lower court. This means that a person who is awarded damages in the lower court and then appeals to the Court of Appeal on the ground that the damages were insufficient will have to pay the costs of both hearings if he loses his appeal.

Anyone appealing to the House of Lords must, unless he has been granted legal aid, give a bond of £1000 as security for costs. If he loses an appeal in the House of Lords he has to pay the costs of all the earlier stages.

# Legal action II : suing to recover a debt

*Applying for a default summons*
*When the debt is admitted*
*When the debt is denied*

*Preparing for a county court hearing*
*Adjournments and appeals*
*Action in the High Court*

TAKING legal action to recover a debt, or resisting such a claim, can be expensive and time-consuming. It is better for creditor and debtor to come to a private agreement about payment. Anyone facing a claim who agrees he owes the money should offer to repay in a lump sum or by instalments. If he disputes the debt, he should explain his reasons to the person making the claim. ☐ Debts and bankruptcy, p. 580.

Anyone owed money should try other methods of collection, such as letters and personal visits, before going to law. Most high-pressure methods of debt collection are illegal, however. ☐ Debts and bankruptcy, p. 580; Recovering business debts, p. 699.

IS A SOLICITOR NECESSARY ? Private agreements on debts can usually be made by the parties themselves. If legal action is taken, the safest course is for each to employ a solicitor. Legal aid is unlikely to be granted towards the costs of claims under about £30. ☐ Help with fees and costs, p. 710.

A claimant who recovers a debt of under £20 cannot obtain his costs from the losing party: he has to pay them himself. Moreover it is often the case that someone trying to recover a debt finds that legal fees come to more than the debt and any costs he may be awarded. He has the choice, therefore, of taking action alone or abandoning the claim. Without legal training he stands a chance of success only if:

**1.** The person from whom he is claiming has a fixed address or can easily be traced.
**2.** The debtor has sufficient resources to pay in a lump sum or in instalments.
**3.** There is adequate evidence to satisfy the court that the claim is genuine.
**4.** The debtor is unlikely to defend the action.

### Applying for a default summons
If all these conditions apply, a creditor can use the instructions here to get a county court default summons. This may force the debtor to offer payment. If he fails to reply within eight days, the court can order him to pay.

Should the debtor defend the action, the creditor normally needs the help of a solicitor. So does anyone resisting an action for debt.

The first step in legal action to recover a debt is for the person making a claim (the plaintiff) to give the person he is suing (the defendant) a court document called a summons. To obtain a default summons, the plaintiff applies to the county court covering the district in which the debtor lives or the district where the claim arose. A default summons cannot be used if the defendant is under 18 or a mental hospital patient.

An application form for a summons, called a request, is available from the court office. The plaintiff must give details of the claim and amount owed, for example '£76 for goods supplied'. He must also enter the court fee which he has to pay for the summons.

PARTICULARS OF CLAIM Detailed particulars of the claim should be given separately. The name of the court should be written at the top left-hand corner of a foolscap sheet and underneath the names of the plaintiff and defendant and precise details of the claim. The plaintiff should sign this and keep two copies. The request and particulars of claim are then sent to the court office, with the fee.

SERVING THE SUMMONS The court office then issues a summons which has to be given or sent to the defendant—in law 'served' on him. The plaintiff can serve the summons himself, but it is easier to ask the court to serve it through a bailiff.

When the plaintiff serves the summons personally, he should hand it to the defendant and say: 'This is a summons issued by (the name of the court) which I am now serving on you.' If the defendant drops it, tries to give it back, or throws it away, the summons has still been served—even if he does not read it.

The summons will not have been served if, for example, the plaintiff gives it to the defendant's wife to pass on, or pushes it through his letter box.

A plaintiff who serves a summons himself must write out a statement (known as an affidavit) confirming that he has done so, swear it before a Commissioner for Oaths, and send it to the court within three days.

A typical affidavit would state: 'I, (name of the plaintiff) hereby swear that at 11 a.m. on July 15, 1972, I did serve a default summons on (name of the defendant) at (place where the summons was served) in my action against him in (name of the court) for repayment of a debt.'

**When the debt is admitted**
A defendant served with a default summons receives three documents—the summons; the particulars of claim; and a form of Admission, Defence or Counterclaim for him to indicate what action he intends taking.

The summons shows the total amount claimed, consisting of the alleged debt, court fees and any other legal charges such as a solicitor's fee for issuing the summons.

If the defendant admits the debt and is able to pay immediately, he should send or take the money to the court office as soon as

possible. By doing so he ends the action against him. The court informs the plaintiff and then pays him the money.

If the defendant admits that he owes the debt but is unable to pay it, he should fill in the Admission section of the form and send it to the court within eight days.

Anyone who ignores a default summons may find that the court has ruled against him in his absence and that a bailiff has been ordered to seize some of his possessions.

In the Admission section of the form, the defendant can offer to pay by instalments or suggest a date when he will pay the whole amount. The plaintiff can either accept or reject the offer. If he accepts, he tells the court which then receives the instalments or lump

## Settling out of court

**D**URING the course of legal action to recover a debt, either the plaintiff or defendant may suggest a settlement which, if accepted, will end the claim and avoid a court hearing.

Approaches about a settlement can be made at any time, from the serving of a summons to the end of a court hearing. In fact many cases are temporarily halted during the hearing, either on the judge's or registrar's direction or at the request of one of the parties, so that the two sides can discuss the possibilities of agreeing on a settlement.

Anyone who wants to suggest a settlement before the hearing should do so in a letter to the other side or to his solicitors. The letter should be clearly marked 'Without Prejudice', so that if a settlement is not agreed and the case is heard in court, the letters cannot be produced as evidence by the other side without the writer's consent.

The settlement of a particular claim will obviously depend on the circumstances surrounding it, but for anyone thinking of accepting the offer of a settlement there are a number of guiding principles.

First, it may be wiser to settle the case early for a sum smaller than the amount claimed, than to risk losing the entire case and incurring substantial costs.

This is particularly so where it is obvious that the defendant intends to fight the case and may be able to throw a doubt on the validity of the claim.

Consider, too, the problems of enforcing any judgment which the court may make.

Even if you win, you may have difficulty in recovering the amount you are awarded, plus costs, from the defendant. ☐ How judgments are enforced, p. 730.

Take into account the cost of a court hearing, even if you have a sound case. If you are employing a solicitor, you will not be able to recover all your costs, even if you win the action. ☐ The cost of legal action, p. 751.

The time spent in bringing proceedings may also have some bearing on a decision.

If there is any doubt about whether a settlement should be offered or accepted, seek the advice of a solicitor. If the defendant's offer seems too low, a solicitor may be able to secure a more realistic offer.

When a settlement is accepted, it should be set out in writing and signed by both parties. The court should then be notified that the action has been settled.

It is also advisable to ask the court to record the settlement as if it were a judgment of the court, although this cannot be done without the consent of both parties.

If the defendant then defaults on his agreement the plaintiff can ask the court to enforce the judgment as if the settlement had been a court decision. ☐ How judgments are enforced, p. 730.

A common and worthwhile kind of settlement makes it a condition that, if the defendant defaults on an agreed rate of instalment payments, the whole sum owing becomes payable immediately and may be obtained through enforcement by the court.

HOW DISPUTES ARE SETTLED

sum from the defendant and pays it to the plaintiff. Should the plaintiff reject the offer, a hearing is fixed for the county court registrar to decide how the debt should be paid.

## When the debt is denied

A defendant who wants to resist a default summons has to decide, preferably with legal advice, whether to defend the claim or to counterclaim against the plaintiff. If he makes the wrong choice he risks losing the case.

DEFENCE If payment is demanded for a loan which was never made, goods never received or work never done, the defendant completes the Defence section of the form. There is no need to give details at this stage—he need write only 'See formal defence which follows'.

COUNTERCLAIM If the defendant thinks he has a claim against the plaintiff—if, for example, he has refused to pay a remover who damaged his furniture—he enters details in the Counterclaim section, and writes 'See Counterclaim' in the Defence section.

If the amount of the counterclaim exceeds the amount of the plaintiff's claim, the defendant may have to pay a court fee before it can be entered on the court register to be dealt with at the same time as the plaintiff's claim.

It is vital that the defendant leaves the Admission section of the form blank if he is making a defence or a counterclaim. If he fills it in he has to pay the amount claimed.

If the defendant enters a defence or counterclaim, the plaintiff knows he will not be paid without a court hearing. He must therefore decide whether to abandon the claim or press it further. To continue the action successfully he needs the advice of a solicitor.

If the case proceeds to a hearing and his claim is dismissed, he may have to pay the defendant's costs as well as his own.

PLAINTIFF'S REPLY When a defendant makes a counterclaim, the plaintiff has to enter a defence to it within eight days if he is to avoid the court ruling against him.

If the debtor files a defence only, the plaintiff may feel he should reply before the court hearing, especially if he has given only brief particulars of the claim.

The plaintiff's solicitor can then serve a reply setting out why the defendant's version of the facts is disputed and which of the facts are admitted.

## Preparing for a county court hearing

Each side should start preparing its case and arrange a meeting with its solicitor once the date of the hearing is fixed.

If the defendant has returned the summons without a detailed reply to the claim his solicitor will send the court a formal defence or defence and counterclaim. A copy is also sent to the plaintiff.

SUGGESTING A SETTLEMENT If the defendant agrees he owes some, but not all, of the money claimed and is able to pay immediately, he can send this sum to the court office. This is known as payment into court and may reduce any costs he eventually has to pay.

The defendant should state clearly that the payment is in *settlement* of the claim, otherwise it will be taken as payment against the whole amount. The court then notifies the plaintiff, who has four days to decide whether to accept it as full settlement. If he does, he is entitled to the costs of his action up to that time.

When such payment is accepted, the claim is regarded as settled. The plaintiff is then entitled to claim costs which, if disputed by the defendant, must be submitted to the court for approval. ☐ The cost of legal action, p. 751.

Once money has been paid into court, the plaintiff should think hard before refusing to accept it in full settlement of the debt.

If he eventually loses the case, he will have lost the money offered, and will probably have to pay his opponent's costs. If he wins, but the amount awarded is less than the sum paid into court, he becomes liable for the defendant's costs from the date when the money was paid in. Usually it is best to take a solicitor's advice on whether to accept or reject money paid into court.

PRELIMINARY HEARING A preliminary hearing is required for the court registrar to consider how to simplify the proceedings.

## Contacting witnesses

Anyone involved in a court case should consider carefully which witnesses he intends asking to give evidence for him. Since he has to pay them for the time they spend away from work, it is important to have only those who are essential.

Generally witnesses fall into three categories—voluntary, reluctant and expert.

VOLUNTARY WITNESSES A solicitor usually takes a written statement from voluntary witnesses to help him to frame questions to put to the witness in court.

RELUCTANT WITNESSES If a witness is reluctant to attend the hearing the court can be asked to issue a summons, called a subpoena, making him attend. Before applying for a subpoena, consider how useful the evidence of a reluctant witness is likely to be and whether he may be unhelpful in court owing to ill-feeling over the subpoena.

EXPERT WITNESSES If policemen, civil servants or local-government officials are required as witnesses they usually have to be subpoenaed, otherwise they could be accused of favouring one party.

Solicitors will also approach any other expert witnesses—such as doctors—and arrange to subpoena them if necessary. An expert's fee will probably have to be paid, possibly before the hearing takes place.

Sometimes, if an expert's report is not disputed by either side, it can be given in evidence as what is called an agreed document without the expert having to attend.

**Applying for an adjournment**

Frequently after a hearing date is fixed one side will want it postponed—perhaps because he wants more time to prepare his case or because a witness is ill.

Usually the side seeking an adjournment contacts the other side suggesting a new

## Who's who in a county court

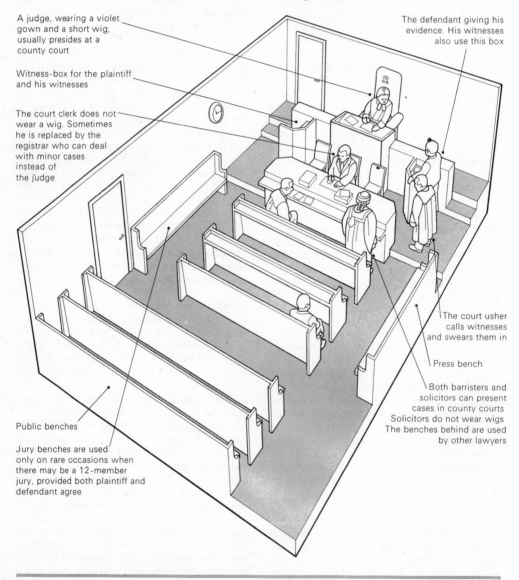

A judge, wearing a violet gown and a short wig, usually presides at a county court

Witness-box for the plaintiff and his witnesses

The court clerk does not wear a wig. Sometimes he is replaced by the registrar who can deal with minor cases instead of the judge

The defendant giving his evidence. His witnesses also use this box

The court usher calls witnesses and swears them in

Press bench

Both barristers and solicitors can present cases in county courts Solicitors do not wear wigs The benches behind are used by other lawyers

Public benches

Jury benches are used only on rare occasions when there may be a 12-member jury, provided both plaintiff and defendant agree

date. If both agree, the court is asked to arrange a new hearing.

When no agreement can be reached, the side requesting the adjournment applies to the court office. A hearing is then held for the *application* at which both sides argue for and against the proposed adjournment.

Late applications for an adjournment—within a day or so of the actual hearing—are not allowed without very good reason.

### The court hearing

The case will be heard by a judge or (where the claim is for less than £75) a registrar. Proceedings begin with the barrister or solicitor for the plaintiff (or the plaintiff himself if he has no lawyer) outlining the facts of the claim.

The plaintiff goes into the witness box and, usually in reply to questions from his lawyer, tells his side of the case. The defendant or the defendant's lawyer may then question him.

When the cross-examination of the plaintiff has ended, his lawyer calls witnesses and questions them. The defendant's lawyer may also cross-examine them in turn. Finally, the plaintiff's lawyer may question the witnesses again—but only on points which have emerged during the other side's cross-examination.

When the plaintiff's case is completed, the defendant's lawyer presents the defence in the same way. The defendant and his witnesses are questioned and cross-examined just as the plaintiff and his witnesses were.

The judge or registrar then decides. He may order the loser to pay the winner's costs as well as his own.

The losing party can apply to pay off the amount owed in instalments. When the judge or registrar has approved an arrangement, a document called a judgment is drawn up by the court and a copy is sent to both parties.

### Appealing against the court's decision

A plaintiff whose claim is dismissed or a defendant who is ordered to pay a claim may consider appealing to get the decision reversed. Appealing is costly, however, and if it fails the appellant usually has to pay the other side's costs as well as his own.

It may be, however, that important new evidence has emerged which could not be given at the hearing. An appeal may also be made on the ground that the judge or registrar misinterpreted the law.

When an appeal is made, the court's decision is suspended until after the appeal has been heard. The procedure for an appeal depends on who heard the original case.

APPEALS OVER REGISTRAR'S DECISION
Appeals against a registrar's decision are heard by a county court judge who considers the points made in the form of sworn statements called affidavits.

After considering the grounds for the appeal and the points put forward by both sides, the judge may confirm the original decision, which means that the appeal has been lost; cancel or vary the judgment, perhaps by reducing the amount which the defendant has to pay; or order the case to be reheard or considered further by the registrar or a judge at a later hearing.

APPEALING AGAINST A JUDGE'S DECISION
When an appeal is made against a county court judge's decision, it is heard by the Court of Appeal which sits at the Royal Courts of Justice, Strand, London WC2A 2LL.

If the *claim*, not the amount awarded, is for less than £20, the county court judge must give his permission before an appeal can be made on a point of law. There is no right of appeal on a question of fact if the claim is for less than £20.

If the claim is for between £20 and £200, either party has the right to appeal on a point of law, but not on a point of evidence or fact. If the claim is for more than £200, either party has the right to appeal both on questions of law and of fact.

### Action in the High Court

Legal action to recover a debt can be taken in a county court only if the amount claimed is less than £750. Legal action to recover any sum can also be taken in the High Court, where the procedure is more formal.

When a defendant in a High Court action admits the claim and wants to pay in instalments or a lump sum on a certain date he has to issue a summons, in effect summoning himself to explain why he is asking for time to pay. He must also supply an affidavit detailing his financial means.

If the defendant contests the claim, known as entering an appearance, and the plaintiff is not satisfied that he has any sound defence, the plaintiff can ask the court to give its judgment for him. A summons is then served on the defendant giving a date on which the application for judgment will be heard.

Affidavits are then sworn by both sides and the court decides whether to give judgment for the plaintiff or whether to let the defendant contest the claim. If the High Court decides that a defence should go ahead, it may sometimes order the county court to hear the case if the claim is for less than £750.

# How judgments are enforced

WHEN a debtor fails to make the payments ordered by a court, the winning side can use a legal process called enforcement to make him pay.

A High Court judgment can be enforced for up to six years after it is given; in a county court the limit is two years. Both periods can be extended with the court's agreement.

Although the extra court and lawyer's fees will be added to the amount owing, anyone considering enforcing a judgment should first satisfy himself that he has a good chance of recovering his money. Only if a plaintiff knows that a debtor has the money to pay is it worth while trying to enforce judgment.

## Execution against goods

The most common method of enforcing judgment is by getting the court to make an order for the debtor's goods to be seized by bailiffs and sold to pay off the debt. This is called executing the judgment against the goods of the defendant.

It is usually best to ask the court to issue a warrant for a smaller sum than the entire amount outstanding, or perhaps for only one of a number of outstanding instalments. There are two reasons for this.

First, a fee has to be paid for the warrant; the smaller the amount the warrant is issued for, the smaller the fee. Secondly, if a debtor is paying by instalments, an order to seize a small amount may persuade him to pay regularly in future instead of having frequent visits from bailiffs.

THE DEBTOR'S CHOICE A debtor is informed when a warrant is issued and if he pays within seven days the bailiffs do not call. If he does not pay, there are three other ways in which he can avoid having his goods seized. He can:
1. Pay the plaintiff or make an arrangement with him so that the warrant is withdrawn.
2. Pay the court bailiff when he arrives.
3. Ask the court to suspend the warrant and allow him to pay by instalments.

If the debtor does not do any of these things the bailiffs enter his home and seize goods to the value of the amount stated in the warrant. The bailiffs can take only goods owned by the debtor himself; but they must not seize his bedding, clothing or tools of his trade worth up to £20. They must not seize anything on hire purchase, or anything belonging to the debtor's wife or to his family.

Sometimes a bailiff lists all the debtor's possessions but takes only one item and leaves the rest behind. The debtor then signs a form agreeing not to dispose of any of the listed goods and to allow the bailiff to return and take them if instalments are not paid.

Seized property is valued and auctioned. After the expenses of the sale have been paid, the proceeds go to the plaintiff.

## Attachment of earnings

A plaintiff who knows that a debtor has an income from a regular job can ask the court to make what is known as an attachment of earnings order.

When an order is granted, the debtor's employer is told to deduct a certain sum from his wages each week or month. The employer pays this money to the court which in turn pays it to the plaintiff.

An attachment of earnings order cannot be made for a judgment debt of less than £5, and while it is in force the court will not allow the plaintiff to take any other steps to recover the amount owing.

Before making an attachment of earnings order, the court asks the debtor to give full details of his income and essential outgoings and other liabilities. It is therefore in his interests to attend the hearing in order to ensure that all his circumstances are fully taken into account.

The sum to be deducted from his wages is then decided—and at the same time what is called a protected-earnings figure is fixed. The employer is not allowed to make a deduction if it would bring the debtor's earnings below this protected amount.

If his earnings drop, and because of the protected-earnings figure no deduction is made, an extra sum is deducted when the earnings are sufficient.

An attachment of earnings order lapses when a debtor changes jobs, but he must notify the court within seven days, giving details of his new earnings.

## Examination of means

A summons can be issued for the debtor to appear before the court to explain why he has not paid. If he is earning or has enough money, a new order for payment is made against him.

# Legal action III : suing for damages

*Damages for death and personal injury*
*Damages for breach of contract*
*Damages for libel and slander*

*Wrongful imprisonment*
*Destruction of property*
*Legal costs and other expenses*

ANYONE whose rights are infringed, or who suffers loss or injury, may have a right to claim damages from any individual or company whom he can show to be partly or wholly to blame. Most claims for damages heard in the courts are concerned with personal injuries, but the right to claim damages arises in a variety of circumstances.

Customers, for example, have a right to claim if the goods they buy or hire are faulty, if repairs are done badly, or if they are served with bad food in restaurants.

Anyone whose reputation is unjustly damaged may have a right to damages for libel or slander. ☐ Dangers of controversy, p. 666.

It is even possible to claim if one suffers loss through bad advice from a professional man—if, for example, a house-buyer loses money because his surveyor is negligent in reporting on the condition of the property. ☐ Engaging a surveyor, p. 199; Claiming damages for bad advice, p. 549.

Anyone who believes he may have grounds for a damages claim needs to take the advice of a solicitor at the earliest possible moment. The procedure for making a claim is complicated, and the layman who tries to act on his own runs the risk of receiving less compensation than he is entitled to, or none at all. ☐ How a damages claim is decided, p. 124.

Most claims for damages are settled without the case coming to court, although the settlement is negotiated on the basis of what a court would be likely to award. The way in which the calculation is made depends on the type of claim.

Damages for breach of contract, for example, cover only the actual loss to the person who is suing. Damages for injury, on the other hand, cover actual loss, probable future loss and compensation for the pain and disability the injured person has suffered.

When the case goes to court, it is the judge alone who decides what award to make. The exceptions are actions involving libel or slander, where he may sit with a jury. It is then the jury's job to assess damages.

The main difference between awards made by judges and those made by juries is that, while the judge bases his award on knowledge of previous cases, the jury has to come to a decision based solely on common sense.

Damages awarded either by a judge or a jury can be changed if the defendant appeals successfully. The Court of Appeal, however, is usually unwilling to alter the amount fixed by a jury except in extreme cases where the court considers the award is much too high or much too low.

Damages reached by negotiation between the two sides can normally be varied only when a court believes that a child's interests have not been properly safeguarded in the settlement that has been reached.

**Damages for death and personal injury**
Damages awarded to the dependants of someone who has been killed are calculated to make good the financial loss they suffer as a result of the death.

If a father has been killed in an accident, for example, the court works out his net annual contribution to the family budget—known as the 'dependency'. Certain types of financial benefit the family may have received from the death are deducted, and the remaining sum is multiplied by a figure based on the estimated working life and earning prospects the dead person would have enjoyed. ☐ Claiming damages for fatal accidents, p. 417.

Damages awarded to someone who is injured are divided into two categories: special damages to compensate for actual loss up to the time of the trial; and general damages to cover probable future loss, and the pain, disability and inconvenience suffered. ☐ How a damages claim is decided, p. 124.

**Damages for breach of contract**
Damages that can be recovered for breach of contract are limited to the losses that were foreseeable when the contract was broken. For example, a seller who fails to deliver goods can be made to pay compensation if, on the day the goods were to be delivered, their market value was higher than the price in the contract. If their market value had dropped, the buyer would have no claim.

Similarly, the seller is not liable for every loss caused by his failure to deliver the goods on time. He would have to pay compensation if a firm had to stop business because he had not provided an important piece of machinery. But he would not be expected to pay for any increase in profit that the firm hoped for as a result of installing improved machinery, unless the loss was a foreseeable result of the failure to deliver on time.

DEFECTIVE GOODS When the subject of the claim is a defective article, the amount of the damages awarded is the difference between its actual value and the value it is stated to have in the contract.

SERVICES When a service contract is broken, the person suing cannot recover the full amount that he has to spend to have the work done by someone else.

He can claim compensation for the expenditure involved, less the amount he would have had to pay under the original contract. If there is no extra cost, he has no claim against the person who breaks the contract.

REDUCING THE LOSS The person who suffers from a breach of contract has a legal duty to reduce his loss if he can. This means, for example, that when a firm hotel booking is cancelled, the hotelier can claim the full cost only if he can show that he made efforts, but failed, to find alternative clients and that the hotel was not full.

If he succeeds in re-letting the room, and his hotel is full, he has a claim against the original holidaymakers only for additional administrative expenses. If he lets the room, but he still has others vacant, he can seek compensation from the holidaymakers because their cancellation has reduced his profits.

The same principle applies when someone breaks a contract to buy goods. A seller can sue for damages only if he can show that he has tried but failed to sell the goods elsewhere. If he does sell them elsewhere, but at a lower price, his claim is for the difference between that and the figure which he had agreed with the original buyer.

## Damages for libel and slander

In actions for libel, the jury—or the judge if no jury is involved—must decide damages on the basis of damage to reputation. The plaintiff does not need to prove that he has suffered any actual loss. There is no kind of scale for such damages, which may be partially punitive if the defamation is exceptionally offensive. They are left to the discretion of the jury (or the judge) in each case.

Only in some slander cases does the plaintiff have to show loss, but it need not be financial or business loss. The loss of friends

or acquaintances is enough to win his case. Damages are then assessed on the value of the food and hospitality he is likely to have received from these people. Moreover, if it can be shown that the slander affected the plaintiff's profession, trade or business, no special or actual financial loss has to be proved.

## Wrongful imprisonment or prosecution

Damages for false imprisonment or malicious prosecution may include a sum for actual loss involved—say, loss of earnings. There may also be a claim for personal injury caused by assault during the false imprisonment. In the main, however, such damages are assessed as compensation for humiliation and loss of dignity. They are at the discretion of the judge—or the jury, if there is one.

## Destruction of property

When property is destroyed, damages are normally awarded to cover the amount by which the value of the property has been reduced. Usually this equals the reasonable cost of repair—but the full price of replacement is not necessarily obtainable. If, for example, a house is burnt down, the owner cannot claim the cost of building a new house on the same site. He can claim only the market value of the property at the time of the fire.

Incidental loss can be claimed only if it can be shown to have been foreseeable when the damage was done. For example, if a house is partly destroyed, the owner or the tenant can claim for cost of repairs plus the cost of renting accommodation while the repairs are made. But if the destruction and consequent upset meant that the owner or tenant had to take another job in another part of the country, this is not foreseeable and the expenses cannot be claimed in damages.

## Legal costs and other expenses

When a claim succeeds, legal costs and other expenses incurred by a plaintiff can be recovered from the defendant. But these do not include the claimant's expenses, or loss of earnings in visiting his lawyer. They do, however, include the expenses and loss of earnings incurred by the claimant in attending medical examinations or in attending court.

A claimant who successfully conducts his own case—unless he is himself a lawyer—may recover only his own and his witnesses' out-of-pocket expenses and lost earnings in attending court, and his own expenses for medical examinations. He cannot recover anything for the time and effort expended in preparing and presenting the case.

# Legal action IV : challenging official decisions

*Three types of action*      *Getting the help of an MP or councillor*
*Grounds for an order*       *Appealing to the Ombudsman*
*The right to a hearing*

W HEN a citizen believes that he has been wrongly or unjustly treated by a Government department, public employee or official body, he may be able to obtain redress in the courts.

If he has been injured in an accident caused by the negligence of someone in the public service he normally has a right to take action for damages against the person directly responsible and that person's employers, who may be the Crown or a local authority.

If he suffers as a result of careless advice or the incompetent performance of professional duties (say, the negligent approval of building plans by a building inspector), the official responsible and his employers may be liable to pay damages.

The principles that apply in such cases are the same as those in ordinary ones against private persons. But there are also special remedies available against public officials. These are High Court orders, known as prerogative orders, granted by the Divisional Court of the Queen's Bench Division.

**Three types of action**
There are three main types of prerogative order:
**1.** *Certiorari* (pronounced sershiorary) to quash an original decision.
**2.** *Mandamus* to compel a body or a person to perform a duty. This could, for instance, be used to make a local council open its accounts for inspection, or compel a tribunal to hear a case or give reasons for its decisions.
**3.** *Prohibition* to stop a body from deciding a case that it has no authority to hear.

Failure to comply with a prerogative order can be punished as contempt of court.

The court can also be asked for a ruling or declaration about the legal position in a dispute involving official action. Failure to follow such a ruling does not carry a penalty, but the public body concerned invariably complies with the court's decision.

**Grounds for an order**
One of the grounds for seeking a court order is that an official body has acted without authority, or exceeded its authority, or failed

to perform duties which it is required by law to carry out.

A body may act outside its powers in several ways. These include not merely doing things it is not empowered to do, but doing them in an improper way. For instance, it may fail to take relevant considerations into account when reaching a decision, or it may exercise discretionary powers in an arbitrary or capricious way.

▶ THE COUNCIL THAT OVERSTEPPED THE MARK *Chertsey Urban District Council granted a licence for a site to be used for caravans—but laid down detailed conditions covering rents, premiums and the rights of caravan dwellers. The site owners, Mixnam's Properties Ltd, appealed against lower-court decisions endorsing the right of the authority to impose such conditions.*
DECISION *In 1964 the House of Lords upheld the appeal, saying that the conditions were valid only in so far as they related to the use of the site. In the words of one of the judges, the conditions involved 'such oppressive or gratuitous interference with the rights of the occupier . . . that they can find no justification in the minds of reasonable men'. (Chertsey Urban District Council v. Mixnam's Properties Ltd.)*◀

If an official body postpones a decision for an unreasonable time or fails to follow the proper procedure in reaching a decision, these would also constitute grounds for seeking a court order.

Anyone affected can also take action if a body exercising judicial functions—for example, transport commissioners deciding whether to grant a licence to a haulage contractor—fails to observe what are called the rules of natural justice. These rules are that the procedure shall be fair, that the authority shall be free from improper interest or bias, and that the people immediately affected by the decision shall have the right to a fair hearing.

The duty to follow the rules of natural justice has been applied to many situations. A Government Minister must observe them, for example, when he decides whether or not

733

to confirm a compulsory purchase order made by a local authority.

Before objections to the order are lodged, the Minister can express tentative approval of the proposed order, or obtain any relevant information. He is not obliged to disclose this information to objectors.

But after the lodging of an objection he must not receive statements from the authority behind the objector's back and without his knowledge.

## The right to a hearing

The rules of natural justice also apply to decisions to dismiss certain public employees and officials. When a public employee—such as a chief constable—can be removed from office only for a specific reason, such as inability or misbehaviour, he has a right to be given notice of the allegations against him and must have an opportunity to be heard in his own defence.

But if he can be dismissed without reasons being given, he normally does not have a right to a hearing.

Members of clubs and trade unions also have a right to fair notice of accusations and an opportunity to reply. So do people threatened with removal from a professional register or revocation of a licence, if such action may result in their being unable to follow their occupation. The courts are particularly ready to invoke the rules of natural justice when a person's ability to earn his living is affected.

The rules have been held to apply to university authorities as well as to professional bodies and voluntary organisations.

➤WHEN STUDENTS MUST BE HEARD *A number of students at the University of Aston in Birmingham were sent down after failing their examinations. In deciding to send them down, the university authorities took into account personal factors concerning the students, as well as their academic performances, and they were not allowed to state their cases. They asked the court to set aside the decision on the grounds that the rules of natural justice had not been followed.*
DECISION *The court said that the students should have been given an opportunity to be heard, though not necessarily in person. But they were not reinstated, since they had taken too long to approach the courts. (R. v. Senate of the University of Aston, ex p. Roffey.)*◄

The situations in which prerogative orders can be granted are still in the process of clarification and alteration, and it is often difficult to predict whether a particular action will succeed.

Prerogative orders are surrounded by many technical rules, and a lawyer's advice will always be necessary before deciding whether to attempt to obtain one. Legal aid can be obtained for this. ☐ Help with legal fees and costs, p. 710.

## Getting the help of an MP or councillor

If no remedy is available in the courts, there is still the possibility of some other form of action. One is a complaint to a Member of Parliament. Many cases of hardship or injustice to people have been put right by this method.

In questions involving the actions of a local authority, a councillor may be able to give help.

## Appealing to the Ombudsman

Anyone whose grievance results from maladministration by central Government bodies exercising administrative functions can ask an MP (not necessarily his own, although MPs do not normally handle cases from other constituencies) to take the matter to the Parliamentary Commissioner for Administration, an official who is popularly known as the Ombudsman.

If the MP agrees to do so (usually after other Parliamentary action has been ineffective), the Ombudsman can call for any papers or witnesses he requires to examine the matter. His report goes to the MP, with a copy to the department complained of.

The Ombudsman has no powers to investigate matters involving the police, State security (including the withholding of passports), the conduct of legal proceedings, or grievances of personnel in the armed forces or the civil service.

Complaints he can examine include those relating to unfair or incompetent administration, corruption, delay in making decisions, the loss of documents, or the giving of misleading information.

The Ombudsman does not hold formal hearings and does not have executive powers. He cannot award damages, nor can he compel a Government department to produce a remedy; but his observations are usually heeded by Ministers.

The Government announced in 1972 that a Health Service Commissioner and Commissioners for Local Administration would be established in April 1974 to help citizens with complaints against the health services and local councils.

# Appearing before a tribunal

*Applying for a hearing*  *The decision*
*How a hearing is conducted*  *How to appeal*

CERTAIN disputes—particularly over decisions by central or local government departments—are dealt with not in the courts but by special bodies called tribunals. Many of these tribunals are permanent; others are set up from time to time to decide special issues. Some have the word 'tribunal' in their titles; but others—the Rent Assessment Committee, for example—do not.

Each tribunal deals with a separate category of dispute—employment, pensions, land, rates, rents, road-traffic licensing, and so on. A tenant complaining about the rent of a furnished flat, for example, can ask a local rent tribunal to rule that it should be reduced.

A tribunal usually consists of a chairman and at least two people with knowledge of the kind of dispute brought before them.

At almost all tribunals the person asking for a decision (the applicant) can have someone else to help him put his case—for example, a trade-union official, a social worker or a friend. If the dispute is involved, it may even be necessary to engage a solicitor or barrister, or an accountant—although legal aid is not available for appearances before any tribunal except the Lands Tribunal, which deals with valuation of properties affected by a compulsory purchase order.

However, tribunals are used to dealing with people who conduct their own cases without expert help, and the chairman will try to ensure that an applicant has a fair hearing.

## Applying for a hearing
A list of tribunals and their addresses is usually available at the relevant Government offices and at main post offices.

Anyone who has a complaint should first find which tribunal will consider his grievance. He should then ask officials of the relevant Government department, or local authority, how to obtain a hearing.

The clerk of the appropriate tribunal or the Government department concerned provides forms on which to state the grounds of the application or appeal, and sets a date for the hearing. An applicant can ask for an adjournment if he needs more time to prepare his case and collect the necessary evidence.

PREPARING THE CASE The relevant evidence may be anything from a letter from a doctor or a statement from an expert, to documents, photographs and sketches. If he is presenting his own case, the applicant should prepare a detailed note of the grounds of his application, to which he can refer at the hearing.

Each side in the dispute must ensure that its own witnesses appear. There is no power to summons witnesses, as in the courts.

Anyone whose case is to be heard by a tribunal should try to attend himself, even if he is proposing to ask for an adjournment.

## How a hearing is conducted
As in a court of law, each side presents its case, calls evidence and examines and cross-examines witnesses. The chairman and members of the panel can ask questions. If information is required which is not immediately available, the chairman may decide to adjourn the hearing until it can be produced.

## The decision
The tribunal may give its decision at the hearing, or it may adjourn to consider its verdict. In either case, both sides are told of the decision in writing.

Reasons for the decision do not have to be given unless they are specifically asked for in advance or at the time of the hearing. Though a statement of reasons is not essential, it is advisable to ask for one, as it will help the applicant to decide whether to appeal.

## How to appeal
The written notification which follows the tribunal's decision normally states whether there is a further right of appeal. If it does not, the applicant can write to the clerk of the tribunal to ask. Action should be taken as quickly as possible, since there is always a time limit for appeals.

The appeal will normally be heard by a higher tribunal. But if an applicant believes that the first hearing was unfair—perhaps because he was not given a proper opportunity to state his case—he may be entitled to make an appeal to the High Court. ☐ Challenging official decisions, p. 733.

# The police and the public

Answering a policeman's questions
The police right to search
Police powers of entry

Going to the police station
The limits on police questioning
Identification parades

MOST people consider it a moral and social duty to co-operate with the police but normally there is no legal obligation to do so. Many everyday police activities—questioning people, interviewing them at the police station and making searches—operate to a considerable degree with the consent of the people concerned.

People who are stopped and questioned, or who are asked to go to a police station, may co-operate with the police under the impression that they must do so. In fact they are often at liberty to refuse.

Similarly, people being questioned at police stations often think they are under an obligation to answer questions, when in fact they are entitled to say nothing if they wish.

The police sometimes have the right to enter homes and make searches without the householder's permission, but these rights are strictly limited.

People who are detained illegally by the police or searched by them without authority can sue for damages.

However, some recent cases have indicated that when the law is not clear, the courts tend to interpret it in favour of the police. The courts increasingly seem to feel that certain sacrifices of individual liberty are required to help the police in the fight against crime.

## Answering a policeman's questions

The police have the right to stop anyone in the street or elsewhere and ask questions, but in most cases there is no obligation to answer or even to give a name and address. The most important exceptions are motoring cases—in which drivers must give their names and addresses on demand—and inquiries made under the Official Secrets Acts. ☐ Powers of the police and traffic wardens, p. 82.

➤ THE MAN WHO WOULD NOT ANSWER *Leonard Rice was stopped by two policemen in the early hours of the morning in 1966 in an area of Grimsby where there had been burglaries during the night. He would not say where he was going or give his name and address. Later he would say only 'Rice, Convamore Road', without giving the number of his house. When he*

*refused to go to the police station he was arrested and charged with obstructing the police in the execution of their duty.*
DECISION *He was found not guilty. The then Lord Chief Justice, Lord Parker, ruled that Mr Rice had been completely within his rights. He had undoubtedly been making it more difficult for the police to carry out their duties, but although there was a moral or social duty to help the police, this was not a legal requirement. The fact that he was sarcastic and truculent did not make his conduct criminal. There was no legal duty to be agreeable or especially polite when accosted by the police. (Rice v. Connolly.)* ◄

Nevertheless, it is usually sensible to help the police, especially when there is no suggestion of a charge being made. Often police officers need to question innocent people who have witnessed accidents or crimes.
IF A CHARGE SEEMS LIKELY People who feel a policeman's questions are directed at them in order to bring a charge are in a more difficult situation. They may feel that they are in danger of incriminating themselves and prefer to say nothing.

## The police right to search

The police have no general right to search people or their houses without a search warrant. Many searches depend on the agreement of the person involved—although he or she may not realise that there is a right to refuse.

In certain cases, though, the police have an absolute right to stop people in the street and search them. They may, for instance, search anyone or any vehicle they reasonably suspect may be carrying dangerous drugs and they may search anyone they reasonably suspect of carrying a gun in a public place.

Additionally, police in the Greater London area and in some other towns can stop and search anyone they reasonably suspect of carrying stolen goods.

If nothing is found, the person searched may be able to sue the police for damages by claiming that they did not have reasonable grounds for suspicion and the search caused embarrassment or inconvenience. The police have not been given clear guidance by the courts on what are 'reasonable' grounds for suspicion. They are obviously more likely to search a shabbily dressed young man for drugs than a conventionally dressed businessman—but it is doubtful if unusual clothing alone is a reasonable ground for suspicion.

It is difficult to obtain redress for being searched. A man stopped in the street and asked to open a suitcase which happened to contain his weekly washing would probably fail if he sued for wrongful search. The police would probably claim they had reason to believe thieves were operating in the area, and it would be hard to convince a court they had exceeded their rights.

But anybody who strongly objects to a search could always refuse to allow it. The police would then have the choice of allowing him to go or of arresting him at the risk of an action for wrongful arrest. If his action was successful any damages awarded would be paid out of police funds.

PRIVATE PROPERTY If the occupier refuses permission, the police are normally entitled to search private property only if a magistrate grants a search warrant. This authorises them to enter and search, using force if necessary.

A search warrant lists what the police are allowed to look for. They are not permitted just to rummage around, though if they do discover evidence of other crimes, they may use it. Generally, a search by warrant may be carried out only during daylight hours.

In some circumstances a senior police officer can authorise a search for stolen goods without the need for a warrant:
**1.** If the occupier has been convicted of handling stolen goods within the last five years, or if he has ever been convicted of an offence involving dishonesty and punishable by imprisonment.
**2.** If any other occupier in the last year has been convicted of handling stolen goods within the last five years.

## A citizen's duty to help the police

THE public has no general duty to help the police unless a policeman specifically asks for assistance. For example, if someone stands and watches a policeman trying to arrest an armed man who gets away in the struggle, he commits no offence. But if the policeman appeals for assistance and the bystander refuses, he could be prosecuted.

However, a person charged with refusing to assist a police officer in the execution of his duty is likely to be acquitted if he can prove that the policeman could have handled the situation without help, or if he can show that he was not physically able to help. For example, someone with a weak heart would be justified in refusing to help.

USE OF FORCE A citizen is entitled to use whatever force is reasonably necessary if he is helping the police to prevent a crime, or to arrest a suspected offender.

He cannot be sued for assault even if the suspect is later found not guilty.

INJURY Anyone who is injured while helping the police to arrest a suspect or prevent a crime is entitled to claim compensation from the Criminal Injuries Compensation Board. A claim can be made even if the person responsible for the injury has not been caught. The Board does not consider claims for less than £50, or claims for injuries that resulted from

traffic offences unless the person injured can prove he was deliberately run down. ☐ Compensation for criminal injuries, p. 547.

**No duty to report a crime**
Failing to report a crime is not an offence. But anyone who accepts a favour for not disclosing such information to the police can be jailed for up to two years.

It is an offence to help an offender avoid arrest or prosecution. Even a husband or wife can be prosecuted for helping a spouse.

But if someone merely continues to provide a criminal with accommodation that he had before the crime, it is unlikely to be considered a criminal offence. It is illegal only if the person intended to hinder the police.

The offence can be committed simply by refusing to tell the truth about what one has seen or heard. But a jury would have to be satisfied that the reason was to impede the prosecution of a guilty person.

FALSE REPORTS If a person knowingly makes a false report that a crime has been committed or gives false information which causes concern for the safety of people or property—say by creating a bomb scare—he can be prosecuted for wasting police time. The penalty is a fine of up to £200 or imprisonment for six months or both.

VEHICLES Cars and lorries may not usually be searched without the consent of the owner, unless the police suspect they are carrying certain articles such as firearms, goods on which duty should be paid, or—in certain parts of the country—stolen goods. ☐ Powers of the police and traffic wardens, p. 82.

SEARCHES AFTER ARREST Once a man has been arrested—that is, told by the police that he is being held for a specific reason—they normally search him, although in law they can do so only to look for evidence of the crime, or a weapon or means of escape. They often search an arrested person's home too, although their right to do so without a warrant has never been established.

## The police right to hold evidence

The police are allowed to keep as evidence items they have found in searches, or otherwise acquired, subject to certain conditions. Provided the items do not prove to be stolen, they must be returned as soon as possible. If necessary, courts will order their return.

Even if an article belongs to a person who has not been charged, the police may retain it as evidence.

This point was established in 1970 when the Court of Appeal ruled that the police may hold items that have come into their possession during an investigation and are needed as evidence in a serious case, provided *either* that they have reasonable grounds for believing the person in possession of the goods was implicated in the offence *or* that it would be wholly unreasonable of him not to allow the police to hold them.

## Police powers of entry

The police have no right to enter a person's home or other private premises without permission—except in special circumstances. An illegal entry can be resisted by reasonable force, although it is obviously extremely risky to rely on one's legal rights in such a situation by using force against the police. If one was in the wrong, the charges that followed would be the more serious.

ARRESTABLE OFFENCES Police are entitled to enter a house to re-arrest someone who has escaped from custody or to arrest someone for an offence carrying a maximum penalty of more than five years. These are known as 'arrestable offences' and include assault, causing actual bodily harm, theft, housebreaking, burglary, rape and false pretences. ☐ When a private citizen can make an arrest, p. 743.

A policeman must first announce his identity and demand entry. Plain-clothes police officers carry a warrant card stating that they are detectives. If entry is refused, a policeman is allowed to use force to break in.

BREACH OF THE PEACE Police have the right to enter a house to stop a breach of the peace they have heard or seen from outside. The police can follow someone who has committed a breach of the peace into a building.

The police may have the right to enter certain private premises where they reasonably suspect that a breach of the peace is about to take place—a private meeting in danger of developing into a fight, for example.

WARRANTS A search warrant or an arrest warrant, granted by a magistrate, allows police to enter private premises without permission, using force if necessary.

A warrant of arrest can be carried out at any time of day or night, but a search warrant can be carried out only during the day, except in certain specified cases. Either warrant may be carried out on a Sunday.

INTERESTS OF STATE A senior police officer is allowed to enter and search without a warrant under the Official Secrets Acts, or if lives are endangered because of explosives.

For instance, police officers would not need a warrant to carry out an emergency search of an office block after receiving a message that a bomb had been planted there.

PUBLIC PLACES A number of Acts of Parliament give the police power to enter buildings without a warrant, but nearly all relate to commercial premises—cinemas, race tracks and places of entertainment for children.

EMERGENCIES The police, and anyone else, can enter private premises in emergencies to save life or prevent serious damage to property.

## Going to the police station

The police can ask anyone to accompany them to a police station for questioning, but there is no obligation to agree unless a formal arrest is made. The police often prefer to question people at a police station without arresting them—particularly when they are not ready to lay a charge.

This is because once a man has been formally arrested by the police he must be told on what charge he is being detained and questioning must cease.

In practice, most people are prepared to go quietly when asked. Those who are innocent often think that going to the station is the best and quickest way of clearing things up.

Nevertheless, some people who are asked to go to the police station may consider it wise to insist on being accompanied by their solicitor. To avoid delay, anybody who wants to do this should telephone the solicitor *before* going with the police to the station. A suspect who is not formally arrested but 'helping the police with their inquiries' may leave the station when he wishes. If he is prevented, an application can be made to a High Court judge for a writ of habeas corpus to free him.

### The limits on police questioning

Police may ask a suspect any questions they like, but there are strict rules on how their questioning should be conducted. Confessions or statements shown to be made after improper questioning are invalid as evidence.

VOLUNTARY STATEMENTS Courts will not accept any statement or confession made after undue pressure. Anything offered in evidence must be a 'voluntary statement'—one that has not been made as a result of any 'fear or prejudice or hope of advantage exercised or held out by a person in authority'.

This definition of a 'voluntary statement' goes much further than a strict ban on threats of violence, or any other form of intimidation. For instance, a statement made after a policeman had suggested that a full confession would

result in lighter punishment could be held to be involuntary. In reality, police often ask suspects for help or strike bargains with them. A suspect who co-operates by giving evidence for the prosecution is not prosecuted or is charged with a lesser offence.

In addition, a defendant is sometimes persuaded to plead guilty to a lesser offence, on condition that the more serious charge is dropped. The danger of this is that he may be convicted where he might have been acquitted of the more serious offence.

JUDGES' RULES There are further restrictions on police questioning under what are known as Judges' Rules. These rules are not law, and judges can use their discretion and admit evidence obtained in breach of them.

The most important of the Judges' Rules is that a suspect must be cautioned as soon as a policeman has reasonable grounds to suspect that he has committed an offence. The policeman uses the traditional phrase 'You are not obliged to say anything, but anything you say may be put into writing and used as evidence'.

A second caution is given when a suspect is charged with an offence, and there should

## Bringing a complaint against the police

COMPLAINTS about the conduct of policemen can be made at any police station. The chief officer of the force involved must investigate every complaint, and in serious cases he can arrange for senior officers from another force to conduct an inquiry.

The investigation is private and when it is completed the complainant is told only the decision, not the reasons for it.

If a complainant believes that no proper investigation has been arranged by the police, he can apply to the Home Secretary, who has power to order an inquiry into the behaviour of any police force in England and Wales.

### Complaints to the court

Anyone who wants to complain about the way he was treated in police custody awaiting trial should raise the matter when he first appears in court. If he claims that he has been beaten by the police or that evidence against him has been fabricated, he or his lawyer is given an opportunity to bring evidence and cross-examine the police witnesses.

When a court accepts that a complainant is telling the truth, the police normally conduct

their own disciplinary inquiry into the conduct of their officers. If they do not, a complaint can be made officially.

### Suing the police

In serious cases the complainant can take civil action for damages for assault, false imprisonment, malicious prosecution or trespass.

It is not necessary to be able to show which individual police officer committed the act. It is enough to show it was an officer belonging to a particular force. When the identity of the police officer is unknown or uncertain, the action is brought against the chief officer of the police force.

POLICEMAN'S RIGHTS Just as a citizen can complain about a policeman's conduct, so the policeman also has certain legal rights. He too can bring an action for defamation. Anyone complaining about the police is covered by qualified privilege. But if the policeman can show that the complaint was brought maliciously—that is, from any ulterior, dishonest or improper motive—the defence of qualified privilege is destroyed. □ The dangers of controversy, p. 666.

normally be no questioning after this—apart from clearing up minor matters of detail. Anyone making a statement must be given the chance to write it in his own words and is usually asked to sign it. If he refuses to sign, the interrogating policeman signs it.

CHILDREN A parent or an adult of the same sex is supposed to be present when children are questioned by the police.

## Physical violence

It is illegal for the police to use physical violence, or the threat of physical violence, to obtain answers to their questions. Policemen are not exempt from the ordinary laws of assault and battery.

In cases where the police have assaulted suspects, substantial damages have been awarded to the victims.

Anyone who believes he has been physically maltreated by the police should always see a doctor as soon as possible. If he is in custody he should ask to see a police surgeon.

The doctor should be asked to carry out a full examination and to make a careful note of any bruises or other injuries in order to give evidence at a later date. ☐ Bringing a complaint against the police, p. 739.

## Asking for a solicitor

Anyone being questioned by the police is entitled to ask to speak to a solicitor. However, the police may refuse to allow a solicitor to be called for a time if they consider it would hinder the administration of justice. In such a case, the person being questioned is entitled to say nothing until his solicitor arrives.

People who go voluntarily to a police station for questioning sometimes complain that their solicitors are not allowed to speak to them. To avoid this happening, anyone who is approached by the police can call his solicitor and then remain silent until he has had an opportunity to consult him.

If a solicitor comes to the police station he is entitled to see his client in private—although many policemen interpret this to mean merely out of earshot.

A difficulty which often arises is that people who have voluntarily agreed to go to a police station for questioning do not know of a solicitor who would act for them. However, some police stations provide a list of solicitors who are prepared to take such cases.

## Identification parades

Many criminal cases revolve round the identification of the person responsible. The conviction of a bank robber may depend entirely on whether passers-by who saw him making his getaway can identify him afterwards—either from photographs in the police rogues' gallery files or by picking him out personally from amongst a group of people of similar appearance.

Many miscarriages of justice have happened because the wrong man was identified, and there are strict Home Office rules covering identification parades.

If a witness has picked out a suspect from photographs he is not normally allowed to confirm his choice at a parade, since there is a serious danger that the witness will pick out not the man he remembers from the scene of the crime, but the man he remembers from the photograph.

THE SUSPECT'S RIGHTS The police can ask anyone suspected of a crime to take part in an identification parade, but they cannot make him do so.

A man who thinks he has been wrongly accused of a crime can *demand* that an identification parade is held.

Suspects should be allowed to have a solicitor or friend present in case there are any complaints afterwards about the way the parade was conducted.

CONDUCT OF PARADES The suspect is allowed to choose his own place in a line of people, who should be of the same general appearance. He can change his position after each witness has been down the line and he may be allowed to alter his dress.

Witnesses have to be taken past one at a time and can ask each member of the line-up to walk a few steps or talk if necessary. They are not allowed to talk to other witnesses and compare notes afterwards.

Parades are not allowed in prison, except in exceptional cases.

## Fingerprints

The police have no automatic right to take fingerprints; the suspect can always refuse. When this happens, a police officer can bring a suspect of 14 or over before a magistrates' court and ask for a fingerprint order, giving the reasons why he needs to take the prints. If the court agrees, fingerprints can then be taken—forcibly if necessary.

But if the man is later acquitted or discharged, the fingerprints, and all copies of them, have to be destroyed. An application can be made to the Home Office to make sure this has been done.

This does not apply if the man who is acquitted gave his fingerprints to the police voluntarily, without a court order.

# How defendants are brought to court

*When a defendant is arrested*      *Committal proceedings*
*Applying for bail*      *Conditions for bail*
*Appearing in a criminal court*      *Trial in a higher court*

A PERSON suspected of having committed a criminal offence can be brought before a court in one of two ways. He may be served with an order called a summons to appear in court on a certain day. Or he may be arrested and held at a police station or prison and taken to court from there.

SUMMONS Magistrates issue a summons after receiving information, usually given by the police, that an offence has been committed. But it must always be given to the defendant in reasonable time—at least a week—before the hearing. If extra time is required to prepare a defence, the defendant may apply to the court for an adjournment.

In cases concerning certain minor offences a defendant may, if he wishes, plead guilty by post. The summons will say whether this course is open to him.

When a defendant ignores a summons and fails to appear in court, the magistrates usually issue the police with a warrant for his arrest, and when he is eventually brought before the court he may be fined for failing to attend. □ What happens if you are prosecuted, p. 100.

## When a defendant is arrested

If the offence is a serious one, or the police think there are circumstances which justify an immediate arrest, a warrant is issued at once, instead of a summons. This may happen when the defendant is likely to leave his usual address or commit further offences. When

---

## Starting a private prosecution

THOUGH almost all prosecutions for criminal offences are brought by the police, a private individual has the right in most cases to follow the same procedure, even if the police have decided not to prosecute.

For instance, shops and stores sometimes prosecute suspected shoplifters when the police are unwilling to do so; and a private individual will occasionally sue for assault after the police have decided that the matter is too trivial to justify prosecution.

APPLYING FOR A SUMMONS Anyone who wants to bring a private prosecution must first apply in person for a summons to the local magistrates. Any magistrates' court office will advise at which court to apply for a summons; magistrates have jurisdiction only over their own court's district.

The person applying must inform the magistrates—'lay an information'—about the offence which he alleges has been committed. It must be an action which constitutes an offence in law and he must give details about where and when he alleges it happened.

If the magistrates decide to issue a summons, they will require the full name and

address of the person to be summonsed and, if possible, his age and job, so that the police can serve the summons on him. If he cannot be found, the hearing cannot take place because anyone accused of a criminal offence must be given the chance to attend court and defend himself against the charge.

The summons tells the defendant what the charge against him is and where and when to appear. At the appointed time, the person who took out the summons can then prosecute him or employ a solicitor to do so. Often, however, it is difficult to find a solicitor willing to take on a private prosecution.

It is then up to the person taking out the summons to conduct the case, just as in police prosecutions the responsibility to prove the crime rests with the police. To secure a conviction, he must show that the defendant is guilty beyond any reasonable doubt.

THE DANGERS OF PROSECUTING If the defendant is later found not guilty, he may be able to claim damages from the person who brought the action if he can show that the prosecution was started maliciously and without a proper reason.

the police ask the magistrates for a warrant, they make a sworn statement in writing, giving their reasons for wanting to make the arrest, the offence with which the defendant is to be charged, and his name and address. Although the warrant is usually granted, the magistrates can refuse it.

The officer who makes the arrest need not have the warrant with him, but the person arrested is entitled to see it as soon as may be reasonably possible.

The police must follow the instructions on the warrant. If they arrest the wrong man, they can be sued for false arrest. Provided the warrant is carried out correctly, however, the police cannot be sued.

ARREST WITHOUT A WARRANT The police can arrest without a warrant in a variety of circumstances. They do not, for example, need a warrant to arrest a person suspected of committing an offence for which the sentence is fixed by law—such as murder—or where a person convicted for the first time would be liable to a sentence of five or more years in prison. They can make an arrest if they reasonably believe that such an offence has been, or is about to be, committed. These are known as 'arrestable offences'. □ When a private citizen can make an arrest, p. 743.

The police may also make arrests without a warrant in certain other circumstances— where someone is believed to be driving while unfit to do so through drink or drugs, for example, or to be in possession of stolen goods. There are also special local provisions; in Greater London, for instance, a police officer may arrest anyone at night if that person is unable, or refuses, to explain what he is doing or where he is going.

A police officer who has made an arrest is not compelled to take the person arrested to a police station immediately. If the police later decide they have no reason to continue holding the suspect, they cannot be sued for false imprisonment unless they delayed an unreasonably long time before releasing him.

A police officer can arrest someone he sees committing, or obviously about to commit, what is known as a breach of the peace. This includes a wide range of offences, such as using or threatening to use violence on another person or using abusive or insulting words or behaviour.

Policemen also have the right to enter private property to make an arrest if they suspect that someone in or on the property is committing, has committed or is about to commit an arrestable offence.

In most circumstances, it is unwise for a member of the public to resist arrest by a police officer, even if the officer is apparently exceeding his powers. It is better to take legal advice later and, if it is considered that the policeman has gone beyond his authority, to sue him for damages.

Anyone who resists arrest by a police officer who is acting within his rights can be prosecuted for resisting arrest.

Within a short time of making an arrest, a police officer must give the person arrested the reason for the arrest—unless he has caught him red-handed.

The explanation need only be in general terms. The officer could, for instance, say: 'I am arresting you for stealing from Mrs Jones.' Failure to give the arrested person information about the reason for his arrest would entitle him to sue the police for damages for false imprisonment.

HOW A DEFENDANT IS CHARGED When people are summonsed to appear in court, the offence with which they are charged is given in full in the summons. Anyone who is arrested must be charged formally at a police station. The charge is read out to him and he is given a copy of it.

## Applying for bail

When magistrates issue a warrant they decide at the same time whether the police should release the accused between the time of his arrest and the hearing—that is, whether he should be given bail. If they decide to allow him to be released, the instructions for giving bail are written on the back of the warrant, which is then said to be 'backed for bail'.

If an arrest has been made without a warrant—or if there are no instructions on the back of the warrant—the police themselves decide whether the accused should be released on bail. The decision must be taken by an officer not below the rank of inspector or by the station officer. Bail must be considered if it is impossible to bring a suspect before the magistrates within 24 hours, for example at a weekend.

When he decides about bail, the officer takes into account the gravity of the alleged offence, the likelihood of the accused's appearing in court and the general circumstances of the person arrested. For example, a married man in regular work who has lived at the same address for a number of years is more likely to be granted bail than a casual worker without a fixed address.

GUARANTEEING BAIL Two kinds of guarantee may be asked for when bail is granted—a guarantee by the arrested person that he will attend court; and a guarantee by someone else to see that the accused attends court.

The arrested person promises to pay a sum of money to the court if he fails to attend the hearing. This is called a recognisance and the defendant is said to have been granted bail in his own recognisance. If the person arrested is under 17 his parents are responsible for negotiating bail with the police.

No money is paid when bail is granted, but if he fails to attend court he may have to pay the amount of the recognisance in addition to any penalty imposed on conviction.

The second kind of guarantee, which may be asked for in addition to a recognisance, is a promise by an individual or individuals other than the arrested person to pay a specified sum of money to the court if the accused fails to appear. This is known as a surety and the people making the promise are known as sureties.

The sureties are responsible for guaranteeing that the accused attends court for his trial and they must be able to pay the amount of the surety if the accused fails to appear. The police usually insist that the surety is someone who owns his own home. ☐ The risks of standing bail, p. 746.

The prisoner can telephone people to ask if they will stand bail for him or the police may contact the people on his behalf. The amount of bail is a matter entirely for the police and there is no effective way of objecting to what seems to be an excessively large amount.

GETTING BAIL FROM THE MAGISTRATES
Once a defendant appears in court the decision to grant bail rests with the magistrates. If the police have fixed an unreasonably

---

## When a private citizen can make an arrest

ANY citizen has the right, in certain circumstances, to make an arrest. But if he tries to do so without proper grounds, he has no legal protection against an action for wrongful arrest, and possibly for assault.

BREACH OF THE PEACE A private citizen is entitled to make an arrest where he sees a breach of the peace or when there are good reasons to believe that there is about to be a breach of the peace.

Although the police interpret a breach to mean no more than abusive or insulting words or behaviour, the ordinary citizen is ill-advised to risk making an arrest unless there is a serious threat of physical violence.

CAUGHT IN THE ACT A private citizen has the right, using reasonable force, to arrest someone whom he reasonably believes to be committing a crime for which the maximum penalty is at least five years' imprisonment, provided the offence has actually been committed. Store detectives, for example, can arrest people they believe to be in the act of shoplifting. If the arrested person is later found not guilty, the person making the arrest cannot be sued for damages if someone else is found guilty of that particular offence.

PAST OFFENCES A citizen can arrest anyone who has committed a crime for which the maximum penalty is at least five years' imprisonment and for which he has not been tried. Again, reasonable force is permitted. But he must be sure of his evidence, for a prisoner who is found not guilty may be able to sue the person who arrested him for damages. These offences are:

| | |
|---|---|
| Assault causing bodily harm | Possessing firearms with intent to endanger life |
| Assault with intent to rob | Using firearms to resist arrest |
| Indecent assault on a girl under 13 | Handling stolen goods |
| Armed assault | Helping prisoners to escape |
| Burglary | Housebreaking |
| Conspiracy to murder | Living off immoral earnings |
| Criminal deception | Manslaughter |
| Causing death by dangerous or reckless driving | Demanding money with menaces |
| Drug offences | Murder |
| Using explosives with intent to do grievous bodily harm, or causing injury by use of explosives | Piracy |
| | Rape |
| | Theft |
| | Treason |
| Possessing firearms while committing another offence | Wounding causing bodily harm or with intent to murder or maim |

☐ ABC of crime and punishment, p. 758.

HANDING OVER TO POLICE Anyone who is arrested privately must be handed over to the police as soon as is reasonably possible.

Anyone injured while making an arrest may be able to claim compensation from the Criminal Injuries Compensation Board. ☐ Compensation for criminal injuries, p. 547.

large figure the magistrates may reduce it. A defendant who is refused bail by the police should ask them if they intend applying to the magistrates for an adjournment—perhaps because they have further inquiries to make—and if so whether they would oppose an application to the magistrates for bail.

If they do not intend to object to his release, he should ask whether sureties are likely to be required and for facilities to arrange for suitable people to be in court.

Even if the police do intend to oppose bail, the accused should still ask to be allowed to arrange for sureties to be present, because the final decision rests with the magistrates.

Anyone whose case is adjourned at any stage by the magistrates is always entitled to ask to be released on bail.

### Appearing in a criminal court

Anyone accused of a criminal offence is well advised to employ a solicitor at least to advise him, and possibly to present his case in court. A defendant who cannot afford to pay legal fees is usually entitled to legal aid and should seek the advice of a solicitor on the Law Society Legal Aid and Advice Panel.
☐ Help with legal fees and costs, p. 710.

Even if a defendant decides not to engage a solicitor the courts are supposed to allow him to be assisted in court by a person other than a lawyer—a friend or colleague, perhaps—who can take notes and make suggestions.

### Deciding how to plead

The most important decision that a person accused of a crime has to make is whether to admit or deny the charge—to plead guilty or not guilty.

A defendant who is innocent should plead not guilty. Sometimes, a defendant who knows he is innocent feels that his defence is too weak to convince a court. He may think it simpler to admit the charge rather than go to the expense and trouble of defending it. When this situation arises, it is advisable to plead not

# How criminal courts are organised

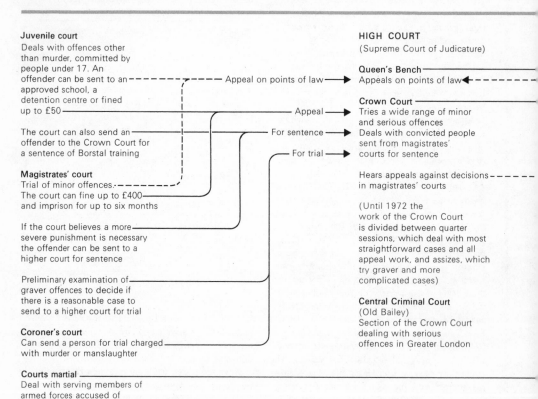

**Juvenile court**
Deals with offences other than murder, committed by people under 17. An offender can be sent to an approved school, a detention centre or fined up to £50

The court can also send an offender to the Crown Court for a sentence of Borstal training

**Magistrates' court**
Trial of minor offences.
The court can fine up to £400 and imprison for up to six months

If the court believes a more severe punishment is necessary the offender can be sent to a higher court for sentence

Preliminary examination of graver offences to decide if there is a reasonable case to send to a higher court for trial

**Coroner's court**
Can send a person for trial charged with murder or manslaughter

**Courts martial**
Deal with serving members of armed forces accused of breaking military law

Appeal on points of law

Appeal

For sentence

For trial

**HIGH COURT**
(Supreme Court of Judicature)

**Queen's Bench**
Appeals on points of law

**Crown Court**
Tries a wide range of minor and serious offences
Deals with convicted people sent from magistrates' courts for sentence

Hears appeals against decisions in magistrates' courts

(Until 1972 the work of the Crown Court is divided between quarter sessions, which deal with most straightforward cases and all appeal work, and assizes, which try graver and more complicated cases)

**Central Criminal Court**
(Old Bailey)
Section of the Crown Court dealing with serious offences in Greater London

guilty or to take legal advice immediately. Even on minor charges an innocent defendant who pleads guilty may risk losing his job or even being sent to prison.

Doubts about what to plead often arise because of the cost of defending a case, for even a person receiving legal aid may have to contribute to this cost (though this is less than many people think). If a defendant pleads not guilty and is later convicted, he may be ordered to pay more towards prosecution costs than if he admits the charge.

Some defendants also believe that if they plead not guilty and are convicted they receive a heavier penalty than if they had pleaded guilty in the first place. This is true only in the sense that the person pleading guilty may get a *lighter* sentence because he has made a full confession.

STRIKING A BARGAIN Sometimes the defendant or his legal representative will be able to 'bargain' with the prosecution. The prosecution may, for instance, agree to drop a serious charge on condition that the defendant pleads guilty to a lesser offence. But the courts are not supposed to accept a guilty plea unless there is evidence to prove that the defendant is in actual fact guilty of the charge.

A defendant should never agree to plead guilty to any charge unless it is certain that he is guilty in law. If he has doubts, he should take legal advice.

### Preparing the case

An accused person who pleads not guilty should try to obtain as much evidence as possible to support his defence. If he does not have sufficient time to prepare his case he should write to the court immediately asking for an adjournment.

A defendant preparing his own case must contact any witnesses he wants to appear and take written statements of their evidence. Although a witness cannot read from a statement in court, the accused can use it

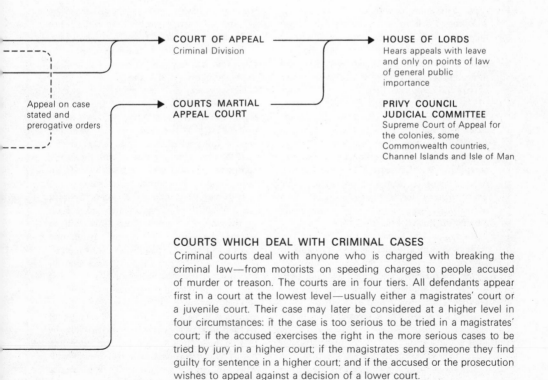

**COURT OF APPEAL**
Criminal Division

**HOUSE OF LORDS**
Hears appeals with leave and only on points of law of general public importance

Appeal on case stated and prerogative orders

**COURTS MARTIAL APPEAL COURT**

**PRIVY COUNCIL JUDICIAL COMMITTEE**
Supreme Court of Appeal for the colonies, some Commonwealth countries, Channel Islands and Isle of Man

**COURTS WHICH DEAL WITH CRIMINAL CASES**
Criminal courts deal with anyone who is charged with breaking the criminal law—from motorists on speeding charges to people accused of murder or treason. The courts are in four tiers. All defendants appear first in a court at the lowest level—usually either a magistrates' court or a juvenile court. Their case may later be considered at a higher level in four circumstances: it the case is too serious to be tried in a magistrates' court; if the accused exercises the right in the more serious cases to be tried by jury in a higher court; if the magistrates send someone they find guilty for sentence in a higher court; and if the accused or the prosecution wishes to appeal against a decision of a lower court.

as a guide when he is questioning his witness in court.

A potential witness who refuses to appear can be made to do so if the court grants the accused an order known as a subpoena.
☐ What happens if you are prosecuted, p. 100.

### Which court tries the case
The court in which a case is tried depends largely on the seriousness of the offence. Offences can be divided into three categories: those which can be tried only in a magistrates' court; those in which the defendant can choose to be tried either by magistrates or by a higher court; and those which can be dealt with only by a higher court.

Crimes which can be tried by the magistrates are known as summary offences; those which can be tried in a higher court are called indictable offences.

The first step in all types of cases is for the accused to appear in a magistrates' court. If he is charged with an indictable offence or a summary offence carrying a maximum penalty of more than three months' imprisonment, the clerk of the court asks whether he wants to be tried by the magistrates, or by a judge and jury in a higher court. If the defendant intends to plead guilty there is little purpose in being tried other than by the magistrates; if he afterwards feels that the sentence they imposed was excessive he can always appeal to a higher court.

If he denies the charge, however, there are several factors to be considered in deciding where to be tried.

Electing to be tried before a jury takes considerably longer than the magistrates' hearing and may be more costly.

If a defendant chooses to be tried in a higher court, there must first be a preliminary proceeding at which the magistrates decide whether there is enough evidence to justify the trial.

If the evidence against the defendant is so strong that he realises he cannot escape

## The risks of standing bail

ANYONE charged with an offence may be refused bail unless he can find one or two other people to guarantee that he appears in court for his trial—that is, to stand bail for him. These people are known as sureties and in giving this guarantee they take on a number of risks and responsibilities.

The police or magistrates fix a sum of money which may be ordered to be paid to the court by each of the sureties if the accused fails to appear for his trial. The people who offer to act as sureties are vetted by the police and accepted only if they seem able to pay the sum fixed if the defendant does not appear. The police usually insist that the surety is a houseowner, and they may want to know his job and his financial position.

If the surety is acceptable, he signs a written agreement which makes him liable to pay the amount fixed if the accused does not appear for his trial. The surety does not have to pay any money, or give any financial security, at the time bail is granted.

Once the defendant is released on bail, the sureties are responsible for ensuring that he does not abscond. They should make arrangements to keep in regular contact with him.

If a surety feels at any time that the person for whom he is standing bail intends to avoid the trial, he has two choices—he can arrest the accused or he can report his fears to the police and ask to be released from his undertaking.

A surety is entitled to make an arrest without a warrant simply by seizing the defendant and handing him over to the police.

This course, however, may be physically dangerous and it is wiser to ask the police to make the arrest, confirming the request in writing later. If the police refuse, the surety can ask to be relieved of his undertaking.

If the police will not release him, the surety can go to the court offices and ask to make an application to the court to be released.

If the sureties continue their guarantee until the trial, all their responsibilities end as soon as the accused attends court. If he fails to appear, the sureties are brought before the court and asked to explain what has happened. The court may then use its discretion in deciding whether to order sureties to forfeit the whole or part of the guaranteed sum.

They may order the whole sum to be paid, especially if the sureties have made no attempt to keep in contact with the accused while he was on bail. In law, this is called estreating bail. The courts often estreat bail even in cases where the surety was not really to blame for the non-appearance of the defendant.

conviction, he can change his plea to guilty at any time. Where appropriate a guilty plea can be changed to not guilty.

In cases where there is a serious conflict between the evidence presented by the prosecution, and that of the defence, the defendant may perhaps consider that he would be better able to persuade a jury of his innocence than convince a magistrate.

### Trial by magistrates
A suspect who has been arrested and charged by the police appears before the magistrates the next day, unless he is arrested on a Saturday, when he must wait until the Monday. If he has been released on bail he is told of the date of the hearing.

The defendant and his witnesses should arrive at the court well before the session is due to begin. He should take with him a writing pad and pen. □ What happens if you are prosecuted, p. 100.

### What happens at committal proceedings
When an accused person elects to go for trial in a higher court or is charged with an offence which must be dealt with in a higher court, a preliminary hearing—called committal proceedings—is held before magistrates.

If the defendant is represented by a lawyer, and the defence, prosecution and magistrates agree, there can be a short, formal hearing called a paper committal. The prosecution submits written statements and no witnesses are called.

When the defendant is not represented, or if he or his lawyer chooses, full committal proceedings have to be held. The defence can question prosecution witnesses, and if the defendant feels that no case has been made against him he can ask the magistrates to dismiss the charge.

The Press is allowed to publish only limited details of the case, such as the name of the court, the names and addresses of the defendand and witnesses, and the charge. If, however, the defence asks the magistrates at the start of the hearing to lift normal reporting restrictions, the hearing can be reported in full.

WHAT HAPPENS IN COURT Full committal proceedings begin with a short opening speech from the prosecution lawyer, after which he calls his witnesses.

The evidence and the answers to questions are written down by the clerk of the court and read back to the witness, who signs the statement, which is known as a deposition.

If the defendant is committed for trial, all the depositions are sent to the higher court.

In practice, the witnesses usually have to give their evidence again at the trial and the depositions are used by the lawyers and the judge to compare what the witnesses say at the trial with what they told the magistrates at the earlier hearing.

The magistrates may allow written statements of witnesses to be presented at full committal proceedings if the accused does not object. Sometimes the magistrates, the prosecution or the defence may want a witness who has made a written statement to give evidence personally; they then issue a witness summons ordering him to come to court.

When all the prosecution witnesses have given evidence the accused, or his lawyer, can claim that there is no case to answer. If the magistrates agree, the charge against the accused is dismissed. If, on the other hand, the magistrates reject the submission, the charge is written down by the clerk of the court, who reads it out to the accused and, if necessary, explains it to him.

The magistrates tell him that he can give evidence on oath in answer to the charge or make a statement which will be taken down and may be given in evidence at his trial. Alternatively, the accused can say nothing. For a defendant who has not had the opportunity of obtaining proper legal advice, this is probably the wisest course.

Whether or not the accused makes a statement, he may call evidence on oath from witnesses, which is also taken down in the form of depositions. When he has completed his evidence he is entitled to address the magistrates and try to persuade them (possibly a second time) that the prosecution has not made out a case against him. The magistrates then decide whether to discharge him or commit him for trial at a higher court.

AFTER THE COMMITTAL After the magistrates have committed the defendant for trial, they make witness orders, requiring all witnesses who have given evidence at the hearing to appear at the trial if they are needed. An order may either be full—which means that a witness must attend when the trial takes place—or conditional, in which case he need attend only if notified later that he is required.

### Conditions for bail
At the end of the committal proceedings the magistrates also decide whether to release the accused on bail until the trial takes place, or whether to keep him in prison.

They also consider bail when a case which they intend to deal with themselves has to be adjourned.

Where the offence is not punishable with more than six months' imprisonment, magistrates must grant bail unless one or more of eight special factors are present. They are:

**1.** Where the accused has previously been sent to prison or to a Borstal institution.

**2.** Where he has previously been on bail and has failed to keep to the conditions, such as reporting to a police station every day.

**3.** Where he is charged with an offence alleged to have been committed while on bail.

**4.** Where it is necessary to detain him to establish his identity or address.

**5.** Where he has no fixed home or lives outside the United Kingdom.

**6.** Where the charge involves violence on another person, explosives, firearms, or an indecent assault on a child under 16.

**7.** Where the court thinks he may commit another offence if he is allowed bail.

**8.** Where a remand in custody is necessary for the accused's own protection—for example, if he is threatening to kill himself.

Even if one or more of these factors are present the magistrates may still grant bail if they wish. When magistrates have a discretion whether to grant bail, the main consideration is whether the accused is likely to appear at his trial. The court also considers whether the defendant is likely to commit other offences while on bail, or interfere with witnesses, or even the fact that the police have not completed their enquiries.

Where the maximum penalty is more than six months' imprisonment, bail is at the discretion of the magistrates.

IF BAIL IS NOT GRANTED When bail is refused and the accused is not represented by a lawyer, the magistrates must tell him that he has a right of appeal to a High Court judge.

Legal aid is not normally available for bail applications. But legal aid granted to someone committed by magistrates for trial in a higher court covers an application for bail.

Otherwise a person with no money can apply for bail from a Crown Court judge through the Official Solicitor. The police station or prison where the accused is detained can supply the necessary forms.

An appeal can be made not only in cases where bail has been refused but also if the accused feels that it has been granted on unreasonable terms or subject to conditions which are unreasonable.

**Trial in a higher court**

Cases that are not tried at the magistrates' court go to the Crown Court.

The Crown Court hears criminal cases, and sentences defendants sent from the magistrates' courts. The Central Criminal Court— the Old Bailey—is the Crown Court for London. Cases are heard before judges and part-time judges called recorders, both sitting with a jury in cases where the defendant pleads not guilty.

## How judges and magistrates are appointed

THE most senior judges are appointed by the Crown on the nomination of the Prime Minister. They are the Lord Chancellor, who as chief law officer comes fifth in order of precedence in the Cabinet, the Lord Chief Justice, the Master of the Rolls, the President of the Family Division, and the judges of the Court of Appeal (known as Lords Justices) and of the House of Lords (known as Lords of Appeal in Ordinary, or more commonly as the Law Lords).

The less senior judges, including the circuit judges and recorders of the Crown Court and the magistrates, are all appointed by the Lord Chancellor. He also nominates the High Court judges, although they are technically appointed by the Crown.

All judges except recorders, circuit judges and the magistrates must have been barristers.

Circuit judges and recorders can be drawn from the ranks of solicitors, although in practice it is more common for them to be barristers.

The 16,000 lay magistrates, known as justices of the peace, are not normally trained as barristers or solicitors and they are not paid. They have to undertake a certain minimal amount of training as magistrates, but they rely chiefly on their experience.

Each magistrates' court also has a clerk, a fully-trained solicitor whose job is to give the magistrates advice and guidance on matters of law and procedure and inform them of the penalties which can be imposed for the various offences.

London and some other large towns have professional paid magistrates, called stipendiary magistrates. They must be barristers or solicitors of at least seven years' standing.

# Deciding whether to appeal

*Appealing from a magistrates' court*
*Appealing from a higher court*
*Appealing to the House of Lords*

*Petitioning the Home Secretary*
*Remedies for wrongful prosecution*
*When a judge or JP can be sued*

ANYONE who is convicted of a crime may have the right to appeal against conviction, or against sentence, or both. A defendant convicted in a magistrates' court has an automatic right to appeal. But if the case is heard at a Crown Court, the defendant has to obtain permission to appeal—from the trial court itself or, more usually, from the Criminal Division of the Court of Appeal.

The Court of Appeal can also grant bail to a convicted person, if he is sentenced to a term of imprisonment, until the result of his appeal is known. Anyone appealing against a fine does not have to pay until his appeal is heard.

GROUNDS FOR APPEALING Possible grounds for appeal include the introduction of new evidence that is favourable to the defendant's case or proof that prosecution witnesses were not telling the truth.

The defendant may think that the judge or magistrates misinterpreted the law, or that there was a defect in the conduct of the trial. He may believe that the sentence is excessive for the offence or that his personal circumstances were not taken into consideration in the sentence. Or he may simply think that the court made the wrong decision on the evidence and that a higher court might draw a different conclusion.

DRAWBACKS OF APPEALING If a defendant loses his appeal against a decision of a magistrates' court, the Crown Court to which he is appealing may increase the original sentence.

The Criminal Division of the Court of Appeal does not have the power to increase a sentence. But it has the power to order that some of the time spent in prison while appealing should not count as part of a sentence.

When deciding whether to appeal, the defendant also has to consider questions of cost and time. If he is legally aided he may be asked to pay a further contribution in addition to what he had to pay as a result of the earlier trial. ☐ Help with legal fees and costs, p. 710.

He has to employ both a solicitor and a barrister to present his case. If the appeal is successful, he will normally not be awarded costs. If the appeal is dismissed he may also be ordered to make a contribution towards the costs of the prosecution, although this is very rare. There are often delays of several months in the hearing of appeals.

## Appealing from a magistrates' court
Appeals against a magistrates' court decision are normally heard by the Crown Court. An appeal must be made within 14 days of the magistrates' decision.

If the defendant was legally aided at the trial, he is entitled to advice about appealing and to help with drafting the notice of appeal. ☐ Help with legal fees and costs, p. 710.

If the appeal is against the entire conviction the case is heard again and witnesses have to give evidence once more. A defendant who pleaded guilty in the lower court is not normally allowed to appeal against conviction.

STATING A CASE An alternative method of appealing is to ask the magistrates to 'state a case'—that is, submit a written summary of the case to the higher court. Such an appeal may be made only on a point of law.

The magistrates' summary is studied by at least two High Court judges in the Divisional Court of the Queen's Bench Division. The judges can uphold the decision of the magistrates, quash it or order a re-hearing of the case. It is advisable to obtain legal advice before making such an appeal.

## Appealing from a higher court
An appeal from a Crown Court is heard by the Criminal Division of the Court of Appeal. It must be lodged within 28 days of the Crown Court's decision.

A person convicted at a Crown Court who was legally aided at the trial is entitled to advice about the appeal from his lawyers. He should complete form 1481 if he is in prison. If not it is advisable to consult a solicitor under the legal-advice scheme. Legal aid is also available for appeals by order of the Court of Appeal.

Unless an appeal concerns a point of law, it needs the permission of the court. The application to appeal is considered by one judge who bases his decision on written documents, including the transcript of evidence given at the lower court. If he refuses the application, it can be renewed to a full court of three judges. If the application is then granted, the case is heard by three judges. The Court of Appeal can dismiss the appeal, quash the conviction, alter or vary (but not increase) the sentence or substitute a conviction for another offence. There is no power to order a retrial unless the appeal succeeds on the ground of fresh evidence.

**Appealing to the House of Lords**
The House of Lords is the supreme court of appeal for the United Kingdom. There is no automatic right of appeal to the Lords. Appeals are heard only on points of law which are considered to be of general importance. A defendant must obtain permission to appeal either from the Court of Appeal or from the House of Lords Appeals Committee.

**Petitioning the Home Secretary**
Anyone who believes that he has been wrongly convicted and has appealed unsuccessfully through all the courts can, as a final resort, petition the Home Secretary.

The Home Secretary has power to ask the Queen to grant a petitioner a free pardon. Alternatively, he can recommend a conditional pardon—an order that the conviction stands, but the punishment is reduced. Sometimes he recommends that the remainder of a sentence need not be served.

The Home Secretary can also refer a case back to the Court of Appeal for further consideration. Finally, he can release a prisoner on licence or on parole.

To obtain a Royal pardon the defendant usually has to prove his innocence. If he does not establish his innocence but manages to throw doubt on the conviction, he may be granted some remission of sentence.

Many prisoners try to get the support of their Member of Parliament, their legal advisers, or the Press in petitioning the Home Secretary. Legal aid is not available after the ordinary appeal process in the courts has been completed.

Someone who has been pardoned has no legal right to claim compensation, but in practice payments are sometimes made.

**Remedies for wrongful prosecution**
Anyone who has been prosecuted on a criminal charge of which he is innocent may feel he would like to take legal action against those who started the prosecution—either the police or a private individual.

In practice this sort of action is rarely possible. Just because an innocent person is prosecuted, it does not mean that the police have acted wrongly—he may have been the victim of mistaken identity, or other evidence may have pointed strongly to his guilt.

If it is clear that a prosecution should never have been brought, the court will sometimes order the prosecution to pay the defendant's costs. If the defendant can prove he was 'framed' he may also have a right to claim damages for malicious prosecution. To succeed, he must be able to show:
**1.** That he has been acquitted.
**2.** That there were no good grounds for the proceedings—even though those who started them thought there were.
**3.** That those who started the proceedings acted from the wrong motives. The desire to have someone prosecuted because he had committed a crime against you would be considered legitimate. But it would be a wrong motive to want to use criminal proceedings, for example, to get even with a personal enemy who is innocent.

An action can be brought only against those who instigate proceedings, not against those who give false information to the police, since this does not automatically start a prosecution. But if the case was based on information known to be false, those responsible might be held to be the instigators.

The amount of damages awarded in an action for malicious prosecution will depend on the degree of loss suffered. If the person acquitted was imprisoned or lost his job, he may get substantial compensation.

**When a judge or JP can be sued**
A defendant who is dissatisfied with the way in which his trial was conducted cannot normally obtain redress by suing the judge. A judge cannot be sued for anything he says or does during a trial unless he commits a crime, such as assaulting a witness.

A magistrate or a lower court judge can be sued only if he exceeds the power given to him by law—by hearing a case over which his court has no jurisdiction, for example, or imposing too high a penalty.

Only when a defendant has suffered loss or inconvenience can he take civil action. To succeed in an action for damages, the person suing must show not only that the magistrates made the mistake, but that there was no reasonable excuse for their doing so.

When a prisoner is sentenced to a longer term than is allowed by the law, he cannot claim damages unless he has served the extra time in prison. In most cases his appeal would have been heard before that happened.

# The cost of legal action

ANYONE involved in civil proceedings—suing for damages after an accident, for example, or resisting such a claim—has to pay certain expenses. These can include his solicitor's fees, witnesses' allowances, the costs of obtaining medical and police reports, and small out-of-pocket expenses.

Costs are worked out differently in the county courts and the High Court. In the county courts, costs are regulated by a set of five scales, which give an upper and lower limit of charges for each item. Which scale is used usually depends on the amount recovered or claimed. For example, Scale 1 applies to amounts between £20 and £50 and Scale 3 runs between £300 and £500.

In the High Court there is a single scale of costs which covers such items as court fees. But for other charges—such as a solicitor's fees for preparing a case—there is no set limit. A solicitor is entitled simply to make a 'reasonable' charge.

### Who pays legal costs
Sometimes after a civil court case each side pays its own costs. It is more common, however, for the judge to award costs to the winning side. This means that the loser pays his own costs and those of his opponent. In the county court the judge also says on which of the five scales payment is to be made.

### How costs are vetted
The fact that someone in a civil action is awarded costs does not mean that he is able to recover from his opponent all his expenses. He is entitled only to those costs which are necessary for the attainment of justice.

The solicitor for the successful party draws up a detailed bill listing all his costs and expenses for the case, and this is presented to the losing party.

A layman who pleads his own case in court is able to recover only his own expenses as a witness and his court fees and, if he has been advised by a solicitor, his solicitor's fee. He cannot claim for preparing and presenting the case himself.

If the unsuccessful party thinks the costs on the bill are not reasonable, he can have them examined—'taxed'—by a court official. County court bills are taxed by the registrar. Bills for High Court actions are scrutinised by an official known as a taxing master in the Supreme Court Taxing Office.

Usually taxation is carried out on what is known as a 'party and party' basis, which aims to ensure that the winner recovers his essential expenses without inflicting on the loser more expense than was necessary to obtain justice. Solicitors for both parties argue the merits of each item on the bill and the taxing master or registrar rejects or reduces any items he considers unreasonable or excessive.

Costs incurred by the plaintiff in deciding whether to bring the action, for example, are unlikely to be allowed. The taxing master or registrar may also reduce the amount the winning side can claim for a barrister's fee if he considers that they chose a more expensive barrister than was necessary to deal with the case.

When the taxation is completed, the costs are totalled and a revised bill is presented to the losing side. The successful party can then ask the court to instruct its bailiffs to enforce payment.

The solicitor for the successful party sends his own client a bill for all the expenses he has incurred (including, if he chooses, the items reduced or disallowed by the taxing master or registrar). From this total is deducted the costs that have been recovered from the other side.

A 'solicitor and own client' bill such as this can also be taxed by the court. □ Complaining about the bill, p. 753.

It is because of this system of taxing costs that the winner of an action to recover a relatively small amount of money can find himself out of pocket.

### Costs in criminal proceedings
In criminal proceedings, courts can order a convicted person to pay the costs of prosecution. They can also order the costs of someone who is acquitted to be paid out of public funds, but this occurs only in exceptional cases—usually when the court thinks that a prosecution was wholly unjustified.

# Complaints against lawyers

*Complaints to professional bodies*
*Suing a lawyer for negligence*

CLIENT who is dissatisfied with the service he has received from either a solicitor or barrister has two possible courses of action open to him. He may complain about unprofessional conduct to the professional body concerned—the Law Society for solicitors or the Bar Council for barristers. Or, if his lawyer's negligence has caused him loss, he may be able to sue for damages.

If the complaint is about the size of the lawyer's bill, the procedure is different.
☐ Complaining about the bill, p. 753.

## Complaints to professional bodies

Normally a client complains first to one of the professional bodies. Solicitors and barristers can be disciplined, and in extreme cases their right to practise can be withdrawn; but neither of the professional bodies has the general power to award financial compensation.

The Law Society, however, administers a compensation fund from which—at the society's discretion—grants may be made to people who suffer loss as a result of the dishonesty of a solicitor or his clerk, or who have suffered or may suffer hardship as a result of a solicitor failing to account for money due.

REPORTING A SOLICITOR The first step in reporting a solicitor is usually to contact the secretary of the local law society, which is an independent body. His address is in the telephone directory or can be obtained from the Citizens' Advice Bureau.

The local society may be able to resolve complaints of delays or failure to answer correspondence, for example.

Alternatively, the client can complain direct to the Law Society at 113 Chancery Lane, London WC2A 1LP. Serious complaints made to local societies are usually referred to the Law Society in London.

Give full details of the complaint, but wherever possible, limit it to facts, rather than comment. A complainant who acts in good faith, and without an ulterior or improper motive, cannot normally be sued successfully for libel; but wild comments could lead the solicitor concerned to take legal action.

Complaints involving matters of law—allegations of negligence, for example—may give the client grounds for taking action in the courts. If the Law Society considers that part or all of the complaint falls into this category, it advises the complainant to contact another solicitor. No complaint of unprofessional conduct can be dealt with until this course has been completed.

If the client complains of unprofessional conduct, the Law Society asks his permission to send the complaint to the solicitor concerned for his comments. No complaint can proceed without this consent.

The solicitor's reply is then considered by the Law Society and, with his consent, a copy is sent to the client. If the society considers the reply disposes of the matter, the client is told; but he has the opportunity of commenting further if he wishes.

If the matter is not settled satisfactorily in this way, it is referred to the Professional Purposes Committee of the Law Society. The client has no right to appear personally before the committee but may be interviewed.

In the case of very serious complaints, disciplinary action may be taken by the society against the solicitor. There is then a formal hearing before a body called the Disciplinary Committee, which is a tribunal set up by Act of Parliament (not a committee of the Law Society). This Committee can remove, fine or suspend a solicitor from practice.

Anyone may apply direct to the Disciplinary Committee, but the advantage for a client in first taking his complaint to the Law Society is that the society will carry out the necessary preliminary investigations without involving a complainant in expense.

REPORTING A BARRISTER Complaints about the conduct of barristers should be made in writing either to the General Council of the Bar, Carpmael Building, Temple, London EC4Y 7AU, or to the Senate of the Four Inns of Court, 5 Essex Court, Temple, London EC4Y 9AH. The complaint is first considered by the chairman of the professional conduct committee of the Bar, and he may dismiss it if he thinks it is frivolous.

Serious complaints are considered by the committee, and the barrister is asked to explain his actions. If he satisfies the committee, no further action is taken. But if he fails to convince the committee that he acted properly, they may reprimand him.

When the committee believes that the complaint is more serious, they refer the matter to the Senate, which can remove the barrister from the list of those allowed to practise.

The only form of financial compensation for the client is that the Senate may order the barrister to return any fees received.

WHEN LEGAL AID IS INVOLVED When the complaint arises out of a case where legal aid was given, the Bar Council or the Law Society can report the matter to a special Legal Aid Tribunal, which can remove the lawyer from the list of those allowed to do legal aid work.

**Suing a lawyer for negligence**

Suing a lawyer—or any professional man—is a difficult matter. First the client must be sure that he has good grounds for the action. This usually means getting advice from another member of the same profession.

THE GROUNDS FOR ACTION To succeed in legal action against a solicitor or barrister, the client needs to prove:

1. That the lawyer has been negligent.
2. That the client has suffered loss as a result.

In law, a lawyer is negligent only if he does something which a reasonably competent lawyer would not have done, or fails to do something which a reasonably competent lawyer would have done.

As a result of this principle, an action will not succeed simply because a lawyer makes a mistake, since reasonably competent lawyers (and people in other walks of life) make mistakes from time to time.

Moreover, neither a barrister nor a solicitor can be sued for negligence for their handling of a court case, and this includes the preparation of the case.

If the lawyer fails to take the necessary legal steps within the time limit for a case, he may be liable to pay damages. ☐ Time limits on claims, p. 720.

If a lawyer has given advice which is later proved wrong, there is no good ground for action against him, unless it can be shown that the advice was given negligently—because, for example, he overlooked legislation or a previous case, called a precedent, which would have affected his client's chances of success.

Similarly, a solicitor who fails to make all the necessary investigations when acting for a house-purchaser may be held liable if his client suffers as a result. Incompetently drafted documents can also give grounds for action.

DECIDING WHO TO SUE The client must take care to sue the correct person. Where a firm of solicitors is involved, he should sue the partners, for they will normally be liable for the defaults of their staff.

GETTING ADVICE If it is difficult to find a local solicitor willing to pursue an action for negligence against another, the client should approach the Law Society. Legal aid may be available if the client cannot afford the professional help he needs. ☐ Help with legal fees and costs, p. 710.

---

## Complaining about the bill

A CLIENT who receives a high bill from a solicitor can take it back to him and ask for a reduction. If the solicitor says that the fee is the correct amount, the client has the right to ask the solicitor to submit the bill to the Law Society for review.

The Law Society charges nothing for this service, and the client is under no obligation to accept its ruling.

A client can also ask for the review of a bill either in the court in which the case has been heard or, if it has not been heard in court, by the High Court. For example, a client can ask the High Court to examine a solicitor's fee for drawing up a will or a commercial agreement.

The High Court has officers called 'taxing masters', who deal with the settlement or 'taxation' of costs. In a county court, the registrar is responsible for taxation of costs. A list of taxation specialists—who can present the client's case to the court—is obtainable from the Law Society.

The client can also seek guidance about procedure from members of staff of the taxing office at the relevant court.

A client's right to ask for taxation applies in all cases, even those in which he has made a written agreement with the solicitor about the fee in advance.

If the court reduces the bill by less than one-sixth, the client must pay the court's taxation costs. If the bill is reduced by more than one-sixth, the solicitor pays the costs. ☐ The cost of legal action, p. 751.

# Serving on a jury

MOST adults in Britain are liable to be summoned to serve on a jury. From the date on which the Criminal Justice Act 1972 comes into force, anyone aged 21 or over but under 65 is eligible. Before that date, jury service was restricted to ratepayers owning or occupying property with certain minimum rateable values.

The property qualification barred from jury service many adults and a majority of women (since they were not responsible for paying rates). It was abolished on the recommendation of a committee under the chairmanship of Lord Morris of Borth-y-Gest.

### Compiling the jury register
A list of people eligible for jury service in each area is compiled every year when the electoral register is drawn up. The registration officer marks the letter 'J' by the names of those who qualify for service, according to the rating valuation list. ☐ The right to vote, p. 675.

The first time an elector is listed as a juror on the electoral register, he is informed and given the opportunity to object. If he fails to make his objection by December 16, he can be summoned to serve on a jury even if, technically, he is ineligible.

### Grounds for objecting to jury service
In law, certain people cannot sit on a jury. There are two categories who are legally disqualified because of their criminal records:
1. Anyone who has served a prison sentence of more than three months at any time during the previous ten years.
2. Anyone who has been sentenced to more than five years' imprisonment.

Others are legally classified as exempt— they have the right to be excused, but if they choose not to exercise that right, they can be summoned to appear. The list of exempt categories is based mainly on the type and importance of the person's work.

The list of people who are entitled to claim exemption from jury service includes those in the following categories:

Peers, Members of Parliament, judges, ministers of religion, nuns, practising barristers, solicitors and clerks, court officials, magistrates, coroners, sheriff's officers, police officers and special constables, councillors, town clerks and borough treasurers, prison governors and officers, practising doctors, surgeons, physicians, pharmacists, dentists, midwives, serving officers in the armed forces, household servants to the Queen, Customs and Inland Revenue officers, mines and quarries inspectors, mental-hospital keepers, Trinity House staff, members of the Mersey Docks and Harbour Board and of the Port of London Authority.

### How to object
When the official notification is received from the electoral registration officer, anyone wanting to be excused from jury service must reply in writing, giving his reasons. He may claim to be in an exempt category, for example, or to be legally disqualified, or he may not meet the age requirements.

If the objection is accepted, he is notified by the electoral registration officer that his name is being deleted from the jury list.

If the electoral registration officer refuses to delete the name from the register, the objector can appeal to a magistrates' court. From there, if necessary, he can make a further appeal to the High Court.

If a person disqualified from jury service does not object, his name stays on the jury list. But should he receive a jury summons, he is asked on the summons whether he has a criminal conviction of the type that would exclude him from jury service.

A person who serves on a jury although disqualified by a previous prison sentence risks a fine, on conviction, of up to £250.

### Receiving a jury summons
Juries are summoned by random selection from the local electoral lists. Normally, 14 days' notice is given before the jury service begins. But there is no indication on the summons as to how long a person is expected to serve on a jury.

A juror has the right to ask to be excused in certain circumstances—for instance, if he is ill; if he is blind or deaf; if he is the owner of a one-man business which would suffer if left unattended; if he is a student with examinations to take; or if he expects to be abroad at the time. A woman who is pregnant also has the right to ask to be excused.

When the summons is received, any juror who wants to be excused should write immediately to the summoning officer, stating the reason for his request.

If the summoning officer accepts the reason, the juror is excused from jury service only at the time given on the summons. He is still liable to be summoned at a later date.

If the request is refused, the objector must attend the court on the date given. There is no limit to the fine that can be imposed for failing to attend. The juror can, however, state his reason for wanting to be excused when he gets to court and can ask the judge to give a ruling in his favour.

JURY PANEL The summoning officer always calls more than the 12 jurors required for any one trial. Their names are put in a box, and the number required is then drawn. Their names, addresses and occupations are listed in a notice in the court.

The juror may find that his name has been drawn to sit on a long case, or he may have to sit on several short cases. Wherever possible, the officials responsible try to ensure that no juror is expected to attend for more than ten days, unless he is sitting on a jury which is hearing one very long case.

## When the jury is chosen
In criminal cases, juries are called to hear serious charges in which the accused pleads not guilty. It is their job to decide from the evidence presented in court whether he or she is guilty 'beyond reasonable doubt'.

When the jurors have been selected, they are led into the courtroom and they take the oath from the jury box. Each juror is sworn in separately, so that he may be challenged. A juror who wishes can take the oath in a nonreligious form, known as affirming. The wording of the oath is read from a printed card held in the hand:

'I swear by Almighty God (or I do solemnly, sincerely and truly declare and affirm) that I will faithfully try the several issues joined between our Sovereign Lady the Queen and the prisoner(s) at the bar and give a true verdict according to the evidence.'

CHALLENGING THE JURY Both the prosecution and the defence have an opportunity to reject a limited number of jurors before they are sworn in.

The defence can challenge seven names without giving a reason—called in law

'peremptory challenges'. Anyone who is challenged in this way may be put into another jury panel for another case. The prosecution is not allowed to make peremptory challenges, but instead it has the right to ask jurymen to 'stand by' which means they will not be required unless a complete jury cannot be chosen from among the other members making up the panel.

In addition, both the prosecution and the defence can reject further jurors, with the judge's permission, for a particular reason, which must be given—for instance, because a juror is related to the victim of the crime.

## The jury during the trial
After the jury has been sworn in, the judge advises the jurors not to discuss the case with anyone other than their fellow jurors until after they have reached their verdict.

If a juror is approached by someone with an interest in the case and offered a bribe to return a particular verdict, the juror has a duty to report the fact to a court official or the police immediately. If he accepts the bribe, he is liable to be prosecuted for perverting the course of justice, and fined or sent to prison for up to two years.

ELECTING A FOREMAN At some point, every jury should elect a foreman, who can act as chairman over its discussions and give its verdict in court. There is no specific procedure laid down. In some courts, the person called first or last in the ballot is automatically foreman. In others, the jury itself elects a foreman during the trial.

The foreman, however, does not have any special position or rights. His vote is no more than equal to that of any other member of the jury. There can be no casting vote in determining a jury's verdict.

TAKING NOTES There is no legal ruling on whether jurymen should be allowed to take notes as the case develops. In some courts they are permitted to do so. In other courts the jury is not allowed to write.

ASKING QUESTIONS There is no reason in law why a juror should not stand up and ask a question of a defendant, his counsel or the prosecution if he does not understand a point in the evidence. He should address his question to the judge.

In practice, embarrassment often prevents jurymen from interrupting a trial.

## How the jury reaches its verdict
As soon as the judge has completed his summing-up of the case, the jury is locked in a jury room to consider its verdict. How a jury

actually reaches its verdict is up to the jury. There is no formal procedure to follow.

But, in reaching its verdict, the jury ought to consider only the evidence—the facts of the case and any ruling that the judge gives in his summing-up on points of law, and his directions on whether to ignore any statements that have been made in court.

If the jury is in any doubt about a question of fact or a ruling given by the judge, it can ask the judge for clarification, either by sending him a note through a court official or policeman or by returning to court.

In most cases, the jurors are able to agree on a verdict. Sometimes a juror only agrees to a particular verdict if a special recommendation, say for leniency, accompanies it. However, the judge is in no way bound by any recommendation given him by a jury.

A verdict may still be returned if a member of a jury dies or is discharged because of illness, provided there are at least nine jurors left to give a verdict.

MAJORITY VERDICTS A jury which has been deliberating for under two hours and ten minutes can return to the court only if it has reached a unanimous verdict. After that time a jury of ten people or more can ask the judge's permission to return a majority verdict.

The majority required is ten of a jury of 11 or 12, or nine of a jury of ten. If the majority verdict is 'guilty', the foreman must state in open court the number of jurors who dissented, but they are not identified.

A jury which cannot reach the required majority must continue to deliberate if the judge considers that there is any possibility that a majority verdict can be reached. The jurors are not allowed to go home and return to the court the next day. Instead, they are kept in isolation and provided with food and sleeping accommodation, perhaps in a nearby school or a hotel.

However, if the jury feels that it will never reach a majority verdict it must report the matter to the judge, who will order a retrial with a new jury. Usually, if the jury at the retrial is also unable to reach a majority verdict, the case is dropped—though in theory a case can be heard as many times as may be necessary in order eventually to bring in a majority verdict.

## Juries in civil cases

The only civil cases normally heard by a jury are those involving libel or slander. In this instance, the jury has to give a verdict on the balance of probabilities. Jurors for civil cases are summoned from the local electoral lists in the same way as for criminal cases, but they take a slightly different oath when being sworn in.

A civil court jury consists of 12 jurors and they are allowed to return a majority verdict according to the same rules as a jury in a criminal court. They can, however, return a majority verdict after any period of time which the judge considers reasonable—not the two hours and ten minutes stipulated in criminal cases.

## Juries in coroners' courts

A coroner holding an inquest must summon a jury if he suspects that the cause of death was murder, a road accident or an industrial disease. In some cases, such as in that of an accident, the coroner summons a jury as soon as he is notified of the death. In other cases, the results of a post mortem may show that the death was in some way unnatural, so the coroner then summons a jury.

There are no legal qualifications for serving on an inquest jury. How the jurors are chosen varies considerably from coroner to coroner.

A coroner's jury usually consists of seven jurors. They can return a variety of verdicts on the cause of death. These include: murder, justifiable homicide, manslaughter, infanticide, suicide, accident, misadventure, death from industrial disease, or death from natural causes. If there is some doubt as to how the death occurred, the jury can return an open verdict. ☐ Investigating a sudden death, p. 410.

---

## Payment for jurors

JURORS are not paid for serving on a jury, and they may lose their normal wages. Firms are encouraged to continue paying an employee who is absent from work as a result of jury service, but no firm is compelled to do so.

Absence from work for jury service is not a valid ground for seeking supplementary benefit.

ALLOWANCES Jurors can, however, claim allowances for travel, subsistence (including meals and board if necessary), and some compensation for loss of earnings.

In 1972, the maximum that could be drawn for lost wages was £4·75 a day, rising to £9·50 a day after more than ten days' service.

# ABC OF CRIME
# AND PUNISHMENT

T HE principal criminal offences with which an individual can be charged are listed in alphabetical order. Each entry explains what the prosecution must prove in order to gain a conviction, and the defences which may be used by the accused to prove his innocence. The entries conclude with the maximum penalties a court can impose on those who are found guilty. In practice, the courts often award lesser sentences, taking into account all the known circumstances of the crime and of the criminal. The main penalties—Borstal training, Life imprisonment, Probation, Suspended sentence and so on—are explained under separate headings. Defences which apply to a number of charges—for instance, Insanity and Diminished responsibility—are also listed separately.

Cross-references in capital letters refer to other entries in the A B C.

# ABC of crime and punishment

## ABDUCTION
Both men and women can be charged with abduction, which involves taking a girl or young woman out of the possession or control of her parent or guardian. It is just as much abduction to talk a girl into leaving home as to kidnap her. Even if she is taken away for as little as one night, the charge can be brought.

Abduction falls into five categories, according to the age of the girl and the intention of the abductor.

**1.** Taking away a girl under 16 against the parent's or guardian's wishes. Main offenders in this category are young men who run away with their girlfriends. It also might include a grandfather who takes his granddaughter away from her parents because he thinks they are not looking after her properly or she is being neglected.
PENALTY Up to two years' imprisonment.

**2.** Taking away an unmarried girl under 18 intending her to have sexual intercourse with a man—not necessarily the abductor himself.
PENALTY Up to two years' imprisonment.

**3.** Taking away an heiress under 21. It must be proved that the abductor took her by fraud, intending her to have sexual intercourse with, or to marry, himself or someone else. The offence is virtually obsolete.
PENALTY Up to 14 years' imprisonment.

**4.** Taking a mentally defective woman of any age out of the possession of her parent or guardian without consent, intending her to have sexual intercourse with a man.
PENALTY Up to two years' imprisonment.

**5.** Taking away or detaining a woman or girl of any age against her will, intending her to marry or have sexual intercourse with anyone. It must be proved that she was taken or detained by force with the intention of gaining control of her property.

A parent can be convicted of this offence if, for example, he locks up his own daughter until she agrees to marry a particular man.
PENALTY Up to 14 years' imprisonment.

Anyone who takes away a child aged under 14 may be charged with CHILD STEALING rather than abduction.

## ABORTION
The destruction of an unborn baby by removing it from the mother's body before it can live on its own is illegal unless the operation is performed in strict compliance with the Abortion Act 1967. ☐ Ending a pregnancy, p. 377.

In all other circumstances, an attempt to procure a miscarriage is a crime. Even if the attempted abortion is not successful, or if the woman proves not to be pregnant in the first place, a crime has been committed.

If the woman proves not to be pregnant, she is not guilty; but anyone who tries to cause her to miscarry, believing her to be pregnant, can be prosecuted.

Proceedings under the Offences Against the Person Act 1861 can be taken against a pregnant woman who allows such an operation to be performed upon her, and also against anyone who operates on her; who knowingly supplies any instrument or drug for the purpose of abortion; who administers a drug to a woman to procure a miscarriage; or who puts a pregnant woman in touch with an abortionist.
PENALTY Any period of imprisonment.

If a woman dies as the result of an unlawful abortion, everyone concerned can be charged with MANSLAUGHTER.

If a baby is killed during its birth, but before it has an independent existence, the person responsible may be guilty of the offence of CHILD DESTRUCTION.

## ABSTRACTING ELECTRICITY
Dishonestly using electricity or causing it to be wasted is an offence. For example, anyone who uses a piece of cable to bypass a meter is liable to prosecution. Similarly, the employee with a grudge against his firm who leaves the lights on so that his employers will have to pay a big electricity bill can be charged with this offence.
PENALTY Up to five years' imprisonment.

Anyone using a public telephone or Telex system intending to avoid payment is charged with a separate offence.
PENALTY Up to two years' imprisonment.

## ABUSIVE WORDS OR BEHAVIOUR
See: BREACH OF THE PEACE.

## AFFRAY
When fighting takes place that might reasonably frighten or intimidate other people, those taking part may be charged with causing an affray. The charge is normally brought where

the fighting includes a number of people—usually gangs of youths in a street, a dance hall, a club or a public house.

PENALTY Any period of imprisonment.

When the fighting is not serious enough to amount to an affray, defendants may be charged only with ASSAULT or with using threatening or INSULTING BEHAVIOUR.

## AIDING AND ABETTING

Anyone who helps an offender to commit a crime is himself guilty of the same offence, and is liable to the same punishment. The chief offender is known as the principal, and the person who helps him is the accessory, accomplice, or aider and abettor (there is no legal difference between these terms).

The accessory is guilty if he gives any encouragement or assistance to the principal, knowing what kind of crime is intended, and the principal actually commits the crime. Anyone who unsuccessfully urges someone to break the law may be guilty of INCITEMENT.

An individual may also be guilty as an accessory if he lends a car to commit a robbery; provides vital information, such as the time when wages will be delivered to a factory; leaves a door unlocked for a burglar; or helps to hold a victim during an assault.

The accessory can be charged only in connection with crimes which he knew the principal intended to commit. If he lent his car to a friend in the belief that he wanted it to go for a drive in the country, and the friend then used the car for the purpose of robbery, the car-owner would not be guilty of aiding and abetting the robbery.

The accessory gives his help or encouragement *before* or *during* the commission of a crime. Help given later may lead to a charge of obstructing the police. □ The police and the public, p. 736.

PENALTY The same as for the main offender.

## ANIMALS, CRUELTY TO □ Cruelty to animals, p. 288.

## ARSON See: CRIMINAL DAMAGE.

## ASSAULT AND BATTERY

Strictly speaking, an assault is a threat to use force, and a battery is the actual use of force. In most cases, however, the accused is charged simply with assault, which covers both.

There can be assault without battery, however, or battery without assault. For example, it is an assault to point a gun—whether it is loaded or not—or to make a threatening gesture with a knife or fist, even if there is no actual intention to shoot or strike, provided there is an intention to frighten the victim.

Battery is usually the culmination of an assault—a victim sees a blow coming before it hits him. But battery can exist by itself: for example, if the victim is struck from behind without warning.

There are many situations in which the use of force is permitted by the law. A parent or schoolteacher can punish a child, provided the punishment is moderate. □ Looking after children, p. 342.

Anyone can use reasonable force in self-defence, or to prevent a crime.

▶ BOYS FOUGHT POLICE—BY MISTAKE *Ian Kenlin, aged 14, and his friend David Sowoolu, both Rugby players, set out one evening to remind their team-mates about a match. They went from house to house, knocking on doors.*

*Two plain-clothes police officers saw them and suspected that they were looking for an empty house to burgle. When the police approached the boys to question them, the boys mistook them for thugs and fought them off. The boys were charged with assaulting the police officers.*

DECISION *The boys were acquitted. The Appeal Court found, among other things, that the boys genuinely believed they were being attacked unlawfully, and had used reasonable force in self-defence. (Kenlin v. Gardner.)* ◀

Only 'reasonable' force is permitted by law, and even then someone who is threatened is expected to try to protect himself nonviolently before resorting to force—by running away, for instance, or by making it clear that he is not looking for a fight.

Provocation can be accepted as a defence to only one charge—murder. In other cases, it is a mitigating factor.

In sport, especially in such games as boxing, wrestling and Rugby, the use of force is made lawful by the implicit consent of the person to whom it is applied. But violence which is outside the rules of the game could amount to assault and battery. Thus, a deliberate, aimed kick at a Rugby player not in possession of the ball would be against the law. □ Accidents at sporting events, p. 131.

As well as common assault, there are a number of more serious offences—assault with intent to rape; assault occasioning actual bodily harm; and assault on a police officer in the execution of his duty.

PENALTY For common assault: up to one year's imprisonment. For assault with intent to rape: up to seven years' imprisonment. For assault occasioning actual bodily harm: up to five years' imprisonment. For assault on a police officer in the course of his duty: up to two years' imprisonment.

## ASSEMBLY, UNLAWFUL
There are three main offences involving public disorder. Unlawful assembly is one of them; the other two are rout and riot.

Traditionally, unlawful assembly is defined as a gathering of three or more people with the common purpose of committing a crime involving violence, or of behaving in such a way as to cause a breach of the peace. It becomes a rout when the assembly moves off to put its plan into action, and it becomes a riot when the action begins.

A violent demonstration in support of a cause may be an unlawful assembly, in spite of the sincerity of the demonstrators.

➤ THE SIT-IN THAT LED TO PRISON *Three demonstrators took over the Greek Embassy in London in 1967, as a protest against the Greek military regime. They were charged with unlawful assembly.*
DECISION *They were sent to prison for periods of between 6 and 15 months, even though the court recognised that they sincerely believed in their cause. (R. v. Foley.)*◄

On the other hand, a purely non-violent demonstration which was not deliberately provocative would be unlikely to be considered an unlawful assembly—even if outsiders reacted violently to it.
PENALTY Any period of imprisonment.

## ATTEMPTING TO COMMIT CRIME
An attempt to commit a crime, even if it does not succeed, carries the same penalty as a successfully completed crime.

Before a man can be convicted of attempting to commit a crime, it must be proved that he intended to commit the completed crime, and that he had made a serious effort to do so.

It must also be proved that the intention behind the attempt was a criminal one. In many cases, there is no direct evidence on this point and courts have to draw their conclusions from the circumstances.

➤ THE ELECTRICIAN'S BOOBY TRAP *Arthur Whybrow, a labourer with an electrical company, connected the bathroom light socket to a soap dish on the side of his wife's bath. He was charged with attempting to murder his wife. The*

*prosecution claimed that he intended to electrocute her. Mr Whybrow said that he had merely intended to give her a shock, to show her who was master in his house.*
DECISION *He was convicted and sentenced to ten years' imprisonment. The Appeal Court held that there was an obvious intention to murder his wife. (R. v. Whybrow.)*◄

## AUTOMATISM
It is a defence against a criminal charge for the accused to claim that he was in a state of mind where he was unaware of his actions—for example, that he was sleep-walking or suffering from concussion.

This behaviour is known as automatism or involuntary conduct. If the plea of automatism is accepted, the accused is acquitted.

➤ THE GIRL WHO DIED IN THE NIGHT *In 1961, United States Air Force Sergeant Boshears, who was stationed in Great Britain, allowed a girl to spend the night in his flat. In the morning he was shocked to find that she was dead. He was tried for murder.*

*Sergeant Boshears said that he and the girl went to sleep and when he woke up his hands were round her throat. He claimed that he did not know how she had died. The trial judge told the jurors that if they thought that Sergeant Boshears had strangled the girl while he was asleep it was not a voluntary act and he was entitled to be acquitted.*
DECISION *The jury found Sergeant Boshears not guilty. (R. v. Boshears.)*◄

**BATTERY** See: ASSAULT AND BATTERY.

## BEGGING
Anyone who begs in a street or public place is liable to be convicted as an 'idle and disorderly person' under the Vagrancy Act 1824. But no offence is committed by people conducting properly licensed street or house-to-house collections with a police permit.
PENALTY Up to one month's imprisonment, or a fine of between £1 and £5.

## BETTING OFFENCES ☐ Betting and gaming, p. 660.

## BIGAMY
A man or woman who marries while a previous marriage is still in existence commits bigamy. Someone who has been married can remarry only in one of five circumstances. These are:
**1.** If the original marriage has been brought to an end by a divorce (decree absolute).

**2.** If the original marriage has been annulled.

**3.** If the first partner is dead.

**4.** If the original marriage was never legally binding—for instance, if one of the partners was already married at the time.

**5.** If the first partner has been continually absent for seven years and there has been no evidence to show that he or she is still alive.

It is a defence for the accused honestly to believe, on reasonable grounds, that he or she was entitled to remarry.

➤ HUSBAND CAME BACK FROM THE DEAD
*In 1881, Martha Ann Tolson was deserted by her husband. The last she heard of him was that the ship in which he had been sailing to America had been lost at sea with all hands.*

*A few years later, she married again. Her first husband, to whom she was still legally married, reappeared and she was charged with bigamy.* DECISION *She was found not guilty because she honestly and reasonably believed that her husband was dead. (R. v. Tolson.)* ◄

Similarly, a person who remarries because he honestly believes that the first marriage is void, or has been terminated, is not guilty. The second marriage, however, is invalid.

PENALTY Up to seven years' imprisonment.

## BINDING OVER
When someone is bound over by a court, he agrees to pay a sum of money to the Crown if he breaks the law at some future time. This is also called 'entering into a recognisance'. No money is deposited at the time of binding over.

To be bound over, a person need not have been convicted of a criminal offence. Courts can bind over anyone whom they fear might break the law or cause a breach of the peace.

No one can be bound over unless he agrees; but if he refuses, he can be imprisoned for up to six months. He can appeal to the Crown Court against the order requiring him to be bound over, or against the penalty imposed.

## BIRDS: KILLING PROTECTED BIRDS
☐ When birds must not be killed, p. 139.

## BLACKMAIL
A blackmailer is somebody who makes an unjustified demand with menaces. He does it for gain or to cause loss to another—to obtain money, for instance, or to get someone sacked.

A demand with menaces which does not involve gain or loss—a demand that someone resigns as a councillor, for example—is not blackmail, although in some circumstances it

may constitute another offence such as corruption or even BRIBERY.

Blackmail is committed the moment that the demand is made, irrespective of whether or not the victim yields to it. It is considered such a serious crime that the police go to considerable lengths to ensure that the victim's name is not disclosed during a trial.

It is not blackmail to make a demand with menaces if a person thinks that he has reasonable grounds for making the demand and if the menaces are a proper method of reinforcing it. For example, it would be lawful for someone to say: 'If you don't pay me the money you owe me by the end of the week, I will take you to court.'

It would, however, be blackmail if a shopkeeper said: 'Pay your bill or I will tell your husband you have been unfaithful to him.' The demand might be justified, but this would not be a proper way of reinforcing it. It would also be blackmail if a shopkeeper threatened to sue someone for a debt that he knew had already been paid. In this case, the demand would be unjustified, even though the means of enforcing it are reasonable.

Obtaining money by violence or by intimidation, which is known as extortion, is also a form of blackmail.

PENALTY Up to 14 years' imprisonment.

## BLASPHEMY
Anyone who attacks the doctrine of the Church of England (but not any other church), denies the truth of the Bible or the Book of Common Prayer or says that God does not exist, is technically guilty of blasphemy. In practice, the charge is obsolete.

Nonetheless, a person who disturbs a church service, or who uses offensive or provocative language against people going into church, might well find himself in the magistrates' court. The charge, however, would be that of INSULTING BEHAVIOUR or disturbing a religious service rather than of blasphemy. This charge applies to the disturbance of a religious service of any denomination, provided it takes place in a building registered as a place of worship.

➤ WHEN CHURCH DEMONSTRATORS WERE
JAILED *In 1966, a demonstration against the British Government's support of American policy in Vietnam took place in a Methodist church in Brighton, when the Labour Party Conference was being held in the town. As Mr George Brown, then Foreign Secretary, was reading the lesson, Mr Nicholas Walter*

*shouted out: 'Oh, you hypocrite, how can you use the word of God to justify your policies!' There were further interruptions which prevented Mr Harold Wilson, then Prime Minister, from reading the second lesson.*

*Mr Walter, and a number of people who took part in the demonstration, were charged with 'indecent behaviour during divine service'.*

DECISION *Mr Walter was found guilty and jailed for two months. His appeal was dismissed because it was held that the offence covered any kind of behaviour which tended to cause a disturbance in a place of public worship. (Abrahams and others v. Cavey.)*◄

PENALTY For blasphemy: any period of imprisonment or fine. For disrupting a religious service: up to two months' imprisonment or a fine of up to £20.

## BORSTAL TRAINING
Any young man over the age of 15 and under 21 who commits an offence for which he could be sent to prison can instead be sentenced to Borstal training—a programme of vocational or educational training under careful supervision at a Borstal institution. The word 'Borstal' refers to the village in Kent where this training was first carried out in 1908.

Although most youths sentenced to Borstal training have committed fairly serious offences —such as housebreaking or taking away a vehicle—the sentence can be imposed for any offence punishable with imprisonment. Only Crown Courts can order Borstal training. If the offender is convicted by a magistrates' court, he may be sent to a Crown Court for the sentence to be imposed.

A youth sentenced to Borstal training may spend a short period waiting in prison. Then he is sent to a Borstal Reception Centre, where his needs and capabilities are assessed. He is then sent to the institution which best fits his needs.

A youth remains in an institution for at least six months, and may be kept there for as long as two years; most stay about 12 months. When the Borstal authorities decide that he has reached a satisfactory point in his progress, the youth is released on licence. This means that he is allowed to leave the institution, but that he is under the supervision of a probation officer.

## BREACH OF THE PEACE
Though the law gives no precise definition, most lawyers would agree that the term 'breach of the peace' includes assaults or woundings, affrays or riots, robberies, and sexual offences involving violence.

It could also be argued that a group of rowdy football supporters would be breaking the peace if they annoyed other train passengers on their way home from a match, or if they damaged other people's property.

In some towns, there is a local Act of Parliament under which there are penalties for those who *disturb* the peace.

If someone is charged with using insulting, abusive or threatening words or behaviour, the prosecution must prove that these words or actions led (or were intended to lead) to a breach of the peace. The words or actions must be shown to have either provoked the insulted person to retaliate, or incited a crowd to behave violently.

Courts frequently BIND OVER anyone who commits a breach of the peace.

## BRIBERY
Anyone who offers any gift or consideration in order to induce someone to show favour in relation to his employer's business is guilty of an offence, and so is the employee if he asks for or accepts the bribe.

PENALTY Up to two years' imprisonment (seven years if the bribe was made to gain business or a favour where any Government contract is involved).

## BROTHELS See: PROSTITUTION

## BURGLARY
Entering a house or shop without permission, intending to steal, is the most common form of burglary. But burglary is also committed by anyone who enters any kind of building without permission intending to steal, to rape, to inflict grievous bodily harm or to cause unlawful damage.

The *intention* of committing one or more of these crimes in the building is all that the prosecution needs to prove; it does not matter whether or not the crime is actually completed. If the accused in fact commits theft or grievous bodily harm, the prosecution does not have to prove that he intended to commit the crime at the time he entered. The building does not necessarily have to be a permanent one, such as a house. It can also be a houseboat or caravan.

A person is guilty of burglary, too, if he goes from one part of a building in which he is permitted to be, to another part where he has no right to be, intending to commit one of the four crimes (theft, grievous bodily harm, rape or unlawful damage). So the workman, authorised to be on the factory floor, who then goes into the factory stores without permission and steals some materials or equipment commits burglary as distinct from theft.

PENALTY Up to 14 years' imprisonment.

If the offender has with him at the time of the crime a gun, imitation gun, explosives or any kind of offensive weapon, the offence is called aggravated burglary.

PENALTY Any period of imprisonment.

## CARNAL KNOWLEDGE See: ILLEGAL INTERCOURSE

## CHILD DESTRUCTION

Anyone who wilfully causes a child which is capable of being born alive to die before it has an independent existence is guilty of the offence of child destruction.

PENALTY Life imprisonment.

## CHILDREN, NEGLECT

Anyone of 16 and over who is in charge of a child of under 16 is guilty of an offence if he assaults, ill-treats, abandons, neglects or exposes the child in a manner likely to cause unnecessary suffering or injury. This includes mental as well as physical injury.

To prove the offence, it is not necessary to show that the child was injured or actually suffered; it is sufficient if the conduct of the person in charge was likely to *lead* to injury or suffering to the child.

Neglecting a child includes failing to provide food, clothing or medical attention. It is no defence for the parents to plead that they could not afford the things the child needed if in fact they had failed to apply for supplementary benefits.

Abandoning a child includes leaving a child to fend for itself in circumstances where suffering or injury is likely to occur.

➤ THE BABY INSIDE THE PARCEL *In 1869, Mary Falkingham put her five-week-old illegitimate child into a hamper, carefully wrapped up, and sent him as a parcel by rail to the man she claimed was the father. The baby arrived safely about an hour later, but Miss Falkingham was charged with abandoning him.* DECISION *Miss Falkingham was found guilty. (R. v. Falkingham.)* ◄

Ill-treatment of children could include excessive punishment, keeping a child awake too long, or even something like making a child wear shoes that are far too small. Anyone who assaults a child in his or her care can be charged not only with the offence of neglect, but also with other offences such as assault and causing bodily harm.

While the courts deal severely with those who callously ill-treat or assault their children, cases of inadequacy on the part of the parent, rather than viciousness, may be treated sympathetically.

PENALTY Up to two years' imprisonment.

## CHILD STEALING

Anyone who takes away a baby may be charged with child stealing. The charge covers the abduction without lawful authority of any child under 14.

A child's mother cannot be charged with this offence. Neither can the father, even if the child is illegitimate. The charge cannot be brought against anyone claiming to be lawfully entitled to possession of the child.

PENALTY Up to seven years' imprisonment.

## COMMUNITY SERVICE

Anyone aged 17 or over who is convicted of an offence punishable with imprisonment can instead be ordered to perform unpaid community work for between 40 and 240 hours. Such an order can be made only if the offender consents. Failure to obey the order can be penalised with a fine of up to £50.

## CONSPIRACY

Two or more people who plan to commit a crime can be charged with conspiracy, as well as with attempting to commit, or committing the crime itself. A group of men who plan a robbery, for example, are guilty of conspiracy to rob, whether or not the robbery actually takes place.

Certain conspiracy offences are specifically laid down by law—conspiracy to murder, to cause an explosion or to pervert the course of justice (by trying to bribe or intimidate a juryman, for example).

But the offence can be extended to new kinds of behaviour. In 1961, a man who published a directory of prostitutes was convicted of conspiracy to corrupt public morals—a new conspiracy offence.

Sometimes two or more people may commit the crime of conspiracy by agreeing to do something which would not be illegal if one of them did it alone. A single individual who spreads false rumours to push up share prices commits no offence; but if a group of people agree to do the same thing they are guilty of conspiracy to defraud.

In law, a man and wife alone cannot commit conspiracy; it becomes conspiracy only if a third person is involved in the agreement.

PENALTY Any fine or term of imprisonment.

## CORRUPTION See : BRIBERY

## CRIMINAL BANKRUPTCY

Anyone convicted of causing loss or damage to property of more than £15,000 can be made criminally bankrupt. This places him under the same restrictions as a normal bankrupt.

☐ What it means to be bankrupt, p. 581.

Only the Director of Public Prosecutions, acting as Official Petitioner, can apply for an offender to be declared criminally bankrupt. The petition is heard by a Crown Court.

If granted, the bankruptcy order names those who have suffered loss or damage to property, and the sums they have lost. Anyone named is entitled to claim that amount in bankruptcy proceedings, but his claim has to take its place with those of other creditors.

☐ Debts and bankruptcy, p. 580.

## CRIMINAL DAMAGE

Destroying or damaging someone else's property intentionally, or with a reckless disregard for the consequences of one's actions, is a criminal offence, however the damage is caused. The offence includes the old crime of arson (damaging buildings by fire).

Anyone convicted of causing criminal damage may be ordered to pay compensation as well as being punished for the offence.

It is also a crime for an individual to damage or destroy his own property if someone else has a legal interest in it. For example, the owner of a house mortgaged to a building society might be guilty if he knocks down the house without first obtaining the society's permission.

PENALTY For damaging someone else's property: up to ten years imprisonment. For damaging property intending to endanger life : any term of imprisonment.

## CRIMINAL DECEPTION

The crime which used to be called 'false pretences' is now known as 'criminal deception'. It involves deception in dishonestly obtaining property with the intention of permanently depriving the owner of it.

In some cases, the deception is verbal. For example, a window cleaner who falsely claims that he has cleaned the windows while the householder was out, and asks for payment, can be charged with the offence.

Criminal deception can also be by conduct. It is committed, for example, by the shopper who obtains goods and writes out a cheque which he knows the bank will not honour.

To be convicted, the defendant accused of criminal deception must have deceived or intended to deceive his victim about an existing fact, or about something in the past. He is not guilty if he states an opinion about the future, as opposed to an intention, even if he knows that his prediction cannot come true. So the stockbroker who persuades a customer to buy shares by falsely claiming that there is a possibility of a take-over bid is not guilty.

On the other hand, the builder who successfully advises a widow to have expensive and unnecessary repairs carried out by saying that, unless the repairs are done, her roof is likely to collapse in a high wind, is guilty of deception. This is because his statement, although on the face of it relating to the future, implies that the roof is in a dangerous condition at the present time.

Even where the statements which mislead the victim are not positively known to be false, the offence is committed if the accused suspects them of being untrue. A man who sells goods which he suspects have been stolen, and does not tell the buyer of his suspicions, is guilty of obtaining money by deception.

It is not enough for the prosecution to prove that a false statement was made after which money or property was obtained. It must be proved that the deception was the cause of the property changing hands, or at least that it was a material factor in persuading the victim to hand over the property.

➤ THE BOGUS BEGGING LETTER *In 1870, Henry Hensler sent a letter to a casual acquaintance called John Hutton saying that he was a 'poor widow', and asking for money. Mr Hutton realised the letter was a fraud, but sent Mr Hensler 5s. so that he could be prosecuted.*

DECISION *It was held that, although Mr Hensler had made a false statement with a dishonest intention, he could not be charged with obtaining money by false pretences because the deception had not been the cause of obtaining the money. He was, however, convicted of attempting to commit the main offence—a decision that would still be valid today. (R. v. Hensler.)* ◄

A dishonest salesman may make a whole series of statements about the product he is selling. Provided that the prosecution can find at least *one* false statement of existing fact or intention which has influenced the buyer to make a purchase, the salesman can be convicted of deception.

Suppose, for instance, that a central-heating salesman offers a householder a cut-price system because he says his company wants a show house in the area to which it can bring potential customers. As an extra inducement, the salesman might say that the householder will be paid £2 each time he allows his central-heating system to be viewed by a visitor.

Suppose, too, that the salesman claims that the system he is offering has certain operating and cost advantages over other systems; and that the householder is convinced by all these claims, and puts down a deposit.

The salesman's description of the merits of the system may well be true, and his claim that the price he is offering is a specially good one is probably a matter of opinion. But if the prosecution can prove that his stories about a show house and a viewing fee are false, and that it was partly because of them that the householder agreed to buy the central-heating system, then the salesman will be guilty.

The charge of criminal deception can be brought only in cases where *property* is involved. A separate offence—obtaining a pecuniary advantage by deception—covers offences such as evading payment of a charge, or giving false information to defer a debt.
PENALTY For criminal deception: up to ten years' imprisonment. For obtaining a pecuniary advantage by deception: up to five years' imprisonment.

## CRUELTY TO ANIMALS ☐ p. 288.

## CRUELTY TO CHILDREN See: CHILD-REN, NEGLECT

## DANGEROUS DRIVING, CAUSING DEATH BY ☐ Death on the road, p. 99.

## DETENTION CENTRES
Offenders under 21 can be sent for short-term training to detention centres. These centres are for boys who do not need BORSTAL TRAINING. The maximum period of detention is six months. An offender under 17 cannot be sentenced to more than three months' detention for any one offence.

## DIMINISHED RESPONSIBILITY
The defence of diminished responsibility can be pleaded only when the charge is murder. The accused must satisfy the jury that he

was suffering from an abnormality of mind which impaired his mental responsibility at the time of the killing. Abnormality of mind includes a wide variety of conditions such as arrested or retarded development, or abnormality caused or induced by disease or injury.

If the defence is successful, the accused is convicted of MANSLAUGHTER, instead of murder, and sentenced in the ordinary way.

## DISCHARGE
A magistrate or judge has the discretion to free an offender unconditionally without punishment. This is known as an absolute discharge, and the offender is treated as if he had never been convicted. Alternatively, the offender may be freed without penalty, but told that if he is convicted within a given period (between one and three years), he will be sentenced for both the fresh and the original offence. This is known as a conditional discharge.

If the offender does not commit any further offence during the period of the conditional discharge, no conviction is recorded. No other penalty (except disqualification from driving for a 'totting-up' offence) can be imposed. ☐ Penalties for motoring offenders, p. 173.

## DRINK AND DRUGS
Anyone accused of a criminal offence has only a limited defence if he claims that he was drunk or under the influence of drugs. He will not be acquitted simply because he claims that he gave way to a temptation that he would normally have resisted. He must show that he was so drunk or drugged that he did not realise what he was doing, or could not possibly have formed the intention of committing the crime.

Such a defence is only effective against a charge which requires an intention to be proved—such as murder—not against one where the intention is immaterial (manslaughter, for example).

➤ THE DRUG EXPERIMENT WHICH ENDED IN DEATH *In 1967, an American, Robert Lipman, and his French girlfriend, Claudie Delbarre, experimented with the drug LSD in a London hotel room. Recovering from the effects of the drug, Mr Lipman found that his girlfriend had been killed. He returned to the United States, but was subsequently extradited to England to be tried for her murder.*

*Mr Lipman's defence was that, although he might have killed her, he could have done so only under the influence of LSD. The jury were told that if they accepted Mr Lipman's story, they should acquit him of murder, as he did not intend to kill her. However, they were told that they could convict him of manslaughter, as that crime did not require intention.*

DECISION *Mr Lipman was convicted of manslaughter and sentenced to six years' imprisonment. (R. v. Lipman.)*◄

## DRUG OFFENCES

The use and possession of 'controlled' drugs, such as amphetamines, cannabis, heroin, LSD, methadone, morphine, opium and pethidine, is restricted by law.

It is an offence for anyone—without lawful authority—to produce a controlled drug; to supply or offer to supply such a drug to another person; to possess a controlled drug; or to have a controlled drug with the intention of supplying it to another. Anyone who allows premises to be used for producing or supplying the drug is also guilty.

Some offences involve specific drugs. For example, it is an offence to grow cannabis, or to let premises be used for smoking it.

These regulations do not apply to someone who has a drug prescribed by a doctor; or to a manufacturer. Anyone charged with unlawful possession of a drug has a defence if he took it to prevent someone else committing an offence.

PENALTY Controlled drugs are graded into classes A, B and C, and penalties vary. For possession of class A drugs, such as heroin: up to seven years' imprisonment; for possession of a class B drug, such as cannabis: up to five years; for possession of a class C drug, such as an amphetamine: up to two years.

For supplying, or possessing with intent to supply, class A or B drugs, up to 14 years' imprisonment; for class C drugs, up to five years' imprisonment.

## EMBRACERY

Anyone who tries to influence a member of a jury by threats, bribery or persuasion is guilty of the crime of embracery.

PENALTY Any fine or term of imprisonment. If more than one person is involved, the people concerned may be guilty of conspiring to PERVERT THE COURSE OF JUSTICE.

## EXPLOSIVES

Anybody using explosives to injure people or damage property faces extremely heavy penalties. In fact, anybody found in posses-

sion of explosives may have to explain why they have it, and can be prosecuted unless they have a lawful reason.

It is a crime to do anything with intent to injure people or damage property and this includes attempting, conspiring or helping anyone else to cause explosions. It is also an offence to make explosives or have them in your possession with intent to do harm.

The law is more severe where human life is endangered or serious damage to property intended—whether the damage is done or not.

If the Attorney-General thinks a crime involving explosives has been committed, he can order an inquiry by a magistrate, and witnesses must attend.

PENALTY Up to 20 years' imprisonment on the lesser charges. Where life or serious damage is involved, the maximum penalty is life imprisonment.

## EXTORTION See: BLACKMAIL

## FALSE ALARMS

Anyone who deliberately misleads the police by giving untrue information is guilty of causing wasteful employment of the police.

It is an offence to give false information in connection with an inquiry which the police are making. It is also an offence to send a false or annoying message—for example, to give a false alarm to a fire department.

A defendant need not have made the false report directly to the police: it would be an offence to tell a mother that her child has been seen getting into a stranger's car, if police waste time seeking a child who is not missing.

But a person who passes information to the police in good faith cannot be convicted of giving a false alarm.

PENALTY Up to six months' imprisonment, or a fine of up to £200.

Penalties are much more severe in cases where someone deliberately misleads the police in their investigations and is found guilty of OBSTRUCTING THE POLICE.

## FALSE PRETENCES See: CRIMINAL DECEPTION

## FIGHTING IN PUBLIC See: AFFRAY

## FIREARMS OFFENCES ☐ Hunting, shooting and fishing, p. 137.

## FORGERY

Making a false document—a bank note, cheque, bank book or receipt, for example—is forgery. It is also forgery to falsify any kind of document, including examination certificates, references for jobs and prescriptions for medicines. It must be proved, however, that the document was forged with the intention to deceive or defraud.

In the case of official documents—applications for Social Security benefits or rate rebates, for example—an intention to deceive is sufficient for a successful prosecution.

Even though a forged document may not subsequently be used, it is an offence to forge it with the intention of deceiving or defrauding. It is illegal, too, to use a document forged by somebody else with the intention of deceiving and defrauding. In this case, the offence is 'uttering a forged document'.
PENALTY Anything from a prison sentence of up to two years to life imprisonment.

## FRAUD See: CRIMINAL DECEPTION

## GOING EQUIPPED FOR CRIME
It is an offence for a person to have in his possession (except at his home) any article for use in the course of or in connection with burglary, theft or fraud.

The offence covers possession of: any housebreaking implement, such as hammers, screwdrivers, or even a pair of plimsolls carried by a cat burglar; any device used for stealing, such as a shoplifter's coat, or car duplicate keys; the props of a confidence trickster; or a cheque book for the issuing of dud cheques.

To succeed, the prosecution must show that the accused intended to use the items 'in the course of or in connection with' burglary, theft or fraud.

The prosecution usually proves intention by showing that the accused was clearly engaged on a criminal expedition.
PENALTY Up to three years' imprisonment.

## GRIEVOUS BODILY HARM, CAUSING
See: WOUNDING

## GUN OFFENCES ☐ Hunting, shooting and fishing, p. 137.

## HANDLING STOLEN GOODS
'Handling' is the new name for a crime which for centuries was known as receiving. Three things must be proved before a person can be convicted of handling stolen goods: first, that the goods were stolen; second, that the handler knew, or believed, they were stolen; and third, that he acted dishonestly.

The expression 'stolen goods' applies not only to goods stolen in the normal sense, but also to those obtained by blackmail or criminal deception, and those stolen abroad. If stolen goods pass through the hands of several people and are then sold cheaply all concerned can be charged.

It is always difficult for the prosecution to prove that the handler knew that the goods were stolen. But it can sometimes be proved that he bought them at such a cheap price that he must have known that they had been obtained illegally.

A charge of handling stolen goods will be dismissed if the accused can show that he intended to return the goods to their true owner or hand them over to the police. The charge will also fail if the accused was legally entitled to the goods.

Anyone who is proved to have taken possession of stolen goods, or arranged or assisted in the removal or disposal of them, is guilty of handling them.

It is not enough for the prosecution to prove that the thief talked over the price at which they were to change hands with the man accused of handling them. The handler must have taken possession of them.

The accused is guilty of handling even if he never sees the goods concerned, but merely allows them to be kept in his premises overnight or finds a possible buyer.
PENALTY Up to ten years' imprisonment.

## HOMICIDE See: MURDER; MANSLAUGHTER; INFANTICIDE; ☐ Causing death on the road, p. 99.

## HOUSEBREAKING IMPLEMENTS
See: GOING EQUIPPED FOR CRIME

## ILLEGAL INTERCOURSE
A man who has sexual intercourse with a girl under the age of 13 is guilty of an offence—whether or not she consents and whether or not he knows her age. It is also illegal to have intercourse with a girl under 16, but here there are limited grounds for defence. Generally, it is no defence for a man to say that he honestly believed the girl to have been over the age of 16.

But this could be a defence only in the case of a man aged under 24 who has never previously been charged with an offence of this kind and who can prove that he had reasonable grounds for believing that the girl was over 16.

A man of any age can defend himself against a charge of illegal intercourse on the ground that he has gone through a ceremony of marriage with a girl under 16 and believes that she is his legal wife;

the marriage itself would normally be regarded as invalid.

PENALTY For intercourse with a girl under 13: up to life imprisonment. With a girl under 16: up to two years' imprisonment.

## INCEST

Sexual intercourse between near blood relatives constitutes the crime of incest. The law is specific about these prohibited relationships. A man is not allowed to have intercourse with a woman he knows to be his mother, sister, daughter or grand-daughter. A woman must not have intercourse with a man whom she knows to be her father, brother, son or grandfather.

Only a woman of 16 or over can be charged with incest; a girl under 16 would probably be brought before a court as being in need of care and protection. □ Children in trouble, p. 356.

The law on incest applies to half-brothers and sisters, to illegitimate children and to relationships traced through illegitimacy.

Apart from being charged with incest, a father who has intercourse with his daughter can be convicted of RAPE if the girl does not consent, and ILLEGAL INTERCOURSE if the child is under the age of 13.

The law presumes that a boy under 14 is incapable of sexual intercourse; he cannot be convicted of incest. Under the same rule, a woman can be convicted only of indecency—not incest—with a boy under 14.

PENALTY For offences committed by a man: with a girl under 13, any term of imprisonment; otherwise up to seven years' imprisonment. For offences committed by a woman: up to seven years' imprisonment.

## INCITEMENT TO COMMIT A CRIME

Anyone who encourages someone else to commit a crime is guilty of incitement—whether or not the person he approaches commits or tries to commit the offence.

PENALTY Any fine or term of imprisonment.

## INDECENT BEHAVIOUR

People acting indecently can be charged with one or more of five offences: indecent assault, indecency with children, gross indecency between males, unnatural offences and indecent exposure.

Assault accompanied by indecency can be committed by either a man or a woman. It is not indecent assault to fondle a woman

over the age of 16 with her consent, but the law does not recognise the validity of such consent by people below that age. Consent by a person over 16 is no defence where the assault is likely to cause serious bodily harm.

PENALTY When the victim is a girl under 13, the maximum imprisonment is five years; for females 13 and over, two years. Where the victim is a man or boy: up to ten years.

A man or woman commits an offence by performing an act of gross indecency with, or towards, a boy or girl under 14, or inciting a child under 14 to perform such an act.

PENALTY Up to two years' imprisonment.

Although the law has never given a precise definition of gross indecency, it covers most forms of sexual behaviour between males. The prosecution must prove that the act involved at least two men (or boys).

The offence can be committed in private or in public. If it is done in private, it is not an offence if both men consent and are 21 or over, and if no one else is present.

PENALTY Up to two years' imprisonment.

Two different kinds of sexual offences can be classed as unnatural offences: intercourse with an animal (bestiality) and anal intercourse with a human being (sodomy).

When the act of sodomy involves two men, no offence is committed if it is done in private and both are over 21 and consent.

There is no defence to proof of unnatural intercourse between a man and a woman—even if they are husband and wife and the act takes place in private and with consent.

PENALTY Any term of imprisonment, including life imprisonment.

The most serious charge that can be brought for indecent exposure is that of outraging public decency. The act must have taken place in such circumstances that it could have disgusted and annoyed at least two people.

The charge of outraging public decency is usually reserved for cases in which there is some kind of sexual behaviour in public.

A lesser charge is that of a man 'wilfully, openly, lewdly and obscenely exposing his person with intent to insult a female'.

PENALTY For exposing the person (Vagrancy Act 1824): up to three months' imprisonment or a £25 fine for a first offence; up to a year for a subsequent offence. For outraging public decency: any term of imprisonment.

## INFANTICIDE

A woman who causes the death of her child under the age of 12 months is unlikely to be guilty of murder. She will be charged with infanticide if, at the time of the death, the balance of her mind was disturbed by the effects of childbirth or of lactation (producing milk) after the birth.

If a mother, depressed or disturbed by the demands of looking after her new baby, kills another of her children—even though the child is under the age of 12 months—she would be charged with murder. She could, however, plead diminished responsibility in her defence.

PENALTY Any term of imprisonment, including life. In many cases the court puts the woman on probation and orders her to undergo treatment in hospital.

## INSANITY

Rules about how the law deals with insanity were drawn up more than a hundred years ago, after a sensational political murder.

➤ THE MURDERER WHO WAS MAD *In 1843, Daniel McNaughten, who was suffering from a mental disorder, shot and killed Edward Drummond, private secretary to Sir Robert Peel, then Prime Minister. He was tried for murder.* DECISION *Mr McNaughten was found 'not guilty on grounds of insanity'. (R. v. McNaughten.)*◄

This decision surprised many and led to a major controversy. The House of Lords put a series of questions to all the judges of England on the subject of insanity and the law. Their answers, known as the McNaughten Rules, have since provided a test of insanity. They are:
1. The accused is regarded in law as sane until the contrary is proved.
2. The accused must produce evidence that he was insane at the time of the offence.
3. The accused must convince the court that he did not know the nature of his act, or that he was doing wrong.
4. If the accused is found to have been insane at the time of the offence, then a verdict of 'not guilty on the grounds of insanity' is returned and ·he is detained in a mental hospital for an indefinite period.
The McNaughten Rules can be applied to all offences, but they are rarely used in anything but murder cases.

The question may arise whether or not an accused person is fit to stand trial. If he cannot understand the proceedings and exercise his rights, he cannot be tried. The accused may be suffering from a serious mental disorder, or he may have been insane at the time of the offence, but if he is mentally competent, then he is fit to stand trial.

The accused himself may claim that he is not able to stand trial. A jury—different from the one which may eventually try the case— must decide, on the basis of medical evidence given by psychiatric experts, whether the accused is able to stand trial.

➤ THE MAN WHO SAID HE FORGOT *In 1960 Gunther Podola killed a policeman. During a struggle with the police officers who arrested him, Mr Podola was injured. He claimed at his trial that as a result of his injuries he could not remember the killing. The prosecution argued that, even if Mr Podola's claim was genuine, he understood his rights and was therefore able to stand trial.*
DECISION *The jury decided that Mr Podola's loss of memory was not genuine. He was eventually convicted of murder. (R. v. Podola.)*◄

## INSULTING BEHAVIOUR

A defendant is guilty of insulting behaviour if he uses threatening, abusive or insulting words or behaviour with the intention of provoking a breach of the peace, or if such a breach does actually take place as a result of these actions.

The charge covers written as well as spoken matter, and the words or actions complained of must have occurred in a public place or at a public meeting.

Even if someone does not intend to cause a breach of the peace, he will be guilty of insulting behaviour if his actions are likely to lead to such a breach in the particular circumstances of the occasion.

➤ THE SPEECH THAT PROVOKED AN UP-ROAR *In 1962, Colin Jordan, then leader of the National Socialist movement in Britain, addressed a meeting in Trafalgar Square and used such expressions as: 'Hitler was right; our real enemies, the people we should have fought, were not Hitler but world Jewry and its associates in this country.'*
*The speech led to serious disorder among the crowd and Mr Jordan was sentenced to two months' imprisonment for 'using insulting words whereby a breach of the peace was likely'.*
*Mr Jordan appealed against the conviction, arguing that the people who caused the disorder belonged to an opposing group who had attended the meeting for the sole purpose of causing trouble. He submitted that his speech would not have provoked 'ordinary, reasonable people' to disorderly behaviour.*
DECISION *The court rejected the appeal. It held*

*that on occasions such as the Trafalgar Square meeting a speaker 'must take his audience as he finds them'. (Jordan v. Burgoyne.)*◄

PENALTY Up to 12 months' imprisonment.

## INTIMIDATION, OBTAINING MONEY BY See: BLACKMAIL

## KIDNAPPING See: ABDUCTION

## LARCENY See: THEFT

## LIBEL, CRIMINAL

Any publication, in printing, writing, painting or any other permanent form, which tends to injure anyone's reputation to an extent likely to cause public disorder, may constitute criminal libel. It need not be 'published'—that is, seen by a third person. It is sufficient for the libel to be communicated to the person defamed. ☐ When libel is a crime, p. 669.

## LITTER

Depositing litter in or from any open-air place to which the public has free access is an offence. In sentencing, the court must have regard to the nature of the litter, and any risk of injury to persons or animals or damage to property.
PENALTY Fine up to £100.

## LOTTERIES, ILLEGAL ☐ Betting and gaming, p. 660.

## MANSLAUGHTER

The law divides manslaughter into two categories: voluntary and involuntary. Voluntary manslaughter includes cases in which the killing is deliberate, but where there is some mitigating factor.

In cases of involuntary manslaughter the killing is accidental or unintentional, but as the accused person has acted in an improper manner to cause the death, it cannot be treated as pure accident.

Someone who kills deliberately may be charged with manslaughter rather than murder in three circumstances:
1. Where there is provocation.
2. Where an individual survives a suicide pact.
3. Where the killer is suffering from diminished responsibility.

The law recognises that a man who kills after grave provocation should not be punished as severely as one who kills in cold blood.

But not every kind of provocation will reduce a charge of murder to one of man-slaughter. A jury must be convinced that:
1. The accused lost his or her self-control and acted in the heat of the moment under the immediate influence of the provocation.
2. An ordinary person, subject to the same provocation, would have acted the same way.

It is no crime to commit or attempt suicide; but it *is* an offence to encourage someone else.

Someone who, in good faith, takes part in a suicide pact with a second person but alone survives the attempt is guilty of manslaughter and not of murder—even if he has killed the other person. He must prove his 'settled intention of dying in pursuance of the pact'.

It is still murder, however, to comply with a request from any person to end his life. The law does not allow killing with consent, nor does it recognise mercy-killing or euthanasia.

But a doctor is not guilty of murder if he gives drugs to alleviate pain, even if he knows they may incidentally shorten life.

Even though an individual kills deliberately, he can still be convicted of manslaughter rather than murder if at the time of the killing his mental responsibility was substantially impaired. This provision covers all major forms of mental illness, and can also include severely subnormal intelligence, brain damage, mental deterioration in old people, and the psychopath's irresistible impulse.

►THE MAN WHO LOST CONTROL *In 1959, Patrick Joseph Byrne strangled a girl of 20 in a YWCA hostel in Birmingham. He was charged with murder and pleaded diminished responsibility. It was said that Mr Byrne suffered from perverted sexual desires which he sometimes found impossible to control, and that he had killed because of these impulses.*

*The judge told the jury that this condition could not be considered sufficient grounds for a defence if the killer was normal in every other respect. Mr Byrne was convicted of murder and sentenced to life imprisonment. He appealed.*
DECISION *The Appeal Court ruled that the jury should have been allowed to make its own decision as to whether Mr Byrne's difficulty in exercising control over his physical acts was such as to impair his mental responsibility for the killing. The court ruled that if the jury had been properly directed they would have concluded that Mr Byrne was suffering from diminished responsibility. The conviction was changed to manslaughter, but the sentence remained the same. (R. v. Byrne.)*◄

Obviously, medical evidence is needed before a jury can bring in a manslaughter verdict based on diminished responsibility.

But the ultimate decision rests with the jury, and not with the doctors.

Someone who kills unintentionally may be convicted of involuntary manslaughter if, in causing the death, he did an unlawful act, such as carrying out an illegal ABORTION, which involved a risk of injury.

➤ PLAYING WITH A LOADED GUN *In 1967, Terence Lamb, aged 25, was playing with a five-chamber revolver in which there were two live bullets—neither of them lined up with the firing hammer. He pointed the gun at a friend and pulled the trigger, not realising that in a revolver the chamber revolves before the hammer strikes. Thus a bullet was in the chamber when the hammer hit it, and the friend was killed.*

*At Mr Lamb's trial, the judge told the jury that the pointing of the gun was either an unlawful or negligent act. He said that the jury could convict Mr Lamb for manslaughter on either or both of these two grounds. Mr Lamb was found guilty and jailed for three years. He appealed.*
DECISION *The Appeal Court quashed the conviction. Pointing the gun would have been an unlawful act if Mr Lamb had wished to frighten or harm his friend. But this was not his intention, so the act was not unlawful. (R. v. Lamb.)*◄

PENALTY For manslaughter of any kind: any period of imprisonment.

## MENACES, DEMANDING MONEY WITH See: BLACKMAIL

## MISTAKE AS A DEFENCE
As a general principle no one can be convicted of a serious crime unless he intended to commit it. In legal terms, there must be an element of *mens rea* (guilty mind or intent) before a person can be found guilty.

If he does not know of the circumstances which make his actions criminal, or does not foresee the results of his behaviour, then generally he is not guilty. A man charged with bigamy, for example, is acquitted if he can satisfy the jury that he honestly believed that his first wife was dead, or his first marriage was void from the start, or that there had been a valid divorce.

There are many crimes, however, for which mistake is no defence. Anyone charged with manslaughter by gross negligence, for example, has no defence if he claims that he did not realise his actions could have caused death. Similarly, anyone who uses force without justification against a member of the police force is guilty of assaulting a policeman even if he did not realise that the victim was a policeman.

It is also rarely a defence for a defendant to claim that he did not know that his behaviour was against the law.

## MOTOR VEHICLE OFFENCES ☐ Law on car safety, p. 39; Speeding, p. 84; Drink and driving, p. 87; Dealing with bad driving, p. 96; Causing death on the road, p. 99; Penalties for motoring offenders, p. 173.

## MURDER
Murder is the deliberate killing of a human being or the intentional inflicting of a serious injury which results in death within a year and a day of the fatal wound or act.

Despite modern developments in medical science—people can now be kept alive for long periods in a state of coma—this 'year and a day' rule still applies.

It is sometimes difficult, in a murder case, to decide whether or not death was caused by an action of the accused.

➤ WRONG DRUG FOR A WOUNDED MAN *In 1956, James Clinton Jordan, an American airman, was charged with murdering Walter Beaumont. Mr Jordan was said to have stabbed his victim in a cafe in Hull. Mr Beaumont died eight days later in hospital. Mr Jordan was convicted of murder, and appealed.*
DECISION *The conviction was quashed. In the Appeal Court, medical evidence was produced which suggested that the real cause of Mr Beaumont's death was not the stab wound but the administration by the hospital of an antibiotic drug to which he was allergic. (R. v. Jordan.)*◄

Evidence that a victim received incorrect or inadequate medical treatment is a complete defence to a murder charge only when the medical treatment itself is the principal or sole cause of death.

At one time, a man could be convicted of murder for killing someone accidentally during a crime of violence such as robbery or rape. Today, the prosecution must prove that the accused actually intended to kill, or to inflict serious injury, or realised that if he persisted in his actions, serious injury or death might result. An individual can be convicted of murder even if the person he kills is not the one he intended to kill.

A mother who kills her own baby is sometimes charged with INFANTICIDE.
PENALTY Life imprisonment. In passing

sentence a judge may recommend to the Home Secretary that the offender should not be released for a specific period. This recommendation is *not* binding.

Until 1965, murder was punishable by hanging. In that year, Parliament decided on an experimental five-year suspension of the death penalty. Hanging for murder was abolished in December 1969.

## OBSCENE PUBLICATIONS

It is not illegal merely to possess an obscene book, film, photograph, picture or gramophone record, but it is an offence to publish it, whether for gain or not. In law, publishing has a wide meaning: anyone who gives or lends an obscene book or picture is publishing it; so is anyone who shows an obscene film, even on private premises, or plays an obscene record, or who distributes, sells, hires out or lends something obscene.

It is also illegal to possess an obscene article with the intention of publishing it for gain. In this case, the prosecution does not need to prove that the article was actually published.

Parliament has defined the term 'obscene' in the Obscene Publications Act 1959 by stating that an article is obscene if its effect is to deprave and corrupt persons who are likely to read, see or hear the matter contained or embodied in it. This definition is not limited to erotic materials. The courts have held that a book which appeared to encourage drug-taking might be obscene.

Even if a book or article is obscene, in the sense that it has the tendency to deprave and corrupt, it is a defence for the accused to prove that publication of the article is justified for the public good in the interests of science, literature, art or learning. Expert evidence can be given on this, but not normally on whether or not the article is obscene.

As an alternative to prosecuting, the police can apply to the magistrates for a warrant to seize obscene articles which someone has in his possession for publication for gain. When seized, if the magistrates decide they are obscene, they are destroyed. In these proceedings it is no defence that the article is justified in the public good.

Sending indecent matter through the post is a separate offence. It is no defence to say that its publication is in the public good, and the prosecution need only prove that the article is indecent, as opposed to obscene. The offence of sending obscene matter through the post is also committed by anyone who *causes* the item to be sent; so anyone who knowingly orders indecent books or films by post can also be prosecuted.

In rare cases there may also be prosecutions for conspiracy to corrupt public morals.

PENALTY For publishing an obscene article: up to three years' imprisonment. For possessing an obscene article for gain: up to three years' imprisonment. For sending indecent articles through the post: up to 12 months.

## OBSTRUCTING THE POLICE □ The police and the public, p. 736.

## OFFENSIVE WEAPONS

Anyone who carries an offensive weapon in a public place is breaking the law, unless he can show that he has lawful authority or reasonable excuse to carry it. The weapon may be ready-made, such as a revolver, or an 'adapted' weapon, such as a bicycle chain.

People with lawful authority to carry offensive weapons include soldiers carrying arms on duty, or security guards carrying truncheons while delivering money.

Even if there is a reason for carrying a weapon on some occasions, it is illegal to carry it when the danger is not actually present.

➤ WHEN SELF-DEFENCE IS NO DEFENCE *In 1964, Mr Evans was stopped by the police while driving. Inside his car was a truncheon; in Mr Evans's pocket was a knuckleduster. He said he needed the weapons for self-defence, as he used his car to collect his firm's payroll from the bank.*

*He was not on his way to the bank, however, when the police stopped him. He was charged with carrying offensive weapons.*
DECISION *He was convicted. (Evans v. Wright.)* ◄

However, it is only if a person carries an offensive weapon *in public* that he can be prosecuted. By 'in public', the law means a street or any place to which members of the public can go, including places where a charge is made for admission—a cinema or a fairground, for example.
PENALTY Up to two years' imprisonment.

## OFFICIAL SECRETS

The most serious offence against the Official Secrets Acts 1911–39 involves a variety of activities 'prejudicial to the safety or interests of the State'. People suspected of spying are often charged with this offence.

Prosecutions for spying are normally brought under Section 1 of the Official Secrets Act 1911; but the provisions of the section are wide-ranging and have been held to cover conduct which would not be thought of as spying in the popular sense. A man will be charged under this section if, for a purpose prejudicial to the safety or interests of the State, he enters or inspects any prohibited place to make any photograph, sketch, plan, model or note which might be useful to an enemy. He is also guilty if, for a similar purpose, he collects, records, publishes or communicates any official code word, document or information which could help an enemy.

The expression 'prohibited place' includes Service establishments, and munitions factories or depots.

The provisions are not directed only against spies, however. In 1962 they were used against nuclear-disarmament demonstrators who had planned to enter a military airfield to prevent aircraft from taking off and landing.

The less serious offence of 'improperly communicating information to an unauthorised person' comes under Section 2 of the Act. This section applies not merely to anyone who communicates any document or information which could help an enemy; it can also apply where any information (not necessarily confidential) has been obtained or communicated in breach of the Act.

The section covers the activities of any person who passes on such information or documents while he is employed in an official position or as a Government contractor.

Such a person is guilty if he passes the information or document to an unauthorised person; if he uses the information to benefit a foreign power or affect the safety of the State; if he retains such a document when he has no right to; or if he fails to take reasonable care of it.

PENALTY For offences under Section 1: up to 14 years' imprisonment. For offences under Section 2: up to two years' imprisonment.

## PAROLE

Anyone sentenced to prison is normally released after serving two-thirds of his or her sentence, provided he or she has behaved well in prison; one-third of the sentence is remitted for good conduct. A prisoner may, however, be released before this time on parole if he convinces the authorities that his case is suitable.

The law allows a prisoner to be considered for parole as soon as he has served one-third of his sentence, or 12 months, whichever is the longer. His application is considered first by a local parole committee attached to the prison where he is serving his sentence. If the committee thinks his case is suitable, it

is considered by the Parole Board in London.

If the prisoner is released, he may still have to comply with conditions imposed by the Parole Board. He can be returned to prison to complete the sentence if he breaks the conditions, or is convicted of a further offence.

The period during which the paroled prisoner is liable to be recalled (the time he is 'on licence') lasts from the date of his release until the time when he would normally have been released on remission for good behaviour—usually after serving two-thirds of his original sentence.

In the case of prisoners serving extended sentences, and certain young offenders, the period of licence may last for the full period of the original sentence.

## PERJURY

Anyone who takes an oath (or makes an affirmation) in a court of law and then gives false evidence is guilty of perjury. To be convicted, he must have known that the statement was false, or not have believed it was true.

➤ FRIENDS PROVIDED A FALSE ALIBI *In 1965, Nigel Pullen was charged with committing a nuisance in a public place. He could have pleaded guilty, in which case he would probably have been fined a pound or two. Instead, he persuaded two friends to give evidence that he was somewhere else with them at the time of the alleged offence. The summons was dismissed.*

*Later, evidence came to light which showed that Mr Pullen's statement had been false, and he was charged with perjury and sentenced to two years' imprisonment. He appealed.*

DECISION *The Court of Appeal upheld the conviction and sentence saying that, even though the original charge of committing a nuisance in public was not an important one, perjury of any kind was a very serious offence. (R. v. Pullen.)* ◄

In cases of perjury, the attempt to deceive the court need not necessarily arise from evidence directly related to the case being heard. For instance, a witness commits perjury if he untruthfully answers material questions about his own background.

The prosecution does not have to prove that the accused positively knew that his statement was false; it is enough to show that he did not believe it to be true. It is a defence that the perjury was induced by a genuinely believed threat of physical injury.

False statements are punishable, too, if they are made before any tribunal which hears witnesses on oath. There is a separate offence called 'subornation of perjury', which consists of helping or persuading someone else to commit perjury by giving false evidence.

PENALTY For perjury or subornation of perjury: up to seven years' imprisonment.

## PERVERTING THE COURSE OF JUSTICE

If two or more people set out to improperly influence a trial, they are guilty of conspiracy to pervert the course of justice.

This offence includes preventing witnesses from giving evidence, or making them give false evidence; bribing, threatening or attempting to dishonestly influence members of a jury; and publishing anything which might interfere with a trial.

PENALTY Any fine or term of imprisonment.

## PIRACY

The passengers, as well as the crew, of a ship can be charged with piracy if they take over, or attempt to take over, a ship on the high seas, put sailors 'in fear of their lives', and steal the cargo. If actual violence is used, the offence is a more serious one.

PENALTY For piracy: life imprisonment. For piracy with violence:-death.

## POACHING ☐ Hunting, shooting and fishing, p. 137.

## POLITICAL UNIFORMS

The Home Secretary or a chief constable can give permission for political uniforms to be worn on certain occasions. Otherwise, it is illegal to wear in a public place or at a public meeting any uniform signifying an association with a political organisation.

The law does not prohibit stewards at political meetings on private premises from wearing badges or objects—such as armlets—which denote a degree of authority.

PENALTY A fine of up to £50 or up to three months' imprisonment.

## PRISON

The length of a prison sentence is to a large extent a matter for the courts. In most cases, Parliament fixes only the maximum, and leaves it to the court to sentence in a particular case within that maximum. But a person may not be sent to prison for the first time unless the court is satisfied that no other method of dealing with him is appropriate

—and if it does send him to prison it must specify its reasons.

Some common-law offences, even trivial ones, have no maximum sentence laid down.

Courts have discretion to impose fines instead of, or in addition to, imprisonment in all cases except murder. Offenders in need of mental treatment can be required to attend a hospital. ☐ Treatment for the mentally ill, p. 380.

In practice, in deciding what punishment to impose, the courts take account of a wide range of matters—the seriousness of the offence, the circumstances of the offender, the reasons why he committed the offence, the effect of the likely sentence on the offender's dependants and the sort of sentences passed on other offenders who have been convicted of similar offences.

When imposing a prison sentence for two years or less, the court has the power to order that the sentence should be suspended for any period up to two years. This means that the offender is free to go, but if he commits any further offence during the suspension period, he will be liable to serve the suspended sentence, as well as any sentence the court may decide to impose on him in respect of the later offence.

When the court passes a suspended sentence of more than six months, it can combine this with a supervision order placing the offender under the supervision of a probation officer. The offender must keep in touch with the probation officer in accordance with instructions he gets from him, and must notify him of any change of address.

A supervision order ceases to have effect if, before the end of the specified period, the court discharges it at the request of either probation officer or offender.

Failure to comply with the terms of the supervision order can be punished by a fine of up to £50.

The sentence of life imprisonment can be imposed at the discretion of the court for a number of offences, including manslaughter, rape, robbery, aggravated burglary, arson and procuring an abortion unlawfully. It is the only sentence which can be passed on a person convicted of murder.

In each case, the effect of the sentence is the same—the offender is legally liable to be detained in prison for the rest of his life. However, the Home Secretary has power to release a person serving a life sentence at any time at his discretion, subject to the approval of the Parole Board. If a prisoner is released he remains under sentence and is liable to be recalled to prison at any time, for the rest of his life, to serve the remainder of his sentence.

He may be released subject to certain conditions, and failure to observe these conditions will also lead to his return to prison.

Most life prisoners are released at some stage in their sentence—some after a very short time, the majority after a more substantial period of seven to ten years. There are a few, however, who are considered so dangerous that they are never released.

In murder cases, the judge is obliged to pass a life sentence, but he may add the recommendation that the prisoner should not be released until a certain period has elapsed. If the judge does make a recommendation of this kind, however, it is not binding upon the Home Secretary.

## PROBATION

Any offender (apart from a murderer) can—with his agreement—be put on probation instead of being sentenced, if the court that finds him guilty thinks fit. The offender has to agree to be placed under the supervision of a probation officer for a period of between one and three years.

In addition, the court may order that the probationer should live for a period in an approved probation hostel, or that he should live at home; that he should not change his job without the consent of the probation officer; that he should not associate with certain people; or that he should comply with any other instruction that appears necessary.

If the probationer fails to keep any of these requirements he can be taken back to court and sentenced as if he had just been convicted of the offence for which he was put on probation. If he commits another criminal offence while on probation, he may be sentenced for both the new and old offences.

## PROSTITUTION

The act of prostitution—taking money for sexual services—is not illegal. But there are several offences linked with it—soliciting, living off the earnings of prostitution and brothel-keeping.

To secure a conviction on any of these charges, the prosecution does not have to prove that the sexual act itself took place: prostitution covers anything which the law defines as 'common lewdness'—that is, most forms of sexual gratification. Both men and women can be charged with soliciting, which

is defined as 'loitering or soliciting as a common prostitute in a street or public place for the purpose of prostitution'.

A man who seeks customers as a homosexual prostitute, or on behalf of a female prostitute, is guilty of soliciting. But if he approaches a woman for the purpose of suggesting normal intercourse, he is charged only with insulting behaviour.

It is also an offence for a man (but not for a woman) to live off the earnings of prostitution. Many people other than a 'pimp' may be guilty of this offence—the shopkeeper who allows a prostitute to advertise her services in his window, or the taxi-driver who takes payment from a prostitute for bringing clients.

A woman cannot be charged with living off the earnings of prostitution; she can, however, be accused of exercising control or influence over a prostitute for gain.

The charge of keeping a brothel can be brought only in cases in which at least two male or female prostitutes use a place for the purpose of prostitution.

Anyone who causes or encourages a woman to be a prostitute is guilty of procuring.
PENALTY For soliciting: £10 maximum fine for a first conviction, rising to £25 for a second. Subsequent convictions carry a penalty of three months' imprisonment. For living on the earnings of prostitution: up to seven years' imprisonment. For a woman exercising control over a prostitute: up to seven years' imprisonment. For brothel-keeping: up to three months' imprisonment on the first conviction; up to six months' on later convictions. For procuring: up to two years' imprisonment.

## 'PROTECTION' See: BLACKMAIL

## RACIAL HATRED, INCITEMENT OF
☐ Meetings, marches, demonstrations, p. 672.

## RAPE
In law, rape takes place when a woman is made to have sexual intercourse *without her consent*. She does not have to be fully aware of what is happening: it is rape to have intercourse with a woman when she is asleep; if she is too drunk to realise what is happening; or if she is too young or ignorant to understand what sexual intercourse is.

➤ THE TEACHER WHO TRICKED HIS PUPIL
*In 1922, Owen Williams, a teacher of singing, told a girl pupil that he could improve her voice if he had intercourse with her. The girl did not know what sexual intercourse was. The act took*

*place, and Mr Williams was charged with rape.*
DECISION *He was found guilty and sentenced to seven years' imprisonment. (R. v. Williams.)* ◄

A man accused of rape can plead in defence that intercourse did not take place, or that he honestly believed the woman had consented.

A husband cannot be convicted of raping his wife unless they are divorced or legally separated. But if he forces her to submit he can be charged with assault.

Rape is committed even though penetration of the woman is only slight. Where there is no penetration at all but the man has clearly set out to commit rape, he may be convicted of attempted rape, assault with intent to commit rape, or indecent assault.

A boy aged under 14 cannot be charged with rape; the law considers him physically too immature. He can, however, be convicted of indecent assault.
PENALTY Any period of imprisonment.

**RECEIVING** See: HANDLING STOLEN GOODS

**RELIGIOUS SERVICE, DISTURBING** See: BLASPHEMY

**RESORTING TO UNAUTHORISED PREMISES TO BET** ☐ Betting and gaming, p. 660.

**RESTITUTION**
Where a person is convicted of an offence involving stolen goods, or where such an offence is taken into consideration, the court can order him to return the goods, or their equivalent in money value.

**RIOT, TAKING PART IN A** See: ASSEMBLY, UNLAWFUL

**ROBBERY**
Robbery is not just another name for theft. It means taking someone's property against his will, and using force or making the victim afraid that force may be used.

To secure a conviction for robbery, the prosecution must prove that theft has taken place. The removal of property does not amount to theft or robbery if the defendant believes that he is entitled to it.

➤COLLECTED WAGES WITH A KNIFE *In 1966, Jim Skivington went to the office where his wife had been working and demanded her wages. He thought he was entitled to the money since, before leaving the firm, she gave him*
*a letter authorising him to collect her wages.*

*To reinforce his demand Mr Skivington threatened the manager and his assistant with a knife. He was given a pay packet. Convicted of robbery, Mr Skivington appealed.*
DECISION *The Appeal Court substituted a conviction for common assault. The court said Mr Skivington's belief that he was entitled to the money was a defence to a robbery charge but did not justify the use of force. (R. v. Skivington.)* ◄

The force which turns theft into robbery must be used before or during the theft.
PENALTY Any period of imprisonment.

**ROUT, TAKING PART IN A**
See: ASSEMBLY, UNLAWFUL

**SCHOOLS, APPROVED** ☐ Children in trouble, p. 356.

**SECRETS, OFFICIAL** See: OFFICIAL SECRETS

**SEDITION**
Anyone who attempts to stir up hostility between different groups within the community, or to provoke discontent among the population at large, may be charged with sedition.

Essentially, the crime of sedition is committed only when there is an intention to provoke protest *through violent means.*
PENALTY Any fine or term of imprisonment.

**SEXUAL OFFENCES** See: INCEST; INDECENT BEHAVIOUR; ILLEGAL INTERCOURSE; OBSCENE PUBLICATIONS; PROSTITUTION; RAPE

**SMUGGLING** ☐ Passports and visas, p. 155; Going through customs, p. 156.

**SOLICITING** See: PROSTITUTION

**STEALING** See: THEFT

**STOLEN PROPERTY** See: HANDLING STOLEN GOODS

**SUICIDE**
It is no longer a crime to commit, or attempt, suicide; but anyone encouraging another to do so may be charged with MANSLAUGHTER or MURDER.

**SUPERVISION ORDER**
Anyone under the age of 17 can be made the subject of a supervision order, which puts them in the care of the local authority

children's officer or a probation officer. The child may remain at home during the period that the order operates. Supervision orders replace the old probation orders for those under 17. They give the children's officer or probation officer wider powers and responsibility for dealing with a child's welfare. □ Children in trouble, p. 356.

A person of any age who is given a suspended prison sentence of more than six months may also be made subject to a supervision order placing him under the supervision of a probation officer. See PRISON

## TAKING AWAY A VEHICLE

Anyone taking a vehicle without the owner's consent may face one of two charges:
**1.** If he intends to keep, sell or otherwise permanently deprive the owner of it, he is charged with theft.
**2.** If he does not intend permanently to deprive the owner of it—if he takes a car to get home after the last bus has gone, and then abandons it, for example—he is charged with taking the vehicle without permission.

A person is not guilty of taking away a vehicle if he believes he has lawful authority to do so, or believes the owner would have consented had he known.

There is a related charge of driving or being carried in a vehicle knowing that it has been taken without authority.

PENALTY For taking a vehicle without permission or being carried in one: up to three years' imprisonment.

## THEFT

Taking someone else's property amounts to theft if the property is taken *dishonestly*, and the intention is to deprive the victim of it *permanently*. The law does not clearly define 'dishonestly', but Parliament has given some guidance on what is *not* dishonest. For instance, anyone taking property is not considered dishonest in law if:
**1.** He believes he is legally entitled to it—even if it turns out that he is not.
**2.** He finds the property and believes that it is not reasonably possible to trace the owner.
**3.** He believes that the owner of the property would consent if he knew.

➤ THE MANAGER WHO 'BORROWED' FROM THE TILL *John Cockburn, the manager of a wine shop in Halifax, was charged with stealing money from the firm's till. He told the court that he had borrowed the money from the till on the*

*Saturday, intending to replace it on the Monday morning with a cheque from his daughter. He said he had no intention to defraud, because he intended to replace the money immediately. His case went to the Appeal Court.*
DECISION *Mr Cockburn was found guilty. The Appeal Court said that Mr Cockburn had no reason to believe that his firm would have agreed to his borrowing the money if he had asked for permission. (R. v. Cockburn.)*◄

The definition of 'intending permanently to deprive' in theft cases was changed by the Theft Act 1968. This laid down that a person can be said to intend to deprive someone of his property permanently even though he intends that the owner should eventually get it back when it is worn out and worthless.

If, for example, someone finds a weekly train ticket on Monday morning and uses it every day until the following Saturday when he returns it, he is guilty of theft.

Not only tangible things—cars, cameras, money, and so on—are involved in theft charges. There are intangibles, too, such as debts and credit balances—it would be theft if a person caused someone else's bank account to be debited and his own credited.

Anyone who, during a walk in the countryside, picks mushrooms, flowers, fruit, or the leaves of any plant *growing wild* is not guilty of theft unless he does so 'for a commercial purpose'—not just for his own use. He would, however, be guilty of theft if he took the plant itself, or dug up a tree, or took anything that was being cultivated by the owner.

The customer with a television set on hire purchase is guilty of theft from the hire-purchase company if he sells the television set before it is fully paid for. The hire-purchase company, on the other hand, will be guilty of stealing the set from the customer if they dishonestly repossess it without having authority to do so.

Technically, theft is the dishonest appropriation of property. The term 'appropriation' covers a wide variety of activities: taking goods away from the owner; selling them; destroying them; consuming them; lending them to someone who is unlikely to return them; giving them away; altering them in such a way that they cannot be restored to their former condition (melting down silverware, for example); pawning them; or dishonestly doing anything with them that only the owner is entitled to do.

In some instances, an individual can even steal his own property. The man who takes back his own property from a pawnshop without redeeming it, for example, is guilty of theft. So is the motorist who leaves his car at a garage for repairs, and then collects it without paying for the repairs or getting the agreement of the garage manager.

PENALTY Up to ten years' imprisonment.

## THREATENING BEHAVIOUR
See: INSULTING BEHAVIOUR

## THREATS, DEMANDING MONEY BY
See: BLACKMAIL

## TREASON
Treason is the oldest surviving criminal offence in the country: it goes back to 1351. There are several ways of committing treason.

In modern times, most people charged with treason are accused of 'levying war on the monarch in his realm'.

➤ THE CRIME OF SIR ROGER CASEMENT *In 1916, Sir Roger Casement, an Irish politician sympathetic to Irish nationalism, was charged with treason. It was said that he had visited British prisoner-of-war camps in Germany to persuade prisoners to join a landing in Ireland and take part in the 1916 uprising.*

*Sir Roger Casement's defence was that the treason law applied only to acts committed in the United Kingdom, and did not cover anything which happened abroad.*

DECISION *This defence was held to be invalid and Sir Roger was executed. (R. v. Casement.)* ◄

PENALTY Life imprisonment or death.

## TRESPASS
It is not a crime simply to trespass on someone else's property—signs which say 'Trespassers will be prosecuted' therefore have no force. All a property owner can do is to sue for damages. ☐ Rights and responsibilities of running a home, p. 280.

Anyone who trespasses intending to commit a crime may, however, be guilty of BURGLARY—in some cases, even if he never manages to carry out his intention. ☐ Hunting, shooting and fishing, p. 137.

## UNIFORMS, POLITICAL  See: POLITICAL UNIFORMS

## UNLAWFUL ASSEMBLY  See: ASSEMBLY, UNLAWFUL

## UNNATURAL OFFENCES  See: INDECENT BEHAVIOUR

## VANDALISM  See: CRIMINAL DAMAGE

## WILD ANIMALS, SNARING  ☐ Hunting, shooting and fishing, p. 137.

## WITNESS, INTERFERING WITH
Anyone who threatens, bribes or persuades a witness not to give evidence, or to give false evidence, is guilty of contempt of court. The offence can also be committed by threatening someone who has already given evidence.

PENALTY Any fine or term of imprisonment.

If two or more people try together to improperly influence a witness, and so affect the course of a trial, they may be charged with conspiracy to PERVERT THE COURSE OF JUSTICE.

## WOUNDING
The law divides wounding into three categories: wounding or causing grievous bodily harm with intent; malicious wounding; and assault occasioning actual bodily harm.

Causing grievous bodily harm by any means amounts to wounding with intent if the accused intended to cause such harm.

A wound is defined in law as a break in the skin, so it would be wounding with intent if an attacker tried to stab his victim but only inflicted a minor cut—provided he *intended* to cause serious harm.

A defendant is also guilty of wounding with intent if he inflicts a wound or grievous bodily harm while trying to prevent a lawful arrest. In these circumstances the prosecution does *not* have to prove that he intended to inflict serious bodily harm—only that he used force in resisting arrest.

The principal difference between wounding with intent and malicious wounding is that, in malicious wounding, the prosecution does not have to prove that the accused intended to inflict a serious injury. He will be guilty if he realised that the action would have caused some injury—even if he did not realise how serious an injury.

To prove a charge of assault occasioning actual bodily harm, all that the prosecution has to show is that there was an assault as a result of which the victim suffered harm—not necessarily of a serious nature. The fact that the accused intended to cause harm, or even realised that he might cause harm, does not have to be proved.

PENALTY For wounding with intent: up to life imprisonment. For malicious wounding and assault occasioning actual bodily harm: up to five years' imprisonment.

# INDEX

Where there are several page references under one entry,
the more important ones are in bold type.
The panels provide a quick guide to solving many of the more common
legal, personal and financial problems.

## All about BORROWING

# C

## All about CHILDREN and YOUNG PEOPLE

| | | |
|---|---|---|
| Before birth | grants for pregnant women | 324–5 |
| | insuring against twins | 324 |
| At birth | grants and allowances | 325–7 |
| | seeing a doctor | 324 |
| | having a baby in hospital | 324 |
| | registering a birth | 327–8 |
| | stillbirth | 327, 411 |
| | nationality | 329 |
| | adoption | 336 |
| | fostering | 334 |
| Nationality | when legitimate | 329 |
| | when illegitimate | 329 |
| | when an alien | 329 |
| Education | in schools | 346–53 |
| | for handicapped children | 347 |
| | in the home | 347 |
| | religious instruction | 345, 349 |
| | sex education | 349 |
| | in universities | 363–5 |
| In trouble | in the home | 354–5 |
| | at school | 351 |
| | with the law | 356–9 |
| | with firearms | 138, 141 |
| Driving a vehicle | a moped | 165 |
| | a motor cycle | 165 |
| | a car | 20 |
| | a tractor | 360 |
| | a lorry | 360 |
| | a bus | 360 |
| Coming of age (minimum age) | for going to school | 346 |
| | for buying a pet | 362 |
| | for film-going | 361 |
| | for owning a gun | 141 |
| | for leaving school | 347 |
| | for taking a job | 593 |
| | for sickness benefit | 362 |
| | for supplementary benefit | 362, 550 |
| | for smoking | 362 |
| | for entering a public house | 656 |
| | for entering a betting shop | 661 |
| | for voting | 675 |
| | for marriage | 312 |
| | for owning land or property | 362 |
| | for inheriting under a will | 431 |
| | for being accused in a juvenile court | 357 |
| | for being charged in a criminal court | 360 |
| | for being sent to prison | 362 |
| Money | maintenance | 387, 388, 391 |
| | owning money and property | 343, 360–1 |
| | income tax allowances | 559–60 |
| | claiming damages | 342–3, 417 |
| | buying goods on credit | 443 |
| Inheriting | for legitimate children | 431–2 |
| | for illegitimate children | 333 |
| | for adopted children | 339 |
| Illegitimacy | State financial help | 331 |
| | money from the father | 331 |
| | registration of birth | 330 |
| | nationality | 329 |
| | custody | 332 |
| | inheriting | 333 |
| | becoming legitimate | 333 |

# D

# E

---

## All about FINANCIAL HELP
### (mainly from the State or local councils)

# F

# G

# H

All about ILLNESS and INJURY

| | | |
|---|---|---|
| Treatment | by a doctor | 368 |
| | by a dentist | 373 |
| | by an optician | 373 |
| | by a surgeon | 377 |
| | in hospital | 376–9 |
| | for infertility | 386 |
| | for drug addiction | 374 |
| | for mental illness | 380 |
| | for deafness | 374 |
| | to end a pregnancy | 375 |
| Financial help | with prescription charges | 369–70 |
| | for those off work through sickness | 602 |
| | for those injured at work | 632 |
| | for the disabled | 635 |
| | for those suffering from an industrial disease | 633 |
| | for injuries inflicted by a criminal | 547 |
| | insuring against illness and injury | 521 |
| | rearranging family finances during illness or injury | 544 |
| Compensation for injuries | in a road accident | 121 |
| | on public property | 547 |
| | on private property | 546 |
| | at school | 352 |
| | at work | 636 |
| | on a bus | 162–3 |
| | on a train | 161–2 |
| | on a ship or in an aircraft | 163–4 |
| | from defective goods | 464 |
| | by neighbours | 286 |
| | by animals | 287 |
| | through a child's carelessness | 344 |
| | in a restaurant | 658 |
| | in hospital | 381 |
| | at sporting events | 131 |
| | at a protest or demonstration | 674 |

# All about INSURANCE

# J

# U

# V

## Acknowledgments

For permission to reproduce copyright material, the publishers wish to thank those credited in the text, and the following: Department of Employment (the Ready Reckoner for Redundancy Payments); The Solicitors' Law Stationery Society Ltd (parts of the National Conditions of Sale); Sweet and Maxwell Ltd (material adapted from *Industrial Injuries* by Vester and Cartwright); and the trade organisations listed on pp. 448–9 and 478–89 (for permission to reproduce their symbols). The publishers also acknowledge their indebtedness to the authors and publishers of the hundreds of works on legal subjects consulted during preparation of this book.

Illustrations drawn by Michael Davidson, Keith Faulkner, Jackson Day Designs and Roger Twinn.

### Paper, printing and binding by:

THE BERKSHIRE PRINTING CO. LTD, READING; BKT PRINTERS LTD, TONBRIDGE; HAZELL, WATSON & VINEY LTD, AYLESBURY; RED BRIDGE BOOK CLOTH CO. LTD, BOLTON; HALE PAPER CO. LTD, LONDON